PSYCHOPATHOLOGY IN ADULTHOOD

SECOND EDITION

Edited by

MICHEL HERSEN

Pacific University

ALAN S. BELLACK

University of Maryland, Baltimore

ALLYN AND BACON
Boston   London   Toronto   Sydney   Tokyo   Singapore

To Vicki—M. H.
To Barbara—A. S. B.

Series Editor: Becky Pascal
Series editorial assistant: Susan Hutchinson
Manufacturing buyer: Suzanne Lareau

Library of Congress Cataloging-in-Publication Data

Psychopathology in adulthood / Michel Hersen and Alan S. Bellack,
    editors. — 2nd ed.
        p.   cm.
    Includes bibliographical references and index.
    ISBN 0-205-20027-3
    1. Psychology, Pathological.   I. Hersen, Michel.   II. Bellack,
Alan S.
    [DNLM: 1. Psychopathology.   2. Mental Disorders.   WM 100 P97488
2000]
RC454.P787   2000
616.89—dc21
DNLM./DLC
for Library of Congress   99-25834
                                                                     CIP

Printed in the United States of America

10   9   8   7   6   5   4   3   2   1   03   02   01   00   99

CONTENTS

ABOUT THE EDITORS

Michel Hersen (Ph.D., State University of New York at Buffalo, 1966) is Professor and Dean, School of Professional Psychology, Pacific University, Forest Grove, Oregon. He is past president of the Association for Advancement of Behavior Therapy. He has coauthored and coedited 120 books, including *Handbook of Prescriptive Treatment for Adults* and *Single Case Experimental Designs*. He has also published more than 222 scientific journal articles and is coeditor of several psychological journals, including *Behavior Modification, Clinical Psychology Review, Journal of Anxiety Disorders, Journal of Family Violence, Journal of Developmental and Physical Disabilities, Journal of Clinical Geropsychology*, and *Aggression and Violent Behavior: A Review Journal*. With Alan S. Bellack, he is coeditor of the recently published eleven-volume work entitled *Comprehensive Clinical Psychology*. Dr. Hersen has been the recipient of numerous grants from the National Institute of Mental Health, the U.S. Department of Education, the National Institute of Disabilities and Rehabilitation Research, and the March of Dimes Birth Defects Foundation. He is a Diplomate of the American Board of Professional Psychology, Distinguished Practitioner and Member of the National Academy of Practice Psychology, and recipient of the Distinguished Career Achievement Award in 1996 from the American Board of Medical Psychotherapists and Psychodiagnosticians.

Alan S. Bellack, Ph.D., ABPP, received his Ph.D. from the Pennsylvania State University in 1970. He currently is Professor of Psychiatry and Director of the Division of Psychology at the University of Maryland School of Medicine. He was formerly Professor of Psychiatry and Director of Psychology at the Medical College of Pennsylvania, and Professor of Psychology and Director of Clinical training at the University of Pittsburgh. He is a past president of the Association for Advancement of Behavior Therapy, and a Diplomate of the American Board of Behavior Therapy and the American Board of Professional Psychology. He is a Fellow of the American Psychological Association, the American Psychological

Society, the Association for Clinical Psychosocial Research, and the American Psychopathological Association. He was the first recipient of the American Psychological Foundation Gralnick Foundation Award for his lifetime research on psychosocial aspects of schizophrenia. Dr. Bellack is coauthor or coeditor of 27 books and has published over 125 journal articles. He received an NIMH MERIT award and has had continuous funding from NIMH for over 20 years for his work on schizophrenia, depression, and social skills training. He currently serves on a NIDA IRG and is an ad hoc reviewer for several NIMH IRGs. He is editor and founder of the journals *Behavior Modification* and *Clinical Psychology Review*, and serves on the editorial boards of nine other journals.

ABOUT THE CONTRIBUTORS

Susan L. Aarestad is a doctoral candidate in clinical psychology at the Ohio State University. Her research interests include sexuality in couples and quality of life among cancer patients. She completed her undergraduate degree at the University of Notre Dame, where she majored in Psychology and Great Books.

Barbara L. Andersen is a Professor in the Department of Psychology and Department of Obstetrics and Gynecology at Ohio State University. She completed her studies at the University of Illinois, where she received the Ph.D. in 1980, and a year of postdoctoral work at the Neuropsychiatric Institute, UCLA. She has written two books and over 100 research articles on behavioral medicine topics. She currently chairs the American Cancer Society's grant study section for Psychosocial and Behavioral Research. She is on several journal editorial boards and is a former associate editor for the *Journal of Consulting and Clinical Psychology* and the *Annals of Behavioral Medicine*.

Christy Barongan received her Ph.D. in clinical psychology from Kent State University in 1998. She received her bachelor's degree in psychology and English from the University of Virginia and completed her internship at the University of Virginia Counseling and Psychological Services. Her research has been on sexual aggression against women. She is currently interested in personality factors in subtypes of eating disorders.

Jack J. Blanchard is Assistant Professor of Psychology and Psychiatry at the University of New Mexico. He received his Ph.D. in Clinical Psychology from the State University of New York at Stony Brook in 1991. His research interests include the role of emotion in the development and course of schizophrenia.

Evelyn J. Bromet, Ph.D., is a Professor of Psychiatry at the State University of New York, Stony Brook. She received her Ph.D. in epidemiology from Yale University and has conducted descriptive and analytic psychiatric epidemiology research. Her work currently focuses on the course of psychosis and the mental health effects of the nuclear accident at Chernobyl.

John F. Clarkin is a Professor of Clinical Psychology in Psychiatry at the Cornell University Medical College, Director of Psychology for The New York Hospital, and Codirector of the Personality Disorder Institute. Dr. Clarkin's academic writing has focused on the phenomenology and treatment of personality disorders and on the theoretical underpinning for differential treatment planning of psychiatric patients. His research activities have focused on the phenomenology of the personality disorders and the treatment of patients with borderline personality disorder and bipolar disorder.

Brett A. Clementz, Ph.D., is an Associate Professor of Psychology at the University of California, San Diego. He was a recipient of the 1998 Distinguished Scientific Award for an Early Career Contribution from the Society for Psychophysiological Research. His research program relies on measures of ocular motor performance, electroencephalography, and magnetoencephalography to study the behavioral neurology and genetics of schizophrenia.

Scott F. Coffey, Ph.D., is a Research Associate and NIDA Postdoctoral Research Fellow at the Medical University of South Carolina. He received his doctorate from the University of Mississippi. His research interests include nicotine dependence, cue reactivity, posttraumatic stress disorder, and variables associated with victimization.

Julie J. Desai, M.A., is the coordinator of the Intensive Outpatient Program at the Toledo Center for Eating Disorders. She has a master's degree in Clinical Psychology from University of Detroit, Mercy. She has experience in individual, group, and family counseling with eating disorders, as well as extensive training in psychoeducational treatment approaches for eating disorders.

Mary Amanda Dew, Ph.D., is Associate Professor of Psychiatry, Psychology, and Epidemiology at Western Psychiatric Institute and Clinic, University of Pittsburgh School of Medicine. She is Codirector of the Training Program in Psychiatric Epidemiology at Western Psychiatric Institute and Clinic and the University of Pittsburgh Graduate School of Public Health. She received her Ph.D. in psychology from Harvard University. Her research interests focus on the epidemiology of mental disorders in populations with chronic physical illness. Her current work concerns mental health, compliance, and quality of life in organ transplantation and in the elderly.

David J. Drobes, Ph.D., is Assistant Professor in the Department of Psychiatry and Behavioral Sciences at the Medical University of South Carolina. He received his doctorate in clinical psychology from Purdue University, then completed postdoctoral training at the University of Florida. His research interests involve psychophysiological aspects of addiction.

Nabila El-Bassel, D.S.W., received her M.A. in social work from Hebrew University. She earned her doctorate from Columbia University School of Social Work, where she is Associate Professor and associate director of the Social Intervention Group. Dr. El-Bassel's research interests include drug abuse, HIV prevention, women's health, family violence, social support, and social problems of recent immigrants.

David M. Garner, Ph.D., is Director of the Toledo Center for Eating Disorders, Adjunct Professor (Psychology) at Bowling Green State University, and Adjunct Professor (Women's Studies) at the University of Toledo. He is a founding member of the Academy for Eating Disorders and a member of the editorial board of the *International Journal of Eating Disorders*. Dr. Garner's primary research interests are in the areas of obesity and eating disorders, including assessment, diagnosis, treatment outcome, psychopathology, and the biology of weight regulation.

Jean S. Gearon, Ph.D., is Assistant Professor of Psychiatry at the University of Maryland School of Medicine, Baltimore. She directs the postdoctoral fellowship program in clinical psychology and was recently honored with the Department of Psychiatry's Outstanding Young Investigators Award for Mental Health Research. Her primary research interests are women with serious mental illness, victimization, and HIV.

Ian H. Gotlib, Ph.D., is a Professor of Psychology at Stanford University. Dr. Gotlib's research focuses on information-processing models of depression in children and adults, the effects of depression on marital and family functioning, and the emotional and behavioral functioning of children of depressed mothers. He is a Fellow of the American Psychological Association and the American Psychological Society. Dr. Gotlib is an Associate Editor of *Cognition and Emotion*, and is on the editorial boards of the *British Journal of Clinical Psychology, Cognitive Therapy and Research*, the *Journal of Abnormal Psychology*, the *Journal of Social and Personal Relationships*, and *Psychological Assessment*.

Gretchen Haas, Ph.D., is an Associate Professor of Psychiatry and director of the Family and Psychosocial Studies Program at the Western Psychiatric Institute and Clinic and the Department of Psychiatry of the University of Pittsburgh School of Medicine. Dr. Haas received her B.A. in Psychology from Cornell University and her doctorate in Clinical Psychology from Wayne State University in Detroit, Michigan. Her early work with children and families in a Pediatric Psychiatry at the Children's Hospital of Michigan generated an abiding interest in developmental factors that influence the onset, treatment response, and course of major psychiatric disorders. In 1984 Dr. Haas joined the faculty of the Cornell University Medical College, where she collaborated with colleagues in research on family interventions for the treatment of major depression and schizophrenia. In 1987 she was awarded funding by the National Institute of Mental Health (NIMH) to conduct a longitudinal study of sex differences in first-episode and chronic schizophrenia. Her pioneering work in this area focuses on the identification of sex differences in clinical, psychosocial and neurocognitive functioning in schizophrenia. In 1990 Dr. Haas moved to the University of Pittsburgh, where she joined the faculty of the Department of Psychiatry and the Center for Neurosciences of Mental Disorders–Schizophrenia (CNMDS) in the study of first-episode psychotic disorders. As associate director of the Clinical Evaluation Core of the CNMDS, Dr. Haas is conducting research on premorbid development and psychosocial functioning in schizophrenia, as well as factors related to sex differences in age at onset of schizo-

phrenia. She is also now completing an NIMH-funded prospective study of risk factors for suicidal behavior in schizophrenia. Dr. Haas is a standing member of the NIMH Internal Review Group (Clinical Psychopathology Review Committee) responsible for review of applications for research funding in the area of clinical psychopathology. She serves as an ad hoc reviewer on over a dozen professional publications that focus on psychiatry and mental health services and she is author and coauthor of over 100 professional publications.

Gordon C. Nagayama Hall is Professor of Psychology at the Pennsylvania State University. His research has been on men who perpetrate sexual aggression. He is currently interested in cultural risk and protective factors associated with sexual aggression. Dr. Hall is Associate Editor of *Cultural Diversity and Ethnic Minority Psychology*.

Martin Harrow, a former chessmaster, is a widely cited expert on schizophrenia and bipolar disorders. He has published over 200 scientific papers and four books in these and related areas, and holds major research grants from NIMH. He is Professor and Director of Psychology in the Department of Psychiatry at the University of Illinois College of Medicine.

Richard G. Heimberg is Professor of Psychology at Temple University. He is actively involved in the study of social phobia and its treatment with cognitive-behavioral and pharmacological methods. Dr. Heimberg has published over 130 papers and two books on these and related topics. He is associate editor of *Cognitive Therapy and Research* and sits on nine other editorial boards. Dr. Heimberg is a member of the board of directors of the Association for Advancement of Behavior Therapy.

Craig S. Holt is currently a psychologist at the Iowa City VA Medical Center and an Associate Clinical Professor of Psychiatry and Psychology at the University of Iowa. His research in anxiety disorders involves information processing, schema development, and emotional regulation in anxious situations.

William G. Iacono, Ph.D., is a Distinguished McKnight University Professor at the University of Minnesota. He is also a Professor and Neuroscience, and an Adjunct Professor of Child Development. Currently director of the clinical psychology training program, he is also director of a training program on neurobehavioral aspects of personality and psychopathology. A past recipient of early scientific career awards from the Society for Psychophysiological Research and the American Psychological Association, he was elected president of the Society for Psychophysiological Research from 1996 to 1997. His research interests include psychophysiological and behavioral genetic studies of schizophrenia, childhood psychopathology, and psychoactive substance use disorders.

Richard C. Josiassen (Ph.D., Clinical Psychology, The Fuller Graduate School of Psychology, 1979), serves as director of the Arthur P. Noyes Clinical Research Center at Norristown State Hospital. Dr. Josiassen has edited two books and published over 70 scientific papers. He served as deputy editor for the journal *Biological Psychiatry* for six years. He heads several research projects that focus on neurophysiological aspects of information processing in schizophrenic patients and their family members.

Danny G. Kaloupek, Ph.D., is a clinical psychologist with expertise in psychophysiological measurement and the health-related effects of psychological trauma. He is currently deputy director of the Behavioral Science Division of the National Center for PTSD at the Boston VA Medical Center and Associate Professor at Boston University School of Medicine.

Terence M. Keane, Ph.D., is Chief of Psychology at the Boston VA Medical Center, director of the National Center for PTSD's Behavioral Science Division, and Professor and Vice-Chairman of Psychiatry at Boston University, Dr. Keane's interests are in the assessment and treatment of PTSD, areas in which he has published extensively.

Patricia R. Koski is Associate Professor and Chair of the Department of Sociology at the University of Arkansas, Fayetteville. Her research interests are in the area of family violence.

Cynthia A. Lease (Ph.D., Virginia Polytechnic Institute and State University, 1994) is a research scientist in the Department of Psychology at Virginia

Tech. Dr. Lease is the project director for an NIMH-funded grant that is investigating posttraumatic stress disorder in children. Dr. Lease also has a private clinical practice in Blacksburg, Virginia, in which she specializes in the treatment of childhood anxiety disorders and children's adjustment to divorce.

William D. Mangold is Professor of Sociology and director of the Center for Social Research at the University of Arkansas. His research current interests include the relationships among social factors and racial differences in mortality and linkages between familial patterns of gender interaction and nonfamily violence.

Douglas S. Mennin is a doctoral student in clinical psychology at Temple University. His research interests include the study of social phobia, generalized anxiety disorder, comorbidity among the anxiety disorders, and emotional processing in anxiety and mood disorders.

Vishwajit Nimgaonkar is Associate Professor of Psychiatry and Human Genetics at the University of Pittsburgh. His training includes medicine with honors (University of Madras), doctoral work at the University of Oxford, and residencies in Psychiatry at the Maudsley Hospital, London, and at WPIC, Pittsburgh. He has received postdoctoral training in molecular biology and in clinical and molecular genetics. His research is focused on the genetic epidemiology of schizophrenia and bipolar disorder.

Susan A. Nolan is a senior graduate student in clinical psychology at Northwestern University in Evanston, Illinois. Her research focuses on interpersonal aspects of depression and anxiety. She began her predoctoral internship at the Vanderbilt University Internship Consortium in September 1998.

Thomas H. Ollendick (Ph.D., Purdue University, 1971) is Professor of Psychology and Director of Training Clinics. His research and teaching interests center on social learning theory and the assessment, treatment, and prevention of child behavior disorders, including the anxiety disorders and the pervasive developmental disorders. He is a Co-PI of a major NIMH grant studying PTSD in traumatized children and adolescents.

Rita Prather, Ph.D., is regional director of the Gulf Coast Texas Region of Senior Psychology Services, Houston. Former Assistant Professor at the University of Texas–Houston Medical School, she continues teaching and consultation in the areas of geropsychology, anxiety disorders, and related topics. Current research area is treatment outcome of the elderly in the long-term care environment.

Cynthia Sanderson, Ph.D., is an Assistant Clinical Professor in Psychology in Psychiatry at Cornell University Medical College, and the Director of the Personality Disorders Program at The New York Hospital–Cornell Medical Center, Westchester Division. She received her Ph.D. from the University of Kentucky, and her career has focused on the etiology of, and treatment methods for, personality disorders.

James R. Sands is a Clinical Assistant Professor at the University of Illinois College of Medicine and director of Clinical Assessment Services, a practice specializing in psychodiagnostic evaluation. Over the past ten years, Dr. Sands has conducted research on major mental illness, including psychosis in affective disorders and depression in schizophrenia. His research has been published in numerous major journals and presented at national conferences.

Robert F. Schilling, Ph.D., received his M.S.W. from the University of Wisconsin–Madison, and his doctorate in social welfare from the University of Washington, Seattle. He is professor at Columbia University School of Social Work, where he directs the Social Intervention Group. His research interests include prevention of HIV/AIDS, substance abuse, and related social problems. Dr. Schilling has a particular interest in the design, development, and testing of interventions in low-income urban communities.

Steven P. Schinke, Ph.D., received his M.S.W. and Ph.D. from the University of Wisconsin–Madison. He is currently professor at Columbia University School of Social Work. Over the past several years, Dr. Schinke has conducted substance abuse prevention and early intervention studies with children, adolescents, and young adults. His research is currently focused on testing intervention models to prevent drug and alcohol abuse, sexually transmitted diseases, HIV infection, and cancer.

Rita A. Shaughnessy (Ph.D., Psychology, University of Illinois at Chicago, 1980; M.D., University of Illinois at Chicago, 1989) is an Assistant Professor of Psychiatry at the MCP/Hahnemann School of Medicine. Dr. Shaughnessy has published numerous book chapters and scientific papers. She currently serves as the director of the Outpatient Clinic at MCP/Hahnemann School of Medicine, and is a consultant on several research projects at the Arthur P. Noyes Clinical Research Center at Norristown State Hospital.

Werner G. K. Stritzke, Ph.D., is a Lecturer in the Psychology Department of the University of Western Australia. He received his doctorate in clinical psychology from Florida State University and completed his clinical internship at the Medical University of South Carolina. His research is in the area of addictive behaviors.

John A. Sweeney, Ph.D., is Associate Professor of Psychiatry at the University of Pittsburgh School of Medicine. He directs the neuropsychology service at Western Psychiatric Institute and Clinic. His research interests are in neurocognitive and neuroimaging abnormalities in schizophrenia, mood disorders, and autism.

Galen E. Switzer, Ph.D., is Research Assistant Professor of Medicine and Psychiatry at the University of Pittsburgh School of Medicine. He received his Ph.D. in sociology from the University of Colorado, Boulder. His research interests include psychometric issues in physical and mental health assessment, and psychosocial and decision-making concerns in organ and bone marrow donation.

Svenn Torgersen, Ph.D., has been a professor in clinical psychology at the University of Oslo since 1986. His main focus in research has been on genetic and environmental factors in the development of psychopathology and personality. Personality disorders have been his main interest in recent years, and he has also been increasingly involved in epidemiological research. He is supervising research at psychiatric clinics for children as well as adults, and he conducts courses for psychologists and psychiatrists in psychiatric classification. He is president of the Norwegian Society for the Study of Personality Disorders and a member of the editorial boards of the *Journal of Personality Disorders* and *Journal of Anxiety Disorders*.

Rose T. Zimering, Ph.D., is Assistant Chief of Psychology at the Boston VA Outpatient Clinic and Associate Professor of Psychiatry at Boston University School of Medicine. Her interests are in the health consequences of posttraumatic stress disorder and in the clinical assessment and treatment of PTSD.

PREFACE AND ACKNOWLEDGMENTS

Study of psychopathology in the late 1990s has become considerably more complex, given discoveries in genetics, improved diagnostic procedures, use of structured interview techniques, and technological advances that, for example, made brain imaging of schizophrenia possible. Our revised text, therefore, is devoted to bringing the reader up to date about these latest developments so that a thorough understanding of increased empiricism of the field will be possible. The second edition of this text, of course, also reflects advances seen in DSM-IV and related research carried out since 1993.

This book is divided into two major sections: Part I, "General Issues and Models," consists of seven chapters that provide the groundwork and context for understanding the issues discussed in the chapters on major disorders in Part II. Included are comprehensive examinations of nosology and diagnosis, epidemiology, genetics, psychobiology, psychophysiological factors, developmental factors, and a sociological perspective.

Part II, "Major Disorders," includes eleven chapters, with two on schizophrenia in order to capture the voluminous literature that has appeared over the last two decades. Chapters in Part II follow a similar format: Description of the Disorder, Epidemiology, Etiology, Course and Complications, Treatment Implications, and a Case Description. A Glossary of terms and definitions appears at the end of the book.

Many individuals have contributed to bringing this project to fruition. First, we are grateful to our experts in psychopathology for contributing chapters to the book. Second, we express appreciation to our technical staff (Eleanor Gil, Lynn J. Harstad, Carole L. Londerée, and Maura Sullivan). Finally, we thank our friends at Allyn and Bacon for their encouragement throughout the process.

Michel Hersen
Forest Grove, Oregon

Alan S. Bellack
Baltimore, Maryland

PART I

GENERAL ISSUES AND MODELS

The psychopathologist of the 21st century must have broad scope and must be fully conversant with the various descriptions that contribute to a comprehensive understanding of this vast topic. No longer will the mere knowledge of psychoanalytic and behavioral perspectives suffice. To the contrary, the complexity of the issues is such that one has to grasp the essentials of nosology and diagnosis, one must have a good knowledge of epidemiology, one needs to evaluate the genetic contribution to various disorders, one must appreciate the psychobiological underpinnings, one requires a keen understanding of development as it relates to pathological behavior, and one needs to understand the sociological context in which psychopathology will be expressed. Indeed, developments in the aforementioned areas are proceeding at remarkably rapid rates, thus requiring the modern-day psychopathologist to have the erudition and knowledge base of the proverbial Renaissance person.

To this end, the general issues and models discussed in Part I of the book provide the foundation for a more enlightened view of the subsequent presentation of individual disorders in Part II. In Chapter 1, Brett A. Clementz and William G. Iacono present a thoughtful discussion of nosology and diagnosis. They comment on nosological nomenclature, classification through the ages, approaches to classifying psychopathology, and current systems of classifica-

tion. The authors present a comprehensive discussion of the interface between DSM-IV and ICD-10 and comment on the need for enhanced validity of the categories. In Chapter 2, Mary Amanda Dew, Evelyn J. Bromet, and Galen E. Switzer define the function of epidemiology as identifying causes of diseases in order to help prevent their expression. In so doing they consider the basic premises of the field, the role of epidemiology in psychopathology, and current knowledge about prevalence, incidence, and risk factors for mental disorders.

Svenn Torgersen, in Chapter 3, clearly delineates both the promises of genetics and its pitfalls as well. He considers quantitative genetics, the family method, the twin method, the adoption method, linkage methods, and the specific role of genetics in psychopathology. He concludes by pointing out that future work will be more concerned with the interaction of environmental variables and genetics. In Chapter 4, Richard C. Josiassen and Rita A. Shaughnessy focus on psychobiological developments as related to adult psychopathology. The predominant focus is on neurons, their unique features, and what can go wrong. The authors document the mounting evidence relating to neuronal abnormality in various forms of psychopathology.

In Chapter 5, David J. Drobes, Werner G.K. Strizke, and Scott F. Coffey argue that psychophysiology is at a crossroads as to its clinical application

1

to adult psychopathology. In their discussion they consider the psychophysiological response systems, conceptual issues, and psychopathological disorders. They underscore that future impact of psychophysiology in clinical practice will depend on increased availability of practical and cost-effective systems of measurement. Cynthia A. Lease and Thomas H. Ollendick, in Chapter 6, examine psychopathology from the developmental perspective. They argue that developmental psychopathology is a nascent area that will require much empirical work in the future. As a model of human behavior, however, the developmental perspective does account nicely for the plasticity of change and variation across time boundaries, while also providing us with a comprehensive framework for looking at longitudinal aspects of disorders.

In Chapter 7, Patricia R. Koski and William D. Mangold provide us with the sociological framework for understanding deviance: namely, antisocial behavior and violence. The authors contrast the sociological model with the medical model, consider interpersonal violence, examine etiology while looking at the empirical data, and outline future directions for the study of violence. Throughout the discussion it is clear that the authors are committed to the notion that neither biology nor psychology alone is able to explain normative or deviant behavior, given that deviance is always relative, situational, and problematic—therefore, the need for the sociological context.

CHAPTER 1

NOSOLOGY AND DIAGNOSIS

Brett A. Clementz
University of California at San Diego
William G. Iacono
University of Minnesota

INTRODUCTION

The classification of psychopathology has long been controversial (e.g., Eysenck, Wakefield, & Friedman, 1983; Kirk & Kutchins, 1992; Rosenhan, 1973; Scheff, 1966; Szasz, 1961). Although the roots of modern classification schemes can be traced back to the mid-19th century, for most of the last hundred years, classification in psychopathology has been largely spurned. Only during the last two to three decades has development of classification systems been pursued in earnest.

Despite their limitations, modern diagnostic systems represent a significant step toward a workable nosology of psychopathology. As we shall highlight, however, there is more to classification than developing diagnoses with high interrater reliability. In fact, an emphasis on reliability to the exclusion of other considerations during development of DSM-III (*Diagnostic and Statistical Manual of Mental Disorders,* third edition; American Psychiatric Association, 1980) through the development of DSM-IV

(American Psychiatric Association, 1994) may have retarded progress in the classification of psychopathology. One consequence of a focus on diagnostic reliability was a chaotic proliferation of diagnoses, from about 100 in DSM-I (American Psychiatric Association, 1952) to 300 in DSM-IV. Most of these diagnoses have unknown validity. Some authorities on this topic (e.g., Goodwin & Guze, 1996) have stated that "there are only about a dozen diagnostic entities in adult psychiatry that have been sufficiently studied to be useful" (p. viii). Diagnostic validity research is sorely needed to determine whether the many diagnoses listed in the DSM-IV will ever be considered useful.

The modern DSM approach (DSM-III; its revision, DSM-III-R, American Psychiatric Association [APA], 1987; and DSM-IV) are reasonable starting points from which to build a diagnostic system (a means for classifying psychopathology the adequacy of which can be scientifically tested; see Morey, 1991). The present chapter, therefore, will not evaluate the DSM approach. Instead, we consider a broad range of issues important for the development and evaluation of a classification system. Our aim is to provide a framework within which to consider nosological issues rather than to give a comprehensive review of this enormous topic (for more extensive reviews, see Blashfield, 1984, and Goodwin & Guze, 1996, for psychopathology; Faber, 1930, for an excellent history of clinical medicine; and Garrison, 1929).[1]

RATIONALE FOR CLASSIFICATION

Some individuals trained in the study of behavior have intimated that classification is neither important nor desirable (Kanfer & Saslow, 1965; Ullman & Krasner, 1975), and have suggested that behavioral descriptions of current and past functioning provide sufficient evaluative information. Unquestionably, in the initial phases of an assessment (whether for diagnostic or for treatment purposes or both), it is advantageous to obtain thorough information about an individual's past and current functioning. Cataloguing behaviors without considering the possibility that certain classes of such characteristics may tend to co-occur with high frequency, however, may neglect potentially valuable information. Merely collecting information without a data reduction (i.e., classification) framework can rapidly lead to the accumulation of an overwhelming and perhaps irrelevant body of knowledge about an individual (e.g., Barker, 1951).

Having a system for classifying psychopathology is desirable. Blashfield and Draguns (1976) and Mayr (1981) discussed the most commonly accepted functions classification can and should serve. The ability of a proposed nosology to fit these objectives is one way in which its utility can in principle be determined (Mayr, 1981).

Among the most widely acknowledged and important virtues of a classification system is its facilitation of information storage and retrieval (Blashfield & Draguns, 1976; Mayr, 1981). Knowledge is organized around diagnostic rubrics, allowing clinicians easy access to information about probabilistic relationships between diagnoses, symptom presentations, treatment options, course, and outcomes. A nosology of psychopathology, for instance, must distinguish between the symptoms associated with major depressive disorder and those of uncomplicated bereave-

ment, although both have depressed mood as one of their defining features. The ability to make these types of distinctions is crucial for both clinicians and researchers.

Perhaps a more important function of classification, related to information retrieval, is the establishment of categories about which generalizations can be made (Blashfield & Draguns, 1976; Mayr, 1981). In the early stages of disease identification, for instance, groups of patients possessing certain common characteristics may be described. These patients are said to have symptoms that fit into a particular diagnostic category. If a patient presents for treatment and has symptoms that also tend to fit this same diagnostic definition, the clinician, on the basis of information gleaned through the study of similar patients, can predict other signs and symptoms such an individual will typically manifest. Such antecedent information, when combined with clinical evaluation, provides a means for either corroborating or refuting a hypothesized diagnosis. If the diagnosis is corroborated, the clinician will be able to make predictions (though perhaps not strong ones) about the course of illness and treatment response.

Accumulation of scientific knowledge and research progress may be greatly facilitated by an appropriate classification system. For example, it may be difficult, if not impossible, to investigate the etiology of a particular disorder without a method for identifying study participants. When investigators are uncertain about the types of patients studied across laboratories, failures to replicate can be expected, making it difficult to advance our knowledge of psychopathology.

NOSOLOGICAL NOMENCLATURE

Before beginning a more detailed discussion of the issues involved, it is important to present a nomenclature appropriate for our task. *Nosology* is the branch of science that deals with the classification of disease(s), with *classification* including both the process and the act of sorting entities, and *taxonomy* referring to the science of classification generally. *Diagnosis* is the act of identifying a disease from its signs (observable indicators of disease, separate from a patient's impressions) and symptoms (perceptible to the patient and known to the interviewer through patient report). The diagnostic enterprise is usually considered to have at least three possible goals: (1) reaching a decision about where to place a particular observation within an existing classification scheme; (2) analyzing the nature and/or cause(s) of a particular condition; and (3) providing a precise technical description of a taxon. Although it is difficult to provide a definition of *taxon,* in psychopathology it can be thought of as an entity, syndrome, disease, or nonarbitrary class (Meehl & Golden, 1982). Later on we will discuss more fully the difference between taxonic (i.e., categorical) and nontaxonic (i.e., dimensional) structures of psychopathological syndromes (complexes of symptoms).

Description of a classification of diseases naturally raises two related questions: "What constitutes a disease?" and "What is the disease entity or 'medical' model?" For the purposes of psychopathological inquiry, given our present state of knowledge, we can consider a *disease* to be an abstract (open) concept (Pap, 1953) that is the outgrowth of clinical observations and around which we organize scientific inquiry. Because of difficulties inherent in providing nonarbitrary definitions of disease, it becomes nearly impossible to define precisely what is meant by the *disease entity* or *medical model* (but see, for instance, Kendell, 1975a; Kraupl Taylor, 1979, 1980; and Meehl, 1977). Nevertheless, medical science has been able to identify some widely recognized diseases, frequently despite symptom heterogeneity, absence of pathognomonic signs, and uncertainty about etiology.

Medical investigators have frequently begun with only vague notions about the nature of a disease (not unlike much of our current understanding of psychopathology). Through careful research, many crude symptom clusters have been refined to provide highly accurate, in some cases exact, definitions or redefinitions of a disease. Such advances have been made both for "genetically simple" disorders like cystic fibrosis, Duchenne muscular dystrophy, and neurofibromatosis, and for "genetically complex" disorders like aganglionic megacolon, Alzheimer's disease, and diabetes mellitus (see Kaufmann, Johnson, & Pardes, 1996, for a discussion and review). This process is essentially the "bootstraps" approach described by Cronbach and Meehl (1955), which is described more fully later in this chapter.[2]

Frequently, discussions about classification issues

in psychopathology revolve around how to define necessarily ambiguous terms like *disease* or *illness,* a tendency that may have limited scientific merit (Meehl, 1972). It is often forgotten (perhaps never recognized) that the meanings of *disease* demonstrate historical change (Faber, 1930). Technological advancements leading to a more sophisticated knowledge base, refinements in our understanding of etiological mechanisms, and even political and social climate will all affect such definitions (see Gould, 1981, for an insightful presentation of how the political and social *Zeitgeist* can influence scientific thinking). Reviewing how some historically significant medical clinicians and scientists have conceptualized nosological issues might provide a valuable background against which to place current classification efforts in psychopathology.

A BRIEF HISTORY OF MEDICAL CLASSIFICATION

A prominent early contributor to medical classification[3] was Thomas Sydenham (1624–1689; see Dewurst, 1966). He believed that the clinician, rather than building "theoretical castles in the sky," should carefully observe patients, record the symptoms that characterized their pathological phenomena (as Hippocrates had recommended), and meticulously follow the course of their illnesses. Clusters of peculiar disease characteristics were hypothesized to result from a specific cause. Pathological changes in organs should be studied (postmortem) and the findings compared with symptom manifestations during life in an effort to refine both symptomatic and anatomical definitions of disease. Sydenham's great descriptive contributions included the classic account of hysteria's psychic manifestations, and its differentiation from chorea minor (also known as Sydenham's chorea or St. Vitus' dance).

For some time, Sydenham's method of clinical medicine maintained its ascendancy, although the focus gradually shifted after his death. When Rene-Theophile-Hyacinth Laennec (1787–1826) invented the stethoscope in 1819, physicians began to *examine* as well as to *observe* patients. With this technological advancement came two important changes: (1) Objective criteria for pathological phenomena and their statistical investigation were demanded, and (2) subjective symptoms became of secondary importance. This was the beginning of a call for the addition of functional (determining the deviation from normal operation of a particular organ system) to structural diagnosis (locating and describing a lesion).

François-Joseph-Victor Broussais (1772–1838) was one who attached more significance to disturbances of function associated with diseased organs than to their anatomical alterations. Broussais argued that there were no symptom clusters that could adequately capture a disease. The symptomatic description of disease Broussais considered to be "ontology" (an epithet of that time, much as "medical model" is today); instead, he believed, it was necessary to study a patient's physiological condition before a disease could be described and understood.

In the mid-19th century, great advances were made in histology, anatomy, physiology, and chemistry. The dramatic turn from Sydenham's descriptive method (a turn clearly evident in the writings of Broussais) received greater impetus from these advancements and found a home in Germany with Rudolf Virchow (1821–1902), the father of cellular pathology. Virchow and his followers eschewed observation for laboratory study. Clinical medicine was redefined as the experimental physiological study of morbid processes. Although great advances were made by German medical researchers of this period, the rejection of clinical observation led to obfuscation concerning certain diseases (e.g., Virchow's splitting of tuberculosis into subentities, despite Laennec's demonstration of this disease's unity some years before) and to a regression in the accurate description and identification of new disease entities (clinical observation was somewhat of a lost art among many of Virchow's followers). With no regard for clinical syndromes, laboratory researchers, working in isolation, lost touch with the phenomenology of disease and did not have a framework within which to place their findings.

Fortunately for clinical medicine, Armand Trousseau (1801–1867) was convincingly and skillfully advocating a more comprehensive approach. He embraced Sydenham's observational method while advocating accurate physiological characterization of pathological phenomena. Like Sydenham, he believed that diseases have taxonic properties: "That

which gives specific diseases their immutable properties is not the quantity but the quality of the morbific cause" (as cited in Faber, 1930, p. 92).

A new series of technological advancements in the mid- to late 19th century, and the recognition of their applicability to patient evaluation, facilitated another important revolution in conceptualizations of disease. Stomach pumps, "stress" tests, and blood pressure examinations, for instance, resulted in vigorous attempts to classify disease according to the nature of the functional disturbance. Through laborious and careful study, several irregularities of the heart, stomach, lungs, and other organ systems were able to be described, in combination with their symptoms and course, as independent "functional diseases" (those defined by alterations in the normal functioning of an organ system).

The most recent advances in the general understanding of disease entities grew out of genetics. Gregor Johann Mendel (1822–1884), isolated from the rest of the scientific community, conducted experiments in an Austrian monastery garden and laid the groundwork for the science of genetics. With the recognition of Mendel's work by the scientific community at the turn of the 20th century, and the realization that his work was applicable to human conditions (see, e.g., Garrod, 1902), constitution became an important consideration for disease classification. When Watson and Crick (1953a, 1953b) described the genetic material, they provided the foundation for a powerful tool that could yield exact definition of certain genetic disorders.

It did not take researchers and clinicians long to recognize, however, that all genetic disorders were not created equal. Whereas some conditions are certain to develop if an individual possessed the necessary (hypothesized) genetic material (e.g., Huntington's disease), other conditions may not develop even if the necessary genetic material is present. For example, a child with the necessary genotype may or may not develop the characteristic phenylketonureic (PKU) phenotypic manifestations depending on the child's phenylalanine intake (see Meehl, 1972, pp. 188–189). "Genes do not simply cause disease; they confer susceptibility" (Kaufmann et al., 1996, p. 12).

It also became clear that some psychiatric disorders, particularly bipolar disorder and schizophrenia, are at least partially genetically determined, although the relationship between genetic predisposition and phenotype is obviously not simple. For schizophrenia, persons almost certainly possessing the necessary genotype (the monozygotic twins of a proband with schizophrenia) only develop the disorder about half the time (Gottesman, Shields, & Hanson, 1982). Some researchers considered the existence of discordant monozygotic twin pairs to indicate that environmental factors may be largely or wholly responsible for schizophrenia susceptibility in some cases. A study by Gottesman and Bertelsen (1989), however, demonstrated that absence of the schizophrenia phenotype was still consistent with being a gene carrier for this illness. They followed up the offspring of monozygotic twin pairs who were discordant for schizophrenia. The morbid risks for schizophrenia among the offspring of both the clinically affected and unaffected monozygotic twins were similar (about 17%) and substantially higher than the population base rate. It is also known that the giant neurons of adult identical twin sea slugs do not have identical dendritic branches (although early in development they are highly similar), demonstrating that factors other than the genetic program influence neurodevelopment (Changeux, 1983). These facts suggest that the concept of *diathesis* (that a person may possess a predisposition for illness without ever manifesting the clinical symptoms, and may even transmit this predisposition to his or her offspring) deserves consideration for the classification, description, and understanding of certain diseases.

To summarize, several themes run through the history of medicine. First, clinical observation and the recognition of symptom clusters have usually been of primary importance. Our current classifications of psychopathology are at this stage (except for cognitive disorders and mental retardation, where laboratory data and test score results are used). When clinical description has not been considered important, investigation and discovery of new disease entities have usually suffered. Second, the usefulness of functional diagnosis increases with technical advances. Eventually, this should also occur with psychopathology (on a related topic, see Hempel, 1965), especially for more severe disorders such as schizophrenia. Use of laboratory measures to assist with schizophrenia diagnosis was considered for DSM-IV, but the work group decided that none of the available alternatives had as yet demonstrated sufficient sensitivity and specificity (Szymanski, Kane, & Lieberman, 1994). Further advances in medical genetics, brain imaging, neuropharmacology, psychometrics, behavior genetics, and psychophysiology, however, may change this conclusion in the near future (see, e.g., Iacono, 1991; McDowell & Clementz, 1997). Third, the meaning and definition of *disease* have not required the pinpointing of pathophysiology. Rather, this meaning has differed both across time and across medical subspecialties. Diseases have variously been defined according to symptom picture, anatomical involvement, function, and even patient strengths and weaknesses.

APPROACHES TO CLASSIFYING PSYCHOPATHOLOGY

As with medicine, different schemes have been advocated as being most appropriate for the description and classification of psychopathology. Among the most commonly discussed strategies are categorical versus dimensional models, prototype classification, and monothetic versus polythetic symptom clusters. Another important, though less frequently discussed, strategy considers the classification of psychopathology to be a construct validation enterprise. We now discuss each of these strategies in turn.

Categorical and Dimensional Schemes

Dimensional classification schemes assume that there are no dichotomies, types, classes, or taxa. Symptoms are considered to reflect quantitative deviations from normal functioning along particular dimensions (e.g., anxiety, introversion, affective stability). Proponents of such an approach for psychopathology believe that mental disorders are currently defined through the implementation of arbitrary cutting scores. They suggest that patients could be more accurately described by evaluating their relative standing on some number of fundamental dimensions. The number of such factors necessary to describe psychopathological phenomena adequately, however, is at present unclear (Clark, Watson, & Reynolds, 1995; Widiger, Frances, Spitzer, & Williams, 1988).

The typical numerical procedures used by dimensional proponents, such as exploratory factor analysis, are correlational in nature (see Blashfield, 1984, for a discussion of this issue). Consider, for instance, the data depicted in Figure 1-1. These are real data obtained from Fisher (1936). They depict the relationship between sepal (the green, leafy part of a flower) length and petal length for two iris species (*versicolor* and *virginica*).[4] The linear regression demonstrated a strong relationship between these two variables, $R^2 = .69$, $p < .001$ on 98 *df*, perhaps suggesting (falsely, as will be shown) that a dimensional rather than a class or dichotomy model best describes these data.

Categorical or taxonic systems, on the other hand, involve the assignment of patients to classes based on the presence of signs and symptoms thought to characterize a particular disease entity. Signs and symptoms of a disorder are interrelated by virtue of their relationship to an underlying (latent) class. Categorical proponents (like Sydenham and Kraepelin, for instance) assume that disorders differ qualitatively both from one another and from normality, although they may show quantitative deviations as well.

There are various numerical methods appropriate to the task of determining taxonicity (i.e., whether a categorical model most accurately describes the data). A set of methods frequently used to solve tax-

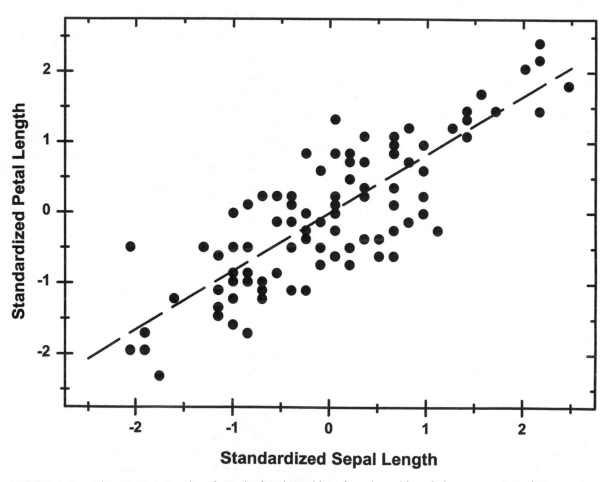

FIGURE 1-1. A bivariate scatterplot of standardized sepal length and petal length for two species of iris, *versicolor* and *virginica* (data from Fisher, 1936). The least-squares regression line is also provided.

onomic problems falls under the general heading of "cluster analysis" (see Sneath & Sokol, 1973). According to Blashfield (1984), "Cluster analysis is best characterized as a loosely organized collection of quasi-statistical procedures that are used to create classificatory systems" (p. 217). Despite the wide applicability of these methods, they also pose numerous problems. First, different clustering methods frequently yield different results for the same data set (a few methods that Monte Carlo trials indicate may be more accurate than others, however, do tend to agree most of the time). Second, some commonly used clustering methods seem to be incapable of accurately solving rather simple taxonomic problems (see, for example, Meehl & Golden, 1982). Third, regardless of whether taxa are in fact present, most clustering methods will generate clusters (Grove, 1990), leaving it for the investigator to determine whether a "true" taxon has been identified (see Blashfield, 1984, and Meehl & Golden, 1982, for more complete presentations of the difficulties with cluster analytic methods).

A novel collection of taxometric methods has been developed by Meehl and colleagues (Golden & Meehl, 1979; Grove & Meehl, 1993; Meehl, 1973, 1995; Meehl & Golden, 1982; Meehl & Yonce, 1994, 1996; see also Meehl, 1996, and Miller, 1996). These methods are appropriate for the detection of a taxon and complement (i.e., nontaxon) class using single indicators, multiple continuously distributed indicators, or multiple dichotomous indicators. They provide accurate estimates of taxon base rate, latent class means, and valid and false-positive rates. These methods do not require a "gold standard" (e.g., a priori knowledge from which group an observation comes) against which to compare the outcome (latent classes are empirically determined through implementation of the procedures, which can then be tested in subsequent studies). Furthermore, they include the use of methods for determining whether a putative taxon is in certain senses spurious (called "consistency tests" by Meehl). The method presented by Grove and Meehl (1993), based on regression procedures with pairs of variables, provides an intuitively and statistically simple approach to the problem of determining whether taxa may be present.

Suppose an experimenter is working with a reasonably well defined criterion group (i.e., it is at least somewhat certain what observations belong to the taxon and complement classes). In this case, discriminant function analysis (Fisher, 1936) might be used to: (1) determine whether two or more variables are helpful for differentiating between classes; and (2) develop a prediction equation suitable for classifying unknown observations into the proper category. Consider our iris species. Both sepal length (*versicolor* mean = −0.49, SD = .78; *virginica* mean = 0.49, SD = .96) and petal length (*versicolor* mean = −0.78, SD = .57; *virginica* mean = 0.78, SD = .67) significantly differentiated between the two species, t's (98) > 5.63, p's < .001. It seemed possible, therefore, that these two variables could help classify plants into one or the other taxa. The data from Figure 1-1 were replotted by including species identifying information (see Figure 1-2). Using a variant of Fisher's (1936) technique, both sepal length (partial R^2 = .21) and petal length (partial R^2 = .60) contributed significantly to the group separation in a stepwise discriminant analysis; the resulting prediction equation correctly classified 94% of the *versicolor* and 94% of the *virginica* cases.

Kendell (1982) has advocated the search for multimodal distributions (see Murphy, 1964). Methods are available for statistically determining whether admixture (more than one distribution characterizes the data better than a single distribution alone) is present when using either single (MacLean, Morton, Elston, & Yee, 1976) or multiple (Titterington, Smith, & Makov, 1985) continuously distributed variables. For instance, forming a linear combination of sepal and petal length that maximally differentiated the two groups produced a new variable, whose distribution is presented in Figure 1-3. The distribution for the linear combination of sepal length and petal length was analyzed using MacLean et al.'s (1976) technique and found to be best characterized by a mixture of two normal distributions, X^2 (2) = 11.1, p < .05. This was true despite the fact that neither sepal length nor petal length demonstrated evidence for mixture (see Figure 1-3, bottom two panels).

The discriminant function and bimodality results support the categorical hypothesis for these data. If one also looks at the "centroids" for the iris species in Figure 1-2 (defined as the intersection of the sepal length and petal length means for the two groups separately), and at the ellipsoids (depicting the group

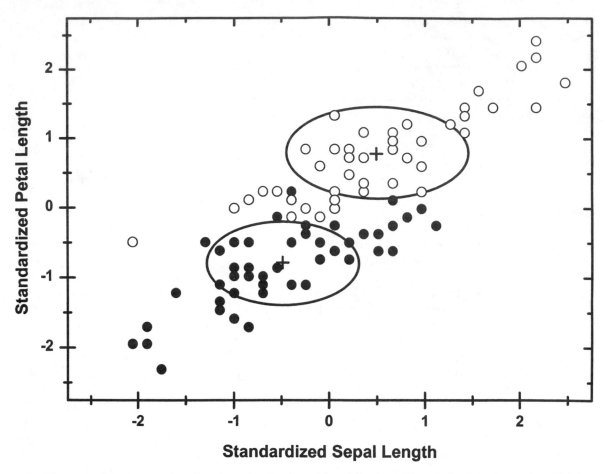

FIGURE 1-2. A bivariate scatter plot of standardized sepal length and petal length for the two species of iris in Figure 1-1, except that the data points have been described by a third variable, species class membership. Filled circles indicate *I. versicolor* (*N* = 50) and hollow circles indicate *I. virginica* (*N* = 50). The centroids (the intersection point of the sepal length and petal length means for the two groups, designated by a "+") and variability around the means (±1 SD, depicted by ellipses) are also provided. This plot shows an example of a taxonic (categorical) situation. We can also see how one observation (the left-most *virginica* case) was probably initially misclassified.

variability, one standard deviation, around those centroids), there appear to be two clearly distinct categories. Nevertheless, the regression results might lead some researchers to conclude that a dimensional scheme most accurately describes the relationship between these two variables. Which model is correct?

In this case, despite the strong correlation observed between sepal length and petal length, the subsequent analyses suggest that a categorical scheme is more accurate (i.e., these are distinct, nonarbitrary classes). This example illustrates the potential danger

of using correlational procedures alone to address such issues (see also Grove & Tellegen, 1991). Manifest correlations (even large ones) and the generation of factors cannot argue for the absence of categories. If, however, discontinuities are not observed in quantitative variable distributions (e.g., there is no multimodality), then the argument that psychopathological disorders are based on arbitrary categorization may have some merit. In fact, demonstration of multimodal distributions for variables related to mental illnesses is rare (but see Clementz, Grove, Iacono, &

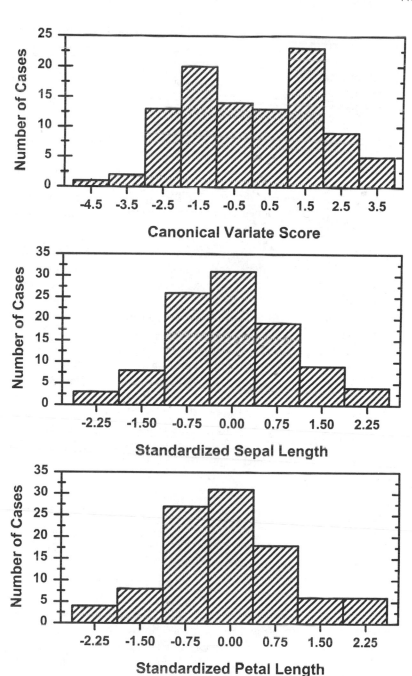

FIGURE 1-3   The distribution of the canonical variate scores (linear combination of sepal length and petal length that maximally discriminated between *I. versicolor* and *I. virginica;* top panel), sepal length (middle panel), and petal length (bottom panel). The canonical variate score was best characterized by a mixture of two nonskewed normal distributions, with modes of –1.5 and 1.5. Sepal length and petal length were best characterized as single, nonskewed normal distributions.

Sweeney, 1992; Iacono & Clementz, 1993; Iacono, Moreau, Beiser, Fleming, & Lin, 1992). Perhaps this reflects the absence of true psychopathology categories, but maybe we have yet to conduct the right kinds of research with informative variables. For instance, the use of either sepal length or petal length alone might lead us to conclude that *I. versicolor* and *I. virginica* were on the same dimensional continuum, a conclusion that would obviously be at odds with considerable additional information.

Prototype Classification

The prototype conception of psychiatric diagnosis (Cantor, Smith, French, & Mezzich, 1980) bears some similarity to taxonic systems. In both approaches, patients are assigned to classes on the basis of overall fit using fallible indicators (rather than on "perfect" inclusion–exclusion rules). In the prototype approach, assignments are made based on the similarity of a patient to the "most typical" patient of a particular class (depicted, for example, as the centroids in Figure 1-2). A more general categorical system, however, assumes that all patients are equally typical of a particular class. The task is the assignment of patients to the correct (nonarbitrary) class rather than assignment specifically based on determining similarity to a class's most "typical" patient. Furthermore, studies of prototype classification typically focus on how patients are assigned to classes (e.g., on how diagnosticians classify) rather than on the construct validity of the classes themselves. Although such studies may illuminate the cognitive activity of diagnosticians, it remains to be established that they can help determine the verisimilitude of hypothesized disease entities (Grove & Tellegen, 1991).

Monothetic versus Polythetic Systems

Different inclusion and exclusion rules have been used for determining when a patient meets the criteria for a particular diagnosis. One method is to require patients to meet a group of jointly necessary and sufficient characteristics, which are called monothetic criteria sets (what Cantor et al., 1980, called *classic* categorical diagnosis). In DSM-III, for instance, a number of personality disorder diagnoses (schizoid, avoidant, and dependent) required all the defining items to be present. Such diagnostic criteria were considered to be excessively restrictive and were eliminated from the DSM-III-R personality disorder section (Widiger et al., 1988), although this approach was preserved for certain disorders (e.g., specific phobia, conversion disorder). Polythetic criteria, on the other hand, specify a number of defining features, with only some potentially being necessary but none being sufficient for making a diagnosis. Such diagnostic criteria are more compatible with the way disorders present themselves. Of note, prototype

classification is necessarily polythetic, but polythetic criteria are not necessarily prototypic. Although it is frequently believed that "true" categorical diagnoses should fit monothetic systems, Meehl and Golden (1982) have pointed out that this is not a logical necessity:

> In the history of medicine it has been repeatedly found upon thorough comprehension of a disease—in all of its important aspects, including its pathology and specific etiology . . . that *there are very few symptoms that are absolutely two-way pathognomonic* [i.e., serving as perfect inclusion and exclusion tests]. (p. 133, emphasis in the original)

Pleiotropy (i.e., one gene, many different manifestations) and variable expressivity (i.e., the same causative agent leading to an effect that varies in degree in different individuals) are commonplaces of nature. Given these well-documented phenomena, it would be surprising to find many symptoms that are two-way pathognomonic even for disorders caused by a single gene. For instance, neurofibromatosis, an autosomal dominant disorder, is sometimes manifest as the full-blown syndrome with systemic involvement and many skin tumors, whereas other cases, even within the same family, manifest only a few, barely noticeable café-au-lait spots, such as freckles confined to the axillae (Vogel & Motulsky, 1986).

Construct Validation Approach

In the absence of preestablished criteria for unambiguously defining particular disorders, researchers may focus on construct validation (Cronbach & Meehl, 1955) to evaluate the utility of diagnostic definitions. This approach is based on testing a postulated system of laws (often involving latent entities) that hypothetically account for the observable phenomena. Suppose, for instance, based on our theoretical understanding of some vague diagnostic category (the construct), we hypothesize that individuals with disorder X will show a poor premorbid adjustment, be academic underachievers, demonstrate a chronic course, and have a necessary but not sufficient genotype. If individuals whom we believe have disorder X manifest these attributes, then we have begun to demonstrate the validity of the construct while also identifying a set of characteristics useful for diagnosing the disorder. If our subjects possess none of these characteristics or only some of them (e.g., the symptoms but not the genotype), this might lead us either to modify our hypothesis (including our conceptualization of the construct) or to doubt the validity of the construct.

The construct validation approach to psychopathology research is central to our ability to refine diagnoses via the "bootstraps effect" (Cronbach & Meehl, 1955). The basic notion here is that one can begin with poor, low-reliability diagnoses (e.g., unskilled clinical examiner ratings) and still develop techniques (e.g., psychometric scales, psychophysiological measures, biochemical tests) that yield more accurate diagnostic definitions than the criteria against which the techniques were developed. Dawes and Meehl (1966) have formally demonstrated how this phenomenon can in principle be utilized and tested in research settings.

Blashfield and Livesley (1991) suggested that "The construct validity of psychiatric classifications has been discussed only rarely, and little research directly related to construct validity has been performed" (p. 267). It is certainly true that the term *construct validity* is rarely uttered by psychiatric researchers, but it is false that there is little research investigating the construct validity of psychiatric diagnoses. We would suggest that there are thousands of such studies in the literature! Every time a researcher attempts to determine if patients with disorder X differ either symptomatically or on some laboratory measure from patients with disorder Y, they are addressing the construct validity of those diagnoses. In fact, a widely cited approach to construct validation of psychopathological classifications was presented by Robins and Guze (1970) over 25 years ago. Robins and Guze advocated investigating the validity of diagnostic categories in five areas: (1) clinical description (as Sydenham had advocated); (2) laboratory investigations (the outcomes of which could then be used to refine clinical-descriptive diagnosis); (3) differentiation from other disorders (discriminant validity); (4) follow-up studies (postulating that patients with a disorder should have similar outcomes and that, if not, perhaps the current definition identifies a heterogeneous patient population); and (5) family studies (if a disorder runs in families, there is more evidence that a meaningful

entity has been identified). Today, with better technology, laboratory investigations may include psychophysiology, neurochemistry, brain imaging, and pharmacological challenge. Family studies may include not only epidemiology but also sophisticated quantitative and molecular genetic research (segregation analysis, linkage studies, and molecular genetic investigations), the latter of which might also investigate gene–environment interaction.

Adopting a construct validation approach to solving classification problems in psychopathology has precedent in the history of medicine. As was previously discussed, however, the ability to perform the requisite studies may depend on the availability of appropriate technology. The remaining chapters will discuss how psychopathologists have applied their tools (including some exciting new technologies) to the understanding of various disorders. To provide a framework for understanding where many contemporary researchers begin their work, we now present some of the more commonly used systems for classifying psychopathology.

CLASSIFICATION OF PSYCHOPATHOLOGY

Nineteenth-Century Pioneers

Compared to the pace and quality of nosological developments in clinical medicine, psychopathological classification has proceeded more slowly and with less satisfying results (see Wallace, 1994, for a comprehensive review of the history of psychiatric classification). The first serious attempts to classify abnormal behavior were not initiated until the late 1800s. Of the many individuals who have worked in this area, perhaps only three figures, Emil Kraepelin (1856–1927), Sigmund Freud (1856–1939), and Adolph Meyer (1866–1950), can be said to have uniquely and substantially influenced present Western psychopathological nosologies (see Blashfield, 1984; Garrison, 1929; and Gay, 1988, for more complete reviews of their work). We discuss their individual contributions in turn.

Kraepelin has properly been called the pioneer of experimental psychiatry. Like Sydenham, whose observational method he embraced, Kraepelin considered psychopathologies attributable to underlying disease states. He also called for the scientific investigation of mental disorders and was optimistic that studies like Diefendorf and Dodge's (1908) investigation of dementia praecox patients' ocular-motor functioning might provide such a foundation (see Kraepelin, 1919/1971, p. 6; and Iacono, 1991, 1998, who reviewed how ocular-motor functioning in schizophrenia may yet serve such a hoped-for purpose). Besides being psychopathology's greatest systematizer, Kraepelin also coalesced various disorders that were previously considered to be distinct entities under the dementia praecox rubric (later renamed "schizophrenia" by Eugen Bleuler).

After abandoning the trauma theory of neurosis, Freud took a very different approach than Kraepelin to classifying mental disorders. Like contemporary German laboratory medicine researchers, Freud placed little emphasis on phenomenology (with some exceptions, such as the obsessive-compulsive triad). He considered an understanding of the latent (psychodynamic) meaning of a patient's manifest symptoms to be essential for accurate classification. A patient's diagnosis, therefore, rather than being based on phenomenology, may be determined only after a thorough psychoanalytic investigation of a patient's unconscious conflicts and utilized defense mechanisms.

The psychoanalytic framework has had considerable influence on past and current classifications of psychopathology. In DSM-II (APA, 1968), for example, there was a separate section for classifying the neuroses. The assessment of these disorders could be based on either symptom presentation or inferred unconscious mechanisms. Although the term *neurosis* was eliminated from modern psychiatric classification with the publication of DSM-III, many disorders with roots in psychoanalysis remained, and continue to be present in DSM-IV (e.g., obsessive-compulsive disorder; conversion disorder; and histrionic, borderline, narcissistic, and obsessive-compulsive personality disorders). In fact, there would appear to be an even greater emphasis on psychoanalytic concepts in DSM-IV, where habitual use of maladaptive defense mechanisms may be indicated on Axis II and a "Defensive Functioning Scale" (pp. 751–757) is included as a "Proposed Axis for Further Study." It is suggested that clinicians list *up to 7* specific defense mechanisms when describing a patient's current functioning (from a list of 27 provided with the scale,

including such classic psychoanalytic defenses as displacement, projection, projective identification, reaction formation, repression, splitting, and sublimation). It would appear that psychoanalytic theory is still considered to be of potential value in psychiatric classification, especially considering that the Defensive Functioning Scale occupies as many pages in the DSM-IV as the description and discussion of depressive episode and manic episode.

Meyer was responsible for popularizing Kraepelin in the United States, although he clearly did not hold Kraepelin's views about disease. Meyer considered psychopathological disorders to be psychobiological reactions to life events. As Broussais did in clinical medicine, he rejected the notion that psychopathologies were disease entities with established courses, although he did seem to believe that they could be characterized by peculiar signs and symptoms. Such anomalies were considered situational disturbances resulting from unsuccessful efforts at adaptation. The history of medicine suggests that Kraepelin might have a more accurate conceptualization of psychopathology than Meyer, although only future research can tell.

Modern Nosologies

Although the first serious attempts to classify abnormal behavior were initiated in the late 1800s, it was not until the mid-20th century that classification systems for mental disorders began to be widely accepted (Kendell, 1975b). Two organizations, the American Psychiatric Association (APA) and the World Health Organization (WHO), have played a major role in the development of present-day diagnostic systems. The WHO classification system evolved through the publication and revision of the International Classification of Diseases (ICD) manuals (WHO, 1948, 1969, 1977, 1992). Mental disorders were added to the ICD system in 1939, and the list of such disorders was expanded and refined with the publication of the sixth edition of the ICD (ICD-6) in 1948 (along with the official formation of the WHO).

Adopted by only a handful of countries, ICD-6 was viewed as somewhat primitive (e.g., personality disorders were not included), a factor that ultimately led the APA to develop its *Diagnostic and Statistical Manual of Mental Disorders* (DSM-I) in 1952. A conscious effort was made to bring these two alternative diagnostic systems into agreement with the "joint" publication of ICD-8 (first introduced in 1966 and formally adopted by the WHO in 1969) and the second edition of the DSM, DSM-II, published in 1968. These two classification schemes diverged again in the late 1970s. ICD-9, published in 1977, was similar to ICD-8 and DSM-II. But DSM-III, released in 1980, represented a radical departure from previous APA and WHO classification efforts. DSM-I, DSM-II, and the ICDs were essentially listings of categories; specific behaviors, symptoms, and signs that might be useful for classification were seldom included. By contrast, DSM-III attempted to provide explicit definitions of disorders, requiring specific types and numbers of symptoms to be present (and often specifying their intensity and duration) before a diagnosis could be made.

The Need for Change: Some Background to the Development of DSM-III

Prior to DSM-III, it had been evident for some time that there were serious problems with both the ICD and DSM classification schemes. For instance, epidemiological research comparing rates of specific forms of psychopathology across countries often revealed large discrepancies even among culturally similar countries (Saugstad, 1985). Such puzzling findings are best understood as due to national differences in how the vague characterizations of psychopathology found in the manuals were interpreted rather than as due to regional variations in prevalence of those affected (Cooper, Kendell, Gurland, Sharpe, Copeland, & Simon, 1972; Sartorius et al., 1986).

An example of an often-cited study used to argue the need for a different diagnostic approach was that of Beck, Ward, Mendelson, Mock, and Erlbaugh (1962). These investigators examined the diagnostic reliability of experienced clinician pairs who had just interviewed the same patients. On average, the clinicians assigned different diagnoses to the patients 46% of the time. Three sources of error were analyzed for their contribution to the diagnostic unreliability observed in this study (Ward, Beck, Mendelson, Mock, & Erlbaugh, 1962). First, variability in the information presented by the patient from one interview to the next accounted for 5% of the disagreement. Second, inconsistencies in diagnostic practices, such as

using different interview techniques and asking different questions, accounted for 32.5% of the disagreement. Third, although the clinicians had met before the study began to review the diagnostic manual and how it would be applied, the greatest source of unreliability, accounting for 62.5% of the disagreement, was attributable to the inadequacies of the diagnostic system (DSM-I). Despite the methodological limitations of such studies, their pessimistic conclusions were largely accepted and exerted a strong influence on subsequent thinking about nosology (Blashfield, 1984). They helped provide the impetus for the development of structured psychiatric interviews and specific diagnostic criteria.

The first influential attempt to provide explicit diagnostic criteria for major forms of psychopathology was made by Feighner, Robins, Guze, Woodruff, Winokur, and Munoz (1972). These authors proposed descriptive criteria for 17 adult psychiatric categories, the validity of which was supported by "precise clinical description, follow-up, and family studies" (p. 57). Definitions for the many other diagnoses listed in DSM-II were not presented "because sufficient clinical criteria for even limited diagnostic validation" (p. 62) were not available. The criteria were proposed as tentative, subject to modification after the collection of new data. The Feighner et al. (1972) criteria were intended for research as well as clinical practice; however, the criteria for various disorders were extremely restrictive, leaving large numbers of individuals undiagnosed (see, e.g., Iacono & Beiser, 1989). As a result, the Feighner system had limited utility for clinical practice.

The Feighner et al. (1972) paper served as a model for the next influential descriptive diagnostic system, the Research Diagnostic Criteria (RDC) of Spitzer, Endicott, and Robins (1975). The RDC is primarily a system for classifying schizophrenia and affective disorders, although criteria for 11 other categories, including some not found in DSM-II (e.g., panic disorder and somatization disorder) were also included. The link between RDC and DSM-III is evident in several respects. The senior author of the RDC, Robert Spitzer, was also the task force chair for DSM-III (and DSM-III-R). In addition, the diagnostic criteria and new disorders introduced in the RDC were incorporated, mostly in only slightly modified form, into DSM-III.

DSM-III and DSM-III-R

In an effort to improve the reliability of psychiatric diagnosis, DSM-III and DSM-III-R provided explicit criteria for over 250 different categories (more than twice the number of DSM-II diagnoses). As others (Feighner et al., 1972; Goodwin & Guze, 1996) have intimated, however, there was then and there remains today little research to justify listing so many disorders. Most of the criteria used to define disorders were thus a product of the somewhat arbitrary but not wholly uninformed decisions by DSM-III and DSM-III-R advisory committee and task force members. This approach to the construction of DSM-III brought controversy to the manual because many clinicians and researchers (justifiably) questioned the validity of various disorders and the criteria used to characterize them.

With respect to these concerns, the new DSM diagnostic definitions, including those of DSM-IV, should be considered as provisional (Frances et al., 1991), tentative starting points in a construct validation enterprise. In this context, DSM-III represented a proposal to enhance reliability while providing a framework within which to investigate empirically, modify, and validate criteria sets and decision rules. The publication of subsequent DSMs, in fact, partially affirmed the provisional nature of DSM-III diagnostic criteria.

Despite the need to update and refine DSM-III, however, the publication of revisions at 7-year intervals may reflect too rapid a change in our diagnostic categories (Zimmerman, 1988, 1990). With several hundred disorders to evaluate, we have neither the resources nor adequate time to investigate the utility of the existing nosology before it is replaced with a new one. With the introduction of DSM-IV, we have had four DSMs in less than 15 years. We may be faced with many patients whose psychopathology has not changed over time but whose diagnostic classification has, with unknown consequences for treatment and conceptual understanding of their disorders.

DSM-IV and ICD-10

To the extent that DSM-III represented an attempt to improve diagnostic reliability, it was hoped that DSM-IV would address issues related to diagnostic validity. Instead, the case for the revision of DSM-III-R, which was led by Allen Frances (Frances, Widiger, & Pincus, 1989; Frances, Pincus, Widiger, Davis, & First, 1990), was based largely on the need to bring the DSM in line with ICD-10 (WHO, 1992). The result, though a clear improvement over DSM-III-R, is another set of provisionally defined disorders, which, ironically, is not closely linked to ICD-10, and which, like its predecessors DSM-III and DSM-III-R, remains quite controversial among mental health professionals (e.g., Caplan, 1995; Clark et al., 1995; Kirk & Kutchins, 1992; Zimmerman, 1990) and the lay public (e.g., Rothman, 1997).

A review of the development of ICD-10 (Kendell, 1991; Thangavelu & Martin, 1995) suggests several reasons that DSM-IV did not achieve full compatibility with ICD-10. The revision of ICD-9 (WHO, 1977) began in 1983, at a time when the worldwide dominance of DSM-III was becoming evident. Early versions of the revision became available before DSM-III-R came out, and these draft versions served as the basis for ICD field trials (described in part in Regier, Kaelber, Roper, Rae, & Sartorius, 1994). As an international classification system, the ICD must attempt to please all of the 140 members of the World Health Organization, a requirement that necessarily complicates its production. The text and categories of ICD-10 were largely set in 1989, five years before DSM-IV was published. The result was a document that was somewhat more closely tied to DSM-III than to DSM-III-R, and one that was little influenced by the development of DSM-IV. Although DSM-IV was influenced by ICD-10, the logical requirement that it build on DSM-III-R, coupled with the fact that the process followed to develop DSM-IV was largely independent of that leading to the development of ICD-10, led to the development of two compatible but different systems (a review of the comparability of the two systems can be found in Thangavelu & Martin, 1995). It is noteworthy that although the U.S. is treaty bound to adopt ICD-10 for coding and reporting health statistics, it will not do so until at least 2000, in part because the alphanumeric system ICD-10 uses to assign diagnostic codes (all behavioral disorders have an "F" prefix) cannot be readily accommodated in the United States. Hence, DSM-IV continues to use ICD-9 numeric codes for reporting purposes.

For much of the time ICD-9 coexisted with DSM-

III and DSM-III-R, the DSM was the preferred diagnostic system, as indicated by the proportion of published research investigations using the DSM scheme and by surveys of the preferences of mental health professionals working outside of the United States (Helzer & Canino, 1992). Although it may be too soon to determine worldwide preference for DSM-IV vs. ICD-10, there is little evidence that ascendance of the DSM will not continue.

In addition to the emphasis on ICD-10 compatibility, development of DSM-IV followed several guidelines (Frances, Mack, First, & Jones, 1995). Changes to DSM-III-R diagnostic criteria were supposed to be made conservatively, based on empirical data. These data were obtained by reviewing the published literature (150 separate literature reviews were carried out), conducting field trials (12 in all) to evaluate diagnostic criteria, and reanalyzing existing data sets (about 50 total) in an effort to answer questions not addressed through the reviews and field trials. Although "advisory" committees responsible for the revision of classes of disorders, such as those used for DSM-III and DSM-III-R, were once again constituted, Frances et al. (1995) characterized these work groups as "expert panels" whose job it was to evaluate and weigh the information from the literature reviews, data reanalyses, and field trials. Despite emphasis on empirically based decision making, a variety of factors contributed to changes being made that were not grounded in empirical findings, including the quality and quantity of data available. As a member of a work group has commented, "there simply are not enough nosologically helpful studies to substantiate all parts of a classification system that has been built on haphazard clinical anecdotes and on observations made over many generations" (Shaffer, 1996, p. 326). Hence, many changes were made to the criteria that could not be supported by empirical documentation. These "numerous small changes were meant to improve the phrasing of the text and criteria sets, not to change the definitions and caseness" (Frances et al., 1995, p. 18).

Eventually, documentation for the decisions made by the work groups is to be published as part of a series of *DSM-IV Sourcebooks*. The first three of these (Widiger, Frances, Pincus, First, Ross, & Davis, 1994; Widiger, Frances, Pincus, Ross, First, & Davis, 1996, 1997) consist largely of chapters authored by work group members that discuss the pros and cons of changes to the diagnostic criteria for the various disorders, issues that were considered but not acted on, future research topics warranting attention, and the recommendations of the work group for modifying the DSM criteria. Future volumes will include the results of the literature reviews, field trials, and data reanalyses. Versions of many of the work group reports have also been archived in the peer-reviewed scientific literature (e.g., field trial summaries for substance use disorders, Cottler et al., 1995; and antisocial personality disorder, Widiger, Cadoret, Hare, Robins, Rutherford, Zanarini, Alterman, Apple, Corbitt, Forth, Hart, Kultermann, Woody, & Frances, 1996).

There are many ways in which DSM-IV differs from its predecessors, only a few of which are noted here. DSM-IV is substantially longer than DSM-III-R, but only a handful of new disorders have been added. Most of the increased length is attributable to the elaborated narrative text, reflecting the fruits of the work group's effort to integrate and evaluate research findings that accompany the criteria defining each disorder. New to DSM-IV are narrative sections for each disorder that describe "associated laboratory" or "physical" findings and "specific culture, age, and gender features." The laboratory and physical findings sections are welcome additions that summarize salient research findings that point to the construct validity of the disorders. The culture, age, and gender sections draw attention to some of the important individual difference factors affecting the expression of psychopathology that were lacking in prior DSMs. Cultural issues also receive substantial attention in Volume 3 of the *DSM-IV Sourcebook* (Widiger et al., 1997), where each major class of disorders is reviewed from a cultural perspective. Many of these brief chapters (7–8 pages is typical) would make useful supplements to courses in psychopathology that wish to beef up their coverage of this area. Also worthy of consideration for this purpose is Castillo's (1997) brief text, which reviews the literature relevant to culture as it pertains to each of the major classes of DSM-IV disorders.

Two other noteworthy changes in DSM-IV both deal with what constitutes a mental disorder. Almost all of the disorders require the presence of clinically significant distress or impaired social-occupational functioning to be diagnosable. This requirement thus has become critical to the DSM-IV definition of what constitutes "abnormality." It was introduced in part to offset concerns that investigations such as the Epidemiologic Catchment Area (ECA) (Robins & Regier, 1991) study were overestimating the prevalence of psychopathology in the absence of severity thresholds (Martin, 1995; Preskorn, 1995). This requirement creates the possibility that two individuals with identical symptoms could be classified differently, with only the one showing distress or impairment receiving a diagnosis. As Shaffer (1996) has noted, such an approach to diagnosis is without parallel in the rest of medicine.

The other change that affects the notion of mental disorder is tied to the introduction of the term *general medical condition* to DSM-IV. This innovation was designed to avoid the problems inherent in past DSMs, which drew distinctions between "organic" and nonorganic syndromes. By implication, if a disorder was not listed in the organic section of the manual, it was presumed to be functional in origin. Modern psychiatry rests comfortably with the notion that biological factors are important to the expression of most if not almost all psychopathologies, thus rendering the organic/functional distinction moot. Also, the use of the modifier *general* reinforces the notion that all the DSM diagnoses represent medical disorders appropriately thought of as "psychiatric" medical conditions (Martin, 1995).

When Will Validity Take Precedence over Reliability?

Reliability offers no guarantee of validity, which ultimately is the most important attribute of a diagnostic system. In their effort to achieve reliability, the authors of DSM-IV have continued to focus on behavioral criteria that can be objectively assessed. Consequently, validity of some disorders that could be well characterized by more subjective criteria may have been compromised.

Consider antisocial personality disorder (ASPD, an attempted objective definition of psychopathy) as a case in point. DSM-IV and DSM-III-R define this disorder by requiring the presence of conduct disorder prior to age 15 and evidence of repeated arrests, lying, physical fights, assaults, and failure to work consistently. Hare, building on Cleckley's (1976) as-

tute observations, defines *psychopathy* by emphasizing, in addition to behavioral criteria, a constellation of personality traits such as glibness, egocentricity, and lack of empathy (Harper, Hare, & Hakstian, 1989). The Cleckley-Hare criteria, though somewhat subjective and difficult to evaluate, are supported by a large body of research attesting to their construct validity (Hare & Schalling, 1978) and excellent interrater reliability (Hare, 1992). It is very telling that for the DSM-IV field trial, which compared Cleckley-Hare and DSM criteria, after showing both to be equivalent in reliability, Widiger et al. (1996) concluded that it was best to deemphasize the Cleckley-Hare traits in DSM-IV because there would be no "guarantee that such items as glib and superficial charm would be assessed as reliably in everyday clinical practice without the explicit guidelines provided by the semistructured interview" (p. 13) used in the field trial. Apparently driven by such reliability considerations, Widiger et al. (1996) did not consider whether the DSM criteria tap the most valid conceptualization of ASPD/psychopathy.

That they might not is indicated by data from field trial and other sources. The DSM-III-R/DSM-IV approach seems to overinclude criminals in the antisocial category to such an extent that most incarcerated felons may qualify for ASPD. For instance, 70% of prison inmates met DSM-III-R criteria for antisocial personality disorder in the DSM-IV field trial, while only 28% satisfied the Cleckley-Hare criteria. This left Widiger et al. (1996) to conclude that the DSM criteria "might not provide a useful differentiation within this [prison] setting" (p. 14). The DSM criteria entirely miss "successful" psychopaths who have managed to avoid contact with the legal system (e.g., Lykken, 1984). In addition, "late bloomers" who show adult antisocial behavior but no evidence of conduct disorder cannot receive this diagnosis. Recent research has shown that these late onset cases who show no evidence of adolescent conduct disorder differ little from those who meet full DSM criteria in self-reported personality traits (including emotional detachment—a core characteristic of psychopathy), comorbid substance dependence, and increased risk for conduct disorder in their offspring (Elkins, Iacono, Doyle, & McGue, 1997).

Although the DSM-IV and ICD-10 emphasis on reliability is commendable and historically justified, much of the controversy surrounding DSMs III–IV has been focused on the lack of attention to the validity of the diagnostic constructs. DSM-IV, with its (as yet unpublished) empirically based justifications for diagnostic criteria revision and its inclusion of narrative text describing laboratory findings associated with each disorder, has only scratched the surface of the need to give more heed to validity. We can only hope for more from DSM-V.

SUMMARY

In an insightful commentary on psychiatric classification, Preskorn (1995) conveyed the following personal experience:

> On surgical pathology, the morning began with review of the histopathological slides from the previous day's surgical cases to establish final diagnoses. . . . As the most junior member, I was called on first. Invariably, I would say: "Looks like inflammation to me." The senior resident would then say: "This section from the pancreas shows an adenocarcinoma blocking the main duct causing inflammation." The junior faculty pathologist would then say: "While it looks like an adenocarcinoma, it is actually a sarcoma." The senior faculty pathologist, who wrote the textbook on surgical pathology, would say, "While it looks like a sarcoma masquerading as an adenocarcinoma, it is actually the third case of histocytosis X. I reported the other two cases last week in *The Journal of Surgical Pathology*." After studying the next slide intently, I would say, "Looks like inflammation to me." (p. 54)

Vis-à-vis depth of understanding regarding psychiatric classification, we are certainly closer to Preskorn in his early days on surgical pathology than to the senior faculty pathologist. This field can and should aspire, however, to be more like the latter. As is true for psychology generally, the study of psychopathology is difficult and is perhaps a more intractable subject matter than, say, the study of astrophysics, genetics, or subatomic particles (see Lykken, 1991, for a scholarly discussion of this and related issues). On the one hand, perhaps Hawking (1993) was correct in suggesting that prediction of behavior is impossible given the complexity of the nervous system. On the other hand, just because physicists have problems precisely describing the gravitational attraction of more than two bodies

simultaneously is no reason for us to be skeptical about the ability to discover a better means for classifying psychopathology. As subsequent chapters will highlight, many promising leads toward this goal are currently being pursued. Of perhaps greater interest to readers of this text, there is considerable room for a new generation of scientists to participate in this critically important endeavor.

NOTES

1. There are a variety of materials available on classification generally and psychiatric classification specifically. Most notably for persons interested in psychopathology, the *Journal of Abnormal Psychology* (1991, Vol. 100, No. 3) and *Psychiatric Annals* (1995, Vol. 25, No. 1) have published issues devoted to the psychiatric classification. The interested reader will find some of the selections in those volumes more helpful than others. We have included references to what we consider to be the more informative contributions in this chapter.
2. Meehl (1972, 1977, 1978) has argued that it is not necessary to have explicit "operational definitions" (Bridgman, 1927) prior to undertaking scientific study of an entity. Furthermore, and contrary to the beliefs of most psychologists, it is simply not possible at present even to formulate such definitions for many terms. Philosophers of science long ago accepted the necessity and desirability of recognizing that we are working with "open concepts" (Pap, 1953). That "disease" and "disease entity" are such fuzzy concepts, therefore, in no way removes them from a field for valid scientific investigation. The use of open concepts will provide the basis for a later discussion of the "construct validation" approach (Cronbach & Meehl, 1955) to classification.
3. The beginning of this section is an abstracted presentation of Faber (1930) and Garrison (1929). Although we will not continually reference these authors, it should be understood that they are, in large measure, the architects of the ideas.
4. How one determines whether categorical versus dimensional approaches to classification are to be preferred is a complex topic, full consideration of which goes beyond the scope of this chapter. To help illustrate this complexity, rather than draw as

an example a classification problem from the psychopathology literature, we have chosen to present an example from botany that nicely illustrates pitfalls that are faced in psychopathological classification. Unlike the situation with psychopathology, where what constitutes a valid category is unknown, the botanical example provides the advantage of knowing that one is dealing with two distinct species that nevertheless have features in common that vary along two quantitative dimensions. The situation is analogous to that facing a psychopathology researcher who is attempting to use individual differences in quantitative scores derived from items tapping personality characteristics to help decide whether DSM personality disorders are better classified using dimensional or categorical systems (e.g., Trull, Widiger, & Guthrie, 1990). We have also used these botanical data in another location (Clementz, Iacono, & Grove, 1996) to discuss an important point vis-à-vis the distribution of ocular-motor performance scores among schizophrenia patients and their first-degree biological relatives. Additionally, Clementz and Iacono (1993) used data from schizophrenia subjects to illustrate these same points. If the reader is interested in a psychopathology-relevant example, it can be found in our earlier publication.

REFERENCES

American Psychiatric Association. (1952). *Diagnostic and statistical manual of mental disorders,* 1st ed. Washington, DC: Author.

American Psychiatric Association. (1968). *Diagnostic and statistical manual of mental disorders,* 2nd ed. Washington, DC: Author.

American Psychiatric Association. (1980). *Diagnostic and statistical manual of mental disorders,* 3rd ed. Washington, DC: Author.

American Psychiatric Association. (1987). *Diagnostic and statistical manual of mental disorders,* 3rd ed. (revised). Washington, DC: Author.

American Psychiatric Association. (1994). *Diagnostic and statistical manual of mental disorders,* 4th ed. Washington, DC: Author.

Barker, R.G. (1951). *One boy's day; a specimen record of behaviour.* New York: Harper.

Beck, A.T., Ward, C.H., Mendelson, M., Mock, J.E., & Erlbaugh, J.K. (1962). Reliability of psychiatric diagnosis: II. A study of consistency of clinical judgments and ratings. *American Journal of Psychiatry, 199,* 351–357.

Blashfield, R.K. (1984). *The classification of psychopathology.* New York: Plenum Press.

Blashfield, R.K., & Draguns, J.G. (1976). Toward a taxonomy of psychopathology: The purpose of psychiatric classification. *British Journal of Psychiatry, 129,* 574–583.

Blashfield, R.K., & Livesley, W.J. (1991). Metaphorical analysis of psychiatric classification as a psychological test. *Journal of Abnormal Psychology, 100,* 262–270.

Bridgman, P.W. (1927). *The logic of modern physics.* New York: Macmillan.

Cantor, N., Smith, E.E., French, R. des., & Mezzich, J. (1980). Psychiatric diagnosis as prototype categorization. *Journal of Abnormal Psychology, 89,* 181–193.

Caplan, P.J. (1995). *They say you're crazy: How the world's most powerful psychiatrists decide who's normal.* Reading, MA: Addison-Wesley.

Castillo, R.J. (1997). *Culture and mental illness: A client-centered approach.* Pacific Grove, CA: Brooks/Cole.

Changeux, J-P. (1983). *Neuronal man,* 7th ed. New York: Pantheon Books.

Clark, L.A., Watson, D., & Reynolds, S. (1995). Diagnosis and classification of psychopathology: Challenges to the current system and future directions. *Annual Review of Psychology, 46,* 121–153.

Cleckley, H. (1976). *The mask of sanity.* St. Louis, MO: Mosby.

Clementz, B.A., Grove, W.M., Iacono, W.G., & Sweeney, J.A. (1992). Smooth-pursuit eye movement dysfunction and liability for schizophrenia: Implications for genetic modeling. *Journal of Abnormal Psychology, 101,* 117–129.

Clementz, B.A., & Iacono, W.G. (1993). Nosology and diagnosis. In A.S. Bellack & M. Hersen (Eds.), *Psychopathology in adulthood* (pp. 3–20). Boston: Allyn and Bacon.

Clementz, B.A., Iacono, W.G., & Grove, W.M. (1996). The construct validity of root-mean-square error for quantifying smooth-pursuit eye tracking abnormalities in schizophrenia. *Biological Psychiatry, 39,* 448–450.

Cooper, J. (1989). An overview of the prospective ICD-10 classification of mental disorders. *British Journal of Psychiatry, 154*(Suppl. 4), 21–23.

Cooper, J.E., Kendell, R.E., Gurland, B.J., Sharpe, L., Copeland, J.R.M., & Simon, R. (1972). *Psychiatric diagnosis in New York and London: A comparative study of mental hospital admissions.* New York: Oxford University Press.

Cottler, L.B., Schuckitt, M.A., Helzer, J.E., Crowley, T., Woody, G., Nathan, P., & Hughes, J. (1995). The DSM-IV field trial for substance use disorders: Major results. *Drug and Alcohol Dependence, 38,* 59–69.

Cronbach, L.J., & Meehl, P.E. (1955). Construct validity in psychological tests. *Psychological Bulletin, 52,* 281–302.

Dawes, R.M., & Meehl, P.E. (1966). Mixed group validation: A method for determining the validity of diagnostic signs without using criterion groups. *Psychological Bulletin, 66,* 63–67.

Dewurst, K. (1966). *Dr. Thomas Sydenham, 1624–1689: His life and original writings.* Berkeley: University of California Press.

Diefendorf, A.R., & Dodge, R. (1908). An experimental study of the ocular reactions of the insane from photographic records. *Brain, 31,* 451–489.

Elkins, I.J., Iacono, W.G., Doyle, A.E., & McGue, M. (1997). Characteristics associated with the persistence of antisocial behavior: Results from recent longitudinal research. *Aggression and Violent Behavior, 2,* 101–124.

Eysenck, H.J., Wakefield, J.A., & Friedman, A.F. (1983). Diagnosis and clinical assessment. *Annual Review of Psychology, 34,* 167–193.

Faber, K. (1930). *Nosography: The evolution of clinical medicine in modern times,* 2nd ed. (revised). New York: Paul B. Hoeber.

Feighner, J.P., Robins, E., Guze, S.B., Woodruff, R.A., Winokur, G., & Munoz, R. (1972). Diagnostic criteria for use in psychiatric research. *Archives of General Psychiatry, 26,* 57–63.

Fisher, R.A. (1936). The use of multiple measurements in taxonomic problems. *Annals of Eugenics, 7,* 179–188.

Frances, A., First, M.B., Widiger, T.A., Miele, G.M., Tilly, S.M., Davis, W.W., & Pincus, H.A. (1991).

An A–Z guide to DSM-IV conundrums. *Journal of Abnormal Psychology, 100,* 407–412.

Frances, A., Mack, A.B., First, M.B., & Jones, C. (1995). DSM-IV: Issues in development. *Psychiatric Annals, 25,* 15–19.

Frances, A., Pincus, H.A., Widiger, T.A., Davis, W.W., & First, M.B. (1990). DSM-IV: Work in progress. *American Journal of Psychiatry, 147,* 1439–1448.

Frances, A., Widiger, T.A., & Pincus, H.A. (1989). The development of DSM-IV. *Archives of General Psychiatry, 46,* 373–375.

Garrison, F.H. (1929). *An introduction to the history of medicine,* 4th ed. (revised and enlarged). Philadelphia: Saunders.

Garrod, A.E. (1902). The incidence of alcaptonuria: A study in chemical individuality. *Lancet, 11,* 1616–1620.

Gay, P. (1988). *Freud: A life for our time.* New York: Norton.

Golden, R., & Meehl, P.E. (1979). Detection of the schizoid taxon with MMPI indicators. *Journal of Abnormal Psychology, 88,* 217–233.

Goodwin, D.W., & Guze, S.B. (1996). *Psychiatric diagnosis,* 5th ed. New York: Oxford University Press.

Gottesman, I.I., & Bertelsen, A. (1989). Confirming unexpressed genotypes for schizophrenia: Risks in the offspring of Fisher's Danish identical and fraternal twins. *Archives of General Psychiatry, 46,* 867–872.

Gottesman, I.I., Shields, J., & Hanson, D. (1982). *Schizophrenia: The epigenetic puzzle.* New York: Cambridge University Press.

Gould, S.J. (1981). *The mismeasure of man.* New York: Norton.

Grove, W.M. (1990). The validity of cluster analysis stopping rules as detectors of taxa. In D. Cicchetti & W.M. Grove (Eds.), *Thinking clearly about psychology: Essays in honor of Paul Everett Meehl.* Minneapolis: University of Minnesota Press.

Grove, W.M., & Meehl, P.E. (1993). Simple regression-based procedures for taxometric investigations. *Psychological Reports, 73,* 707–737.

Grove, W.M., & Tellegen, A. (1991). Problems in the classification of personality disorders. *Journal of Personality Disorders, 5,* 31–41.

Hare, R.D. (1992). *The Hare psychopathy checklist—Revised*. Toronto: Multi-Health Systems.

Hare, R.D., & Schalling, D. (1978). *Psychopathic behavior: Approaches to research*. New York: Wiley.

Harper, T.J., Hare, R.D., & Hakstian, A.R. (1989). Two-factor assessment of psychopathy: Assessment implications. *Psychological Assessment: A Journal of Consulting and Clinical Psychology, 1,* 6–17.

Hawking, S. (1993). *Black holes and baby universes and other essays*. New York: Bantam Books.

Helzer, J.E., & Canino, G.J. (1992). Comparative analysis of alcoholism in 10 cultural regions. In J.E. Helzer & G.J. Canino (Eds.), *Alcoholism in North America, Europe, and Asia*. New York: Oxford University Press.

Hempel, C.G. (1965). *Aspects of scientific explanation*. New York: Free Press.

Iacono, W.G. (1991). Psychological assessment of psychopathology. *Psychological Assessment: A Journal of Consulting and Clinical Psychology, 3,* 309–320.

Iacono, W.G. (1998). Identifying genetic risk for psychopathology. In D.K. Routh & R.J. DeRubeis (Eds.), *The science of clinical psychology: Accomplishments and future directions* (pp. 3–22). Washington, DC: American Psychological Association.

Iacono, W.G., & Beiser, M. (1989). Age of onset, temporal stability, and eighteen-month course of first-episode psychosis. In D. Cicchetti (Ed.), *The emergence of a discipline: Rochester symposium on developmental psychopathology* (Vol. 1, pp. 221–260). Hillsdale, NJ: Lawrence Erlbaum.

Iacono, W.G., & Clementz, B.A. (1993). A strategy for elucidating genetic influences on complex psychopathological syndromes (with special reference to ocular motor functioning and schizophrenia). In L.J. Chapman, J.P. Chapman, & D. Fowles (Eds.), *Progress in experimental personality and psychopathology research* (Vol. 16, pp. 11–65). New York: Springer.

Iacono, W.G., Moreau, M., Beiser, M., Fleming, J.A.E., & Lin, T-Y. (1992). Smooth-pursuit eye tracking in first-episode psychotic patients and their relatives. *Journal of Abnormal Psychology, 101,* 104–116.

Kanfer, F.H., & Saslow, G. (1965). Behavioral analysis: An alternative to diagnostic classification. *Archives of General Psychiatry, 12,* 529–538.

Kaufmann, C.A., Johnson, J.E., & Pardes, H. (1996). Evolution and revolution in psychiatric genetics. In L.L. Hall (Ed.), *Genetics and mental illness: Evolving issues for research and society*. New York: Plenum Press.

Kendell, R.E. (1975a). The concept of disease and its implications for psychiatry. *British Journal of Psychiatry, 127,* 305–315.

Kendell, R.E. (1975b). *The role of diagnosis in psychiatry*. London: Blackwell.

Kendell, R.E. (1982). The choice of diagnostic criteria for biological research. *Archives of General Psychiatry, 39,* 1344–1339.

Kendell, R.E. (1991). Relationship between the DSM-IV and the ICD-10. *Journal of Abnormal Psychology, 100,* 297–301.

Kirk, S., & Kutchins, K. (1992). *The selling of DSM: The rhetoric of science in psychiatry*. Hawthorne, NY: Aldine de Gruyter.

Kraepelin, E. (1971). *Dementia praecox and paraphrenia* (R. M. Barklay, Trans.). Huntington, NY: Krieger. (Original work published 1919).

Kraupl Taylor, F. (1979). *The concepts of illness, disease, and morbus*. London: Cambridge University Press.

Kraupl Taylor, F. (1980). The concepts of disease. *Psychological Medicine, 10,* 419–424.

Lykken, D.T. (1984). Psychopathic personality. In R.I. Corsini (Ed.), *Encyclopedia of psychology* (pp. 165–167). New York: Wiley.

Lykken, D.T. (1991). What's wrong with psychology anyway? In D. Cicchetti & W.M. Grove (Eds.), *Thinking clearly about psychology: essays in honor of Paul E. Meehl: Vol. 1. Matters of public interest*. Minneapolis: University of Minnesota Press.

MacLean, C.J., Morton, N.E., Elston, R. C., & Yee, S. (1976). Skewness in commingling distributions. *Biometrics, 32,* 695–699.

Martin, R.L. (1995). DSM-IV: The baby is born. *Psychiatric Annals, 25,* 11–14.

Mayr, E. (1981). Biological classification: Toward a synthesis of opposing methodologies. *Science, 214,* 510–516.

McDowell, J.E., & Clementz, B.A. (1997). The effect of fixation condition manipulations on antisaccade performance in schizophrenia: Studies of diagnostic specificity. *Experimental Brain Research,* in press.

Meehl, P.E. (1972). Specific genetic etiology, psychodynamics and therapeutic nihilism. *International Journal of Mental Health, 1,* 10–27.

Meehl, P.E. (1973). MAXCOV-HITMAX: A taxonomic search method for loose genetic syndromes. In P.E. Meehl (Ed.), *Psychodiagnosis: Selected papers* (pp. 200–224). New York: Norton.

Meehl, P.E. (1977). Specific etiology and other forms of strong influence: Some quantitative meanings. *Journal of Medicine and Philosophy, 2,* 33–53.

Meehl, P.E. (1978). Theoretical risks and tabular asterisks: Sir Karl, Sir Ronald, and the slow progress of soft psychology. *Journal of Consulting and Clinical Psychology, 46,* 806–834.

Meehl, P.E. (1995). Bootstraps taxometrics. Solving the classification problem in psychopathology. *American Psychologist, 50,* 266–275.

Meehl, P.E. (1996). MAXCOV pseudotaxonicity. *American Psychologist, 51,* 1184–1185.

Meehl, P.E., & Golden, R.R. (1982). Taxometric methods. In P.E. Kendall & J.N. Butcher (Eds.), *Handbook of research methods in clinical psychology* (pp. 127–181). New York: Wiley.

Meehl, P.E., & Yonce, L.J. (1994). Taxometric analysis: 1. Detecting taxonicity with two quantitative indicators using means above and below a sliding cut (MAMBAC procedure). *Psychological Reports, 74,* 1059–1274.

Meehl, P.E., & Yonce, L.J. (1996). Taxometric analysis: 2. Detecting taxonicity using covariance of two quantitative indicators in successive interval of a third indicator (MAXCOV procedure). *Psychological Reports, 78,* 1091–1227.

Miller, M.B. (1996). Limitations of Meehl's MAXCOV-HITMAX procedure. *American Psychologist, 51,* 554–556.

Morey, L.C. (1991). Classification of mental disorder as a collection of hypothetical constructs. *Journal of Abnormal Psychology, 100,* 289–293.

Murphy, E.A. (1964). One cause? Many causes? The argument from the bimodal distribution. *Journal of Chronic Diseases, 17,* 301–324.

Pap, A. (1953). Reduction-sentences and open concepts. *Methodos, 5,* 3–30.

Preskorn, S.H. (1995). Beyond DSM-IV: What is the cart and what is the horse? *Psychiatric Annals, 25,* 53–62.

Regier, D.A., Kaelber, C.T., Roper, M.T., Rae, D.S., & Sartorius, N. (1994). The ICD-10 clinical field trial for mental and behavioral disorders: Results in Canada and the United States. *American Journal of Psychiatry, 151,* 1340–1350.

Robins, E., & Guze, S.B. (1970). Establishment of diagnostic validity in psychiatric illness: Its application to schizophrenia. *American Journal of Psychiatry, 126,* 107–111.

Robins, L.N., & Regier, D.A. (1991). *Psychiatric disorders in America: The Epidemiologic Catchment Area Study.* New York: Free Press.

Rosenhan, D.L. (1973). On being sane in insane places. *Science, 179,* 250–258.

Rothman, S.M. (1997, April 21). There's a name for what ails you. *The Washington Post National Weekly Edition,* p. 25.

Sartorius, N., Jablensky, A., Korten, A., Ernberg, G., Anker, M., Cooper, J.E., & Day, R. (1986). Early manifestations and first-contact incidence of schizophrenia in different cultures. *Psychological Medicine, 16,* 909–928.

Saugstad, L. (1985). In defense of international classification. *Psychological Medicine, 15,* 1–2.

Scheff, T.J. (1966). *Being mentally ill: A sociological theory.* Chicago: Aldine.

Shaffer, D. (1996). A participant's observations: Preparing DSM-IV. *Canadian Journal of Psychiatry, 41,* 325–329.

Sneath, P.H.E., & Sokol, R.R. (1973). *Numerical taxonomy.* San Francisco: Freeman.

Spitzer, R.L., Endicott, J., & Robins, E. (1975). *Research diagnostic criteria (RDC) for a selected group of functional disorders.* New York: New York State Psychiatric Institute.

Szasz, T.S. (1961). *The myth of mental illness.* New York: Hoeber-Harper.

Szymanski, S., Kane, J., & Lieberman, J. (1994). Trait markers in schizophrenia. Are they diagnostic? In T.A. Widiger, A.J. Frances, H.A. Pincus, M.B. First, R. Ross, & W. Davis (Eds.), *DSM-IV Sourcebook* (Vol. 1). Washington, DC: American Psychiatric Association.

Thangavelu, R., & Martin, R.L. (1995). ICD-10 and DSM-IV: Depiction of the diagnostic elephant. *Psychiatric Annals, 25,* 20–28.

Titterington, D.M., Smith, A.F.M., & Makov, U.E. (1985). *Statistical analysis of finite mixture distributions*. New York: Wiley.

Trull, T.J., Widiger, T.A., & Guthrie, P. (1990). Categorical versus dimensional status of borderline personality disorder. *Journal of Abnormal Psychology, 99*, 40–48.

Ullman, L.P., & Krasner, L.A. (1975). *A psychological approach to abnormal behavior*. Englewood Cliffs, NJ: Prentice-Hall.

Vogel, F., & Motulsky, A.G. (1986). *Human genetics: Problems and approaches*. Berlin: Springer-Verlag.

Wallace, E.R. IV. (1994). Psychiatry and its nosology: A historico-philosophical overview. In J.Z. Sadler, O.P. Wiggins, & M.A. Schwartz (Eds.), *Philosophical perspectives on psychiatric diagnostic classification*. Baltimore, MD: Johns Hopkins University Press.

Ward, C.H., Beck, A.T., Mendelson, M., Mock, J.E., & Erlbaugh, J.K. (1962). The psychiatric nomenclature: Reasons for diagnostic disagreement. *Archives of General Psychiatry, 7*, 198–205.

Watson, J.D., & Crick, F.H.C. (1953a). General implications of the structure of deoxyribose nucleic acid. *Nature, 171*, 964–967.

Watson, J.D., & Crick, F.H.C. (1953b). A structure for deoxyribose nucleic acid. *Nature, 171*, 737–738.

Widiger, T.A., Cadoret, R., Hare, R., Robins, L., Rutherford, M., Zanarini, M., Alterman, A., Apple, M., Corbitt, E., Forth, A., Hart, S., Kultermann, J., Woody, G., & Frances, A. (1996). DSM-IV antisocial personality disorder field trial. *Journal of Abnormal Psychology, 105*, 3–16.

Widiger, T.A., Frances, A.J., Pincus, H.A., First, M.B., Ross, R., & Davis, W.W. (1994). *DSM-IV Sourcebook* (Vol. 1). Washington, DC: American Psychiatric Press.

Widiger, T.A., Frances, A.J., Pincus, H.A., Ross, R., First, M.B., & Davis, W.W. (1996). *DSM-IV Sourcebook* (Vol. 2). Washington, DC: American Psychiatric Press.

Widiger, T.A., Frances, A.J., Pincus, H.A., Ross, R., First, M.B., & Davis, W.W. (1997). *DSM-IV Sourcebook* (Vol. 3). Washington, DC: American Psychiatric Press.

Widiger, T.A., Frances, A., Spitzer, R.L., & Williams, J.B.W. (1988). The DSM-III-R personality disorders: An overview. *American Journal of Psychiatry, 145*, 786–795.

World Health Organization. (1948). *Manual of the international statistical classification of diseases, injuries, and causes of death, 6th revision*. Geneva: Author.

World Health Organization. (1969). *Manual of the international statistical classification of diseases, injuries, and causes of death, 8th revision*. Geneva: Author.

World Health Organization. (1977). *Manual of the international statistical classification of diseases, injuries, and causes of death, 9th revision*. Geneva: Author.

World Health Organization. (1992). *The ICD-10 classification of mental and behavioural disorders: Clinical descriptions and diagnostic guidelines*. Geneva: Author.

Zimmerman, M. (1988). Why are we rushing to publish DSM-IV? *Archives of General Psychiatry, 45*, 1135–1138.

Zimmerman, M. (1990). Is DSM-IV needed at all? *Archives of General Psychiatry, 47*, 974–976.

CHAPTER 2

EPIDEMIOLOGY

Mary Amanda Dew
University of Pittsburgh Schools of Medicine and Public Health

Evelyn J. Bromet
State University of New York at Stony Brook

Galen E. Switzer
University of Pittsburgh School of Medicine

INTRODUCTION

No mass disorder afflicting mankind has ever been eliminated or brought under control by attempts at treating the affected individual, nor by training large numbers of individual practitioners.

—*John E. Gordon*

Gordon's words, arising from decades of his own work on factors associated with health and illness (Gordon, 1958; Plunkett & Gordon, 1960), provide the reason that basic research is fundamental to preventive medicine and public health. The basic science of both of these disciplines is *epidemiology,* the study of patterns of illness in the population and of the factors that affect these patterns (Lilienfeld & Stolley, 1994). With respect to psychopathology in particular, a subspecialty of epidemiology—psychiatric epidemiology—focuses on mental disorders and symptoms in the population and on the risk factors that influence their onset and course.

Mental disorders occur in every sociocultural group in the world. In the United States, an estimated 12% of children (Institute of Medicine, 1989) and 28% to 29% of adults currently suffer from one or more disorders (Kessler et al., 1994; Regier et al., 1993). International estimates are similarly high or higher (Aderibigbe & Adityanjee, 1995). Mental illness constitutes a significant burden to the affected individual in terms of reduced quality of life (Hays et al., 1995; Revicki & Murray, 1994). A recent landmark study by the World Health Organization concluded that one mental illness, major depression, accounted for 5.1% of the total global burden of disease in 1990 with respect to disability-adjusted life years lost to the individual and society; depression was ranked as the fourth most important cause of global disease burden (Murray & Lopez, 1996).

Yet, only a minority of mentally ill individuals, 30% to 40% on average (Regier et al., 1993; Vernon & Roberts, 1982; Weissman, Myers, & Thompson, 1981), are treated within the health care system. It is

25

this minority on which traditional research techniques of clinical observation and laboratory experimentation are typically based. While this research has improved our understanding of factors associated with psychopathology, the role of such factors in the larger ill but untreated population remains less clear. By focusing on psychopathology under natural conditions in whole populations, the psychiatric epidemiologist thus provides an empirical base that complements and extends data gathered through traditional clinical and laboratory techniques.

Psychiatric epidemiology, as practiced today, is a relatively young discipline. Nevertheless, considerable strides have been made in the past several decades in understanding the epidemiology of, for example, suicide, depression, schizophrenia, substance abuse, and disorders of childhood and old age. While the etiology of most conditions remains unknown, the risk factors identified in this recent research suggest avenues for control and prevention of psychopathology, as well as potential directions for etiologic study. Psychiatric epidemiologists have focused primarily on personal and environmental risk factors, although new research on genetic epidemiology is beginning to make important contributions to our understanding of many disorders. The core of this chapter focuses on current knowledge about personal and environmental risk factors for three of the most common and/or widely studied mental disorders—depression, substance abuse, and schizophrenia. Where relevant, recent findings from genetic epidemiology are incorporated as well. Although we de-

vote the most attention to recent diagnostic studies, important earlier results from classic studies are also described.

BASIC PREMISES

Psychiatric epidemiologic research is conducted at three levels: descriptive, analytic, and experimental. Table 2-1 summarizes key terms and study designs relevant to each of these research levels.

Descriptive Epidemiology

Descriptive epidemiology aims at ascertaining the occurrence of disorder by time, place, and person. The *prevalence* rate (the ratio of all existing cases during a given time period to the defined population) and the *incidence* rate (the ratio of newly diagnosed cases during a given time period to the population at risk for developing a first episode of an illness) are two basic tools of descriptive epidemiology. Determination of these rates depends on three factors:

1. An accurate count of the number of *cases* of illness or disorder in the study population (i.e., the numerator of the rate) is required. As discussed later in this chapter, the issue of case definition has been one of special significance for psychiatric epidemiology.
2. The *population at risk* (i.e., the denominator) must be specified, and denotes the group of individuals from whom the cases were identified. For preva-

TABLE 2-1   Key concepts in epidemiologic research.

Level of Research	Basic Terms	Common Study Designs
I. Descriptive epidemiology	Prevalence rate Incidence rate Case Population at risk Cohort	Prevalence study Incidence study
II. Analytic epidemiology	Risk factor	Cross-sectional survey Retrospective cohort study Prospective study Follow-back study
III. Experimental epidemiology	Random assignment	Clinical trial Natural experiment

lence rates, the entire group of individuals—regardless of whether they have had the illness previously—is considered to constitute the population at risk. For incidence rates, the denominator excludes those individuals with the disorder of interest at the beginning of the period of observation.

3. These rates are calculated for a specified *time frame*—for example, incidence during a 12-month period, prevalence at one point in time (point prevalence), or prevalence during a given period of time (period prevalence).

Descriptive epidemiologic studies are often referred to as *prevalence studies* when they utilize cross-sectional, survey designs in which a group of individuals—a *cohort*—are interviewed at one point in time and prevalence rates for current and past periods of time are estimated. In *incidence studies,* a cohort is followed forward for a given period of time and new cases are identified. A landmark descriptive epidemiologic study that incorporated both of these study designs is the Epidemiologic Catchment Area (ECA) research program. In this ECA study, close to 20,000 adults from catchment areas in New Haven, St. Louis, Baltimore, Los Angeles, and Durham, NC, were interviewed with a structured diagnostic instrument, the Diagnostic Interview Schedule (DIS; Robins, Helzer, Croughan, & Ratcliff, 1977). The DIS obtains information on a specific set of mental disorders. For the ECA study, the DIS was scored according to the criteria in use at the time in the United States for psychiatric disorders, as specified in the third edition of the *Diagnostic and Statistical Manual of Mental Disorders* (DSM-III; American Psychiatric Association, 1980). (The DIS has subsequently been revised and updated as the DSM has been revised.) Six-month and lifetime prevalence rates were determined from the interview. Then, in order to estimate incidence rates, a follow-up interview using the DIS was conducted with respondents one year after their original assessment. Later in this chapter, basic findings on prevalence and incidence rates are presented.

We will also present some findings from a second, more recent descriptive epidemiologic study conducted in the United States. This National Comorbidity Survey (NCS) built upon the experiences in the earlier ECA effort and provides the most up-to-date estimates of 6-month, 12-month, and lifetime prevalence rates of a range of psychiatric disorders (Kessler et al., 1994). The NCS included a nationally representative sample of over 8,000 young and middle-aged adults, each of whom was interviewed with a version of the Composite International Diagnostic Interview (CIDI). (The CIDI grew out of the DIS and shares numerous features with it.) The NCS determined rates of psychiatric disorders according to DSM-III-R criteria (American Psychiatric Association, 1987).

Analytic Epidemiology

The second level of epidemiologic research, analytic epidemiology, examines why a rate is high or low in a given population. Studies under this rubric test hypotheses about whether specific variables serve as *risk factors* for particular disorders. Risk factors are characteristics whose presence increases the risk, or likelihood, of developing a disorder. In addition to its role as a prevalence study, the NCS is a prime example of analytic epidemiologic research. It was designed to examine a comprehensive risk factor battery in relation to psychopathology. Thus, respondents were questioned in detail about their parents' mental health history, family adversity, social networks and supports, and recent life events and difficulties. Analyses were then conducted to determine which risk factors were most strongly associated with specific psychiatric disorders.

True risk factors exist prior to the onset of a disorder. This is easy to establish for some variables, such as gender and ethnicity. However, the insidious nature of many psychiatric disorders makes it difficult to determine whether many variables, such as social class, marital status, and social supports, are risks or consequences of disorder. Thus, while the NCS and many other analytic epidemiologic studies have yielded a great deal of data on the size and nature of associations between risk factors and disorder, they have less convincingly demonstrated that these associations have a causal component.

Four types of study designs are often employed at the level of analytic epidemiology. First, *cross-sectional survey studies,* such as the NCS, enroll individuals on the basis of a sampling plan without regard to whether potential respondents do or do not have the psychiatric disorder(s) of interest. Respondents who are found to meet criteria to be considered as "cases" are then compared to the remaining noncases on one or more risk factors of interest. In cross-sectional surveys, information about respondents' psychiatric status is obtained at the same point in time as information about possible risk factors. Although this means that cause cannot be distinguished from effect, many cross-sectional surveys, including the NCS, at least attempt to determine the ordering of onset of risk factors versus psychiatric disorder. This is typically accomplished by relying on respondents' recollections of the past. While such recollections may be inaccurate or incomplete for a variety of reasons, elaborate techniques for probing life history have partially mitigated this problem (Kessler & Wethington, 1991; Lyketsos et al., 1994).

A second type of study design is the *retrospective cohort* design, in which a cohort of psychiatric cases is identified on the basis of existing records, and a comparison group of individuals without disorder is selected to be studied. Individuals in both groups are then examined for the presence of hypothesized antecedent risk factors for the disorder. Risk factors may be determined on the basis of respondents' recollections and/or by using archival data such as medical records. When risk factor information is available from records collected in the past, retrospective cohort studies may allow cause and effect to be better disentangled than in studies that rely exclusively on respondents' recall. One drawback, however, is that archival data may be incomplete or of lower quality than information collected in the context of ongoing research.

The Iowa 500 study employed a retrospective cohort design (Morrison, Clancy, Crowe, & Winokur 1972; Tsuang, Woolson, & Fleming, 1979). Psychiatric cases were identified using psychiatric hospital admission records; a comparison sample was assembled from records of nonpsychiatric surgery patients. Individuals in both groups were contacted and interviewed. Medical record data were also examined. One interesting finding to emerge from this study and others using the retrospective cohort design is that loss of a parent during childhood is more common among depressed adults than among nondepressed controls (Pfohl, Stangl, & Tsuang, 1983; Roy, 1981).

A third study design is considerably stronger than these other designs for examining prediction and pos-

sible causal direction. This is the *prospective* design, which identifies one of two types of cohorts and follows them over time. Prospective studies aimed at identifying risk factors that predict the *onset* of a disease identify and follow an initially *healthy* cohort. An example of such a study is Vaillant's (1983) 40-year effort to follow a group of initially healthy Harvard undergraduates in order to examine their subsequent health and social functioning. The British Birth Cohort Studies provide other well-known examples: These investigations continue to follow cohorts of all persons born in England, Scotland, and Wales during one week in the years 1946, 1958, and 1970 in order to examine numerous physical and mental health outcomes (e.g., Power, 1992). Prospective studies of factors associated with the *course* of illness identify representative cohorts of *cases* at the start of their illness and follow them naturalistically over time. Thus, several recent studies have followed first-episode schizophrenic patients for periods as long as 5 years in order to examine various parameters of outcome (Biehl et al., 1986; Shepherd, Watt, Falloon, & Smeeton, 1989; for recent reviews, see Bromet, Dew, & Eaton, 1995, and Ram et al., 1992).

The fourth important study design within analytic epidemiology is the *follow-back* design, also referred to as an anterospective or a mixed prospective–retrospective approach. With this strategy, a cohort is selected on the basis of archival data—for example, agency records—collected many years previously. The rate of disorder during the interval from the time the early records were created until the present is then examined and compared to the rate in a selected control group. Robins (1966) conducted a particularly noteworthy study utilizing this design. She reviewed 30-year-old child guidance clinic records in order to identify a cohort at risk for future psychiatric impairment. She then retrieved data on the following 30-year interval in order to trace individuals' subsequent natural history of childhood disorder and the development of antisocial behavior relative to a control group.

Experimental Epidemiology

The third level of epidemiologic research attempts to establish a causal relationship between a variable of interest and a specific psychiatric outcome. This may involve *randomly assigning* individuals to treatment or control groups in the case of a clinical trial of a drug, or to exposure and nonexposure groups in the case of an environmental agent or intervention (e.g., an education program in the workplace). The basic principle behind random assignment is that all participants begin with an equal probability of receiving the exposure or treatment of interest. This is essential in order to determine whether participants' responses in the study are brought about by the experimental agent—the exposure—rather than merely by individual differences between respondents or other factors in the environment.

In one area of epidemiology, sometimes referred to as clinical epidemiology, a growing number of such trials have been successfully completed. Clinical epidemiology generally encompasses studies of well-defined patient populations, or populations of individuals with diagnosed medical conditions (Cooper, 1993; Feinstein, 1985). When those populations are studied in order to chart the prevalence or incidence of psychiatric disorders, clinical epidemiology and psychiatric epidemiology intersect. For example, cohorts of patients with heart disease, HIV infection, diabetes, or cancer have been systematically assessed to determine rates of depression and anxiety-related psychiatric disorders (e.g., Dew et al., 1996, Dew et al., 1997; Frasure-Smith, Lesperance, & Talajic, 1993; Maj et al., 1994; Popkin et al., 1993; Razavi, Delvaux, Farvacques, & Robaye, 1990; Schleifer et al., 1989; see Dew, 1998, for a recent review). Findings of dramatically elevated rates of these disorders in such populations have provided the impetus for specific clinical trials to test whether patients will benefit from therapeutic interventions designed to improve mental health (Chesney & Folkman, 1994; Fawzy, Fawzy, Arndt, & Pasnau, 1995). The rationale behind these trials is that the intervention will lessen the impact of physical health status and other hypothesized risk factors on patients' mental health.

In many nonmedical field settings with nonpatient populations, however, random assignment to a specific treatment or exposure may not be possible or ethical. This is often the case when potential respondents have never been identified on the basis of any characteristic or antecedent risk factor (such as "patienthood"), or when a researcher's interest focuses on the mental health consequences of exposures that are likely to be harmful rather than therapeutic. The more common design in such circumstances is the *natural experiment*. In this situation, the investigator has (often fortuitously) collected data from a population, only some of whom go on to receive exposure to an environmental agent. The previously collected data thus become baseline data, and the population can be followed forward through time to examine differences between exposed and nonexposed groups. If the groups were similar in every respect (except for the subsequent exposure) at baseline, then follow-up differences are likely to be attributable to the exposure.

We were presented with such a situation in an ongoing longitudinal study of a cohort of mothers of young children residing in western Pennsylvania (Dew, Bromet, & Schulberg, 1987; Penkower, Bromet, & Dew, 1988). During the course of the field work, we learned that some of these women's husbands had lost their jobs during a period of massive recession in the steel industry. Other women were not exposed to job loss in their immediate family during this period. We used data collected prior to the onset of layoffs as baseline data, and followed both exposed and nonexposed groups forward in time to chart the long-term mental health effects of husband's job loss.

In sum, the methodologies used at the three levels of epidemiologic research were developed to provide data relevant for prevention and control of illness. Two additional requirements for research at any of the three levels are *representative sampling* and a *reliable and valid case definition*. The importance of these requirements, and how they have been met within psychiatric epidemiology, are best understood in a historical context. A historical perspective also helps to define psychiatric epidemiology's current contribution to the understanding of adult psychopathology.

ROLE IN UNDERSTANDING PSYCHOPATHOLOGY

A Brief History

The growth of psychiatric epidemiologic research has been described as evolving through three periods, or generations (Dohrenwend & Dohrenwend, 1982), each characterized by its views on the sampling and case definition issues. First-generation studies, conducted prior to World War II, relied on key informants' reports and agency records for case ascertainment. The first prevalence study of this sort was conducted in Massachusetts in 1854 by Edward Jarvis, who undertook a census on the "insane" by gathering information from general practitioners, other key informants such as clergymen, and records of mental hospitals and other official agencies (Jarvis, 1971). He identified 2,632 "lunatics" and 1,087 "idiots" needing "the care and protection of their friends or of the public for their support, restoration or custody" (p. 17).

A classic first-generation study was conducted by Faris and Dunham (1939), who compared rates of mental illness across geographical areas. After reviewing medical records from four state hospitals serving the Chicago area between 1922 and 1934 in order to identify cases, they determined the rate per 100,000 of the adult population for different sections of Chicago. They found that rates of mental illness, and of schizophrenia in particular, decreased progressively as one moved away from the city center. Thus, 46% of the cases of schizophrenia were from the inner-city area, compared to 13% from the outermost districts. Faris and Dunham argued that the inner-city environment was conducive to mental illness, and their findings have been replicated many times (see Giggs, 1986, for a review).

As in most first-generation studies, Faris and Dunham relied on medical records rather than a community survey approach in order to identify cases. However, U.S. Army experiences during World War II, in which large numbers of presumably healthy recruits scored in the impaired range on a psychological symptom screen (Stouffer et al., 1950), suggested that treated cases represented only the tip of the iceberg. (Extensive subsequent work has confirmed that not only do treated cases represent only a minority of psychiatrically ill individuals, but that a number of factors are systematically associated with treatment seeking. For example, individuals seeking outpatient professional help have been found more likely to be female, younger, better educated, divorced, urban dwellers, Jewish, frequent church or temple attenders, residing in Pacific states, and to have divorced

parents and fathers with professional occupations [Veroff, Kulka, & Douvan, 1981].)

The Army findings during World War II prompted a series of community studies—second-generation studies—on the extent of psychiatric impairment in the general population. These studies were designed to use sophisticated probabilistic sampling techniques and symptom-based face-to-face interview schedules derived in part from the Neuropsychiatric Screening Adjunct, the psychological screening tool developed by the Army. These studies focused on psychiatric "impairment" rather than specific diagnostic categories, which during the 1950s and 1960s could not be reliably operationalized. The hypothesis that treated cases represented a minority of all cases was strongly supported. Indeed, community sample impairment rates in studies such as the Midtown Manhattan Project (Srole et al., 1962) and the Nova Scotia study (Leighton et al., 1963) were considerably higher than those found in first-generation pre–World War II research. Thus, while the median current prevalence rate of disorder was estimated to be 3.6% in the first-generation studies (Dohrenwend & Dohrenwend, 1982), the median rate from second-generation studies was 20%.

Important questions arose concerning possible reasons for this marked difference in rates. For example, it was unclear how much of the rate difference was attributable to improved case-finding techniques. Alternatively, given their focus on symptom counts and continuous measures of impairment, it was possible that disorder rates in second-generation studies were inflated by counting as "cases" those respondents who were symptomatic yet not so severely impaired that they would warrant a psychiatric diagnosis. There was ample evidence that psychiatric *impairment,* as defined by the instruments used in these studies, was not comparable to *disorder* as defined by psychiatrist clinicians (Leighton et al., 1963; Srole et al., 1962). An additional issue in attempting to interpret the impairment rates from second-generation studies was that the instruments utilized did not assess the full range of clinical diagnostic categories—largely excluding, for example, behavior disorders and substance abuse. These have been key issues for the current third generation of psychiatric epidemiologic studies, which rely on psychometric advances in the area of diagnosis accomplished in the 1970s. Thus, unlike their predecessors, many of today's third-generation studies are characterized by the use of semi- or fully structured diagnostic interview schedules embodying the most recent psychiatric nomenclature (although studies of symptom impairment are still being conducted as well).

Psychometric work leading to structured clinical interviewing was initially stimulated by Kramer's (1961) earlier observation that first-admission rates for schizophrenia were higher in the United States, whereas those for depression and manic-depressive illness were higher in England. He questioned whether these differences reflected true differences in morbidity or were artifacts of diagnosis. This simple observation led to the first major scientific study of the determinants of diagnosis, which demonstrated that the application of systematic interviewing techniques and comparable diagnostic criteria resulted in similar diagnostic distributions (Cooper et al., 1972). Several years later, the International Pilot Study of Schizophrenia demonstrated that patients could be reliably diagnosed in countries worldwide, including the United States, with structured diagnostic interview schedules (Sartorius et al., 1986; World Health Organization, 1975).

In the United States, the need to define homogeneous patient populations for clinical drug trials and multicenter collaborative research prompted further developments in structured interviewing techniques and reliable diagnostic criteria. Rejecting the use of general clinical descriptions to make diagnoses, Feighner, Robins, and Guze (1972) published the first set of specific research criteria, which listed the symptoms and their duration required for each diagnosis. Six years later, the Research Diagnostic Criteria (RDC) (Spitzer, Endicott, & Robins, 1978)—which represent revisions of the Feighner criteria—and an accompanying semistructured interview schedule, the Schedule for Affective Disorders and Schizophrenia (SADS) (Endicott & Spitzer, 1978) were published. Weissman and Myers (1980) first applied the SADS to a community population, showing that diagnoses could be systematically made in the field. The RDC and the SADS went on to widespread use in the next 10 years. With the publication of DSM-III and DSM-III-R, Spitzer, Williams, Gibbon, and First (1987) developed the Structured Clin-

ical Interview for DSM-III (SCID). The SCID built upon its predecessor, the SADS, and both require clinically experienced raters. The SCID was revised in conjunction with the publication of DSM-IV, and it and other semistructured interviews based on current DSM or ICD criteria (e.g., the Schedules for Clinical Assessment in Neuropsychiatry, SCAN; Wing et al., 1990; WHO, 1994) continue to be widely used today.

Utilizing highly experienced clinicians can be costly; in epidemiologic studies of large community samples, training lay interviewers to conduct the field work is often more cost-effective than hiring experienced mental health professionals. Thus, in the late 1970s, the National Institute of Mental Health (NIMH) decided to sponsor the development of a fully structured interview that could be administered by lay interviewers. Their ultimate goal was to estimate the rates of discrete psychiatric disorders in unbiased, community populations. The new instrument was the Diagnostic Interview Schedule (DIS), a fully structured DSM-III-based schedule (Robins et al., 1977). The DIS has been administered in many community surveys, including the ECA study. It has been adapted and updated to reflect not only current DSM criteria, but criteria in the International Classification of Diseases (ICD-10; WHO, 1992). It has been translated into several languages and used in other countries as well (Aderibigbe & Adityanjee, 1995; Robins & Regier, 1991). Several structured instruments have also been developed and validated for children (Angold & Costello, 1995; Boyle et al., 1993; Shaffer et al., 1993).

The fact that the DIS was shown to be feasible to use in a variety of settings led to the development of a series of other fully structured instruments. One of the most notable is the CIDI (Robins et al., 1988; WHO, 1993), the instrument that was adapted for use in the NCS. The CIDI was specifically developed for cross-cultural research, and it has been employed in a variety of WHO-sponsored efforts worldwide (Sartorius, 1993; Wittchen et al., 1991).

Like any tool that relies solely on respondents' memories and understanding of the questions being posed, the instruments we have discussed are far from being perfectly valid or reliable diagnostic techniques (see Üstün & Tien, 1995, for a review). These difficulties were illustrated by a study of women's reports of lifetime depression using SADS interviews, which found that over an 18-month period, women often failed to recall earlier lifetime episodes that they had previously described at the first interview, or provided new information about lifetime episodes that they had not mentioned originally (Bromet et al., 1986). This phenomenon of altered reporting of the past has been noted with other diagnostic instruments, including the DIS and the SCID, as well (Robins, Helzer, Ratcliff, & Seyfried, 1982; Williams, 1992). On the other hand, the significance of the shift from impairment ratings to diagnostic categories in epidemiologic studies cannot be underestimated. The shift has helped to bridge the gap between psychiatric epidemiology and clinical psychiatry and psychology by providing clinical outcomes—diagnoses—that are understood across disciplines.

Current Knowledge about Prevalence and Incidence of Mental Disorders

The ECA and NCS studies, described earlier, have been among the most comprehensive prevalence studies using modern assessment techniques. They also provided extensive information regarding incidence (in the ECA study) and risk factors (in the NCS) for psychiatric disorders. The range of 12-month and lifetime prevalence rates, and the 12-month incidence rates of disorders assessed across both studies, are reported in Table 2-2. The ECA study generally reported lower rates of the disorders than the NCS. Speculation as well as additional analyses (Regier et al., 1998) on the reasons for this difference center on the following:

1. Differences between the structured interviews that were employed—for example, the use of memory probes in the NCS to improve respondents' recall
2. The fact that ECA sampling focused on five specific geographical areas and that these areas were not selected to necessarily represent the U.S. population, whereas the NCS used a national probability sample
3. Inclusion of somewhat different age ranges—in the ECA, respondents were aged 18 to over 75 (with oversampling at some sites among elder persons), whereas the NCS was restricted to persons aged 15 to 55

4. Important changes in the diagnostic criteria for some disorders between the DSM-III used in the ECA study and the DSM-III-R used in the NCS
5. The fact that the studies were separated by over 10 years, a period in which the true rates of some disorders may have changed

Despite the differences in disorder rates across these two studies, and their possible explanations, it is clear that the most prevalent disorders in both studies were substance abuse/dependence, major depression, and phobias. Posttraumatic stress disorder, examined only in the NCS, was also relatively prevalent. The least common disorders were schizophrenia and schizophreniform disorder, mania, and somatization. Both the ECA and the NCS prevalence data have begun to be compared to international prevalence studies. ECA data have been examined relative to results of community-based studies using the DIS conducted in European, Asian, and North American countries, and ECA prevalence rates for affective disorders (mania, major depression, dysthymia), anxiety disorders (phobia, panic, and obsessive-compulsive disorders), substance use disorders, and psychosis were within the range of rates reported in the international studies (Aderibigbe & Adityanjee, 1995; Regier et al., 1988a). Recently, Weissman et al. (1997) reported that both the ECA and NCS lifetime prevalence rates for panic disorder were similar to the rates found in the majority of 10 international community surveys using structured assessment instruments.

One of the most important contributions of psychiatric epidemiology to the understanding of psychopathology has been the identification of risk factors for mental disorders. We review data regarding the two major classes of such factors: personal and environmental variables. We focus, as noted earlier, primarily on three of the most common and/or widely studied mental disorders—major depression, substance abuse, and schizophrenia.

Current Knowledge about Risk Factors for Mental Disorders

Personal Risk Factors

As shown in the upper section of Table 2-3, risk factors in this class may be characterized either as gen-

TABLE 2-2   Prevalence and incidence rates of DSM-III/DSM-III-R disorders in the United States among adults in the Epidemiologic Catchment Area (ECA) study (N = 18,571) and the National Comorbidity Survey (NCS) (N = 8,098).[a]

Disorder[b]	Rate Estimates		
	Lifetime Prevalence	12-month Prevalence	12 month Incidence
Alcohol abuse/dependence	13.3–23.5[c]	6.8–9.7	1.8
Drug abuse/dependence	5.9–11.9	2.7–3.6	1.1
Any affective disorder	7.8–19.3	3.7–11.3	—[d]
Major depressive episode	5.8–17.1	2.7–10.3	1.6
Dysthymia	3.3–6.4	2.5 (NCS)	—
Manic episode	0.8–1.6	0.6–1.3	—
Phobic disorders	12.5 (ECA)	11.8 (ECA)	4.0
Agoraphobia	5.6–6.7	2.8 (NCS)	—
Simple phobia	11.2–11.3	8.8 (NCS)	—
Social phobia	2.7–13.3	7.9 (NCS)	—
Obsessive-compulsive disorder	2.5 (ECA)	1.6 (ECA)	0.7
Panic	1.6–3.5	0.9–2.3	0.6
Generalized anxiety	5.1 (NCS)	3.1 (NCS)	—
Posttraumatic stress disorder[e]	7.8 (NCS)	—	—
Antisocial personality	2.5–3.5	1.2 (ECA)	—
Schizophrenia[e]	1.3–1.1	0.1 (ECA)	—
Schizophreniform disorder[e]	0.1–0.2	0.1 (ECA)	—
Cognitive impairment (severe)[f]	—	1.3 (ECA)	1.2
Somatization	0.1 (ECA)	0.1 (ECA)	—

[a]The ECA sample included persons aged 18 and older. The NCS sample included persons aged 15 to 55.
[b]Disorders were assessed with the Diagnostic Interview Schedule/DSM-III in the ECA and with the University of Michigan revision of the Composite International Diagnostic Interview/DSM-III-R in the NCS.
[c]Except for disorders for which only one study reported rates, in each pair of numbers the ECA rate is listed first, followed by the NCS rate. ECA prevalence rates are adapted from Regier et al. (1988a) and Robins and Regier (1991). ECA incidence rates are adapted from Eaton et al. (1989) and do not include the New Haven site. NCS prevalence rates are adapted from Kendler, Gallagher, Abelson, and Kessler (1996), Kessler et al. (1994), Kessler et al. (1995), and Wittchen et al. (1994).
[d]Rate was not examined.
[e]The NCS rates for this disorder are based on a subsample of 5,877 persons.
[f]Only current impairment at time of interview was assessed.

erally fixed, unmodifiable features of an individual, or as factors more amenable to change. This distinction is important because intervention efforts to prevent or ameliorate mental disorder will be quite different in the presence of each of the two types of risk factors. For example, prevention efforts in the case of unmodifiable factors may aim to alter other features of the individual's environment so as to minimize the impact of unmodifiable factors. In contrast, prevention efforts for modifiable factors may focus on changing the factors themselves.

Gender.   Although men and women have been found to have very similar overall rates of mental disorder in the United States (Kessler et al., 1994; Regier et al., 1988a), there appear to be marked gender differences in lifetime and period prevalence rates of specific disorders, including depression, substance

TABLE 2-3   Widely studied personal and environmental risk factors for the onset of mental disorder.

Personal Factors	
Unmodifiable	*Modifiable*
Gender	Social class
Age	Marital status
Ethnicity/race and culture of origin	Physical illness
Personal history of mental disorder	
Genetics and family history of mental disorder	

Environmental Factors	
Macroenvironmental	*Microenvironmental*
Community-wide stressors	Individual stressful life events
	Multiple life events and chronic strains
	Physical and psychosocial conditions of the environment

abuse, anxiety, and personality disorders. Such differences have appeared in general population studies, in studies conducted in primary medical care settings, and in studies of psychiatric patients. In the ECA study, for example, the male:female ratios were approximately 1:2 for depression, 6:1 for alcohol abuse/dependence, 2:1 for drug abuse/dependence, 1:2 to 1:3 for phobias, and 4:1 for antisocial personality disorder (Regier et al., 1988a; Robins et al., 1984). Both social and biological factors are likely to contribute to these differences. Gender differences in social roles and role performance, drinking habits, expression of emotional problems, and tendency to seek treatment may largely account for them (Briscoe, 1982).

The prevalence of schizophrenia and bipolar disorder do not appear to differ dramatically by gender (Bromet et al., 1995; Egeland & Hostetter, 1983). However, it has long been asserted that the risk period for schizophrenia occurs at an earlier age in men than in women (Lewine, 1988). Recent epidemiologic evidence suggests that the apparent gender difference in risk may be largely accounted for by gender differences in age of first hospitalization for this disorder: Men tend to present for treatment in their late teens and early twenties, whereas women are more likely to have their first treatment contact in their late twenties and early thirties (Eaton, Day, & Kramer, 1988). When indicators other than age of first hospitalization are used to define age of onset of schizophrenia (e.g., age of first prominent psychotic symptom), men and women both have been found to have the highest risk for developing this disorder in their early twenties (Beiser, Erickson, Fleming & Iacono, 1993).

Age.   ECA and NCS data indicate that lifetime and period prevalence rates for all psychiatric disorders, as well as specific rates for depression and anxiety disorders and for bipolar disorder, were generally higher in adults aged 44 or less than in older individuals (Kessler et al., 1994; Lasch, Weissman, Wickramaratne, & Bruce, 1990; Regier et al., 1988a; Robins et al., 1984). The rates of both alcohol and drug abuse/dependence were highest among individuals aged 24 or less, consistent with findings from national surveys of drinking patterns, which suggest that the peak period for heavy drinking and associated serious problems, such as driving or fighting while intoxicated, is in the early twenties (Cahalan & Cisin, 1980). The manifestations of schizophrenia also appear to vary with age, with prevalence rates generally dropping, particularly among women, after age 45 (Regier et al., 1988a).

The marked elevation of depression in younger versus older cohorts has received particular attention. Klerman and his colleagues analyzed data from several prevalence studies and noted that depression rates are consistently higher, with earlier reported age of onset, in generations born since World War II (Klerman, 1976; Klerman & Weissman, 1989). The possibility that various biologic, social, or economic factors may have increased recent generations' risk for depression means that, in order to disentangle the true impact of age per se versus other period- or cohort-related risk factors, it will be necessary to focus on longitudinal rather than cross-sectional studies of prevalence.

Ethnicity/race and culture of origin.   In the United States, there are mixed findings concerning ethnic/racial differences in prevalence rates. The ECA study found few striking ethnic differences once the effects of social class had been taken into account. For example, lifetime prevalence rates for most of the disorders assessed in the study were similar among African American and non–African American respondents (Robins et al., 1984). Exceptions to this pattern in the ECA data concerned major depression, for which white men tended to have higher prevalence rates than black men, but black women had higher prevalence rates that white women (Sommervell et al., 1989). In addition, African Americans had nearly twice the lifetime prevalence of simple phobia and agoraphobia (Eaton, Dryman, & Weissman, 1991). In contrast, the NCS reported that phobia rates were similar across African American and white groups and that blacks had significantly lower prevalence rates of affective disorder (major depression, dythymia, bipolar disorder), and substance use disorders (Kessler et al., 1994). The differences noted earlier between the ECA study and the NCS may have contributed to the inconsistency in findings, particularly those differences related to sampling.

Similar to black–white comparisons, comparisons of Hispanic Americans and non-Hispanic white Americans in the Los Angeles ECA revealed relatively similar rates of most disorders (Burnam et al., 1987; Karno et al., 1987). The three exceptions were drug abuse/dependence, major depression, and panic disorder, for which Hispanic Americans had lower prevalence rates than non-Hispanic whites. In contrast, Hispanics in the NCS had significantly higher rates of affective disorder than non-Hispanic whites but did not differ in any other diagnostic category.

Ethnic/racial differences in schizophrenia have been studied for many years. Early prevalence studies of treated samples within the United States suggested that, compared to whites, Hispanic Americans were at lower risk for schizophrenia (Jaco, 1959), while African Americans were disproportionately diagnosed with schizophrenia, and were hospitalized at a younger age and for longer periods of time (Fried, 1975). Given the ECA and NCS findings of no differences between whites and either of these other groups in prevalence rates of schizophrenia in the community, it is possible that ethnic differences in

earlier studies primarily reflected treatment differences between social groups.

International data suggest that schizophrenia may be concentrated in certain ethnic subgroups among Caucasians: elevated rates have been found in parts of Croatia (Lemkau, Kulcar, Kesic, & Kovacic, 1980) and Ireland (Walsh et al., 1980; Youssef, Kinsella, & Waddington, 1991). These high rates cannot be explained by differential emigration. Possible explanations relate to genetic transmission in relatively isolated population groups, or exposures to environmental agents such as viruses (see further discussion below). However, because differences in study design and diagnostic criteria varied in tandem with differences in observed rates in these community prevalence studies, it is difficult to reach firm conclusions regarding etiology.

It is noteworthy that ethnic differences in suicide rates have been consistently reported throughout the 20th century, with whites of all ages—particularly white men—having higher rates than both African Americans and some other ethnic groups, including Japanese Americans (Kramer, Pollack, Redick, & Locke, 1972; National Center for Health Statistics [NCHS], 1994). However, age-adjusted suicide rates for American Indians and Chinese Americans are higher than those for whites (Kramer et al., 1972). Indeed, the rate among American Indian and Alaskan native youths is over three times that for the U.S. population of the same age (Indian Health Service [IHS], 1993; NCHS, 1994).

An issue that overlaps, but is not synonymous, with ethnicity is one's culture of origin. Many of the ethnic group comparisons described here pertain to groups residing within one country, the United States. These comparisons, while informative for the U.S. population, may be of limited usefulness for understanding more broadly defined cultural differences. Consider, for example, Hispanics residing in Central and South American countries versus Western Europeans in North America or Europe. There is evidence that some psychiatric illnesses (e.g., *ataques de nervios*) and types of somatic symptoms and complaints are unique to non-U.S. Hispanic populations and are not observed in persons of Western European origin (Escobar, Gomez, & Tuason, 1983; Guarnaccia, Good, & Kleinman, 1990). Because cultural and ethnic group definitions often overlap, but are not synonymous, both comparisons of distinct ethnic groups within a given country *and* comparisons of those groups across cultural and political boundaries are needed in order to understand possible differences in risk and/or expression of psychiatric disorders.

Personal history of mental disorder. In addition to the well-known fact that a positive history of a disorder increases one's risk for new episodes of the disorder (e.g., Amenson & Lewinsohn, 1981), an important finding in psychiatric epidemiology is that individuals with one disorder often also meet criteria for a second, different disorder. Although both disorders may begin simultaneously, it has often been observed in treated populations that new disorders arise among individuals previously diagnosed with another disorder. Thus, patients with alcohol abuse/ dependence often develop a secondary depression during the course of the alcoholism. Schizophrenic patients discharged after their first lifetime admission often develop depression during the subsequent year. Recent epidemiologic findings have confirmed the relatively common co-occurrence of multiple psychiatric disorders in the general population, such as alcohol abuse/dependence with drug abuse/dependence (measure of association, Odds Ratio [OR] ranging from 10 to 16), alcohol abuse/dependence with antisocial personality (ORs ranging from 12.7 to 16), obsessive-compulsive disorder with panic disorder (OR = 20.6), major depression with somatization (OR = 27), and generalized anxiety disorder with dysthymia (OR = 14) (Boyd et al., 1984; Kessler et al., 1996, 1997; Wittchen et al., 1994).

Genetics and family history of mental disorder. Considerable research on familial aggregation of psychopathology is underway, and seeks to identify both sociocultural and biological familial risk factors. Although family, twin, and adoption studies have established that genetic factors are involved in the etiology of a variety of disorders, the precise degree of heritability and mode of genetic transmission remains to be specified (Merikangas, 1987). With respect to depression and bipolar disorders, a review of family studies indicated that there is an approximately threefold increase in the disorder in first-degree adult relatives of individuals with these illnesses (Ciaranello & Ciaranello, 1991). A study of

the offspring of depressed patients also found a threefold increase in risk of psychiatric disorder (though not depression per se) among these children (Weissman et al., 1984). Twin studies have shown that monozygotic twins have a concordance rate of approximately 67% for affective disorders, ranging from 54% for major depression to 74% for bipolar disorder. In contrast, dizygotic twins have only about a 20% concordance rate for these disorders (Ciaranello & Ciaranello, 1991). The most extensive recent studies of twins' risk for a variety of psychiatric disorders has been published by Kendler and colleagues and indicates that genetic factors account for substantial portions of the variability in risk for affective disorders (Kendler et al., 1995).

The preponderance of evidence regarding alcohol abuse/dependence also points to a genetic vulnerability to this disorder (Kendler et al., 1995; Merikangas, 1990). The risk of developing this disorder in the presence of an affected parent is 25% for men and 5% for women (Goodwin, 1984; Merikangas, 1987). Anxiety disorders such as panic and obsessivecompulsive disorder are also found at elevated rates in co-twins and in first-degree adult relatives and offspring of affected individuals (Ciaranello & Ciaranello, 1991; Kendler et al., 1995).

In schizophrenia, monozygotic twins have a concordance rate for the disorder of approximately 50%, compared to 8% to 28% for dizygotic twins (Gottesman, 1991; Kendler, 1988). The risk of developing schizophrenia in the presence of an affected firstdegree relative is approximately 10% to 12% (compared to an overall prevalence of less than 1%) (Kendler, 1988; Kety et al., 1994).

The 1990s have been a period of great growth in the field of psychiatric genetics. Excitement initially focused on several early results from genetic linkage studies (i.e., research designed to identify specific genes involved in transmission) of schizophrenia and bipolar disorder, but their results were not confirmed in subsequent replications. However, since these initial apparently false positive results, there is now emerging some evidence indicating replicated linkages on several chromosomes for both schizophrenia and bipolar disorder (Kendler, 1997).

Social class. In his prevalence study described earlier, Jarvis noted in 1855 that "the pauper class furnishes, in ratio of its numbers, sixty-four times as many cases of insanity as the independent class" (Jarvis, 1971, pp. 52–53). Since then, the relationship between social class and mental illness has been one of the most extensively documented associations within the epidemiology of mental disorders. Lower social-class status has been consistently found to be associated with depressive symptoms, substance abuse/dependence, antisocial personality disorder, and, especially, schizophrenia (Dohrenwend & Dohrenwend, 1974; Faris & Dunham, 1939; Schwab & Schwab, 1978). However, it has rarely been possible to draw strong inferences about the causal direction of this relationship. Some, notably Faris and Dunham (1939), have argued for a "social causation" explanation—that the stressful conditions of being in the lowest class foster illness onset. However, the alternative, "social selection" explanation, that vulnerable people drift downward into the lowest class, is often equally plausible.

One of the most influential studies supporting a social causation interpretation was conducted by Hollingshead and Redlich (1958), who demonstrated that among psychiatric patients, higher rates of schizophrenia occurred in lower social classes. Most of these patients had lived in poor areas of the city all of their lives. Moreover, 90% of their families of origin were in the same social class, suggesting that downward social mobility could not explain the findings.

More recent studies of individuals' social class backgrounds, however, have indicated that the direction of the social class–psychiatric disorder relationship strongly depends on the specific disorder under consideration. Despite the earlier findings by Hollingshead and Redlich, subsequent work has shown that social selection is the most compelling explanation for schizophrenia (Dohrenwend et al., 1992; Turner & Gartrell, 1978). For example, schizophrenic patients' occupational attainment is typically lower than that of their fathers and lower than that predicted from their school careers (e.g., Goldberg & Morrison, 1963). In contrast, at least one study demonstrated that social causation is more plausible for depression (particularly among women), and for antisocial personality and substance use disorders (particularly in men) (Dohrenwend et al., 1992).

Marital status. Both marital status and quality of the relationship have been associated with psychiatric disorder. In the ECA study, for example, both men and women were two to three times more likely to have had a recent psychiatric disorder if they were unmarried rather than married (Leaf et al., 1984). Even more striking was the finding that, among married individuals, the rate of disorder was four times higher among those who did not get along very well with their spouses compared to more happily married persons.

These relationships have been observed not only for total rates of any disorder, but for specific diagnoses such as major depression, dysthymia, and social phobia (Leaf et al., 1986; Schneier et al., 1992). The causal direction of these associations remains unclear because of the cross-sectional nature of most studies. However, at least for depression, a growing body of longitudinal evidence suggests that causality flows in both directions: Marriage affects one's mental health, which, in turn, influences the future of the marriage (Brown & Harris, 1978; Dew & Bromet, 1991; Krantz & Moos, 1987).

With respect to schizophrenia, being unmarried is associated with an elevated risk of the disorder (Eaton et al., 1988), and, among schizophrenics, being single at the time of first hospital admission is associated with a poorer prognosis (e.g., Bland, Parker & Orn, 1978). It is difficult, however, to determine the effects of marital status independent of known gender differences in schizophrenia: It is usually male patients who are likely to be unmarried, since, as noted earlier, males tend to be hospitalized in their late teens and early twenties, before many individuals get married.

Physical illness. Convergent evidence from general population, primary medical care, and specialty care samples indicates that physical illness and psychiatric disorder are reliably associated. In community-based studies, from 23% to 32% of respondents with either self-reported or medically verified physical illnesses met criteria for psychiatric disorders, compared to an average of about 15% among physically healthy respondents (Dilling & Weyerer, 1984; Kramer, Simonsick, Lima, & Levav, 1992; Vazquez-Barquero et al., 1987; Wells, Golding, & Burnam, 1989). Depression, anxiety, and substance use disorders were among the most common diagnoses among ill respondents.

The association between physical and mental illness becomes stronger as one moves from general population studies to studies of individuals receiving medical care. Thus, whereas physically ill persons in community samples are up to three times more likely to have psychiatric disorders than physically healthy persons, rates of psychiatric disorders in studies of physically ill persons in treated samples are up to 8.5 times higher than prevalence rates in healthy, non-patient populations (Dew, 1998; Rodin, Craven, & Littlefield, 1991). Although this increase may be partially due to "Berkson's bias"—the fact that individuals in treated populations are more likely to have multiple, comorbid conditions (Berkson, 1946)—there are considerable data showing that the more important element is increasing severity of physical illness (Weyerer, 1990; Dew, 1998, provides an extensive review). Even among medically ill inpatient groups, for example, rates of mental disorders increase with severity of the medical condition.

Certain types of psychiatric disorder appear to be more strongly associated with certain types of physical illnesses. For example, panic disorder has been found to be the most common psychiatric disorder among individuals with lung disease (e.g., Yellowlees & Ruffin, 1989), while major depression and dysthymia are more common than other disorders among individuals with cancer, HIV, and heart disease (Dean, 1987; Dew et al., 1997; Forrester et al., 1992).

Physical illness appears to act as a significant risk factor for mental disorder through both psychosocial and biological pathways. Psychosocially, an illness may elevate risk of mental disorder by affecting body image, self-esteem, and capacity to function at work and socially (Dew, 1998). Biologically, there is evidence that patients' risk for depression, for example, is elevated by certain endocrine disorders, nutritional or electrolyte abnormalities, some viral disorders, and drug effects (Hall, 1980; Klerman, 1981; Rodin et al., 1991).

As for the other risk factors we have discussed, it is also likely that the comorbidity of physical and psychiatric disorder is explained in some cases by the psychiatric disorder leading to physical health changes. Depression in physically ill persons is sometimes predictive of a shortened life expectancy (Frasure-Smith et al., 1993; Wai, Burton, Richmond, & Lindsay, 1981). Indeed, the mortality rate among psychiatrically ill individuals in general is higher than that expected for the general population (Babigian & Odoroff, 1969; Bruce & Leaf, 1989; Muñoz, Marten, Gentry, & Robins, 1971).

Environmental Risk Factors

Stressful events and circumstances have been demonstrated to elevate significantly an individual's risk of psychiatric disorder as well as subclinical psychiatric symptoms. As shown in the lower section of Table 2-3, these environmental stressors may be macroenvironmental events (e.g., natural and technological disasters) that affect large segments of the population and are relatively cataclysmic disruptors of social life (Hough, 1982). Alternatively, they may be microenvironmental factors that, while potentially devastating, affect relatively small portions of a given population.

Community-wide stressors.   These stressors expose large numbers of people to uncontrollable events. Both the acute and the long-term mental health effects of many such events have been studied, including natural disasters like volcanic eruptions (Shore, Tatum, & Vollmer, 1986), floods (Canino, Bravo, Rubio-Stipec, & Woodbury, 1990), firestorms (Koopman, Classen, & Spiegel, 1994), and earthquakes (Murphy, 1988). Technological accidents and events related to warfare have also been shown to produce significant mental health effects. Examples include missile attacks (Solomon et al., 1993), oil spills (Palinkas, Russell, Downs, & Patterson, 1992), and our own study of the psychiatric sequelae of a technological disaster, the 1979 accident at the Three Mile Island (TMI) nuclear power plant in Pennsylvania (Bromet, Parkinson, Dunn, & Gondek, 1982; Dew & Bromet, 1993).

Although each disaster has particular characteristics, and studies vary in design and instrument selection, a recent meta-analysis indicated that disasters increase the prevalence rate of psychopathology by about 17%, on average (Rubonis & Bickman, 1991). While most studies have focused on psychiatric symptom levels rather than diagnosable disorders, the few that have employed structured assessments and diagnostic criteria have noted two- to threefold increases in rates of major depression and generalized anxiety (e.g., Bromet et al., 1982), and posttraumatic stress disorder (PTSD; Palinkas et al., 1992) in exposed persons, relative to unexposed comparison samples.

Community-wide stressors vary in intensity and duration, and these elements appear to be among the most critical determinants of mental health effects. Recent reviews have emphasized that additional features of such events that also appear to be responsible for inducing psychiatric distress are their speed of onset, community residents' degree of involvement in terms of loss of life or property, and whether or not the events were precipitated by human actions (as opposed to being natural disasters) (Bromet & Dew, 1995; Green, 1994).

Individual stressful life events.   Single traumatic events, though perhaps as personally devastating as community-wide stressors, typically occur at a more individual level in the population. Thus, life events such as job loss (Dew, Bromet, & Penkower, 1992; Penkower et al., 1988), death of a loved one (Mendes de Leon, Kasl, & Jacobs, 1994), and physical injury (Perry et al., 1992) have been noted to produce changes in mental health. Most studies show initial increases in psychiatric disturbance and somatic complaints. Although some studies have noted few effects extending beyond an initial acute period, others have found these effects to persist for months and sometimes years. Indeed, recent reviews have concluded that a large minority of individuals—20% to 40%—do not recover fully from major life stressors despite the passage of many years (Kessler, Price, & Wortman, 1985). Extended stress effects have been noted primarily in the areas of somatic complaints and mood and anxiety disorders and associated symptoms.

Some of the earliest observations of deleterious mental health effects following stressful life events occurred during the two world wars, when many previously mentally healthy soldiers suffered from "shell shock," or combat stress reactions, when faced with extreme combat stress or deprivation. Since the Vietnam War, there has been considerable interest in establishing the prevalence of PTSD among combat veterans. This, in turn, has led to concern over risk for

this disorder in individuals experiencing a wide range of traumatic events, including the community disasters noted before as well as more individualized life stressors such as violent crime and sexual assault (Resnick et al., 1993; Rothbaum et al., 1992) and life-threatening illnesses and their treatments (Alter et al., 1996; Stukas, Dew, Switzer, DiMartini, Kormos, & Griffith, in press). PTSD is defined as a response to an unusual stressor in which an individual reexperiences the traumatic event through recurrent thoughts or dreams, experiences psychic numbing, and has symptoms such as sleep disturbance, survivor guilt, difficulty concentrating, hyperalertness, avoidance of activities associated with the event, and/or an intensification of symptoms if exposed to a similar event. A recent national study of male Vietnam combat veterans reported a point prevalence rate of 15.2% and a lifetime rate of 31% (Kulka et al., 1988). The NCS found a lifetime rate of 8.1% for men and 20.4% for women in the subset of its community-based sample who were exposed to trauma (Kessler et al., 1995).

Multiple life events and chronic strains.   The most extensive body of literature on environmental stress focuses on the mental health effects of multiple stressors, conceptualized as either acute, discrete life events or chronic strains (or, occasionally, some combination of the two (e.g., Turner, Wheaton, & Lloyd, 1995). In contrast to studies of the aftermath of single traumatic events, the multiple life events literature focuses not so much on the nature of specific events, but on whether the occurrence of *any* stressful event, as well as the total *number* of events that an individual experiences, is associated with certain mental health outcomes. In general, the occurrence of multiple discrete stressful life events is prognostic for depressive disorders and symptomatology (Kessler et al., 1985). For example, Shrout et al. (1989) found that "fateful" events (stressful events that were unlikely to have been brought about by the individual him- or herself) occurred 2.5 times more frequently in persons who then developed depressive illness than in community controls who did not experience such events. There appears to be some association between such events and the onset of schizophrenia as well. In a frequently cited report, Brown and Birley (1968) found that 46% of a sample of patients experiencing a first episode or recurrence of schizophrenia had had at least one "independent" life event in the previous 3 weeks, compared to only 14% of a comparison sample. Subsequent studies have not uniformly confirmed this finding for schizophrenia onset (see additional comments below regarding recurrence), although some reviewers have concluded that the evidence generally suggests that life events play some role in precipitating this disorder (Lukoff, Snyder, Ventura, & Nuechterlein, 1984).

Adverse life events may play a stronger causal role in the occurrence of depression, schizophrenia, and other disorders in particular individuals already made vulnerable by other factors. For example, Brown and Harris (1978) have shown that threatening life events precipitate episodes of depression in middle- to lower-class women who already lack a confiding relationship with their husbands, are unemployed, have three or more children under the age of 6, and/or have lost a parent in childhood. Several large literatures have developed around the issues of whether or not factors such as poor social support and poor coping strategies elevate one's vulnerability to psychiatric distress in the face of stressful life events (see Cohen & Wills, 1985, and Kessler et al., 1985, for reviews).

The effects of stressful life events may also be somewhat larger in patient populations than in community samples. For example, among individuals with schizophrenia, the occurrence of stressful life events may trigger psychotic episodes, particularly in patients with inadequate social network supports (Zubin, Steinhauer, Day, & Van Kammen, 1985). In bipolar patients, new episodes of mania and/or depression can also be provoked by the occurrence of multiple major life events (Ambelas, 1987; Cassano et al., 1989).

Some stressful occurrences are more appropriately characterized as chronic, ongoing strains, rather than discrete events. There is evidence that such strain arising from one's social roles, from the marriage, from occupational demands, and the like elevates psychological distress—and depressed mood in particular—in community samples (e.g., Pearlin, Lieberman, Menaghan, & Mullen, 1981; Pearlin & Schooler, 1978; Phelan et al., 1991). Moreover, the combination of multiple discrete life events with ongoing chronic strains dramatically elevates risk for

depressive symptomatology and diagnosable disorder (Turner et al., 1995). Additional studies of occupational samples have noted that employees in jobs characterized by high levels of demand, little autonomy over decision making, conflicting requirements, and ambiguity experience higher levels of psychological symptoms and alcohol abuse than employees experiencing less occupational stress (Kasl, 1978). The combination of high demands and low decision latitude has been shown to be particularly stressful (Bromet, Dew, Parkinson, & Schulberg, 1988; Karasek, 1979).

In sum, there is strong evidence that chronic strains—alone or in combination with acute stressors—are associated with mental health. However, causal interpretation of this association remains problematic: Most chronic strain measures are based on subjective assessments and thus may sometimes be symptoms of, rather than risk factors for, respondents' psychiatric impairment.

Physical and psychosocial conditions of the environment. With respect to the physical environment, an extensive clinical literature has demonstrated that intense exposure to lead, mercury, carbon monoxide, carbon disulphide, and the like can cause serious central nervous system (CNS) disturbances (Feldman, Ricks, & Baker, 1980). In *Alice in Wonderland,* Lewis Carroll immortalized the well-known hallucinations, delusions, and mania produced by high-level mercury exposure in the character of the Mad Hatter. Since the 19th century, dramatic case reports have described cognitive and neurasthenic symptoms, and even suicide, in workers exposed to a variety of solvents. As late as the 1940s, a significantly elevated suicide rate was reported in workers exposed to carbon disulphide (Mancuso & Locke, 1972). Outbreaks of neurotoxic disorders, with affected individuals manifesting a variety of symptoms of severe mental disorder, have continued to occur following exposures to contaminated foodstuffs and pharmaceuticals in numerous industrialized countries (Cooper, 1993). More subtle infiltrations of viruses into certain population groups have also been linked to mental illness (e.g., Lipkin, Schneemann, & Solbrig, 1995). Cooper (1993) provides an interesting account of the role of epidemiologists in identifying the neuropsychiatric symptoms and their etiology.

An issue of current concern is potential neuropsychiatric effects of low-level exposure to chemicals that have become widely distributed in the environment. Two such exposures that have been investigated extensively are inorganic lead and solvents. In addition to the documented developmental effects of low-level lead exposure in children (Needleman et al., 1979; Rutter, 1980), clinical studies of low-level lead exposure among male workers have noted effects on neuropsychological functioning, personality, and anxiety (e.g., Haenninen et al., 1978; Hogstedt, Hane, Agrell, & Bodin, 1983). However, epidemiologic research has been unable to detect significant effects of low-level lead exposure on either neuropsychological or psychiatric status (Parkinson, Ryan, Bromet, & Connell, 1986). With respect to solvents, several large epidemiologic studies of both male and female workers chronically exposed at threshold or subthreshold levels have reported significantly more depressive symptomatology, CNS disturbances (headaches, dizziness, memory disturbances), nonspecific somatic complaints (nausea, abdominal pain, skin problems), and/or impaired performance on cognitive tasks compared to unexposed workers (e.g., Axelson, Hane, & Hogstedt, 1976; Parkinson et al., 1990).

Other more social-structural facets of the physical environment also appear to affect risk for psychiatric disorders and symptomatology. First, whether an individual resides in an urban versus a rural area has been consistently related to rates of mental illness. In a comprehensive review of community prevalence studies, Dohrenwend and Dohrenwend (1974) showed that total rates of mental illness were higher in urban than in rural areas, although whether this resulted from the stresses of living in an urban environment or from ill individuals migrating to an urban environment remains unresolved. The elevated urban rates appeared to be due to an excess of "neurosis" (which encompasses many of the current DSM-IV mood and anxiety disorders) and personality disorder in urban areas. In fact, total rates for psychoses tended to be higher in rural settings, although schizophrenia in particular appeared equally frequent in rural and urban settings. Subsequent studies have generally confirmed these findings. For example, in the ECA study, rates of major depression and bipolar disorder were two to four times higher in urban versus rural areas (Blazer et al., 1985; Weissman et al., 1991). However, recent reports have shown that schizophrenia, as well, may show an urban excess (Eaton, 1974; Lewis, David, Andreasson, & Allebeck, 1992).

A second structural aspect of the physical environment that has been studied extensively, particularly in England after World War II, is housing characteristics. For example, studies of effects of high-rise housing have shown an association between living on higher floor levels and heightened psychological strain (Gillis, 1977). Apartment dwellers have been found to be more depressed and lonely than demographically similar individuals residing in single-family houses (Richman, 1974). A large literature on density and crowding suggests that measures of "social pathology" (e.g., juvenile delinquency rates, admissions to mental hospitals, and public assistance rates) may be associated with environmental factors such as the number of residents per room and the number of rooms per housing unit (e.g., Galle, Gove, & McPherson, 1972; Williams, 1994).

A third important aspect of the residential environment concerns the effects of *lack* of a permanent residence, and the associated rising pandemic of homelessness. Rates of mental illness among homeless adults are alarmingly high. For example, Koegel, Burnam, and Farr (1988) reported that more than one-quarter of homeless individuals in a Los Angeles sample had a major chronic mental illness, such as schizophrenia or substance abuse. North, Smith, and Spitznagel (1994) found that two-thirds of their sample in St. Louis met DSM-III-R criteria for one or more mental disorders, with rates of substance use disorders, antisocial personality, major depression, PTSD, and schizophrenia being particularly high. While evidence from some of these studies suggest that homelessness provoked mental illness or new episodes of a chronic disorder, other work has shown that having a mental disorder also increases the risk of homelessness. Thus, in some U.S. cities, deinstitutionalization of the mentally ill from state institutions has significantly contributed to the problem of homelessness. The risk of homelessness among discharged state hospital patients is 25% to 50%, which is 10 to 20 times higher than the risk of homelessness for the general population (Jahiel, 1992; Susser, Moore, & Link, 1993)

It is clear that some of the characteristics that we have described as structural, physical factors (e.g., residential status or lack thereof), or as personal factors (e.g., marital status, family psychiatric history) also reflect the psychosocial nature of one's environment. In other words, the way in which such characteristics operate as risk factors for mental disorders involves, in part, the degree to which they facilitate formal and informal social ties and supports. Both one's specific connections with others (by virtue of being married, having children, living alone or with others) and the quality of those relationships have been widely demonstrated to affect likelihood of incident and recurrent psychiatric disorder (for reviews, see Cohen & Wills, 1985; Thoits, 1995).

SUMMARY AND FUTURE DIRECTIONS

An ultimate goal of epidemiology is to identify causes of disease so as to provide information useful in disease prevention. For a given disorder, epidemiologic work begins with the assessment of the distribution of the disorder in the population, followed by delineation of risk factors associated with that distribution, leading to experimental efforts to intervene on one or more such factors in order to prevent or control the disorder. Notions of representative sampling and a reliable and valid case definition are fundamental to this process, and psychiatric epidemiology has advanced through three stages in attempting to incorporate these notions: First-generation studies defined cases on the basis of treatment seeking; second-generation studies relied on global impairment scales to assess community populations; and third-generation studies employ methods of diagnostic categorization to examine cases in the population. All three approaches continue to be used today.

Much of psychiatric epidemiology has focused on the identification of personal characteristics and/or social-environmental risk factors for psychiatric disorder. Which of these risk factors are causally linked to disorder is unknown, although the etiologies of most mental disorders are believed to be multifactorial. One task for future research is to build and test causal models that further integrate the variety of individually identified risk factors. Evaluation of these models will require more frequent use of longitudinal

study designs capable of disentangling predictors of disorder from the disorder and its consequences, as well as the wider application of experimental and quasi-experimental methods, with prospective data, to examine how much of the link between a risk factor and a disorder is due to a causal component (Kessler et al., 1985). Application of experimental methods is difficult, but not impossible, to employ in psychiatric epidemiologic research, as evidenced by, for example, studies taking advantage of "natural experiments."

Even in the absence of knowledge about the etiology of a given disorder, experimental intervention efforts aimed at changing a known risk factor may effectively lead to a reduction in the rate of disorder in a population (Earls, 1987). Indeed, one of the central challenges for the field of psychiatric epidemiology is to accelerate the development and—particularly—the evaluation of prevention efforts for the major psychiatric disorders. As will be summarized briefly, some prevention efforts, developed on the basis of psychiatric epidemiologic data, have already been undertaken at primary, secondary, and tertiary prevention levels.

Primary prevention refers to efforts to reduce the incidence of a disorder, and has been successfully applied in the few situations where the etiology of a psychiatric disorder was understood and the environmental cause could be eliminated. Thus, psychoses resulting from pellagra and brain damage from measles and rubella have essentially been eradicated in the United States through primary prevention efforts. In the workplace, application of standards such as the United States Occupational Safety and Health Administration's Lead Standard have reduced many chemical exposures to levels at which neuropathy, encephalopathy, or other mental disorders rarely occur.

What warrants greater recognition is the fact that primary prevention efforts can begin even when etiology is unknown. Such efforts can target asymptomatic individuals in groups already shown by epidemiologic research to be at high risk for a disorder. For example, several such programs have been aimed at reducing psychological difficulties in recently separated couples; substance abuse and delinquency in young adolescents with a history of poor academic performance and disruptive behaviors; depression in low-income mothers and in adults undergoing major life changes; depression and anxiety levels in persons with chronic physical illnesses; and psychiatric problems in occupational groups (Price & Smith, 1984; Snow & Kline, 1995; Williams & Chesney, 1993). While many such programs have been grassroots efforts and have not included a research component, there is a growing trend for these efforts to receive systematic evaluation of their effectiveness. Examples include some school-based teenage suicide prevention programs, and programs to maximize the mental health of caregivers to the elderly, the goals of which are to heighten awareness of the mental health issues involved, to provide information about mental health resources, and to help in referring individuals for care and assistance (e.g., Goodman & Pynoos, 1990; Shaffer et al., 1988).

The focus of third-generation psychiatric epidemiologic studies on case finding in the general population provides the necessary framework for the expansion of secondary prevention efforts, which refer to the treatment of populations who are in the early stages of a disorder in order to prevent episode recurrence or resulting disability. Currently, the workplace and both general and specialty medical settings have become focal points for secondary intervention programs. Although their effectiveness has not been determined, many companies have established Employee Assistance Programs to counsel troubled employees. The goal of these programs is to detect mental health problems at an early stage and offer an intervention that might help to avert a full-blown psychiatric episode. Similarly, because psychopathology has been found to impede recovery from concurrent physical illnesses or provoke continued physical morbidity, interventions have been implemented to treat mild to moderate levels of distress in such patients before the distress further complicates the patients' medical picture (Schulberg et al., 1996).

Finally, tertiary prevention is designed to minimize long-term disability and handicap in patients with a history of mental illness. An important example, developed on the basis of both clinical and epidemiologic work, is the NIMH Depression/Awareness, Recognition and Treatment program (Regier et al., 1988b). The program is a mixed secondary and tertiary prevention effort aimed at educating mental health professionals, nonpsychiatric general medical practitioners, and the lay public about the symptoms and treatments for affective disorder.

In addition to the continued application of epidemiologic data to the development of prevention programs, the future of psychiatric epidemiology is likely to involve closer ties with clinical research and practice (Cooper, 1993; Feinstein, 1985). Epidemiology and clinical research already share many study designs and analytic strategies. However, as suggested previously, epidemiology could be enriched by continuing beyond the enumeration of risk factors, to incorporating and testing clinically developed models of *how* risk factors come to affect psychopathology. Clinical research, on the other hand, could benefit from more extensive consideration of traditionally epidemiologic concerns with representative sampling and standardized diagnostic assessment. For example, representative sampling issues are relevant not only to the selection of general community samples, but also to the selection of individuals from *patient* populations.

With respect to the connection of epidemiology with clinical practice, closer ties may help to reduce the number of epidemiologic studies which, though well designed, continue to focus on a narrow range of often unmodifiable risk factors (e.g., gender, age, social class) and yield findings of limited relevance to actually improving the health of sick people (Weissman, 1987). Alternatively, clinical understanding of psychopathology may be enriched by incorporating the epidemiologic fact that data about mental disorder obtained from patients often does not represent the full spectrum of the disorder and its prognosis (Cohen & Cohen, 1984; Weissman, 1987).

In sum, though a relatively young discipline, psychiatric epidemiology has developed and applied important case finding techniques in community samples and, once cases are identified, has described an array of risk factors that are associated with psychopathology. Although the etiology of most disorders remains unknown, epidemiologic data provides valuable clues as to appropriate interventions to avert and/or minimize the effects of mental disorders. Increased integration of psychiatric epidemiology with clinical research and practice will afford new opportunities to test clinically derived models of the development and progression of mental disorders in community populations. This epidemiologic work will lead, in turn, to an enriched clinical understanding of psychopathology.

REFERENCES

Aderibigbe, Y.A., & Adityanjee, S.K. (1995). Psychiatric epidemiology in cross-cultural perspective: A review. *European Archives of Psychiatry and Clinical Neuroscience, 246,* 37–46.

Alter, C.L., Pelcovitz, D., Axelrod, A., Goldenberg, B., Harris, H., Meyers, B., Grobois, B., Mandel, F., Septimus, A., & Kaplan, S. (1996). Identification of PTSD in cancer survivors. *Psychosomatics, 37,* 137–143.

Ambelas, A. (1987). Life events and mania: A special relationship. *British Journal of Psychiatry, 150,* 235–240.

Amenson, C.S., & Lewinsohn, P.M. (1981). An investigation into the observed sex difference in prevalence of unipolar depression. *Journal of Abnormal Psychology, 90,* 1–13.

American Psychiatric Association. (1980). *Diagnostic and statistical manual of mental disorders,* 3rd ed. Washington, DC: Author.

American Psychiatric Association. (1987). *Diagnostic and statistical manual of mental disorders,* 3rd ed. (revised). Washington, DC: Author.

Angold, A., & Costello, E.J. (1995). A test–retest reliability study of child-reported psychiatric symptoms and diagnoses using the Child and Adolescent Psychiatric Assessment (CAPA-C). *Psychological Medicine, 25,* 755–762.

Axelson, O., Hane, M., & Hogstedt, C. (1976). A case referent study on neuropsychiatric disorders among workers exposed to solvents. *Scandinavian Journal of Work, Environment and Health, 2,* 14–20.

Babigian, H.M., & Odoroff, C.L. (1969). The mortality experience of a population with psychiatric illness. *American Journal of Psychiatry, 126,* 470–480.

Beiser, M., Erickson, D., Fleming, J., & Iacono, W. (1993). Establishing the onset of psychotic illness. *American Journal of Psychiatry, 150,* 1349–1354.

Berkson, J. (1946). Limitations of the application of fourfold table analysis to hospital data. *Biometrics Bulletin, 2,* 47–53.

Biehl, H., Maurer, K., Schubart, C., Krumm, B., & Jung, E. (1986). Prediction of outcome and utilization of medical services in a prospective study of first onset schizophrenics: Results of a prospective 5-year follow-up study. *European Archives of Psychiatry and Neurological Sciences, 236,* 139–147.

Bland, R.C., Parker, J.H., & Orn, H. (1978). Prognosis in schizophrenia. Prognostic predictors and outcome. *Archives of General Psychiatry, 35,* 72–77.

Blazer, D.G., George, L.K., Landerman, R., Pennybacker, M., Melville, M.L., Woodbury, M., Manton, K.G., Jordan, D., & Locke, B.Z. (1985). Psychiatric disorders: A rural/urban comparison. *Archives of General Psychiatry, 42,* 651–656.

Boyd, J.H., Burke, J.D., Jr., Holzer, C.E. III, Rae, D.S., George, L.K., Karno, M., Stoltzman, R., McEvoy, L., & Nestadt, G. (1984). Exclusion criteria of DSM-III. A study of co-occurence of hierarchy-free syndromes. *Archives of General Psychiatry, 41,* 983–989.

Boyle, M.H., Offord, D.R., Racine, Y., Sanford, M., Szatmari, P., Fleming, J.E., & Price-Munn, N. (1993). Evaluation of the Diagnostic Interview for Children and Adolescents for use in general population samples. *Journal of Abnormal Child Psychology, 21,* 663–681.

Briscoe, M. (1982). Sex differences in psychological well-being. *Psychological Medicine, 12*(Suppl. 1), 1–46.

Bromet, E.J., & Dew, M.A. (1995). Review of psychiatric epidemiologic research on disasters. *Epidemiologic Reviews, 17,* 113–119.

Bromet, E.J., Dew, M.A., & Eaton, W.W. (1995). Epidemiology of psychosis with special reference to schizophrenia. In M.T. Tsuang, M. Tohen, & G.E.P. Zahner (Eds.), *Textbook in psychiatric epidemiology* (pp. 283–300). New York: Wiley-Liss.

Bromet, E.J., Dew, M.A., Parkinson, D.K., & Schulberg, H.C. (1988). Predictive effects of occupational and marital stress on the mental health of a male workforce. *Journal of Organizational Behavior, 9,* 1–13.

Bromet, E.J., Dunn, L.O., Connell, M., Dew, M.A., & Schulberg, H.C. (1986). Long-term reliability of lifetime major depression in a community sample. *Archives of General Psychiatry, 43,* 435–440.

Bromet, E.J., Parkinson, D.K., Dunn, L.O., & Gondek, P.C. (1982). Mental health of residents near the TMI reactor: A comparative study of selected groups. *Journal of Preventive Psychiatry, 1,* 225–275.

Brown, G., & Birley, J.L.T. (1968). Crises and life changes and the onset of schizophrenia. *Journal of Health and Social Behavior, 9,* 203–214.

Brown, G., & Harris, T. (1978). *The social origins of depression: A study of psychiatric disorder in women.* New York: Free Press.

Bruce, M.L., & Leaf, P.J. (1989). Psychiatric disorders and 15-month mortality in a community sample of older adults. *American Journal of Public Health, 79,* 727–730.

Burnam, M.A., Hough, R.L., Escobar, J.I., Karno, M., Timbers, D.M., Telles, C.A., & Locke, B.Z. (1987). Six-month prevalence of specific psychiatric disorders among Mexican Americans and non-Hispanic whites in Los Angeles. *Archives of General Psychiatry, 44,* 687–694.

Cahalan, D., & Cisin, I.H. (1980). American drinking practices: Summary of findings from a national probability sample: I. Extent of drinking by population subgroups. In D.A. Ward (Ed.), *Alcoholism: Introduction to theory and treatment* (pp. 101–118). Dubuque, Iowa: Kendall/Hunt.

Canino, G., Bravo, M., Rubio-Stipec, M., & Woodbury, M. (1990). The impact of disaster on mental health: Prospective and retrospective analyses. *International Journal of Mental Health, 19,* 51–69.

Cassano, G.B., Akiskal, H.S., Musetti, L., Perugi, G., Soriani, A., & Mignoni, V. (1989). Psychopathology, temperament, and past course in primary major depressions: II. Toward a redefinition of bipolarity with a new semistructured interview for depression. *Psychopathology, 22,* 278–288.

Chesney, M.A., & Folkman, S. (1994). Psychological impact of HIV disease and implications for inter-

vention. *Psychiatric Clinics of North America, 17,* 163–182.

Ciaranello, R.D., & Ciaranello, A.L. (1991). Genetics of major psychiatric disorders. *Annual Review of Medicine, 42,* 151–158.

Cohen, P., & Cohen, J. (1984). The clinician's illusion. *Archives of General Psychiatry, 41,* 1178–1182.

Cohen, S., & Wills, T.A. (1985). Stress, social support and the buffering hypothesis. *Psychological Bulletin, 98,* 310–357.

Cooper, B. (1993). Single spies and battalions: The clinical epidemiology of mental disorders. *Psychological Medicine, 23,* 891–907.

Cooper, J.E., Kendell, R.E., Gurland, B.J., Sharpe, L., & Copeland, J.R.M. (1972). *Psychiatric diagnosis in New York and London: A comparative study of mental hospital admissions.* London: Oxford University Press.

Dean, C. (1987). Psychiatric morbidity following mastectomy: Preoperative predictors and types of illness. *Journal of Psychosomatic Research, 31,* 385–392.

Dew, M.A. (1998). Psychiatric disorder in the context of physical illness. In B.P. Dohrenwend (Ed.), *Adversity, stress, and psychopathology* (pp. 177–218). New York: Oxford University Press.

Dew, M.A., Becker, J., Sanchez, R., Caldararo, R., Lopez, O.L., Wess, J., Dorst, S.K., & Banks, G. (1997). Prevalence and predictors of depressive, anxiety and substance use disorders in HIV-infected and uninfected men: A longitudinal evaluation. *Psychological Medicine, 27,* 395–409.

Dew, M.A., & Bromet, E.J. (1991). Effects on depression and social support in a community sample of women. In J. Eckenrode (Ed.), *The social context of coping* (pp. 189–211). New York: Plenum Press.

Dew, M.A., & Bromet, E.J. (1993). Predictors of temporal patterns of psychiatric distress during 10 years following the nuclear accident at Three Mile Island. *Social Psychiatry and Psychiatric Epidemiology, 28,* 49–55.

Dew, M.A., Bromet, E.J., & Schulberg, H.C. (1987). A comparative analysis of two community stressors' long-term mental health effects. *American Journal of Community Psychology, 15,* 167–184.

Dew, M.A., Roth, L.H., Schulberg, H.C., Simmons, R.G., Kormos, R.L., Trzepacz, P.T., & Griffith, B.P. (1996). Prevalence and predictors of depression and anxiety-related disorders during the year after heart transplantation. *General Hospital Psychiatry, 18,* 48S–61S.

Dew, M.A., Bromet, E.J., & Penkower, L. (1992). Mental health effects of job loss in women. *Psychological Medicine, 22,* 751–764.

Dilling, H., & Weyerer, S. (1984). Prevalence of mental disorders in the small-town–rural region of Traunstein (Upper Bavaria). *Acta Psychiatrica Scandinavia, 69,* 60–79.

Dohrenwend, B.P., & Dohrenwend, B.S. (1974). Social and cultural influences on psychopathology. *Annual Review of Psychology, 25,* 417–452.

Dohrenwend, B.P., & Dohrenwend, B.S. (1982). Perspectives on the past and future of psychiatric epidemiology: The 1981 Rema Lapouse Lecture. *American Journal of Public Health, 72,* 1271–1279.

Dohrenwend, B.P., Levav, I., Shrout, P.E., Schwartz, S., Naveh, G., Link, B.G., Skodol, A.E., & Stueve, A. (1992). Socioeconomic status and psychiatric disorders: The causation-selection issue. *Science, 255,* 946–952.

Earls, F. (1987). Toward the prevention of psychiatric disorders. In R.E. Hales & A.J. Francis (Eds.), *Psychiatry update* (Vol. 6, pp. 664–675). Washington, DC: American Psychiatric Press.

Eaton, W.W. (1974). Residence, social class, and schizophrenia. *Journal of Health and Social Behavior, 15,* 289–299.

Eaton, W.W., Day, R., & Kramer, M. (1988). The use of epidemiology for risk factor research in schizophrenia: An overview and methodologic critique. In M.T. Tsuang & J.C. Simpson (Eds.), *Nosology, epidemiology, and genetics of schizophrenia* (pp. 169–204). New York: Elsevier.

Eaton, W.W., Dryman, A., & Weissman, M.M. (1991). Panic and phobia: The diagnosis of the panic disorder and phobic disorder. In L.N. Robins & D.A. Regier (Eds.), *Psychiatric disorders in America: The Epidemiologic Catchment Area Study* (pp. 155–179). New York: Free Press.

Eaton, W.W., Kramer, M., Robins, L.N., Blazer, D.G., Hough, R.L., & Locke, B.Z. (1989). The incidence of specific DIS/DSM-III mental disorders: Data from the NIMH Epidemiologic Catchment Area Program. *Acta Psychiatrica Scandinavica, 79,* 163–178.

Egeland, J.A., & Hostetter, A.M. (1983). Amish study, I: Affective disorders among the Amish, 1976–1980. *American Journal of Psychiatry, 140,* 56–61.

Endicott, J., & Spitzer, R. (1978). A diagnostic interview: The Schedule for Affective Disorders and Schizophrenia. *Archives of General Psychiatry, 35,* 837–844.

Escobar, J.I., Gomez, J., & Tuason, V.G. (1983). Depressive phenomenology in North and South American patients. *American Journal of Psychiatry, 140,* 47–51.

Faris, R., & Dunham, H. (1939). *Mental disorders in urban areas: An ecological study of schizophrenia and other psychoses.* New York: Hafner.

Fawzy, F.I., Fawzy, N.W., Arndt, L.A., & Pasnau, R.O. (1995). Critical review of psychosocial interventions in cancer care. *Archives of General Psychiatry, 52,* 100–113.

Feighner, J.P., Robins, E., & Guze, S.B. (1972). Diagnostic criteria for use in diagnostic research. *Archives of General Psychiatry, 26,* 57–63.

Feinstein, A.R. (1985). *Clinical epidemiology: The architecture of clinical research.* Philadelphia: W.B. Saunders.

Feldman, R., Ricks, N., & Baker, E. (1980). Neuropsychological effects of industrial toxins: A review. *American Journal of Industrial Medicine, 1,* 211–227.

Forrester, A.W., Lipsey, J.R., Teitelbaum, M.L., DePaulo, J.R., Andrzejewski, P.L., & Robinson, R.G. (1992). Depression following myocardial infarction. *International Journal of Psychiatry in Medicine, 22,* 33–46.

Frasure-Smith, N., Lesperance, F., & Talajic, M. (1993). Depression following myocardial infarction: Impact on 6-month survival. *Journal of the American Medical Association, 270,* 1819–1825.

Fried, M. (1975). Social differences in mental health. In J. Kosa & I. Zola (Eds.), *Poverty and health: A sociological analysis* (pp. 113–167). Cambridge, MA: Harvard University Press.

Galle, O.R., Gove, W.R., & McPherson, J.M. (1972). Population density and pathology: What are the relations for man? *Science, 176,* 23–30.

Giggs, J.A. (1986). Mental disorders and ecological structure in Nottingham. *Social Science in Medicine, 23,* 945–961.

Gillis, A.R. (1977). High-rise housing and psychological strain. *Journal of Health and Social Behavior, 18,* 418–431.

Goldberg, E., & Morrison, S. (1963). Schizophrenia and social class. *British Journal of Psychiatry, 109,* 785–802.

Goodman, C.C., & Pynoos, J. (1990). A model telephone information and support program for caregivers of Alzheimer's disease. *Gerontologist, 30,* 399–404.

Goodwin, D.W. (1984). Studies of familial alcoholism: A review. *Journal of Clinical Psychology, 45,* 14–17.

Gordon, J.E. (1958). Medical ecology and the public health. *American Journal of the Medical Sciences, 235,* 337–359.

Gottesman, I.I. (1991). *Schizophrenia epigenesis: The origins of madness.* New York: W H Freeman.

Green, B.L. (1994). Psychosocial research in traumatic stress: An update. *Journal of Traumatic Stress, 7,* 341–362.

Guarnaccia, P.J., Good, B.J., & Kleinman, A. (1990). A critical review of epidemiological studies of Puerto Rican mental health. *American Journal of Psychiatry, 147,* 1449–1456.

Haenninen, H., Hernberg, S., Mantere, P., Vesanto, R., & Jalkanen, M. (1978). Psychological performance of subjects with low exposure to lead. *Journal of Occupational Medicine, 20,* 683–689.

Hall, R.C. (1980). Depression. In R.C. Hall (Ed.), *Psychiatric presentations of medical illness* (pp. 37–63). New York: Spectrum Publications.

Hays, R.D., Wells, K.B., Sherbourne, C.D., Rogers, W., & Spritzer, K. (1995). Functioning and well-being outcomes of patients with depression compared with chronic general medical illnesses. *Archives of General Psychiatry, 52,* 11–19.

Hogstedt, C., Hane, M., Agrell, A., & Bodin, L. (1983). Neuropsychological test results and symptoms among workers with well-defined long-term exposure to lead. *British Journal of Industrial Medicine, 40,* 99–105.

Hollingshead, A.B., & Redlich, F.C. (1958). *Social class and mental illness: A community study.* New York: Wiley.

Hough, R.L. (1982). Psychiatric epidemiology and prevention—An overview of the possibilities. In R.L. Hough, P.A. Gongla, V.B. Brown, & S.E. Gordon (Eds.), *Psychiatric epidemiology and prevention: The possibilities* (pp. 1–28). Los Angeles: Neuropsychiatric Institute, University of California.

Indian Health Service. (1993). *Trends in Indian health—1993.* Rockville, MD: U.S. Department of Health and Human Services, Public Health Service.

Institute of Medicine. (1989). *Research on children and adolescents with mental, behavioral, and developmental disorders: Mobilizing a national initiative.* Washington, DC: National Academy Press.

Jaco, E.G. (1959). Mental health of the Spanish American in Texas. In M.K. Opler (Ed.), *Culture and mental health: Cross-cultural studies* (pp. 467–485). New York: Macmillan.

Jahiel, R.I. (Ed.). (1992). *Homelessness: A prevention-oriented approach.* Baltimore: The Johns Hopkins University Press.

Jarvis, E. (1971). *Insanity and idiocy in Massachusetts: Report of the Commission on Lunacy, 1855.* Cambridge, MA: Harvard University Press.

Karasek, R. (1979). Job demands, job decision latitude, and mental strain: Implications for job redesign. *Administrative Science Quarterly, 24,* 285–306.

Karno, M., Hough, R.L., Burnam, M.A., Escobar, J.I., Timbers, D.M., Santana, F., & Boyd, J.H. (1987). Lifetime prevalence of specific psychiatric disorders among Mexican Americans and non-Hispanic whites in Los Angeles. *Archives of General Psychiatry, 44,* 695–701.

Kasl, S. (1978). Epidemiological contributions to the study of work stress. In C. Cooper & R. Payne (Eds.), *Stress at work* (pp. 3–48). New York: Wiley.

Kendler, K.S. (1988). The genetics of schizophrenia: An overview. In M.T. Tsuang & J.C. Simpson (Eds.), *Nosology, epidemiology and genetics of schizophrenia* (pp. 437–462). New York: Elsevier.

Kendler, K.S. (1997). The genetic epidemiology of psychiatric disorders: A current perspective. *Social Psychiatry and Psychiatric Epidemiology, 32,* 5–11.

Kendler, K.S., Gallagher, T.J., Abelson, J.M., & Kessler, R.C. (1996). Lifetime prevalence, demographic risk factors, and diagnostic validity of nonaffective psychosis as assessed in a U.S. community sample: The National Comorbidity Survey. *Archives of General Psychiatry, 53,* 1022–1031.

Kendler, K.S., Walters, E.E., Neale, M.C., Kessler, R.C., Heath, A.C., & Eaves, L.J. (1995). The structure of the genetic and environmental risk factors for six major psychiatric disorders in women. Phobia, generalized anxiety disorder, panic disorder, bulimia, major depression, and alcoholism. *Archives of General Psychiatry, 52,* 374–383.

Kessler, R.C., Crum, R.M., Warner, L.A., Nelson, C.B., Schulenberg, J., & Anthony, J.C. (1997). Lifetime co-occurrence of DSM-III-R alcohol abuse and dependence with other psychiatric disorders in the National Comorbidity Survey. *Archives of General Psychiatry, 54,* 313–321.

Kessler, R.C., McGonagle, K.A., Zhao, S., Nelson, C.B., Hughes, M., Eshleman, S., Wittchen, H-U., & Kendler, K.S. (1994). Lifetime and 12-month prevalence of DSM-III-R psychiatric disorders in the United States: Results from the National Comorbidity Survey. *Archives of General Psychiatry, 51,* 8–19.

Kessler, R.C., Nelson, C.B., McGonagle, K.A., Edlund, M.J., Frank, R.G., & Leaf, P.J. (1996). The epidemiology of co-occurring addictive and mental disorders: Implications for prevention and service utilization. *American Journal of Orthopsychiatry, 66,* 17–31.

Kessler, R.C., Price, R.H., & Wortman, C.B. (1985). Social factors in psychopathology. *Annual Review of Psychology, 36,* 531–572.

Kessler, R.C., Sonnega, A., Bromet, E., Hughes, M., & Nelson, C.B. (1995). Posttraumatic stress disorder in the National Comorbidity Survey. *Archives of General Psychiatry, 52,* 1048–1060.

Kessler, R.C., & Wethington, R.C. (1991). The reliability of life event reports in a community survey. *Psychological Medicine, 21,* 723–738.

Kety, S.S., Wender, P.H., Jacobsen, B., Ingraham, L.J., Jansson, L., Faber, B., & Kinney, D.K. (1994). Mental illness in the biological and adoptive relatives of schizophrenic adoptees: Replication of the Copenhagen Study in the rest of Denmark. *Archives of General Psychiatry, 51,* 442–455.

Klerman, G.L. (1976). Age and clinical depression: Today's youth in the twenty-first century. *Journal of Gerontology, 31,* 318–323.

Klerman, G.L. (1981). Depression in the mentally ill. *Psychiatric Clinics of North America, 4,* 301–317.

Klerman, G.L., & Weissman, M.M. (1989). Increasing rates of depression. *Journal of the American Medical Association, 261,* 2229–2235.

Koegel, P., Burnam, A., & Farr, R.K. (1988). The prevalence of specific psychiatric disorders among homeless individuals in the inner city of Los Angeles. *Archives of General Psychiatry, 45,* 1085–1092.

Koopman, C., Classen, C., & Spiegel, D. (1994). Predictors of posttraumatic stress symptoms among survivors of the Oakland/Berkeley, Calif., firestorm. *American Journal of Psychiatry, 151,* 888–894.

Kramer, M. (1961). Some problems for international research suggested by observations on differences in first admission rates to the mental hospitals of England and Wales and of the United States. *Proceedings of the Third World Congress of Psychiatry* (Vol. 3, pp. 153–160). Montreal, Canada.

Kramer, M., Pollack, E., Redick, R., & Locke, B. (1972). *Mental disorders/suicide.* Cambridge, MA: Harvard University Press.

Kramer, M., Simonsick, E., Lima, B., & Levav, I. (1992). The epidemiological basis for mental health care in primary care: A case for action. In B. Cooper & R. Eastwood (Eds.), *Primary health care and psychiatric epidemiology* (pp. 69–98). London: Routledge.

Krantz, S.E., & Moos, R.H. (1987). Functioning and life context among spouses of remitted and non-remitted depressed patients. *Journal of Consulting and Clinical Psychology, 55,* 353–360.

Kulka, R.A., Schlenger, W.E., Fairbank, J.A., Hough, R.L., Jordan, B.K., Marmar, C.R., & Weiss, D.S. (1988). *Contractual report on findings from the National Vietnam Veterans Readjustment Study: Vol. I. Executive summary, description of findings, and technical appendices*. Research Triangle Park, NC: Research Triangle Institute.

Lasch, K., Weissman, M.M., Wickramaratne, P.J., & Bruce, M.L. (1990). Birth-cohort changes in the rates of mania. *Psychiatry Research, 33,* 31–37.

Leaf, P.J., Weissman, M.M., Myers, J.K., Holzer, C.E. III, & Tischler, G.L. (1986). Psychosocial risks and correlates of major depression in one United States urban community. In J. Barrett & R.M. Rose (Eds.), *Mental disorders in the community: Findings from psychiatric epidemiology* (pp. 47–66). New York: Guilford Press.

Leaf, P.J., Weissman, M.M., Myers, J.K., Tischler, G.L., & Holzer, C.E. III. (1984). Social factors related to psychiatric disorder: The Yale Epidemiologic Catchment Area Study. *Social Psychiatry, 19,* 53–61.

Leighton, D.C., Harding, J.S., Macklin, D., Macmillan, A.M., & Leighton, A.H. (1963). *The character of danger: Vol. III. The Sterling County study of psychiatric disorder and socio-cultural environment.* New York: Basic Books.

Lemkau, P.V., Kulcar, Z., Kesic, B., & Kovacic, L. (1980). Selected aspects of the epidemiology of psychoses in Croatia, Yugoslavia. *American Journal of Epidemiology, 112,* 661–674.

Lewine, R.R.J. (1988). Gender and schizophrenia. In M.T. Tsuang & J.C. Simpson (Eds.), *Handbook of schizophrenia: Vol. 3. Nosology, epidemiology and genetics* (pp. 379–397). Amsterdam: Elsevier Science Publishers.

Lewis, G., David, A., Andreasson, S., & Allebeck, P. (1992). Schizophrenia and city life. *Lancet, 340,* 137–140.

Lilienfeld, D.E., & Stolley, P.D. (Eds.). (1994). *Foundations of epidemiology,* 3rd ed. New York: Oxford University Press.

Lipkin, W.I., Schneemann, A., & Solbrig, M.V. (1995). Borna disease virus: Implications for neuropsychiatric illness. *Trends in Microbiology, 3,* 64–69.

Lukoff, D., Snyder, K., Ventura, J., & Nuechterlein, K H. (1984). Life events, familial stress, and coping in the developmental course of schizophrenia. *Schizophrenia Bulletin, 12,* 258–292.

Lyketsos, C.G., Nestadt, G., Cwi, J., Heithoff, K., & Eaton, W.W. (1994). The life chart interview: A standardized method to describe the course of psychopathology. *International Journal of Methods in Psychiatric Research, 4,* 143–155.

Maj, M., Janssen, R., Starace, F., Zaudig, M., Satz, P., Sughondhabirom, B., Luabeya, M., Riedel, R., Ndetei, D., Calil, H.M., Bing, E.G., St. Louis, M., & Sartorius, N. (1994). WHO Neuropsychiatric AIDS Study, cross-sectional Phase I: Study design and psychiatric findings. *Archives of General Psychiatry, 51,* 39–49.

Mancuso, T., & Locke, B.Z. (1972). Carbon disulphide as a cause of suicide: Epidemiologic study of viscose rayon workers. *Journal of Occupational Medicine, 14,* 595–606.

Mendes de Leon, C.F., Kasl, S.V., & Jacobs, S. (1994). A prospective study of widowhood and changes in symptoms of depression in a community sample of the elderly. *Psychological Medicine, 24,* 613–624.

Merikangas, K.R. (1987). Genetic epidemiology of psychiatric disorders. In R.E. Hales & A.J. Francis (Eds.), *Psychiatry Update* (Vol. 6, pp. 625–646). Washington, DC: American Psychiatric Press.

Merikangas, K.R. (1990). The genetic epidemiology of alcoholism. *Psychological Medicine, 20,* 11–22.

Morrison, J., Clancy, J., Crowe, R., & Winokur, G. (1972). The Iowa 500: I. Diagnostic validity in mania, depression and schizophrenia. *Archives of General Psychiatry, 27,* 457–461.

Muñoz, R.A., Marten, S., Gentry, K.A., & Robins, E. (1971). Mortality following a psychiatric emergency room visit: An 18-month follow-up study. *American Journal of Psychiatry, 128,* 220–224.

Murphy, S.A. (1988). Mediating effects of intrapersonal and social support on mental health 1 and 3 years after a natural disaster. *Journal of Traumatic Stress, 1,* 155–172.

Murray, C.J.L., & Lopez, A.D. (1996). *The global burden of disease: A comprehensive assessment of mortality and disability from diseases, injuries, and risk factors in 1990 and projected to 2020.* Cambridge, MA: Harvard University Press.

National Center for Health Statistics. (1994). Advance report of final mortality statistics, 1991. *Monthly Vital Statistics Report* (Vol. 42, No. 2, Suppl.). Hyattsville, MD: Public Health Service.

Needleman, H.L., Gunnoe, C., Leviton, A., Reed, R., Peresie, H., Maher, C., & Barrett, P. (1979). Deficits in psychologic and classroom performance of children with elevated dentine lead levels. *New England Journal of Medicine, 300,* 689–695.

North, C.S., Smith, E.M., & Spitznagel, E.L. (1994). Violence and the homeless: An epidemiologic study of victimization and aggression. *Journal of Traumatic Stress, 1,* 95–110.

Palinkas, L.A., Russell, J., Downs, M.A., & Patterson, J.S. (1992). Ethnic differences in stress, coping, and depressive symptoms after the Exxon Valdez oil spill. *Journal of Nervous and Mental Disease, 180,* 287–295.

Parkinson, D., Bromet, E.J., Cohen, S., Dunn, L., Dew M.A., Ryan, C., & Schwartz, J.E. (1990). Health effects of long-term solvent exposure among women in a blue collar population. *American Journal of Industrial Medicine, 17,* 661–675.

Parkinson, D., Ryan, C., Bromet, E.J., & Connell, M. (1986). A psychiatric epidemiologic study of occupational lead exposure. *American Journal of Epidemiology, 123,* 261–269.

Pearlin, L.I., Lieberman, M.A., Menaghan, E.G., & Mullen, J.T. (1981). The stress process. *Journal of Health and Social Behavior, 22,* 337–356.

Pearlin, L.I., & Schooler, C. (1978). The structure of coping. *Journal of Health and Social Behavior, 19,* 2–21.

Penkower, L., Bromet, E.J., & Dew, M.A. (1988). Spouse layoff and wives' mental health: A prospective analysis. *Archives of General Psychiatry, 45,* 994–1000.

Perry, S., Difede, J., Musngi, G., Frances, A.J., & Jacobsberg, L. (1992). Predictors of posttraumatic stress disorder after burn injury. *American Journal of Psychiatry, 149,* 931–935.

Pfohl, B., Stangl, D., & Tsuang, M.T. (1983). The association between early parental loss and diagnosis in the Iowa 500. *Archives of General Psychiatry, 40,* 965–967.

Phelan, J., Schwartz, J.E., Bromet, E.J., Dew, M.A., Parkinson, D.K., Schulberg, H.C., Dunn, L.O., Blane, H., & Curtis, E.C. (1991). Work stress, family stress and depression in professional and managerial employees. *Psychological Medicine, 21,* 999–1012.

Plunkett, R.J., & Gordon, J.E. (1960). *Epidemiology and mental illness.* New York: Basic Books.

Popkin, M.K., Callies, A.L., Colon, E.A., Lentz, R.D., & Sutherland, D.E. (1993). Psychiatric diagnosis and the surgical outcome of pancreas transplantation in patients with type I diabetes mellitus. *Psychosomatics, 34,* 251–258.

Power, C. (1992). A review of child health in the 1958 birth cohort: National Child Development Study. *Paediatric and Perinatal Epidemiology, 6,* 81–110.

Price, R.H., & Smith, S.S. (1984). *A guide to evaluating prevention programs in mental health.* Washington, DC: U.S. Government Printing Office.

Ram, R., Bromet, E.J., Eaton, W.W., Pato, C., & Schwartz, J. (1992). The natural course of schizophrenia: A review of first-admission studies. *Schizophrenia Bulletin, 18,* 185–207.

Razavi, D., Delvaux, N., Farvacques, C., & Robaye, E. (1990). Screening for adjustment disorders and major depressive disorders in cancer in-patients. *British Journal of Psychiatry, 156,* 79–83.

Regier, D., Boyd, J.H., Burke, J.D., Rae, D.S., Myers, J.K., Kramer, M., Robins, L.N., George, L.K., Karno, M., & Locke, B.Z. (1988a). One-month prevalence of mental disorders in the United States based on five epidemiologic catchment area sites. *Archives of General Psychiatry, 45,* 977–986.

Regier, D., Hirschfeld, R., Goodwin, F., Burke, J., Lazar, J., & Judd, L. (1988b). The NIMH Depression/Awareness, Recognition, and Treatment Program: Structure, aims, and scientific basis. *American Journal of Psychiatry, 145,* 1351–1357.

Regier, D.A., Kaelber, C.T., Rae, D.S., Farmer, M.E., Knauper, B., Kessler, R.C., & Norquist, G.S. (1998). Limitations of diagnostic criteria and assessment instruments for mental disorders: Implications for research and policy. *Archives of General Psychiatry, 55,* 109–115.

Regier D.A., Narrow, W.E., Rae, D.S., Manderscheid, R.W., Locke, B.Z., & Goodwin, F.K. (1993). The de facto U.S. mental and addictive disorders service system. *Archives of General Psychiatry, 50,* 85–94.

Resnick, H.S., Kilpatrick, D.G., Dansky, B.S., Saunders, B.E., & Best, C.L. (1993). Prevalence of civilian trauma and posttraumatic stress disorder in a representative national sample of women. *Journal of Consulting and Clinical Psychology, 61,* 984–991.

Revicki, D.A., & Murray, M. (1994). Assessing health-related quality of life outcomes of drug treatments for psychiatric disorders. *CNS Drugs, 6,* 465–476.

Richman, N. (1974). The effects of housing on preschool children and their mothers. *Developmental Medicine and Child Neurology, 16,* 53–58.

Robins, L.N. (1966). *Deviant children grown up.* Baltimore: Williams & Wilkins.

Robins, L.N., Helzer, J.E., Croughan, J., & Ratcliff, K.S. (1977). National Institute of Mental Health Diagnostic Interview Schedule. *Archives of General Psychiatry, 34,* 129–133.

Robins, L.N., Helzer, J.E., Ratcliff, K.S., & Seyfried, W. (1982). Validity of the Diagnostic Interview Schedule, Version II: DSM-III diagnoses. *Psychological Medicine, 12,* 855–870.

Robins, L.N., Helzer, J.E., Weissman, M.M., Orvaschel, H., Gruenberg, E., Burke, J.D., Jr., & Regier, D.A. (1984). Lifetime prevalence of specific psychiatric disorders in three sites. *Archives of General Psychiatry, 41,* 949–958.

Robins, L.N., & Regier, D.A. (Eds.). (1991). *Psychiatric disorders in America: The Epidemiologic Catchment Area Study.* New York: Free Press.

Robins, L.N., Wing, J.K., Wittchen, H.U., Helzer, J.E., Babor, T.F., Burke, J., Farmer, A., Jablenski, A., Pickens, R., Regier, D.A., Sartorius, N., & Towle, L.H. (1988). The Composite International Diagnostic Interview: An epidemiologic instrument suitable for use in conjunction with different diagnostic systems and in different cultures. *Archives of General Psychiatry, 45,* 1069–1077.

Rodin, G., Craven, J., & Littlefield, C. (1991). *Depression in the medically ill: An integrated approach.* New York: Brunner/Mazel.

Rothbaum, B.O., Foa, E.B., Riggs, D.S., Murdock, T., & Walsh, W. (1992). A prospective examina-

tion of posttraumatic stress disorder in rape victims. *Journal of Traumatic Stress, 5,* 455–475.

Roy, A. (1981). Role of past loss in depression. *Archives of General Psychiatry, 38,* 301–302.

Rubonis, A.V., & Bickman, L. (1991). Psychological impairment in the wake of disaster: The disaster–psychopathology relationship. *Psychological Bulletin, 109,* 384–399.

Rutter, M. (1980). Raised lead levels and impaired cognitive/behavioural function: A review of the evidence. *Developmental Medicine and Child Neurology, 22* (Suppl. 42).

Sartorius, N. (1993). WHO's work on the epidemiology of mental disorders. *Social Psychiatry and Psychiatric Epidemiology, 28,* 147–155.

Sartorius, N., Jablensky, A., Korten, A., Ernberg, G., Anker, M., Cooper, J.E., & Day, R. (1986). Early manifestations and first-contact incidence of schizophrenia in different cultures: A preliminary report on the initial evaluation phase of the WHO Collaborative Study on Determinants of Outcome of Severe Mental Disorders. *Psychological Medicine, 16,* 909–928.

Schleifer, S.J., Macari-Hinson, M.M., Coyle, D.A., Slater, W.R., Kahn, M., Gorlin, R., & Zucher, H.D. (1989). The nature and course of depression following myocardial infarction. *Archives of Internal Medicine, 149,* 1785–1789.

Schneier, F.R., Johnson, J., Hornig, C.D., Liebowitz, M.R., & Weissman, M.M. (1992). Social phobia: Comorbidity and morbidity in an epidemiological sample. *Archives of General Psychiatry, 49,* 282–288.

Schulberg, H.C., Block, M.R., Madonia, M.J., Scott, C.P., Rodriguez, E., Imber, S.D., Perel, J., Lave, J., Houck, P.R., & Coulehan, J.L. (1996). Treating major depression in primary care practice: Eight-month clinical outcomes. *Archives of General Psychiatry, 53,* 913–919.

Schwab, J.J., & Schwab, M.E. (1978). *Sociocultural roots of mental illness: An epidemiologic survey.* New York: Plenum Press.

Shaffer, D., Garland, A., Gould, M., Fisher, P., & Trautman, P. (1988). Preventing teenage suicide: A critical review. *American Academy of Child and Adolescent Psychiatry, 27,* 675–687.

Shaffer, D., Schwab-Stone, M., Fisher, P., Cohen, P., Piacentini, J., Davies, M., Conners, C.K., & Regier, D. (1993). The Diagnostic Interview Schedule for Children—Revised Version (DISC-R): I. Preparation, field testing, interrater reliability, and acceptability. *Journal of the American Academy of Child and Adolescent Psychiatry, 32,* 643–650.

Shepherd, M., Watt, D., Falloon, I., & Smeeton, N. (1989). The natural history of schizophrenia: A five-year follow-up study of outcome and prediction in a representative sample of schizophrenics. *Psychological Medicine, 19,* 1–46.

Shore, J.H., Tatum, E.L., & Vollmer, W.M. (1986). The Mount St. Helens stress response syndrome. In J.H. Shore (Ed.), *Disaster stress studies: New methods and findings* (pp. 76–97). Washington, DC: American Psychiatric Press.

Shrout, P.E., Link, B.G., Dohrenwend, B.P., Skodol, A.E., Stueve, A., & Mirotznik, J. (1989). Characterizing life events as risk factors for depression: The role of fateful loss events. *Journal of Abnormal Psychology, 98,* 460–467.

Snow, D.L., & Kline, M.L. (1995). Preventive interventions in the workplace to reduce negative psychiatric consequences of work and family stress. In C.M. Mazure (Ed.), *Does stress cause psychiatric illness?* (pp. 221–270). Washington, DC: American Psychiatric Press.

Solomon, Z., Laor, N., Weiler, D., Muller, U.F., Hadar, O., Waysman, M., Kozlowsky, M., Ben Yakar, M., & Bleich, A. (1993). The psychological impact of the Gulf War: A study of acute stress in Israeli evacuees (Letter). *Archives of General Psychiatry, 50,* 320–321.

Sommervell, P.D., Leaf, P.J., Weissman, M.M., Blazer, D.G., & Bruce, M.L. (1989). The prevalence of major depression in black and white adults in five United States communities. *American Journal of Epidemiology, 130,* 725–735.

Spitzer, R., Endicott, J., & Robins, E. (1978). Research diagnostic criteria: Rationale and reliability. *Archives of General Psychiatry, 35,* 773–782.

Spitzer, R., Williams, J.B., Gibbon, M., & First, M. (1987). *Structured Clinical Interview for DSM-III-R.* New York: Biometrics Research Department, New York State Psychiatric Institute.

Srole, L., Langner, T.S., Michael, S.T., Kirkpatrick, P., Opler, M.K., & Rennie, T.A.C. (1962). *Mental health in the metropolis: The Midtown Manhattan Study.* New York: Harper & Row.

Stouffer, S.A, Guttman, L., Suchman, E.A., Lazarsfeld, P.F., Star, S.A., & Clausen, J.A. (1950). *The American soldier: Measurement and prediction* (Vol. IV). Princeton, NJ: Princeton University Press.

Stukas, A.A., Dew, M.A., Switzer, G.E., DiMartini, A., Kormos, R.L., & Griffith, B.P. (in press). Post-traumatic stress disorder in heart transplant recipients and their primary family caregivers. *Psychosomatics.*

Susser, E., Moore, R., & Link, B. (1993). Risk factors for homelessness. *Epidemiologic Reviews, 15,* 546–556.

Thoits, P.A. (1995). Stress, coping, and social support processes: Where are we? What next? *Journal of Health and Social Behavior,* 53–79.

Tsuang, M.T., Woolson, R.F., & Fleming, J.A. (1979). Long term outcome of major psychoses: I. Schizophrenia and affective disorders compared with psychiatrically symptom-free surgical conditions. *Archives of General Psychiatry, 36,* 1295–1301.

Turner, R.J., & Gartrell, J.W. (1978). Social factors in psychiatric outcome: Toward the resolution of interpretive controversies. *American Sociological Review, 43,* 368–382.

Turner, R.J., Wheaton, B., & Lloyd, D.A. (1995). The epidemiology of social stress. *American Sociological Review, 60,* 104–125.

Üstün, T.B., & Tien, A.Y. (1995). Recent developments for diagnostic measures in psychiatry. *Epidemiologic Reviews, 17,* 210–220.

Vaillant, G.E. (1983). *The natural history of alcoholism.* Cambridge, MA: Harvard University Press.

Vazquez-Barquero, J.L., Diez-Manrique, J.F., Pena, C., Aldama, J., Samaniego-Rodriquez, C., Menendez-Arango, J., & Mirapeix, C. (1987). A community mental health survey in Cantabria: A general description of morbidity. *Psychological Medicine, 17,* 227–241.

Vernon, S.W., & Roberts, R.E. (1982). Prevalence of treated and untreated psychiatric disorder in three ethnic groups. *Social Science in Medicine, 16*, 1575–1582.

Veroff, J., Kulka, R.A., & Douvan, E. (1981). *Mental health in America*. New York: Basic Books.

Wai, L., Burton, H., Richmond, J., & Lindsay, R.M. (1981). Influence of psychosocial factors on survival of home-dialysis patients. *Lancet, 2*, 1155–1156.

Walsh, D., O'Hare, A., Blake, B., Holpenny, J., & O'Brien, P., (1980). The treated prevalence of mental illness in the Republic of Ireland—The Three County Case Register Study. *Psychological Medicine, 10*, 465–470.

Weissman, M.M. (1987). Epidemiology overview. In R.E. Hales & A.J. Francis (Eds.), *Psychiatry update* (Vol. 6, pp. 574–588). Washington, DC: American Psychiatric Press.

Weissman, M.M., Bland, R.C., Canino, G.J., Faravelli, C., Greenwald, S., Hwu, H-G., Joyce, P.R., Karam, E.G., Lee, C-K., Lellouch, J.P., Lepine, J-P., Newman, S.C., Oakley-Browne, M.A., Rubio-Stipec, M., Wells, J.E., Wickramaratne, P.J., Wittchen, H-U., & Yeh, E-K. (1997). The cross-national epidemiology of panic disorder. *Archives of General Psychiatry, 54*, 305–309.

Weissman, M.M., Bruce, M.L., Leaf, P.J., Florio, L.P., Holzer, C. III. (1991). Affective disorders. In L.N. Robins & D.A. Regier (Eds.), *Psychiatric disorders in America: The Epidemiologic Catchment Area Study* (pp. 53–80). New York: Free Press.

Weissman, M.M., & Myers, J.K. (1980). Psychiatric disorders in a U.S. community. The application of Research Diagnostic Criteria to a resurveyed community sample. *Acta Psychiatrica Scandinavica, 62*, 99–111.

Weissman, M.M., Myers, J.K., & Thompson, W.D. (1981). Depression and its treatment in a U.S. urban community, 1975–1976. *Archives of General Psychiatry, 38*, 417–421.

Weissman, M.M., Prusoff, B.A., Gammon, G.D., Merikangas, K.R., Leckman, J.F., & Kidd, K.K. (1984). Psychopathology in the children (ages 6–18) of depressed and normal parents. *Journal of the American Academy of Child Psychiatry, 23*, 78–84.

Wells, K.B., Golding, J.M., & Burnam, M.A. (1989).

Affective, substance use, and anxiety disorders in persons with arthritis, diabetes, heart disease, high blood pressure, or chronic lung conditions. *General Hospital Psychiatry, 11*, 320–327.

Weyerer, S. (1990). Relationships between physical and psychological disorders, In N. Sartorius, D. Goldberg, G. de Girolamo, J.A. Costa e Silva, Y. Lecrubier, & H-U. Wittchen (Eds.), *Psychological disorders in general medical settings* (pp. 34–46). Toronto: Hogrefe and Huber.

Williams, D.G. (1994). Population density and mental illness. *Journal of Social Psychology, 134*, 545 546.

Williams, J.B.W. (1992). The Structured Clinical Interview for DSM-III-R (SCID): II. Multisite test–retest reliability. *Archives of General Psychiatry, 49*, 630–636.

Williams, R.B., & Chesney, M.A. (1993). Psychosocial factors and prognosis in established coronary artery disease: The need for research on interventions. *Journal of the American Medical Association, 270*, 1860–1861.

Wing, J.K., Babar, T., Brugha, T., Burke, J., Cooper, J.E., Giel, R., Jablenski, A., Regier, D.A., & Sartorius, N. (1990). SCAN: Schedule for Clinical Assessment in Neuropsychiatry. *Archives of General Psychiatry, 47*, 589–593.

Wittchen, H.U., Robins, L.N., Cottler, L., Sartorius, N., Burke, J., Regier, D., Altamura, A.C., Andrews, G., Dingemanns, R., Droux, A., Essau, C.A., Farmer, A., Halikas, J., Ingebrigsten, G., Isaac, M., Jenkins, P., Kuhne, G.E., Krause, J., Lepine, J.P., Lyketsos, K.G., Maier, W., Miranda, C.T., Pfister, H., Pull, C., Rubio-Stipec, M., Sandanger, I., Smeets, R., Tacchini, G., & Tehrani, M. (1991). Cross-cultural feasibility, reliability and sources of variance of the Composite International Diagnostic Interview (CIDI)—Results of the multicentre WHO/ADAMHA field trials (wave I). *British Journal of Psychiatry, 159*, 645–653.

Wittchen, H-U., Zhao, S., Kessler, R.C., & Eaton, W.W. (1994). DSM-III-R generalized anxiety disorder in the National Comorbidity Survey. *Archives of General Psychiatry, 51*, 355 364.

World Health Organization. (1975). *Schizophrenia: A multinational study*. Geneva, Switzerland: Author.

World Health Organization. (1992). *International statistical classification of diseases and related health problems: ICD-10,* Vol. 1, 10th ed. (revised). Geneva, Switzerland: Author.

World Health Organization. (1993). *The Composite International Diagnostic Interview, Core Version 1.1.* Washington, DC: American Psychiatric Press.

World Health Organization. (1994). *Schedules for Clinical Assessment in Neuropsychiatry (SCAN).* Washington, DC: American Psychiatric Press.

Yellowlees, P.M., & Ruffin, R.E. (1989). Psychological defenses and coping styles in patients following a life-threatening attack of asthma. *Chest, 95,* 1298–1303.

Youssef, H.A., Kinsella, A., Waddington, J.L. (1991). Evidence for geographical variations in the prevalence of schizophrenia in rural Ireland. *Archives of General Psychiatry, 48,* 254–258.

Zubin, J., Steinhauer, R., Day, R., & Van Kammen, D. (1985). Schizophrenia at the crossroads: A blueprint for the '80s. *Comprehensive Psychiatry, 26,* 217–240.

CHAPTER 3

GENETICS

Svenn Torgersen
University of Oslo

INTRODUCTION

Prevailing attitudes toward genetic determination of behavior have varied throughout history. In the past, genes have been seen as equal to fate and degeneration. A counterreaction appeared in the 20th century, when genetic influence was discarded and environment was looked upon as the sole origin of behavior. Hereby an optimistic point of view arose: By changing environment, behavior problems could be prevented or alleviated.

Today, a more realistic attitude prevails. Environment is not so easy to monitor, and a given environment does not seem to have the same effect on different individuals. We have to realize that we have various endowments. This understanding has been reached in part because modern genetic research has moved us away from speculation and toward more true knowledge.

This chapter deals with these modern genetic methods and the results we have obtained in the field of psychopathology. The basic mechanisms, con-

cepts, models, and theories in human behavioral genetics will be presented first. Next, methods in genetic research will be described. Finally, some results pertaining to psychopathological conditions will be examined.

BASIC PREMISES

It is usually held that certain behavior patterns can be inherited. In reality, however, *behavior* cannot be inherited. What is inherited are certain molecular chains located on the chromosomes. The genetic code influencing the development of human behavior is situated on 23 pairs of chromosomes. One of these pairs contains the sex chromosomes: two X-chromosomes for females and one X- and one Y-chromosome for males. Spread around the chromosome pairs we find the sites or loci for different *genes*. Genes may exist in different versions, or *alleles*. Such allelic diversification creates the variation among human individuals. With more than 100,000 genes with alternative alleles, we can easily imagine how unlikely it is to find two people with the same genetic endowment. The exception is the case of identical twins, who stem from the same fertilized egg cell. Sometimes, both alleles of the chromosome pair are identical (*homozygous*), but often they are different (*heterozygous*).

The allele's variation is due to differences in their building blocks: the molecules of DNA (deoxyribonucleic acid). The DNA molecule is composed of four different nucleotides; the *nucleotide* is a base attached to sugar as bonding material. The sequence of these four different nucleotides and the strands of different nucleotides define the property of the allele. The allele may influence behavior by means of the DNA structure, which is stamped on a molecule of RNA (ribonucleic acid). The RNA molecule monitors the construction of a polypeptide: a protein. The sequence of specific amino acids in the polypeptide is dependent on the base sequence in RNA, which in turn depends on the base sequence in DNA. In this way, DNA in the allele determines the polypeptides. These peptides can then eventually influence the central nervous system and hence our behavior.

Genes are transmitted to the offspring in a way that makes them partly similar and partly dissimilar to their parents and sibs. Sex cells in the parents are created by the process of meiosis. Without going into detail, we can emphasize the following: One cell consists of 23 pairs of chromosomes, one of each pair inherited from the mother and one from the father. The cell is divided into two new cells, each containing only 23 single chromosomes, partly maternal and partly paternal. One cell will never be identical to another cell. The two new cells are again split into four cells, with 23 single chromosomes: the sex cells. Two pairs of these four cells are generally identical. However, often a so-called crossing over takes place. A part of the chromosome in the new sex cells stems from the mother's chromosome in the original allele; a part stems from the father's chromosome. This phenomenon is the basis for the so-called *linkage method,* which will be presented later.

Offspring and parents share 50% of the genes. On the average the same is true for siblings. Identical or *monozygotic* (MZ) twins are an exception because they stem from the same fertilized egg. Fraternal or *dizygotic* (DZ) twins, on the other hand, are the result of two different fertilized eggs. Genetically, they are no more similar than any other two sibs.

Genes may affect behavior in different ways. We may have so-called simple *Mendelian inheritance,* in which one gene is responsible for the development of a disorder. If the disorder-producing allele is dominant, the individual needs only one such allele in the gene pair in order to develop the disorder. He or she can be *heterozygotic* for the disorder. If the allele is recessive, however, the individual must have the disorder-producing allele on both chromosomes. He or she must be *homozygotic* in order to develop the disorder.

Usually, genetic transmission is not that simple. Several separate genes may be independently responsible for the disorder (so-called *oligogenic inheritance*). In that case, the disorder is heterogeneous. There could be an interaction or epistasis among the genes. For instance, one gene may be important in creating the biochemical basis for the disorder. However, unless another gene also occurs, the disorder-producing gene will have no effect. On the other hand, some genes may be protective. It is possible that a person must both have the disorder-producing gene and lack the protective one in order to develop the disorder.

Most common behavior patterns may be due to several additive, independent genes: a so-called *polygenic inheritance*. Each gene is replaceable, and the sum total of genes determines whether a behavior pattern is likely to develop. Finally, we may have a complex inheritance, whereby presence of any of a variety of single rare genes could be a necessary but not a sufficient condition for the development of the disorder. In addition, other more common genes must occur together, and perhaps even a sufficient number of independent additive genes are necessary for development of the disorder.

If some specific or general provocation is necessary in addition to the genes, we then get a multifactorial-polygenic inheritance. We may also assume that some individuals will develop the disorder without any genetic basis. If the disorder is phenomenologically identical to the disorder created by genes, we call it a *phenocopy* or a sporadic disorder.

To add even more complexity, one and the same gene may be responsible for many different disorders: a so-called *pleiotropy*. In many instances, we have to assume that more or less qualitatively different variants of the same disorder of varying severity might be due to a variation in the same genetic background. We will deal with this in more detail in connection with quantitative genetics.

So far we have discussed genetic transmission by means of chromosomes other than sex chromosomes, the so-called *autosomal inheritance*. However, genes may also be located on the sex chromosomes. This has important implications for genetic transmission. If the locus of the gene is on the Y-chromosome, the only transmission is from father to son. A recessive X-linked transmitted disorder is much more likely to occur among men because women must be homozygous for the allele to cause the disorder. If the disorder is lethal in early age and is X-linked, recessive, it can be transmitted only from the mother. She can be heterozygous and thus unaffected, whereas a man will not survive with the allele. With an X-linked recessive inheritance, the genetic basis for the disorder is generally transmitted from a healthy mother to the offspring, with consequences only for the son. However, a healthy heterozygous daughter may cause the disorder in her future son.

Quantitative Genetics

Geneticists have increasingly turned away from descriptions of specific genetic disorders in individuals and toward calculation of the impact of genetic variation on populations. The reason is that one can assess the effects of the allele on the individuals only for single-gene transmitted disorders. Because most disorders and behaviors are considered to be polygenetic, it would be better to speak about genetic variation in a population. This has important implications. It means that we speak about heredity as a percentage of the variance of the behavior or disorder accounted for by genetic factors. The rest has to be due to environmental variance.

Environmental variance is usually divided in two parts, One part is a variance that affects only all first-degree members of a family to the same degree. This is called *common family variance* or *shared-in-families variance*. The other environmental part is a variance due to factors that make close family members dissimilar; a *unique* or *non-shared-in-families variance*. These three types of variance may change over time and may become different from culture to culture. This means that it is not possible to speak

about heritability as a fixed attribute of a disorder. If the environmental variance increases, then the genetic variance, heredity, must decrease, because the sum total is unity, or 100%.

Recently, several quantitative models have been developed to make assumptions about monogenetic or polygenetic inheritance, dominance, epistasis, and so on. The concept of *penetrance,* which says something about the likelihood that the disorder will emerge, is also of importance. Another important point is *selective mating* (the tendency of a person to choose a similar or dissimilar spouse). This has important implications for the kind of offspring they will produce. If spouses often are dissimilar with respect to a specific behavior pattern, then their children can be more dissimilar than unrelated children. By means of chi-square tests, it is possible to test which models will fit the data and which will have to be rejected.

The so-called *multithreshold model* of disease transmission is particularly interesting. This model states that all individuals in a population are liable to develop a certain disorder, to varying degrees. The liability is the sum total of all genetic and environmental influences on the disorder. If the liability is greater than a certain threshold, then the individual will have the disorder. Milder variants of the disorder may occur at lower thresholds, and the most severe variants require that a high threshold of liability be passed. Relatives of individuals with a severe variant will have a higher frequency of the disorder and are also more likely to have the more severe subtypes of the disorder. Relatives of individuals with a milder variant of the disorder have the disorder less frequently and have a milder type of the disorder. Exact mathematical predictions can be made and tested.

Recently, models have been developed that describe alternative joint effects of genotype and environment. It is assumed that the genetic influence is monogenetic and that the environment contributes to development of the disorder. There are three possibilities:

1. Genotype and environmental provocation are simply additive. If the genotype is severe, then less provocation is required for the disorder to develop. An individual who has a benign genotype needs a strong stressor to develop the disorder.

2. The gene determines the sensitivity of the individual to a certain negative environment. If he has both sensitive alleles, he will be vulnerable in a provocative environment but safe in a protective one. If he has one sensitive allele, he will show the same tendency to a lesser degree. If he lacks both sensitive alleles, however, the environment is of no importance for his likelihood of developing the disorder.

3. The gene may be unrelated to the development of the disorder in itself because the disorder is due to a certain life event, but the genotype affects the likelihood of experiencing the live event. Thus, without the provocation, no disorder develops irrespective of genotype, and, given the provocation, the disorder occurs independently of genotype. However, the genotype makes the provocation more or less likely.

Given frequency of the allele and the provocative environment, it is possible to make precise predictions of the frequency of the disorder among relatives who are exposed to a protective or provocative environment and then to test which of the models best fits the data.

RESEARCH METHODS

Having presented the basic principles of human behavior genetics, I will now turn to research methods in genetics.

The Family Method

The most straightforward method in genetic studies is the family method, whereby one simply records frequency of a disorder among the biological relatives of the proband (identified case). It is important to differentiate between first-, second-, and third-degree relatives. First-degree relatives share, on average, half of the genetic variation, second-degree relatives 25%, and so on. Pedigree studies, in which family trees are studied, may provide valuable information about the mode of inheritance.

There are many ways to collect data about relatives. The easiest way, the family history method, is to ask the proband about the relatives. Although the proband may be well informed about emotional prob-

lems among his children, he may not know as much about parents, older sibs, cousins, aunts, uncles, and grandparents. Although this method may give some underestimation, it has proved to be more accurate than one might expect, especially for the more serious psychiatric disorders.

The best method, however, is the family interview method, in which relatives are interviewed directly. In that way, one can apply the same structured interview methods to the relatives as to the probands. The biggest problem with the direct family interview is that it is expensive and time consuming, especially in countries where people move a lot. One way to reduce the costs can be to conduct the interviews by telephone. Then, however, some information about the relatives' emotional reactions and contact abilities will be lost.

Frequency of a certain disorder among relatives may be compared to its frequency in the general population. However, the best strategy is also to study the relatives of a control group. The control group can be patients with another mental disorder, patients with a medical disease, random individuals from the general population, or screened individuals without any disorder or disease.

It is important to match the control group for age, sex, education, and rural versus urban living, but multivariate techniques can also be applied to rule out these third variables. In any case, morbidity risk is better than mere frequency of a disorder. *Morbidity risk* means the risk for an individual of developing a disorder in his lifetime. If he is young, he still has the chance, but as he ages, the chance decreases. If the disorder usually has an early debut, the chance decreases more rapidly. Most commonly, number of individuals at risk is calculated. This means that the individual is counted as less than one if he is younger than the age of the end of the risk period for the disorder; the younger the person is, the smaller the fraction. In this way the number of relatives at risk will usually be lower than the actual number of relatives. Hence, morbidity risk—number of cases divided by the number at risk—will usually be higher than the frequency of cases among the relatives.

The sampling procedure is important in family studies. Most studies deal with probands who have been treated in psychiatric facilities. The possibility exists that the likelihood of seeking help for treatment may be related to the number of relatives with psychiatric disorders. In that case, the morbidity risk will be too high in studies of this kind. The best study would be one that dealt with the common population. Because only 10% of the individuals with nonpsychotic mental disorders attend psychiatric facilities, however, the possibility of biased results is considerable.

Even though the family method seems straightforward, it is not easy to draw conclusions about genetic factors. One might say that if no higher morbidity risk is observed among relatives of probands with a certain disorder, then genetic factors cannot be of any importance, but this is not certain. Selective mating can cause individuals with opposite characteristics to marry. This means that offspring can be very different even if genetic factors contribute to the development of the characteristics. The wish to be different from parents and sibs might also counteract an eventual genetic tendency to be similar. That this is not a trivial objection is shown by many twin studies in which the correlations between MZ twins can be considerable, whereas the DZ twin correlations are zero or even negative. Even when a higher morbidity risk is obtained among relatives, evidence does not prove that genetic factors are important in the etiology of the disorder. Results may be due to common environment, identification, imitation, or learning.

Why then perform family studies? In part, family studies are interesting in themselves. To find a similarity between family members can tell us something about risk factors for disorders. Furthermore, establishment of a familial link can provide an impetus to go further with more powerful genetic methods. Finally, given that the importance of genetic factors is established, pedigree studies can tell us something about the mode of inheritance.

If we find that the morbidity risk is halved every time we move one degree away from the proband, the inheritance might be a simple Mendelian one, with only one gene. If it decreases more rapidly, then we probably are dealing with interacting genes. If the morbidity risk is lower among parents than among sibs, recessive genes are likely. We have commented earlier on how family studies can reveal sex-linked inheritance.

A modern technique made possible by the frequency of divorce today is to study so-called blended families (families in which not only the spouses but also some of the children are not biologically related). Some children may be half-sibs, whereas others are full sibs. The family method has been applied more frequently not to study genetic factors but to examine environmental factors and the interaction between genetic and environmental influences.

I have discussed the family method in detail because it illustrates many of the problems that are also found in the application of the other methods.

The Twin Method

The blended family design gives several opportunities to study the effect of having a different amount of genetic similarity while growing up in the same family. However, half-sibs and social sibs who are genetically unrelated have usually not lived together for very long. Twins are more like ordinary sibs in that respect; they usually grow up together. If they are monozygotic (MZ) twins, they not only have a very similar environment but are genetically identical as well. Dizygotic (DZ) twins, by contrast, are no more similar genetically than ordinary sibs. Given that the environment is not more similar for MZ than for DZ twins, an eventual higher similarity or concordance in MZ twins compared to DZ twins is considered a proof of the influence of genes.

However, studies uniformly show that MZ twins spend more time together, are closer, and more frequently have the same friends and the same activities than DZ twins. So the equal environment similarity premise in the twin study is not true. Then how can the twin method be applied? It is argued that a more similar environment for MZ twin partners does not make the MZ twins more similar than DZ twin partners. Furthermore, one way to solve the problem is to see whether similarity in environment is related to similarity in the characteristics studied within the group of MZ twins.

Another problem with twin studies is the extent to which twins are representative of the population at large. A twin delivery is a physically risky event, and twins are more prone to head injuries than singletons. Perhaps environmental factors, less important to singletons, might be important to twins. To grow up with a sib of the same age, to compete for attention, to share everything, to be able to develop your dependency or reclusiveness to a greater degree than other children, to be dominated and bullied, or to express your own domineering tendencies, all may make the environment of twins very special.

Even so, most of what we know about genetic factors comes from twin studies. The usual formula for expressing the relative contribution of heredity and environment is

$$H + V_c + V_u = 1$$

where H is heredity, V_c is common or shared environment, and V_u is unique or nonshared environment.

These three variances are usually calculated from the correlation R_{mz} between MZ twins and the correlation R_{dz} between DZ twins, in this way:

$$H = 2(R_{mz} - R_{dz})$$

$$V_c = 2R_{dz} - R_{mz}$$

$$V_u = 1 - R_{mz}$$

We observe that if the twin relationship makes the MZ twins too similar, the hereditability, H, will be too high, and V_c and V_u too low. If in addition DZ twins are pushed in the direction of being dissimilar in order to develop their separate identities, V_c will be even more reduced. A twin relationship in which one of the MZ twins has a strong tendency to domineer the other may increase V_u unduly.

Generally, these factors most likely lead to an overestimation of H and V_u, heredity and nonshared environment, and an underestimation of V_c; in other words, individual and not collective factors are the source of variance.

It is also important to note that this model is based on an assumption of additive genes. If the genetic etiology is based on a single recessive gene or on several genes that all have to be there, R_{dz} will be very small compared to R_{mz}, and again H will be overestimated and V_c underestimated.

The Adoption Method

One limitation of the twin method is the fact that although genetic factors vary, the family environment is more constant. The adoption method makes it possible to also study the effect of the family variation.

Two procedures are employed. One consists of starting with an adopted-away proband with a certain disorder and then looking at the disorders among both biological and social relatives. A higher frequency or morbidity risk among the biological than the social adoptive relatives speaks for the stronger effect of heredity than of family environment for the development of the disorder.

Another approach is to start with parents who have placed their offspring for adoption. One proband group consists of parents without the disorder. Frequency of the disorder among the adopted-away offspring of disordered parents is contrasted to frequency among the adopted-away offspring of the normal controls.

The adoption method may demonstrate the effects of heredity by showing a striking similarity among relatives even if they never have lived together. However, some limitations do exist. The method is perhaps less effective in studying the effect of variation in environment, because the adoptive homes may be relatively similar. Requirements for being accepted as adoptive parents are rather stringent, and the home must meet at least current middle-class standards.

Furthermore, characteristics of the adoptive home often are not recorded thoroughly. In this way, the design disregards important information. Another problem is that many children have been in residential placement before adoption, often with bad care. One can also imagine that conditions in pregnancy and shortly after birth were not always optimal for children of mothers with severe psychiatric disorders. To give up a child for adoption means that parents are far from average in the first place, and thus adopted children may not be representative of the population at large. A lack of genetically determined personality match between adopted child and adoptive relatives may also create problems.

Many of these shortcomings of the adoption method are solved by using an adequate control group. Even so, one has to make a careful search for alternative explanations for the often striking findings in adoption studies.

Twins Reared Apart

An interesting design is a combination of the twin method and the adoption method, whereby one studies twins who are reared apart. It is particularly interesting to look at MZ twins reared apart. An eventual positive correlation or a concordance between twin partners cannot be due to common upbringing. Theoretically, prenatal and perinatal factors may contribute. However, the twins-reared-apart design may solve some problems of the classical twin design. One problem is to find enough twins reared apart who have rare disorders. Another problem is the fact that twins reared apart cannot give us the opportunity to study the effect of shared environment in a positive way. Rather, this method may tell us what we find when the possibility of shared environment does not exist.

An alternative design that is much more feasible is to study twins with variable contact. In that way the shared environment will be a gradual variable, and its effect on behavior can be studied more reliably.

Linkage Methods

All of these methods are indirect ways of studying genetics by estimating the effects of genetic variance. The direct method is to study the gene itself. The linkage studies seem to make this possible.

As mentioned before, frequent recombinations during meiosis make it possible to trace the site of the gene for a specific disorder. A positive result of a linkage study tells two things: that a simple gene is important for development of the disorder and that the gene has a specific location on a certain part of the chromosome. The first achievement may be the most important for understanding the etiology for the disorder and the second for treatment of the disorder. The exact location of the gene may in future make it possible to study the biochemical process from the DNA molecule, via RNA and amino acids, and eventually the central nervous system effects of the allele. This may make it possible to create the right therapeutic drug for the disorder. Today, however, this goal is far from being achieved.

Basically, the linkage method requires either large pedigrees with many affected individuals or a number of sibships. Here there is a source of nonrepresentation, in that many individuals with severe mental disorders have few sibs.

The claim of monogeneity is more problematic. Although positive confirmed results do tell us that a major gene is in operation, negative results may tell either that we have not located the gene or that it is not any single gene that is responsible for the disorder. Many believe that psychopathology seldom is due to only one major gene. This means that the ability of the linkage method is limited.

Another problem has to do with the statistics. Although the logic of the linkage studies is relatively simple, the statistical models and assumptions behind the calculation of LOD (logarithm of the odds ratio) scores, the standard for representing the strength of association or probability of a genetic linkage, are very complicated. The robustness of the calculation methods seems questionable.

Molecular Genetics

Having found out that genetic factors are important for the development of behavior, the next step is to detect the specific gene and the allele variant. This has already been done for a number of medical diseases as a result of the remarkable progress in the techniques of the direct inspection of the alleles. Also, the allelic variants influencing the development of some types of mental retardation, Alzheimer's disease, and rare forms of violence have been detected. Such a procedure is relatively attainable today with single-gene diseases and behaviors.

However, when we deal with behavior and disorders involving many genes, the task is more complicated. Plomin et al. (1994) advocate the concept of "quantitative trait loci" (QTL). This means that multiple genes of varying effect may be responsible for the genetic influence on the disorder. Each gene may have too small an effect to be detected by the linkage method. However, if, for instance, animal genetic studies have given a clue to a candidate gene, then molecular genetics applied on a blood sample can tell us whether the same gene is of some importance for humans. If the effect is small, we have to study a large sample. However, patient work may bring us closer to the aim of directly identifying the genes responsible for the genetic effect on development of the disorder. As the biochemical effects of more and more genes on the human genome are disclosed, the procedure to chose the right candidate genes are increasingly simple.

In the following section, I shall discuss the relative importance of genetic factors in the development of different types of psychopathology.

ROLE IN PSYCHOPATHOLOGY

Personality Disorders

Modern empirical personality research has shown that commonly studied personality traits are clustered in five general factors or dimensions, the so-called Big Five: neuroticism, extraversion–introversion, openness to experience, agreeableness, and conscientiousness. These dimensions seem to be correlated to the various personality disorders, being assessed either by interview (Soldz, Budman, Demoy, & Merry, 1993; Trull, 1992) or by questionnaire (Costa & McCrae, 1990; Soldz et al., 1993; Trull, 1992).

In the absence of genetic research on most of the personality disorders (PDs) it may be of interest to look at the genetic and environmental contribution to development of these personality dimensions.

All five dimensions are studied in a Swedish study of twins reared apart and together (Bergeman et al., 1993; Pedersen et al., 1991). In a U.S. study, three dimensions that are close to three of these five have been studied: *negative affectivity,* which is close to neuroticism; *positive affectivity,* which is similar to extraversion; and *constraint,* analogous to conscientiousness (Tellegen et al., 1988). If we look at the results together, we find evidence of heredity for all dimensions except agreeableness. The non-shared-in-families environmental variance is, however, higher than the genetic variance, and the shared-in-families environmental variance is very low. However, the nonshared variance also includes error variance due to unreliability of the personality scales. Such unreliability decreases the calculated genetic and shared environmental variance to the same degree as it inflates the nonshared variance. Fortunately, the articles state the reliability of the instruments. If we control for unreliability, we find a heritability close to 50% for four of the dimensions, excluding agreeableness. The shared environmental variance is around 10%, and the nonshared variance is around 40%. These results are in accordance with other twin and adoption studies of similar personality dimensions and probably represent the truth concerning the development of these broad personality dimensions. Agreeableness is the exception; here, the heritability is probably only 10% to 20%, shared environment 33%, and nonshared environment more than 50%.

Recently a gene on chromosome 16, which influences dopamine regulation, is found to be related to extraversion, conscientiousness, and novelty seeking (Benjamin et al., 1996; Ebstein et al., 1996). Individuals high on extraversion, low on conscientiousness, and high on novelty seeking are more likely to have the long 7-repeat allele of this gene.

Even more recently, another gene, which influences neuroticism, has been found (Lesch, Bengel, Heils, et al., 1996).

However, even if the regression correlations between the Big Five and PDs, measured by interview, are around .40, and around .60 when PDs are measured with questionnaires, the personality disorders may have a somewhat different etiology from the personality dimensions.

Because PDs measured by questionnaires are strongly correlated to the broad personality measures, one may expect a similar etiology for personality disorders measured in that way.

Livesley, Jang, Jackson, and Vernon (1993) have measured (by means of a questionnaire) personality deviances that are similar to the PDs in DSM-III. They observed that most of their types of personality deviances showed heritability. The heritability (when additive and nonadditive were combined) ranged from .64 to 0, with a median of .49. Narcissism, identity problems (analogous to borderline) and social avoidance (similar to avoidant-schizoid), callousness (antisocial), and oppositionality (passive-aggressive) were most heritable. Conduct problems did not show heritability. Submissiveness (dependent), self-harm (borderline), insecure attachment (dependent), and intimacy problems (avoidant) showed a relatively low heritability. Correspondingly, conduct problems showed a very high shared environment variance; submissiveness also had such a high variance. The nonshared environmental variance was highest for self-harm, followed by intimacy problems. As is the case for most twin studies, only 7 of the 18 traits displayed any shared-in-families variance. These estimates are probably too low, resulting from more similar environments for MZ twin partners compared to DZ twin partners and possibly to gene–environment interaction.

The pattern of heritability does not follow that of the PDs in the study by Livesley et al. (1993). Personality deviance (close to borderline, antisocial, and avoidant) shows both high and low heritability. The reason may be the heterogeneity of the PDs defined by DSM (Torgersen, Skre, Onstad, Edvardsen, & Kringlen, 1993a). Another reason may be that Livesley et al. (1993) used a questionnaire, and thus other delineation of disorders may appear than proposed in the clinical DSM approach.

Very few additional twin studies exist. Kendler, Heath, and Martin (1987) used four items from Eysenck's personality inventory (intending to measure suspiciousness) in a large Australian sample. They obtained a heritability of .41, with no shared environmental variance, as common in twin studies, so the rest, .59, was non-shared-in-families variance.

More recently, Kendler and Hewitt (1992) have studied heritability of schizotypal features using 9 scales intended to measure schizotypi. They found that for 7 of the scales, heritability was relatively high, from .40 to .68, and with no shared environmental variance. The highest heritability was found for anhedonia, picturing the so-called negative features of schizotypi. On the other hand, for two scales measuring perceptual aberration and "positive" schizotypi, no heredity was observed. There was a high shared environmental variance (.25–.29) and a very high nonshared variance (.71–.75).

These studies suggest, as expected from the high correlations between the Big Five and PDs measured by questionnaires, that heritability contributes considerably to development of PDs. However, as correlations between PDs measured by questionnaires and by interviews are moderate to low (Zimmermann, 1994), we do not know whether interview PDs are also genetically transmitted.

Most of the genetic research that has to do with personality disorders assessed by interview or records has applied to antisocial personality disorder or an important aspect of this disorder, criminal behavior. In 1976, Dalgard and Kringlen published a twin study of criminality. With a very broad definition of criminality, they observed only a slightly higher concordance for MZ twin pairs compared to DZ pairs. A more strict concept of crime yielded a concordance of 26% for MZ and 15% for DZ twin pairs. Some will consider this difference impressive; others will be more skeptical, taking into account the fact that MZ partners spend more time together than DZ twins. To study the effect of similarity in environment, the authors analyzed separately twin pairs who were close and other pairs who were distant. They made the surprising discovery that the closer MZ twins showed lower concordance and the closer DZ twins showed higher concordance. Thus, the concordance difference appeared only among twin pairs who were distant. In disagreement with Dalgard and Kringlen, I do not think that this result disproved genetic influence. However, results may show that an environmental factor in the twin relationship modifies the effect of genes in criminality.

McGuffin and Gottesman (1984) reviewed a number of relatively systematic ascertained twin studies of crime. They concluded that a fairly high difference in concordance was found between MZ and DZ twin pairs. However, the same was not true for juvenile delinquency. A U.S. study of discharges for dishonesty in the U.S. Army also showed a clearly higher concordance for MZ twin partners compared to DZ partners (Centerwall & Robinette, 1989). All these studies share the problem that MZ twins often make offenses together. Consequently, some data from the Minnesota Study of Twins Reared Apart are important. By implying the Diagnostic Interview Survey (DIS) to twins reared apart, the investigators observed a heritability for child antisocial features of .41 and for adult antisocial features of .28 (Grove et al., 1990). Thus, this study did not find that the genetic influence is higher for antisociality in older age.

Several adoption studies of antisocial features and criminality have been performed. Crowe (1974) studied offspring of female offenders who had been given up for adoption in infancy. Offspring of the offenders more often had antisocial personality (but not other personality deviations or psychiatric disorders) when compared with control adopted-away offsprings. Length of time spent in temporary care prior to final placement was important for development of antisocial personality, pointing to the interaction between genetic factors and environment.

Cadoret has published a number of articles from his adoption study of antisocial personality. In a more recent article (Cadoret & Stewart, 1991), it is shown that not only antisocial personality but also attention deficit hyperactivity disorder (ADHD) were found among adopted-away offspring of criminals. However, this was true only when offspring had been placed in lower-socioeconomic-status homes.

Psychiatric problems in the adoptive home were related to aggressivity in the offspring, and such aggressivity syndrome in its turn predicted antisocial adult personality. The study does show important interaction between environment and genetics in the development of antisocial personality. In addition, ADHD seems to be an alternative outcome of genetic factors influencing development of antisociality.

Other adoption studies (Cloninger, Sigvardson, & Bohman, 1982; Sigvardson, Cloninger, & Bohman, 1982) have also shown that prolonged institutional care before adoption and the socioeconomic status of the adoptive home influences the likelihood of criminality in the adopted-away offspring of criminals.

In addition to antisocial disorder, schizotypal disorder is the most studied personality syndrome in the realm of genetics. An early twin study of 25 MZ and 34 DZ twin pairs showed a concordance of 28% for the MZ twins and 3% for the DZ twin partners (Torgersen, 1984). Genetic factors seem to play a part in the development of schizotypal personality disorder. A more recent twin study has demonstrated the heterogeneity of the schizotypal personality disorder. Only the odd, eccentric, and affect-constricted features of the schizotypal personality disorder seem to be genetically influenced (Torgersen et al., 1993a).

Kendler, Gruenberg, and Kinney (1994) have recently updated the famous Danish Adoption Study of Schizophrenia. Among their adopted-away probands were also some (13) whom they diagnosed (based on interview) as having a schizotypal personality disorder. It turned out that 5 (21.7%) of their first-degree biological relatives and 2 (8.3%) of their second-degree biological relatives also had schizotypal personality disorder. Frequencies were significantly higher than for biological relatives of control adoptees (3.7% and 1.6%, respectively). Therefore, an adoption study also confirms the genetic influence on development of schizotypal PD.

As for other types of personality disorders, very little genetic research has been performed. A twin study did not find any concordance for borderline personality disorder among 7 MZ pairs (Torgersen, 1984). On the other hand, 2 of 18 DZ pairs were concordant, pointing to some shared-in-families environmental variance.

A more recent twin study yielded moderate genetic influence on PD features (Torgersen et al.,

1993a). Syndromes close to the self-defeating PD seemed to be genetically influenced, in addition to affect-constricted, eccentric schizotypal syndrome. A tendency was also observed for genetic factors influencing development of passive-aggressive, obsessive, paranoid, and narcissistic features. On the other hand, histrionic, borderline, and avoidant traits were more influenced by shared-in-families environmental variance. All in all, the median genetic variance for the 12 personality disorder syndromes was around 20%, the shared-in-families variance 10%, and the non-shared-in-families environmental variance around 70%. Using a reliability factor of about .70, we would have to conclude that around 30% of the variance may be accounted for by heredity, 15% by shared environment, and 55% by unshared environment. Shared-in-families environmental variance may be more important, and heredity less important, in development of personality disorders compared to common personality dimensions. To date, however, we know too little about the genetic transmission of personality disorders other than antisocial and schizotypal disorders.

Given the power of studies of twins reared apart, one has to conclude that most broad personality dimensions are genetically influenced. Perhaps half the variance is explained by genes. Studies of twins reared together have usually disconfirmed that shared-in-families environmental variance has any importance. The reason may be that the higher similarity in environment for MZ twins compared with DZ twin partners inflates estimates of heredity at the expense of shared family environment. A tendency to show opposite behavior in DZ twin pairs may also be the reason. The studies of twins reared apart demonstrate that at least one-tenth of the variance in the personality dimensions may be due to shared family environment.

As for the personality disorders proper, we may be able to state firmly that genes influence development of antisocial personality disorder. The adoptive studies clearly demonstrate the importance of environment. Whether aspects of the family environment, indicated in the adoption studies, interact with genes, constitute unique nonshared environmental influence, or represent shared environmental influence is difficult to determine. To make that evaluation, we should have explicit information about whether eventual adoptive siblings also develop antisocial traits. No adoption study has evaluated this factor.

Schizotypal personality disorder, especially the eccentric and affect-constricted aspects of the disorder, also seems to be influenced by genes. Yet we do not know enough about the kind of environmental influence that exists. To adduce information about aggregation of schizotypal cases in the Danish adoptive families would have been informative.

As for the other personality disorders, we do not have sufficient data. We know that borderline and also some fearsome personality disorders (cluster C) co-occur in families, but we can only speculate whether such aggregation is due to genes or to shared environment. If the scattered evidence that exists today is taken as a point of departure, it would appear that genes influence development of personality disorders a little less than is the case for most broad personality dimensions, and that the influence of shared-in-families environment is a bit more. However, the less-than-ideal reliability of the assessment of personality disorders may deflate estimates of familial transmission of such disorders.

Substance Abuse and Dependency

Family studies uniformly show that relatives of individuals with problems involving alcohol and drug use also show substance abuse and dependency. The question arises whether such familial aggregation is due to genes or shared environment. Twin studies may provide the answer.

In the Virginia Twin Study, more than 1,000 female twin pairs and most of their biological parents were investigated (Kendler, Neale, Heath, et al., 1994). The study yielded an estimate of heritability of more than 50%, and no evidence of shared-in-families environmental variance for alcoholism in females. Genetic vulnerability was transmitted to daughters equally from their fathers and from their mothers.

Another twin study showed results at variance with the Virginia study (McGue, Pickens, & Svikis, 1992). This study showed that females did not display a heritability for alcohol. However, men showed a heritability of more than 50%. Furthermore, early-onset alcoholism yielded a heritability of above 70%, versus only 30% for later-onset alco-

holism. Moreover, shared-in-families environmental variance was substantial: around 30% for males and 60% for females.

A problem of twin studies is that MZ twins spend more time together than DZ twin partners; therefore, the higher concordance in MZ pairs compared to DZ pairs may be due to common twin environment and not to identified genes. Rose, Kaprio, Williams, Viken, and Obrenski (1990) showed that MZ twins having much contact seem to have more similar alcohol consumption than twins seeing very little of each other. Studies of twins reared apart have yielded mixed results in American and Scandinavian studies (Grove et al., 1990; Kaprio, Koskenuvo, & Langinvaino, 1984; Pedersen, Friberg, Floderins-Myrhed, McClean, & Plomin, 1984). So, without completely ruling out results from twins reared together, the evidence is questionable.

It is fortunate, then, that we have some adoption studies of alcoholism. A Swedish adoption study demonstrated some effect of genetic factors in the development of alcoholism (Bohman, Sigvardsson, & Cloninger, 1981). The same held true for a U.S. adoption study (Cadoret, Yates, Woodworth, & Stewart, 1995). The latter study showed through a path analysis that alcohol abuse and dependency in adoptees were also influenced by alcohol problems and other psychiatric conditions in the adoptive family.

Recently a gene has been discovered that influences the likelihood of developing alcoholism (Hsu et al., 1996). This gene on chromosome X has to do with the A-form of monoamine oxidase (MAO-A). MAO-A is related to degradation of neurotransmitters such as dopamine and serotonin. It is interesting that this result was obtained for the Han Chinese but not for four aboriginal groups on Taiwan. Thus, cultural aspects may moderate the effect of genes.

As for drug abuse, the Minnesota Study of Twins Reared Apart observed a heritability of 45% for this kind of substance abuse (Grove et al., 1990). The U.S. adoption study mentioned before (Cadoret et al., 1995) indicated that genes also were of importance for development of drug problems, in combination with adverse adoptive family environment.

Alcohol abuse and dependency in biological parents, as well as disturbed adoptive parents, contribute to development of alcohol problems in adoptees. In fact, the study showed the alcohol problems' development via drug abuse and dependency. Thus, drug problems and alcohol problems may have the same genetic roots.

In DSM-III and DSM-IV, smoking also is classified as a substance disorder. The Virginia Twin Study also investigated smoking in females, and the authors observed a heritability above 50% (Kendler, Neale, et al., 1993). In this case, the shared-in-families environmental variance was above 25%, unusual in twin studies.

Taken together, the various methods applied to study the genetics of alcohol problems suggest that heritability does play a role in the development of abuse or dependency. However, the fact that more of the studies are negative indicates that the genetic etiology in some populations may be weak. Cultural factors play a large role in alcohol consumption and may reduce the potential effects of genes in some populations. If Muslim and Christian families were mixed in the same samples, heritability of alcohol abuse would tend to be close to zero because of the high between-family variance in alcohol consumption. Furthermore, some twin studies showing no effect of shared-in-families environmental variance are very likely biased by the close ties between MZ twin partners. Studies of twins reared apart and adoption studies document the importance of the family environment.

The same limitations that have been noted about alcohol disorders may also hold true for drug abuse and dependency. These two groups of disorders seem to be linked both genetically and in terms of family environment. Smoking as well seems to be influenced by both hereditary and family environmental factors.

Somatoform Disorders

Little is known about genetic factors in the development of somatoform disorders. Family studies have shown a weak aggregation of somatization or multiple-somatic-symptom disorders in families.

Although some older twin studies have included cases with what they called "hysteria," only one twin study has applied DSM-III criteria for somatoform disorders (Torgersen, 1986b). Both the older study and the new one show relatively similar results, however, with a moderately high concordance in MZ twin

pairs (29%–21%) and a clearly lower concordance (10%–0%) in DZ twin pairs. The concordance difference between MZ and DZ pairs suggests a genetic etiology; the relatively moderate concordance in MZ pairs speaks for the limits of such genetic influence. The twin study also showed that the more the MZ twins had been together in childhood, the more concordant they were. The same was true for DZ twins. Thus, environmental factors that influence sibs in a similar way seem to contribute to development of somatoform disorders.

Indirect evidence for inheritance of somatoform disorders is also observed in a Swedish adoption study, where female offspring of antisocial and alcoholic biological fathers had an increased risk of developing somatoform disorders (Bohman, Cloninger, von Knorring, & Sigvardson, 1984). These results will be discussed more thoroughly under the section about the genetic relationship between different psychiatric disorders.

Anxiety Disorders

Today, we know more about the influence of genetic factors on the development of the various anxiety disorders than is the case for any other group of psychiatric disorders. Several family studies have shown that anxiety disorders run in families. The question arises: Is this familial transmission genetic, environmental, or both? A Norwegian twin study from the early 1980s (Torgersen, 1983) suggested that genetic factors play a role in the development of anxiety disorders.

More interesting than the etiology of anxiety disorders in general are the genetics of the specific anxiety disorders. The Norwegian twin study suggested that panic disorders and anxiety disorders with panic attacks were more strongly influenced by genetic factors than anxiety disorders in general. For generalized anxiety disorder, when strict criteria were applied (i.e., the individual had never experienced any other anxiety or affective disorder higher in the hierarchy), genetic factors were of no importance.

The Virginia Twin Study, comprising more than 1,000 female twin pairs from the general population, made it possible to study the genetics of a number of anxiety disorders (Kendler, Neale, Kessler, Heath, & Eaves, 1993c). Study of panic disorders revealed a heritability above .40 when a strict definition of the disorder was applied, and below that when subclinical cases also were included. A multiple-threshold model, with panic disorders with phobic avoidance as a more severe variant, yielded a heritability a little below .40. As Kendler et al. note, their results are very much in agreement with the Norwegian study.

What about the generalized anxiety disorders in the Virginia Twin Study? Different definitions of generalized anxiety disorders and different hierarchies yielded heritabilities of .30 and lower. Applying a hierarchy with major depression reduced heritability with 6-month duration to zero (Kendler, Neale, Kessler, Heath, & Eaves, 1992a). However, a multiple-threshold model with 1 and 6 months' duration evaluating generalized anxiety disorders without major depression yielded a heritability of 19%.

Kendler, Neale, Kessler, Heath, and Eaves (1992b) also studied the etiology of phobias in women. They obtained a heredity of .32 for any phobia, .39 for agoraphobia, .32 for animal phobia, and .30 for social phobia. The rest of the variance was explained by a nonshared environment. Situational phobias (claustrophobia, fear of nature, etc.) constitute an exception, as heredity seemed to be of no importance; surprisingly, however, there was a shared-in-families environmental variance of 27%, but the investigators viewed this as a chance finding.

Especially interesting was an analysis disclosing common and specific genetic and non-shared-in-families environmental variance. Agoraphobia was the phobic disorder that shared most etiology with other phobias, but the common variance was almost exclusively non-shared-in-families variance. Social phobia and animal phobia were in a middle position. For social phobia, the common variance was environmental, and for animal phobia, genetic. Situational phobia was mainly due to specific non-shared-in-families environmental variance, but little etiology was shared with other phobias. As for all results from the Virginia Twin Study, the fact that MZ twins seemed to spend more time together in childhood and later did not influence the results.

An exceptional study of 4,000 male twin pairs who served in the armed forces in the Vietnam War has evaluated the etiology of posttraumatic stress symptoms (True et al., 1993). Although intuitively one would think posttraumatic stress disorder to be environmentally determined, the twin study shows that heredity contributes. MZ twins were more often concordant for posttraumatic stress symptoms than DZ twin partners. However, MZ twin partners were also more concordant for combat exposure, so some might think that this provided the explanation However, difference in concordance for PTSD between MZ and DZ partners survived the connection for such exposure. After such correction, the adjusted heritability varied between .13 and .35, with a median of .30, for 15 symptoms. Thirteen of the 15 showed a heritability of .26 or higher. Shared-in-families environmental variance only slightly influence symptoms.

Taken together, genetic factors seem to be of importance for all types of anxiety disorders. The exception is obsessive-compulsive disorders, where we have insufficient data. The difference is small between the various anxiety disorders. Perhaps panic disorder is most strongly influenced by heredity, followed by agoraphobia, animal phobia, social phobia, and posttraumatic stress disorder Generalized anxiety disorder also seems to be influenced by genes. However, if a strict hierarchy is applied, the influence becomes trivial. The genetic contribution to development of situational phobias seems questionable.

Most of the genetic variance lies between .30 and .40. As reliability problems reduce the genetic variance, a qualified guess may be that the "real" genetic variance for these disorders is between .40 and .55. Shared-in-families environmental variance, such as social class, parental upbringing methods, and neighborhood, does not seem to be of much importance.

Mood Disorders

It is well known that mood disorders run in families. Furthermore, major depression is observed among biological relatives of individuals with bipolar disorder, and dysthymic disorder among relatives of individuals with major depression.

A twin study confirms that bipolar depression is genetically transmitted in families. As for dysthymic disorder, the evidence is less compelling (Torgersen, 1986a). Moreover, results of this study suggest a genetic relationship between bipolar disorder and major depression and between major depression and dysthymic disorder. Heritability for major depression was calculated at more than 50%.

Recently, the large population-based Virginia Twin Study indicated a heredity of more than 40% when DSM-III-R definition of major depression was applied (Kendler, Neale, Kessler, Heath, & Eaves, 1992d). As in the Norwegian twin study, shared-in-families environmental variance was of little importance.

In an additional sample of close to 20,000 individuals, twins and their relatives were also studied (Kendler et al., 1994). Both samples yielded a heritability between 30% and 40%. Correction for unreliability brought heritability up to 50% (Kendler, Neale, Kessler, Heath, & Eaves, 1993a).

Results from the twin studies are confirmed by a Danish adoption study, showing a higher morbidity risk of bipolar disorder major depression among the biological relatives of adopted-away mood disorder probands (Wender et al., 1986). A Swedish adoption study yields weak evidence for genetic transmission among milder nonpsychotic mood disorders (von Knorring, Cloningen, Bohman, Sigvardson, 1983). On the other hand, depression in the adoptive father seemed to be related to depression in the adopted child, pointing to the importance of environmental familial transmission of minor depression.

Linkage studies offer more direct evidence of the genetic influence on the development of mood disorders. A linkage study among the Amish people in the United States showed promising clues to the location of a gene for bipolar disorder on chromosome 11 (Egeland et al., 1987). However, as new cases appeared among the studied families, such evidence was no longer apparent. Other linkage studies have not been able to confirm a site for such a gene on chromosome 11.

Twin and adoption studies suggest that genetic factors are of importance in the transmission of bipolar depression. Twin studies also point to a high—possibly 50%—heritability of major depression. As for the milder dysthymic disorder, the evidence is weak.

The possible genetic relationship between bipolar disorder and major depression, and between major depression and dysthymic disorder, may be understood in two ways: either by a multiple-threshold theory or by heterogeneity. A multiple-threshold theory would state that all three mood disorders are due to the same continuous liability for mood disorders. A severe condition such as bipolar disorder is more likely to appear if the liability is high, major depression if the liability is moderate, and dysthymic disorder if the liability is low. Among relatives, especially MZ co-twins of individuals with bipolar disorder, distribution of liability includes high, moderate, and low levels. Distribution of liability is somewhat more restricted among relatives of individuals with major depression. Consequently, bipolar disorder occurs less frequently. However, dysthymic disorder, in addition to major depression, will often be observed. Finally, among relatives of individuals with dysthymic disorder, the low average liability will preclude disorders other than dysthymic disorder.

Against this theory speaks the fact that we do not find more major depression among the relatives (especially MZ co-twins) of individuals with bipolar disorder than among other relatives, nor do we find more dysthymic disorder among the relatives of individuals with more severe mood disorders than among relatives of dysthymic individuals.

The heterogeneity theory seems more promising; among the major disorder cases, some are in reality cases of bipolar disorder who have not yet experienced the manic phase. The rest are "true" unipolar major depressives. Correspondingly, among the dysthymic disorders, some are in the prodromal stage of major depression. Further research, of course, will confirm whether this heterogeneity hypothesis is right.

Nothing is known about the mode of genetic transmission—whether it is additive, polygenetic, nonadditive with one or more genes, or mixed. In the case of additive heritability, linkage studies are very difficult, as it is unlikely that one of many genes has a major impact. To locate a series of genes at the same time is not possible with known linkage methodology.

Schizophrenia

It has been known for many years that schizophrenia, to some extent, runs in families. Relatives of individuals with a schizophrenic disorder have an increased risk of developing schizophrenia. The risk for first-degree relatives is around 10%, half of that for second-degree relatives, and, again, half of that figure for third-degree relatives. The risk for parents of individuals with schizophrenia is somewhat lower than the risk for siblings and children. Individuals who are schizophrenic, or about to become schizophrenic, are less likely to marry and in general have less contact with the opposite sex. To the extent that schizophrenia is genetically transmitted, parents of schizophrenics may sometimes "transfer" some genes to the offspring without themselves being influenced by those genes. However, almost 9 of 10 individuals who become schizophrenic have no relatives with schizophrenia.

Is it true that schizophrenia is genetically transmitted? Family studies cannot confirm this; twin studies may be more informative. Modern studies with good sampling techniques, interview methods, and DSM-III/DSM-III-R criteria show that half of the MZ co-twins of individuals with schizophrenia also develop schizophrenia, compared to about 13% of DZ co-twins (Farmer, McGuffin, & Gottesman, 1987; Onstad, Skre, Torgersen, & Kringlen, 1991). With a population risk under 1%, these results yield a heritability between 80% and 90%, with the rest being nonshared environment.

However, twin studies have a tendency to produce too high a heritability factor. The reason can be attributed to nonadditive genetic transmission. MZ twins will have all the necessary genes; DZ twins will not, especially if the genes are rare. Another reason can be attributed to interaction between genes and environment. If schizophrenia is caused by an interaction between some genes and specific environmental factors, twin studies show us only the product of these genes and environment. We do not see the cases in which only the genes are present, or only the adverse environment, as the separate set of factors does not lead to schizophrenia. This fact will exaggerate concordance in MZ pairs determined through a schizophrenic index twin and will decrease concordance in DZ pairs. Furthermore, MZ twin partners, in fact, experience more similar environment than DZ twins. When twin and family studies are combined, a more likely estimate of heritability is 60% to 70% (McGue, Gottesman, & Rao, 1985).

The best strategy to avoid the problem of correlation between similarity in genes and environment in twin pairs is to apply the adoption method. The best adoption study of schizophrenia is the Danish Adoption Study, which started in the 1960s, looking at the adopted-away children of schizophrenic mothers and the biological and adoptive relatives of adoptees with schizophrenia. Recently, results for the total sample, comprising the whole of Denmark, were published (Kendler, Gruenberg, & Kinney, 1994). DSM-III diagnoses were applied to the interview material collected 40 years ago. Investigators observed a high frequency of schizophrenia among biological relatives of adopted-away individuals with schizophrenia. Such frequency was, in fact, the same as one observes among relatives of schizophrenics who are not adopted away and are living with their biological families (Onstad, Skre, Torgersen, & Kringlen, 1991). No schizophrenia was observed among adoptive relatives. Biological relatives of adoptees without schizophrenia displayed a very low rate of schizophrenia. Therefore, the most likely interpretation is that schizophrenia is genetically and not environmentally transmitted in families.

Different subtypes of schizophrenia show both different symptomatology, different age of onset, and different course and progression. The question arises as to whether these subtypes have the same or different etiology. One way to answer this question is to look at biological relatives of probands with schizophrenia, and see whether subtypes of schizophrenia breed true in families and whether the various schizophrenic members of the family have the same type of schizophrenia. If one looks at ordinary first-degree relatives, one does not find such a pattern. However, among MZ twin partners, the same subtype of schizophrenia is displayed (Onstad, Skre, Edvardsen, Torgersen, & Kringlen, 1991).

Furthermore, nonparanoid schizophrenia, disorganized, and catatonic showed more evidence of genetic influence than paranoid schizophrenia. One may interpret these results in two ways. One interpretation may be according to a multiple-threshold theory. Nonparanoid schizophrenia appears when the highest threshold of liability for schizophrenia is passed. Nonparanoid schizophrenia is on a lower threshold of liability. If an index twin has nonparanoid schizophrenia, the high liability will then predict a high number of schizophrenia among the MZ co-twins. Some of them will have the same subtype of schizophrenia. If the index twin has paranoid schizophrenia, the MZ co-twin is less likely to have schizophrenia and very unlikely to have nonparanoid schizophrenia. Another explanation may be that different genes are responsible for the inheritance of schizophrenia generally and the subtype specifically.

The delineation between schizophrenia and other psychoses has been debated. A way to solve the problem is to see whether schizophrenia and other psychoses have similar etiology. Kendler, McGuire, Gruenberg, and O'Hare (1993) investigated the familial relationship between schizophrenia and other nonaffective psychoses and affective illness in the Roscommon Family Study. Their conclusion was that schizophrenia shares a familial predisposition with schizoaffective disorder and other nonaffective psychoses (schizophreniform and delusional disorder, atypical psychoses) and probably psychotic affective disorder, but not nonpsychotic affective disorder.

One twin study (Farmer et al., 1987) suggested a genetic relationship between schizophrenia and affective psychoses, but another one did not (Onstad, Skre, Torgersen, & Kringlen, 1991). The Danish Adoption Study confirmed a genetic relationship between schizophrenia and schizophrenic-like schizoaffective disorder, but no other kind of psychoses or affective disorders.

The genetic linkage studies have proved to be useful in detecting site of the genes for some somatic and neurological disorders. Several researchers hoped that the same would happen for schizophrenia. One promising study was published by Sherrington et al. (1988). Strong evidence was observed for a site for a schizophrenia gene on chromosome 5. However, other studies have disconfirmed such localization of a gene for schizophrenia (McGuffin et al., 1990). Either the Sherrington et al. results appeared by chance, or some few cases of schizophrenia have such an etiology.

There is little doubt that genetic factors influence development of schizophrenia. However, we do not know the mode of transmission—whether there is one dominant or recessive gene, more nonadditive genes, or a number of additive genes. One gene is unlikely (a factor that also makes it difficult to perform linkage studies).

The different subtypes of schizophrenia may possibly have some specific genetic etiology. The schizophrenic-like schizoaffective disorder may share genetic etiology with schizophrenia. Other types of psychoses may have environmental factors, possibly familial, in common with schizophrenia.

GENETIC RELATIONSHIP BETWEEN DISORDERS

An interesting question is whether different disorders have some similarity in etiology. Different disorders may be variants of the same underlying pathology, genetic or environmental. Some milder disorders may be within the spectrum of more serious disorders. Genetic research methods are a good way to identify such relationships.

The Virginia Twin Study has also made a great contribution in this area. Kendler, Neale, Kessler, Heath, and Eaves (1992c) showed that the same genetic factors seemed to influence the development of major depression and generalized anxiety disorders. Their conclusion was that environmental nonshared experiences determine whether a genetically vulnerable woman shall develop major depression or generalized anxiety disorder, or both. However, if the diagnosis of generalized anxiety disorder is applied only if no major depression exists, then the genetic factors (which were the same as those for major depression) were *unimportant* in the development of generalized anxiety disorder (i.e., less than 20%). Generally, the study demonstrated how much more important genetic variables are for major depression as contrasted to generalized anxiety disorder.

Kendler, Neale, Kessler, Heath, and Eaves (1993b) also looked at the genetic relationship between major depression and phobias. They found that the common genetic influence was modest—and perhaps nonexistent—for simple situational phobias. On the other hand, shared-in-families environmental variance seemed to be common for major depression and situational phobias. Nonshared environmental variance seemed to some extent to be common for major depression and agoraphobia. In addition, smoking (Kendler, Neale, et al., 1993) and alcoholism (Kendler, Neale, Kessler, & Eaves, 1993) shared to some extent genetic vulnerability with major depression.

Kendler, Walters, Neale, Kessler, et al. (1995) finally attempted to delineate the genetic and environmental relationship between major depression and all of the aforementioned anxiety disorders plus bulimia.

By means of multivariate genetic analyses, they discovered two common genetic factors and one disorder-specific factor. The first factor apparently influences development of phobias, panic disorder, and bulimia. The second is mainly responsible for development of major depression but also contributes to development of generalized anxiety disorder. Both factors have a modest influence on development of alcoholism. However, the disorder-specific factor was the really important one in the etiology of alcoholism. One shared-in-families environmental factor had a strong influence on bulimia, which is rarely confirmed in genetic research. Furthermore, one non-shared-in-families factor was of importance for both major depression and generalized anxiety disorder and, to a lesser extent, for phobias and panic disorder. All disorders had some specific non-shared-in-families variance. We see that major depression and generalized anxiety have a common etiology, which may account for high comorbidity between these disorders.

The Swedish Adoption Study shows a genetic and environmental relationship between antisociality, alcoholism, and somatization disorders (Bohman et al., 1984). The investigators observed a genetic relationship in females between what they called "high-frequency somatizers" and antisociality. Antisociality, on the other hand, was genetically related to what they named "diversiform somatizers" in females. In addition, alcohol abuse in the adoptive family contributed to the development of "diversiform somatizers." Names of these disorders were based on discriminant analysis of information from health registers. Therefore, it is difficult to say for sure what kinds of disorders the name subsumes, except that both groups suffered from abdominal pain, backache, and nervous complaints. The "diversiform" group had more headaches and the "high-frequency" had greater use of sick leave. The study is in accordance with an early family study showing the relationship between antisocial personality disorder and somatization disorder (Cloninger, Reich, & Guze, 1975).

Other adoption studies have demonstrated a genetic relationship between substance abuse and antisociality. Cadoret et al. (1995) discovered a pathway from antisocial personality in biological parents to aggressivity in adoptees. If the adoptive parents were psychiatrically disturbed, such aggressivity had a higher likelihood to develop into antisocial personality as well in adoptees. The antisocial personality may develop further to drug abuse/dependency in adoptees, especially if the biological parents also suffered from alcohol abuse or dependency. Drug abuse and dependency may finally lead to alcohol abuse and dependency in the adoptees—so-called early-onset alcoholism. Thus, a genetic tendency to antisociality, combined with a disturbed family environment, seems to increase the risk for substance abuse and dependency.

In the last decade we have seen a growing interest in studying the genetic relationship between personality disorders and schizophrenia. Kendler, Gruenberg, and Kinney (1994) discovered in the Danish Adoption Study a genetic relationship between schizotypal personality disorder and schizophrenia. A twin family study has shown the same (Torgersen, Skre, Onstad, Edvardsen, & Kringlen, 1993b). However, it seems as if only the affect-constricted, eccentric aspects of the schizotypal personality disorder are related to schizophrenia. The schizotypal personality disorder is highly heterogeneous, and it is likely that most cases of schizotypal personality disorder are completely outside the realm of the schizophrenia spectrum.

We see that the same genes seem to affect the development of a large range of various psychiatric disorders.

SUMMARY

In the course of the last decade we have been able to detect the genetic contribution to many psychiatric disorders. The more severe disorders, such as schizophrenia and bipolar disorder, seem to be highly influenced by genes. Major depression and panic disorder may be in a middle position, and the rest of the mood and anxiety disorders seem to be influenced to a lesser degree by genes. Least genetically influenced are dysthymic disorder and generalized anxiety disorder without a life history of major depression. The strength of the genetic determination of alcoholism is a bit unclear, but the confirmative twin and adoption studies suggest that genes may be of importance.

Less is known about the personality disorders, with the exception of the antisocial and schizotypal disorders, where the genetic influence is established. However, the marked genetic influence on development of broad personality dimensions, as well as a few studies of relevance for the other personality disorders, suggests that at least some of the other personality disorders are also influenced by genes.

Twin studies generally show little effect of shared-in-families environmental variance. (Bulimia is an apparent exception; this disorder seems to be highly influenced by familial variance.) The reason may be that the equal environmental assumptions, which state that MZ and DZ twins have similar environment, are often violated. Adoption studies demonstrate more effect of shared family environmental variance. However, even these studies, together with studies of twins reared apart, suggest that such environmental variance is seldom more than 10%. That means that socioeconomic factors, living conditions, rural versus urban environment, parental rearing practice, and so on are of less importance. However, it is likely that sampling limitations (which may mean that individuals from the most adverse childhood environments have not agreed to participate in the studies) may deflate the family environmental variance.

The non-shared-in-families environmental variance may sometimes be estimated too high, leaving too little to the other types of variance, because of unreliability of the measurement instruments.

We know very little, if anything, about the mode of inheritance—additive or nonadditive. Interaction effects between genes, or between genes and environment, are also unidentified at this juncture.

Linkage studies have not yet yielded what we once expected in the field of psychiatric disorders. One reason may be the painstaking work of searching through the whole genome, given the numerous possible sites for genes. Another reason may be the likely fact that the disorders are influenced by a number of genes, each of limited importance. Even so, there is reason to believe that in the future the locations of genes for some disorders will be identified. This is likely to happen if new technology is able to handle many genes at the same time in linkage or microbiological genetic studies. When this materializes, studies of the interaction between genes and environment will take place with increased speed.

The fact that disorders are genetically influenced does not mean that the children of a parent who has a disorder will evidence it. Indeed, in schizophrenia, only 5% to 10% of children of a parent with schizophrenia will also develop that disorder. The reason is that a rare combination of genes is difficult to inherit from the parents. However, studies of the genetics of psychiatric disorders tell us that an individual can develop the disorder without any adverse childhood environment. Unique experiences are of much higher importance than experiences shared by the rest of the family, and it is likely that such experiences may be of little importance for other individuals without the requisite genetic vulnerability. The experience may be psychological but can also be somatic (e.g., physical trauma or virus in pregnancy).

Modern genetic research has, paradoxically, taught us a lot about how the environment operates. Not only have we realized that the unique environment is more important for development of psychopathology than the shared-in-families environment, but this research has also shown us that what we earlier thought was pure environment are, in reality, gene–environment interactions. Studies of MZ twins brought up apart demonstrates that the reports about the family climate are highly correlated between MZ twins who have grown up in completely unrelated families (Plomin, 1994). How can two twin partners describe their parents as similarly warm or cold, even if these parents are unrelated, live in different areas, and have never seen each other? First, it may be in the eyes of the beholder. If one has a strong need of care from the start, then it is likely that one will feel that one does not get enough, and one will describe the parents as cold. On the other hand, a self-sufficient person may be content with almost any attitude from the parents. Furthermore, the memory of the childhood may be influenced by the present state of emotionality. To the extent that the need for warmth, the indifference to care, or the adult affectivity is influenced by genes, reports about the parents' attitudes also may be genetically influenced.

Second, children of different mood and different amount of sociability may elicit different behavior in the parents. In that way, an infant creates to some extent his or her own environment. To the extent that the mood and the sociability of the child are genetically influenced, the treatment the child receives also is genetically influenced.

Studies of twins reared apart have shown that a

number of "environmental" factors throughout the whole life cycle are reported to be rather similar in MZ, but not in DZ twin partners brought up apart.

In addition to these reactive and active gene–environment interactions, a passive gene–environment interaction also exists. Parents share genes with their biological children. To the extent that some of these genes are the cause of specific behavior, the children receive both the genes and the treatment based on the genes. For example, children who are beaten in childhood may be more often aggressive as youth and adults. This has often been explained by learning and imitation. But if aggressivity is genetically influenced, another possibility exists: The parents may beat the child "because of" their genes, and the child may be aggressive because of the same genes. Thus, there may be a spurious correlation between the treatment of the child and the subsequent behavior of the child. To entangle such relationships and rule out the spurious correlation, one needs an adoption design. The best procedure is to study twins reared apart. Today, as we are increasingly able to study the genes directly, we do not necessarily need twins and adoptive families. We can directly inspect the behavior in individuals with specific alleles.

The new knowledge from studies of twins reared apart, other adoptive families, and molecular genetics means that we have to rewrite our theories about development of behavior. We cannot any longer believe so strongly in learning, imitation, and identification. We have to realize that, in reality, we were studying gene–environmental interactions when we believed that we were studying pure environment.

In the future, the task will be to figure out which environmental factors still can be proved to influence the development of psychopathology, when genes are controlled for. We have to study what kind of environment interacts, in what way, with which types of genes. All these aims will come closer as the larger part of the human genome is mapped, and as we become more clever in the even more difficult task of studying environment in a reliable and valid way.

We must be aware that major cultural changes can have a profound effect on behavior that may overrule many of the effects of genes. For example, times of war may lower the threshold of all kinds of evil behavior and mental instability. Economic depression and major social changes may have a similar effect.

Thus, most results of studies of the relative contribution of genes and environment to the development of psychopathology are limited to the current cultural situation at the place when the studies are performed. In that way, we have to look upon results concerning causes of development of most types of psychopathology as relative. This fact, though good for the research, may be bad for the reader who wants the final truth.

REFERENCES

Benjamin, L., Li, L., Patterson, C., Greenberg, B.D., Murphy, D.L., & Hamer, D.H. (1996). Population and familial association between the D4 dopamine receptor and measures of novelty seeking. *Nature Genetics, 12,* 81–84.

Bergeman, C.S., Chipuer, H.M., Plomin, R., Pedersen, N.L., McClearn, G.E., Nesselroade, J.R., Costa, P.T. Jr., & McCrae, R.R. (1993). Genetic and environmental effects on openness to experience, agreeableness, and conscientiousness: An adoption/twin study. *Journal of Personality, 61,* 159–178.

Bohman, M., Cloninger, R.C., von Knorring, A.L., & Sigvardson, S. (1984). An adoption study of somatoform disorders: III. Cross-fostering analysis and genetic relationship to alcoholism and criminality. *Archives of General Psychiatry, 41,* 872–878.

Bohman, M., Sigvardsson, S., & Cloninger, C.R. (1981). Maternal inheritance of alcohol abuse: Cross-fostering analysis of adopted women. *Archives of General Psychiatry, 38,* 965–969.

Cadoret, R.J., & Stewart, M.A. (1991). An adoption study of attention deficit/hyperactivity/aggression and their relationship to adult antisocial personality. *Comprehensive Psychiatry, 32,* 73–82.

Cadoret, R.J., Yates, W.R., Woodworth, G., & Stewart, M.A. (1995). Adoption study demonstrating two genetic pathways to drug abuse. *Archives of General Psychiatry, 52,* 42–52.

Centerwall, B.S., & Robinette, C.D. (1989). Twin concordance for dishonorable discharge from the military: With a review of the genetics of antisocial behavior. *Comprehensive Psychiatry, 30,* 442–446.

Cloninger, C.R., Reich, T., & Guze, S.B. (1975). The multifactorial model of disease transmission: III. Familial relationship between sociopathy and hysteria (Briquet's syndrome). *British Journal of Psychiatry, 127,* 11–22.

Cloninger, C.R., Sigvardson, S., & Bohman, M. (1982). Predisposition to petty criminality in Swedish adoptees: III. Cross-fostering analysis of gene–environment interaction. *Archives of General Psychiatry, 39,*1242–1253.

Costa, P.T. Jr., & McCrae, R.R. (1990). Personality disorders and the five factor model of personality. *Journal of Personality Disorders, 4,* 362–371.

Crowe, R.R. (1974). An adoption study of antisocial personality. *Archives of General Psychiatry, 31,* 785–791.

Dalgard, O.S., & Kringlen, E. (1976). A Norwegian twin study of criminality. *British Journal of Criminology, 16,* 213–232.

Ebstein, R.P., Novick, O., Umansky, R., Priel, B., Osher, Y., Blaine, D., Benett, E.R., Nemanov, L., Katz, M., & Belamker, R.H. (1996). Dopamine D4 receptor (D4DR) exon III polymorphism associated with the human personality trait of novelty seeking. *Nature Genetics, 12,* 78–80.

Egeland, J.A., Gerhard, D.S., Pauls, D.L., Susser, J.N., Kidd, K.K., Allen, C.R., Hostetter, A.M., & Housman, D.E. (1987). Bipolar affective disorders linked to DNA markers on chromosome 11. *Nature, 325,* 783–787.

Farmer, A.E., McGuffin, P., & Gottesman, I.I. (1987). Twin concordance for DSM-III schizophrenia: Scrutinizing the validity of the definition. *Archives of General Psychiatry, 44,* 634–641.

Grove, W.M., Eckert, E.D., Heston, L., Bouchard, T.J., Jr., Segal, N., & Lykken, D.T. (1990). Heritability of substance abuse and antisocial behavior: A study of monozygotic twins reared apart. *Biological Psychiatry, 27,* 1293–1304.

Hsu, Y-P.P., Chen, W.J., Chen, C-C., Yu, J-M., & Cheng, T.A. (1996). Association of monoamine oxidase A alleles with alcoholism among male Chinese in Taiwan. *American Journal of Psychiatry, 153,* 1209–1211.

Kaprio, J., Koskenuvo, M., & Langinvaino, H. (1984). Finnish twins reared apart: IV. Smoking and drinking habits: A preliminary analysis of heredity and environment. *Acta Geneticae Medicae et Gemellologiae, 33,* 425–433.

Kendler, K.S., Gruenberg, A.M., & Kinney, D.K. (1994). Independent diagnoses of adoptees and relatives as defined by DSM-III in the Provincial and National sample of the Danish Adoption Study of Schizophrenia. *Archives of General Psychiatry, 51,* 456–468.

Kendler, K.S., Heath, A., & Martin, N.G. (1987). A genetic epidemiologic study of self-report suspiciousness. *Comprehensive Psychiatry, 28,* 187–196.

Kendler, K.S., Heath, A.C., Neale, M.C., Kessler, R.C., & Eaves, L.J. (1993). Alcoholism and major depression in women: A twin study of the causes of comorbidity. *Archives of General Psychiatry, 50,* 690–698.

Kendler, K.S., & Hewitt, J.K. (1992). The structure of self-report schizotypi in twins. *Journal of Personality Disorders, 6,* 1–17.

Kendler, K.S., McGuire, M., Gruenberg, A.M., & O'Hare, A. (1993). The Roscommon Family Study: I. Methods, diagnosis of probands, and risk of schizophrenia in relatives. *Archives of General Psychiatry, 50,* 527–540.

Kendler, K.S., Neale, M.C., Heath, A.C., Kessler, R.C., & Eaves, L.J. (1994). A twin-family study of alcoholism in women. *American Journal of Psychiatry, 151,* 707–715.

Kendler, K.S., Neale, M.C., Kessler, R.C., Heath, A.C., & Eaves, L.J. (1992a). Generalized anxiety disorder in women: A population-based twin study. *Archives of General Psychiatry, 49,* 267–272.

Kendler, K.S., Neale, M.C., Kessler, R.C., Heath, A.C., & Eaves, L.J. (1992b). The genetic epidemiology of phobias in women. The interrelationship of agoraphobia, social phobia, situational phobia and simple phobia. *Archives of General Psychiatry, 49,* 273–281.

Kendler, K.S., Neale, M.C., Kessler, R.C., Heath, A.C., & Eaves, L.J. (1992c). Major depression and generalized anxiety disorder: Same genes, (partly) different environments? *Archives of General Psychiatry, 49,* 716–722.

Kendler, K.S., Neale, M.C., Kessler, R.C., Heath, A.C., & Eaves, L.J. (1992d). A population-based twin study of major depression in women: The impact of varying definitions of illness. *Archives of General Psychiatry, 49,* 257–266.

Kendler, K.S., Neale, M.C., Kessler, R.C., Heath, A.C., & Eaves, L.T. (1993a). The lifetime history of major depression in women: Reliability of diagnosis and heritability. *Archives of General Psychiatry, 50,* 863–870.

Kendler, K.S., Neale, M.C., Kessler, R.L., Heath, A.C., & Eaves, L.J. (1993b). Major depression and phobias: The genetic and environmental sources of comorbidity. *Psychological Medicine, 23,* 361–371.

Kendler, K.S., Neale, M.C., Kessler, R.L., Heath, A.C., & Eaves, L.J. (1993c). Panic disorder in women: A population-based twin study. *Psychological Medicine, 23,* 397–406.

Kendler, K.S., Neale, M.C., MacLean, C.J., Heath, A.C., Eaves, L.J., & Kessler, R.C. (1993). Smoking and major depression: A casual analysis. *Archives of General Psychiatry, 50,* 36–43.

Kendler, K.S., Walters, E.E., Neale, M.C., Kessler, R.C., et al. (1995). The structure of the genetic and environmental risk factors for six major psychiatric disorders in women: Phobia, generalized anxiety disorder, panic disorder, bulimia, major depression and alcoholism. *Archives of General Psychiatry, 52,* 374–383.

Kendler, K.S., Walters, E.E., Truett, K.R., Heath, A.C., Neale, M.C., Martin, N.G., & Eaves, L.J. (1994). Sources of individual differences in depression symptoms: Analysis of two samples of twins and their families. *Archives of General Psychiatry, 151,* 1605–1614.

Knorring, A.L. von, Cloningen, C.R., Bohman, M., & Sigvardson, S. (1983). An adoption study of depressive disorders and substance abuse. *Archives of General Psychiatry, 40,* 943–950.

Lesch, K-P., Bengel, D., Heils, A., Sabol, S.Z., Greenberg, B.D., Petri, S., Benjamin, J., Müller, C.R., Harner, D.H., & Murphy, D.L. (1996, November 29). Association of anxiety-related traits with a polymorphism in the serotonin transporter gene regulatory region. *Science, 274,* 1527–1537.

Livesley, W.J., Jang, K.L., Jackson, D.N., & Vernon, P.A. (1993). Genetic and environmental contributions to dimensions of personality disorder. *American Journal of Psychiatry, 150,* 1826–1831.

McGue, M., Gottesman, I.I., & Rao, D.C. (1985). Resolving genetic models for the transmission of schizophrenia. *Genetic Epidemiology, 2,* 99–110.

McGue, M., Pickens, R., & Svikis, D. (1992). Sex and age effects on the inheritance of alcohol problems: A twin study. *Journal of Abnormal Psychiatry, 101,* 3–17.

McGuffin, P., & Gottesman, I.I. (1984). Genetic influence on normal and abnormal development. In M. Rutter & L. Hersou (Eds.), *Child psychiatry: Modern approaches,* 2nd ed. London: Blackwell.

McGuffin, P., Sargeant, M., Hetti, G., Tidmarsh, S., Whatley, S., & Marchbanks, R.M. (1990). Exclusion of a schizophrenia susceptibility gene from the chromosome 5Q11–Q13 region: New data and a reanalysis of previous reports. *American Journal of Human Genetic, 47,* 524–535.

Onstad, S., Skre, I., Edvardsen, J., Torgersen, S., & Kringlen, E. (1991b). Mental disorders in first-degree relatives of schizophrenics. *Acta Psychiatrica Scandinavia, 83,* 463–467.

Onstad, S., Skre, I., Torgersen, S., & Kringlen, E. (1991a). Twin concordance for DSM-III-R schizophrenia. *Acta Psychiatrica Scandinavia, 83,* 395–401.

Pedersen, N.L., Friberg, L., Floderins-Myrhed, B., McClean, G.E., & Plomin, R. (1984). Swedish early separated twins: Identification and characterization. *Acta Geneticae Medicae et Gemellologiae, 33,* 243–250.

Pedersen, N.L., McClearn, G.E., Plomin, R., Nesselroade, J.R., Berg, S., & De Faire, U. (1991). The Swedish Adoption/Twin Study of Ageing: An update. *Acta Geneticae Medicae et Gemellologiae, 40,* 7–20.

Plomin, R. (1994). *Genetics and experience. The interplay between nature and nurture.* London: Soge Publications.

Plomin, R., Owen, M.J., & McGuffin, P. (1994). The genetic basis of complex human behaviors. *Science, 264,* 1733–1739.

Rose, R.J., Kaprio, J., Williams, C.J., Viken, R., & Obrenski, K. (1990). Social contact and sibling similarity: Facts, issues and red herrings. *Behavior Genetics, 20,* 763–778.

Sherrington, R., Brynjolfsson, J., Pettersen, A., Potter, M., Dadlesten, K., Barrachlough, B., Wasmuth, J., Dobbs, M., & Gruling, H. (1988). Localization of a susceptibility locus for schizophrenia on chromosome 5. *Nature, 336,* 164–167.

Sigvardson, S., Cloninger, C.R., & Bohman, M. (1982). Predisposition to petty criminality in Swedish adoptees: III. Sex differences and validation of the male typology. *Archives of General Psychiatry, 39,* 1248–1253.

Soldz, S., Budman, S., Demoy, A., & Merry, J. (1993). Representation of personality disorders in circumplex and five-factor space: Exploration with a clinical sample. *Psychological Assessment, 5,* 41–52.

Tellegen, A., Lykken, T.D., Bouchard, T.J., Wilcox, K.J., Segal, N.L., & Rich, S. (1988). Personality similarity in twins reared apart and together. *Journal of Personality and Social Psychology, 54,* 1031–1039.

Torgersen, S. (1983). Genetic factors in anxiety disorders. *Archives of General Psychiatry, 40,* 1085–1089.

Torgersen, S. (1984). Genetic and nosological aspects of schizotypal and borderline personality disorders. A twin study. *Archives of General Psychiatry, 41,* 546–554.

Torgersen, S. (1986a). Genetics of somatoform disorders. *Archives of General Psychiatry, 43,* 502–505.

Torgersen, S. (1986b). Genetic factors in moderately severe and mild affective disorders. *Archives of General Psychiatry, 43,* 222–226.

Torgersen, S., Skre, I., Onstad, S., Edvardsen, I., & Kringlen, E. (1993a). The psychometric-genetic structure of DSM-III-R personality disorder criteria. *Journal of Personality Disorders, 7,* 196–213.

Torgersen, S., Skre, I., Onstad, S., Edvardsen, I., & Kringlen, E. (1993b). "True" schizotypal personality disorder: A study of co-twins and relatives of schizophrenic probands. *American Journal of Psychiatry, 150,* 1661–1667.

True, W.R., Rice, J., Eisen, S.A., Heath, A.C., Goldberg, J., Lyons, M.J., & Nowak, J. (1993). A twin study of genetic and environmental contributions to liability for posttraumatic stress symptoms. *Archives of General Psychiatry, 50,* 257–264.

Trull, T.J. (1992). DSM-III-R personality disorders and the five-factor model of personality: An empirical comparison. *Journal of Abnormal Psychology, 101,* 553–560.

Wender, P.H., Kety, S.S., Rosenthal, D., Shalzinger, F., Oreman, J., & Lund, I. (1986). Psychiatric disorders in the biological and adoption families of adopted individuals with affective disorders. *Archives of General Psychiatry, 43,* 923–929.

Zimmermann, M. (1994). Diagnosing personality disorders. A review of issues and research methods. *Archives of General Psychiatry, 51,* 225–242.

CHAPTER 4

PSYCHOBIOLOGICAL REFLECTIONS OF ADULT PSYCHOPATHOLOGY

Richard C. Josiassen
Arthur P. Noyes Research Foundation

Rita A. Shaughnessy
MCP/Hahnemann School of Medicine

INTRODUCTION

For many hundreds of years there have been beliefs and strong hints that psychopathology is associated with abnormalities of the central nervous system (CNS).[1] As early as the fourth century B.C., Hippocrates turned his mind toward speculations about psychopathology and boldly introduced its relation to the human brain:

> Men ought to know that from the brain, and from the brain only, arise our pleasures, joys, laughter, and jests, as well as our sorrows, pains, griefs, and fears. Through it, in particular, we think, see, hear, and distinguish the ugly from the beautiful, the bad from the good, the pleasant from the unpleasant. . . . It is the same thing which makes us mad or delirious, inspires us with dread and fear, whether by night or by day, brings sleepless-

ness, inopportune mistakes, aimless anxieties, absent-mindedness, and acts that are contrary to habit. These things that we suffer all come from the brain, when it is not healthy, but becomes abnormally hot, cold, moist, or dry, or suffers from any other unnatural affection to which it was not accustomed. Madness comes from its moistness.

The assertion that madness comes from a moist brain was further elaborated by Hippocrates to considerations of the importance of bile. Yellow and black bile were thought to play a predominant role in mental disease, with a sudden change of bile to the brain bringing on disturbing dreams and states of anxiety.

These first approximations dominated Greek and Roman medical thinking and culminated in the scientific positivism of Galen (130–200 A.D.), who centered all mental functions, sensations, and motion in the human brain. With the death of Galen, interest in psychopathology surrendered to demonology and supernatural explanations in the Dark Ages. The terms *devil sickness* and *witch disease* were frequently used, and the idea became crystallized that

The technical assistance of Paul E. Rapp and Donald A. Overton is gratefully acknowledged. Their timely interventions and corrective thinking prevented the needless loss of numerous hours. The editorial assistance of Susan Jensen is greatly appreciated.

psychopathology was mostly supernatural.[2] The seven centuries between Hippocrates and Galen were the first pages of a story that was not strongly raised again until the 17th and 18th centuries, when philosopher-scientists began to ponder over the brain and work upon its puzzle.

The speculations of Hippocrates and Galen, launched with no basis in proven fact, established a long tradition of philosophical thought that grew into an orderly and coherent collection of scientific findings. From the psychophysiological dualism of Descartes (1596–1650), who believed that mind and body are different forms of existence that interact and influence each other, came the mechanistic formulation that human beings perceive and move by virtue of nerves that act as message cables to and from the brain. Hobbes (1599–1679) argued the theory of a radical materialism, in which reality is a physical entity and any form of mental phenomena are epiphenomena, emerging merely as secondary effects of physical processes. From the early philosopher-scientists, struggling with the relationship between mind and body, to the fanciful attempts of Franz Joseph Gall (1758–1828) to chart individual feelings on the skull and underlying cerebral cortex, and the

systematic studies of François Magendie (1783–1855), Charles Bell (1774–1842), Johannes Müller (1801–1858), Paul Broca (1824–1880), Hughlings John Jackson (1835–1911), Emil Kraepelin (1856–1926), Wilder Graves Penfield (1891–1976), John Eccles (b. 1903), Roger Sperry (b. 1913), and countless others, it has become widely believed that *all* behavior is constrained within the structural and functional capacities of the CNS.

Hippocrates, Galen, and Descartes had provided primitive explanations of mechanisms subserving reflex movement and sensation. But gradually, and with more clarity, scientists began to demonstrate that it is within the aggregated networks of nerve cells that memory and learning also occur, which in turn influence higher cognitive functions, including the human capacity for reasoning and understanding. At the same time, our knowledge of particular forms of psychopathology increased, and, with the steady accumulation of basic information, it became widely believed that these aggregated neural systems and their electrochemical interrelationships also provide the underpinnings for *all abnormal* human experience and behavior. It was probably Adolph Meyer (1928) who first used *psychobiological* as the inte-

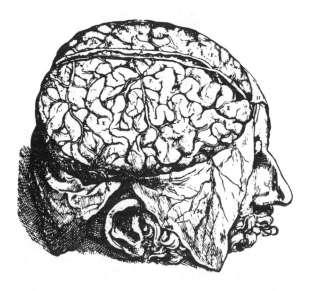
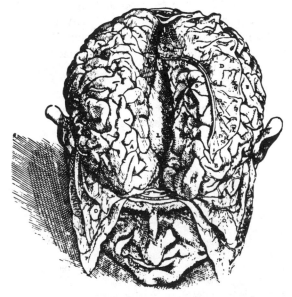

FIGURE 4-1. Plate 67 from *Illustrations from the Works of Andreas Vesalius of Brussels,* originally published by the World Publishing Company. Courtesy of the New York Academy of Medicine Library.

grating term for the emerging dynamic physiological views of mental illness that, in their own ways, Freud and many of his contemporaries held.

This psychobiological viewpoint has led some to a reductionistic belief that mental illness is caused by "nothing but a broken brain," fostering a search for specific regions of the CNS or for the activity of neurotransmitters and their receptors as causes or correlates of psychopathology. As a practical necessity, this reductionism continues to be reflected within the scientific literature, yielding spectacular details that have shed light on the fundamental pathophysiology of certain forms of mental illness. But in taking an inventory of these spectacular advances, there lies an invitation to pretentiousness that at times has run roughshod over one of the oldest and most widely addressed issues in the history of thought: the mind–body problem.[3] On this very point, Freedman (1992) writes:

> . . . for our forefathers, as for us, the core issue is no more or less than the nature of human nature . . . there is an underlying complex question actuating psychiatric thought—how mind and body are linked. For we ask how it is that living matter can accommodate the links of bodily function, subjective experience, and overt behavior. (p. 860)

Even with the technological wonders in hand, this underlying complex question of mind and body, though embarrassing, is intrinsic to our work. It stands at the heart of the matter even as we more deliberately focus our intellectual business on CNS structure and function and the many things that can go wrong.

To avoid an excessive reductionism, it might be helpful to suggest that psychobiology represents more of a bridging discipline. It has a perspective and technology that are well positioned to observe the summation or interaction of genetic and environmental factors contributing to psychiatric conditions. Both environmental and genetic theories have been advanced in efforts to explicate the causality of various mental illnesses; for the most part, however, the numerous proposals still continue to represent antagonistic rather than complementary viewpoints. Nevertheless, whether one's conceptual orientation gives more emphasis to environmental factors over genetic factors, or vice versa, it is generally believed the psychopathology reflects the interaction of genetic and environmental influences, and that this synthesis of influences occurs within the cells and cellular assemblies of the human brain. Certain psychopathological conditions have been regarded as resulting from a preponderance of genetic factors (e.g., transmission of schizophrenia), whereas others result from more obviously environmental factors (e.g., uncontrolled family violence in dissociative disorders). However, each of the putative causal factors must somehow have a direct impact on neural activity or be transduced into neural activity in order to produce transient or lasting influence on the experience and behavior of the human being.[4] Therefore, the task for psychobiological research into mental illness is to explicate how causal factors, whether genetic or environmental, affect neural activity, and to provide a detailed specification of how these altered neuronal events underlie psychopathologic experience and behavior.

From this viewpoint, then, it becomes essential to understand as much as possible about brain cells (called *neurons*) and their unique capacity as fundamental building blocks of the brain. Brain cells have the same genes and the same functional organization as other cells throughout the body. However, neurons have several unique features that allow the brain to function in a very different way from any other body organ. These unique neuronal features include a *distinctive cell shape*, an *outer excitable membrane* capable of generating nerve impulses, *synaptic structures* that transfer information from one neuron to the next, and *neural plasticity* providing the capacity for neurons to be modified in transient or lasting ways as information-processing units. Each of these four unique neuronal features is firmly established in the minds of neuroscientists, and they have begun to serve in varying degrees as organizing frameworks for research into the nature of psychopathology.

The psychobiological approach into the function and structure of the human CNS has greatly accelerated in recent years, and the mounting evidence of CNS involvement in psychopathology has become much more explicit and convincing. However, this approach brings with it a vast number of confounding subject variables that need to be fully untangled. These include gender differences, hemispheric specialization, aging, cellular types, genetic and environmental impact on neural development, effects of neurotransmitters and neuromodulators, and the long-lasting influences of psychoactive medication on cell membranes. Most existing psychobiological studies of mental illness can be seriously criticized for ignoring some of these relevant variables. Yet, though imperfect, the developing psychobiological insights have begun to unlock fundamental questions and bring relief from mental suffering.

What follows in this chapter is a selective sketch of some high points in the ongoing investigation of *cell shape, membrane excitability, synaptic activity,* and *plasticity* in this long tradition of attempting to relate psychopathology to the multitude of things that can go wrong within the structural architecture or the electrical and chemical processes of the human CNS. A cautionary comment is needed here: In view of the fact that this chapter is intended to be a selective sketch, it was often impossible to indulge in many qualifying statements or the luxury of numerous details. Instead, the aim of the chapter is to convey a picture of the present state of psychobiological study of mental illness, and a framework within which to encounter the alluring tradition that continues to evolve even into the present day. If, indeed, psychopathology is rooted within the interwoven connective neural pathways of the human central nervous system, then it is highly likely that the theories, concepts, and findings of psychobiology will have considerable influence on the study of mental illness.

ON THE SHAPE OF NEURONS (ANATOMY)

Some Basic Anatomy

The human brain weighs about three pounds and contains some 10^{12} (1,000 billion) or 10^{14} *neurons.* The neurons are surrounded, supported, and nourished by *glial* cells, which are more plentiful (10:1) than the neurons. Although the compound microscope had been invented by Hans Jansen in the period around 1590–1609, neurons and glial cells are so densely packed together that the microscope yielded only a useless smeared image when postmortem tissue was examined. Even the largest human neuron is exceedingly small and lies outside the range of unaided

vision; therefore, the characterization of individual brain cells was a slow and arduous process.

Without the necessary tools, early brain scientists were limited to unaided visual observation of gross postmortem tissue using gross anatomical divisions: (1) the *telencephalon,* consisting of two cerebral hemispheres that give the appearance of convolutions (*gyrus* and *sulcus*) folded together to stay within the confines of the skull; (2) the *diencephalon,* comprising the thalamus and hypothalamus; (3) the *mesencephalon* or midbrain; (4) the *metencephalon,* consisting of the cerebellum and the pons; and (5) the *myelencephalon,* also known as the medulla oblongata. With the naked eye, early investigators were able to recognize gross damage resulting from hemorrhage, displacement, trauma, infectious diseases, degeneration, and atrophy, and to relate the gross neuropathology to abnormal behavior. The writings of Bain in *The Senses and the Intellect* (1855) and *The Emotions and the Will* (1859) summed up the achievements of physiological work up to the mid-19th century, demonstrating that psychology was beginning to think of experimental physiology as fundamental to serious explanations of the science of human behavior.

One landmark study during this period came from Broca (1861), who, in the brain of a patient with speech loss, found that the second and third frontal convolutions on the left side were destroyed. This finding attracted attention and soon came into wide acceptance as one of the first case studies definitely showing cortical localization of a specific function, and antedating by 20 years the definite location of any of the sensory centers. The work of Fritsch and Hitzig (1870) laid the groundwork for localizing the motor functions, and Wernicke (1874) published the finding of a second major center for language located on the first and second temporal convolutions. Ribot, in *Diseases of Memory* (1881) and *Diseases of Personality* (1885), regarded brain physiology as the basis of personality and personality disorders as the product of disordered brain functions. But he thought in terms of gross lesions, not in terms of the disorganization of microscopic elements. More fine-grained anatomical progress awaited the development of staining procedures.

Although the microscope had been available for more than two hundred years, it was the development of an ingenious selective staining procedure by the anatomist Golgi (1875; see Golgi, 1883) that made it possible for researchers to examine directly the fundamental units of the brain. To this day, no one knows why the Golgi method works. But the procedure *completely* stains approximately 1% to 2% of the neurons in a given region, while leaving all of the surrounding neurons and glial cells unaffected, thus making it possible to contrast individual neurons with their surroundings. By looking at stained cells under a microscope, Golgi concluded that neurons are independent units and that each nerve cell is in some way connected physiologically, but not anatomically, with other neurons. This was important in confirming the belief that the most significant relation between neurons was to be found not in their anatomical interconnections but, rather, in the ways in which neurons influence one another in function. This view was named the *neuron theory* by Waldeyer (1891). Anatomists during this period began to build up an inventory of various kinds of cell shapes and sizes. Ramon y Cajal devoted his professional life to applying the new Golgi stain to virtually every part of the human nervous system. His monumental work, *Histology of the Nervous System of Humans and Vertebrates,* originally published in Spanish in 1904, is still recognized as one of the most important single works in neurobiology, bringing together the central conception of anatomical independence of neurons and their physiological interconnection. During that same period, Brodmann (1909) partitioned the brain into 50 distinct regions on the basis of cytoarchitectural criteria; the Brodmann numbers are still commonly used.

Using microscopy with Golgi-stained cells, and later Nissl-stained cells (this stain picks out only individual cell bodies, not axons and dendrites), it became clear that there is considerable variation in the shape of neurons. However, each neuron has two main parts: the cell body or *soma,* and the *processes,* which extend out from the soma and transmit excitation. These processes are usually distinguished as *axons* and *dendrites,* with axons functioning as the major output apparatus for the soma, and dendrites receiving and integrating information from other neurons. The soma, axons, and dendrites are all parts of the neuron proper and share a single nucleus. A single axon generally protrudes from the soma, and commonly it will branch out extensively toward its end. In contrast, a dense arborization of dendrites often extends from the soma, and in many types of neurons the dendrites are covered with *dendritic spines* that serve as the dominant points of contact with other neurons. With microscopy and staining procedures coupled at the end of the 19th century, the cellular investigation of the brain became possible (see Figure 4-2 on page 87).

Early Cellular Studies

This opportunity for microscopic scrutiny of stained brain cells was seized by the Munich School of Kraepelin and led to many potent attempts at establishing cellular abnormalities in both neurologic and psychiatric patients. Some of the first fruits came from Alzheimer (1897), who reported severe cellular changes in cerebral cortex of patients with *dementia praecox* (later to be called schizophrenia), with disorganization of the ganglion cells and extensive glial reactions. In a later study, Alzheimer (1913) reviewed the pathological anatomy of 55 cases of dementia praecox and found the changes to be most pronounced in layers II and III of the cerebral cortex. He also found *cell loss* and *gliosis* (excessive growth of glial tissue) in the outer layers of the frontal cortex. Kraepelin (1907) attributed *dementia praecox, catatonia,* and *dementia paranoids* to histopathological changes within the cerebral cortex.

The reports of Alzheimer and Kraepelin were particularly important to the scientific community. They made careful statements and reported detailed observations of swollen nuclei and shrunken neurons, with the frequent loss (termed *falling out*) of groups of cells. These early findings were closely followed by numerous neuropathological postmortem studies showing dark shrunken nerve cells in layers III and V of the cerebral cortex of patients with dementia praecox. These were considered *sclerotic* cells reflecting chronic, nonrecoverable change. Southard (1919) suggested that histological abnormalities of the temporal and parietal lobes were correlated with auditory hallucinations and catatonia, respectively. Early cellular studies examined the CNS extensively, with particular interest in the cortex, thalamus, basal ganglia, and reticular system.

One of the earliest *controlled microscopic studies* using a semiquantitative approach was carried out by

Dunlap (1924), who compared cell counts in frontal lobe tissue from patients with dementia praecox to cell counts in control cases. Dunlap concluded that

> . . . nerve cell reactions in dementia praecox seem in no way specific and are not constant or uniform from case to case; since they do not differ materially in degree or in kind from the changes seen in the cells of control cases, we feel justified, at present, in believing that the changes are dependent on the same general causes that operate in the controls and are not dependent on any special conditions existent in dementia praecox. (p. 416)

The early microscope studies of postmortem cellular pathology produced a number of positive findings of importance, particularly in neurodegenerative diseases. But to a large extent, the findings of cellular pathology in mental illness proved to be nonspecific, and their possible relevance remained obscure (for review, see Spielmeyer, 1930).

Early Imaging Studies

The development of *X-ray procedures* allowed investigators to move beyond postmortem studies to gross observation of the living brain. In addition to nonspecific cellular pathology, prior postmortem studies had already documented that psychiatric patients displayed an unexpectedly high prevalence of *brain tumors* (for review, see Waggoner & Bagchi, 1954). Many writers expressed uncertainty as to whether the observed tumors were directly related to psychosis or were merely activating a latent disease that was unrelated to the tumor.[5] However, with the advent of X-ray procedures came the opportunity to examine gross brain anatomy of living patients, and this became a routine procedure at admission to many psychiatric hospitals. The general findings with X-ray revealed tumors in 1% to 2% of psychiatric inpatients, which exceeded the estimated prevalence of cerebral tumors (0.5%) in the general population at that time.

Gross structural defects in the ventricular system also began to be detected by *pneumoencephalography (PEG)*, an X-ray technique in which the cerebral spinal fluid that normally surrounds the brain and fills the ventricular system is replaced with air to reveal the shape of the ventricles. Jacobi and Winkler (1927) were the first to report PEG abnormalities in schizophrenia. Following this original observation there were numerous reports showing gross structural defects in the ventricular system of various patient groups. The report of Haug (1962) merits particular attention. His study involved the analysis of PEG images from 270 patients taken from three global diagnostic groups, which were labeled as "organic mental disorders," "the group of schizophrenics," and "nonorganic mental disorders." Within this heterogeneous population, "definite cerebral atrophy" was observed in 60% of the patients and was the most consistent abnormal finding. The cerebral atrophy included "definitely pathological dilatation" of the ventricles (focal or general) in 48% of the cases and varying degrees of atrophy in brain surface of 35% of the cases. Although cortical atrophy was thought to occur in 60% to 80% of schizophrenic patients, Haug found evidence of ventricular dilatation and cortical atrophy across all of the diagnostic groups, and concluded that there is "probably no causal connection between the patient's mental disturbance and the demonstrated cerebral abnormalities" (p. 33).

The first half of the 20th century was a classical period for neuroanatomical study. The distinction was made between gradual cellular atrophy and the more rapid forms of neural degeneration. Several neurodegenerative diseases were characterized, as well as inflammatory processes. Studies of brain mechanisms and emotion were advanced, particularly by the work of Papez (1937), who proposed a neural circuit of emotions involving a set of interconnected pathways within the *limbic system*. But with regard to particular forms of psychopathology, the review of Dastur (1959) made it clear that the available cellular and gross anatomical findings among psychiatric patients were nonspecific and had become progressively controversial. Many of the postmortem studies involved psychiatric patients with other significant medical illness that may have contributed to the observed brain pathology. The resolution of X-ray and PEG images was poor. Concerns also emerged regarding the technical limitations of postmortem microscopic findings, due to confounding variables such as age, hypoxia, postmortem deterioration of tissue, and variations among fixation and staining procedures. These methodological limitations probably accounted for the demise of this era of neuroanatomical study of mental illness.

The field had become lost in controversy, and the major focus of psychopathological research was drawn away from neuroanatomical anomalies (for a time) into neurochemistry with the discovery that neural transmission was susceptible to the influence of medications.[6]

Contemporary Cellular Study

Renewed interest in neuroanatomy was stimulated by Stevens (1973), who reintroduced the limbic system as a promising brain region for cellular changes in schizophrenia. On postmortem study of 25 schizophrenic patients, she found increased gliosis in neural circuits that converge on and project to major tracts and nuclei of the limbic system. This was followed shortly thereafter by several postmortem brain studies showing evidence of subtle morphological anomalies, mainly in the limbic temporal lobe regions of schizophrenic patients. The evidence included smaller hippocampal and parahippocampal gyrus volume (Bogerts, Meertz, & Schonfeldt-Bausch, 1985; Bogerts et al., 1990; Jeste & Lohr, 1989), reduced cell numbers and cytoarchitectural alterations in hippocampus, entorhinal cortex, and cingulate gyrus (Arnold et al., 1991, 1995; Benes et al., 1986; Benes, 1993; Hecker, Heinsen, Heinsen, & Beckmann, 1990; Kovelman & Scheibel, 1984), but these findings have not been consistently observed (Benes, 1997; Christison et al., 1989). Although it was initially tempting to conclude that these findings were consistent with a neurodegenerative process playing a major role in schizophrenia, several systematic quantitative analyses have failed to show evidence of an increased density of reactive glial cells in patients with schizophrenia. However, there is a recent report of "inflammatory" changes (Korschenhausen et al., 1996), as would be expected in the presence of a neurodegenerative process.

Of recent postmortem studies, the work of Brown, Akbarian, and Freedman warrants particular attention. Brown et al. (1986) investigated structural changes in the brains of 232 patients with chart diagnoses of schizophrenia or affective disorder who had died in one mental hospital between 1956 and 1978. From this sample were eliminated the brains of patients whose illnesses either did not meet contemporary research diagnostic criteria applied retrospec-

tively to hospital chart information, or showed significant histopathologic evidence of Alzheimer's disease or cerebrovascular disease. When age, gender, and year of birth were controlled, the main differences between these large study groups were as follows:

1. Brain weight was reduced (by 5%–6%) in schizophrenic patients.
2. Lateral ventricular area was modestly increased (by 15%) in schizophrenic patients.
3. Temporal horn area was dramatically increased (by 80%) in schizophrenic patients.
4. Parahippocampal gyrus width was reduced in schizophrenic patients.

It is also noteworthy that these structural differences were greater on the left side. Crow (1990) suggests that this array of postmortem findings supports the hypothesis that schizophrenia is in some way associated with neurodevelopmental alterations in the emergence of hemispheric asymmetries in the human brain, an idea presented in several earlier theoretical publications (Crow et al., 1989; Flor-Henry, 1969; Geschwind & Galaburda, 1985; Torrey & Peterson, 1974; Weinberger, 1987).

The possibility of a more specific neurodevelopmental alteration in schizophrenia has been suggested in the postmortem cellular studies of Akbarian et al. (1993, 1996), which focused on the cortical subplate. The cortical subplate is a transitory structure involved in the formation of neuronal connections as cells migrate in the developing cortex. With normal neurodevelopment, most of the neurons within the subplate are eventually eliminated through programmed cell death (known as *apoptosis*) once cell migration is completed. Akbarian has shown selective displacement of three neuronal populations in the frontal lobe of brains from schizophrenic patients, which indicates alteration in the migration patterns of subplate neurons or in the pattern of programmed cell death. This could lead to the development of defective cortical circuitry in the brains of persons with schizophrenia.

Another interesting line of ongoing work is found in the studies of Freedman and colleagues (Freedman, Hall, Adler, & Leonard, 1995; Freedman, Waldo, Bickford-Wimer, & Nagamoto, 1991; Leonard et al.,

1996), who have focused on a specific neurophysiological deficit observed in the processing of auditory information among persons with schizophrenia. This deficit (lack of inhibition in the auditory P50) in patients is transiently normalized with nicotine use. Based on these findings, along with an important series of animal studies (Freedman et al., 1993), it was speculated that this neurophysiological deficit may be related to a decrease in nicotinic cholinergic receptors within the hippocampus. Freedman et al. (1995) examined postmortem sections of hippocampus in schizophrenic and in age-matched nonschizophrenic sample patients and, in fact, observed a significant reduction of nicotinic receptors among the schizophrenic patients. Interestingly, these results were not related to generalized hippocampal cell loss, drug exposure at time of death, or smoking history.

Contemporary Structural Imaging

The introduction of contemporary in vivo brain-imaging techniques, such as the computerized axial tomographic (CT) brain scan and magnetic resonance imaging (MRI), has further fueled neuroanatomical study. With the CT scan, an X-ray source rotates around the head and is coupled with a synchronously moving X-ray detector on the other side to yield a faithful representation of the internal structure of the living brain in a cross-sectional image. The CT image may reveal enlarged and atrophied structures. Abnormal masses also may be visualized, although these masses may not show up until they are in an advanced stage. Small tumors and demyelinating diseases are often missed.

Johnstone et al. (1976) were the first to report CT evidence of lateral ventricular enlargement in a group of older chronic schizophrenic patients as compared with control subjects, and to note a preponderance of "negative" symptoms in patients with enlarged ventricles. Weinberger, Cannon-Spoor, Potkin, and Wyatt (1980) also reported ventricular pathology along with prominent sulci, and further suggested that lateral ventricular enlargement was correlated with poor premorbid adjustment. These findings of ventricular pathology and cortical atrophy in schizophrenia have been extensively replicated by other workers (for recent review, see Lewis, 1990), al-

though there have been divergent reports that found no ventricular abnormality (Iacono et al., 1988; Jernigan, Zatz, Moses, & Berger, 1982). The clinical correlates of these structural changes and their meaning remain unresolved. However, the recent reports of Davis et al. (1998) and DeLisi et al. (1992, 1995, 1997) may suggest some clarification. In the Davis et al. (1998) study, 53 male patients with schizophrenia and 13 healthy controls were examined using CT scan on two occasions at least four years apart. The patients were subtyped as "Kraepelinian" (showing a classic degenerative course) and "non-Kraepelinian." Using semiautomated computer measurements, they found a bilateral increase in ventricular size over the four-year interval in the Kraepelinian subgroup, more marked in the left hemisphere than in the right. In contrast, neither the non-Kraepelinian nor the healthy controls showed CT changes. DeLisi et al. (1992) reported a follow-up study of first-episode schizophrenia patients. At a two-year follow-up there was no evidence of ventricular enlargement, however, progressive enlargement did become apparent at four years (DeLisi et al., 1995) and five years (DeLisi et al., 1997).

Enlargement of the ventricular system has also been observed in patients with other forms of psychopathology, including several studies of patients with affective disorder (Jacoby & Levy, 1980; Schlegel & Kretschmar, 1987), mania (Nasrallah, McCalley-Whitters, & Pfohl, 1984; Pearlson & Veroff, 1981), and alcoholism (Pfefferbaum, Rosenbloom, Crusan, & Jernigan, 1988). For a recent review, see Soares and Mann (1977). A limited number of controlled CT studies have directly compared schizophrenic and affective disorder populations, and the majority find no significant differences between the two diagnostic groups (Luchins, Levine, & Meltzer, 1984; Nasrallah, Jacoby, & McCalley-Whitters, 1981; Pearlson & Veroff, 1981; Pearlson et al., 1984; Rieder et al., 1983). These initial studies revealed nonspecific findings of brain atrophy in depressed patients, including lateral ventricular enlargement, increased ventricular–brain ratio, increased cerebrospinal fluid volummes, and sulcal atrophy. These findings were particularly relevant for elderly depressed patients. In one recent study of the temporal lobe, patients with late-onset depression had significantly more left medial temporal atrophy than did early-onset patients of similar age (Greenwald et al., 1997). In this study, temporal atrophy was significantly correlated with cognitive impairment and was not related to physical illness.

In addition to the well-established findings of ventricular abnormality and widespread cortical atrophy in schizophrenia, CT studies have focused on specific brain regions of interest. The focal findings have included aqueduct stenosis (Reveley & Reveley, 1983), arachnoid and septal cysts (Lewis & Mezey, 1985), and agenesis of the corpus callosum (Lewis et al., 1988). Owens, Johnstone, Bydder, and Kreel (1980) reported unsuspected focal lesions in 12 of 136 (9%) of their schizophrenic patients. Unfortunately, because of the limited image resolution, CT scans are not able to provide reliable delineation of limbic temporal lobe structures such as hippocampus, amygdala, and temporal horn; hence, many of the more provocative postmortem findings have not been replicated in the living brain using CT procedures.

The more recent magnetic resonance imaging (MRI) technology provides much better anatomical resolution. MRI technology is based on the ability to measure the random spinning behavior of hydrogen nuclei (or protons), the most common nucleus in biological tissue. When the spinning protons are placed in a static magnetic field, they align themselves in the direction of that magnetic field, and this realignment can be measured. The imaging of brain structure has gradually shifted to MRI because of the inherently superior resolution of images.[7] The basic principles of MRI have been described very clearly by Andreasen (1988), and a recent review of its application in psychopathology is available (Besson, 1990).

MRI studies have continued to demonstrate that many patients with schizophrenia have enlargement of the ventricular system, although the findings have again been inconsistent. Among seven controlled quantitative MRI studies that investigated lateral ventricular size (Andreasen et al., 1986, 1990; Johnstone et al., 1989; Kelsoe, Cadet, Pickar, & Weinberger, 1988, Rossi et al., 1989; Smith, Baumgartner, & Calderon, 1987; Smith, Baumgartner, & Ravichandran, 1984), four studies have found enlarged ventricles, while three have not. There have also been MRI findings of focal brain abnormalities in the corpus callosum (Andreasen et al., 1990; Smith et al., 1984)

and the temporal lobe complex of the hippocampus/amygdala and parahippocampal gyrus (DeLisi, Dauphinais, & Gershon, 1988; Suddath et al., 1989, 1990), although Kelsoe et al. (1988) found no differences either in temporal lobe or in hippocampus or amygdala. The recent report of Pearlson et al. (1997) warrants particular comment. Pearlson and colleagues examined 46 schizophrenic patients, 60 healthy controls, and 27 bipolar disorder patients. Entorhinal cortex, not previously assessed using MRI in schizophrenia, was bilaterally smaller among schizophrenic patients as compared to healthy controls, although no difference was found when the schizophrenic patients were compared to the bipolar disorder patients. Schizophrenia was also associated with an alteration in the superior temporal gyrus, as well as with reductions in the left anterior superior temporal gyrus and right amygdala. The only MRI measurements suggesting abnormality among the bipolar disorder patients were smaller left amygdala and larger right anterior superior temporal gyrus. Thus, although quantitative MRI findings to date have been somewhat mixed, the improved resolution of MRI resulting in enhanced anatomical definition holds considerable promise for the current generation of ongoing studies that are highly focused on specific brain sites or interconnected brain regions.

Focus on Ventricular Abnormality

One important consequence of this anatomical research has been to focus attention on the natural history of ventricular abnormality. It is clear that structural alterations in limbic brain regions and/or enlargement of the ventricular system occurs in subsets of schizophrenic and affective disorder populations, but controversy exists as to whether an increase in ventricular size represents a failure of neural development, a loss of surrounding tissue, or a more obstructive process causing structural abnormality (Mesulam, 1990). The suggestion that ventricular changes are the result of somatic treatments (e.g., medication or electroconvulsive therapy) has not been supported (Bogerts et al., 1990; Owens et al., 1985; Weinberger, Torrey, Neophytides, & Wyatt, 1979). Lewis (1990) and Crow (1990) have argued that ventricular enlargement might well be a long-standing and nonprogressive change, similar to abnormalities seen in other disorders that are characterized as a failure of neural development. In contrast, the DeLisi et al. studies (1992, 1997) do point to progressive enlargement that becomes apparent over time. The natural history of these changes remains unclear; evidence for both progressive degeneration and alteration in neural development may be noted. Discussion of neuroplastic effects and even apoptosis (cell death) have enriched the discussion. It could be reasonably questioned whether ventricular system pathology in schizophrenia and affective illness reflect the same process or a variety of heterogeneous processes. However, it is generally agreed that an increase in the size of cerebral ventricles results in a corresponding decrease in cerebral tissue, especially in medial temporolimbic structures such as the hippocampal complex.

Considerations

Contemporary interest in both postmortem anatomy and in vivo imaging labors within more clearly understood limitations and greater caution than was the case in the late 19th and early 20th centuries. Recent postmortem investigation may reflect considerable refinement in staining and visualization technique, but all of the studies are based on brain specimens collected decades ago from heterogeneous populations of chronically ill patients who were not diagnosed by contemporary nosologic criteria. Even when modern diagnostic criteria are applied retrospectively, the validity of classification is open to question and limited by the quality and detail of hospital records. More recent postmortem cellular and in vivo brain imaging studies are compromised to an unknown degree by three to four decades of somatic therapy, which might conceivably lead to subtle morphological alterations. In contrast, recent MRI study of Bogerts et al. (1990) found that reduced temporal limbic structures could be detected in young first-episode schizophrenic patients. DeLisi et al. (1992) reported MRI findings on 50 first-episode schizophreniform patients and controls who had 3-year follow-up MRIs. Significant ventricular enlargement and reduced temporal lobe, hippocampus, and amygdala volummes were not initially present, but on follow-up, patients showed greater change in ventricular size than did controls. Taken together, these findings are very encouraging and suggest that certain known neural anomalies in schizophrenia may not be secondary to medication treatment but, rather, a progressive brain defect.

An important next step in cellular studies may be found in the recent single-cell work on living human olfactory neurons from both healthy control and patient samples (Josiassen et al., 1997). Figures 4-2 and 4-3 show olfactory neurons from a healthy control. Small numbers of olfactory neurons are biopsied from the nasal pathway; they are subtyped on the basis of the physiological response to "smell" molecules, and the physiological response of the single cells is recorded. Using this technique, it appears to be possible to detect abnormalities in single-cell physiology, particularly intracellular calcium regulation in unmedicated patients with bipolar disease.

The anatomical framework for understanding psychopathology has again captured the imagination of many researchers and remains a powerful point of view guiding the focus of research and interpretation of results. It is a viewpoint consistent with what is known about the degree of specialization of brain tissue and which points to an orderly relationship between human brain and human behavior. However, the very precision of newer cellular staining techniques and in vivo MRI may itself highlight previously unappreciated problems. The precision may yield subtle and diverse morphological pathology that underscores the heterogeneous nature of psychopathology as well as the presence of inherent individual subject differences which in the past have been obscured. There is considerable promise for the next generation of anatomical studies, but these findings will have to be framed within a context wherein all technical limitations and interpretive complications are taken into full account; otherwise, the breezy nature of Gall's phrenology will come back to haunt us.

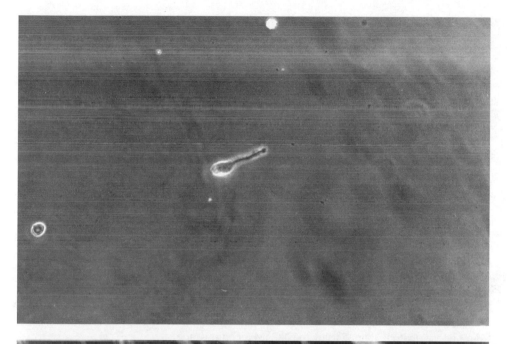

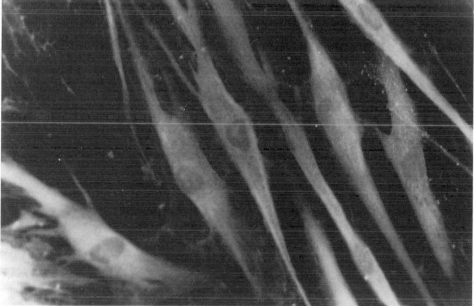

FIGURE 4-2.   A single olfactory neuron photographed through electron microscope. The cell body, axon, and dendrites can be clearly observed. Photograph provided courtesy of Nancy E. Rawson, Ph.D., Monell Institute, Philadelphia, Pennsylvania.

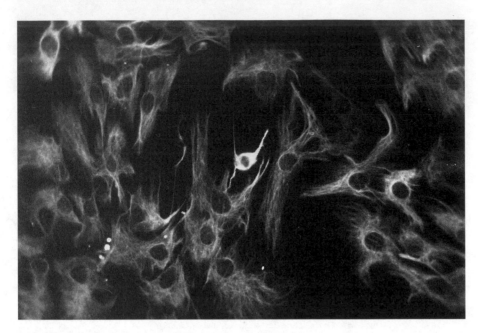

FIGURE 4-3.   Cultured olfactory neurons stained using the NCAM technique and photographed through electron microscope. The developing cell is seen in the center of the image in yellow. The stain shows the developing axons and cell body. Photograph provided courtesy of Chang Gyu Hahn, M.D., Ph.D., Allegheny University of the Health Sciences, Philadelphia, Pennsylvania.

ON THE EXCITABLE MEMBRANE OF NEURONS (PHYSIOLOGY)

Some Basic Physiology

Functional activity throughout various human brain regions involves the flow of electrical activity through elaborate networks of single neurons, each encased in an *excitable membrane,* with an accompanying background of constant oxygen and glucose utilization sustaining the enormous level of electrical activity. The membrane of each neuron acts as a boundary between its chemical contents and the surrounding tissue composed of glial cells and extracellular space, but it is the excitability of this membrane that is unique to brain cells. Along the membrane are specialized points of contact (the *synapse*), and it is at these unique points that informational excitement can be transferred from one neuron to another neuron.

Two very different forms of electrical activity take place along the excitable membrane: *graded signals* and *action potentials*. The graded signals represent information flowing into a single neuron from nu-merous other neurons, and these signals can have either excitatory or inhibitory influences on the cell membrane. The excitatory graded signal (termed the *excitatory postsynaptic potential* or *EPSP*) is intense and of short duration (in the range of 50 msec), and is most often transferred through synapses located in distal dendritic regions. The arborization of dendrites receives excitatory information from thousands of EPSP synapses, which are integrated and transmitted toward the body of the neuron. The inhibitory graded signal (termed the *inhibitory postsynaptic potential* or *IPSP*) is of much longer duration (up to 600 msec in cortical neurons) and is typically located on the cell bodies and along the trunk of the dendrites.

Single neurons within the human cortex are highly interconnected with other neurons and in certain instances the cell membrane may be covered with 10^5 (100,000) synapses that transmit EPSPs and/or IPSPs from other neurons (see Figure 4-3). The net effect of the EPSP and IPSP combinations summate algebraically to determine the likelihood that electrical excitement will continue toward the body of the neuron and actually initiate cell firing. When an individual cell body becomes sufficiently excited, it produces an *all-or-nothing signal* known as an *action potential,* which is transmitted down the axon and away from the cell body toward other neurons. While our understanding of neuroelectrical functioning ultimately rests on studying active single cells and elaborate cellular networks, the insertion of indwelling electrodes into the human brain to provide direct recording of neural activity has been extremely rare in psychiatric research.[8] Thus, contemporary research in limited to scalp recordings, with the full awareness that scalp electrical activity represents from large aggregates of neurons, with action potentials, EPSPs, IPSPs and other slow electrical potential shifts all combining in a number of ways to produce a scalp record. For extensive reviews of human electrophysiology and brain metabolism, see Greitz, Ingvar, and Widen (1985), Niedermeyer and da Silva (1987), and Nuñez (1981).

Early Functional Studies

To put the study of scalp-recorded electrical activity into some context, it is important to go back to the work of Caton (1875), who is credited with the demonstration that, as nerve impulses flow in and out of the brain, these "feeble currents" are detectable from the exposed cortex. He observed electrical activity in cats, rabbits, and monkeys from direct recording of the brain, and at the same time provided a method for mapping the localization of cerebral electrical potentials evoked by sensory stimulation. These were to become the two general categories of electrical activity available from the human scalp: the *electroencephalogram* and *event-related potentials.*

At first, there was little interest in these revelations. Nearly half a century passed before Berger (1929) followed up the work of Caton and demonstrated for the first time that electrical activity from the human brain could actually be recorded at the scalp through the intact skull. Linking scalp electrodes to the terminals of a galvanometer, Berger noted that the electrical potentials of the neurons varied constantly, but with sufficient synchronization to create observable differences. These differences of electrical potential and their temporal variations constituted "das Elektrenkephalogram," and almost immediately *EEG* became a quantitative tool for the

measurement of brain electricity, with obvious applications demonstrated for brain tumors, epileptic conditions, head injury, drug overdose, and even brain death. These techniques also made it possible to begin to study the relationship between electrical brain processes and various psychopathological conditions.

EEG Studies

From the earliest studies, it was known that the scalp-recorded EEG contains a wide range of frequencies (oscillations per second). The synchronous rhythm of these frequencies, as well as the actual voltage, wave morphology, and spatial distribution across the scalp all became important visual guides for evaluating these brain signals. The original EEG literature in psychopathology derived from simple compilations of abnormal findings based solely on *qualitative visual interpretation* by a trained electroencephalographer. Visual evaluation of these signals resulted in reports of a high incidence of abnormal waveforms in psychiatric patients, particularly patients with schizophrenia, although in many of the early studies the exact nature of the EEG abnormality was not specified. Incidence of EEG abnormalities ranged from 5% to 80%, with the lowest incidence of abnormality usually found in the largest and most representative schizophrenic samples (Colony & Willis, 1956). It has been suggested that samples with a high incidence of abnormality were biased by overrepresentation of patients referred for a clinical EEG examination because they showed signs of brain disease, such as convulsive disorder. However, one consistent qualitative EEG finding seemed to distinguish chronic from acute cases of schizophrenia: unusually regular resting EEG tracings (termed *hyperstable* or *hypernormal*) were found more frequently in chronic than in acute patients. With regard to affective disorders, most early workers concluded that there were no specific clinical EEG abnormalities (for review of the early EEG findings in psychopathology, see Small, 1987).

The introduction of computers into electrophysiology drew attention to the possibility that EEG signals may contain useful information that it not evident to the naked eye. *Computer-assisted quantitative* EEG studies began to reveal a number of interesting findings. The analysis of EEG frequencies of schizophrenic patients showed more energy outside of the alpha frequency band and less energy in the alpha band than those of normals. When multiple scalp-recording sites from patients and controls were analyzed quantitatively, the evidence suggested differences in EEG organization across the scalp leads (electrodes) or in the relations between the hemispheres. Lifshitz and Gradijan (1974) showed regional EEG frequency differences in chronic schizophrenia. Abrams and Taylor (1979) showed that schizophrenic patients had twice as many EEG abnormalities (especially in the temporal lobe) as did patients with affective disorders. Quantitative studies of affective disorder patients also suggested functional abnormality. Dalen (1965) studied patients with recurrent manic conditions that probably met DSM-III criteria for bipolar disorder. Some patients were found to have a positive family history of affective disorder and a normal EEG, whereas others had EEG abnormalities along with a history of perinatal complications and a negative family history of affective disorder. This suggested a correlation between perinatal hazard, abnormal or borderline EEGs, and absence of familial affective disease. Recently, Cook, Shukla, and Hoff (1986) reported comparable findings in patients with bipolar illness. Although it is often lost sight of in our quest for better answers with more advanced techniques, knowledge of brain electrical functioning greatly stimulated the belief that pathophysiology was detectable in major mental disorders. Quantitative EEG research generated a huge stockpile of data, but what remained elusive were the specific etiology and pathogenesis of these disorders to focus scientific activity.

Event-Related Potential Studies

EEG studies proceeded for some time without seriously raising the question of the other category of electrical activity, the *event-related potentials (ERPs)*. Caton had demonstrated that electrical potentials can be stimulated in the brain by a sensory stimulus and that there is a degree of cortical localization of the sensory area activated. ERPs should not be confused with the spontaneous EEG or with action potentials occurring in single axons. When a sensory stimulus is presented, a series of electrical events is initiated at the receptor organ, conducted into the

brain, and propagated through the various sensory pathways. However, ERP signals recorded from the intact scalp are so much smaller in amplitude than the continuously changing EEG background ($.1-30\mu V$ versus $10-100\mu V$) that they are essentially buried within the ongoing spontaneous EEG "noise." Thus, scalp-recorded ERPs require computer-assisted signal averaging, in which EEG epochs that are time-locked to repeated presentations of specific stimuli are algebraically averaged together. In this way, the random EEG activity is averaged out, and the ERP signal emerges as a composite waveform made up of distinct components that offer the opportunity to map the temporal features and spatial distribution of underlying neural mechanisms involved in sensory and cognitive processing.

The pioneering sensory ERP work of Shagass and Schwartz (1961) focused on the possibility that reduction in neural excitability underlies psychopathology. Pairs of weak sensory stimuli were administered to patients, with the paired stimuli separated by varying time intervals (interstimulus intervals). ERP amplitudes and latencies were measured. When the second stimulus of the pair yielded the same ERP response as the first stimulus, it was taken as an indication that neural recovery was complete. Related recovery functions were assessed by comparing diagnostic groups and healthy controls. The results suggested that psychopathology is accompanied by a reduction in brain excitability but that the pattern of reduced excitability may differ among various diagnostic groups. Sensory ERPs evoked with the presentation of distinct sensory stimuli have been described extensively in various psychopathologic groups (for review of ERPs in psychopathology, see Friedman & Bruder, 1992; Vaughan, 1978). Abnormalities of these obligatory sensory ERPs are thought to be a sign of physiological deviance reflecting impaired neural processing of sensory and perceptual input.

ERP signals have also been recorded in conjunction with performance of complex cognitive tasks (e.g., selective attention, short-term memory). Systematic changes in ERP activity are considered representative of the engagement of different neural processes mediating the cognitive task. Sutton, Braren, Zubin, and John (1965) were the first to show that a portion of the auditory ERP was sensitive to how a subject perceived the probability of an event. When a rare event was presented, the auditory ERP showed a prominent positive deflection called a *P300 wave,* having a latency of approximately 300 msec poststimulus. Roth and Cannon (1972) were the first to demonstrate that the cognition-related P300 component is attenuated in schizophrenic patients as compared with normal controls and patients with other psychiatric disorders. There has been remarkable consistency in this observation despite differences in paradigms, instructional sets, diagnostic criteria, sensory modality, medication status, strategies of matching patients and control groups, and data analysis techniques (Blackwood & Muir, 1990; Mirsky & Duncan, 1986).

Further studies have shown that P300 amplitude reduction is observed in major affective disorders (Roth et al., 1981), alcoholism (Porjesz & Begleiter, 1981), and nonpsychotic dysphoric patients (Josiassen, Roemer, Shagass, & Straumanis, 1986), though to a lesser degree than usually seen in symptomatic schizophrenic patients. P300 anomalies also can be found in higher than expected rates among unaffected siblings of schizophrenic probands (Saitoh et al., 1984), as well as other groups thought to be at high risk for schizophrenia (Josiassen, Shagass, Roemer, & Straumanis, 1985). At present the mechanism underlying P300 abnormality is uncertain.

Another interesting paradigm was recently developed by Guterman, Josiassen, Bashore, and Lubow (1996) showing the utility of studying paired associative learning with cognitive ERPs, specifically the contingent negative variation (CNV). Guterman and colleagues demonstrated that CNV amplitude developed as subjects learned the experimental task and, moreover, that the development of CNV varied among patients with schizophrenia. The extent that these cognitive ERP effects can be experimentally manipulated, the findings will have heuristic impact on cognitive and informational processing models of psychopathology.

Measurement of Cerebral Metabolism (Cerebral Blood Flow and Glucose Utilization)

The constant flow of neuroelectric activity causes the human brain to be an active energy consumer, more so than any other body organ, and yet the brain contains almost no energy reserves of its own. Energy resources (glucose and oxygen) must constantly be transported to the brain. Roy and Sherrington (1890) had speculated over a century ago that neuroelectric activity is coupled with the utilization of energy, and that the measurement of the consumption of metabolic substrates (glucose and oxygen) or their transportation (cerebral blood flow) might provide a reflection of local neural activity. The ability to make these measurements, however, awaited technological development.

Cerebral Blood Flow Studies

Early work by Dameshek and Myerson (1935) provided the first approximations for inferring total *cerebral blood flow (CBF)*. Kety and Schmidt (1948) offered a quantitative CBF measurement known as the *nitrous oxide technique*. Using this technique, Kety et al. (1948) found no group CBF differences between controls and schizophrenic patients, although they did report CBF changes following treatment with insulin hypoglycemia and coma, and electroshock.

More recently, Lassen and Ingvar (Lassen, Ingvar, & Skinhoj, 1978) developed a technique to measure *regional cerebral blood flow (rCBF)*, which involves the use of xenon[133], a radioactive isotope of the inert gas xenon. Xenon[133] may be inhaled or dissolved in sterile saline solution and injected as a bolus into one of the main arteries. The arrival and subsequent washout of the radioactivity from brain regions is then tracked with a gamma-ray camera. Changes in circulation and distribution of blood flow in specific cortical regions can then be monitored in response to different mental activities or clinical states. Ingvar and Franzen (1974) applied this technique and found increased parietal CBF in schizophrenic patients compared to increased frontal CBF in normals. This finding suggested a differential pattern (*hypofrontality*) of cortical energy utilization in schizophrenia.

Hypofrontality in schizophrenia has found empirical support along several lines. Lower rCBF in left frontal areas of the brain were positively correlated with negative symptoms in schizophrenic patients, while elevated rCBF in parietal regions was associated with positive symptoms (Ingvar, 1980). Another study (Ariel et al., 1983) compared intrahemispheric and bilateral rCBF in gray and white matter and found the schizophrenic group to have significantly lower rCBF values in all areas as compared to healthy controls, especially in anterior regions.

Patients with affective disorder have also been investigated using rCBF techniques, although to a lesser degree. Schlegel et al. (1989) measured rCBF during rest and cognitive activation and found that patients with major depression had significantly lower rCBF during rest across the entire right hemisphere and in the left frontal region as compared to healthy controls. During mental activation, patients showed significantly lower values in all right and left parietal regions. Moreover, rCBF in the Schlegel study was correlated with scores on various clinical rating scales of depression.

In the majority of rCBF studies to date, subjects were studied in a resting state, and the actual between-group differences were not dramatically different (though statistically significant). The use of a cognitive or behavioral task, however, increases cerebral activity and has worked to enhance between-group differences in rCBF. Using xenon[133] inhalation to measure rCBF linked to the performance of the Wisconsin Card Sort Test, Weinberger, Berman, and Illkowsky (1988) found that chronic schizophrenic patients fail to activate the dorsolateral prefrontal cortex during task performance. Warkentin et al. (1989) coupled xenon inhalation measurements of rCBF with performance of a verbal-fluency task. The most marked effect of this activation paradigm in normals was seen in the left prefrontal area, but in the schizophrenic group this increase was attenuated. These studies illustrate how cerebral activation approaches may reveal patient differences that appeared to be only modest or hidden using resting measures.

Positron Emission Tomography Studies

Sokolov (1977) laid the groundwork for yet another technique to measure the consumption of metabolic substrates and their transport, known as *positron emission tomography (PET scan)*. With the original PET scan approach (Reivich et al., 1979; Phelps et al., 1979), a synthetic and radioactively labeled derivative of glucose, 2-[^{18}F] fluoro-2-deoxy-D-glucose (often simply called *FDG*), was introduced into the blood supply. As energy metabolism in the brain requires increases in glucose uptake, FDG is transported across the blood–brain barrier and into brain tissue as if it were unlabeled glucose. However, the synthetic isotope cannot be fully metabolized, and it essentially remains trapped within the cerebral tissue for several hours. The extent of radiation accumulation can be detected outside the brain with gamma-ray cameras. Levels of isotope concentration reflect changes in glucose metabolism in different cortical and subcortical brain regions. Currently, PET provides the means for measuring rates of cerebral blood volume and flow; transport and metabolism of oxygen, glucose, and various amino acids; protein synthesis; and receptor system activity. In addition to FDG, carbon, nitrogen, and oxygen can be replaced with the short-lived radioisotopes ^{11}carbon, ^{13}nitrogen, and ^{15}oxygen. ^{18}Fluorine is used as a substitute for hydrogen. The use of compounds labeled with positron-emitting radionuclides also provide the means for in vivo estimation of dopaminergic, cholinergic, benzodiazepine, opiate, and adrenergic receptor system activity (for extensive overviews, see Phelps & Mazziotta, 1985; Bench, Dolan, Friston, & Frackowiak, 1990).

In one of the first PET applications in psychopathology, Farkas, Reivich, and Alavi (1980) observed a 40% reduction in measures of glucose metabolism in frontal cortex, with a concomitant increase in right temporal and parietal cortices in one unmedicated schizophrenic patient studied over several months. Following treatment with neuroleptic drugs, the frontal glucose metabolism increased to within 25% of normal levels, accompanied by a clinical improvement with fewer hallucinations and improved social behavior. Baxter et al. (1985) studied glucose utilization changes in a rapid-cycling bipolar patient, showing sets of PET images obtained during depressed and manic states. Global reduction in glucose utilization was seen in the scans obtained in the depressed state relative to the scan obtained during a manic phase. These two case studies illustrate the potential of PET to provide pathophysiological insights into abnormal behavior that occurs in psychiatric disorders.

To date PET technology has been used to study schizophrenia more than any other psychiatric disorder. Most of the studies have tried to isolate a regional cerebral dysfunction associated with the illness. Buchsbaum et al. (1984) examined glucose metabolism using FDG in a small sample of schizophrenic patients, affective disorder patients, and healthy controls, and found a significant anterior–posterior gradient in both patient groups. The highest FDG values were observed posteriorly and this was interpreted as being consistent with the hypofrontal pattern seen with rCBF. This pattern was nonspecific insofar as it was observed in both patient groups. Brodie et al. (1984) took FDG scans before and after neuroleptic drug treatment and found a 25% elevation of glucose activity in basal ganglia following drug administration. Gur et al. (1987a, 1987b) described abnormalities of the subcortical-cortical metabolic gradient, and Szechtman et al. (1988) examined whether duration of neuroleptic treatment influenced the patterns of regional metabolism.

A few studies in schizophrenia have gone beyond the search for regional dysfunction to correlate PET measures of regional activity with clinical ratings and psychological test performance. Other investigators have used activation designs. DeLisi et al. (1985) studied chronic schizophrenic patients and reported significant correlations between hypofrontality and clinical symptom ratings for emotional withdrawal, disorientation, distractibility, and helplessness/hopelessness. Cohen et al. (1987) studied cerebral metabolism during an auditory discrimination task and found a direct relationship between metabolic rate in the prefrontal cortex and accuracy of performance.

In contrast to schizophrenia, there have been relatively few PET studies of patients with affective disorders. Buchsbaum et al. (1984) found no FDG difference between affective disorder and schizophrenic groups, a finding that was interpreted as resulting from a small sample with high diagnostic heterogeneity among the groups. In a later study of affective illness, Buchsbaum et al. (1986) reported significantly lower frontal-to-occipital glucose metabolic ratios and significantly lower metabolic rates in basal ganglia for the depressed patients compared to normal controls. In a detailed series of related PET studies (Phelps, Mazziotta, Baxter, & Gerner, 1984; Schwartz et al., 1987; Baxter et al., 1989), affectively ill patients were found to have consistently decreased inferior frontal lobe metabolism during depressed states. Patterns of cerebral metabolism have also been evaluated in other forms of psychopathology, including obsessive-compulsive disorder (Baxter et al., 1988), bulimia (Hagman et al., 1990), and panic disorder (Reiman et al., 1986).

Focus on Measurement Stability

An enormous amount has been learned about neuroelectrical differentiation between clinically defined psychopathologic groups, and an impressive literature has begun to develop showing altered patterns of cerebral blood flow, as well as alterations in oxygen and glucose consumption. For the most part, however, what has been learned with these functional approaches has centered around statistical group differences, and there has been considerable difficulty moving beyond group differences to understanding individuals. The situation is clearly illustrated in two large population comparisons using EEG and ERP measurements. Shagass, Roemer, Straumanis, and Josiassen (1985) and Josiassen, Shagass, and Roemer (1988) showed highly significant between-group differences on quantitative EEG (population $N = 336$) and ERP (population $N = 836$) measures, respectively. In both cases, however, nearly half the functional measures from schizophrenic patients fell within the range of nonpatients, and there was considerable overlap between diagnostic categories. Comparable large population studies using rCBF and PET approaches have not yet been attempted, but smaller population studies with these newer measures reflect a similar level of measurement overlap.

The technological aspects of functional brain measurement are extremely advanced, but the basic psychometric characteristics of most of these measures are understood only at rudimentary levels. Even if one assumes adequate stability of a functional measurement, the clinical stability of any patient group or the stability of their underlying biology cannot be assumed. Neuroelectric activity and accompanying cerebral metabolism are both exquisitely sensitive to transient fluctuations in clinical symptoms, drug treatment, and numerous secondary consequences of the illness, but to a large extent, experimental methods have yet to be devised that control adequately for these sources of artifact. This problem strikes at the heart of all functional brain measurement in psychopathology and limits scientific progress.

Considerations

Modern brain-imaging techniques allow in vivo assessment of functional brain organization in living patients with a minimal degree of intrusiveness. Findings of functional abnormality in adult psychopathology are intriguing. The tacit assumption that there may be a single salient functional marker for each diagnostic category is probably incorrect, and linking functional measures (e.g., ERP and PET) is uncharted territory. Putting several sources of functional data together could provide a more complete picture of normal and abnormal brain functioning than either measure by itself. However, the demonstration of a tight coupling between neuroelectric activity and metabolism has so far proved to be difficult, primarily because of the difficulty in assessing the levels of functional and metabolic activities within the same components of the brain at the same point in time. Linkages between brain electricity, cerebral blood flow, glucose utilization, and oxygen consumption are probably more complex than previously realized (Fox, Raichle, Mintun, & Dence, 1988). However, the principle is robust: Brain activity involves the utilization of energy, and the level of glucose and/or oxygen consumption or their transport reflects local neural activity. Many unanswered questions remain, and major breakthroughs are yet to be made, but the functional properties of the neuron are no longer a mystery.

ON THE POINTS OF CONTACT AMONG CELLS (SYNAPSES AND NEUROTRANSMITTERS)

Some Basics of Synaptic Transmission

Functional activity within a single neuron involves the flow of electrical information across an excitable membrane. This informational excitement is transferred from one neuron to another neuron across a gap, known as the *synapse*. Sherrington (1906) was the first to use the word *synapse* as the name for a specialized electrical or chemical mechanism by which one neuron can transmit a signal across a gap to another neuron. He knew the velocity of nerve conduction (200 feet/second) and reasoned that it would be possible to predict the response latency of a simple reflex in a dog because the length of the reflex arc was known. If nerve conduction was the only mode of transmission along the reflex arc, the response latency should have been about 10 millisec-

onds, but instead it was much longer—about 100 milliseconds. Thus, Sherrington reasoned that electrical conduction along the neural membrane was not the only mode of transmission; instead, the signal must be transmitted across a gap between sensory neurons and motor neurons by a different and slower process. Shortly thereafter, it was postulated that synaptic transmission was accomplished by releasing a *receptive substance* across the gap that induced a response in neighboring neurons.

Direct observation of the synapse did not become possible until the 1950s, with the development of electron microscopy. Using staining procedures and piecing together micrographs of serial sections a few microns thick, it became possible to visualize the intricate synaptic structures from which neural signals are sent and received. The synapse shows up in the electron microscope as a darkened smudge on the membrane, and a large congregation of minute round *vesicles* can be seen milling about the membrane on the sending side (*presynaptic membrane*). The vesicles may contain some 10,000 or more molecules of a specific *neurotransmitter substance*. When a neuroelectric impulse reaches the synapse, a train of events is set in motion that culminates with the fusion of the vesicle on the neuronal membrane and the spilling of neurotransmitter molecules into the extracellular space. The transmitter molecules diffuse across the synaptic cleft and bind at specialized sites (*receptors*) on the receiving cell (*postsynaptic membrane*), with the unused molecules broken down by the activity of *monoamine oxidase and other enzymes*. Most of the products of the neurotransmitter breakdown (*metabolites*) are retrieved by a pumplike mechanism that takes the products back (*reuptake*) into the presynaptic membrane from which they had been released, although some of the breakdown metabolites become free to circulate within the cerebral spinal fluid and eventually the blood supply. The transmitter molecule that is bound to the receptor site is also quickly removed by enzymatic activity; otherwise, it would continue to have prolonged and disruptive effects on the receiving cell (Axelrod, 1965).

Neurotransmitters

It might have been predicted that just two chemical substances would be needed to serve as neurotransmitters—one for neural excitation (EPSPs) and the other for neural inhibition (IPSPs). But developments in analytical chemistry allowed identification of transmitter substances and soon demonstrated that there are many more than two neurotransmitters. Indeed, there are currently 11 known neurotransmitter substances: *acetylcholine, dopamine, norepinephrine, epinephrine, serotonin, histamine, gamma-aminobutyric acid, glycine, glutamate, aspartate,* and *taurine.* Another 30 or more active neuromodulators are known to circulate within the nervous system, with various kinds of interacting neuronal influence.[9]

Each of the identified neurotransmitters seems to interact with a specific type (or types) of receptor(s) on the postsynaptic membrane, and in return each receptor on the postsynaptic membrane has a high degree of affinity for a particular neurotransmitter substance. As a result, each receptor site appears to be specific to a particular neurotransmitter and does not respond to the effects of other neurotransmitters (Snyder, Banerjee, Yamamura, & Greenberg, 1974). Another influential development has been evidence that, within a given neurotransmitter system, there can be more than one kind of receptor site. Dopamine (also called *DA*) has at least two well-established types of receptors (D_1 and D_2), with two more (D_3 and D_4) under intensive study; gamma-aminobutyric acid (also called *GABA*) has two known receptor sites ($GABA_A$ and $GABA_B$), and serotonin (also called *5-HT*) has as many as a dozen distinct receptors. Thus, the mechanism of *synaptic transmission* Sherrington had inferred from careful observation of simple reflexes in dogs has now been elucidated in detail.

Studies in Dopamine Function

Dopamine (*DA*) appears to produce inhibitory postsynaptic potentials. The dopaminergic (*DAergic*) system has yielded two of the more celebrated lines of clinical investigation, with the study of DA and its relationship to both Parkinson's disease and schizophrenia. Degeneration of neurons in the substantia nigra causes Parkinson's disease, a neurodegenerative disorder characterized by tremors, rigidity of the limbs, poor balance, and difficulty in initiating movements. The substantia nigra is rich in DA neurons, which became crucial information suggesting that DAergic deficiency was the root of Parkinson's dis-

ease. Shortly thereafter, the discovery was made that the motor dysfunctions could be alleviated by giving patients the drug L-dopa (which converts to dopamine in the brain). The intervention was tried with considerable success, and L-dopa became the drug of choice for reducing the effects of Parkinson's disease.

At approximately this same point in time, Delay and Deniker (1952) had heard that the drug *chlorpromazine* was useful in sedating patients before surgical anesthesia and speculated that it might also be effective in calming schizophrenic patients. In their initial uncontrolled study, Delay and Deniker found that chlorpromazine reduced florid schizophrenic symptoms and possibly even activated withdrawn patients. In addition to its therapeutic effectiveness in the reduction of psychotic symptoms, however, it was soon noticed that chlorpromazine produced motor symptoms (tremor, rigidity of limbs) in schizophrenic patients resembling those seen in Parkinson's disease. With the prior discovery that Parkinson's disease is related to degeneration of the nigrostriatal tract, which results in low levels of DA within the basal ganglia, the speculation arose that neuroleptic drugs produced therapeutic effects in schizophrenia by means of lowering DA levels. With the evidence that chlorpromazine may intervene in the synaptic affairs of neurons, it was only a short leap to suggest that schizophrenia was caused by a primary disturbance of DAergic transmission or metabolism resulting in an increase in DA function. This became the *dopamine hypothesis of schizophrenia,* which has been the dominant view on the pathogenesis of schizophrenia for more than two decades.

Apart from the obvious treatment effect of early neuroleptic drugs, there were several other lines of support for the dopamine hypothesis. Support came from the amphetamine psychosis literature, which provided three important pieces of information—amphetamine (a dopamine agonist) can produce a state that closely resembles paranoid schizophrenia, amphetamines can exacerbate the symptoms of schizophrenia, and neuroleptic medication can be therapeutically effective in the treatment of amphetamine psychosis (Angrist, Lee, & Gershon, 1974). Meltzer and Stahl (1976) demonstrated that the potency of antipsychotic drugs was directly correlated with dopamine receptor binding and blockade. Other studies examined homovanillic acid (a product of dopamine metabolism) levels in the cerebrospinal fluid and plasma of schizophrenic patients and found increased levels suggesting increased dopaminergic activity (Davidson & Davis, 1988). Levels of prolactin (one of the hormones controlled by the DA-ergic system) were also found to be increased in schizophrenia and to decrease with neuroleptic treatment (Meltzer & Sacher, 1974).

With the effectiveness of neuroleptics related to their ability to antagonize the action of the DA system, D_1 and D_2 receptors began to be studied in schizophrenia. In a postmortem receptor binding study, Lee and Seeman (1977) analyzed normal and schizophrenic brains to determine the binding sites of neuroleptic molecules. They found increased binding sites in the caudate, putamen, and nucleus accumbens of patients, which suggested either increased numbers or activity of DAergic receptors in schizophrenia. Further postmortem receptor studies by Owen et al. (1978) showed increased D_2 receptors in schizophrenia, which supported the idea that the basic problem resulted from too many dopamine receptors. However, these findings were controversial because neuroleptic drugs appear to induce the actual development of D_2 receptors (Reynolds, 1983). Because most schizophrenic patients have been exposed to neuroleptics, the postmortem findings were indeterminate; the elevated D_2 receptor densities found in schizophrenia could either be related to the disorder itself or to previous neuroleptic treatment.

Compounds have now been labeled with positron-emitting radionuclides that allow PET scan estimation of DAergic receptor system activity down to a spatial resolution of 3 to 4 millimeters in the living human brain. In one PET study of neuroleptic-naive patients, D_2 receptor density was elevated on postsynaptic membrane in the caudate nucleus (Wong et al., 1986), suggesting an increase in dopamine receptor number that is unrelated to medication treatment. However, in another PET study using a different radionuclide (Farde et al., 1987), D_2 receptor density was not elevated. Recently, Moises et al. (1991) examined the D_2 receptor gene region and failed to find strong linkage for this gene region and schizophrenia. These findings do not provide clear support for the dopamine hypothesis, although they do not exclude the possibility that a defect in other genes that regulate aspects of D_2 receptor expression might be involved in schizophrenia.

The dopamine hypothesis of schizophrenia remains the dominant neurochemical model of this illness, although it has been shown that certain antipsychotics (e.g., chlorpromazine, thioridazine, and clozapine) have a high affinity for *serotonin receptors* as well as dopamine receptors. It has become increasingly apparent that conventional antipsychotic treatment of schizophrenia is only partially effective, and that some of the novel antipsychotics with a high affinity for serotonin receptors can diminish psychotic symptoms in patients who have not responded to conventional neuroleptics. This raises the possibility that several neurotransmitter mechanisms are involved in the pathogenesis of schizophrenia (Bleich, Brown, Kahn, & Van Praag, 1988).

Studies in Monoamine Function

The rapid development of neuroleptics raised the hope that analogous work with antidepressants would lead to comparable knowledge regarding the etiology of depression. It had been known for several hundred years that an alkaloid extract from the shrub Rauwolfia serpentia, later to be named *reserpine,* was useful for treating high blood pressure, and it became widely used as an antihypertensive drug. But reserpine also *caused* symptoms closely resembling those of severe depression, and 15% of the cases were indistinguishable from severe depression. The fact that reserpine could virtually produce depressive symptoms was an important observation, although the neurotransmitter system involved was not identified for some time.

While Delay and Deniker were working with chlorpromazine in schizophrenia, Crane (1957) was following up the clinical observation that certain drugs used in the treatment of tuberculosis seemed to serve as mood elevators. He isolated *iproniazid* as the active agent, and it soon became used widely in the treatment of psychotic depression. This represented the first class of antidepressant medications, known as *monoamine oxidase (MAO)* inhibitors. Shortly thereafter, a second class of antidepressant drugs, known as *tricyclic antidepressants,* was discovered (Kuhn, 1958).

The neurotransmitter systems that have been implicated with reserpine, MAO inhibitors, and tricyclic antidepressants are *serotonin* (5-hydroxytryptamine or *5-HT*) and *norepinephrine (NE),* both of which belong to a family of compounds known as *monoamines.* Glowinski and Axelrod (1964) demonstrated that tricyclics inhibit the reuptake of monoamines (MA) into MAergic neurons, and the monoamine hypothesis of depression was proposed (Schildkraut, 1965). MAO inhibitors block the activity of the enzyme monoamine oxidase, which can destroy both NE and 5-HT at the synapse. As a result, the administration of MAO inhibitors results in the build up of 5-HT and NE concentrations, causing greater activity at the respective receptor sites. Tricyclic antidepressants exert their effects by preventing the inactivation of 5-HT and NE molecules that have been released in the synapse through normal nerve impulse flow. These neurotransmitters are usually inactivated after synaptic release primarily by taking them back (reuptake) by a pumplike mechanism into the nerve ending from which they have been released. The tricyclic antidepressants block this reuptake mechanism, building up (potentiating) the action of released neurotransmitters; and, like the MAO inhibitors, these drugs produce an excess of 5-HT and NE synaptic activity.

Given the observation that reserpine (a monoamine antagonist) produces depression and the therapeutic effectiveness of MAO inhibitors and tricyclic antidepressants (monoamine agonists), the monoamine hypothesis of depression became the dominant biochemical view of the pathogenesis of depression. Several studies found that suicidal depression is related to decreased cerebral spinal fluid levels of *5-hydroxyindoleacetic acid* (also called *5-HIAA*), a metabolite of serotonin that is produced when serotonin is destroyed by monoamine oxodase. Traskmann, Asberg, Bertilsson, and Sjostrand (1981) found that CSF levels of 5-HIAA in people who had attempted suicide were significantly lower than those of controls. More recent studies have confirmed these results (Roy, De Jong, & Linnoila, 1989). Sedvall et al. (1980) analyzed the CSF of healthy, nondepressed volunteers. The families of subjects with unusually low levels of 5-HIAA were more likely to include people with family members with depression, suggesting that serotonin metabolism or release is genetically influenced. These findings lend support to the monoamine hypothesis.

Complexity of Synaptic Affairs

Clearly, the symptoms of schizophrenia and major affective disorders can be modulated by altering the level of specific neurotransmitter activity. Neuroleptics alter DAergic transmission, and antidepressants modify 5-HT and NE activity, making DA and monoaminergic neurons prime sites of investigation. But powerful as these pieces of evidence have been in focusing intensive study on particular neurotransmitter systems, many puzzles still remain. Schizophrenia consists of both positive and negative symptoms, the former involving the presence of unusual behavior (hallucinations, delusions) and the latter involving the absence of normal behavior (social involvement, affect). Yet, current evidence suggests that DAergic antagonists only alleviate the positive symptoms in a significant proportion of schizophrenic patients. The negative symptoms of schizophrenia seem not to be affected by standard DAergic antagonists, although Kane et al. (1988) report that the novel antipsychotic Clozaril may be effective with negative symptoms. Clozaril has a high affinity for 5-HT receptors as well as DA receptors. Adding to the puzzle is the longstanding awareness that neuroleptics do not "cure" schizophrenia in the same sense that penicillin cures some infections, even though the DA theory of schizophrenia suggests that they should (Snyder, 1980). Moreover, it is clear that the brain does not consist of isolated synapses, and drug treatment effects do not occur immediately. DAergic projections have a high degree of reciprocal regulation, and DA modulation may be enhanced in some projections and (given the reciprocal regulation) reduced in others (Simon et al., 1988). This same concern can be raised regarding the monoamine hypothesis of depression. It has been known for a long time that the symptoms of depression do not respond immediately to monoamine increases. Often, the relevant treatment effects may take several weeks (or months) to develop, even though an increase of 5-HT and NE at the synapse begins immediately. Perhaps the acute effects of antidepressants are not the pharmacological effects that relieve the symptoms of depression. Sulser and Sanders-Bush (1989) suggest that the therapeutic effect of antidepressants is *not* the building up of excess 5-HT and NE but, rather, a subsensitization of postsynaptic noradrenergic receptors.

Considerations

The vulnerability of synaptic activity to modification through neurochemicals has stimulated intense research into the nature of synaptic transmission at the cellular level. Investigation of the neurochemicals that have some role in the synaptic transmission is considerably important, not only for determining what is going on at the cellular level, but in leading to effective treatment of CNS disorders. Considerable progress has been made in the study of neurotransmitter systems and psychopathology.

Although there are 40 or so endogenous substances within the brain, each found to have some neural effect, the linking of neuroleptic action to dopaminergic transmission and antidepressant action to monoaminergic transmission makes these two neurotransmitter systems prime suspects. The trouble is that even if these hypotheses are generally accurate, there is an assortment of ways in which the neurotransmitter systems might be malfunctioning. For example, Olney and Farber (1995) have advanced a unified hypothesis pertaining to combined dopamine and N-methyl-D-aspartate receptor hypofunction as a key mechanism to explain the clinical and pathophysiological aspects of schizophrenia. It is also entirely possible that some other biochemical impropriety (e.g., an intracellular second- or third-messenger action) further upstream in the intracellular activity is the underlying cause. Additionally, it is likely that other complex factors play a role in altering the nature of neurotransmission. As an example of this complexity, consider the study of Bloom (1977), who evaluated the effects of NE using direct recording of hippocampal cells and found that NE could produce either EPSPs or IPSPs in the same target cell, depending on the experimental task (i.e., the NE effects were state-dependent). Clearly, the subtlety of interneuronal communication within and between neurotransmitter systems still outstrips the technological repertoire. We are only beginning to

understand the complex roles of even the well-known DAergic and monoaminergic systems in mental illness, not to mention the impact of other recognized neurotransmitters, second- and third-messenger systems, and neuromodulators—and those that are yet to be discovered.

ON THE MODIFICATION OF CELLS (PLASTICITY)

Brief Orientation to Plasticity

The intensive work of the 19th and 20th centuries brought about an increased understanding of the anatomical and physiological mechanisms of human behavior, particularly the short-term electrochemical effects of sensorimotor impulses within and between cell groups of the CNS. Sherrington (1906) had inferred the mechanism of synaptic transmission, and almost immediately a steady stream of hypotheses broadened their focus beyond sensory-motor processing to target the synapse as the CNS site where learning and memory are stored. It was speculated that, in one way or another, experience modifies the facilitation and inhibition of neural impulses between two or more neurons to form the basis of memory and learning. Kappers (1917) argued that the growth of neural tissue could be explained on the basis of electrical attracting forces. His postulate of *neurobiotaxis* stated that electrical activity along the neural membrane generates electromagnetic fields, which in turn influence the direction of neural growth. Electrical negativity in a group of active neurons, according to Kappers, would exert attraction for the growth of neighboring neurons, and these electrical field forces over time would establish patterns of synaptic facilitation and inhibition. Although the specific details of this electrical force argument were not borne out by subsequent study, the idea of neurobiotaxis had considerable heuristic impact. Others of this period, Ramon y Cajal (1911/1904) the most influential among them, proposed chemotropic processes within the neural environment rather than electrical forces as the primary directive influence on neural modification.

The idea that learning and memory, as well as experience in general, might have an impact on the formation of new synaptic contacts has had its ups and downs. It was only in the last quarter century that experiments with laboratory animals produced evidence to test the hypothesis that differential environments and formal training alter brain anatomy and chemistry. In a well-known series of studies by Rosenzweig and his associates (Rosenzweig et al., 1961, 1962, 1967, 1972), rats were assigned to differential environmental conditions at weaning (about 25 days after birth), and kept in these conditions for 80 days. The conditions included a *standard colony* of 3 rats per cage (*SC*), an *impoverished environment* with only 1 rat per cage (*IC*), and an *enriched environment* with 10 to 12 rats per cage, as well as a variety of stimulus objects (*EC*). At the end of the differential environmental experience, each brain was dissected into standard samples for analysis. Scrutiny of the data revealed that the EC animals differed from the IC animals in several important ways: The EC animals developed greater weight of the cerebral cortex, which was later related to cortical thickness. The EC animals developed greater levels of cortical acetylcholinesterase (AChE), an enzyme related to the total flux of cholinergic nerve impulses, which in previous studies had been shown to correlate with problem-solving ability (Rosenzweig et al., 1961). More refined neuroanatomical measures were made of specific brain sites and included counts of dendritic spines, measures of dendritic branching, and measurement of the size of synaptic contacts. All three measures showed significant effects of differential experience (Diamond et al., 1975; Globus, Rosenzweig, Bennett, & Diamond, 1973; Greenough & Volkmar, 1973). The rigorous study of neural plasticity has only recently begun, and already important lines of investigation have documented that learning and memory, and the more general environmental milieu, affect brain anatomy, chemistry, and electrophysiology (for extensive reviews, see Changeux & Konishi, 1987; Rosenzweig & Bennett, 1976; Thompson, 1986). Simplistically, it might be said that an experience that lasts a few seconds may result in neural changes that last a lifetime.

Role of Neural Plasticity in Psychopathology

In light of the potential etiological significance of environmental factors on mental illness, a fruitful line of research in psychopathology may concern the adaptation of neuronal circuitry to environmental milieu. Although psychopathologists have yet to define a precise role for neural plasticity in CNS dysfunction, the possibility has been appreciated. Many turn-of-the-century thinkers attempted to exploit the CNS as the setting for disordered mental life, although the part played by environmental factors on CNS development was inevitably vague. The remarkable document from Freud, *Project for a Scientific Psychology* (1895; in Pribram and Gill, 1976), embodied a scheme for reference to the CNS and its function as the basis for the understanding of psychopathology. The period of neurological and neurophysiological investigation offered Freud the possibility that specific anatomical and physiological detail, such as the diameters of the axons of neurons, might hold the secret of memory and forgetfulness. The *Project* defined the psychic regulatory principles as biochemical and neurochemical, and the controlling signals as neuroelectric. But since Freud never published the document, it seems that he was more concerned with building up a psychological system, not in dabbling in speculative neurophysiology.

Plasticity in Depression

More recent attempts have been made to provide an orientation that takes into account the plasticity of neurons, particularly with regard to depression and schizophrenia. A series of studies by Brier and associates (Brier et al., 1988; Brier, 1989) attempted to bridge two parallel bodies of knowledge within the depression literature: (1) clinical studies indicating that early childhood trauma is associated with onset of adult depressive illness, and (2) preclinical studies in several animal species indicating that early parental separation and deprivation have enduring neurobiological effects, which also may be seen in humans. On the clinical side, several early studies (Brown, 1961; Dehhehy, 1966; Forrest, Fraser, & Priest, 1965) have shown a significant relationship between parental loss in childhood and the subsequent development of affective illness in adulthood. How early loss specifically leads to the development of adult affective illness is not known, but one hypothesis is that the stress associated with early loss results in long-term neurobiological alterations that predispose to the development of affective illness later in life.

The feasibility of this notion is supported by a growing body of preclinical studies demonstrating that early parental separation in several animal species results in enduring alterations in neurobehavioral development (Hinde & Spencer-Booth, 1971), including specific effects on tissue growth (Butler, Suskind, & Schanberg, 1978), immune function (Landenslager, Capitanio, & Reite, 1985), central catecholaminergic activity (Kraemer, Ebert, Lake, & McKinney, 1984), and autonomic physiology (Hofer, 1983).

Taking these lines of investigation together, Brier (1989) examined the hypothesis of altered neurobehavioral function in 90 adult humans who experienced parental separation during childhood. He found that those who developed psychopathology in later adulthood were neurobiologically different from those with no history of adult psychopathology. The neurobiological measurement of interest was hypothalamus-pituitary-adrenal (HPA) activity, which showed that those who experienced the greatest emotional trauma as children had the highest levels of adult HPA activity. These findings suggest that early life stress, particularly during periods of high neuronal plasticity, could affect neurohumoral systems, resulting in enduring molecular and functional alterations.

Plasticity in Schizophrenia

Neural plasticity also may have relevance to developmental models of schizophrenia. Some investigators have suggested that emotionally stressful experiences during early development could modify neuronal circuitry and predispose the child to future psychopathology. Along this line, Brody (1981) and Scheflen (1981) speculated that the mother–infant relationship might have an especially significant impact on vulnerability to later schizophrenia. Kafka et al. (1980) suggested that patterns of synaptic formation, including the extent and location of axonal and dendritic terminal arborizations, may have been altered in schizophrenia by the actions of environmental stress or deprivation. This notion finds some support from findings of Feldon and Weiner (1988) and Feldon, Avnimelech-Gigus, and Weiner (1990), who reared laboratory animals in two housing conditions: *isolated* and *grouped*. At maturity, the isolated animals showed an attentional deficit related to a DAergic dysfunction; neuroleptic treatment was shown to enhance attentional functioning. Haracz (1985) evaluated the explanatory potential of neural plasticity concepts in relation to schizophrenia.

Considerations

The implications of neural plasticity for psychopathology are necessarily speculative. At present, it is difficult to evaluate the hypotheses relating neural plasticity to depression (Brier et al., 1988), and studies relating neural plasticity to the pathophysiology of schizophrenia have yet to be undertaken. However, it was nearly a quarter century ago that Kety (1978) pointed out that it is highly likely that environmental factors of a complex nature play a significant role in altering the balance of the "neurochemical soup," even as such alterations in the "soup" in turn affect the psychological states. Thus, any fully developed account of schizophrenia, depression, sociopathy, and so forth will eventually need to integrate biological and environmental descriptions.

SUMMARY

This brief historical sketch has touched on only some of the psychobiological developments related to adult psychopathology. The sketch was intentionally narrowed to provide a glimpse of neurons and their unique features, and of the many things that can go wrong. At the same time, intensive efforts are underway from other psychobiological points of view, including studies in neuropsychology, neuroendocrinology, psychoneuroimmunology, peripheral psychophysiology, and cellular physiology, each with procedures that are appropriate for the phenomena being examined. The neuronal point of view was selected as an organizing framework because of the conviction that neurons provide the opportunity to observe the summation of interaction of both genetic and environmental factors contributing to psychopathologic conditions. Genetic influence and environmental impact meet at the level of neurons.

The mounting evidence of neuronal abnormality in major forms of psychopathology has become much more explicit and convincing, and has provided empirical findings and testable hypotheses. Advances at the psychobiological level have raised many questions leading in quite different directions, but as Adolph Meyer (1928) noted nearly three quarters of a century ago, it is often difficult to know which are the "facts that count." Many conflicts and puzzles remain unresolved, and the overall effort has not yet yielded the correlative "grand scheme" for understanding psychopathology. But the hope still remains that this vast array of accumulating neuronal information will yield valid and useful knowledge regarding the mound of biological stuff under the skull. Clearly, the brain does not give up its secrets easily.

NOTES

1. Numerous scientific reports are cited throughout this chapter, but the work of Churchland (1986), Kety (1979), and Zilboorg and Henry (1941) has been utilized extensively in the hope of providing an orderly and coherent structure for the chapter.

2. The surrender of psychopathology to concepts of demonology and the supernatural are illustrated in the invocation taken from Zilboorg and Henry (1941, p. 132), which suggests that demons had provoked the wandering of the uterus over the body, resulting in psychopathology:

> *I conjure thee, O womb, by our Lord Jesus Christ, who walked over the sea with dry feet, who cured the sick, who expelled demons, who brought the dead back to life, by whose blood we were redeemed, by whose wound we were cured, by whose plight we were healed, by Him, I conjure thee not to harm that maid of God, N., not to occupy her head, throat, neck, chest, ears, teeth, eyes, nostrils, shoulderblades, arms, hands, heart, stomach, spleen, kidneys, back, sides, joints, navel, intestines, bladder, thighs, shins, heels, nails, but to lie down quietly in the place which God chose for thee, so that this maid of God N. be restored to health.*
>
> *May He, who lives as one in Trinity and as three in unity, the Lord who rules through all the centuries, consider this as worthy of His mercy. Amen.*

3. Goodman (1991) has extensively argued that the relationship between mind and body has assumed a heightened practical significance in contemporary scientific efforts to define the nature of psychopathology and the proper role of treatment.

4. Kety (1979) suggests that much of the discussion regarding biological and environmental factors is predicated on the erroneous equation of genetic with biological and environmental with psychological. Because causal factors that are not strictly genetic must be environmental, the array of possible environmental influences spans a wide spectrum and differs in quality, intensity, and time of influence in the life of an individual. Environmental factors come into play at the moment of conception within the uterine environment; in the development from fertilized ovum to newborn infant, chemical and physical processes operate at every stage to allow the expression of the genetic program. Any number of environmental deficiencies and disturbances can interfere with this expression and thwart the normal development of the central nervous system. Hormonal disorders in the mother and exposure to certain drugs and other foreign substances can give rise to abnormalities in the fetus. Malnutrition and exposure to alcohol and toxins all can disturb the normal development of the fetal brain. Certainly, each event or process involved in the etiology, pathogenesis, symptomatic manifestation, and treatment of psychopathology occurs within the context of both genetic and environmental factors.

5. An interesting historical note is contributed by Brill (1941) who reports the opinions of two committees of eminent psychiatrists (including Carl Jung) in the early 1920s who were asked to decide, for insurance purposes, whether schizophrenia could be caused by CNS trauma. The two committees did not reach agreement on the matter.

6. Methodological limitations are usually discussed in regard to the demise of this classical period of neuroanatomical research in mental illness. However, Kolb and Whishaw (1980) have raised the more perplexing theoretical question of how to actually establish a link between brain abnormality and psychopathology. Careful lesion studies in animals and "naturally occurring" lesions in humans suggested that in many cases there may be no direct, simple link between brain areas and overt behavioral change. Lesions in comparable

brain regions could result in quite different and contradictory behavioral effects (e.g., loss of behavior, release of behavior, or disorganization of behavior). The effects of a lesion can vary depending on the age of the person at the time of onset; however, time of onset is often difficult to pinpoint. The situation is further complicated by the often seen restoration of behavioral function following lesion onset, although the degree of restoration varies considerably from patient to patient.

7. The hydrogen-1 nuclei have been the object of most recent MRI innovations, although other nuclei in biological tissue that have magnetic characteristics can also be influenced by magnetic field, including phosphorus-31, fluorine-19, and oxygen-17. These magnetic nuclei are currently under investigation using a state-of-the-art technology known as *magnetic resonance spectroscopy (MRS)*. A good introduction to the use of MRS has been given by Lock, Abou-Saleh, and Edwards (1990). For recent review of the theory and application of magnetic resonance imaging, see Besson et al. (1990).

8. There was a brief period of direct neural recording in psychiatric research following along with the wave of interest in psychosurgical procedures. Sem-Jacobsen (1957) showed that focal slow discharges observed with depth electrodes, but not seen in simultaneous scalp recordings, were associated with hallucinations and agitation. Heath (1962) recorded spiking in the septal regions during hallucinatory and other psychotic manifestations of schizophrenia. However, these findings have not been replicated, and ethical restrictions have limited contemporary psychopathologic research to scalp recordings (for a review of depth electroencephalography, as well as the relationship between scalp recordings and their underlying intracellular sources, see Nuñez, 1981, and Niedermeyer & da Silva, 1987).

9. To be considered a neurotransmitter, a substance must satisfy four conditions: (1) It must be synthesized in the presynaptic neurons, (2) it must be released from the presynaptic terminal, (3) it must be shown to cause EPSPs or IPSPs, and (4) there must be mechanisms for its removal from the site of neural action.

REFERENCES

Abrams, R., & Taylor, M.A. (1979). Differential EEG patterns in affective disorder and schizophrenia. *Archives of General Psychiatry, 36,* 1355–1358.

Akbarian, S., Kim, J.J., Potkin, S.G., Hetrick, W.P., Bunney, W.E., & Jones, E.G. (1996). Maldistribution of interstitial neurons in prefrontal white matter of the brains of schizophrenic patients. *Archives of General Psychiatry, 53,* 425–436.

Akbarian, S., Vinuela, A., Kim, J.J., Potkin, S.G., Bunney, W.E., & Jones, E.G. (1993). Distorted distribution of nicotinamide-adenine dinucleotide phosphate diaphorase neurons in temporal lobe in schizophrenics implies anomalous cortical development. *Archives of General Psychiatry, 50,* 178–187.

Alzheimer, A. (1897). Beitrage zur pathologischen Anatomie der Hirnrinde und zur anatomischen Grundlage einiger Psychosen. *Monatsschr Psychiatric Neurology, 2,* 82–120.

Alzheimer, A. (1913). Beitrage zur pathologischen Anatomie der Dementia praecox. *Allg. Ztschr. Psychiat., 70,* 810.

Andreasen, N.C. (1988). Brain imaging: Application in psychiatry. *Science, 239,* 1381–1388.

Andreasen, N.C., Ehrhardt, J.C., Swayze, V.W. II, Alliger, R.J., Yuh, W.T.C., Cohen, G., & Ziebell, S. (1990). Magnetic resonance imaging of the brain in schizophrenia. *Archives of General Psychiatry, 47,* 35–44.

Andreasen, N.C., Nasrallah, H.A., Dunn, V.D., Olson, S.C., Grove, W.M., Ehrhardt, J.C., Coffman, J.A., & Crossett, J.H. (1986). Structural abnormalities in the frontal system in schizophrenia: A magnetic resonance imaging study. *Archives of General Psychiatry, 43,* 136–144.

Angrist, B., Lee, H.K., & Gershon, S. (1974). The antagonism of amphetamine-induced symptomatology by a neuroleptic. *American Journal of Psychiatry, 131,* 817–819.

Ariel, R.N., Golden, C.J., Berg, R.A., Quiafe, M.A., Dirksen, J.W., Forsell, T., Wilson, J., & Graber, B. (1983). Regional cerebral blood in schizophrenia. *Archives of General Psychiatry, 40,* 258–263.

Arnold, S.E., Franz, B.R., Gur, R.C., et al. (1995). Smaller neuron size in schizophrenia in hippocampal subfields that mediate cortical–hippocampal interactions. *American Journal of Psychiatry, 152,* 138–748.

Arnold, S.E., Hyman, B.T., Hoesen, G.W.V., & Damasio, A.R. (1991). Some cytoarchitectural abnormalities of the entorhinal cortex in schizophrenia. *Archives of General Psychiatry, 48,* 625–632.

Arnold, S.E., Ruscheinsky, D.D., & Han, L.Y. (1997). Further evidence of abnormal cytoarchitecture of the entorhinal cortex in schizophrenia using spatial point pattern analyses. *Biological Psychiatry, 48,* 639–647.

Axelrod, J. (1965). The metabolism, storage and release of catecholamines. *Recent Progress in Hormonal Research, 21,* 597–622.

Bain, A. (1855). *The senses and the intellect.* London: Parker.

Bain, A. (1859). *The emotions and the will.* London: Parker.

Baxter, L.R., Phelps, M.E., Mazziotta, J.C., Schwartz, J.M., Gerner, R.H., Selin, C.E., & Sumida, R.M. (1985). Cerebral metabolic rate for glucose in mood disorders. *Archives of General Psychiatry, 42,* 441–447.

Baxter, L.R., Schwartz, J.M., Mazziotta, J.C., Phelps, M.E., Pahl, J.J., Guze, B.H., & Fairbanks, L. (1988). Cerebral glucose metabolic rates in obsessive-compulsive disorder. *American Journal of Psychiatry, 145,* 1560–1563.

Baxter, L.R., Schwartz, J.M., Phelps, M.E., Mazziotta, J.C., Guze, B.H., Selin, C.E., Gerner, R.H., & Sumida, R.M. (1989). Reduction of prefrontal cortex glucose metabolism common to three types of depression. *Archives of General Psychiatry, 46,* 243–250.

Bench, C.J., Dolan, R.J., Friston, K.J., & Frackowiak, S.J. (1990). Positron emission tomography in the study of brain metabolism in psychiatric and neuropsychiatric disorders. *British Journal of Psychiatry, 157,* 82–95.

Benes, F.M. (1993). The relationship between structural brain imaging and histopathologic findings in schizophrenia research. *Harvard Review of Psychiatry, 1,* 100–109.

Benes, F.M. (1997). Is there evidence for neuronal loss in schizophrenia? *International Review of Psychiatry, 9,* 429–436.

Benes, F.M., Davidson, J., & Bird, E.D. (1986).

Quantitative cytoarchitectural studies of the cerebral cortex of schizophrenics. *Archives of General Psychiatry, 43,* 31–35.

Berger, H. (1929). Über das Elektrenkephalogram des Menschen. *Archives für Psychiatrie und Nervenhrankheiten, 87,* 527–570.

Besson, J.A.O. (1990). Magnetic resonance imaging and its applications in neuropsychiatry. *British Journal of Psychiatry, 157,* 25–37.

Blackwood, D.H.R., & Muir, W.J. (1990). Cognitive brain potentials and their application. *British Journal of Psychiatry, 157,* 96–101.

Bleich, A., Brown, S.L., Kahn, R., & Van Praag, H.M. (1988). The role of serotonin in schizophrenia. *Schizophrenia Bulletin, 14,* 297–315.

Bloom, F.E. (1977). Norepinephrine: Central synaptic transmission and hypotheses of psychiatric disorders. In E. Usdin, D. Hamburg, & J.D. Barchas (Eds.), *Neuroregulators and psychiatric disorders.* New York: Oxford University Press.

Bogerts, B., Ashtari, M., Degreef, G., Ma, J.A., Bilder, R.M., & Lieberman, J.A. (1990). Reduced temporal limbic structure volumes on magnetic resonance images in first episode schizophrenia. *Psychiatry Research: Neuroimaging, 35,* 1–13.

Bogerts, B., Meertz, E., & Schonfeldt-Bausch, R. (1985). Basal ganglia and limbic system pathology in schizophrenia: A morphometric study of brain volume and shrinkage. *Archives of General Psychiatry, 42,* 784–791.

Brier, A. (1989). Experimental approaches to human stress research: Assessment of neurobiological mechanisms of stress in volunteers and psychiatric patients. *Biological Psychiatry, 26,* 438–462.

Brier, A., Kelsoe, J.R., Kirwin, P.D., Bellar, S.A., Wolkowitz, O.M., & Pickar, D. (1988). Early parental loss and the development of adult psychopathology. *Archives of General Psychiatry, 45,* 987–993.

Brill, A.A. (1941). The etiological relationship of trauma to schizophrenia. *Medical Records, 153,* 159–162.

Broca, P. (1861). Remarques sur le siège de la faculté du langage articule; suivies d'une observation d'aphemie (perte de la parole). *Bulletin de la société anatomique de Paris, 36,* 330–357.

Brodie, J.D., Christman, D.R., Corona, J.F., Fowler, J.S., Gomez-Mont, F., Jaeger, J., Micheels, P.A.,

Rotrosen, J., Russell, J.A., & Volkow, N.D. (1984). Patterns of metabolic activity in the treatment of schizophrenia. *Annals of Neurology, 15,* 166–169.

Brody, E.B. (1981). Can mother-infant interaction produce vulnerability to schizophrenia? *Journal of Nervous and Mental Disease, 169,* 72–81.

Brodmann, K. (1909). *Vergleichende Lokalisationlehre der Grosshirnrinde in ihren Prinzipien dargastellt auf Grund des Zellenbaues.* Leipzig: J.A. Barth.

Brown, F. (1961). Depression and childhood bereavement. *Journal of Mental Science, 107,* 754–777.

Brown, R., Colter, N., Nicholas Corsellis, J.A., Crow, T.J., Frith, C.D., Jagoe, R., Johnstone, E.C., & Marsh, L. (1986). Postmortem evidence of structural brain changes in schizophrenia: Differences in brain weight, temporal horn area, and parahippocampal gyrus compared with affective disorder. *Archives of General Psychiatry, 43,* 36–42.

Buchsbaum, M.S., DeLisi, L.E., Holcomb, H.H., Cappelletti, J., King, A.C., Johnson, J., Hazlett, E., Dowling-Zimmerman, S., Post, R.M., & Morihisa, J. (1984). Anteroposterior gradients in cerebral glucose use in schizophrenia and affective disorders. *Archives of General Psychiatry, 41,* 1159–1166.

Buchsbaum, M.S., Wu, J., DeLisi, L.E., Holcomb, H., Kessler, R., Johnson, J., King, A.C., Hazlett, E., Langston, K., & Post, R.M. (1986). Frontal cortex and basal ganglia metabolic rates assessed by positron emission tomography with [^{18}F]2-deoxyglucose in affective illness. *Journal of Affective Disorders, 10,* 137–152.

Butler, S.R., Suskind, M.R., & Schanberg, S.M. (1978). Maternal behavior as a regulator of polyamine biosynthesis in brain and heart of the developing rat pup. *Science, 199,* 455–457.

Caton, R. (1875). The electric currents of the brain. *British Medical Journal, 2,* 278.

Changeux, J.P., & Konishi, M. (Eds.). (1987). *The neural and molecular bases of learning.* Chichester: John Wiley and Sons Limited.

Christison, G.W., Casanova, M.F., Winberger, D.R., Rawlings, R., & Kleinman, J.E. (1989). A quantitative investigation of hippocampal pyramidal cell size, shape, and variability of orientation in schizophrenia. *Archives of General Psychiatry, 46,* 1027–1032.

Churchland, P.S. (1986). *Neurophilosophy: Toward a unified science of the mind/brain.* Cambridge, MA: MIT Press.

Cohen, R.M., Semple, W.E., Gross, M., Nordahl, T.E., DeLisi, L.E., Holcomb, H.H., King, A.C., Morihisa, J.M., & Pickar, D. (1987). Dysfunction in a prefrontal substrate of sustained attention in schizophrenia. *Life Sciences, 40,* 2031–2039.

Colony, H.S., & Willis, S.E. (1956). Electroencephalographic studies of 1,000 schizophrenic patients. *American Journal of Psychiatry, 113,* 163–169.

Cook, B.L., Shukla, S., & Hoff, A.L. (1986). EEG abnormalities in bipolar affective disorder. *Journal of Affective Disorders, 11,* 147–149.

Crane, G.E. (1957). Iproniazid (Marsilid) phosphate, a therapeutic agent for mental disorders and debilitating diseases. *Psychiatry Research Reports, 8,* 142–152.

Crow, T.J. (1990). Temporal lobe asymmetries as the key to the etiology of schizophrenia. *Schizophrenia Bulletin, 16,* 433–443.

Crow, T.J., Ball, J., Bloom, S.R., Brown, R., Burton, C.J., Colter, N., Frith, C.D., Johnstone, E.C., Owens, D.G.C., & Roberts, G.W. (1989). Schizophrenia as an anomaly of development of cerebral asymmetry in early onset schizophrenia. *Archives of General Psychiatry, 46,* 1145–1150.

Dalen, P. (1965). Family history, the electroencephalogram and perinatal factors in manic conditions. *Acta Psychiatric Scandinavica, 41,* 527–563.

Dameshek, W., & Myerson, A. (1935). Insulin hypoglycemia: Mechanism of neurologic symptoms. *Archives of Neurology and Psychiatry, 33,* 1–18.

Dastur, D.K. (1959). The pathology of schizophrenia. *Archives of Neurology, 81,* 601–614.

Davidson, M., & Davis, K.L. (1988). A comparison of plasma homovanillic acid concentrations in schizophrenic patients and normal controls. *Archives of General Psychiatry, 45,* 561–563.

Davis, K.L., Bucksbaum, M.S., Shihabuddin, L., Spiegel-Cohen, J., Metzger, M. Frecska, E., Keefe, R.S., & Powchik, P. (1998). Ventricular enlargement in poor-outcome schizophrenia. *Biological Psychiatry, 43,* 781–782.

Dehhehy, C. (1966). Childhood bereavement and psychiatric illness. *British Journal of Psychiatry, 212,* 1049–1069.

Delay, J., & Deniker, P. (1952). Le traitement des psychoses par une méthode neurolytique derivée d'hibernotherapie; le 4560 RP utilisé seul en cure prolongée et continuée. *Congres des Medecins Alienistes et Neurologistes de France et des Pays du Langue Française, 50,* 503–513.

DeLisi, L.E., Buchsbaum, M.S., Holcomb, H.H., Dowling-Zimmerman, S., Pickar, D., Boronow, J., Morihisa, J.M., van Kammen, D.P., Carpenter, W., & Kessler, R. (1985). Clinical correlates of decreased anteroposterior metabolic gradients in positron emission tomography (PET) of schizophrenic patients. *American Journal of Psychiatry, 142,* 78–81.

DeLisi, L.E., Dauphinais, I.D., & Gershon, E. (1988). Perinatal complications and reduced size of brain limbic structures in familial schizophrenia. *Schizophrenia Bulletin, 14,* 185–191.

DeLisi, L.E., Sakuma, M., Tew, W., Kushner, M., Hoff, A.L., & Grimson, R. (1997). Schizophrenia as a chronic active brain process: A study of progressive brain structural change subsequent to the onset of schizophrenia. *Psychiatry Research, 7,* 129–140.

DeLisi, L.E., Stritzke, P., Kushner, M., Neale, C., Boccio, A., & Anand, A. (1992). A longitudinal MRI study of brain developmental and progressive changes in schizophrenia and clinical outcome. *Journal of Biological Psychiatry, 31,* 63.

DeLisi, L.E., Tew, W., Xie, S., et al. (1995). A prospective follow-up study of brain morphology and cognition in first-episode schizophrenic patients: Preliminary findings. *Biological Psychiatry, 38,* 459–360.

Diamond, M.C., Lindner, B., Johnson, R., Bennett, E.L., & Rosenzweig, M.R. (1975). Differences in occipital cortical synapses from environmentally enriched, impoverished, and standard colony rats. *Journal of Neuroscience Research, 1,* 109–119.

Dunlap, C.B. (1924). Dementia praecox: Some preliminary observations on brains from carefully selected cases, and a consideration of certain sources of error. *American Journal of Psychiatry, 80,* 403–421.

Farde, L., Wiesel, F., Hall, H., Halldin, C., Stone-Elander, S., & Sedvall, G. (1987). PET determination of striatal D_2 dopamine receptors in drug-naive schizophrenics. *Science, 234,* 1558–1563.

Farkas, T., Reivich, M., & Alavi, A. (1980). Application of [^{18}F] 2-deoxy-2-fluoro-D-glucose and positron emission tomography in the study of psychiatric condition. In Passonneau et al. (Eds.), *Cerebral metabolism and neural function.* Baltimore: Williams & Wilkins.

Feldon, J., Avnimelech-Gigus, N., & Weiner, I. (1990). The effects of pre- and postweaning rearing conditions on latent inhibition and partial reinforcement extinction effect in male rats. *Behavioral and Neural Biology, 53,* 189–204.

Feldon, J., & Weiner, I. (1988). Long-term attentional deficit in nonhandled males: Possible involvement of the dopaminertic system. *Psychopharmacology, 95,* 213–236.

Flor-Henry, P. (1969). Psychosis and temporal lobe epilepsy: A controlled investigation. *Epilepsia, 10,* 363–395.

Forrest, A.D., Fraser, R.H., & Priest, R.G. (1965). Environmental factors in depressive illness. *British Journal of Psychiatry, 111,* 243–253.

Fox, P.T., Raichle, M.E., Mintun, M.A., & Dence, C. (1988). Nonoxidative glucose consumption during focal physiologic neural activity. *Science, 241,* 462–464.

Freedman, D.X. (1992). The search: Body, mind, and human purpose. *American Journal of Psychiatry, 149,* 858–866.

Freedman, R., Hall, M., Adler, L.E., & Leonard, S. (1995). Evidence in post-mortem brain tissue for decreased number of hippocampal nicotinic receptors in schizophrenia. *Biological Psychiatry, 38,* 22–33.

Freedman, R., Waldo, M., Bickford-Wimer, P., & Nagamoto, H. (1991). Elementary neuronal dysfunctions in schizophrenia. *Schizophrenia Research, 4,* 233–243.

Freedman, R., Wetmore, C., Strömberg, I., Leonard, S., & Olson, L. (1993). α-Bungarotoxin binding to hippocampal interneurons: Immunocytochemical characterization and effects on growth factor expression. *Journal of Neuroscience, 13,* 1965–1975.

Friedman, D., & Bruder, G. (1992). *Psychophysiology and experimental psychopathology*. New York: New York Academy of Sciences.

Fritsch, G., & Hitzig, E. (1870). Uber die elektrische Erregharkeit des Grosshirns. *Archiv für Anatomie und Physiologie, 300–332.*

Geschwind, N., & Galaburda, A.M. (1985). Cerebral lateralization—biological mechanisms, associations, and pathology. *Archives in Neurology, 42,* 428–651.

Globus, A., Rosenzweig, M.R., Bennett, E.L., & Diamond, M.C. (1973). Effects of differential experience on dendritic spine counts in rat cerebral cortex. *Journal of Comparative and Physiological Psychology, 82,* 175–181.

Glowinski, J., & Axelrod, J. (1964). Inhibition of uptake of tritiated noradrenaline in the intact rat brain by imipramine and structurally related compounds. *Nature (London), 204,* 1318–1319.

Goodman, A. (1991). Organic unity theory: The mind–body problem revisited. *American Journal of Psychiatry, 148,* 553–563.

Golgi, C. (1883). Récherches sur l'histologie des centres nerveux. *Archives Ital. Biology, 3,* 285–317.

Greenough, W.T., & Volkmar, F.R. (1973). Pattern of dendritic branching in occipital cortex of rats reared in complex environments. *Experimental Neurology, 40,* 491–504.

Greenwald, B., Kramer-Ginsberg, E., Krishnan, K.R.R., Ashtari, M., Auerbach, C., & Patel, M. (1997). Neuroanatomical localization of magnetic resonance imaging signal hyperintensities in geriatric depression. *Stroke, 29,* 613–617.

Greitz, T., Ingvar, D.H., & Widen, L. (Eds.). (1985). *The metabolism of the human brain studied with positron emission tomography*. New York: Raven Press.

Gur, R.E., Resnick, S.M., Alavi, A., Gur, R.C., Caroff, S., Dann, R., Silver, F.L., Saykin, A.J., Chawluk, J.B. Kushner, M., et al. (1987a). Regional brain function in schizophrenia: I. A positron emission study. *Archives of General Psychiatry, 44,* 119–125.

Gur, R.E., Resnick, S.M., Gur, R.C., Alavi, A., Caroff, S., Kushner, M., Reivich, M., et al. (1987b). Regional brain function in schizophrenia: II. Repeated evaluation with positron emission tomography. *Archives of General Psychiatry, 44,* 126–129.

Guterman, Y., Josiassen, R.C., Bashore, T.E., & Lubow, R.E. (1996). Latent inhibition effects reflected in event-related brain potentials in healthy controls and schizophrenics. *Schizophrenia Research, 20,* 315–326.

Hagman, J.O., Buchsbaum, M.S., Wu, J.C., Rao, S.J., Reynolds, C.A., & Blinder, B.J. (1990). Comparison of regional brain metabolism in bulimia nervosa and affective disorder assessed with positron emission tomography. *Journal of Affective Disorders, 19,* 153–162.

Haracz, J.L. (1985). Neural plasticity in schizophrenia. *Schizophreia Bulletin, 11,* 191–229.

Haug, J.O. (1962). Pneumoencephalographic studies in mental disease. *Acta Psychiatrica Scandinavica, 38,* 1–114.

Heath, R.G. (1962). Common characteristics of epilepsy and schizophrenia: Clinical observation and depth electrode studies. *American Journal of Psychiatry, 118,* 1013–1026.

Hecker, S., Heinsen, H., Heinsen, Y.C., & Beckmann, H. (1990). Limbic structures and lateral ventricle in schizophrenia. *Archives of General Psychiatry, 47,* 1016–1022.

Hinde, R.A., & Spencer-Booth, Y. (1971). Effects of brief separation from mother on rhesus monkey. *Science, 173,* 111–118.

Hofer, M.A. (1983). On the relationship between attachment and separation processes in infancy. In R. Plutchik & H. Kellerman (Eds.), *Emotions: Theory, research and experience*. New York: Academic Press.

Iacono, W.G., Smith, G.N., Morean, M., Beiser, M., Fleming, J.A.E., Lin, T., & Flak, B. (1988). Ventricular and sulcal size at the onset of psychosis. *American Journal of Psychiatry, 145,* 820–824.

Ingvar, D.H. (1980). Abnormal distribution of cerebral activity in chronic schizophrenia: A neurophysiological interpretation. In C.F. Baxter & T. Melnechuk (Eds.), *Perspectives in schizophrenia research*. New York: Raven Press.

Ingvar, D.H., & Franzen, G. (1974). Abnormalities of cerebral blood flow distribution in patients with chronic schizophrenia. *Acta Psychiatrica Scandinavica, 165,* 425–462.

Jacobi, W., & Winkler, H. (1927). Encephalographischen Studien an Schiziophrenen. *Archives of Psychiatry Nervenkr, 84,* 208–226.

Jacoby, J.R., & Levy, R. (1980). Computed tomography in the elderly: III. Affective disorder. *British Journal of Psychiatry, 136*, 270.

Jernigan, T.L., Zatz, L.M., Moses, J.A., & Berger, P.A. (1982). Computed tomography in schizophrenics and normal volunteers. *Archives of General Psychiatry, 39*, 765–770.

Jeste, D.V., & Lohr, J.B. (1989). Hippocampal pathologic findings in schizophrenia: A morphometric study. *Archives of General Psychiatry, 45*, 1019–1024.

Johnstone, E.C., Crow, T.J., Frith, C.D., Husband, J., & Kreel, J.L. (1976). Cerebral ventricular size and cognitive impairment in chronic schizophrenia. *Lancet, 2*, 924–926.

Johnstone, E.C., Owens, D.G.C., Crow, T.J., Frith, C.D., Alexandropolis, K., Bydder, G., & Colter, N. (1989). Temporal lobe structure as determined by nuclear magnetic resonance in schizophrenia and bipolar affective disorder. *Journal of Neurology, Neurosurgery, and Psychiatry, 52*, 736–741.

Josiassen, R.C., Restrepo, D., Rawson, N.E., Gomez, G., Bloom, F.E., & Hahn, C.G. (1997). *Workshop: Olfactory neurons as "in vitro" model for the study of psychiatric illnesses.* Symposium presented at the 52nd Annual Scientific Meeting of the Society of Biological Psychiatry. San Diego, May.

Josiassen, R.C., Roemer, R.A., Shagass, C., & Straumanis, J.J. (1986). Attention-related effects on somatosensory evoked potentials in nonpsychotic dysphoric psychiatric patients. In C. Shagass, R.C. Josiassen, & R.A. Roemer (Eds.), *Brain electrical potentials and psychopathology.* New York: Elsevier Science.

Josiassen, R.C., Shagass, C., & Roemer, R.A. (1988). Dealing with differential gender and age effects in evoked potential studies of psychopathology. *Biological Psychiatry, 23*, 612–621.

Josiassen, R.C., Shagass, C., Roemer, R.A., & Straumanis, J.J. (1985). Attention-related effects on somatosensory evoked potentials in college students at high risk for psychopathology. *Journal of Abnormal Psychology, 94*, 507–518.

Kafka, M.S., van Kammen, D.P., Kleinman, J.E., Nurnberger, J.I., Siever, L.J., Uhde, T.W., & Polinsky, R.J. (1980). Alpha-adrenergic receptor function in schizophrenia, affective disorder and some neurological diseases. *Communications in Psychopharmacology, 4*, 477–486.

Kane, J., Honigfeld, G., Singer, J., Meltzer, H., et al. (1988). Clozapine for the treatment-resistant schizophrenic: A double-blind comparison with chlorpromazine. *Archives of General Psychiatry, 45*, 789–796.

Kappers, C.U.A. (1917). Further contributions on neurobiotaxis: IX. An attempt to compare the phenomena of neurobiotaxis with other phenomena of taxis and tropism. The dynamic polarization of the neurone. *Journal of Comparative Neurology, 27*, 261–298.

Kelsoe, J.R., Cadet, J.L., Pickar, D., & Weinberger, D.R. (1988). Quantitative neuroanatomy in schizophrenia: A controlled magnetic resonance imaging study. *Archives of General Psychiatry, 45*, 533–541.

Kety, S.S. (1978). The biological roots of mental illness: Their ramifications through cerebral metabolism, synaptic activity, genetics, and the environment. *Harvey Lecture, 71*, 1–22.

Kety, S.S. (1979). Disorders of the human brain. *Scientific American, 241*, 120–127.

Kety, S.S., & Schmidt, C.F. (1948). The nitrous oxide method for quantitative determination of cerebral blood flow in man: Theory, procedure and normal values. *Journal of Clinical Investigation, 27*, 476–483.

Kety, S.S., Woodford, R.B., Harmel, M.H., Freyhan, F.A., Appel, K.E., & Schmidt, C.F. (1948). Cerebral blood flow and metabolism in schizophrenia: Effects of barbiturate seminarcosis, insulin coma and electroshock. *American Journal of Psychiatry, 104*, 765–770.

Kolb, B., & Whishaw, I.Q. (1980). *Fundamentals of human neuropsychology.* San Francisco: W.H. Freeman.

Korschenhausen, D.A., Hampel, Ackenheil, M., Penning, R., & Muller, N. (1996). Fibrin degradation products in post mortem brain tissue of schizophrenics: A possible marker for underlying inflammatory process. *Schizophrenic Research, 19*, 103–110.

Kovelman, J.A., & Scheibel, A.B. (1984). A neurohistological correlate of schizophrenia. *Biological Psychiatry, 19*, 1601–1621.

Kraemer, G.W., Ebert, M.H., Lake, C.R., & McKinney, W.T. (1984). Hypersensitivity to d-amphetamine several years after early social deprivation in rhesus monkeys. *Psychopharmacology, 82,* 266–271.

Kraepelin, E. (1907). *Introduction à la psychiatrie clinique: Edition 2,* A. Devaux & P. Merklen (Eds.). Paris: Vigot Frères.

Kuhn, R. (1958). The treatment of depressive states with G2235 imipramine hydrochloride. *American Journal of Psychiatry, 115,* 459–464.

Landenslager, M., Capitanio, J.P., & Reite, M. (1985). Possible effects of early separation experiences on subsequent immune function in adult macaque monkeys. *American Journal of Psychiatry, 142,* 862–864.

Lassen, N.A., Ingvar, D.H., & Skinhoj, E. (1978). Brain function and blood flow. *Scientific American, 239,* 62–71.

Lee, T., & Seeman, P. (1977). Dopamine receptors in normal and schizophrenic human brains. *Proceedings of the Society of Neurosciences, 3,* 443.

Leonard, S., Adams, C., Breese, C.R., Adler, L.E., Bickford, P., Byerley, W., et al. (1996). Nicotinic receptor function in schizophrenia. *Schizophrenia Bulletin, 22,* 432–445.

Lewis, S.W. (1990). Computerized tomography in schizophrenia 15 years on. *British Journal of Psychiatry, 157,* 16–24.

Lewis, S.W., & Mezey, G.C. (1985). Clinical correlates of septum pellucidum cavities: An unusual association with psychosis. *Psychological Medicine, 15,* 43–54.

Lewis, S.W., Reveley, M.A., David, A.S., et al. (1988). Agenesis of the corpus callosum and schizophrenia. *Psychological Medicine, 18,* 341–347.

Lifshitz, K., & Gradijan, J. (1974). Spectral evaluation of the electroencephalogram: Power and variability in chronic schizophrenics and control subjects. *Psychophysiology, 11,* 479–490.

Lock, T., Abou-Saleh, M.T., & Edwards, R.H.T. (1990). Psychiatry and the new magnetic resonance ear. *British Journal of Psychiatry, 157,* 38–55.

Luchins, D.J., Levine, R.R., & Meltzer, H.Y. (1984). Lateral ventricular size, psychopathology and medication response in the psychoses. *Biological Psychiatry, 19,* 29–44.

Meltzer, H.Y., & Sacher, E.J. (1974). Serum prolactin levels in unmedicated schizophrenic patients. *Archives of General Psychiatry, 31,* 564–569.

Meltzer, H.Y., & Stahl, S.M. (1976). The dopamine hypothesis: A review. *Schizophrenia Bulletin, 2,* 19–76.

Mesulam, M.M. (1990). Schizophrenia and the brain. *New England Journal of Medicine, 322,* 842–845.

Meyer, A. (1928). Presidential address: Twenty-five years of psychiatry in the United States and our present outlook. *American Journal of Psychiatry, 85,* 1–31.

Mirsky, A.F., & Duncan, C.C. (1986). Etiology and expression of schizophrenia: Neurobiological and psychosocial factors. *Annual Review of Psychology, 37,* 291–319.

Moises, H.W., Gelernter, J., Giuffra, L.A., Zarcone, V., Wetterberg, L., Civelli, O., Kidd, K.K., & Cavalli-Sforza, L.L. (1991). No linkage between D2 dopamine receptor gene region and schizophrenia. *Archives of General Psychiatry, 48,* 643–647.

Nasrallah, H.A., Jacoby, C.G., & McCalley-Whitters, M. (1981). Cerebellar atrophy in schizophrenia and mania. *Lancet, 1,* 1102.

Nasrallah, H.A., McCalley-Whitters, M., & Pfohl, B. (1984). Clinical significance of large cerebral ventricles in manic males. *Psychiatry Research, 13,* 151–156.

Niedermeyer, E., & da Silva, F.L. (1987). *Electroencephalography: Basic principles, clinical applications and related field,* 2nd ed. Munich: Urban und Schwarzenerg.

Nuñez, P.L. (1981). *Electric fields of the brain.* New York: Oxford University Press.

Olney, F.W., & Farber, N.B. (1995). Glutamate receptor dysfunction and schizophrenia. *Archives of General Psychiatry, 52,* 998–1007.

Owen, F., Cross, A.J., Crow, T.J., Longden, A., Poulter, M., & Riley, G.J. (1978). Increased dopamine receptor sensitivity in schizophrenia. *Lancet, 2,* 223.

Owens, D.G.C., Johnstone, E.C., Bydder, G.M., & Kreel, L. (1980). Unsuspected organic disease in chronic schizophrenia demonstrated by computed tomography. *Journal of Neurology, Neurosurgery and Psychiatry, 43,* 1065–1069.

Owens, D.G.C., Johnstone, E.C., Crow, T.J., Frith, C.D., Jagoe, J.R., & Kreel, L. (1985). Lateral ventricular size in schizophrenia: Relationship to the disease process and its clinical manifestations. *Psychological Medicine, 15,* 27–41.

Papez, J.W. (1937). A proposed mechanism of emotion. *Archives of Neurology, 38,* 725–743.

Pearlson, G.D., Barta, P.E., Powers, R.E., Menon, R.R., Richards, S.S., Aylward, E.H., Federman, E.B., Chase, G.A., Petty, R.G., & Tien, A.Y. (1997). Medial and superior temporal gyral volumes and cerebral asymmetry in schizophrenia versus bipolar disorder. *Biological Psychiatry, 41,* 1–14.

Pearlson, G.D., Garbacz, D.J., Tompkins, R.H., Ahn, H.S., Gutterman, D.R., Veroff, A.E., & DePaulo, R., Jr. (1984). Clinical correlates of lateral ventricular enlargement in bipolar affective disorder. *American Journal of Psychiatry, 141,* 253–256.

Pearlson, G.D., & Veroff, A.E. (1981). Computerized tomographic scan changes in manic-depressive illness. *Lancet, 2,* 470.

Pfefferbaum, A., Rosenbloom, M., Crusan, K., & Jernigan, T.L. (1988). Brain CT changes in alcoholics: The effects of age and alcohol consumption. *Alcoholism: Clinical and Experimental Research, 12,* 81–87.

Phelps, M.E., Huang, S.C., Hoffman, E.J., Selin, C., Sokoloff, L., & Kuhl, D.E. (1979). Tomographic measurement of local glucose metabolic rate in humans with (F-18) 2-fluoro-2-deoxy-D-glucose: Validation of method. *Annals of Neurology, 6,* 371–388.

Phelps, M.E., & Mazziotta, J. (1985). Positron emission tomography: Human brain function and biochemistry. *Science, 228,* 799–809.

Phelps, M.E., Mazziotta, J.C., Baxter, L.R., & Gerner, R. (1984). Positron emission tomography study of affective disorders: Problems and strategies. *Annals of Neurology, 15,* 149–156.

Porjesz, B., & Begleiter, H. (1981). Human evoked brain potentials and alcohol. *Alcoholism: Clinical and Experimental Research, 5,* 304–317.

Pribram, K.H., & Gill, M.M. (1976). *Freud's "Project for a Scientific Psychology": Preface to contemporary cognitive theory and neuropsychology.* New York: Basic Books.

Ramon y Cajal, S. (1911/1904). *Histologie dy système nerveux de l' homme et des vertebres.* Paris: Maloine.

Reiman, E.M., Raichle, M.E., Robins, E., Butler, F.K., Herscovitch, P., Fox, P., & Perlmutter, J. (1986). The application of positron emission tomography to the study of panic disorder. *American Journal of Psychiatry, 143,* 469–477.

Reivich, M., Kuhl, D., Wolf, A., Greenberg, J., Phelps, M., Ido, T., Casella, V., Fowler, J., Hoffman, E., Alavi, A., Som, P., & Sokoloff, L. (1979). The F-fluorodeoxyglucose method for the measurement of local cerebral glucose utilization in man. *Circulation Research, 44,* 127–137.

Reveley, A.M., & Reveley, M.A. (1983). Aqueduct stenosis and schizophrenia. *Journal of Neurology, Neurosurgery and Psychiatry, 46,* 18–22.

Reynolds, G.P. (1983). Increased concentrations and lateral asymmetry of amygdala dopamine in schizophrenia. *Nature, 305,* 527–529.

Ribot, T. (1881). *A. les maladies de la mémoire.* Paris: Alcan.

Ribot, T. (1885). *Les maladies de la personnalité.* Paris: Germer-Balliere.

Rieder, R.O., Mann, L.S., Weinberger, D.R., VanKammen, D.P., & Post, R.M. (1983). Computed tomographic scans in patients with schizophrenia, schizoaffective, and bipolar affective disorder. *Archives of General Psychiatry, 40,* 735–739.

Rosenzweig, M.R., & Bennett, E.L. (Eds.). (1976). *Neural mechanisms of learning and memory.* Cambridge: MIT Press.

Rosenzweig, M.R., Bennett, E.L., & Diamond, M.C. (1967). Effects of differential environments on brain anatomy and brain chemistry. In J. Zubin & G. Jervis (Eds.), *Psychopathology of mental development.* New York: Grune & Stratton.

Rosenzweig, M.R., Bennett, E.L., & Diamond, M.C. (1972). Brain changes in response to experience. *Scientific American, 226,* 22–29.

Rosenzweig, M.R., Krech, D., & Bennett, E.L. (1961). Heredity, environment, brain biochemistry, and learning. In *Current trends in psychological theory.* Pittsburgh: University of Pittsburgh Press.

Rosenzweig, M., Krech, D., Bennett, E.L., & Diamond, M. (1962). Effects of environmental complexity and training on brain chemistry and anatomy: A replication and extension. *Journal of Comparative and Physiological Psychology, 55,* 429–437.

Rossi, A., Stratta, P., Gallucci, M., Passarellio, R., & Cassachia, M. (1989). Quantification of corpus callosum and ventricles in schizophrenia: A preliminary follow-up study. *American Journal of Psychiatry, 146,* 99–101.

Roth, W.T., & Cannon, E.H. (1972). Some features of the auditory evoked response in schizophrenics. *Archives of General Psychiatry, 27,* 466–471.

Roth, W.T., Pfefferbaum, A., Kelly, A.F., Berger, P.A., & Kopell, B.S. (1981). Auditory event-related potentials in schizophrenia and depression. *Psychiatry Research, 4,* 199–212.

Roy, A., De Jong, J., & Linnoila, M. (1989). Cerebrospinal fluid monoamine metabolites and suicidal behavior in depressed patients. *Archives of General Psychiatry, 46,* 609–612.

Roy, C.S., & Sherrington, C.S. (1890). On the regulation of the blood-supply of the brain. *Journal of Physiology, 11,* 85–108.

Saitoh, O., Niwa, S.I., Hiramatsu, K.I., Kameyama, T., Rymar, K., & Itoh, K. (1984). Abnormalities in late positive components of even-related potentials may reflect a genetic predisposition to schizophrenia. *Biological Psychiatry, 19,* 293–303.

Scheflen, A.E. (1981). *Levels of schizophrenia.* New York: Brunner/Mazel.

Schildkraut, J.J. (1965). The catecholamine hypothesis of affective disorders: A review of supporting evidence. *American Journal of Psychiatry, 122,* 509–522.

Schlegel, S., Aldenhoff, J.B., Eissner, D., Lindner, P., & Nickel, O. (1989). Regional cerebral blood flow in depression: Associations with psychopathology. *Journal of Affective Disorders, 17,* 211–218.

Schlegel, S., & Kretschmar, K. (1987). Computerized tomography in affective disorders: I. Ventricular and sulcal measurements. *Biological Psychiatry, 22,* 4–14.

Schwartz, J.M., Baxter, L.R., Mazziotta, J.C., Gerner, R.H., & Phelps, M.E. (1987). The differential diagnosis of depression: Relevance of positron emission studies of cerebral glucose metabolism to the bipolar–unipolar dichotomy. *Journal of the American Medical Association, 258,* 1368–1374.

Sedvall, G., Fyro, B., Gullberg, B., Nyback, H., Wiesel, F-A., & Wode-Helgodt, B. (1980). Relationship in healthy volunteers between concentrations of monoamine metabolites in cerebrospinal fluid and family history of psychiatric morbidity. *British Journal of Psychiatry, 136,* 366–374.

Sem-Jacobsen, C.W. (1957). Intra-cerebral electrographic studies in schizophrenic patients. *Report of Second International Psychiatric Congress,* Zurich, Vol. 2, pp. 247–248.

Shagass, C., Roemer, R.A., Straumanis, J.J., & Josiassen, R.C. (1985). Combinations of evoked potential amplitude measurements in relation to psychiatric diagnosis. *Biological Psychiatry, 20,* 701–722.

Shagass, C., & Schwartz, M. (1961). Reactivity cycle of somatosensory cortex in humans with and without psychiatric disorder. *Science, 134,* 1757–1759.

Sherrington, C.S. (1906). *The integrative action of the nervous system.* New Haven: Yale University Press.

Simon, H., Taghzouti, K., Gozlan, H., Studler, J.M., Louilot, A., Herve, D., Glowinski, J., Tassin, J.P., & LeMoal, M. (1988). Lesion of dopaminergic terminals in the amygdala produces enhanced locomotor response to D-amphetamine and opposite changes in dopaminergic activity in prefrontal cortex and nucleus accumbens. *Brain Research, 447,* 335–340.

Small, J.G. (1987). Psychiatric disorders and EEG. In E. Niedermeyer & F. Lopes da Silva (Eds.), *Electroencephalography: Basic principles, clinical applications and related fields,* 2nd ed. Munich: Urban und Schwarzenerg.

Smith, R.C., Baumgartner, R., & Calderon, M. (1987). Magnetic resonance imaging studies of the brains of schizophrenic patients. *Psychiatry Research, 20,* 33–46.

Smith, R.C., Baumgartner, R., & Ravichandran, G.K. (1984). Lateral ventricular enlargement and clinical response in schizophrenia. *Psychiatric Research, 14,* 241–253.

Snyder, S.H. (1980). *Biological aspects of mental disorder.* New York: Oxford University Press.

Snyder, S.H., Banerjee, S.P., Yamamura, H.I., & Greenberg, D. (1974). Drugs, neurotransmitters, and schizophrenia. *Science, 184,* 1243–1253.

Soares, J.C., & Mann, J.J. (1997). The anatomy of mood disorders—review of structural imaging studies. *Biological Psychiatry, 41,* 86–106.

Sokolov, L. (1977). The [^{14}C] deoxyglucose method for the measurement of local cerebral glucose utilization: Theory, procedure and normal values in the conscious and anesthetized albino rat. *Journal of Neurochemistry, 28,* 897–916.

Southard, E.E. (1919). On the focality of microscopic brain lesions found in dementia praecox. *Archives of Neurology and Psychiatry, 1,* 172–192.

Spielmeyer, W. (1930). The problem of the anatomy of schizophrenia. *Journal of Nervous and Mental Disturbances, 72,* 241–244.

Steffens, D.C. (1998). Structural neuroimaging and mood disorders: Recent findings, implications for classification, and future directions. *Biological Psychiatry, 43,* 705–712.

Stevens, J.R. (1973). An anatomy of schizophrenia? *Archives of General Psychiatry, 29,* 177–189.

Suddath, R.L., Casanova, M.F., Goldberg, T.E., Daniel, D.G., Kelsoe, J.R., & Weinberger, D.R. (1989). Temporal lobe pathology in schizophrenia: A quantitative magnetic resonance imaging study. *American Journal of Psychiatry, 146,* 464–472.

Suddath, R.L., Christison, G.W., Torrey, E.F., Casanova, M.F., et al. (1990). Anatomical abnormalities in the brains of monozygotic twins discordant for schizophrenia. *New England Journal of Medicine, 322,* 789–794.

Sulser, F., & Sanders-Bush, E. (1989). From neurochemical to molecular pharmacology of antidepressants. In E. Costa (Ed.), *Tribute to B.B. Brodie.* New York: Raven Press.

Sutton, S., Braren, M., Zubin, J., & John, E.R. (1965). Evoked potential correlates of stimulus uncertainty. *Science, 150,* 1187–1188.

Szechtman, H., Nahmias, C., Garnett, S., Firnau, G., Brown, G.M., Kaplan, R.D., & Cleghorn, J.M. (1988). Effect of neuroleptics on altered cerebral glucose metabolism in schizophrenia. *Archives of General Psychiatry, 45,* 523–532.

Thompson, R.F. (1986). The neurobiology of learning and memory. *Science, 233,* 941–947.

Torrey, E.F., & Peterson, M.R. (1974). Schizophrenia and the limbic system. *Lancet, 2,* 942–946.

Traskman, L., Asberg, M., Bertilsson, L., & Sjostrand, L. (1981). Monoamine metabolites in CSF and suicidal behavior. *Archives of General Psychiatry, 38,* 631–636.

Vaughan, H.G. (1978). *The nature of schizophrenia: Toward a neurophysiology of schizophrenia.* New York: Wiley.

Waggoner, R.W., & Bagchi, B.K. (1954). Initial masking of organic brain changes by psychic symptoms. *American Journal of Psychiatry, 110,* 904–910.

Waldeyer, H.W. von. (1891). Ueber einige neuere Forschungen im gebiete der Anatomie des Centralnervensystems. *Deutsche Medizinische Wochenschrift, 17,* 1213–1218, 1244–1246, 1287–1289, 1331–1332, 1352–1356.

Warkentin, S., Nilsson, A., Risberg, J., et al. (1989). Absence of frontal lobe activation in schizophrenia. *Journal of Cerebral Blood Flow and Metabolism, 9,* 354.

Weinberger, D.R. (1987). Implications of normal brain development for the pathogenesis of schizophrenia. *Archives of General Psychiatry, 44,* 660–669.

Weinberger, D.R., Berman, K.F., & Illowsky, B.P. (1988). Physiological dysfunction of the dorsolateral prefrontal cortex in schizophrenia. *Archives of General Psychiatry, 45,* 609–615.

Weinberger, D.R., Cannon-Spoor, E., Potkin, S.G., & Wyatt, R.J. (1980). Poor premorbid adjustment and CT scan abnormalities in chronic schizophrenia. *American Journal of Psychiatry, 137,* 1410–1413.

Weinberger, D.R., Torrey, E.F., Neophytides, A.N., & Wyatt, R.J. (1979). Lateral cerebral ventricular enlargement in chronic schizophrenia. *Archives of General Psychiatry, 36,* 735–739.

Wernicke, C. (1874). *Der aphasische Symptomenkomplex.* Breslau: Cohn und Weigert.

Wong, D.F., Wagner, H.N. Jr., Tune, L., et al. (1986). Positron emission tomography reveals elevated D$_2$ dopamine receptors in drug-naive schizophrenics. *Science, 234,* 1558–1563.

Zilboorg, G., & Henry, G.W. (1941). *A history of medical psychology.* New York: Vail-Ballou Press.

CHAPTER 5

PSYCHOPHYSIOLOGICAL FACTORS

David J. Drobes
Medical University of South Carolina

Werner G.K. Stritzke
University of Western Australia

Scott F. Coffey
Medical University of South Carolina

INTRODUCTION

Psychophysiology is at a crossroads with respect to its clinical application toward adult psychopathology. Our current understanding of mental disorders has undoubtedly been enriched by psychophysiological data and theories, yet transfer of this information to clinical settings has been relatively limited. Areas in which applied psychophysiology is particularly advanced (e.g., biofeedback, behavioral medicine) tend to focus on disorders that have clear physical manifestations (e.g., pain), rather than on disorders that are seemingly more psychological in nature. However, the rapid pace of technological innovations in recording of biological signals, along with development of more user-friendly equipment, has broadened the scope of psychophysiological applications to psychopathology.

Preparation of this chapter was supported in part by NIH grants DA10595 and AA10761.

The focus of this chapter is on psychophysiological research that may have received less attention by individual service providers because it is less commonly encountered in clinical practice than, for example, use of biofeedback in multidisciplinary pain programs (e.g., Kee, Redpath, & Middaugh, 1994). We hope that by selectively reviewing relevant findings in this area, we will enable more clinicians to appreciate the unique contribution of psychophysiology to assessment and classification of mental disorders, identification of at-risk populations, and evaluation of treatment outcome.

We begin with an overview of psychophysiological response systems commonly studied in relation to adult psychopathology. We then discuss some conceptual issues of which one needs to be mindful when relating activity in these systems to clinical phenomena. In the following sections, we selectively review psychophysiological findings pertinent to several major disorders. We conclude by highlighting areas in adult psychopathology in which the potential of psychophysiological methods has yet to be fully realized.

PSYCHOPHYSIOLOGICAL RESPONSE SYSTEMS

Psychophysiological measurement generally involves noninvasive recording of biological signals. A defining feature of psychophysiology is that measures of activity in the physiological domain are used to make inferences about psychological phenomena, including those classifiable as abnormal in the current version of the *Diagnostic and Statistical Manual of Mental Disorders* (DSM-IV; American Psychiatric Association, 1994). In this section, we will briefly describe several of the most frequently studied psychophysiological response systems and how these may be related to psychological functioning. For a more comprehensive treatment of these issues, the reader is referred to several excellent texts (e.g., Cacioppo & Tassinary, 1990; Coles, Donchin, & Porges, 1986; Hugdahl, 1995).

Before describing specific response systems, an important distinction must be made between *tonic* and *phasic* physiological activity. Tonic activity refers to ongoing "baseline" or "background" levels of physiological activity, and it may be recorded over brief or relatively lengthy periods of time. The primary feature of tonic activity is that it occurs without the influence of any immediate eliciting stimuli. In contrast, phasic activity involves a response to a discrete stimulus and typically involves a shorter period of measurement. Both tonic and phasic activity are of interest in the study of adult psychopathology. In addition, tonic activity can serve as a context for interpreting phasic responses, in that level of tonic activity may limit the range of stimulus-induced, phasic changes in activity (Wilder, 1967).

We now turn to a brief overview of four major psychophysiological response systems.

Cardiovascular. Measurement of the cardiovascular system has been a mainstay in psychophysiological research since formal inception of the field over three decades ago. The essential function of this system is to regulate blood flow throughout the body in the face of changing metabolic demands. These functions are controlled primarily by the heart and the vast network of blood vessels that extends throughout the body. Electrocardiography (ECG) involves measurement of electrical potentials at the surface of the skin that are produced by each cardiac cycle. ECG can involve the simple recording of heart rate (HR) or more complex analyses of the cardiac waveform. HR provides a sensitive index for many forms of motor or cognitive activity, yet it lacks specificity in terms of differentiating processes.

Electrodermal. Electrodermal activity (EDA) was one of the earliest applications of psychophysiology to psychopathology and remains one of the most widely used measures. Formerly referred to as *galvanic skin response,* EDA is primarily a measure of sympathetic nervous system activation and is therefore often used as an index of general arousal. It is commonly measured as changes in a small, constant voltage passed over the skin's surface. Skin conductivity is influenced largely by activity in the eccrine sweat glands near the surface of the skin, which are thought to serve a thermoregulatory function. Contemporarily, this activity is most often indexed as skin conductance, expressed either in terms of tonic skin conductance level (SCL) or phasic skin conductance response (SCR).

Skeletomotor. The skeletomotor system can be thought of as the final common pathway though which humans interact and modify their environment (e.g., Cacioppo, Tassinary, & Fridlund, 1990). This system therefore has important implications for understanding deviant patterns of emotion, cognition, and behavior. The primary psychophysiological measure of this system is surface electromyography (EMG). As a general indicator of tension and arousal, it is usually measured along the forehead, neck, or trapezius muscle regions. As a specific indicator of emotional processes, facial EMG readings are often taken. For instance, zygomatic muscle activity over the cheek region has been associated with smiling and positive affect, whereas corrugator muscle activity over the brow region has associated with frowning and negative affect. Recently, the startle eyeblink reflex, as measured by EMG activity in the orbicularis oculi muscle surrounding the eye, has gained popularity as a measure of attentional and emotional processing. We will review how this measure has been used to study features of several forms of adult psychopathology, including anxiety disorders, schizophrenia, antisocial personality disorder, and alcoholism.

Electrocortical.   For well over 50 years, there has been considerable interest in relating normal and abnormal psychological processes to electrical recordings taken over the surface of the scalp. At a recent scientific conference of the Society for Psychophysiological Research, the largest proportion of paper presentations involved use of electrocortical measures, relative to other psychophysiological measures (Patrick, 1997). Analysis of slow-wave electroencephalogram (EEG) and event-related potentials (ERPs) has led to important theoretical and practical advances in the area of adult psychopathology. The EEG is a record of spontaneous rhythmic oscillations in voltage, whereas ERPs involve measurement of phasic responses in reaction to, or in anticipation of, a discrete stimulus. Components of the ERP waveform are typically described in terms of their polarity and latency, and are referenced to a specific scalp location. Components with particular relevance for adult psychopathology will be reviewed in this chapter. However, some important conceptual issues need to be considered before relating psychophysiological data to psychological disorders.

CONCEPTUAL ISSUES

Psychophysiological Inference Making

One critical issue to which all psychophysiologists must attend is the extent to which inferences about psychological processes can be made on the basis of physiological data. Such inferences can be perilous when based on simple one-to-one relations between a particular psychophysiological response and the psychological phenomenon of interest (e.g., Cacioppo & Tassinary, 1990). Most physiological systems subserve more than one function, thereby making it difficult to assert that a given physiological event is attributable to a particular psychological state or process. For instance, when an increase in heart rate is attributed to a fearful reaction to a stimulus, it must also be taken into account that the heart is busy pumping blood in service of many other bodily demands, and it does not stop doing this for the convenience of the researcher who may only be interested

in measuring an emotional response. Thus, the process of making inferences from psychophysiological data is complex and may often require the interpretation of response *patterns,* integrating data from several physiological as well as nonphysiological response domains (cf. Stritzke, Lang, & Patrick, 1996).

Three-Systems Integration

For the past three decades, progress in understanding normal and abnormal emotional processes has been guided by a "three-systems" perspective (see Lang, 1968). That is, emotional states (e.g., fear, anger, depression) are best conceptualized and assessed with reference to three loosely related response systems: verbal report, overt behavior, and expressive physiology (e.g., autonomic, cortical, somatic). Expressive physiology is the least readily observed of these systems. However, increasing technological sophistication, together with a growing appreciation for the importance of multisystem assessment, has led to a better integration of psychophysiology in the study and treatment of adult psychopathology.

One of the advantages of multisystem assessment is a greater appreciation for subtle differences between similar diagnostic categories, as well as differences in the patterns of responses across the three systems that can be observed in individual patients. Lang (1971), among others, has argued that an important benefit of a multisystem approach is that it allows clinicians to tailor their treatments according to individual response patterns. For example, a fearful patient who experiences strong physiological responses in a fear-eliciting situation should benefit from procedures geared directly toward reducing physiological arousal (e.g., progressive muscle relaxation). Conversely, a patient who primarily avoids fearful stimuli should benefit from treatments based on gradual exposure whereby the threshold of physiological arousal is kept deliberately at a low level. Despite the inherent logic of this argument, studies that have explicitly attempted to demonstrate an improved effectiveness of therapy when techniques were geared toward individual response profiles have yielded mixed results (e.g., Michelson, 1986; Öst, Jerremalm, & Johansson, 1981, 1984; Öst, Johansson, & Jerremalm, 1982).

With respect to diagnostic criteria and accuracy of

differential diagnosis, multisystem assessment incorporating psychophysiological measures has been especially useful. It must be noted, though, that diagnostic schemes are constantly evolving. This raises the problem that psychophysiological findings generated within one diagnostic system may not generalize to a revised set of criteria for a particular disorder in a new classification scheme. We will discuss findings as they pertain to the most recent version of the DSM (APA, 1994). We will describe how psychophysiological data have helped to support current diagnostic categories and, in some instances, have raised issues that need to be addressed in future refinements of the DSM.

PSYCHOPATHOLOGICAL DISORDERS

In the following sections, we will review psychophysiological research within six broad categories of disorders. This review is meant to be illustrative rather than exhaustive. For the interested reader, more detailed or comprehensive sources are cited where appropriate. We limit our discussion to disorders that are primarily "psychological" in nature; that is, we will not focus on disorders with symptoms primarily due to a medical condition, or on physiological complications of psychopathology (e.g., digestive tract sequelae of an eating disorder). Detailed descriptions of the disorders discussed here can be found in other chapters of this volume.

Substance Use Disorders

Fundamental questions as to use and abuse of psychoactive substances are deceptively simple: What motivates people to drink alcohol or use drugs? Why do some users become addicted while others do not? What are the processes that contribute to relapse after a period of nonproblematic use or abstinence? Despite a voluminous research literature, straightforward answers to these questions have been elusive. The scope of this chapter allows for only a brief illustration of how psychophysiological approaches have been used to address these questions, with the primary focus here on alcohol use and abuse.

A commonly held expectation is that drinking alters emotional response (Goldman, Brown, & Chris-

tiansen, 1987), and many people report that they drink to obtain this effect (Cooper, Russell, Skinner, & Windle, 1992). Until recently, most laboratory investigations of alcohol–emotion relations focused on the purported anxiolytic or stress-reducing effects of alcohol in response to some physical or social stressors (see Stritzke et al., 1996, for a review). Although evidence of alcohol-induced stress response dampening was found in a number of studies, contradictory findings have also been reported (Cappell & Greeley, 1987; Sher, 1987). To the extent that psychophysiological measures were included in these studies, they were typically limited to nonspecific indices of autonomic arousal. In addition, most designs did not include pleasantly valenced, affective control conditions, thereby confounding negative affect and general arousal. Thus, even when alcohol was found to attenuate physiological stress responses, it is impossible to determine whether this effect is specific to aversive stimuli or is secondary to a general dampening of all emotional processing (Stritzke et al., 1996).

In the only experiment to date that manipulated positive as well as negative affect, participants consumed either a moderate dose of alcohol or a nonalcoholic beverage before viewing pleasant, neutral, and unpleasant slide stimuli (Stritzke, Patrick, & Lang, 1995). Eyeblink reactions to auditory startle probes were used to index the valence of the affective response evoked by the slides, whereas EDA indexed emotional arousal. Results indicated that alcohol diminished the overall magnitude of both startle and skin conductance response, regardless of the valence of the foreground stimuli. However, the typical affective modulation of startle, with greater reactions to aversive slides and smaller reactions to pleasant slides (see Lang, Bradley, & Cuthbert, 1990), remained intact in the alcohol condition. In other words, alcohol did not selectively attenuate reactions to aversive slides as predicted by stress-response dampening models. These findings suggest that theories of motivation for drinking that are based on mood alteration need refinement. Recent reviews of this literature (Sayette, 1993; Stritzke et al., 1996) conclude that, while alcohol may exert an overall dampening effect on arousal, it appears to selectively modulate emotional response through its disruptive effects on higher order associative processes (see also Curtin, Lang, Patrick, & Stritzke, 1998).

Another important area of alcohol research, one that has traditionally incorporated psychophysiological methods, has been identification of individuals at high biological risk for alcoholism (McGue, 1994; Newlin & Thomson, 1990). Research over the past two decades has provided compelling evidence for a genetic vulnerability to alcoholism (Anthenelli & Schuckit, 1992; Searles, 1988). For example, Finn and Pihl (1987, 1988) found that cardiovascular response to aversive stimuli, and sensitivity to alcohol-mediated dampening of this response, distinguished sons of alcoholic fathers with extensive transgenerational family histories of alcoholism from sons of families in which alcoholism is limited to a single member, as well as from normal controls. Men in the highest risk group showed the greatest autonomic reactivity to a laboratory stressor, and alcohol reduced this hyperarousal more so than for the lower risk groups. This alcohol-induced attenuation of stress reactivity in high-risk men appears to be dose-dependent (Stewart, Finn, & Pihl, 1992). Furthermore, enhanced cardiovascular arousal during stressful tasks was recently observed in high-risk preadolescent boys and thus appears to predate experimentation with alcohol (Harden & Pihl, 1995). Consequently, drinking may serve to normalize states of hyperarousal in these individuals, which may be experienced as reinforcing and, over time, may escalate to problem drinking and alcohol dependence. However, reviewers of this literature (Newlin & Thomson, 1990; Sher, 1991) have noted that there are about as many studies showing that individuals with a family history of alcoholism are more sensitive to the effects of alcohol as there are studies reporting the opposite finding (i.e., less sensitivity). Efforts to integrate these diverse findings are likely to benefit from fresh theoretical perspectives, along with refinements in methodology and experimental design (Finn, 1994; Newlin, 1994).

Most of those who attempt abstinence from addictions ultimately relapse (Brownell, Marlatt, Lichtenstein, & Wilson, 1986). Conditioning models of relapse propose that interoceptive or exteroceptive cues previously associated with drug intake acquire the capacity to elicit drug-related responses, which, in turn, can act as triggers for drug use (e.g., Coffey & Lombardo, 1998; Drobes, Saladin, & Tiffany, in press; Drummond, Tiffany, Glautier, & Remington,

1995). Some have argued that the often observed increases in cardiac and electrodermal activity in the presence of drug stimuli can be construed as a response pattern indicative of a pleasantly valenced, appetitive motivational state (e.g., Niaura, Rohsenow, Binkoff, Monti, Pedraza, & Abrams, 1988). More recently, there has been a growing recognition that the autonomic response profiles found in many cue reactivity studies are compatible with several alternative interpretations (Glautier & Remington, 1995; Tiffany, 1995). For example, increases in skin conductance and HR can be viewed as evidence for an appetitive motivational model, but they may also be suggestive of an aversive, withdrawal-like state (Glautier & Drummond, 1994). Furthermore, directionality of a given psychophysiological response may be affected by the modality of cue presentation (e.g., Drobes & Tiffany, 1997; Glautier, Drummond, & Remington, 1992). Thus, where psychophysiological assessment in cue reactivity is concerned, there is a critical need to avoid the now common practice of portraying any physiological reaction to drug-relevant cues as invariably indicative of a classically conditioned response (Glautier & Tiffany, 1995). Used properly, psychophysiological methods have the potential to yield fruitful indicators of important psychological processes in cue reactivity, such as the immediate cognitive (e.g., attention) and behavioral demands (e.g., approach/avoidance) of the stimulus situation (Stritzke, Lang, Patrick, Curtin, & Breiner, 1997; Tiffany, 1990).

Eating Disorders

In recent years, the shift toward understanding eating disorders as multidetermined, heterogeneous syndromes yielded notable refinements in the DSM-IV diagnostic criteria for anorexia nervosa and bulimia nervosa (Garner, 1993). The growing interest in the clearer specification of particular features that may differentiate between meaningful subgroups of eating-disordered patients has prompted several investigators to explore psychophysiological response profiles, although data are still limited and often conflicting.

Salivation to the sight and thought of food was one of the first psychophysiological responses systematically studied as a quantitative and objective index of "appetite" (Wooley & Wooley, 1973). Early findings were contradictory, with some showing that low-calorie dieting decreased salivary flow (e.g., Wooley & Wooley, 1981), and others reporting an increase of the salivary response to food following dietary restraint (e.g., Herman, Polivy, Klajner, & Esses, 1981). Further evidence suggested that dietary restraint alone, without considering dietary patterns, is insufficient to account for differences in salivary response to food (LeGoff, Leichner, & Spigelman, 1988). Results from that study indicated that, before treatment, anorexics salivated less than controls, whereas bulimics salivated more than controls. After treatment, the salivary responses of both eating-disordered groups were similar to those of controls.

Wardle (1990) proposed that changes in salivation reflect conditioned associations between eating and environmental cues such as the sight and smell of food. From this perspective, excessive eating patterns in bulimics should be amenable to extinction through systematic unreinforced exposure to food stimuli. This hypothesis was recently tested in a study with normal-weight women, comparing the effect of repeatedly tasting versus not tasting a highly desired chocolate stimulus on anticipatory salivation and subjective craving (Lappalainen, Sjödén, Karhunen, Gladh, & Lesinska, 1994). Although prevention of tasting during exposure to the chocolate cues inhibited salivary response, it did not affect craving for the chocolate.

To summarize, analysis of salivary responses to food cues has been useful in validating distinctions between diagnostic subgroups and measuring treatment outcome. However, data in support of this conclusion are few, and many inconsistencies remain. In part, this may be due to limitations of the methods traditionally used to measure saliva flow (e.g., cotton swab absorption), which are invasive, low in sensitivity, and potentially reactive. Noninvasive recording of salivary activity in the parotid salivary glands from surface electrodes was recently introduced as a possible alternative approach (Davis, Bauslaugh, & Wintrup, 1996; LeGoff, Davis, & Bauslaugh, 1996), but this measure has not yet been validated using a clinical population.

In addition to salivary response, psychophysiological analysis of diagnostic criteria and etiological factors in the development and maintenance of eating disorders have included various autonomic and EMG measures. In a series of studies using multiple psychophysiological measures, Williamson and his colleagues (Williamson, Goreczny, Davis, Ruggiero, & McKenzie, 1988; Williamson, Kelley, Davis, Ruggiero, & Veitia, 1985) tested an anxiety model of bulimia, which proposes that binge eating produces anxiety due to the bulimic's worry regarding weight gain, and that purging then serves to reduce that anxiety. Following consumption of a test meal, psychophysiological response patterns generally did not support predictions derived from the anxiety model. In another comparison of bulimics, anorexics, and controls, Buree (1990) also failed to find differences in anxious arousal during eating as measured by HR and skin conductance. Williamson et al. (1988) concluded that uncontrolled influences during a complex eating task and an hour-long postconsumption recording period are likely to generate considerable noise, which may interfere with reliable psychophysiological assessment within the context of this type of experimental manipulation.

In contrast, psychophysiological recordings of phasic reactivity to discrete eating-related cues are less susceptible to many of the potential confounds associated with the measurement of tonic activity. There is evidence that eating-disordered individuals may process stimuli associated with food or body image differently than normal controls. Restrained eaters, for example, may have developed cognitive strategies to suppress or ignore normal reactions to food-relevant situations (Herman & Polivy, 1980; Stunkard & Messik, 1985). In support of this hypothesis, Piacentini, Schell, and Vanderweele (1993) found that restrained eaters had diminished skin conductance orienting responses to food odors as compared to nonrestrained eaters. Similarly, restrained eaters (Drobes, Miller, & Lang, 1993) and college students who reported highly conflicting approach and avoidance reactions to photographic images of food (Stritzke, Drobes, Lang, Patrick, & Lang, 1997) showed elevated HR responses to food slides, a response that has been described as an index of defensive or inhibitory stimulus processing (Graham & Clifton, 1966). In the same studies, individuals who were not restrained or conflicted with respect to food stimuli reacted with significant heart rate deceleration to the food cues, a response believed to be related to greater orienting or attention (Jennings, 1986). Furthermore, other researchers found that, following a negative mood induction, bulimics showed greater heart rate deceleration to food slides than restrained eaters, reflecting increased orienting in the bulimic patients only (Laberg, Wilson, Eldredge, & Nordby, 1991). In sum, results from different laboratories converge on the conclusion that phasic autonomic response patterns to olfactory and visual food cues differentiate restrained eaters from other eating-disordered diagnostic subtypes, as well as from normal controls.

Anxiety Disorders

Anxiety disorders represent an extremely important area of study for psychophysiological researchers interested in psychopathology, primarily due to the pervasiveness of these disorders and the potential for integrating research findings into assessment and treatment protocols. Unfortunately, many early psychophysiological studies of anxiety disorders did not use strict diagnostic guidelines when forming experimental groups, but tended to lump together patients with multiple types of anxiety problems (e.g., Bond, James, & Lader, 1974; Goldstein, 1964; Hart, 1974; Raskin, 1975). This type of classification makes earlier data difficult to interpret in light of DSM-IV diagnostic criteria. Therefore, this section will focus on studies using diagnostic entities that bear some correspondence with the current DSM-IV taxonomy (APA, 1994).

Over the past several years, psychophysiological indices have assisted in differentiating among anxiety disorders. In one study (Cook, Melamed, Cuthbert, McNeil, & Lang, 1988), patients who were diagnosed as simple phobic, social phobic, or agoraphobic participated in an imagery assessment in which physiological responding and subjective reports were obtained during standardized and personally relevant clinical fear scripts. The most notable finding was that simple phobics displayed significantly greater HR and EDA changes during imagery of personalized phobic material, as compared to the other groups. Whereas social phobics showed smaller responses to their personalized clinical fear scenes than simple phobics, they showed larger responses to a standardized "speech fear" scene than simple phobics or agoraphobics. Cook et al. (1988) speculated that

the personalized social-phobic scenes had been experienced many times by these patients and thus were associated with a diminished or naturally desensitized response when these cues were presented during imagery. The standardized "speech" scene, on the other hand, presented these subjects with salient fear cues to which they had not yet become desensitized. Using a similar methodology, Zander and McNally (1988) attempted to introduce increasing amounts of information into imagery scripts for agoraphobics. These findings confirmed that agoraphobics are not physiologically reactive during fear imagery, nor were there any differences in responding based on the amount of information contained in the scripts. In general, the autonomic data collected in these studies supports the contention that there is a continuum of anxiety disorders, in which lower psychopathology but increased cue specificity represent one end (specific phobia); the other end is characterized by greater psychopathology and an absence of cue specificity (panic disorder/agoraphobia). Social phobia appears to be more closely aligned with specific phobia, and it is a reasonable speculation that generalized anxiety disorder would be more like panic disorder on this continuum (see Drobes & Lang, 1995).

Despite the lack of cue specificity in terms of eliciting physiological responses, panic disorder is clearly characterized by pronounced physiological changes occurring at the time of panic attacks. Cohen, Barlow, and Blanchard (1985) presented data from two anxiety disorder patients who experienced panic attacks during a psychophysiological assessment session. The patients showed decreases in HR and frontalis EMG during a relaxation period, followed by a rapid increase in both measures at the onset of a reported panic attack. In an effort to systematically identify and characterize the physiology of panic attacks occurring in naturalistic settings, some investigators have employed ambulatory monitoring techniques (e.g., Freedman, Ianni, Ettedgui, & Puthezhath, 1985; Taylor et al., 1986). In the Taylor et al. study, 12 panic disorder patients and 12 matched control subjects were monitored continuously for six days. The authors found that panic attacks occurred most frequently between 1:30 and 3:30 A.M. and could be identified by sharp increases in HR not attributable to increased physical activity. The subjects also reported panic attacks that were not accompanied by elevated HR, but these panic attacks were rated as less severe than those that included elevated HR. These data suggest that there is less than perfect concordance between the subjective aspects of panic and those that can be measured physiologically.

Ley (1992) has proposed three subcategories of panic based largely on psychophysiological indicators. "Classic" panic attacks are marked by a sharp drop in CO_2 production; sharp increases in respiration, HR, and EDA; and decreased finger temperature. "Anticipatory" panic attacks may or may not involve a sharp increase in HR and EDA, while other physiologic symptoms are absent. Finally, physiological symptoms are absent in "cognitive" panic attacks.

Posttraumatic stress disorder (PTSD) has been the focus of a great deal of psychophysiological research. Recent studies have shown that psychophysiological measures can be used to distinguish PTSD veterans accurately from non-PTSD veterans and nonveterans. For instance, Blanchard and colleagues have demonstrated that elevated HR, forehead EMG, and systolic blood pressure responses to combat sounds among Vietnam veterans with PTSD, relative to matched non-PTSD veteran or nonveteran groups (Blanchard, Kolb, Gerardi, Ryan, & Pallmeyer, 1986; Blanchard, Kolb, Pallmeyer, & Gerardi, 1982; Blanchard, Kolb, & Prins, 1991). In these studies, between 70% and 95% of the subjects were correctly classified as PTSD or non-PTSD according to their autonomic responses. This body of literature clearly supports the use of autonomic measures as a diagnostic aid and for identifying characteristics of PTSD.

Several studies have measured the startle reflex as a potential diagnostic index in anxiety disorder patients. In particular, PTSD researchers have been interested in this psychophysiological measure, as exaggerated startle is listed as a formal diagnostic criteria for this disorder in the DSM-IV (APA, 1994). Unfortunately, results have not confirmed startle as a consistent part of the PTSD symptom picture, with some studies showing augmented startle reactions in PTSD patients (e.g., Morgan, Grillon, Southwick, Davis, & Charney, 1996; Orr, Lasko, Shalev, & Pitman, 1995), and others obtaining null or equivocal effects (e.g., Butler et al., 1990; Ross et al., 1989; Shalev, Orr, Peri, Schreiber, & Pitman, 1992), or even a diminished response (e.g., Ornitz & Pynoos, 1989).

One recent study assessed startle responding in four categories of anxiety patients—specific phobia, social phobia, panic disorder, and PTSD—and in a group of normal controls (Cuthbert, Drobes, Patrick, & Lang, 1994). The results supported the hypothesis that augmented base startle reactivity is associated with anxiety disorders. However, the hypothesis that a high base startle is *specific* to PTSD, when compared to diagnoses with a comparable level of psychopathology, was not supported, with panic disorder patients showing the largest base startle response. Furthermore, the less severe anxiety patients (i.e., those with specific and social phobia) showed the most elevated responses during fear imagery, further refuting the notion that elevated startle response is a specific diagnostic marker for PTSD. This finding is also consistent with the continuum of anxiety disorders discussed earlier in relation to autonomic data; that is, phobic patients appear to show more cue specificity in startle responding, whereas panic disorder appears to involve a more tonic elevation in responding.

The startle reflex also appears to have potential as a measure of treatment outcome in the anxiety disorders. Two recent studies have reported that animal phobics treated with exposure-based therapy display a reduction in startle responding when presented with phobic cues after treatment (de Jong, Arntz, & Merckelbach, 1993; Vrana, Constantine, & Westman, 1992). In the Vrana et al. (1992) study, the startle reduction was accompanied by verbal and behavioral indices of reduced fear. Investigation with pharmacological anxiety reduction agents has shown that these drugs also reduce fear-potentiated startle responses in animals (e.g., Berg & Davis, 1984).

From the data reviewed in this section, it is clear that psychophysiological indices have added much to our understanding of anxiety disorders. In particular, we have suggested that the startle response can be added to the arsenal of more traditional psychophysiological measures that have demonstrated value in differentiating anxiety disorder categories and understanding treatment responses among anxiety patients.

Affective Disorders

Diagnostic criteria for affective disorders have undergone substantial revision over the years. In this section, we will illustrate how autonomic, skeleto-motor, and electrocortical measures have been instrumental in clarifying symptom profiles, severity, course, and differential diagnosis of these disorders.

Several studies have explored whether autonomic measures could serve as a marker for depression. Ward and Doerr (1986), for example, found that resting electrodermal activity (EDA) was lower in depressed than in nondepressed individuals and correctly identified 95% of depressed women and 93% of depressed men. In another study, both electrodermal and cardiovascular measures distinguished depressed from nondepressed controls (Dawson, Schell, Braaten, & Catania, 1985). Cardiovascular measures discriminated better than EDA in this study, and phasic responses discriminated better than tonic levels of activity in both response systems.

Autonomic activity has also been found to vary across diagnostic categories. In an early study, Lader and Wing (1969) found that EDA discriminated agitated depressed patients from depressed patients who were behaviorally slowed. Often, a single autonomic index is not sufficient for distinguishing categories within or across broad symptom clusters. For example, when depressed patients were compared to schizophrenics in one study, electrodermal reactivity was similar for both groups (Bernstein et al., 1988). However, depressed patients could be differentiated from schizophrenic patients and normal controls when electrodermal reactivity was combined with changes in finger-pulse volume, another measure of autonomic reactivity. Nonetheless, diminished electrodermal responding in depressed patients has been found to persist for up to one year following remission, which suggests that it may be a traitlike characteristic in individuals at risk for the disorder (Iacono, Tuason, & Johnson, 1984).

Facial EMG activity can also provide an objective index of mood states (Tassinary & Cacioppo, 1992). For example, depressed patients have been shown to differ from nondepressed individuals on measures of facial EMG, even in the absence of group differences in overt facial responding (e.g., Schwartz, Fair, Salt, Mandel, & Klerman, 1976). In that study, participants were instructed to imagine either happy, sad, or angry situations that had strongly evoked these specific emotions in the past, or to imagine "what you do on a typical day" with no requirement to reexperience

any particular emotion. Depressed patients showed lower EMG responses in muscle regions associated with smiling (*zygomatic*), and higher EMG responses in muscle regions associated with frowning (*corrugator*). Moreover, EMG patterns of depressed patients during "typical day" imagery were similar to those evoked by "sad" imagery, whereas EMG patterns of nondepressed participants during "typical day" imagery were similar to those evoked by "happy" imagery.

One of the most active current areas of psychophysiological research on depression is the examination of EEG sleep profiles. Depressed patients have recently been found to show abnormal EEG sleep patterns relative to nondepressed controls (Dew et al., 1996). In addition, EEG sleep profiles of depressed patients appear to vary as a function of gender, severity and course of the disorder, and diagnostic subgroup. Comparisons between depressed men and women suggest significant differences in EEG sleep patterns particularly in the right hemisphere (Armitage, Hudson, Trivedi, & Rush, 1995). Furthermore, patients with a longer, more severe, and recurrent history of depression tend to have poorer EEG sleep patterns than patients with shorter, less severe, single-episode depression (Dew et al., 1996; Pozzi, Golimstock, Petracchi, Garcia, & Starkstein, 1995). It is noteworthy, though, that there are also similarities between EEG sleep profiles of patients suffering from dysthymia and those of patients diagnosed with major depression, suggesting that the two disorders are variants of the same underlying clinical syndrome (Arriaga, Cavaglia, Matos-Pires, Lara, & Paiva, 1995).

Schizophrenia

Schizophrenia is a disorder characterized by major disturbances in thought, affect, and social functioning. An essential feature of schizophrenia is that it involves a mixture of symptoms affecting multiple domains of functioning. Positive symptoms (e.g., hallucinations) reflect an exaggeration or distortion of normal functions, and negative symptoms (e.g., affective flattening) reflect a decrement or loss of normal functions. Because no single symptom or response system is pathognomonic of schizophrenia (APA, 1994), psychophysiological indicators can add valuable insights into basic mechanisms, subtypes, and risk factors associated with the disorder.

Psychophysiological evidence consistently supports the long-held view that information-processing impairments are a defining feature of schizophrenia (Bleuler, 1911/1950; Kraepelin, 1913/1919). For example, irregularities in attentional processing have been found across a number of different measures including ERPs, SC orienting response, and startle reflex modulation.

Several investigators have found that schizophrenic patients show diminished or delayed responses in the P300 component of the ERP (Mitchie, 1995; Pfefferbaum, Wenegrat, Ford, Roth, & Koppel, 1984). These findings reflect primarily a deficit during attention-demanding, resource-limited, controlled information processing, although automatic processing also is affected by schizophrenia (Mitchie, 1995; Neuchterlein & Dawson, 1984). In addition to providing insights into the mechanisms of cognitive dysfunction in schizophrenia, the amplitude of the P300 response also appears to be predictive of social functioning. For instance, in one prospective longitudinal study, current social functioning was correlated with P300 amplitude measured more than 2 years earlier (Strik, Dierks, Kulke, Maurer, & Fallgatter, 1996). Moreover, abnormal P300 responses may have differential diagnostic utility. Recent studies found that P300 amplitudes were diminished in schizophrenics but not in patients with schizotypal personality disorder (Trestman et al., 1996) or bipolar affective disorder (Souza et al., 1995).

The longer latency finding of the P300 component of the event-related potential is consistent with other data showing delayed autonomic orienting responses in schizophrenics (e.g., Hazlett, Dawson, Filion, Schell, & Neuchterlein, 1997). Together, these findings suggest that schizophrenia is characterized by reduced availability of processing resources and/or delayed allocation of resources. Interestingly, similar patterns of abnormal SC orienting responses were observed in individuals putatively at risk for schizophrenia (Hazlett et al., 1997). This suggests that these deficits may be indicative of a traitlike vulnerability factor.

Additional evidence for predispositional attentional processing deficits in schizophrenia comes from studies investigating startle reflex modulation (Dawson, Schell, Hazlett, Filion, & Neuchterlein, 1995). The amplitude of the eyeblink reflex to a startling noise can be either inhibited or facilitated depending on the stimulus event (prepulse) immediately preceding the startle probe, the interval between the two stimuli, and the task demands. At short lead intervals (< 250 msec), startle amplitude is typically diminished relative to the blink elicited by the startle probe alone. At longer lead intervals (>1000 msec), startle amplitude is enhanced. In the context of an auditory selective-attention task, prepulse inhibition and prepulse facilitation are greater following a to-be-attended tone than following a to-be-ignored tone (Filion, Dawson, & Schell, 1993). Impairments in this attentional modulation of the startle reflex have been found in schizophrenic patients and psychosis-prone individuals, but not in matched control groups (e.g., Dawson, Hazlett, Filion, Neuchterlein, & Schell, 1993; Schell, Dawson, Hazlett, & Filion, 1995).

Another psychophysiological response that has shown promise in the classification and differential diagnosis of schizophrenia is smooth-pursuit eye movement (SPEM). SPEM, the ability to track a moving target closely using slow, sweeping movements of the eye, is typically measured by placing electrodes at the outer canthi of the eyes. The initial finding of disturbed SPEMs in schizophrenics was made by Holzman, Proctor, and Hughes (1973) and has been subsequently supported in a number of studies (e.g., Holzman, Solomon, Levin, & Waternaux, 1984; Iacono et al., 1981; Spohn & Larson, 1983). It is estimated that 50% to 85% of schizophrenics show impaired SPEM, and this deficit appears to be fairly specific to schizophrenia (e.g., Holzman & Levy, 1977). In addition, first-degree relatives and monozygotic twins of schizophrenics show a higher rate of concordance for impaired SPEM performance than do nonrelatives and dizygotic twins, respectively, which provides further evidence for a genetic contribution to the disorder (Holzman et al., 1984; Holzman & Levy, 1977). Given the relatively high rate of impaired SPEM in schizophrenia, the general lack of this deficit in other disorders and in normals, and its apparent genetic transmission, SPEM appears to have great potential as a reliable psychophysiological marker of schizophrenia risk (Iacono & Ficken, 1989).

In summary, psychophysiological data across different response systems show a remarkable convergence with respect to cognitive impairments in schizophrenia. Some of the evidence suggests that these information-processing deficits may constitute a marker of an underlying cognitive-attentional vulnerability factor.

Antisocial Personality Disorder

Psychophysiological analysis of Axis II disorders has figured most prominently in the study of antisocial personality disorder (APD). Empirical findings consistently suggest that standardized psychophysiological tests may be useful in identifying important subcategories of APD that are not adequately differentiated by current DSM-IV diagnostic criteria (Lykken, 1995). As defined in DSM-IV, criteria for this disorder rely too heavily on socially deviant and criminal behaviors and neglect the core emotional deficits (e.g., poverty of affect, absence of nervousness, lack of remorse or shame, and incapacity to love) central to Cleckley's (1941) classic description of psychopathy (Hare, Hart, & Harpur, 1991). An alternative assessment system (the Revised Psychopathy Checklist, PCL-R) developed by Hare (1991) accounts for both of these symptom patterns and identifies emotional detachment and antisocial behavior as two correlated but distinct factors. Psychophysiological studies have been instrumental in validating the emotional factor as described by Cleckley and operationalized by Hare, though this factor is not accounted for in the current DSM nosology.

A longstanding hypothesis has been that the psychopath's affective insensitivity and inability to profit from experience reflect a primary deficit in anxiety or fear reactivity (Fowles, 1980; Gray, 1987; Hare, 1970; Lykken, 1957; Patrick, 1994). In an early experiment, Lykken (1957) tested the prediction that psychopaths should show weaker physiological signs of a fear reaction in an aversive-conditioning paradigm. A group of psychopaths who met all of Cleckley's criteria was compared to a group of persons who also had extensive records of antisocial behavior but did not meet the Cleckley criteria. In addition, a group of normal individuals matched for age, education, and gender with the other two groups was also recruited. Participants were conditioned to anticipate an electric shock following termination of a brief buzzing sound. Consistent with the prediction, the psychopaths who had exhibited the classic signs of emotional deficits described by Cleckley showed smaller conditioned electrodermal responses during the shock anticipation periods than did individuals in the other two groups. Similar results have since been reported in other aversive-conditioning studies with psychopaths (e.g., Hare & Quinn, 1971; Ziskind, Syndulko, & Maltzman, 1978).

Hare and his colleagues (Hare, 1965, 1966; Hare, Frazelle, & Cox, 1978) also recorded change in skin conductance as an index of fear-elicited arousal, but introduced a simpler anticipation paradigm. In this procedure, participants monitor a counter advancing steadily toward a point at which they are certain to receive an aversive stimulus. Whether anticipating electric shock or an aversive noise burst, psychopaths showed increased latency and marked attenuation of EDA as compared to controls. Fowles (1993) recently reviewed the many findings that support the notion of an electrodermal hyporeactivity among psychopaths and concluded that there is a diminished response to the anticipation of punishment in this group.

An intriguing explanation for this subnormal EDA in psychopaths during the Hare *countdown* derives from studies monitoring not only skin conductance but also HR. In those studies, the same psychopaths who showed relatively low EDA and, by inference, experienced less anticipatory anxiety while awaiting aversive stimuli, simultaneously produced greater cardiac acceleration than nonpsychopathic controls (e.g., Hare, 1978; Hare & Quinn, 1971). HR acceleration is generally thought to reflect the operation of a defensive or inhibitory control mechanism that reduces the impact of an aversive stimulus (Graham & Clifton, 1966; Sokolov, 1960). Thus, a reduction in concurrent EDA might indicate the success of that coping response (Hare, 1978). This interpretation is supported by further evidence that when psychopaths were provided with an operant response opportunity to prevent the aversive stimulus from occurring, which de facto preempted the need for a coping response as signaled by HR increase, cardiac acceleration did not occur (Ogloff & Wong, 1990).

Perhaps the most compelling evidence yet that APD is a heterogeneous disorder, including an emotional subcategory that is distinct from antisociality or common criminality, emerged from the innovative integration of startle probe methodology into this area of research (Patrick, 1994; Patrick, Bradley, & Lang, 1993). In this paradigm (cf., Lang, 1995; Lang et al., 1990), eyeblink startle reactions elicited by sudden noise probes are recorded while participants view a series of pleasant, neutral, and unpleasant slides. Unlike traditional autonomic measures, which provide only a nonspecific index of emotional activation, the strength of the blink reflex is modulated by the emotional valence of the slide being viewed. Thus, blink reactions are potentiated during exposure to unpleasant slides (e.g., snakes, mutilations, aimed guns) as compared with neutral slides, whereas startle responses are reduced during exposure to pleasant slides (e.g., happy babies, erotica). Patrick et al. (1993) hypothesized that if psychopathy were truly characterized by an absence of fear reactivity, then only criminal offenders who present the core affective and interpersonal qualities of the Cleckley psychopath should exhibit a deficit in startle reflex potentiation during processing of aversive stimuli. Results confirmed that only felons with high scores on the emotional detachment features of the PCL-R showed an abnormal startle pattern, with blink responses diminished during both pleasant and unpleasant slides relative to neutral. In other words, the *detached* psychopaths reacted to the unpleasant slides in the same manner as to the pleasant slides, without the kind of unpleasant affect that in the other offenders increased their startle response. This deviant pattern of startle modulation has been replicated in a follow-up study involving anticipation of an aversive noise blast (see Patrick, 1994).

SUMMARY AND FUTURE DIRECTIONS

As stated at the outset, clinical application of psychophysiological methods and findings has been quite limited. Psychophysiology will only enter the mainstream of clinical practice if practitioners understand how psychophysiological measures relate to clinical processes and outcome for the disorders they are dealing with. By reviewing response systems, conceptual issues, and relevant data, a central goal of this chapter was to foster an appreciation of psychophysiological contributions toward our under-

standing of adult psychopathology. Expanding the impact of psychophysiology on clinical practice will also depend on the increased availability of practical and cost-effective measurement systems. In this final section, we will mention a few additional areas in which further work may enrich the link between psychophysiology and adult psychopathology.

Much research discussed in this chapter has involved phasic measurement in response to situational or affective cue presentations, such as standardized pictures or text-prompted images. Recent work has begun to expand the range of stimuli that can be used in these studies, such as emotionally evocative sounds (Bradley, Zack, & Lang, 1994) or motivationally relevant smells (Miltner, Matjak, Braun, Diekmann, & Brody, 1994; Saladin, Drobes, Libet, & Anton, 1996). Psychophysiological research will benefit from additional standardization of relevant stimuli that can be used in phasic research paradigms. In addition, technological advancements should permit multisensory cue paradigms that are directly relevant to psychopathological conditions, or that can be personalized for individual patients or research subjects. Limitations will come to be based less on technology and more on the ingenuity of the researcher.

We have described the use of the startle reflex as an index of emotional functioning in the context of several of the disorders discussed in this chapter. Further work might productively incorporate measurement of other reflex systems for the study of a variety of psychopathological disorders. For example, an appetitive reflex probe (e.g., phasic salivary response to an appetitive taste probe) may be used to elucidate more directly features of addictive and eating disorders, and perhaps other types of impulse-control disorders (e.g., pathological gambling, paraphilias).

Many fundamental questions concerning brain–behavior relationships and psychopathology can be addressed with more assurance by combining traditional psychophysiological indices with other developing technologies. Integrating psychophysiological methods and measures with findings from molecular biology and brain-imaging studies will improve the interpretability of responses and may lead to new insights regarding various forms of adult psychopathology. For example, electrocortical measurement, when combined with studies of regional blood flow or glucose utilization in specific brain regions, can be interpreted with greater certainty than surface scalp measurements taken in isolation.

In conclusion, the formal inception of the field of psychophysiology is still a fairly recent event. There remain innumerable possibilities in which the study of adult psychopathology may benefit from psychophysiological investigation. The prospects for a fertile amalgam of these disciplines appear promising and will depend on technological and theoretical advancement, as well as attention to scientific rigor and clinical applicability.

REFERENCES

American Psychiatric Association. (1994). *Diagnostic and statistical manual of mental disorders,* 4th ed. Washington, DC: Author.

Anthenelli, R.M., & Schuckit, M.A. (1992). Genetics. In J.H. Lowinson, P. Ruiz, R.B. Millman, & J.G. Langrod (Eds.), *Substance abuse: A comprehensive textbook,* 2nd ed. Baltimore, MD: Williams & Wilkins.

Armitage, R., Hudson, A., Trivedi, M., & Rush, A.J. (1995). Sex differences in the distribution of EEG frequencies during sleep: Unipolar depressed outpatients. *Journal of Affective Disorders, 34,* 121–129.

Arriaga, F., Cavaglia, F., Matos-Pires, A., Lara, E., & Paiva, T. (1995). EEG sleep characteristics in dysthymia and major depressive disorder. *Neuropsychobiology, 32,* 128–131.

Berg, W.K., & Davis, M. (1984). Diazepam blocks fear-enhanced startle elicited electrically from the brainstem. *Physiology and Behavior, 32,* 333–336.

Bernstein, A.S., Riedel, J.A., Graae, F., Seidman, D., Steele, H., Connolly, J., & Lubowsky, J. (1988). Schizophrenia is associated with altered orienting activity: Depression with electrodermal (cholinergic?) deficit and normal orienting response. *Journal of Abnormal Psychology, 97,* 3–12.

Blanchard, E.B., Kolb, L.C., Gerardi, R.J., Ryan, P., & Pallmeyer, T.P. (1986). Cardiac response to relevant stimuli as an adjunctive tool for diagnosing post-traumatic stress disorder in Vietnam veterans. *Behavior Therapy, 17,* 592–606.

Blanchard, E.B., Kolb, L.C., Pallmeyer, T.P., & Gerardi, R.J. (1982). A psychophysiological study of posttraumatic stress disorder in Vietnam veterans. *Psychiatric Quarterly, 54,* 220–229.

Blanchard, E.B., Kolb, L.C., & Prins, A. (1991). Psychophysiological responses in the diagnosis of posttraumatic stress disorder in Vietnam veterans. *Journal of Nervous and Mental Diseases, 179,* 97–101.

Bleuler, E. (1950). *Dementia praecox or the group of schizophrenias* (J. Zinkin, Trans.). New York: International Universities Press. (Original work published 1911).

Bond, A.J., James, C., & Lader, M.H. (1974). Physiological and psychological measures in anxious patients. *Psychological Medicine, 4,* 364–373.

Bradley, M.M., Zack, J., & Lang, P.J. (1994). Cries, screams, and shouts of joy: Affective responses to environmental sounds. *Psychophysiology, 31,* S29 [Abstract].

Brownell, K., Marlatt, G.A., Lichtenstein, E., & Wilson, G.T. (1986). Understanding and preventing relapse. *American Psychologist, 41,* 765–782.

Buree, B.U. (1990). Eating in anorexia nervosa and bulimia nervosa: An application of the tripartite model of anxiety. *Canadian Journal of Behavioral Science, 22,* 207–218.

Butler, R.W., Braff, D.L., Rausch, J.L., Jenkins, M.A., Sprock, J., & Geyer, M.A. (1990). Physiological evidence of exaggerated startle response in a subgroup of Vietnam veterans with combat-related PTSD. *American Journal of Psychiatry, 147,* 1308–1312.

Cacioppo, J.T., & Tassinary, L.G. (1990). *Principles of psychophysiology: Physical, social, and inferential elements.* New York: Cambridge University Press.

Cacioppo, J.T., Tassinary, L.G., & Fridlund, A.J. (1990). In J.T. Cacioppo & L.G. Tassinary (Eds.), *Principles of psychophysiology: Physical, social, and inferential elements* (pp. 413–455). New York: Cambridge University Press.

Cappell, H., & Greeley, J. (1987). Alcohol and tension reduction: An update on research and theory. In H. Blane & K. Leonard (Eds.), *Psychological theories of drinking and alcoholism* (pp. 15–54). New York: Guilford Press.

Cleckley, H. (1941). *The mask of sanity.* St. Louis: C.V. Mosby.

Coffey, S.F., & Lombardo, T.W. (1998). Effects of smokeless tobacco-related sensory and behavioral cues on urge, affect, and stress. *Experimental and Clinical Psychopharmacology, 6,* 406–418.

Cohen, A.S., Barlow, D.H., & Blanchard, E.B. (1985). Psychophysiology of relaxation-associated panic attacks. *Journal of Abnormal Psychology, 94,* 96–101.

Coles, M.G.H., Donchin, E., & Porges, S.W. (1986). *Psychophysiology: Systems, processes, and applications.* New York: Guilford Press.

Cook, E.W., Melamed, B.G., Cuthbert, B.N., McNeil, D.W., & Lang, P.J. (1988). Emotional imagery and the differential diagnosis of anxiety. *Journal of Consulting and Clinical Psychology, 56,* 734–740.

Cooper, M.L., Russell, M., Skinner, J.B., & Windle, M. (1992). Development and validation of a three-dimensional measure of drinking motives. *Psychological Assessment, 4,* 123–132.

Curtin, J.J., Lang, A.R., Patrick, C.J., & Stritzke, W.G.K. (1998). Alcohol and fear-potentiated startle: The role of competing cognitive demands in the stress-reducing effects of intoxication. *Journal of Abnormal Psychology, 107,* 547–557.

Cuthbert, B.N., Drobes, D.J., Patrick, C.J., & Lang, P.J. (1994). Autonomic and startle responding during affective imagery among anxious patients. *Psychophysiology, 31,* S37 [Abstract].

Davis, C., Bauslaugh, T., & Wintrup, A. (1996). Noninvasive recording of human salivary activity from surface electrodes: Logic, method, and application. *Psychophysiology, 33,* S33.

Dawson, M.E., Hazlett, E.A., Filion, D.L., Neuchterlein, K.H., & Schell, A.M. (1993). Attention and schizophrenia: Impaired modulation of the startle reflex. *Journal of Abnormal Psychology, 102,* 633–641.

Dawson, M.E., Schell, A.M., Braaten, J.R., & Catania, J.J. (1985). Diagnostic utility of autonomic measures for major depressive disorders. *Psychiatry Research, 15,* 261–270.

Dawson, M.E., Schell, A.M., Hazlett, E.A., Filion, D.L., & Neuchterlein, K.H. (1995). Attention, startle eye-blink, and psychosis proneness. In A. Raine, T. Lencz, & S.A. Mednick (Eds.), *Schizotypal personality* (pp. 250–271). New York: Cambridge University Press.

de Jong, P.J., Arntz, A., & Merckelbach, H. (1993). The startle probe response as an instrument for evaluating exposure effects in spider phobia. *Advances in Behaviour Research and Therapy, 15,* 301–316.

Dew, M.A., Reynolds, C.F. III, Buysse, D.J., Houck, P.R., Hoch, C.C., Monk, T.H., & Kupfer, D.J. (1996). Electroencephalographic sleep profiles during depression: Effects of episode duration and other clinical and psychosocial factors in older adults. *Archives of General Psychiatry, 53,* 148–156.

Drobes, D.J., & Lang, P.J. (1995). Bioinformational theory and behavior therapy. In W.T. O'Donohue & L. Krasner (Eds.), *Theories of behavior therapy: Exploring behavior change* (pp. 229–257). Washington, DC: American Psychological Association.

Drobes, D.J., Miller, E.J., & Lang, P.J. (1993). Effects of food deprivation and eating patterns on psychophysiological responses to slides. *Psychophysiology, 30,* S23. [Abstract].

Drobes, D.J., Saladin, M.E., & Tiffany, S.T. (in press). Classical conditioning mechanisms in alcohol dependence. In N. Heather, T.J. Peters, & T. Stockwell (Eds.), *Handbook of alcohol dependence and alcohol-related problems.* Chichester: John Wiley & Sons.

Drobes, D.J., & Tiffany, S.T. (1997). Induction of smoking urge through imaginal and in vivo procedures: Physiological and self-report manifestations. *Journal of Abnormal Psychology, 106,* 15–25.

Drummond, D.C., Tiffany, S.T., Glautier, S., & Remington, B. (Eds.). (1995). *Addictive behaviour: Cue exposure theory and practice.* New York: Wiley.

Filion, D.L., Dawson, M.E., & Schell, A.M. (1993). Modification of the acoustic startle-reflex eyeblink: A tool for investigating early and late attentional processes. *Biological Psychology, 35,* 185–200.

Finn, P.R. (1994). Alcohol challenge in high-risk individuals: A discussion of Newlin's biobehavioral model. In R. Zucker, G. Boyd, & J. Howard (Eds.), *The development of alcohol problems: Exploring the biopsychosocial matrix of risk* (NIAAA Research Monograph No. 26). Rockville,

MD: National Institutes of Health (NIH Publication No. 94-3495)

Finn, P.R., & Pihl, R.O. (1987). Men at high risk for alcoholism: The effect of alcohol on cardiovascular response to unavoidable shock. *Journal of Abnormal Psychology, 96,* 230–236.

Finn, P.R., & Pihl, R.O. (1988). Risk for alcoholism: A comparison between two different groups of sons of alcoholics on cardiovascular reactivity and sensitivity to alcohol. *Alcoholism: Clinical and Experimental Research, 12,* 742–747.

Fowles, D.C. (1980). The three arousal model: Implications of Gray's two-factor learning theory for heart rate, electrodermal activity, and psychopathy. *Psychophysiology, 17,* 87–104.

Fowles, D.C. (1993). Electrodermal activity and antisocial behavior: Empirical findings and theoretical issues. In J.C. Roy, W. Boucsein, D. Fowles, & J. Gruzelier (Eds.), *Progress in electrodermal research* (pp. 223–237). London: Plenum Press.

Freedman, R.R., Ianni, P., Ettedgui, E., & Puthezhath, N. (1985). Ambulatory monitoring of panic disorder. *Archives of General Psychiatry, 42,* 244–250.

Garner, D.M. (1993). Eating disorders. In A.S. Bellack & M. Hersen (Eds.), Psychopathology in adulthood (pp. 319–336). Boston: Allyn and Bacon.

Glautier, S., & Drummond, D.C. (1994). Alcohol dependence and cue reactivity. *Journal of Studies on Alcohol, 55,* 224–229.

Glautier, S., Drummond, D.C., & Remington, B. (1992). Different drink cues elicit different physiological responses in non-dependent drinkers. *Psychopharmacology, 106,* 550–554.

Glautier, S., & Remington, B. (1995). The form of responses in drug cues. In D.C. Drummond, S.T. Tiffany, S. Glautier, & B. Remington (Eds.), *Addictive behaviour: Cue exposure theory and practice* (pp. 21–46). New York: Wiley.

Glautier, S., & Tiffany, S.T. (1995). Methodological issues in cue reactivity research. In D.C. Drummond, S.T. Tiffany, S. Glautier, & B. Remington (Eds.), *Addictive behaviour: Cue exposure theory and practice* (pp. 75–97). New York: Wiley.

Goldman, M.S., Brown, S.A., & Christiansen, B.A. (1987). Expectancy theory: Thinking about drinking. In H. Blane & K. Leonard (Eds.), *Psychological theories of drinking and alcoholism* (pp. 181–226). New York: Guilford Press.

Goldstein, I.B. (1964). Physiological responses in anxious women patients: A study of autonomic activity and muscle tension. *Archives of General Psychiatry, 10,* 382–388.

Graham, F.K., & Clifton, R.K. (1966). Heart rate change as a component of the orienting reflex. *Psychological Bulletin, 65,* 305–320.

Gray, J.A. (1987). *The psychology of fear and stress,* 2nd ed. Cambridge: Cambridge University Press.

Harden, P.W., & Pihl, R.O. (1995). Cognitive function, cardiovascular reactivity, and behavior in boys at high risk for alcoholism. *Journal of Abnormal Psychology, 104,* 94–103.

Hare, R.D. (1965). Psychopathy, fear arousal and anticipated pain. *Psychological Reports, 16,* 499–502.

Hare, R.D. (1966). Temporal gradient of fear arousal in psychopaths. *Journal of Abnormal and Social Psychology, 70,* 442–445.

Hare, R.D. (1970). *Psychopathy: Theory and research.* New York: Wiley.

Hare, R.D. (1978). Psychopathy and physiological responses to threat of an aversive stimulus. *Psychophysiology, 15,* 165–172.

Hare, R.D. (1991). *The Hare Psychopathy Checklist—Revised.* Toronto: Multi-Health Systems.

Hare, R.D., Frazelle, J., & Cox, D.N. (1978). Psychopathy and physiological responses to threat of an aversive stimulus. *Psychophysiology, 15,* 165–172.

Hare, R.D., Hart, S.D., & Harpur, T.J. (1991). Psychopathy and the proposed DSM-IV criteria for antisocial personality disorder. *Journal of Abnormal Psychology, 100,* 391–398.

Hare, R.D., & Quinn, M.J. (1971). Psychopathy and autonomic conditioning. *Journal of Abnormal Psychology, 71,* 223–235.

Hart, J.D. (1974). Physiological responses of anxious and normal subjects to simple signal and non-signal auditory stimuli. *Psychophysiology, 11,* 443–451.

Hazlett, E.A., Dawson, M.E., Filion, D.L., Schell, A.M., & Neuchterlein, K.H. (1997). Autonomic orienting and the allocation of processing resources in schizophrenia patients and putatively at-risk individuals. *Journal of Abnormal Psychology, 106,* 171–181.

Herman, C.P., & Polivy, J. (1980). Restrained eating. In A.B. Stunkard (Ed.), *Obesity* (pp. 647–660). Philadelphia: Saunders.

Herman, C.P., Polivy, J., Klajner, F., & Esses, V.M. (1981). Salivation in dieters and non-dieters. *Appetite, 2,* 356–361.

Holzman, P.S., & Levy, D.L. (1977). Smooth pursuit eye movements and functional psychosis: A review. *Schizophrenia Bulletin, 3,* 15–27.

Holzman, P.S., Proctor, L.R., & Hughes, D.W. (1973). Eye tracking patterns in schizophrenia. *Science, 181,* 179–181.

Holzman, P.S., Solomon, C.M., Levin, S., & Waternaux, C.S. (1984). Pursuit eye movement dysfunctions in schizophrenia. *Archives of General Psychiatry, 41,* 136–139.

Hugdahl, K. (1995). *Psychophysiology: The mind–body perspective.* Cambridge, MA: Harvard University Press.

Iacono, W.G., & Ficken, J.W. (1989). Research strategies employing psychophysiological measures: Identifying and using psychophysiological markers. In G. Turpin (Ed.), *Handbook of clinical psychophysiology* (pp. 45–70). New York: Wiley.

Iacono, W.G., Tuason, V.B., & Johnson, R.A. (1981). Dissociation of smooth-pursuit and saccadic eye tracking in remitted schizophrenics. *Archives of General Psychiatry, 38,* 991–996.

Jennings, J.R. (1986). Bodily changes during attending. In M.G.H. Coles, E. Donchin, & S.W. Porges (Eds.), *Psychophysiology: Systems, processes, and applications* (pp. 268–289). New York: Guilford Press.

Kee, W.G., Redpath, S., & Middaugh, S.J. (1994). The chronic pain patient. In J.M. Conroy & B.H. Dorman (Eds.), *Anesthesia for orthopedic surgery.* New York: Raven Press.

Kraepelin, E. (1919). *Dementia praecox and paraphrenia* (R.M. Barclay, Trans.). Edinburgh: E. & S. Livingston. (Original work published 1913).

Laberg, J.C., Wilson, G.T., Eldredge, K., & Nordby, H. (1991). Effects of mood on heart rate reactivity in bulimia nervosa. *International Journal of Eating Disorders, 10,* 169–178.

Lader, M.H., & Wing, L. (1969). Physiological measures in agitated and retarded depressed patients. *Journal of Psychiatric Research, 7,* 89–100.

Lang, P.J. (1968). Fear reduction and fear behavior: Problems in treating a construct. In J.M. Shlien (Ed.), *Research in psychotherapy* (Vol. 3, pp. 90–103). Washington, DC: American Psychological Association.

Lang, P.J. (1971). The application of psychophysiological methods to the study of psychotherapy and behavior modification. In A.E. Bergin & S.L Garfield (Eds.), *Handbook of psychotherapy and behavior change* (pp. 75–125). New York: Wiley.

Lang, P.J. (1995). The emotion probe: Studies of motivation and attention. *American Psychologist, 50,* 372–385.

Lang, P.J., Bradley, M.M., & Cuthbert, B.N. (1990). Emotion, attention, and the startle reflex. *Psychological Review, 97,* 377–395.

Lappalainen, R., Sjödén, P., Karhunen, L., Gladh, V., & Lesinska, D. (1994). Inhibition of anticipatory salivation and craving in response to food stimuli. *Physiology and Behavior, 56,* 393–398.

LeGoff, D.B., Davis, C., & Bauslaugh, T. (1996). Electrophysiological measurement of parotid response to food in fasted and nonfasted subjects. *Psychophysiology, 33,* S54.

LeGoff, D.B., Leichner, P., & Spigelman, M.N. (1988). Salivary responses to olfactory food stimuli in anorexics and bulimics. *Appetite, 11,* 15–25.

Ley, R. (1992). The many faces of Pan: Psychological and physiological differences among three types of panic attacks. *Behaviour Research and Therapy, 30,* 347–357.

Lykken, D.T. (1957). A study of anxiety in the sociopathic personality. *Journal of Abnormal and Social Psychology, 55,* 6–10.

Lykken, D.T. (1995). *The antisocial personalities.* Hillsdale, NJ: Lawrence Erlbaum.

McGue, M. (1994). Genes, environment, and the etiology of alcoholism. In R. Zucker, G. Boyd, & J. Howard (Eds.), *The development of alcohol problems: Exploring the biopsychosocial matrix of risk* (NIAAA Research Monograph No. 26, pp. 1–40). Rockville, MD: National Institutes of Health. (NIH Publication No. 94-3495).

Michelson, L. (1986). Treatment consonance and response profiles in agoraphobia: The role of individual differences in cognitive, behavioral and physiological treatments. *Behaviour Research and Therapy, 24,* 263–275.

Miltner, W., Matjak, M., Braun, C., Diekmann, H., & Brody, S. (1994). Emotional qualities of odors and their influence on the startle reflex in humans. *Psychophysiology, 31,* 107–110.

Mitchie, P.T. (1995). Cognitive deficits in psychopathology: Insights from event-related potentials. In F. Boller & J. Grafman (Eds.), *Handbook of neuropsychology* (Vol. 10, pp. 299–327). Amsterdam: Elsevier.

Morgan, C.A., Grillon, C., Southwick, S.M., Davis, M., & Charney, D.S. (1996). Exaggerated acoustic startle reflex in Gulf War veterans with posttraumatic stress disorder. *American Journal of Psychiatry, 153,* 64–68.

Neuchterlein, K.H., & Dawson, M.E. (1984). Information processing and attentional functioning in the developmental course of schizophrenic disorders. *Schizophrenia Bulletin, 10,* 160–203.

Newlin, D.B. (1994). Alcohol challenge in high-risk individuals. In R. Zucker, G. Boyd, & J. Howard (Eds.), *The development of alcohol problems: Exploring the biopsychosocial matrix of risk* (NIAAA Research Monograph No. 26, pp. 47–68). Rockville, MD: National Institutes of Health. (NIH Publication No. 94-3495).

Newlin, D.B., & Thomson, J.B. (1990). Alcohol challenge with sons of alcoholics: A critical review and analysis. *Psychological Bulletin, 108,* 383–402.

Niaura, R.S., Rohsenow, D.J., Binkoff, J.A., Monti, P.M., Pedraza, M., & Abrams, D.B. (1988). The relevance of cue reactivity to understanding alcohol and smoking relapse. *Journal of Abnormal Psychology, 97,* 133–152.

Ogloff, J.R., & Wong, S. (1990). Electrodermal and cardiovascular evidence of a coping response in psychopaths. *Criminal Justice and Behavior, 17,* 231–245.

Ornitz, E.M., & Pynoos, R.S. (1989). Startle modulation in children with posttraumatic stress disorder. *American Journal of Psychiatry, 146,* 866–870.

Orr, S.P., Lasko, N.B., Shalev, A.Y., & Pitman, R.K. (1995). Physiologic responses to loud tones in Vietnam veterans with posttraumatic stress disorder. *Journal of Abnormal Psychology, 104,* 75–82.

Öst, L., Jerremalm, A., & Johansson, J. (1981). Individual response patterns and the effects of different behavioral methods in the treatment of social phobia. *Behaviour Research and Therapy, 19,* 1–16.

Öst, L., Jerremalm, A., & Johansson, J. (1984). Individual response patterns and the effects of different behavioral methods in the treatment of agoraphobia. *Behaviour Research and Therapy, 22,* 697–707.

Öst, L., Johansson, J., & Jerremalm, A. (1982). Individual response patterns and the effects of different behavioral methods in the treatment of claustrophobia. *Behaviour Research and Therapy, 20,* 445–460.

Patrick, C.J. (1994). Emotion and psychopathy: Startling new insights. *Psychophysiology, 31,* 415–428.

Patrick, C.J. (1997). *Program committee chair report,* Annual Meeting of the Society for Psychophysiological Research, Cape Cod, Massachusetts.

Patrick, C.J., Bradley, M.M., & Lang, P.J. (1993). Emotion in the criminal psychopath: Startle reflex modulation. *Journal of Abnormal Psychology, 102,* 82–92.

Pfefferbaum, A., Wenegrat, B.G., Ford, J.M., Roth, W.T., & Koppel, B.S. (1984). Clinical application of the P3 component of event-related potentials. II. Dementia, depression, and schizophrenia. *Electroencephalography and Clinical Neurophysiology, 59,* 104–124.

Piacentini, A., Schell, A.M., & Vanderweele, D.A. (1993). Restrained and nonrestrained eaters' orienting responses to food and nonfood odors. *Physiology and Behavior, 53,* 133–138.

Pozzi, D., Golimstock, A., Petracchi, M., Garcia, H., & Starkstein, S. (1995). Quantified electroencephalographic changes in depressed patients with and without dementia. *Biological Psychiatry, 38,* 677–683.

Raskin, M. (1975). Decreased skin conductance response habituation in chronically anxious patients. *Biological Psychology, 2,* 309–319.

Ross, R.J., Ball, W.A., Cohen, M.E., Silver, S.M., Morrison, A.R., & Dinges, D.F. (1989). Habituation of the startle reflex in posttraumatic stress disorder. *Journal of Neuropsychiatry, 1,* 305–307.

Saladin, M.E., Drobes, D.J., Libet, J.M., & Anton, R.F. (1996). Startle responding to alcohol cues among alcoholics. *Psychophysiology, 33,* S72. [Abstract].

Sayette, M.A. (1993). An appraisal–disruption model of alcohol's effects on stress responses in social drinkers. *Psychological Bulletin, 114,* 459–476.

Schell, A.M., Dawson, M.E., Hazlett, E.A., & Filion, D.L. (1995). Attentional modulation of startle in psychosis prone college students. *Psychophysiology, 32,* 266–273.

Schwartz, G.E., Fair, P.L., Salt, P., Mandel, M.R., & Klerman, G.L. (1976). Facial expression and imagery in depression: An electromyographic study. *Psychosomatic Medicine, 38,* 337–347.

Searles, J.S. (1988). The role of genetics in the pathogenesis of alcoholism. *Journal of Abnormal Psychology, 97,* 153–167.

Shalev, A.Y., Orr, S.P., Peri, T., Schreiber, S., & Pitman, R.K. (1992). Physiological responses to loud tones in Israeli patients with posttraumatic stress disorder. *Archives of General Psychiatry, 49,* 870–875.

Sher, K.J. (1987). Stress response dampening. In H. Blane & K. Leonard (Eds.), *Psychological theories of drinking and alcoholism* (pp. 227–271). New York: Guilford Press.

Sher, K.J. (1991). *Children of alcoholics: A critical appraisal of theory and research.* Chicago: University of Chicago Press.

Sokolov, E.N. (1960). Neuronal models and the orienting reflex. In M.A.B. Brazier (Ed.), *CNS and behavior* (Vol. 3, pp. 70–93). New York: Josiah Macey, Jr., Foundation.

Souza, V.B., Muir, W.J., Walker, M.T., Glabus, M.F., Roxborough, H.M., Sharp, C.W., Dunan, J.R., & Blackwood, D.H. (1995). Auditory P300 event-related potentials and neuropsychological performance in schizophrenia and bipolar affective disorder. *Biological Psychiatry, 37,* 300–310.

Spohn, H.E., & Larson, J. (1983). Is eye tracking dysfunction specific to schizophrenia? *Schizophrenia Bulletin, 9,* 50–55.

Stewart, S.H., Finn, P.R., & Pihl, R.O. (1992). The effects of alcohol on the cardiovascular stress response in men at high risk for alcoholism: A dose response study. *Journal of Studies on Alcohol, 53,* 499–506.

Strik, W.K., Dierks, T., Kulke, H., Maurer, K., & Fallgatter, A. (1996). The predictive value of P300-amplitudes in the course of schizophrenic disorders. *Journal of Neural Transmission, 103,* 1351–1359.

Stritzke, W.G.K., Drobes, D.J., Lang, A.R., Patrick, C.J., & Lang, P.J. (1997). Cardiac reactivity during appetitive picture processing: Dietary restraint and ambivalence. *Psychophysiology, 34,* S87. [Abstract].

Stritzke, W.G.K., Lang, A.R., & Patrick, C.J. (1996). Beyond stress and arousal: A reconceptualization of alcohol–emotion relations with reference to psychophysiological methods. *Psychological Bulletin, 120,* 376–395.

Stritzke, W.G.K., Lang, A.R., Patrick, C.J., Curtin, J.J., & Breiner, M.J. (1997). Toward a topography of craving. *Alcoholism: Clinical and Experimental Research, 21,* 112A [Abstract].

Stritzke, W.G.K., Patrick, C.J., & Lang, A.R. (1995). Alcohol and human emotion: A multidimensional analysis incorporating startle-probe methodology. *Journal of Abnormal Psychology, 104,* 114–122.

Stunkard, A.J., & Messick, S. (1985). The three-factor eating questionnaire to measure dietary restraint, disinhibition, and hunger. *Journal of Psychosomatic Research, 29,* 71–83.

Tassinary, L.G., & Cacioppo, J.T. (1992). Unobservable facial actions and emotion. *Psychological Science, 3,* 28–33.

Taylor, C.B., Sheikh, J., Agras, W.S., Roth, W.T., Margraf, J., Ehlers, A., Maddock, R.J., & Gossard, D. (1986). Self-report of panic attacks: Agreement with heart rate changes. *American Journal of Psychiatry, 143,* 478–482.

Tiffany, S.T. (1990). A cognitive model of drug urges and drug-use behavior: Role of automatic and nonautomatic processes. *Psychological Review, 97,* 147–168.

Tiffany, S.T. (1995). The role of cognitive factors in reactivity to drug cues. In D.C. Drummond, S.T. Tiffany, S. Glautier, & B. Remington (Eds.), *Addictive behaviour: Cue exposure theory and practice* (pp. 75–97). New York: Wiley.

Trestman, R.L., Horvath, T., Kalus, O., Peterson, A.E., Coccaro, E., Mitropoulou, V., Apter, S., Davidson, M., & Siever, L.J. (1996). *Journal of Neuropsychiatry and Clinical Neurosciences, 8,* 33–40.

Vrana, S.R., Constantine, J.A., & Westman, J.S. (1992). Startle reflex modulation as an outcome measure in the treatment of phobia: Two case studies. *Behavioral Assessment, 14,* 279–291.

Ward, N.G., & Doerr, H.O. (1986). Skin conductance: A potentially sensitive and specific marker for depression. *Journal of Nervous and Mental Disease, 174,* 553–559.

Wardle, J. (1990). Conditioning processes and cue exposure in the modification of excessive eating. *Addictive Behaviors, 15,* 387–393.

Wilder, J. (1967). *Stimulus and response: The law of initial value.* Bristol: Wright.

Williamson, D.A., Goreczny, A.J., Davis, C.J., Ruggiero, L., & McKenzie, S.J. (1988). Psychophysiological analysis of the anxiety model of bulimia nervosa. *Behavior Therapy, 19,* 1–9.

Williamson, D.A., Kelley, M.L., Davis, C.J., Ruggiero, L., & Veitia, M.C. (1985). The psychophysiology of bulimia. *Advances in Behavior Research and Therapy, 7,* 163–172.

Wooley, O.W., & Wooley, S.C. (1981). Relationship of salivation in humans to deprivation, inhibition and the encephalization of hunger. *Appetite, 2,* 331–350.

Wooley, S.C., & Wooley, O.W. (1973). Salivation to the sight and thought of food: A new measure of appetite. *Psychosomatic Medicine, 35,* 136–142.

Zander, J.R., & McNally, R.J. (1988). Bio-informational processing in agoraphobia. *Behaviour Research and Therapy, 26,* 421–429.

Ziskind, E., Syndulko, K., & Maltzman, I. (1978). Aversive conditioning in the sociopath. *Pavlovian Journal, 13,* 199–205.

CHAPTER 6

DEVELOPMENT AND PSYCHOPATHOLOGY

Cynthia A. Lease
Thomas H. Ollendick
Virginia Polytechnic Institute and State University

INTRODUCTION

Psychopathology can be defined and understood from several different perspectives. In this chapter, we will address psychopathology from a developmental perspective. In doing so, we will borrow heavily from principles of developmental psychology and, more broadly, developmental psychopathology (Cicchetti, 1989a; Kazdin, 1989; Lease & Ollendick, 1993; Lerner, Hess, & Nitz, 1990). Developmental psychopathology has been defined as "the study of the origins and course of individual patterns of behavioral maladaptation, whatever the age of onset, whatever the causes, whatever the transformations in behavioral manifestations, and however complex the course of developmental pattern may be" (Sroufe & Rutter, 1984, p. 18). Implicit in this definition is concern with development and developmental deviations that occur throughout and across the life span. The study of psychopathology, from this perspective, is organized around milestones and sequences in physical, cognitive, and social-emotional development (Achenbach, 1990a). Presumably, a clearer understanding of maladaptive behavior is best achieved by considering it in relation to patterns of adaptation associated with salient developmental issues. It is, therefore, important to implement the theories, perspectives, and methods of developmental psychology in both clinical and empirical investigations (Sroufe & Rutter, 1984).

BASIC PREMISES

Developmental Psychology

Within the field of developmental psychology, considerable theoretical and philosophical differences remain as to how best to conceptualize changes that occur in individuals across their life span. Historically, two primary models have been invoked to account for these changes: an "organismic" model and a "mechanistic" model. The organismic model (Erikson, 1968; Freud, 1949; Piaget, 1950) asserts that basic structures and functions change across age (e.g., Piaget's stages of cognitive development) and that they reflect emerging, qualitatively different ways of interacting with the environment (i.e., the doctrine of epigenesis; see Gottlieb, 1970). In its most radical form, this model assumes that behavioral development results from maturational processes that are determined largely by intrinsic organismic factors rather than by environmental forces (Ollendick & King, 1991a). Moreover, the organism is assumed to be an active constructor of its environment, rather than a passive responder. Conversely, the mechanistic model of development (Baer, 1982; Bijou, 1976; Skinner, 1938) posits that behavior changes across time result from alterations in stimuli, and explanations for behavior development are derived largely from principles of learning theory (Ollendick & King, 1991a). In contrast to the organismic model, the mechanistic view, in its most radical form, assumes that the organism, regardless of age, is a relatively passive responder to stimulus input.

In recent years, recognition of the limitations of these models has led to their integration into what has come to be known as "developmental contextualism." According to this model, developmental changes occur as a result of continuous reciprocal interactions (i.e., transactions) between an active organism and an active environmental context (Lerner, et al., 1990; Zenah, Anders, Seifer, & Stern, 1989). Organisms affect their own development by being both producers and products of their environment.

Although some differences remain, developmentalists of all persuasions generally agree that development involves systematic, successive, and adaptive changes within and across all life periods in the structure, function, and content of the individual's mental, behavioral, and interpersonal/social characteristics (Lerner et al., 1990). Because developmental changes are assumed to occur in an orderly fashion (e.g., they are systematic and successive), it is inferred that changes observed at one point in time will influence subsequent events (Lerner, 1986). With regard to research, these changes require special attention to the selection of appropriate methods of inquiry and analysis, particularly when studying developmental psychopathology.

Developmental Psychopathology

Developmental psychopathology has much in common with developmental psychology; however, there are important differences. First, developmental psychology—at least historically—has focused on universals in development; that is, species-typical developmental patterns (Plomin, Nitz, & Rowe, 1990). Normative patterns are important in the study of psychopathology, but they serve primarily as a point of contrast to illustrate deviations in development.

Second, developmental psychology has generally assumed continuity in functioning (Rutter, 1986) so that, for example, debilitating anxiety as evidenced in anxiety disorders is regarded as being on the same continuum as "normal" anxiety (e.g., nervousness, apprehension, mild or moderate fears and worries), with both extending from heightened concern and vigilance to an absence of anxiety. On the other hand, abnormal psychology and clinical psychiatry tend to define dysfunctional behavior and emotions as "conditions" or "disorders," as if they were encapsulated entities that people either have or do not have (Achenbach, 1990a). Implicit in this dichotomy is the assumption of discontinuity, with illness on one side of the demarcation line and normality or health on the other (Rutter, 1986). Both of these viewpoints are probably valid; that is, there are mental illnesses that are qualitatively distinct from normality (e.g., autism disorder), and there are other disorders that represent no more than quantitative variations on a healthy state (e.g., oppositional defiant disorder, separation anxiety disorder). From the point of view of developmental psychopathology, there is no a priori assumption that either must be the case (Rutter, 1986). Rather, the focus is on the continuities and discontinuities between adaptive and maladaptive processes and on the complex relationships between child and adult behavior (functional and dysfunctional).

Psychopathology Defined

How then is psychopathology to be defined from a developmental perspective? In essence, psychopathology may be defined as developmental deviations or as a distortion of the developmental process (Sroufe & Rutter, 1984). From a transactional perspective, development is seen as a series of qualitative reorganizations among and within behavioral systems. The character of these reorganizations is determined by factors at various levels of analysis (e.g., genetic, constitutional, physiological, behavioral, psychological, environmental, and sociological) which are in dynamic transaction with one another (Cicchetti & Schneider-Rosen, 1986; Lerner, 1978, 1979; Lerner et al., 1990).

Healthy psychological development may be defined as a series of interlocking social, emotional, and cognitive competencies that tend to make the individual broadly adapted to his or her environment. Thus, good mental health exists when there is an adequate relation between psychological and social functioning—that is, between a child and his or her environment (Lerner et al., 1990).

Conversely, pathological development is understood as a lack of integration of social, emotional, and cognitive competencies that contribute to adaptation at a particular developmental level (Cicchetti & Schneider-Rosen, 1986; Sroufe, 1979). The development of psychopathology involves the "emergence of unadaptive, or inadequate characteristics in the psychosocial system" (Lerner et al., 1990, p. 10). Therefore, from a developmental contextual view, psychopathology exists and develops when, and only when, an inadequate relation exists between psychological and sociological functioning—that is, between an individual child and her or his environmental context. Changes that do not involve this relation are not developmental ones and, in addition, do not involve the development of psychopathology. It is a malfunctional child–context relation that defines developmental psychopathology; from the changing nature of this relation, either adaptive or maladaptive and, hence, healthy or psychopathological behaviors emerge.

Relevant to the issue of pathology is the distinction among perturbation, disturbance, and disorder (Emde & Sameroff, 1989):

The concept of perturbation is implicit in development. Development advances through the meeting of challenges and the overcoming of problems. Rolling over, sitting and standing, getting attention and communicating, and sleeping through the night, [as well as forming attachments with caregivers, mastery of the environment] are all major challenges that each child must struggle with. Frustration, overinvolvement, and nega-

tive affect associated with each of these developmental milestones reflect normative perturbations in behavior. For most children, these perturbations are soon resolved as competence is reached in the new area. For others, however, a failure to attain a given developmental milestone becomes a disturbance if it interferes with other areas of adaptation and a disorder if it persists far beyond normative bounds. (p. 9)

Table 6-1 outlines a series of developmental issues that are broadly integrative and include affective, cognitive, and social domains. From a developmental perspective, not only do various aspects of functioning interact at any one point in time, but, more important, issues experienced at one period are also seen as laying the groundwork for subsequent issues (Sroufe & Rutter, 1984). For instance, the quality of

TABLE 6-1 Salient developmental issues.

Age (Years)	Issues
0–1	Biological regulation Harmonious dyadic interaction Formation of effective attachment relationship
1–2½	Exploration, experimentation, and mastery of the object world (caregiver as secure base) Individuation and autonomy Responding to external control of impulses
3–5	Flexible self-control Self-reliance Initiative Identification and gender concept Establishing effective peer contacts (empathy)
6–12	Social understanding (equity, fairness) Gender constancy Same-sex chumships Sense of "industry" (competence) School adjustment
13+	"Formal operations" (flexible perspective taking; "as if" thinking) Loyal friendships (same sex) Beginning heterosexual relationships Emancipation Identity

Source: L.A. Sroufe & M. Rutter, "The Domain of Developmental Psychopathology," *Child Development,* 55 (1984), 17–29. Reprinted with permission.

exploration, experimentation, and mastery during the second year of life is related to the nature of the attachment relationship developed in the first year of life (Arend, Gove, & Sroufe, 1979; Bowlby, 1988; Cassidy & Berlin, 1994; Lamb, Thompson, Gardner, & Charnov, 1985; Matas, Arend, & Sroufe, 1978). Thus, normal development involves the integration of earlier competencies into later modes of functioning, whereas pathological development is marked by early deviation or disturbance in functioning that may be linked to the emergence of disturbances (or disorders) later on (Cicchetti & Schneider-Rosen, 1986). The significance of the interdependence among levels is stressed by Tobach and Greenberg (1984). These authors note that "the dialectic nature of the relationship among levels is one in which lower levels are subsumed in higher levels so that any particular level is an integration of preceding levels. . . . In the process of integration, or fusion, new levels with their own characteristics result" (p. 2).

The assumption that development at one level affects later functioning does not necessarily imply isomorphic continuity of behavior. Rather, because the process of both healthy and pathological development is seen as resulting from individually distinct transactions between a changing organism and his or her changing context, there are multiple pathways by which developmental outcomes may be achieved. It is therefore important to identify and understand intra- and extraindividual characteristics that promote or inhibit early deviations or maintain or disrupt early adaptation (Cicchetti & Schneider-Rosen, 1986). Toward this end, the field of developmental psychopathology is primarily concerned with the origins and course of a given disorder, its precursors and sequelae, its variations in manifestation with development, and, more broadly, its relations to nondisordered behavior patterns.

THE ROLE OF DEVELOPMENT IN PSYCHOPATHOLOGY

Developmental psychopathology focuses on change and development in maladaptive behavior and processes. "From a developmental perspective, it introduces the problems of change and transformation, and from a psychopathological perspective, it introduces the concept of individual difference, and with

it, the variety of possible processes and outcomes" (Lewis & Miller, 1990, p. xiv). The process of development emerges from individually unique interactions between a changing organism and his or her changing context, thus there are a number of potential child–context combinations (i.e., pathways) along which development may proceed (Lerner et al., 1990). This does not imply that outcomes are random and unpredictable; rather, it emphasizes the necessity for a comprehensive investigation of those factors that influence the nature of individual differences, the continuity of adaptive or maladaptive behavioral patterns, and the various pathways by which similar outcomes may result (Cicchetti & Schneider-Rosen, 1986).

Origins and Course of Psychopathology

Because psychopathology is defined in terms of competence and adaptation, interest is focused on ascertaining the internal and external factors that are related to the development of competence or resiliency in children and adults (Cicchetti, 1989b). Adaptive changes throughout development are those that allow the organism to meet the demands of its environment. *Adaptation,* then, refers to the child's active engagement of the environment, fitting and shaping herself or himself to that environment and effecting changes in the environment to satisfy emerging needs. Neither the child nor the adult (i.e., the parent) merely reacts to environmental events; rather, they seek stimulation and select and organize behavior in terms of their own goals (Sroufe, 1979). To the extent that an individual's behavior fails to serve in shaping him or her to the environment and fails to promote satisfaction of needs and developmental advances, it can be characterized as maladaptive or incompetent. Adaptational solutions at given developmental periods, however, must be examined in their own terms (Sroufe & Rutter, 1984). For example, separation anxiety, characterized by the clingy overdependence of a child on his or her parent(s) is one form of maladaptation in the preschool years, but such dependency is the norm in infancy. In fact, it has been shown that infants who actively seek physical contact, mold, cling, and derive comfort from such contact with their caregiver (i.e., are "functionally" dependent) when threatened or distressed are more effectively autonomous as toddlers and more competent as preschoolers (Arend et al., 1979; Main, 1977; Matas et al., 1978; Waters, Wippman, & Sroufe, 1979; Speltz, Greenberg, & Deklyen, 1990).

Moreover, the goal is to move beyond mere identification of risk factors for and precursors of psychopathology to an increased understanding of the mechanisms and processes by which such factors lead to the emergence of a disorder (Rutter, 1985). This does not necessarily mean less emphasis on observable behavior; rather, it suggests that more emphasis be placed on the meaning and organization of behavior (Sroufe, 1979). This emphasis on the process and organization of development broadens the investigation for etiology of pathology away from phenotypically similar patterns of behavior in early life toward particular adaptational failures that are defined in terms of salient issues of a given age period. The strongest predictors of later pathology are not likely to be early replicas of behavioral indicators of adult pathology but, rather, adaptational failures defined in age-appropriate terms (Sroufe & Rutter, 1984). For example, as noted earlier, overdependency is not a salient issue during infancy and therefore would not be expected to bear much relation to later pathology. In the preschool years, however—at a time when one important developmental task for the child is to progress from emotional dependency to instrumental dependency—overdependency does predict later behavior.

Precursors and Sequelae of Psychopathology

Early patterns of adaptation influence later adaptation, not in a simple, straightforward or linear manner, but rather in terms of how they equip the child to face subsequent developmental issues. Rutter (1981, 1983) has suggested a number of ways in which early adaptation or experience might be connected to later disorder. These include three direct and four less direct pathways. First, early experience may lead to disorder at the time, which then persists for reasons that are largely independent of the initial causation or provocation. An example of this would be the persistence of a conditioned fear response in the form of a phobia initially provoked by some acute stressful event. Second, experience may lead to bodily changes

that influence later functioning. Some aversive experiences in infancy produce changes in the neuroendocrine system that promote resistance to later stressors (Hennessy & Levine, 1979; Hunt, 1979; Thompson & Grusec, 1970), whereas other more traumatic experiences produce physiological changes that increase vulnerability to later stressors, as in the case of posttraumatic stress disorder (van der Kolk & van der Hart, 1989).

Third, early events may lead directly to altered patterns of behavior, which, though changed at the time of the event, take the form of an overt disorder only some years later. For instance, Crittenden (1985) has noted that maltreated children who become aware of a parent's hostility toward them may protect themselves from further abuse by avoiding or withdrawing from the abusive caregiver and/or by blunting or controlling their emotional experiences. Although this may be adaptive in "dealing with" the immediate situation and at that particular point in the child's development, avoidance behavior and the denial of strong emotions may, in the long run, be maladaptive in terms of the child's mental health. Further, this response pattern may lead to problems in subsequent cognitive, linguistic, educational, and/or socioemotional development (Erickson, Egeland, & Pianta, 1989; Schneider-Rosen, Braunwald, Carlson, & Cicchetti, 1985).

Fourth, early events may lead to changes in the family context, which in turn may indirectly predispose to later disorder. Longitudinal studies, such as the British National Survey (Wadsworth, 1984), for example, confirm that people who experience parental divorce, death, or permanent separation before the age of 5 years have a substantially increased risk of both psychiatric illness and delinquency in early adult life. Later disorder may result not so much from the experienced loss as such but, rather, from the psychosocial adversities that accompany the loss (Rutter, 1981). For example, it appears that early parental loss predisposes to depression only if it leads to inadequate care of the children and to lack of emotional stability in the family (Birchnell, 1980; Brown, Harris, & Bifulco, 1986; Kennard & Birchnell, 1982; Parker, 1983).

Fifth, early experiences may operate through means of altering sensitivities to stress or in modifying styles of coping that then protect from (resiliency) or predispose to (vulnerability) disorder in later life, but only in the presence of later stressful events. To illustrate, Lewis and his colleagues (Lewis, Feiring, McGuffog, & Jaskir, 1984) examined the relationship between the quality of early attachment relationship and later psychopathology. They followed 114 children from ages 1 to 6 years and obtained measures of parent–child attachment and behavior adjustment using the Strange Situation Test (Ainsworth, Blehar, Waters, & Wall, 1978) and the Child Behavior Profile (Achenbach, 1978), respectively. Additional variables examined included birth order, birth planning, stressful life events, and number of friends. Findings of this study showed that insecurely attached males who experienced negative environmental factors were more likely to develop subsequent pathology than were insecurely attached males who did not experience these adverse factors. Secure males who were exposed to the same negative environmental factors did not themselves develop psychopathology. These results suggest that early secure attachment renders males somewhat impervious to the effects of stress and places them at low risk for psychopathology. Secure attachment might be thought of as an invulnerability or protective factor; that is, with an early secure attachment relationship, the individual may be better at coping with later life stress (Lewis et al., 1984).

On the other hand, Lewis and his colleagues (1984) found that although insecure attachment alone was insufficient to predict later psychopathology, when coupled with other negative environmental factors it appeared to increase vulnerability to the effects of stress and to later psychopathology (also see Rutter, 1995). This finding has been supported by numerous contemporary studies. In general, it has been shown that insecure attachment status constitutes a significant risk factor for later childhood aggressive disorders (Lyons-Ruth, 1996). Studies examining the more specific effects of attachment status (i.e., whether particular styles of insecure attachment are related to particular psychiatric disorders) have produced a rich array of findings. For instance, in several studies utilizing various populations, individuals with dismissing attachment organization, in which childhood attachment to parents is minimized, were more likely to be diagnosed with a psychiatric disorder in which stress tends to be minimized, such as substance abuse and conduct disorders, and with narcissistic or antisocial personality disorders (Rosenstein & Horowitz, 1996; Pianta, Egeland, & Adam, 1996) and eating disorders (Cole-Detke & Kobak, 1996). Conversely, those with a preoccupied attachment organization, in which attachments are of supreme importance, were more likely to be diagnosed with psychiatric disorders reflecting high levels of subjective distress, such as affective (e.g., depression), histrionic, or borderline personality disorders (Cole-Detke & Kobak, 1996; Fonagy et al., 1996; Pianta et al., 1996; Rosenstein & Horowitz, 1996). Finally, a strong finding on the link between unresolved/disorganized responses to loss, trauma, or separation from attachment figures and severe adolescent psychopathology (e.g., suicidality) has been reported (Adam, Sheldon-Keller, & West, 1996; Allen, Hauser, & Borman-Spurrell, 1996).

Other research has also suggested that a secure relationship with at least one parent (or other significant adult) serves as a protective factor against the effects of stress and later psychopathology (Main & Weston, 1981; Rutter, 1971, 1979). Although the exact mechanism of protection is unclear, a secure attachment appears to be related to successful coping by the child. Rutter (1981) has suggested that the long-term effects of experiencing stressful life events depends not so much on the number of stressors encountered as on how the stressors are dealt with at the time and, perhaps more important, on whether the outcome was successful adaptation or humiliating failure. Similarly, the child's emotional reaction to a stressor is influenced by the degree of control exercised by the child (Gunnar-Vugnchten, 1978).

A secure infant–caregiver attachment relationship is one in which the child is confident that her or his parent will be available, responsive, and helpful should she or he encounter adverse or frightening (i.e., stressful) situations. This pattern is promoted by a parent being readily and consistently available; sensitive to the child's signals; and responsive when the child seeks protection, comfort, and/or assistance (Bowlby, 1988). It may be speculated that repeated interactions of this kind set up an organizational pattern by which the child develops beliefs of self-worth and expectancies of successfully overcoming stressful situations (i.e., self-efficacy). To quote Rutter (1985):

. . . it matters greatly how people deal with adversities and life stressors—not so much in the particular coping strategy, but in the fact that they do act and not simply react . . . people's ability to act positively is a function of their self-esteem and feelings of self-efficacy as much as their range of problem solving skills . . . such a cognitive set seems to be fostered by features as varied as secure stable affectional relationships and success, achievement, and positive experiences, as well as by temperamental attributes. (p. 608)

This leads to the sixth way in which early experiences may be linked to later psychopathology; that is, they may alter the individual's self-efficacy for successful experiences or, more broadly, their self-concept, which then in turn influence response to later situations. In a follow-up study into adult life of institution-reared women, for example, it was shown that compared to non-institution-reared women, the institution-reared women had a substantially worse outcome with respect to psychosocial functioning and parenting (Quinton, Rutter, & Liddle, 1984; Rutter & Quinton, 1984). The influence of such an early experience was, however, indirect. A subgroup of institution-reared women who, unlike their counterparts, had good adult outcome, were found to be in harmonious marriages with supportive husbands. The protective factor against vulnerability to stressors and psychopathology was presumably a good marital relationship. Inquiry about what enabled some women to make a successful marriage, despite prolonged family discord in early life and an upbringing in an institution, revealed that the most influential prior protective factor was some form of good experiences in school. Good school experiences were in the form of social relationships, athletic prowess, musical success, or scholastic achievement. These experiences appeared to increase the likelihood that these women would exert foresight and "planning," with respect to both their choice of a marriage partner and their choice of work. It is assumed that an experience of success in one area of life led to enhanced self-esteem and a feeling of self-efficacy, enabling them to cope more successfully with subsequent life challenges and adaptations (Rutter, 1981).

Finally, early events may have an indirect impact on later behavior through effects on the selection of environments or on the opening up or closing down of opportunities. Events leading to an infant being placed in an institution may eliminate opportunity to form selective attachments in the first 3 years of life. This lack of opportunity may have enduring effects; institutional rearing in early years tends to increase the likelihood that peer relationships will lack a certain closeness and emotional intensity (Rutter, 1987). Moreover, it has been shown that inadequacy of peer relations is a powerful predictor of later psychopathology (John, Mednick, & Schulsinger, 1982; Kohlberg, LaCrosse, & Ricks, 1972; Ollendick, Weist, Borden, & Greene, 1992; Roff & Ricks, 1970). An additional example of this kind is that children raised in institutions lack parental care, which, in turn, is associated with an increased risk of adolescent pregnancy; this makes it less likely that the girl will be upwardly socially mobile, and the consequent social disadvantage in adult life may increase the risk of depression (Brown et al., 1986).

Discussion of the ways in which early adaptation of experience might be related to subsequent psychopathology raises important issues about the continuities and discontinuities in the development of psychopathology. Moreover, this discussion highlights the concept of individual differences and the variable processes and variable outcomes associated with development. Against the backdrop of the preceding examples, we will attempt to integrate and summarize these two key issues.

Variable Processes/Variable Outcomes
Because basic developmental theory generally takes a normative approach, there is a tendency to make the assumption that each developmental process has a single path leading to a specific outcome. A developmental psychopathology perspective, however, invites us to consider the possibility for multiple models of development, where process as well as outcome can be variable (Lewis & Miller, 1990). Recall, for example, the study of institution-reared women cited earlier. Compared with a general-population control group, institutional rearing was associated with poor outcome; however, marital support in early adult life reduced the adverse effect of the institutional upbringing (Rutter, 1987). Recall further that harmonious relationships with a supportive husband were associated with earlier protective factors, namely some form of success or achievement in the school setting. Thus, although institutional

rearing made it less likely that the women would achieve a successful and supportive marriage, differences existed among the women. This illustrates that variant processes operating along the developmental pathway (in this case, those resulting from experiences in school) were functional in leading to different outcomes.

Another example comes from the investigation of the relationship between institutional rearing and peer relationships (Rutter, 1987). Although institutional rearing in the early years was linked with poor peer relationships, a period of institutional care at a later age, when children had already experienced longer lasting attachments, did not have the same debilitating effects. This finding seems to reflect the general rule that the effects of severe traumata (physical or psychological) tend to be greatest during developmental phases of rapid growth, when skills are becoming established (Rutter, 1987). Therefore, the timing and meaning of events influence the effects of stress as well as the developmental outcome.

Continuities and Discontinuities

A full discussion of the various concepts of continuity is beyond the scope of this chapter (for a review, see Rutter, 1987). However, the notion of *coherence* may be employed to integrate ideas of both continuity and discontinuity (i.e., change). From a developmental perspective, a central proposition is that the course of development is lawful (Sroufe & Rutter, 1984). It is assumed that there exists a common general course of development followed by normal and "abnormal" individuals alike (Cicchetti & Sroufe, 1978), and that there is coherence to the course of each individual's development. However, the prediction of coherence is different from a prediction of behavioral stability over time; the search is actually for qualitative similarities in behavior patterns over time, not behavioral identities (Kohlberg et al., 1972; Sroufe, 1979). Thus, continuity can be demonstrated by measures of how well the child is meeting developmental challenges and of the quality of the child's adaptation.

The notion of coherence is not incompatible with discontinuity; that is, both change and continuity are incorporated by this concept. For example, even though developmental reorganization and behavioral transformations occur, this does not mean that earlier

individual differences will necessarily disappear or are unimportant (Hinde & Bateson, 1985). "Even metamorphosis does not necessarily erase previous memories. In certain moth species whose larvae can feed on more than one foodstuff, it has been shown that the adult females are prone to lay eggs on the substrate on which they were reared. It seems that experience during the larval phase can affect the behavior of the adult. Comparable effects have also been demonstrated in amphibians" (Rutter, 1987, p. 1268). Equally complex examples have been cited for humans. Although relatively little is known about the mechanisms that maintain characteristic behavioral patterns, relevant findings indicate that individuals tend to maximize congruent patterns of interpersonal behavior by selecting and interacting with people whose behavior requires minimal change from previous interpersonal situations (Carson, 1969; Swann, 1983). Furthermore, once established, interpersonal styles can become self-perpetuating (Elder, Caspi, & Downey, 1986). For instance, in the institutional study mentioned earlier (Quinton et al., 1984; Rutter & Quinton, 1984), it was found that 51% of the young girls reared in institutions (compared to 15% of the control subjects) later married men with psychosocial problems. The main point is that continuity does not exist in isomorphic behaviors over time, but in lawful relations to later behavior, however complex the link. At any point in time, the individual's behavior may be strongly influenced by the current environment; but the fact that the individual is in that particular environment will have been influenced by the person's earlier behavior and experiences.

DEVELOPMENTAL PSYCHOPATHOLOGY: THE CASE OF CHILDHOOD ANXIETY DISORDERS

As evident in the preceding discussion, the concept of developmental psychopathology does not prescribe particular theoretical explanations for disorders (e.g., psychodynamic theory, social learning theory) nor does it supplant particular theories; rather, it is intended to sharpen awareness about the connections among phenomena that may otherwise seem haphazard and unrelated (Achenbach, 1990b). The foci of developmental psychopathology (i.e., normal developmental patterns, individual differences, continuities and discontinuities in functioning, and longitudinal research on relations between characteristics evident in particular developmental periods and the favorable versus unfavorable outcomes of these characteristics) may be viewed as a common core of questions and phenomena by which to integrate different theoretical approaches. In this sense, Achenbach (1990b) suggests that it can be viewed as a "macroparadigm" that functions to coordinate models (or microparadigms) that emphasize particular subsets of variables, methods, and explanations (see Figure 6-1).

A variety of theories have been put forth to explain the development and maintenance of anxiety disorders in children and adolescents (including those depicted in Figure 6-1). However, no one theory alone adequately accounts for the development of anxiety disorders in youth or for the subsequent expression of these disorders across age and into adulthood. Recent research suggests the need to explore a host of factors including genetics, temperament, attachment security, and parental psychopathology, as well as direct and indirect learning experiences (see reviews by Hagopian & Ollendick, 1997; Ollendick, Hagopian, & King, 1997). Here, we shall briefly review findings associated with temperament and attachment security to illustrate the value of these different influences and to illustrate a developmental psychopathological approach to disorder.

In recent years, Kagan and his colleagues (Kagan, 1989, 1994; Kagan, Reznick, & Gibbons, 1989; Kagan, Reznick, & Snidman, 1987) have demonstrated that 10% to 15% of American Caucasian children are born predisposed to be irritable as infants; shy and fearful as toddlers; and cautious, quiet, and introverted when they reach school age. In contrast, 10% to 15% of the population show the opposite profile, with the remainder of the population intermediate on these dimensions. Kagan hypothesized that inhibited children, compared with uninhibited children, have a low threshold for arousal in the amygdala and hypothalamic circuits, especially to unfamiliar events and that they react under such conditions with sympathetic arousal (Kagan, Reznick, & Snidman, 1988). Sympathetic activation is indicated by high heart rate under stressful conditions. Indeed, inhibited children have been shown to evince higher and more stable heart rates and to show greater heart-rate acceleration under stressful and novel conditions than uninhibited children. Collectively, these findings indicate a more reactive sympathetic influence on cardiovascular functioning in inhibited children. The behavioral response of withdrawal and avoid-

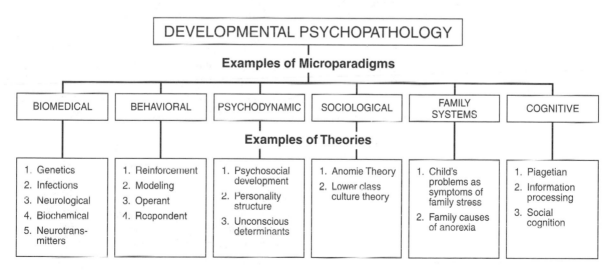

FIGURE 6-1. Schematic overview of developmental psychopathology as a macroparadigm in relation to other conceptual levels. From T.M. Achenbach, "What Is 'Developmental' about Development Psychopathology?" In J. Rolf, A. Masten, D. Cicchetti, K. Nuechterlein, & S. Weintraub (Eds.), *Risk and Protective Factors in the Development of Psychopathology* (New York: Cambridge University Press, 1990). Reprinted with permission.

ance shown by children with behavioral inhibition, along with considerable evidence of increased arousal in the limbic–sympathetic axes, fits well with current hypotheses of the neurophysiological underpinnings of anxiety disorders (see Gray, 1982, and Davis, 1992, for discussions).

The sample of inhibited and uninhibited children studied by Kagan and colleagues has been described in detail elsewhere (see Kagan et al., 1987, 1988). Initially, from a pool of 305 children who were 21 months of age, 28 children were identified as the most extremely inhibited and 30 as the most extremely uninhibited. Subsequent to identification, 22 inhibited and 19 uninhibited children were available for follow-up at ages 4, $5\frac{1}{2}$, and $7\frac{1}{2}$ years of age (details of behavioral evidence of inhibition at the various ages can be found in the original studies). Mothers of the inhibited and uninhibited children were interviewed by Biederman and colleagues (1990) with a structured diagnostic interview when the children were between 7 and 8 years of age. Although a variety of measures were obtained in this study, only the results of diagnosis for common childhood anxiety disorders (overanxious disorder, separation anxiety disorder, avoidant disorder, and phobic disorder) will be presented here. Findings revealed that rates of all anxiety disorders were higher in inhibited children than uninhibited children: overanxious disorder (13.6% vs. 10.5%), separation anxiety disorder (9.1% vs. 5.3%), avoidant disorder (9.1% vs. 0%), and phobic disorders (31.8% vs. 5.3%). Although all disorders favored the inhibited group for presence of disorder, only differences for phobic disorders were statistically significant. Clearly, the inhibited group was found to be at risk for anxiety disorder, particularly phobic disorder. It should be recalled that designation of inhibited and uninhibited group status occurred when the children were 21 months of age and that the assessment for psychopathology occurred at $7\frac{1}{2}$ years of age.

In a subsequent study, Hirshfeld and colleagues (1992) reanalyzed these findings by contrasting children who remained inhibited or uninhibited throughout childhood with those who were less stable across the four assessment periods (21 months, 4 years, $5\frac{1}{2}$ years, and $7\frac{1}{2}$ years). Four groups of children were formed: stable inhibited ($n = 12$), unstable inhibited ($n = 10$), stable uninhibited ($n = 9$), and unstable un-

inhibited ($n = 10$). As is evident, 54.5% of the inhibited children and 47.4% of the uninhibited children maintained stable group status across the four assessment periods (girls tended to remain more stably inhibited and boys more stably uninhibited). The four groups differed in the presence of any one anxiety disorder, of multiple anxiety disorders, and of simple phobias at $7\frac{1}{2}$ years of age. Stable inhibited children had significantly higher rates of any anxiety disorder, multiple anxiety disorders, and phobic disorders than the other three groups. Moreover, rates of anxiety disorders in unstable inhibited children did not differ from those in stable and unstable uninhibited children. Finally, with the exception of one case of phobia, all of the anxiety disorders among inhibited children occurred in children from the stable inhibited group. Thus, children who remained inhibited throughout childhood demonstrated increased risk of anxiety disorder relative to children who were not persistently inhibited or were not inhibited at 21 months of age.

Behavioral inhibition has also been examined in children of clinical samples of anxiety-disordered parents. In one study (Rosenbaum et al., 1988), children (2 to 7 years of age) of parents with panic disorder with agoraphobia (with or without a depressive disorder; PDAG/MDD and PDAG parents, respectively) were found to be more likely to demonstrate this temperamental characteristic than children of parents with a depressive disorder alone (MDD) or some other psychiatric disorders (non-PDAG/non-MDD). Findings indicated a progression of increasing rates of behavioral inhibition from 15.4% in the non-PDAG/non-MDD group to 50.0% in the MDD group to 70.0% in the comorbid PDAG/MDD group to 84.6% in the PDAG group of parents. Comorbidity of MDD with PDAG did not confer additional risk status. As can be seen in these findings, behavioral inhibition as defined and measured by Kagan and colleagues (1987, 1988) is highly prevalent in the offspring of adults in treatment for PDAG, with or without MDD. As will be recalled, behavioral inhibition occurs at a rate of approximately 10% to 15% in normal, nonclinical samples.

Subsequently, Biederman et al. (1990) explored the presence of anxiety disorder in the older children (4 to 7 years of age) of PDAG parents with or without MDD who were first examined in the Rosenbaum et al. (1988) study. Children who were found to be behaviorally inhibited in the earlier study were found to have higher rates of anxiety disorders than children at the time of follow-up. In particular, and in contrast with findings from Hirshfeld et al. (1992) who found higher rates of phobic disorder in behaviorally inhibited children from a nonclinical sample, inhibited children of PDAG parents were characterized by the presence of overanxious disorder. Almost 30% of the inhibited children of PDAG parents were so diagnosed; 0% of the uninhibited children of PDAG parents received this diagnosis.

The findings from these studies are provocative. Essentially, they suggest that a majority of children of parents with anxiety disorders (PDAG, in particular) are at risk for behavioral inhibition and that a significant number of the behaviorally inhibited children, in turn, are at risk for anxiety disorder (especially overanxious disorder). Moreover, findings from the nonclinical sample suggest that, whereas only a minority of children are at risk for behavioral inhibition (10% to 15%), a significant number of the stably inhibited children are at risk for anxiety disorder (especially phobic disorder, and especially girls). Thus, behavioral inhibition is associated with anxiety disorder in children of both normal and clinical parents. Yet, it is obvious that not all children of PDAG parents are behaviorally inhibited and that not all behaviorally inhibited children develop anxiety disorder. There is an obvious need to consider influences other than temperament to account for these variable outcomes.

Variable outcomes might be related to parental psychopathology and to gender of the child, for example. In their study of the original cohort of Kagan et al.'s inhibited and uninhibited children, Hirshfeld et al. (1992) observed that parents of those children who were stably inhibited from 21 months to $7\frac{1}{2}$ years of age reported a childhood history of ongoing anxiety symptoms. That is, they reported being anxious as children themselves and as remaining generally anxious into adulthood. It was suggested that exposure to a parent's anxious symptoms might induce a child to remain cautious and fearful in novel situations, especially those characterized by uncertainty. Phobic parents, for example, might model phobic avoidance and may have difficulty encouraging their children to take risks in such situations.

Indeed, retrospective reports of phobic adults have suggested their parents were overly protective; moreover, and in turn, parental protective behavior appears to be associated with parental anxiety (Hirshfeld et al., 1992; Ollendick et al., 1997). Interestingly, and consistent with this thesis, Kagan et al. (1987) indicated that children in their study who stopped being inhibited seemed to come from families in which children were encouraged to be more sociable and outgoing. Moreover, the observed gender difference between the stable inhibited (more girls) and stable uninhibited (more boys) raises the possibility that family members and others (i.e., peers, teachers) may be more likely to accept girls who are inhibited (shy, withdrawn) and boys who are uninhibited (bold, aggressive) and to try to alter the behavior of children who do not meet these gender stereotypes.

Variable outcomes associated with anxiety disorder may, of course, be related to a variety of other influences, including attachment security of the child (Manassis, Bradley, Goldberg, Hood, & Swinson, 1995; Mattis & Ollendick, 1997; Warren, Huston, Egeland, & Sroufe, 1997). As we have noted earlier, a secure attachment relationship is one in which the child is confident that his or her parent will be available, responsive, and helpful should he or she encounter adverse or frightening situations. If the caregiver routinely comes to the child's aid when the child is in need, the child develops confidence that the caregiver will help and protect him or her. Early on, Bowlby (1973) noted that once infants become attached to the caregiver (during the second half-year of life, see Table 6-1), there is a period in which they are made anxious by even brief separations. This response is said to be adaptive and to serve the evolutionary purpose of protecting the infant by prompting proximity with the caregiver and reducing the likelihood of harm. A child who has a secure attachment relationship is less likely to feel anxious upon separation because the child has confidence that the caregiver will return and will be protective should harm arise or danger ensue. A child who has not experienced sensitive and responsive care, however, and who thus does not believe that the caretaker will come to his or her aid, is said to have an "insecure" attachment relationship. Such a child may become anxious more frequently, even in relatively benign circumstances, compared to his or her "secure" counterpart. Chronic vigilance and anxiety, in turn, may set the stage for development of an anxiety disorder in insecure infants (Warren et al., 1997).

Ainsworth and colleagues (1978) described two types of insecure attachment relationships and the mother–child interactions that preceded them. Infants whose mothers frequently rejected them when the infant sought contact later tended to avoid their caretaker upon reunion after a brief separation. These infants were thought to avoid their mother as a way of avoiding the feelings they experienced in relation to their mother's unavailability (Sroufe, 1996). Avoidant infants appeared to displace or preempt their anxious feelings. The second type of insecure attachment relationship has been labeled "anxious/resistant" (Ainsworth et al., 1978). Mothers of these infants showed inconsistent or intrusive (i.e., either overly protective or overly demanding) caregiving. Infants of these mothers showed angry, resistant, and ambivalent feelings upon reunion. They appeared to display both anger at and anxiety toward their mothers. In marked contrast to avoidant infants, anxious/resistant infants appeared to "overtly experience and display their anxiety in a chronic manner" (Warren et al., 1997, p. 638). It is this latter group of insecure infants who are thought to be most at risk for development of anxiety disorder (Cassidy & Berlin, 1994; Manassis & Bradley, 1994; Mattis & Ollendick, 1997). Space permits only brief exploration of this literature in this chapter (see Sroufe, 1996, for a detailed discussion).

In one of the most interesting and informative studies in this area, Warren et al. (1997) followed a cohort of 172 children (91 males, 81 females) and their mothers over a 17.5-year period. Parents were primiparous mothers who were receiving prenatal care through a public health clinic; at the time of delivery, they ranged in age from 12 to 37 years (mean age was approximately 20 years), 62% were not married, 41% had not completed high school, and 84% were Caucasian (11% were African American and 5% were Native American or Hispanic). Mothers were of low socioeconomic status, and their lives were marked by a high degree of stress. These high-risk sociodemographic variables should be recalled in interpreting the findings that follow.

Quality of attachment relationship was assessed using the Strange Situation Test when the infants were 12 months of age (Ainsworth et al., 1978). This procedure consisted of eight episodes, including two brief separations from and reunions with the mother. The attachment classification is based primarily on reactions to the mother's return. Measures of temperament were obtained from nurses in the newborn nursery during the first few days of the infants' lives and again at home 7 and 10 days after birth (indices of "high reactivity," as described by Kagan, 1994, including motor activity, arousability, and regulation of responsiveness following arousal were obtained). Basically, children at risk show high levels of motor activity and crying in response to novel stimuli. Approximately 60% of these children later display behavioral inhibition (as described above; Kagan, 1994). Finally, past and present anxiety disorders (separation anxiety disorder, overanxious disorder, panic disorder, agoraphobia, social phobia, avoidant disorder, and obsessive-compulsive disorder) were assessed with a structured diagnostic interview when the 172 youth were 17.5 years of age.

Findings were complex, with 15% of the youth having at least one past or current anxiety disorder: 20 had one anxiety disorder, 5 had two anxiety disorders, and 1 had five anxiety disorders based on the structured diagnostic interview. Youth with anxiety disorder were, as infants, classified as anxious/resistant more frequently than youth without anxiety disorder (of interest, youth classified as avoidant as infants were more likely to present with other disorders). Of the adolescents who were not anxiously/resistantly attached, 13% developed anxiety disorders. In contrast, 28% of the youth who were anxiously/resistantly attached developed anxiety disorder, a twofold increase in risk. Zero-order correlations revealed that childhood and adolescent anxiety disorders were significantly related to nurses' temperament rating obtained during the first days of life and to temperament ratings of arousability obtained at 7 and 10 days of age, as well as anxious/resistant attachment style measured at 12 months of age. Hierarchical regression analyses indicated that measures of both infant temperament and attachment style predicted anxiety disorder. Anxious/resistant attachment specifically and consistently predicted anxiety disorder in children and adolescents, above and beyond the variables indexing temperament. Although the amount of variance accounted for in these regression analyses was modest (Multiple Rs ranged from .22 to .31), the findings are remarkable inasmuch as they were obtained approximately 17 years after the temperament measures were obtained and 16 years after the measurement of attachment style.

In a related study, Manassis et al. (1995) explored relations among behavioral inhibition, attachment style, and anxiety in children of 18 mothers with anxiety disorders, including 14 mothers with a primary diagnosis of panic disorder, 3 diagnosed with generalized anxiety disorder, and 1 with obsessive-compulsive disorder. All were Caucasian married women (mean age of 34) from varied socioeconomic backgrounds, and all were in treatment for anxiety disorder. Their children included 14 boys and 6 girls with a mean age of 36 months (with a standard deviation of 15 months). Behavioral inhibition and attachment security were measured in standard laboratory ways. Anxiety in the children was assessed with diagnostic criteria and a parent completed checklist.

Results of this interesting study revealed that 13 of the children of these anxious mothers were classified as inhibited and 7 as uninhibited (65% inhibited) and that 16 were classified as insecurely attached (unfortunately, avoidant and anxious/resistant insecure types were not differentiated) and 4 as securely attached (80% insecurely attached). Somewhat surprisingly, no significant relationship was found between behavioral inhibition and security of attachment (possibly because avoidant and anxious/resistant types were not specified, as in Warren et al., 1997). Three children met criteria for anxiety disorder: all three were classified as insecurely attached, with only one classified as behaviorally inhibited. However, mothers of inhibited children did report significantly more somatic problems on the parent checklist (and fewer destructive behaviors) than did mothers of uninhibited children. Finally, mothers of insecurely attached children reported more somatic problems, depression, and social withdrawal than did mothers of securely attached children on this same checklist. Thus, although insecurity of attachment was more closely related to anxiety disorder outcome than behavioral inhibition in this preliminary study, it appears these two risk factors exist independently, with no increased risk of inhibition in children who were insecurely attached and vice versa (although again it

should be recalled that Manassis and colleagues did not, unfortunately, differentiate between avoidant and anxious/resistant attachment styles in this study). Within this limitation, both behavioral inhibition and insecurity of attachment appear to confer risk, and independently so. It is not clear at this time whether or how behavioral inhibition and insecure attachment interact to increase risk of early anxiety (Manassis et al., 1995).

Results of these studies illustrate the developmental psychopathology approach to understanding deviance. They reveal the role of development in psychopathology, its origin and course, and its precursors and sequelae. Invariant relations are not obtained; rather, continuities and discontinuities prevail. Initial conditions such as behavioral inhibition and anxious/resistant attachment in infancy are not early manifestations of disorder and do not necessarily cause pathology in a direct, linear fashion. Rather, interactively or alone, they initiate a developmental pathway that is probabilistically related to later disorder and dependent on subsequent experiences that support or fail to support maintenance of the pathway (Warren et al., 1997). Children showing behavioral inhibition and/or anxious/resistant attachment relationships are at risk for anxiety problems. Such risk status, manifest in the transactions between the infant and the caregiver, is relational in nature. It is a malfunctional parent–child relationship context (as illustrated here with mothers) that defines developmental psychopathology. It is from the changing nature of this relationship that either adaptive or maladaptive behaviors emerge.

FUTURE DIRECTIONS

The field of developmental psychopathology is in its infancy, still more of a speculative, conceptual venture than an exacting science. Although it has enjoyed considerable success in the identification of risk factors for and precursors of psychopathology, understanding must be obtained regarding the mechanisms and processes by which such factors lead to emergence of disorder. To achieve this goal, considerable empirical research must be pursued. In what follows, we explore the issues requiring our concerted attention.

Mechanisms

A variety of mechanisms are involved in continuities and discontinuities of development, including biological or structural factors; habits, attitudes, and self-concepts; vulnerabilities and sensitivities; and environmental factors (Lease & Ollendick, 1993; Rutter, 1987). Developmental psychopathology is a comprehensive approach that strives to integrate these elements, a task that can best be accomplished by examining the person–environment transaction. Disordered behavior cannot be conceptualized as a static condition; rather, it is viewed in dynamic transaction with both intra- and extraorganismic forces. With regard to competence in negotiating developmental tasks, a transactional analysis would not propose that early competence predicts later competence in a rigid, deterministic fashion. Nor would it presuppose that if, at an early age, children do not adequately resolve a stage-salient developmental task (e.g., forming a secure attachment with the primary caregiver, developing autonomy, establishing effective peer relationships), they are destined to "fail" at subsequent tasks (Cicchetti & Schneider-Rosen, 1986). Capturing this dynamic transaction, however, is not an easy task.

The transactional analysis incorporates the notions of continuity and discontinuity and, at the same time, attempts to account for the factors that maintain, or lead to alterations in, the individual's capacity to resolve developmentally salient tasks. In extending this analysis to the assessment of competence at various states of the life span, Cicchetti and Schneider-Rosen (1986) have emphasized several important points that make our task somewhat easier. First, competence at one developmental period will positively influence the achievement of competence at the next period. Second, early competencies exert subtle influence toward adaptation throughout the life span because each developmental issue, though most important during one developmental period, is of continuing importance throughout the life cycle. Third, failure to achieve adaptation at one period makes adaptation more difficult at the next and, to a lesser extent, more difficult throughout the life span, because each issue continues to assume importance throughout the individual's development. Finally, various factors mediate early and later adaptation or maladaptation and

allow for the occurrence of alternative outcomes; in other words, early problems or deviations in the successful resolution of a developmental task may be countered by major changes in the individual's experience that result in the successful negotiation of subsequent developmental tasks. Conversely, mediating factors may also serve to dissipate the benefits of positive developmental experiences (Rutter, 1987).

Moreover, a transactional approach assumes that behavioral development occurs as a consequence of reciprocal relations between an active organism and an active environmental context (Lerner, 1986; Lerner et al., 1990; also see Bandura, 1977, 1986). For example, although acute stressors and chronic adversities can have a great impact on psychological functioning, the experiences impinge upon an active rather than a passive organism, and the effects are influenced by how individuals appraise the situation and respond to the adaptations involved. Individual differences in response originate in constitutional variations in susceptibility, in vulnerabilities, and resilience created in the social context and, in specific, characteristics of person–environment interactions (Kagan, 1994; Rutter, 1987; Sroufe, 1996). Experiences and contexts can change the individual, but individuals also create their own environments and thus affect their own development (Rutter, 1987; Ollendick & King, 1991b). It is in this bidirectional process that complex patterns of stability and change are found. The study of this process is, however, only in its infancy.

Processes

Developmental psychopathology emphasizes the study of the processes involved in continuity and discontinuity. This, too, is a complicated task. First, different concepts of continuity predict rather different patterns of statistical associations; therefore, there is no one direct way of testing for the strength of continuities and discontinuities from the infancy period to later phases in development (Rutter, 1987). Second, it is evident that many of the protective and risk factors operate through their effect, both direct and indirect, on chain reactions over time. This implies that the analysis of protective and risk processes must examine each of the individual links in such longitudinal chains (Rutter, 1985). Third, interactive processes must be considered over time as part of development and not just as some kind of chemistry at a single point in time when an individual encounters stress or adversity. Thus, cross-sectional multivariate analysis that treats all variables as if they interact at one point in time cannot test hypotheses regarding influences of protective and risk factors (Rutter, 1985). Rutter (1987) argues that traditional univariate and multivariate correlational analysis may either exaggerate or conceal continuities and discontinuities and suggests that if the processes involved in developmental linkages are to be identified, it will be necessary to undertake analyses appropriate for the detection of indirect chain effects and circular causal processes as well as direct main effects.

In a similar fashion, Lerner and his colleagues (1990), focusing on the plasticity of human development across the life span, suggest that research must reflect the nature of dynamic, interlevel interactions across time. This "requires a temporal/longitudinal and a relational/comparative orientation to research . . ." (p. 26). Examples of this type of research include the goodness-of-fit model of person–context relations (Thomas & Chess, 1977) and the intergenerational model of problem behavior and family relationships (Caspi & Elder, 1988; Elder et al., 1986). Although empirical support has been found for these and other models consistent with a developmental contextual or life-span perspective (e.g., Baltes, 1987; Featherman, 1985; Perlmutter, 1988), additional verification of this approach is sorely needed.

In conclusion, the field of developmental psychopathology will require considerable advances in the years ahead. Still, it puts forth a model of human behavior, and its variations, that, in a complex fashion, incorporates development as a central feature. Surely, greater understanding of the processes and mechanisms associated with variable developmental outcomes will be a key to the advancement of this young discipline. Much remains to be learned; however, as we noted in the first edition of this book (Lease & Ollendick, 1993), the model shows considerable promise.

REFERENCES

Achenbach, T.M. (1978). The Child Behavior Profile: I. Boys aged 6–11. *Journal of Consulting and Clinical Psychology, 46,* 478–488.

Achenbach, T.M. (1990a). Conceptualization of developmental psychopathology. In M. Lewis & S.M. Miller (Eds.), *Handbook of developmental psychopathology* (pp. 3–14). New York: Plenum Press.

Achenbach, T.M. (1990b). What is "developmental" about developmental psychopathology? In J. Rolf, A. Matsen, D. Cicchetti, K. Neuchterlein, & S. Weintraub (Eds.), *Risk and protective factors in the development of psychopathology* (pp. 29–48). New York: Cambridge University Press.

Adam, K.S., Sheldon-Keller, A.E., & West, M. (1996). Attachment organization and history of suicidal behavior in clinical adolescents. *Journal of Consulting and Clinical Psychology, 64,* 264–272.

Ainsworth, M.D.S., Blehar, M.C., Waters, E., & Wall, S. (1978). *Patterns of attachment: A psychological study of the strange situation.* Hillsdale, NJ: Lawrence Erlbaum.

Allen, J.P., Hauser, S.T., & Borman-Spurrell, E. (1996). Attachment theory as a framework for understanding sequelae of severe adolescent psychopathology: An 11-year follow-up study. *Journal of Consulting and Clinical Psychology, 64,* 254–263.

Arend, R., Gove, F.L., & Sroufe, L.A. (1979). Continuity of individual adaptation from infancy to kindergarten: A predictive study of ego-resiliency and curiosity in preschoolers. *Child Development, 50,* 950–959.

Baer, D.M. (1982). Behavior analysis and developmental psychology: Discussant comments. *Human Development, 25,* 357–361.

Baltes, P.B. (1987). Theoretical propositions of life span developmental psychology: On the dynamics between growth and decline. *Developmental Psychology, 23,* 611–626.

Bandura, A. (1977). *Social learning theory.* Englewood Cliffs, NJ: Prentice-Hall.

Bandura, A. (1986). *Social foundations of thought and action: A social cognitive theory.* Englewood Cliffs, NJ: Prentice-Hall.

Biederman, J., Rosenbaum, J.F., Hirshfeld, D.R., Faraone, S.V., Bolduc, M.G., Meminger, S.R., Kagan, J., Sniderman, N., & Reznick, S. (1990). Psychiatric correlates of behavioral inhibition in young children of parents with and without psychiatric disorders. *Archives of General Psychiatry, 47,* 21–26.

Bijou, S.W. (1976). *Child development: The basic stage of early childhood.* Englewood Cliffs, NJ: Prentice-Hall.

Birchnell, J. (1980). Women whose mothers die in childhood: An outcome study. *Psychological Medicine, 10,* 699–713.

Bowlby, J. (1973). *Attachment and loss: Separation, anxiety, and anger.* New York: Basic Books.

Bowlby, J. (1988). Developmental psychiatry comes of age. *American Journal of Psychiatry, 145,* 1–10.

Brown, G.W., Harris, T.O. & Bifulco, A. (1986). Long-term effects of early loss of parent. In M. Rutter, C.E. Izard, & P.B. Read (Eds.), *Depression in young people: Developmental and clinical perspectives* (pp. 251–296). New York: Guilford Press.

Carson, R.C. (1969). *Interaction concepts of personality.* Chicago: Aldine.

Caspi, A., & Elder, G.H., Jr. (1988). Childhood precursors of the life course: Early personality and life disorganization. In E.M. Hetherington, R.M. Lerner, & M. Perlmutter (Eds.), *Child development in lifespan perspective* (pp. 115–142). Hillsdale, NJ: Lawrence Erlbaum.

Cassidy, J., & Berlin, L.J. (1994). The insecure/ambivalent pattern of attachment: Theory and research. *Child Development, 65,* 971–991.

Cicchetti, D. (1989a). Developmental psychopathology: Past, present, and future. In D. Cicchetti (Ed.), *The emergence of a discipline: The Rochester symposium on developmental psychopathology* (Vol. 1, pp. 1–12). Hillsdale, NJ: Lawrence Erlbaum.

Cicchetti, D. (1989b). Developmental psychopathology: Some thoughts on its evolution. *Development and Psychopathology, 1,* 1–4.

Cicchetti, D., & Schneider-Rosen, K. 1986). An organizational approach to childhood depression. In M. Rutter, C.E. Izard, & P.B. Read (Eds.), *Depression in young people: Developmental and clinical perspectives* (pp. 71–134). New York: Guilford Press.

Cicchetti, D., & Sroufe, L.A. (1978). An organizational view of affect: Illustration from the study of Down's syndrome infants. In M. Lewis & L. Rosenblum (Eds.), *The development of affect* (pp. 309–350). New York: Plenum Press.

Cole-Detke, H., & Kobak, R. (1996). Attachment processes in eating disorder and depression. *Journal of Consulting and Clinical Psychology, 64,* 282–290.

Crittenden, P.M. (1985). *Children's strategies for coping with adverse home environments: Abuse and neglect.* Paper presented at the meeting of the Society for Research in Child Development, Toronto, Ontario, April 25–28.

Davis, M. (1992). The role of the amygdala in fear and anxiety. *Annual Review of Neuroscience, 15,* 353–375.

Elder, G.H., Jr., Caspi, A., & Downey, G. (1986). Problem behavior and family relationships: Life course and intergenerational themes. In A. Sorensen, F.E. Weinert, & L.R. Sherrod (Eds.), *Human development and the life course: Multidisciplinary perspectives* (pp. 293–340). Hillsdale, NJ: Lawrence Erlbaum.

Emde, R.N., & Sameroff, A.J. (1989). Understanding early relationship disturbances. In A.J. Sameroff & R.N. Emde (Eds.), *Relationship disturbances in early childhood* (pp. 3–16). New York: Basic Books.

Erickson, M.F., Egeland, B., & Pianta, R. (1989). The effects of maltreatment on the development of young children. In D. Cicchetti & V. Carlson (Eds.), *Child maltreatment: Theory and research on the causes and consequences of child abuse and neglect* (pp. 647–684). New York: Cambridge University Press.

Erikson, E.H. (1968). *Identity, youth, and crisis.* New York: Norton.

Featherman, D.M. (1985). Individual development and aging as a population process. In J.R. Nesselroade & A. von Eye (Eds.), *Individual development and social change: Explanatory analysis* (pp. 213–241). New York: Academic Press.

Fonagy, P., Leigh, T., Steele, M., Steele, H., Kennedy, R., Mattoon, G., Target, M., & Gerber, A. (1996). The relation of attachment status, psychiatric classification, and response to psychotherapy. *Journal of Consulting and Clinical Psychology, 64,* 22–31.

Freud, S. (1949). *Outline of psychoanalysis.* New York: Norton.

Gottlieb, G. (1970). Conceptions of prenatal behavior. In L.R. Aronson, E. Tobach, D.S. Lehrman, & J.S. Rosenblatt (Eds.), *Developmental evolution of behavior: Essays in memory of T.C. Schneirla* (pp. 111 137). San Francisco: W.H. Freeman.

Gray, J.A. (1982). *The neuropsychology of anxiety.* New York: Oxford University Press.

Gunnar-Vugnchten, M.R. (1978). Changing a frightening toy into a pleasant toy by allowing the infant to control its actions. *Developmental Psychology, 14,* 157–162.

Hagopian, L.P., & Ollendick, T.H. (1997). Anxiety disorders. In R.T. Ammerman & M. Hersen (Eds.), *Handbook of prevention and treatment with children and adolescents: Intervention in the real-world context.* New York: Wiley.

Hennessy, J.W., & Levine, S. (1979). Stress, arousal, and the pituitary-adrenal system: A psychoendocrine hypothesis. In J.M. Sprague & A.N. Epstein (Eds.), *Progress in psychobiology and physiological psychology* (pp. 133–178). New York: Academic Press.

Hinde, R.A., & Bateson, P. (1985). Discontinuities versus continuities in behavioral development and the neglect of process. *International Journal of Behavioral Development, 7,* 129–143.

Hirshfeld, D.R., Rosenbaum, J.F., Biederman, J., Bolduc, E.A., Faraone, S.V., Snidman, N., Reznick, J.S., & Kagan, J. (1992). Stable behavioral inhibition and its association with anxiety disorder. *Journal of the American Academy of Child and Adolescent Psychiatry, 31,* 103–111.

Hunt, J.McV. (1979). Psychological development: Early experience. *Annual Review of Psychology, 30,* 103–143.

John, R., Mednick, S. & Schulsinger, F. (1982). Teacher reports as a predictor of schizophrenia and borderline schizophrenia: A Bayesian decision analysis. *Journal of Abnormal Psychology, 91,* 399–413.

Kagan, J. (1989). Temperamental contributions to social behavior. *American Psychologist, 44,* 668–674.

Kagan, J. (1994). *Galen's prophecy.* New York: Basic Books.

Kagan, J., Reznick, J.S., & Gibbons, J. (1989). Inhibited and uninhibited types of children. *Child Development, 60,* 838–845.

Kagan, J., Reznick, J.S., & Snidman, N. (1987). The physiology and psychology of behavioral inhibition in children. *Child Development, 58,* 1457–1473.

Kagan, J., Reznick, J.S., & Snidman, N. (1988). Biological bases of childhood shyness. *Science, 240,* 167 171.

Kazdin, A.E. (1989). Developmental psychopathology: Current research, issues, and directions. *American Psychologist, 44,* 180–187.

Kennard, J., & Birchnell, J. (1982). The mental health of early separated women. *Acta Psychiatrica Scandinavia, 65,* 388–402.

Kohlberg, L., LaCrosse, J., & Ricks, D. (1972). The predictability of adult mental health from childhood behavior. In B. Wolman (Ed.), *Manual of child psychopathology.* New York: McGraw-Hill.

Lamb, M.E., Thompson, R.A., Gardner, W., & Charnov, E.L. (1985). *Infant–mother attachment: The origins and developmental significance of individual differences in strange situation behavior.* Hillsdale, NJ: Lawrence Erlbaum.

Lease, C.A., & Ollendick, T.H. (1993). Development and psychopathology. In A.S. Bellack & M. Hersen (Eds.), *Psychopathology in adulthood* (pp. 89–103). Boston: Allyn and Bacon.

Lerner, R.M. (1978). Nature, nurture, and dynamic interactionism. *Human Development, 21,* 1–20.

Lerner, R.M. (1979). A dynamic interactional concept of individual and social relationship development. In R. Burgess & T. Huston (Eds.), *Social exchange in developing relationships* (pp. 271–305). New York: Academic Press.

Lerner, R.M. (1986). *Concepts and theories of human development,* 2nd ed. New York: Random House.

Lerner, R.M., Hess, L.E., & Nitz, K. (1990). A developmental perspective on psychopathology. In M. Hersen & C.G. Last (Eds.), *Handbook of child and adult psychopathology: A longitudinal perspective* (pp. 9–32). New York: Pergamon Press.

Lewis, M., & Miller, S.M. (Eds.) (1990). *Handbook of developmental psychopathology.* New York: Plenum Press.

Lewis, M., Feiring, C., McGuffog, C., & Jaskir, J. (1984). Predicting psychopathology in six-year-olds from early social relations. *Child Development, 55,* 123–136.

Lyons-Ruth, K. (1996). Attachment relationships among children with aggressive behavior problems: The role of disorganized early attachment patterns. *Journal of Consulting and Clinical Psychology, 64,* 64–73.

Main, M. (1977). Analysis of a peculiar form of reunion behavior seen in some daycare children: Its history and sequelae in children who are home-reared. In R. Webb (Ed.), *Social development in daycare.* Baltimore: Johns Hopkins University Press.

Main, M.B., & Weston, & D.R. (1981). Security of attachment to mother and father: Related to conflict behavior and the readiness to establish new relationships. *Child Development, 52,* 932–940.

Manassis, K., & Bradley, S.J. (1994). The development of childhood anxiety disorders: Toward an integrated model. *Journal of Applied Developmental Psychology, 15,* 345–366.

Manassis, K., Bradley, S., Goldberg, S., Hood, J., & Swinson, R.P. (1995). Behavioural inhibition, attachment and anxiety in children of mothers with anxiety disorders. *Canadian Journal of Psychiatry, 40,* 87–92.

Matas, L., Arend, R.A., & Sroufe, L.A. (1978). Continuity of adaptation in the second year: The relationship between quality of attachment and later competence. *Child Development, 49,* 547–556.

Mattis, S.G., & Ollendick, T.H. (1997). Children's cognitive responses to the somatic symptoms of panic. *Journal of Abnormal Child Psychology, 25,* 47–57.

Ollendick, T.H., Hagopian, L.P., & King, N.J. (1997). Specific phobias in children. In G. Davey (Ed.), *Phobias: A handbook of description, treatment, and theory* (pp. 201–224). Oxford: Wiley.

Ollendick, T.H., & King, N. (1991a). Developmental factors in child behavioral assessment. In P.R. Martin (Ed.), *Handbook of behavior therapy and psychological sciences: An integrated approach* (pp. 57–72). New York: Pergamon Press.

Ollendick, T.H., & King, N.J. (1991b). Origins of childhood fears: An evaluation of Rachman's theory of fear acquisition. *Behaviour Research and Therapy, 29,* 117–123.

Ollendick, T.H., Weist, M.D., Borden, M.C., & Greene, R.W. (1992). Sociometric status and academic, behavioral, and psychological adjustment: A five-year longitudinal study. *Journal of Consulting and Clinical Psychology, 60,* 80–87.

Parker, G. (1983). *Parental overprotection: A risk factor for psychosocial development.* New York: Grune & Stratton.

Perlmutter, M. (1988). Cognitive development in lifespan perspective: From description of differences to explanation of changes. In E.M. Hetherington, R.M. Lerner, & M. Perlmutter (Eds.), *Child development in lifespan perspective* (pp. 191–214). Hillsdale, NJ: Lawrence Erlbaum.

Piaget, J. (1950). *The psychology of intelligence.* New York: Harcourt Brace.

Pianta, R.C., Egeland, B., & Adam, E.K. (1996). Adults' attachment classification and self-reported psychiatric symptomatology as assessed by the Minnesota Multiphasic Personality Inventory—2. *Journal of Consulting and Clinical Psychology, 64,* 273–281.

Plomin, R., Nitz, K., & Rowe, D.C. (1990). Behavioral genetics and aggressive behavior in children. In M. Lewis & S.M. Miller (Eds.), *Handbook of developmental psychopathology* (pp. 119–134). New York: Plenum Press.

Quinton, D., Rutter, M., & Liddle, C. (1984). Institutional rearing, parenting difficulties, and marital support. *Psychological Medicine, 14,* 102–124.

Roff, M., & Ricks, D. (Eds.). (1970). *Life history research in psychopathology* (Vol. 1). Minneapolis: University of Minnesota Press.

Rosenbaum, J.F., Biederman, J., Gersten, M., Hirshfeld, D., Meminger, S.R., Herman, J.B., Kagan, J., Reznick, S., & Snidman, N. (1988). Behavioral inhibition in children of parents with panic disorder and agoraphobia: A controlled study. *Archives of General Psychiatry, 45,* 463–470.

Rosenstein, D.S., & Horowitz, H.A. (1996). Adolescent attachment and psychopathology. *Journal of Consulting and Clinical Psychology, 64,* 244–253.

Rutter, M. (1971). Parent–child separation: Psychological effect on the children. *Journal of Child Psychology and Psychiatry, 12,* 233–260.

Rutter, M. (1979). Protective factors in children's responses to stress and disadvantage. In M.W. Kent & J.E. Rolf (Eds.), *Primary prevention of psychopathology: Vol. 3. Social competence in children* (pp. 49–74). Hanover, NH: University Press of New England.

Rutter, M. (1981). Stress, coping and development: Some issues and come questions. *Journal of Child Psychology and Psychiatry, 22,* 323–356.

Rutter, M. (1983). Continuities and discontinuities in socio-emotional development: Empirical and conceptual perspective. In R. Emde & R. Harmon (Eds.), *Continuities and discontinuities in development* (pp. 105–144). Hillsdale, NJ: Lawrence Erlbaum.

Rutter, M. (1985). Resilience in the face of adversity: Protective factors and resistance to psychiatric disorder. *British Journal of Psychiatry, 147,* 498–611.

Rutter, M. (1986). The developmental psychopathology of depression: Issues and perspectives. In M. Rutter, C.E. Izard, & P.B. Read (Eds.), *Depression in young people: Developmental and clinical perspectives* (pp. 3–32). New York: Guilford Press.

Rutter, M. (1987). Continuities and discontinuities from infancy. In J.D. Osofsky (Ed.), *Handbook of infant development,* 2nd ed. (pp. 1256–1296). New York: Wiley.

Rutter, M. (1995). Clinical implications of attachment concepts: Retrospect and prospect. *Journal of Clinical Psychology and Psychiatry, 36,* 549–571.

Rutter, M., & Quinton, D. (1984). Long-term follow-up of women institutionalized in childhood: Factors promoting good functioning in adult life. *British Journal of Developmental Psychology, 18,* 225–234.

Schneider-Rosen, K., Braunwald, K.G., Carlson, V., & Cicchetti, D. (1985). Current perspectives in attachment theory: Illustration from the study of maltreated infants. In I. Bretherton & E. Waters (Eds.), *Monographs of the Society for Research in Child Development, 50*(1–2), 194–210.

Skinner, B.F. (1938). *The behavior of organisms.* New York: Appleton.

Speltz, M.L., Greenberg, M.T., & Deklyen, M. (1990). Attachment in preschoolers with disruptive behavior: A comparison of clinic-referred and nonproblem children. *Development and Psychopathology, 2,* 31–46.

Sroufe, L.A. (1979). The coherence of individual development: Early care, attachment, and subsequent developmental issues. *American Psychologist, 34,* 834–841.

Sroufe, L.A. (1996). *Emotional development.* New York: Cambridge University Press.

Sroufe, L.A., & Rutter, M. (1984). The domain of developmental psychopathology. *Child Development, 55,* 17–29.

Swann, W.B., Jr. (1983). Self-verification: Bringing social reality into harmony with the self. In J. Suls & A.G. Greenwald (Eds.), *Psychological perspectives on the self* (Vol. 2). Hillsdale, NJ: Lawrence Erlbaum.

Thomas, A., & Chess, S. (1977). *Temperament and development.* New York: Brunner/Mazel.

Thompson, W.R., & Grusec, J.E. (1970). Studies of early experience. In P.H. Mussen (Ed.), *Carmichael's manual of child psychology* (pp. 565–654). New York: Wiley.

Tobach, E., & Greenberg, G. (1984). The significance of T.C. Schnerila's contribution to the concept of levels of integration. In G. Greenberg & E. Tobach (Eds.), *Behavioral evolution and integrative levels* (pp. 1–7). Hillsdale, NJ: Lawrence Erlbaum.

van der Kolk, B.A., & van der Hart, O. (1989). Pierre Janet and the breakdown of adaptation in psychological trauma. *American Journal of Psychiatry, 146,* 1530–1538.

Wadsworth, M.E.J. (1984). Early stress and associations with adult health, behavior, and parenting. In N.R. Butler & B.D. Corner (Eds.), *Stress and disability in childhood: The long-term problems* (pp. 100–104). Bristol: John Wright.

Warren, S.L., Huston, L., Egeland, B., & Sroufe, L.A. (1997). Child and adolescent anxiety disorders and early attachment. *Journal of the American Academy of Child and Adolescent Psychiatry, 36,* 637–644.

Waters, E., Wippman, J., & Sroufe, L.A. (1979). Attachment, positive affect, and competence in the peer group: Two studies in construct validation. *Child Development, 50,* 821–829.

Zenah, C.H., Anders, T.F., Seifer, R., & Stern, D.N. (1989). Implications of research on infant development for psychodynamic theory and practice. *Journal of the American Academy of Child and Adolescent Psychiatry, 28,* 657–668.

CHAPTER 7

A SOCIOLOGICAL PERSPECTIVE: ANTISOCIAL BEHAVIOR AND VIOLENCE

Patricia R. Koski
William D. Mangold
University of Arkansas

INTRODUCTION

In this chapter, we summarize contemporary sociological perspectives on antisocial behavior, with special emphasis on interpersonal violence. We will treat concepts of antisocial behavior and deviance synonymously as behaviors that violate the commonly accepted standards of a culture. The sine qua non of social life is conformity to what anthropologists call the "rules of living" (Linton, 1936). However, not everyone conforms to all of the rules all of the time. Some rules are trivial and are broken at one time or another by everyone. Serious violations occur less often but are committed occasionally by large numbers of individuals. Frequent serious acts of deviance, however, are committed by a relatively small number of individuals. In fact, when all forms of serious deviance are considered, a relatively small number of individuals are responsible for the bulk of the total volume of the serious offenses (Wolfgang, 1987; Wolfgang, Sellin, & Figlio, 1972).

The main emphasis of this chapter is on the violation of rules that are important to a large number of people in society and on those violations that are subject to formal pressures to prevent their occurrence. We will first examine the general sociological perspective on antisocial behavior, then contrast it with the medical perspective as expressed in the *Diagnostic and Statistical Manual of Mental Disorders* (DSM) (American Psychiatric Association, 1994). In the remaining sections, we will illustrate the sociological perspective by focusing specifically on violence.

BASIC PREMISES

The Sociological Perspective

Whereas a psychological or psychiatric model emphasizes the characteristics of the individual, the sociological perspective stresses the importance of social interactions in understanding any human behavior. This is particularly relevant to the study of deviance in two ways. First, sociology reminds us that norms and laws are human creations, and so is the definition of what constitutes "devance." Second, the sociological assumption is that individual characteristics are not sufficient to explain the etiology of deviance. We discuss each of these ideas in this section.

Stated simply, the cause of deviance is social norms. Because it is the social group that defines the rules for what is and what is not acceptable behavior and applies sanctions to particular people who violate them, deviance is not a quality inherent in the behavior of the individual but, rather, a consequence of the application by others of rules and sanctions to an "offender." A deviant is a person to whom the label has been successfully applied (Becker, 1963, p. 91). The key issue, then, is not the behavior per se, but the audience that confers a deviant status (Erickson, 1962). Because of the subjective nature of judgments about deviance, there is no way for a scientific "referee" to establish the correctness of the response (Schur, 1980, p. 10).

Sociologists and anthropologists find that while many norms arise from the need to regulate behaviors that can disrupt the social order, the definitions of the social order that needs regulation and of the behaviors that threaten it are highly variable from one culture to another and even within a particular culture. Even so-called cultural universals, such as prohibitions against incest or killing another person, are subject to a near infinite variety of cultural and circumstantial exceptions. For example, although homicide is regarded as an extreme act of deviance in all societies, the exact definition of what constitutes homicide varies from culture to culture. Even in a single society, legitimate exceptions from the norm are also variable; the notion of justifiable homicide in the United States is a case in point.

Emile Durkheim was among the first to observe that deviance is necessary to preserve the moral order of a society. Deviance, rather than being a destructive social force, is essential for societies because it affords the opportunity for nondeviants to reaffirm their shared sense of morality. Thus, public awareness of deviance and the application of sanctions produce a sense of shared outrage and solidarity among nondeviants (Durkheim, 1964, p. 102). Moreover, there is an intimate connection between deviance and social power: To the extent that some social groups have

more power, they will have a better chance of having their definitions of deviance imposed on others. What is deviant, then, to use Schur's (1980) terminology, is the "objectionableness" of an act as perceived by the powerful. In a very real sense, the definition of deviance can be viewed as the outcome of a power struggle between groups who hold competing definitions of morality.

This perspective insists that "deviance" and "normality" are relative and situational, not absolute. However, people often engage in deviance even when the norms are well defined and the label of "deviance" is likely to be applied. This raises the issue of etiology. As mentioned previously, the sociological lens focuses not on the characteristics of the individual, but on interpersonal interactions, the society, and the culture. This emphasis will be illustrated in the last part of the chapter in our discussion of violence.

The Sociological versus the DSM or Medical Model

In its purest form, the medical model of psychopathology assumes that the source of disorder is within the individual and that, through the systematic observation of behavior patterns, biological or psychological sources can be discovered and cured (Draguns & Phillips, 1971; McCaghy, 1976). Many sociologists (e.g., Schur, 1980; also see the review of this literature by Conrad, 1992) are highly critical of psychiatric classification and argue that it should be abandoned entirely for two reasons: It does not take into account the definitional and power issues discussed previously, nor does it adequately consider the role of social factors in producing deviance (Wheaton, 1978). Sociologists are not alone in their criticism. Draguns and Phillips (1971, p. 4), in their critique of the DSM model, go so far as to claim that "the evidence of biological correlates of maladaptation, neurosis and characterological disorders, is for the most part fragmentary, controversial, or negative." Thomas Szasz, a psychiatrist, argues:

Every "ordinary" illness that persons have, cadavers also have. A cadaver may thus be said to "have" cancer, pneumonia, or myocardial infarction. The only illness a cadaver surely cannot "have" is a mental illness. Bodily illness is something the patient has, whereas mental illness is really something he *is* or *does*. The mind (whatever it is) is not an organ or part of the body. Hence, it cannot be diseased in the same sense as the body can. When we speak of mental illness, then, we speak metaphorically. To say that a person's mind is sick is like saying that the economy is sick or that a joke is sick. When metaphor is mistaken for realities and used for social purposes, then we have the making of myth. (Szasz, 1974, pp. 99–100; emphasis in original)

Of course, there is a range of applicability of the medical model: Organic bases do exist for many disorders; biochemical factors do affect behavior; and genetic factors have been identified for various disorders. However, if disorders could be arrayed on a continuum reflecting the extent to which identifiable genetic or biologic factors are involved, then there is a wide variety of behaviors that may be called maladaptive but whose origins are unknown. At the opposite end of the continuum are many forms of deviance that are clearly biological in origin but are too trivial for serious debate. Our concern in this chapter is not with either end of the continuum, but with the broad range of behaviors that have serious consequences for both the individual and society but are not known to have any medical origin. Given that only a small fraction of entries in the DSM can be linked to known organic, biological, or genetic factors, then there is ample opportunity for disagreement with the utility of the DSM to classify many forms of behavior.

The area of greatest conflict between the sociological and medical models of deviance is where symptoms are ideational and behavioral. Sociologists argue that these symptoms cannot adequately be interpreted and classified without knowledge of the norms of the culture or subculture to which the individual belongs. Whereas physical disorders remain the same from one culture to another, mental disorders do not. Different cultures simply have sharply differing definitions of deviance (Kleinman, 1979). As discussed earlier, deviation is not a purely objective phenomenon. Because the distinction between deviant and nondeviant is always socially constructed, the meaning of behavior is never inherent in the behavior itself. Moreover, the relationship between power and deviance has important implications for the medical model of antisocial behavior. To the extent that physicians are in a position of power to define what is and what is not antisocial, behaviors

once regarded as "wrong" or "immoral" are now explained by medical models (Conrad & Schneider, 1980). Starr (1982) and Zola (1972), among others, argue that the medicalization of deviance serves to extend the influence and control of physicians in society. In this sense, the physician replaces the theologian or the judge as an agent of social control. Three examples will clarify the relationship between the power to define and resulting social labels of deviance. Hyperkinesis can be treated with Ritalin, but, like many disorders, the hyperkinetic disorders were in fact "discovered" only after it was learned that Ritalin could calm overactive children. Simply stated, the "cure" caused the "disorder." Similarly, millions of homosexuals were "cured" in 1973 when the American Psychiatric Association eliminated homosexuality as a specific disorder (Bayer, 1981). Finally, "drapetomania" was once seriously proposed as a medical condition of slaves; the major "symptom" of the disorder was running away from the master (Szasz, 1973).

This issue is not simply an intellectual one, but an ideological one as well. To the extent that deviance springs from the individual, then its treatment is directed toward the individual. However, if the source of deviance involves the larger social environment, then the environment as well as the individual must be "treated." However, the latter involves social reform and intervention, which are likely to be resisted by individuals and institutions with a vested interest in preserving the status quo.

In the rest of the chapter, we focus on violent behavior, rather than on deviant behavior in general. This will allow us to demonstrate the use of a sociological perspective with a specific example of behavior, and to examine a relevant body of literature.

INTERPERSONAL VIOLENCE

What is interpersonal violence? Even a brief overview of this question will leave little doubt about the complexity of the concept. Although definitional issues will not be considered in detail, it is necessary to delineate some salient differences among violence, interpersonal violence, and aggression (a detailed treatment of definitional issues can be found in Megargee, 1969, or Toch, 1969). It is important to keep in mind that what constitutes interpersonal violence in general, and criminal violence in particular, is socially defined. In addition to the nature of the act, all of the following will help determine whether the act is defined as violence: the personal and social characteristics of the victim, the offender, the observer, and the setting in which the act occurs.

For our purposes, *violence* is the application of force that is intended to cause injury or destruction to property or another person—interpersonal violence targets people exclusively (Megargee, 1969). Unintended personal injury is excluded, but an intentional act, successful or not, is included. Thus, arson or bombing directed exclusively toward property will not be regarded as interpersonal violence, but a punch that misses its target is. Although terrorism, genocide, lynchings, and police brutality are frequently regarded as interpersonal violence, these will not be considered here because they involve political issues that would take us too far afield.

Aggression refers to a wide range of assertive and intrusive behaviors and/or characteristics. While aggression may lead to violence, it can also find expression in a variety of other forms, such as business, athletic competition, and the like. Aggression can be covert, but violence cannot. A final difference between violence and aggression has important implications for study: Because violence involves injury and often is a criminal act, it cannot be studied experimentally. This limits research to naturalistic and correlational studies that use readily available variables that may not be specifically tailored to important theoretical issues (Megargee, 1982, p. 89).

Types of Interpersonal Violence

Because of the bewildering array of violent behaviors and the methodological limitations cited here, classification schemes that are based on reported offenses abound. Perhaps the simplest and most common means of classifying violence is in terms of the illegality of the act, such as presented in the Uniform Crime Reports (e.g., murder and nonnegligent manslaughter, aggravated assault, forcible rape). Similarly, there are categorizations that cut across criminal law, such as the various types of family or domestic violence (spouse, child, sibling, and elderly abuse). Nonetheless, although subcategories exist (gang rape, prison rape, date rape), little analytic ad-

vantage is gained from creating detailed categories of violent acts because, although the characteristics of victims may be made more homogeneous, offender characteristics remain too diverse for meaningful interpretation (Megargee, 1982, p. 91).

Types of Violent Offenders

Alternatively, classification schemes may be based on the characteristics of the offender. The motivation of the violent person is one widely used criterion to create typologies of interpersonal violence. At a high level of abstraction, the distinction between instrumental and expressive (or angry) violence is perhaps the most common. Thus, violent acts are classified in terms of the extent to which they are a response to an emotion (a response intended to injure) or are a means to an end, such as robbery.

The distinction between "internal" and "external" motivation also is frequently used. The presence, severity, and nature of psychopathology provides a major continuum for the analysis of internal motivation. Other researchers view the control over aggressive drives as the primary axis for delineating internal sources of violence. Megargee's "overcontrolled" and "undercontrolled" types are well-known examples (Megargee, 1966). Numerous syndromes exist for internally motivated individuals (see Megargee, 1982). Cultural or subcultural elements and situational factors are the primary explanatory variables for external sources of violence. The assumed propensity toward violence among lower-class persons is an example. Some variables, such as the use of alcohol, are treated as both internal and external factors (this is discussed at length later on). Even where the internal motivation of the actor is the focus, however, we must remember that this motivation is always embedded in social meanings. Thus, the person's actions must be seen in the larger context of norms and values. For example, the male who responds violently to an insult to his wife may be conforming to subcultural norms; if he did not respond in such a manner, people would consider him deviant. Although motivation may appear to be internal (the man feels the insult and chooses to respond with violence because he is unable to control himself), the "internal urge" producing violence is, actually, behavior that conforms to socially defined norms.

An important methodological issue cuts across all classifications of violence and illustrates a basic issue in any attempt to count deviance and crime. That is, violence in general, and specific forms of violence, such as rape and domestic violence in particular, are selectively reported. This means that the characteristics of victims and offenders in the general population will differ from the characteristics of those who come to the attention of authorities. Unless the characteristics (social and economic as well as psychodynamic) of both victims and offenders are obtained from representative samples, and not only from those receiving some form of intervention, then both classification schemes and causal factors will be misunderstood. For example, use of self-selected or clinical samples of abused women guarantees the conclusion that not only do poor women experience more domestic violence than their more affluent counterparts, but also that they differ in terms of other characteristics as well. This is because women from middle- and upper-income families have more private alternatives available and are less likely to use public institutions such as police and domestic abuse centers. In a similar vein, the extent of psychopathology among different types of violent offenders may also be an artifact because only the most serious or bizarre offenses are likely to attract the attention of clinicians.

EPIDEMIOLOGY

How much violence is there in the United States, and who are the violent? To answer these questions, we must immediately make a choice—whether to discuss violence in general or violent *criminal* behavior. Of course, there are good reasons to make either choice. Here, we will discuss violent criminal behavior. Estimates of criminal behavior can be made on the basis of official reports of crimes known to the police, such as the Uniform Crime Reports published by the Federal Bureau of Investigation, victimization reports such as the National Crime Victimization Survey, or official reports of convictions or incarcerations published by the Bureau of Justice Statistics. In addition, self-reports by offenders may be used. A primary issue in the counting of violent crime, then, is in deciding whether to use official reports on offenders, official reports of victimization, or self-reports. Caution is needed when interpreting the meaning of interpersonal violence from statistics on those processed through the criminal justice system, as only a fraction of violent acts come to the attention of authorities. For example, victimization studies based on representative samples find that only 37% of completed rapes and about 6 in 10 aggravated assaults are reported to the police (Dobrin, Wiersema, Loftin, & McDowall, 1996). Because the characteristics of both victim and offender are related to the likelihood that an offense will be reported (Reid, 1990), the number and characteristics of individuals appearing in official statistics are the result of a series of decisions about the nature of the offender and offense. Because control groups (persons not processed through the criminal justice system) are not studied, causal variables are likely to be confounded by the self-selective nature of the criminal justice system. The mistaken identification of body build as a cause of crime by early criminologists (e.g., Lombroso, 1911; Glueck & Glueck, 1956) provides a clear example of this problem. Even imputing "seriousness" or "dangerousness" from the Uniform Crime Reports is risky. The difference between assault and homicide may simply be that the victim dies—perhaps a chance consequence of an available weapon, an injury to a vulnerable part of the body, or a delay in receiving medical attention. Moreover, official statistics reflect decisions made by social control officials, such as determining if an offense has even occurred. Only a fraction of violent behaviors result in arrest, and an even smaller proportion result in prosecution. The likelihood of arrest is further reduced if the victim and offender are known to each other (Buzawa, Austin, & Buzawa, 1995). This issue is of paramount importance when considering specific forms of violence such as domestic violence and rape, where the perceived credibility of the victim as a witness is an important determinant of whether the violence will be defined as an official offense.

This discussion has implications not only for the study of violence, but for all deviance. When we rely on official counts of crime, the issues of definition we discussed previously are made very real. In order for behavior to become a crime, it must be defined as and responded to as criminal by someone who has the power to attach that label. Given that not all potential acts of deviance will be so labeled, characteristics of the offender, the social control official, the situation, and the social control bureaucracies will all play a role.

Keeping these limitations in mind, we use official statistics of crimes known to the police (the Uniform Crime Reports, or UCR) and the National Crime Victimization Survey (NCVS). From the UCR we refer to only aggravated assault, robbery, nonnegligent manslaughter, murder, and forcible rape; the NCVS reports only on robbery, rape, and assault. Keep in mind that this discussion of epidemiology refers only to these crimes. Using arrest data (UCR) for 1996, these violent crimes tend to be committed by young, minority males: 46% of arrests were of people under 25, 85% were of males, and 45% were members of minority groups (Maguire & Pastore, 1998). These offenders are also more likely to be poor (U.S. Department of Justice, 1997). Moreover, victimization data indicate that the victims of violent crime have the same characteristics as the offenders: They tend to be young, male, poor and members of minority groups (U.S. Department of Justice, 1997).

Homicide and assault are both class endogamous (e.g., poor against poor) and are structured in terms of primary group relationships (victim and offender are frequently members of the same primary group). The incidence of violent crime follows a different pattern over the life cycle than that of other offenses. Property crime (burglary) reaches its peak at age 17 and drops to half of its maximum by age 21. However, aggravated assault reaches its maximum at age 21 but falls to half its maximum at age 46 (*Science,* 1986, p. 26).

Thus, it is a criminological truism that these street crimes, and violent crimes in general, are done by poor, young, usually minority males (Hagan, 1994). It is important to note that because African Americans tend to be overrepresented among the poor, there is a correlation between race and poverty that is not controlled for in official data. Additionally, police practices are likely to lead to more arrests in lower-class neighborhoods than in middle- and upper-class neighborhoods, so the ways in which race is causally associated with crime are still the subject of much debate. Pilivian and Briar (1964) found that the primary determinant of juvenile arrest was *not* the nature of the offense but whether the youth was hostile or cooperative when questioned by an officer. To the extent that minority youth and police interact in an arena of mutual suspicion or even hostility, then, dif-

ferential rates of arrest are to be expected even if minority youths are no more likely to commit an offense than other youths.

The reader is again reminded to use data on the epidemiology of crime with caution. Many transformations are required to get from the occurrence of a crime to the ability to count it; each of those transformations (e.g., an officer's decision to arrest, a victim's ability to remember) involves unknown factors that are difficult to control, and it is impossible to know how they affect the count. For example, in their review of 35 studies of the relationship between crime and social class, Tittle, Villemez, and Smith (1978) found a stronger correlation between social class and crime in studies using official statistics than among those based on self-reported offenses. Even nearly 20 years later, the social class and crime debate is far from settled (Hagan, 1994).

Data from other sources both provide support for and suggest modifications of official arrest and victimization reports. In a representative national sample, Straus, Gelles, and Steinmetz (1980) found an inverse relationship between family violence and income, with households in which the male was employed part time or unemployed having the most severe violence. This relationship was reconfirmed in a study done 9 years later (Gelles, 1992). However, Shields, McCall, and Hanneke (1988) and Kandel-Englander (1992) found that men who were only violent toward family members had higher occupational status than men who were violent only toward nonfamily members or violent toward both family and nonfamily members.

ETIOLOGY: THEORETICAL PERSPECTIVES AND EMPIRICAL RESEARCH

In this section, we develop a typology of theories and discuss relevant empirical findings. It is important to keep in mind the previous discussions about the definition of violence and the difficulties in establishing epidemiology. How one defines violence and where one thinks it is most likely to occur will both affect and be affected by one's assumptions about human nature, and by whether one is attempting to explain crime or noncriminal behavior.

There are so many theories of violence that it is virtually impossible to describe them all concisely,

Consequently, we develop a typology of theories that allows us to address the major research orientations and summarize typical research findings through the use of representative theories in each category.

Explanations for human behavior typically incorporate a set of assumptions about what it means to be human in a biological sense. Sociologists often do not make these assumptions explicit, and usually it is not necessary to do so because biological capacities are largely irrelevant to what we are seeking to explain. For example, the fact that humans feel hunger does not explain why some are vegetarians and some not. In explaining aggressive and violent behavior, however, many sociologists implicitly or explicitly incorporate biological assumptions. Thus, in developing a typology of theories, it is useful to start here, even though the focus of any sociological theory is on interpersonal and environmental variables.

Another dimension necessary for developing a typology of theories is whether the theorist is explaining deviant or conforming violence. Often we take for granted that violence is deviant and explain it in that way. However, it is obvious that there is much violence that is not deviant and, indeed, is often admired, as Blumenthal, Kahn, Andrews, and Head (1972) clearly document.

On the basis of these two dimensions, it is possible to develop a three-by-two categorization scheme that allows us to group theories with similar explanations of human violence. The first dimension, biological assumptions, consists of three mutually exclusive beliefs: (a) that humans are biologically or genetically violent; (b) that humans are biologically or genetically nonviolent; (c) that humans are biologically neutral. The second dimension consists of two parts: that the behavior being explained is (a) deviant or (b) conforming. Combining these two dimensions produces the following:

	Violence Is:	
Humans are:	Deviant	Conforming
Biologically violent	1	2
Biologically nonviolent	3	4
Biologically neutral	5	6

Categories 1 and 2

These theorists make the assumption that people are biologically violent—that is, that violence can best be explained by reference to innate biological mechanisms. Although there is also recognition that society is important in explaining violence, the impetus to violence is in the genes or hormones (Daly & Wilson, 1988; Hernstein, 1995; but see Gelles, 1991; Gelles & Harrop, 1991). Society is important in terms of providing opportunity for the violence, but, more important, society constructs "dams" against illegitimate violence. The image to be used with these theories is that of a force being held back (as in Freud's theory that aggression is a means to reduce tension but cannot always be indulged; Hall, 1954). These dams, being socially constructed, are necessarily weaker than the biological predispositions but are usually successful in controlling the aggression. Thus, a significant difference between theories in category 1 and category 2 is that theories in the first category pay attention to social prohibitions, whereas those in category 2 need not, because such prohibitions do not exist. Society is primarily important, then, in whether it allows the violence or prohibits it. Instances of deviant violence occur when the aggressive impulses of "the human animal" overcome the weaker social barriers. Instances of conforming violence occur because people are aggressive and use available outlets for that aggression. A corollary assumption is that there must be an outlet for human aggression, a catharsis, or the aggression will break down the dam and occur in deviant ways.

A variation on this assumption is that some groups or types of individuals are biologically violent and some are not. For example, often these theorists assume that men, but not women, have these instincts or hormones for violence. Another version is Eysenck's argument that there are differences in the autonomic nervous system that biologically predispose some people to crime (Kraska, 1989).

Alternatively, theorists such as E.O. Wilson (1978) see an important interplay between biology and the environment: "innateness refers to the measurable probability that a trait will develop in a specified set of environments, not to the certainty that the trait will develop in all environments" (p. 100). Rather than the "drive–discharge" or catharsis theory suggested before, Wilson argues that aggression is an inherent trait or "potential" that is realized through learning.

Those who start with the assumption that people are biologically violent necessarily assume that we are all capable of violence under conditions that break down the socially constructed barriers holding back the aggressive drives, or under conditions in which there are no social barriers against the violence. These theories may be biological, psychological, or sociological. We focus on those theories that aid in the understanding of a sociological or social-psychological perspective, regardless of the discipline of the author.

Zoologist Wilson (1975) argues that there are nine basic forms of aggression: territorial, dominance, sexual, parental, disciplinary, weaning, moralistic, predatory, and antipredatory. Sociologists working in this area typically are not as explicit about when aggression will occur. However, there are exceptions, such as van den Berghe (1974), who argues that resource competition is the key variable that affects aggression both directly and indirectly through territoriality and hierarchy.

For other sociologists, the impetus for violence is taken as a given—humans are violent unless constrained by social norms—and explaining the violence, then, focuses mostly on the relative strength of biological urges and the social barriers. Where social barriers do not exist, the biological urges will be given free play. Where barriers do exist, either the social norms have been weakened or the urges made stronger so as to overcome the barriers. Thus, there will be two general categories of theories: those that focus on the presence or absence and strength of social barriers and those that focus on the strength of the biological urges. In either case, no sociologist will argue that biology, by itself, produces aggression.

Where social barriers are either absent or weak, there are no constraints on violent or antisocial behavior. One example of such a category is found in some versions of anomie theory (Lee, 1995), in which it is assumed that society is in a condition of normlessness or that people are not sufficiently committed to the values of society. Another example is a version of Wolfgang and Ferracuti's (1967) "subculture of violence" hypothesis. Although Wolfgang and Ferracuti did not start with the assumption that hu-

mans are biologically violent, others interpret their theory in this way. Wolfgang and Ferracuti suggest that a subculture exists within the lower classes in which norms and values reinforce and encourage the use of violence in interpersonal interactions. In his reference to this theory, Elliott (1983), an M.D., argues that some people do not "learn to [reduce their primitive drives to a socially acceptable level] because they have been brought up in a subculture where violent behavior is condoned or even encouraged as a means of survival" (p. 85). Note that such an interpretation of Wolfgang and Ferracuti does not suggest that subcultural norms teach violence but, rather, that they allow it because social barriers against the violence have been weakened or made nonexistent by the subculture.

In contrast, other theories focus on the strength of the violent urges (e.g., Daly & Wilson, 1988). When the urge to violence is sufficiently strong, it may overcome almost any social barrier. Some theorists speak of hormonal changes, such as those caused by changes in temperature (e.g., Michael & Zumpe, 1983). Another important set of theories focuses on the link between alcohol use and violence. There appears to be a well-established correlation between alcohol use and some types of aggression (e.g., Collins, 1988; Taylor & Leonard, 1983). However, the explanation for the correlation will differ with the underlying assumptions about human nature. Keep in mind that theories in this category see the link in this way: Alcohol must somehow reduce the social inhibitions against violence; thus, alcohol is seen as a disinhibitor. Collins (1988) argues that the disinhibition theory has not received empirical support and suggests that it is simplistic because it does not take adequate notice of social and cultural variables. Indeed, not all individuals react to alcohol in the same way (Taylor & Leonard, 1983). One could consider this a challenge to the assumption that all humans are potentially violent, because an explanatory model that sees alcohol as physiologically reducing the inhibitions against violence should see this as invariant (cf. Taylor & Leonard, 1983).

However, although we should all become aggressive at some level of intoxication, given this theory, the exact mix of biological and social factors that produces violence may well differ among individuals. Moreover, both an increase in the urge to violence and a decrease in barriers may be required. For example, Taylor and Leonard (1983) discuss a study in which "intoxicated subjects behaved more aggressively than the nonintoxicated subjects under threatening conditions" (p. 87). Presence of a threat might be enough to increase the "floodwaters" behind the "dam" and overflow the dam when the height of the dam is also lowered by the use of alcohol.

Another category of theories with sociological implications includes those theories suggesting that stress increases the propensity to violence. Such stress may be heat, overcrowding, noise, air pollution, violation of space, or something else (see Mueller, 1983). The variability in the research results suggests, again, that simple physiological explanations are not adequate to explain the relationship between stress and violence (Mueller, 1983). Rather, the theorists must explain why the stress increases the violent urges in some people in some situations (but not all) or why it decreases the social barriers for some people in some situations (but not all), or both. One extremely important theory is frustration-aggression (Berkowitz, 1962), which suggests that aggression is an invariant response to frustration of a goal drive. In essence, frustration-aggression theorists suggest that frustration increases aggressive urges, which then overflow existing social barriers. Such a theory is more psychological than sociological, however.

Finally, there are theories suggesting that observing violence, as in sports or the media, either increases the biological urges themselves or increases excitement, which results in aggression. Unlike theories suggesting that watching violence may teach one to engage in violence, these theories, instead, argue that watching violence increases already existing predispositions to violence. However, Huesmann (1982) argues that this model has not been well enough developed to make sense of the research results. Moreover, again, this is not a sociological perspective, because the focus is on the internal condition of the individual.

Categories 3 and 4

These theories start with the assumption that people are biologically nonviolent. It follows, then, that violence is caused by something that is alien to human nature. Thus, violence must be the result of an individual, interpersonal, or societal pathogen (e.g., Wolfe & Jaffe, 1991). In contrast to the image of a force being held back by a dam, these theories view violence as a dark force created by some unhealthy agent. Because of the belief that humans are biologically passive or even altruistic, all violence is seen as unnatural. Thus, whether such violence is culturally deviant or conforming is important primarily for understanding whether the explanatory factor is to be found in the individual or in society. Consider the role of alcohol, for example, and contrast this with the first assumption. If we assume that people are biologically violent, then alcohol breaks down the socially constructed dams. But if we assume that people are biologically nonviolent and the violence is deviant, then alcohol is seen as creating an abnormal, pathogenic condition. If the violence is conforming, then we point to both the pathogenic condition of a society that holds norms allowing violence and the condition of the individual under the influence of alcohol.

The classic example of a theory within this category, of course, is Rousseau's "noble savage." It is also possible to incorporate this assumption with a Marxist orientation, although we believe that Marxism is more compatible with the assumption that people are biologically neutral. Certainly the Marxist assumption about alienation inherent in class-divided societies presumes a pathological condition that could lead to violence. A representative quote along these lines is that by Gil (1989), who writes that "human development will proceed healthily only when people live in natural and social environments compatible with their developmental needs. Consistent frustration of these needs 'violates' human development, blocks constructive, developmental energy, and transforms it into destructive energy" (p. 40).

Theorists in any field who point to personality disorders and mental disease as the cause of violence, and who are therefore suggesting that violence is the result of a pathology, are implicitly assuming that people in general are not biologically aggressive. That is to say that although there may be biological explanation for aggression, *people* are not inherently violent. The two images, as we suggested earlier, are very different. In one case, violence is a strong force being held back by (potentially weaker) social barriers; in the other case, violence is a force created by a pathogenic condition in the individual or society. Although the differences are sometimes subtle when expressed in theoretical form, there necessarily would be profound differences in prescriptions for responding to the violence.

Again, the relationship between alcohol or other drugs and violence is important in these categories of theories. Here, the focus is on the ways in which alcohol or other drugs disrupt normal brain functioning, leading to aggression. Goldstein (1989) reviews this literature for drugs, and Taylor and Leonard (1983) review the literature with regard to alcohol. Taylor and Leonard's general conclusion is that alcohol reduces the ability to attend to subtle cues in the environment and makes individuals more responsive to superficial cues such as threats or social pressure, thereby increasing the probability of violence. Again, it is important to understand the importance of the situation, not just the pharmacological effects of alcohol. It is a combination of the alcohol and the cues in the environment that produces the aggression; a simple biological explanation has not held up under research.

Keep in mind that the major difference between categories 3 and 4 is in the role of society. These theorists assume that violence is always *pathological* in that it is contrary to the nature of humans. However, it may not always be *deviant* from the perspective of a culture or subculture. From the perspective of category 4 (violence is conforming), it is society itself that is creating the pathological condition. Wolfgang and Ferracuti's (1967) subculture of violence thesis is recast, under this assumption, as a pathological subculture of poverty that creates violence among the people living within it. Contrast this formulation to that discussed previously. Under the assumption that violence is inherent in people, a subculture of violence argument suggests that society removes the barriers and lets those violent urges out. But if we assume that people are inherently nonviolent, then a subculture of violence is caused by the pathology of poverty, which actually creates an "illness" within the people who live there. Prescriptions for reducing the violence would differ dramatically: In the first case, society must reinforce social controls to make the social barriers stronger; in the second case, we must address the underlying pathological conditions

of poverty. In both cases, however, it is not enough to focus on either the biological or the psychological conditions of the individual. Rather, the immediate social situation, the society, and the culture must be taken into account.

Categories 5 and 6

Finally, it is possible to start with the assumption that people are biologically neutral with regard to violence—that violence, like any behavior, is learned. Of course, people have the biological equipment to engage in violence, just as they have the equipment to eat or laugh, but these theorists assume that explanations that resort to biological factors are reductionist and incorrect. Society, culture, interpersonal interactions, definitions of self, and the like are the focus in these theories. Thus, violence is considered to be both learned and situationally restricted. Whether the violence is considered deviant or conforming is very important, not because the basic mechanisms of learning vary, but because learning deviant behavior involves different content than learning conforming behavior.

Theorists working from assumptions in categories 1 through 4 assume that human behavior can be predicted in the absence of social norms. For example, those who believe that humans are biologically violent (categories 1 and 2) would argue that, in the absence of social norms to the contrary and given the appropriate stimuli, people will be violent. Those who believe that humans are biologically nonviolent (categories 3 and 4) would argue that in the absence of social (and individual) pathogens, people will be nonviolent. Unlike these theorists, however, those who start with the assumption that people are biologically neutral with regard to violence also assume that there is no condition in which society fails to exert an influence. Thus, we cannot refer to the absence of social norms, because there are always social norms. However, sometimes the difference between categories 1 and 2, on the one hand, and 5 and 6, on the other, is a matter of emphasis. Theories in categories 1 and 2 emphasize the biological basis of learning, whereas those in categories 5 and 6 emphasize the social nature of learning (Bandura, 1973, 1983).

A sociological focus is on either (a) the culture or society (macro level), or (b) the interpersonal interactions that teach a particular set of norms (micro level). Durkheim's (1964) anomie theory is a classic example of those working at the cultural level. Durkheim argued that during times of transition between folk and urban societies, old norms break down and produce a condition of anomie (normlessness). Given that the old norms no longer operate to constrain behavior, the moral boundaries of society also break down. Merton (1938) and the subcultural theorists (e.g., Cohen, 1955) suggested that a variety of responses may follow; one such possibility is the substitution of deviant norms for the conforming norms (what Merton called "innovation"). Cloward and Ohlin (1960), following the same tradition, argued that juveniles in street gangs, unable to achieve social recognition through legitimate *or* illegitimate means, would turn to violence as a way to achieve status and prestige within their subculture. These theories do not argue that biological urges are turned loose by the absence of social constraints, nor that pathological conditions are created. Rather, they suggest that people learn norms and that sometimes those norms reinforce the use of violence.

An example of a micro perspective in this category is that of Athens (1977), who argues that people engage in violence when their self-concepts include the perceived capacity for violence and when they define a particular situation as one requiring violence. Self-concepts are not purely individual characteristics but are created through comparison with a "generalized other," a composite of cultural/subcultural norms and values.

A comparison of these categories with the others can be made through an examination of social control theory (Agnew, 1993; Hirschi, 1969). Hirschi argues that juveniles engage in deviant behavior when their ties to conventional society are weak. Someone working from the assumptions of categories 1 or 2 would suggest that such weak bonds allow the underlying aggressive and antisocial urges to erupt. Someone working from the assumptions of categories 3 and 4 would suggest that such weak bonds would create unhealthy mental conditions leading to violence. Those working from categories 5 and 6, however, would say that when bonds to conventional society are weak, bonds to a deviant society will replace them. It isn't human nature that is erupting or being corrupted, it is just the learning of alternative norms.

There are four categories of variables that are particularly important in this body of literature: familial, other interpersonal, societal, and cultural/subcultural. *Familial variables* focus on the role of the family in teaching and reinforcing violence. Much of the literature in family violence takes this perspective; an example is the importance of role models, whereby children who grow up in abusive families are more likely to be violent toward siblings (Straus, 1994), tend to create violence in their own adult homes (MacEwen, 1994; Rosenbaum & O'Leary, 1981), and tend to be more violent outside the home (Forsstrom-Cohen & Rosenbaum, 1985; Mangold & Koski, 1990). Compare this to the perspective that sees the dysfunctioning home as creating pathological mental conditions that lead to violence—a theory focusing on the family but starting with the assumption that people are biologically nonviolent. A typical phrase used by those who believe that people are biologically neutral will be "socialization to violence" (Fagan & Wexler, 1987a, 1987b), and such authors will seek to explain how that socialization occurs. The assumption is that socialization always occurs; it is just the content of the learning that differs.

We use the term *other interpersonal variables* to refer to those socializing influences outside the family. Peer groups are particularly important, but so are schools (Toby, 1995) and the media (Donnerstein & Linz, 1995). Fagan and Wexler (1987b) argue that these variables may be more important than family variables and that a combination of family and nonfamily variables may be necessary to explain why someone learns antisocial and violent behavior. For example, Heath, Kruttschnitt, and Ward (1986) found an association between childhood television viewing and adult violent crime only when there also was family violence in the juvenile's home.

When we speak of interpersonal variables, it is again necessary to consider the role of alcohol in aggressive behavior. Taylor and Leonard (1983) report several studies in which intoxicated subjects failed to act aggressively or reduced their aggression when social norms prescribed such actions. Again, this suggests that a simple physiological explanation for the alcohol–violence link is not sufficient, but it also suggests that even with a drug that alters the functioning of the brain, people are constrained by and respond to social norms. Similarly, in some situations, there are norms which indicate that if one is "drunk" it is acceptable to be violent. These are situations in which we should expect to see more alcohol-related violence and antisocial behavior. In his review of the literature, Coid (1982) points to some research showing that the social and physical characteristics of the drinking situation influence the rate of aggression. For example, Coid (1982) says that the "most violence-prone bars were in skid-row districts, had permissive decorum expectations and unpleasant, unsanitary and inexpensive physical surroundings" (p. 3).

Societal conditions are also very important in explaining violence. For example, as mentioned previously, it is a sociological truism that rates of interpersonal violence are higher among the lower classes. Consequently, much attention has focused on explaining this association. Important theories include these:

1. The condition of the neighborhoods in which the lower classes live, particularly the transitional, anomic state of those neighborhoods (Bursik, 1988; Shaw & McKay, 1942)
2. The substitution of deviant, sometimes violent, norms for conforming norms in the absence of any real ability to "make it" through conventional behavior (Cloward & Ohlin, 1960)
3. The poorer quality of the schools
4. The influence of strong anticonventional forces such as street gangs and successful criminal role models (e.g., organized crime figures; Silberman, 1978)
5. Racial discrimination (Silberman, 1978)
6. Racial inequalities in social and economic standing (Balkwell, 1990; Blau & Golden, 1986; Golden & Messner, 1987)
7. Stress (Gelles, 1989)

In addition, many theories focus on the interaction between the family and the neighborhood and on the functioning of the family in poverty (Fagan & Wexler, 1987a).

Finally, *cultural and subcultural variables* are important. Here the assumption is that there are norms that actually promote and teach the use of violence in interpersonal relations (Shields et al., 1988). The "subculture of violence" idea (Wolfgang & Ferracuti, 1967) discussed earlier is one example. Another ex-

ample is a study by Landau and Pfeffermann (1988) that examined the effect of wars on violent crime rates in Israel. Two competing hypotheses were tested: the "legitimation-habituation hypothesis," which suggests that war increases violent crime because it legitimates violence through modeling, and the "cohesion hypothesis," which suggests that war decreases violence because it promotes in-group solidarity. The data supported the legitimation-habituation hypothesis (cultural influences) for homicide, but neither hypothesis for robbery. Rather, for robbery, inflation and unemployment (social influences) were more important.

In the area of family violence and rape, some authors focus on the patriarchal nature of society, which reinforces norms allowing the use of violence (Brownmiller, 1975; Fagan & Wexler, 1987a). For example, Scully and Marolla (1984) found that a sample of convicted rapists used a "vocabulary of motives" that sometimes held the woman accountable for the violence done to her. As Scully and Marolla point out, such "vocabularies" are only possible within a cultural framework that gives them credibility.

FUTURE DIRECTIONS FOR THE STUDY OF VIOLENCE

The question "What remains to be done in the study of violence?" illustrates, again, the general sociological perspective on deviance. Current public issues, particularly the concern with drugs and violent crime, indicate that understanding violence is of national interest. There is much we know about violence, as the review of literature has suggested, but there is also much we do not know. However, some of the issues we have raised have been well examined by sociologists, and the urgent task is to communicate these debates to the lay public for consideration in public policy decision making. For example, the controversies over the definition and measurement of violence, and the fact that the difference between conventional and deviant violence is often qualitative rather than quantitative, should inform all public debates. Moreover, the idea that even a definition of violent crime is not obvious would improve public discussion. Our culture tends to emphasize the characteristics of the individual and tends to assume that definitions of deviance are absolute, rather than relative. It would be helpful for the understanding of deviance in general, and violence in particular, if these assumptions were tempered by the considerations we have mentioned in this chapter.

A final issue has to do with the epidemiology of violence. Our discussion suggests that violence is more likely among poor, minority males. Many people take this to mean that violence is a norm among the lower classes because of the breakdown of social barriers, the creation of pathogenic conditions of poverty, or the learning of subcultural norms and values. However, if we assume that violence is situational, regardless of human nature, then we have to consider the likelihood that there may be different opportunities for violence in the different social classes and age groups. It is possible that pro-violence norms are very similar throughout our culture and that some groups have more opportunities to express that violence in more conventional ways (e.g., in sports) than do other groups. Moreover, some groups may have the power to define their behaviors as "aggression" rather than violence. The issue of power in defining violence is relevant and important here. More work needs to be done on the incidence and acceptance of violence in nondeviant settings.

SUMMARY

From a sociological perspective, it seems very clear that no behavior, whether considered normative or deviant, can be explained by biology or psychology alone. As we have suggested, this is true for two reasons. First, deviance is often equated with pathology, leading to the search for pathogens. But the very designation of a behavior as deviant—and the equation of deviance with pathogenesis—is a social construction of reality. What is considered to be deviant or conforming is a product not only of individual behavior, but also of the power of the labeling agent, the characteristics of the bureaucracy imposing the label, the interactions between the potential deviant and the labeling agent, the characteristics of witnesses (such as complainants who have brought the matter to the attention of the police), and societal and cultural characteristics. In other words, deviance is always rela-

tive, situational, and problematic. If we focus only on the characteristics of the individual, we take the larger social context for granted; we assume that norms are universal and that such norms have the same meanings for all groups in society. From a sociological perspective, these assumptions make it impossible truly to understand deviant (or conforming) behavior. Our discussion of violence has examined the same behavior from the perspective of different assumptions in order to illustrate how these differences have consequences for the theoretical view of violence and its causes.

Second, interpersonal, societal, and cultural factors are also important in understanding why someone engages in deviance, given the existence of social norms. Again, our discussion of violence has suggested the importance of social factors such as interactional cues, subcultures, generalized others, societal characteristics (e.g., racism, poverty, income inequality, quality of the schools), and cultural/subcultural values. Violence is a behavior that seems, superficially, to be particularly amenable to a purely biological or psychological explanation. However, the research suggests that explanations of violence are enhanced when social factors are also considered.

Biological, psychological, and sociological explanations are not substitutes for one another. No one explanation is superior to another; no one field should replace the others. Rather, these explanations are different, in that they emphasize different aspects of human behavior. Contrast the psychological and sociological explanations, for example. If we use the analogy of a camera, a psychological lens focuses on the internal characteristics of the individual. Given that focus, the social factors, while present in the background, are blurred. A sociological lens, on the other hand, focuses on the background—the social factors. In the process, the internal characteristics of the individual (while present) are blurred. We have argued in this chapter that a sociological lens is important for the understanding of deviant behavior because it brings into focus those characteristics that are often blurred, and thus completes the picture. An individual, with all of his or her internal characteristics, acts and reacts in a complex network of social interactions.

REFERENCES

Agnew, R. (1993). Why do they do it? An examination of the intervening mechanisms between "social control" variables and delinquency. *Journal of Research in Crime and Delinquency, 30,* 245–266.

American Psychiatric Association. (1994). *Diagnostic and Statistical Manual of Mental Disorders* (4th ed.). Washington, DC: American Psychotic Association.

Athens, L.H. (1977). Violent crime: A symbolic interactionist study. *Symbolic Interaction, 1,* 56–70.

Balkwell, J.W. (1990). Ethnic inequality and the rate of homicide. *Social Forces, 69,* 53–70.

Bandura, A. (1973). *Aggression: A social learning analysis.* Englewood Cliffs, NJ: Prentice-Hall.

Bandura, A. (1983). Psychological mechanisms of aggression. In R.G. Green & E.I. Donnerstein (Eds.), *Aggression, theoretical and empirical reviews: Vol. 1. Theoretical and methodological issues.* New York: Academic Press.

Bayer, R. (1981). *Homosexuality and American psychiatry: The politics of diagnosis.* New York: Basic Books.

Becker, H.S. (1963). *Outsiders.* New York: Free Press.

Berkowitz, L. (1962). *Aggression: A social-psychological analysis.* New York: McGraw-Hill.

Blau, P.M., & Golden, R.M. (1986). Metropolitan structure and criminal violence. *The Sociological Quarterly, 27,* 15–26.

Blumenthal, M.D., Kahn, R.L., Andrews, F.M., & Head, K.B. (1972). *Justifying violence: Attitudes of American men.* Ann Arbor, MI: Institute for Social Research.

Brownmiller, S. (1975). *Against our will: Men, women and rape.* New York: Bantam.

Bursik, R.J. (1988). Social disorganization and theories of crime and delinquency, *Criminology, 26,* 519–551.

Buzawa, E., Austin, T.L., & Buzawa, C.G. (1995). Responding to crimes of violence against women: Gender differences versus organizational imperatives. *Crime and Delinquency, 41,* 443–466.

Cloward, A.K., & Ohlin, L.E. (1960). *Delinquency and opportunity.* New York: Free Press.

Cohen, A.K. (1955). *Delinquent boys.* New York: Free Press.

Coid, J. (1982). Alcoholism and violence. *Drug and Alcohol Dependence, 9,* 1–13.

Collins, J.J. (1988). Suggested explanatory frameworks to clarify the alcohol use/violence relationship. *Contemporary Drug Problems, 15,* 107–121.

Conrad, P. (1992). Medicalization and social control. *American Review of Sociology, 18,* 209–232.

Conrad, P., & Schneider, J.W. (1980). *Deviance and medicalization: From baldness to sickness.* St. Louis: Mosby.

Daly, M., & Wilson, M. (1988). *Homicide.* New York: Aldine.

Dobrin, A., Wiersema, B. Loftin, C., & McDowall, D. (1996). *Statistical handbook on violence in America.* Phoenix, AZ: Oryx Press.

Donnerstein, E., & D. Linz. (1995). The media. In J.Q. Wilson & J. Petersilia (Eds.), *Crime* (pp. 237–264). San Francisco: ICS Press.

Draguns, J.G., & Phillips, L. (1971). *Psychiatric classification and diagnosis: An overview and critique.* New York: General Learning Press.

Durkheim, E. (1964). *Suicide.* Glencoe, IL: Free Press. (Original work published 1897).

Elliott, F.A. (1983). Biological roots of violence. *Proceedings of the American Philosophical Society, 127,* 84–94.

Erickson, K.T. (1962). Notes on the sociology of deviance. *Social Problems, 9,* 307–314.

Fagan, J., & Wexler, S. (1987a). Crime at home and in the streets: The relationship between family and stranger violence. *Violence and Victims, 2,* 5–23.

Fagan, J., & Wexler, S. (1987b). Family origins of violent delinquents. *Criminology, 25,* 643–669.

Forsstrom-Cohen, B., & Rosenbaum, A. (1985). The effects of parental marital violence on young adults: An exploratory investigation. *Journal of Marriage and the Family, 47,* 467–472.

Gelles, R. (1989). Child abuse and violence in single-parent families: Parent absence and economic deprivation. *American Journal of Orthopsychiatry, 59,* 492–501.

Gelles, R. (1991). Physical violence, child abuse and child homicide: A continuum of violence, or distinct behaviors? *Human Nature, 2,* 59–72.

Gelles, R. (1992). Poverty and violence toward children. *American Behavioral Scientist, 35,* 258–274.

Gelles, R., & Harrop, J.W. (1991). The risk of abusive violence among children with nongenetic caretakers. *Family Relations, 40,* 78–83.

Gil, D.G. (1989). Work, violence, injustice and war. *Journal of Sociology and Social Welfare, 16,* 39–53.

Glueck, S., & Glueck, E. (1956). *Physique and delinquency.* New York: Harper & Row.

Golden, R.M., & Messner, S.F. (1987). Dimensions of racial inequality and rates of violent crime. *Criminology, 25,* 525–541.

Goldstein, P.J. (1989). Drugs and violent crime. In N.A. Weiner & M.E. Wolfgang (Eds.), *Pathways to criminal violence* (pp. 16–48). Newbury Park: Sage.

Hagan, F.E. (1994). *Introduction to criminology,* 3rd ed. Chicago: Nelson-Hall.

Hall, C.S. (1954). *A primer of Freudian psychology.* New York: World.

Heath, L., Kruttschnitt, C., & Ward, D. (1986). Television and violent criminal behavior: Beyond the bobo doll. *Victims and Violence, 1,* 177–190.

Hernstein, R.J. (1995). Criminogenic traits. In J.Q. Wilson & J. Petersilia (Eds.), *Crime* (pp. 39–63). San Francisco: ICS Press.

Hirschi, T. (1969). *Causes of delinquency.* Berkeley: University of California Press.

Huesmann, L.R. (1982). *Television violence and aggressive behavior.* In National Institute of Mental Health, Television and Behavior (DHHS Publication No. ADM 82-1196 (Vol. 2, pp. 126–137). Washington, DC: U.S. Government Printing Office.

Kandel-Englander, E. (1992). Wife battering and violence outside the family. *Journal of Interpersonal Violence, 7,* 462–470.

Kleinman, A. (1979). *Patients and healers in the context of culture.* Berkeley: University of California Press.

Kraska, P.B. (1989). *The sophistication of Hans Jurgen Eysenck: An analysis and critique of contemporary biological criminology* (Vol. 4, No. 5). Huntsville, TX: Sam Houston State University, Criminal Justice Center.

Landau, S.F., & Pfeffermann, D. (1988). A time series analysis of violent crime and its relation to prolonged states of warfare: The Israeli case. *Criminology, 26,* 489–504.

Lee, R. (1995). Machismo values and violence in America: An empirical study. In L.L. Adler & F.L. Denmark (Eds.), *Violence and the prevention of violence* (pp. 11–31). Westport, CT: Praeger.

Linton, R. (1936). *The study of man.* New York: Appleton-Century-Crofts.

Lombroso, C. (1911). *Crime: Its causes and remedies.* Boston: Little, Brown.

MacEwen, K. (1994). Refining the intergenerational transmission hypothesis. *Journal of Interpersonal Violence, 9,* 350–365.

Maguire, K., & A. Pastore (Eds.). (1998). *Sourcebook of criminal justice statistics—1997.* Washington, DC: U.S. Government Printing Office.

Mangold, W.D., & Koski, P.R. (1990). Gender comparisons in the relationship between parental and sibling violence and nonfamily violence. *Journal of Family Violence, 5,* 225–235.

McCaghy, C.H. (1976). *Deviant behavior: Crime, conflict and interest groups.* New York: Macmillan.

Megargee, E. (1966). Undercontrolled and overcontrolled personality types in extreme antisocial aggression. *Psychological Monographs, 80,* (3, Whole No. 611).

Megargee, E. (1969). The psychology of violence: A critical review of theories of violence. In D.J. Mulvihill & M.M. Tumin (Eds.), *Crime and violence: A staff report to the National Commission on the Causes and Prevention of Violence.* NCCPV Report (Vol. 13). Washington, DC: U.S. Government Printing Office.

Megargee, E. (1982). Psychological determinants and correlates of criminal violence. In M.E. Wolfgang & N.A. Weiner (Eds.), *Criminal violence* (pp. 81–170). Beverly Hills, CA: Sage.

Merton, R.K. (1938). Social structure and anomie. *American Sociological Review, 3,* 672–682.

Michael, R.P., & Zumpe, D. (1983). Annual rhythms in human violence and sexual aggression in the United States and the role of temperature. *Social Biology, 30,* 263–278.

Mueller, C.W. (1983). Environmental stressors and aggressive behavior. In R.G. Geen & E.I. Donnerstein (Eds.), *Aggression, theoretical and empirical reviews: Vol. 2. Issues in research* (pp. 51–76). New York: Academic Press.

Pilivian, I., & S. Briar. (1964). Police encounters with juveniles. *American Journal of Sociology, 70,* 206–214.

Reid, S.T. (1990). *Criminal Justice,* 2nd ed. New York: Macmillan.

Rosenbaum, A., & O'Leary, K.D. (1981). Children: The unintended victims of marital violence. *American Journal of Orthopsychiatry, 51,* 692–699.

Schur, E.M. (1980). *The politics of deviance.* Englewood Cliffs, NJ: Prentice-Hall.

Science. (1986). The growing focus on criminal careers. *News and Comments,* p. 1377.

Scully, D., & Marolla, J. (1984). Convicted rapists' vocabulary of motive: Excuses and justifications. *Social Problems, 31,* 530–544.

Shaw, C.R., & McKay, H.T. (1942). *Juvenile delinquency in urban areas.* Chicago: University of Chicago Press.

Shields, N.M., McCall, G.J., & Hanneke, C.R. (1988). Patterns of family and nonfamily violence: Violent husbands and violent men. *Violence and Victims, 3,* 83–97.

Silberman, C.E. (1978). *Criminal violence, criminal justice.* New York: Vintage.

Starr, P. (1982). *The transformation of American medicine.* New York: Basic Books.

Straus, M.A. (1994). *Beating the devil out of them.* New York: Lexington.

Straus, M.A., Gelles, R.J., & Steinmetz, S.K. (1980). *Behind closed doors.* Garden City, NY: Anchor.

Szasz, T. (1973). The sane slave. In J.A. Goodman (Ed.), *Dynamics of racism in social work practice* (pp. 66–79). Washington, DC: National Association of Social Workers.

Szasz, T. (1974). *The myth of mental illness.* New York: Harper & Row.

Taylor, S.P., & Leonard, K.E. (1983). Alcohol and human physical aggression. In R.G. Geen & E.I.

Donnerstein (Eds.), *Aggression, theoretical and empirical reviews: Vol. 2. Issues in research.* New York: Academic Press.

Tittle, C.R., Villemez, W.J., & Smith, D.A. (1978). The myth of social class and criminality. *American Sociological Review, 43,* 643–656

Toby, J. (1995). The schools. In J.Q. Wilson & J. Petersilia (Eds.), *Crime* (pp. 141–170). San Francisco: ICS Press.

Toch, H. (1969). *Violent man: An inquiry into the psychology of violence.* Chicago: Aldine.

U.S. Department of Justice (1997). *Criminal victimization 1996.* Report No. NCJ-165812, Washington, DC: U.S. Department of Justice.

van den Berghe, P.L. (1974). Bringing beasts back in: Toward a biosocial theory of aggression. *American Sociological Review, 39,* 777–788.

Wheaton, B. (1978). The sociogenesis of psychological disorder. *American Sociological Review, 43,* 383–403.

Wilson, E.O. (1975). *Sociobiology.* Cambridge, MA: Harvard University Press.

Wilson, E.O. (1978). *On human nature.* Cambridge, MA: Harvard University Press.

Wolfe, D.A., & Jaffe, P. (1991). Child abuse and family violence as determinants of child psychopathology. *Canadian Journal of Behavioural Science, 23,* 282–299.

Wolfgang, M.E. (1987). *From boy to man, from delinquency to crime.* Chicago: University of Chicago Press.

Wolfgang, M.E., & Ferracuti, F. (1967). *The subculture of violence.* London: Tavistock.

Wolfgang, M.E., Sellin, T., & Figlio, R. (1972). *Delinquency in a birth cohort.* Chicago: University of Chicago Press.

Zola, I.K. (1972). Medicine as an institution of social control. *Sociological Review, 20,* 480–504.

PART II

MAJOR DISORDERS

In Part II of this textbook, the major disorders that frequently come to the attention of mental health professionals are given close scrutiny by the respective experts in the field. In examining 11 such disorders (because of its importance, and in consideration of the voluminous literature, two chapters are devoted to schizophrenia), the authors include a definition of the disorder, examine its etiology and pathogenesis, consider the nature of the disorder, and point to future directions that researchers should pursue. In each chapter the relationship to other disorders is presented, thus alerting the reader to the overlaps and complexities of adult psychopathology.

Douglas S. Mennin, Richard G. Heimberg, and Craig S. Holt (Chapter 8) discuss panic, agoraphobia, phobias, and generalized anxiety disorders. They point out that despite advances in understanding these disorders in the 1980s, some definitional problems remain. It is clear, however, that improved methodology and diagnostic procedures, coupled with better theories, have led to testable hypotheses. Terence M. Keane, Rose T. Zimering, and Danny G. Kaloupek (Chapter 9) review the most current literature on posttraumatic stress disorder. Most of the studies conducted to date have considered exposure to natural disasters, sexual abuse, and technological accidents. Although these are frequently identified victims and sufferers who have been studied, it is recommended that future research should include randomly selected subjects and appropriate comparison groups. Also, further work examining the role of gender in response to traumatic events is warranted.

Rita C. Prather (Chapter 10) examines obsessive-compulsive disorder. Although we have increased understanding of this disorder, many questions remain unanswered about its etiology and treatment. The role of genetic components needs to be clarified, as does the role of neurochemical correlates. In addition, the etiological role of specific conditioning experiences awaits clarification. Ian H. Gotlib and Susan A. Nolan (Chapter 11) detail the depressive disorders. They review the two major behavioral theories accounting for onset of depressive disorders: Beck's cognitive vulnerability model and the reformulated learned helplessness model. Although data do not provide support for the causal hypotheses of these models, Gotlib and Nolan feel that they should not be discarded out of hand, given their heuristic value. These authors also emphasize that in future research a distinction should be made between variables that predict *onset* and those that predict *relapse* in depression.

John A. Sweeney, Gretchen L. Haas, and Vishwajit Nimgaonkar (Chapter 12), in the first chapter on schizophrenia, consider the major scientific questions facing the area: the psychobiology of the disorder, genetic factors, environmental factors, and the identification of "marker" variables. Although a wealth of data about schizophrenia are available, the etiology of the disorder is still poorly understood. However, availability of imaging techniques has added some understanding of morphological changes associated with schizophrenia. Recent data suggest that the cause of ventricular and neuropsychological abnormalities may be more a reflection of the progression of the illness or of some environmental insult rather than a genetic factor. Alan S. Bellack and Jean S. Gearon (Chapter 13), in the second chapter on schizophrenia, consider the definition of the disorder, examine the notion of a core deficit, and review the issues surrounding social competence, including the stress/vulnerability model. The chapter is devoted to giving the reader an understanding of the uncertainties and controversies faced by clinical researchers interested in schizophrenia.

James R. Sands and Martin Harrow (Chapter 14), discuss the interesting research issues in bipolar disorders. They are especially concerned about definitional issues and identifying the specific subtypes of the disorder. They argue that advances in brain imaging and biochemical assays will lead to better understanding of diagnostic heterogeneity. John F. Clarkin and Cynthia Sanderson (Chapter 15) examine the personality disorders in light of the criteria established by the American Psychiatric Association. They note the high prevalence (11%) of these 10 disorders in the nonclinical population. The authors point out

the need for longitudinal studies to track the long-term stability of these disorders.

Robert F. Schilling, Stephen P. Schinke, and Nabila El-Bassel, in Chapter 16, review the complicated issues related to substance abuse, noting improved understanding of the biological, psychological, and social determinants. However, they astutely point out that enhanced understanding of the precursors, nature, correlates, and consequences of drug dependence has to date not been accompanied by similar advances in prevention or treatment.

Gordon C. Nagayama Hall, Barbara L. Andersen, Susan L. Aarestad, and Christy Barongan (Chapter 17) present a comprehensive review of sexual dysfunction and deviation. Examined in detail are the sexual response cycle, individual differences, hypoactive sexual desire disorders, sexual aversion disorder, female arousal disorder, orgasmic disorders, and sexual pain disorders.

David M. Garner and Julie J. Desai (Chapter 18) emphasize throughout the chapter that the eating disorders are multidetermined and heterogeneous syndromes that result from the combination of biological, psychological, familial, and sociocultural factors. In presenting their comprehensive view of the issues, the authors have considered the diagnostic issues, major etiological formulations, and associated psychopathology.

CHAPTER 8

PANIC, AGORAPHOBIA, PHOBIAS, AND GENERALIZED ANXIETY DISORDER

Douglas S. Mennin
Richard G. Heimberg
Temple University

Craig S. Holt
University of Iowa

INTRODUCTION

Anxiety disorders are the most common of mental disorders (Kessler et al., 1994) and are associated with significant suffering and impairment in functioning. They also put substantial pressure on the nation's health care system and economy (DuPont et al., 1996; Simon, Ormel, VonKorff, & Barlow, 1995). Individuals with anxiety disorders overutilize the medical health care system (Pollard, Henderson, Frank, & Margolis, 1989) and account for twice the per capita health care expenditures of those without an anxiety disorder (Simon et al., 1995). In 1990, anxiety disorders cost $46.6 billion, or 31.5% of the total U.S. expenditures for mental health (DuPont et al., 1996). Although many of these dollars were directly associated with health care utilization, substantial costs were also associated with decreased productivity in the workplace (DuPont et al., 1996; Salvador-Carulla, Segui, Fernandez-Cano, & Canet, 1995).

Interest in the study of anxiety disorders has increased dramatically since advent of the third edition of the *Diagnostic and Statistical Manual of Mental Disorders* (DSM-III; American Psychiatric Association [APA], 1980). The 1980s witnessed a tenfold increase in the number of published articles devoted to the study of anxiety disorders (Norton, Cox, Asmundson, & Maser, 1995), which also accounted for 14% of the papers in clinical psychological and psychiatric journals between 1990 and 1992 (Cox, Wessel, Norton, Swinson, & Direnfeld, 1995). The large majority of these studies focused on panic disorder. However, research on social phobia has advanced significantly in the present decade (see Heimberg, Liebowitz, Hope, & Schneier, 1995). Following recognition of the construct of worry, examinations of the nature of generalized anxiety disorder have also appeared with increasing frequency (Borkovec, Shadick, & Hopkins, 1991; Brown & Barlow, 1992; Wittchen, Zhao, Kessler, & Eaton, 1994).

Overall, the importance of anxiety disorders as the focus of theory and research has been reaffirmed. One contribution to recent growth has been development of more descriptive and homogeneous diagnostic categories. Indeed, a fundamental problem in summarizing research on the anxiety disorders is that there have been major shifts in both the prevailing system of diagnosis and the nature of the disorders classified. The second edition of DSM (APA, 1968) divided the anxiety disorders into phobic and anxiety neuroses, based in part on presumed underlying psychoanalytic mechanisms. DSM-III took a less theoretically biased and more rigorous approach, providing a specific descriptive nosology for classification of anxiety disorders, based on an increasingly empirical database, according to known or suspected differences in symptomatology, epidemiology, etiology, phenomenology, and treatment outcome. Classification of anxiety disorders was further refined in DSM-III-R (APA, 1987), retaining the five principal categories of anxiety disorders outlined in DSM-III: phobic disorders, agoraphobia/panic disorder, generalized anxiety disorder, obsessive-compulsive disorder, and posttraumatic stress disorder. Notably, panic disorder became the primary diagnosis in patients with both panic disorder and agoraphobia. Previously, agoraphobia was considered primary, with frequent panic attacks as a secondary condition.

DSM-IV's (APA, 1994) classification of anxiety disorders featured only a few significant changes. Childhood diagnoses of avoidant disorder and overanxious disorder were subsumed under social phobia and generalized anxiety disorder, respectively. Diagnostic criteria were also modified to be more compatible with the tenth revision of the *International Statistical Classification of Diseases and Related Health Problems* (ICD-10; World Health Organization, 1993). For the most part, these diagnostic systems have become more similar. However, ICD-10 has retained the primary status of agoraphobia and does not require that worry in generalized anxiety disorder be difficult to control. Finally, panic attack criteria were separated from panic disorder criteria and presented before the specific anxiety disorder categories in recognition of occurrence of panic in all anxiety disorders.

This chapter examines the phobias, panic disorder, and generalized anxiety disorder. In summarizing a diverse and intricate literature, two limitations must be noted. First, theory and research across the anxiety disorders is unevenly developed. For example, panic disorder has stimulated more theory and re-

search related to biological mechanisms than have phobic or generalized anxiety disorders. Several books (e.g., Barlow, 1988; Heimberg et al., 1995; McNally, 1994; Rapee & Barlow, 1991) provide more in-depth coverage of the theoretical issues and research findings pertaining to the anxiety disorders than can be attempted in the limited scope of this chapter. Second, the revisions of the DSM system highlight many issues that remain unresolved, and promising results need to be replicated using more recently specified criteria. As the DSM-IV has been available only since 1994, much of the literature discussed herein is based on earlier diagnostic systems.

The following discussion examines the existing literature with a focus on the underlying nature of anxiety. The section on the description of disorders provides a general overview of the individual diagnostic categories in DSM-IV including case descriptions. A brief review of the most recent prevalence data for the anxiety disorders is provided in the epidemiology section. In order to gain a better understanding of the nature of these disorders, characteristics, such as age at onset, gender distribution, course, impairment, and comorbidity, are examined in the following section. The etiology and pathogenesis section is broadly inclusive of research that supports various theories of etiology, but, as a whole, this section says more about the nature of anxiety disorders than about their pathogenesis. The final section summarizes the current state of our understanding of phobic, panic, and generalized anxiety disorders; offers possible directions for future research; and briefly examines the treatment implications of recent psychopathological findings.

DESCRIPTION OF THE ANXIETY DISORDERS

The hallmarks of anxiety disorders are physiological arousal and subjective apprehension. Physiological arousal includes symptoms of autonomic hyperactivity, such as sweating, flushing, breathing difficulties, or changes in heartbeat (e.g., palpitations, tachycardia), or other physiological sensations such as twitches, aches and pains, or tremor. Subjective symptoms of anxiety include worry, apprehension, inability to concentrate, subjective tension, restlessness, and "feelings" of fear, panic, or dread (a future-oriented sense of threat or danger). These disorders may also have an external focus toward a more or less specific stimulus and may therefore have an additional behavioral component of avoidance, escape, or disruption of response.

The DSM-II diagnosis of phobic neurosis was retained in DSM-III but renamed "phobic disorder." It was subdivided into specific diagnoses of agoraphobia, social phobia, and simple phobia, based on the particular patterns of situations or objects that evoke anxiety. Furthermore, agoraphobia with a history of panic disorder was distinguished from agoraphobia without such a history. DSM-III also provided a hierarchical system of exclusionary diagnoses that minimized concurrent (comorbid) diagnoses. For example, anxiety disorders were not diagnosed in the presence of pathology presumed to be more pervasive, such as depressive disorders or schizophrenia. DSM-III-R and DSM-IV retained the overall structure of the original DSM-III diagnostic system but modified it in ways that have an important bearing on the present discussion. First, DSM-III-R modified the hierarchical rules for assignment of concurrent diagnoses, as follows:

(a) A more pervasive disorder takes precedence over a less pervasive one if both would account for the symptomatology and there is further evidence for the more pervasive disorder.
(b) Additional Axis I diagnoses may be assigned if the focus of the secondary concern is not related to the first disorder.

DSM-IV then added:

(c) The condition is not due to the direct physiological effects of a substance (e.g., a drug of abuse, a medication) or a general medical condition.

These revisions allow concurrent diagnoses that might previously have been excluded, a change that has permitted a more complete empirical investigation of the overlap of diagnostic entities. DSM-IV allows more heterogeneous anxiety phenomenology within a diagnostic category and aids study of the comorbidity of anxiety disorders with each other and with other disorders as well.

Second, DSM-III-R and DSM-IV refined the diagnostic criteria for most of the anxiety disorders. Although hierarchical exclusions were deemphasized, the revised criteria redefine the relationship between panic disorder and agoraphobia, such that panic disorder is the primary diagnostic determinant if both are present. In addition, criteria for panic disorder were broadened and could exclude other anxiety disorder diagnoses if they were not clearly distinct. Furthermore, the diagnosis of panic disorder now assigns a central role to presence of "spontaneous panic attacks." The criteria for generalized anxiety disorder were also specified more clearly, allowing it to become more than a residual category (as will be discussed). In addition, cognitive components were further stressed, and autonomic hyperactivity was removed from the generalized anxiety disorder criteria set. DSM-III-R also modified the social phobia criteria to include the generalized subtype (if a person fears most social situations) and a note to consider the concurrent diagnosis of avoidant personality disorder. Changes from DSM-III-R to DSM-IV and the diagnostic features for the anxiety disorders reviewed in this chapter are summarized in Table 8-1. For specific diagnostic criteria, the reader is referred to DSM-IV.

Specific Phobia

Both specific and social phobia belong to the category of phobias. The diagnosis of specific phobia (renamed in DSM-IV; previously "simple phobia") is marked by two components: intense anxiety when exposed to a specific stimulus and persistent fear and/or avoidance of that stimulus between exposures. Physiologically, the symptoms of specific phobia may become so extreme as to meet the criteria for a panic attack. However, unlike the uncued and unexpected attacks of panic disorder (to be discussed), panic attacks or episodes of intense anxiety in specific phobia are elicited by presentation or anticipation of the phobic stimulus. The experience of these episodes produces a persistent fear of the phobic stimulus, which is either avoided or endured with intense discomfort. The anticipatory anxiety and avoidance behavior may generalize to a range of situations associated with the phobic stimulus, leading to interference with general activities and, in severe cases, a very restricted lifestyle. In other instances, individu-

TABLE 8-1 Diagnostic features, rule-outs, and modifications from DSM-III-R for selected DSM-IV anxiety disorders.

Specific Phobia

Diagnostic features: Marked and persistent fear of a specific object or situation that is recognized to be excessive or unreasonable. Exposure to the phobic situation(s) almost invariably provokes an immediate anxiety response. Marked distress or interference with usual activities. No minimum duration needed for diagnosis unless under the age of 18, in which case a 6-month duration is required.

Rule-outs: Phobic anxiety due primarily to another Axis I disorder (esp. fears in the context of panic disorder, agoraphobia, or social phobia).

Modifications: For compatibility with ICD-10, the name of the category has been changed from simple phobia. In addition, the threshold of anxiety has been raised by requiring that it be marked and excessive or unreasonable (as well as persistent). Common types of phobias are also described.

Social Phobia (Social Anxiety Disorder)

Diagnostic features: A marked or persistent fear of one or more social or performance situations in which the person is exposed to unfamiliar people or to possible scrutiny by others and fears that he or she may act in a way that will be humiliating or embarrassing or show anxiety symptoms. Fear is recognized as excessive or unreasonable. Exposure to the phobic situation(s) almost invariably provokes an immediate anxiety response. Marked distress or interference in occupational or social activities. Generalized subtype is specified if phobic concerns include most social situations (an additional diagnosis of avoidant personality disorder may also be considered). No minimum duration required for diagnosis.

Rule-outs: Phobic anxiety due primarily to another Axis I disorder, general medical condition, or physiological effects of a substance.

Modifications: The disorder now subsumes DSM-III-R avoidant disorder of childhood, and criteria have been modified for childhood presentations.

Panic Disorder

Diagnostic features: Recurrent unexpected panic attacks (discrete periods of intense fear or discomfort) with at least one of the attacks being followed by one or more months of persistent concern about future attacks, worry about the implications of the attack, or a significant change in behavior related to the attacks.

Rule-outs: Disturbance due to a general medical condition or a substance. Generalized anxiety disorder should be considered if apprehensive anxiety is present and not due to fear of having a panic attack. Additional diagnoses of specific or social phobia should be considered if some attacks occur upon presentation of a phobic stimulus.

Modifications: DSM-IV definition no longer requires four attacks in a 4-week period or one attack followed by a month of persistent fear of having another attack. Attacks must be recurrent and followed by a month of concern about future attacks, worry about the implications of the attack, or a significant change in behavior related to the attacks.

Agoraphobia

Diagnostic features: Fear of being in places or situations from which escape might be difficult (or embarrassing), or in which help might not be available in the event of a panic attack. As a result of this fear, the person either restricts travel, needs companionship when away from home, or endures the situations with intense anxiety.

Rule-outs: Anxiety and avoidance due to another mental disorder such as social phobia, specific phobia, obsessive-compulsive disorder, posttraumatic stress disorder, or separation anxiety disorder. A diagnosis of panic disorder with agoraphobia should be given if there is a history of panic disorder (even if in full remission).

Modifications: The definition of agoraphobia has been modified to emphasize that agoraphobic fears typically involve a characteristic cluster of situations. Furthermore, specific criteria for mild, moderate, and severe that were provided in DSM-III-R have been deleted.

Generalized Anxiety Disorder

Diagnostic features: Excessive anxiety and worry (apprehensive expectation) about a number of events or activities, for at least 6 months, during which the person has been bothered by these concerns more days than not. The person finds it difficult to control the worry. The anxiety and worry are associated with at least 3 of 6 possible symptoms from general categories of restlessness, fatigue, concentration difficulties, irritability, muscle tension, or sleep disturbance.

Rule-outs: Focus of anxiety and worry due to another Axis I disorder; anxiety symptoms present only during the course of a mood disorder, psychotic disorder, or pervasive developmental disorder. In addition, the disorder is not due to a general medical condition or the direct physiological effects of a substance.

Modifications: The disorder now subsumes DSM-III-R overanxious disorder of childhood. Worry is no longer described as unrealistic. A requirement that the person must find it difficult to control the worry has been added. Symptom criteria include a simpler, more reliable, and more coherent 6-item set rather than the 18-item set in DSM-III-R.

Source: Adapted with permission from the *Diagnostic and Statistical Manual of Mental Disorders,* Fourth Edition. Washington, DC, American Psychiatric Association, 1994.

als suffering from specific phobia can maintain a normal routine that excludes the phobic stimulus, and it is only when some life change disrupts this routine that the person seeks treatment. Maser (1985) provided a listing of different phobias that spans several pages. In practice, however, DSM-IV specifies only a few particular subcategories of specific phobia, including animal type, natural environment type, blood–injection–injury type, situational type, and other type (APA, 1994; for a discussion of the differences between these subtypes, see Merckelbach, de Jong, Muris, & van den Hout, 1996).

Case Description
Robert is a 41-year old man who has had a fear of elevators since the age of 10. Specifically, he fears that the cables will break and the car will come "crashing down." He has worked as a computer technician for more than 17 years. His present position is in an office on the ground floor of a small office building. While he is quite comfortable there, he would like to seek employment at a larger corporation which would offer more opportunities for advancement and greater financial reward. However, most of these companies operate out of high-rise office buildings. As a result, Robert has avoided seeking a new position. He reports that he is "O.K. most of the time" because he has successfully avoided elevators. However, if he is confronted with a situation in which he needs to use an elevator, he becomes quite anxious and often experiences panic attacks in these situations which are marked by difficulty breathing, chest pain, and tachycardia. Robert reports that his mother was "always anxious" and had a number of panic attacks. Robert reports no other significant mental or emotional difficulties. However, a recent divorce increased his need to earn more money to pay for legal matters and child support. As a result, Robert entered a behavioral treatment program to address his fear of elevators.

Social Phobia

The essential feature of this disorder is a persistent fear of situations in which the phobic stimulus is perceived scrutiny by others or exposure to unfamiliar people and in which the person fears displaying anxiety symptoms or behaving in a manner that would be embarrassing or humiliating. As with specific phobia, the phobic stimulus (in this case a social or performance situation) is avoided or endured only with intense anxiety. The inclusion of social interaction as a possible phobic situation substantially changed the

diagnostic criteria from DSM-III to DSM-III-R. Also, a diagnosis of avoidant personality disorder no longer supercedes social phobia, and persons who experience more pervasive distress related to social or performance situations may now receive a diagnosis of social phobia. These changes in diagnostic criteria have been an important contributing factor to the increase in reported prevalence of social phobia since the advent of DSM-III-R (Kessler et al., 1994).

The social phobic stimulus may reside in a single or limited set of situations (akin to a specific phobia), as portrayed in DSM-III. However, subsequent research (Holt, Heimberg, Hope, & Liebowitz, 1992b; Turner, Biedel, & Larkin, 1986b) has demonstrated that most persons with social phobia report fear of more than one type of social situation. DSM-III-R first specified a generalized subtype in which the phobic stimulus extends to most social situations, although the subtype diagnosis is poorly defined. Common situations feared by social phobics include public speaking, assertive interactions, group or dyadic conversations, dating interactions, and non-interactional behavior which may be observed by others (e.g., writing or eating in public; Holt et al., 1992b).

Case Description
Heather is a 30-year-old unmarried woman who was employed as a nurse at a local hospital. After working at the hospital for several years, she attained the position of head nurse on the overnight shift of the hospital's cardiac intensive care unit. She excelled at the clinical and administrative aspects of this new position, but as time passed she became increasingly depressed. It was a regular part of the daily routine for the head nurse to present during morning rounds each of the patients on the unit and any procedures required by patients since the end of the previous day shift. However, Heather was extremely frightened by the prospect of speaking in front of other people and being the center of their attention. Her anxiety was heightened when the audience was comprised of authority figures, as it was in the present situation (i.e., the physicians and occasionally the medical director), and medical rounds soon became the focus of her day. She would experience increasing anxiety as the time for rounds grew near, suffer through the experience with high anxiety, and leave work angry at herself, frustrated, and increasingly demoralized. As a medical professional, however, she had access to a powerful, if maladaptive, method of managing her anxiety. One morning, in a burst of anticipatory panic about upcoming rounds, she

opened the controlled substances cabinet and injected herself with morphine, which effectively quelled her anxiety. Unfortunately, this behavior became increasingly frequent. She soon developed an addiction to morphine. Furthermore, her drug-taking behavior was detected, leading to her arrest and the loss of her professional license. It was only after a stint in an addiction rehabilitation unit that she was referred for cognitive-behavioral treatment of her social phobia.

Panic Attacks and Panic Disorder (with and without Agoraphobia)

According to the DSM-IV, a panic attack is defined as a "discrete period of intense fear or discomfort that is accompanied by at least 4 of 13 somatic or cognitive symptoms" (APA, 1994, p. 394). Common physical symptoms experienced during attacks include tachycardia (rapid pulse), dyspnea (shortness of breath), chest pains or constriction, sweating, smothering, choking, faintness, hot or cold flashes, tremor, and nausea. Common phenomenological symptoms include experiences of depersonalization or derealization, and fears of dying, going crazy, or doing something uncontrolled. The attack is sudden, usually peaks in intensity within 10 minutes, and is often associated with a sense of impending harm and desire to escape.

The hallmark symptom of panic disorder is spontaneous panic attacks. Although panic attacks are often reported as random or unpredictable, additional attacks may occur that are cued or triggered, such as in stressful situations, and there may be extreme apprehension about the possibility of having an attack (Barlow, 1988). Some degree of anticipatory apprehension may develop between attacks, with the patient then presenting typical anxiety symptoms, including hypervigilance, apprehensive expectation (usually focused on the next attack), muscle tension, and autonomic hyperactivity. Between attacks, symptoms often may be difficult to distinguish from those of generalized anxiety disorder, or may be nonexistent.

Criteria for panic disorder were broadened in DSM-IV so that a person who has experienced panic attacks in the past month would meet criteria if there is also persistent fear of having a second attack, worry about the implications of the attack (e.g., "What if I panic during the staff meeting?"), or a sub-stantial behavioral change due to the attacks (e.g., avoidance of previously enjoyed activities such as seeing a movie).

In addition, the panic disorder patient may develop avoidance behavior associated with spontaneous panic attacks that occur in specific situations. In many cases, the avoidance behavior leads to a diagnosis of panic disorder with agoraphobia, the fear of being alone in public places, especially in situations from which a rapid exit would be difficult. Agoraphobic dread and avoidance behavior are primarily focused on concern about physical sensations and losing control, rather than features of a phobic stimulus, such as public scrutiny or small enclosed places (Mannuzza, Fyer, Liebowitz, & Klein, 1990). The situations commonly associated with agoraphobia include being in crowds, going out alone, being in tunnels or on bridges, and using public transportation (Eaton & Keyl, 1990). The patient, fearful of becoming incapacitated or humiliated by the anticipated loss of control, may find it difficult to leave home or other "safe" places. As a result, the agoraphobic person may develop an extremely constricted lifestyle in which she rarely leaves her home. In addition, there may be ritualistic or superstitious behaviors that are necessary to reduce anxiety before being able to leave home, such as being accompanied by a "safe" person or bringing a talisman (e.g., a vial of medication).

Agoraphobia without History of Panic Disorder

Agoraphobia may also develop without a prior history of panic disorder, although this presentation is relatively rare in clinical practice. In this case, the patient either is likely to experience only limited symptom attacks (episodes of panic-like arousal, which, however, do not include 4 of the 13 symptoms necessary to be considered a panic attack) or may react with similar avoidance behavior to other symptoms, such as irritable bowel (to be discussed).

Case Description: Panic Disorder with Agoraphobia
Cheryl was a 34-year-old married African American woman from a rural community in the deep South. It was a difficult period in her life, as her common-law husband had just left her with three young children to care for and, despite considerable emotional support from her family, there

were few resources available with which to provide for her children. Cheryl soon found herself working three jobs, all physically exhausting and unrewarding, and "running around like a crazy person" to care for the children and meet other family responsibilities. One night, after midnight, when Cheryl finally allowed herself to rest, she was overcome with a "spell." She reported difficulty breathing, extreme fear that she would suffocate, tachycardia, as well as derealization and a number of other panic symptoms, and she became certain she was going to die. She ran out of her house and kept running, as if trying to outrun her demons. Medical examination was negative, but Cheryl became convinced that any substance she put into her body might have been responsible for her attack and might precipitate another. She developed phobias of several foods, resulting in precipitous weight loss, and of taking medications, which resulted in a near-fatal relapse of her asthmatic condition. She found herself unable to leave the house without being accompanied by one of her daughters or, later in life, by her relationship partner. She became unable to drive her car more than a short distance from home, even when accompanied. Twenty years later (at age 54), she was still symptomatic and, despite the fact that she had experienced a panic attack almost every day, still strongly believed that an attack signaled her imminent demise. Cognitive-behavioral treatment for panic disorder, consisting of exposure to feared situations and to feared interoceptive (bodily) cues paired with relaxation and breathing retraining procedures, was successful in reducing the frequency of her panic attacks and overcoming her agoraphobic avoidance.

Case Description: Agoraphobia without History of Panic Disorder

Joe was a 35-year-old Caucasian man who was happily married and the father of a newborn son. Everything should have been perfect, but it was not. Although he was successful in his home-based marketing business and provided a very high standard of living for his family, he rarely left his house. Joe's specific concern was that he felt nauseated on frequent occasions and feared that he would lose control of his bowels in a public place (as had actually happened on one recent occasion). Joe's medical doctor had given him the diagnosis of irritable bowel syndrome, but it had been difficult to treat with traditional medical treatments. Although he did not have panic attacks, his avoidance behavior was similar to that of the patient with panic attacks and agoraphobia. He would leave the house only after escalating conflict with his wife, and then only accompanied by her, and to places he could "scope out in advance" to assess the availability and accessibility of public restrooms. He would not go to sporting events or concerts because he was afraid that he would lose control and embarrass himself either by soiling himself or by running out of the hall and making a scene. He became increasingly tense and dysphoric, and he and his wife began to fight with increasing frequency and intensity. Joe sought cognitive-behavioral treatment when he began to think that his symptoms might endanger his marriage. Treatment consisting of stress management training and relaxation for his physical symptoms and in vivo exposure for his avoidance behavior resulted in a positive outcome.

Generalized Anxiety Disorder

The main feature of generalized anxiety disorder is excessive worry occurring more days than not for at least 6 months. Such worry may concern a number of different domains or activities (e.g., work, finances, family, and health) and must be difficult to control. In addition, the worry or anxiety must be associated with at least three of the following six symptoms: (1) restlessness, (2) fatigue, (3) impaired concentration, (4) irritability, (5) muscle tension, and (6) sleep disturbance. Finally, the worry must lead to significant distress or impairment.

In DSM-III, generalized anxiety disorder was primarily a residual category, considered only when other anxiety disorders had been ruled out (Spitzer & Williams, 1985). As such, it was poorly defined and tended to be assigned to those patients who experienced significant anxiety but did not evidence phobic avoidance or panic attacks. As Barlow (1988, p. 567) noted, "the category of generalized anxiety disorder in DSM-III produced so much confusion that few clinicians or investigators could agree on individuals who would meet this definition." However, once generalized anxiety disorder was more fully delineated, evidence began to emerge that supported its existence as a separate and distinct category. For example, one study (Anderson, Noyes, & Crowe, 1984) found generalized anxiety disorder to be distinct from panic disorder in pattern of symptoms, family history of psychopathology, and type of onset. Subjects with generalized anxiety disorder had fewer bodily symptoms than those with panic disorder. Onset of symptoms was more gradual and occurred at an earlier age.

Generalized anxiety disorder has been rigorously defined in DSM-IV. However, the determination of excessive worry is often problematic, and no sharp dividing line separates generalized anxiety disorder from the anxiety of everyday life. The minimum duration of the disorder was lengthened from 1 to 6 months to eliminate more transitory anxiety reactions. The criteria list differentiates generalized anxiety disorder from nonclinical anxiety in duration, magnitude, and number of symptoms, but not in quality of the anxiety experience (Lipschitz, 1988).

Case Description

Jennifer is a 20-year old woman who is enrolled as a sophomore in a state university. She complains that she is "constantly anxious and worries about everything." Jennifer reports that she remembers "always being this way" and states that it has interfered greatly with her daily functioning. Although she is a good student, Jennifer worries about most of her assignments until she receives a positive grade. In addition to worrying, Jennifer complains of constant headaches and tension in her shoulders. Recently, Jennifer experienced her first panic attack, which occurred after a fight with her boyfriend. In addition, she reports feeling depressed since the age of 12. She attributes her difficulties with her boyfriend to her constant anxiety and depression. Jennifer also reports that her mother has a history of depression and her father a history of substance dependence.

EPIDEMIOLOGY OF ANXIETY DISORDERS

Anxiety disorders are among the most prevalent categories of mental disorder. However, reported rates have varied widely. Lifetime prevalence rates for any anxiety disorder have ranged from 10.4% to 25.1% in the general population (Bourdon et al., 1988; Kessler et al., 1994). In part, these discrepant rates may be the result of revisions in DSM criteria (Barlow, 1988; Marks, 1987; Weissman, 1985). Although a comprehensive examination of DSM-IV prevalence rates has not yet been undertaken, large-scale studies of DSM-III and DSM-III-R prevalence rates have been conducted.

The two largest epidemiological studies of the prevalence of mental disorders in the United States are the Epidemiological Catchment Area Study (ECA; Robins et al., 1984) and the National Comorbidity Survey (NCS; Kessler et al., 1994). The ECA study examined over 18,000 participants in five communities (New Haven, Baltimore, St. Louis, Durham, and Los Angeles). However, only three sites (Durham, St. Louis, and Los Angeles) assessed the full range of anxiety disorders. DSM-III diagnoses were assigned after administration of the Diagnostic Interview Schedule (DIS; Robins, Helzer, Croughan, & Ratcliff, 1981). In the NCS, DSM-III-R diagnoses were assigned to 8,098 individuals between the ages of 15 and 54 after the administration of the Composite International Diagnostic Interview (CIDI; World Health Organization, 1990). Both the DIS and the CIDI were designed for administration by lay interviewers.

Lifetime prevalence rates for the anxiety disorders examined in this chapter are listed in Table 8-2. Specific phobias were among the most common anxiety diagnoses reported in the ECA and NCS studies. However, only a small fraction of those affected ever seek mental health services. Lifetime prevalence rates for specific (simple) phobias in the two studies were comparable (see Table 8-2). Lifetime rates of generalized anxiety disorder ranged from 4.1% to 6.6% in the ECA study (no national projection was computed), and a similar figure was reported in the NCS. Rates for agoraphobia without a history of panic disorder were surprisingly high given that clin-

TABLE 8-2 Lifetime prevalence rates of selected anxiety disorders in the ECA and NCS studies.

Disorder	ECA Study (DSM-III)	NCS Study (DSM-III-R)
Panic disorder	0.9	3.5
Agoraphobia (without panic disorder)	4.2	5.3
Social phobia	2.8	13.3
Generalized anxiety disorder	4.1–6.6	5.1
Simple phobia	11.2	11.3
Any anxiety diagnosis[a]	10.4–25.1	24.9

Note: ECA study: Epidemiological Catchment Area Study (Bourdon et al., 1988; Robins et al., 1984); NCS study: National Comorbidity Survey (Kessler et al., 1994).

[a] "Any anxiety diagnosis" refers to all possible anxiety diagnoses, including obsessive-compulsive disorder and posttraumatic stress disorder. Rates in the ECA study are based on only three of the five cities

ical studies typically report that agoraphobia without panic disorder is rare (Barlow & Cerny, 1988). These conflicting findings may reflect the low rates with which "pure" agoraphobics seek treatment.

The lifetime prevalence rate of panic disorder in the ECA study was notably lower than the rate reported in the NCS study. However, the former rate represents only persons who met criteria for panic disorder without agoraphobia, as appropriate to DSM-III criteria. Whereas DSM-III subsumed panic disorder under agoraphobia, DSM-III-R subsumed agoraphobia under panic disorder. The most striking difference in rates between these two studies is in lifetime rates of social phobia. In the NCS, social phobia (13.3%) was the third most prevalent lifetime disorder, after alcoholism and depression. This value was more than four times the rate of 2.8% reported in the ECA study. Chapman, Manuzza, and Fyer (1995) suggest that this discrepancy may be due to the increase in the scope of social phobia from DSM-III to DSM-III-R. In particular, avoidant personality disorder was no longer considered an exclusion for the diagnosis of social phobia. Also, the generalized subtype of social phobia, introduced in DSM-III-R, targeted individuals with pervasive social anxiety. In addition, the rates found in the ECA sample may be low as only 3 social situations relevant to social phobia were assessed (Turk, Fresco, & Heimberg, in press).

Epidemiological investigations of the anxiety disorders have become increasingly sensitive to the impact on prevalence rates of person characteristics such as gender and race. Women have been found to be at increased risk for most of the anxiety disorders (Kessler et al., 1994; Robins et al., 1984; Weissman, 1985). Kessler et al. (1994) reported that 71% of persons with panic disorder (with or without agoraphobia) were female. Generalized anxiety disorder was twice as common in women than men in the NCS study (Kessler et al., 1994). Simple phobias were almost three times more common in women than men in the NCS sample. Finally, social phobia was more common in women than in men by a 3:2 ratio in both the ECA and NCS samples (Bourdon et al., 1988; Kessler et al., 1994). However, studies of treatment seeking samples have typically reported equal or slightly male-biased gender distributions for social phobia (Mannuzza et al., 1990). This inconsistency

may reflect differences in the impact of social phobia on the gender role specific behaviors of men and women (Turk, Heimberg, et al., in press).

The ECA and NCS studies also examined prevalence rates in African American populations. In the ECA study, rates of simple phobia were higher in African Americans than in any other ethnic group (Robins et al., 1984). Lifetime rates of agoraphobia were also higher in African Americans than Caucasians at four of the five ECA sites (Blazer et al., 1984). However, major concerns about sampling bias have been raised (Neal & Turner, 1991). The ECA study included a large sample of African Americans by targeting a poor East Baltimore community and a severely disadvantaged St. Louis neighborhood. Both areas were characterized as predominately African American and low income. In addition, these areas were home to many elderly persons but relatively few African American men (Williams, 1986). The NCS study yielded no significant differences between African Americans and Caucasians for any anxiety disorder (Kessler et al., 1994). Clearly, more research is needed to examine rates of mental disorders in minority populations.

COURSE AND COMPLICATIONS

Age at Onset

Ages at onset for specific (simple) and social phobias have consistently been found to be earlier than for other anxiety disorders such as panic disorder (Magee, Eaton, Wittchen, McGonagle, & Kessler, 1996; Scheibe & Albus, 1992). Marks and Gelder (1966) suggested that various phobic disorders have different ages of onset because there may be periods of development that facilitate the acquisition of fear and avoidance responses for limited classes of objects or situations, analogous to critical developmental periods that potentiate imprinting phenomena in very young animals. Using DSM-III criteria, Öst (1987) reported that animal phobics had the earliest average age at onset (7 years), followed by blood phobics (9 years), dental phobics (12 years), and claustrophobics (20 years). Overall, the NCS study found a median age at onset of 15 years of age for simple phobics.

Age at onset for social phobia appears to occur most often during the mid- to late teens (Hazen &

Stein, 1995; Magee et al., 1996; Mannuzza et al., 1990; Marks, 1987). However, it has been suggested that this pattern of onset may be skewed (Amies, Gelder, & Shaw, 1983; Schneier, Johnson, Hornig, Liebowitz, & Weissman, 1992). Almost half the subjects in one social phobic sample reported having the disorder all their lives (Schneier et al., 1992). It may be that there is a bimodal distribution whereby most cases occur in the teenage years, but other individuals have early-onset social phobia (Juster & Heimberg, 1998). In fact, a number of studies have reported that those meeting criteria for the generalized subtype of social phobia were more likely to have an earlier age at onset (Brown, Heimberg, & Juster, 1995; Holt, Heimberg, & Hope, 1992; Mannuzza et al., 1995).

Generalized anxiety disorder has been found to begin most often before the age of 20 (Brown, Barlow, & Liebowitz, 1994). However, the disorder is commonly reported to affect individuals for the majority of their lives. This finding has led many researchers (e.g., Sanderson & Wetzler, 1991) to conceptualize generalized anxiety disorder as a trait dysfunction or personality disorder. Although most studies find ages at onset in the teens and early twenties, changes in the diagnostic criteria may lead to the discovery of earlier ages at onset. In particular, DSM-IV subsumes the DSM-III-R childhood category of overanxious disorder under generalized anxiety disorder. A recent investigation of the overanxious and generalized anxiety disorder categories supports the convergence of these diagnoses in children (Kendall & Warman, 1996). Hoehn-Saric et al. (in an unpublished report noted in Brown et al., 1994) found that early-onset generalized-anxiety-disordered subjects could be distinguished from later-onset subjects by a greater predominance of women, a history of frequent or severe childhood fears, prior psychiatric conditions, and marital or sexual disturbances. In contrast, late-onset subjects were more likely to report the emergence of the disorder after a stressful life event.

Panic disorder and agoraphobia appear to most often begin in the late teens to late twenties (Burke, Burke, Regier, & Rae, 1990; Magee et al., 1996). The ECA and NCS studies found mean ages at onset of approximately 25 years for panic disorder. Agoraphobia was found to have a median age at onset of 29 years (Magee et al., 1996). A later age at onset for agoraphobia makes intuitive sense given theories of agoraphobia pathogenesis in avoidance of panic attacks, but little is known about the age at onset for agoraphobia without panic disorder. Recently, investigators have begun to examine the minority of patients who have an early onset of panic disorder. Biederman, Faraone, Marrs, and Moore (1997) found that panic-disordered subjects with a prepubertal age at onset had a more severely disturbed presentation. These authors suggested that early onset of panic disorder may be a marker for poor prognosis.

Persistence across the Life Span

Once developed, there is evidence that anxiety disorders remain a problem throughout one's life. The course of anxiety disorder is typically either chronic or recurrent (Wittchen, 1988), and one-year recovery rates tend to be low (Bland, Newman, & Orn, 1988; Oakley-Browne et al., 1989). ECA data displayed a trend toward chronicity (Robins et al., 1981). Angst and Vollrath (1991) found recovery rates between 12% and 25% for anxiety disorders in community samples. Overall, it would appear that anxiety disorders, though somewhat episodic, persist throughout the life span.

There is some variability of persistence across the different anxiety disorders. Generalized anxiety disorder has been found to follow a chronic course but often fluctuates in severity according to life stressors (Brown et al., 1994). Furthermore, elderly persons can also suffer from debilitating generalized anxiety, suggesting that this disorder may persist into late adulthood (Beck, Stanley, & Zebb, 1996). Social phobia has been found to persist into adulthood (Campbell & Rapee, 1994; Lovibond & Rapee, 1993). This seems to be the case for both generalized and nongeneralized subtypes (Reich, Goldenberg, Vasile, Goisman, & Keller, 1994a). Furthermore, early childhood shyness and behavioral inhibition have been associated with onset of social phobia in later life (Rosenbaum et al., 1991). Panic disorder is often persistent but may follow a more episodic course. However, many panic-disordered patients report continuous severe symptoms. Krieg et al. (1987) found that 53% of an inpatient sample had a chronic course of panic disorder. Ehlers (1995), in a one-year prospective study of panic attacks, found that 92% of panic-disordered patients continued to experience panic attacks. In addition, 41% of the initially remitted patients had relapsed at follow-up. In contrast, Noyes et al. (1990), in reviewing a number of clinical studies, reported that 41% to 59% of subjects recovered. Often, agoraphobia will subside when panic disorder remits. However, in some cases, agoraphobia persists despite the remission of panic attacks. Overall, naturalistic follow-up studies have found that at 6 to 10 years posttreatment, about 30% of panic disorder patients are well, 40% to 50% are symptomatic but show improvement, and 20% to 30% have similar or worse clinical presentations (APA, 1994).

Life Quality and Interference

Anxiety disorders can place a substantial burden on affected persons. Because anxiety disorders often persist throughout the life span, patients may be quite impaired and demoralized by their anxiety. Interpersonal relationships, work, finances, and health can be affected by the existence of anxiety disorders. In addition, people with anxiety disorders are often less satisfied with the quality of their lives than those without anxiety disorders.

Impact of the phobias on functioning varies widely with the specific diagnosis. Specific phobias are rarely significantly impairing. However, the severity of impairment depends on the nature of the exposure to the phobic stimulus. For example, a person who has no reason to travel may not be affected by her fear of flying. However, a person whose occupation requires frequent travel may face significant work and social disruption because of her flying phobia. Specific phobias often appear more debilitating when they co-occur with other disorders. Presumably, however, this severity is largely due to the comorbid condition.

Social phobia has been related to significant impairment in education, employment, family relationships, marriage/romantic relationships, friendships, and other interests (Schneier et al., 1994). Turner, Beidel, Dancu, and Keys (1986a) found that 69% of a group of social phobics reported their anxiety interfering with social relationships. Shyness, a construct that is often characteristic of persons with social phobia, has been found to be associated with low ratings of friendliness and sociability, increased loneliness, and low rates of daily social interactions (Anderson & Harvey, 1988; Caspi, Elder, & Bem, 1988). A recent report by Wittchen and Beloch (1996) also found significant impairment in friendships and family functioning in social phobia. However, romantic relationships were most affected. This finding is consistent with a number of reports that social phobic individuals are less likely to be married than non–social phobics (Amies et al., 1983; Sanderson, DiNardo, Rapee, & Barlow, 1990b; Schneier et al., 1992; Solyom, Ledwidge, & Solyom, 1986). Lelliot, McNamee, and Marks (1991) found that patients with social phobia have fewer children than patients with other anxiety disorders. In addition, Wittchen and Beloch (1996) reported that social phobics were more likely to be divorced than were control subjects. Recent evidence also suggests that social phobics often mate assortively with other social phobics (Chapman, 1993). Assortative mating refers to the likelihood that patients will marry and reproduce with other similarly disordered patients.

Panic disorder is commonly quite debilitating. Interference from panic disorder may increase with the frequency and intensity of panic attacks. In addition, the presence of agoraphobia increases the impact of panic disorder. Work, social relationships, income, and health are all significantly affected by avoidance of public environments for fear of panic attacks. Recent reports have found evidence for increased functional impairment in a sample of panic-disordered patients when compared with controls (Fyer et al., 1996; Hollifield et al., 1997). In particular, subjects reported increased difficulty with physical and emotional functioning. A majority of panic-disordered patients have also endorsed social impairment and marital dysfunction (Markowitz, Weissman, Ouellette, Lish, & Klerman, 1989; Massion, Warshaw, & Keller, 1993). Panic disorder was associated with greater social impairment than major depression. Educational and occupational functioning was also impaired by panic disorder (Markowitz et al., 1989). Panic-disordered patients have been found to be significantly more socially and occupationally impaired than medical patients with hypertension (Shelbourne, Wells, & Judd, 1996).

Since it first appeared in DSM-III, generalized anxiety disorder has been perceived as a relatively mild condition (APA, 1980, 1987). However, many generalized anxiety-disorder patients report that they worry more than 50% of their waking day (Sanderson & Barlow, 1990). Recent research suggests that, contrary to earlier conceptualizations, generalized anxiety disorder is associated with significant impairment. Wittchen et al. (1994) found that 82% of NCS respondents with lifetime generalized anxiety disorder met criteria for significant role impairment. An earlier study utilizing ECA data found that generalized anxiety disorder was associated with increased mental health care utilization (Blazer, Hughes, & George, 1991). Massion et al. (1993), examining subjects from the Harvard/Brown Anxiety Disorders Research Program, found low levels of emotional health, role functioning, social life, and overall functioning in patients with generalized anxiety disorder.

In addition to clinician-rated and self-report judgments of functional impairment, investigators have begun to examine subjective ratings of quality of life to determine the impact of anxiety disorders. Most ratings of life interference focus on the effect of the disorder on the person's ability to perform or behave within the range of the normal population. In contrast, quality-of-life assessments measure the dissatisfaction with being ill from the perspective of the individual with the disorder or significant others (Bech & Angst, 1996). Wittchen and Beloch (1996) examined both impairment and quality-of-life ratings in a sample of social phobics. They found that social phobics reported significantly greater dissatisfaction with their general health, physical function, emotional role limitations, social function, vitality, and perceived mental health than control subjects. Importantly, ratings of quality of life were significantly related to ratings of functional impairment. Safran, Heimberg, Brown, and Holle (1997) found that both the generalized subtype of social phobia and avoidant personality disorder were indicators of poorer quality of life. Furthermore, quality of life improved following cognitive-behavioral group treatment for social phobia. Fyer et al. (1996) found that subjects with DSM-III-R or DSM-IV panic disorder rated themselves as having greater difficulty with physical function, bodily pain, social function, emotional role, perceived mental health, general health, and vitality than control subjects. Generalized-anxiety-disorder subjects have also been found to endorse poor per-

ceptions of emotional health when compared with panic-disordered subjects (Massion et al., 1993). In addition, wives with generalized anxiety disorder perceived their marriages to be less satisfying than did other wives (McLeod, 1994). Suicide can be viewed as an indicator of extreme life dissatisfaction, and high rates of suicide has been found in patients with both social phobia and panic disorder (Cox, Direnfeld, Swinson, & Norton, 1994; Johnson, Weissman, & Klerman, 1990; Schneier et al., 1992).

Comorbidity

Since the advent of DSM-III-R, anxiety disorders are no longer subsumed hierarchically under other Axis I disorders. Removal of these hierarchical exclusions has permitted researchers to examine co-occurrence of disorders. *Comorbidity* refers to the occurrence of at least two different disorders in the same individual (Brown & Barlow, 1992). Anxiety disorders are frequently comorbid with other disorders, with as many as 50% to 70% of patients having an additional Axis I disorder (deRuiter, Rijken, Garssen, van Schaik, & Kraaimaat, 1989; Moras, DiNardo, Brown, & Barlow, 1994; Sanderson, Beck, & Beck, 1990a). Comorbidity has major implications for our understanding of the nosology, etiology, course, severity, and treatment of anxiety disorders. In the following paragraphs, studies examining the prevalence and implications of comorbid disorders are presented for each diagnostic category.

Comorbidity among the Anxiety Disorders

Anxiety disorders rarely present as "pure" diagnoses (Brown & Barlow, 1992; Goldenberg et al., 1996; Sanderson et al., 1990a). Rather, they frequently co-occur in the same individual. Comorbidity rates may be so high that some theorists have suggested that these disorders not be viewed as distinct entities but, rather, as different expressions of the same underlying diathesis (Andrews, 1996; Clark, Watson, & Mineka, 1994). Social phobia and panic disorder are often comorbid. Approximately 50% of panic patients may have social phobia (Stein, Shea, & Uhde, 1989), and panic disorder occurs in roughly 5% to 20% of persons with social phobia (Moras et al., 1994; Sanderson et al., 1990a). Generalized anxiety disorder often occurs in the presence of another anxiety disorder. Only 20% to 26% of cases with generalized anxiety disorder did not meet criteria for an additional diagnosis, as reported by Brown et al. (1994). The disorder most commonly comorbid with generalized anxiety disorder is social phobia, with rates ranging from 30% to 60% (Moras et al., 1994; Sanderson et al., 1990a). In addition, about one-third of social phobics meet criteria for generalized anxiety disorder (Turner, Beidel, Borden, Stanley, & Jacob, 1991). Despite these high rates of comorbidity, little research has examined the frequent co-occurrence of generalized anxiety disorder and social phobia. In addition to comorbid diagnoses, the symptoms of panic and worry are common in all the anxiety disorders (DiNardo & Barlow, 1990).

Comorbidity among the anxiety disorders raises the issue of classification. As noted earlier, some investigators have argued that these diagnoses do not represent clearly delineated pathologies. Achenbach (1995) suggests that high rates of comorbidity may be artifactual, for several reasons:

1. The disorders are manifestations of an underlying condition.
2. The disorders reflect a higher order taxon that includes both disorders.
3. The taxonomic borders between the disorders are not clearly specified.
4. Assessment materials do not clearly differentiate the disorders.
5. A referral bias exists in which cases with two disorders are more likely to be referred than individuals with only one disorder (commonly known as Berkson's bias).

Recent studies have begun to investigate the latent structure of anxiety disorders to determine if a higher order factor may have explanatory power in defining the anxiety disorders (Kenardy, Evans, & Oei, 1992; Zinbarg & Barlow, 1996). These authors have empirically demonstrated that existing anxiety disorders can be subsumed under a higher order factor of negative affectivity. This factor is often viewed as a trait vulnerability. Biederman, Rosenbaum, and colleagues have begun to provide evidence for *behavioral inhibition* as such a temperamental characteristic that may predispose individuals to anxiety disorders (for a review, see Biederman, Rosenbaum, Chaloff, &

Kagan, 1995). It is hoped that further research into the common pathways of the anxiety disorders will shed light on the trait vulnerability hypothesis.

Mood Disorders

Some researchers have argued that mood and anxiety disorders may also be considered variable expressions of the same underlying condition (e.g., Clark et al., 1994). Indeed, major depression does occur in a large proportion of patients with anxiety disorders. Moras et al. (1994) reported rates ranging from 20% to 55% for major depression or dysthymia in patients with social phobia, panic disorder, or generalized anxiety disorder. In the NCS (Magee et al., 1996), 41% of respondents with social phobia had a history of at least one mood disorder. Munjack and Moss (1981) found that one-third of their social phobia patients had a lifetime diagnosis of depression. Amies et al. (1983) reported that approximately 50% of their social phobia sample had a comorbid depressive disorder. In addition, efficacy of monoamine oxidase inhibitors for social phobia was first demonstrated with atypical depressive patients, who share with social phobics the characteristic of interpersonal rejection sensitivity (Liebowitz et al., 1984b; Nies, Howard, & Robinson, 1982). Both depressive and social-phobic patients are characterized by the core symptoms of social withdrawal and avoidance, but clinicians should be careful not to diagnosis social phobia unless it occurs outside of a depressive episode (Dilsaver, Qamar, & del Medico, 1992).

According to ECA data, the risk of major depression is six times greater in persons with panic disorder than in control respondents with no disorder (Boyd et al., 1984). Rates of comorbid major depression in panic-disordered patients range from 30% to 70% (Lesser et al., 1988, 1989; Moras et al., 1994; Sanderson et al., 1990a). Frequency of comorbid depression may also vary as a function of illness duration and severity. Those patients with a more severe expression of panic disorder may be more susceptible to depression. Alternatively, depression may precipitate a protracted and unremitting expression of panic disorder. Depression, however, is not solely a demoralized response to having panic disorder. It often may precede the onset of panic disorder (McNally, 1994). Several studies have shown that when major depression is present, panic disorder is more severe and has a longer course and poorer prognosis (Keller et al., 1993; Lesser et al., 1988; Noyes et al., 1990).

Generalized anxiety disorder is often comorbid with mood disorders, with rates ranging from 8% to 39% (Brawman-Mintzer et al., 1993; Brown & Barlow, 1992). In addition, 22% of a sample of major depressive patients met criteria for generalized anxiety disorder (Sanderson et al., 1990a). DiNardo and Barlow (1990) found a higher rate of generalized anxiety disorder in major depression, with 45% meeting criteria. These authors also found that 33% of dysthymic cases had generalized anxiety disorder. With such high rates of comorbidity, investigators have examined common pathways of origin. Kendler, Neale, Kessler, Heath, and Eaves (1992a) found that genetic factors were completely shared for major depression and generalized anxiety disorder in a twin study. In addition, there were moderate nonfamilial environmental risk factors shared by the two disorders. However, no effect was found for a shared familial environmental factor for the pathogenesis of major depression and generalized anxiety disorder.

Alcohol Abuse and Dependence

Several studies have shown a relationship between anxiety disorders and alcoholism. However, this relationship appears to vary according to the particular anxiety diagnosis (Kushner, Sher, & Beitman, 1990). Alcoholism has appeared in 6% to 36% of social-phobic patients in a number of separate samples (e.g., Amies et al., 1983; Schneier, Martin, Liebowitz, Gorman, & Fyer, 1989). Otto, Pollack, Sachs, O'Neil, and Rosenbaum (1992) reported histories of DSM-III-R alcohol dependence in 24% of panic-disordered patients, most of whom also had agoraphobia. Alcoholism may also complicate the clinical presentation of generalized anxiety disorder. However, it is not as prevalent as in other anxiety disorders and the abuse is often brief and intermittent (Brawman-Mintzer et al., 1993). Studies of temporal relationships have found that social phobia often precedes alcohol use disorders (Smail, Stockwell, Canter, & Hodgson, 1984). However, Otto et al. (1992) found that 80% of panic-disordered patients reported their alcohol disorders *preceded* their panic. Alcohol may be used to alleviate anticipatory anxiety and may become reinforcing in terms of tension reduction. Alcohol appears to be used as a "self-medication"

even before presence of acute anxiety states such as panic occurs.

Personality Disorders

Studies have recently begun to examine the occurrence of Axis II disorders in patients with anxiety disorders. Social phobia and generalized anxiety disorder have been found to have a stronger relationship with personality disorders than panic disorder or agoraphobia, and this relationship is strengthened when major depression is also present (Reich et al., 1994b). Avoidant personality disorder is commonly comorbid with social phobia, especially the generalized subtype (Holt et al., 1992a; Schneier, Spitzer, Gibbon, Fyer, & Liebowitz, 1991). In fact, in six studies reviewed by Heimberg (1996), a median of 57.6% of patients with generalized social phobia, compared to only 17.5% of patients with nongeneralized social phobia, also received a diagnosis of avoidant personality disorder. Most patients receiving a diagnosis of avoidant personality disorder also have social phobia. However, there remains substantial controversy over the nature of the relationship between social phobia and avoidant personality disorder. Although the presence of avoidant personality disorder is associated with increased severity of social phobia, the symptomatic profile of these patients does not differ from that of social-phobic patients without avoidant personality disorder (Heimberg, 1996). Furthermore, treatment for social phobia does not seem to be compromised by comorbid avoidant personality disorder (Brown et al., 1995). Dependent and obsessive personality disorders have also been reported in various samples of patients with social phobia (Jansen, Arntz, Merckelbach, & Mersch, 1994; Turner et al., 1991).

Avoidant, dependent, and histrionic personality disorders are the most common Axis II diagnoses in patients with panic disorder, with rates ranging from 40% to 65% (Brooks, Baltazar, & Munjack, 1989). Panic-disordered patients with a personality disorder are twice as likely as those without a personality disorder to have a chronic, persistent course and past histories of both depression and childhood anxiety disorders (Pollack, Otto, Rosenbaum, & Sachs, 1992). In addition, treatment is often refractory in the presence of a personality disorder (Chambless, Renneberg, Goldstein, & Gracely, 1992; Reich, 1988).

Sanderson and Wetzler (1991) found avoidant, dependent, and not otherwise specified to be the most common personality disorder diagnoses in 32 patients with generalized anxiety disorder. These authors suggest that generalized anxiety disorder may best be conceptualized as a personality disorder because of its chronicity and pervasiveness. Further research on the relationship of generalized anxiety disorder to personality disorders is necessary.

ETIOLOGY AND PATHOGENESIS

Although this section outlines research findings that hint at the possible etiology of anxiety disorders, little is known about the actual causes of anxiety. There are many theories of etiology, but most research simply examines current pathology and then posits potential etiological mechanisms. Other prominent limitations include retrospective data collection, lack of adequate comparison groups, contrived or reductionist experimental analogs, small sample sizes, outdated or nonstandard diagnostic practices, and cross-sectional or correlational research designs. Viewed in this cautious light, however, theory and research have produced consistent findings most supportive of multimodal (encompassing both biological and experiential factors) and heterogeneous pathogeneses for each of the anxiety disorders. Most probably, there are multiple paths to development of any anxiety disorder. No single etiological factor has emerged as a sufficient unitary cause of current pathology.

In general, the existing research on possible mechanisms has focused on the two broad categories of anxiety: phobic reactions (focusing on cued physiological arousal, anticipatory anxiety, and avoidance behavior) and anxiety states (focusing on uncued physiological arousal and anxious apprehension). Research related to the etiology of phobic disorders (specific phobia, social phobia, and agoraphobia without history of panic disorder) have focused more narrowly on the cognitive and behavioral aspects of the disorder, whereas research on the anxiety states (panic disorder and generalized anxiety disorder) has also addressed more biological aspects. Researchers have investigated anxiety mechanisms that implicate theories of developmental facilitation, family transmission, biological function and structures, behavioral learning, cognitive appraisal, and environmental stress.

Specific Phobias

Familial Transmission

The study of the familial aggregation of anxiety disorders encompasses both genetic and family environmental theories of etiology. That is, an observed increase in risk for anxiety disorders among family members (i.e., familial transmission) could be due to genetic factors or to factors related to the shared environment, such as diet or emotional climate. In general, there does appear to be support for familial transmission of anxiety disorders from both genetic and environmental perspectives. Both lines of research have methodological limitations that are inherent in the types of questions asked of the population. For example, genetic research would benefit from the greater use of samples of twins reared apart, and environmental research could adopt a more longitudinal focus, following the subject from birth to adulthood. Nevertheless, studies have consistently demonstrated familial transmission of the anxiety disorders.

Specific phobias appear to have a modest familial component. Fyer et al. (1990) found that first-degree relatives of 15 patients who sought treatment for DSM-III-R simple phobias had a higher rate of anxiety disorders than did family members of control subjects. These results are somewhat limited in that individuals with a simple phobia severe enough to seek treatment may differ from those simple phobics who do not seek treatment. In fact, relatively few simple (specific) phobics seek treatment (Barlow, 1988). Large-scale twin studies also have examined a genetic contribution to the development of specific phobias (Kendler, Neale, Kessler, Heath, & Eaves, 1992b; Philips, Fulker, & Rose, 1987). These studies have also found a modest heritable component in simple (specific) phobias. However, concordance of anxiety disorders in siblings is not limited to a diagnosis of specific phobia. Rather, twins often have another anxiety disorder such as social phobia or agoraphobia. Although there is a modest familial component to specific phobia, it appears to be non-specific in anxiety transmission.

Several studies have focused on the environmental aspects of familial transmission of specific phobia.

Gerlsma, Emmelkamp, and Arrindell (1990) conducted a meta-analytic review of retrospective studies of early family environment of persons with anxiety or depressive disorders. Limiting themselves to studies conducted between 1970 and 1988 with measures demonstrated to be psychometrically sound, Gerlsma et al. reviewed six studies that examined the early parenting of anxiety-disordered subjects compared to nonpsychiatric comparison subjects. Subjects with phobic disorders were more likely to report an early parenting environment with less affection and greater parental control (i.e., overprotection) than control subjects. In contrast, obsessive-compulsive disorder and "anxiety neurosis" did not produce consistent differences across studies comparing these target groups with normative control groups.

Behavioral and Cognitive Theories

According to classical learning theory, phobias are acquired through association of a previously neutral (phobic) stimulus (CS) with a stimulus (UCS) that is "hard-wired" to elicit a response such as pain, discomfort, or fear (the unconditioned response or UCR). If this pairing occurs strongly or frequently, then the CS may come to elicit the response in the absense of the UCS. This conditioned response (CR) constitutes the phobic reaction. In a recent paper on etiological factors in specific phobia, Merckelbach et al. (1996) reviewed studies that examined the occurrence of conditioning events in nonexperimental settings. One study found that 21 of 55 (38%) victims of motor vehicle accidents (UCS) developed a phobia (CR) of driving a car (CS; Kuch, Cox, Evans, & Shulman, 1994).

In addition to fear acquisition, learning theory has postulated a cause for the avoidance often associated with specific phobia. Mowrer (1960) first developed a two-stage theory of the development and maintenance of phobias. First, individuals become anxious in the presence of the phobic object via the classically conditioned associations described here. Thereafter, phobias are maintained through avoidance of the phobic object. Avoidance reduces fear levels, which subsequently reinforces avoidance. Thus, avoidance is a hallmark symptom of specific phobia. Mowrer's theory includes both classical and operant conditioning elements.

Criticisms of this theory have pointed out that many phobic individuals have never had an aversive experience with the phobic stimulus (i.e., no UCS–CS pairing). Conversely, many individuals who are confronted with aversive experiences with spiders, snakes, dogs, and heights do not become phobic of these objects or situations (Wolpe, Lande, McNally, & Schotte, 1985). Alternative behavioral formulations address these criticisms. First, individuals can develop a phobia based on vicarious learning or *modeling*. Mineka and her colleagues (Cook & Mineka, 1989; Mineka, Davidson, Cook, & Keir, 1984) have illustrated this phenomenon with adolescent rhesus monkeys that were reared with parents who had an intense fear of snakes. These young monkeys witnessed their parents interact fearfully with both real and fake snakes. After six sessions, these adolescent monkeys also appeared anxious when confronted with snakes.

Another revision of learning theory offered by Rachman (1991) and Mineka (1985), among others, states that most phobic learning is stimulus–stimulus learning rather than stimulus–response learning. In other words, the CS predicts occurrence of the UCS rather than the CR. Integral to this "neoconditional" approach is the phenomenon of "latent inhibition," whereby a commonly confronted CS is not often followed by a UCS. At the time of the pairing of the CS and the aversive UCS, there is unlikely to be a lasting association given that the person has experienced that CS a number of times without aversive consequences. "UCS inflation" occurs when the UCS is mild in strength and becomes weakly associated with the CS. A subsequent pairing of the CS with a strong UCS can then inflate the association to create aversive consequences. In both instances, a person's perceptions of the stimulus plays a role in the learning of the phobic reaction. As a result, these theories are often considered to have a cognitive component. Tomarken, Mineka, and Cook (1989) have also examined cognitive factors in specific phobias. Subjects high in snake or spider fears were much more likely to associate fear-relevant slides (e.g., a snake hissing) with an aversive outcome (e.g., an electric shock) than low-fear subjects (the so-called covariation bias). This suggests that phobic individuals may hold extreme beliefs regarding the likelihood of aversive outcomes when confronted with their phobic objects or situations.

Biological and Evolutionary Theories

Another criticism of the two-stage learning theory concerns the differential strengths of possible phobic stimuli. For example, fear of spiders occurs more often than fear of guns despite the fact that guns pose a larger threat to modern-day humans. Seligman (1971) has offered a theory to explain why certain stimuli often become aversively conditioned. He considers fears of phobic stimuli such as snakes and spiders to be "prepared"—biologically determined through evolutionary processes. At one time, fears of such creatures were adaptive and kept individuals from confronting these creatures when they could be life-threatening. In the present day, these fears are mental "appendices" that no longer serve a direct purpose but remain "hard-wired" to our nervous systems such that these stimuli are more easily associated with aversive outcomes than other stimuli. A number of studies have provided substantial evidence for this theory (for a review, see Merckelbach et al., 1996). Most of this research has employed a paradigm in which animals or humans are confronted with different stimuli (CSs) and associated aversive outcomes (UCSs) to determine which become most easily conditioned. In most cases, the evolutionary stimuli are more associated with aversion than are commonly expected fear stimuli such as an attacker, rapist, or murderer.

Although this theory is considered a genetic and biological theory, little neuroanatomical evidence has been provided in its support. Firstly, genetic studies, as evidenced here, do not show that specific phobias breed true. In other words, phobias do not appear to be specifically transmitted, suggesting that genetic influences may not have such specific effects on the nervous system. In addition, few biological substrates have been suggested as the foci of such evolutionary processes. Öhman (1993) has postulated that subcortical areas of the brain such as the thalamus and the amygdala may play a role in rapid conditioning and processing of fear-evoking stimuli. These are the oldest areas of the brain and thought to be involved in biologically determined motivations for survival (LeDoux, 1992). In addition, Kelley (1987) combined conditioning theory with knowledge of neurohormones. They suggested that high levels of adrenocorticotropic hormone (ACTH) and vasopressin enhance the effects of CS UCS pairings.

In contrast, endorphins attenuate these effects. Another active area of research into evolutionarily prepared stimuli concerns the role of disgust in fear acquisition (e.g., Davey, 1994). Disgust, rather than fear, is often the outcome of confrontation with aversive stimuli and may play a role in the avoidance of objects such as spiders.

Social Phobia

Familial Transmission

Reich and Yates (1988) examined 17 probands with DSM-III social phobia, 88 probands with panic disorder, and 10 non-ill control subjects. Although a family history method was used (i.e., relatives were not interviewed directly), these authors did find that the rates of social phobia were higher in the 76 relatives of the social phobia probands (6.6%) than in either the 46 relatives of control subjects (2.2%) or the 471 relatives of the panic-disordered probands (0.4%). Fyer, Manuzza, Chapman, Liebowitz, and Klein (1993), utilizing a family study method in which relatives were interviewed, examined 30 probands with social phobia and 77 never-ill control subjects. Thirteen of the 83 first-degree relatives of social-phobic probands (16%) had a diagnosis of social phobia, compared with 12 of the 231 relatives of the control subjects (5%). Male and female relatives had similar rates of social phobia. In addition, social phobia was more common in siblings than in parents. An expansion of the Fyer et al. work has shown that social phobia is more prevalent in relatives of probands with generalized social phobia than in relatives of probands with nongeneralized social phobia or in control subjects (Mannuzza et al., 1995). A recent family study of social phobia replicated these findings but demonstrated familial aggregation only for generalized social phobia in the relatives of probands with generalized social phobia (Stein et al., 1998). Kendler et al. (1992b) found a 24.4% concordance rate for social phobia in monozygotic twins compared to 15.3% in dizygotic twins in a large sample of female twin pairs. These studies suggest that social phobia is a familial disorder, has a modest genetic component, and most probably breeds true.

As mentioned earlier, behavioral inhibition is a proposed trait vulnerability to the anxiety disorders (Biederman et al., 1995). In particular, behavioral inhibition has been conceptualized as a temperamental precursor to shyness and the development of anxiety disorders. In addition, shyness has been shown to be positively related to social phobia in adulthood (Bruch & Cheek, 1995). Parental factors have been associated with shyness and, through retrospective report, social phobia. Parents of social phobics have been retrospectively reported to express less affection and be more controlling than parents of agoraphobic and control subjects in several studies (Arrindell, Emmelkamp, Monsma, & Brilman, 1983; Arrindell et al., 1989; Parker, 1979). Bruch, Heimberg, Berger, and Collins (1989b) reported that generalized social phobics described their parents as having greater concern about the opinions of others, isolating them from activities involving other children, and being less inclined to socialize with other families than the parents of agoraphobics. Bruch and Heimberg (1994) compared generalized social phobics, nongeneralized social phobics, and normal controls on these dimensions in addition to the use of shame as a method of discipline. Generalized and nongeneralized social phobics differed from normal controls, but not from each other, in reporting greater parental concern with the opinions of others and the use of shame. However, generalized social phobics reported more isolated and less sociable families of origin than nongeneralized social phobics.

Biological Theories

Little is known about the specific neurobiology of social phobia (Nickell & Uhde, 1995). A number of reports have shown evidence of increased heart rate in social phobics during socialization or public speaking (Öst, Jerremalm, & Johansson, 1981). In addition, systolic blood pressure appears to be elevated in social phobics during social interaction and public speaking (Turner et al., 1986b). This increased heart rate, in addition to trembling, sweating, and blushing, are symptoms often associated with catecholamine activity in the peripheral nervous system. Elevated plasma catecholamines, especially epinephrine and norephinephrine, have been reported in unscreened normals during public speaking (Taggart, Carruthers, & Somerville, 1973) and musical performance (Neftel et al., 1982). Catecholamine secretion may be related to the change in heart rate and blood pressure found when subjects speak publicly and interact so-

cially. A recent report has also provided evidence for lower striatal dopamine reuptake site densities in comparison with matched comparison subjects (Tihonen et al., 1997). In other words, social phobia may be associated with decreased dopaminergic activity in the central nervous system. The greatest evidence for the role of the catecholamines in social phobia comes from the established efficacy of monoamine oxidase inhibitors such as phenelzine (Nardil) with social phobic patients (Nickell & Uhde, 1995). Selective serotonin uptake inhibitors have also been found to be effective for social phobia in several empirical studies (e.g., Katzelnick et al., 1995; Stein et al., 1996; van Vliet, den Boer, & Westenberg, 1994).

Behavioral and Cognitive Theories

A number of related cognitive models have been proposed to account for the occurrence of social phobia (e.g., Beck & Emery, 1985; Clark & Wells, 1995; Rapee & Heimberg, 1997). Common to these theories is the notion that social-phobic individuals believe that social situations pose a threat because of the possibility that their behavior will lead to negative evaluation by others. This negative evaluation, in turn, is perceived to lead to distressing consequences such as rejection, loss of social status, self-worth, and embarrassment. Once the individual interprets a situation in this manner, she or he will begin to experience cognitive, affective, somatic, and behavioral symptoms of anxiety. These symptoms then become sources of information about how the individual is perceived by others, which in turn feeds back into a cycle of anxiety that, inevitably, competes for the person's attentional resources. This process causes the person with social phobia to judge the social situation as a failure. Integral to this anxiety process is the presence of others. For some social phobics, these others may be an audience during a presentation. Other social phobics may fear interactions with strangers at a party. According to cognitive theory, individuals with social phobia will form a mental representation of their behavior and how it is perceived by others. Often, this mental representation is distorted and biased toward negative evaluation (Rapee & Heimberg, 1997). Commonly, social phobics engage in "emotional reasoning" in which they determine their impression they make on others by the level of anxiety they experience (Burns, 1980). A number of studies have provided empirical support for the existence of distorted schemata of social phobics, including judgment of their performance as poor regardless of its actual quality (Heimberg, Hope, Dodge, & Becker, 1990) and overestimation of the visibility of their anxiety to others (Bruch, Gorsky, Collins, & Berger, 1989a). In addition, social-phobic individuals have been found to focus attention preferentially on threatening social cues (Hope, Rapee, Heimberg, & Dombeck, 1990; Mattia, Heimberg, & Hope, 1993). As a result, they may be prone to perceive ambiguous social cues as negative. Persons with social phobia may believe that others are judging them by extreme and perfectionistic standards (Alden & Wallace, 1995). When these standards are not met, the social phobic will interpret the outcome as negative and will begin the cycle in which catastrophic thoughts elicit a myriad of anxiety symptoms. Biological, evolutionary, genetic, and developmental theories of the acquisition of social phobia are not inconsistent with these formulations.

Behavioral conditioning and ethological models of the origins of social phobia have also been advanced (Mineka & Zinbarg, 1995; Öhman, 1986). These authors contend that social phobia originates in the same manner as specific phobias. In this formulation, the development of a social or specific phobia would be dependent on the nature of the CS. A CS of public speaking would lead to social phobia, whereas a CS of a snake would spur the development of a specific phobia. Mineka and Zinbarg also hypothesize that the UCS in each situation would probably differ as well. In the case of the social phobic, the UCS would involve a negative social experience. Specific phobias, on the other hand, would develop from the perception of physical threat associated with a circumscribed object or environment. However, like the specific phobias, social phobia may develop through modeling or observational learning. These conditioning models have been combined with preparedness theory to explain the phenomenon of social phobia (Bond & Siddle, 1996; Öhman, 1986). Some theorists have suggested that social phobia evolved as a result of dominance hierarchies that develop and change as a result of frequent encounters. In these encounters, the individual fears aggressive action from a dominant other. Experiences in which the person is confronted with a dominant other will cause the person to display submissive behaviors often associated with social fears. Much of the empirical evidence for this theory focuses on the perceptions of facial expressions of others (Cloitre & Shear, 1995; Trower & Gilbert, 1989).

Panic Disorder and Agoraphobia

Familial Transmission

Using the family study method, Crowe, Noyes, Pauls, and Slymen (1983) reported morbidity risk rates (i.e., percentage of families in a group with at least one affected member) of 24.7% for the first-degree relatives of patients with panic disorder, compared to 2.3% of the first-degree relatives of control patients. This represents a twelvefold increase in the likelihood of developing panic. Noyes et al. (1986) examined rates of panic disorder and agoraphobia in first-degree relatives of agoraphobic, panic-disordered and control subjects. They reported panic disorder morbidity risk rates of 17.3% for relatives of panic disordered probands, 8.3% for relatives of agoraphobic probands, and 4.2% for relatives of control probands. Other researchers (e.g., Moran & Andrews, 1985) have obtained similar results with differing diagnostic criteria, patient populations, and designs. Overall, family studies suggest a strong familial component of panic disorder. However, for conclusions about genetic etiology, twin and linkage studies must be examined.

Torgersen (1983) reported concordance rates in a sample of 13 MZ and 16 DZ twins. He found concordance rates for panic disorder of 31% and 0% in the MZ and DZ twins, respectively. In a more recent study, Kendler, Neale, Kessler, Heath, and Eaves (1993) reported concordance rates of 24% in MZ twins and 11% in DZ twins. Using a broader definition of panic disorder, Kendler et al. reported a concordance rate of close to 50% in the MZ twins. Even with this definition, however, genetic factors played a modest role in the etiology of panic disorder. In other words, environmental influences must be present for the disorder to appear.

Recently, linkage studies have been used to examine possible genetic factors in mental disorders such as panic disorder. These studies typically involve examining the cosegregation of panic disorder with a known genetic marker within a pedigree. This marker can be a phenotypic trait or a mapped DNA sequence on a particular chromosome. Most linkage studies appear to find weak evidence for varying chromosomal locations or genetic mutations at any of these loci as the cause of panic disorder (Crowe, 1994; McNally, 1994). This may, however, be due to the reliance on Mendelian models of transmission. If panic is inherited, it may be best studied through a model of polygenic inheritance. Taken together, the studies reviewed suggest that genetic factors play a role in the etiology of panic disorder.

The role of early environment in the pathogenesis of panic disorder has also been examined (Crowe, 1994; McNally, 1994). A number of studies have shown that panic-disordered patients often have a history of childhood separation anxiety disorder (Pollack et al., 1996; Weissman, Leckman, Merikangas, Gammon, & Prusoff, 1984). However, conflicting studies have shown that a history of separation anxiety disorder may not be greater in panic disorder than in other anxiety disorders (e.g., Thyer, Nesse, Cameron, & Curtis, 1986). Other studies suggest that agoraphobic patients rate their parents as less caring and more overprotective than normal control subjects (Faravelli et al., 1991; Leon & Leon, 1990). However, they did not differ from the parents of depressed and patients or those with generalized anxiety disorder. These factors may have nonspecific effects on development of anxiety disorders in general, rather than panic disorder in particular (McNally, 1994).

Biological Theories

A number of areas of research point toward biological dysfunction in individuals with panic disorder. Research has focused on neural substrates, abnormal anatomical structures, physical effects of medication, and biological challenges in the generation of panic attacks (McNally, 1994). Many different physical and biological challenges have been used to provoke anxiety-like symptoms in the laboratory (for a review, see Papp & Gorman, 1995). These provocations produce physiological changes that often elicit panic or panic-like symptoms in persons with a history of panic attacks but less frequently do so in persons without such a history (Barlow, 1988). Provocation of panic-like symptomatology has occurred with infusions of sodium lactate, norepinephrine, and isoproterenol. Oral administration of

caffeine and yohimbine have also been effective, as have CO_2 inhalation, hyperventilation, and aerobic exercise. Other laboratory stressors have not successfully induced panic. For example, mental arithmetic (Kelly, Mitchell-Heggs, & Sherman, 1971), peripherally generated pain (Uhde, Roy-Byrne, Vittone, Boulenger, & Post, 1985), insulin reaction (Schweizer, Winokur, & Rickels, 1986), and hypoglycemia during the glucose tolerance test (Uhde, Vittone, & Post, 1984) all failed to induce panic symptoms, although subjects frequently became anxious.

Methods for eliciting panic in the laboratory have been proposed as diagnostic markers for panic disorder and as indications of the biological mechanisms involved. Some etiological theories have adhered closely to the provocation mechanism. For example, Ley (1985) proposed a theory of panic disorder based on hyperventilation, in which persons who are predisposed to hyperventilate do so in response to stress. Thus, subjective sensations of anxiety are viewed in this theory as a result of this abnormal breathing pattern, and rapid breathing leading to hyperventilation during an attack may be responsible for many panic symptoms. However, hyperventilation cannot reliably evoke panic attack symptoms in panic-disordered patients, who typically begin to hyperventilate only after the onset of a naturally occurring panic attack (Barlow, 1988).

The intravenous infusion of sodium lactate is one of the most widely studied provocation challenges in studies of panic disorder. Panic response to lactate infusion is seen in a higher proportion of panic-disordered patients than in normal controls or patients with other mental disorders, although the exact mechanism for this result remains unclear (Liebowitz et al., 1985b; McNally, 1994). Lactate infusion can produce a sudden onset of panic symptoms (e.g., tachycardia, dyspnea, sweating, and faintness) and other biological changes, such as increased systolic and diastolic blood pressure, lowered pCO_2 (exhaled carbon dioxide pressure), and other changes consistent with hyperventilation (Liebowitz et al., 1985b).

Positive response to lactate infusion as a marker for panic disorder is problematic on several counts: Not all panic-disordered patients respond to infusion; a proportion of subjects with another or no mental disorder also respond symptomatically to lactate infusion; and some subjects (whether panic-disordered or not) respond to infusions of control substances, such as dextrose (Knott & Lapierre, 1986). Barlow (1988) reported a range of 54% to 90% of panic-disordered patients who experience "panic," compared to 0% to 25% of nonpsychiatric control subjects. Additionally, 5% to 36% of panic-disordered patients experience panic when given placebo infusions. Attempting to differentiate panic disorder from other anxiety disorders or depression via lactate provocation has also yielded mixed results. Panic-disordered patients experienced lactate-induced panic more frequently than social phobics (Liebowitz et al., 1985a) or patients with major depression (Cowley, Dager, & Dunner, 1987), but not more frequently than patients with generalized anxiety disorder (Cowley, Dager, McClellan, Roy-Byrne, & Dunner, 1988). Subjects reporting panic attacks too infrequently to meet DSM-III criteria for panic disorder responded similarly to panic disordered patients when infused with sodium lactate (Cowley et al., 1987). A second widely used provocation challenge is the inhalation of CO_2. Similar to lactate infusion, CO_2 inhalation produces a panic response in a higher proportion of panic-disordered patients than normal controls or patients with other mental disorders (Griez, deLoof, Pols, & Zandbergen, 1990; Woods, Charney, Goodman, & Heninger, 1988). The proportion of CO_2 in the air mixture used in these studies has varied from 5% to 65%.

Studies of panic provocation in the laboratory do not point to a single underlying biological mechanism. However, two factors emerge as common across all provocation procedures. First, procedures with very different physiological consequences, such as exercise, hyperventilation, CO_2 inhalation, and lactate infusion, have common somatic signs and symptoms, such as rapid breathing and increased heart rate. A mechanism that has been proposed to account for the commonality of effect is a physiologically based suffocation alarm mechanism (Gorman, Liebowitz, Fyer, & Stein, 1989). Second, a high level of apprehension or basal anxiety seems a consistent predictor of panic in the laboratory across different procedures. For example, patients who panicked during provocation had a greater sense of anxiety (Liebowitz et al., 1984a) and higher resting heart rate (Liebowitz et al., 1985b) prior to lactate infusion than

patients who did not panic. As a result of these findings, investigators have examined neurobiological sources for these anxiety reactions associated with panic disorder.

Gorman et al. (1989) proposed a three-component neuroanatomical model for panic disorder in an attempt to organize biological research regarding neuroanatomy, biological provocation tests, and pharmacological treatment effects. Each neuroanatomical structure is meant to be the focus of a particular type of anxiety phenomenology, and their model may serve as a useful heuristic to direct further investigation, both biologically and psychologically, into the relations among the various anxiety disorders. First, *panic* is said to originate in the brainstem (in the locus coeruleus), and definition of the panic symptomatology is primarily somatic. Second, *anticipatory anxiety* (defined in terms of the affective response) is said to arise from the limbic system. Finally, *phobic avoidance* (defined as a primarily cognitive phenomenon) is said to originate in the prefrontal cortex in recognition of the learned nature of phobic avoidance. Gorman et al. (1989) do not suggest that the three anatomical regions operate independently of each other and have taken care to document the known and hypothesized interconnections between them. Indeed, their model of panic disorder depends on the interdependence of the three components. For example, discharge from the locus coeruleus during the actual panic attack is probably interpreted by areas of the prefrontal cortex, the area of the higher brain most involved with learning and complex emotion. It is there that sensations are labeled as dangerous, whereas it is in the prefrontal cortex that associations are made between the autonomic storm of the attack itself and the environmental situations and cognitions that happened to accompany the attack. Not only are these beliefs strengthened by anticipatory anxiety, representing discharge from the limbic lobe; but they reciprocally act through descending pathways to further stimulate the limbic areas and maintain anticipatory anxiety. Afferent pathways from the frontal cortex to the brainstem enable learned associations and catastrophizing cognitions originating in the prefrontal cortex to stimulate brainstem areas and cause panic attacks. Specifically, the corticoreticular pathway that terminates on the nuclei pontis oralis in the pons and on the nucleus reticularis gigantocellularis of the medulla may be the mechanism for cognitively generated panic. One potential contribution of this model is that it could make theoretically useful distinctions by assuming multiple levels of processing. For example, a panic attack may be elicited through prefrontal cortex stimulation of the brainstem ("cognitively") versus originating in the brainstem ("spontaneously"). In that way it may serve a broader organizational role beyond the biological aspects of anxiety disorders.

Several lines of evidence point to the involvement of the locus coeruleus in panic disorder (Gorman et al., 1989). It contains nearly half of the brain's noradrenergic neurons and produces 70% of the brain's norepinephrine. Early researchers found that electrical stimulation of the locus coeruleus in monkeys caused physiological and behavioral stimulation identical to those provoked by threatening stimuli. They concluded that the locus coeruleus controls alarm, fear, and anxiety reactions (Redmond, 1979; Redmond & Huang, 1979).

This research prompted examinations of yohimbine, an α-2 adrenergic antagonist that stimulates locus coeruleus firing (Charney & Heninger, 1986; Charney et al., 1990b). Normally, increased norepinephrine release stimulates presynaptic inhibitory α-2 adrenergic autoreceptors and sympathetic activity is decreased through this negative feedback loop. However, yohimbine antagonizes these receptors and interrupts this loop producing disinhibition of sympathetic activity. Evidence for this effect in humans comes from levels of the norepinephrine metabolite, 3-methoxy-4-hydroxyphenylglycol (MHPG). Panic patients have higher baseline levels of MHPG and have stronger increases of MHPG when given yohimbine than do psychiatric or normal control subjects (Charney et al., 1990b). This would suggest that panic-disordered patients have an overactive locus coeruleus/norepinephrine system.

Proponents of the overactive system theory have attempted to integrate findings concerning the locus coeruleus with the false-alarm theory of suffocation (Klein, 1993). Specifically, a faulty locus coeruleus may stimulate an alarm reaction at a lower threshold than normal, causing hyperventilation and subsequent panic. In support of this view is the fact that the respiratory centers that regulate CO_2 intake lie in the medulla near the locus coeruleus. CO_2 inhalation is involved in a complex system of respiration and neuronal functioning (Barlow, 1988).

There is also conflicting evidence regarding the role of the locus coeruleus in panic disorder. Some studies have found that panic-disordered patients have exaggerated decreases in levels of MHPG following administration of α-2 adrenergic agonists such as clonidine (Charney, Woods, Krystal, & Heninger, 1990a). This seems inconsistent with the preceding findings that panic-disordered patients have increased levels of MHPG. If the locus coeruleus is a central player in the causation of panic, it would seem odd that it increases and decreases normal norepinephrine functioning in these patients. Researchers have suggested that the locus coeruleus may be dysregulated in response to dysfunction in other systems such as the gamma-aminobutyric acid (GABA)/benzodiazepine system (Gorman et al., 1989).

Recently, the Food and Drug Administration approved the use of paroxetine (Paxil) in the treatment of panic disorder. This drug is among a growing class of medications that block the reuptake of serotonin (5-HT) and are called *selective serotonin reuptake inhibitors*. A number of studies have also begun to examine the role of the 5-HT system in panic disorder (Kahn, Westenberg, & Moorse, 1995). Overall, it would appear that presynaptic 5-HT functioning is normal in panic-disordered patients but that some panic patients may have hypersensitive postsynaptic 5HT receptors—possibly for $5HT_{1A}$ (Lesch et al., 1992). Studies of 5-HT may provide a link between this system and the norepinephrine and GABA systems. For example, 5-HT neurons project from the dorsal raphe to the locus coeruleus. Destruction of the mesencephalic part of the raphe system causes an increase in norepinephrine turnover in the locus coeruleus (Belin et al., 1983). Also, there may be a link between 5-HT and GABA (Belin et al., 1983). Specifically, certain neurons of the raphe contain both 5-HT and GABA. Benzodiazepines may exert their anxiolytic effect by indirectly decreasing 5-HT functioning through GABA facilitation.

A naturally occurring physiological phenomenon worth noting is nocturnal panic, reported by about one-fourth of panic-disordered patients (Barlow, 1988; Craske & Rowe, 1997). Presence of nocturnal panic suggests a possible subtype of panic disorder.

Panic-disordered patients with nocturnal panic have a faster respiration rate in response to mild stressors (Craske & Barlow, 1988) and report shortness of breath more frequently as a symptom during attacks (Barlow & Craske, 1988) than panic-disordered patients without nocturnal panic. Although this might suggest hyperventilation-related causation (Ley, 1985), response to CO_2 challenge failed to differentiate the two panic disorder groups (Craske & Barlow, 1990). Nocturnal panic remains an interesting anomaly to most comprehensive models of panic.

Behavioral and Cognitive Theories

Goldstein and Chambless (1978) suggested a hypothesis based on "fear of fear" to explain the origin of agoraphobia with panic. They noted that *agoraphobia* was defined as a fear of impending panic symptoms rather than of the agoraphobic situation itself. Fear-of-fear was originally described as the result of conditioning of neutral internal cues (CS) to the aversive physical sensations of a panic attack (UCS). That is, panic attacks arise from an interoceptively conditioned response, in which internal stimuli of panic-like symptoms come to elicit the full panic response. In the interoceptive conditioning formulation, internal sensations that may present as panic symptoms (e.g., palpitations due to any cause) serve as the CS, cueing the onset of other anxiety symptoms (e.g., dizziness) as the CR. Although this paradigm has stimulated interesting research, particularly in the treatment of panic disorder and agoraphobia (Barlow, 1988), a Pavlovian-conditioning explanation of panic attacks has serious theoretical limitations. As McNally (1994) notes, a strict interoceptive conditioning model lacks the distinctiveness of anxiety symptoms that serve as separate UCS and CS in the paradigm and results in the CS and CR being defined in terms of relative and arbitrary degrees of anxiety (i.e., CS = little arousal and few symptoms; CR = more arousal and more symptoms). Also interoceptive conditioning does not explain the initial panic attack—the UCS–UCR association. Some theorists (e.g., Seligman, 1988) have suggested that the initial panic episode may result from an event or state not related to panic, such as an increase in lactate level, and that subsequent episodes are cued by anxiety symptoms. To date however, there is little evidence to address this proposal.

A variation on the fear-of-fear hypothesis is that of anxiety sensitivity (McNally, 1994; Reiss, Peterson, Gursky, & McNally, 1986). Anxiety sensitivity refers to the fear of anxiety symptoms, which reflects a belief that anxiety symptoms are harmful. Thus, it plays a role in heightening the anxiety experienced in a given situation through an additional alarm reaction to extant anxiety symptoms. In its modifier role, anxiety sensitivity can be seen as a necessary but not sufficient factor in eliciting panic attacks. Rapee (1986) found nonclinical subjects reporting high anxiety sensitivity resembled panic-disorder patients in their anxious response to a hyperventilation challenge. A recent study supports the role of anxiety sensitivity in the pathogenesis of panic (Schmidt, Lerew, & Jackson, 1997). This study, using a prospective design, followed a nonclinical sample of 1,000 young adults over a 5-week period during military basic training. Anxiety sensitivity predicted development of uncued panic attacks after controlling for actual history of panic attacks and trait anxiety. Lilienfeld (1996) has questioned whether anxiety sensitivity is truly distinct from trait anxiety. He suggests that researchers focus on the associations of these constructs rather than work to distinguish them. In either case, the anxiety sensitivity construct provides an important psychological marker for the occurrence of panic attacks.

Clark (1986) proposed a cognitive variation of the fear-of-fear model based on the appraisal of physical symptoms, in which panic disorder is a result of catastrophic misinterpretation of bodily sensations. In this view, catastrophic misinterpretation is necessary for production of a panic attack. Even the occurrence of fear per se would not provoke a full panic attack without the addition of the construal of the fear to indicate impending danger. That is, Clark's model states that it is the catastrophic misinterpretation of immediate symptoms and the fear of these symptoms that elicits the panic response. In particular, sensations that elicit misinterpretation are common anxiety responses such as palpitations, breathlessness, dizziness, and numbness. These sensations are viewed as signaling extremely threatening and dangerous physical or mental events. For example, heart palpitations may be mistaken for a heart attack. As a result of these sensations being viewed as dangerous, an apprehensive state ensues, during which the panicker experiences further bodily sensations. If these sensations are then viewed catastrophically, further apprehension occurs, which in turn increases bodily sensations, and a vicious cycle is set in motion. An individual can develop a tendency to become hypervigilant to bodily sensations. As he or she continually scans the body for physical sensations, the panic-prone individual will begin to catastrophically misinterpret these sensations and view these occurrences as evidence of serious threat. Panic-disordered individuals also will engage in subtle and overt avoidance techniques in order to circumvent situations that may cause them physical distress. As a result, these individuals reinforce their negative beliefs about the danger associated with these sensations and the situations in which they are likely to occur. A recent investigation supports the notion that panic-disordered individuals misinterpret benign bodily sensations (Clark et al., 1997). In a series of studies, these authors found that panic-disordered patients were more likely to interpret ambiguous autonomic sensations as signs of impending physical or mental threat and were more likely than other anxiety-disordered patients and nonpatients to believe these interpretations. Furthermore, misinterpretations of bodily sensations predicted follow-up relapse in patients who were panic-free at the end of treatment (Clark et al., 1994). This model has produced interesting research, but a cognitive theory of panic disorder has its own limitations. For example, nocturnal panic attacks force cognitive theorists to invoke concepts of automatic processing (i.e., cognitive processing outside of awareness) that are less accessible to the researcher. Further, even panic attacks during full wakefulness are not always preceded, or accompanied, by fearful or catastrophic cognitions (Rachman, Lopatka, & Levitt, 1988). Cognitive and behavioral theories are not inconsistent with existing biological theories of panic disorder. Panic patients who knew that they were going to breathe CO_2 demonstrated greater physiological arousal than when they knew they were going to breathe room air in the same setting. Patients who also had an illusion of control in their ability to regulate CO_2 intake were less likely to panic (Sanderson, Rapee, & Barlow, 1988). Panzarella (1995) suggests that suffocation false alarm theory and cognitive theory of panic disorder can be integrated. She explains that the physiological mechanisms involved in a false alarm system may be distal causes of present cognitions which can serve as proximal causes of panic disorder. Barlow (1988; Antony & Barlow, 1996) has presented a model that uses emotion theory to integrate cognitive, behavioral, and biological formulations of panic disorder. He cites emotion theorists Lang (1988) and Zajonc (1984), who argue that cognitive appraisals may not be necessary for the experience of emotion and presents a model of panic disorder that addresses the criticisms of these emotion theorists. In this model, an initial panic attack often occurs following a stressful life event in individuals who are prone (i.e., possess a genetic vulnerability for biological malfunction) to experiencing surges of fear in the absence of clear situational triggers. In addition, some individuals possess a psychological vulnerability in which they perceive their emotions as uncontrollable and unpredictable. This vulnerability instigates an increase in arousal and self-focused attention. This shift in focus begins the process of anxious apprehension that is associated with the onset of a panic attack. In this manner, conscious appraisal is not necessary for a panic attack to occur.

Generalized Anxiety Disorder

Familial Transmission

Early studies from both the human and animal literatures suggest that emotionality and neuroticism—constructs related to generalized anxiety—are at least partially heritable (Barlow, 1988). Noyes, Clarkson, Crowe, Yates, and McChesney (1987) examined rates of disorder in 20 probands with DSM-III generalized anxiety disorder without a history of panic attacks. Of 123 first-degree relatives, 24 (19.5%) met criteria for generalized anxiety disorder, compared with only 4 of 113 (3.5%) of the relatives of control probands and 13 of 241 (5.4%) of the relatives of panic-disordered probands. Panic disorder was not more common in relatives of GAD patients than in relatives of control probands. Torgersen (1983), using DSM-III criteria, did not find support for a genetic model of generalized anxiety disorder in twins with anxiety disorders. However, this study used the hierarchical structure of the DSM-III diagnosis of generalized anxiety disorder, which precludes present-day interpretations of its results. A more recent twin study of generalized anxiety disorder was presented by Kendler, Neale, Kessler, Heath, and Eaves (1992a), who examined concordance of this disorder in a sample of 1,033 female–female twin pairs. Generalized anxiety disorder had a modest genetic component, with heritability rates ranging from 19% to 30% for various definitions. In addition, environmental factors unshared by the twins seemed to account for more of the remaining liability than early shared environment. A number of recent reports have also suggested that there is a genetic relationship between major depression and generalized anxiety disorder (Kendler, Neale, Kessler, Heath, & Eaves, 1992c; Mendlewicz, Papdimitriou, & Wilmotte, 1993; Roy et al., 1995). These authors found that genetic factors were completely shared between major depression and generalized anxiety disorder. In addition, a modest proportion of the nonfamilial environmental risk factors were shared between these two disorders. Shared familial environmental factors did not play a role in either condition. These findings suggest that a "neuroticism trait" may be inherited and expressed as different emotional disorders.

Few studies have examined the role of family environmental factors in the onset of generalized anxiety disorder. Some studies have compared early childhood factors in patients with generalized anxiety disorder and patients with panic disorder. Few differences were found on variables such as early separations, child abuse, separation disorder, disturbed environments, divorce, or ill health (Raskin, Peeke, Dickman, & Pinsker, 1982). Torgersen (1986) found that individuals with generalized anxiety disorder were more likely to report the death of a parent prior to age 16. Consistent with this finding, a recent study has found retrospective reports of dysfunctional attachment styles in patients with generalized anxiety disorder (Zuellig, Newman, Kachin, & Constantino, 1997). Furthermore, results from studies examining DSM-III-R overanxious disorder, a developmental precursor to generalized anxiety disorder, have shown that this disorder occurs persistently throughout childhood, beginning quite early (Bernstein & Borchardt, 1991). Further research is necessary to examine the role of developmental variables in the pathogenesis of generalized anxiety disorder.

Biological Theories

Research into the biological underpinnings of generalized anxiety disorder has been neglected (Cowley & Roy-Byrne, 1991). Most existing knowledge of the biology of generalized anxiety disorder comes from examinations of the physical effects of benzodiazepines (e.g., alprazolam, diazepam) on patients with generalized anxiety disorder. Benzodiazepines attach to specific "benzodiazepine-binding" sites that are associated with GABA receptors. GABA is the major inhibitory neurotransmitter in the human nervous system. Benzodiazepine receptor agonists increase the frequency of available chloride ion channels in the GABA receptor system. As a result, the inhibitory strength of GABA is increased. Karp, Weizman, Tyano, and Gavish (1989) have shown that patients with generalized anxiety disorder have a decreased number of platelet benzodiazepine-binding sites. In addition, diazepam works to increase activity of the benzodiazepine-GABA receptor complex (Roy-Byrne et al., 1991).

In addition to the GABA system, other neurotransmitters may play a role in generalized anxiety disorder. The efficacy of buspirone, a 5-HT_{1A} receptor agonist, in patients with generalized anxiety disorder suggests the involvement of serotonin. In particular, the dorsal raphe system may be involved in the production of chronic anxiety (File, 1984). In addition, there may be a slight abnormality of catecholamine activity such as norepinephrine. However, results are inconclusive at this time (Cowley & Roy-Byrne, 1991). Other possible candidates for exploration are adenosine receptors, N-methyl-asparate (NMDA) receptors, and cholecystokinin-B (CCK-B) receptors, all of which have shown abnormality associated with chronic anxiety. In addition, a recent study has examined autonomic characteristics of worry in patients with generalized anxiety disorder (Thayer, Friedman, & Borkovec, 1996). These investigators reported that, relative to baseline and relaxation conditions, worry in these patients was associated with decreased cardiac vagal control. Finally, patients with generalized anxiety disorder have been shown to exhibit sleep abnormalities including increased stage 2 sleep, lower levels of rapid eye movement (REM), longer REM latency, and less REM activity than patients with major depression (Reynolds, Shaw, Newton, Coble, & Kupfer, 1983).

Behavioral and Cognitive Theories

Most psychological models of generalized anxiety disorder have relied on cognitive information-processing formulations (Rapee, 1991). Mathews and colleagues (Butler & Mathews, 1983; Mathews & MacLeod, 1985, 1986) have shown that individuals with generalized anxiety disorder allocate extensive attentional resources to threatening information, and, subsequently, are able to detect this information in an accelerated manner. This process has been demonstrated using a number of different procedures including the modified Stroop task, a dichotic listening task, and a visual detection task. Rapee (1991) suggests that once threat information is processed, it is encoded into elaborate schemas that may be easily accessed by persons with generalized anxiety disorder. These schemas consist of "anxiety nodes" containing information on potential responses to threat and information about the likelihood of controlling the threat. Information concerning successful control of the threat will inhibit anxiety. However, individuals with generalized anxiety disorder may have little experience with personal control. As a result, threat processing is strengthened and perceptions of control are further decreased. For the most part, Rapee explains, this process is automatic. However, a more controlled process in generalized anxiety disorder is worry.

Worry in generalized anxiety disorder must be excessive and difficult to control (APA, 1994). However, knowledge concerning the process of worry has only recently begun to accumulate (Borkovec et al., 1991). Patients with generalized anxiety disorder seem to spend most of their day worrying (Craske, Rapee, Jackel, & Barlow, 1989; Sanderson & Barlow, 1990). In addition, Craske et al. found that patients with generalized anxiety disorder believed their worries to be less controllable, less realistic, and less successfully reduced by corrective actions than control subjects. Borkovec et al. (1991) conclude that the nature of worry in these patients is not significantly different than in normal subjects. However, individuals with generalized anxiety disorder may worry excessively.

These findings suggest that worry processes are distinct cognitive phenomena that are elevated in patients with generalized anxiety disorder. However, they do not address the utility of the worry process for the individual with generalized anxiety disorder. Worry in generalized anxiety disorder is primarily a verbal and linguistic activity (Borkovec & Inz, 1990). Borkovec et al. (1991) propose that worry is a means of avoidance of other types of thought, such as imaginal processes, that may be more closely associated with negative emotion. Generalized-anxiety-disorder patients may use worry to avoid emotional processing. Borkovec and Roemer (1995) have shown that patients with generalized anxiety disorder were more likely to cite "distraction from emotional topics" as a reason for worrying than comparison groups. Such cognitive avoidance is likely to be reinforced, given the likely release from displeasing emotion. As a result, full emotional processing may be blocked (Foa & Kozak, 1986). Worry, then, may reduce anxiety in the short term, but it may increase anxiety or prevent its extinction in the long term. Wells (1995) has extended this line of reasoning in his description of "meta-worry," in which the individual negatively appraises the recurrent process of worry (i.e., worries about worrying). As a result, the generalized anxiety-disordered patient is then motivated to simultaneously worry (to avoid emotional activation) and to reduce the worry (to avoid the unpleasant cognitive consequence associated with worry). Wells suggests that the concept of meta-worry can distinguish worriers with generalized anxiety disorder from normal worriers. However, empirical investigation of this theory is still forthcoming.

Environmental Stress

Apart from traumatic learning in cases of phobic disorders, environmental stress may contribute to the onset of anxiety disorders (Endler & Edwards, 1988; Monroe & Wade, 1988). For example, one study found that in a large number of cases of generalized anxiety disorder, patients had experienced important negative and unexpected events in the months prior to their anxiety reaching clinical proportions (Blazer, Hughes, & George, 1987). Also, many patients experience significant stressors in the months preceding their first panic attack (Faravelli, 1985; Roy-Byrne, Gerzci, & Uhde, 1986). The types of stressors mentioned in these and similar studies range from interpersonal problems, to difficulties at work, adjustment to new environments, personal loss, or physical illness. Care was taken in DSM-III to differentiate normal stress reactions and adjustment disorders from more enduring anxiety disorders, and more prospective research needs to document the increased risk for anxiety disorders that may follow environmental stress. The evidence to date has not established a specific anxiogenic effect. Depressive effects following stress have also been noted (e.g., Brown & Harris, 1978; Monroe & Steiner, 1986), and panic disorder preceded by a major life event did not differ from panic disorder that was not preceded by such an event on clinical presentation or demographics (Garvey, Noyes, & Cook, 1987). On the whole, results do support the promise of a diathesis–stress model, but the actual linkages are not yet clear.

TREATMENT IMPLICATIONS AND SUMMARY

The study of anxiety disorders has made great advances in the closing decades of the 20th century, due in part to increasingly rigorous diagnostic procedures, improved methodology, and coherent theories that yield testable predictions. On the other hand, many basic issues will require further research before an integrative understanding of the pathology of anxiety can be achieved. The most basic of these issues is definitional. The continuous revisions in DSM over that past decade have helped researchers appreciate the complexity of anxiety disorders, but they make comparison across studies employing different diagnostic systems difficult. On the whole, changes in diagnostic procedure have been based on empirical evidence, and the revision of DSM-III was more a clarification than a redefinition, aiding the continuity of research. DSM-III-R and DSM-IV facilitated the investigation of comorbid pathology, further enhancing the validity or revision of diagnostic categories.

It is perhaps uninformed to believe that any one theory can encompass the whole of anxiety disorder pathology. Perhaps the most influential theories to date are biological and cognitive, and the integration of these perspectives will surely proceed. Clearly no viable theories of anxiety can ignore the interplay of response domains. In particular, vulnerability hypotheses, such as the behavioral inhibition model (Biederman et al., 1995), will aid in the integration of these differing theoretical formulations. Similarly, more research is needed directly comparing specific anxiety disorders and contrasting anxiety with other disorders to address the similarities and dissimilarities of underlying pathology. Without psychiatric comparison groups, most investigations are open to alternative hypotheses related to the presence of general psychopathology.

Research on the phenomenology of anxiety should also go beyond immediate clinical presentation. The life interference of anxiety disorders is poorly understood. Studies of panic disorder generated epidemiologic evidence for reduced quality of life, such as increased health system usage, substance abuse, suicide attempts, and financial dependency. Only a handful of studies (e.g., Safran et al., 1997) have examined the quality of social or work relationships, which should be a cornerstone of quality of life assessment, for any of the anxiety disorders.

The treatment of anxiety disorders was not discussed in this chapter but the success of psychological and pharmacological interventions, and the manner in which successfully treated patients maintain normative functioning or relapse after treatment, may yield very important information about the nature of anxiety disorders. For this purpose, treatment studies might include assessment that is not directly related to symptom alleviation. Similarly a better understanding of the nature and etiology of anxiety pathology should lead to earlier detection of persons at risk and more efficient treatment implementation. Thus, the study of treatment efficacy and the nature of anxiety disorders have a reciprocal relationship that should be beneficial to both.

REFERENCES

Achenbach, T. (1995). Diagnosis, assessment, and comorbidity in psychosocial treatment research. *Journal of Abnormal Child Psychology, 23,* 45–65.

Alden, L.E., & Wallace, S.T. (1995). Social phobia and social appraisal in successful and unsuccessful social interactions. *Behaviour Research and Therapy, 33,* 497–505.

American Psychiatric Association. (1968). *Diagnostic and statistical manual of mental disorders,* 2nd ed. Washington DC: Author.

American Psychiatric Association. (1980). *Diagnostic and statistical manual of mental disorders,* 3rd ed. Washington DC: Author.

American Psychiatric Association. (1987). *Diagnostic and statistical manual of mental disorders,* 3rd ed. (revised). Washington DC: Author.

American Psychiatric Association. (1994). *Diagnostic and statistical manual of mental disorders,* 4th ed. Washington DC: Author.

Amies, P.L., Gelder, M.G., & Shaw, P.M. (1983). Social phobia: A comparative clinical study. *British Journal of Psychiatry, 142,* 174–179.

Anderson, C.A., & Harvey, R.J. (1988). Discriminating between problems in living: An examination of measures of depression, loneliness, shyness, and social anxiety. *Journal of Social and Clinical Psychology, 6,* 482–491.

Anderson, D.J., Noyes, R., & Crowe, R.R. (1984). A comparison of panic disorder and generalized anxiety disorder. *American Journal of Psychiatry, 141,* 572–575.

Andrews, G. (1996). Comorbidity in neurotic disorders: The similarities are more important than the differences. In R.M. Rapee (Ed.), *Current controversies in the anxiety disorders* (pp. 3–20). New York: Guilford Press.

Angst, J., & Vollrath, M. (1991). The natural history of anxiety disorders. *Acta Psychiatrica Scandinavica, 84,* 446–452.

Antony, M.M., & Barlow, D.H. (1996). Emotion theory as a framework for explaining panic attacks and panic disorder. In R.M. Rapee (Ed.), *Current controversies in the anxiety disorders* (pp. 55–76). New York: Guilford Press.

Arrindell, W.A., Emmelkamp, P.M.G., Monsma, A., & Brilman, E. (1983). The role of perceived parental rearing practices in the etiology of phobic disorders: A controlled study. *British Journal of Psychiatry, 143,* 183–187.

Arrindell, W.A., Kwee, M.G.T., Methorst, G.J., Van Der Ende, J., Pol, E., & Moritz, B.J.M. (1989). Perceived parental rearing styles of agoraphobic and socially phobic inpatients. *British Journal of Psychiatry, 155,* 526–535.

Barlow, D. (1988). *Anxiety and its disorders.* New York: Guilford Press.

Barlow, D.H., & Cerny, J.A. (1988). *Psychological treatment of panic.* New York: Guilford Press.

Barlow, D.H., & Craske, M.G. (1988). The phenomenology of panic. In S.J. Rachman & J.D. Maser (Eds.), *Panic: Psychological perspectives* (pp. 11–36). Hillsdale, NJ: Lawrence Erlbaum.

Bech, P., & Angst, J. (1996). Quality of life in anxiety and social phobia. *International Clinical Psychopharmacology, 11(Suppl. 3),* 97–100.

Beck, A.T., & Emery, G. (1985). *Anxiety disorders and phobias.* New York: Basic Books.

Beck, J.G., Stanley, M.A., & Zebb, B.J. (1996). Characteristics of generalized anxiety disorder in older adults: A descriptive study. *Behaviour Research and Therapy, 34,* 225–234.

Belin, M.F., Nanopoulos, D., Didier, M.I., Aguera, M., Steinbusch, H., Verhofstad, A., Maite, M., & Pujol, J.F. (1983). Immunohistochemical evidence for the presence of gamma-aminobutyric acid and serotonin in one nerve cell. A study on the raphe nuclei of the rat using antibodies to glutamate decarboxylase and serotonin. *Brain Research, 275,* 329–339.

Bernstein, G.A., & Borchardt, C.M. (1991). Anxiety disorders of childhood and adolescence: A critical review. *Journal of the American Academy of Child and Adolescent Psychiatry, 30,* 519–532.

Biederman, J., Faraone, S.V., Marrs, A., & Moore, P. (1997). Panic disorder and agoraphobia in consecutively referred children and adolescents. *Journal of the American Academy of Child and Adolescent Psychiatry, 36,* 214–223.

Biederman, J., Rosenbaum, J., Chaloff, J., & Kagan, J. (1995). Behavioral inhibition as a risk factor for anxiety disorders. In J. March (Ed.), *Anxiety disorders in children and adolescents* (pp. 61–81). New York: Guilford Press.

Bland, R.C., Newman, S.C., & Orn, H. (1988). Age of onset of psychiatric disorders. *Acta Psychiatrica Scandanavica, 77(Suppl. 338),* 43–49.

Blazer, D., George, L.K., Landerman, R., Pennybaker, M., Melville, M.L., Woodbury, M., Manton, K.G., Jorden, K., & Locke, B. (1984). Psychiatric disorders: A rural/urban comparison. *Archives of General Psychiatry, 42,* 651–656.

Blazer, D., Hughes, D., & George, L.D. (1987). Stressful life events and the onset of a generalized anxiety syndrome. *American Journal of Psychiatry, 144,* 1178–1183.

Blazer, D., Hughes, D., George, L.K. (1991). Generalized anxiety disorder. In L.N. Robins & D.A. Regier (Eds.), *Psychiatric disorders in America: The Epidemiological Catchment Area Study* (pp. 180–203). New York: Free Press.

Bond, N.W., & Siddle, D.A.T. (1996). The preparedness account of social phobia: Some data and alternative explanations. In R.M. Rapee (Ed.), *Current controversies in the anxiety disorders* (pp. 291–316). New York: Guilford Press.

Borkovec, T.D., & Inz, J. (1990). The nature of worry in generalized anxiety disorder: A predominance of thought activity. *Behaviour Research and Therapy, 28,* 153–158.

Borkovec, T.D., & Roemer, L. (1995). Perceived functions of worry among generalized anxiety disorder subjects: Distraction from more emotionally distressing topics? *Journal of Behavior Therapy and Experimental Psychiatry, 26,* 25–30.

Borkovec, T.D., Shadick, R.N., & Hopkins, M. (1991). The nature of normal and pathological worry. In R.M. Rapee & D.H. Barlow (Eds.), *Chronic anxiety: Generalized anxiety disorder and mixed anxiety-depression* (pp. 29–51). New York: Guilford Press.

Bourdon, K.H., Boyd, J.H., Rae, D.S., Burns, B.J., Thompson, J.W., & Locke, B.Z. (1988). Gender differences in phobias: Results of the ECA Community Study. *Journal of Anxiety Disorders, 2,* 227–241.

Boyd, J.H., Burke, J.D., Gruenberg, E., Holzer, C.E. III, Rae, D.S., George, L.K., Karno, M., Stoltzman, R., McEvoy, L., & Nestadt, G. (1984). Exclusion criteria of DSM-III: A study of co-occurrence of hierarchy-free syndromes. *Archives of General Psychiatry, 41,* 983–989.

Brawman-Mintzer, O., Lydiard, R.B., Emmanuel, N., Payeur, R., Johnson, M., Roberts, J., Jarrell, M.P., & Ballenger, J.C. (1993). Psychiatric comorbidity in patients with generalized anxiety disorder. *American Journal of Psychiatry, 150,* 1216–1218.

Brooks, R.B., Baltazar, P.L., & Munjack, D.J. (1989). Co-occurrence of personality disorders with panic disorder, social phobia, and generalized anxiety disorder: A review of the literature. *Journal of Anxiety Disorders, 3,* 259–285.

Brown, E.J., Heimberg, R.G., & Juster, H.R. (1995). Social phobia subtype and avoidant personality disorder: Effect on severity of social phobia, impairment, and outcome of cognitive behavioral treatment. *Behavior Therapy, 26,* 467–486.

Brown, G.W., & Harris, T. (1978). *Social origins of depression.* New York: Free Press.

Brown, T.A., & Barlow, D.H. (1992). Comorbidity among anxiety disorders: Implications for treatment and DSM-IV. *Journal of Consulting and Clinical Psychology, 60,* 835–844.

Brown, T.A., Barlow, D.H., & Liebowitz, M.R. (1994). The empirical basis of generalized anxiety disorder. *American Journal of Psychiatry, 151,* 1272–1280.

Bruch, M.A., & Cheek, J.M. (1995). Developmental factors in childhood and adolescent shyness. In R.G. Heimberg, M.R. Liebowitz, D.A. Hope, & F.R. Schneier (Eds.), *Social phobia: Diagnosis, assessment, and treatment* (pp. 163–184). New York: Guilford Press.

Bruch, M.A., Gorsky, J.M., Collins, T.M., & Berger, P.A. (1989). Shyness and sociability reexamined: A multicomponent analysis. *Journal of Personality and Social Psychology, 57,* 904–915.

Bruch, M.A., & Heimberg, R.G. (1994). Differences in perceptions of parental and personal characteristics between generalized and nongeneralized social phobics. *Journal of Anxiety Disorders, 8,* 155–168.

Bruch, M.A., Heimberg, R.G., Berger, P., & Collins, T.M. (1989). Social phobia and perceptions of early parental and personal characteristics. *Anxiety Research, 2,* 57–65.

Burke, K.C., Burke, J.D., Jr., Regier, D.A., & Rae, D.S. (1990). Age at onset of selected mental disorders in five community populations. *Archives of General Psychiatry, 47,* 511–518.

Burns, D.D. (1980). *Feeling good: The new mood therapy.* New York: Avon.

Butler, G., & Mathews, A. (1983). Cognitive processes in anxiety. *Advances in Behaviour Research and Therapy, 5,* 51–62.

Campbell, M.A., & Rapee, R.M. (1994). The nature

of feared outcome representations in children. *Journal of Abnormal Child Psychology, 22,* 99–111.

Caspi, A., Elder, G.H., & Bem, D.J. (1988). Moving away from the world: Life-course patterns of shy children. *Developmental Psychology, 24,* 824–831.

Chambless, D.L., Renneberg, B., Goldstein, A., & Gracely, E. (1992). MCMI-diagnosed personality disorders among agoraphobic outpatients: Prevalence and relationship to severity and treatment outcome. *Journal of Anxiety Disorders, 6,* 193–211.

Chapman, T.F. (1993). *Assortative mating and mental illness.* Unpublished doctoral dissertation, Yale University.

Chapman, T.F., Manuzza, S., & Fyer, A.J. (1995). Epidemiology and family studies of social phobia. In R.G. Heimberg, M.R. Liebowitz, D.A. Hope, & F.R. Schneier (Eds.), *Social phobia: Diagnosis, assessment, and treatment* (pp. 21–40). New York: Guilford Press.

Charney, D.S., & Heninger, G.R. (1986). Noradrenergic function and the mechanism of action of antianxiety treatment: The effects of long-term alprazolam treatment. *Archives of General Psychiatry, 43,* 1042–1054.

Charney, D.S., Woods, S.W., Krystal, J.H., & Heninger, G.R. (1990a). Serotonin function and human anxiety disorders. *Annals of the New York Academy of Sciences, 600,* 558–573.

Charney, D.S., Woods, S.W., Nagy, L.M., Southwick, S.M., Krystal, J.H., & Heninger, G.R. (1990b). Noradrenergic function in panic disorder. *Journal of Clinical Psychiatry, 51(Suppl. A),* 5–11.

Clark, D.M. (1986). A cognitive approach to panic. *Behaviour Research and Therapy, 24,* 461–470.

Clark, D.M., Salkovskis, P.M., Hackmann, A., Middleton, H., Anastasiades, P., & Gelder, M. (1994). A comparison of cognitive therapy, applied relaxation and imipramine in the treatment of panic disorder. *British Journal of Psychiatry, 164,* 759–769.

Clark, D.M., Salkovskis, P.M., Öst, L.G., Breitholtz, E., Koehler, K.A., Westling, B.E., Jeavons, A., & Gelder, M. (1997). Misinterpretation of body sensations in panic disorder. *Journal of Consulting and Clinical Psychology, 65,* 203–213.

Clark, D.M., & Wells, A. (1995). A cognitive model of social phobia. In R.G. Heimberg, M.R. Liebowitz, D.A. Hope, & F.R. Schneier (Eds.), *Social phobia: Diagnosis, assessment, and treatment* (pp. 69–93). New York: Guilford Press.

Clark, L.A., Watson, D., & Mineka, S. (1994). Temperament, personality, and the mood and anxiety disorders. *Journal of Abnormal Psychology, 103,* 103–16.

Cloitre, M., & Shear, M.K. (1995). Psychodynamic perspectives. In M.B. Stein (Ed.), *Social phobia: Clinical and research perspectives* (pp. 163–187). Washington, DC: American Psychiatric Press.

Cook, M., & Mineka, S. (1989). Observational conditioning of fear to fear-relevant versus fear-irrelevant stimuli in rhesus monkeys. *Journal of Abnormal Psychology, 98,* 448–459.

Cowley, D.S., Dager, S.R., & Dunner, D.L. (1987). Lactate infusions in major depression without panic attacks. *Journal of Psychiatric Research, 21,* 243–248.

Cowley, D.S., Dager, S.R., McClellan, J., Roy-Byrne, P.P., & Dunner, D. L. (1988). Response to lactate infusion in generalized anxiety disorder. *Biological Psychiatry, 24,* 409–414.

Cowley, D.S., & Roy-Byrne, P.P. (1991). The biology of generalized anxiety disorder and chronic anxiety. In R.M. Rapee & D.H. Barlow (Eds.), *Chronic anxiety: Generalized anxiety disorder and mixed anxiety-depression* (pp. 52–75). New York: Guilford Press.

Cox, B.J., Direnfeld, D.M., Swinson, R.P., & Norton, G.R. (1994). Suicidal ideation and suicide attempts in panic disorder and social phobia. *American Journal of Psychiatry, 151,* 882–887.

Cox, B.J., Wessel, I., Norton, G.R., Swinson, R.P., & Direnfeld, D.M. (1995). Publication trends in anxiety disorders research: 1990–1992. *Journal of Anxiety Disorders, 9,* 531–538.

Craske, M.G., & Barlow, D.H. (1988). A review of the relationship between panic and avoidance. *Clinical Psychology Review, 8,* 667–685.

Craske, M.G., & Barlow, D.H. (1990). Nocturnal panic: Response to hyperventilation and carbon dioxide challenges. *Journal of Abnormal Psychology, 99,* 302–307.

Craske, M.G., Rapee, R.M., Jackel, L., & Barlow, D.H. (1989). Qualitative dimensions of worry in

DSM-III-R generalized anxiety disorder subjects and nonanxious controls. *Behaviour Research and Therapy, 27,* 397–402.

Craske, M.G., & Rowe, M.K. (1997). Nocturnal panic. *Clinical Psychology: Science and Practice, 4,* 153–174.

Crowe, R.R. (1994). The Iowa linkage study of panic disorder. In E.S. Gershon & C.R. Cloninger (Eds.), *Genetic approaches to mental disorders* (pp. 291–310). Washington, DC: American Psychiatric Press.

Crowe, R.R., Noyes, R., Pauls, D.L., & Slymen, D. (1983). A family study of panic disorder. *Archives of General Psychiatry, 40,* 1065–1069.

Davey, G.C.L. (1994). Self-reported fears to common indigenous animals in an adult UK population: The role of disgust sensitivity. *British Journal of Psychology, 85,* 541–554.

deRuiter, C., Rijken, H., Garssen, B., van Schaik, A., & Kraaimaat, F. (1989). Comorbidity among the anxiety disorders. *Journal of Anxiety Disorders, 3,* 57–68.

Dilsaver, S.C., Qamar, A.B., & del Medico, V.J. (1992). Secondary social phobia in patients with major depression. *Psychiatry Research, 44,* 33–40.

DiNardo, P.A., & Barlow, D.H. (1990). Syndrome and symptom comorbidity in the anxiety disorders. In J.D. Maser & C.R. Cloninger (Eds.), *Comorbidity in anxiety and mood disorders* (pp. 205–230). Washington, DC: American Psychiatric Press.

DuPont, R.L., Rice, D.P., Miller, L.S., Shiraki, S.S., Rowland, C.R., & Harwood, H.J. (1996). Economic costs of anxiety disorders. *Anxiety, 2,* 167–172.

Eaton, W.W., & Keyl, P.M. (1990). Risk factors for the onset of Diagnostic Interview Schedule/DSM-III agoraphobia in a prospective, population-based study. *Archives of General Psychiatry, 47,* 819–824.

Ehlers, A. (1995). A one-year prospective study of panic attacks: Clinical course and factors associated with maintenance. *Journal of Abnormal Psychology, 104,* 164–172.

Endler, N.S., & Edwards, J.M. (1988). Stress and vulnerability. In C.G. Last & M. Hersen (Eds.), *Handbook of anxiety disorders* (pp. 278–292). New York: Pergamon Press.

Faravelli, C. (1985). Life events preceding the onset of anxiety disorders. *Journal of Affective Disorders, 9,* 103–105.

Faravelli, C., Panichi, C., Pallanti, S., Paterniti, S., Grecu, L.M., & Rivelli, S. (1991). Perception of early parenting in panic and agoraphobia. *Acta Psychiatrica Scandanavica, 84,* 6–8.

File, S.F. (1984). The neurochemistry of anxiety. In G.D. Burrows, T.R. Norman, & B. Davies (Eds.), *Anti-anxiety agents* (pp. 13–14). Amsterdam: Elsevier.

Foa, E.B., & Kozak, M.J. (1986). Emotional processing of fear: Exposure to corrective information. *Psychological Bulletin, 99,* 20–35.

Fyer, A., Katon, W., Hollifield, M., Rassnick, H., Manuzza, S., Chapman, T., & Ballenger, J. (1996). The DSM-IV panic disorder field trial: Panic attack frequency and functional disability. *Anxiety, 2,* 157–166.

Fyer, A.J., Mannuzza, S., Chapman, T.F., Liebowitz, M.R., & Klein, D.F. (1993). A direct interview family study of social phobia. *Archives of General Psychiatry, 50,* 286–293.

Fyer, A.J., Mannuzza, S., Gallops, M.S., Martin, L.Y., Aaronson, C., Gorman, J.M., Liebowitz, M.R., & Klein, D.F. (1990). Familial transmission of simple phobias and fears: A preliminary report. *Archives of General Psychiatry, 47,* 252–256.

Garvey, M., Noyes, R., & Cook, B. (1987). Does situational panic disorder represent a specific panic disorder subtype? *Comprehensive Psychiatry, 28,* 329–333.

Gerlsma, C., Emmelkamp, P.M.G., & Arrindell, W.A. (1990). Anxiety, depression, and perception of early parenting: A meta-analysis. *Clinical Psychology Review, 10,* 251–277.

Goldenberg, I.M., White, K., Yonkers, K., Reich, J., Warshaw, M.G., Goisman, R.M., & Keller, M.B. (1996). The infrequency of "pure culture" diagnoses among the anxiety disorders. *Journal of Clinical Psychiatry, 57,* 528–533.

Goldstein, A.J., & Chambless, D.L. (1978). A reanalysis of agoraphobia. *Behavior Therapy, 9,* 47–59.

Gorman, J.M., Liebowitz, M.R., Fyer, A.J., & Stein, J. (1989). A neuroanatomical hypothesis for panic disorder. *American Journal of Psychiatry, 146,* 148–161.

Griez, E., deLoof, C., Pols, H., & Zandbergen, J. (1990). Specific sensitivity of patients with panic attacks to carbon dioxide inhalation. *Psychiatry Research, 31,* 193–199.

Hazen, A.L., & Stein, M.B. (1995). Social phobia: Prevalence and clinical characteristics. *Psychiatric Annals, 25,* 544–549.

Heimberg, R.G. (1996). Social phobia, avoidant personality disorder and the multiaxial conceptualization of interpersonal anxiety. In P.M. Salkovskis (Ed.), *Trends in cognitive and behavioural therapies* (Vol. 1, pp. 43–61). West Sussex, England: John Wiley & Sons Ltd.

Heimberg, R.G., Hope, D.A., Dodge, C.S., & Becker, R.E. (1990). DSM-III-R subtypes of social phobia: Comparison of generalized social phobics and public speaking phobics. *Journal of Nervous and Mental Disease, 178,* 172–179.

Heimberg, R.G., Liebowitz, M.R., Hope, D.A., & Schneier, F.R. (Eds.). (1995). *Social phobia: Diagnosis, assessment, and treatment.* New York: Guilford Press.

Hoehn-Saric, R. (1981). Characteristics of chronic anxiety patients. In D.F. Klein & J. Rabkin (Eds.), *Anxiety: New research and changing concepts.* New York: Raven Press.

Hollifield, M., Katon, W., Skipper, B., Chapman, T., Ballenger, J.C., Mannuzza, S., & Fyer, A.J. (1997). Panic disorder and quality of life: Variables predictive of functional impairment. *American Journal of Psychiatry, 154,* 766–772.

Holt, C.S., Heimberg, R.G., & Hope, D.A. (1992a). Avoidant personality disorder and the generalized subtype of social phobia. *Journal of Abnormal Psychology, 101,* 318–325.

Holt, C.S., Heimberg, R.G., Hope, D.A., & Liebowitz, M.R. (1992b). Situational domains of social phobia. *Journal of Anxiety Disorders, 6,* 63–77.

Hope, D.A., Rapee, R.M., Heimberg, R.G., & Dombeck, M.J. (1990). Representations of the self in social phobia: Vulnerability to social threat. *Cognitive Therapy and Research, 14,* 177–189.

Jansen, M.A., Arntz, A., Merckelbach, H., & Mersch, P.P.A. (1994). Personality disorders and features in social phobia and panic disorder. *Journal of Abnormal Psychology, 103,* 391–395.

Johnson, J., Weissman, M.M., & Klerman, G.L. (1990). Panic disorder, comorbidity, and suicide attempts. *Archives of General Psychiatry, 47,* 805–808.

Juster, H.R., & Heimberg, R.G. (1998). Social phobia. In P. Salkovskis (Volume Ed.), *Comprehensive clinical psychology: Volume 6. Adults: Clinical formulation and treatment* (M. Hersen & A.S. Bellack, Series Eds.). New York: Elsevier.

Kahn, R.S., Westenberg, H.G.M., & Moorse, C. (1995). Increased serotonin function and panic disorder. In G.M. Asnis & H.M. van Praag (Eds.), *Panic disorder: Clinical, biological, and treatment aspects* (pp. 151–180). New York: Wiley.

Karp, L., Weizman, A., Tyano, S., & Gavish, M. (1989). Examination stress, platelet peripheral benzodizepine binding sites, and plasma hormone levels. *Life Sciences, 44,* 1077–1082.

Katzelnick, D.J., Kobak, K.A., Greist, J.H., Jefferson, J.W., Mantle, J.M., & Serlin, R.C. (1995). Sertraline for social phobia: A double-blind, placebo-controlled crossover study. *American Journal of Psychiatry, 152,* 1368–1371.

Keller, M.B., Lavori, P.W., Goldenberg, I.M., Baker, L.A., et al. (1993). Influence of depression on the treatment of panic disorder with imipramine, alprazolam and placebo. *Journal of Affective Disorders, 28,* 27–38.

Kelley, M.J. (1987). Hormones and clinical anxiety: An imbalanced neuromodulation of attention. In J. Eysenck & I. Martin (Eds.), *Theoretical foundations of behavior therapy.* New York: Plenum Press.

Kelly, P., Mitchell-Heggs, N., & Sherman, D. (1971). Anxiety in the effects of sodium lactate assessed clinically and physiologically. *British Journal of Psychiatry, 119,* 468–470.

Kenardy, J., Evans, L., & Oei, T.P. (1992). The latent structure of anxiety symptoms in anxiety disorders. *American Journal of Psychiatry, 149,* 1058–1061.

Kendall, P.C., & Warman, M.J. (1996). Anxiety disorders in youth: Diagnostic consistency across DSM-III-R and DSM-IV. *Journal of Anxiety Disorders, 10,* 452–463.

Kendler, K.S., Neale, M.C., Kessler, R.C., Heath, A.C., & Eaves, L.J. (1992a). Generalized anxiety disorder in women: A population-based twin study. *Archives of General Psychiatry, 49,* 267–272.

Kendler, K.S., Neale, M.C., Kessler, R.C., Heath, A.C., & Eaves, L.J. (1992b). The genetic epidemiology of phobias in women: The interrelationship of agoraphobia, social phobia, situational phobia, and simple phobia. *Archives of General Psychiatry, 49,* 273–281.

Kendler, K.S., Neale, M.C., Kessler, R.C., Heath, A.C., & Eaves, L.J. (1992c). Major depression and generalized anxiety disorder: Same genes, (partly) different environments? *Archives of General Psychiatry, 49,* 716–722.

Kendler, K.S., Neale, M.C., Kessler, R.C., Heath, A.C., & Eaves, L.J. (1993). Panic disorder in women: A population-based twin study. *Psychological Medicine, 23,* 397–406.

Kessler, R.C., McGonagle, K.A., Zhao, S., Nelson, C.B., Hughes, M., Eshleman, S., Wittchen, H.U., & Kendler, K.S. (1994). Lifetime and 12-month prevalence of DSM-III-R psychiatric disorders in the United States: Results from the National Comorbidity Survey. *Archives of General Psychiatry, 51,* 8–19.

Klein, D. (1993). False suffocation alarms, spontaneous panics, and related conditions: An integrative hypothesis. *Archives of General Psychiatry, 50,* 306–318.

Knott, V.J., & Lapierre, Y.D. (1986). Effects of lactate-induced panic attacks on brain stem auditory evoked potentials. *Neuropsychobiology, 16,* 9–14.

Krieg, J.C., Bronischt, T., Wittchen, H.U., & von Zerssen, D. (1987). Anxiety disorders: A long-term prospective and retrospective follow-up study of former inpatients suffering from an anxiety neurosis or phobia. *Acta Psychiatrica Scandanavica, 76,* 36–47.

Kuch, K., Cox, B.J., Evans, R.E., & Shulman, I. (1994). Phobias, panic, and pain in 55 survivors of road vehicle accidents. *Journal of Anxiety Disorders, 8,* 181–187.

Kushner, M.G., Sher, K.J., & Beitman, B.D. (1990). The relation between alcohol problems and the anxiety disorders. *American Journal of Psychiatry, 147,* 685–695.

Lang, P.J. (1988). Fear, anxiety, and panic: Context, cognition, and visceral arousal. In S. Rachman & J.D. Maser (Eds.), *Panic: Psychological perspectives.* Hillsdale, NJ: Lawrence Erlbaum.

LeDoux, J. (1992). Emotion as memory: Anatomical systems underlying indelible neural traces. In S.A. Christianson (Ed.), *The handbook of emotion and memory: Research and theory* (pp. 269–288). Hillsdale, NJ: Lawrence Erlbaum.

Lelliott, P., McNamee, G., & Marks, I. (1991). Features of agora-, social, and related phobias and validation of the diagnoses. *Journal of Anxiety Disorders, 5,* 313–322.

Leon, C.A., & Leon, A. (1990). Panic disorder and parental bonding. *Psychiatric Annals, 20,* 503–508.

Lesch, K.P., Wiesmann, M., Hoh, A., Müller, T., Disselkamp-Tierze, J., Osterheider, M., & Schulte, H.M. (1992). 5-HT1A receptor-effector system responsivity in panic disorder. *Psychopharmacology, 106,* 111–117.

Lesser, I.M., Rubin, R.T., Pecknold, J.C., Rifkin, A., et al. (1988). Secondary depression in panic disorder and agoraphobia: I. Frequency, severity, and response to treatment. *Archives of General Psychiatry, 45,* 437–443.

Lesser, I.M., Rubin, R.T., Rifkin, A., Swinson, R.P., et al. (1989). Secondary depression in panic disorder and agoraphobia: II. Dimensions of depressive symptomatology and their response to treatment. *Journal of Affective Disorders, 16,* 49–58.

Ley, R. (1985). Blood, breath, and fears: A hyperventilation theory of panic attacks and agoraphobia. *Clinical Psychology Review, 5,* 271–285.

Liebowitz, M.L., Fyer, A.J., Gorman, J.M., Dillon, D., Appleby, I.L., Levy, G., Anderson, S., Levitt, M., Palij, M., Davies, S.O., & Klein, D.F. (1984a). Lactate provocation of panic attacks: I. Clinical and behavioral findings. *Archives of General Psychiatry, 41,* 764–770.

Liebowitz, M.R., Fyer, A.J., Gorman, J.M., Dillon, D., Davies, S., Stein, J.M., Cohen, B.S., & Klein, D.F. (1985a). Specificity of lactate infusions in social phobia versus panic disorder. *American Journal of Psychiatry, 142,* 947–50.

Liebowitz, M.L., Gorman, J.M., Fyer, A.J., Levitt, M., Dillon, D., Levy, G., Appleby, I.L., Anderson, S., Palij, M., Davies, S.O., & Klein, D.F. (1985b). Lactate provocation of panic attacks: II. Biochemical and physiological findings. *Archives of General Psychiatry, 42,* 709–719.

Liebowitz, M.R., Quitkin, F.M., Steward, J.W., McGrath, P.J., Harrison, W., Rabkin, J., Tricamo, E., Markowitz, J.S., & Klein, D.F. (1984b). Phenelzine vs. imipramine in atypical depression: A preliminary report. *Archives of General Psychiatry, 41,* 669–677.

Lilienfeld, S.O. (1996). Anxiety sensitivity is not distinct from trait anxiety. In R.M. Rapee (Ed.), *Current controversies in the anxiety disorders* (pp. 228–244). New York: Guilford Press.

Lipschitz, A. (1988). Diagnosis and classification of anxiety disorders. In C.G. Last & M. Hersen (Eds.), *Handbook of anxiety disorders* (pp. 41–65). New York: Pergamon Press.

Lovibond, P.F., & Rapee, R.M. (1993). The representation of feared outcomes. *Behaviour Research and Therapy, 31,* 595–608.

Magee, W.J., Eaton, W.W., Wittchen, H.U., McGonagle, K.A., & Kessler, R.C. (1996). Agoraphobia, simple phobia, and social phobia in the National Comorbidity Survey. *Archives of General Psychiatry, 53,* 159–68.

Mannuzza, S., Fyer, A.J., Liebowitz, M.R., & Klein, D.F. (1990). Delineating the boundaries of social phobia: Its relationship to panic disorder and agoraphobia. *Journal of Anxiety Disorders, 4,* 41–59.

Mannuzza, S., Schneier, F.R., Chapman, T.F., Liebowitz, M.R., Klein, D.F., & Fyer, A.J. (1995). Generalized social phobia: Reliability and validity. *Archives of General Psychiatry, 52,* 230–237.

Markowitz, J.S., Weissman, M.M., Ouellette, R., Lish, J.D., & Klerman, G.L. (1989). Quality of life in panic disorder. *Archives of General Psychiatry, 46,* 984–992.

Marks, I.M. (1987). *Fears, phobias, and rituals: Panic, anxiety and their disorders.* New York: Oxford University Press.

Marks, I.M., & Gelder, M.G. (1966). Different ages of onset in varieties of phobias. *American Journal of Psychiatry, 123,* 218–221.

Maser, J.D. (1985). List of phobias. In A.H. Tuma & J.D. Maser (Eds.), *Anxiety and the anxiety disorders* (pp. 805–814). Hillsdale, NJ: Lawrence Erlbaum.

Massion, A.O., Warshaw, M.G., & Keller, M.B. (1993). Quality of life and psychiatric morbidity in panic disorder and generalized anxiety disorder. *American Journal of Psychiatry, 150,* 600–607.

Mathews, A., & MacLeod, C. (1985). Selective processing of threat cues in anxiety states. *Behaviour Research and Therapy, 23,* 563–569.

Mathews, A., & MacLeod, C. (1986). Discrimination of threat cues without awareness in anxiety states. *Journal of Abnormal Psychology, 95,* 131–138.

Mattia, J.I., Heimberg, R.G., & Hope, D.A. (1993). The revised Stroop color-naming task in social phobics. *Behaviour Research and Therapy, 31,* 305–313.

McLeod, J.D. (1994). Anxiety disorders and marital quality. *Journal of Abnormal Psychology, 103,* 767–776.

McNally, R.J. (1994). *Panic disorder: A critical analysis.* New York: Guilford Press.

Mendlewicz, J., Papdimitriou, G., & Wilmotte, J. (1993). Family study of panic disorder: Comparison with generalized anxiety disorder, major depression and normal subjects. *Psychiatric Genetics, 3,* 73–78.

Merckelbach, H., de Jong, P.J., Muris, P., & van den Hout, M.A. (1996). The etiology of specific phobias: A review. *Clinical Psychology Review, 16,* 337–361.

Mineka, S. (1985). Animal models of anxiety-based disorders: Their usefulness and limitations. In A.H. Tuma & J. Maser (Eds.), *Anxiety and the anxiety disorders* (pp. 199–244). Hillsdale, NJ: Lawrence Erlbaum.

Mineka, S., Davidson, M., Cook, M., & Keir, R. (1984). Observational conditioning of snake fear in rhesus monkeys. *Journal of Abnormal Psychology, 93,* 355–372.

Mineka, S., & Zinbarg, R. (1995). Conditioning and ethological models of social phobia. In R.G. Heimberg, M.R. Liebowitz, D.A. Hope, & F.R. Schneier (Eds.), *Social phobia: Diagnosis, assessment, and treatment* (pp. 134–162). New York: Guilford Press.

Monroe, S.M., & Steiner, S.C. (1986). Social support and psychopathology: Interrelations with preexisting disorder, stress, and personality. *Journal of Abnormal Psychology, 95,* 29–39.

Monroe, S.M., & Wade, S.L. (1988). Life events. In C.G. Last & M. Hersen (Eds.), *Handbook of anxiety disorders* (pp. 293–305). New York: Pergamon Press.

Moran, C., & Andrews, G. (1985). The familial occurrence of agoraphobia. *British Journal of Psychiatry, 146,* 262–267.

Moras, K., Di Nardo, P.A., Brown, T.A., & Barlow,

D.H. *Comorbidity and depression among the anxiety disorders.* Submitted for publication.

Mowrer, O. (1960). *Learning theory and behaviour.* New York: Wiley.

Munjack, D.J., & Moss, H.B. (1981). Affective disorder and alcoholism in families of agoraphobics. *Archives of General Psychiatry, 38,* 869–871.

Neal, A.M., & Turner, S.M. (1991). Anxiety disorders research with African Americans: Current status. *Psychological Bulletin, 109,* 400–410.

Neftel, K.A., Adler, R.H., Kappell, L., Rossi, M., Dolder, M., Kaser, H.E., Bruggesser, H.H., & Vorkauf, H. (1982). Stage fright in musicians: A model illustrating the effects of beta-blockers. *Psychosomatic Medicine, 44,* 461–469.

Nickell, P.V., & Uhde, T.W. (1995). Neurobiology of social phobia. In R.G. Heimberg, M.R. Liebowitz, D.A. Hope, & F.R. Schneier (Eds.), *Social phobia: Diagnosis, assessment, and treatment* (pp. 113–162). New York: Guilford Press.

Nies, A., Howard, D., & Robinson, D.S. (1982). Antianxiety effects of MAO inhibitors. In R.J. Mathew (Ed.), *The biology of anxiety* (pp. 123–133). New York: Brunner/Mazel.

Norton, G.R., Cox, B.J., Asmundson, G.J.G., & Maser, J.D. (1995). The growth of research on anxiety disorders in the 1980s. *Journal of Anxiety Disorders, 9,* 75–85.

Noyes, R., Clarkson, C., Crowe, R.R., Yates, W.R., & McChesney, C.M. (1987). A family study of generalized anxiety disorder. *American Journal of Psychiatry, 144,* 1019–1024.

Noyes, R., Crowe, R., Harris, E., Hamra, B., McChesney, C., & Chaudhry, D. (1986). Relationship between panic disorder and agoraphobia: A family study. *Archives of General Psychiatry, 43,* 227–232.

Noyes, R., Reich, J., Christiansen, J., Suelzer, M., Pfohl, B., & Coryell, W.A. (1990). Outcome of panic disorder: Relationship to diagnostic subtypes and comorbidity. *Archives of General Psychiatry, 47,* 809–818.

Oakley-Browne, M.A., Joyce, P.R., Wells, J.E., Bushnell, J.A., & Hornblow, A.R. (1989). Christchurch psychiatric epidemiology study: II. Six month and other period prevalences for specific psychiatric disorders. *Australian and New Zealand Journal of Psychiatry, 23,* 327–340.

Öhman, A. (1986). Face the beast and fear the face: Animal and social fears as prototypes for evolutionary analyses of emotion. *Psychophysiology, 23,* 123–145.

Öhman, A. (1993). Fear and anxiety are emotional phenomena: Clinical phenomenology, evolutionary perspectives, and information processing mechanisms. In M. Lewis & J.M. Haivland (Eds.), *Handbook of emotions* (pp. 511–536). New York: Guilford Press.

Öst, L.G. (1987). Age of onset in different phobias. *Journal of Abnormal Psychology, 96,* 223–229.

Öst, L.G., Jerremalm, A., & Johansson, J. (1981). Individual response patterns and the effects of different behavioral methods in the treatment of social phobia. *Behaviour Research and Therapy, 19,* 1–16.

Otto, M.W., Pollack, M.H., Sachs, G.S., O'Neil, C.A., & Rosenbaum, J.F. (1992). Alcohol dependence in panic disorder patients. *Journal of Psychiatry Research, 26,* 29–38.

Panzarella, C. (1995). Klein's suffocation false alarm theory: Another perspective. *Anxiety, 1,* 144.

Papp, L.A., & Gorman, J.M. (1995). Respiratory neurobiology of panic. In G.M. Asnis & H.M. van Praag (Eds.), *Panic disorder: Clinical, biological, and treatment aspects* (pp. 255–275). New York: Wiley.

Parker, G. (1979). Reported parental characteristics of agoraphobics and social phobics. *British Journal of Psychiatry, 135,* 555–560.

Philips, K., Fulker, D.W., & Rose, R.J. (1987). Path analysis of seven fear factors in adult twin and sibling pairs and their parents. *Genetic Epidemiology, 4,* 345–355.

Pollack, M.H., Otto, M.W., Rosenbaum, J.F., & Sachs, G.S. (1992). Personality disorders in patients with panic disorder: Association with childhood anxiety disorders, early trauma, comorbidity, and chronicity. *Comprehensive Psychiatry, 33,* 78–83.

Pollack, M.H., Otto, M.W., Sabatino, S., Majcker, D., Worthington, J.J., McArdle, E.T., & Rosenbaum, J.F. (1996). Relationship of childhood anxiety to adult panic disorder: Correlates and influence on course. *American Journal of Psychiatry, 153,* 376–381.

Pollard, C.A., Henderson, J.G., Frank, M., & Margolis, R.B. (1989). Help-seeking patterns of anxiety-disordered individuals in the general population. *Journal of Anxiety Disorders, 3,* 131–138.

Rachman, S. (1991). Neoconditioning and the classical theory of fear acquisition. *Clinical Psychology Review, 11,* 155–173.

Rachman, S., Lopatka, C., & Levitt, K. (1988). Experimental analyses of panic: II. Panic patients. *Behaviour Research and Therapy, 26,* 33–40.

Rapee, R.M. (1986). Differential response to hyperventilation in panic disorder and generalized anxiety disorder. *Journal of Abnormal Psychology, 95,* 24–28.

Rapee, R.M. (1991). Generalized anxiety disorder: A review of clinical features and theoretical concepts. *Clinical Psychology Review, 11,* 419–440.

Rapee, R.M., & Barlow, D.H. (Eds.). (1991). *Chronic anxiety: Generalized anxiety disorder and mixed anxiety-depression.* New York: Guilford Press.

Rapee, R.M., & Heimberg, R.G. (1997). A cognitive-behavioral model of anxiety in social phobia. *Behaviour Research and Therapy, 35,* 741–756.

Raskin, M., Peeke, H.V.S., Dickman, W., & Pinsker, H. (1982). Panic and generalized anxiety disorders. *Archives of General Psychiatry, 39,* 687–689.

Redmond, D.E. (1979). *Alterations in the function of the nucleus locus coeruleus: A possible model for studies in anxiety.* Oxford: Pergamon Press.

Redmond, D.E., & Huang, Y.H. (1979). New evidence for a locus coeruleus-norepinephrine connection with anxiety. *Life Sciences, 25,* 2149–2162.

Reich, J. (1988). DSM-III personality disorders and the outcome of treated panic disorder. *American Journal of Psychiatry, 145,* 1149–1152.

Reich, J., Goldenberg, I., Vasile, R., Goisman, R., & Keller, M. (1994a). A prospective follow-along study of the course of social phobia. *Psychiatry Research, 54,* 249–258.

Reich, J., Perry, J.C., Shera, D., Dyck, I., Vasile, R., Goisman, R.M., Rodriguez-Villa, F., Massion, A.O., & Keller, M. (1994b). Comparison of personality disorders in different anxiety disorder diagnoses: Panic, agoraphobia, generalized anxiety, and social phobia. *Annals of Clinical Psychiatry, 6,* 125–134.

Reich, J., & Yates, W. (1988). Family history of psychiatric disorders in social phobia. *Comprehensive Psychiatry, 29,* 72–75.

Reiss, S., Peterson, R.A., Gursky, D.M., & McNally, R.J. (1986). Anxiety sensitivity, anxiety frequency and the prediction of fearfulness. *Behaviour Research and Therapy, 24,* 1–8.

Reynolds, C.F., Shaw, D.H., Newton, T.F., Coble, P.A., & Kupfer, D.J. (1983). EEG sleep in outpatients with generalized anxiety: A preliminary comparison with depressed outpatients. *Psychiatry Research, 8,* 81–89.

Robins, L.N., Helzer, J.E., Croughan, J., & Ratcliff, K.S. (1981). National Institute of Mental Health Diagnostic Interview Schedule: Its history, characteristics, and validity. *Archives of General Psychiatry, 38,* 381–389.

Robins, L.N., Helzer, J.E., Weissman, M.M., Orvaschel, H., Gruenberg, E., Burke, J.D., & Regier, D.A. (1984). Lifetime prevalence of specific psychiatric disorders in three sites. *Archives of General Psychiatry, 41,* 949–958.

Rosenbaum, J.F., Biederman, J, Hirshfeld, D.R., Bolduc, E.A. & Chaloff, J. (1991). Behavioral inhibition in children: Possible precursor to panic disorder or social phobia. *Journal of Clinical Psychiatry, 52*(Suppl. 11), 5–9.

Roy, M.A., Neale, M.C., Pedersen, N.L., Mathe, A.A., et al. (1995). A twin study of generalized anxiety disorder and major depression. *Psychological Medicine, 25,* 1037–1049.

Roy-Byrne, P.P., Cowley, D.S., Hommer, D., Ritchie, J., et al. (1991). Neuroendocrine effects of diazepam in panic and generalized anxiety disorders. *Biological Psychiatry, 30,* 73–80.

Roy-Byrne, P.P., Gerzci, M., & Uhde, T.W. (1986). Life events and the onset of panic disorder. *American Journal of Psychiatry, 143,* 1424–1427.

Safran, S.A., Heimberg, R.G., Brown, E.J., & Holle, C. (1997). Quality of life in social phobia. *Depression and Anxiety, 4,* 126–133.

Salvador-Carulla, L., Segui, J., Fernandez-Cano, P., & Canet, J. (1995). Costs and offset effect in panic disorder. *British Journal of Psychiatry, 166*(Suppl. 27), 23–28.

Sanderson, W.C., & Barlow, D.H. (1990). A description of patients diagnosed with DSM-III-R generalized anxiety disorder. *Journal of Nervous and Mental Disease, 178,* 588–591.

Sanderson, W.C., Beck, A.T., & Beck, J. (1990a). Syndrome comorbidity in patients with major depression or dysthymia: Prevalence and temporal relationships. *American Journal of Psychiatry, 147,* 1025–1028.

Sanderson, W.C., DiNardo, P.A., Rapee, R.M., & Barlow, D.H. (1990b). Syndrome comorbidity in patients diagnosed with a DSM-III-R anxiety disorder. *Journal of Abnormal Psychology, 99,* 308–312.

Sanderson, W.C., Rapee, R.M., & Barlow, D.H. (1988). Panic induction via inhalation of 5.5% CO_2 enriched air: A single subject analysis of psychological and physiological effects. *Behaviour Research and Therapy, 26,* 333–335.

Sanderson, W.C., & Wetzler, S. (1991). Chronic anxiety and generalized anxiety disorder: Issues in comorbidity. In R.M. Rapee & D.H. Barlow (Eds.), *Chronic anxiety: Generalized anxiety disorder and mixed anxiety-depression* (pp. 119–135). New York: Guilford Press.

Scheibe, G., & Albus, M. (1992). Age at onset, precipitating events, sex distribution, and co-occurrence of anxiety disorders. *Psychopathology, 25,* 11–18.

Schmidt, N.B., Lerew, D.R., & Jackson, R.J. (1997). The role of anxiety sensitivity in the pathogenesis of panic: Prospective evaluation of spontaneous panic attacks during acute stress. *Journal of Abnormal Psychology, 106,* 355–364.

Schneier, F.R., Heckelman, L.R., Garfinkel, R., Campeas, R., Fallon, B.A., Gitow, A., Street, L., Del Bene, D., & Liebowitz, M.R. (1994). Functional impairment in social phobia. *Journal of Clinical Psychiatry, 55,* 322–331.

Schneier, F.R., Johnson, J., Hornig, C.D., Liebowitz, M.R., & Weissman, M.M. (1992). Social phobia: Comorbidity and morbidity in an epidemiologic sample. *Archives of General Psychiatry, 49,* 282–288.

Schneier, F.R., Martin, L.Y., Liebowitz, M.R., Gorman, J.M., & Fyer, A.J. (1989). Alcohol abuse in social phobia. *Journal of Anxiety Disorders, 3,* 15–23.

Schneier, F.R., Spitzer, R.L., Gibbon, M., Fyer, A.J.,

& Liebowitz, M.R. (1991). The relationship of social phobia subtypes and avoidant personality disorder. *Comprehensive Psychiatry, 32,* 1–5.

Schweizer, E.E., Winokur, A., & Rickels, K. (1986). Insulin-induced hypoglycemia and panic attacks. *American Journal of Psychiatry, 143,* 654–655.

Seligman, M.E. (1971). Phobias and preparedness. *Behavior Therapy, 2,* 307–320.

Seligman, M.E.P. (1988). Competing theories of panic. In S. Rachman & J.D. Maser (Eds.), *Panic: Psychological perspectives* (pp. 321–330). Hillsdale, NJ: Lawrence Erlbaum.

Shelbourne, C.D., Wells, K.B., & Judd, L.L. (1996). Functioning and well-being of patients with panic disorder. *American Journal of Psychiatry, 153,* 213–218.

Simon, G., Ormel, J., VonKorff, M., & Barlow, W. (1995). Health care costs associated with depressive and anxiety disorders in primary care. *American Journal of Psychiatry, 152,* 352–357.

Smail, P., Stockwell, T., Canter, S., & Hodgson, R. (1984). Alcohol dependence and phobic anxiety states. I. A prevalence study. *British Journal of Psychiatry, 144,* 53–57.

Solyom, L., Ledwidge, B., & Solyom, C. (1986). Delineating social phobia. *British Journal of Psychiatry, 149,* 464–470.

Spitzer, R.L., & Williams, J.B.W. (1985). Proposed revisions in the DSM-III classification of anxiety disorders based on research and clinical experience. In A.H. Tuma & J.D. Maser (Eds.), *Anxiety and the anxiety disorders* (pp. 759–773). Hillsdale, NJ: Lawrence Erlbaum.

Stein, M.B., Chartier, M.J., Hazen, A.L., Kozak, M.V., Tancer, M.E., Lander, S., Furer, P., Chubaty, D., & Walker, J.R. (1998). A direct-interview family study of generalized social phobia. *American Journal of Psychiatry, 155,* 90–97.

Stein, M.B., Chartier, M.J., Hazen, A.L., Kroft, C.D.L., Chale, R.A., Coté, D., & Walker, J.R. (1996). Paroxetine in the treatment of generalized social phobia: Open-label treatment and double-blind placebo-controlled discontinuation. *Journal of Clinical Psychopharmacology, 16,* 218–222.

Stein, M.B., Shea, C.A., & Uhde, T.W. (1989). Social phobic symptoms in patients with panic disorder:

Practical and theoretical implications. *American Journal of Psychiatry, 146,* 235–238.

Taggart, P., Carruthers, M., & Somerville, W. (1973). Electrocardiogram, plasma catecholamines and lipids, and their modification by oxprenolol when speaking before an audience. *Lancet, 2,* 341–346.

Thayer, J.F., Friedman, B.H., & Borkovec, T.D. (1996). Autonomic characteristics of generalized anxiety disorder and worry. *Biological Psychiatry, 39,* 255–266.

Thyer, B.A., Nesse, R.M., Cameron, O.G., & Curtis, G.C. (1986). Panic disorder: A test of the separation anxiety hypothesis. *Behaviour Research and Therapy, 24,* 209–211.

Tiihonen, J., Kuikka, J., Begstrom, K., Lepola, U., Koponen, H., & Leinonen, E. (1997). Dopamine reuptake site densities in patients with social phobia. *American Journal of Psychiatry, 154,* 239–242.

Tomarken, A.J., Mineka, S., & Cook, M. (1989). Fear-relevant selective associations and covariation bias. *Journal of Abnormal Psychology, 98,* 381–394.

Torgersen, S. (1983). Genetic factors in anxiety disorders. *Archives of General Psychiatry, 40,* 1085–1089.

Torgersen, S. (1986). Childhood and family characteristics in panic and generalized anxiety disorders. *American Journal of Psychiatry, 143,* 630–632.

Trower, P., & Gilbert, P. (1989). New theoretical conceptions of social anxiety and social phobia. *Clinical Psychology Review, 9,* 19–35.

Turk, C., Fresco, D., & Heimberg, R.G. (in press a). Social phobia: Cognitive behavior therapy. In M. Hersen & A.S. Bellack (Eds.), *Handbook of comparative treatments of adult disorders,* 2nd ed. New York: Wiley.

Turk, C.L., Heimberg, R.G, Orsillo, S.M., Holt, C.S., Gitow, A., Street, L.L., Schneier, F.R., & Liebowitz, M.R. (In press b). An investigation of gender differences in social phobia. *Journal of Anxiety Disorders.*

Turner, S.M., Beidel, D.C., Borden, J.W., Stanley, M.A., & Jacob. (1991). Social phobia: Axis I and II correlates. *Journal of Abnormal Psychology, 100,* 102–106.

Turner, S.M., Beidel, D.C., Dancu, C.V., & Keys, D.J. (1986a). Psychopathology of social phobia and comparison to avoidant personality disorder. *Journal of Abnormal Psychology, 95,* 389–394.

Turner, S.M., Biedel, D.C., & Larkin, K.T. (1986b). Situational determinants of social anxiety in clinic and nonclinic samples: Physiological and cognitive correlates. *Journal of Consulting and Clinical Psychology, 54,* 523–527.

Uhde, T.W., Roy-Byrne, P.P., Vittone, B.J., Boulenger, J-P., & Post, R.M. (1985). Phenomenology and neurobiology of panic disorder. In A.H. Tuma & J.D. Maser (Eds.), *Anxiety and the anxiety disorders* (pp. 557–576). Hillsdale, NJ: Lawrence Erlbaum.

Uhde, T.W., Vittone, B.M., & Post, R.M. (1984). Glucose tolerance listing in panic disorder. *American Journal of Psychiatry, 14,* 1461–1463.

van Vliet, I.M., den Boer, J.A., & Westenberg, H.G.M. (1994). Psychopharmacological treatment of social phobia: A double blind controlled study with fluvoxamine. *Psychopharmacology, 115,* 128–134.

Weissman, M.M. (1985). The epidemiology of anxiety disorders: Rates, risks and familial patterns. In A.H. Tuma & J.D. Maser (Eds.), *Anxiety and the anxiety disorders* (pp. 275–296). Hillsdale, NJ: Lawrence Erlbaum.

Weissman, M.M., Leckman, J.F., Merikangas, K.R., Gammon, G.D., & Prusoff, B.A. (1984). Depression and anxiety disorders in parents and children: Results from the Yale Family Study. *Archives of General Psychiatry, 41,* 845–852.

Wells, A. (1995). Meta-cognition and worry: A cognitive model of generalised anxiety disorder. *Behavioural and Cognitive Psychotherapy, 23,* 301–320.

Williams, D.H. (1986). The epidemiology of mental illness in Afro-Americans. *Hospital and Community Psychiatry, 37,* 42–49.

Wittchen, H.U. (1988). Natural course and spontaneous remissions of untreated anxiety disorders: Results of the Munich Follow-up Study. In I. Hand & H.U. Wittchen (Eds.), *Panic and phobias: Treatments and variables affecting course and outcome* (pp. 3–17). New York: Springer-Verlag.

Wittchen, H.U., & Beloch, E. (1996). The impact of social phobia on quality of life. *International Clinical Psychopharmacology, 11*(Suppl. 3), 15–23.

Wittchen, H.U., Zhao, S., Kessler, R.C., & Eaton, W.W. (1994). DSM-III-R generalized anxiety disorder in the National Comorbidity Survey. *Archives of General Psychiatry, 51,* 355–364.

Wolpe, J., Lande, S.D., McNally, R.J., & Schotte, D. (1985). Differentiation between classically conditioned and cognitively learned anxiety. *Journal of Behavior Therapy and Experimental Psychiatry, 12,* 35–42.

Woods, S.W., Charney, D.S., Goodman, W.K., & Heninger, G.R. (1988). Carbon dioxide-induced anxiety: Behavioral physiologic, and biochemical effects of carbon dioxide in patients with panic disorder and healthy subjects. *Archives of General Psychiatry, 45,* 43–52.

World Health Organization. (1990). *Composite International Diagnostic Interview (CIDI), Version 1.0.* Geneva: World Health Organization.

World Health Organization. (1993). *The international statistical classification of diseases and related health problems, tenth revision.* Geneva: World Health Organization.

Zajonc, R.B. (1984). On the primacy of affect. *American Psychologist, 39,* 117–123.

Zinbarg, R.E., & Barlow, D.H. (1996). Structure of anxiety and the anxiety disorders: A hierarchical model. *Journal of Abnormal Psychology, 105,* 181–193.

Zuellig, A.R., Newman, M.G., Kachin, K.E., & Constantino, M.J. (1997, November). *Differences in parental attachment profiles in adults diagnosed with generalized anxiety disorder, panic disorder, or nondisordered.* Paper presented at the annual meeting of the Association for Advancement of Behavior Therapy, Miami, Florida.

CHAPTER 9

POSTTRAUMATIC STRESS DISORDER

Terence M. Keane
Rose T. Zimering
Danny G. Kaloupek
Boston Veterans Affairs Medical Center
Boston University School of Medicine

INTRODUCTION

Characteristics of the Disorder

Posttraumatic stress disorder (PTSD) is uniquely characterized by the intense reliving of a life threatening, traumatic event. This reexperiencing occurs through intrusive thoughts, nightmares, and/or flashbacks and is accompanied by psychological numbing and avoidance, and by symptoms indicative of hyperarousal or physiological dysregulation. PTSD may be observed following one of a host of extremely stressful life experiences, and is often psychologically and vocationally debilitating. It is also one of the few disorders currently in the diagnostic nomenclature (American Psychiatric Association, 1994) that includes the presumed etiology as one of the diagnostic criteria. As we shall see later, the need to identify a causal experience presents numerous challenges to both clinicians and researchers who work with traumatized populations.

PTSD has been the subject of considerable empir-ical study since its inclusion in the DSM-III in 1980. Much of the initial research related to the diagnosis was supported by the Department of Veterans Affairs to examine the adjustment of veterans who served in Vietnam and other war zones. Subsequent studies have expanded the focus and described PTSD as a consequence of rape, natural disaster, technological disaster, motor vehicle accidents, torture, and criminal victimization, among other events.

Symptomatology

The preeminent symptoms that are observed when evaluating a patient with PTSD are anxiety and depression. For this reason, traumatized patients often have been misdiagnosed, and this continues to be a risk unless an appropriate evaluation of potentially traumatic experiences is included in the assessment.

Apart from anxiety and depression, patients with PTSD report core symptoms that are assigned to three clusters: (1) reexperiencing of the traumatic event in

TABLE 9-1   Diagnostic criteria for posttraumatic stress disorder.

A. The person has been exposed to a traumatic event in which both of the following were present:
   (1) The person experienced, witnessed, or was confronted with an event or events that involved actual or threatened death or serious injury, or a threat to the physical integrity of self or others.
   (2) The person's response involved intense fear, helplessness, or horror. In children this may be expressed instead by disorganized or agitated behavior.

B. The traumatic event is persistently reexperienced in at least one of the following ways:
   (1) Recurrent and intrusive distressing recollections of the event (in young children, repetitive play in which themes or aspects of the trauma are expressed)
   (2) Recurrent distressing dreams of the event
   (3) Acting or feeling as if the traumatic event were recurring (includes a sense of reliving the experience, illusions, hallucinations, and dissociative [flashback] episodes, even those that occur upon awakening or when intoxicated)
   (4) Intense psychological distress at exposure to internal or external cues that symbolize or resemble an aspect of the traumatic event

C. Persistent avoidance of stimuli associated with the trauma or numbing of general responsiveness (not present before the trauma), as indicated by at least three of the following:
   (1) Efforts to avoid thoughts or feelings or conversations associated with the trauma
   (2) Efforts to avoid activities, places, or people that arouse recollections of the trauma
   (3) Inability to recall an important aspect of the trauma
   (4) Markedly diminished interest or participation in significant activities
   (5) Feeling of detachment or estrangement from others
   (6) Restricted range of affect, e.g., unable to have loving feelings
   (7) Sense of a foreshortened future, e.g., does not expect to have a career, marriage, or children, or a normal life span

D. Persistent symptoms of increased arousal (not present before the trauma), as indicated by at least two of the following:
   (1) Difficulty falling or staying asleep
   (2) Irritability or outbursts of anger
   (3) Difficulty concentrating
   (4) Hypervigilance
   (5) Exaggerated startle response

E. Duration of the disturbance (symptoms in B, C, and D) of at least 1 month.

Specify delayed onset if the onset of symptoms was at least 6 months after the trauma

the form of intrusive thoughts, distressing nightmares, physiological arousal, and, possibly, feeling as if the event were occurring again (flashbacks); (2) avoidance of stimuli resembling the traumatic event or cues associated with it, and emotional numbing of responsiveness; and (3) persistent symptoms of excessive arousal, such as disturbed sleep, exaggerated startle, and heightened vigilance. Table 9-1 presents the full list of symptom criteria.

ASSESSMENT METHODS

Multimethod Assessment of PTSD

Assessment instruments for evaluating an individual for a history of exposure to traumatic stressors and for the development of PTSD are numerous (see Wilson & Keane, 1997). This growth in assessment methods has contributed enormously to the burgeoning new knowledge in the field of psychological trauma. The quality of the instruments generally is very high in terms of demonstrated reliability and validity (Norris & Riad, 1997). The selection of instruments to be employed depends largely on the purpose of the evaluation. The goal of this section is to encourage clinicians and researchers to consider using a multimethod approach in their assessment of PTSD.

A multimethod approach to assessing PTSD was initially developed in an innovative clinical research program for Vietnam veterans with combat-related PTSD at the Jackson, Mississippi, VA Medical Center in the early 1980s (Keane, Fairbank, Caddell, Zimering, & Bender, 1985; Keane & Kaloupek, 1982). It advocated the use of multiple measures for evaluating the presence of PTSD in order to increase the accuracy of the diagnostic process that was so fundamental to the clinical and research missions of the program.

At that time, few measures of PTSD were available, and those that were available were experimental in nature. These clinical researchers reasoned that no single measure of PTSD could ever function as the definitive indicator of PTSD and that there is a need for the use of multiple assessment formats in order to maximize the possibility of appropriately assessing all individuals. For example, some individuals will be more comfortable and forthcoming with a clinically oriented diagnostic interview, some will prefer self-report questionnaires, and still others will be most comfortable with a computer-administered questionnaire. An approach that incorporates all of these formats may be optimal for identifying cases of PTSD. Because of the high rates of trauma exposure and PTSD among women and minorities, such an approach may also address the gender and cultural limitations of psychological assessment for PTSD (Keane, Kaloupek, & Weathers, 1996; Wolfe, Brown, Furey, & Levin, 1993).

Structured Diagnostic Interviews

Perhaps the most frequently employed diagnostic measures are structured diagnostic interviews that derive their content directly from the DSM criteria. There are multiple available interviews and all have excellent psychometric properties. The Clinician Administered PTSD Scale (Blake et al., 1990; Weathers

et al., 1996), developed in the National Center for PTSD–Boston, measures all symptoms of PTSD and its associated features, requiring attention to both the frequency and the intensity of the expressed symptom. Moreover, it explores the impact of the symptomatology on both social and vocational functioning, features that are unavailable in any other assessment instrument. Because of its comprehensiveness, it has become one of the most widely used measures of PTSD both in the clinic and in the research laboratory.

Other instruments developed expressly for the assessment of PTSD include the PTSD Diagnostic Scale by Foa (1997), the Davidson PTSD Interview (Davidson, Smith, & Kudler, 1989), the Structured Clinical Interview for the DSM (First, Spitzer, Gibbon, & Williams, 1997), and the Anxiety Disorders Interview Schedule—Revised (DiNardo & Barlow, 1988). Each has distinct strengths, and the needs of a particular clinic or research study will determine which diagnostic interview is best.

Self-Report Instruments

The field has experienced a proliferation of self-report measures of PTSD over the past 15 years. Included among them are scales and questionnaires that are quite reliable and, when compared to a clinical diagnosis of PTSD, work very effectively in identifying people who have PTSD (i.e., high sensitivity) and people who do not (i.e., high specificity). Some of these scales directly measure the DSM criteria, while others purport to measure the construct of PTSD more broadly. Still others are empirically derived from existing measures of personality such as the Minnesota Multiphasic Personality Inventory–2 (MMPI-2) or symptomatology, such as the 90-item Symptom Checklist–Revised (SCL-90-R).

The PTSD Checklist (Weathers, Litz, Herman, Huska, & Keane, 1993), also developed at the National Center for PTSD–Boston, provides a continuous measure of the 17 symptoms of the diagnostic criteria for PTSD. It has strong psychometric properties and has been validated against clinicians' diagnosis and other known measures of PTSD. A measure with many of the same attributes, developed by Foa and her colleagues, is the PTSD Symptom Scale—Self-Report Version (Foa, Riggs, Dancu,

& Rothbaum, 1993). It, too, has strong psychometric properties.

The PTSD Scale of the MMPI-2 (PK; Keane, Malloy, & Fairbank, 1984) was empirically derived from the full MMPI administered to veterans with and without PTSD. The scale consists of 46 items of the MMPI-2 taken from across the standard clinical scales of the instrument. It was initially validated and cross-validated on war veterans; more recent work on civilian trauma indicates that it is a good measure of PTSD across traumatic events (Koretzky & Peck, 1990). Further, the use of the MMPI-2 in assessments of PTSD capitalizes on the many validity scales contained therein, items of particular importance when forensic issues and compensation are pivotal in the evaluation.

Similarly, Saunders, Arata, and Kilpatrick (1990) developed a crime-related PTSD scale from the SCL-90-R, as did Weathers et al. (1996) for combat-related PTSD. These scales can be especially valuable because existing data sets that contain these measures can be used to address questions regarding posttraumatic symptomatology. Several research projects utilizing these measures are now underway.

The Mississippi Scale for Combat-Related PTSD (Keane, Caddell, & Taylor, 1988) and its civilian counterpart measure broadly the construct of PTSD. When this scale was first developed, DSM-III and III-R criteria were in use clinically. That research group recognized that any scale that strictly measured the DSM criteria would necessarily have a short life as a result of the major advances in the field of trauma. As a result, the group focused on the construct of PTSD broadly so that items selected would provide enduring contribution to the measurement of the disorder, regardless of modifications in the criteria themselves. The strategy was successful in that the Mississippi Scale has been in continuous use for 15 years and has successfully crossed three versions of the diagnosis (Newman, Kaloupek, & Keane, 1996).

Psychophysiology of PTSD

Numerous research studies have documented that individuals with PTSD respond to cues reminiscent of the traumatic event with heightened psychophysiological arousal. An early demonstration of this re-

activity by Malloy, Fairbank, and Keane (1983) involved the presentation of a series of pictures and sounds depicting combat to veterans with combat-related PTSD, combat veterans without PTSD, and non–combat veteran controls diagnosed with other psychiatric conditions. The investigators compared each individual's responding to the combat cues with their responding to an audiovisual series of control cues that were unrelated to combat. Measuring heart rate and skin conductance (a reflection of emotion-triggered sweating), they found that the PTSD veterans showed differentially high rates of physiological arousal to the combat relative to the control cues. This pattern of responding was specific to the PTSD group; neither the well-adjusted combat veterans nor the psychiatric controls showed much physiological responding to either set of cue presentations. Using only auditory combat cues, Blanchard, Kolb, Pallmeyer, and Gerardi (1982) also observed greater heart rate, skin conductance, electromyographic (i.e., muscle tension), and blood pressure responses among Vietnam veterans compared with nonveteran controls. A systematic series of studies by this research group also indicated that heart rate reactivity was a particularly sensitive index of the PTSD diagnosis in over 200 subjects tested.

Similarly, Pitman, Orr, Forgue, deJong, and Claiborn (1987) employed a procedure involving emotional imagery (based on the work of Peter Lang) and found that PTSD patients with combat-related PTSD were more aroused than veterans without PTSD when images of their own stressful combat experiences were presented to them. This physiological arousal to trauma imagery was more directly observable in skin conductance responses, although other response channels showed some differential reactivity as well.

In addition to the heightened psychophysiological reactivity to combat cues found in these studies, PTSD patients have sometimes demonstrated greater physiological arousal during baseline (rest) periods at the beginning of their test session than have comparison groups employed in the studies. Gerardi, Keane, Cahoon, and Klauminzer (1994) also found greater arousal outside the experimental laboratory when they examined the resting heart rate of veterans with and without PTSD in a medical (nonpsychiatric) setting.

It is tempting to interpret these differences at rest as an indication that individuals with PTSD have higher levels of sustained arousal, but such does not appear to be the case. McFall, Veith, and Murburg (1992) demonstrated that the resting heart rate and blood pressure readings for combat veterans with a PTSD diagnosis did not differ from the readings for combat veterans without the diagnosis when care was taken to ensure that the circumstances of testing were not threatening or stressful. Prins, Kaloupek, and Keane (1995) have reviewed the findings associated with baseline readings and concluded that differences between PTSD and non-PTSD groups reflect apprehension on the part of the individuals with PTSD. From this perspective, the psychophysiological differences at rest are comparable to those demonstrated in response to trauma cues, although they are evoked by the *anticipation* of encountering such cues rather than by direct contact with the cues themselves. These anticipatory reactions highlight the potential for fear conditioning to generalize beyond concrete stimuli to abstract mental representations.

This body of research findings suggests that objective psychophysiological hyperreactivity is strongly associated with the diagnosis of PTSD. The strength of this association was tested in a recent, study of over 1200 military veterans (Keane et al., 1998). One aim of the study was to examine the correspondence between the diagnosis of PTSD based on clinical interview and psychophysiological responses measured under several conditions that included rest, presentation of standardized combat pictures and sounds, and presentation of individually determined imagery scenes of combat. The study replicated many of the previously documented differences between PTSD and non-PTSD groups. It also used advanced statistical methods to demonstrate that the diagnostic status of approximately two-thirds of the subjects could be identified correctly on the basis of individual psychophysiological reactivity. This outcome supports the importance of psychophysiological responding as a feature of PTSD, but it also makes it clear that the diagnostic interview and psychophysiological challenge test are measuring different domains that do not fully overlap. However, both provided useful information about the nature of PTSD, and both offer important targets for its assessment and treatment (Keane,

Fairbank, Caddell, & Zimering, 1989; Keane & Kaloupek, 1982).

Finally, although the bulk of evidence regarding psychophysiological response to trauma-related cues has involved combat veterans, recent efforts are addressing other traumatized populations. The work of Blanchard and his colleagues, in particular, has demonstrated the applicability of psychophysiological challenge testing with individuals who have experienced serious motor vehicle accidents (Blanchard et al., 1996; Blanchard, Hickling, Taylor, & Loos, 1994). The studies have thus far demonstrated the expected differences in responding between individuals who qualify for a PTSD diagnosis and those who do not. In addition, Blanchard et al. (1996) found that they could use psychophysiological responding to imagery scenes depicting the individual's accident to predict the diagnostic status for over 75% of those with accident-related PTSD. They administered an imagery procedure within 4 months of the accident and found that those who continued to meet diagnostic criteria for PTSD 1 year later showed greater initial physiological response than those who became less symptomatic over the 1-year period. This preliminary attempt to predict the course of PTSD demonstrates the potential value of psychophysiological challenge testing for both research and clinical applications. Further study will determine whether this potential can be realized.

DIAGNOSTIC ISSUES

To meet diagnostic criteria for PTSD, an individual must first endorse the presence of a traumatic event in which the person experienced, witnessed, or was confronted with an event that involved actual or threatened death or serious injury, or a threat to the physical integrity of self or others. The person's response to the event typically involves intense fear, horror, or helplessness. Individuals must report at least one symptom of reexperiencing, three avoidance or numbing symptoms, and two of the hyperarousal symptoms. Both the overarching symptom clusters (i.e., reexperiencing, numbing, and hyperarousal) and the stressor criterion have stimulated considerable debate and controversy in the field. DSM workgroups have focused on these issues with an eye toward resolving the concerns of various scholars and clinicians. Here we will attempt to out-line some of these controversies.

The Stressor Criterion

Among the most frequently debated of the diagnostic issues surrounding PTSD is the inclusion of an iden-tified stressor within the criteria for the disorder. This feature is problematic for several reasons. First, struc-turally PTSD is one of a very few disorders (adjust-ment disorder is another) that requires a nonsymptom event as a key feature of the disorder. In creating the DSM-III, great care was exerted by the authors to be atheoretical and phenomenological in orientation to-ward diagnosis. This meant an emphasis on the ob-servable and, in particular, on the psychological condition of the patient. PTSD is thus at odds with the format used for other psychological disorders. Re-moving the stressor criterion would at least make PTSD comparable to most other disorders on this di-mension. However, some scholars advocate the in-clusion of the stressor in order to emphasize the connection of the event to the symptoms.

A second issue that centers on the stressor crite-rion is definitional. The problem has at least two ele-ments. First, events that are extremely stressful for some are not necessarily devastating for others. For instance, some combat veterans found that their experiences in Vietnam prepared them to lead suc-cessful lives (Hendin & Haas, 1984). Was their ex-perience, then, a traumatic one? Presumably, past learning history, biological factors, and personality style must play a role in who appraises an event as traumatic and who develops PTSD. At the opposite end of the spectrum, a woman in our clinic whose en-tire family had died in a car accident, when she was later involved in a relatively mild accident herself (i.e., cars colliding at 10 mph), developed a dramatic case of PTSD. Clearly, not all people would experi-ence marked distress at a relatively minor car acci-dent; yet it is quite understandable that this woman did develop PTSD because of her past experience with automobile accidents.

Second, there is little evidence to substantiate the assertion that events must be outside the range of usual human experience to cause traumatic symp-toms. Breslau and Davis (1987) have provided some data indicating that PTSD symptomatology occurs following a wide range of common stressors, not sim-ply those that are unusual. Virtually everyone would agree that the imprisonment and slaughter of Euro-pean Jews by the Nazis or inflicted upon the Cambo-dians by the Khmer Rouge are traumatic for the survivors. However, there is active debate among re-searchers and clinicians about whether less dramatic events such as the loss of a job, sexual harassment, an illness, or the natural death of a loved one qualify as traumatic stressors, sufficient to fulfill this criterion for PTSD.

The problems with the stressor criterion, there-fore, may be inherently unresolvable unless one adopts a transactional perspective on the develop-ment of behavioral disorders. Such a model empha-sizes the interaction of both person and environment factors in the development of psychopathology. Other similar models of psychopathology, including the diathesis–stress model and the vulnerability–stress model, all recognize a biological or psycholog-ical predisposition on which a significant stressor is superimposed. Theoretically, there is no apparent empirical justification for PTSD to be distinguished from other forms of psychopathology with respect to the primacy and importance of the psychological stressor or the type of stressor that might be respon-sible for someone developing the disorder. There remains considerable controversy regarding the in-clusion of the stressor criterion and its precise defin-ition in the PTSD diagnosis. Future research should provide an empirical foundation for continuing this diagnostic convention. Unfortunately, there are no data that decisively support either the inclusion or ex-clusion of the stressor criterion at this time.

Symptom Clustering

The three sets of PTSD symptoms include the cate-gories of reexperiencing, numbing/avoidance, and hyperarousal. This classification scheme was derived from a conceptual article by Brett and Ostroff (1985) that described the phenomena associated with psy-chological trauma from a psychoanalytic standpoint. Borrowing and expanding on Horowitz's (1976) work, this article proposed an opponent-process model of the major symptoms of PTSD, such that the stressful reliving experiences and numbing balance each other while the individual attempts to cope with or master overwhelming life experiences. This process is characterized by behavioral, physiological, and cognitive components that, over time, result in affective numbing for those who suffer PTSD. Like Horowitz, Brett and Ostroff (1985) felt that there was an oscillating dimension of the reliving and numbing features of the disorder, such that people passed from one phase into another and back. On the basis of this perspective, the DSM-III-R organized the symptoms of PTSD into the reliving and numbing/avoidance categories. In addition, the numerous studies on the psychophysiology of PTSD (e.g., Blanchard et al., 1982; Malloy et al., 1983) helped to identify a third major cluster of arousal symptoms to be included in the diagnostic criteria.

To date, there is substantial empirical support for the clusters of reliving symptomatology and hyper-arousal as key features of PTSD (Gleser, Green, & Winget, 1981; Kilpatrick et al., 1985; Shore, Tatum, & Vollmer, 1986). In contrast, there is growing skepticism about the inclusion of the numbing/avoidance criterion at its current high level (three necessary symptoms; Kulka et al., 1988). This skepticism derives from the observation that a major coping strategy employed by some traumatized individuals during the course of their recovery is involvement with many groups and experiences designed to assist in recovery and promote social and psychological change (e.g., Mothers against Drunk Driving; Veterans Service Organizations, Rape Centers). In addition, no precise definition of emotional numbing has as yet appeared in the literature, leading to inconsistent operationalization of this term and hindering systematic research (Litz, 1991). Innovative research on the numbing symptoms associated with trauma would be a significant contribution to our clinical and conceptual knowledge of the disorder.

In addition, several recent studies have found considerable reliving and hyperarousal symptomatology following high-level stressors, but little avoidance or numbing (e.g., Helzer, Robins, & McEvoy, 1987). Consequently, the DSM working group on PTSD is reconsidering the emphasis currently placed on the numbing and avoidance characteristics in arriving at the diagnosis. The primary concern is that many possible cases of PTSD are not being identified because of an overly restrictive set of criteria. Unfortunately, the data are not yet available to determine what the differences in rates of PTSD might be when diagnostic criteria are modified or when different criteria are used. Although most experts agree that PTSD frequently has a numbing and avoidant component, the universality of this symptom cluster is now being reconsidered in light of both conceptual and empirical work.

Prolonged Stressors

Another concern of researchers and clinicians in the PTSD field is the extent to which the diagnostic criteria are adequate for the identification of people who have survived certain types of prolonged, aversive life experiences. The psychological condition of incest survivors (Herman, 1981) and of women who have been battered or abused by their partners (Koss, Gidycz, & Wisniewski, 1987) emphasizes more of the withdrawal, numbing, and avoidant symptoms associated with PTSD, coupled with low self-esteem, confidence, and feelings of inadequacy. Reliving experiences and flashbacks are less salient among victims of prolonged stress. The applicability of the PTSD diagnosis to these groups is currently being examined (see disorders of extreme stress in the DSM-IV), but to date there is no consensus on the best approach to handling this issue.

Categorization of the Disorder

Currently PTSD is considered an anxiety-related disorder and, accordingly, is placed within the anxiety disorder category in the DSM. Indeed, PTSD shares many common elements with other disorders, including affective disorder, as mentioned earlier, and dissociative disorder. Because one of the diagnostic features of PTSD is psychogenic amnesia, and because the backgrounds of dissociative disorder patients routinely contain childhood, sexual, and physical abuse (Braun, 1987), many have suggested that PTSD should be a variant of the category dissociative disorder. Although there appears to be a fundamental relationship between PTSD and dissociative disorders, the precise nature of this relationship has not been very well delineated. Given that some PTSD patients have dissociative experiences (Brett & Ostroff, 1985), but not all PTSD patients have these experiences (Helzer et al., 1987; Kulka et al., 1988), perhaps a more accurate strategy would have dissociative disorder classified as a variant of PTSD. Such a proposal will be particularly compelling if the high rates of psychological trauma in the histories of dissociative disorder patients are replicated in additional empirical studies.

At present, PTSD's placement will likely remain within the anxiety disorders. This is appropriate given our current state of knowledge, but also because PTSD has benefited immensely from the sophisticated research methodology that has developed in the anxiety disorders field (Keane, 1989). Presumably, association with other anxiety disorders like panic disorder, obsessive-compulsive disorder, and generalized anxiety disorder will continue to stimulate high-quality research on PTSD. In the future, as more evidence is collected, we can perhaps consider a separate traumatic stress disorder category. Included under this rubric might be all types of disorders that have traumatic etiology (e.g., borderline personality disorder, dissociative disorder, psychogenic amnesia, traumatic phobias, etc.). This emphasis on etiology is not now appropriate given our current state of knowledge, but may ultimately prove to be the most accurate scheme for classification.

EPIDEMIOLOGY

Exposure to Potentially Traumatic Experiences

When PTSD was originally incorporated into the diagnostic nomenclature (APA, 1980), exposure to traumatic events was thought to be unusual and rare. Recent studies of exposure have seriously challenged this assumption. In the National Comorbidity Survey (NCS), the first truly representative study of mental health problems among adults in the United States, Kessler and his colleagues (Kessler, Sonnega, Bromet, Hughes, & Nelson, 1995) learned that 61% of men and 51% of women reported at least one event that could potentially lead to PTSD. Importantly, the majority of people who reported one traumatic event had actually been exposed to multiple events of a potentially traumatic nature. Studies by other researchers have confirmed these high rates of exposure in contemporary U.S. society (Kilpatrick, Edmonds, & Seymour, 1992; Norris, 1992).

What types of events are most likely to lead to PTSD? In the NCS, a series of 12 questions posed to study participants elucidated the individual's history of exposure to potentially traumatic events. The events included combat, life-threatening accidents, natural disasters, witnessing injury or death, rape, sexual molestation, physical assault, child abuse, neglect, kidnapping or other forms of violent life threat, and other forms of severe stressors. The results varied to some extent by gender, with men indicating that rape, combat, and child abuse most often led to PTSD, whereas for women the events most likely to lead to PTSD were: rape, child abuse, molestation, and physical assault. Clearly, exposure to traumatic events is more common than anyone ever suspected.

PTSD Prevalence

Studies on the prevalence of PTSD have appeared in the research literature with increasing frequency since the publication of the DSM-III. These studies, often focusing on the prevalence of PTSD in the general U.S. population (Breslau, Davis, Andreski, & Peterson, 1991; Kessler et al., 1995), have also examined the rate of this disorder following combat (e.g., Kulka et al., 1988), among survivors of a natural disaster (e.g., Mount St. Helens; Shore et al., 1986), among those who have experienced criminal victimization (e.g., Kilpatrick et al., 1985; Resnick et al. 1993), among survivors of sexual assault and rape (Kilpatrick et al., 1992) and technological disasters (e.g., Buffalo Creek; Gleser et al., 1981). In each study, persistent mental health disturbances were found among some of the people who endured these extreme life experiences. In several of these studies, PTSD was measured directly by structured diagnostic interviews (e.g. Kilpatrick et al., 1992; Kulka et al., 1988), while in others only general disturbance and symptomatology were examined (Gleser et al., 1981). Unfortunately, rates varied substantially in many of the earliest studies, and it was difficult to compare the rates of PTSD across studies because of the utilization of different measurement instruments, sampling procedures, and methodologies. Indeed, the procedures for case identification used in many of the initial epidemiological studies suffered from a wide variety of methodological shortcomings. These may account for the differences in prevalence rates found for PTSD in early studies. Yet, there has been a remarkable consistency in the findings regarding incidence and prevalence of PTSD since the development and use of standardized, reliable, and valid measurement tools.

General Population Estimates

The best estimates of the prevalence of PTSD in the general population of America come from two studies conducted in the early 1990s. Breslau et al. (1991) reported that 39% of a sample of young adults had been exposed to one or more traumatic events and that fully 25% of them developed PTSD as a result. This suggested a 9% rate of PTSD in the United States.

Similarly, the NCS, which reported much higher rates of exposure than the Breslau study (50%–61% vs. 39%), found a prevalence rate of 8% for PTSD. These estimates translate into approximately 20 to 25 million cases of PTSD across the United States alone. These estimates place PTSD among the most prevalent of all mental disorders, ranking below only substance abuse, social phobia, and depression.

Others have found different rates of PTSD in their studies. Helzer et al. (1987) found that one to two percent of the general population suffered from PTSD. In this study, a component of the Epidemiological Catchment Area study, PTSD was measured using the Diagnostic Interview Schedule (DIS) constructed by Robins and her colleagues (Robins et al., 1981). However, relying on a single diagnostic instrument to confirm psychiatric diagnoses and the employment of a regionally specific (St. Louis) sample for this study renders the results somewhat less convincing than those of the NCS.

Rates Following Specific Events

The most methodologically rigorous epidemiological study of PTSD ever conducted in the United States was the National Vietnam Veterans Readjustment Study (NVVRS; Kulka et al., 1988). These researchers, employing the multimethod approach to case identification initially proposed by Dohrenwend and Shrout (1981), selected a two-stage case identification process. From interviews conducted by trained lay interviewers, they identified high-risk individuals who were then interviewed by an experienced mental health clinician to verify diagnosis. To ascertain cases, these authors used multiple measures of PTSD—standardized interviews and psychological tests—which determined the probability of any individual having the PTSD diagnosis. Given the lack of a gold standard and the acknowledged problems in measuring any psychological construct, this multimethod approach was sound and continues to influence the conduct of epidemiological studies in mental health.

At the time it was conducted, the NVVRS was unique for at least two separate reasons: because it was the first time that any country sought to understand the psychological and social consequences of participation in a war, and because it employed a nationally representative sampling procedure. This sampling methodology is routinely employed in other medical areas but had never been applied in the mental health arena largely because of the complex logistics of such an attempt and the costs of conducting the interviews on a nationwide sample.

The NVVRS found that the current prevalence rate for PTSD among Vietnam veterans was 15%. Having oversampled several minority groups, this study was also able to report differential effects of the war on these groups. Among African Americans, 21% had PTSD; among Hispanics 28% had PTSD. Nearly 9% of female veterans (of whom there were some 7,000 who served in the Vietnam theater) also had current PTSD. Lifetime rates were essentially twice the current rate for both males and females. These findings indicated that a substantial number of the 3.14 million American men and women who served in the Vietnam War suffered PTSD at some point since their return from the war.

This study also suggested that rates of PTSD differed by service and gender variables. Specifically, the 15% rate of PTSD found in theater veterans is contrasted with a 4% rate in Vietnam-era veterans (those who did not go to Vietnam but did serve in the military). Among the female veterans, the 9% rate of PTSD is contrasted with approximately 2% of Vietnam-era female veterans.

In examining prevalence rates, it was determined that those who were exposed to high war-zone stressors had a current rate of PTSD of 36%, compared to those exposed to low/moderate war zone stressors, whose rate of PTSD was 9%. These findings indicated that those individuals who were involved in the most gruesome aspects of the war were the most likely to develop significant and persistent psychological problems as a function of that experience. Clearly, the findings of this well-designed study indicated that the psychological effects of participation in the Vietnam War were long lasting for a very large number of its combatants.

PTSD can also occur following other life-threatening and stressful experiences. Resnick et al. (1993) employed a national sample of women and studied exposure to criminal victimization and its psychological consequences. They found that lifetime exposure to any traumatic event was 69%, with 12% of the total population of women developing PTSD at some point afterwards. Similarly, in the National Women's Study, Kilpatrick et al. (1992) found that fully 13% of U.S. women had been the target of a completed rape at some point in their life, with 31% of these women subsequently developing PTSD, yielding a national rate of 4% of U.S. women experiencing rape-related PTSD.

Following the eruption of the Mount St. Helen's volcano, Shore et al. (1986) examined the presence of postdisaster psychological disorders in three groups stratified by stress exposure. Among those exposed to the highest levels of stress, 40% reported major psychological disturbance for 3 to 4 years after the disaster. Similarly, McFarlane (1986) followed firefighters who were involved in extinguishing the Ash Wednesday bushfires in Australia and found that 21% of these people had PTSD symptoms 29 months after the event; little change had occurred longitudinally in these symptoms over this period.

The aftermath of the Beverly Hills Supper Club Fire in Kentucky was examined by Green and her colleagues (1983) in an elegant sequence of studies. They found high rates of psychological morbidity and established important conceptual links among preexisting traits, components of the stressor, and the posttrauma environment in identifying people who were at greatest risk of long-term impairment. This study served as an important model for future investigation of factors responsible for the development of PTSD.

In summarizing the epidemiology of PTSD, two things are eminently clear: first, the rates of exposure to potentially traumatic events is nothing short of epidemic in U.S. society. Seven out of 10 people have been exposed to at least one such event. Second, the rates of PTSD place it among the most common of all mental disorders. With rates of rape, criminal victimization, natural disaster, technological disaster, and war all continuing unabated, public policy must place a high priority on improving access to care for affected citizens and on providing sufficient resources to enhance our scientific understanding of this disorder and its treatment. In any case, with war, disaster, and victimization all reaching startling proportions worldwide, it is clear that PTSD is a major international public health concern.

ETIOLOGY OF PTSD

Conceptual Models

There are at least three general models of PTSD that rely on psychological processes and concepts. The three approaches can be characterized by their use of psychoanalytic (e.g., Horowitz, 1977), behavioral (e.g., Keane, Zimering, & Caddell, 1985), or information-processing formulations (e.g., Chemtob et al., 1988; Foa, Steketee, & Rothbaum, 1989). Although they are derived from independent theories, the models are somewhat compatible with one another in the sense that they focus on and explicate different components of the disorder. To the degree that each approach has been able to generate distinct, testable hypotheses for investigation, each has contributed to our understanding of the disorder.

Psychodynamic Model

Although there is no single psychodynamic model for PTSD, an influential view is that of Horowitz (1976) who proposed that trauma occurs when an external event exceeds the ego's ability to tolerate the negative emotion associated with it. According to Horowitz, traumatic experiences produce "information overload" that must be processed psychologically in order to attain emotional equilibrium and behavioral adjustment. The individuals' personal schema, their beliefs and attitudes about themselves (i.e., self-concept) and the world around them, somehow must be altered to incorporate the occurrence of the extreme event and its meaning for them (see Janoff-Bulman, 1992).

Horowitz (1973) views PTSD as a disorder characterized by stages of undercontrol and overcontrol.

That is, periods of intrusive repetition of the traumatic event (i.e., flashbacks, nightmares, ruminative thinking) are seen as a consequence of undercontrol. Correspondingly, phases of denial and numbing are the products of defensive overcontrol. These stages can alternate with each other or, at times, can coexist. Thus, someone with PTSD might have intrusive memories of parts of the event (reflecting undercontrol), be emotionally constricted and numb toward other people in his or her life, and be unable to recall specific details of the most intense aspects of the memory (reflecting overcontrol).

Behavioral Model

Two-factor learning theory (Mowrer, 1960) has served as a useful animal model for many of the components of PTSD. This theory proposes that fear is learned via classical conditioning as the first stage of a process that can sustain emotional learning despite the impact of naturally occurring processes that would otherwise reduce it. The key is a second stage marked by avoidance behavior that minimizes the duration of contact with conditioned cues alone (i.e., without painful consequences) and thereby retards the extinction of the learned fear. Extending this framework to humans, Keane, Zimering, and Caddell (1985) proposed that an extreme stressor acts as an unconditioned stimulus (UCS) that is capable of producing learned associations with internal and external cues (visual, auditory, olfactory, and tactile) that are present when the stressor occurs. After such conditioned associations are established, previously neutral cues can evoke strong autonomic and physiological responses that resemble those that occurred at the time of the stressful event. These responses are so aversive that individuals may begin to systematically avoid the triggering cues as a way to limit their own fear. Thus, the impact of classical conditioning is considered especially important for the development of PTSD, and instrumental avoidance is viewed as critical to its maintenance (i.e., the two factors).

Cognitive or Information-Processing Model

Several prominent features of PTSD reflect attentional, perceptual, and memory processes (nightmares, intrusive thoughts, hypervigilance, concentration problems, and psychogenic amnesia). For this reason, the application of information-processing models of

psychopathology (Lang, 1977, 1979) has been a welcome addition to the PTSD literature (e.g., Foa et al., 1989). This set of theories proposes highly organized, semantic "fear networks" containing stimulus propositions (i.e., representations of cues that evoke fear), response propositions (i.e., representations of psychophysiological, cognitive, and behavioral responses), and meaning propositions attached to both the stimulus and response components. Trauma networks are postulated by Foa et al. (1989) to have unusually stable and coherent stimulus, response, and meaning components. Accordingly, trauma networks may be fully activated by less intense input than other propositional networks because of the increased likelihood that many elements in the network will be active at the same time.

Similarly, Chemtob et al. (1988) proposed that representations of danger, fear, and threat (especially among those who have been exposed to life-and-death experiences) are stored in a rich, multidimensional semantic framework so that a wide variety of cues can activate the network easily. They extended the information-processing approach by hypothesizing that trauma memory networks in people who have PTSD are so well organized that, when activated, they can affect behavior, attention, and arousal in a feedback cycle that promotes severe symptomatic responses.

These information-processing models of PTSD prompt important questions regarding cognitive processes in PTSD patients. For example, do PTSD patients perceive their environments differently than others do? Do they interpret ambiguous stimuli as inherently threatening? Is their physiological reactivity more easily triggered by environmental cues than it is for others? Are they particularly attentive to stimuli that are threatening—even mildly so? These questions, among others, frame some of the current issues of interest to trauma investigators and provide a useful template for research on this disorder.

Neurobiological Models

There is no single neurobiological model for PTSD. Many research teams have investigated single physiological systems in an effort to define the neurobiological basis and correlates of PTSD. In the last 10 years there has been excellent progress in this area. From the beginning, PTSD was viewed by most authorities as a stress response sharing many biological characteristics with responses to lower magnitude stressors. Recent research has challenged that assumption suggesting that the overwhelming nature of exposure to a life threatening stressor can lead, in some people, to marked physiological changes that differ in fundamental ways from the normal stress response (Yehuda, Giller, Levengood, Southwick, & Siever, 1995). One of the most consistent findings in the psychobiological research on PTSD is the unexpected observation that individuals with PTSD frequently display alterations in the hypothalamic–pituitary–adrenocorticotropic (HPA) axis marked by lower levels of cortisol; one of the main by-products of the production of catecholamines during the stress response. This finding is a consistent one across several forms of PTSD and is surprising because most authorities predicted elevations in this hormonal system. The implications of this finding are now being investigated and may yield compelling new information for understanding the biological basis of trauma.

Further, several studies have preliminarily demonstrated that individuals with PTSD may have a smaller hippocampus, an area of the brain central to the processing and relaying of information, the formation and retrieval of memory, and the promotion of contextual learning. Coupled with some fascinating infrahuman findings on the role of stress in the dysregulation of the HPA and in the morphology of the hippocampus, scholars are now beginning to propose a coherent psychobiological theory of the development and maintenance of PTSD. Although the precise changes and mechanisms are imperfectly understood at this time, researchers are building a sound evidentiary base for PTSD that involves the HPA axis, catecholamines, receptor sites, neurotransmitter systems, and specific brain regions that might account for the development of PTSD (Yehuda & McFarlane, 1997).

It is clear that stress alters a wide range of neurobiological systems down to the cellular level of functioning. It is also becoming increasingly clear that prior stress exposure alters the body's response to subsequent stressors, so that an individual who has experienced child abuse does not respond in the same way psychobiologically to a rape as does a rape victim without such a background (Resnick, Yehuda,

Pitman, & Foy, 1995). These findings may account for the epidemiological data suggesting that people with PTSD often have experienced multiple traumatic events (Kessler et al., 1995). There may be a sensitization that occurs following exposure to an overwhelming event that alters biological functioning and that places one at increased risk for developing PTSD when exposed to another traumatic event.

At the present time, many of the details of these dynamic biological processes are being elucidated by researchers (e.g., McEwen & Magarinos, 1997), and psychobiological models and theories for explaining the etiology of PTSD are in the nascent stage of development. At present, the task is to understand further the psychobiological underpinnings and correlates of PTSD so that cogent theoretical models and mechanisms can be proposed to help us understand why some people develop PTSD when exposed to overwhelming stressors and others do not (Yehuda & McFarlane, 1995). Ultimately, a comprehensive biopsychosocial theory that emphasizes person or constitutional variables (biological, cognitive, and personality factors), the characteristics of the event itself, and the postevent environment will account for the most variance in predicting outcomes.

Individual Differences in Risk or Vulnerability, Coping, and Social Support

As noted at the beginning of this chapter, etiological factors are a component of the diagnostic criteria for PTSD (i.e., the traumatic event: criterion A). It has been assumed that the magnitude of acute traumatic response and chronic symptom severity is a direct function of the frequency, intensity, and duration of the traumatic event, with the most extreme events yielding the most disabling symptoms for most people. In broad terms, this relationship is substantiated by available data; yet other factors are needed to account for the development of PTSD.

The most compelling evidence that other factors are involved in the development of PTSD is the frequent observation that only a proportion of the people exposed to a particular traumatic experience develop PTSD. Moreover, some people develop PTSD symptoms to events that appear to be low-level stressors. Person factors—that is, individual differences in life history, personality, biological constitution, and behavior—are often introduced to explain these discrepancies.

Freud, Ferenczi, Simmel, and Jones (1921) proposed that soldiers whose psychosexual development was marked by unresolved conflicts were likely to develop war neuroses. A more physiological substrate of vulnerability for such dysfunction was reflected by the World War I term *shell shock* and the World War II term *combat fatigue*. More recent conceptualizations of psychopathology have emphasized diathesis–stress models (Zubin & Spring, 1977) which posit a chronic vulnerability combined with acute stress to produce mental and behavioral disorders. Barlow (1988), for example, has proposed that vulnerability can be genetic, physiological, psychological, social, or even a combination of these factors. A similar, biopsychosocial model of vulnerability has been applied to the etiology of PTSD (Foy, Carroll, & Donahoe, 1987; Keane, 1989).

Most recent work on the etiology of PTSD has occurred with Vietnam veterans. Egendorf et al. (1981) found that combat exposure was the strongest predictor of postmilitary adjustment, although minority status and poor family stability both accounted for significant variance. In a clinical sample of veterans, Foy, Sipprelle, Rueger, and Carroll (1984) found that combat exposure variables accounted for significantly more variance than did a host of premilitary variables in predicting current PTSD symptomatology. Similarly, Penk et al. (1981) identified combat exposure as more important than demographic, family environment, or other premilitary variables among help-seeking substance-abusing veterans. In a group of officer candidate school graduates, Frye and Stockton (1982) again identified military variables and post-Vietnam experiences as more important than premilitary variables in the development of PTSD.

As mentioned earlier, the NVVRS found that warzone stress exposure was a strong predictor of psychological adjustment in general and PTSD in particular. Subsequent analyses of these data employing structural equation modeling (a contemporary multivariate statistical procedure) suggested that components of the war experience were deeply associated with who did and who didn't develop PTSD (King, King, Gudanowski, & Vreven, 1995). Traditional combat experiences coupled with exposure to

atrocities or abusive violence, perception of a threat to life, and the harsh, malevolent environment of Vietnam accounted for much of the outcome observed in these veterans 20 years after their service. The availability of high levels of social support upon return home buffered the effects of the war, while the occurrence of additional traumatic events contributed to deleterious outcomes (King, King, Fairbank, Keane, & Adams, 1998).

Taken together, these results indicate the role of individual differences as important risk factors for the development of PTSD. They also point to the difficulty in retrospectively attributing current-day functioning to a single traumatic event, given that multiple traumatic events can occur to a single individual over the course of a lifetime. Conceptually, it is not surprising that people who are already exhibiting psychological distress will be at greater risk for PTSD once exposed to an extreme life event. Similarly, it is not at all surprising that, in aggregate, people who experience multiple traumatic events will have more adverse psychosocial outcomes.

Whereas the Vietnam veteran research literature has provided critical data in understanding the linkage between the stressor and symptomatology, it is not the only empirical data confirming this relationship. Shore, Tatum, and Vollmer's (1986) evaluation of the Mount St. Helen's explosion indicated that those subjects who were exposed to the greatest amount of destruction and devastation reported the most psychological distress, both in the short term and over the next several years. In confirming the relationship of disasters to PTSD, Rubonis and Bickman (1991) employed a meta-analytic strategy and found a distinct relationship between the extent of various disasters and the subsequent negative effects on the long-term mental health of survivors.

Although many variables contribute to the ultimate development of PTSD, it appears reasonable to conclude that the dominant contributor to the development of PTSD is the traumatic stressor. Person factors such as biological, psychological, and social variables also play a role, but the exact mechanism of this role is not fully understood at this time (e.g., Yehuda & McFarlane, 1995). Future studies might also examine pretrauma, trauma, and posttrauma factors in a systematic way so that the relative contributions of each can be more precisely understood.

Many studies have found that the most vulnerable and disenfranchised people suffer disproportionately as a function of exposure to extreme events. However, this does not imply that individuals who have greater resources, a different biological constitution, or disproportionate levels of power are not vulnerable to the negative effects of such life experiences. Once exposed to extreme events, all are at risk for the development of psychological distress. For each individual it is simply a matter of how extreme the event (or series of events) is before he or she will begin to suffer a traumatic response. However, certain segments of our population clearly are at greater risk for exposure to extreme events and thus for the development of persistent adverse psychological reactions.

Many studies have demonstrated that minority-group members and women are at greater risk for the development of PTSD (see, e.g., the NVVRS). Future research studies might address the factors responsible for placing these individuals at higher risk for PTSD. Issues to be examined would include differential levels of vulnerability, both biologically and psychologically, as well as cultural, educational, and socioeconomic factors.

Coping and Social Support

The psychological condition of individuals appears to be enhanced or impaired as a result of the coping strategies employed and the social support systems available. For this reason, Fairbank, Hansen, and Fitterling (1991) examined the coping style of former prisoners of war with and without PTSD. They learned that the coping styles of both groups were similar for standard everyday stressors, but that when traumatic memories were considered, the PTSD ex–prisoners of war displayed unique characteristics. They used more self-isolation, wishful thinking, self-blame, and social support in an effort to cope with the traumatic memories.

Many theoreticians have offered a stress-buffering hypothesis to explain the positive effects of strong social support systems (Cobb, 1976; Rabkin & Struening, 1976). Keane, Scott, Chavoya, Lamparski, and Fairbank (1985) explored changes in social support systems among patients with PTSD through a period of some 15 years beginning immediately prior to trauma. On all dimensions of social support (including sources of material support, advice, physical sup-

port, financial support, and positive social interactions), the PTSD groups showed a decline from pre-trauma to posttrauma and onward to the time of the current assessment. This reported decline in the dimensions of social support was mirrored in measures of social support network size and of individuals' levels of satisfaction with their support systems.

It appears that individuals with PTSD suffer a wide range of psychological symptoms that are accompanied by dramatic reductions in social support over time. This decline in support may place them at continued risk for an exacerbation of distress when they encounter new life stressors. In addition, one might hypothesize from these data that those individuals who maintained and used their social support systems would be the most likely ones to recover from PTSD during the time following a traumatic experience. For whatever reasons, those unable to use their support systems or those who lack support systems continue to be symptomatic.

Information Processing in PTSD

As mentioned earlier, many current studies of information processing stem from the cognitive network conceptualization of anxiety developed by Lang (1977, 1979). This model hypothesizes that the cognitive representation of fear involves stimulus and response propositions that relate to the fear-eliciting cues, on one hand, and the motoric and physiological reactions they elicit on the other, as well as meaning propositions that contain personally relevant information. Cognition, motoric behavior, and physiology are response channels that can represent activation of the fear network.

Studies by McNally and his colleagues (McNally et al., 1987; McNally, Kaspi, Riemann, & Zeitlin, 1990) have elucidated some of the cognitive mechanisms associated with PTSD. In an initial study, PTSD veterans were compared with non-PTSD combat veteran psychiatric patients and with noncombat psychiatric veteran controls on a learning and memory task containing fear-relevant and control words. Although all three groups were equally sensitive to the detection of threat-related words, only the PTSD group demonstrated any emotional processing (e.g., increased skin conductance) as a function of the presentation of the combat threat words. This study provided additional support for the emotional reactivity of PTSD patients when fear-relevant stimuli were presented to them. Moreover, it demonstrated that simple semantic presentations were capable of activating the trauma or fear network (compared to studies using more intense nonsemantic cues).

In a second sequence of studies, this research group employed the Stroop interference task (Stroop, 1935), wherein words of varying levels of threat are presented in different colors. The experimental task is to identify the color of each word as quickly as possible. Selective processing of information is reflected by relative response latency for color naming as well as response accuracy per se. Longer latency and poorer accuracy in color naming are presumed to represent interference with information processing. Consistent with the author's hypotheses, combat veterans and rape victims with PTSD took significantly longer to color-name the PTSD-threat words than the control words. In addition, PTSD subjects were distinguished from an array of control groups (e.g., rape victims without PTSD) in their performance on this task. These findings are consistent with the notion that PTSD patients have cognitive representations of their traumatic experiences that can influence their interpretation of stimuli and events in their lives (Litz & Keane, 1989).

Research on attentional and memory processes in PTSD has also yielded valuable information about the disorder. Zimering, Caddell, Fairbank, and Keane (1993) found that, compared to well-adjusted combatants, PTSD patients showed attentional deficits on continuous performance tasks and poorer performance on affect recognition tasks (auditory). These findings were coupled with intact immediate memory for two verbally presented paragraphs (the Wechsler Memory Scale). These preliminary findings further demonstrate the selective nature of cognitive defects associated with PTSD.

Studies of information processing seem to hold great promise for understanding the nature of this disorder and for assisting in identifying the underlying cognitive and emotional components of PTSD. With increased research attention, information processing will provide a more complete functional analysis of the disorder and will more accurately describe the perceptual, emotional, and cognitive features of PTSD. These features may become targets for the development of assessment techniques (i.e., psychological markers) or treatment interventions.

COURSE AND COMPLICATIONS OF PTSD: LONGITUDINAL FINDINGS

Most PTSD research consists of cross-sectional studies that examine symptoms of the disorder at a single point in time following exposure to a traumatic event. To date, no long-term, prospective studies have been designed for the explicit purpose of examining fluctuations of symptom intensity and frequency across time in PTSD patients. Nonetheless, several retrospective studies do provide useful information on the course and duration of PTSD.

Retrospective studies that assessed individuals long after exposure to a traumatic stressor have documented the presence of PTSD over periods of 14 years (Green, Lindy, Grace, & Leonard, 1992) and 17 years (Desivilya, Gal, & Ayalon, 1996). The NVVRS evaluated PTSD symptomatology retrospectively by asking subjects about both lifetime and current occurrences of the disorder. They found that 30% of Vietnam veterans had PTSD at some point since military discharge, with 15% of the total sample reporting current PTSD. This 50% reduction over time was true for both male and female veterans over a period of approximately 15 to 20 years.

Several prospective studies have evaluated individuals at limited intervals following a traumatic experience and offer information about the short-term course of PTSD. Rothbaum, Foa, Riggs, Murdock, and Walsh (1992) assessed women for PTSD symptoms over 12 consecutive weeks following a sexual assault. At the time of the initial assessment, 94% of the women met criteria for PTSD. Three weeks later, 65% of the women endorsed PTSD symptoms, and by the 3-month evaluation, the number of women with PTSD had dropped to 47%. In a similar study of individuals who experienced nonsexual assault, Riggs, Rothbaum, and Foa (1995) examined PTSD symptoms weekly for 3 months and again found a sharp decline in PTSD symptomatology between the 1-month evaluation at which PTSD status was first established and the 3-month evaluation.

Prospective research that extends the assessment time frame beyond 3 months is found in a series of studies by McFarlane, who assessed PTSD symptomatology in 469 firefighters who were involved in the 1983 Australian bushfires. McFarlane (1986) found that PTSD was still evident in 41 cases and had resolved in 59 cases at a point 11 months after the fires. At the 29-month follow-up, PTSD had emerged in another 52 cases and resolved in 35. Only 53% of those who were diagnosed with PTSD at the 4-month evaluation met full diagnostic criteria at the 29-month evaluation. At 42 months, only a subgroup of 147 subjects (from the original 469) who had characteristics that placed them at high risk for PTSD were interviewed again. A total of 70 subjects were found to have PTSD (Spurrell & McFarlane, 1993). On the basis of this evidence, McFarlane concluded that PTSD as a result of a natural disaster can have a chronic course for some and a recurrent course for others, and that delays in the onset of the disorder are not uncommon. At the symptom level, McFarlane (1988) also noted that the reliving symptoms dissipated over time for many individuals, whereas the numbing and arousal symptoms seemed to be more persistent.

Additional information regarding the course of PTSD comes from studies of Israeli war veterans. Solomon (1988) followed soldiers who developed acute combat stress reactions during the 1983 Lebanon War. At the 2-year follow-up, 56% of the combatants who had an acute reaction also met criteria for PTSD, whereas only 18% of the nonreacting controls had developed PTSD. Those with PTSD suffered significant marital, social, and vocational impairment. Most individuals in this sample who developed PTSD met all symptom criteria for the disorder at the time of their acute reaction.

Finally, a prospective longitudinal study by Ronis et al. (1996) examined mental health service utilization by patients with PTSD in Veterans Health Administration (VHA) inpatient and outpatient facilities over a 56-month period. Their analysis was based on the assumption that the pattern of utilization reflects the course of the disorder. They found that PTSD patients used substantial amounts of mental health services and that their utilization was both persistent and episodic. On the basis of these data, the authors concluded that PTSD remissions are typically followed by relapse and that the absence of symptoms does not mean the disorder has fully resolved. Current VHA mental health policy reflects a similar view in that it characterizes combat-related PTSD as a chronic mental condition that cannot be expected to show stable improvement without sustained intervention.

The course of PTSD appears to be variable in terms of onset, chronicity, and recurrence. However, it does appear that PTSD symptoms develop acutely in many individuals following a traumatic stressor and that this can become a chronic condition in a significant minority of affected individuals. Studies have shown that individuals who experience a chronic course of PTSD may be distinguished by greater traumatic experience (e.g., criminal victimization; Desivilya et al., 1996), a higher level of dissociation in response to the traumatic event (Bremner & Brett, 1997), more severe initial symptoms (Riggs et al., 1995), and a predisposing family history (Solomon, Kotler, & Mikulincer, 1989). PTSD symptoms also may be reactivated by the anniversary date of a traumatic event or other life stressors (e.g., death of a loved one, serious medical illness, retirement, etc.; Davidson & Fairbank, 1993). Future research that contains more comprehensive examinations of factors influencing the course of the disorder, such as type and severity of trauma, age at the time of traumatic exposure, gender, and ethnicity, will undoubtedly broaden our understanding of the longitudinal course of this complex disorder.

COMORBID CONDITIONS

Studies of PTSD in the clinical setting and in the community suggest that PTSD is associated with a number of other disorders. For example, Keane and his colleagues (Keane et al., 1983) found high rates of substance abuse, including alcohol and drug abuse, in a clinical sample of Vietnam veterans. Similarly, Sierles and his colleagues (1983, 1986) in both an inpatient and an outpatient medical setting found high rates of alcohol abuse, depression, and antisocial personality disorder in addition to the primary diagnosis of PTSD.

In addition, Keane and Wolfe (1990) examined comorbidity among 50 help-seeking PTSD veterans using the Structured Clinical Interview for DSM-III-R (Spitzer & Williams, 1985). This study indicated that 84% of the sample met criteria for substance abuse or dependence and that 68% met lifetime criteria for major depression, with 34% reaching criteria for dysthymic disorders. Further, 26% of the sample were diagnosed with an Axis II personality disorder, generally an antisocial personality disorder. These patients averaged 3.8 diagnoses, including PTSD.

In the NVVRS, Kulka et al. (1988) also found high rates of comorbidity among community-residing veterans. Using the DIS (Robins, Helzer, Groughan, & Ratcliff, 1981), they found that virtually all PTSD cases also met criteria for another disorder at some time in their lives and that 50% had another disorder within the past 6 months. Alcohol abuse or dependence (73%) was the most prevalent coexisting disorder, while antisocial personality disorder was found among 30% of the community sample. Depression (26%) and dysthymia (21%) were also frequently associated diagnoses.

These clinical and community studies have consistently found that PTSD is associated with high rates of comorbid substance abuse (particularly alcohol abuse), depression, and antisocial personality disorder. However, all studies reviewed here studied PTSD in veterans; thus, these findings may be specific to PTSD in that population.

Helzer et al. (1987) studied the general population in the St. Louis catchment area and also observed that individuals with PTSD were twice as likely to have another disorder as were individuals without PTSD. Depression, dysthymia, and obsessive-compulsive disorders were frequently seen in this sample. Moreover, Kilpatrick, Saunders, Veronen, Best, and Von (1987) used the DIS to examine the consequences of criminal victimization and also reported high rates of comorbidity. Sexual dysfunction (41%), major depression (32%), obsessive-compulsive disorder (27%), social phobia (18%), and agoraphobia (18%) were all found to be associated with PTSD.

Indeed, PTSD rarely occurs in isolation. Among women who have been raped and are seeking treatment, high rates of comorbidity are typically observed (Cashman, Foa, & Molnar, 1995; Griffin, Resick, & Mechanic, 1996). Major depression and substance abuse are the most frequently observed concurrent conditions in PTSD patients, and data from the National Comorbidity Study clearly indicate that PTSD often precedes the onset of depression and substance abuse (Kessler et al., 1995). The presence of this degree of comorbidity often contributes to the complexity involved in conducting research on PTSD as well as in its clinical assessment and treatment (Keane & Kaloupek, 1997).

Analyzing these high rates of comorbidity presents a challenge. Are these separate, independent disorders? Are they secondary to PTSD? Do they predispose one to develop PTSD? Or are these findings a function of the limitation of our classification scheme or our measurement tools? Some authors have suggested that PTSD is characterized by diffuse symptomatology beyond the reliving, numbing, and hyperarousal criteria (Keane & Wolfe, 1990) and that the high rate of symptom endorsement is due in part to the distress felt by sufferers. Others have identified the symptom overlap between PTSD and other disorders as an artifact that produces this high rate of comorbidity. Future research on developmental histories, family genealogies, and genetics may help us disentangle the puzzle underlying the high rates of comorbidity in PTSD. At present there appears to be some evidence to suggest both that the presence of other psychological disorders is a risk factor for developing PTSD (Breslau et al., 1991) and that the development of PTSD leads inexorably to the development of other conditions such as substance abuse and depression (Kessler, et al., 1995).

IMPLICATIONS FOR TREATMENT OF PTSD

The psychological treatment of PTSD has advanced considerably since the development of reliable and valid assessment methods. Successful treatment of PTSD secondary to a wide variety of traumatic events typically includes anxiety management methods, such as stress inoculation, in addition to one or more of the exposure therapies, including systematic desensitization, flooding, graduated in vivo exposure, or implosive therapy (see Keane, 1997, for a full evaluation of the treatment outcome literature). Studies on combat veterans (Keane et al., 1989), rape victims (Foa, Rothbaum, Riggs, & Murdock, 1991; Resick & Schnicke, 1992), and civilian trauma (Brom, Kleber, & Defares, 1989) support the use of these methods.

Yet, the psychological treatment of PTSD can be complicated as a result of its chronic course, the high levels of comorbidity frequently observed, the development of character problems secondary to living under extreme duress for sustained periods of time, the presence of numerous psychosocial problems, and its resistance to a wide range of psychopharmacological interventions. Further information is needed about the biological correlates of PTSD and the specific structural, hormonal, and neurotransmitter systems that suffer dysregulation as a function of exposure to life-threatening traumatic events and the development of PTSD. This will guide the development of additional, innovative treatments for the disorder.

As researchers head into the next millennium, the clear priority for research foci will be on the provision of treatment services in the most effective way, in the most accessible settings, and with an emphasis on combining treatments that have empirical documentation for positive treatment outcome, whether those treatments are psychological or psychopharmacological in nature. Increasingly, resources are being directed on a national, regional, and local level to the treatment of victims of violence and other forms of psychological trauma. This trend can be expected to continue indefinitely in response to the high rates of trauma exposure in contemporary society, the high prevalence of PTSD, and the tremendous social and economic costs associated with this disorder.

PTSD Case Description

Mr. J is a 26-year-old single white male referred by his psychiatrist for desensitization therapy of intrusive memories surrounding a traumatic event that occurred two years earlier. At the time he presented for therapy, the patient was experiencing intense PTSD symptoms secondary to a near fatal automobile accident.

Exposure to a traumatic event: *On his return home from work one evening, Mr. J stopped and then proceeded into a four-way stop intersection. In the middle of the intersection, his car was broadsided on the left by a speeding car. The force of the impact spun his car around twice and overturned the car. When his car stopped moving, Mr. J was crushed between the car door, the steering wheel, and the roof. He remained conscious and attempted to free himself from the wreckage, but pain from his legs and chest increased with each attempt. He felt his blood on his face and chest but could not specifically pinpoint his injuries. Moments later, in this trapped position, Mr. J heard a loud pressured hissing noise from the car's engine and was terrified that the engine would explode. Then, when the noise abated, Mr. J became filled with dread that he would bleed to death before he could be freed from the car. When he heard the siren of the ambulance, he felt relief and horror simultaneously because he feared he would lose a limb in order to be freed from the car. Mr. J was finally freed by the Jaws of Life 2 hours later and made a near-full medical recovery.*

Reexperiencing symptoms: *The patient's intrusive thoughts began immediately after the accident and persisted 2 years following the event. He had frequent nightmares of the accident (from which he would awake screaming), daily intrusive thoughts and images of his entrapment, kinesthetic flashbacks in which he could feel blood on his skin, and auditory flashbacks of the loud noise of the crash and the hissing sound of steam. He was particularly plagued by the physical and psychological feeling of being trapped and experienced this sensation in a wide array of settings where he was in small, enclosed spaces, including cars, elevators, and small rooms. Additionally, the sound of any siren resulted in an intense anxiety reaction.*

Avoidance of stimuli associated with the trauma: *Following his serious motor vehicle accident, Mr. J began to avoid driving or riding in an automobile. It was difficult for him to walk (because of a leg injury from the accident), and he avoided using public transportation because of the small enclosed space of a bus or subway. As a result, Mr. J severely curtailed his activities. He quit his job and greatly decreased his once active social life. Furthermore, it became increasingly uncomfortable for him to be in public because he could not predict when something in his environment (e.g., an ambulance siren) would trigger an intrusive thought of the accident and a significant anxiety reaction. Interpersonally, his commitment to his girlfriend and plans for marriage made him feel trapped (evoking images of the accident), and he ended their engagement. Thus, in order to avoid exposure to both internal and external cues of the accident, Mr. J isolated himself physically from the external environment and numbed his feelings emotionally.*

Symptoms of increased arousal: *Mr. J endorsed all symptoms of increased arousal. He was unable to sleep without medication and had difficulty concentrating on simple tasks. He had frequent outbursts of anger, and he harbored a rage toward drivers who did not obey all traffic laws. On one occasion, when he witnessed a driver make an incomplete stop at a flashing red light, he became incensed and threw a large rock at the car, shattering the rear window. On the rare occasions when Mr. J had to drive, his extreme levels of hypervigilance negatively affected his driving because he tried to be aware of everything in his environment and did not concentrate sufficiently on the road and other drivers. The patient frequently showed an exaggerated startle response to loud, sudden noises that closely resembled the auditory characteristics of the accident.*

Desensitization treatment for the traumatic reexperiencing symptoms was very effective and resolved distressing images and perceptions quickly. Unfortunately, Mr. J continued to experience symptoms of avoidance and increased arousal, which were much more difficult to resolve. These required additional treatment that focused on stress management skills and cognitive strategies that promoted a change in his views of himself, the world, and his relationship with others, as well as an understanding of his avoidant behavior.

SUMMARY AND FUTURE DIRECTIONS

Although we have learned a great deal about the psychological effects associated with exposure to extreme stressors, much work remains to be done. Many of the studies that have been conducted on exposure to disasters, sexual abuse, and technological accidents indicate that psychological impairment can result as a function of these experiences. Unfortunately, many studies suffer from methodological weaknesses that preclude firm conclusions with respect to tying the psychological stress directly to the traumatic events. Future research in this area needs to continue to include randomly selected samples of subjects, appropriate comparison groups, and psychological test instruments that have documented reliability and validity. By improving the methodological quality of these studies, we will enable policymakers to develop comprehensive public policy toward victims and survivors so that justice is provided to all those affected by these experiences.

Psychophysiological arousal and reactivity have been documented among veterans with combat-related PTSD. Recent research has documented that individuals with PTSD from different events, such as moving vehicle accidents and terrorist attacks, also manifest this heightened psychophysiological pattern. In addition to the diagnostic importance of this arousal pattern, it is distinctly likely that this sustained, heightened cardiovascular reactivity places these individuals at substantial risk for the development of health-related problems including cardiovascular disease. Future research studies examining the association between PTSD and cardiovascular disease would, therefore, be both timely and important. Similarly, studies of stress, anger, and immune system functioning are also theoretically important to examine in this population. Theoretical models of health and disease would indicate that individuals with high levels of stress, depression, and anger are

at risk for the development of neoplastic disease as well as cardiovascular disease.

Much work needs to be done to understand more fully the gender differences in response to traumatic events. Currently, there is an opportunity to begin to examine more closely the psychological effects of war-zone stress exposure in men and women. The Persian Gulf War provided an experience where for the first time males and females served in many similar roles and were exposed to many of the same overwhelming stressors. As a result of this experience, we may be able to examine the extent to which gender influences the expression and manifestation of traumatic symptoms (Ursano & Norwood, 1996).

Further, there is some reason to believe that there may well be a genetic component that helps determine who does and who does not develop PTSD. Future work on this topic will help researchers to understand more fully the role of biological determinants and how they interact with developmental course and environmental events to yield symptoms of PTSD.

REFERENCES

American Psychiatric Association. (1980). *Diagnostic and statistical manual of mental disorders,* 3rd ed. Washington, DC: Author.

American Psychiatric Association. (1987). *Diagnostic and statistical manual of mental disorders,* 3rd ed.—revised. Washington, DC: Author.

American Psychiatric Association. (1994). *Diagnostic and statistical manual of mental disorders,* 4th ed. Washington, DC: Author.

Blake, D.D., Weathers, F.W., Nagy, L.M., Kaloupek, D.G., Klauminzer, G., Charney, D.S., & Keane, T.M. (1990). A clinical rating scale for assessing current and lifetime PTSD: The CAPS-1. *The Behavior Therapist, 18,* 187–188.

Blanchard, E.B., Hickling, E.J., Buckley, T.C., Taylor, A.E., Vollmer, A., & Loos, W.R. (1996). The psychophysiology of motor vehicle accident related post-traumatic stress disorder: Replication and extension. *Journal of Consulting and Clinical Psychology, 64,* 742–751.

Blanchard, E.B., Hickling, E.J., Taylor, A., & Loos, G.R.J. (1994). The psychophysiology of motor vehicle accident related posttraumatic stress disorder. *Behavior Therapy, 25,* 453–467.

Blanchard, E.B., Kolb, L.C., Pallmeyer, T.B., & Gerardi, R.J. (1982). The development of a psychophysiological assessment procedure for posttraumatic stress disorder in Vietnam veterans. *Psychiatric Quarterly, 54,* 220–229.

Braun, B.G. (1984). The role of the family in the development of Multiple Personality Disorder. *International Journal of Family Psychiatry, 5*(4), 303–313.

Braun, B.G. (1987). *Treatment of multiple personality disorder.* Washington, DC: American Psychiatric Press.

Bremner, J.D., & Brett, E. (1997). Trauma-related dissociative states and long-term psychopathology in posttraumatic stress disorder. *Journal of Traumatic Stress, 10,* 37–49.

Breslau, N., & Davis, G.C. (1987). Posttraumatic stress disorder: The stressor criterion. *Journal of Nervous and Mental Disease, 175,* 255–264.

Breslau, N., Davis, G.C., Andreski, P., & Peterson, E. (1991). Traumatic events and posttraumatic stress disorder in an urban population of young adults. *Archives of General Psychiatry, 48,* 216–222.

Brett, E.A., & Ostroff, R. (1985). Imagery and posttraumatic stress disorder: An overview. *American Journal of Psychiatry, 142,* 417–424.

Brom, D., Kleber, R.J., & Defares, P.B. (1989). Brief psychotherapy for posttraumatic stress disorders. *Journal of Consulting and Clinical Psychology, 57*(5), 607–612.

Chemtob, C., Roitblat, H., Hamada, R., Carlson, J., & Twentyman, C. (1988). A cognitive action theory of post-traumatic stress disorder. *Journal of Anxiety Disorders, 2,* 253–275.

Cobb, S. (1976). Social support as a moderator of life stress. *Psychosomatic Medicine, 38,* 301–314.

Davidson, J.R.T., & Fairbank, J.A. (1993). The epidemiology of posttraumatic stress disorder. In J.R. Davidson & E.B. Foa (Eds.), *Posttraumatic stress disorder: DSM-IV and beyond* (pp. 147–169). Washington DC: American Psychiatric Press.

Davidson, J., Smith, R., & Kudler, H. (1989). Validity and reliability of the DSM-III criteria for posttraumatic stress disorder: Experience with a structured interview. *Journal of Nervous and Mental Disease, 177,* 336–341.

Desivilya, H.S., Gal, R., & Ayalon, O. (1996). Extent of victimization, traumatic stress symptoms, and adjustment of terrorist assault survivors: A long-term follow-up. *Journal of Traumatic Stress, 9,* 881–889.

DiNardo, P.A., Brown, T.A., & Barlow, D.H. (1994). *Anxiety Disorders Interview Schedule for DSM-IV: Lifetime Version (ADIS-IV-L).* New York: Phobia and Anxiety Disorders Clinic, Center for Stress and Anxiety Disorders, University at Albany, State University of New York.

Dohrenwend, B.D., & Shrout, P.B. (1981). Toward the development of a two-stage procedure for case identification and classification in psychiatric epidemiology. *Research in Community and Mental Health, 2,* 295–323.

Egendorf, A. et al. (1981). *Legacies of Vietnam.* Washington, DC: U.S. Government Printing Office.

Foa, E.G. (1997) *Posttraumatic Stress Disorder Diagnostic Scale,* (Available from author.)

Foa, E.B., Molnar, C., & Cashman, L. (1995). Change in rape narratives during exposure therapy for posttraumatic stress disorder. *Journal of Traumatic Stress, 8*(4), 675–690.

Foa, E.G., Riggs, D., Dancu, C., & Rothbaum, B. (1993). Reliability and validity of a brief instrument for assessing posttraumatic stress disorder. *Journal of Traumatic Stress, 6,* 459–474.

Foa, E.G., Rothbaum, B.O., Riggs, D., & Murdock, T.B. (1991). Treatment of posttraumatic stress disorder in rape victims: A comparison of cognitive behavioral approaches and counseling. *Journal of Consulting and Clinical Psychology, 59,* 715–723.

Foa, E.G., Steketee, G., & Rothbaum, B.O. (1989). Behavioral/cognitive conceptualization of posttraumatic stress disorder. *Behavior Therapy, 20,* 155–176.

Foy, D.W., Carroll, E.M., & Donahoe, C.P. (1987). Etiological factors in the development of PTSD in clinical samples of Vietnam combat veterans. *Journal of Clinical Psychology, 43,* 17–27.

Foy, D.W., Sipprelle, R.C., Rueger, D.B., & Carroll, E.M. (1984). Etiology of PTSD in Vietnam veterans: Analysis of premilitary, military, and combat exposure influences. *Journal of Consulting and Clinical Psychology, 52,* 79–87.

Freud, S., Ferenczi, A.K., Simmel, E., & Jones, E.

(1921). *Psychoanalysis and the war neurosis.* New York: International Psychoanalytic Press.

Frye, J.S., & Stockton, R.A. (1982). Discriminant analysis of post-traumatic stress disorder among a group of Vietnam veterans. *American Journal of Psychiatry, 139,* 52–56.

Gerardi, R.J., Keane, T.M., Klauminzer, G.W., & Cahoon, B.J. (1994). An in-vivo assessment of psychophysiological arousal in Vietnam veterans. *Journal of Abnormal Psychology, 103,* 825–827.

Gleser, G.C., Green, B.L., & Winget, C. (1981). *Buffalo Creek revisited: Prolonged psychosocial effects of disaster.* New York: Simon & Schuster.

Goodwin, D.W., & Guze, S.B. (1984). *Psychiatric diagnosis.* New York: Oxford University Press.

Green, B.L., et al. (1983). Levels of functional impairment following a civilian disaster: The Beverly Hills Supper Club fire. *Journal of Consulting and Clinical Psychology, 51*(4), 573–580.

Green, B.L., Lindy, J.D., Grace, M.C., & Leonard, A.C. (1992). Chronic posttraumatic stress disorder and diagnostic comorbidity in a disaster sample. *Journal of Nervous and Mental Disease, 180,* 760–766.

Griffin, M.G., Resick, P.A., & Mechanic, M.B. (1997). Objective assessment of peritraumatic dissociation: Psychophysiological indicators. *American Journal of Psychiatry, 154*(8), 1081–1088.

Helzer, J.E., Robins, L.N., & McEvoy, L. (1987). Post-traumatic stress disorder in the general population: Findings of the Epidemiological Catchment Area Survey. *New England Journal of Medicine, 317,* 1630–1634.

Hendin, H., & Haas, A.P. (1984). Combat adaptations of Vietnam veterans without posttraumatic stress disorders. *American Journal of Psychiatry, 141*(8), 956–960.

Herman, J.L. (1981). *Father–daughter incest.* Cambridge, MA: Harvard University Press.

Herman, J.L., Perry, J.C., & van der Kolk, B.A. (1989). Childhood trauma in borderline personality disorder. *American Journal of Psychiatry, 146,* 490–495.

Horowitz, M. (1973). Phase oriented treatment of stress response syndromes. *American Journal of Psychotherapy, 27,* 506–515.

Horowitz, M. (1976). *Stress response syndromes.* New York: Jason Aronson.

Janoff-Bulman, R. (1992). *Shattered assumptions.* New York: Free Press.

Keane, T.M. (1989). Post-traumatic stress disorder: Current status and future directions. *Behavior Therapy, 20,* 149–153.

Keane, T.M. (1997). Psychological and behavioral treatments for PTSD. In P. Nathan & J. Gorman (Eds.), *Treatments that work,* London: Oxford University Press.

Keane, T.M., et al. (1983). Substance abuse among Vietnam veterans with posttraumatic stress disorders. *Bulletin of the Society of Psychologists in Addictive Behaviors, 2*(2), 117–122.

Keane, T.M., Caddell, J.M., & Taylor, K.L. (1988). Mississippi Scale for Combat-Related Posttraumatic Stress Disorder: Three studies in reliability and validity. *Journal of Consulting and Clinical Psychology, 56,* 85–90.

Keane, T.M., Fairbank, C.L., Caddell, J.M., & Zimering, R.T. (1989). Implosive (flooding) therapy reduces symptoms of post-traumatic stress disorder in Vietnam combat veterans. *Behavior Therapy, 20,* 245–260.

Keane, T.M., Fairbank, J.A., Caddell, J.M., Zimering, R.T., & Bender, M.E. (1985). A behavioral approach to assessing and treating post-traumatic stress disorder in Vietnam veterans. In C.R. Figley (Ed.), *Trauma and its wake* (pp. 257–294). New York: Brunner/Mazel.

Keane, T.M., & Kaloupek, D.G. (1982). Imaginal flooding in the treatment of post-traumatic stress disorder. *Journal of Consulting and Clinical Psychology, 50,* 138–140.

Keane, T.M., & Kaloupek, D.G. (1997). Comorbid psychiatric disorders in PTSD: Implications for research. In R. Yehuda, A.C. McFarlane, et al. (Eds.), *Psychobiology of Posttraumatic Stress Disorder* (Vol. 821, pp. 24–34). New York: Annals of the New York Academy of Sciences.

Keane, T.M., Kaloupek, D.G., & Weathers, F.W. (1996). Ethnocultural considerations in the assessment of PTSD. In A.J. Marsella, M.J. Friedman, et al. (Eds.), *Ethnocultural aspects of posttraumatic stress disorder: Issues, research, and clinical applications* (pp. 183–205). Washington, DC: American Psychological Association.

Keane, T.M., Kolb, L.C., Kaloupek, D.G., Orr, S.P., Blanchard, E.B., Thomas, R.G., Hsieh, F.Y., &

Lavori, P.W. (1998). Utility of psychophysiological measurement in the diagnosis of posttraumatic stress disorder: Results from a Department of Veterans Affairs cooperative study. *Journal of Consulting and Clinical Psychology, 66,* 914–923.

Keane, T.M., Malloy, P.F., & Fairbank, J.A. (1984). Empirical development of an MMPI subscale for the assessment of combat-related posttraumatic stress disorder. *Journal of Consulting and Clinical Psychology, 52,* 888–891.

Keane, T.M., Scott, W.O., Chavoya, G.A., Lamparski, D.M., & Fairbank, J.A. (1985). Social support in Vietnam veterans with posttraumatic stress disorder: A comparative analysis. *Journal of Consulting and Clinical Psychology, 53,* 95–102.

Keane, T.M., & Wolfe, J. (1990). Comorbidity in post-traumatic stress disorder: An analysis of community and clinical studies. *Journal of Applied Social Psychology, 20,* 1176–1788.

Keane, T.M., Zimering, R.T., & Caddell, J.M. (1985). A behavioral formulation of post-traumatic stress disorder in Vietnam veterans. *The Behavior Therapist, 8,* 9–12.

Kessler, R.C., Sonnega, A., Bromet, E., Hughes, M., & Nelson, C.B. (1995) Posttraumatic stress disorder in the National Comorbidy Survey. *Archives of General Psychiatry, 52,* 1048–1060.

Kilpatrick, D.G., Best, C.L., Veronen, L.J., Amick, A.E., et al. (1985). Mental health correlates of criminal victimization: A random community survey. *Journal of Consulting and Clinical Psychology, 53,* 866–873.

Kilpatrick, D.G., Edmonds, C.N., & Seymour, A.K. (1992). *Rape in America: A report to the nation.* Arlington, VA: National Victim Center.

Kilpatrick, D.G., Saunders, B.E., Veronen, L.J., Best, C.L., & Von, J.M. (1987). Criminal victimization: Lifetime prevalence, reporting to police and psychological impact. *Crime and Delinquency, 33,* 479–489.

King, D.W., King, L.A., Gudanowski, D.M., & Vreven, D.L. (1995). Alternative representations of war-zone stressors: Relationships to posttraumatic stress disorder in male and female Vietnam veterans. *Journal of Abnormal Psychology, 104*(1), 184–196.

King, L.A., King, D.W., Fairbank, J.A., Keane, T.M., & Adams, G.A. (1998). Resilience/recovery factors in posttraumatic among female and male Vietnam veterans: Hardiness, postwar social support, and additional stressful life events. *Journal of Personality and Social Psychology, 74,* 420–434.

Koss, M.P., Gidycz, C.A., & Wisniewski, N. (1987). The scope of rape: Incidence and prevalence of sexual aggression and victimization in a national sample of higher education students. *Journal of Consulting and Clinical Psychology, 55,* 162–170.

Koretzky, M.B., & Peck, A.H. (1990). Validation and cross-validation of the PTSD subscale of the MMPI with civilian trauma victims. *Journal of Clinical Psychology, 46*(3), 296–300.

Kulka, R.A., Schlenger, W.E., Fairbank, J.A., Hough, R.L., Jordan, B.K., Marmar, C.R., & Weiss, D.S. (1988). *National Vietnam veterans readjustment study (NVVRS): Description, current status, and initial PTSD prevalence estimates.* Washington, DC: Veterans Administration.

Lang, P.J. (1977). Imagery in therapy: An information processing analysis of fear. *Behavior Therapy, 8,* 862–886.

Lang, P.J. (1979). A bioinformational theory of emotional imagery. *Psychophysiology, 16,* 495–512.

Litz, B.T. (1991). *The parameters of emotional processing in combat-related post-traumatic stress disorder.* Unpublished manuscript.

Litz, B.T., & Keane, T.M. (1989). Information processing in anxiety disorders: Application to the understanding of post-traumatic stress disorder. *Clinical Psychology Review, 9,* 243–257.

Malloy, P.F., Fairbank, J.A., & Keane, T.M. (1983). Validation of a multimethod assessment of posttraumatic stress disorders in Vietnam veterans. *Journal of Consulting and Clinical Psychology, 51,* 488–494.

McFall, M.E., Veith, R.C., & Murburg, M.M. (1992). Basal sympathoadrenal function in posttraumatic stress disorder. *Biological Psychiatry, 34,* 311–320.

McEwen, B.S., & Magarinos, A.M. (1997). Stress effects on morphology and function of the hippocampus. In R. Yehuda & A.C. McFarlane (Eds.), *Psychobiology of postraumatic stress disorder* (pp. 271–284), New York: Annals of the New York Academy of Science.

McFarlane, A.C. (1986). Long-term psychiatric morbidity after a natural disaster: Implications for disaster planners and emergency services. *Medical Journal of Australia, 145,* 561–563.

McFarlane, A.C. (1988). The longitudinal course of posttraumatic morbidity: The range of outcomes and their predictors. *Journal of Nervous and Mental Disease, 176,* 30–39.

McNally, R.J., Kaspi, S.P., Riemann, B.C., & Zeitlin, S.B. (1990). Selective processing of threat cues in posttraumatic stress disorder. *Journal of Abnormal Psychology, 99*(4), 398–402.

McNally, R.J., Luedke, D.L., Besyner, J.K., Peterson, R.A., Bohn, K., & Lips, O.J. (1987). Sensitivity to stress relevant stimuli in post-traumatic stress disorder. *Journal of Anxiety Disorders, 1,* 105–116.

Mowrer, O.H. (1960). *Learning theory and behavior.* New York: Wiley.

Newman, E., Kaloupek, D.G., & Keane, T.M. (1996). Assessment of posttraumatic stress disorder in clinical and research settings. In B. van der Kolk, A.C. McFarlane, & L. Weisaeth (Eds.), *Traumatic stress: The effects of overwhelming experiences on mind, body, and society.* New York: Guilford Press.

Norris, F.H. (1992). Epidemiology of trauma: Frequency and impact of different potentially traumatic events on different demographic groups. *Journal of Consulting and Clinical Psychology, 60,* 409–418.

Norris, F.H., & Riad, J.K. (1997). Standardized self-report measures of civilian trauma and posttraumatic stress disorder. In J.P. Wilson & T.M. Keane (Eds.), *Assessing psychological trauma and PTSD* (pp. 7–42), New York: Guilford Press.

Orr, S.P., Claiborn, J.M., Altman, B., Forgue, D.F., et al. (1990). Psychometric profile of posttraumatic stress disorder, anxious, and healthy Vietnam veterans: Correlations with psychophysiologic responses. *Journal of Consulting and Clinical Psychology, 58*(3), 329–335.

Penk, W.E., Robinowitz, R., Roberts, W.R., Patterson, E.T., et al. (1981). Adjustment differences among male substance abusers varying in degree of combat experience in Vietnam. *Journal of Consulting and Clinical Psychology, 49,* 426–437.

Pitman, R.K., Orr, S.P., Forgue, D.F., deJong, J.B., & Claiborn, J.M. (1987). Psychophysiologic assessment of post-traumatic stress disorder imagery in Vietnam combat veterans. *Archives of General Psychiatry, 44*(11), 970–975.

Prins, A., Kaloupek, D.G., & Keane, T.M. (1995). Psychophysiological evidence for autonomic arousal and startle in traumatized adult populations. In M.J. Friedman, D. Charney, & A. Deutch (Eds.), *Neurobiological and clinical consequences of stress: From normal adaptation to PTSD* (pp. 291–314). New York: Raven.

Rabkin, J.G., & Struening, G.S. (1976). Life events, stress, and illness. *Science, 194,* 1013–1020.

Resick, P.A., & Schnicke, M.K. (1992). Cognitive processing theory for sexual assault victims. *Journal of Consulting and Clinical Psychology, 60*(5), 748–756.

Resnick, H.S., Kilpatrick, D.G., Dansky, B.S., Saunders, B.E., & Best, C.L. (1993). Prevalence of civilian trauma and posttraumatic stress disorder in a representative national sample of women. *Journal of Consulting and Clinical Psychology, 61,* 984–991.

Resnick, H.S., Yehuda, R., Pitman, R.K., & Foy, D.W. (1995). Effect of previous trauma on acute plasma cortisol level following rape. *American Journal of Psychiatry, 152*(11), 1675–1677.

Riggs, D.S., Rothbaum, B.O., & Foa, E.B. (1995). A prospective examination of symptoms of posttraumatic stress disorder in victims of nonsexual assault. *Journal of Interpersonal Violence, 10,* 201–214.

Robins, L.N., Helzer, J.E., Groughan, J., & Ratcliff, K. (1981). National Institute of Mental Health Diagnostic Interview Schedule. *Archives of General Psychiatry, 38,* 381–389.

Ronis, D.L., Bates, E.W., Garfein, A.J., Buit, B.K., Falcon, S.P., & Liberzon, I. (1996). Longitudinal patterns of care for patients with posttraumatic stress disorder. *Journal of Traumatic Stress, 9,* 763–781.

Rothbaum, B.O., Foa, E.B., Riggs, D.S., Murdock, T., & Walsh, W. (1992). A prospective examination of post-traumatic stress disorder in rape victims. *Journal of Traumatic Stress, 5,* 455–475.

Rubonis, A.V., & Bickman, L. (1991). Psychological impairment in the wake of disaster: The disaster–psychopathology relationship. *Psychological Bulletin, 109,* 384–399.

Saunders, B., Arata, C., & Kilpatrick, D.G. (1990). Development of a crime-related posttraumatic stress disorder scale for women within the Symptom Checklist 90-R. *Journal of Traumatic Stress, 3,* 439–448.

Shore, J., Tatum, E., & Vollmer, W. (1986). Psychiatric reactions to disaster: The Mount St. Helen's Experience. *American Journal of Psychiatry, 143,* 590–595.

Sierles, F.S., Chen, J., McFarland, R.E., & Taylor, M.A. (1983). Post-traumatic stress disorder and concurrent psychiatric illness. *American Journal of Psychiatry, 140,* 1177–1179.

Sierles, F.S., Chen, J., Messing, M.L., Besyner, J.K., & Taylor, M.A. (1986). Concurrent psychiatric illness in non-Hispanic outpatients diagnosed as having posttraumatic stress disorder. *Journal of Nervous and Mental Disease, 174,* 171–173.

Solomon, Z. (1988). Somatic complaints, stress reaction, and posttraumatic stress disorder: A three-year follow-up study. *Behavioral Medicine, 14*(4), 179–185.

Solomon, Z., Kotler, M., & Mikulincer, M. (1989). Combat-related post-traumatic stress disorder among the second generation of Holocaust survivors: Transgenerational effects among Israeli soldiers. *Psychologia Israel Journal of Psychology, 1,* 113–119.

Spitzer, R.L., & Williams, J.B. (1985). *Structured clinical interview for DSM-III.* Unpublished manuscript, Biometrics Research Department, New York State Psychiatric Institute.

Spitzer, R.L., Williams, J.B., Gibbon, M., & First, M. (1997). *Structured clinical interview for DSM-IV.* New York: Biometrics Research Department, New York State Psychiatric Institute.

Spurrell, M.T., & McFarlane, A.C. (1993). Posttraumatic stress disorder and coping after a natural disaster. *Social Psychiatry and Psychiatric Epidemiology, 28*(4), 194–200.

Stroop, J.R. (1935). Studies of interference in serial verbal reactions. *Journal of Experimental Psychology, 18,* 643–661.

The Tenth International Psychoanalytic Congress. (1928). *Psychoanalytic Review, 15,* 85–107.

Ursano, R.J., & Norwood, A.E. (1996). *Emotional aftermath of the Persian Gulf war.* Washington, DC: American Psychiatric Press.

Weathers, F.W., Litz, B.T., Herman, D., Huska, J., & Keane, T.M. (1993). *The PTSD Checklist (PCL): Reliability, validity, and diagnostic utility.* Paper presented at the International Society for Traumatic Stress Studies, San Antonio, TX.

Weathers, F.W., Litz, B.T., Herman, D., Keane, T.M., Steinberg, H., Huska, J., & Kraemer, H.C. (1996). The utility of the SCL-90-R for the diagnosis of war-zone related PTSD. *Journal of Traumatic Stress, 9,* 111–128.

Wilson, J.P. (1977). *Forgotten warrior project.* Cincinnati: Disabled American Veterans.

Wilson, J.P., & Keane, T.M. (1997). *Assessing psychological trauma and PTSD.* New York: Guilford Press.

Wolfe, J., Brown, P.J., Furey, J., & Levin, K. (1993). Development of a wartime stressor scale for women. *Psychological Assessment: Journal of Consulting and Clinical Psychology, 5,* 330–335.

Yehuda, R., Giller, E.L. Jr., Levengood, R.A., Southwick, S.M., & Siever, L.J. (1995). Hypothalamic-pituitary-adrenal functioning in post-traumatic stress disorder: Expanding the concept of the stress response spectrum. In M.J. Friedman, D.S. Charney, et al. (Eds.), *Neurobiological and clinical consequences of stress: From normal adaptation to post-traumatic stress disorder* (pp. 351–365). Philadelphia: Lippincott-Raven.

Yehuda, R., & McFarlane, A.C. (1995). Conflict between current knowledge about posttraumatic stress disorder and its original conceptual basis. *American Journal of Psychiatry, 152,* 1705–1713.

Yehuda, R., & McFarlane, A.C. (1997). *Psychobiology of posttraumatic stress disorder.* New York: Annals of the New York Academy of Science.

Zimering, R.T., Caddell, J.M., Fairbank, J.A., & Keane, T.M. (1993). PTSD in Vietnam veterans: An empirical evaluation of the diagnostic criteria. *Journal of Traumatic Stress, 6,* 327–342.

Zubin, J., & Spring, B. (1977). Vulnerability: A new view of schizophrenia. *Journal of Abnormal Psychology, 86,* 103–126.

CHAPTER 10

OBSESSIVE-COMPULSIVE DISORDER

Rita C. Prather
Senior Psychology Services, Regional Director
University of Houston/Downtown, Adjunct Faculty

DESCRIPTION OF THE DISORDER

The clinical description of obsessive-compulsive disorder (OCD) has varied somewhat in detail but very little in generalities since the mid-1800s. The current description according to DSM-IV (APA, 1994) includes the following components:

A. The presence of obsessions or compulsions with content unrelated to any other psychiatric disorders present.

Obsessions are described as:
1. Recurrent, persistent thoughts, images, or impulses that are not simply excessive worries about real-life problems.
2. Experienced as intrusive and inappropriate.
3. Result in marked anxiety or distress.
4. Efforts are made to ignore, suppress, or neutralize the thoughts, images, or impulses with other thoughts or actions.
5. Recognized by the patient as a product of his/her own mind.

Compulsions are described as:
1. Repetitive physical or mental behaviors performed in response to an obsession or performed rigidly according to rules.
2. The purpose of the behaviors is to prevent or reduce distress and/or prevent the occurrence of an event.
3. The behaviors are not realistically connected to what they are meant to prevent or neutralize or are clearly excessive.

B. At some point during the course of the disorder the adult patient recognizes that the obsessions and compulsions are excessive or unreasonable. If for most of the time during a current episode the person does not have this recognition a specification of "with poor insight" is given.

C. The obsessions or compulsions result in marked distress, take more than one hour per day, or significantly interfere with normal routine or functioning.

Although OCD is characterized by presence of *either* obsessions or compulsions, 80% of patients diagnosed with OCD report both types of symptoms (Welner, Reich, Robins, Fishman, & VanDoren, 1976). Additionally, a subgroup of patients does not believe that the symptoms are irrational; rather, the individuals in this subgroup are described as having "overvalued ideas" and believe such rituals are necessary to prevent future feared events (Foa, 1979; Jenike, 1990).

Mere presence of obsessional thought or compulsive behavior is not adequate for a diagnosis of OCD. Experiencing some level of obsessions and compulsions is not uncommon in the general population. For instance, it is not unusual to have a phrase, word, or lyric get "stuck" in one's thoughts for a period of time. The difference between normal and pathological obsessions and compulsions appears to be quantitative. Clinical and nonclinical symptoms seem to be similar in form and content, but clinical symptoms have been described as being more intense, more frequent, and of longer duration than nonclinical symptoms (Rachman & deSilva, 1978; Salkovskis & Harrison, 1984).

The most prevalent forms of obsessions include doubting, thinking, impulses, fears, and images (Akhtar, Wig, Verma, Pershod, & Verma, 1975; Khanna & Channabasavanna, 1988; Welner et al., 1976). The most prevalent forms of compulsions include washing and cleaning, checking, counting, and ordering (Rachman & Hodgson, 1980; Turner & Beidel, 1988). There appear to be common themes and patterns associated with obsessions and compulsions. The most frequent content of obsessions involves themes of dirt and contamination, aggression and violence, religion, and sex (Akhtar et al., 1975; Jenike, Baer, & Minichiello, 1986). The most predominant patterns include washing and cleaning compulsions or rituals associated with contamination obsessions, and checking rituals are frequently paired with doubting obsessions (Insel, 1990; Khanna & Mukherjee, 1992; Turner & Beidel, 1988).

Differential diagnosis and comorbidity can present a significant challenge to the clinician. It is common for OCD patients to meet criteria for other diagnoses within the anxiety or depression disorders (Sanderson, DiNardo, Rapee, & Barlow, 1990; Stanley, Swann, Bowers, Davis, & Taylor, 1992). It also appears that as many as 50% of OCD patients meet criteria for at least one personality disorder (Baer et

al., 1990; Stanley, Turner, & Borden, 1990). Although research is not yet conclusive, the co-occurrence of Gilles de la Tourette's syndrome and OCD in some patients presents further challenge to diagnosis and intervention decisions.

EPIDEMIOLOGY

Although the general description of OCD has varied little over time, what has been learned regarding prevalence and characteristics of those experiencing OCD has grown considerably.

Actual prevalence of OCD in the general population is uncertain, but estimates suggest a lifetime prevalence to be approximately 2.5% (Henderson & Pollard, 1988; Karno, Golding, Sorenson, & Burnam, 1988, Robins et al., 1984). The actual prevalence may be somewhat higher given that persons with OCD are often reluctant to reveal their symptoms to others, and routine assessments frequently do not explore for OCD.

There do not appear to be differences in prevalence rates across ethnic groups (Karno et al., 1989); however, Karno et al. (1988) suggest that OCD is more common in young, divorced, separated, or unemployed persons and may be somewhat less common among African Americans than Caucasians. A recent study by Weissman et al. (1994) also documents little effect of geographical location on prevalence. They found prevalence rates to be similar in the United States, Canada, Puerto Rico, Germany, Taiwan, Korea, and New Zealand.

Onset of the disorder tends to occur during later adolescence or young adulthood. However, earlier indicators of OCD may be present sooner (Rasmussen & Eisen, 1990b). Rasmussen and Eisen (1990a) found the average age of onset of clinical symptoms to be 19.8 years, ±9.6 years. Weissman et al. (1994) found a slightly higher mean age at onset in the international OCD population (range 21.9–35.5 years). There is also evidence to suggest that females have a later mean onset age than do males (Castle, Deale, & Marks, 1995).

Although some studies have suggested that more females than males suffer from OCD, research using large samples has consistently found no gender differences in adult prevalence rates (Castle et al., 1995; Gray, 1978; Ingram, 1961; Karno et al., 1988). In contrast, clinical presentation may be related to gender, as Rachman and Hodgson (1980) found most of the "cleaners" and "washers" to be female, whereas there was no gender difference in the incidence of "checkers." A more recent study supported the female gender expression of OCD as washers, but found more checkers to be male (Khanna & Mukherjee, 1992).

ETIOLOGY

The etiology of OCD has been explored from multiple theoretical perspectives, with biological (genetic, neuroanatomical, neurochemical) and behavioral models receiving the most empirical attention (Stanley & Prather, 1993). In this section, the main principles and relevant empirical data from biological and behavioral perspectives are presented. Two other theories also will be reviewed, including an interaction model that integrates both biological and environmental components, and a cognitive perspective.

Biological Theories

Genetic Models

In addressing the theory of the genetic etiology of OCD, several studies have assessed family history characteristics. In particular, these studies looked at the prevalence of OCD and obsessive-compulsive personality traits in family members of OCD patients. Some of these studies found higher percentages of OCD in these families than would be expected in the general population (Carey & Gottesman, 1981; Pauls, 1992). Others reported no increase in the incidence of OCD but greater frequency of obsessional traits, other anxiety disorders, or general psychiatric disturbance in families of OCD patients (Black, Noyes, Goldstein, & Blum, 1992; Insel, Hoover, & Murphy, 1983; McKeon & Murray, 1987). Although current studies offer mixed support for family patterns of psychiatric diagnoses, it is difficult to confirm unequivocally the genetic hypothesis because of the inability to isolate effects of environmental variables.

Another line of research addressing genetic models includes twin studies, in which comparisons are made between concordance rates of OCD (how often OCD occurs in both individuals) in monozygotic (MZ) and dizygotic (DZ) twin pairs. In these studies,

it is assumed that environmental family variables are similar for all twins, but that genetic makeup is identical for MZ but not for DZ pairs. Thus, higher concordance in MZ than in DZ twins could be evidence of a genetic model. A review of early studies supported this type of pattern (Inouye, 1972), although, as the author himself and others suggested (Turner, Beidel, & Nathan, 1985), data included were based on brief chart reviews and thus were not conclusive. Subsequent data collected via interviews with identified patients and their twins, however, confirmed higher concordance rates for MZ (33%) than for DZ (7%) twins among identified patients receiving treatment (Carey & Gottesman, 1981). Other data suggest a genetic pattern less specific to OCD (Torgersen, 1983), with MZ twins exhibiting higher concordance rates than DZ twins for anxiety disorders in general (excluding generalized anxiety disorder). Further study of twins by Andrews, Stewart, Allen, and Henderson (1990) found no evidence to support inheritence of the specific disorder; rather, their data suggest a genetic role in the predisposing trait.

Although these data suggest the importance of a genetic factor in the development of OCD, further study of the contribution of such a factor would come from adoption studies of concordance rates of OCD in MZ twins who are raised from birth in separate environments. These individuals have the same genetic makeup but develop under the influence of different environmental conditions.

Even though evidence to date suggests some importance of a genetic factor in the development of OCD, the fact that concordance rate among MZ twins is not 100% suggests that genetic factors alone are not sufficient to account for onset of the disorder. Following from Andrews et al. (1990), the data suggest a genetic vulnerability hypothesis. That is, this hypothesis suggests that the pathogenesis begins with a biological predisposition to develop OCD, which may be inherited, but that development of the disorder depends further on the interaction of such vulnerability with environmental variables.

Neuroanatomical Models

Impetus for studies addressing the neuroanatomical correlates of OCD comes from literature suggesting an overlap between OCD symptoms and neurological disorders, such as encephalitis, temporal lobe tumors, temporal lobe epilepsy, and various head injuries (Jenike, 1986). In all studies evaluating possible neuroanatomical mechanisms of OCD, however, it is important to note that data are collected with patients currently experiencing the disorder; thus, it is unclear whether or not the neuroanatomical correlates investigated are causes or results of the disorder. Regardless, a significant amount of data have pointed to associated pathology in a number of areas (Stanley & Prather, 1993).

First, cerebral functioning in OCD patients has been examined in some studies by measuring evoked potentials (EP) that occur in response to various cognitive processing tasks. In general, studies have reported a unique pattern of EP amplitudes and latencies in OCD patients compared to normal and psychiatric controls (e.g., Beech, Ciesielski, & Gordon, 1983; Malloy, Rasmussen, Braden, & Haier, 1989; Shagass, Roemer, Straumanis, & Josiassen, 1984). These data suggest that some type of arousal mechanism may account for onset and/or maintenance of OCD. However, statistical differences have not always reached accepted confidence levels (e.g., Shagass et al., 1984), and reported EP pattern distinctions have varied, perhaps as a result of differences in patient populations and the choice of cognitive tasks. As concluded in a review by Turner et al. (1985), it still is not clear whether specific EP differences are unique to OCD or are instead associated with some generalized psychopathological deficit.

Electroencephalogram (EEG) patterns associated with OCD also have been examined. Although some data have suggested a unique pattern of EEG response in OCD patients indicative of left frontal dysfunction (Flor-Henry, Yeudall, Koles, & Howarth, 1979), in other studies only approximately 10% of OCD patients exhibit EEGs in the abnormal range (Insel, Donnelly, Lalakea, Alterman, & Murphy, 1983). A report by Jenike and Brotman (1984) suggested a higher percentage (33%), but the subject sample was small and the data were retrospective. Furthermore, data were collected only on patients for whom an EEG had been requested, so the sample may have been biased toward patients for whom EEG disturbances were suspected on the basis of presenting symptoms. Thus, although there is some evidence of abnormal EEG functioning in OCD, the data do not present a clear and consistent pattern.

A third group of studies has attempted to identify neuroanatomical correlates of OCD through neuropsychological testing. Several of these reports have suggested frontal lobe dysfunction, with early data indicating a loss of inhibitory function from the dominant left frontal lobe (Flor-Henry et al., 1979). Subsequent studies failed to support this pattern, reporting instead data suggestive of deficits in spatial orientation (Insel et al., 1983) and right-hemisphere dysfunction (Behar et al., 1984). More recent data have suggested specific difficulties with set shifting during complex spatial tasks (Head, Bolton, & Hymas, 1989). In addition, although global memory deficits have not been reported in heterogeneous groups of OCD patients (e.g., Flor-Henry et al., 1979), level of performance on memory tasks has correlated fairly consistently with the presence and severity of checking behavior in both nonclinical and clinical samples (Sher, Frost, Kushner, Crews, & Alexander, 1989; Sher, Frost, & Otto, 1983). In summary, there appear to be multiple neuropsychological correlates of OCD, although these are not consistent across reports and require further research to clarify.

A final body of neuroanatomical literature has attempted to localize cerebral dysfunction associated with OCD via measurement techniques that produce pictures of brain structure and activity. These techniques include X-ray computerized tomography (CT), positron emission tomography (PET), and single photon emission computed tomography (SPECT). CT studies have suggested that OCD is associated with larger ventricle:brain ratios (Behar et al., 1984; Stein et al., 1993) and smaller caudate nuclei volumes (Luxenberg, Swedo, Flament, Friedland, Rapoport, & Rapoport, 1988) relative to normal controls. Studies utilizing PET procedures have demonstrated elevated metabolic rates in the orbital cortex and the striatum of OCD patients (Baxter, 1990; Baxter et al., 1988; Swedo, Rapoport, Leonard, Lanane, & Cheslow, 1989) as well as the cingulate cortex (Perani et al., 1995). In comparison to PET studies, SPECT technology has produced inconsistent results with regard to increased activity in the orbital frontal region (Adams, Warneke, McEwan, & Fraser, 1993; Machlin et al., 1991; Rubin, Villanueva-Meyer, Ananth, Trajmar, & Mena, 1992). Studies utilizing the SPECT approach also have suggested the possibility of a higher ratio of medial-frontal to whole cortex blood flow in OCD (Machlin et al., 1991), as well as increased activity in the high dorsal parietal cortex and the left posterior frontal cortex (Rubin et al., 1992). Though encouraging, this body of literature is small, reflecting the relatively recent development of these technologies and the expense associated with them. Much of the inconsistency could be related to the variance in methodology. There is a paucity of large-sample studies, although case studies of clinical patients have provided intriguing data (Simpson & Baldwin, 1995; Stein, Prohovnik, Goldman, & Hollander, 1994). This is, however, a very promising area of research, and future studies should help address the unanswered questions. In particular, functional neuroimaging may provide the most useful data on the pathophysiology of OCD (Rauch & Savage, 1994).

Neurochemical Models

Investigations into the neurochemistry of OCD have focused largely on the role of serotonin (5-HT). This line of research developed out of treatment outcome studies demonstrating the selective response of OCD symptoms to the serotonergic antidepressants (e.g., clomipramine, fluoxetine, fluvoxamine) (Zak, Miller, Shuhan, & Fanous, 1988). Support for the theory comes from studies demonstrating correlations between treatment response and levels of serotonin metabolites in blood platelets and cerebrospinal fluid (Insel & Winslow, 1990), and from a correlation between changes in the cingulate cortex and improvement of OCD symptoms in patients treated with serotonin-specific reuptake inhibitors (SSRIs) (Perani et al., 1995). In addition, serotonin agonists administered under double-blind conditions elicit increases in OCD symptoms that are blocked following long-term treatment with clomipramine (e.g., Zohar, Insel, Zohar-Kadouch, Hill, & Murphy, 1988). Also, Piccinelli, Pini, Bellantuono, and Wilkinson (1995) conducted a meta-analytic review and found clomipramine and fluoxetine treatments to be superior to antidepressant medications without SSRI properties. Inconsistent findings have been reported, however, with regard to blood serotonin levels in untreated OCD patients (Insel & Winslow, 1990), and the treatment literature suggests that examination of the serotonergic system alone may be insufficient. In a review by Rauch and Jenike (1993), they point out that even though antiobsessional agents may have therapeutic effects via the 5-HT system, there is little evidence to suggest an underlying abnormality in the 5-HT system. Others suggest that an interaction between serotonergic and dopaminergic systems may be more central in the onset and maintenance of at least some forms of OCD (Goodman et al., 1990; Kustermann & Bersani, 1991). Research into the neurochemical pathogenesis of OCD is in the early stages but is growing; thus, subsequent data may provide useful information.

Behavioral Theories

Behavioral models of OCD have changed little over the years. Their basic premise is that environmental variables and principles of learning theory play a prominent role in the onset and maintenance of OCD (Stanley & Prather, 1993). First, the influence of environmental variables is suggested by clinical observations of the frequency with which onset of OCD follows occurrence of a life stressor (Turner & Beidel, 1988). Also, severity of the syndrome seems to increase and decrease in response to environmental stressors (Turner & Beidel, 1988).

Second, onset and maintenance of OCD often is explained using basic learning principles. In particular, Mowrer's two-factor theory about acquisition of fear seems relevant (Mowrer, 1939; Dollard & Miller, 1950). In this theory, it is proposed that learning occurs via a two-step process: First, a neutral stimulus acquires fear-producing properties through a process of classical conditioning. Second, avoidance or escape behaviors, which are performed in response to the fear, tend to persist and to maintain the fear given the negative reinforcement that occurs when the behaviors reduce anxiety.

In the application of this theory to OCD, rituals or compulsive behaviors are conceptualized as avoidance or escape behaviors, given that they typically reduce anxiety associated with obsessive thinking. Although this theoretical conceptualization can apply to avoidance behaviors for all phobic disorders, avoidance and escape in OCD are less situation-specific given that feared stimuli (i.e., obsessive thoughts) are internal and therefore become paired with any number of stimuli and anxiety-reducing be-haviors (Foa, Steketee, & Ozarow, 1985). Empirical support for this perspective comes from both physio-logical and subjective data, demonstrating increases in anxiety following contact with obsession-related stimuli and reductions in anxiety following perfor-mance of ritualistic behavior (e.g., Hodgson & Rach-man, 1972). Additional support comes from outcome studies investigating efficacy of behavioral tech-niques, wherein behavior therapy was found to be su-perior to or equally effective as other treatment modalities (Cox, Swinson, Morrison, & Lee, 1993; vanBlakom et al., 1994). However, the behavioral perspective may be more useful in addressing the maintenance of ritualistic behaviors than in ade-quately accounting for the etiology of obsessive and compulsive symptoms (Foa et al., 1985).

Cognitive Theories

Cognitive conceptualizations of OCD have only recently received much attention; therefore, the em-pirical literature is sparse. Given the success of cog-nitive therapy in treating depression and some anxiety disorders (e.g., panic disorder) it seems logi-cal to suggest applications of cognitive approaches to OCD (James & Blackburn, 1995). One cognitive the-ory developed from Lang's (1979) bioinformational theory and was elaborated and applied to OCD by Foa and Kozak (1986). In this cognitive model, it is suggested that fear is represented via a cognitive net-work of information about threatening events or stim-uli, behavioral and physiological responses to those stimuli, and the meanings attached to each. Within this conceptualization, OCD is maintained by the in-ability to process disconfirming evidence available to the patient to discount the information in the cogni-tive network.

Other more general cognitive theories suggest that OCD is maintained by unrealistic perceptions of re-sponsibility for obsessive thoughts and other dys-functional beliefs about the meaning of these thoughts (e.g., "having a thought about an action is like performing the action") (Salkovskis, 1985, p. 579). Several theorists have suggested that either the patient has unrealistically high expectations of nega-tive outcome or consequences (Carr, 1974), or the pa-tient has an excessive need for predictability or cer-tainty (Beech & Liddell, 1974), or the patient devel-ops a belief system that requires perfectionism and punishment for failure to retain perfectionism; there-fore these patients develop erroneous perceptions of threat (McFall & Wollersheim, 1979). In a similar line of thought, research by Main and Hesse (1990) suggests that consistent exposure to an anxious or frightened attachment figure during early develop-ment may lead to a sense of confused fear and an in-ability to develop a schema of self-competency.

As stated earlier, empirical data for cognitive con-ceptualizations of OCD are lacking, and further re-search is needed prior to deciding the efficacy of such a perspective. Additionally, like Mowrer's two-factor theory of OCD, cognitive theories seem to apply more directly to explanations of maintenance of the disorder than to etiology.

In summary, just as the biological theories dis-cussed earlier were insufficient to explain etiology of OCD, none of the behavioral or cognitive theories alone accounts for why similar environmental stres-sors may precipitate OCD in some individuals but not in others, nor do they explain how obsessional think-ing, which occurs commonly in "normal" popula-tions (Rachman & deSilva, 1978), develops into a dysfunctional syndrome for some individuals but not for others. Therefore, it is more likely that there is an interaction among the theories, and an integration of these perspectives is necessary.

Interaction Model

Conclusions from the biological, behavioral, and cognitive models of the etiology of OCD suggest that none of the perspectives alone is sufficient to ex-plain development of the syndrome. Rather, an in-teraction model that combines the biological and psychological theories may be needed. In an interac-tion model, some genetically determined neuroana-tomical and/or neurochemical factor(s) can create a predisposition to traits associated with the develop-ment of the disorder (Andrews et al., 1990), but OCD develops for these individuals only in combi-nation with certain patterns of learning or experi-ences. Thus, a vulnerability to developing the disorder is suggested.

Barlow (1988) has outlined a related model that focuses on an attempt to differentiate occurrence of "normal" versus "abnormal" obsessional thinking. In this model, Barlow suggests that obsessional thoughts, increased anxiety, and perceptions of loss of control are common reactions to stressful situations, and therefore occur with some frequency in the majority of any identified population. The frequency with which obsessional thinking occurs in normal populations has been documented empirically (Rachman & deSilva, 1978; Salkovskis & Harrison, 1984) and was discussed in an earlier section. Barlow proposes that a pathological expression of obsessional thinking develops when these stress reactions occur along with biological or psychological vulnerabilities and a learning history that leads the individual to perceive the thoughts as unacceptable. As a result of this perception, avoidance behaviors and rituals develop to reduce anxiety and to reinstate a sense of control. Given the inherent inability to control thoughts completely, however, the behaviors persist or increase in such a way that functioning becomes disturbed. Empirical support for the model comes indirectly from the literature reviewed previously, as well as from data concerning the relationships between guilt and intrusive thinking (Niler & Beck, 1989) and between personality style and negative cognitions in the experience of obsessional thoughts (Clark & Hemsley, 1985; Rachman, 1971). Barlow further suggests that the specific content of obsessive thoughts is environmentally determined on the basis of the nature of thoughts that an individual has learned are unacceptable. Empirical data supporting this position come from Steketee, Grayson, and Foa (1985). In this study, "washers" and "checkers" were compared on a variety of variables, and it was found that the latter described their parents as more meticulous and demanding, suggesting that, as a result of this parenting style, "checkers" may develop a style of responding to stress by becoming meticulous. Given the retrospective nature of these reports, however, the data are only indirectly supportive of Barlow's (1988) hypothesis.

In summary, an interaction or vulnerability model seems to explain onset of OCD more adequately than the data from either the biological, behavioral learning, or cognitive theories. The specific mechanisms of the vulnerability model are not yet clear, however,

and these questions provide opportunity for further research.

COURSE AND COMPLICATIONS

Course

In a 1965 long-term follow-up study of OCD patients, Kringlen found that nearly one-third of the patients evidenced unvarying, chronic symptoms. Kringlen (1965) also found that in nearly another third of the patients the symptoms remained unchanged for some time and then improved gradually. While slightly less than one-third of the patients evidenced a fluctuating increase in severity of symptoms, about 8% of the patients got worse (Kringlen, 1965). These data are discouraging and suggest that OCD patients are rarely free of symptoms beyond the short-term. Given the advent of psychological and pharmacological interventions available to treat OCD, one might expect better outcomes than pre-1965. However, recent follow-up studies have not produced any more promising outcome data. Thomsen and Mikkelsen (1995) found that only 4 of 23 patients treated were asymptomatic at an 18-month to 5-year follow-up. Bolton, Luckie, and Steinberg (1995) reported that 7 of 14 patients followed for 9 to 14 years showed "improvement." Most outcome studies of OCD report short follow-up of only 6 months or so, and often report percentage of patients improved. These "improvement" scores usually are obtained by administration of instruments, such as the Yale–Brown Obsessive-Compulsive Scales (Y-BOCS) (Goodman et al., 1989). The lack of better long-term follow-up data and the lack of reported "cure" rates from the available studies preclude making definitive statements about the true course of OCD.

Although we might not be able to ascertain a true cure rate, some predictors of outcome have been identified. In a review of retrospective studies looking at factors predictive of outcome in OCD, Steketee and Shapiro (1995) found that most demographic variables, severity of symptoms, depression, general anxiety, assertiveness, expectancy and motivation, and treatment context were not consistently correlated with outcome. However, Turner and Beidel (1988) stated that episodes of stress were found to be associated with an exacerbation of OCD symptoms.

Rachman and Hodgson (1980) demonstrated that the course of OCD was associated with the patient's ability to exert some control over the symptoms. Individuals who spent most of the day obsessing or performing rituals showed a poorer treatment response and a more chronic clinical course than individuals who demonstrated more defined or limited symptom expression.

In summary, the course of OCD appears to be chronic and persistent in at least one-third of patients receiving treatment, and those patients showing reduction in symptoms often become symptomatic again during times of stress. Although it is difficult to determine from the current literature how likely one is to reach a goal of "cure," it appears that, over the long term, OCD is a recalcitrant disorder, and that the poor outcome could be related to the complications that accompany this disorder.

Complications

Complications of OCD most frequently suggested include interference with family, occupational, and interpersonal functioning, although it has not been demonstrated whether these associated problems occur before or after the onset of symptoms (Turner & Beidel, 1988). In fact, Coryell (1981) found no differences in marital dysfunction between a matched group of depressed patients and OCD patients. Although the nature of the OCD symptoms would lead one intuitively to think that patients are occupationally dysfunctional, research supporting such a notion is not available. The concept of interpersonal dysfunction or personality style is an important one and will be discussed further. Other syndromes complicate OCD, with the most problematic being depressive symptomatology. Although it cannot be clearly demonstrated that the associated syndromes occur because of OCD, the comorbidity and complicating capacity of personality and depressive disorders can be supported empirically.

Personality Disorders

At one time it was thought that obsessive-compulsive personality disorder (OCPD) and OCD were part of the same syndrome and that the former preceded the latter. However, research has not supported this view (Baer & Jenike, 1992). In a review of the literature,

Baer and Jenike (1992) found that OCPD was actually present only in a minority of OCD patients and that it was less common than other personality pathology. The most common personality structures found to be associated with OCD fall in the avoidant, dependent, and histrionic categories (Baer & Jenike, 1992; Joffe, Swinson, & Regan, 1988).

In a recent study of personality characteristics and OCD (Fals-Stewart & Lucente, 1993), it was found that OCD patients with no evident personality pathology and those with dependent personality features demonstrated the best overall outcome. In this same study, OCD patients with personality features leading to interpersonal interaction difficulties were most likely to refuse behavior therapy, and those who did participate in treatment evidenced no reduction in OCD symptoms. Patients with histrionic and borderline traits evidenced some improvement but did not maintain the improvement at a 6-month follow-up. Serious consideration of the interaction between the DSM-IV (APA, 1994) Axis II pathology and OCD and its impact on outcome seems essential given that research has suggested that approximately 50% of OCD patients meet criteria for a coexisting personality disorder (Baer et al., 1990; Stanley et al., 1990).

Depression

Most OCD patients experience some degree of generalized depression, typically reporting greater levels of distress in this area than patients with other anxiety disorders (Turner, McCann, Beidel, & Mezzich, 1986). Rasmussen and Eisen (1994) suggest that at least two-thirds of OCD patients evidence a lifetime history of major depression. At least one-third of OCD patients meet criteria for a coexisting secondary diagnosis of major depression or dysthymia (Sanderson et al., 1990; Stanley et al., 1992), and a larger percentage report the presence of some significant depressive symptoms (Barlow, 1988; Rasmussen & Tsuang, 1986). Although there is agreement on the degree of overlap between OCD and depression, there is disagreement among researchers as to which disorder is primary. Turner and Beidel (1988) have suggested that in differentiating OCD and affective disorders, the primary disorder should generally be considered the one with the earlier onset. In fact, these authors review data suggesting that in the majority of cases where OCD and depression co-occur, symptoms of OCD preceded depression (Welner et al., 1976). Even when OCD is determined to be the primary diagnosis, however, if accompanying symptoms of depression are severe, these symptoms may require initial attention with pharmacological treatment before OCD symptoms can be addressed with behavioral interventions (Foa et al., 1985).

Given the significant overlap between symptoms of OCD and depression, as well as data supporting the efficacy of antidepressant medications in the treatment of OCD (Piccinelli, Pini, Bellantuono, & Wilkinson, 1995; Pigott et al., 1990), it has been suggested that OCD actually may be conceptualized as a variant of affective disorder (Insel, Zahn, & Murphy, 1985). Some empirical support for this position has come from studies demonstrating common biological correlates of the two disorders. For example, some OCD patients demonstrate a nonsuppression response on the dexamethasone suppression test (DST) that is similar to the pattern exhibited by a subset of depressed patients. In addition, similar EEG patterns have been reported in the two disorders (Turner et al., 1985). However, difficulties in interpretation of these studies arise given that OCD patients with secondary depression have not always been excluded from these studies, and specific response patterns on the two measures generally are identified for only a subset of patients with either disorder. Thus, although depression often accompanies OCD, it seems to be an oversimplification to assume that the two syndromes should be classified together. However, it also is unclear that the two are completely distinct. In some views, various anxiety and depressive syndromes are hypothesized to be different expressions of a common biological mechanism (e.g., Barlow, 1988). This perspective has received some support from multivariate genetic analyses that suggested common genetic pathways for the expression of depression and anxiety, with the specific form of the disorder influenced more strongly by environmental factors (Kendler, Heath, Martin, & Eaves, 1987). Certainly, substantiation of these hypotheses with prospective, longitudinal data is needed.

In summary, OCD is a disorder that is usually accompanied by a variety of distressing clinical symptoms of depression as well as personality disorders. As a result, the relationship between these sets of symptoms is of interest. Regardless of the relationship, however, it appears that the accompanying symptoms can complicate the presentation and the outcome of OCD and need to be considered during the assessment and intervention phases.

Other Disorders

Conceptual links also have been made between OCD and other disorders, such as hypochondriasis, body dysmorphic disorder, and eating disorders (Stanley & Prather, 1993). Patients with hypochondriasis exhibit an excessive preoccupation with fears of having a serious illness; these thoughts and fears persist despite repeated reassurances from medical professionals that no signs of serious illness are present. An overlap between these symptoms and OCD is apparent given the repetitive, intrusive quality of the hypochondriacal patient's thoughts. Also, the repetitive visits to physicians typically encountered in hypochondriasis can be conceptualized as ritualistic behavior given the subsequent reduction in anxiety about obsessional fears of illness (Salkovskis & Warwick, 1986).

Conceptualization of hypochondriasis as a variant of OCD has led to the use of treatment with exposure and response prevention for this disorder (Salkovskis & Warwick, 1986) and to a more detailed cognitive-behavioral conceptualization of the disorder (Warwick & Salkovskis, 1990). Overlap in the pharmacotherapy for OCD and hypochondriasis also has been noted (Fallon, Javitch, Hollander, & Liebowitz, 1991). However, the empirical literature addressing the OCD–hypochondriasis relationship has only begun to emerge, and stronger support for current hypotheses is needed. Given the frequency with which somatic obsessions occur in OCD (Rasmussen & Tsuang, 1986) and some suggestion that hypochondriasis may often be accompanied by "obsessional traits" (Kenyon, 1964), more information also is needed about differential diagnosis of the disorders.

Body dysmorphic disorder, currently classified as a somatoform disorder in the DSM-IV, shares with hypochondriasis an excessive preoccupation with the physical body. Patients with body dysmorphic disorder exhibit excessive concern with an imagined defect in some body part that appears to others to be normal. Like hypochondriasis, this disorder has been viewed recently as a variant of OCD (Tynes, White, & Steketee, 1990), particularly given the intrusive and repetitive quality of thoughts about an imagined bodily defect. In addition, body dysmorphic patients often exhibit ritualized behavior (e.g., visually checking their appearance in the mirror) or avoidance symptoms that decrease anxiety regarding imagined defects (Hollander, Liebowitz, Winchel, Klumker, & Klein, 1989).

The relationship between OCD and body dysmorphic disorder also has received only slight empirical attention. Hardy and Cotterill (1982) reported higher levels of obsessional symptoms in dysmorphophobic patients than in normal controls, but the former group did not differ on this dimension from patients with psoriasis. No direct comparison with OCD was made. Other data from clinical case studies have suggested the utility of serotonergic antidepressants (fluoxetine, clomipramine) in the treatment of body dysmorphic disorder (Hollander et al., 1989). Again, however, empirical data addressing the relationship between these disorders are extremely limited, and future investigations in this area are certainly needed.

Finally, an overlap between OCD and the eating disorders anorexia nervosa and bulimia nervosa has been posited. A lifetime prevalence of eating disorders in OCD patients was found by Rubenstein, Pigott, L'Heureux, Hill, and Murphy (1992) to be as high as 12.9%. Anorexia and bulimia nervosa are eating disorders characterized by excessive concern about body shape and weight. These thoughts are accompanied by ritualistic interactions with food or repetitive binge eating, which generally is followed in turn by drastic attempts to reduce weight (e.g., vomiting, laxative use, a period of severe food restriction, or excessive exercising). Again, the intrusive, persistent thoughts about food and body weight in anorexia and bulimia seem analogous to obsessive ideation in OCD, and the drastic behaviors that follow eating have a ritualistic quality; that is, they occur repetitively and serve to decrease anxiety regarding feared weight gain. These apparent similarities have led to an "anxiety disorder" model of eating disorders and to the use of exposure and response prevention in the treatment of the disorders (Rosen & Leitenberg, 1982; Williamson, Prather, Goreczny, Davis, & McKenzie, 1989). Although use of this intervention has provoked some controversy in the literature (e.g., Agras, Schneider, Arnow, Raeburn, & Telch, 1989), the model is appealing and suggests that additional work needs to be done regarding the relationship between eating disorders and OCD.

TREATMENT IMPLICATIONS

The literature addressing the treatment of OCD is exceptionally large. For example, a recent MEDLINE search (Goldberg, 1995) produced 130 citations referring just to the treatment of OCD patients with fluoxetine. Given the large body of data available, it is beyond the scope of this book to provide an exhaustive review. Instead, results will be summarized across four modalities: pharmacotherapy, behavior therapy, cognitive therapy, and group therapy.

Pharmacological Therapy

The efficacy of pharmacological treatment of OCD has been demonstrated across several double-blind controlled studies. The medications that have proved most useful include a tricyclic antidepressant, clomipramine, and three serotonin reuptake inhibitors: fluoxetine, fluvoxamine, and sertraline. In a meta-analytic review of 47 randomized, double-blind clinical trials conducted between 1975 and 1994, Piccinelli et al. (1995) determined that all four of these medications resulted in greater reductions than placebo of OCD symptoms. They also documented that clomipramine provided the greatest improvement on a measure of OCD symptoms (Y-BOCS). Clomipramine resulted in 61.3%, fluoxetine 28.5%, fluvoxamine 28.2%, and sertraline 21.6% improvement of obsessions occurring alone, compulsions occurring alone, or obsessions and compulsions occurring together (Piccinelli et al., 1995). In addition, clomipramine and fluoxetine were found to be more effective than other antidepressants without serotonin reuptake inhibitor properties. Further support of the efficacy of these medications was provided in a double-blind comparison of clomipramine and fluvoxamine (Koran et al., 1996). These authors found that 54% of patients receiving clomipramine (100–250 mg) and 56% of patients treated with fluvoxamine (100–300 mg) achieved greater than a 25% reduction in symptoms over a 10-week trial. Of interest, however, are the long-term results of treatment with these medications. Several studies have documented consistent return of symptoms or relapse once medication is withdrawn (Stanley & Turner, 1995). Another problem with medication therapy, however, is the dropout rate due to side effects. For example, clomipramine may produce uncomfortable anticholinergic effects as well as sexual dysfunction and seizures, while fluoxetine may lead to tachycardia, initial weight loss, agitation, tremors, sexual difficulties, and skin rash. Koran et al. (1996) documented that dropout rates due to adverse side effects were similar for clomipramine and fluvoxamine. Dewulf, Hendericks, and Lesaffre (1995) found that the main reason for dropout from fluvoxamine therapy in treating OCD was the adverse side effects before week 8. There are two important issues related to treatment of OCD with medications. Those include the dropout rate of one-quarter of patients entering treatment (Beck & Bourg, 1993) and the relapse or return of symptoms when the medication is terminated. Therefore, it seems likely that other treatment options are necessary.

Behavior Therapy

Interventions for OCD using behavioral techniques stem from the conceptual model of negative reinforcement—that is, the process whereby an obsession leads to a ritual to reduce the distress or anxiety associated with the content of the obsession. The behavioral strategy of exposure with response prevention (ERP) has provided the most promise in treating OCD patients thus far. In ERP the patient is exposed to the obsession content and prevented from performing the ritual or compulsion. For example, a patient who obsesses about contamination might be prescribed prolonged contact with objects that produce contamination distress. Over time, as the patient "learns" that nothing untoward happens, the anxiety associated with the fear subsides and eventually goes away on its own. The patient also develops self-efficacy in that he or she experiences an ability to survive the anxiety and exert control over the compulsion.

Outcome data considering the success of ERP have produced favorable results. In early studies, ERP was found to be effective for approximately 75% of OCD patients, and dropout rates ran about 20% (Marks, 1981; Rachman & Hodgson, 1980; Rasmussen & Tsuang, 1986). Current research continues to support the effectiveness of behavior therapy. One

study investigating outcome over a 6-year follow-up documented that improvements were maintained for longer periods when more sessions of ERP were administered (6 weeks as compared to 3 weeks), while the use of antiobsessional agents made no difference in the long-term outcome (O'Sullivan, Noshirvani, Marks, Monteiro, & Lelliott, 1991). A meta-analysis of 111 studies employing behavior therapy, medications, or cognitive therapy reported that patients' self-ratings of improvement supported the superiority of behavior therapy over medications and cognitive therapy (vanBlakom et al., 1994). However, it is important to note that while Cox et al. (1993) found ERP therapy to be significantly effective in reducing overall severity of OCD, the procedure was not effective in reducing the depressed mood that frequently accompanies OCD. As discussed previously, the long-term maintenance of treatment gains for OCD patients has been discouraging. Addressing this issue, Hiss, Foa, and Kozak (1994) conducted a controlled study investigating the usefulness of relapse prevention strategies. In their study, patients completing a standard ERP program were followed by either a relapse prevention (RP) program or an attention-control program. At 6-month follow-up assessment by independent evaluators, these authors demonstrated that RP was effective in preventing relapse, while the patients in the attention-control program showed some return of symptoms. These data are encouraging, and further research is warranted.

Cognitive Therapy

Cognitive interventions for OCD are hypothesized to reduce either the irrationality or the frequency of obsessions. Following Beck's (1976) model, compulsions or rituals are performed to alleviate the doubt rather than the anxiety. Anxiety is proposed to stem not from the content of the obsessions but, rather, from thinking the thought. Given this conceptualization, cognitive techniques are aimed at controlling the obsession. The most commonly reported components used in cognitive therapy with OCD patients have been thought stopping and thought replacement. Recent reviews of cognitive studies with OCD have not provided support for the inclusion of these techniques. In a study evaluating efficacy of medications, behavior therapy, and cognitive therapy (vanBlakom et al., 1994), cognitive therapy was found not to differ in effect size from either attention placebo or pill placebo. James and Blackburn (1995) examined 15 clinical studies using cognitive therapy. Eleven of the 15 studies were case reports, and the remaining 4 studies reported small sample sizes, with the largest sample being 24 OCD patients. Although all of the case studies reported effective outcome using cognitive techniques, there was little support for the application of cognitive therapy provided by the other 4 studies using a larger sample of patients (James & Blackburn, 1995). These authors concluded that there is little evidence of improvement when cognitive therapy is used alone or added to other therapeutic techniques such as medication or behavior therapy. However, few studies exist to date, and those that are available suffer from methodological problems. It is clear that further study is needed to evaluate the usefulness of using cognitive therapy alone or in conjunction with other treatment modalities.

Group Therapy

Very little work has been published to assist in determining the value of group interventions for OCD. Two reports have suggested that group treatment should not generally be the treatment of choice (Enright, 1991; Espie, 1986), however, a controlled comparison study of group behavior to individual behavior therapy found the two to be equally effective (Fals-Stewart, Marks, & Schafer, 1993). It should be noted, however, that patients receiving individual therapy improved faster than patients in the group therapy setting (Fals-Stewart et al., 1993). These authors also note that the patient pool was limited to mild to moderate OCD symptom severity and excluded those with major depression or diagnosable personality disorders. It is likely that with the more severe and complicated cases, individual therapy may be more efficacious. A recent review supported this view stating that group treatment of OCD shows promise but may be limited to less complicated clinical presentations of OCD (Kobak, Rock, & Greist, 1995).

In summary, pharmacological and behavioral interventions are currently the treatments of choice for OCD symptom reduction. Complete cure seems elusive, however. Depression and personality features can severely complicate treatment progress, and these variables need to be assessed and actively treated. Other predictors of outcome include the patient's expectations regarding the treatment modality (either medication or behavioral); therefore, identifying the strength of the patient expectations may assist in matching patients to treatment (Cottrauz et al., 1993). Improvements in treatment options available for OCD patients have resulted in better short-term prognosis, but long-term results suggest that patients may continue to evidence some level of symptoms and may have periods of exacerbation or relapse. Although research considering the usefulness of relapse prevention strategies is just emerging, the procedure appears to have promise in improving long-term outcome. Cognitive interventions as well as group therapy show promise, but further study is needed.

Case Description: M.T., a Case of Complicated OCD

M.T. arrived at his first appointment accompanied by his wife. It had taken them three hours to drive the 12 miles from their home to the office. M.T. was 38 years old and refused to drive alone because several times during a trip he would become obsessed with the thought that he had just run over a person. He would then return to the area to "check." On his way to check the site of the first obsession, he would develop another belief that he had run over another person. He would then be entangled in a maze of "visions" and "thoughts" of persons he had hit with his vehicle lying on the roadside needing help, and with "checking" to make sure he had not struck anyone. He would at times spend hours circling within a radius of a few miles. Needless to say, this behavior severely interrupted his social and occupational performance. M.T. had withdrawn from a well-respected, high-salaried professional career as a result of his symptoms.

Assessment revealed that M.T. began experiencing obsessional thoughts by age 24, although he recalled earlier behaviors that suggested rigid and inflexible beliefs and behaviors and an intolerance for ambiguity. A thorough investigation of M.T.'s history did not reveal a particular precipitating factor. He did present a developmental history, however, that suggested an emotionally confusing environment. He described his father as emotionally distant, his mother as emotionally labile, and both as judgmental and righteous. M.T. was an only child and was prevented from interacting with his peers because his mother thought other children were beneath his status. He described an environment in which he could do no wrong but also could not get anything right. He stated that he usually had a feeling of absolute confidence paired with feeling totally unsure.

It is likely that the lack of interactions with peers and others besides his parents prevented M.T. from developing a more integrated self-concept. He also presented a history that strongly indicated he had an intolerance to criticism and a fear of his own anger. He stated that he would get so angry at people when they said or did anything he could interpret as criticism that he would fantasize their demise by "horrible" means. He denied acting on any of these fantasies. He stated that even though he knew his thoughts and images while driving were irrational, he would become incensed if anyone else dared to tell him the thoughts were senseless.

The Y-BOCS documented a severe level of OCD, with a score of 35. M.T.'s self-monitoring documented avoidance of driving due to the overwhelming anxiety he experienced when the obsessions started. During a 2-week period, he drove only once, and although the destination was only 2 miles away from his home, he drove 10 miles and it took him 3 hours to arrive. Upon arrival, it took another hour for M.T. to gather enough "courage" to attempt the return trip to his home. The details of the trip home were similar. M.T. had spent over 7 hours of his day trying to complete a simple 15-minute errand. His self-report also documented that he believed his thoughts were irrational, but he could not resist the compulsion. M.T. stated that even though he was relatively sure the thoughts were senseless, he became very angry if anyone else pointed out the irrational nature of his obsessions.

Complicating M.T.'s clinical presentation was the presence of narcissistic traits. He wanted to be in control of himself and others all the time; he became excessively angry when not treated as he believed he should be. M.T. was currently employed in a seasonal job that was very rule-oriented and allowed him to be in total control. The salary was minimal, and he spent considerable time and money on transportation. M.T. had withdrawn from a highly respected and well-paid professional career shortly after the onset of his obsessions. His parents and wife were all quite displeased with his decision to withdraw.

Intervention was not straightforward with M.T. because of his narcissistic inability to relinquish control of himself to another. He resisted the usual recommended modalities such as antiobsessional medications or exposure with response prevention. A combination of therapy techniques were used, including supportive "talk." After rapport was developed with M.T. (2 months, 15 sessions), cognitive therapy using rational-emotive techniques targeting his beliefs about anger were employed next (6 months, 24 sessions). The method used for cognitive therapy was bibliotherapy so that M.T. could retain control. A variety of

books addressing irrational beliefs was recommended. He was free to choose any text and read any sections he desired. He would then discuss his readings during the next therapy session rather than being assigned readings.

Exposure was initiated in an indirect manner as well. At first, he would ride with his wife (whom he trusted) and, regardless of how obsessed he became, she agreed not to go back to check on M.T.'s imagined victims. After 4 sessions, he reported decreases in obsessional thoughts while his wife drove. The next step was for M.T. to drive while his wife was a passenger. To prepare for this next step, behavioral rehearsal during office sessions targeted the potential anger he would feel when he could not do as he wanted during the exposure sessions. As expected, he had considerable difficulty responding to someone else's request that he not turn back to check on an imagined victim. He was able to resist but reported that it required all of his mental strength to not turn the car around during these sessions.

After another 4 sessions, M.T. again reported a decrease in the obsessional thoughts and images. The final step was for M.T. to drive on his own without giving in to the obsessions. Behavioral rehearsal was used to assist him. With 5 self-exposure and response prevention sessions, M.T. began to drive without acting on the obsessions; however, the thoughts continued. Seventeen sessions over 17 weeks were required to complete this "exposure with response prevention" schedule. Even though M.T. had refused to consider medications at the beginning of therapy, he subsequently agreed to be evaluated for pharmacotherapy. The psychiatrist placed him on clomipramine. Although M.T. complained frequently about the side effects, he honored his commitment to a fair trial of medications. In 3 weeks' time, M.T. reported a further decrease in obsessional thought. At the time of discharge from individual therapy (14-month course), M.T. was able to drive successfully but reported he would rather not drive as he continued to experience the "thought" even though it no longer had the "obsessive" quality. His score on the Y-BOCS decreased to a mild level. He also reported improvement in anger management; he stated that he continued to get angry when he felt he was being evaluated by another, but that he no longer plotted the destruction of that person. He felt more in control and less fearful that his anger was uncontrollable. He had no plans to return to his former professional career and intended to retain his current job. At the time of discharge, it was mutually agreed that it would be up to M.T. to initiate further therapy sessions in the future at any time he thought it useful. Over a 2-year period, he called about twice a year and attended a few "booster" sessions of cognitive-behavioral therapy. He continued to take the medication on an intermittent basis.

The case of M.T. demonstrates a classic obsessive-compulsive pattern of OCD symptoms. The obsessions were thoughts and images that were intrusive and were experienced by the patient as senseless. He avoided situations that exacerbated the OCD symptoms; otherwise, he would spend several hours a day engaged in obsessing and performing rituals. Rituals were aimed at reducing anxiety associated with the content of the obsession. Further, M.T.'s occupational functioning was severely disrupted. He responded well to cognitive-behavioral therapy techniques as well as to clomipramine. However, his narcissistic personality characteristics complicated the intervention process and prevented the usual application of these modalities, and therapy took more sessions than would normally be expected. These personality traits required finding strategies for which this patient could retain the control during therapy and protect his sense of self. Once the strategies were identified and accepted by the patient, the success was consistent, with the outcome literature addressing behavioral, cognitive, and medication interventions with OCD.

SUMMARY

Although a number of questions about the epidemiology of OCD have been addressed over the last decade, many questions remain unanswered about the etiology and treatment of OCD. It is obvious that additional research is required before decisive conclusions can be drawn. With regard to etiology, although an interaction model appears to be the most appropriate one for interpretation of currently available data, the separate and integrative roles of biological, behavioral, and cognitive mechanisms within the model are unclear. The role of genetic components can be clarified only with data from adoption studies, and neuroanatomical correlates of OCD will be understood more thoroughly only with continued use and further development of recently available techniques and strategies for functional brain imaging (e.g., SPECT, PET). The possible etiological role of neurochemical correlates will be clarified further as more empirical work examines phathophysiology of the interaction of serotonergic and other neurochemical systems. It is hoped that increasing advances in and availability of affordable medical technology will enhance investigations in this area.

The etiological impact of environmental and behavioral variables is another area needing further study. Longitudinal, prospective studies will be necessary to clarify the impact of environmental events on the onset and course of OCD, and to examine the role of psychological vulnerability factors. The role of learning history and the role of patterns of thinking and interacting will be most clear following implementation of longitudinal investigations. The role of specific conditioning experiences in the onset of OCD, and the mechanism by which any etiological cognitive networks develop, also may await longitudinal studies or more sophisticated laboratory examinations of the differential development of clinical and nonclinical obsessions and compulsions.

In addition, the relationship between OCD and other disorders with prominent obsessional ideation (e.g., hypochondriasis, body dysmorphic disorder, and eating disorders) is not clear.

Finally, OCD has a chronic, episodic course that is complicated by the presence of affective problems and by certain personality characteristics. There is hope that further advances in pharmacological and behavioral treatments for OCD will result in improved long-term prognosis; to date, however, it appears that OCD patients may require lifetime access to mental health services in order to retain initial treatment gains. One treatment component showing promise for retention of symptom reduction achieved during behavior therapy is relapse prevention, but only further research will confirm the usefulness of adding this modality.

REFERENCES

Adams, B.L., Warneke, L.B., McEwan, A.J., & Fraser, B.A. (1993). Single photon emission computerized tomography in obsessive compulsive disorder: A preliminary study. *Journal of Psychiatry and Neuroscience, 18*, 109–112.

Agras, W.S., Schneider, J.A., Arnow, B., Raeburn, S.D., & Telch, C.F. (1989). Cognitive-behavioral treatment with and without exposure plus response prevention in the treatment of bulimia nervosa: A reply to Leitenberg and Rosen. *Journal of Consulting and Clinical Psychology, 57*, 778–779.

Akhtar, S., Wig, N.H., Verma, V.K., Pershod, D., & Verma, S.K. (1975). A phenomenological analysis of symptoms in obsessive-compulsive neurosis. *British Journal of Psychiatry, 127,* 342–348.

American Psychiatric Association. (1994). *Diagnostic and statistical manual of mental disorder,* 4th ed., Washington, DC: Author.

Andrews, G., Stewart, G., Allen, R., & Henderson, A.A. (1990). The genetics of six neurotic disorders: A twin study. *Journal of Affective Disorders, 19,* 23–29.

Baer, L., & Jenike, M.A. (1992). Personality disorders in obsessive compulsive disorder. *Psychiatric Clinics of North America, 15,* 803–812.

Baer, L., Jenike, M.A., Ricciardi, J.N., Holland, A.D., Seymour, R.J., Minichiello, W.E., & Buttolph, M.L. (1990). Standardized assessment of personality disorders in obsessive-compulsive disorder. *American Journal of Psychiatry, 47,* 826–830.

Barlow, D. (1988). *Anxiety and its disorders.* New York: Guilford Press.

Beck, A.T. (1976). *Cognitive therapy and the emotional disorders.* New York: International Universities Press.

Beck, J.G., & Bourg, W. (1993). Obsessive-compulsive disorder in adults. In R.T. Ammerman & M. Hersen (Eds.), *Handbook of behavior therapy with children and adults: A developmental perspective* (pp. 167–186). Boston: Allyn and Bacon.

Baxter, L.R. (1990). Brain imaging as a tool in establishing a theory of brain pathology in obsessive-compulsive disorder. *Journal of Clinical Psychiatry, 51,* 32–35.

Baxter, L.R., Schwartz, J.M., Mazziotta, J.C., Phelps, M.E., Pahl, J.J., Guze, B.H., & Fairbanks, L. (1988). Cerebral glucose metabolic rates in non-depressed patients with obsessive-compulsive disorder. *American Journal of Psychiatry, 145,* 1560–1563.

Beech, H.R., Ciesielski, K.T., & Gordon, P.K. (1983). Further observations of evoked potentials in obsessional patients. *British Journal of Psychiatry, 142,* 605–609.

Beech, H.R., & Liddell, A. (1974). Decision making, mood, and ritualistic behavior among obsessional patients. In H.R. Beech (Ed.), *Obsessional states* (pp. 143–160). London: Methuen.

Behar, D., Rapoport, J.L., Berg, C.J., Denckla, M.B., Mann, L., Cox, C., Fedio, P., Zahn, T., & Wolf-

man, M.G. (1984). Computerized tomography and neuropsychological test measures in adolescents with obsessive-compulsive disorder. *American Journal of Psychiatry, 141,* 363–369.

Black, D.W., Noyes, R., Goldstein, R.B., & Blum, N. (1992). A family study of obsessive-compulsive disorder. *Archives of General Psychiatry, 49,* 362–368.

Bolton, D., Luckie, M., & Steinberg, D. (1995). Long-term course of obsessive-compulsive disorder treated in adolescence. *Journal of the American Academy of Child and Adolescent Psychiatry, 34,* 1441–1450.

Carey, G., & Gottesman, I.I. (1981). Twin and family studies of anxiety, phobic, and obsessive disorders. In D.F. Klein & J.G. Rabkin (Eds.), *Anxiety: New research and changing concepts* (pp. 117–135). New York: Raven Press.

Carr, A.T. (1974). Compulsive neurosis: A review of the literature. *Psychological Bulletin, 81,* 311–318.

Castle, D.J., Deale, A., & Marks, I.M. (1995). Gender differences in obsessive-compulsive disorder. *Australian and New Zealand Journal of Psychiatry, 24,* 114–117.

Clark, D.A., & Hemsley, D.R. (1985). Individual differences in the experience of depressive and anxious, intrusive thoughts. *Behaviour Research and Therapy, 23,* 625–633.

Coryell, W. (1981). Obsessive-compulsive disorder and primary unipolar depression: Comparison of background, family history, course, and mortality. *Journal of Nervous and Mental Disorders, 169,* 220–224.

Cottrauz, J., Messy, P., Marks, I.M., Mollard, E., et al. (1993). Predictive factors in the treatment of obsessive-compulsive disorders with fluvoxamine and/or behaviour therapy. *Behavioural Psychotherapy, 21,* 45–50.

Cox, B.J., Swinson, R.P., Morrison, B., & Lee, P.S. (1993). Clomipramine, fluoxetine, and behavior therapy in the treatment of obsessive-compulsive disorder: A meta-analysis. *Journal of Behavior Therapy and Experimental Psychiatry, 24,* 149–153.

Dewulf, L., Hendricks, B., & Sesaffre, E. (1995) Epidemiological data of patients treated with fluvoxamine: Results from a 12-week noncomparative multicentre study. *International Clinical Psychopharmacology, 9,* 67–72.

Dollard, J., & Miller, N.E. (1950). *Personality and psychotherapy: An analysis in terms of learning, thinking, and culture.* New York: McGraw-Hill.

Enright, S.J. (1991). Group treatment for obsessive compulsive disorder: An evaluation. *Behavior Psychotherapy, 19,* 183–192.

Espie, C.A. (1986). The group treatment of obsessive-compulsive ritualizers: Behavioral management of identified patterns of relapse. *Behavior Psychotherapy, 14,* 21–33.

Fallon, B.A., Javitch, J.A., Hollander, E., & Liebowitz, M.R. (1991). Hypochondriasis and obsessive-compulsive disorder: Overlaps in diagnosis and treatment. *Journal of Clinical Psychiatry, 52,* 457–460.

Fals Stewart, W., & Lucente, S. (1993). An MCMI cluster typology of obsessive-compulsives: A measure of personality characteristics and its relationship to treatment participation, compliance, and outcome in behavior therapy. *Journal of Psychiatric Research, 27,* 139–154.

Fals-Stewart, W., Marks, A.P., & Schafer, J. (1993). A comparison of behavioral group therapy and individual behavior therapy in treating obsessive-compulsive disorder. *Journal of Nervous and Mental Disease, 181,* 189–193.

Flor-Henry, P., Yeudall, L.T., Koles, A.J., & Howarth, B.G. (1979). Neuropsychological and power spectral EEG investigations of the obsessive-compulsive syndrome. *Biological Psychiatry, 14,* 119–130.

Foa, E.B. (1979). Failure in treating obsessive-compulsives. *Behaviour Research and Therapy, 17,* 169–176.

Foa, E.B., & Kozak, M.S. (1986). Emotional processing of fear: Exposure of corrective information. *Psychological Bulletin, 99,* 20–35.

Foa, E.B., Steketee, G.S., & Ozarow, B.J. (1985). Behavior therapy with obsessive-compulsives: From theory to treatment. In M. Mavissakalian, S.M. Turner, & L. Michelson (Eds.), *Obsessive-compulsive disorder: Psychological and pharmacological treatment* (pp. 49–129). New York: Plenum Press.

Goldberg, I. (1995). *MEDLINE search on fluoxetine and obsessive compulsive disorder* (E-mail). Bibliographic database from MEDLINE: I. Goldberg producer and distributor, ikgl@columbia.edu.

Goodman, W.K., McDougle, C.J., Price, L.H., Riddle, M.A., Pauls, D.L., & Leckman, J.F. (1990). Beyond the serotonin hypothesis: A role for dopamine in some forms of obsessive compulsive disorder. *Journal of Clinical Psychiatry, 51,* 36–43.

Goodman, W., Price, L.H., Rasmussen, S.A., Mazure, C., Fleischmann, R.L., Hill, C.L., Heninger, G.R., & Charney, D.S. (1989). The Yale–Brown Obsessive-Compulsive Scales. *Archives of General Psychiatry, 46,* 1006–1011.

Gray, M. (1978). *Neuroses: A comprehensive and critical review.* New York: Van Nostrand Reinhold.

Hardy, G.E., & Cotterill, J.A. (1982). A study of depression and obsessionality in dysmorphophobic and psoriatic patients. *British Journal of Psychiatry, 140,* 19–22.

Head, D., Bolton, D., & Hymas, N. (1989). Deficit in cognitive shifting ability in patients with obsessive-compulsive disorder. *Biological Psychiatry, 25,* 929–937.

Henderson, J.G., & Pollard, C.A. (1988). Three types of obsessive-compulsive disorder in a community sample. *Journal of Clinical Psychology, 44,* 747–752.

Hiss, H., Foa, E.B., & Kozak, M.J. (1994). Relapse prevention program for treatment of obsessive-compulsive disorder. *Journal of Consulting and Clinical Psychology, 62,* 801–808.

Hodgson, J. & Rachman, S. (1972). The effects of contamination and washing in obsessional patients. *Behaviour Research and Therapy, 10,* 111–117.

Hollander, E., Liebowitz, M.R., Winchel, R., Klumker, A., & Klein, D.F. (1989). Treatment of body-dysmorphic disorder with serotonin reuptake blockers. *American Journal of Psychiatry, 146,* 768–770.

Ingram, I.M. (1961). Obsessional illness in mental hospital patients. *Journal of Mental Science, 107,* 382–407.

Inouye, E. (1972). Genetic aspects of neurosis: A review. *International Journal of Mental Health, 1,* 176–189.

Insel, T. (1990). Phenomenology of obsessive-compulsive disorder. *Journal of Clinical Psychiatry, 51,* 4–9.

Insel, T.R., Donnelly, E.F., Lalakea, M.L., Alterman, I.S., & Murphy, D.L. (1983). Neurological and neuropsychological studies of patients with obsessive-compulsive disorder. *Biological Psychiatry, 18,* 741–751.

Insel, T.R., Hoover, C., & Murphy, D.L. (1983). Parents of patients with obsessive compulsive disorder. *Psychological Medicine, 13,* 807–811.

Insel, T.R., & Winslow, J.T. (1990). Neurobiology of obsessive-compulsive disorder. In M.A. Jenike, L. Baer, & W.E. Minichiello (Eds.), *Obsessive-compulsive disorders: Theory and management,* 2nd ed. (pp. 118–131). Chicago: Year Book Medical Publishers.

Insel, T.R., Zahn, T., & Murphy, D.L. (1985). Obsessive-compulsive disorder: An anxiety disorder. In A.H. Tuma & J.D. Maser (Eds.), *Anxiety and the anxiety disorders* (pp. 577–590). Hillsdale, NJ: Lawrence Erlbaum.

James, I.A., & Blackburn, I.-M. (1995). Cognitive therapy with obsessive-compulsive disorder. *British Journal of Psychiatry, 166,* 444–450.

Jenike, M.A. (1990). Theories of etiology. In M.A. Jenike, L. Baer, & W.E. Minichiello (Eds.), *Obsessive-compulsive disorders: Theory and management* (pp. 99–117). Littleton, MA: PSG.

Jenike, M.A., & Brotman, A.W. (1984). The EEG in obsessive-compulsive disorder. *Journal of Clinical Psychiatry, 45,* 122–124.

Joffe, R.T., Swinson, R.P., & Regan, J.J. (1988). Personality features of obsessive-compulsive disorder. *American Journal of Psychiatry, 145,* 1126–1129.

Karno, M., Golding, J.M., Burnam, M.A., Hough, R.L., Escobar, J.I., Wells, K.M., & Boyer, R. (1989). Anxiety disorders among Mexican Americans and non-Hispanic whites in Los Angeles. *Journal of Nervous and Mental Disease, 177,* 202–209.

Karno, M., Golding, J., Sorenson, S., & Burnam, M.A. (1988). The epidemiology of obsessive-compulsive disorder in five U.S. communities. *Archives of General Psychiatry, 45,* 1094–1099.

Kendler, K.S., Heath, A.C., Martin, N.G., & Eaves, L.J. (1987). Symptoms of anxiety and symptoms of depression: Same genes, different environ-

ments. *Archives of General Psychiatry, 44,* 451–457.

Kenyon, F.E. (1964). Hypochondriasis: A clinical study. *British Journal of Psychiatry, 110,* 478–488.

Khanna, S., & Channabasavanna, S. (1988). Phenomenology of obsessions in obsessive-compulsive neurosis. *Psychopathology, 21,* 12–18.

Khanna, S., & Mukherjee, D. (1992). Checkers and washers: Valid subtypes of obsessive-compulsive disorder. *Psychopathology, 25,* 283–288.

Kobak, K.A., Rock, A.L., & Greist, J.H. (1995). Group behavior therapy for obsessive-compulsive disorder. *Journal for Specialists in Group Work, 20,* 26–32.

Koran, L.M., McElroy, S.L., Davidson, J., Rasmussen, S.A., Hollander, E., & Jenike, M.A. (1996). Fluvoxamine versus clomipramine for obsessive-compulsive disorder: A double-blind comparison. *Journal of Clinical Pharmacology, 16,* 121–129.

Kringlen, E. (1965). Obsessional neurotics: A long-term follow-up. *British Journal of Psychology, 111,* 709–722.

Kustermann, S., & Bersani, G. (1991). Response to pharmacological treatment of obsessive-compulsive disorder and hypotheses on its neurobiology. *Rivista di Psichiatria, 26,* 219–233.

Lang, P.J. (1979). A bio-information theory of emotional imaging. *Psychophysiology, 16,* 495–512.

Luxenberg, J.S., Swedo, S.E., Flament, M.F., Friedland, R.P., Rapoport, J., & Rapoport, S.I. (1988). Neuroanatomical abnormalities in obsessive-compulsive disorder detected with quantitative X-ray computed tomography. *American Journal of Psychiatry, 145,* 1089–1093.

Machlin, S.R., Harris, G.J., Pearlson, G.D., Hoehn-Saric, R., Jeffery, P., & Camargo, E.E. (1991). Elevated medial-frontal cerebral blood flow in obsessive-compulsive patients: ASPECT study. *American Journal of Psychiatry, 148,* 1240–1242.

Main, M., & Hesse, E. (1990). Parents' unresolved traumatic experiences are related to infants' disorganized attachment status: Is frightened and/or frightening parental behavior the linking mechanism? In M.T. Greenbert, D. Cicchetti, & E.M. Cummings (Eds.), *Attachment in the preschool years* (pp. 161–182). Chicago: University of Chicago Press.

Malloy, P., Rasmussen, S., Braden, W., & Haier, R.J. (1989). Topographic evoked potential mapping in obsessive-compulsive disorder: Evidence of frontal lobe dysfunction. *Psychiatry Research, 28,* 63–71.

Marks, I.M. (1981). Review of behavior psychotherapy, obsessive-compulsive disorders. *American Journal of Psychiatry, 138,* 584–592.

McFall, M.E., & Wollersheim, J.P. (1979). Obsessive-compulsive neurosis: A cognitive behavioral formulation and approach to treatment. *Cognitive Therapy and Research, 3,* 333–348.

McKeon, P., & Murray, R. (1987). Familiar aspects of obsessive-compulsive neurosis. *British Journal of Psychiatry, 151,* 528–534.

Mowrer, O. (1939). A stimulus-response analysis of anxiety and its role as a reinforcing agent. *Psychological Review, 46,* 553–565.

Niler, E.R., & Beck, S.J. (1989). The relationship among guilt, dysphoria, anxiety, and obsessions in a normal population. *Behaviour Research and Therapy, 27,* 213–220.

O'Sullivan, G., Noshirvani, H., Marks, I., Monteiro, W., & Lelliott, P. (1991). Six-year follow-up after exposure and clomipramine therapy for obsessive compulsive disorder. *Journal of Clinical Psychiatry, 52,* 150–155.

Pauls, D.L. (1992). The genetics of obsessive-compulsive disorder and Gilles de la Tourette's syndrome. *Psychiatric Clinics of North America, 15,* 759–766.

Perani, D., Colombo, C., Bressi, S., Bonfanti, A., et al. (1995). (-SUP-1-SUP-8F) FDG PET study of obsessive-compulsive disorder: A clinical/metabolic correlation study after treatment. *British Journal of Psychiatry, 166,* 244–250.

Piccinelli, M., Pini, S., Bellantuono, C., & Wilkinson, G. (1995). Efficacy of drug treatment in obsessive-compulsive disorder: A meta analytic review. *British Journal of Psychiatry, 166,* 424–443.

Pigott, T.A., Pato, M.T., Bernstein, S.E., Grover, G.N., Hill, J.L., Tolliver, T.J., & Murphy, D.L. (1990). Controlled comparisons of clomipramine and fluoxetine in the treatment of obsessive-compulsive disorder. *Archives of General Psychiatry, 47,* 926–932.

Rachman, S. (1971). Obsessional ruminations. *Behaviour Research and Therapy, 9,* 229–235.

Rachman, S., & deSilva, P. (1978). Abnormal and normal obsessions. *Behaviour Research and Therapy, 16,* 233–248.

Rachman, S.J., & Hodgson, R.J. (1980). *Obsessions and compulsions.* Englewood Cliffs, NJ: Prentice-Hall.

Rasmussen, S., & Eisen, J. (1990a). Epidemiology and clinical features of obsessive-compulsive disorder. In M.A. Jenike, L. Baer, & W. Minichiello (Eds.), *Obsessive-compulsive disorders: Theory and management* (pp. 10–27). Chicago: Year Book Medical Publishers.

Rasmussen, S.A., & Eisen, J. (1990b). Epidemiology of obsessive-compulsive disorder. *Journal of Clinical Psychiatry, 51,* 10–14.

Rasmussen, S.A., & Eisen, J.L. (1994). The epidemiology and differential diagnosis of obsessive compulsive disorder. *Journal of Clinical Psychiatry, 55,* 5–10.

Rasmussen, S.A., & Tsuang, M.T. (1986). DSM-III obsessive-compulsive disorder: Clinical characteristics and family history. *American Journal of Psychiatry, 143,* 317–322.

Rauch, S.L., & Jenike, M.A. (1993). Neurobiological models of obsessive-compulsive disorder. *Psychosomatics, 34,* 20–32.

Rauch, S.L., & Savage, C.R. (1994). Functional neuroimaging of obsessive-compulsive disorder: New paradigms and models. *Chinese Mental Health Journal, 8,* 181–185.

Robins, N., Helzer, J.E., Weissman, M., Orvaschell, H., Gruenberg, E., Burke, J., & Reigier, D. (1984). Prevalance of specific psychiatric disorders in a community sample. *Journal of Clinical Psychology, 44,* 747–752.

Rosen, J.C., & Leitenberg, H. (1982). Bulimia nervosa: Treatment with exposure and response prevention. *Behavior Therapy, 13,* 117–124.

Rubin, R.T., Villanueva-Meyer, J., Ananth, J., Trajmar, P.G., & Mena, I. (1992). Regional xenon 133 cerebral blood flow and cerebral technetium 99 m HMPAO uptake in unmedicated patients with obsessive-compulsive disorder and matched normal control subjects. *Archives of General Psychiatry, 49,* 695–702.

Rubenstein, C.S., Pigott, T.A., L'Heureux, F., Hill,

J.L., & Murphy, D.L. (1992). A preliminary investigation of the lifetime prevalence of anorexia and bulimia nervosa in patients with obsessive-compulsive disorder. *Journal of Clinical Psychiatry, 53,* 309–314.

Salkovskis, P.M. (1985). Obsessional-compulsive problems: A cognitive-behavioural analysis. *Behaviour Research and Therapy, 23,* 571–583.

Salkovskis, P.M., & Harrison, J. (1984). Abnormal and normal obsessions—A replication. *Behaviour Research and Therapy, 22,* 549–552.

Salkovskis, P.M., & Warwick, H.M.C. (1986). Morbid preoccupations, health anxiety, and reassurance: A cognitive-behavioural approach to hypochondriasis. *Behaviour Research and Therapy, 24,* 597–602.

Sanderson, W.C., DiNardo, P.A., Rapee, R.M., & Barlow, D.H. (1990). Syndrome comorbidity in patients diagnosed with a DSM-III-R anxiety disorder. *Journal of Abnormal Psychology, 99,* 308–312.

Shagass, C., Roemer, R.A., Straumanis, J.T., & Josiassen, R.C. (1984). Distinctive somatosensory evoked potential features in obsessive-compulsive disorder. *Biological Psychiatry, 19,* 1507–1524.

Sher, K.J., Frost, R.O., Kushner, M., Crews, T.M., & Alexander, J.E. (1989). Memory deficits in compulsive checkers: Replication and extension in a clinical sample. *Behaviour Research and Therapy, 27,* 65–69.

Sher, K.J., Frost, R.O., & Otto, R. (1983). Cognitive deficits in compulsive checkers: An exploratory study. *Behaviour Research and Therapy, 21,* 357–363.

Simpson, S., & Baldwin, B. (1995). Neuropsychiatry and SPECT of an acute obsessive-compulsive syndrome patient. *British Journal of Psychiatry, 166,* 390–392.

Stanley, M.A., & Prather, R.C. (1993). Obsessive-compulsive disorders. In A. Bellack & M. Hersen (Eds.), *Psychopathology in adulthood.* Boston: Allyn and Bacon.

Stanley, M.A., Swann, A.C., Bowers, T.C., Davis, M.L., & Taylor, D.J. (1992). A comparison of clinical features in obsessive-compulsive disorder and trichotillomania. *Behaviour Research and Therapy, 30,* 39–44.

Stanley, M.A., & Turner, S.M. (1995). Current status of pharmacological and behavioral treatment of obsessive-compulsive disorder. *Behavior Therapy, 26,* 163–186.

Stanley, M.A., Turner, S.M., & Borden, J.W. (1990). Schizotypal features in obsessive-compulsive disorder. *Comprehensive Psychiatry, 31,* 511–518.

Stein, D.J., Hollander, E., Chan, S., DeCarla, C.M., et al. (1993). Computed tomography and neurological soft signs in obsessive-compulsive disorder. *Psychiatry Research: Neuroimaging, 50,* 143–150.

Stein, D.J., Prohovnik, T., Goldman, R.G., & Hollander, E. (1994). Cingulate cortex in compulsivity and impulsivity: A case report. *Neuropsychiatry Neuropsychology and Behavioral Neurology, 7,* 308–312.

Steketee, G.S., Grayson, J.B., & Foa, E.B. (1985). Obsessive-compulsive disorder: Differences between washers and checkers. *Behaviour Research and Therapy, 23,* 197–201.

Steketee, G., & Shapiro, L.J. (1995). Predicting behavioral treatment outcome for agoraphobia and obsessive-compulsive disorder. *Clinical Psychology Review, 15,* 317–346.

Swedo, S.E., Rapoport, J., Leonard, H., Lanane, M., & Cheslow, D. (1989). Obsessive-compulsive disorder in children and adolescents: Clinical phenomenology of 70 consecutive cases. *Archives of General Psychiatry, 46,* 335–341.

Thomsen, P.H., & Mikkelsen, H.U. (1995). Course of obsessive-compulsive disorder in children and adolescents: A prospective follow-up study of 23 Danish cases. *Journal of the American Academy of Child and Adolescent Psychiatry, 34,* 1432–1440.

Torgersen, S. (1983). Genetic factors in anxiety disorders. *Archives of General Psychiatry, 40,* 1085–1089.

Turner, S.M., & Beidel, D.C. (1988). *Treating obsessive-compulsive disorder.* New York: Pergamon Press.

Turner, S.M., Beidel, D.C., & Nathan, R. (1985). Biological factors in obsessive-compulsive disorders. *Psychological Bulletin, 97,* 430–450.

Turner, S.M., McCann, B.S., Beidel, D.C., & Mezzich, J.E. (1986). DSM-III classification of the anxiety disorders: A psychometric study. *Journal of Abnormal Psychology, 95,* 168–172.

Tynes, L.L., White, K., & Steketee, G.S. (1990). Toward a new nosology of obsessive-compulsive disorder. *Comprehensive Psychiatry, 31,* 465–480.

VanBlakom, A., vanOppen, P., Vermeulen, A., vanDyck, R., et al. (1994). A meta-analysis on the treatment of obsessive-compulsive disorder: A comparison of antidepressants, behavior, and cognitive therapy. *Clinical Psychology Review, 14,* 359–381.

Warwick, H.M.C., & Salkovskis, P.M. (1990). Hypochondriasis. *Behaviour Research and Therapy, 28,* 105–117.

Weissman, M.M., Bland, R.C., Canino, G.J., Greenwald, S., et al. (1994). The Cross-National Collaborative Group. *Journal of Clinical Psychiatry, 55,* 5–10.

Welner, A., Reich, R., Robins, E., Fishman, R., & VanDoren, T. (1976). Obsessive-compulsive neurosis: Record, follow-up, and family studies: I. Inpatient record study. *Comprehensive Psychiatry, 17,* 527–539.

Williamson, D.A., Prather, R.C., Goreczny, A.J., Davis, C.J., & McKenzie, S.J. (1989). A comprehensive model of bulimia nervosa: Empirical evaluation. In W.G. Johnson (Ed.), *Advances in eating disorders—bulimia nervosa: Perspectives on clinical research and therapy.* Greenwich, CT: JAI Press.

Zak, J.P., Miller, J.A., Shuhan, D.V., & Fanous, B.S.L. (1988). The potential role of serotonin reuptake inhibitors in the treatment of obsessive-compulsive disorder. *Journal of Clinical Psychiatry, 49,* 23–29.

Zohar, J., Insel, T.R., Zohar-Kadouch, R.C., Hill, J.L., & Murphy, D.L. (1988). Serotonergtic responsivity in obsessive-compulsive disorder. *Archives of General Psychiatry, 45,* 167–172.

CHAPTER 11

DEPRESSIVE DISORDERS

Ian H. Gotlib
Stanford University
Susan A. Nolan
Northwestern University

INTRODUCTION

Depression is the most common of all the psychiatric disorders. Each year, more than 100 million people worldwide develop clinically recognizable depression. The costs of depression are significant. For example, in terms of economic costs, Rice and Miller (1995) estimate that depression places a burden of over $30 billion per year on the U.S. economy. Depression also has a significant personal cost: Hirschfeld and Davidson (1988) estimate that as many as 15% of individuals with severe recurrent depression attempt to commit suicide.

This chapter presents an overview of the nature of depression. We begin with a description of the psychological symptoms and characteristics of depression, and the criteria necessary for a diagnosis of depression. We continue with a discussion of some commonly described and discussed subtypes of depressive disorder, and an extended description of the nature of unipolar depression, the primary focus of this chapter. Next, we discuss epidemi-

ologic aspects of depression. We then present psychological theories of the etiology of depression, as well as representative research examining these theories. Following this presentation, we describe the course and complications of unipolar depression. We then examine treatment options for depression, followed by a case description. Finally, we discuss several directions for future research in the area of unipolar depression. Before we begin this chapter, however, we must note that, because of space limitations, our focus here will be primarily on the psychological aspects of depression. It is absolutely clear that a consideration of biological, genetic, and neurological factors is crucial in gaining a comprehensive understanding of depression; in this context, the interested reader is referred to recent reviews of these literatures (e.g., Ferrier, 1991; Mann & Kupfer, 1993). Similarly, the research reviewed in this chapter must by necessity be representative rather than exhaustive. Nevertheless, whenever possible, we will cite relevant review articles.

SYMPTOMATOLOGY

The term *depression* has a number of meanings, covering a wide range of emotional states that range in severity from normal sadness to psychotic depressive episodes. Certainly, everyone has at some time felt "sad" or "blue"—feelings of despondency and disappointment are nearly universal experiences. In fact, Bradburn (1977) notes that, over the course of a year, approximately 40% of the population report feelings of depression, disappointment, and unhappiness. Although the differentiation of these common emotions from psychiatrically significant disorder is often difficult, there are specific symptoms that, in the context of a syndrome, distinguish clinically significant, diagnosable depression from normal, occasional feelings of sadness. These symptoms cover a range of functioning, including affective, behavioral, cognitive, and physiological functioning.

With respect to affective symptoms, depressed persons demonstrate a pronounced and persistent dysphoric affect, most often characterized by depression, disappointment, or, for some individuals, hostility. Moreover, between 50% and 70% of depressed persons also report experiencing anxiety, a co-occurrence or comorbidity that clearly creates difficulties with respect to differential diagnosis (cf. Kendall & Watson, 1989). Although these emotions resemble the unhappiness experienced in normal everyday life, they appear to be both quantitatively and qualitatively distinct. Episodes of weeping, for example, often accompany depression, at least in its early stages. With increasing severity of depression, however, patients may become incapable of weeping and state that although they feel like crying, they cannot.

Depressed persons may also demonstrate behavioral disturbances involving either agitated or retarded psychomotor activity and retarded or pressured speech. Behavioral agitation, likely associated with the anxiety component of depression, is relatively uncommon. Although some depressed patients may fidget, more obvious signs of agitation, such as pacing and pressured speech, are rare. In contrast, psychomotor retardation is a significantly more common symptom of depression, frequently exhibited as stooped posture, delay in responding to questioning, reduced activity levels, sluggish behavior, and monotonous voice pitch.

With respect to cognitive functioning, depressed individuals often find it difficult to concentrate; thoughts are slowed and confused, and effective problem solving becomes virtually impossible. Depressed persons may also report problems with short-term memory. Thoughts concerning the self are often centered on themes of hopelessness, helplessness, and self-devaluation. In severe cases, delusions and hallucinations congruent with these themes may be present, and the individual may experience extreme cognitive confusion or demonstrate a preoccupation with suicide.

Finally, many depressed persons exhibit vegetative or physiological symptoms of depression. Of these physical manifestations of depression, sleep disturbances are the most prominent, being experienced by 80% to 90% of depressed patients. Indeed, some investigators have suggested that sleep disturbance may be a biological marker of a vulnerability to depression (e.g., Rush et al., 1986). Most depressed persons experience insomnia combined with early morning awakening, but this symptom may be reversed in the early stages of depression. Disturbances in gastrointestinal functioning are common and, combined with loss of appetite, often result in considerable weight loss. Depressed individuals frequently report tiredness and fatigue, even in the absence of any physical exertion, and experience a loss of sexual energy, often manifested in men by impotence and in women by sexual unresponsiveness or amenorrhea.

In essence, therefore, it is the severity, pervasiveness, and persistence of the alteration in day-to-day functioning that distinguishes clinical depression from more common but less intense feelings of sadness.

DIAGNOSTIC CRITERIA

The current diagnostic system in North America, the *Diagnostic and Statistical Manual of Mental Disorders,* fourth edition (DSM-IV; American Psychiatric Association, 1994) divides mood disorders into depressive disorders and bipolar disorders, as well as two additional disorders based on their assumed causes, "mood disorder due to a general medical condition" and "substance-induced mood disorder." Whereas a diagnosis of bipolar disorder requires presence of one or more manic, mixed, or hypomanic episodes, a diagnosis of depressive disorder, the focus of this chapter, requires one or more periods of clinically significant depression without a history of manic, mixed, or hypomanic episodes. Because of the absence of manic episodes, depressive disorders are often referred to as *unipolar depression*.

Bipolar Disorders

Bipolar disorders are divided into four categories: (1) bipolar I disorder, which consists of one or more manic or mixed episodes and is usually also accompanied by major depressive episodes; (2) bipolar II disorder, which consists of at least one major depressive episode along with at least one hypomanic episode; (3) cyclothymic disorder, in which there are numerous hypomanic episodes and numerous periods with depressive symptoms; and (4) bipolar disorder not otherwise specified, which consists of bipolar features not meeting the criteria for the above disorders. Because a diagnosis of bipolar disorder requires presence of a manic episode, it is possible that some patients who are diagnosed initially with major depression must later be rediagnosed with bipolar disorder if they experience a subsequent manic episode. Indeed, in a 40-year follow-up of patients from the Iowa 500 study, Winokur, Tsuang, and Crowe (1982) found that 10% of patients initially diagnosed with unipolar depression were rediagnosed with bipolar disorder.

Unipolar Disorders

Three unipolar depressive disorders are described in DSM-IV: major depressive disorder, dysthymic disorder, and depressive disorder not otherwise specified. For a diagnosis of major depression, occurrence of one or more major depressive episodes must be established. DSM-IV lists nine symptoms describing disturbances in affective, motivational, somatic, and cognitive functioning that may be present during a major depressive episode. These symptoms must represent a change from the previous functioning of the individual and must be present most of the day, nearly every day, for at least a 2-week period. Typically, no one patient will report all of the symptoms listed in DSM-IV. During a major depressive episode, at least five of the following symptoms must be pre-

sent, one of which must be either depressed mood or a loss of interest in, or failure to obtain pleasure from, most daily activities (anhedonia):

1. Persistent depressed mood most of the day
2. Loss of interest or pleasure in all, or almost all, activities
3. Significant weight loss or weight gain not due to dieting or binge eating, or decreased or increased appetite
4. Insomnia or hypersomnia
5. Psychomotor agitation or retardation
6. Fatigue or loss of energy
7. Feelings of worthlessness or inappropriate guilt
8. Diminished ability to concentrate or make decisions
9. Recurrent thoughts of death or suicidal ideation

Specifiers

DSM-IV delineates a number of specifiers of both the current episode and the longitudinal course of mood disorders. First, severity is noted as mild, moderate, severe, in partial remission, or in full remission. Second, the mood disorder can be classified as being characterized by psychotic features. If an episode has persisted for at least two years, it may be classified as chronic. An episode that includes either an excess of purposeless motor activity or a severe lack of motor activity may be labeled with catatonic features. A depressive episode that is characterized by a number of specific symptoms, or by particular patterns of co-morbid functioning, may be classified as having melancholic features. These symptoms and patterns include loss of interest or pleasure, lack of reactivity to usually pleasurable stimuli, a worsening of depressed mood in the morning, early-morning awakening, psychomotor retardation or agitation, significant weight loss, good premorbid personality functioning, one or more previous major depressive episodes followed by complete or near complete recovery, and a previous good response to somatic antidepressant therapy (see Young, Scheftner, Klerman, Andreason, & Hirschfeld, 1986). Similarly, a depressive episode may be classified as having atypical features if it includes mood reactivity, weight gain, hypersomnia, and hypersensitivity to rejection.

Numerous other classifiers are delineated in

DSM-IV. For example, if an episode occurs within 4 weeks of a woman's giving birth, it may be labeled "with postpartum onset." It is also possible to specify whether there is interepisode recovery and whether the disorder is recurrent or single-episode. The specifier "with seasonal pattern" is used when the onset of the particular mood disorder is related to the time of year, typically winter. Seasonal mood disorders generally include overeating, weight gain, lack of energy, hypersomnia, and carbohydrate craving. A depressive disorder that includes at least four episodes of mania, hypomania, or depression within 12 months is referred to as "with rapid cycling." Finally, a mood disorder may be labeled as "superimposed" on another disorder.

Dysthymia

Dysthymic disorder, previously labeled *depressive neurosis,* is a chronic, nonpsychotic disturbance defined by presence of sustained or intermittent depressed mood for a period of 2 or more years, and by presence of at least two major symptoms of depression. For a diagnosis of dysthymic disorder to be made, the individual must have been in full remission from any previous episodes of major depression for at least 2 months prior to onset of the current condition, and cannot have been free of depressive symptoms for more than 2 months during the 2-year period. In addition, there cannot have been a major depressive episode during this initial 2-year period. Following this initial period, major depressive episodes may be superimposed upon a diagnosis of dysthymia, a disorder known as "double depression" (Keller & Lavori, 1984). A distinction is also made between secondary dysthymia, in which the mood disturbance is apparently related to a preexisting, nonmood disorder or medical condition, and primary dysthymia, in which the mood disturbance does not appear to be related to a preexisting disorder.

It is clear that there is substantial symptom overlap between major depressive disorder and dysthymic disorder. Indeed, there has been considerable debate in the literature as to whether dysthymia represents a distinct type of mood disorder, or if major depressive episode and dysthymia simply represent two points along a continuum of severity (e.g., Goldstein & Anthony, 1989). Results of recent studies suggest that these disorders can be differentiated by specific criteria, such as loss of pleasure or interest, sleep disturbance, and reports of intense despair and discouragement (e.g., Clark, Beck, & Beck, 1994).

It is important to recognize, however, that this specific issue reflects a more general longstanding controversy in the area of depressive disorders. Investigators have long argued about whether depression is a single disorder that varies in severity along a continuum, or whether it is more accurately conceptualized as a number of subtypes that differ in etiology, symptomatology, and course (cf. Kendell, 1976). Although this issue is far from resolved, there is nevertheless reasonable consensus that depression is a heterogeneous disorder or group of disorders. In an effort to reduce such heterogeneity, researchers and clinicians have attempted to subclassify major depression into types. Thus, in addition to the diagnostic categories discussed previously, several subtypes of depression also have been described (e.g., psychotic, neurotic, reactive, involutional, agitated, presenile, acute, chronic, and seasonal affective disorder). Three of the most widely acknowledged subtypes are unipolar–bipolar depression, endogenous–nonendogenous depression, and primary–secondary depression.

SUBTYPES OF DEPRESSION

Unipolar–Bipolar

The unipolar–bipolar dichotomy, first proposed by Leonhard (1957), is one of the most widely accepted subdivisions of depression. This distinction rests on the proposition that depressions with and without manic periods should be viewed as different types of depressions. *Unipolar disorder* is commonly defined as one depressive episode or a history of only depressive episodes. In contrast, *bipolar disorder* is characterized by both manic and depressive episodes, either separately or concurrently. Clearly, manic episodes and depressive episodes differ significantly with respect to phenomenology. Arguably, the more interesting question concerns possible differences between the depressive phase of bipolar disorder and unipolar depression.

In examining these differences, researchers have assessed a number of diverse aspects of depressive disorders. For example, although both unipolar and bipolar depression are determined, at least in part, by genetic factors, this effect appears to be stronger for bipolar disorder (e.g., Perris, 1966; Winokur, Coryell, Endicott, & Akiskal, 1993a). In this context, it is interesting to note that identical twins tend to be concordant for the same disorder (i.e., unipolar or bipolar depression) rather than manifesting two disorders (Bertelsen, Harvald, & Hauge, 1977). Investigators have also demonstrated consistently that the gender difference that is evident for unipolar depression is absent in bipolar depression (e.g., Perris, 1966; Winokur et al., 1993a). Other researchers have found differences between unipolar and bipolar depression with respect to age of onset (e.g., Perris, 1966) and number of episodes (e.g., Winokur, Coryell, Keller, Endicott, & Akiskal, 1993b). Despite these specific differences between unipolar and bipolar depression, however, it is important to note that other investigators have failed to differentiate these two types of depressions on the basis of the degree to which patients experience stress prior to the onset of the disorder (Rice et al., 1984), the patients' proneness to suicide (Black, Winokur, & Nasrallah, 1988), and general responsivity to treatment (e.g., Coppen, Metcalfe, & Wood, 1982).

Endogenous–Reactive

Another distinction is that between endogenous and nonendogenous, or reactive, depression. Originally, the term *endogenous depression* was used to describe depressions that were assumed to have a biological etiology and to be independent of precipitating life events. More recently, however, this term has been used to describe depressions characterized by a particular cluster of symptoms, such as severely depressed mood; depressive delusions and/or hallucinations; psychomotor retardation or agitation; pathological guilt; and disorders of sleep, appetite, and other bodily functions, without regard to the presence or absence of precipitating life events (Beckham, Leber, & Youll, 1995). In contrast, *reactive depression* generally refers to a depression that follows a stressful environmental event and is not typically characterized by the constellation of symptoms noted here.

Several investigators have found significant differences between endogenous and reactive depressions. For example, Prusoff, Weissman, Klerman, and Rounsaville (1980) found that endogenous depressions seem to respond better to antidepressant medication and more poorly to psychological treatment than do nonendogenous depressions. Similarly, both Fairchild, Rush, Vasavada, Giles, and Khatami (1986) and Peselow, Sanfilipo, Difiglia, and Fieve (1992) reported that endogenous depressives do not respond to placebo as well as do nonendogenous depressives. Moreover, most factor-analytic studies of depressive symptoms typically find a factor that corresponds to the endogenous–reactive dimension (e.g., Parker, Hadzi-Pavlovic, & Boyce, 1989).

Despite the promising results of these studies, it is important to bear in mind that other investigations have not supported the validity of the endogenous–reactive distinction. Benjaminsen (1981), for example, found that endogenous and nonendogenous depressives could not be differentiated on the basis of the number of stressful life events experienced prior to onset of the depressive episode. Moreover, other investigators have failed to differentiate melancholic or endogenous depressives from their nonendogenous counterparts with respect to genetic loading, family aggregation, cognitive functioning, or course of illness (cf. Zimmerman & Spitzer, 1989). It is unclear, therefore, whether the endogenous–nonendogenous distinction is useful for researchers or clinicians, although, given its long history (cf. Kendell, 1976) and some of the intriguing results described here, it is likely that this distinction will remain in widespread use.

Primary–Secondary

The distinction between primary and secondary depression was originally advanced by Munro (1966) and later developed by Robins and Guze (1972). The crux of this distinction essentially involved presence or absence of a preexisting, nonaffective psychiatric disorder or incapacitating medical illness. *Primary depression* was defined as a full depressive syndrome that met the criteria for major depression in the absence of other psychiatric or medical disorders. In contrast, *secondary depression* referred broadly to depressive symptoms occurring subsequent to, or superimposed on, any other psychiatric or medical disorder. This distinction was based on the recognition that depressive syndromes frequently accompany or follow certain psychiatric or physical disorders, such as anxiety disorder or alcoholism.

The primary secondary distinction has received support from a number of investigators. For example, Faravelli and Poli (1982) reported that diagnoses of primary and secondary depression were stable over a 4-year follow-up period. Several investigators have noted symptom differences between primary and secondary depressives. Brim et al. (1984), for example, found psychomotor retardation to be more common in primary than in secondary depression, and Reveley and Reveley (1981) found that suicide attempts were more common among patients with secondary than with primary depression. Weissman et al. (1977) reported that patients with secondary depression tend to have less severe depressions, to have their first episode at a younger age, and to have histories of more psychiatric illness in their families. Costello and Scott (1991) noted that, compared to individuals with primary depression, secondary depressives have been found to have a more suicidal thoughts, a greater tendency to experience chronic dysphoria even in the absence of a major depressive episode, and a poorer prognosis following pharmacological treatment. Furthermore, Keller, Shapiro, Lavori, and Wolfe (1982) reported that those individuals with primary depression are less likely to relapse than are those with secondary depression. Nevertheless, as Beckham et al. (1995) note, because of its generally low utility in clinical contexts, the concept of primary and secondary depression is more widely used in research endeavors than in clinical practice.

It is apparent that diagnostic criteria in the area of affective disorders are continually evolving. As Sinaikin (1985) recently stated, ". . . at this point in time the clinician cannot possibly hope to glean from the literature a set of discrete, mutually exclusive, and valid diagnostic categories. Rather, the clinician must be willing to tolerate some degree of diagnostic overlap, forego considerations of ultimate nosological validity, and instead judge each diagnostic category on the basis of the therapeutic and prognostic information that it conveys" (p. 199).

EPIDEMIOLOGY

As noted earlier, depression is the most common of all psychiatric disorders. Data from the NIMH Epidemiologic Catchment Area (ECA) study indicate that about 30% of the population reports experiencing "dysphoria" lasting at least 2 weeks at some point during their lifetime (Weissman, Bruce, Leaf, Florio, & Holzer, 1991). Importantly, Horwath, Johnson, Klerman, and Weissman (1994) found that individuals who are experiencing symptoms of depression are almost five times more likely than are nonsymptomatic persons to develop diagnosable depression over the next year (see Gotlib, Lewinsohn, & Seeley, 1995, for similar data for adolescents). With respect to diagnosable depression, the ECA data indicated that about 4% of men and 9% of women met diagnostic criteria for major depressive episode at some point during their lifetime. Moreover, data from a more recent epidemiologic study, the National Comorbidity Survey (NCS), yielded higher lifetime prevalence estimates for major depressive episode: 21% of women and 13% of men (Kessler et al., 1994). Finally, depression is a recurrent disorder, with up to 75% of depressed patients experiencing more than one episode over the course of their lives (Belsher & Costello, 1988; Keller, 1985).

Depression has a critical personal cost. For a significant proportion of these individuals, the depressive episode will result in suicide. Hirschfeld and Davidson (1988), for example, report that up to 15% of severely depressed individuals will attempt suicide. From a somewhat different perspective, Rice and Miller (1995) estimate that 60% of suicides are due to mood disorders. Indeed, the mortality risk from all causes appears to be considerably elevated in depressed individuals. For example, in a 16-year prospective study, Murphy, Monson, Olivier, Sobol, and Leighton (1987) found that depressed persons have death rates that are 1.5 to 2 times that of their nondepressed counterparts. When one considers the various medical and diagnostic categories of which depression is an integral part or with which it is frequently associated, it is clear that the problem of depression is considerable, and its consequences potentially lethal.

A number of investigators have identified subsets

of the population who are at particular risk for developing depression. For example, as noted, women are between 1.5 and 3 times as likely to experience depression as are men (Blehar & Oren, 1995; Frank, Carpenter, & Kupfer, 1988). Thus, of the 11 million individuals estimated to have suffered from depression in 1990, an estimated 7.8 million were women (Greenberg, Stiglin, Finkelstein, & Berndt, 1993). Weissman and Klerman (1977) reviewed the literature examining this gender difference and concluded that the difference is not a result of an artifact, such as increased help-seeking behavior, but is veridical. More recently, Kessler, McGonagle, Swartz, Blazer, and Nelson (1993) examined the NCS data and developed a measure of chronicity of depression by computing the ratio of 12-month prevalence estimates to lifetime prevalence estimates. Interestingly, this ratio was almost identical for males (60.1%) and females (60.5%), suggesting that although women have an increased risk of first onset of major depression, their risk of chronicity or recurrence is not greater than is the case for men.

Several investigators have documented an elevated prevalence of depressive symptoms among the elderly (e.g., Blazer, 1989; Romanoski et al., 1992). Interestingly, however, such elevation of relatively mild levels of depressive symptoms appears to be accompanied by a decrease in the prevalence of more major depressive diagnoses in this age group. For example, in the ECA study, lifetime prevalence rates of major depression were lowest among those aged 65 or older (Romanoski et al., 1992; Weissman et al., 1991). Kessler et al. (1994) also reported a declining prevalence of major affective disorders with age in the NCS data set. Henderson (1994) and Ernst and Angst (1995) offer several explanations for the decrease in prevalence estimates of major depression in the elderly. For example, life events may be less common in the elderly, and social interactions more satisfactory. In addition, physical illness, frailty, and disability have been identified as predictors of depression (e.g., Jorm, 1995), and the mortality of elderly persons with such comorbidity may contribute to their decreased rates of diagnosable depression. Finally, Ernst and Angst suggest that "subthreshold" depression may be more common with age as symptoms of depression become more transient and less variable.

Finally, a number of investigators have noted a change in rates of depression over time. In several studies, for example, the incidence and lifetime prevalence rates of depression appear to be increasing across successive generations (Cross-National Collaborative Group, 1992; Lewinsohn, Rohde, Seeley, & Fischer, 1991). Generally, these investigators argue that, because genetic factors could not change at such a rapid pace, the reasons underlying these changes are environmental. Nevertheless, no specific factors for this change have been consistently identified. Klerman and Weissman (1989) reviewed a number of large epidemiologic studies using similar methods and diagnostic procedures. They concluded that age of onset of depression has become earlier, and that prevalence of depression for successive birth cohorts has increased since World War II. Klerman and Weissman suggested that, although an increase in depressive symptoms across generations could account for this pattern of results, it is also possible that it is due to other factors, such as an increased mortality among older persons with depression, changing diagnostic criteria over time, and biases in memory. Clearly, more prospective studies are required to examine this issue more explicitly.

ETIOLOGY

Psychological Theories of Depression

Several diverse theoretical frameworks have been advanced to explain the etiology and maintenance of depression. These theories can be organized with respect to their reliance on psychoanalytic, cognitive, or behavioral concepts.

Psychoanalytic Theories

Psychoanalytic conceptualizations of depression regard as central to this disorder the imagined or real loss of a valued or loved object, through death, separation, or rejection, or symbolically through the loss of some ideal or abstraction. Moreover, loss in early childhood is postulated to serve as a vulnerability factor for depression later in adulthood. In one of the earliest psychoanalytic formulations of depression, Abraham (1911/1927) postulated that the depressed individual is dominated by feelings of loss of a loved object. For the depressed person, unconscious feelings of hostility toward the lost person are internalized and directed toward the self, as are the deficiencies and weaknesses the depressed individual had unconsciously attributed to the lost person. Finally, Abraham postulates that the unconscious destructive wishes of the depressed individual leads to overwhelming feelings of guilt.

In a subsequent but similar formulation, Freud (1917) expanded upon Abraham's postulations and compared depression with grief in order to emphasize the concept of loss of self-esteem. Freud noted that depressed persons exhibit symptoms similar to those present when one experiences a significant loss. Unlike those in mourning, however, depressed persons appeared to lack self-esteem, an observation that led Freud to hypothesize that the anger and disappointment that had previously been directed toward a lost object leads to a loss of self-esteem and a tendency to engage in self-criticism.

Finally, utilizing an object-relations perspective, Jacobson (1971) hypothesized that a fusion of the individual's self- and object representations early in childhood result in the self-condemnation and self-reproach characteristic of depression. Anger and hostility are directed at the lost object and its internal representation, but, through the process of fusion, the internal representations of the object and the self become indistinguishable. Consequently, the anger and hostility initially directed toward the lost object are experienced as self-condemnation and self-hate.

In essence, therefore, psychoanalytic theorists view depression as a failure of the normal mourning process, and describe a depressive syndrome composed of self-criticism, loss of libido, guilt, and low self-esteem. Furthermore, psychoanalytic theorists also emphasize the importance of loss in early childhood as a vulnerability factor for subsequent depression. Indeed, consistent with this formulation, several investigators have found that an elevated proportion of depressed persons report early loss of a parent (e.g., Brown, Harris, & Bifulco, 1986) and a negative early family environment (e.g., Gotlib, Mount, Cordy, & Whiffen, 1988).

Cognitive Theories

A number of models of depression have implicated cognitive factors in the etiology of this disorder. The first major cognitive theory of depression was formulated by Beck (1967, 1976). Beck's cognitive theory focuses on three interrelated aspects of depressed individuals' cognitions. Beck postulates the operation of a "cognitive triad," in which depressed persons are hypothesized to be characterized by negative views of themselves, of their experiences, and of the future. Beck further suggests that depressed individuals exhibit "cognitive distortions" through engaging in faulty information processing. More specifically, Beck contends that depressed persons are characterized by several systematic errors in thinking, including arbitrary inference, selective abstraction, overgeneralization, and all-or-none thinking.

The most important construct in Beck's cognitive model of depression, however, is the "negative self-schema." Schemata are "chronically atypical" cognitive processes that represent "a stable characteristic of [the depressed individual's] personality" (Kovacs & Beck, 1978, p. 530). Moreover, schemata are postulated to play a causal role in depression by influencing the selection, encoding, categorization, and evaluation of stimuli in the environment, processes that lead to depressive affect. Extending a psychoanalytically oriented formulation, Beck postulates that schemata develop from early negative experiences in childhood, and that they become activated when the individual is exposed to a current stressor, particularly if this current stressor is related in some important way to the early negative experiences. These activated schemata take the form of excessively rigid and inappropriate beliefs or attitudes about the self and the world. When these schemata are active, the depressed person attempts to interpret information from the environment so that it is consistent with the schemata, even if it means distorting the information to achieve congruence. Thus, Beck suggests that depressed persons selectively filter out positive stimuli and perceive negative or neutral information as being more negative than is actually the case.

In the reformulated learned-helplessness model of depression, Abramson, Seligman, and Teasdale (1978) maintain that vulnerability to depression derives from a habitual style of explaining the causes of life events, known as *attributional* or *explanatory style*. Explanatory style is viewed as a trait that has its origins in early childhood experiences; thus, individuals are expected to exhibit cross-situational and temporal consistency in their causal explanations for events (cf. Brewin, 1985). Individuals with a "depressogenic" attributional style not only have learned through early experiences to believe that previous events in their lives were uncontrollable, but also expect that future outcomes will similarly be out of their control. Onset of a depressive episode is precipitated by occurrence of a negative event that triggers the expectation of the uncontrollability of future negative events. Abramson et al. postulate that persons who are prone to depression tend to attribute negative outcomes to internal, global, and stable factors and, to a lesser extent, tend to attribute positive outcomes to external, specific, and unstable causes (cf. Sweeney, Anderson, & Bailey, 1986). As in Beck's model, these patterns of attributions are hypothesized to play a causal role in the development of depression.

In a revision of the reformulated learned-helplessness theory, Abramson, Metalsky, and Alloy (1989) propose a subtype of depression they refer to as "hopelessness depression." According to this theory, hopelessness depression results from the expectation that desired outcomes will not occur, that undesired outcomes will occur, and that nothing the individual could do would influence the likelihood of these outcomes. Similar to the reformulated learned-helplessness model, hopelessness depression is expected to occur when people attribute negative life events to stable and global causes. In addition, the likelihood of experiencing hopelessness depression rises with increases in the individual's perception that he or she is unable to affect outcomes in his or her environment. Thus, individuals' resulting views of themselves, including their own worth, abilities, and personality, following a negative event are hypothesized to affect the likelihood that they will experience hopelessness. Finally, Abramson et al. hypothesized that individuals may have domain-specific depressogenic attributional styles. That is, individuals may be especially sensitive to experiencing depression following achievement-oriented events or interpersonal events, in which case a particular type of negative life event would be necessary for hopelessness to occur. This "matching" hypothesis, in which individuals may be vulnerable to depression following one particular type of negative life event but not another, resembles Beck's (1983) subtyping of sociotropic and autonomous individuals.

A third cognitive model of depression is that formulated by Bower (1981, 1987). Bower's associative network theory postulated that in a given mood state individuals are more likely to recall events that have been linked with that mood in the past. Bower predicts that this "linkage" will lead to a tendency to interpret current events in a negative manner when in a negative mood. Bower further suggests that, because feelings related to failure and loss have likely been associated with depression in the past, these feelings will emerge each time an individual enters a depressive mood. Thus, Bower hypothesizes that negative cognitions result because current depressed mood enhances the accessibility of negative memories and negative ways of interpreting events.

Although Bower (1981) sees negative cognitions as both antecedents and consequences of depression, their role as consequences of depression are particularly important in his model. Bower suggests that a depressed mood leads to negative thinking in the manner outlined here; however, he also believes that these negative cognitions can then serve to maintain the depression. Furthermore, a negative interpretation of any event, regardless of current mood state, can activate a depressed mood. Thus, although Bower, like Beck and Abramson et al., postulates an antecedent role for negative cognitions in the etiology of depression, he places a greater emphasis on their role as a consequence of this disorder than as factors that affect the course of depression.

Teasdale's (1983, 1988) differential activation hypothesis was formulated as an extension of Bower's associative network model. Teasdale hypothesized that individuals' risk for depression stems from their accessibility of negative cognitions *once they have entered a depressed mood state*. Contrary to earlier models, Teasdale postulates that negative cognitions are almost entirely mood-state dependent. Indeed, he suggests that they arise only in the presence of depressed mood, rather than representing more stable, traitlike, constructs. Teasdale emphasizes empirical evidence demonstrating that there are no differences in cognitive functioning between nondepressed individuals with and without a history of depression, as long as they are not currently depressed. He suggests further that differences between these two groups may be found if negative cognitive constructs are assessed when the individuals are in a depressed mood.

There is a very large body of literature assessing these cognitive formulations, and it is clearly beyond the scope of this chapter to review these studies. The interested reader is referred to reviews by Gotlib and Abramson (1999); Gotlib, Gilboa, and Sommerfeld (in press); Gotlib and McCabe (1992); and Haaga, Dyck, and Ernst (1991). In general, there is considerable evidence that depressed persons, while they are in episode, are indeed characterized by presence of negative cognitions (e.g., Gotlib, 1984; Hollon, Kendall, & Lumry, 1986) and by an increased "readiness" to attend to negative information in their environment (e.g., Gotlib, MacLachlan, & Katz, 1988; McCabe & Gotlib, 1995). Depressed persons also have been found to attribute causes of negative events to internal, stable, and global factors (see Sweeney et al., 1986). There is some question, however, concerning the specificity of these negative cognitions and negative attributions to depression (e.g., Hollon et al., 1986).

Results of investigations examining the causal aspects of these cognitive formulations of depression and the temporal stability of these negative cognitions are more equivocal. For example, Lewinsohn, Steinmetz, Larson, and Franklin (1981) found no differences between causal attributions of individuals who became depressed over the course of a year and the attributions of individual subjects who remained nondepressed. This result clearly suggests that a self-deprecating attributional style does not precede onset of a depressive episode, although it may prolong or intensify dysphoria among nondepressed individuals (e.g., Metalsky, Joiner, Hardin, & Abramson, 1993). Similarly, Gotlib, Whiffen, Wallace, and Mount (1991) found that negative cognitions measured during pregnancy did not significantly predict the subsequent onset of a diagnosable episode of depression during the postpartum period. Finally, a significant number of studies have reported that negative cognitions found in depressed persons decrease following symptomatic recovery, to the extent that remitted depressives in these studies do not differ in their cognitive functioning from nondepressed controls (e.g., Gotlib & Cane, 1987; Hollon et al., 1986; McCabe & Gotlib, 1993).

Recall that Teasdale (1988) suggests that vulnerable and nonvulnerable individuals should differ with respect to their negative functioning while they are in

a sad mood. Interestingly, results of a small number of recent investigations support this formulation, suggesting that the cognitive functioning of formerly or remitted depressed individuals can look as negative as that of depressed persons if they are found to be (or induced to be) in a negative mood. Miranda, Persons, and their colleagues, for example, have found elevated scores on the Dysfunctional Attitudes Scale in formerly depressed individuals while they are in a negative mood; never-depressed persons in a negative mood do not show these same elevations in negative cognitive functioning (e.g., Miranda & Persons, 1988; Miranda, Persons, & Byers, 1990; see Miranda & Gross, 1997, for a recent review of this literature).

It appears, therefore, that although cognitive formulations of depression have been supported by cross-sectional research in terms of "concomitants" of this disorder, there is little consistent evidence from longitudinal investigations of a stable cognitive vulnerability to depression, particularly in the absence of a negative mood state. Although negative cognitions are evident in symptomatic depressed patients, they do not appear to precede the onset of depression, to predict the course of the disorder in depressed individuals, or to be evident following remission. There is some evidence that procedures that "prime" negative mood may activate negative cognitive functioning in individuals with a history of depression, but more research needs to be done in this area before firm conclusions can be drawn. As Barnett and Gotlib (1988) concluded, the causal formulations of existing cognitive models of depression do not seem to fit accurately the majority of the accumulated relevant data.

Behavioral Theories

Twenty-five years ago, Ferster (1973) conceptualized depression as a generalized reduction of rates of response to external stimuli. Essentially, the depressed individual was postulated to be on an extinction schedule, with a reduced rate of reinforcement. Costello (1972), however, argued that it was not a reduction in the *number* of reinforcers available to the depressed individual but, rather, in the *quality* of reinforcers.

Lewinsohn and his colleagues (e.g., Lewinsohn, 1974; Lewinsohn, Youngren, & Grosscup, 1979) refined these positions by hypothesizing that a low rate of response-contingent positive reinforcement leads to dysphoria and a reduction in behavior, resulting in the experience of depression. Factors that may lead to this low rate of reinforcement include a paucity of potential reinforcers in the individual's environment, deficits in the behavioral repertoire of the individual that prevent attainment of reinforcers, and a change in the individual's responsiveness to positive and/or negative events. Thus, Lewinsohn posited that depressed individuals may lack adequate social skills and may therefore find it difficult to obtain reinforcement from their social environment, leading them to experience a reduced rate of positive reinforcement. Because of such insufficient positive reinforcement, depressed persons find it difficult to initiate or maintain instrumental behavior and, consequently, they become increasingly passive and inactive. Lack of rewarding interchanges with the environment is also assumed to result in the subjective experience of dysphoria (cf. Feldman & Gotlib, 1993).

Segrin (1992) also has identified a repertoire of behaviors and cognitions used and communicated by depressed persons that may lead to negative reactions in others. Framed in terms of social skill deficits, this collection of communication behaviors includes low social expressivity and low behavioral involvement, especially in unstructured interpersonal situations. These deficits, most obvious in the self-reports of the depressed individuals, also appear to be present in observer ratings, albeit to a smaller degree. Segrin suggests that these behaviors and cognitions will affect the impressions formed by those with whom depressed persons interact.

Complementing this formulation, Coyne (1976) contends that depression is maintained by the negative responses of significant others to the depressive person's symptomatic behavior. Coyne postulates a sequence of behavior that begins with the depressed person's initial demonstration of depressive symptoms. Individuals in the depressed person's social environment initially respond with genuine concern and support. If the depressive's symptomatic behavior continues, however, those with whom he or she interacts begin themselves to feel depressed, anxious, and frustrated. These feelings are communicated subtly to the depressed person, who in turn becomes

increasingly symptomatic. Coyne suggests that this "deviation-amplifying" process continues until people ultimately withdraw completely from the depressed person or have him or her withdrawn through hospitalization.

According to behavioral models of depression, therefore, essential features of the disorder include a reduced rate of reinforcement, diminished behavioral output, and a loss of motivation to engage in behaviors that may serve as potential sources of reinforcement. Research has generally supported these models of depression. For example, compared with their nondepressed counterparts, depressed individuals have been found to have lower activity levels, report receiving less pleasure from positive events, and are less socially skilled (e.g., Gotlib, 1982; Gotlib & Meltzer, 1987; Lewinsohn, Mischel, Chaplin, & Barton, 1980). Perhaps not surprisingly, given these deficits, depressed persons also report having smaller and less supportive social networks (e.g., George, Blazer, Hughes, & Fowler, 1989) and engaging in fewer social activities (e.g., Gotlib & Lee, 1989). Importantly, these social deficits not only are a concomitant of depression, but appear to precede the onset of this disorder and to persist following recovery from a depressive episode (e.g., Barnett & Gotlib, 1988; Gotlib & Lee, 1989). Thus, lending support to behavioral theories, deficits in social skill and social support may play an etiologic role in depression.

Consistent with Coyne's (1976) theory, persons interacting with depressed individuals have been found to experience negative affect and to react negatively to the depressed persons (e.g., Gotlib & Robinson, 1982; Hokanson, Loewenstein, Hedeen, & Howes, 1986; see Gotlib & Hammen, 1992, for a more detailed review of these studies). More recently, Segrin (1993) reported that depressed persons were rejected in interactions with both strangers and friends, an indication that they are behaving in a manner that leads to negative reactions from others. Interestingly, Segrin also found that depressives were accurate in their perceptions of rejection, lending support to Coyne's hypothesis that depressives are aware of others' negative feelings toward them. Results such as these have led to a recent expansion of behavioral theories of depression to include an explicit consideration of depressed individuals' social environment and cognitions concerning their social interactions (e.g., Gotlib, 1990; Lewinsohn & Gotlib, 1995; Lewinsohn, Hoberman, Teri, & Hautzinger, 1985).

In an effort to examine the social functioning of depressed persons in more intimate relationships, several investigators have recently begun to examine the marriages and family interactions of depressed persons. At a broad level, there is little question that depression is characterized by low marital satisfaction. Indeed, Merikangas (1984) reported that the divorce rate in depressed patients 2 years after discharge is nine times that of the general population. At a more molecular level, a number of researchers have demonstrated that interactions of depressed patients and their spouses are characterized by complaints, conflict, tension, and hostility (e.g., Biglan et al., 1985). Ruscher and Gotlib (1988), for example, found that couples in which one spouse was depressed emitted a greater proportion of negative verbal and nonverbal behaviors than did nondepressed control couples. Similarly, Gotlib and Whiffen (1989) reported that interactions of depressed male and female psychiatric inpatients and their spouses were characterized by negative affect and hostility. In an examination of the effects of marital functioning on the course of depression, Rounsaville, Weissman, Prusoff, and Herceg-Baron (1979) found that presence of marital disputes was an important determinant of treatment outcome. Those women who came to treatment and who also had marital disputes demonstrated less improvement in their symptoms and social functioning and were more likely to relapse after a course of individual therapy (see Gotlib & Beach, 1995, for a more detailed review of this literature).

Finally, given these difficulties in the marital functioning of depressed persons, it is not surprising that children of depressed patients have been found to exhibit emotional and behavioral difficulties. Whiffen and Gotlib (1989), for example, reported that infants of depressed mothers demonstrated deficits in both motor and mental functioning on the Bayley Scales of Infant Development. Older children of depressed patients, too, have been found to exhibit disturbed psychosocial functioning. Welner, Welner, McCrary, and Leonard (1977), for example, found that children of depressed parents had more depressed mood, death wishes, frequent fighting, and disturbed classroom behavior than did children of nondepressed controls. More recently, Hammen et al. (1987) reported simi-

lar findings in a sample of unipolar depressed psychiatric patients, but emphasized the importance of the role of psychosocial stresses in mediating the relation between parental depression and child disturbance. Finally, Lee and Gotlib (1989) found that children of depressed mothers were rated both by their mothers and by a clinician as having a greater number of both internalizing and externalizing problems than were the children of the nondepressed control mothers; indeed, two-thirds of the children of the depressed mothers were placed in the clinical range on the Child Behavior Checklist, an incidence three times greater than that observed in the nondepressed controls. Interestingly, these difficulties in the children were also evident at a one-year follow-up assessment, even though mothers were no longer symptomatic (see Gotlib & Goodman, 1999; Gotlib & Lee, 1996).

In summary, therefore, it is clear that there are strong interpersonal aspects to depression, lending support to behavioral models of this disorder. Depressed persons are more likely than are their nondepressed counterparts to have experienced a difficult early family environment and to report having less social support and smaller social networks. The marital relationships of depressed persons have been found to be characterized by tension and hostility, and there is now a sizable literature attesting to the difficulties in psychosocial functioning exhibited by children of depressed parents. The functional role played by these interpersonal deficits in the onset and maintenance of depression, however, is still unclear, and much research remains to be done.

COURSE AND COMPLICATIONS

Describing the course of unipolar depression accurately is difficult because investigators are not consistent in their definitions of onset, recovery, and relapse. For example, as Zis and Goodwin (1979) note, if hospitalization is the criterion used to determine onset, incidence of single-episode patients may be unreliable. Clearly, there are a variety of factors, such as desire to be hospitalized, demands of the home situation, presence of suicidal ideation, and availability of hospital beds, among others, that influence decisions regarding hospitalization of patients who are depressed. Similarly, Belsher and

Costello (1988) have criticized use of vague definitions of *recovery,* which can range from a low score on a depression measure, to release from hospital, to a 2-month period of freedom from depressive symptoms (cf. Keller et al., 1982). Definitions of *relapse,* too, are also dramatically different across studies, ranging from rehospitalization, to recurrence of symptoms, to diagnosis of any psychiatric disorder. Finally, as Keller (1988) has observed, much of our knowledge concerning the course of depression has been obtained through the study of patients who are treated at clinics or university treatment centers. Thus, the generalizability of this information to untreated depressed persons in the community is unclear.

Despite these difficulties, however, we do have a considerable accumulation of information concerning the course of unipolar depression. For example, although a severe depression can develop in only 2 to 3 weeks, it can last for up to a year or more (cf. Clayton, 1983; Lewinsohn, Fenn, Stanton, & Franklin, 1986). Between 80% and 90% of patients with an episode of major depression recover within 5 years (Keller et al., 1992). It is important to note, however, that the likelihood of recovery decreases with the length of the depressive episode; that is, the longer a patient remains depressed, the less likely she or he is to demonstrate a complete recovery. Indeed, whereas 64% of depressed patients will recover in the 6 months following onset of a depressive episode, only 10% of those still depressed will recover in the 18th to 24th months following an episode (Keller et al., 1982). Mueller et al. (1996) reported that, among a sample of patients who remained depressed for 5 years following onset of a depressive episode, the median annual rate of recovery over the next 5 years was 9%. Robins and Guze (1972) report that between 10% and 20% of all patients diagnosed with major depression will have a chronic course.

Several investigators have examined factors that predict recovery from a depressive episode. Keller (1988), for example, noted that acuteness of onset and severity of major depressive disorder were strong predictors of recovery. In fact, Keller found that protracted illness prior to seeking treatment was the most powerful predictor of a slow time to recovery and a higher rate of chronicity. Other variables that have been found to be associated with the speed of recovery from depression include "double depression" (a major depressive episode superimposed on a dysthymic disorder that preceded the onset of the major depression by at least 2 years), secondary (as opposed to primary) depression, and age, with earlier onset of depression predicting a slower recovery from a depressive episode (Keller & Shapiro, 1982). In an important analysis of data from the NIMH Treatment of Depression Collaborative Research Program, Sotsky et al. (1991) examined patient predictors of response to psychotherapy and pharmacotherapy. These investigators found that six patient characteristics, in addition to depression severity, predicted response to treatment across psychotherapy, pharmacotherapy, and combined conditions: social dysfunction, cognitive dysfunction, expectation of improvement, endogenous depression, double depression, and duration of current episode. Although there was some indication of specificity of predictors of outcome to type of treatment, those results were more tenuous and clearly warrant replication.

Finally, it is now apparent that depression is a recurrent disorder (Zis & Goodwin, 1979). Between 50% and 90% of patients with one major depressive episode will have at least one subsequent episode of depression in their lifetimes (Clayton, 1983). Indeed, Angst et al. (1973) reported that the mean number of lifetime episodes in patients with unipolar depression is five to six. As with recovery, the longer an individual remains symptom free the less likely he or she is to relapse. Data from the NIMH Collaborative Study (e.g., Keller et al., 1982) indicate that whereas 40% of unipolar depressed patients relapsed within the first year following recovery, only an additional 14% relapsed in the second year, and 10% in the third (see also Lewinsohn, Zeiss, & Duncan, 1989).

As with recovery, investigators have also examined factors that predict relapse of depression. Interestingly, it appears that factors identified as predictive of relapse may be different from those responsible for recovery from depression. For example, Keller and Shapiro (1982) found that whereas duration of illness predicted recovery from a depressive episode but not relapse, the number of previous depressive episodes was found to be a significant predictor of relapse but not of recovery. Investigators have also found that patients with primary depression are less likely to relapse than are those with secondary depression (e.g., Keller et al., 1982), and that patients who live with hostile or critical relatives are more likely to relapse than are patients who return to more positive family environments (Hooley, Orley, & Teasdale, 1986). Finally, equivocal results have been obtained in investigations examining the impact on relapse of double depression (Keller et al., 1982), negative life events (Paykel & Tanner, 1976), previous psychiatric history (Lewinsohn et al., 1989; Simons, Murphy, Levine, & Wetzel, 1986), and age of the patient (Keller & Shapiro, 1982; Zis & Goodwin, 1979; see Belsher & Costello, 1988, for a detailed review of this literature).

TREATMENT IMPLICATIONS

Psychoanalytic and Psychodynamic Therapies

As we discussed earlier, psychoanalytic theorists conceptualize depression as the self-criticism and the loss of self-esteem that develop when one has internalized unconscious feelings of hostility toward a lost person or object. On the basis of this premise, psychoanalytic therapy aims to guide the depressed individual in his or her search for insight into these unconscious hostilities. The formulation is that if one can uncover these repressed feelings, one may have a glimpse into the motivations and dynamics of the mood disorder.

There are few studies on the effectiveness of psychoanalytic or psychodynamic therapies. Klerman (1978) reviewed treatments for depression and failed to find systematic or controlled studies of the outcome of psychoanalytically oriented therapy in the treatment of depression. In one of the few studies that did examine either psychoanalytic or psychodynamic treatment, Covi, Lipman, Derogaris, Smith, and Pattison (1974) randomly assigned chronically depressed women to medication, biweekly brief supportive therapy, or psychodynamically oriented weekly group therapy. The results of this study indicated that psychodynamic group therapy was not superior to brief supportive therapy.

Interpersonal Psychotherapy

Although psychodynamic and psychoanalytic therapies have received little empirical support, several other psychotherapeutic methods have been demonstrated to be effective in the treatment of depression. One such treatment, interpersonal psychotherapy (IPT; Klerman, Weissman, Rounsaville, & Chevron, 1984), grew out of the psychodynamic tradition but focuses specifically on interpersonal relationships. This treatment aims to guide patients in identifying and understanding their interpersonal problems and conflicts. The ultimate goal is to help patients relate to others in a more adaptive manner. Among the techniques employed in this process are discussion of problems in relating to others, training in verbal and nonverbal communication skills, problem-solving improvement, and explorations of the accuracy of patients' views concerning their interpersonal experiences.

IPT is a relatively brief psychoeducational therapy that focuses on both symptom relief and improvement in interpersonal relations. Symptom relief is achieved in part through the provision of didactic information that helps patients to understand their depression. Patients are informed about possible ways to treat depression and are told that depression has a good prognosis. Patients are occasionally given antidepressants in addition to IPT to quickly alleviate symptoms of depression. At the same time, the IPT therapist attempts to isolate the interpersonal etiology of the individual's depression. Potential problem areas include grief, role disputes, role transitions, and interpersonal deficits. When the particular problem is identified, the therapist and patient collaborate to examine the problem issue, particularly as it affects their depression.

IPT was one of the treatments examined in the NIMH multisite Treatment of Depression Collaborative Research Program. This project compared IPT with Beck's cognitive therapy for depression, pharmacotherapy (imipramine hydrochloride) plus clinical management, and placebo plus clinical management (see Elkin et al., 1989, for an overview of this project). Two hundred forty depressed outpatients were randomly assigned to one of these four conditions and were followed for 16 weeks. One of the most important aspects of this study was its careful selection and training of therapists. Each therapist received months of intensive training, ensuring standardization of the therapy administered in each condition (see Hollon, Shelton, & Davis, 1993).

Results of this project indicated that IPT was an effective treatment for depression. Those patients who received IPT demonstrated a substantial decrease in their depressive symptoms over the 16 weeks of the study. Importantly, however, differences between IPT and the other conditions in the study (cognitive-behavior therapy, imipramine with brief supportive "clinical management," and placebo pill with "clinical management") were minimal. Elkin et al. (1989) concluded that, although IPT appeared to be highly effective, it did not appear to offer specific or additional effectiveness over other common treatments for depression. Moreover, Shea et al. (1992) reported a similar pattern of results over an 18-month naturalistic follow-up of these patients.

In a more recent investigation of IPT, Frank et al. (1990) followed a sample of depressed patients who had responded to a combination of antidepressants and IPT over three years. Frank et al. concluded from their results that IPT was an effective therapeutic tool for maintaining patients who do not respond to other forms of treatment. Thus, in patients who were not receiving medication during maintenance treatment, monthly sessions of IPT appeared to prolong the interval between depressive episodes.

Cognitive-Behavior Therapies

A number of cognitive-behavior therapies have been developed over the last few decades. In fact, most treatments that are considered primarily either behavioral or cognitive have elements of both theoretical approaches. Consequently, we have combined our discussion of these treatments into a single section. The most frequently cited and evaluated of these therapies is Aaron Beck's cognitive therapy for depression (Beck, Rush, Shaw, & Emery, 1979). Although a number of other cognitive-behavior treatments exist, because of space limitations we will focus in this section on Beck's cognitive therapy for depression.

As we described earlier, Beck's (1967, 1976) cognitive theory posits that individuals' cognitions are based in large part on their *schemata,* belief systems that are derived from past experiences. These schemata color the way in which individuals interpret the world around them. Individuals whose schemata, and the cognitions that are based on these schemata, are maladaptive, interpret their world in a negative man-

ner, leading to an emotional disorder such as depression or anxiety. Cognitive therapy, therefore, attempts to identify patients' dysfunctional beliefs and attitudes, guide the patients in real-life experiments to test the validity of these beliefs, and then correct these erroneous and/or maladaptive beliefs. Behavioral strategies also are used to enhance the effectiveness of the treatment. For example, depressed patients may be asked to monitor their weekly activities in an attempt to increase pleasurable activities and challenge dysfunctional beliefs, both of which should have the effect of reducing feelings and symptoms of depression.

Typically, cognitive therapy begins with a didactic presentation to patients of the theoretical background and foundation of cognitive therapy. Patients learn to monitor their "automatic thoughts," negative cognitions that arise when they encounter specific situations. Patients then learn to examine their automatic thoughts for faulty logic, such as overgeneralization or all-or-none thinking. They learn to test hypotheses about these cognitions and to replace dysfunctional thoughts with more adaptive cognitions and ways of thinking. Finally, patients are guided in the identification of the underlying beliefs that guide their automatic thoughts on a daily basis.

Cognitive therapy has been subjected to extensive empirical validation. The first major investigation of the effectiveness of cognitive therapy for depression was conducted by Rush, Beck, Kovacs, and Hollon (1977). Results of this study indicated that cognitive therapy was more effective than antidepressant medication in the treatment of depression, leading to greater decreases in depressive symptoms. Although other studies have failed to replicate this pattern of results, a number of investigations have provided evidence, nevertheless, that cognitive therapy is highly effective and at least equivalent to antidepressants in reducing depressive symptomatology. For example, findings from the NIMH Treatment of Depression Collaborative Research Program (Elkin et al., 1989), described earlier, suggest that cognitive therapy is as effective as IPT and imipramine hydrochloride in reducing depressive symptomatology. More recent reviews support the finding that cognitive therapy is as effective as pharmacological treatment (e.g., Persons, 1993) or that it may be even more effective than pharmacotherapy (e.g., Scott, 1996).

In addition to its effectiveness in reducing depressive symptoms, cognitive therapy appears to be highly effective in reducing the likelihood of relapse. Rush et al. (1977) found that individuals treated with cognitive therapy had a decreased relapse rate over the 6 months following treatment. More recent research has supported this finding. Simons et al. (1986) found that depressed patients treated with cognitive therapy had lower rates of relapse than did patients treated with antidepressants. Similarly, Blackburn, Eunson, and Bishop (1986) reported that addition of cognitive therapy to medication maintenance led to lower rates of relapse than did medication alone. Finally, results of studies reported by Evans et al. (1992) and Shea et al. (1992) suggest a trend for cognitive therapy, either alone or in combination with pharmacotherapy, to be slightly better than maintenance pharmacotherapy in preventing relapse of depression over an 18- to 24-month interval.

Because it now seems clear from the empirical data that cognitive therapy is an effective treatment for depression, a number of investigators have now turned their attention to the *mechanisms* of cognitive therapy that might be responsible for producing change in levels of depression. For example, Jacobson et al. (1996) reported results of a study conducted to compare the effects of the behavioral components of Beck's cognitive therapy with the effects of the full treatment on patients with major depression. Cognitive information in the behavioral treatment was limited to automatic thought modification, with no focus on the maladaptive underlying beliefs of the patients. Interestingly, despite the participating therapists' clear bias toward the full treatment, there were no differences in outcome. In addition, the two treatments were equally effective in the reduction of negative cognitions. Persons (1993) has also discussed mechanisms that may underlie change as a result of cognitive therapy. She suggests that two approaches—changing patients' schemata and teaching patients new behavioral skills—both may lead directly to clinical improvement. Clearly, this is an important new direction that warrants continued investigation.

Case Description

Ms. X is a 29-year-old Caucasian female referred for feelings of hopelessness subsequent to relationship problems.

On the day of the initial interview, she was well groomed and was casually dressed in faded oversized jeans and a sweater. Ms. X was pleasant and cooperative, though quiet and reserved. She displayed appropriate affect, crying when discussing her failing relationship. Her primary complaint was, "Nobody loves me."

Ms. X's boyfriend recently ended their relationship with no explanation. Now he refuses to talk to her or see her. Ms. X explained that this was a pattern in her life, in which her boyfriends would leave her and she would have enormous difficulty letting go. She stated that she had no other relationship prospects and thus clung to old boyfriends in the hope that they would reconsider.

Ms. X had moved to the city in which she now lives to escape from her mother. Her father had left the family when Ms. X was an infant, and her mother had never remarried. Ms. X described her mother as entering into a string of "bad relationships." Her mother frequently blamed Ms. X for her troubles, contending that Ms. X's father had left because he was not ready for fatherhood and the unexpected birth of Ms. X. Three years ago, irritated with what she described as her mother's constant demands for attention, Ms. X decided to move to a city several states away. In the process, she incurred a great deal of debt both from the move and from living with no paycheck for the 3 months it took her to find work. Her financial problems were compounded by a roommate who moved out unexpectedly and refused to pay her part of the rent, despite having signed a lease.

Ms. X has a degree in English from a small liberal arts university. She is currently working as a receptionist in a dentist's office, and is aware that her current job does not fully utilize her talents and abilities. She has few friends, preferring instead to spend time with her pets, three dogs.

When asked specifically about symptoms that she may be experiencing, Ms. X stated that she had been feeling very depressed and has lost interest in many of her usual activities. For example, she rarely socializes, and she quit her job as a volunteer at a local animal shelter. Her appetite is markedly reduced; although she has lost no weight, she reported little interest in food. She sleeps fewer hours than she did previously; she often awakens in the early morning and is unable to fall back asleep. During the day, she experiences fatigue and low energy. Ms. X reported feelings of guilt, worthlessness, and hopelessness; she stated that she felt like a failure. Although she occasionally has suicidal ideation, she denied that she would ever hurt herself. Ms. X reported that she has had previous bouts of depression, and that she has twice before been treated successfully with psychotherapy.

Ms. X's symptoms clearly meet DSM-IV criteria for major depressive disorder. In addition, her symptoms are consistent with a picture of a melancholic subtype of depression. Ms. X began individual psychotherapy that had a cognitive-behavioral emphasis. The therapist first attempted to establish an empathic therapeutic relationship with Ms. X, one in which she would feel comfortable working collaboratively with the therapist on decreasing her symptoms. For the first several sessions, the therapist worked on establishing the therapeutic relationship and outlined the rationale for cognitive-behavioral therapy. During this time, Ms. X, in collaboration with the therapist, formulated treatment goals. Consistent with the aim of cognitive-behavioral treatments, Ms. X was guided in the formulation of goals involving specific ways of acting or thinking. Ms. X identified as goals for therapy a decreased reliance on romantic relationships for her happiness, elucidating concrete career plans, and improving her social life.

Over the course of the therapeutic sessions, Ms. X learned to identify her automatic thoughts surrounding the situation. For example, she often found herself calling her ex-boyfriend to no avail, then thinking, "He clearly hates me, and if he hates me, I can't get anyone." She also frequently thought, "I am almost 30 years old and I haven't gotten anywhere in my career." Ms. X learned to question the logic behind these thoughts. For example, she was taught to ask herself, "How could anyone have a chance to like me if I continue chasing my ex-boyfriend?" and, "Because I have never really been serious about finding a career, I really don't know for sure whether I can or cannot achieve what I want to." Ms. X then learned to test hypotheses related to these cognitions and learned to think in a more functional manner. Over time, the underlying beliefs governing these automatic thoughts were identified. Ms. X realized that she had categorized herself as a failure in both the interpersonal and work worlds.

Behavioral strategies were used in conjunction with the cognitive techniques. For example, Ms. X was asked to refrain from calling her ex-boyfriend for several weeks; through this process, she discovered that she had several social options. It was decided that she pursue some of these social options, and she went out on several occasions with groups of friends. Eventually, Ms. X decided, on her own, to answer a personal ad. She went on two dates with this person and stated that he was "a jerk"; however, she was able to blame this failure on situational factors, particularly on this specific individual, rather than on her own shortcomings.

With respect to her career, Ms. X was asked to examine potential career opportunities. She decided that her degree in English did not directly enable her to enter any jobs in business, her area of choice. Consequently, she began to examine ways to enhance her education. She wrote for course catalogs at area universities and made appointments with financial aid counselors. She is in the process of selecting a potential evening course for the spring semester.

Over the course of therapy, it became clear that Ms. X had difficulty asserting herself. In particular, she had difficulty refusing others, even when they made unreasonable requests, such as asking Ms. X to stay late at work several nights in a row, or asking her to adopt an unwanted pet. Her acceptance of her roommate's refusal to pay her rent in the face of a signed lease was the therapist's first hint of this pattern, but additional examples of this behavior emerged in almost every session. As part of her treatment, therefore, the therapist examined Ms. X's automatic thoughts regarding assertiveness. Ms. X felt that if she were assertive, there would be "a scene," and Ms. X wanted to avoid any type of conflict. She was afraid that she would cry, and she stated that she would be very embarrassed and upset if she were put in such a position. The therapist worked with Ms. X to examine these assumptions, and Ms. X began to test hypotheses that she generated with the therapist. For example, Ms. X began to say no in small, inconsequential situations. When she saw the general acceptance of her refusals in these situations, she began to attempt this behavior in more meaningful situations. More recently, she was able to tell her mother that the upcoming holiday was a bad time to visit, and that they would have to work out another time. She is now able to incorporate this successful experience into evidence that her prior feelings regarding assertiveness were unreasonable.

After approximately 24 sessions, Ms. X's symptoms of depression have diminished significantly. In addition, she has attained her goals of an improved social life and a decreased reliance on romantic relationships for her happiness. She has begun the process necessary to achieve her career goals. Ms. X and her therapist terminated therapy when it was clear that Ms. X not only was solidly on the way to achieving these goals but, further, had increased her assertiveness and self-esteem. Ms. X now appears to have the tools necessary to maintain the gains that she has made in therapy.

SUMMARY

It is apparent from the literature reviewed in this chapter that a number of unanswered questions and unresolved issues remain in the study of the depressive disorders. Indeed, a circumscribed discussion focusing only on these controversies and their implications for future research could itself fill an entire chapter. In this final section, therefore, we will touch briefly on three issues in particular that we think are important in the area of depression: the role played by cognitive variables in the onset of depression, the role played by interpersonal variables in the onset of depression, and the differentiation of variables implicated in the onset of depression from variables predictive of relapse. In discussing these issues, we will elucidate some directions for further work in this field.

With respect to the role played by cognitive variables in the onset of depression, the results of the studies reviewed earlier suggest that negative cognitive functioning is a concomitant of depression that waxes and wanes with the onset and remission of a depressive episode. There is currently little support for the causal hypotheses of either Beck's cognitive vulnerability model or the reformulated learned-helplessness model. Nevertheless, it is important that these models not be dismissed too readily. Both these models are diathesis–stress conceptualizations of depression; that is, both posit that it is the interaction of a cognitive vulnerability and a relevant stressor that leads to onset of depression. One reason for the lack of consistent evidence in support of cognitive theories of depression, therefore, is that both sides of this interaction may not have been tested appropriately in a sufficient number of studies. There is no question that measures of "schemata" (diathesis) are becoming increasingly sophisticated (cf. Gotlib & McCabe, 1992; Gotlib & MacLeod, 1997; Miranda et al., 1990), as are measures of stressful life events (cf. Hammen, 1991). Investigators are beginning to utilize information-processing paradigms to assess schematic functioning and to adopt a more idiographic approach to the measurement of life events. Future research examining cognitive vulnerability to depression will undoubtedly benefit from these refinements, as well as from a more precise matching of diathesis and stress. For example, Hammen, Ellicott, Gitlin, and Jamison (1989) examined the relation between specific types of life events and two classes of schemata in unipolar depressed patients. These investigators found that those patients whose symptoms worsened over the 6 months of the study had experienced stressful life events that were congruent with their schematic functioning. This move away from a conceptualization of depressogenic cognitions as global traitlike entities, and toward a view of cog-

nitions and stressors as specific and dynamic constructs that have reciprocal effects, will undoubtedly continue to be an important foundation for future research.

Investigations examining interpersonal aspects of depression, too, have evolved from cross-sectional "snapshots" of the social functioning of currently depressed persons to more informative longitudinal "movies" of the relation between interpersonal difficulties and depression. There is little question from cross-sectional studies that depressed persons experience difficulties with their social networks, spouses, and children. The results of longitudinal investigations, however, suggest more importantly that some areas of problematic interpersonal functioning may precede the onset of depression, or persist following recovery from this disorder (cf. Barnett & Gotlib, 1988). Findings such as these should inform hypotheses concerning the nature of the association between interpersonal functioning and depression, and should provide direction for further research. For example, Barnett and Gotlib (1988) recently hypothesized that depression may be caused by the disruption or loss of a central interpersonal relationship among individuals who do not have satisfying alternative sources of self-esteem. Thus, among vulnerable individuals, the disruption of a primary relationship, such as the marital relationship, may lead to depression (see Roberts, Gotlib, & Kassel, 1996). It is not yet clear, however, how such vulnerability is defined, or how this disruption leads to depression. It may be, for example, that marital conflict is the "final straw" that precipitates depression. Alternatively, chronic marital distress may gradually erode self-esteem and coping resources, leading to the onset of a depressive episode by decreasing the individual's capacity to cope effectively with other stresses. Similarly, although it is clear that children of depressed mothers exhibit a range of problematic behaviors, the mechanisms underlying the transmission of risk for psychopathology from depressed mother to child is unknown (cf. Goodman & Gotlib, 1997). It is clear, however, that delineation of the relation between interpersonal functioning and depression is a critical direction for future research.

Finally, it is important in future research to distinguish between variables implicated in the onset of depression and factors that predict relapse of this disorder. Studies reviewed by Belsher and Costello (1988) indicate that half of recovered depressed patients will relapse within 2 years. Clearly, there are factors that represent an elevated and continuing vulnerability for certain individuals. Although it is possible that these factors are present before the onset of a first episode of depression, as is hypothesized in most current cognitive and behavioral models of depression, it is also reasonable to postulate that these factors may be a result of a depressive episode itself (cf. Rohde, Lewinsohn, & Seeley, 1990). Distinguishing between these two formulations has important implications not only for theory, but for intervention as well. For example, most psychotherapy outcome studies to date have focused primarily on the onset and treatment phases of the depressive episode, with relatively little attention given to long-term outcome (i.e., beyond one year). Thus, we have relatively little information concerning those psychosocial variables that are associated with relapse. A delineation of these variables would contribute to the development of intervention strategies aimed specifically at preventing or mitigating future depressive episodes, and might also have implications for the early detection and prevention of depression.

There are numerous issues in the study of psychosocial aspects of depression that call for further research. There is no doubt that significant advances in this field will come from efforts to integrate cognitive and interpersonal variables into a more comprehensive theory of depression. Attempts in this direction have been initiated (e.g., Gotlib, 1990; Gotlib & Hammen, 1992; Lewinsohn et al., 1985), but it is clear that this is a difficult endeavor, and that much work remains to be done. The rewards of these efforts, however, should be considerable.

REFERENCES

Abraham, K. (1911/1927). Notes on the psycho-analytic investigation and treatment of manic-depressive insanity and allied conditions. In *Selected papers on psycho-analysis* (pp. 137–156). London: Hogarth Press, 1927. (Original work published 1911)

Abramson, L.Y., Metalsky, G.I., & Alloy, L.B. (1989). Hopelessness depression: A theory-based subtype of depression. *Psychological Review, 96,* 358–372.

Abramson, L.Y., Seligman, M.E.P., & Teasdale, J. (1978). Learned helplessness in humans: Critique and reformulation. *Journal of Abnormal Psychology, 87,* 49–74.

American Psychiatric Association. (1994). *Diagnostic and statistical manual of mental disorders,* 4th ed. Washington, DC: Author.

Angst, J., Baastrup, P.C., Grof, P., Hippius, H., Poeldinger, W., & Weiss, P. (1973). The course of monopolar depression and bipolar psychoses. *Psychiatrie, Neurologie, et Neurochirurgie, 76,* 246–254.

Barnett, P.A., & Gotlib, I.H. (1988). Psychosocial functioning and depression: Distinguishing among antecedents, concomitants, and consequences. *Psychological Bulletin, 104,* 97–126.

Beck, A.T. (1967). *Depression: Clinical, experimental, and theoretical aspects.* New York: Harper & Row.

Beck, A.T. (1983). Cognitive therapy of depression: New perspectives. In P.J. Clayton & J.E. Barrett (Eds.), *Treatment of depression: Old controversies and new approaches* (pp. 265–284). New York: Raven Press.

Beck, A.T., Rush, A.J., Shaw, B.F., & Emery, G. (1979). *Cognitive therapy of depression.* New York: Guilford Press.

Beckham, E.E., Leber, W.R., & Youll, L.K. (1995). The diagnostic classification of depression. In E.E. Beckham & W.R. Leber (Eds.), *Handbook of depression* (pp. 36–60). New York: Guilford Press.

Belsher, G., & Costello, C.G. (1988). Relapse after recovery from unipolar depression: A critical review. *Psychological Bulletin, 104,* 84–96.

Benjaminsen, S. (1981). Primary non-endogenous depression and features attributed to reactive depression. *Journal of Affective Disorders, 3,* 245–259.

Bertelsen, A., Harvald, B., & Hauge, M. (1977). A Danish twin study of manic-depressive disorders. *British Journal of Psychiatry, 130,* 330–351.

Biglan, A., Hops, H., Sherman, L., Friedman, L.S., Arthur, J., & Osteen, V. (1985). Problem-solving interactions of depressed women and their husbands. *Behavior Therapy, 16,* 431–451.

Black, D.W., Winokur, G., & Nasrallah, A. (1988). Effect of psychosis on suicide risk in 1,593 patients with unipolar and bipolar affective disorders. *American Journal of Psychiatry, 145,* 849–852.

Blackburn, I.M., Eunson, K.M., & Bishop, S. (1986). A two-year naturalistic follow-up of depressed patients treated with cognitive therapy, pharmacotherapy and a combination of both. *Journal of Affective Disorders, 10,* 67–75.

Blazer, D.G. (1989). The epidemiology of depression in late life. *Journal of Geriatric Psychiatry, 22,* 35–52.

Blehar, M.C., & Oren, D.A. (1995). Women's increased vulnerability to mood disorders: Integrating psychobiology and epidemiology. *Depression, 3,* 3–12.

Bower, G.H. (1981). Mood and memory. *American Psychologist, 36,* 129–148.

Bradburn, N.M. (1977). The measurement of psychological well-being. In J. Ellison et al. (Eds.), *Health goals and health indicators* (pp. 84–94). Washington, DC: American Association for the Advancement of Science.

Brewin, C.R. (1985). Depression and causal attributions: What is their relation? *Psychological Bulletin, 98,* 297–309.

Brim, J., Wetzel, R.D., Reich, T., Wood, D., Viesselman, J., & Rutt, C. (1984). Primary and secondary affective disorder: III. Longitudinal differences in depressive symptoms. *Journal of Clinical Psychiatry, 45,* 64–69.

Brown, G.W., Harris, T.O., & Bifulco, A. (1986). Long-term effects of early loss of parent. In M. Rutter, C.E. Izard, & P.B. Read (Eds.), *Depression in young people: Clinical and developmental perspectives* (pp. 251–296). New York: Guilford Press.

Clark, D.A., Beck, A.T., & Beck, J.S. (1994). Symptom differences in major depression, dysthymia, panic disorder, and generalized anxiety disorder. *American Journal of Psychiatry, 151,* 205–209.

Clayton, P.J. (1983). The prevalence and course of the affective disorders. In J.M. Davis & J.W. Maas (Eds.), *The affective disorders* (pp. 193–201). Washington, DC: American Psychiatric Press.

Coppen, A., Metcalfe, M., & Wood, K. (1982). Lithium. In E.S. Paykel (Ed.), *Handbook of affective disorders* (pp. 276–285). New York: Guilford Press.

Costello, C.G. (1972). Depression: Loss of reinforcers or loss of reinforcer effectiveness? *Behavior Therapy, 3,* 240–247.

Costello, C.G., & Scott, C.B. (1991). Primary and secondary depression: A review. *Canadian Journal of Psychiatry, 36,* 210–217.

Covi, L., Lipman, R.S., Derogaris, L.R., Smith, J.E., & Pattison, J.H. (1974). Drugs and group psychotherapy in neurotic depression. *American Journal of Psychiatry, 131,* 191–198.

Coyne, J.C. (1976). Toward an interactional description of depression. *Psychiatry, 39,* 28–40.

Cross-National Collaborative Group. (1992). The changing rate of major depression: Cross-national comparisons. *Journal of the American Medical Association, 268,* 3098–3105.

Davidson, J., Turnbull, C., Strickland, R., & Belyea, M. (1984). Comparative diagnostic criteria for melancholia and endogenous depression. *Archives of General Psychiatry, 41,* 506–511.

Elkin, I., Shea, M.T., Watkins, J.T., Imber, S.D., Sotsky, S.M., Collins, J.F., Glass, D.R., Pilkonis, P.A., Leber, W.R., Docherty, J.P., Fiester, S.J., & Parloff, M.B. (1989). National Institute of Mental Health Treatment of Depression Collaborative Research Program: General effectiveness of treatments. *Archives of General Psychiatry, 46,* 971–983.

Ernst, C., & Angst, J. (1995). Depression in old age: Is there a real decrease in prevalence? A review. *European Archives of Psychiatry and Clinical Neuroscience, 245,* 272–287.

Evans, M., Hollon, S., DeRubeis, R., Piasecki, J., Grove, W., Garvey, M., & Tuason, V. (1992). Differential relapse following cognitive therapy and pharmacotherapy of depression. *Archives of General Psychiatry, 49,* 802–808.

Fairchild, C.J., Rush, A., Vasavada, N., Giles, D.E., & Khatami, M. (1986). Which depressions respond to placebo? *Psychiatric Research, 18,* 216–226.

Faravelli, C., & Poli, E. (1982). Stability of the diagnosis of primary affective disorder: A four-year follow-up study. *Journal of Affective Disorders, 4,* 35–39.

Feldman, L., & Gotlib, I.H. (1993). Social dysfunction. In C.G. Costello (Ed.), *Symptoms of depression* (pp. 85–112). New York: Wiley.

Ferrier, I.N. (1991). Chronic depression: Future prospects from recent research. *International Clinical Psychopharmacology, 6,* 83–89.

Ferster, C.B. (1973). A functional analysis of depression. *American Psychologist, 28,* 857–870.

Frank, E., Carpenter, L.L., & Kupfer, D.J. (1988). Sex differences in recurrent depression: Are there any that are significant? *American Journal of Psychiatry, 145,* 41–45.

Frank, E., Kupfer, D.J., Perel, J.M., et al. (1990). Three-year outcomes for maintenance therapies in recurrent depression. *Archives of General Psychiatry, 47,* 1093–1099.

Freud, S. (1917). Mourning and melancholia. In *Complete psychological works: Standard edition,* Vol. 14. (Trans. & ed. J. Strachey). London: Hogarth Press.

George, L.K., Blazer, D.G., Hughes, D.C., & Fowler, N. (1989). Social support and the outcome of major depression. *British Journal of Psychiatry, 154,* 478–485.

Goldstein, W.N., & Anthony, R.N. (1989). DSM-III and depression. In J.G. Howells (Ed.), *Modern perspectives in the psychiatry of the affective disorders* (pp. 150–167). New York: Brunner/Mazel.

Goodman, S.H., & Gotlib, I.H. (1997). *Risk for psychopathology in the children of depressed parents: A developmental approach to the understanding of mechanisms.* Unpublished manuscript, Emory University.

Gotlib, I.H. (1982). Self-reinforcement and depression in interpersonal interaction: The role of performance level. *Journal of Abnormal Psychology, 91,* 3–13.

Gotlib, I.H. (1984). Depression and general psychopathology in university students. *Journal of Abnormal Psychology, 93,* 19–30.

Gotlib, I.H. (1990). An interpersonal systems approach to the conceptualization and treatment of depression. In R.E. Ingram (Ed.), *Contemporary psychological approaches to depression: Theory, research, and treatment* (pp. 137–154). New York: Plenum Press.

Gotlib, I.H., & Abramson, L.Y. (1999). Attributional theories of emotion. In T. Dalgleish & M. Power (Eds.), *The handbook of cognition and emotion* (pp. 613–636). Chichester: John Wiley & Sons.

Gotlib, I.H., & Beach, S.R.H. (1995). A marital/family discord model of depression: Implications for therapeutic intervention. In N.S. Jacobson & A.S. Gurman (Eds.), *Clinical handbook of couple therapy* (pp. 411–436). New York: Guilford Press.

Gotlib, I.H., & Cane, D.B. (1987). Construct accessibility and clinical depression: A longitudinal investigation. *Journal of Abnormal Psychology, 96,* 199–204.

Gotlib, I.H., Gilboa, E., & Sommerfeld, B.K. (in press). Cognitive functioning in depression: Nature and origins. In R.J. Davidson (Ed.), *Wisconsin symposium on emotion* (Vol. 1). New York: Oxford University Press.

Gotlib, I.H., & Goodman, S.H. (1999). Children of parents with depression. In W.K. Silverman & T.H. Ollendick (Eds.), *Developmental issues in the clinical treatment of children and adolescents* (pp. 415–432). Boston: Allyn and Bacon.

Gotlib, I.H., & Hammen, C.L. (1992). *Psychological aspects of depression: Toward a cognitive-interpersonal integration.* Chichester: Wiley.

Gotlib, I.H., & Lee, C.M. (1989). The social functioning of depressed patients: A longitudinal assessment. *Journal of Social and Clinical Psychology, 8,* 223–237.

Gotlib, I.H., & Lee, C.M. (1996). Impact of parental depression on young children and infants. In C. Mundt, M.J. Goldstein, K. Hahlweg, & P. Fiedler (Eds.), *Interpersonal factors in the origin and course of affective disorders* (pp. 218–239). London: Royal College of Psychiatrists.

Gotlib, I.H., Lewinsohn, P.M., & Seeley, J.R. (1995). Symptoms versus a diagnosis of depression: Differences in psychosocial functioning. *Journal of Consulting and Clinical Psychology, 63,* 90–100.

Gotlib, I.H., MacLachlan, A.L., & Katz, A.N. (1988). Biases in visual attention in depressed and nondepressed individuals. *Cognition and Emotion, 2,* 185–200.

Gotlib, I.H., & MacLeod, C. (1997). Information processing in anxiety and depression: A cognitive developmental perspective. In J. Burack & J. Enns (Eds.), *Attention, development, and psychopathology* (pp. 350–378). New York: Guilford Press.

Gotlib, I.H., & McCabe, S.B. (1992). An information-processing approach to the study of cognitive functioning in depression. In E.F. Walker, B.A. Cornblatt, & R.H. Dworkin (Eds.), *Progress in experimental personality and psychopathology research* (Vol. 15, pp. 131–161). New York: Springer.

Gotlib, I.H., & Meltzer, S.J. (1987). Depression and the perception of social skill. *Cognitive Therapy and Research, 11,* 41–54.

Gotlib, I.H., Mount, J.H., Cordy, N.I., & Whiffen, V.E. (1988). Depressed mood and perceptions of early parenting: A longitudinal investigation. *British Journal of Psychiatry, 152,* 24–27.

Gotlib, I.H., & Robinson, L.A. (1982). Responses to depressed individuals: Discrepancies between self-report and observer-rated behaviour. *Journal of Abnormal Psychology, 91,* 231–240.

Gotlib, I.H., & Whiffen, V.E. (1989). Depression and marital functioning: An examination of specificity and gender differences. *Journal of Abnormal Psychology, 98,* 23–30.

Gotlib, I.H., Whiffen, V.E., Wallace, P.M., & Mount, J.H. (1991). A prospective investigation of postpartum depression: Factors involved in onset and recovery. *Journal of Abnormal Psychology, 100,* 122–132.

Greenberg, P.E., Stiglin, L.E., Finkelstein, S.F., & Berndt, E.R. (1993). Depression: A neglected major illness. *Journal of Clinical Psychiatry, 54,* 419–424.

Haaga, D.A.F., Dyck, M.J., & Ernst, D. (1991). Empirical status of cognitive theory of depression. *Psychological Bulletin, 110,* 215–236.

Hammen, C. (1991). Generation of stress in the course of unipolar depression. *Journal of Abnormal Psychology, 100,* 555–561.

Hammen, C., Adrian, C., Gordon, D., Burge, D., Jaenecke, C., & Hiroto, D. (1987). Children of depressed mothers: Maternal strain and symptom predictors of dysfunction. *Journal of Abnormal Psychology, 96,* 190–198.

Hammen, C., Ellicott, A., Gitlin, M., & Jamison, K.R. (1989). Sociotropy/autonomy and vulnerability to specific life events in unipolar and bipolar patients. *Journal of Abnormal Psychology, 98,* 154–160.

Henderson, A.S. (1994). Does aging protect against depression? *Social Psychiatry and Psychiatric Epidemiology, 29,* 107–109.

Hirschfeld, R.M.A., & Davidson, L. (1988). Risk factors for suicide. In A.J. Frances and R.E. Hales (Eds.), *Review in psychiatry* (pp. 307–333). Washington, DC: American Psychiatric Press.

Hokanson, J.E., Loewenstein, D.A., Hedeen, C., & Howes, M.J. (1986). Dysphoric college students and roommates: A study of social behaviors over a three-month period. *Personality and Social Psychology Bulletin, 12,* 311–324.

Hollon, S.D., Kendall, P.C., & Lumry, A. (1986). Specificity of depressotypic cognitions in clinical depression. *Journal of Abnormal Psychology, 95,* 52–59.

Hollon, S.D., Shelton, R.C., & Davis, D.D. (1993). Cognitive therapy for depression: Conceptual issues and clinical efficacy. *Journal of Consulting and Clinical Psychology, 61,* 270–275.

Hooley, J.M., Orley, J., & Teasdale, J.D. (1986). Levels of expressed emotion and relapse in depressed patients. *British Journal of Psychiatry, 148,* 642–647.

Horwath, E., Johnson, J., Klerman, G.L., & Weissman, M.M. (1994). What are the public health implications of subclinical depressive symptoms? *Psychiatric Quarterly, 65,* 323–337.

Jacobson, E. (1971). *Depression: Comparative studies of normal, neurotic, and psychotic conditions.* New York: International Universities Press.

Jacobson, N.S., Dobson, K.S., Truax, P.A., Addis, M.E., Koerner, K., Gollan, J.K., Gortner, E., & Prince, S.E. (1996). A component analysis of cognitive-behavioral treatment for depression. *Journal of Consulting and Clinical Psychology, 64,* 295–304.

Jorm, A.F. (1995). The epidemiology of depressive states in the elderly: Implications for recognition, intervention, and prevention. *Social Psychiatry and Psychiatric Epidemiology, 30,* 53–59.

Keller, M.B. (1985). Chronic and recurrent affective disorders: Incidence, course and influencing factors. *Advances in Biochemical Psychopharmacology, 40,* 111–120.

Keller, M.B. (1988). Diagnostic issues and clinical course of unipolar illness. In A.J. Frances & R.E. Hales (Eds.), *Psychiatry update: The American Psychiatric Association annual review* (Vol. 7, pp. 188–212). Washington, DC: American Psychiatric Press.

Keller, M.B., & Lavori, P.W. (1984). Double depression, major depression, and dysthymia: Distinct entities or different phases of a single disorder? *Psychopharmacology Bulletin, 20,* 399–402.

Keller, M.B., Lavori, P.W., Mueller, T.I., Endicott, J., Coryell, W., Hirschfeld, R.M.A., & Shea, T. (1992). Time to recovery, chronicity, and levels of psychopathology in major depression: A five-year prospective follow-up of 431 subjects. *Archives of General Psychiatry, 49,* 809–816.

Keller, M.B., & Shapiro, R.W. (1982). "Double depression": Superimposition of acute depressive episodes on chronic depressive disorders. *American Journal of Psychiatry, 139,* 438–442.

Keller, M.B., Shapiro, R.W., Lavori, P.W., & Wolfe, N. (1982). Relapse in major depressive disorder. *Archives of General Psychiatry, 39,* 911–915.

Kendall, P.C., & Watson, D. (Eds.). (1989). *Anxiety and depression: Distinctive and overlapping features.* San Diego, CA: Academic Press.

Kendell, R.E. (1976). The classification of depression: A review of contemporary confusion. *British Journal of Psychiatry, 129,* 15–28.

Kessler, R.C., McGonagle, K.A., Swartz, M., Blazer, D.G., & Nelson, C.B. (1993). Sex and depression in the National Comorbidity Survey: I. Lifetime prevalence, chronicity, and recurrence. *Journal of Affective Disorders, 29,* 85–96.

Kessler, R.C., McGonagle, K.A., Zhao, S., Nelson, C.B., Hughes, M., Eshleman, S., Wittchen, H-U., & Kendler, K.S. (1994). Lifetime and 12-month prevalence of DSM-III-R psychiatric disorders in the United States: Results from the National Comorbidity Survey. *Archives of General Psychiatry, 51,* 8–19.

Klerman, G.L. (1978). Affective disorders. In A.M. Nicholi, Jr. (Ed.), *The Harvard guide to modern psychiatry* (pp. 253–280). Cambridge, MA: Harvard University Press.

Klerman, G.L., & Weissman, M.M. (1989). Increasing rates of depression. *Journal of the American Medical Association, 261,* 2229–2235.

Klerman, G.L., Weissman, M.M., Rounsaville, B.J., & Chevron, E.S. (1984). *Interpersonal psychotherapy of depression.* New York: Basic Books.

Kovacs, M., & Beck, A.T. (1978). Maladaptive cognitive structures in depression. *American Journal of Psychiatry, 135,* 525–533.

Lee, C.M., & Gotlib, I.H. (1989). Clinical status and emotional adjustment of children of depressed mothers. *American Journal of Psychiatry, 146,* 478–483.

Leonhard, K. (1957). *Aufteilung der endogenen Psychosen.* Berlin: Akademieverlag.

Lewinsohn, P.M. (1974). A behavioral approach to depression. In R.J. Friedman & M.M. Katz (Eds.), *The psychology of depression: Contemporary theory and research* (pp. 157–185). New York: Wiley.

Lewinsohn, P.M., Fenn, D.S., Stanton, A.K., & Franklin, J. (1986). Relation of age at onset to duration of episode in unipolar depression. *Journal of Psychology and Aging, 1,* 63–68.

Lewinsohn, P.M., & Gotlib, I.H. (1995). Behavioral theory and treatment of depression. In E.E. Beckham & W.R. Leber (Eds.), *Handbook of depression* (pp. 352–375). New York: Guilford Press.

Lewinsohn, P.M., Hoberman, H.M., Teri, L., & Hautzinger, M. (1985). An integrative theory of depression. In S. Reiss & R. Bootzin (Eds.), *Theoretical issues in behavior therapy* (pp. 331–359). New York: Academic Press.

Lewinsohn, P.M., Mischel, W., Chaplin, C., & Barton, R. (1980). Social competence and depression: The role of illusory self-perceptions. *Journal of Abnormal Psychology, 89,* 203–217.

Lewinsohn, P.M., Rohde, P., Seeley, J.R., & Fischer, S.A. (1991). Age-cohort changes in the lifetime occurrence of depression and other mental disorders. *Journal of Abnormal Psychology, 102,* 110–120.

Lewinsohn, P.M., Steinmetz, J.L., Larson, D.W., & Franklin, J. (1981). Depression related cognitions: Antecedent or consequence? *Journal of Abnormal Psychology, 91,* 213–219.

Lewinsohn, P.M., Youngren, M.A., & Grosscup, S.J. (1979). Reinforcement and depression. In R.A. Depue (Ed.), *The psychobiology of the depressive disorders: Implications for the effects of stress* (pp. 291–315). New York: Academic Press.

Lewinsohn, P.M., Zeiss, A.M., & Duncan, E.M. (1989). Probability of relapse after recovery from an episode of depression. *Journal of Abnormal Psychology, 98,* 107–116.

Mann, J.J., & Kupfer, D.J. (1993). *Biology of depressive disorders, Part B: Subtypes of depression and comorbid disorders.* New York: Plenum Press.

Merikangas, K.R. (1984). Divorce and assortative mating among depressed patients. *American Journal of Psychiatry, 141,* 74–76.

Metalsky, G.I., Joiner, T.E., Hardin, T.S., & Abramson, L.Y. (1993). Depressive reactions to failure in a naturalistic setting: A test of the hopelessness and self-esteem theories of depression. *Journal of Abnormal Psychology, 102,* 101–109.

Miranda, J., & Gross, J.J. (1997). Cognitive vulnerability, depression, and the mood-state dependent hypothesis: Is out of sight out of mind? In I.H. Gotlib, H.S. Kurtzman, & M.C. Blehar (Eds.), *The cognitive psychology of depression: A special issue of Cognition and Emotion, 11,* 585–605.

Miranda, J., & Persons, J.B. (1988). Dysfunctional attitudes are mood-state dependent. *Journal of Abnormal Psychology, 97,* 76–79.

Miranda, J., Persons, J.B., & Byers, C.N. (1990). Endorsement of dysfunctional beliefs depends on current mood state. *Journal of Abnormal Psychology, 97,* 251–264.

Mueller, T.I., Keller, M.B., Leon, A.C., Solomon, D.A., Shea, M.T., Coryell, W., & Endicott, J. (1996) Recovery after 5 years of unremitting major depressive disorder. *Archives of General Psychiatry, 53,* 794–799.

Munro, A. (1966). Some familial and social factors in depressive illness. *British Journal of Psychiatry, 112,* 429–441.

Murphy, J.M., Monson, R.R., Olivier, D.C., Sobol, A.M., & Leighton, A.H. (1987). Affective disorders and mortality. *Archives of General Psychiatry, 44,* 473–480.

Parker, G., Hadzi-Pavlovic, D., & Boyce, P. (1989). Endogenous depression as a construct: A quantitative analysis of the literature and a study of clinician judgements. *Australian and New Zealand Journal of Psychiatry, 23,* 357–368.

Paykel, E.S., & Tanner, J. (1976) Life events, depressive relapse, and maintenance treatment. *Psychological Medicine, 6,* 481–485.

Perris, C. (1966). A study of bipolar and unipolar recurrent depressive psychoses. *Acta Psychiatrica Scandinavica, 42*(Suppl. 194), 172–188.

Persons, J.B. (1993). Outcome of psychotherapy for unipolar depression. In T.R. Giles (Ed.), *Effective psychotherapy: A handbook of comparative research.* New York: Plenum Press.

Peselow, E.D., Sanfilipo, M.P., Difiglia, C., Fieve, R.R. (1992). Melancholic/endogenous depression and response to somatic treatment and placebo. *American Journal of Psychiatry, 149,* 1324–1334.

Prusoff, B.A., Weissman, M.M., Klerman, G.L., & Rounsaville, B.J. (1980). Research diagnostic criteria subtypes of depression. *Archives of General Psychiatry, 38,* 902–907.

Reveley, A.M., & Reveley, M.A. (1981). The distinction of primary and secondary affective disorders: Clinical implications. *Journal of Affective Disorders, 3,* 273–279.

Rice, D.P., & Miller, L.S. (1995). The economic burden of affective disorders. *British Journal of Psychiatry, 166*(Suppl. 27), 34–42.

Rice, J., Reich, T., Andreasen, N.C., Lavori, P.W., Endicott, J., Clayton, P.J., Keller, M.B., Hirschfeld, R.M., & Klerman, G.L. (1984). Sex-related differences in depression: Familial evidence. *Journal of Affective Disorders, 7,* 199–210.

Roberts, J.E., Gotlib, I.H., & Kassel, J.D. (1996). Adult attachment security and symptoms of depression: The mediating roles of dysfunctional attitudes and low self-esteem. *Journal of Personality and Social Psychology, 70,* 310–320.

Robins, E., & Guze, S.B. (1972). Classification of affective disorders: The primary–secondary, the endogenous–reactive, and the neurotic–psychotic concept. In T.A. Williams, M.M. Katz, & J.A. Shield (Eds.), *Recent advances in the psychobiology of the depressive illnesses* (pp. 283–293). DHEW Publication No. (HSM) 79-9053. Washington, DC: U.S. Government Printing Office.

Rohde, P., Lewinsohn, P.M., & Seeley, J.R. (1990). Are people changed by the experience of having an episode of depression? A further test of the scar hypothesis. *Journal of Abnormal Psychology, 99,* 264–271.

Romanoski, A.J., Folstein, M.F., Nestadt, G., Chahal, R., Merchant, A., Brown, C.H., Gruenberg, E.M., & McHugh, P.R. (1992). The epidemiology of psychiatrist-ascertained depression and DSM-III depressive disorders: Results from the Eastern

Baltimore Mental Health Survey clinical reappraisal. *Psychological Medicine, 22,* 629–655.

Rounsaville, B.J., Weissman, M.M., Prusoff, B.G., & Herceg-Baron, R.L. (1979). Marital disputes and treatment outcome in depressed women. *Comprehensive Psychiatry, 20,* 483–489.

Ruscher, S.M., & Gotlib, I.H. (1988). Marital interaction patterns of couples with and without a depressed partner. *Behavior Therapy, 19,* 455–470.

Rush, A.J., Beck, A.T., Kovacs, M., & Hollon, S. (1977). Comparative efficacy of cognitive therapy and pharmacotherapy in the treatment of depressed outpatients. *Cognitive Therapy and Research, 1,* 17–37.

Rush, A.J., Erman, M.K., Giles, D.E., Schlesser, M.A., Carpenter, G., Nishendu, V., & Roffwarg, H.P. (1986). Polysomnographic findings in recently drug-free and clinically remitted depressed patients. *Archives of General Psychiatry, 43,* 878–884.

Scott, J. (1996). Cognitive therapy of affective disorders: A review. *Journal of Affective Disorders, 37,* 1–11.

Segrin, C. (1992). Specifying the nature of social skill deficits associated with depression. *Human Communication Research, 19,* 89–123.

Segrin, C. (1993). Interpersonal reactions to dysphoria: The role of relationship with partner and perceptions of rejection. *Journal of Social and Personal Relationships, 10,* 83–97.

Shea, M.T., Elkin, I., Imber, S.D., Sotsky, S.M., Watkins, J.T., Collins, J.F., Pilkonis, P.A., Beckham, E., Glass, D.R., Dolan, R.T., & Parloff, M.B. (1992). Course of depressive symptoms over follow-up: Findings from the National Institute of Mental Health Treatment of Depression Collaborative Research Program. *Archives of General Psychiatry, 49,* 782–787.

Simons, A.D., Murphy, G.E., Levine, J.L., & Wetzel, R.D. (1986). Cognitive therapy and pharmacotherapy for depression: Sustained improvement over one year. *Archives of General Psychiatry, 43,* 43–49.

Sinaikin, P.M. (1985). A clinically relevant guide to the differential diagnosis of depression. *Journal of Nervous and Mental Disease, 173,* 199–211.

Sotsky, S.M., Glass, D.R., Shea, M.T., Pilkonis, P.A., Collins, J.F., Elkin, I., Watkins, J.T., Imber, S.D., Leber, W.R., Moyer, J., & Oliveri, M.E. (1991). Patient predictors of response to psychotherapy and pharmacotherapy: Findings in the NIMH Treatment of Depression Collaborative Research Program. *American Journal of Psychiatry, 148,* 997–1008.

Sweeney, P.D., Anderson, K., & Bailey, S. (1986). Attributional style in depression: A meta-analytic review. *Journal of Personality and Social Psychology, 50,* 974–991.

Teasdale, J.D. (1983). Negative thinking in depression: Cause, effect, or reciprocal relationship? *Advances in Behaviour Research and Therapy, 5,* 3–25.

Weissman, M.M, & Klerman, G.L. (1977). Sex differences and the epidemiology of depression. *Archives of General Psychiatry, 34,* 98–111.

Weissman, M.M., Pottenger, M., Klebver, H., Reuben, H.L., Williams, D., & Thompson, W.D. (1977). Symptom patterns in primary and secondary depression. *Archives of General Psychiatry, 34,* 98–111.

Weissman, M.M., Bruce, M.L., Leaf, P.J., Florio, L.P., & Holzer, C. III. (1991). Affective disorders. In L.N. Robins & D.A. Regier (Eds.), *Psychiatric disorders in America* (pp. 53–80). New York: Free Press.

Welner, Z, Welner, A, McCrary, M.D., & Leonard, M.A. (1977). Psychopathology in children of inpatients with depression: A controlled study. *Journal of Nervous and Mental Disease, 164,* 408–413.

Whiffen, V.E., & Gotlib, I.H. (1989). Infants of postpartum depressed mothers: Temperament and cognitive status. *Journal of Abnormal Psychology, 98,* 274–279.

Winokur, G., Coryell, W., Endicott, J., & Akiskal, H. (1993a). Further distinctions between manic-depressive illness (bipolar disorder) and primary depressive disorder (unipolar depression). *American Journal of Psychiatry, 150,* 1176–1181.

Winokur, G., Coryell, W., Keller, M., Endicott, J., & Akiskal, H. (1993b). A prospective follow-up of patients with bipolar and unipolar affective disorder. *Archives of General Psychiatry, 50,* 457–465.

Winokur, G., Tsuang, M.T., & Crowe, R.R. (1982). The Iowa 500: Affective disorder in the relatives of manic and depressed patients. *American Journal of Psychiatry, 139,* 209–212.

Young, M.A., Scheftner, W.A., Klerman, G.L., Andreason, N.C., & Hirschfeld, R.M.A. (1986). The endogenous sub-type of depression: A study of its internal construct validity. *British Journal of Psychiatry, 148,* 257–267.

Zimmerman, M., & Spitzer, R.L. (1989). Melancholia: From DSM-III to DSM-III-R. *American Journal of Psychiatry, 146,* 20–28.

Zis, A.P., & Goodwin, F.K. (1979). Major affective disorder as a recurrent illness: A critical review. *Archives of General Psychiatry, 36,* 835–839.

CHAPTER 12

SCHIZOPHRENIA: ETIOLOGY

John Sweeney
Gretchen Haas
Vishwajit Nimgaonkar
University of Pittsburgh Medical School

INTRODUCTION

Efforts to identify the causes of schizophrenia have been one of the most active areas of psychopathology research. Following the confident assertions of several prominent neurologists (Alzheimer, 1897; Griesinger, 1857), it was generally accepted early in the 20th century that schizophrenia was a direct result of degenerative abnormalities in the brain. In the 1950s and 1960s, after several decades of inconclusive biological studies, the question of interest turned to whether disturbances in family interaction were the primary cause of this disorder (Bateson, Jackson, Haley, & Weakland, 1956; Lidz, Cornelison, & Fleck, 1958). Currently available data do not support this causal hypothesis, although psychosocial factors such as critical and overinvolved family interaction patterns appear to influence the course of the illness.

Most currently accepted etiological models of schizophrenia emphasize biological factors such as genetics, abnormalities of brain physiology or anatomy in adult life, and abnormalities in brain devel-

opment (Feinberg, 1983; Weinberger, 1987). Brain-imaging research has provided persuasive evidence in support of biological models of the pathophysiology of the disorder. The fact that antipsychotic medications reduce psychotic symptoms and prevent relapse, together with the demonstration that the efficacy of neuroleptics is mediated largely by their impact on the dopamine neurotransmitter system, offer convincing evidence that biological dysfunctions are central to the illness.

The idea that the etiology of schizophrenia rests in a brain dysfunction, together with data from twin and other family studies showing an increased risk for illness in family members of affected patients, has stimulated interest in heritable/genetic factors that might increase risk for the illness. Clinical observations of social and cognitive problems in close relatives of schizophrenic patients also have contributed to hypotheses about a genetic cause of the illness. In fact, soon after Kraepelin argued for the separation of the clinical syndromes of schizophrenia and affective disorders, one of his students conducted the first family study of schizophrenia (Rudin, 1916). Over three-quarters of a century of work, the role of a familial/genetic contribution to risk for schizophrenia has received widespread support.

The relative importance and interrelationship of genetic, central nervous system (CNS) trauma, and psychosocial factors in the etiology of this disorder are not now known. Progress toward answering these questions, however, has proceeded at a rapid pace in recent years. The focus of this chapter will be on reviewing this literature and on introducing key concepts pertaining to neurobiological, genetic, and psychosocial models of schizophrenia.

MAJOR SCIENTIFIC QUESTIONS

In recent years, many significant advances have been achieved through biological and psychosocial studies of schizophrenia, and these offer several promising leads about the etiology of schizophrenia. In several areas, advances have followed from the availability of new scientific methods and enhanced knowledge about brain function. Sophisticated neuroimaging techniques have offered increased potential for noninvasive study of the brain in living humans, including the study of brain anatomy, metabolism, neurotransmitter systems, and changes in neuronal activity during cognitive operations. Other technical developments have permitted the study of a wider array of biochemical measures in blood and cerebrospinal fluid, and the identification and localization of genetic abnormalities. At the same time, however, unanswered questions regarding the fundamental nature of schizophrenia, and about normal brain physiology and development, continue to limit our ability to answer questions about the etiology of the illness. Questions regarding biological processes and abnormalities related to schizophrenia may need to be addressed, and at least partially answered, before a systematic progression of studies will identify the ultimate causes of this illness. Examples of such questions follow.

1. *How does the normal brain function?* Explanatory biological models attempting to define the etiology of gross clinical phenomena such as thought disorder and delusions on the basis of a specific isolated biochemical abnormality, such as high levels of a particular neurotransmitter (e.g., dopamine) or low levels of cerebral metabolic activity in a specific area of the brain, are limited by the complexity and interaction of neural systems. More detailed understanding from the basic neurosciences about normal brain development and physiology, and more refined knowledge from cognitive neuroscience regarding the biological substrate of cognitive processes, are needed to develop a comprehensive model of schizophrenia that explains the disorder from the level of molecular biology; to brain physiology; to disturbances in specific cognitive, behavioral, and emotional processes; and, ultimately, to symptom expression. Efforts to explain the causes of schizophrenia by attempting to leap across the gap from the level of molecular biology or biochemistry to that of clinical syndromes may require more than a fair amount of good fortune to be successful (Holzman, 1987).

2. *Is schizophrenia a single disorder, or is it a syndrome caused by several different disease processes with different etiologies?* Questions about the heterogeneity (both clinical and etiological) of schizophrenia need to be resolved. It is not yet clear whether the syndrome of schizophrenia has a single major cause or whether it is a final common pathway for different disease processes. Studies are needed to determine whether there are large and distinguishable subgroups of patients with different primary etiologic factors. If such etiological heterogeneity exists, studies of any specific cause(s) of the disorder will need first to identify the specific subgroups of patients in which the parameter of interest is etiologically important. Developments in statistical methodologies for determining whether qualitatively different subgroups of patients comprise a clinically defined syndrome are needed to facilitate this effort (Pauler, Escobar, Sweeney, & Greenhouse, 1996).

3. *What clinical criteria should be used to identify an individual as affected with schizophrenia?* With the development of criteria-based diagnoses in DSM-III, the clinical diagnosis of schizophrenia became more reliable and standardized across settings. However, even the best available conventional clinical diagnostic procedures still define crudely characterized syndromes having "fuzzy" boundaries with other disorders. In selecting affected cases for etiological studies (i.e., individuals meeting criteria for schi-

zophrenia), it is not yet clear whether the definition should include cases with serious personality disorders (such as schizotypal personality disorder), or all cases of nonaffective psychoses (which would include, for example, delusional disorder), or only cases with more narrowly defined schizophrenia.

Modifications in diagnostic practice (such as the addition of negative symptoms to the diagnosis of schizophrenia in DSM-III-R) cause some inconsistency across etiological studies, because conclusions are derived from the use of different diagnostic classification systems. Shifts in diagnostic practice from DSM-II, to DSM-III, to DSM-III-R, and ultimately to DSM-IV, have progressively changed the diagnostic criteria for schizophrenia so as to include a smaller group of more severely ill individuals with higher levels of chronicity and severity of functional impairment. Changes that significantly redefine the diagnostic classification of schizophrenia, together with ongoing uncertainty as to what clinical characteristics define the schizophrenic phenotype, complicate interpretation of etiological research.

Several basic questions related to diagnostic classification need to be resolved. For example, current diagnostic practice emphasizes serious positive symptoms (such as hallucinations and delusions) more than long-standing pervasive negative symptoms (e.g., impairments in social and other functional aspects of role functioning). These two clinical dimensions of schizophrenia may not prove to be caused by the same factors (as proposed by Crow, 1982). If diagnostic practice emphasizes one aspect of the syndrome more than others, then etiological research studying correlates of a schizophrenic diagnosis may determine the causes of one aspect of the syndrome but not others, or of some cases more than others.

4. *What psychobiological abnormalities are primary in schizophrenia?* The development of knowledge regarding basic psychobiological abnormalities associated with the disorder is needed to focus etiological studies. In simple terms, the yield of etiologic studies is likely to be increased if they are undertaken to identify the cause of a specific pathological process rather than the presence of a broadly defined clinical syndrome.

Advances in studies of the etiology of this disorder will depend on improved clinical classification procedures, determining whether there are large subgroups of patients with different causes of illness, and the development of well-validated psychobiological markers of risk for the illness that can identify high-risk individuals prior to illness onset. An integrated multidisciplinary effort is needed to bring expertise from many areas of scientific research to bear on efforts to understand the causes of schizophrenia. For the same reasons, acquiring a broad understanding of the origins of schizophrenia has come to require familiarity with neuroscience; molecular and behavioral genetics; epidemiology; and cognitive, clinical, and social psychology. For psychologists, this commonly involves learning basic concepts of neurobiology and genetics in order to evaluate evidence bearing on what etiological factors play a role in causing this illness. Among geneticists, there is a growing recognition that phenotypic characterization and identification of psychobiologic risk markers can be a complex multistage process.

PSYCHOBIOLOGY OF SCHIZOPHRENIA

Developments in biomedical research technology over the past two decades have provided tools that neuroscientists can use to conduct detailed noninvasive studies of the central nervous system. Investigators have utilized increasingly more accurate neuroimaging procedures to identify structural anatomic brain abnormalities using computed tomography (CT) (Weinberger, 1984) and, more recently, magnetic resonance imaging (MRI) (Andreasen et al., 1990; Gur & Pearlson, 1993; Shenton et al., 1992).

CT scanning uses radiation (X-rays) to provide brain images. MRI, which has higher resolution than CT, uses a high-strength magnetic field to orient hydrogen atoms in the brain, permitting their resonant echo to radio frequency pulses to be detected and used to construct images of brain anatomy. The high resolution of MRI is important for studying subtle neuroanatomic abnormalities associated with psychiatric disorders, particularly those in small structures of the limbic system, thalamus, and basal ganglia (Andreasen et al., 1994; Bogerts et al., 1993).

The physiological dysfunctions of the brain in schizophrenia have been studied by a range of techniques, including: regional cerebral blood flow (rCBF) with xenon inhalation, positron emission tomography (PET) used to localize abnormalities in cerebral glucose metabolism and to study specific neurotransmitter receptors, studies of regional changes in brain activity in different cognitive conditions with functional magnetic resonance imaging (fMRI) or PET, and computerized studies of EEG to study localization of evoked cortical responses to sensory stimuli. In addition, sophisticated quantitative neurohistology has been performed on postmortem brain samples to search for neuronal abnormalities in different brain regions.

Neuroanatomic/Neuroimaging Studies

The degree of resolution available with brain imaging procedures has been greatly enhanced over the past decade. CT and MRI scanning procedures are commonly available in hospital settings for medical diagnostic purposes. They generate a series of two-dimensional images of brain tissue from one end of the brain to the other, as if segments of brain were progressively sliced off, leaving the remaining internal structure of the brain to be viewed. If contiguous slices are acquired, the images can be combined into a three-dimensional structure permitting true volumetric measurement of brain regions of interest.

The most common initial methodology used in studies using CT and MRI brain-scanning studies was to measure the lateral ventricles of the brain. The cerebral ventricles hold cerebrospinal fluid and play an important role in removing metabolic by-products from the brain. They are C-shaped structures, one in each hemisphere, which are large and have relatively easily distinguished boundaries with adjacent brain tissue so they can be easily measured. Because ventricular fluid is under pressure, the ventricles enlarge to fill space once occupied by neural tissue when neural cell loss occurs. For this reason, aggregate ventricle size serves as a gross index of degenerative changes, or perhaps neurodevelopmental abnormality, in brain. The degree of ventricular enlargement has been shown to have a moderate relationship to severity of cognitive and behavioral deficits in schizophrenic patients (Andreasen et al., 1986; Keilp et al., 1988).

While the presence of ventricular enlargement has been reported in many studies, definitive interpretation of the finding is mitigated by several factors

(Weinberger, 1984). First, many schizophrenic patients do not show any clear signs of structural brain abnormalities, which raises the possibility that enlargement of cerebral ventricles may be an abnormality associated with a subgroup of perhaps more chronically ill deteriorated schizophrenic patients. Second, similar observations have been reported in cases of bipolar affective disorder (Rieder, Mann, Weinberger, van Kammen, & Post, 1983), which raises questions as to the specificity of this abnormality to schizophrenia. Third, it is unclear what the origin of this apparently static brain change may be. Although the finding played an important role by providing the first widely replicated direct observation of a brain abnormality in schizophrenia, it is not clear whether the observation represents early-life periventricular pathology, or some degenerative change that may occur either as part of an abnormal brain development during adolescence or over the early course of illness.

The higher resolution of MR images has permitted more detailed analyses of brain anatomy than were possible with CT scans. For example, Zipursky and colleagues (Zipursky, Lim, Sullivan, Brown, & Pfefferbaum, 1992) reported widespread reduction of gray matter (cell bodies and local circuit axons and dendrites), but not in white matter (the pathways of connectivity across brain regions). Specific abnormalities have been identified in temporal cortex (Suddath et al., 1989), particularly the left superior temporal gyrus (Barta, Pearlson, Powers, Richards, & Tune, 1990), amygdala-hippocampal formation (Bogerts et al., 1993; Marsh, Suddath, Higgins, & Weinberger, 1994), basal ganglia (Jernigan et al., 1991), and thalamus (Andreasen et al., 1994). Some of these anatomic abnormalities have been related to cognitive, clinical and electrophysiological abnormalities in the disorder (McCarley et al., 1993; Seidman et al., 1994).

Neurohistology Studies

Studying postmortem brain tissue from schizophrenic patients has the advantage of permitting fine microscopic analysis of brain neurons, and more detailed biochemical investigation of receptors for different neurotransmitter systems in different brain regions. Brown et al. (1986) reported that brains of schizophrenics were 6% lighter and had lateral ventricles larger in both the anterior (by 19%) and temporal (by 97%) horn cross-sections than control brains—a finding that parallels the findings of neuroimaging studies.

Bogerts et al. (Bogerts, Meertz, & Schonfeldt-Bausch, 1985) conducted volumetric studies of myelin-stained serial sections of brains from 13 schizophrenic patients, and demonstrated considerable shrinkage of limbic structures (hippocampal formation, amygdala, and parahippocampal gyrus). These brain areas are important in short-term memory and the mediation of emotional experience. This group of investigators later reported a 27% reduction of volume in entorhinal cortex (cortex of the temporal lobe adjacent to the hippocampus) in schizophrenic cases that was associated with a 37% reduction in the number of neurons, but not with any increase in the number of glial cells (Falkai, Bogerts, & Rozumek, 1988). Glial cells, which surround and support neurons in brain, proliferate in areas where neuronal cell loss occurs to essentially fill the space once occupied by the nerve cells. The absence of glial proliferation suggests that the neuronal changes represent an abnormality of brain development (such as the migration of neurons to the correct location in brain or excessive developmental pruning of neurons) in medial temporal lobe structures rather than a degenerative loss of brain neurons. This inference is consistent with reports by Arnold and colleagues (Arnold, Hyman, Van Hoesen, & Damasio, 1991) of aberrant invaginations of the cortical surface and disruption of cortical layers in this region, and the Jakob and Beckmann (1986) report of abnormal sulcal and gyral configurations of temporal cortex that probably represent neurodevelopmental anomalies.

Significant abnormalities have been reported in several other brain areas. Weinberger, Kleinman, Luchins, Bigelow, and Wyatt (1980) and others have reported a reduction in the size of the cerebellar vermis. Pakkenberg (1990) reported reduced cell number in the nucleus accumbens and mediodorsal thalamic nucleus. Cell disorientation disarray (an abnormal orientation of neuronal processes relative to local anatomy) has been observed in the hippocampus (Conrad, Abebe, Austin, Forsythe, & Scheibel, 1991). Benes and colleagues (Benes, McSparren, Bird, SanGiovanni, & Vincent, 1991) reported a reduction of inhibitory interneurons in prefrontal and cingulate cortex. Questions about areas where localized changes in brain structure and function are most pronounced, and about the clinical significance of such changes, are only beginning to be addressed.

A relatively small number of postmortem neurochemistry studies have been completed to examine regional disturbances in neurotransmitter systems. Studies have identified abnormalities in dopamine receptors from the striatum (Kornhuber et al., 1989), serotonin receptors in prefrontal cortex (Laruelle et al., 1993), GABA receptors in cingulate cortex (Benes, Vincent, Alsterberg, Bird, & SanGiovanni, 1992), and cortical NMDA-associated glycine binding sites (Ishimaru, Kurumaji, & Toru, 1994).

Brain Metabolism Studies

PET studies of resting-state glucose utilization have been conducted to localize areas of regional hypometabolism—that is, reduced regional resting-state neuronal activity. Reduced metabolism in prefrontal cortex has been associated with negative symptom severity (Wolkin et al., 1992; Dolan et al., 1993), and it appears to be related to metabolic disturbances in the striatum (Buchsbaum et al., 1992). This reduced frontal activity has been referred to as *hypofrontality*. Liddle and colleagues have proposed that psychomotor poverty is related to reduced flow in left dorsolateral frontal cortex and cingulate, that a right ventral prefrontal syndrome is associated with psychological disorganization, and that a left parahippocampal abnormality is associated with reality distortion (Liddle et al., 1992). The abnormality in frontal activation appears greatest when patients are performing a cognitive task requiring activation of prefrontal cortex (Franzen & Ingvar, 1975; Weinberger, Berman, & Zec, 1986), such as the Wisconsin Card Sorting Test. In discordant monozygotic twins, abnormal frontal activation during the card sort test, in unaffected twins, was related to their left hippocampal volume; in affected twins, it was related to both left and right hippocampal volume. This suggests a relationship between anatomic changes in the hippocampus and physiologic abnormalities in prefrontal cortex. Some data suggests that disrupted dopaminergic modulation may contribute to disruption of task-related activation in the anterior cingulate region of frontal cortex (Dolan et al., 1995). Daniel et al. (1991) reported that administration of an amphetamine dopamine agonist increased task-related activation in prefrontal cortex in schizophrenic patients during the Wisconsin Card Sort Test. Not all studies have identified frontal lobe pathology. Gur et al. (1995) reported increased midtemporal metabolism, not hypofrontality, in acutely ill schizophrenic patients, as well as an increased overall subcortical-to-cortical metabolism ratio.

Dopamine Studies

Probably the most widely accepted biochemical abnormality of schizophrenia is that increased activity in dopaminergic neurons (neurons using dopamine as a neurotransmitter) is associated with acute psychosis (positive symptoms such as delusions and hallucinations). The strongest support for this model is indirect and pharmacological. Antipsychotic medications are believed to exert their therapeutic action by binding to postsynaptic dopamine receptors, reducing the rate of neurotransmission across synapses and thereby preventing dopamine from binding to adjacent neurons. Parallel data indicate that drugs that increase dopaminergic activity (e.g., amphetamine) can produce a paranoid psychosis similar in many ways to that seen in acute paranoid schizophrenia (Angrist, 1983). Because reducing dopaminergic activity reduces hallucinations and delusions, and dopamine agonists (drugs which increase dopamine activity) increase these symptoms, many have inferred that increased dopaminergic activity is probably a major component of the biology of psychosis.

More direct evidence for a dopaminergic dysfunction in schizophrenia comes from clinical studies showing increased levels of the dopamine metabolite, homovanillic acid (HVA) in cerebral spinal fluid (CSF) and blood plasma (Davis et al., 1985; Pickar et al., 1984), and from PET studies and postmortem studies of brain tissue showing increased numbers of dopamine receptors in brain. Relatively few PET studies of dopamine receptors have been conducted in schizophrenia. Wong et al. (1986) reported elevated dopamine receptor density in the striatum of a sample of subjects with schizophrenia, but this effect has not been consistently replicated (Sedvall, 1992).

In sum, evidence regarding dopamine in schizo-

phrenia is overwhelmingly supportive of the role of this system as the site of therapeutic action of antipsychotic drugs, but is less convincing with regard to whether this abnormality is involved in the primary pathology of the illness. To some extent, this uncertainty about the role of dopaminergic abnormalities in schizophrenia results from the complexity of the dopamine system. The neurobiology of dopaminergic brain systems involves different types of dopamine receptors that have different patterns of distribution throughout the brain. For example, D_1 receptors are more common in frontal cortex, and D_2 receptors are more common in the basal ganglia. Also, although some neurotransmitters have a relatively homogeneous presence throughout the cerebral cortex, dopaminergic innervation is more prominent in anterior cortex (particularly the frontal lobes) than in posterior cortex. However, the specific physiologic functions of dopaminergic tracts in frontal cortex, and how these might be associated with schizophrenia, are not yet understood.

Several neurobiological questions remain to be answered:

1. Do the structural neuroanatomic changes occurring in schizophrenia represent a developmental disturbance or a degenerative one?
2. Are structural anatomic changes or physiologic dysfunctions limited primarily to specific areas of the brain?
3. Do positive symptoms of the disorder (e.g., hallucinations and delusions) and negative or deficit symptoms (e.g., reduced volition and social interest) result from different disease processes?
4. Are dopaminergic disturbances central to the pathophysiology of the illness, or are they secondary responses to other primary brain abnormalities?

GENETIC FACTORS

Genetic studies are attractive in the search for the etiology of schizophrenia because their role as causative agents is unquestioned. Classical genetic investigations of human diseases follow a logical sequence: (1) evidence that genetic factors have an etiological role for the disease in question; (2) information about the mode of inheritance; (3) search for genetic markers located physically close to the disease gene, using information about the mode of inheritance; and (4) identification of the disease gene. Such an orderly sequence is not always followed. For example, a genetic etiology for schizophrenia is well accepted, but the mode of inheritance is unclear. In spite of this difficulty, the search for genetic markers is continuing apace.

Traditionally, etiological investigations pit genetic factors against nongenetic (environmental) factors in a simplistic dichotomy. Such an approach has stimulated a vigorous ongoing debate in relation to schizophrenia, often at the cost of ignoring possible gene–environment interactions (Gottesman, 1991). Even so, the genetic etiology of schizophrenia has been established following family, twin, and adoption studies.

Family studies have been unanimous in demonstrating familial clustering for schizophrenia. Approximately 15% to 25% of individuals diagnosed with schizophrenia have a first- and/or a second-degree relative with a history of schizophrenia (Kendler et al., 1993b; Baron, 1985). Because the risk for schizophrenia is dependent on age, morbid risk—a measure that reflects the prevalence corrected for the age of the relative in question—is more appropriate. The morbid risk among first-degree relatives such as children, parents, and siblings varies between 6% and 17%. It falls off significantly to approximately 2% to 6% among second-degree relatives such as uncles and aunts, grandchildren, grandparents, and half-siblings (Gottesman, 1991).

Interestingly, a range of other psychiatric conditions is also encountered more frequently among relatives of individuals with schizophrenia. These include psychotic illnesses such as schizoaffective disorder, other affective and nonaffective psychoses, and severe personality disorders such as schizotypal personality disorder (Kendler et al., 1993a). On the assumption that the familial clustering reflects an inherited predisposition, it has even been argued that all psychotic disorders have a common genetic etiology (Crow, 1986). This simplistic formulation has been widely disputed. The view that separate genetic factors for schizophrenia and bipolar disorder exist is more favored (McGuffin, Owen, O'Donovan, Thapar, & Gottesman, 1994). However, etiological relationships between schizophrenia and schizoaffective

disorder remain conjectural. On the other hand, the increased clustering of schizotypal, schizoid, and paranoid personality disorder among relatives of probands with schizophrenia is thought to be due to shared genetic factors, since such aggregation is not observed among relatives of unscreened controls or cases with affective psychoses (Kendler et al., 1993a; Webb & Levinson, 1993). The term *schizophrenia spectrum disorders* has been coined to include such conditions.

An increased prevalence of neurobehavioral abnormalities among unaffected relatives of schizophrenic patients has also been observed. These include deficits in smooth pursuit eye movements (Levy, Holzman, Matthysse, & Mendell, 1994; Clementz & Sweeney, 1990), attention (Erlenmeyer-Kimling, 1987), and neurological abnormalities called *soft neurological signs* (Kinney, Woods, & Yurgelun-Todd, 1986). These findings are persuasive not only because they have been replicated, but because the observed abnormalities among relatives are not confounded by factors such as psychoactive medication. Because these abnormalities are quantifiable, they have added considerable impetus to genetic studies in schizophrenia. They have helped crystallize the notion of *latent trait* markers for schizophrenia—characteristics that occupy an intermediate position in the chain of events initiated by the underlying genetic abnormality and culminating in the observed psychopathology among clinical cases. Such markers may also occur in lieu of the psychiatric abnormalities, as seen among relatives of affected probands (Matthysse, Holzman, & Lange, 1986).

Intriguingly, familial clustering of nonpsychiatric diseases within families with a schizophrenic patient may also exist. For example, studies have suggested an increased prevalence of autoimmune diseases such as insulin-dependent diabetes mellitus (IDDM) and thyrotoxicosis among relatives of probands with schizophrenia (DeLisi et al., 1991; Ganguli, Rabin, Kelly, Lyte, & Ragu, 1987; Wright et al., 1995b). Taken together with the numerous reports suggesting an inverse relationship in the prevalence of schizophrenia and rheumatoid arthritis, another autoimmune disease (Vinogradov, Gottesman, Moises, & Nicol, 1991), as well as diverse reports suggesting an autoimmune pathology in schizophrenia, it has been suggested that schizophrenia may share etiologic factors with established autoimmune diseases (Ganguli, Brar, & Rabin, 1994; Heath & Krupp, 1967; Knight, 1982).

Claims for a genetic etiology based solely on family studies ignore the likelihood that families share environmental factors. Studies among twins have been helpful in this regard. Monozygotic (MZ) twins share virtually all their genetic characteristics, and dizygotic (DZ) twins share half, on average. If the first of a series of MZ and DZ twins are affected with a disease caused solely by a genetic mutation, the concordance rates for the disease would be 100% among the MZ twins and 50% among the DZ twins. Assuming similar environments for the twins, the difference in concordance rates would reflect the difference in shared genetic factors between MZ and DZ twins. On the basis of published data on Caucasians in Europe and the United States, Gottesman concluded that the overall concordance rates for MZ and DZ twins are 48% and 17%, respectively (Gottesman, 1991). Indeed, all published studies to date have detected significant MZ–DZ differences in concordance rates, providing compelling evidence for a genetic etiology.

The observed MZ–DZ concordance rates fall short of the predictions solely on the basis of a genetic etiology. What can be made of this? The discrepancies support a significant role for environmental factors. In a recent study, the offspring of MZ twins discordant for schizophrenia were followed up (Gottesman & Bertelsen, 1989). The morbid risks for schizophrenia were similar among the offspring of affected and unaffected members of these pairs, in support of an earlier study (Fischer, 1971). Thus, even the unaffected MZ twins appear to have transmitted an increased predisposition to schizophrenia. Failure to manifest the illness among such individuals may be attributable to lack of exposure to "toxic" environmental factors or, alternatively, to exposure to "protective" environmental factors.

Other twin studies have highlighted a genetic basis for abnormalities associated with schizophrenia. The most commonly investigated variable is age at onset of the illness. There is a significant correlation for age of onset among members with schizophrenia in multiply affected pedigrees (Taylor, 1990). The correlation is stronger among affected siblings (Abe, 1966) and even stronger among monozygotic twins concor-

dant for schizophrenia (Kendler, Tsuang, & Hays, 1987). On the basis of these findings, it has been concluded that a significant genetic predisposition to age of onset exists and is probably independent of the gene or genes predisposing to schizophrenia per se (Neale et al., 1989). Twin studies have also suggested that genetic factors may influence brain ventricular size (Reveley, Reveley, & Murray, 1984), another abnormality that is increased among patients with schizophrenia, as was discussed.

Twin studies have also clarified another important controversy. Early family studies did not use reliable operationalized diagnostic criteria, a shortcoming that has been criticized. It has even been suggested that samples selected using prototypic diagnostic criteria do not yield significant evidence for a genetic etiology (Pope, Jonas, Cohen, & Lipinski, 1982). Although more recent studies using DSM-III criteria have contradicted this view (Kendler, Gruenberg, & Tsuang, 1985), the validity of newer diagnostic criteria from a genetic standpoint may be questioned. In a novel strategy, differences in concordance between MZ and DZ twins using different diagnostic criteria for schizophrenia have been made (Farmer, McGuffin, & Gottesman, 1987; McGuffin, Farmer, Gottesman, Murray, & Reveley, 1984). The most valid diagnostic scheme from the genetic perspective would yield the highest heritability values calculated from the concordance values. The Research Diagnostic Criteria (RDC; Spitzer, Endicott, & Robins, 1977) provided the highest values, whereas the Schneiderian First Rank Symptoms were unsatisfactory. DSM-III criteria yielded values comparable to RDC if the following diagnoses were included along with schizophrenia: affective disorder with mood incongruent delusions, atypical psychosis, and schizotypal personality disorder. This analysis has been extended to DSM-III-R criteria, but not yet to DSM-IV criteria (Onstad, Skre, Torgersen, & Kringlen, 1991).

Twin studies presume that MZ and DZ twins have similar environments. This unproved assumption may be resolved by investigating concordance rates among twins reared apart. Such studies are difficult, but the available evidence does not negate the MZ–DZ difference in concordance (Gottesman, 1991). The role of the shared environment in disease predisposition is investigated more easily through adoption studies. Adoption studies investigate the risk of schizophrenia among biological relatives of affected probands from whom they were separated through adoption. Such studies include studies of adopted-away offspring of ill individuals and analyses of biological relatives of individuals who became ill following adoption. The cross-fostering design involves investigation of risk to individuals adopted into households with an affected foster parent (Wender et al., 1974). Adoption studies to date have unanimously supported a genetic predisposition (see review by Gottesman, 1991). A recently concluded adoption study of a national sample of adoptees in Denmark is particularly compelling (Kety & Ingraham, 1992).

If the genetic basis for schizophrenia is accepted, the next step is to identify the mode of inheritance. Here, considerable disagreement exists. Autosomal dominant and recessive modes of inheritance have been suggested (Slater, 1958; Hurst, 1972). The possibility of genetic heterogeneity (i.e., the same psychopathology being produced by different genes) cannot be excluded (Baron, 1985). Such competing hypotheses may be resolved by comparing the observed patterns of illness among selected pedigrees with patterns predicted by each model. This method, called *complex segregation analysis,* has consistently rejected the monogenic models when published family and twin data are analyzed (Carter & Chung, 1980; Rao, Morton, Gottesman, & Lew, 1981). Therefore, alternatives such as the multifactorial polygenic threshold (MFPT) model have to be considered.

The polygenic model proposes the presence of several disease genes that interact. The closely related MFPT model proposes, in addition, a threshold of liability beyond which the illness occurs. In a given individual, the threshold can be attained by the presence of varying combinations of alleles at different disease-predisposing loci, with or without the presence of environmental stressors (Falconer, 1965). It is important to note that in the MFPT model, each gene individually may not be necessary or sufficient to produce disease (Hodge, 1993). Several findings in schizophrenia support the MFPT model: e.g., the absence of full concordance among monozygotic twins, a gradation in severity of the illness among probands, a sharp drop in frequency of illness from first- to second- to third-degree relatives, increased frequency of illness among relatives of more severely ill probands, and

the increased risk to offspring with larger number of ill members in a pedigree (Gottesman & Shields, 1967). Although the MFPT model has substantial explanatory power, it does not predict the number of susceptibility genes a priori. Finally, a combined or "ecumenical" model has been suggested (Gottesman, 1991). This model envisages monogenic, polygenic/MFPT, and nongenetic causes in different groups of ill individuals. Under this scenario, polygenic/MFPT modes of inheritance would be attributable to the majority of patients. Such a formulation lacks parsimony but, on balance, appears most likely.

Uncertainty about the mode of inheritance is compounded by the enormity of the task at hand. The human genome is estimated to have perhaps 1,000,000 genes, one or more of which may be involved in schizophrenia genesis. On the other hand, breathtaking advances in molecular genetic techniques, availability of DNA markers, and advances in computing techniques have occurred over the past 3 decades (DeLisi & Lovett, 1990; Gejman & Gelernte, 1993; Kaufmann & Malaspina, 1991). Such advances have enabled the dissection of the genetic etiology of diseases with complex modes of inheritance, such as insulin-dependent diabetes mellitus and Hirschsprung's disease (Angrist et al., 1993; Davies et al., 1994). Therefore, it is not unreasonable to be optimistic about similar success with regard to schizophrenia.

Broadly, two strategies are available in the search for disease-predisposing genes: linkage studies and association studies. If an allele (variant) of a marker gene segregates with the illness (i.e., is inherited along with the illness in a family), it is said to be *linked* to the disease gene. In other words, the locus for the marker gene probably occurs close to the disease gene locus. This technique has been spectacularly successful for diseases with monogenic inheritance, such as Huntington's disease and cystic fibrosis (Gusella et al., 1983; Kerem et al., 1989). Presuming a single gene model for schizophrenia, some workers have used large multigenerational families with multiple affected members for linkage studies. Several groups are currently conducting linkage and analysis using highly polymorphic markers throughout the genome. This strategy is dogged by methodological problems, such as uncertainties about the mode of inheritance and the possibility of genetic heterogeneity (Pauls, 1993). Despite its shortcomings, however, the classical linkage approach may be useful for localizing rare monogenic variants of schizophrenia, especially among genetically isolated populations. Of note is a recent report of linkage to markers on the long arm of chromosome 22 (22q12–q13), which was first reported from linkage studies in multigenerational U.S. families (Pulver, Karayiorgou, & Wolyniec, 1994). However, this effect could not be replicated in two other studies.

Faced with uncertainties about the mode of inheritance of schizophrenia, workers have resorted to "model-free" linkage methods. These strategies do not require assumptions about the mode of inheritance. The *affected sib-pair* method, which is currently popular, is restricted to nuclear families with two or more affected siblings (Penrose, 1935; Weeks & Lange, 1988). Allele sharing at a given locus is measured among pairs of affected siblings. Deviation from expected frequencies suggests linkage to the locus. The affected sib-pair strategy has several advantages over conventional linkage analysis of large multigenerational pedigrees, besides being free of assumptions about the mode of inheritance. Because only affected members are included in the analysis, problems related to uncertainties about the future status of currently well members does not arise. Unlike linkage analysis involving large pedigrees, it also can be used to study disorders with a presumed polygenic form of inheritance, provided the contribution from a given locus is relatively large (Suarez, Van Eerdewegh, & Hampe, 1991). It has been used for analysis of quantitative traits (Fulker, Cherny, & Cardon, 1995). Finally, this method can be used even when there is assortative mating in the parental generation (Sribney & Swift, 1992).

The affected sib-pair method has already proved fruitful in the analysis of linkage between HLA haplotypes and insulin-dependent diabetes mellitus (Davies et al., 1994). Other diseases examined thus include Hodgkin's disease, multiple sclerosis, coeliac disease, leprosy, and hemochromatosis (Risch, 1987). Using this method, a pseudoautosomal telomeric locus for the schizophrenia susceptibility gene has been proposed, but replication has been difficult (Collinge et al., 1991; d'Amato et al., 1991).

Great excitement has been engendered by recent reports of linkage to markers on the short arm of chromosome 6 (6p22–p24), which was first detected

in a large sample of small nuclear Irish families (Wang et al., 1995). Supportive evidence has since been presented in an enlarged cohort and by other groups using the affected sib-pair method (Straub, Maclean, Walsh, & Kendler, 1995; Maier et al., 1996). Other groups have not detected linkage, but this may arguably be due to insufficient sample size. Refinement of the linkage findings is in progress (Pulver et al., 1996). Nevertheless, linkage to the chromosome 6 markers accounts for only 20% to 30% of the variance attributable to genetic factors, and the region of susceptibility extends over a large genetic distance (20 cM) (Maier et al., 1996). Parenthetically, linkage analysis of a large German pedigree suggested linkage between abnormalities in smooth pursuit eye movements (SPEM) and markers in this region (Arolt et al., 1995). These findings lend support to the notion that SPEM abnormality may be a latent trait marker for schizophrenia (Matthysse et al., 1986).

The association strategy, which complements the linkage approach, involves the study of genetic markers in ill individuals compared with matched controls (Mourant, Kopec, & Domaniewska-Sobczak, 1978). Unlike linkage studies, association studies involve unrelated individuals. If the allele frequency of a marker gene is significantly different in the disease state, the allele is said to be "associated" with the disease. Associations can occur either because the marker gene itself is the disease gene, or because an allele of the marker gene and the mutant gene are so close physically that they are inherited together at the population level.

Association studies have used numerous inherited traits before the availability of molecular genetic markers (McGuffin & Sturt, 1986). Recently, polymorphisms of genes have been examined directly, e.g., genes regulating dopamine and serotonin receptors, pro-opiomelanocortin, neuropeptide Y, porphobilinogen deaminase, and GABA receptor subunits (Coon et al., 1994; Feder, Gurling, Darby, & Cavalli-Sforza, 1985; Nimgaonkar et al., 1995; Nimgaonkar, Zhang, Brar, DeLeo, & Ganguli, 1996). No robust association with the illness or its subgroups has yet been demonstrated (Owen, 1992), but, inconsistencies may be due to relatively small samples or inappropriate genetic markers (Kidd, 1993).

Because the precise pathophysiology of schizophrenia is unknown, it is difficult to identify markers for candidate genes that have a high probability of association. In this context, recent studies of human leukocyte antigen (HLA) markers have shown promise. Associations between HLA markers and several autoimmune diseases have been reported (Tiwari & Terasaki, 1985). Since abnormalities suggestive of autoimmune pathology have been reported (see above), an association between HLA and schizophrenia is plausible. Numerous early studies failed to detect consistent effects, possibly because accurate molecular genetic assays were unavailable. Recently, evidence for an association with the HLA DQB1 locus has been reported and replicated (Nimgaonkar, Rudert, Zhang, Trucco, & Ganguli, 1996). Others have reported associations with HLA DPB1 and HLA DRB1 loci (Wright et al., 1995a). These genes are physically close on the short arm of chromosome and are strongly linked. Interestingly, these loci are within the region of susceptibility identified from the chromosome 6 linkage studies described previously.

Inconsistencies in some of the association studies may also be due to inadequately matched controls. A case-control approach may help to avoid spurious associations. Matching with respect to racial origin and even socioeconomic status may be important. Even so, spurious associations can occur as a result of stratification following admixture between two or more populations with different gene frequencies. In the United States, this is a serious problem. For example, the proportion of Caucasian genes among African Americans has been estimated at 25% (Chakraborty, Kamboh, Nwankwo, & Ferrell, 1992).

To overcome such difficulties, Rubinstein has proposed a hypothetical control group: the alleles not inherited by the proband from his or her parents (Falk & Rubinstein, 1987). An unselected sample of cases are investigated, along with their parents. At each locus, the two parental alleles inherited, as well as the pair *not* inherited by the proband, can be identified. The noninherited alleles serve as controls. This simple *haplotype relative risk* strategy (HRR) ensures that both cases and controls come from the same genetic group. The HRR strategy is gaining popularity in psychiatric research (e.g., Todd, Chakraverty, & Parsian, 1994). However, some of the requirements for this approach, such as absence of assortative mating among the probands' parents and lack of differential fertility among the disease phenotype, may not be fulfilled in schizophrenia. Assortative mating has been well documented in this illness, and fertility among ill individuals may be related to both gender and illness severity (Slater, Hare, & Price, 1971). Finally, familial fragmentation and uncertain paternity may reduce the number of eligible family units.

In summary, a number of approaches are being used to pinpoint the genes that increase susceptibility to schizophrenia. Consistent patterns are beginning to emerge and regions of susceptibility on the human genome are being identified. Disease susceptibility loci on the long arm of chromosome 22 and on the short arm of chromosome 6 are promising given currently available data. The combined linkage/ association approach has been useful for the genetic dissection of neuropsychiatric disorders like Alzheimer's disease (Roses, 1995). Such successes augur well for research into genetic etiologic factors in schizophrenia.

ENVIRONMENTAL FACTORS

It has been recognized among genetic researchers that comprehensive etiologic models must take into account the joint contribution of genetic and environmental factors (Kendler & Eaves, 1986). Thus, contemporary models posit at least three fundamental pathways along which environmental factors could contribute to the etiology of one or more forms of schizophrenia:

1. As environmental *triggers,* physical and psychosocial stressors may precipitate onset of familial forms of the disorder.
2. As *causal agents,* deleterious organic or physical conditions or environmental events may produce a pathophysiologic abnormality that is causal in nonfamilial forms of schizophrenia (i.e., phenocopies; Kinney & Jacobsen, 1978).
3. As *moderating factors,* physical and psychosocial stressors may modulate the severity or phenotypic expression of the disorder.

Research on environmental risk factors in schizophrenia can be broadly divided into two general categories—*neurodevelopmental* and *psychosocial* factors. Neurodevelopmental factors of interest are those that can alter the course of normal brain development, such as biochemical toxins, psychoactive chemicals, viruses, and physical factors (e.g., extremes of temperature, geophysical events, variation in climate, season of birth). Psychosocial factors include both sociocultural conditions (e.g., cultural and socioeconomic factors) that may modulate the expression of the disorder and psychosocial stressors (e.g., stressful life events or more enduring psychosocial stressors) that are presumed to potentiate onset of illness in a genetically vulnerable individual.

Physical Environmental Factors

Epidemiologic studies have identified a number of nongenetic "risk" factors that tend to be observed more commonly among the histories of individuals with schizophrenia than among those from the general population. These include an elevated incidence of winter births, obstetric complications, and exposure to environmental toxins (e.g., influenza virus) that may be associated with increased vulnerability of the fetus to developmental deviation. Contemporary neurodevelopmental models of schizophrenia have implicated several of these variables as putative causal factors in the etiology of a subgroup of nonfamilial cases of schizophrenia.

Season of Birth

One of the oldest and most robust findings regarding environmental factors in the etiology of schizophrenia comes from data indicating that an excess of schizophrenic patients are born in the first 3 to 4 months of the year (January through April) (Dalen, 1975; McNeil, 1987). The excess of winter births (8% to 10%) among individuals who go on to develop schizophrenia has been presumed to represent a season-related risk for prenatal or perinatal complications (due to cold temperature, nutritional deficiencies, or infectious agents) that predispose to later schizophrenia.

However, the specific nature of the linkage of winter birth to schizophrenia has not been established. Kinney and Jacobsen (1978) observed that winter births were more common among cases at low genetic risk—and especially among those with *neither* known family history of schizophrenia *nor* postnatal brain injury. These investigators carried out comparisons of data from probands, biological siblings, par-

ents, and other psychiatric disorders to determine whether the season-of-birth finding was a spurious one related to some general factor. Their results indicated that season-of-birth effects were restricted to schizophrenic cases and were concentrated among cases with a low familial risk for schizophrenia. Several investigators have now replicated the Kinney and Jacobsen findings of disassociation between winter birth and family history of schizophrenia (McNeil, 1987; O'Callaghan et al., 1991; Roy, Flaum, & Andreasen, 1995).

Viral Disease Models of Schizophrenia

A growing body of data suggests that viral infections may act as triggering agents in some cases of schizophrenia—whether by directly producing a pathologic change in the brain or by triggering an autoimmune process in which antibodies to brain form and produce biochemical dysfunction. The season-of-birth data are often presented in association with the viral disease model, the argument being that individuals born during the winter months are more susceptible to diseases of viral origin. Given their potential for generating encephalitic illnesses, common viruses associated with influenza, mumps, and measles have been long regarded as possible etiologic agents for psychoses (Menninger, 1928). Evidence of deficient immune response to mumps virus in schizophrenia (King et al., 1985) and viral triggering of autoimmune disease have suggested that an autoimmune disorder may underlie some cases of schizophrenia.

Obstetric Complications

Obstetric complications (OCs) represent a heterogeneous group of irregularities occurring over the course of pregnancy, during labor and delivery, or in the early neonatal period of development. Substantial evidence suggests that OCs can have adverse effects on the normal growth and development of the human brain. Though controversial, a rather consistent finding is that OCs are associated with increased risk for the development of schizophrenia (Kendell, Juszczak, & Cole, 1996). McNeil (1987) reported an increased frequency of OCs among childhood schizophrenic patients as compared with a group of healthy (nonpsychiatric) control children. He also found a higher rate of OCs in the histories of adult schizophrenic patients as compared with their normal siblings. Finally, in a study of monozygotic twins discordant for schizophrenia, birth complications were more frequent in the more severely ill twin (Reveley, Reveley, & Murray, 1984).

The nature of the OC events among schizophrenic cases vary, although recent studies indicate an excess of preeclampsia and neonatal complications (Kendell et al., 1996). Specific OCs tend to occur with low frequency; hence, the presence or absence of a history of any OC and quantitative summary scores of OC severity have generally been used in research investigations. The pathogenic mechanism underlying the association between obstetric complications and schizophrenia is not known. Speculations vary and hypotheses include: anoxia due to obstetric complications causing damage to the hippocampus (Mednick, 1970); exposure to influenza causing developmental abnormalities during the first and second trimesters of gestation (Von Euler et al., 1985); a loss of brain tissue in the limbic areas resulting from trauma during prenatal development (Bogerts et al., 1985); and persistent biochemical abnormalities due to anoxia (Von Euler et al., 1985) brought on by prolonged labor (McNeil, 1987).

Cerebral Infections

Cases presenting with a schizophrenia-like disorder during or after viral or bacterial encephalitis appear to be of low frequency; however, they exceed chance association and thus support the notion of an etiologic relationship between cerebral trauma and the psychosis (Davison, 1983). Davison and Bagley (1969) examined case reports on a series of 113 patients reported to have developed psychoses following encephalitis lethargica during the epidemics of the 1920s. They found that 16% of the cases developed psychoses. Cases of schizophrenia-like psychoses are also observed in an estimated 3% to 20% of cases of tertiary syphilis with general paresis (Davison, 1983).

Other Organic Disorders

Schizophrenia-like psychoses with late-life onset have been observed in association with several cerebral disorders, including cerebrovascular disease, motor neuron diseases, degenerative ataxias, and dementing processes (Davison, 1983; Davison & Bagley, 1969). There is also increased risk for schizophrenia-like psychoses in association with various endocrine disorders (e.g., abnormalities of the adrenal, thyroid, and parathyroid glands) (Davison, 1987). The implications of these findings for understanding the etiology of schizophrenia are as yet unclear, although reviewers of these data suggest that psychoses associated with neurologic and other medical conditions may be related to abnormalities of temporolimbic cortex (Torrey & Peterson, 1974) or various subcortical regions (Cummings, 1985).

Drug-Related Psychoses

Schizophrenia-like syndromes also have been observed in cases of LSD abuse, and psychoses represent up to 63% of the adverse reactions to LSD (Davison, 1976). Paranoid hallucinatory psychoses and schizophreniform psychoses have been observed in association with other hallucinogens, cannabis, and psychostimulants such as amphetamines (Angrist, 1983). These drug-related psychoses tend to occur in close temporal association with ingestion of drug and typically are of relatively short duration. Animal studies designed to identify the mechanisms for drug-related psychoses may have relevance to enhancing understanding the pathogenesis of some forms of schizophrenia.

Recent clinical and epidemiologic studies indicate a high prevalence of alcohol and drug use in schizophrenia (Dixon, Haas, Weiden, Sweeney, & Frances, 1991; Mueser et al., 1990). Retrospective data collected on a sample of 232 first-admission schizophrenia patients suggest that in a minority (roughly one-third) of drug-abusing patients, alcohol or drug abuse was initiated before the first sign of schizophrenia; in roughly one-third of these cases, the alcohol and/or drug use coincided with the first signs of the disorder (Hambrecht & Hafner, 1996). Such data do not indicate whether or not drug use is causal or even potentiating in the etiology of schizophrenia, but, they do identify a need for further investigation of the possible influence of drug use on the risk and expression of schizophrenia-like conditions.

Psychosocial Environmental Factors

A number of psychosocial factors such as stressful life events and problematic family behavior are associated with increased risk for psychotic episodes, though not established as direct causes of the illness itself. Early psychosocial theories of intergenerational transmission of schizophrenia viewed the disorder as the product of pathogenic child rearing (Fromm-Reichman, 1948), including notions such as the "schizophrenogenic" mother. Such ideas are not widely accepted today.

Dysfunctional Parental Communication as a Risk Predictor

Common to the family communication theories is the assumption that schizophrenia is a psychosocially transmitted disorder (i.e., learned within a social-learning context), developing out of the child's repeated exposure to faulty communication or to ambiguous and confusing structural characteristics of family relations. Wynne and Singer (1963) hypothesized that a specific type of dysfunctional communication within the family, reflecting an inability to establish and maintain a shared focus of attention (referred to as *communication deviance* or CD), disrupts the cognitive development of the child. Wynne's theory subsumes both genetic and psychosocial factors, suggesting that exposure to dysfunctional patterns of family interaction may provoke and maintain schizophrenia in individuals with a genetic predisposition to schizophrenia.

Goldstein (1985) tested a diathesis–stress model in which Wynne and Singer's parental communication deviance (CD) construct was evaluated as a predictor of schizophrenia-spectrum disorders. In one of the few prospective studies examining family interaction factors among children "at risk" for psychiatric disorder, Goldstein (1985) followed a sample of adolescents with behavior problems who had been referred for outpatient psychiatric care. They found that a combination of parental CD and negative affective communication predicted over 50% of the variance in the diagnosis of schizophrenia spectrum disorders (schizophrenia, schizophreniform, schizotypal, and borderline disorders) among individuals at 5-year follow-up (Goldstein, 1985; Rodnick, Goldstein, Lewis, & Doane, 1984). Though supportive of a vulnerability–stress model of schizophrenia, results of this study suggest that the specificity of the model to narrowly defined schizophrenia is questionable. Also, references to causality should be minimized, as the possibility that family members were reacting to

the affected member's abnormal behavior cannot be ruled out.

Because CD is a multidimensional construct that reflects difficulties in perceptual-cognitive organization as well as deviant patterns of language use, it has been interpreted both as a behavioral mediator — linking pathologic parental communication patterns with the information-processing deficits of patients (Wynne & Singer, 1963)—and as a possible *indicator of gene–environment interaction* or cross-generational transmission of genetic vulnerability (Nuechterlein, Goldstein, Ventura, Dawson, & Doane, 1989). Studies that have examined the relationship between parental CD and information-processing deficits in schizophrenic offspring have suggested that it is specifically the perceptual distortion rather than the deviant language component of parental communication that is associated with the information processing deficits in offspring (e.g., Nuechterlein et al., 1989).

Expressed Emotion

A particularly active area of research on family environment factors in schizophrenia focuses on a measure of familial attitudes toward the patient referred to as *expressed emotion* (EE). This construct refers to varying levels of critical attitudes, hostility, and emotional overinvolvement of relatives in relation to individuals with schizophrenia. EE is measured via a semistructured psychiatric history interview (the Camberwell Family Interview) conducted with household relatives (Brown, Birley, & Wing, 1972). The Camberwell Family Interview focuses on patient symptomatology, chronology of illness, and interpersonal relations between patient and relative. Ratings of relative's criticism, hostility, and overinvolvement are based on content and tone of voice during the interview.

Leff and Vaughn (1985) have described a theoretical model in which frequent contact with a high-EE relative predisposes the biologically vulnerable individual to the onset and recurrence of episodes of illness. Convergent evidence from multiple investigations in the United States, Great Britain, and elsewhere indicate that among individuals in frequent (35 hours or more per week) contact with relatives, EE is a strong predictor of *relapse* in schizophrenia (see Kuipers & Bebbington, 1988, and Kavanaugh, 1992, for reviews), such that risk of relapse among patients returning to high-EE homes is approximately two- to threefold that of individuals returning to low-EE homes (Leff & Vaughn, 1985).

Testing the contribution of patient psychopathology and other variables to the association between EE and relapse, Vaughn and Leff (1976) found that such factors as behavioral disturbance, lack of antipsychotic drug treatment, and other features of psychiatric history could not account for the relationship between EE and relapse. In fact, these investigators found that EE was at least as closely related to relapse ($r = 0.45$) as was noncompliance with antipsychotic medication ($r = 0.39$). Pooling the data from two studies, Vaughn and Leff (1976) examined the relative contribution of EE, maintenance medication, and hours of contact between patient and relative to relapse rate. The investigators found that the three factors interacted in an interesting fashion: among patients returning home to low-EE families, relapse rates were relatively low (12%–15%), and maintenance medication afforded no greater protection against relapse. In contrast, among high-EE patients, maintenance medication *and* less frequent family contact (less than 35 hours per week) were *each* associated with lower relapse rates.

Finally, in addition to longitudinal studies of EE as an indicator of risk for relapse, many of the advances in empirically based family treatments over the past 20 years have aimed to reduce the critical and overinvolved behaviors found to be associated with high-EE attitudes (reviewed by Barrowclough & Tarrier, 1992). Family interventions targeted at reducing EE among family members suggests that reducing EE may moderate course of the illness (Falloon et al., 1985; Leff, Kuipers, Berkowitz, Eberlein-Fries, & Sturgeon, 1982).

In summary, recent findings suggest that high-EE critical attitudes reflect a traitlike cognitive and/or temperamental disposition to respond in a critical or rejecting manner to certain symptoms of schizophrenia; the expression of critical attitudes toward the patient and his or her symptoms appears to vary with the severity of symptoms and the acute (versus chronic) phase of illness. Observational studies of patient–family discourse indicate that critical remarks on the part of a relative tend to be reciprocally related to disordered communications of the proband. These find-

ings suggest that high-EE behaviors—whether criticism or emotional overinvolvement—may induce symptom exacerbation and relapse among individuals who have had their first episode of schizophrenia.

Whether high-EE behaviors increase the likelihood of schizophrenia onset among genetically vulnerable individuals is not yet known. To date, the most credible model of the relationship of family environment variables to schizophrenia is one that identifies chronic familial stress (e.g., relatives' criticism and overinvolvement) as a *priming agent* for onset and illness episodes in an individual with a genetic or biologic vulnerability to schizophrenia.

Life Events

The notion that stressful life events are causal in the onset of psychiatric disorders such as schizophrenia has had broad intuitive appeal but little empirical support (Day, 1981, 1986; Rabkin, 1980). A sizable empirical literature indicates a causal role of life events in the onset of depression and various physical illnesses. With regard to schizophrenia, however, it has been generally concluded that stressful life events have a *triggering,* rather than a *formative* (i.e., etiologic) influence on the onset of the disorder (Brown & Harris, 1987). Proponents of a "vulnerability model" of schizophrenia, Zubin and Spring (1977), hypothesized that life events "trigger" the onset of episodes of illness in "vulnerable" individuals. In this model, life events are viewed as necessary, but not sufficient, precursors of an illness episode.

The most convincing evidence for a role of life events in provoking onset of schizophrenia comes from two studies conducted by Brown and colleagues of the Bedford College in London. In a case-controlled study of life events reported by 50 acute-onset, first-episode schizophrenic patients, Brown and Birley (1968) found a significantly higher incidence of life events during the 3 weeks prior to admission, as compared to a comparable period in a sample of 325 community control cases. Birley and Brown (1970) examined the clinical characteristics of patients in the 1968 Brown and Birley study and found that history of illness, type of onset, and differences in symptomatology were not related to the occurrence/nonoccurrence of life events during the 3 weeks prior to onset of the episode. Reduction and/or discontinuation of maintenance medication during the 11 months prior to onset was associated with a higher incidence of life events. Birley and Brown (1970) concluded that medication discontinuation and life events have an independent and additive contribution to the onset of an episode of illness. A more recent study conducted by the World Health Organization (WHO) replicated the methods and procedures of Brown and Birley's original study (Day et al., 1987), and found an increased incidence of independent life events during the 3 weeks prior to onset of first psychotic episodes in schizophrenia. Most remarkable was that the findings were cross-replicated in 6 of the 9 centers in which the study was conducted.

Finally, several studies (Beck & Worthen, 1972; Harris, 1985; Jacobs & Myers, 1976) suggest that among schizophrenic patients, medication status and the degree of threat or hazardousness of life events is of particular importance. For example, based on the results of their controlled treatment studies, Leff, Hirsch, Gaind, Rhode, and Stevens (1973) have argued that patients on maintenance medication are better protected against the exigencies of daily life, and are unlikely to relapse unless exposed to an acute increase in stress associated with a life event. Ventura, Nuechterlein, Lukoff, and Hardesty (1989) tested this hypothesis in a prospective study of 30 first-episode schizophrenic patients maintained on standardized medication over a 1-year follow-up period. As predicted, they found a significant elevation in the number of independent and non-illness-related life events among the relapsing patients during the month preceding relapse.

Similarly, Bebbington et al. (1993) observed an excess of independent life events during the 3 months preceding the onset of the first episode of schizophrenia. Bebbington and colleagues pointed out the potential importance of so-called minor as well as major events in the lives of individuals with schizophrenia. In research that investigates the role of life events in the onset of psychosis, sensitivity to events that do not meet threshold criteria for major threats is particularly characteristic of unmedicated individuals (Leff et al., 1973).

Testing Diathesis–Stress Models

Some of the more interesting attempts to investigate a possible linkage between social and biological fac-

tors in the etiology of schizophrenia focus on a hypothesized relationship between abnormalities of autonomic arousal and exposure to acute (life event) and/or enduring stress (e.g., high levels of expressed emotion in relatives). Electrodermal arousal of schizophrenic patients appears to vary with psychosocial stressors such as the presence of a high-EE relative (Tarrier & Turpin, 1992) or the recent exposure to an independent life event (Nuechterlein et al., 1989). These findings are consistent with a vulnerability–stress model (e.g., Nuechterlein & Dawson, 1984) which proposes that individual vulnerability to environmental stressors may be mediated by a predisposition to the disorganizing influence of states of autonomic hyperarousal. Exposure to a high-EE relative may represent a chronic stressor that activates and/or predisposes the individual to autonomic nervous system hyperarousal. Likewise, acute environmental stressors appear to have some potential for activating states of autonomic hyperactivity in schizophrenia (Nuechterlein et al., 1989). Such models offer a potential heuristic for further investigation of the impact of psychological stressors on the communication and information-processing deficits of schizophrenia. Beyond this, research on the pathophysiology of stress response mechanisms will have important implications for further evaluation of the possible role of psychosocial environmental factors in the etiology of schizophrenia.

Conclusions Regarding Environmental Factors

The list of potential nongenetic, so-called environmental factors in schizophrenia is indeed long. No single factor has been found to predominate in a majority of cases of apparently low genetic risk. In their review of environmental etiologic factors in schizophrenia, DeLisi (1987) note that the cumulative findings on environmental factors point to a heterogeneity of etiologies of schizophrenia, and the need for broad-based, clinical-epidemiologic approaches that combine careful behavioral assessment with epidemiologic statistical models of risk in the study of larger samples than heretofore studied. We have entered an age in which etiologic models must accommodate complex interactions of individuals with their physical, social, and biochemical environment.

Whether as etiologic agents with a disruptive impact on neurodevelopment, or as triggering mechanisms that activate pathologic developmental or metabolic processes, environmental factors are likely to continue to play an important role in our working models of schizophrenia etiology.

THE IDENTIFICATION OF MARKER VARIABLES

Concerns about the possible heterogeneity of schizophrenia and the use of clinical diagnosis as the sole indicator of the presence of illness, together with efforts to leap the gap from molecular biology to symptom expression, have led many investigators to seek cognitive, psychophysiological, and biochemical "markers" for the illness. The issue of etiologic heterogeneity is important because, if the clinical syndrome of schizophrenia turns out to have several frequent but distinct causes, efforts to study the role of any single causative factor will be slow and unlikely to be productive unless quite large samples are recruited. This may be particularly important in family studies, where milder social and cognitive/perceptual aberrations must be used to identify cases affected with phenomenologically similar but less severe characteristics than are seen in schizophrenia. The clinical assessment of such traits, which may vary over time, has lower reliability than the diagnosis of schizophrenia, which is based on the presence of severe psychotic symptoms. Typical family/genetic analyses require individuals to be classified as either affected or not affected with the illness in question, and it is not yet clear where on the severity dimension of schizotypal traits this boundary should be drawn, or whether schizotypal characteristics in the idiosyncratic thought content domain should have more or less weight than poor social relations or blunted affect. The identification of reliable and valid markers for schizophrenia risk, however, would make the reliance on uncertain symptom ascertainments less necessary. The third issue is that the mechanisms by which an abnormality of genes or neurotransmitters might lead to the clinical expression of schizophrenia is not clear. Most marker variables that have been studied to date probably assess subclinical expressions of illness, such as attention disturbances. Studying these abnormalities in unaffected and untreated relatives may help clarify the mechanisms by which genetic factors alter brain function to disrupt particular cognitive, emotional, and social processes to increase risk for illness.

Studies of marker variables associated with schizophrenia often have the twofold purpose of attempting to learn about possible biological causes of the condition, as well as to validate a biological marker for the illness that can be used to identify high-risk cases in etiological studies. Meehl (1962/1973, 1989), and many others, have advocated the use of psychobiological markers to identify individuals at risk for schizophrenia. Most markers used for this purpose (attentional and biochemical disturbances) were selected because the dimension they evaluate is hypothesized to be related to illness processes per se. It is hoped that such measures will provide a quantitative evaluation of a specific psychobiological characteristic, and therefore will identify a homogeneous subset of patients who share a common etiology.

One difficulty faced by researchers attempting to discover the mode of genetic inheritance for schizophrenia is illustrated by Gottesman and Bertelson's (1989) study. In their study, as in other twin studies, clinically unaffected MZ co-twins were identified. If one accepts that genetic factors contributed to the cause of the ill twin's disorder, then the well twins would be undetected carriers of the same high-risk genotype. Such individuals possess the genotype (the hereditary factors that predispose to illness) but do not manifest the phenotype (the clinical expression of illness to a degree that surpasses the diagnostic threshold for the illness). This suggests that a substantial number of false negatives (i.e., failure to identify cases carrying the high-risk genotype) may occur in pedigree analyses when the psychiatric diagnosis of schizophrenia spectrum disorders is the sole method of case classification. Marker variables may help to reduce the number of false negatives and identify factors leading to increased risk for the illness (not just factors causing full expression of the condition). In this way, they may elucidate mechanisms by which genetic and biochemical changes disturb psychological processes and cause expression of the illness.

Several potential markers were studied in a recent investigation directed at the NIMH by E. Fuller Torrey. In this study, pairs of monozygotic twins were studied in which only one twin was affected with schizophrenia. The main advantage of this design was in separating environmental and familial etiologies of these marker abnormalities. If the cause of an abnormality in the affected patient was familial, both individuals should manifest the characteristic because they have the same genes. If the cause was environmental and related to the presence of the illness, only the ill twin would show the marker characteristic.

In studies of cerebral ventricular enlargement (Suddath, Christison, Torrey, Casanova, & Weinberger, 1990) and neuropsychological abnormalities (Goldberg et al., 1990) in these twin pairs, the principal finding was that the ill twins were more abnormal than their unaffected twins, and the unaffected twins were similar to other monozygotic twin controls from families without a positive history for schizophrenia. These findings suggest that the cause of ventricular and neuropsychological abnormalities is to a significant degree not genetic, and that these impairments may reflect the progression of the illness or some environmental insult.

To be useful, valid marker variables for schizophrenia need to have several properties, including: (1) reasonably high specificity for the disorder in question, (2) segregation with illness in relatives of affected probands, (3) a low base rate of the marker in the general population, (4) stability over time, and (5) high prevalence in persons from the general population who are at high risk for the disorder. In addition, because genetic factors contribute meaningfully to risk for illness, evidence should exist that the marker can be genetically transmitted.

The validation of markers for an illness is a complicated and time-consuming process, requiring several progressive steps. These include efforts to: (1) identify the abnormality in patients, (2) show that it is stable irrespective of clinical state and medication treatment, (3) determine that it is significantly more frequent in patients affected with schizophrenia than in individuals with other psychiatric disorders, (4) show that the characteristic is more prevalent in relatives of schizophrenics, and (5) determine whether it segregates with illness in relatives and is associated with any specific DNA anomaly in linkage studies.

Among the most promising and best studied marker variables for schizophrenia are smooth pursuit eye movement dysfunction (Holzman, Proctor, &

Hughes, 1973), deficient sensory gating in an auditory evoked potential paradigm (Freedman et al., 1987), and impaired performance on complex vigilance tasks (see Erlenmeyer-Kimling, 1987, for a review). Several studies have shown that abnormalities on these measures are more frequent in schizophrenic patients and their unaffected first-degree relatives than in the general population (Keefe et al., 1997). Identifying deficits that are present in schizophrenic patients but not other psychiatric disorders has proved to be a particularly difficult aspect of the marker validation process (Sweency et al., 1994).

The use of such marker variables may help to advance molecular genetic investigations of complex disorders like schizophrenia. Such complex disorders, manifest in multiple domains and not having clear Mendelian patterns of inheritance, are likely to have complex genetic and environmental causes. On the other hand, traits that are manifest in only one domain, like disturbed-pursuit eye movements, seem more likely to have simpler causes (including genetic ones). Using traits with simpler (perhaps Mendelian) inheritance patterns may yield greater power in quantitative efforts to determine mode of inheritance, and may help determine whether there is heterogeneity in the clinical phenotype defined by schizophrenia-related behavior.

Further, markers may facilitate linkage analyses, perhaps leading to the identification of major genes predisposing specific subgroups of individuals to schizophrenia. Ultimately, better understanding of the etiology of this illness may lead to the development of improved treatment strategies for schizophrenic patients. Although social skills training and medications that block dopamine receptors are helpful in the clinical management of patients, the majority of affected patients have markedly reduced quality of life, and many do not benefit appreciably from available treatments. As more is learned about the causes of the illness, clinicians may be better prepared to intervene to help their patients, and perhaps ultimately to engage in preventive interventions with individuals known to be at risk for the disorder.

REFERENCES

Abe, K. (1966). Susceptibility to psychosis and precipitating factor: A study of families with two or more psychotic members. *Psychiatry and Neurology, 151,* 276.

Alzheimer, A. (1897). Beitrage zur pathologischen Anatomie der Hirnrunde und zur anatomischen Grund-lage einiger Psychosen: Monatsschrift. *Psychiatry and Neurology, 2,* 82–120.

Andreasen, N.C., Arndt, S., Swayze, V., Cizadlo, T., Flaum, M., O'Leary, D., Ehrhardt, J.C., & Yuh, W.T.C. (1994). Thalamic abnormalities in schizophrenia visualized through magnetic resonance image averaging. *Science, 266,* 294–298.

Andreasen, N.C., Ehrhardt, J.C., Swayze, V.W., Allider, R.J., Yuh, W.T.C., Cohen, G., & Ziebell, S. (1990). Magnetic resonance imaging of the brain in schizophrenia: The pathophysiologic significance of structural abnormalities. *Archives of General Psychiatry, 47,* 35–44.

Andreasen, N.C., Nasrallah, H.A., Dunn, V., Olson, S.C., Grove, W.M., Erhardt, J.C., Coffman, J.A., & Crossett, J.H.W. (1986). Structural abnormalities in the frontal system in schizophrenia. *Archives of General Psychiatry, 43,* 134–144.

Angrist, B. (1983). Psychoses induced by CNS stimulants and related drugs. In I. Creese (Ed.), *Stimulants: Neurochemical, behavioral and clinical perspectives* (pp. 1–30). New York: Raven Press.

Angrist, M., Kauffman, E., Slaughenhaupt, S.A., Matise, T.C., Puffenberger, E.G., Washington, S.S., Lipson, A., Cass, D.T., Reyna, T., Weeks, D.E., Sieber, W., & Chakravarti, A. (1993). A gene for Hirschsprung disease (megacolon) in the pericentromeric region of human chromosome 10. *Nature Genetics, 4,* 351–356.

Arnold, S.E., Hyman, B.T., Van Hoesen, G.W., & Damasio, A.R. (1991). Some cytoarchitectural abnormalities of the entorhinal cortex in schizophrenia. *Archives of General Psychiatry, 48,* 625–632.

Arolt, V., Purmann, S., Nolte, A., Lencer, R., Leutelt, J., Muller, B., Schurmann, M., & Schwinger, E. (1995). Possible linkage of ETD and markers on chromosome 6p. *Psychiatric Genetics, 5*(Suppl. 1), S33.

Baron, M. (1985). The genetics of schizophrenia: New perspectives. *Acta Psychiatrica Scandinavica, Supplementum, 319,* 85–92.

Barrowclough, C., & Tarrier, N. (1992). Interventions with families. In M. Birchwood & N. Tarrier (Eds.), *Innovations in the psychological management of schizophrenia* (pp. 79–102). Chichester: Wiley.

Barta, P.E., Pearlson, G.D., Powers, R.E., Richards, S.S., & Tune, L.E. (1990). Auditory hallucinations and smaller superior temporal gyral volume in schizophrenia. *American Journal of Psychiatry, 147,* 1457–1462.

Bateson, G., Jackson, D., Haley, J., & Weakland, J.H. (1956). Toward a theory of schizophrenia. *Behavioral Science, 1,* 251–264.

Bebbington, P., Wilkins, S., Jones, P., Foerster, A., Murray, R., Toone, B., & Lewis, S. (1993). Life events and psychosis: Initial results from the Camberwell collaborative psychosis study. *British Journal of Psychiatry, 162,* 72–79.

Beck, J., & Worthen, K. (1972). Precipitating stress, crisis theory, and hospitalization in schizophrenia and depression. *Archives of General Psychiatry, 26,* 123–129.

Benes, F.M., McSparren, J., Bird, E.D., SanGiovanni, J.P., & Vincent, S.L. (1991). Deficits in small interneurons in prefrontal and cingulate cortices of schizophrenic and schizoaffective patients. *Archives of General Psychiatry, 48,* 996–1001.

Benes, F.M., Vincent, S.L., Alsterberg, G., Bird, E.D., & SanGiovanni, J.P. (1992). Increased GABA receptor binding in superficial layers of cingulate cortex in schizophrenics. *Journal of Neuroscience, 12,* 924–929.

Birley, J.L.T., & Brown, G.W. (1970). Crises and life changes preceding the onset or relapse of acute schizophrenia: Clinical aspects. *British Journal of Psychiatry, 116,* 327–333.

Bogerts, B., Lieberman, J.A., Ashtari, M., Bilder, R.M., Degreef, G., Lerner, G., Johns, C., & Masiar, S. (1993). Hippocampus–amygdala volumes and psychopathology in chronic schizophrenia. *Biological Psychiatry, 33,* 236–246.

Bogerts, B., Meertz, E., & Schonfeldt-Bausch, R. (1985). Basal ganglia and limbic system pathology in schizophrenia: A morphometric study of brain volume and shrinkage. *Archives of General Psychiatry, 42,* 784–791.

Brown, G.W., & Birley, J.L.T. (1968). Crises and life changes and the onset of schizophrenia. *Journal of Health and Social Behavior, 9,* 203–214.

Brown, G.W., Birley, J.L.T., & Wing, J.K. (1972). Influence of family life on the course of schizophrenic disorder: Replication. *British Journal of Psychiatry, 121,* 241–258.

Brown, G.W., & Harris, T.O. (1987). *Illness and life events.* New York: Guilford Press.

Brown, R., Colter, N., Corsellis, J., Crow, T.J., Frith, C.D., Jagoe, R., Johnstone, E.C., & Marsh, L. (1986). Postmortem evidence of structural brain change in schizophrenia. *Archives of General Psychiatry, 43,* 36–42.

Buchsbaum, M.S., Haier, R.J., Potkin, S.G., Nuechterlein, K., Bracha, H.S., Katz, M., Lohr, J., Wu, J., Lottenberg, S., Jerabek, P.A., Trenary, M., Tafalla, R., Reynolds, C., & Bunney, W.E. (1992). Frontostriatal disorder of cerebral metabolism in never-medicated schizophrenia. *Archives of General Psychiatry, 49,* 935–942.

Carter, C.L., & Chung, C.S. (1980). Segregation analysis of schizophrenia under a mixed genetic model. *Human Heredity, 30,* 350–356.

Chakraborty, R., Kamboh, M.I., Nwankwo, M., & Ferrell, R.E. (1992). Caucasian genes in American Blacks: New data. *American Journal of Human Genetics, 50,* 145–155.

Clementz, B.A., & Sweeney, J.A. (1990). Is eye movement dysfunction a biological marker for schizophrenia? A methodological review. *Psychological Bulletin, 108,* 77–92.

Collinge, J., Delisi, L.E., Boccio, A., Johnstone, E.C., Lane, A., Larkin, C., Leach, M., Lofthouse, R., Owen, F., Poulter, M., Shah, T., Walsh, C., & Crow, T.J. (1991). Evidence for a pseudo-autosomal locus for schizophrenia using the method of affected sibling pairs. *British Journal of Psychiatry, 158,* 624–629.

Conrad, A.J., Abebe, T., Austin, R., Forsythe, S., & Schiebel, A.B. (1991). Hippocampal pyramidal cell disarray in schizophrenia as a bilateral phenomenon. *Archives of General Psychiatry, 48,* 413–417.

Coon, H., Sobell, J., Heston, L., Sommer, S., Hoff, M., Holik, J., Umar, F., Robertson, M., Reimherr, F., Wender, P., Vest, K., Myles-Worsley, M., Gershon, E.S., DeLisi, L.E., Shields, G., Dale, P.W., Polloi, A., Waldo, M., Leonard, S., Sikela, J., Freedman, R., & Byerley, W. (1994). Search for mutations in the beta 1 GABA-A receptor subunit gene in patients with schizophrenia. *American Journal of Medical Genetics, 54,* 12–20.

Crow, T.J. (1986). The continuum of psychosis and its implication for the structure of the gene. *British Journal of Psychiatry, 149,* 419–429.

Cummings, J.L. (1985). Organic delusions: Phenomenology, anatomical correlations and review. *British Journal of Psychiatry, 146,* 184–197.

Dalen, P. (1975). *Season of birth: A study of schizophrenia and other mental disorders.* Amsterdam: North-Holland.

d'Amato, T., Campion, D., Gorwood, P., Jay, M., Sabate, O., Waksman, G., Malafosse, A., Leboyer, M., & Mallet, J. (1991). Linkage analysis using four RFLP markers of the pseudoautosomal region in schizophrenia. *Psychiatric Genetics, 2,* 30–38.

Daniel, D.G., Weinberger, D.R., Jones, D.W., Zigun, J.R., Coppola, R., Handel, S., Bigelow, D.B., Goldberg, T.E., Berman, K.F., & Kleinman, J.E. (1991). The effect of amphetamine on regional cerebral blood flow during cognitive activation in schizophrenia. *Journal of Neuroscience, 11,* 1907–1917.

Davies, J.L., Kawaguchi, Y., Bennett, S.T., Copeman, J.B., Cordell, H.J., Pritchard, L.E., Reed, P.W., Gough, S.C., Jenkins, S.C., Palmer, S.M., Balfour, K.M., Rowe, B.R., Farrall, M., Barnett, A.H., Bain, S.C., & Todd, J.A. (1994). A genome-wide search for human type 1 diabetes susceptibility genes. *Nature, 371,* 130–136.

Davis, K.L., Davidson, M., Mohs, R.C., Kendler, K.S., Davis, B.M., Johns, C.A., DeNigris, Y., & Horvath, T.G. (1985). Plasma homovanillic acid concentrations and the severity of schizophrenic illness. *Science, 227,* 1601–1602.

Davison, K. (1976). Drug-induced psychoses and their relationship to schizophrenia. In D. Kemali, G. Bartholini, & D. Richter (Eds.), *Schizophrenia today* (pp. 105–133). Oxford: Pergamon Press.

Davison, K. (1983). Schizophrenia-like psychoses associated with organic cerebral disorders: A review. *Psychiatric Developments, 1,* 1–33.

Davison, K. (1987). Organic and toxic concomitant of schizophrenia: Association or chance? In H. Helmchen & F.A. Henn (Eds.), *Biological perspectives on schizophrenia* (pp. 139–160). New York: Wiley.

Davison, K., & Bagley, C.R. (1969). Schizophrenia-like psychoses associated with organic disorders of the CNS: A review of the literature. In R.N.

Herrington (Ed.), Current problems in neuropsychiatry. *British Journal of Psychiatry (Special Publication), 4,* 113–184.

Day, R. (1981). Life events and schizophrenia: The "triggering" hypothesis. *Acta Psychiatrica Scandinavica, 64,* 97–122.

Day, R. (1986). Social stress and schizophrenia: From the concept of recent life events to the notion of toxic environments. In G.D. Burrows & T.R. Norman (Eds.), *Handbook of studies of schizophrenia* (pp. 71–82). Amsterdam: Elsevier.

Day, R., Neilsen, J.A., Korten, A., Ernberg, G., Dube, K.C., Gebhart, J., Jablensky, A., Leon, C., Marsella, A., Olatawura, M., Sartorius, N., Stromgren, E., Takahashi, R., Wig, N., & Wynne, L.C. (1987). Stressful life events preceding the acute onset of schizophrenia: A cross-national study from the World Health Organization. *Culture, Medicine and Psychiatry, 11,* 123–206.

DeLisi, L.E. (1987). Nongenetic etiological factors: Group report. In H. Helmchen & F.A. Henn (Eds.), *Biological perspectives in schizophrenia* (pp. 167–184). New York: Wiley.

DeLisi, L.E., Boccio, A.M., Riordan, H., Hoff, L.A., Dorfman, A., McClelland, J., Kushner, M., Van Eyl, O., & Oden, N. (1991). Familial thyroid disease and delayed language development in first admission patients with schizophrenia. *Psychiatric Research, 38,* 39–50.

DeLisi, L.E., & Lovett, M. (1990). The reverse genetic approach to the etiology of schizophrenia. In H. Hafner & W.F. Gattaz (Eds.), *Search for the causes of schizophrenia* (Vol. 2, pp. 144–170). New York: Springer-Verlag.

Dixon, L., Haas, G.L., Weiden, P.J., Sweeney, J., & Frances, A.J. (1991). Drug abuse in schizophrenic patients: Clinical correlates and reasons for use. *American Journal of Psychiatry, 148,* 224–230.

Dolan, R.J., Bench, C.J., Liddle, P.F., Friston, K.J., Frith, C.D., Grasby, P.M., & Frackowiak, R.S.J. (1993). Dorsolateral prefrontal cortex dysfunction in the major psychoses: Symptom or disease specificity? *Journal of Neurology, Neurosurgery and Psychiatry, 56,* 1290–1294.

Dolan, R.J., Fletcher, P., Frith, C.D., Friston, K.J., Frackowiak, R.S., & Grasby, P.M. (1995). Dopaminergic modulation of impaired cognitive activation in the anterior cingulate cortex in schizophrenia. *Nature, 378,* 180–182.

Erlenmeyer-Kimling, L. (1987). Biological markers for the liability to schizophrenia. In H. Helmchen & F.A. Henn (Eds.), *Biological perspectives of schizophrenia* (pp. 33–56). New York: Wiley.

Falconer, D.S. (1965). The inheritance of liability to certain diseases estimated from the incidence among relatives. *Annals of Human Genetics (London), 29,* 51–76.

Falk, C.T., & Rubinstein, P. (1987). Haplotype relative risks: An easy reliable way to construct a proper control sample for risk calculations. *Annals of Human Genetics, 51*(Part 3), 227–233.

Falkai, P., Bogerts, B., & Rozumek, M. (1988). Limbic pathology in schizophrenia: The entorhinal region—a morphometric study. *Biological Psychiatry, 24,* 515–521.

Falloon, I.R.H., Boyd, J.L., McGill, C.W., Williamson, M., Razani, J., Moss, G.B., Gilderman, A.M., & Simpson, G.M. (1985). Family management in the prevention of morbidity of schizophrenia. Clinical outcome of a two-year longitudinal study. *Archives of General Psychiatry, 42,* 887–896.

Farmer, A.E., McGuffin, P., & Gottesman, I.I. (1987). Twin concordance for DSM-III schizophrenia. Scrutinizing the validity of the definition. *Archives of General Psychiatry, 44,* 634–641.

Feder, J., Gurling, H.M., Darby, J., & Cavalli-Sforza, L.L. (1985). DNA restriction fragment analysis of the proopiomelanocortin gene in schizophrenia and bipolar disorders. *American Journal of Human Genetics, 37,* 286–294.

Feinberg, I. (1983). Schizophrenia caused by a fault in programmed synaptic elimination during adolescence? *Journal of Psychiatric Research, 17,* 319–334.

Fischer, M. (1971). Psychoses in the offspring of schizophrenic monozygotic twins and their normal co-twins. *British Journal of Psychiatry, 118,* 43–52.

Franzen, G., & Ingvar, D.H. (1975). Absence of activation in frontal structures during psychological testing of chronic schizophrenics. *Journal of Neurology, Neurosurgery, and Psychiatry, 38,* 1027–1032.

Freedman, R., Adler, L.E., Gerhardt, G.A., Waldo, M., Baker, N., Rose, G.M., Drebing, C., Nagemoto, H., Bickford-Wimer, P., & Franks, R. (1987). Neurobiological studies of sensory gating in schizophrenia. *Schizophrenia Bulletin, 13,* 670–677.

Fromm-Reichmann, F. (1948). Notes on the development of treatment of schizophrenics by psychoanalytic psychotherapy. *Psychiatry, 11,* 263–273.

Fulker, D.W., Cherny, S.S., & Cardon, L.R. (1995). Multipoint interval mapping of quantitative trait loci using sib pairs. *American Journal of Human Genetics, 56,* 1224–1233.

Ganguli, R., Brar, J.S., & Rabin, B.S. (1994). Immune abnormalities in schizophrenia: Evidence for the autoimmune hypothesis. *Harvard Review of Psychiatry, 2,* 2–70.

Ganguli, R., Rabin, B.S., Kelly, R.H., Lyte, M., & Ragu, U. (1987). Clinical and laboratory evidence of autoimmunity in acute schizophrenia. *Annals of the New York Academy of Sciences, 496,* 676–685.

Gejman, P.V., & Gelernte, J. (1993). Mutational analysis of candidate genes in psychiatric disorders. *American Journal of Medical Genetics, 48,* 184–191.

Goldberg, T.E., Ragland, J.D., Torrey, E.F., Gold, J.M., Bigelow, L.B., & Weinberger, D.R. (1990). Neuropsychological assessment of monozygotic twins discordant for schizophrenia. *Archives of General Psychiatry, 47,* 1066–1072.

Goldstein, M.J. (1985). Family factors that antedate the onset of schizophrenia and related disorders: The results of a fifteen-year prospective longitudinal study. *Acta Psychiatric Scandinavia, 71,* 7–18.

Gottesman, I.I. (1991). *Schizophrenia genesis: The origins of madness.* New York: W.H. Freeman.

Gottesman, I.I., & Bertelsen, A. (1989). Confirming unexpressed genotypes for schizophrenia. Risks in the offspring of Fischer's Danish identical and fraternal discordant twins. *Archives of General Psychiatry, 47,* 867–872.

Gottesman, I.I., & Shields, J. (1967). A polygenic theory of schizophrenia. *Proceedings of the National Academy of Sciences, 58,* 199–205.

Griesinger, W. (1857). *Mental pathology and therapeutics* (C. Lockhart Robertson & J. Rutherford, Trans.). London: New Sydenham Society.

Gur, R.E., Mozley, P.D., Resnick, S.M., Mozley, L.H., Shtasel, D.L., Gallacher, F., Arnold, S.E., Karp, J.S., Alavi, A., Reivich, M., & Gur, R.C. (1995). Resting cerebral glucose metabolism in first-episode and previously treated patients with schizophrenia relates to clinical features. *Archives of General Psychiatry, 52,* 657–667.

Gur, R.E., & Pearlson, G.D. (1993). Neuroimaging in schizophrenia research. *Schizophrenia Bulletin, 19,* 337–353.

Gusella, J.F., Wexler, N.S., Conneally, P.M., Naylor, S.L., Anderson, M.A., Tanzi, R.E., Watkins, P.C., Ottina, K., Wallace, M.R., Sakaguchi, A.Y., Young, A.B., Shoulson, I., Bonilla, E., & Martin, J.B. (1983). A polymorphic DNA marker genetically linked to Huntington's disease. *Nature, 306,* 234–238.

Hambrecht, M., & Hafner, H. (1996). Substance abuse and the onset of schizophrenia. *Biological Psychiatry, 40,* 1155–1163.

Harris, T. (1985). Recent developments in the study of life events in relation to psychiatric and physical disorders. In B. Cooper (Ed.), *The epidemiology of psychiatric disorders* (pp. 81–102). Baltimore: Johns Hopkins University Press.

Heath, R.G., & Krupp, I.M. (1967). Schizophrenia as an immunologic disorder: I. Demonstration of antibrain globulins by fluorescent antibody techniques. *Archives of General Psychiatry, 16,* 1–9.

Hodge, S.E. (1993). Linkage analysis versus association analysis: Distinguishing between two models that explain disease–marker associations. *American Journal of Human Genetics, 53,* 367–384.

Holzman, P.S. (1987). Recent studies of psychophysiology in schizophrenia. *Schizophrenia Bulletin, Special Report 1987,* 65–91.

Holzman, P.S., Proctor, L.R., & Hughes, D.W. (1973). Eye-tracking patterns in schizophrenia. *Science, 181,* 179–180.

Hurst, L.A. (1972). Hypothesis of a single-locus recessive genotype for schizophrenia. In A.R. Kaplan (Ed.), *Genetic factors in "schizophrenia"* (pp. 219–245). Springfield: Charles C Thomas.

Ishimaru, M., Kurumaji, A., & Toru, M. (1994). Increases in strychnine-insensitive glycine binding sites in cerebral cortex of chronic schizophrenics:

Evidence for glutamate hypothesis. *Biological Psychiatry, 35,* 84–95.

Jacobs, S., & Myers, J. (1976). Recent life events and acute schizophrenia psychosis: A controlled study. *Journal of Nervous and Mental Disease, 162,* 75–87.

Jakob, H., & Beckmann, H. (1986). Prenatal developmental disturbances in the limbic allocortex in schizophrenics. *Journal of Neural Transmission, 65,* 303–326.

Jernigan, T.L., Zisook, S., Heaton, R.K., Moranville, J.T., Hesselink, J.R., & Braff, D.L. (1991). Magnetic resonance imaging abnormalities in lenticular nuclei and cerebral cortex in schizophrenia. *Archives of General Psychiatry, 48,* 881–890.

Kaufmann, C.A., & Malaspina, D. (1991). Molecular genetics of schizophrenia. *Psychiatric Annals, 23,* 111–122.

Kavanaugh, D.J. (1992). Recent developments in expressed emotion and schizophrenia. *British Journal of Psychiatry, 160,* 601–620.

Keefe, R.S.E., Silverman, J.M., Mohs, R.C., Siever, L.J., Harvey, P.D., Friedman, L., Roitman, S.E.L., Dupre, R.L., Smith, C.J., Schmeidler, J., & Davis, K.L. (1997). Eye tracking, attention, and schizotypal symptoms in nonpsychotic relatives of patients with schizophrenia. *Archives of General Psychiatry, 54,* 169–176.

Keilp, J.G., Sweeney, J.A., Jacobsen, P., Solomon, C., St. Louis, L., Deck, M., Frances, A., & Mann, J.J. (1988). Cognitive impairment in schizophrenia: Specific relations to ventricular size and negative symptomatology. *Biological Psychiatry, 24,* 47–55.

Kendell, R.E., Juszczak, E., & Cole, S.K. (1996). Obstetric complications and schizophrenia: A case control study based on standardised obstetric records. *British Journal of Psychiatry, 168,* 556–561.

Kendler, K.S., & Eaves, L.J. (1986). Models for the joint effect of genotype and environment on liability to psychiatric illness. *American Journal of Psychiatry, 143,* 279–289.

Kendler, K.S., Gruenberg, A.M., & Tsuang, M.T. (1985). Psychiatric illness in first-degree relatives of schizophrenic and surgical control patients. A family study using DSM-III criteria. *Archives of General Psychiatry, 42,* 770–779.

Kendler, K.S., McGuire, M., Gruenberg, A.M., O'Hare, A., Spellman, M., & Walsh, D. (1993a). The Roscommon Family Study: III. Schizophrenia-related personality disorders in relatives. *Archives of General Psychiatry, 50,* 781–788.

Kendler, K.S., McGuire, M., Gruenberg, A.M., Spellman, M., O'Hare, A., & Walsh, D. (1993b). The Roscommon family study: II. The risk of nonschizophrenic nonaffective psychoses in relatives. *Archives of General Psychiatry, 50,* 645–652.

Kendler, K.S., Tsuang, M.T., & Hays, P. (1987). Age at onset in schizophrenia. A familial perspective. *Archives of General Psychiatry, 44,* 881–890.

Kerem, B., Rommens, J.M., Buchanan, J.A., Markiewicz, D., Cox, T.K., Chakravarti, A., Buchwald, M., & Tsui, L.C. (1989). Identification of the cystic fibrosis gene: Genetic analysis. *Science, 245,* 1073–1080.

Kety, S.S., & Ingraham, L.J. (1992). Genetic transmission and improved diagnosis of schizophrenia from pedigrees of adoptees. *Journal of Psychiatric Research, 26,* 247–255.

Kidd, K.K. (1993). Associations of disease with genetic markers: Déjà vu all over again. *American Journal of Medical Genetics, 48,* 71–73.

King, D.J., Cooper, S.J., Earle, J.A.P., Martin, S.J., McFerran, N.V., Rima, B.K., & Wisdom, G.B. (1985). A survey of serum antibodies to eight common viruses in psychiatric patients. *British Journal of Psychiatry, 147,* 137–144.

Kinney, D.K., & Jacobsen, B. (1978). Environmental factors in schizophrenia: New adoption study evidence. In L.C. Wynne, R.L. Cromwell, & S. Matthysse (Eds.), *The nature of schizophrenia: New approaches to research and treatment* (pp. 38–52). New York: Wiley.

Kinney, D.K., Woods, B.T., & Yurgelun-Todd, D. (1986). Neurologic abnormalities in schizophrenic patients and their families: II. Neurologic and psychiatric findings in relatives. *Archives of General Psychiatry, 43,* 665–668.

Knight, J.G. (1982). Dopamine-receptor-stimulating autoantibodies: A possible cause of schizophrenia. *Lancet, 2,* 1073–1076.

Kornhuber, J., Riederer, P., Reynolds, G.P., Beckmann, H., Jellinger, K., & Gabriel, E. (1989). 3H-Spiperone binding sites in post-mortem brains from schizophrenic patients: Relationship to neuroleptic drug treatment, abnormal movements, and positive symptoms. *Journal of Neural Transmission, 75,* 1–10.

Kuipers, L., & Bebbington, P. (1988). Expressed emotion research in schizophrenia: Theoretical and clinical implications. *Psychological Medicine, 18,* 893–909.

Laruelle, M., Abi-Dargham, A., Casanova, M.F., Toti, R., Weinberger, D.R., & Kleinman, J.E. (1993). Selective abnormalities of prefrontal serotonergic receptors in schizophrenia. *Archives of General Psychiatry, 50,* 810–818.

Leff, J.P., Hirsch, S., Gaind, R., Rhode, P., & Stevens, B. (1973). Life events and maintenance therapy in schizophrenic relapse. *British Journal of Psychiatry, 123,* 659–660.

Leff, J.P., Kuipers, L., Berkowitz, R., Eberlein-Fries, R., & Sturgeon, D. (1982). A controlled trial of social intervention in schizophrenic families. *British Journal of Psychiatry, 141,* 594–600.

Leff, J.P., & Vaughn, C. (1985). *Expressed emotion in families.* New York: Guilford Press.

Levy, D.L., Holzman, P.S., Matthysse, S., & Mendell, N.R. (1994). Eye tracking and schizophrenia— a selective review. *Schizophrenia Bulletin, 20,* 47–62.

Liddle, P.F., Friston, K.J., Frith, C.D., Hirsch, S.R., Jones, T., & Frackowiak, R.S.J. (1992). Patterns of cerebral blood flow in schizophrenia. *British Journal of Psychiatry, 160,* 179–186.

Lidz, T., Cornelison, A.R., & Fleck, S. (1958). The transmission of irrationality. *Archives of Neurology and Psychiatry, 79,* 305–316.

Maier, W., Albus, M., Schwab, S., Hallmayer, J., Ebstein, P., Risch, N., Lerer, B., & Wildenauer, D. (1996). Evaluation of a susceptibility gene for schizophrenia on chromosome 6p. *Schizophrenia Research, 18,* 167.

Marsh, L., Suddath, R.L., Higgins, N., & Weinberger, D.R. (1994). Medial temporal lobe structures in schizophrenia: Relationship of size to duration of illness. *Schizophrenia Research, 11,* 225–238.

Matthysse, S., Holzman, P.S., & Lange, K. (1986). The genetic transmission of schizophrenia: Application of Mendelian latent structure analysis to eye tracking dysfunctions in schizophrenia and affective disorder. *Journal of Psychiatric Research, 20,* 57–67.

McCarley, R.W., Shenton, M.E., O'Donnell, B.F., Faux, S.F., Kikinis, R., Nestor, P.G., & Jolesz, F.A. (1993). Auditory P300 abnormalities and left posterior superior temporal gyrus volume reduction in schizophrenia. *Archives of General Psychiatry, 50,* 190–197.

McGuffin, P., Farmer, A.E., Gottesman, I.I., Murray, R.M., & Reveley, A.M. (1984). Twin concordance for operationally defined schizophrenia. Confirmation of familiality and heritability. *Archives of General Psychiatry, 41,* 541–545.

McGuffin, P., Owen, M.J., O'Donovan, M.C., Thapar, A., & Gottesman, I.I. (1994). *Seminars in psychiatric genetics.* London: Gaskell.

McGuffin, P., & Sturt, E. (1986). Genetic markers in schizophrenia. *Human Heredity, 36,* 65–88.

McNeil, T.F. (1987). Obstetric factors and perinatal injuries. In M.T. Tsuang & J.C. Simpson (Eds.), *Handbook of schizophrenia: Nosology, epidemiology and genetics* (pp. 319–344). Amsterdam: Elsevier.

Mednick, S.A. (1970). Breakdown in individuals at high risk for schizophrenia: Possible predispositional perinatal factors. *Mental Hygiene, 54,* 50–63.

Meehl, P.E. (1962/1973). Schizotaxia, schizotypy, and schizophrenia. *American Psychologist, 17,* 827–838.

Meehl, P.E. (1989). Schizotaxia revisited. *Archives of General Psychiatry, 46,* 935–944.

Menninger, K.A. (1928). The schizophrenic syndrome as a product of acute infectious disease. *Archives of Neurology and Psychiatry, 20,* 464–481.

Mourant, A.E., Kopec, A.C., & Domaniewska-Sobczak, K. (1978). *Blood groups and diseases.* Oxford: Oxford University Press.

Mueser, K.T., Yarnold, P.R., Levinson, D.F., Singh, H., Bellack, A.S., Kee, K., Morrison, R.L., & Yadalam, K.G. (1990). Prevalence of substance abuse in schizophrenia: Demographic and clinical correlates. *Schizophrenia Research, 16,* 31–56.

Neale, M.C., Eaves, L.J., Hewitt, J.K., MacLean, C.J., Meyer, J.M., & Kendler, K.S. (1989). Analyzing the relationship between age at onset and risk to relatives. *American Journal of Human Genetics, 45,* 226–239.

Nimgaonkar, V.L., Rudert, W.A., Zhang, X.R., Trucco, M., & Ganguli, R. (1996). Negative association of schizophrenia with HLA DQB1*0602: Evidence from a second African-American cohort. *Schizophrenia Research, 23,* 81–86.

Nimgaonkar, V.L., Sanders, A.R., Ganguli, R., Zhang, X.R., Brar, J.S., Hogge, W., Fann, W.E., Patel, P.I., & Chakravarti, A. (1995). Association study of schizophrenia and the dopamine D3 receptor gene locus in two independent samples. *American Journal of Medical Genetics, 48,* 214–217.

Nimgaonkar, V.L., Zhang, X.R., Brar, J.S., DeLeo, M., & Ganguli, R. (1996). 5-HT2 receptor gene locus: Association with schizophrenia or treatment response not detected. *Psychiatric Genetics, 6,* 23–28.

Nuechterlein, K.H., & Dawson, M.E. (1984). A heuristic vulnerability/stress model of schizophrenic episodes. *Schizophrenia Bulletin, 10,* 300–312.

Nuechterlein, K.H., Goldstein, M.J., Ventura, J., Dawson, M.E., & Doane, J.A. (1989). Patient-environment relationships in schizophrenia: Information processing, communication deviance, autonomic arousal, and stressful life events. *British Journal of Psychiatry, 155*(Suppl. 5), 84–89.

O'Callaghan, E., Gibson, T., Colohan, H.A., Walshe, D., Buckley, P., Larkin, C., & Waddingtion, J.L. (1991). Season of birth in schizophrenia: Evidence for confinement of an excess of winter births to patients without a family history of mental disorder. *British Journal of Psychiatry, 158,* 764–769.

Onstad, S., Skre, I., Torgersen, S., & Kringlen, E. (1991). Subtypes of schizophrenia—evidence from a twin-family study. *Acta Psychiatrica Scandinavica, 84,* 203–206.

Owen, M.J. (1992). Will schizophrenia become a graveyard for molecular geneticists? *Psychological Medicine, 22,* 289–293.

Pakkenberg, B. (1990). Pronounced reduction of total neuron number in mediodorsal thalamic nucleus and nucleus accumbens in schizophrenics. *Archives of General Psychiatry, 47,* 1023–1028.

Pauler, D.K., Escobar, M.D., Sweeney, J.A., & Greenhouse, J. (1996). Mixture models for eye-tracking data: A case study. *Statistics in Medicine, 15,* 1365–1376.

Pauls, D.L. (1993). Behavioural disorders: Lessons in linkage. *Nature Genetics, 3,* 4–5.

Penrose, L.S. (1935). The detection of autosomal linkage in data which consists of pairs of brothers and sisters of unspecified parentage. *Annals of Eugenics, 6,* 133–138.

Pickar, D., Labarca, R., Linniola, M., Roy, A., Hommer, D., Everett, D., & Paul, S.M. (1984). Neuroleptic induced decrease in plasma homovanillic acid and antipsychotic activity in schizophrenic patients. *Science, 225,* 954–957.

Pope, H., Jr., Jonas, J.M., Cohen, B.M., & Lipinski, J.F. (1982). Failure to find evidence of schizophrenia in first-degree relatives of schizophrenic probands. *American Journal of Psychiatry, 139,* 826–828.

Pulver, A.E., Antonarakis, S., Blouin, J., Ton, C., Housman, D., Karayiorgou, M., Wolyniec, P., Lasseter, V., Nestadt, G., DeMarchi, N., Loetscher, E., Luebbert, H., Kazazian, H., & Williams, S. (1996). Schizophrenia loci: Data of the JHU collaborative group. *Biological Psychiatry, 39,* 614.

Pulver, A.E., Karayiorgou, M., & Wolyniec, P.S. (1994). Sequential strategy to identify a susceptibility gene for schizophrenia: Report of a potential linkage on chromosome 22q12-q13.1: Part I. *American Journal of Medical Genetics, 54,* 36–43.

Rabkin, J.G. (1980). Stressful life events and schizophrenia. A review of the research literature. *Psychology Bulletin, 87,* 408–425.

Rao, D.C., Morton, N.E., Gottesman, I.I., & Lew, R. (1981). Path analysis of qualitative data on pairs of relatives: Application to schizophrenia. *Human Heredity, 31,* 325–333.

Reveley, A.M., Reveley, M.A., & Murray, R.M. (1984). Cerebral ventricular enlargement in nongenetic schizophrenia: A controlled twin study. *British Journal of Psychiatry, 144,* 89–93.

Rieder, R.O., Mann, L.S., Weinberger, D.R., van Kammen, D., & Post, R.M. (1983). Computed tomographic scans in patients with schizophrenia, schizoaffective and bipolar disorder. *Archives of General Psychiatry, 40,* 735–739.

Risch, N. (1987). Assessing the role of HLA-linked and unlinked determinants of disease. *American Journal of Human Genetics, 40,* 1–14.

Rodnick, E.H., Goldstein, M.J., Lewis, J.M., & Doane, J.A. (1984). Parental communication style, affect, and role as precursors of offspring schizophrenia-spectrum disorders. In N.F. Watt, J.

Anthony, L.C. Wynne, & J.E. Rolf (Eds.), *Children at risk for schizophrenia* (pp. 81–92). New York: Cambridge University Press.

Roses, A.D. (1995). Apolipoprotein E and Alzheimer disease. *Science and Medicine, 2,* 16–25.

Roy, M.A., Flaum, M., & Andreasen, N.C. (1995). No difference found between winter- and non-winter-born schizophrenic cases. *Schizophrenia Research, 17,* 241–248.

Rudin, E. (1916). *Zur Vererbung und Neuentstehung der Dementia Praecox.* Berlin and New York: Springer-Verlag.

Sedvall, M.D. (1992). The current status of PET scanning with respect to schizophrenia. *Neuropsychopharmacology, 7,* 41–54.

Siedman, L.J., Yurgelun-Todd, D., Kremen, W.S., Woods, B.T., Goldstein, J.M., Faraone, S.V., & Tsuang, M.T. (1994). Relationship of prefrontal and temporal lobe MRI measures to neuropsychological performance in chronic schizophrenia. *Biological Psychiatry, 35,* 235–246.

Shenton, M.E., Kikinis, R., Jolesz, F.A., Pollak, S.D., LeMay, M., Wible, C.G., Hokama, H., Martin, J., Metcalf, D., Coleman, M., & McCarley, R.W. (1992). Abnormalities of the left temperal lobe and thought disorder in schizophrenia. *New England Journal of Medicine, 327,* 604–612.

Slater, E. (1958). The monogenic theory of schizophrenia. *Acta Genetics and Statistics in Medicine, 8,* 50–60.

Slater, E., Hare, E.H., & Price, J.S. (1971). Marriage and fertility of psychiatric patients compared with national data. *Social Biology, 18,* S60–S73.

Spitzer, R., Endicott, J., & Robins, E. (1977). *Research diagnostic criteria for a selected group of functional disorders,* 3rd ed. New York: New York State Psychiatric Institute.

Sribney, W.M., & Swift, M. (1992). Power of sib-pair and sib-trio linkage analysis with assortative mating and multiple disease loci. *American Journal of Human Genetics, 51,* 773–784.

Straub, R.E., Maclean, C.J., Walsh, D., & Kendler, K.S. (1995). A potential susceptibility locus for schizophrenia on chromosome 6p: Evidence for genetic heterogeneity. *Psychiatric Genetics, 5,* S26–S27.

Suarez, B.K., Van Eerdewegh, P., & Hampe, C.L. (1991). Detecting loci for oligogenic traits by link-age analysis. *American Journal of Human Genetics, 49,* 14.

Suddath, R.L., Casanova, M.F., Goldberg, T.E., Daniel, D.G., Kelsoe, J.R., & Weinberger, D.R. (1989). Temporal lobe pathology in schizophrenia. A quantitative magnetic resonance imaging study. *American Journal of Psychiatry, 146,* 464–472.

Suddath, R.L., Christison, G.W., Torrey, E.F., Casanova, M.F., & Weinberger, D.R. (1990). Anatomical abnormalities in the brains of monozygotic twins discordant for schizophrenia. *New England Journal of Medicine, 322,* 789–794.

Sweeney, J.A., Clementz, B.A., Haas, G.L., Escobar, M.D., Drake, K., & Francis, A.J. (1994). Eye tracking dysfunction in schizophrenia: Characterization of component eye movement abnormalities, diagnostic specificity, and the role of attention. *Journal of Abnormal Psychology, 103,* 222–230.

Tarrier, N., & Turpin, G. (1992). Psychosocial factors, arousal and schizophrenic relapse. *British Journal of Psychiatry, 161,* 3–11.

Taylor, C. (1990). Evidence for independent transmission of genetic vulnerability and age of onset in schizophrenia. *Schizophrenia Research, 3,* 13.

Tiwari, J.L., & Terasaki, P.I. (1985). *HLA and disease associations.* New York: Springer-Verlag.

Todd, R.D., Chakraverty, S., & Parsian, A. (1994). Possible association between the dopamine D3 receptor gene and bipolar affective disorder. *American Journal of Human Genetics, 55,* A167.

Torrey, F.F., & Peterson, M.R. (1974). Schizophrenia and the limbic system. *Lancet, 2,* 942–946.

Vaughn, C.E., & Leff, J.P. (1976). The measurement of expressed emotion in the families of psychiatric patients. *British Clinical and Social Psychology, 15,* 157–165.

Ventura, J., Nuechterlein, K.H., Lukoff, D., & Hardesty, J.P. (1989). A prospective study of stressful life events and schizophrenic relapse. *Journal of Abnormal Psychology, 98,* 407–411.

Vinogradov, S., Gottesman, I.I., Moises, H.W., & Nicol, S. (1991). Negative association between schizophrenia and rheumatoid arthritis. *Schizophrenia Bulletin, 17,* 669–678.

Von Euler, C., Forssberg, H., Hedner, F., Johnson, G., Lagercrantz, H., Lundborg, P., Olson, L., &

Seiger, A. (1985). Det centrala nervsystemets utveckling—inre och yttre miljopaverkan (The CNS development—internal and external environmental influence). *Lakartidningen, 82,* 3177–3190.

Wang, S., Sun, C., Walczak, C.A., Ziegle, J.S., Kipps, B.R., Goldin, L.R., & Diehl, S.R. (1995). Evidence for a susceptibility locus for schizophrenia on chromosome 6pter-p22. *Nature Genetics, 1,* 41–46.

Webb, C.T., & Levinson, D.F. (1993). Schizotypal and paranoid personality disorder in the relatives of patients with schizophrenia and affective disorders: A review. *Schizophrenia Research, 11,* 81–92.

Weeks, D.E., & Lange, K. (1988). The affected-pedigree-member method of linkage analysis. *American Journal of Human Genetics, 42,* 315–326.

Weinberger, D.R. (1987). Implications of normal brain development for the pathogenesis of schizophrenia. *Archives of General Psychiatry, 44,* 660–669.

Weinberger, D.R., Berman, K.F., & Zec, R.F. (1986). Physiological dysfunction of dorsolateral prefrontal cortex in schizophrenia. *Archives of General Psychiatry, 43,* 114–124.

Weinberger, D.R., Kleinman, J.E., Luchins, D.J., Bigelow, L.B., & Wyatt, R.J. (1980). Cerebellar pathology in schizophrenia—a controlled postmortem study. *American Journal of Psychiatry, 137,* 359–361.

Wender, P.H., Rosenthal, D., Kety, S.S., Schulsinger, F., & Welner, J. (1974). Crossfostering: A research strategy for clarifying the role of genetic and experiential factors in the etiology of schizophrenia. *Archives of General Psychiatry, 30,* 121–128.

Wolkin, A., Sanfilipo, M., Wolf, A.P., Angrist, B., Brodie, J.D., & Rotrosen, J. (1992). Negative symptoms and hypofrontality in chronic schizophrenia. *Archives of General Psychiatry, 49,* 959–965.

Wong, D.F., Wagner, H.N., Tune, L.E., Dannals, R.F., Pearlson, G.D., Links, J.M., Tamminga, C.A., Broussolle, E.P., Ravert, H.T., Wilson, A.A., Toung, J.K.T., Malat, J., Williams, J.A., O'Tuama, L.A., Snyder, S.H., Kuhar, M.J., & Gjedde, A. (1986). Positron emission tomography reveals elevated D_2 dopamine receptors in drug-naive schizophrenics. *Science, 234,* 1558–1563.

Wright, P., Donaldson, P., Underhill, J., Doherty, D., Choudhuri, K., & Murray, R.M. (1995a). Schizophrenia: A HLA class I and II association study. *Psychiatric Genetics, 5*(S35).

Wright, P., Gilvarry, C.M., Jones, P.B., Cannon, M., Sham, P.C., & Murray, R.M. (1995b). Insulin dependent diabetes mellitus is commoner in first degree relatives of schizophrenic patients. *Psychiatric Genetics, 5,* S68–S69.

Wynne, L.C., & Singer, M.T. (1963). Thought disorder and family relations of schizophrenics: II. A classification of forms of thinking. *Archives of General Psychiatry, 9,* 191–206.

Zipursky, R.B., Lim, K.O., Sullivan, D.V., Brown, B.W., & Pfefferbaum, A. (1992). Widespread cerebral gray matter volume deficits in schizophrenia. *Archives of General Psychiatry, 49,* 195–205.

Zubin, J., & Spring, B. (1977). Vulnerability—a new view of schizophrenia. *Journal of Abnormal Psychology, 8,* 103–126.

CHAPTER 13

SCHIZOPHRENIA: PSYCHOPATHOLOGY

Alan S. Bellack
Jean S. Gearon
University of Maryland School of Medicine

Jack J. Blanchard
University of New Mexico

INTRODUCTION

Schizophrenia is perhaps the most pernicious of all psychiatric disorders. It generally begins in late adolescence or young adulthood and has a lifelong course. Most patients suffer periodic exacerbations that require inpatient care. Although some—a fortunate minority—have a relatively benign course between acute psychotic episodes, most schizophrenia patients experience continued discomfort and disability throughout their lives. Psychotic symptoms such as delusions and hallucinations often persist, albeit at a milder level. Many patients also experience persistent negative symptoms, such as anergia and blunted affect, that impede their ability to care for themselves or fulfill social roles. Between one-half and two-thirds of patients are unable to work, live on their own, or maintain adequate social relationships (Goldstrom & Manderscheid, 1981). Consequently, they tend not to marry and to have a high rate of divorce if they do. They have higher rates of morbidity (prevalence of illness) and earlier mortality than their peers, and have become one of the highest risk groups for HIV (Cournos, 1996). People with schizophrenia also are disproportionately the victims of crime; women with schizophrenia seem especially vulnerable to physical and sexual abuse (Goodman, Rosenberg, Mueser, & Drake, 1997).

Viewed from afar, schizophrenia patients may seem bizarre, frightening, unmotivated, or distasteful, and they fail to elicit sympathy from the community at large. However, the human tragedy of the illness cannot be overemphasized. Promising young lives are destroyed; normal adult goals, such as independence, career, and marriage, generally are unreachable. Despite their "craziness," schizophrenia patients often have a painful awareness of their disability and suffer tremendous depression and anguish. The suicide rate among young schizophrenia patients is 10% to 30%, as high as for patients with affective disorder (Caldwell & Gottesman, 1990). They experience extreme social anxiety and discomfort, and their hallucinations and delusions are frequently terrifying. The economic and psychological toll on families is also

305

dramatic. Parents and siblings endure their own fear, anger, and frustration over adult children who cannot function on their own, who drain family resources, and who periodically become verbally or physically disruptive to the household. While people with schizophrenia are sometimes portrayed as violent by the mass media, they are much more often the victims of violence than perpetrators. The discussion in this and the preceding chapter has a technical flavor, but the reader should not forget that the material pertains to a tragic and painful human condition.

Schizophrenia has been a source of great controversy and confusion in the scientific literature. Despite almost one hundred years of study, its cause is still unknown, and even its definition is the subject of ongoing debate and development. The literature on schizophrenia is so voluminous that even a book-length manuscript would be unable to do justice to the broad range of issues that have been studied. Given the space limitations in this book, we have chosen to highlight some of the most important current themes in the literature. As a concession to the amount of material, two chapters are devoted to schizophrenia. The previous chapter dealt primarily with etiology. This chapter will focus on the nature of the disorder: diagnostic criteria and primary symptoms, prevalence and course, and primary areas of dysfunction, including deficits in information processing and social competence. There is a broad consensus in the field that schizophrenia is a biological disorder whose pathophysiology lies in the structure and/or function of the brain. Hence, discussion will focus on genetics, neurophysiology, and neurochemistry, and related biological issues.

DEFINITION OF THE DISORDER

Schizophrenia is marked by a wide array of symptoms involving multiple aspects of functioning. Each case is unique, but there characteristically are disturbances in several of the following domains:

1. The content of thought may be distorted by delusions and bizarre beliefs.
2. The form of thought is disrupted by loosening of associations or poverty of the content of speech.
3. There are distortions in perception, such as hallucinations.

4. Affect may be flat or blunted, or inappropriate.
5. There is often a distorted or vague sense of self.
6. Many patients experience a loss of volition (e.g., motivation or drive).
7. The quality and range of social relationships are often severely disrupted.
8. There may be disturbances in psychomotor behavior, such as catatonic posturing or odd movements and gestures.

The acute stages of the illness are characteristically marked by extreme thought disturbance and severe behavioral disorganization (e.g., florid psychosis). Many of these symptoms, however, are also present in milder form during prodromal periods prior to acute episodes and/or in residual stages after the episode subsides. As will be indicated, many patients remain substantially dysfunctional between exacerbations; this is especially true of those suffering from high levels of negative symptoms (e.g., avolition, blunted affect, poverty of speech).

Although there is general agreement about the definition of most symptoms, there is considerable controversy over precisely which symptoms are necessary and sufficient to reach the diagnosis. Few patients exhibit all of the characteristic symptoms, and most exhibit different symptoms at different times. There also is no "gold standard," such as a biological test, by which to identify the illness. Hence, the diagnostic criteria or definition of the disorder must be derived by consensus. Not surprisingly, the definition has varied over time and across geographical boundaries. The most widely accepted definition in the United States appears in the *Diagnostic and Statistical Manual of Mental Disorders,* fourth edition (DSM-IV; American Psychiatric Association [APA], 1994). It is a relatively narrow or restrictive definition, which attempts to apply the label to a relatively homogeneous group of patients. This is in marked contrast to earlier periods in our history, when the label was used to describe a broad range of conditions that now receive other diagnoses (e.g., manic-depressive illness, schizotypal personality). As is illustrated in this and the previous chapter, seemingly subtle changes in the criteria can have profound effects on which patients receive the diagnosis. Changes in the makeup of the diagnosed cohort can lead to markedly different conclusions about etiology, response to treatment, genetic risk, and so on.

DSM criteria are based on several implicit assumptions about schizophrenia that have varying degrees of empirical support and are subject to ongoing debate, First, it is assumed that there are no pathognomonic indicators or symptoms. One could arbitrarily define schizophrenia on the basis of a particular symptoms, such as delusions that one's thoughts have been removed or that specific thoughts have been inserted into one's head. To date, however, no such symptom(s) have proved useful in delineating a homogeneous group of patients (e.g., having a common course, response to treatment, family history, etc.). Consequently, as discussed in Chapter 1, DSM criteria are polythetic. While the DSM-III and III-R gave primacy to positive symptoms (e.g., delusions and hallucinations), DSM-IV gives more prominence to negative symptoms. Specifically, alogia (poverty of speech) and avolition (lack of interest or motivation) have been included in the list of diagnostic criteria. This shift in emphasis is in response to current research findings indicating that negative symptoms account for a substantial degree of the morbidity associated with schizophrenia. Indeed, some researchers argue that negative symptoms play such a prominent role in schizophrenia that they demarcate a distinct subtype of the illness (to be discussed below).

Psychotic symptoms are exhibited by patients suffering from a variety of disorders in addition to schizophrenia (e.g., manic-depressive illness, organic psychoses). Thus, a diagnosis of schizophrenia cannot be made on the basis of a cross-sectional snapshot of the patient. The DSM requires that acute symptoms persist for at least 1 month, and there must be continuous signs of the illness (e.g., a prodrome) for at least 6 months before the diagnosis can be made. In the case of a chronic patient, the diagnosis can be made by reference to the previous history, but a so-called first-break patient cannot receive the diagnosis until at least 6 months have passed (the interim diagnosis is schizophreniform disorder).

One additional assumption made by the DSM also warrants brief mention. DSM infers that schizophrenia is a discrete disease entity: Either one has it (i.e., meets the criteria) or one does not have it. As is discussed in this and the previous chapter, this assumption is subject to considerable debate. The polythetic DSM criteria acknowledge that schizophrenia is a heterogeneous disorder. This heterogeneity may pertain to etiology, course, and treatment, as well as to the manner of symptom presentation (to be discussed), For example, not everyone with schizophrenia has a chronic course, or evidence of excessive dopamine activity. If subsequent research indicates that the current heterogeneous definition is not a useful predictor or is not consistent with, say, new findings on genetic linkage, the category might best be replaced by two or more categories that are more homogeneous. An example might be positive schizophrenia, an inherited disorder of the dopamine system, and negative schizophrenia, an acquired structural brain disease (Crow, 1985).

Schizophrenia also may be an extreme form of a continuum of psychopathology or neurophysiological dysfunction. DSM reflects this possibility indirectly with the category of schizotypal personality disorder. DSM assumes that schizotypals and schizophrenics share some symptoms but have a different etiology and pathophysiology. However, there is considerable research to suggest an underlying commonality, referred to as schizotypy or schizophrenia spectrum (Meehl, 1990). The spectrum concept infers that what is inherited is a neurophysiological impairment that makes the individual vulnerable to a range of interrelated symptoms, not schizophrenia per se (see later in this chapter and in the previous chapter for a more extensive discussion of this issue). Although some individuals develop the full schizophrenic syndrome, others are somehow protected and remain asymptomatic or develop milder disorders. This issue is still not resolved and requires much further study.

PREVALENCE AND COURSE

To appreciate fully the clinical, social, and economic impact of schizophrenia, it is necessary to begin with an overview of the epidemiology and course of this disorder. A small but significant percentage of individuals will suffer from schizophrenia during their lifetime. Prevalence rates of schizophrenia obtained from the National Institute of Mental Health (NIMH) Epidemiologic Catchment Area (ECA) Program, based on 18,571 persons in five community samples, indicate 1-month, 6-month, and lifetime prevalence rates of 0.6%, 0.8%, and 1.3%, respectively (Reiger et al., 1988). These prevalence rates translate into approximately 1.5 million persons with schizophrenia in a 6-month period (Rosenstein, Milazzo-Sayre, & Manderscheid, 1989). Lifetime prevalence rates appear to be equivalent for males and females (Regier et al., 1988); however, as will be discussed, there may be gender differences in age of onset and the course of the illness.

Onset of schizophrenia typically occurs in late adolescence or early adulthood. There is some evidence that there may be gender differences in age of onset (see Anger-Myer et al., 1990; Flor-Henry, 1985; and Lewine, 1981, for reviews), with males having an earlier age of onset or hospitalization (Loranger, 1984; Dworkin, 1990). Rates of onset for males are concentrated in the twenties, whereas females have higher rates in the thirties (Lewine, 1981; Loranger, 1984; Rosenthal, 1971). We will return to the issue of gender differences later on.

Although schizophrenia has a lower lifetime prevalence rate than such disorders as major depression or phobia (5.8% and 12.5%, respectively; Regier et al., 1988), its impact is perhaps best reflected in the proportion of mental health services that are devoted to patients with schizophrenia. Findings from the National Reporting Program for Mental Health Statistics (Rosenstein et al., 1989) provide an overview of characteristics of patient care for individuals with a diagnosis of schizophrenia or schizophreniform disorder prior to the managed-care era. Of the 4.2 million admissions to inpatient, outpatient, and partial care programs in the United States in 1986, 495,000 (12%) were for schizophrenia. Additionally, of an estimated 1.8 million individuals under care in these settings on April 1, 1986, approximately 390,000 (22%) had a diagnosis of schizophrenia. Thirty-eight percent of the entire inpatient population consisted of schizophrenics, of whom 92% had received prior psychiatric inpatient care (Rosenstein et al., 1989). These data are reflective of psychiatric hospitalization practices prior to the advent of managed care in the United States. Admission criteria for inpatient psychiatric care have become much more stringent since the mid-1990s, and lengths of stay have declined precipitously. Nevertheless, the overall proportion of health care dollars expended on schizophrenia remains grossly out of proportion to the percentage of cases in the population.

An understanding of the course and outcome of schizophrenia is important, as the prognosis of this disorder has, historically, been central in definitions of this diagnostic construct. For Kraepelin, a deteriorating course was the core identifying feature of schizophrenia (the *dementia* of dementia praecox). The relevance of the course of schizophrenia continues to be reflected in its use in various diagnostic concepts, as well as in theories of schizophrenia.

Although there has been much debate over Kraepelin's formulation of a deteriorating course in schizophrenia, accumulating evidence suggests little optimism as to the prognosis of individuals suffering from the disease. Of those patients successfully stabilized on medication, approximately 25% to 40% will relapse in the first year following hospitalization, and 50% to 60% will have relapsed by the second year (Hogarty et al., 1986; Hogarty, Anderson, & Reiss, 1987). Recent reports (Breier, Schreiber, Dyer, & Pickar, 1991; Harrow, Sands, Silverstein, & Goldberg, 1997), with follow-up periods of 2 to 12 years, further indicate that few patients show complete remission; only a minority (approximately 20%) show a good outcome; and over 50% will have a poor outcome with continued symptomatology and poor social and work functioning. One notable exception comes from a long-term follow-up of chronic patients discharged from a state psychiatric hospital in Vermont. Harding, Brooks, Ashikaga, Strauss, and Breier (1987) found that 32 years after discharge, between one-half and two-thirds of the ex-patients were symptom-free and had made a reasonable adjustment to life in the community. These data suggest that the course of schizophrenia may be variable rather than uniformly downward. It should also be noted that the data presented above reflect treatment with the traditional antipsychotic medications (e.g., haloperidol, fluphenazine). There has been a dramatic change in medication treatment in the 1990s with the advent of the so-called atypical antipsychotics such as clozapine and risperidone. These new medications seem to have different modes of action (i.e., they are less potent dopamine blockers), have much more favorable side effect profiles, and may produce better outcomes (Buchanan, 1995). For example, clozapine appears to have significant benefits for about 30% of severely ill patients who are not responsive to the traditional drugs (Kane et al., 1988). However, while some patients have had their lives turned around by these new drugs, most continue to suffer and remain unable to fulfill social roles successfully.

In addition to the potential effects of new medications, the course of the illness also may be ameliorated by earlier intervention than has been the case in the past. Most people with schizophrenia do not come to the attention of mental health professionals until the illness is well established: e.g., after several psychiatric episodes and periods of hospitalization. There often is a reluctance to assign this label to young people because of the difficulty of making the diagnosis among adolescents and the stigma associated with the diagnosis. However, the difficulty of reversing the course in well-established cases has stimulated increasing interest in early intervention. As discussed at length in a recent issue of the *Schizophrenia Bulletin* (Volume 22, No. 2, 1996) there are promising data from several programs around the world that are engaged in outreach to identify prepsychotic and "first-break" cases, and to provide pharmacotherapy, skills training, and family counseling to reduce stress, modulate the neurobiology of the disorder, and prevent social isolation.

In addition to the earlier age of onset noted previously, males may also display a more chronic course of schizophrenia than females. Males represent a larger proportion of the inpatient population (64%; Rosenstein et al., 1989), are rehospitalized more often (Goldstein, 1988; Salokangas, 1983), and have longer stays in the hospital (Goldstein, 1988; Salokangas, 1983). In a 2-year follow-up of patients participating in the International Pilot Study of Schizophrenia (World Health Organization, 1979), male gender predicted longer duration of the episode of inclusion and a higher percentage of the follow-up period spent in psychotic episode(s), and was associated with the incidence of an unremitting course (still in episode of inclusion at time of follow-up). The reasons for these gender differences are unclear. However, neurobiological differences between the sexes (e.g., hormonal factors, functional organization of the brain) as well as social or environmental factors may act as protective agents for females or may place males at greater risk. Gender differences remain enigmatic, however, and are the focus of much current research.

THE HETEROGENEITY OF SCHIZOPHRENIA

Perhaps one of the most outstanding features of schizophrenia is its heterogeneity. Within the diagnosis of schizophrenia, symptoms vary widely between patients and even within the same patient across time. Such heterogeneity is also seen in the variance of performance across tasks utilized in psychopathology research (measures of attention, memory, etc.), with some patients performing well below normal while others evince little impairment.

This heterogeneity is problematic in that it may reflect the misdiagnosis of patients or may be the result of diverse etiologies that, while sharing some common symptoms, nevertheless represent different disease entities. Furthermore, such diversity in symptomatology introduces an additional explanatory burden on theories that seek to account for the clinical manifestations of this disorder. In the early stages of theory building and testing it may be useful to focus on a central feature or subtype of the disorder prior to accounting for the entire array of possible expressions of the diagnostic construct. For these reasons, various attempts have been made to delimit the phenotypic heterogeneity of the illness. Two such strategies that seek to obtain more homogeneous diagnostic groups are (1) refinement of diagnosis to delineate more clearly diagnostic boundaries between schizophrenia and other disorders, as well as to reduce method error, and (2) use of subtypes within the diagnosis of schizophrenia.

Introduction of operational diagnostic criteria, such as the Research Diagnostic Criteria (RDC; Spitzer, Endicott, & Robins, 1978) in the late 1970s, in conjunction with structured diagnostic interviews such as the Schedule for Affective Disorders and Schizophrenia (SADS; Endicott & Spitzer, 1978), increased the reliability of diagnosis (see Matarazzo, 1983) and helped demarcate schizophrenia from other disorders. With provision of explicit inclusion and exclusion criteria, accuracy of diagnosis was greatly enhanced. These advances in diagnosis provided purer diagnostic categories by minimizing diagnostic error and addressing (but not eliminating) symptom overlap between diagnostic categories. Although the boundaries of schizophrenia have been clarified and the error related to the diagnosis of schizophrenia reduced, phenotypic heterogeneity remains within the confines of this diagnosis.

Another approach to resolve the problem of phenotypic heterogeneity has been to identify distinct subtypes of the disease. As Bleuler (1911/1950) noted, the possible "symptom combinations are endless. . . ." (p. 227); however, Bleuler and Kraepelin differentiated four primary subtypes: paranoid, catatonia, hebephrenic, and schizophrenia simplex. Three of these subtypes have endured to be reflected in the DSM-IV schizophrenia diagnoses of paranoid type, catatonic type, and disorganized type (the equivalent of hebephrenic). In the nosological history of schizophrenia, numerous other subtypologies have been proposed, typically in the form of dichotomous distinctions such as paranoid–nonparanoid, acute–chronic, process–reactive, and active–withdrawn. These dichotomies have enjoyed various degrees of empirical support and have waxed and waned in importance. For the most part they have had mixed success in predicting course or treatment response. Most patients exhibit symptoms of different subtypes at different times. We will focus our discussion on the two dichotomies that are of greatest contemporary interest: positive versus negative schizophrenia and deficit and nondeficit schizophrenia.

The Positive–Negative Symptom Distinction

As illustrated in Table 13-1, the so-called *positive* symptoms of schizophrenia reflect behavioral excesses (e.g., hallucinations, delusions), whereas *negative* symptoms reflect behavioral deficits (e.g., poverty of speech, flat affect). Although the origins of the positive–negative terminology are often attributed to the neurologist John Hughlings Jackson (1835–1911), Berrios (1985) has identified the origins as pre-Jacksonian, originating instead in the writings of John Russell Reynolds (1828–1896). Contemporary use of these terms in schizophrenia is based largely on the proposed two-syndrome concept of Crow (1980, 1983, 1985).

Crow (1985) proposed two "dimensions of pathology" underlying schizophrenia. These dimensions reflect the positive–negative distinction and are referred to as Type I (characterized by positive symptoms) and Type II (characterized by negative symp-

toms). As shown in Table 13-2, this model proposes that the two syndromes of positive and negative symptoms differ not only in the constellation of symptoms by which they can be identified, but also with respect to underlying pathological processes (though sharing the same pathogen), course, and treatment response.

Positive-symptom schizophrenia is hypothesized to reflect a neurotransmitter (dopaminergic) disturbance that is responsive to neuroleptic treatment. Negative-symptom schizophrenia is hypothesized to reflect neuroanatomical changes (such as enlarged ventricles) that, because of the structural anomalies involved, are not amenable to neuroleptic treatment. Crow (1983, 1985) did not view these two subtypes as independent. Rather, these syndromes of subtypes are conceptualized as "overlapping constellations of symptoms" (1983, p. 81) that may co-occur in the same patient. Crow further suggested that the temporal relationship between the two syndromes may be characterized by a progression over time from predominantly positive symptoms, to mixed, to predominantly negative symptoms.

The distinction between positive and negative schizophrenia has received a great deal of attention from researchers, in part because of the testability of the predictions derived from the model. For example, positive symptoms are hypothesized to be the expression of a neurotransmitter disturbance, which responds to medication and thus is related to a good outcome; negative symptoms are hypothesized to result from structural changes in the brain, are refractory to pharmacological treatment, and are differentially associated with cognitive impairment and poor prognosis. Initial research findings about these differences have been quite promising.

Some of the most compelling data in support of the positive–negative distinction involve demonstration of the association between negative symptoms and neurological abnormalities such as enlarged ventricles (e.g., Andreasen, Olsen, Dennert, & Smith, 1982; Besson, Corrigan, Cherryman, & Smith, 1987; Johnstone, Crow, Frith, Husband, & Kreel, 1976). Further support for the positive–negative distinction has been provided by studies that have purported to demonstrate the response of positive symptoms to neuroleptics and the nonresponsiveness of negative symptoms (Johnstone, Crow, Frith, Carney, & Price,

TABLE 13-1 Positive and negative symptoms in schizophrenia.

Negative Symptoms

Affective flattening	Paucity of affective behavior, including lack of facial and vocal expression and gestures
Alogia	Poverty of speech or speech content
Avolition–apathy	Decreased motivation, interest, or energy
Anhedonia–asociality	Lack of interest or pleasure typically associated with activities or social relations
Attention	Deficits in attention as evidenced during social interactions or in formal cognitive testing

Positive Symptoms

Delusions	Beliefs that are unreasonable, illogical, or absurd
Hallucinations	Sensory experiences that are not based on real stimuli
Psychomotor behavior	Bizarre or excessive mannerisms, posture, excitability, and so on
Formal thought disorder	Disturbances in the form of thought, such as tangentiality or loosening of associations, neologisms, and perseverations

TABLE 13-2 Crow's two-syndrome model of schizophrenia.

Defining symptoms	Flat affect, poverty of speech, anhedonia (negative symptoms)	Hallucinations, delusions thought disorder (positive symptoms)
Underlying pathology	Neuroanatomical abnormalities (e.g., enlarged ventricles)	Increased number of sensitivity of D_2 dopamine receptors)
Treatment response	Poor response to medication	Relatively good response to medication

1978; Angrist, Rotrosen, & Gershon, 1980). Also, negative symptoms have been shown to be related to poor outcome (Pogue-Geile & Harrow, 1985).

The accumulating research evidence has not been all positive, however, and a number of critical inconsistencies have arisen. First, several studies have failed to find an association between negative symptoms and neuroanatomical abnormalities such as enlarged ventricles (Andreasen, Flaum, Swayze, Tyrrell, & Arndt, 1990; DeLisi, Goldin, Hamovit, Maxwell, Kurtz, & Gershon, 1986; Nasrallah, Kuperman, Hamara, & McCalley-Whitters, 1983). Second, cognitive deficits have been demonstrated to be related to both negative and positive symptoms (Green & Walker, 1985; Johnstone, Owens, Gold, Crow, & Macmillan, 1981), although the pattern of deficits may differ for each symptom type (Green & Walker, 1985). Third, the temporal stability and treatment-refractory nature of negative symptoms, and the responsiveness of positive symptoms, proposed by Crow has not been established. Negative symptoms

have been shown to decrease over time (Pogue-Geile & Harrow, 1985) and do show at least some degree of response to neuroleptic treatment (Meltzer, 1985; Kay & Singh, 1989). Additionally, in some cases positive symptoms do not respond or respond poorly to neuroleptics (Brown & Herz, 1989; Keefe et al., 1988). Finally, negative symptoms are not invariably associated with poor prognosis (Kay, 1990), whereas positive symptoms have been shown to be related to poor outcome (Kay, 1990; Pogue-Geile & Harrow, 1985).

The positive–negative distinction may reflect important differences between patients but may not be sufficiently comprehensive to categorize all patients diagnosed with schizophrenia. A series of factor-analytic studies suggests that the illness may be better represented by three symptom domains: hallucinations and delusions, negative symptoms, and cognitive impairment (Buchanan & Carpenter, 1994). The precise symptom composition of the cognitive impairment factor has varied somewhat across studies but generally includes positive formal thought disorder and attentional impairments. Bizarre behavior and disorganization are also sometimes included. The fact that this three-dimensional factor-analytic solution has been replicated, in whole or in part, across multiple studies from different laboratories and with different patient populations makes it quite promising. Conversely, this model could reflect a measurement artifact, as the data are primarily derived from the same set of semistructured clinical interviews that focus on a specific set of symptoms. Different assessment techniques or assessments with a different focus (e.g., social role functioning) could yield a different factor structure or include a different set of behaviors.

Are these inconsistencies sufficient to refute the positive–negative symptom distinction? Although these conflicting findings do pose very serious challenges to the theory, they suggest the need to evaluate this distinction more critically and refine it, rather than its demise. A review of this literature suggests the need to address a variety of methodological issues that may contribute to these inconsistent findings:

1. Use of varying definitions of symptoms and methods of symptom assessment clearly impedes the comparison of results across studies.
2. The almost exclusive reliance on cross-sectional designs has been problematic in that such designs may yield unstable assessments of symptoms. Additional studies utilizing longitudinal assessments are required.
3. The vast majority of studies have used medicated patients, which introduces confounds because medicated patients may exhibit drug side effects that are potentially indistinguishable from negative symptoms.
4. The comparison of acute and chronic patient samples also may impede comparisons between studies.

This is not an exhaustive list of the problems in this research, but it does highlight fundamental methodological issues that must be addressed.

The positive and negative subtypology may also be showing the same weaknesses that have hobbled past subtype schemes. That is, the positive–negative distinction may retain the very problem of symptom heterogeneity that it sought to address. For example, the positive symptom complex, depending on the rating system employed, may include such diverse symptoms as delusions, conceptual disorganization, hallucinatory behavior, excitement, grandiosity, suspiciousness/persecution, and hostility. Given this diversity of symptoms, patients with equivalent global positive or negative symptom scores may differ greatly in the individual symptoms on which the global score is based. More important, however, the majority of schizophrenics evince a mixture of both positive and negative symptoms. Andreasen et al. (1990) recently failed to replicate the incidence of "predominantly" negative- or positive-symptom schizophrenics reported in earlier studies (Andreasen & Olsen, 1982). That is, rather than finding an approximately equal proportion of patients in the negative-, positive-, and mixed-symptom categories, these investigators found the majority of patients to have mixed symptoms (76%) while only a small minority had exclusively positive (16%) or negative symptoms (8%). These issues, in addition to the inconsistent findings outlined previously, suggest the need to consider alternative approaches to the study of schizophrenia. One such alternative approach has been proposed by Carpenter and colleagues (Carpenter, Heinrichs, & Wagman, 1988): deficit and non-deficit schizophrenia.

The Deficit Syndrome

Clinical manifestations of negative symptoms can result from a number of factors in addition to schizophrenia per se. For example, depression, side effects of antipsychotic medications, and social withdrawal can all present as loss of interest and energy, decreased speech, and decreased pleasure from social activities. Medication side effects such as pseudo-Parkinsonism can also produce the wooden facial expression, motoric rigidity and slowness often seen in patients with prominent negative symptoms. These "secondary" negative symptoms can be just as debilitating as "primary" negative symptoms that result from schizophrenia, but they often are transient (increasing or decreasing in conjunction with the precipitating factor) and do not result from the same underlying pathophysiology. Moreover, the diagnostic distinction is difficult, if not impossible, to make in a brief, cross sectional interview, it requires more information about the patient over time. Carpenter argues that the effort to use negative symptoms to define a putative subtype of schizophrenia has failed because no clear distinction has been made between the primary, *enduring* negative symptoms (labeled *deficit* symptoms) and the more transient negative symptoms secondary to other factors in the assessment process.

By definition, deficit symptoms are present during and between episodes of symptom exacerbation, are considered to be independent of medical status, and are not necessarily responsive to anticholinergic drugs (i.e., medications used to control the side effects of antipsychotics) or antipsychotic drug withdrawal. Criteria for a diagnosis of deficit syndrome include: (1) DSM-IV criteria for schizophrenia, and (2) two of the following negative symptoms must have been present for the preceding 12 months and during periods of clinical stability or recovery from psychotic exacerbation: *affective flattening* (restricted affect and diminished emotional range), *alogia* (poverty of speech), and/or *avolition* (diminished sense of purpose and social drive). Furthermore, the negative symptoms cannot be fully accounted for by depression or anxiety, drug effects, or environmental deprivation. Initial validity research examining this subtype of schizophrenia is promising and indicates that deficit syndrome patients have neuropsychological and eye-tracking impairments that distinguish them from other chronic schizophrenic patients (Wagman, Heinrichs, & Carpenter, 1987; Thacker, Buchanan, Kirkpatrick, & Tamminga, 1988). Ongoing research, however, is needed to further validate this subtype of schizophrenia.

Symptoms versus Subtypes

Our understanding of schizophrenia may benefit from a symptom approach rather than exclusive reliance on diagnostic categories or subtypologies within these categories, as with the positive–negative distinction (Neale, Oltmanns, & Harvey, 1985; Persons, 1986; also see Chapman & Chapman, 1973, pp. 335–337). With the symptom approach, an individual symptom is the focus of study rather than a heterogeneous class of symptoms. Thus, a researcher may study the symptom of thought disorder or flat affect rather than the global positive or negative symptom score.

There are several advantages to this symptom oriented approach (see Neale et al., 1985, and Persons, 1986, for a full discussion). First, it is conceptually easier to formulate and test theories regarding the underlying mechanisms of a *single* symptom rather than a phenotypically heterogeneous *class* of symptoms. Second, the symptom approach ensures that the symptom of interest is indeed present in the patient sample studied. In contrast, the assignment of a subtype label (e.g., positive or negative) provides only general information regarding the individual symptoms that may be present. Third, this approach offers the advantage of studying psychological phenomena that are not explicitly included or required in diagnostic categories or subtypes. Finally, given the specificity involved in the study of a symptom, this approach facilitates the comparison of results across studies, avoiding the interpretive difficulty encountered in the positive–negative symptom literature.

The symptom approach has been applied to such symptoms as thought disorder (e.g., Harvey, 1983) and flat affect (e.g., Mayer, Alpert, Stastny, Perlick, & Empfield, 1985). In the study of thought disorder, for example, use of traditional diagnostic or subtyping approaches fails to acknowledge that thought disorder is not present in all schizophrenics, ignores the various forms of thought disorder (incoherence, derailment, illogical thinking, poverty of content of speech, neologisms), and does not account for the fact that thought disorder is a transient phenomenon. Thus, in adopting a symptom approach, Harvey (1983) was able to compare thought-disordered speech segments with non-thought-disordered speech segments in schizophrenics and to demonstrate the specificity of language deficits to thought disordered segments.

A CORE DEFICIT OF SCHIZOPHRENIA?

Yet another method to understand the diverse symptom picture of schizophrenia has been the attempt to specify a core deficit that underlies the varied symptoms of this disorder. For example, Bleuler (1911/1950) postulated a single underlying cognitive deficit that was responsible for what Kraepelin and Bleuler considered to be the hallmark symptom of disordered thinking. Bleuler proposed the construct of associative threads to understand normal thinking. Associative threads were hypothesized to link ideas, topics, sentences, and words in a goal-directed fashion. It is the "disconnecting of associative threads" (Bleuler, 1911/1950, p. 21) that results in the confused and bizarre thinking of schizophrenia. This disturbance in associations was considered by Bleuler to be the only symptom that was both fundamental—occurring in all cases—and primary being a direct result of the supposed underlying organic pathology.

Bleuler's theory of associative disturbance represents the first attempt to specify a primary cognitive deficit that is theorized to underlie a constellation of diverse symptoms (i.e., the various manifestations of thought disorder). Bleuler's theory serves as the precursor of contemporary cognitive theories to which we will now turn. We will focus our discussion on information-processing theories (and related psychophysiological research), given the historical and contemporary prominence of such theories.

Attention and Information Processing

There is an extensive body of literature documenting that patients with schizophrenia have prominent cognitive impairments, including deficits in attention, memory, and higher level cognitive processes, such as abstract reasoning, maintenance of set, the ability to integrate situational context or previous experience into ongoing processing, and other "executive" functions (Gray, Feldon, Rawlins, Hemsley, & Smith, 1991). As discussed in the preceding chapter, there are several lines of evidence which suggest that cognitive impairment is largely independent of symptoms, and that many of these higher level deficits may result from a neurodevelopmental problem that results in subtle dysfunction of a neural system in the frontal and temporal lobes of the brain (Goldberg & Gold, 1995; Saykin et al., 1994). Moreover, cognitive performance deficits are not substantially ameliorated by treatment with typical antipsychotic medications (Spohn & Strauss, 1989). We will focus the following discussion on problems in attention to highlight this research area, as attention has occupied a central place in cognitive models of the disorder. However, it should be noted that equal attention could be devoted to problems in memory or executive function.

Attentional theories of schizophrenia are rooted in clinical accounts of the disorder and have been further refined with the advances of cognitive psychology, Kraepelin (1919/1971) offered the first account of disordered attention in schizophrenia:

This behavior is without doubt nearly related to the disorder of attention which we very frequently find conspicuously developed in our patients. It is quite common for them to lose both inclination and ability on their own initiative to keep their attention fixed for any length of time. It is often difficult for them to attend at all. (pp. 5–6)

Personal accounts from people with schizophrenia further suggest the centrality of attentional deficits.

My concentration is poor. I jump from one thing to another. If *I am* talking to someone they only need to cross their legs or scratch their heads and I am distracted and forget what I was saying. I think I could concentrate better with my eyes shut. (McGhie & Chapman, 1961, p. 104)

Theorizing about attentional or information-processing deficits in schizophrenia was facilitated by the emergence of models of information processing in cognitive psychology. For example, Broadbent (1958) contended that there were limits on the amount and speed of information that could be processed at one time and that a filter mechanism first screens out, or attenuates (Broadbent, 1971) irrelevant information prior to processing. In the processing-capacity model of Kahneman (1973), attention is viewed as a finite processing capacity that can be exclusively devoted to one task or distributed among several. The manner in which processing capacity is allocated is dependent on such factors as enduring dispositions, momentary intentions, perceived demands on processing capacity, and level of arousal (Kahneman, 1973).

Nuechterlein and Dawson (1984b) followed the processing capacity model developed by Kahneman, and proposed that a reduced amount of processing capacity available for cognitive tasks may be the primary deficit responsible for a variety of performance deficits in schizophrenia. At least four factors may contribute to the reduction of available processing capacity in schizophrenics (Nuechterlein & Dawson, 1984b):

1. The actual processing capacity is limited.
2. Although there may be a normal amount of processing capacity, it is allocated inefficiently.
3. Processing capacity is allocated to task-irrelevant stimuli, leaving less capacity available for task-relevant stimuli.
4. Rather than using automatic, resource-efficient processing for some cognitive operations, active, conscious processing is used, placing further demands on available processing resources.

With the foregoing discussion as background, we will now turn to an overview of one of the more prominent methods employed to study information processing in schizophrenia. Our review of methods is limited by space; for more extensive discussions of the various paradigms employed, the reader should consult Neale and Oltmanns (1980), and Nuechterlein and Dawson (1984b).

Tasks demonstrating information-processing deficits in schizophrenics and their offspring all impose a high momentary processing load (Nuechterlein & Dawson, 1984b). One such task, the Continuous Performance Task (CPT), is one of the most widely used measures of sustained attention in clinical research. Although a number of versions of the CPT have been employed, the typical protocol requires the subject to view a series of stimuli (letters or digits) on a rear projected screen or computer monitor. The subject is required to respond to a target stimulus (e.g., the number zero) with a button press. Stimuli are rapidly presented with a constant interstimulus interval, ranging from 100 to 1,500 milliseconds. Stimulus presentation times are brief, 40 to 200 milliseconds, and target presentation is relatively infrequent, with the proportion of target stimuli ranging from 0.10 to 0.25. Demands on processing capacity may be increased by degrading the stimuli (blurring them) or by introducing a memory component to the task by requiring *response to a two* trial sequence of letters or numbers, such as a 3 followed by a 7 (Nuechterlein, Edell, Norris, & Dawson, 1986).

Performance deficits have been found in medicated and drug-free schizophrenics and across clinical state. Drug-free schizophrenics have shown lower target hit rates on the CPT than normals and alcoholics (Orzack & Kornetsky, 1966). However, neuroleptics do appear to improve performance (e.g.,

Spohn, Lacoursiere, Thompson, & Coyne, 1977). Decreased target hit rates have also been observed in clinically remitted schizophrenics (Asarnow & MacCrimmon, 1976; Wohlberg & Kornetsky, 1973). Additionally, Nuechterlein et al. (1990) report preliminary findings from a longitudinal study of schizophrenics indicating stable performance deficits across actively psychotic and remitted states.

Deficits in information processing also may serve as markers of vulnerability to schizophrenia. CPT performance deficits have also been shown in populations at risk for the development of schizophrenia (i.e., the offspring of schizophrenics). These deficits are specific to versions of the CPT that have increased processing load because of either a memory component (Erlenmeyer-Kimling & Cornblatt, 1978) or degraded stimuli (Nuechterlein, 1983). Performance deficits on these versions of the CPT appear to be specific to the offspring of schizophrenics. Offspring of parents with psychiatric disorders other than the schizophrenia spectrum do not show CPT deficits (Nuechterlein, 1983). Although children with attention deficit disorder also display performance deficits on the CPT, their pattern of performance differs from that of the offspring of schizophrenics, suggesting an impulsive cognitive style (Nuechterlein, 1983).

The CPT has been demonstrated to be a powerful tool in the investigation of information processing in schizophrenia. Data from this task have been utilized in generating and testing models of vulnerability to schizophrenia (Nuechterlein, 1987; Nuechterlein & Dawson, 1984a). It has also been proposed that the CPT may be useful in genetic linkage analysis (Holzman & Matthysse, 1990). However, several issues concerning the CPT (which are likely to be applicable to other measures of information processing) should be noted. First, deficient performance on the CPT is not present in all schizophrenics. Depending on the criteria of performance employed, approximately 40% to 50% of schizophrenics display deficits (Orzack & Kornetsky, 1966; Walker & Shaye, 1982). Second, the functional relationship between CPT deficits and symptomatology in schizophrenia has been poorly articulated. Only recently have investigators gone beyond the correlation between CPT deficits and the diagnosis of schizophrenia to look at specific symptoms such as thought disorder that may be related to information-processing deficits by the

CPT (Nuechterlein et al., 1986). Third, there is evidence that poor performance on the CPT not only may reflect information-processing abnormalities but also may be the result of poor motor functioning (Walker & Green, 1982). Finally, performance deficits on the CPT may not reflect deficits in sustained attention but may result from other, as yet uninvestigated, processing deficits (Nuechterlein, 1991).

Psychophysiological Abnormalities

In addition to use of cognitive measures as putative indices of central deficits, schizophrenia researchers have also looked to psychophysiological measures, such as electrodermal responding (Bernstein, 1987; Dawson, 1990). Electrodermal activity poses an attractive variable for study because it reflects sympathetic nervous system activity associated with arousal and attentional processes (Bernstein, 1987; Dawson & Nuechterlein, 1984). Additionally, psychophysiological paradigms allow for the study of patients who may be too ill to participate in more demanding cognitive tasks (Bernstein, 1987).

One electrodermal response that has received much study is the phasic increase in skin conductance level elicited by novel or psychologically meaningful stimuli such as innocuous tones. These skin conductance responses (SCRS) reflect sympathetic nervous system arousal and are a component of the orienting response (OR), a pattern of physiological response that is viewed as an index of attentional processes involved in information intake (Bernstein, 1987).

In general, two deviant patterns of electrodermal response have been noted in schizophrenics: (1) the failure to display skin conductance orienting responses, or SCORs (reflecting hypoarousal), and (2) in patients who do evince SCORS, the failure of these responses to habituate (hyperarousal). Approximately 40% to 50% of schizophrenics can be classified as SCOR nonresponders (Bernstein, 1987; Bernstein et al., 1982). Nonresponding in these schizophrenics may indicate a failure "to allocate central attentional capacity as, and when, most normal people do" (Bernstein et al, 1988, p. 9), suggesting an inefficient deployment of cognitive resources (Ohman, Nordby, & d'Elia, 1986).

In those patients who are SCOR responders, a subgroup fails to habituate and continues to display a pattern of responses indicative of sympathetic nervous system hyperarousal. Sympathetic hyperresponsivity is also present in high-risk children and may be an indicator of those children at highest risk for later developing schizophrenia (Bernstein, 1987; Dawson & Nuechterlein, 1984). It has been suggested (Nuechterlein & Dawson, 1984a) that such hyperarousal may be related to sensitivity to aversive social stimuli and may contribute to information-processing impairments at higher levels of arousal.

Electrodermal nonresponders and responders (schizophrenics who are slow to habituate) appear to differ in a number of ways, including brain metabolism, types of attentional deficits, behavioral characteristics, and prognosis. Preliminary data suggest that nonresponders may have lower brain metabolic activity (assessed using positron emission tomography) than do responders during performance on the CPT (Dawson, 1990). Regarding attentional deficits, Dawson (1990) has recently speculated that performance on attentional tasks suggests that nonresponders "may be deficient in the ability to actively allocate attentional resources to environmental stimuli," while responders "may be deficient in the ability to inhibit the allocation of attentional resources to irrelevant environmental stimuli" (p. 249). Behaviorally, nonresponders have been characterized as socially and emotionally withdrawn, whereas responders have been described as more excited and active (Bernstein, 1987; Dawson & Nuechterlein, 1984). Both nonresponse and slow habituation have been shown to be related to poor prognosis, although each may be related to a different dimension of outcome. Specifically, SCOR nonresponse may predict poor social functioning (Ohman, Ohlund, Alm, Wieselgren, Ost, & Lindstrom, 1989), whereas slow habituation may be related to poor symptom response to treatment (particularly for positive symptoms) (Bernstein, 1987).

Although electrodermal responding is a powerful method of study in schizophrenia, some qualifications to the foregoing generalizations should be noted, There is debate as to whether the available empirical evidence actually supports the theoretical link between psychophysiological measures and performance on attentional tasks. Psychophysiological measures have been shown to be poorly or imperfectly correlated with performance (Bernstein, 1987;

Ohman et al., 1986). Additionally, the relationship between electrodermal nonresponding and symptomatology has not been consistently replicated (Ohman et al., 1989). Finally, the status of electrodermal measures as stable vulnerability markers is in question, as recent evidence indicates that electrodermal measures may be state-dependent (Dawson, 1990). Despite these issues, however, this area continues to hold great promise, and the domain of psychophysiological activity has been incorporated into a stress/vulnerability model to be discussed.

SOCIAL COMPETENCE

Schizophrenia is ordinarily associated with severe psychotic symptoms, but the only symptom that DSM IV requires of all cases is a deterioration (or failure to achieve adequate levels) of social competence. As indicated previously, as many as two-thirds of schizophrenia patients are unable to fulfill basic social roles, such as spouse, parent, and worker, even when psychotic symptoms are in remission. Most patients have significant impairments in social relationships; they often are isolated, and when they do interact with others, they have difficulty maintaining appropriate conversations, expressing their needs and feelings, achieving social goals, or developing close relationships. Schizophrenia patients are not grossly odd or impaired as children, but subtle signs of interpersonal difficulty are often present in childhood or adolescence (Dworkin et al., 1996). These problems tend to become more apparent during the early stages of the disorder, when many patients become progressively more isolated and have increasing difficulty maintaining previous levels of social adjustment. Premorbid social competence is among the best predictors of long-term outcome (Zigler & Phillips, 1961), either because poor premorbid adjustment is a marker of a more pernicious form of illness or because social competence is a coping skill that helps the individual achieve goals and avoid stress.

Historically, social dysfunction has often been regarded as a correlate or consequence of more fundamental aspects of the illness, such as negative symptoms. However, recent research has shown that poor social competence persists even in the relative absence of other symptoms (Mueser, Bellack, Dou-glas, & Morrison, 1991), and social dysfunction is now considered to be a critical domain in its own right (Strauss, Carpenter, & Bartko, 1974). The precise basis of the social impairment (or any other symptom, for that matter) is not known. The most widely accepted hypothesis is based on the behavioral model of social skills (Bellack & Morrison, 1982; Hersen & Bellack, 1976).

Effective social behavior depends on the ongoing integration of a number of specific component elements, including production of appropriate and clear speech content; modulation of the voice via paralinguistic characteristics such as volume, pace, tone, and inflection; nonverbal behavior, including facial expression, gestures, and posture; and social perception, which includes the identification and interpretation of the behavior of others (Bellack & Morrison, 1982). These component elements are integrated to create complex performance repertoires, such as assertiveness (e.g., arguing with a professor about a grade), social sexual skills (e.g., asking someone for a date), and employment skills (e.g., interviewing for a job). The ability to implement these repertoires is a function of social skills, a set of learned performance capacities that is acquired in the course of development. From this perspective, poor social performance in schizophrenia results from specific social skill deficits rather than from a generic social defect. In comparison to normal controls and patients with other disorders, schizophrenia patients have been found to have a list of specific deficits, including the form of speech (e.g., paralinguistics), the amount and content of speech, facial expression of affect, use of gestures, and ability to maintain appropriate eye contact (Bellack, Morrison, Wixted, & Mueser, 1990).

It has been hypothesized that schizophrenia patients either fail to learn requisite skills or lose them as a result of long periods of isolation, hospitalization, and psychotic withdrawal. Evidence is accumulating that the precursors of adult social disability often can be discerned in childhood (Lewine, Watt, Prentky, & Fryer, 1980), and may be associated with early attentional impairments (Cornblatt, Lenzenweger, Dworkin, & Erlenmeyer-Kimling, 1992). Similarly, poor premorbid social competence has been found to be related to deficits in information processing, and recent studies with adult patients have also noted significant relationships between measures of social competence and diverse measures of cognitive functioning (Green, 1996).

There is not complete consistency across these studies in terms of which specific cognitive measures correlate with which specific measures of social skill, but this literature is consistent with the hypothesis that an impairment of basic cognitive functions (especially verbal memory and visual information processing) may be an important determinant of both social skill level and the ability to profit from skills-training interventions. Social interchange involves a constant and rapid flow of information: verbal content of speech, illustrative gestures and changes in voice inflection, subtle changes in facial expression, and the like flow in machine gun fashion. The social participant must continually monitor and translate these social stimuli, screen out irrelevant information (a partner scratching her neck, a noise from behind, etc.), determine an appropriate response, and emit the response. As previously indicated, schizophrenia patients have pronounced difficulties in sustaining attention, memory, and speed of processing. Hence, they may not be able to manage the rapid flow of social information. They also have difficulty in sensorimotor gating: the ability to screen out irrelevant stimuli and focus attention on relevant input (Braff & Geyer, 1990). Consequently, they are overwhelmed by environmental stimuli and may miss relevant cues, respond to the wrong cues, or misinterpret cues. Some patients apparently react to this bombardment of stimuli by defensively "turning down" the sensory control mechanism and screening the environment out (Ohman et al., 1989). Either excessive screening or inadequate screening can have a profound impact on social perception and social learning. Moreover, lack of adequate skill development and continuing problems in social perception lead to social failure, anxiety, and frustration, which further impedes information processing and increases the inclination to avoid or withdraw from social interactions.

THE STRESS–VULNERABILITY MODEL

Research concerning the etiology and expression of schizophrenia has historically followed one of two broad models—the genetic, or biological, and the environmental (Zubin & Spring, 1977). Each of these models has enjoyed its own empirical successes. For example, twin studies have provided the most compelling data supporting the heritability of schizophrenia, with concordance rates of approximately 45% to 50% for monozygotic (MZ) twins and 9% for dizygotic (DZ) twins (Gottesman & Shields, 1972; Holzman & Matthysse, 1990). On the other hand, data concerning the role of the environment in schizophrenia have demonstrated that exposure to critical family members (e.g., Vaughn & Leff, 1976) or stressful life events (Brown, Birley, & Wing, 1972) greatly increases the likelihood of relapse.

Despite these successes, however, each model appears to have failed to provide a full understanding of the phenomenon of schizophrenia. The episodic course of the illness, with waxing and waning symptoms, has proved to be problematic (Zubin & Spring, 1977). The failure of MZ concordance rates to reach 100% has suggested to some that genes may not tell the whole story. However, environmental models have not been able to compete with genetics in the prediction of who will develop schizophrenia—genetics remain the best bet (Meehl, 1962). As observed by Zubin and Spring (1977), "just as no model has been in danger of being refuted by findings that support another, neither has it been enriched by the interaction of differing views" (p. 108). In the last two decades, however, researchers have sought to study the interaction of these models within a superordinate model that encompasses both—the stress/vulnerability model (Nuechterlein, 1987; Nuechterlein & Dawson, 1984a; Zubin & Steinhauer, 1981).

Vulnerability, defined as the likelihood that an individual will develop schizophrenia, comprises both inborn and acquired components (Zubin & Spring, 1977). Inborn vulnerability is the result of genetic processes, whereas acquired vulnerability may result from such factors as prenatal or perinatal trauma, toxins, disease, or social-developmental events. An individual's vulnerability will be a function of the presence and severity of these various putative factors. An individual's degree of vulnerability will interact with stressors to determine the ultimate risk of exceeding some threshold and moving from normal functioning to the onset or relapse of illness.

Nuechterlein and colleagues (Nuechterlein, 1987; Nuechterlein & Dawson, 1984a) have proposed an elegant model that seeks to incorporate findings concerning personal and environmental factors. Specifically, the stress–vulnerability model comprises four general domains that are involved in the development of schizophrenic symptomatology: personal vulnerability factors, personal protective factors, environmental potentiators and stressors, and environmental protectors (Nuechterlein, 1987).

Personal factors can either place a person at risk (vulnerability) or assist in protecting the individual. Personal vulnerability factors include dopaminergic anomalies, reduced available processing capacity (information-processing deficits), autonomic hyperactivity to aversive stimuli, and schizotypal personality traits (social impairments and related cognitive anomalies). Personal factors that may protect an individual are coping abilities, which may include both cognitive and behavioral abilities to attenuate the impact of stressors (Lukoff, Snyder, Ventura, & Nuechterlein, 1984).

Environmental factors also can be divided into risk and protective categories. Environmental potentiators and stressors include an unsupportive or highly critical family environment, an overstimulating social environment, and stressful life events (see Lukoff et al., 1984). Environmental protectors include a supportive family and psychosocial interventions (e.g., see Hogarty et al., 1987).

In this model, personal and environmental vulnerability factors are seen as interacting to lead to intermediate states of processing capacity overload, tonic autonomic hyperarousal, and impaired processing of social stimuli. As the intermediate states emerge, with attendant prodromal symptoms, they interact in a feedback fashion to amplify personal and environmental vulnerabilities further and to tax protective factors. Thus, intermediate states might further impair the perception and processing of social cues, disrupt coping abilities, and result in dysfunctional behaviors that potentiate or create environmental stressors. Unless interrupted by protective factors, this process escalates to a psychotic episode.

In summary, the stress vulnerability model attempts to integrate environmental models with biological models in an effort to provide a fuller understanding of the development and course of schizophrenia. This model remains "heuristic" (Nuechterlein & Dawson, 1984a), and its individual elements continue to be elevated. However, the model provides great promise for the integration of various scientific disciplines in the study of this vexing disorder.

SUBSTANCE ABUSE

We have focused our discussion on problems and illness manifestations that are part of the inherent nature of schizophrenia. Before concluding our discussion some mention is warranted about a problem that results from an interaction of the illness and the environment: substance abuse. Drug and alcohol abuse by schizophrenia patients is one of the most pressing problems currently facing the mental health system. The lifetime prevalence rate of substance abuse in schizophrenia is close to 50% (Mueser, Bennett, & Kushner, 1995; Regier et al., 1990) and estimates of recent or current substance abuse range from 20% to 65% (Mueser, Yarnold, & Bellack, 1992). Excessive substance use by people with schizophrenia has most of the same adverse social, health, economic, and psychiatric consequences as it does for other individuals. Moreover, it has additional serious consequences for these multiply handicapped patients. It increases the risk of symptom exacerbation and relapse, may compromise the efficacy of neuroleptics, and decreases compliance with treatment. It is often a source of conflict in families—a pernicious circumstance for schizophrenia patients, who are highly vulnerable to heightened stress. Substance use also has deleterious cognitive effects that are superimposed on the information-processing deficits we have already discussed.

One of the most common hypotheses about the reasons for substance abuse in schizophrenia is self-medication: the desire to control frightening thoughts and unpleasant symptoms. While *all* substance use can be defined as self-medication, studies of substance abusing schizophrenia patients have not documented a consistent relationship between substance use and specific forms of symptomatology (Dixon, Haas, Weiden, Sweeney, Frances, 1991). Alcohol is the most commonly abused substance in schizophrenia, as well as in the general population. Following alcohol, drug choice for schizophrenia patients varies over time and as a function of the demographic characteristics of the sample. For example, Mueser et al. (1992) reported that in 1983–1986 cannabis was the most commonly abused illicit drug among schizophrenia patients, whereas in 1986–1990 cocaine became the most popular drug, a change in pattern similar to that in the general population. For many patients, availability of substances appears to be more relevant than the specific CNS effects. The most common reasons given for use of alcohol and other drugs are to "get high" and to reduce negative affective states including social anxiety and tension, dysphoria and depression, and boredom (Dixon et al., 1991). Overall, the data suggest that substance abuse by schizophrenia patients is motivated by the same factors that drives excessive use of harmful substances. However, the data also suggest that substance use may be associated with a desire to seem "normal" and be accepted by peers, as well as help to reduce social anxiety and compensate for social skill deficits.

SUMMARY

This chapter has provided an introduction to schizophrenia. We have attempted to give the reader a sense of the disorder and the many uncertainties and controversies that characterize it. We have emphasized issues that are current and that have a base of empirical support, even if there is considerable disagreement in the literature. We have provided few definitive answers, as few are justified. However, we have tried to illustrate the rapid growth of knowledge about the disorder and have stimulated the reader to think about the controversies in the field rather than memorize a litany of unsupported "facts."

We first described the nature of the disorder, including primary symptoms, diagnostic criteria and controversies, and data about prevalence and course. The heterogeneity of the disorder was then considered, including the literature on subcategories. Emphasis was placed on the distinction between positive and negative schizophrenia and the deficit syndrome. The next section examined the possibility of a core deficit that might underlie the range of symptoms and impairments. The role of information-processing deficits and impairments in electrophysiological functions was highlighted. The next section examined the vulnerability–stress model, which is the most widely accepted hypothesis of how and the symptom exacerbations occur. Finally, we discussed the importance of social dysfunction in schizophrenia and

provided an overview the social skills model. As previously indicated, our goal was not to provide encyclopedic coverage of the field or of the multiple theories currently under investigation. The interested student is urged to peruse back issues of the *Schizophrenia Bulletin* or *Schizophrenia Research,* journals that provide up-to-date reviews and empirical papers on current topics of interest to the field. Numerous specialty texts and anthologies are also available in most university and medical school libraries.

REFERENCES

American Psychiatric Association. (1994). *Diagnostic and statistical manual of mental disorders,* 4th ed. Washington, DC: Author.

Andreasen, N.C., Flaum, M., Swayze, V.W., Tyrell, G., & Arndt, S. (1990). Positive and negative symptoms in schizophrenia: A critical reappraisal. *Archives of General Psychiatry, 47,* 615–621.

Andreasen, N.C., & Olsen, S.A. (1982). Negative versus positive schizophrenia: Definition and validation. *Archives of General Psychiatry, 39,* 789–794.

Andreasen, N.C., Olsen, S.A., Dennert, J.W., & Smith, M.R. (1982). Ventricular enlargement in schizophrenia: Relationship to positive and negative symptoms. *American Journal of Psychiatry, 139,* 297–302.

Anger-Myer, M.C., Kuhn, L., & Goldstein, J.M. (1990). Gender and the course of schizophrenia: Differences in treatment outcomes. *Schizophrenia Bulletin, 16,* 293–307.

Angrist, B., Rotrosen, J., & Gershon, S. (1980). Positive and negative symptoms in schizophrenia—differential response to amphetamine and neuroleptics. *Psychopharmacology, 72,* 17–29.

Asarnow, R.F., & MacCrimmon, D.J. (1976). Residual performance deficit in clinically remitted schizophrenics: A marker of schizophrenia? *Journal of Abnormal Psychology, 87,* 597–608.

Bellack, A.S., & Morrison, R.L. (1982). Interpersonal dysfunction. In A.S. Bellack, M. Hersen, A.E. Kazdin (Eds.), *International handbook of behavior modification and therapy* (pp. 717–748). New York: Plenum Press.

Bellack, A.S., Morrison, R.L., Wixted, J.T., & Mueser, K.T. (1990). An analysis of social competence in schizophrenia. *British Journal of Psychiatry, 156,* 809–818.

Bernstein, A.S. (1987). Orienting response research in schizophrenic: Where we have come and where we might go. *Schizophrenia Bulletin, 13,* 623–641.

Bernstein, A.S., Frith, C., Gruzelier, J., Patterson, T., Straube, E., Venables, P., & Zahn, T. (1982). An analysis of the skin conductance orienting response in samples of American, British, and German schizophrenics. *Biological Psychiatry, 14,* 155–211.

Bernstein, A.S., Riedel, J.A., Graae, F., Seidman, D., Steele, H., Connolly, J., & Lubowsky, J. (1988). Schizophrenia is associated with altered orienting activity; depression with electrodermal (cholinergic?) deficit and normal orienting response. *Journal of Abnormal Psychology, 97,* 3–12.

Berrios, G.E. (1985). Positive and negative symptoms and Jackson: A conceptual history. *Archives of General Psychiatry, 42,* 95–97.

Besson, J.A.O., Corrigan, F.M., Cherryman, G.R., & Smith, F.W. (1987). Nuclear magnetic brain imaging in chronic schizophrenia. *British Journal of Psychiatry, 150,* 161–163.

Bleuler, E. (1950). *Dementia praecox or the group of schizophrenias.* (J. Zinkin, Trans.). New York: International Universities Press. (Original work published in 1911.)

Braff, D.L., & Geyer, M.A. (1990). Sensimotor gating and schizophrenia: Human and animal model studies. *Archives of General Psychiatry, 47,* 181–188.

Breier, A., Schreiber, J.L., Dyer, J., & Pickar, D. (1991). National Institute of Mental Health longitudinal study of chronic schizophrenia: Prognosis and predictors of outcome. *Archives of General Psychiatry, 48,* 239–246.

Broadbent, D.E. (1958). *Perception and communication.* London: Pergamon Press.

Broadbent, D.E. (1971). *Decision and stress.* London: Academic Press.

Brown, G.W., & Birley, J.L., & Wing, J.K. (1972). Influence of family life on the course of schizophrenic disorders: A replication. *British Journal of Psychiatry, 121,* 241–258.

Brown, W.A., & Herz, L.R. (1989). Response to neuroleptic drugs as a device for classifying schizophrenia. *Schizophrenia Bulletin, 15,* 123–129.

Buchanan, R.W. (1995). Clozapine: Efficacy and safety. *Schizophrenia Bulletin, 21,* 579–591.

Buchanan, R.W., & Carpenter, W.T. (1994). Domains of psychopathology. *Journal of Nervous and Mental Disease, 182,* 193–204.

Caldwell, C.B., & Gottesman, I.I. (1990). Schizophrenics kill themselves too: A review of risk factors for suicide. *Schizophrenia Bulletin, 16,* 571–589.

Carpenter, W.T., Heinrichs, D.W., & Wagman, A. (1988). Deficit and nondeficit forms of schizophrenia: The concept. *American Journal of Psychiatry, 145,* 578–583.

Chapman, L.J., & Chapman, J.P. (1973). *Disordered thought in schizophrenia.* New York: Appleton-Century-Crofts.

Cornblatt, B.A., Lenzenweger, M.F., Dworkin, R.H., & Erlenmeyer-Kimling, L. (1992). Childhood attentional dysfunctions predict social deficits in unaffected adults at risk for schizophrenia. *British Journal of Psychiatry.*

Cournos, F. (1996). Epidemiology of HIV. In F. Cournos & N. Bakalar (Eds.), *AIDS and people with serious mental illness* (pp. 3–16). New Haven: Yale University Press.

Crow, T.J. (1980). Molecular pathology of schizophrenia: More than one disease process? *British Medical Journal, 280,* 66–68.

Crow, T.J. (1983). Schizophrenic deterioration (discussion). *British Journal of Psychiatry, 143,* 80–81.

Crow, T.J. (1985). The two-syndrome concept: Origins and current status. *Schizophrenia Bulletin, 11,* 471–485.

Dawson, M.E. (1990). Psychophysiology at the interface of clinical science, cognitive science, and neuroscience. *Psychophysiology, 27,* 243–255.

Dawson, M.E., & Nuechterlein, K.H. (1984). Psychophysiological dysfunctions in the developmental course of schizophrenic disorders. *Schizophrenia Bulletin, 10,* 204–232.

DeLisi, L.E., Goldin, L.R., Hamovit, J.R., Maxwell, M.E., Kurtz, D., & Gershon, E.S. (1986). A family study of the association of increased ventricular size with schizophrenia. *Archives of General Psychiatry, 43,* 148–153.

Dixon, L., Haas, G., Weiden, P.J., Sweeney, J., & Frances, A.J. (1991). Drug abuse in schizophrenic patients: Clinical correlates and reasons for use. *American Journal of Psychiatry, 148,* 224–230.

Dworkin, R.H. (1990). Patterns of sex differences in negative symptoms and social functioning consistent with separate dimensions of schizophrenic psychopathology. *American Journal of Psychiatry, 147,* 347–349.

Dworkin, R.H., Bernstein, G., Kaplansky, L.M., Lipsitz, J.D., Rinaldi, A., Slater, S.L., Cornblatt, B.A., & Erlenmeyer-Kimling, L. (1991). Social competence and positive and negative symptoms: A longitudinal study of children and adolescents at risk for schizophrenia and affective disorder. *American Journal of Psychiatry, 148*(9), 1182–1188.

Endicott, J., & Spitzer, R.L. (1978). A diagnostic interview. *Archives of General Psychiatry, 35,* 837–844.

Erlenmeyer-Kimling, L., & Cornblatt, B. (1978). Attentional measures in a study of children at high risk for schizophrenia. In L.C. Wynne, R. Cromwell, & S. Matthysse (Eds.), *Nature of schizophrenia: New approaches to research and treatment* (pp. 359–365). New York: Wiley.

Flor-Henry, P. (1985). Schizophrenia: Sex differences. *Canadian Journal of Psychiatry, 30,* 319–322.

Goldberg, T.E., & Gold, J.M. (1995). Neurocognitive deficits in schizophrenia. In S.R. Hirsch & D.R. Weinberger (Eds.), *Schizophrenia* (pp. 146–162). Cambridge, England: Blackwell Science.

Goldstein, J.M. (1988). Gender differences in the course of schizophrenia. *American Journal of Psychiatry, 145,* 684–689.

Goldstrom, I.D., & Manderscheid, R.W. (1981). The chronically mentally ill: A descriptive analysis from the uniform client data instrument. *Community Support Service Journal, II,* 4–9.

Goodman, L., Rosenberg S., Mueser, K., Drake, R. (1997). Physical and sexual assault history in women with serious mental illness: Prevalence, impact, treatment, and future research. *Schizophrenia Bulletin, 23,* 685–696.

Gottesman, I., & Shields, J. (1972). *Schizophrenia and genetics: A twin study vantage point.* New York: Academic Press.

Gray, J.A., Feldon, J., Rawlins, J.N.P., Hemsley, D.R., & Smith, A.D. (1991). The neuropsychology of schizophrenia. *Behavioral and Brain Sciences, 14,* 1–84.

Green, M., & Walker, E. (1985). Neuropsychological performance and positive and negative symptoms in schizophrenia. *Journal of Abnormal Psychology, 94,* 460–469.

Green, M.F. (1996). What are the functional consequences of neurocognitive deficits in schizophrenia? *American Journal of Psychiatry, 153,* 321–330.

Harding, C.M., Brooks, G.W., Ashikaga, T., Strauss, J.S., & Breier, A. (1987). The Vermont longitudinal study of persons with severe mental illness: II. Long-term outcome of subjects who retrospectively met DSM-III criteria for schizophrenia. *American Journal of Psychiatry, 144,* 727–735.

Harding, C.M., Zubin, J., & Strauss, J.S. (1992). Chronicity in schizophrenia revisited. *British Journal of Psychiatry, 161,* 27–37.

Harrow, M., Sands, J.R., Silverstein, M.L., & Goldberg., J.F. (1997). Course and outcome for schizophrenia versus other psychotic patients: A longitudinal study. *Schizophrenia Bulletin, 23,* 287–303.

Harvey, P.D. (1983). Speech competence in manic and schizophrenic psychosis: The association between clinically rated thought disorder and cohesion and reference performance. *Journal of Abnormal Psychology, 92,* 368–377.

Hersen, M., & Bellack, A.S. (1976). Social skills training for chronic psychiatric patients: Rationale, research findings, and future directions. *Comprehensive Psychiatry, 17,* 559–580.

Hogarty, G.E., Anderson, C.M., & Reiss, D.J. (1987). Family psychoeducation, social skills training, and medication in schizophrenia: The long and the short of it. *Psychopharmacology Bulletin, 23,* 12–13.

Hogarty, G.E., Anderson, C.M., Reiss, D.J., Kornblith, S.J., Greenwald, D.P., Javna, C.D., & Madonia, M.J. (1986). Family psychoeducation, social skills training, and maintenance chemotherapy in the aftercare treatment of schizophrenia: I. One-year effects of a controlled study on relapse and expressed emotion. *Archives of General Psychiatry, 43,* 633–642.

Holzman, P.S., & Matthysse, S. (1990). The genetics of schizophrenia: A review. *Psychological Science, 1,* 279–286.

Johnstone, E.C., Crow, T.J., Frith, C.D., Carney,

M.W.P., & Price, J.S. (1978). Mechanism of the antipsychotic effect in the treatment of acute schizophrenia. *Lancet, 1,* 848–851.

Johnstone, E.C., Crow, T.J., Frith, C.D., Husband, J., & Kreel, L. (1976). Cerebral ventricular size and cognitive impairment in chronic schizophrenia. *Lancet, 2,* 924–926.

Johnstone, E.C., Owens, D.G.C., Gold, A., Crow, T.J., & Macmillan, J.F. (1981). Institutionalization and the defects of schizophrenia. *British Journal of Psychiatry, 139,* 195–203.

Kahneman, D. (1973), *Attention and effort.* Englewood Cliffs, NJ: Prentice-Hall.

Kane, J.M., Honigfeld, G., Singer, J., Meltzer, H.Y., & the Clozapine Collaborative Study Group. (1988). Clozapine for the treatment-resistant schizophrenic: A double-blind comparison with chlorpromazine. *Archives of General Psychiatry, 45,* 789–796.

Kay, S.R. (1990). Significance of the positive–negative distinction in schizophrenia. *Schizophrenia Bulletin, 16,* 635–652.

Kay, S.R., & Singh, M.M. (1989). The positive–negative distinction in drug-free schizophrenic patients: Stability, response to neuroleptics, and prognostic significance. *Archives of General Psychiatry, 46,* 711–718.

Keefe, R.S.E., Mohs, R.C., Davidson, J., Losonczy, M.F., Silverman, J.M., Lesser, J.C., Horvath, T.B., & Davis, K.L. (1988). Kraepelinian schizophrenia: A subgroup of schizophrenia? *Psychopharmacology Bulletin, 24,* 56–61.

Kirkpatrick, B., Buchanan, R.W., McKenney, P.D., Alphs, L.D., & Carpenter, W.T. (1989). The schedule for the deficit syndrome: An instrument for research in schizophrenia. *Psychiatry Research,* (30), 119–123.

Kirkpartrick, B., Buchanan, R.W., McKenney, P.D., Alphs, L.D., & Carpenter, W.T. (1993). *The schedule for the deficit syndrome manual.* Unpublished manuscript, University of Maryland.

Kraepelin, E. (1971). *Dementia praecox and paraphrenia.* Translated by R.M. Barclay & G.M. Robertson. Huntington, NY: Robert E. Krieger. (Original work published in 1919.)

Lewine, R.R. (1981). Sex differences in schizophrenia: Timing or subtypes? *Psychological Bulletin, 90,* 432–444.

Lewine, R.J., Watt, N F., Prentky, R.A., & Fryer, J.H. (1980). Childhood social competence in functionally disordered psychiatric patients and in normals. *Journal of Abnormal Psychology, 89,* 132–138.

Loranger, A.W. (1984). Sex difference in age at onset of schizophrenia. *Archives of General Psychiatry, 41,* 157–161.

Lukoff, D., Snyder, K., Ventura, J., & Nuechterlein, K.H. (1984). Life events, familial stress, and coping in the developmental course of schizophrenia. *Schizophrenia Bulletin, 10,* 258–292.

Matarazzo, J.D. (1983). The reliability of psychiatric and psychologic diagnosis. *Clinical Psychology Review, 3,* 103–145.

Mayer, M., Alpert, M., Stastny, P., Perlick, D., & Empfield, M. (1985). Multiple contributions to clinical presentation of flat affect in schizophrenia. *Schizophrenia Bulletin, 11,* 420–426.

McGhie, A., & Chapman, J. (1961). Disorders of attention and perception in early schizophrenia. *British Journal of Medical Psychology, 34,* 103–116.

Meehl, P.E. (1962). Schizotaxia, schizotypy, schizophrenia. *American Psychologist, 17,* 827–838.

Meehl, P.E. (1990). Toward an integrated theory of schizotaxia, schizotypy, and schizophrenia. *Journal of Personality Disorders, 4,* 1–99.

Meltzer, H.Y. (1985). Dopamine and negative symptoms in schizophrenia: Critique of the Type I–II hypothesis. In M. Alpert (Ed.), *Controversies in schizophrenia: Changes and constancies* (pp. 110–136). New York: Guilford Press.

Mueser, K.T., Bellack, A.S., Douglas, M.S., & Morrison, R.L. (1991). Prevalence and stability of social skill deficits in schizophrenia. *Schizophrenia Research, 5,* 167–176.

Mueser, K.T., Yarnold, P.R., & Bellack, A.S. (1992). Diagnostic and demographic correlates of substance abuse in schizophrenia and major affective disorder. *Acta Psychiatrica Scandinavica, 85,* 48–55.

Mueser, K.T., Bennett, M., & Kushner, M.G. (1995). Epidemiology of substance use disorders among persons with chronic mental illnesses. In A.F. Lehman & L.B. Dixon (Eds.), *Double jeopardy: Chronic mental illness and substance use disorders.* Harwood Academic Publishers, *56,* 520–528.

Nasrallah, H.A., Kuperman, S., Hamara, B.J., & McCalley-Whitters, M. (1983). Clinical differences between schizophrenic patients with and without large cerebral ventricles. *Journal of Clinical Psychiatry, 44,* 407–409.

Neale, J.M., & Oltmanns, T.F. (1980). *Schizophrenia.* New York: Wiley.

Neale, J.M., Oltmanns, T.F., & Harvey, P.D. (1985). The need to relate cognitive deficits to specific behavioral referents of schizophrenia. *Schizophrenia Bulletin, 11,* 286–291.

Nuechterlein, K.H. (1983). Signal detection in vigilance tasks and behavioral attributes among offspring of schizophrenic mothers and among hyperactive children. *Journal of Abnormal Psychology, 92,* 4–28.

Nuechterlein, K.H. (1987). Vulnerability models for schizophrenia: State of the art. In H. Hafner, W.F. Gattaz, & W. Janzarik (Eds.), *Search for the causes of schizophrenia* (pp. 297–316). Berlin: Springer-Verlag.

Nuechterlein, K.H. (1991). Vigilance in schizophrenia and related disorders. In S. Steinhauer, J.H. Gruzelier, & J. Zubin (Eds.), *Handbook of schizophrenia: Vol. 5. Neuropsychology, psychophysiology, and information processing.* Amsterdam: Elsevier.

Nuechterlein, K.H., & Dawson, M.E. (1984a). A heuristic vulnerability/stress model of schizophrenic episodes. *Schizophrenia Bulletin, 10,* 300–312.

Nuechterlein, K.H., & Dawson, M.E. (1984b). Information processing and attentional functioning in the developmental course of schizophrenic disorders. *Schizophrenia Bulletin, 10,* 160–203.

Nuechterlein, K.H., Dawson, M.E., Ventura, J., Fogelson, D., Gitlin, M., & Mintz, J. (1990). Testing vulnerability models: Stability of potential vulnerability indicators across clinical state. In H. Hafner & W.F. Gattaz (Eds.), *Search for the causes of schizophrenia* (Vol. 2, pp. 177–191). Heidelberg: Springer-Verlag.

Nuechterlein, K.H., Edell, W.S., Norris, M., & Dawson, M.E. (1986). Attentional vulnerability indicators, thought disorder, and negative symptoms. *Schizophrenia Bulletin, 12,* 408–426.

Ohman, A., Nordby, H., & d'Elia, G. (1986). Orienting and schizophrenia: Stimulus significance, attention, and distraction, in a signaled reaction time task. *Journal of Abnormal Psychology, 95,* 326–334.

Ohman, A., Ohlund, L.S., Alm, T., Wieselgren, I-M., Ost, L-G., & Lindstrom, L.H. (1989). Electrodermal nonresponding, premorbid adjustment, and symptomatology as predictors of long-term social functioning in schizophrenics. *Journal of Abnormal Psychology, 98,* 426–435.

Orzack, M.H., & Kornetsky, C. (1966). Attention dysfunction in chronic schizophrenia. *Archives of General Psychiatry, 14,* 323–326.

Persons, J.B. (1986). The advantages of studying psychological phenomena rather than psychiatric diagnoses. *American Psychologist, 41,* 1252–1260.

Pogue-Geile, M.F., & Harrow, M. (1985). Negative symptoms in schizophrenia: Their longitudinal course and prognostic importance. *Schizophrenia Bulletin, 11,* 427–439.

Regier, D.A., Boyd, J.H., Burke, J.D., Rae, D.S., Myers, J.K., Kramer, M., Robins, L.N., George, L.K., Karno, M., & Locke, B.Z. (1988). One-month prevalence of mental disorders in the United States: Based on five epidemiologic catchment area sites. *Archives of General Psychiatry, 45,* 977–986.

Rosenstein, M.J., Milazzo-Sayre, L.J., & Manderscheid, R.W. (1989). Care of persons with schizophrenia: A statistical profile. *Schizophrenia Bulletin, 15,* 45–58.

Rosenthal, D. (1970). *Genetic theory and abnormal behavior.* New York: McGraw-Hill.

Rosenthal, D. (1971). *Genetics and psychopathology.* New York: McGraw-Hill.

Salokangas, R.K.R. (1983). Prognostic implications of the sex of schizophrenic patients. *British Journal of Psychiatry, 142,* 145–151.

Saykin, A.J., Shtasel D.L., Gur R.E., Kester, D.B., Mozley, L.H., Stafiniak, P., & Gur, R.C. (1994). Neuropsychological deficits in neuroleptic naive patients with first-episode schizophrenia. *Archives of General Psychiatry, 51,*124–131.

Spitzer, R.L., Endicott, J., & Robins, E. (1978). Research diagnostic criteria. *Archives of General Psychiatry, 35,* 773–782.

Spohn, H.E., & Strauss, M.E. (1989) Relation of neuroleptic and anticholinergic medication to cognitive functions in schizophrenia. *Journal of Abnormal Psychology, 4,* 367–380.

Spohn, H.E., Lacoursiere, R., Thompson, K., & Coyne, L. (1977). Phenothiazine effects on psychological and psychophysiological dysfunction in chronic schizophrenics. *Archives of General Psychiatry, 34,* 633–644.

Strauss, J.S., Carpenter, W.T., Jr., & Bartko, J.J. (1974). The diagnosis and understanding of schizophrenia: Part III. Speculations on the processes that underlie schizophrenic symptoms and signs. *Schizophrenia Bulletin, 11,* 61–69.

Thacker, G., Buchanan, R, Kirkpatrick, B., & Tamminga, C. (1988). Eye movements in schizophrenia: Clinical and neurobiological correlates. *Society for Neuroscience Abstracts, 14,* 339.

Vaughan, C., & Leff, J. (1976). The influence of family and social factors on the course of psychiatric illness: A comparison of schizophrenic and depressed neurotic patients. *British Journal of Psychiatry, 129,* 125–137.

Wagman, A.M.I., Heinrichs, D.W., & Carpenter, W.T. (1987). Deficit and nondeficit forms of schizophrenia: Neuropsychological evaluation. *Psychiatry Research, 22,* 319–330.

Walker, E., & Green, M. (1982). Motor proficiency and attentional task performance by schizophrenics. *Journal of Abnormal Psychology, 91,* 261–268.

Walker, E., & Shaye, J. (1982). Familial schizophrenia: A predictor of neuromotor and attentional abnormalities in schizophrenia. *Archives of General Psychiatry, 39,* 1153–1156.

Wohlberg, G.W., & Kornetsky, C. (1973). Sustained attention in remitted schizophrenics. *Archives of General Psychiatry, 28,* 533–537.

World Health Organization. (1979). *Schizophrenia: An international follow-up study.* New York: Wiley.

Zigler, E., & Phillips, L. (1961). Social competence and outcome in psychiatric disorder, *Journal of Abnormal and Social Psychology, 63,* 264–271.

Zubin, J., & Spring, B. (1977). Vulnerability—a new view of schizophrenia. *Journal of Abnormal Psychology, 86,* 103–126.

Zubin, J., & Steinhauer, S. (1981). How to break the logjam in schizophrenia: A look beyond genetics. *Journal of Nervous and Mental Disease, 169,* 477–492.

CHAPTER 14

BIPOLAR DISORDER: PSYCHOPATHOLOGY, BIOLOGY, AND DIAGNOSIS

James R. Sands
Martin Harrow
University of Illinois, College of Medicine

INTRODUCTION

Our understanding of bipolar disorder is evolving with recent advances in knowledge of its pathophysiology, psychology, and treatment (Bunney, Goodwin, & Murphy, 1992; Dunner, 1992; Goodwin & Jamison, 1990; Keller & Baker, 1991; Klerman, 1981). The most obvious factor driving this evolution is the rapidly increasing sophistication of research methods at all levels of analysis. Refined approaches to biochemical methods, brain imaging, and neuropsychological assessment have replaced much of the clinical lore and anecdotal knowledge about bipolar disorder. Modern paradigms, such as chaos dynamics, are being applied to an understanding of mood changes in bipolar patients (Ehlers, 1995; Gottschalk, Bauer, & Whybrow, 1995). The accumulation of longitudinal data has brought a new life-course perspective on the disorder, thus integrating modern scientific methods and the longitudinal observational studies of Kraepelin (1919).

Finally, standardized and reliable diagnostic methods have facilitated more consistent, homogeneous research samples.

Another factor in our evolving understanding of bipolar disorder is the continual interplay between nosology, diagnosis, and psychiatric research. Psychiatric nosology is a construct—a theoretical position that attempts to articulate, but does not completely mirror, the variations of psychopathology extant in nature. Formal diagnostic systems are the concretizations of nosological theory and are revised periodically as nosological theory evolves. Diagnostic criteria define the patient samples used in psychopathology research. Those sampling criteria have a bearing on the data obtained in psychiatric research—research that is subsequently incorporated into psychiatric nosology. This is particularly important for research on bipolar disorders, especially in light of continued, unresolved debate regarding the nosological relationships of bipolar disorder to other major psychiatric illnesses such as unipolar major depression, schizoaffective disorder, and schizophrenia, and the delineation of possible discrete subtypes of bipolar disorder.

RECENT DEVELOPMENTS IN DIAGNOSTIC CRITERIA

As of this writing, the most current, widely used American diagnostic system, reflecting the most recent nosological theory, is the *Diagnostic and Statistical Manual of Mental Disorders,* fourth edition (DSM-IV; American Psychiatric Association, 1994). Compared to the DSM-III-R, the DSM-IV now reflects greater nosological complexity for bipolar disorder and its variants. Prominent among these changes include the delineation of bipolar II (major depression with hypomania) and the inclusion of specifiers to indicate subgroups of patients with seasonal variants, postpartum onset, rapid cycling, and interepisodic course types. Incorporation of these variations constitutes increased recognition for the multifaceted nature of bipolar disorders and a greater emphasis on longitudinal concepts in defining the disorder (Dunner, 1992).

The DSM-IV has made several changes to the criteria for a manic episode, which pertain to psychotic symptoms. One important change incorporated in the DSM-IV is the elimination of the criterion that excludes a bipolar diagnosis when the patient has experienced psychotic symptoms for at least 2 weeks in the absence of prominent mood symptoms (DSM-III-R Criterion D). However, this is implicit in DSM-IV Criterion B for the diagnosis of bipolar I disorder, which precludes a diagnosis of bipolar disorder for cases that meet criteria for schizoaffective disorders, schizophrenia, or other psychotic disorders. DSM-IV Criterion D, which pertains to the severity of impairment, now adds the presence of psychosis as indicative of a diagnosis of manic episode when the differential is between mania and hypomania.

Another important change in the DSM-IV is the inclusion of specific criteria for a hypomanic episode. These criteria allow for explicit definition of a heretofore poorly defined syndrome. The essential difference between hypomania and a full mania is the duration and severity of the episode (with manic episode requiring a longer duration and more severe

disruption), and the absence of psychotic symptoms in hypomania.

Concomitant with the inclusion of explicit criteria for hypomanic episode, the DSM-IV now delineates bipolar II disorder (recurrent major depression with hypomania) as a distinct nosological entity (to be discussed). Bipolar II has been the object of much research over the past several years, but, until the DSM-IV, patients with that symptom constellation have been formally diagnosed as having an atypical bipolar disorder, bipolar disorder not otherwise specified (NOS). By definition, psychotic symptoms during hypomanic periods preclude a diagnosis of bipolar II diagnosis, although psychosis during depressive phases does not preclude a bipolar II diagnosis.

SUBTYPES OF BIPOLAR DISORDER AND DIFFERENTIAL DIAGNOSIS

As noted, based on the DSM-IV, two main subtypes of bipolar disorder are recognized as nosological entities: bipolar I and bipolar II disorders. Bipolar I is the most commonly conceptualized subtype of bipolar disorder and involves both full manic and full depressive syndromes. This is the manic–depressive psychosis characterized by Kraepelin (1919). Most bipolar patients have this pattern. Bipolar II, on the other hand, involves full depressive syndromes in conjunction with hypomanic episodes. The etiological relationship between bipolar I and bipolar II is not entirely resolved. Research indicates that bipolar II is intermediate between bipolar I and unipolar disorder with regard to gender, familial bipolar history, and age at onset; but its course characteristics generally support its closer relationship to bipolar I disorder (Cassano et al., 1992).

Other, less widely recognized forms of bipolar disorder, exist, reflecting multidimensional aspects of the illness. The issue of whether to define phenomenologically homogeneous subtypes of bipolar disorder or to group all bipolar patients into a larger heterogeneous category is a matter of debate (Bowden, 1993; Klerman, 1981). Other variants that have not achieved recognition as discrete diagnostic entities are nonetheless the object of study and theoretical speculation. These include rapid cycling, unipolar mania and pediatric bipolar disorder.

Rapid Cycling

Over the past 20 years, increasing attention has been paid to a subgroup of bipolar patients who evidence rapid cycling. Rapid cycling was included as a (specified) variant of bipolar disorder in the DSM-IV for patients who have four or more discrete episodes of mood disorder within a 12-month period. Although at face value the term *rapid cycling* connotes shifts in polarity, the DSM-IV indicates that episodes can occur in any combination as long as the episodes are discrete (demarcated by either 2 months of remission or by a subsequent episode of opposite polarity). The definition and assessment of rapid-cycling bipolar disorder is problematic, and the development of criteria for the DSM-IV was the focus of some debate (Ananth, Wohl, Ranganath, & Beshay, 1993; Bauer & Keller, 1994; Bauer & Whybrow, 1993; Maj et al., 1994). Rapid cycling may be characterized by an increased frequency of depressive phases rather than increased frequency of manic episodes, compared to other bipolar patients. In much of the literature, however, rapid cycling refers to a pattern of frequent shifts from mania to depression or from depression to mania. Some researchers use the term *rapid cycling* to refer only to very rapid shifts between poles, often within a matter of days or hours (Calabrese & Delucchi, 1989).

The nature of rapid cycling is poorly understood. Rapid mood fluctuations between mania and depression could be a phenomenon that has emerged only in the past 20 years. Wolpert and colleagues analyzed case records of 570 patients hospitalized for affective disorders in 1960, 1975, or 1985 (Wolpert, Goldberg, & Harrow, 1990). They found that rapid cycling was absent in case records of patients hospitalized in 1960 but was present in those of patients hospitalized in 1975 and 1985. Some researchers, noting a similar trend, suggest that the increase in rapid cycling has coincided with the rapid increase in cocaine use in society, even though such an association cannot prove a causal relationship (Ananth et al., 1993). Rapid cycling has been associated with reactions to tricyclic antidepressants and other agents (such as propranolol and levodopa). It has been suggested that rapid cycling could emerge out of comorbid metabolic or neuroendocrine illness, such as hypothyroidism and hyperthyroidism (Ananth et al.,

1993). It has also been suggested that the development of Graves' disease in patients with preexisting bipolar disorder may lead to an excess mobilization of thyroid hormones and, subsequently, to an increased vulnerability for rapid cycling (Khouzam, Bhat, Boyer, & Hardy, 1991).

Between 13% and 20% of patients with bipolar disorder have rapid cycling (Bowden, 1993). Some researchers suggest that bipolar patients are most likely to show rapid cycling during the early phase of their disorder and later to show more extended cycles; however, other research suggests that rapid cycling is usually a persistent characteristic (Tomitaka & Sakamoto, 1994). There is some evidence to suggest that rapid-cycling bipolar disorder occurs with greater frequency in female patients (Coryell, Endicott, & Keller, 1992).

The association of rapid cycling with kindling is a matter of current investigation (Goldberg & Harrow, 1994; Post, 1992; Post et al., 1982). Some of the earliest research and most replicated findings on rapid cycling is its association with poor lithium prophylaxis (Dunner & Fieve, 1974). Rapid cycling also has been associated with poor outcome during the early years of the disorder (Goldberg & Harrow, 1994; Goldberg, Harrow, & Grossman, 1995a, 1995b), although its relationship to outcome beyond the early years is not clear (Coryell et al, 1990).

Unipolar Mania

Unipolar mania, a condition characterized by repeated manic episodes without previous or subsequent depressed episode, is controversial. Contemporary theory is that these patients should be incorporated in the bipolar disorder diagnosis, because of the expectation that they will eventually have a depression. Given the longitudinal requirement for delineating this illness, diagnosis is relatively speculative until a considerable length of time has passed without a depressive phase. Pfohl and colleagues developed a mathematical model to predict patterns of hospital admission for unipolar mania patients given that such patients might actually be bipolar patients (Pfohl, Vasquez, & Nasrallah, 1981). These authors support the classification of patients with unipolar mania as having bipolar disorder.

The existing empirical work on unipolar mania is

quite limited, particularly in the last decade. Early estimates of the prevalence of unipolar mania suggested that it occurred for less than 25% of bipolar patients, and probably for well below 10%. The duration of unipolar illness (or frequency of unipolar manic episodes without a depressive phase) is probably a major factor in the variability of base rates across studies (Abrams & Taylor, 1974). Unipolar mania may have a prominence among males as compared to bipolar mania (Abrams, Taylor, Hayman, & Krishna, 1979; Kubacki, 1986), although this has not been consistently replicated (Pfohl, Vasquez, & Nasrallah, 1982). Most studies show a similarity of clinical presentation, family history and treatment response between unipolar manic and bipolar manic patients (Abrams & Taylor, 1974; Nurnberger, Roose, Dunner, & Fieve, 1979). Rare cases of patients with extended histories of unipolar mania are most likely associated with specific limbic neuropathology (Berthier, Starkstein, Robinson, & Leiguarda, 1990) or orbitofrontal and basotemporal cortical involvement (Starkstein, Fedoroff, Berthier, & Robinson, 1991). The potential for specific neuropathology in unipolar mania could be one reason that some researchers call for the reconsideration of unipolar mania as a distinct clinical entity (Shulman & Tohen, 1994).

Juvenile-Onset (Pediatric) Bipolar Disorder

Juvenile-onset or pediatric bipolar disorder has come to the attention of clinical researchers in the past decade. Emerging during childhood or adolescence, pediatric bipolar disorder is a complex clinical phenomenon that is easily misdiagnosed and often does not receive clinical attention (Weller, Weller, & Fristad, 1995). Pediatric bipolar disorder occurs among about 1% of the population (Lewinsohn, Klein, & Seeley, 1995). These rates are higher if subsyndromal clinical profiles are assessed. Research indicates that many adult bipolar patients have onset of illness during childhood or adolescence (Faedda et al., 1995). Among prepubertal children with a history of a major depressive episode, as many as one-third will have a bipolar course of illness (Geller, Fox, & Clark, 1994). Some researchers suggest that bipolar patients have increased traits of hyperactivity as children even though the illness does not emerge until early adulthood (Winokur, Coryell, Endicott, & Akiskal, 1993a).

Certain comorbid illnesses in pediatric bipolar disorder, and its symptomatic similarity to other pediatric psychopathology, make the differential diagnosis of pediatric bipolar disorder challenging (Ballenger, Reus, & Post, 1982; Borchardt & Bernstein, 1995; Kovacs & Pollock, 1995; Lewinsohn et al., 1995; Weller et al., 1995; West et al., 1995). High rates of comorbidity between bipolar disorder and attention deficit hyperactivity disorder have been observed (Wozniak et al., 1995). Differentiating pediatric bipolar disorder from attention deficit hyperactivity disorder is particularly difficult because of similarity in both the motoric symptoms (hyperactivity) and cognitive symptoms (distractibility and poor attention). Optimal discrimination between these disorders is facilitated by focusing on key behavioral manifestations of the two disorders. Researchers suggest that behaviors associated with "classic" manic symptoms (e.g., elevated mood, increased sexual interest, pressured speech, and racing thoughts) can effectively discriminate between pediatric bipolar patients and those with attention deficit hyperactivity; whereas behaviors such as increased activity level and irritability may not (Fristad, Weller, & Weller, 1995).

CLINICAL PRESENTATION

The Manic or Hypomanic Syndrome

The cornerstone for the diagnosis of a manic or hypomanic episode is the presence of an elated, expansive, or irritable mood (APA, 1994). Though overtly simple, the emotional component of bipolar disorder can run the gamut from normal happiness to gross elation and euphoria (Klerman, 1981). The effective demarcation of normal happiness from emotional states that are abnormal, inappropriate, or excessive is a subjective clinical judgment. Unfortunately, despite scientific advances in many areas of psychopathology, our understanding of basic emotional processes has not kept pace with the more easily measured (and quantified) aspects of psychopathology. Moreover, although the presence of elation or expansive mood is an essential feature of the bipolar disorder, the underlying pathological processes that form the physiologic and psychological basis of aberrant emotional experience remains unknown.

Concomitant with the emotional component of elation, euphoria, or manic irritability are other behavioral and cognitive features. Diagnostic criteria specify that the manic or hypomanic syndrome must also include three or four of the following: grandiosity, decreased need for sleep, excessive talkativeness or pressured speech, flight of ideas or racing thoughts, distractibility, increased goal-directed behavior or psychomotor agitation, and excessive involvement in pleasurable activities that have potential negative consequences. The syndromal consistency of these multifaceted components is high. Thus, although subjective clinical judgment is required to ascertain whether a patient's mood is disordered, there are several convergent behavioral features that facilitate additional certainty when diagnosing the affective syndromes of mania and hypomania.

Bipolar Disorder in the Depressed Phase

Is the depressed phase of bipolar disorder similar to the depressed phase of unipolar depression? Research from our own group has begun to suggest that the depressive syndrome in bipolar disorder is more severe and disruptive than that in unipolar depression, and is much more likely to lead to rehospitalization (Goldberg et al., 1995a, 1995b). Another study found that bipolar depressed patients had shorter episodes of depression and were less likely to demonstrate slowed movements than unipolar patients (Mitchell et al., 1992). However, other research has suggested that bipolar depressed and unipolar depressed patients do not have significantly different motor activity during depressed periods (Kuhs & Reschke, 1992). Bipolar patients in a depressed phase could have more cognitive slippage compared to unipolar depressed patients as well as other idiosyncrasies of information processing (Sinnger & Brabender, 1993). Despite these potential differences, there are more similarities when comparing the depressive features of unipolar and bipolar patients.

The similarity between the depressed phase of bipolar disorder and primary unipolar major depression could point to the nosological affinity between these two disorders. Specifically, the pathogenic processes resulting in bipolar patients becoming depressed are likely to be similar to those in primary unipolar depression. However, Katz and associates found that the pattern of relationships between changes in serotinergic derivatives and observed mood states in the unipolar subtype was different from that in the bipolar subtype (Katz et al., 1994). This provides support for the presence of some unique pathogenic processes for bipolar and unipolar depressions. This issue is far from resolved and warrants additional research.

Mixed States

For some bipolar patients, both manic and depressive symptoms occur simultaneously. Mixed states may be more prevalent than previously recognized because the dysphoric symptoms go unnoticed during manic episodes. Research has suggested that dysphoric symptoms are continuously rather than bimodally distributed, and that the prevalence of these symptoms varies widely depending on the definition used (Bauer et al., 1994). Mixed states are easily confused with very rapid cycling, during which elation and dysphoria alternate with such frequency that manic and depressive states cannot be clearly differentiated.

Nosological theorists propose that the status of mixed states might depend on the presence or absence of psychosis, with psychotic mixed states being more closely related to bipolar I disorder and nonpsychotic mixed states being more related to bipolar II disorder (DellOsso et al., 1993). Longitudinal research has suggested that mixed manic and depressive states have negative prognostic implications. Dysphoric mania may be a distinct form of affective disruption, but research also suggests that mixed states may be a transitional state between mania and depression (McElroy et al., 1992).

As noted in our discussion of rapid cycling, a clinical picture involving mixed or rapid-cycling affective patterns has been associated with significantly poorer outcomes, including less symptomatic improvement with treatment and more frequent relapses, compared to discrete manic or depressive episodes (Goldberg & Harrow, 1994; Keller & Baker, 1991; Keller et al., 1993). Mixed affective states may be associated with suboptimal response to lithium (Frye et al., 1996; Himmelhoch & Garfinkel, 1986; Maj, Pirozzi, & Starace, 1989; Prien, Himmelhoch, & Kupfer, 1988).

Suicide

Although suicide is typically associated with major depression, there is little research addressing suicide in bipolar disorder. Some research suggests that bipolar patients are more vulnerable to suicide than patients with unipolar major depression (Rihmer, Barsi, Arato, & Demeter, 1990). Among bipolar patients, suicidal behavior is more frequent during the depressed phase than during the manic phase. Some research finds that most suicides occur late in the course of illness (Isometsa, Henriksson, Aro, & Lonnqvist, 1994), but other research finds that bipolar patients with an early age at onset may be at greatest risk for suicide (Sharma & Markar, 1994). Although rapid cycling is often a poor prognostic feature among bipolar patients (see the section on rapid cycling), it is not associated with higher suicide attempt rates (Wu & Dunner, 1993). Given the seriousness of suicide, there is a need for more research assessing any potential unique aspects of suicidality among bipolar patients.

Formal Thought Disorder

Formal thought disorder was once considered the hallmark of schizophrenia. In the 1970s and 1980s, however, research emerged that showed that thought disorder is very common among hospitalized manic patients. The prevalence of thought disorder has been estimated to be over 70% among hospitalized manic patients (Andreasen, 1979; Andreasen & Grove, 1986; Andreasen & Powers, 1974, 1975; Harrow, Grossman, Silverstein, & Meltzer, 1982; Marengo, Harrow, Lanin-Kettering, & Wilson, 1985). The frequency and severity of thought disorder in acute mania is not substantially different than that found among schizophrenia patients. Longitudinal research, looking at the course of bipolar disorder from the acute inpatient phase through the posthospital period, indicates that, despite overall reductions in disordered thinking, thought disorder is not uncommon during the early years following hospital discharge (Grossman, Harrow, & Sands, 1986; Sands, Marengo, & Harrow, 1987).

Some researchers suggest that the quality of formal thought disorder among bipolar patients is different than among schizophrenia patients (Shenton,

Solovay, & Holzman, 1987). Others suggest that the mechanisms underlying thought disorder may be different, although the overt presentation by the patient's verbalizations may be similar for both disorders. For example, Docherty and colleagues propose that impairments in working memory are involved in the thought disorder found among schizophrenia patients but not the thought disorder among bipolar patients (Docherty et al., 1996). Other researchers suggest that bipolar patients with mixed affective symptoms (as discussed earlier) have different types of thought disorder than those with pure mania (Sax et al., 1995).

Clinical lore portrays disordered thinking in bipolar disorder as a product of (and hence secondary to) the manic affective disruption, particularly the euphoric mood and its accompanying excitation and overactivity. This has received some empirical support. For example, Grossman and associates found a relationship between manic behavioral signs and thought disorder among previously hospitalized bipolar patients (Grossman et al., 1986).

Although there is evidence to suggest that thought disorder occurs frequently in the context of a manic or hypomanic syndrome, other evidence suggests that it also occurs during the interepisodic interval and even among some bipolar patients who are in a depressed phase (Sands et al., 1987). The potential of bipolar patients to manifest thought disorder during various phases of illness was also reported by Sinnger and colleagues, who found greater elevations of cognitive slippage among bipolar patients in a depressed phase compared to unipolar depressed patients (Sinnger & Brabender, 1993). One inference is that thought pathology or a vulnerability to thought disorder under internal or external stresses may be an index of the active disease process. Hence, thought pathology is quite likely to occur in conjunction with other psychopathology, but is not necessarily dependent on manic symptoms or other symptoms to occur. Relevant longitudinal research has been reported for schizophrenia and has indicated an association between severely disordered thinking and a persistent course of illness (Harrow & Marengo, 1986; Marengo, Galloway, Sands, Koeber, & Harrow, 1986; Marengo & Harrow, 1987). This formulation has been used to explain the persistence of formal thought-disordered thinking among schizophrenia patients whose psychosis is in remission (Marengo et al., 1985).

Psychosis

Psychotic symptoms, specifically delusions and hallucinations, occur frequently among manic patients. Research has shown that, during the acute phase of mania (e.g., during episodes often requiring hospitalization), between 50% and 80% of patients have psychotic symptoms (Carlson & Goodwin, 1973; Harrow, Grossman, Silverstein, Meltzer, & Kettering, 1986; Kolb, 1968; Sands et al., 1987). Though less intense, psychosis frequently persists into the posthospital course of manic disorders (Grossman et al., 1986; Sands et al., 1987). Although the occurrence of psychotic symptoms in bipolar disorder has not received much recent empirical attention, several main issues regarding psychosis in bipolar disorder warrant empirical attention and theoretical consideration.

The antecedent causes of psychosis in bipolar disorder are not understood, and it is unclear to what extent the pathogenesis of psychosis in bipolar disorder is unique from that in other psychotic disorders, especially schizophrenia. Clearly, given the relatively high prevalence of psychosis during acute mania, one possible factor is the intensity of the manic affective disruption. (The relationship of manic affect to formal thought disorder has been described.) The relationship of affect to psychosis is a topic of significant theoretical (nosological) and clinical importance. The classical view of psychosis in the affective disorders is that psychosis is an outgrowth of the severity of affective disruption. This view has been questioned with regard to unipolar major depression (Glassman & Roose, 1981; Sands & Harrow, 1994; Shatzberg & Rothschild, 1992); but, despite its important clinical implications, the issue has received little empirical research regarding psychosis in bipolar disorder. One of the few exceptions is the research of Abrams and Taylor, who demonstrated only a trend toward an association between severity of mania and presence of psychosis (Abrams & Taylor, 1981). Others found a positive relationship between presence of psychotic symptoms and a scale of manic affective disruption (Young, Abrams, Taylor, & Meltzer, 1983).

A second important issue when considering psychotic features in bipolar disorder (as well as other affective disorders) is the mood congruence of the patient's delusions or hallucinations. Psychotic features that have a content that is consistent with the patient's prevailing affect state (mood-congruent psychosis) are distinguished from psychotic symptoms that are inconsistent or divergent from the patient's affect state (mood-incongruent psychosis). An example of a mood-congruent delusion might be the case of an acute manic patient with prominent elation who believes that he is an astronaut or has discovered a major scientific advance. An example of a mood-incongruent psychotic symptom might be that of a similarly elated patient who believes (falsely) that he has an incurable cancer. The DSM-IV has a particular designation for mood-congruent psychosis versus mood-incongruent psychosis during manic and depressive episodes.

The implications of mood congruence in psychotic bipolar disorder has received much less attention than in primary major depression, particularly in more modern research. Clinical lore and early anecdotal accounts depict mood-incongruent psychosis as relatively frequent compared to mood-congruent psychotic symptoms. An earlier literature review by Pope and Lipinski reported that between 20% and 50% of manic patients exhibited schizophrenic symptoms such as first-rank symptoms, auditory and visual hallucinations, catatonia, or delusions (Pope & Lipinski, 1978). Among the few recent studies of the issue, Tohen and colleagues have suggested that patients with psychotic mania display equal rates of mood-incongruent psychosis and mood-congruent psychosis (Tohen, Tsuang, & Goodwin, 1992). Among first-admission psychotic bipolar patients, most who show mood-incongruent psychotic symptoms also concurrently evidence mood-congruent psychotic symptoms (Fennig et al., 1996).

The relative prominence of mood-incongruent psychotic symptoms is particularly relevant for its prognostic implications. This issue has been studied primarily with regard to major depression (Coryell & Tsuang, 1985; Coryell, Tsuang, & McDaniel, 1982) but has received less empirical attention in bipolar disorder. The existing modern research targeting bipolar patients suggests that mood incongruence is associated with poorer clinical outcome (Davies & Harrow, 1994; Fennig et al., 1996; Tohen et al., 1992).

Diagnostic and Nosological Considerations of Concomitant Affective and Psychotic Symptoms

For patients with both psychosis and acute mania, the differential diagnosis of bipolar disorder, on the one hand, and schizoaffective disorder (and, to a lesser extent, schizophrenia), on the other hand, can be challenging. This is particularly salient when diagnosis is based solely on cross-sectional clinical data. Indeed, the differential diagnosis of bipolar disorder from schizoaffective disorder and schizophrenia must be based not only on presenting clinical symptoms, but also on longitudinal information and the temporal relationship of affective and psychotic symptoms. With the DSM-IV criteria, this differential diagnosis is based on two factors: (1) the relative timing and persistence of psychotic and affective symptoms and (2) the qualitative features of the psychotic symptoms, particularly the salience of mood-incongruent or bizarre psychotic features.

For a diagnosis of bipolar disorder among patients who have co-occurring psychosis and mania, the psychosis must be present only when affective symptoms are present. If the psychosis, particularly mood-incongruent psychosis, is present for any sustained period in the absence of prominent mood symptoms, then a diagnosis of schizoaffective disorder must be seriously considered. Some argue that diagnosis can be clarified by examining the longer course of illness. Most research has shown that patients with bipolar disorder have better outcomes than those with either schizoaffective disorder or schizophrenia (DellOsso et al., 1993; Harrow & Grossman, 1984; Tsuang & Dempsey, 1979). Yet other studies comparing outcome in schizoaffective disorder with outcome in bipolar disorder find no significant differences (Clayton, 1982; Coryell et al., 1990).

The nosological differentiation of bipolar disorder from schizophrenia is further complicated by the presence of affective disruption, including cyclothymic mood swings and depression, in schizophrenia (Fitchner, Grossman, Harrow, & Klein, 1989; Harrow, Yonan, Sands, & Marengo, 1994; Sands & Harrow, 1999; Sax, Strakowski, Keck, & Upadhyaya, 1996; Siris, 1991). According to DSM-IV criteria for schizophrenia, the duration of full syndromal affective disruption must be brief relative to the ac-

tive phases of the primary schizophrenic symptoms. Additional research is needed to clarify whether the mechanisms leading to affective disruption in schizophrenia are the same as those leading to affective disruption in bipolar disorder.

Dysfunction of the dopamine system has been implicated in the pathogenesis of schizophrenia, particularly because neuroleptic medications that block dopamine receptors are the most effective medications for reducing the psychotic symptoms of schizophrenia. Still, the issue of dopamine system pathology in the etiology of psychotic affective disorders has received only scant attention. Some researchers suggest that patients with psychotic bipolar disorder have an increased density of dopamine receptors, comparable to that hypothesized by some researchers for schizophrenia patients (Pearlson et al., 1995). Others argue that there is no compelling evidence that a defect in the dopamine system is an essential part of the pathogenisis of bipolar disorder. For example, Craddock and colleagues studied the functional mutation of the dopamine D2 receptor gene in bipolar disorder and a control sample (Craddock et al., 1995). Their results failed to find a genetic association with the dopamine receptor. This is consistent with other evidence arguing against a genetic abnormality of the dopamine receptor as a factor in susceptibility to bipolar disorder (Kelsoe et al., 1993).

Although diagnostic criteria can optimally facilitate the distinction between bipolar disorders and schizophrenia, the concomitance of both affective disruption and psychosis presents interesting nosological and etiological questions. Is the affective disruption experienced by patients with psychotic affective disorders, including bipolar disorder and psychotic unipolar depression, central, or even necessary, to the pathogenesis of the psychotic symptoms in these patients? To the extent that nosology expresses etiological assumptions, this question seems to be answered in the affirmative. However, although the work of researchers has shown some relationship between affect and psychosis, there is currently no compelling evidence for unique pathogenesis of psychosis in the primary affective disorders compared to schizoaffective disorder or even schizophrenia. It is likely that this controversy will be resolved as psychiatric nosology comes to be based more on empirically verified etiological considerations and less reliant on phenomenological descriptions.

EPIDEMIOLOGY

Research on the epidemiology of bipolar disorder varies depending on the specific criteria used, the measure of occurrence (incidence, point prevalence, lifetime morbidity, etc.), and the means of assessment (Goodwin & Jamison, 1990). Even when considering its variants, however, research shows that bipolar disorder is far less prevalent than unipolar major depression. Most recent epidemiological studies place the lifetime morbidity at approximately 1%. In a prospective study, Angst and associates (Angst, 1992) estimate the lifetime morbidity of depression at 15%, while the lifetime morbidity for bipolar disorder is less than 3%. The same study suggested that hypomania is even less prevalent than bipolar mania. Fogarty and associates place the lifetime prevalence of mania at 0.6% for both sexes combined (Fogarty, Russell, Newman, & Bland, 1994). They report a lifetime morbidity risk of 1.4% for men and 0.6% for women. Cassano and associates found that among patients who have had major depressive episodes, 5.1% gave a past history of mania (bipolar I), and 13.7% met the authors' operational criteria for hypomania (bipolar II) (Cassano et al., 1992).

Sex differences in the major affective disorders have been the object of much empirical study. Although it is well known that the rate of unipolar depression is higher among women than among men, some researchers suggest that there is no sex difference among bipolar patients (Weissman et al., 1984). Winokur and colleagues looked at this issue from the perspective of sex differences in the ratio of unipolar depression to bipolar disorder (Winokur & Crowe, 1983). They report that the ratio of unipolar to bipolar disorder was higher among women than among men.

An emerging variant of epidemiological research is epidemiological economics, assessing the costs associated with psychiatric disorders. In a recent report, Wyatt and associates state that the direct and indirect economic costs of bipolar disorder in the United States is considerable (Wyatt & Henter, 1995). They report that direct costs, including expenditures for both inpatient and outpatient care as well as non-treatment-related costs (such as use of the criminal justice system by individuals with bipolar disorder) total approximately $7 billion. When indirect costs, such as the lost productivity of bipolar patients and of the family members who care for them, are considered, the economic impact of bipolar disorder rises an additional $37 billion. Thus, it is apparent that the economic impact of bipolar disorder extends beyond that of the afflicted patients and their families to have an impact on the United States economy as a whole.

COMORBIDITY

Comorbidity with other disorders occurs for a high percentage of patients with bipolar disorder (Fogarty et al., 1994; Strakowski et al., 1992; Winokur, 1994). These include alcohol abuse, substance abuse, antisocial or criminal behavior, and phobias. Personality disorders, including bipolar disorder and obsessive compulsive disorder (OCD) syndrome, have been clinically observed in bipolar disorder (Kruger et al., 1995). Large epidemiological studies have shown the lifetime prevalence of panic disorder among bipolar disorder to be about 20%, twice as high as it is in unipolar depression and much higher than among the general population (Chen & Dilsaver, 1995). Among many adolescent bipolar patients, comorbid conduct disorder confuses its clinical presentation and could obscure the underlying affective disorder (Kovacs & Pollock, 1995).

DISEASE PROCESS AND ETIOLOGICAL CONSIDERATIONS

Clinical Phenomenon and Disease Process

The signs and symptoms of a disease are not to be equated with the disease process itself (Carpenter, Strauss, & Bartko, 1974). Bridging the gap between hypothetical underlying disease processes and the overt symptoms of mania appears a distant but important objective. The specific underlying etiology of manic and bipolar disorders has not been conclusively identified. Biochemical hypotheses appear to be the current object of focus, typically focusing on various neurotransmitters or their metabolites (Belmaker & van Praag, 1980; Goodwin & Jamison, 1990). Several studies present strong evidence of a genetic component for bipolar disorder (Fischer, 1980). Psychoanalytic perspectives, reviewed by Aleksandrowicz (1980), focus on the defensive nature of mania (a means of mitigating against depression) and also on the narcissistic aspects of the manic personality (Aleksandrowicz, 1980).

Whether the etiological origin of bipolar disorders lies in the biochemical, neuroanatomical, or psychodynamic realm, or some combination thereof, the overt symptoms reflect disruption along psychological dimensions. Disturbances of mood (e.g., elation and irritability), behavior (e.g., hyperarousal, increased goal-directed behavior, spending sprees, and hypersexuality), and ideation (e.g., grandiosity and delusional thinking) can be viewed with respect to dysfunctions of affective modulation, impulse control, failure of inhibition, conation, cognition, and reality testing among other possible psychological functions. The presence of an underlying disease process is shown through overt symptoms, which are thus mediated by psychological processes. The examination of the relationships of overt symptoms to one another and to dysfunction along various psychological dimensions can be viewed as a step in tracing the manifestations of bipolar disorder back to underlying disease processes.

Genetics

Some genetic transmission of bipolar disorder is fairly well established. Research has shown that there are significantly higher rates of positive family history of mental illness among bipolar patients. Estimates have ranged as high as 48% (Alexander et al., 1995). Others have found family history of affective illness between 20% and 30% (Gershon et al., 1982). However, the rates of familial illness vary substantially as a result of a number of methodological factors. When the focus is on bipolar I disorders in first-degree relatives of bipolar I patients, the reported morbid risk is between 3% and 5% (Gershon, 1990).

Genetic factors could also contribute to predispositions for the dimensions that contribute to the variability in bipolar disorder. Family history of mania in bipolar patients was associated with more recurrences over a 10-year follow-up period than if such a history were absent (Winokur et al., 1994). Morbid risk for children is much higher if two parents have

bipolar disorder than if only one parent has the disorder (Gershon et al., 1982). New research suggests that there could be a genetic factor in the degree of therapeutic response of some bipolar patients to lithium (Abou-Saleh & Coppen, 1986; Maj et al., 1984; Mendlewicz, Fieve, & Stallone, 1973; Prien, Caffey, & Klett, 1974), although others have failed to observe this association (Dunner, Fliess, & Fieve, 1976; Taylor & Abrams, 1981). Paternal transmission has been found to be significantly associated with age of onset among bipolar patients (Grigoroiu et al., 1995).

Family and genetic research also provides data relevant to the basic nosological relationship of bipolar disorder to unipolar depression, on the one hand, and to schizophrenia, on the other. The occurrence of relatives with unipolar depression among families of bipolar patients can cause conceptual difficulties in understanding the genetic linkage for bipolar disorder (Blacker & Tsuang, 1993). Winokur and colleagues report that familial bipolar I or schizoaffective mania is significantly higher in the first-degree relatives of patients with bipolar I or schizoaffective mania than in relatives with unipolar depression (Winokur, 1995). This finding supports the nosological distinction of bipolar disorder from unipolar depression (Heun & Maier, 1993). Other research suggests that schizophrenia was no more prevalent in first-degree relatives of manic-depressives than it is in the population at large, supporting the view that manic-depression and schizophrenia are genetically unrelated diseases.

Genetic research, targeting the possible genetic locus of bipolar disorder, is making rapid advances as a result of new technology and methodology. A crucial issue will be the determination of whether bipolar disorder is due to a single major gene, a small number of genes, or multifactorial polygenic inheritance. Much of the research has narrowed potential factors to fewer than 10 possible genes. This research, based on the analysis of bipolar patients and their relatives, has tentatively identified several areas, chromosomes 18, 11, and the X chromosome, as possible loci for bipolar disorder (Craddock & Owen, 1994; Marshall, 1994). Research is continuing on a potential multigene theory; but, despite advances in technology, there are still problems in currently available methodologies. Researchers have explored the possible linkage between bipolar disorder and specific genetic foci, such as chromosome 18, but this research has not found any definitive association (Baron, 1995). Controversy also surrounds the potential influence of the X chromosome, be it the possession of an extra X chromosome or other defects associated with the X chromosome (Craddock & Owen, 1994; Crow, 1994; Mendlewicz & Hirsch, 1991)

Pathophysiological and Biochemical Theories

Major advances in structural brain imaging, functional brain imaging and related techniques allow for new data on possible structural abnormalities in bipolar disorders. Some of this new data are identifying striking similarities of bipolar disorder to schizophrenia. Neurodevelopmental abnormalities have long been proposed in schizophrenia (Weinberger, 1987), and studies of early neuromotor abnormalities and deficits in affect expression have been implicated in schizophrenia (Walker, 1994; Walker, Grimes, Davis, & Smith, 1993; Walker, Savoie, & Davis, 1994). Whether a neurodevelopmental model could be applicable to both bipolar disorder and schizophrenia is uncertain. Indeed the presence of specific defects in both disorders is controversial (Jurjus, Nasrallah, Brogan, & Olson, 1993; Nasrallah, 1991). Modern imaging studies have shown that, while bipolar patients show some ventricular enlargement, it is less than that observed in schizophrenia (Andreasen et al., 1990; Swayze et al., 1990). Thus, although a structural neurodevelopmental model may provide a useful model for understanding the pathogenesis of bipolar disorder and schizophrenia, these processes may be quite different in the two disorders (Swayze et al., 1992).

A major theoretician in bipolar disorder, Robert Post described possible mechanisms underlying the development of bipolar disorder over time. He suggests that behavioral sensitization and electrophysiological kindling could be key factors in the development of bipolar disorder (Post, 1990). He hypothesized that frequent episodes of bipolar illness, early in the course of the disorder, predisposes the individual to more frequent episodes later during the course. In this view, pathophysiolgical changes, at the level of the individual neuron, occurring in response to stress during the early stages of illness, re-

sult in increased morbidity over subsequent years and in treatment resistance, particularly to lithium. Evidence that could be seen as supportive of this view has emerged from some outcome studies (Goldberg & Harrow, 1994; Goodnick, 1987), including studies of patients with pediatric-onset bipolar disorder (Strober et al., 1995). In a related series of studies, Altshuler and colleagues have reported that cognitive deficits during episodes of mania could result in structural changes that increase patients' vulnerability to future episodes of illness (Altshuler, 1993). The formulations of Post and Altshuler suggest the possibility of physical changes arising subsequent to the emergence of the bipolar illness.

Neuropsychology

Over the past decade, neuropsychological assessment has gained popularity as a means of investigating possible pathogenic processes in major mental illnesses. Much research has been conducted on various cognitive and neuropsychological factors in bipolar disorder, with comparisons to schizophrenia patients, medical patients, and/or normal controls (Hoff et al., 1990; Jones et al., 1994; Serper, 1993). Bipolar patients' laterality of function, memory and learning processes, attentional processing, psychomotor speed, and visual-spatial functioning all have been the object of focus.

In studying motor abnormalities, schizophrenia and bipolar patients exhibited opposite asymmetries, with greater right-hand dyscontrol in schizophrenia and greater left-hand dyscontrol in bipolar disorder (Lohr & Caligiuri, 1995). This has been viewed as suggesting greater pathological involvement of the dominant hemisphere in schizophrenia and of the nondominant hemisphere in bipolar disorder. Other neuropsychological researchers have also reported evidence suggesting differential hemispheric activation as a possible factor in manic states (Kaprinis et al., 1995; Stratta et al., 1995).

Attentional deficits are of central importance because of their far-reaching impact on other areas of functioning. Some attentional deficits in bipolar manic patients are similar to those seen in schizophrenia patients (Serper, 1993). Hoff and colleagues compared acute schizophrenia patients to bipolar patients during a manic episode (Hoff et al., 1990) and found no significant differences on a variety of standard neuropsychological and cognitive tests.

Some researchers suggest that abnormal cognitive functioning is not dependent on the presence of an active manic state or depressed state. Compared to controls, bipolar patients show worse performance on backward masking tasks, both during acute mania and following remission of the mania (Fleming & Green, 1995). These researchers suggest that some of these cognitive problems could be due to the effect of lithium on cognitive function (to be discussed). Others (Sands et al., 1987) found signs of abnormal thinking and formal thought disorder among previously hospitalized bipolar patients, even though many of these patients had no other manic affective symptoms at the time of assessment.

One possible factor involved in postacute neuropsychological deficits among bipolar patients is lithium. Though commonly prescribed and effective in stabilizing mood for a number of bipolar patients, lithium has been associated with impairments in a variety of cognitive functions. The most frequently noted neuropsychological effects of lithium is on patients' memory, psychomotor slowing, and verbal productivity (Fleming & Green, 1995; Kocsis et al., 1993).

Stress Modulation and Precipitating Factors

The role of precipitating stress or environmental–person interactions has always been controversial in the study of psychopathology. This issue has been the subject of much debate regarding bipolar disorder. Although bipolar disorder has typically been construed to run an autonomous course, some researchers suggest that stress could play a role in relapse rate (Akiskal et al., 1995; Pichot, 1995). Prospective research has found a significant association between life events and relapse or recurrence of the disorder (Ellicott et al., 1990; Hunt, Bruce, & Silverstone, 1992). These effects could not be explained by differences in levels of medication or compliance. On the other hand, a number of researchers have found no statistically significant association between life events and the likelihood of relapse among bipolar patients (McPherson, Herbison, & Romans, 1993).

Stressful environmental factors, difficulties adjusting to environmental stress, and lack of social supports all contribute to relapse and outcome among bipolar patients (O'Connell et al., 1985, 1991). One study suggested that systemic family therapy, purportedly one way of reducing environmental stress or increasing support for patients, was effective in reducing relapse rates among patients with bipolar disorder (Retzer et al., 1991). As noted previously, Post's theory of kindling places an emphasis on stress during the early phases of illness, with subsequent pathophysiological changes resulting in increased vulnerability to relapse regardless of stress.

LONGITUDINAL COURSE AND OUTCOME

Onset Patterns and Prodromal Characteristics

The overall pattern of onset and prodrome is fairly well documented. Age of onset is typically before 30 (Fogarty et al., 1994). Newer research on these characteristics in the past decade has focused on patterns in younger age groups. As noted previously, approximately 10% to 15% of adult bipolar patients have onset in childhood or adolescence (Weller et al., 1995). Relatively few bipolar patients have onset before age 10 (Fogarty et al., 1994). Some researchers suggest that patients whose bipolar illness emerges during childhood or adolescence may have a more pernicious course of illness (Strober et al., 1995). Onset occurs in later life for a small subgroup of bipolar patients; unfortunately, our understanding of manic syndromes and bipolar disorders in the elderly is very limited (Young & Klerman, 1992).

Research on bipolar disorder has suggested that prodromal symptoms may precede the full syndrome by weeks or months (Fava & Kellner, 1991). In one major report, the mean duration of manic prodromes was slightly longer than that of depressive prodromes—28.9 days and 18.8 days, respectively (Smith & Tarrier, 1992). One investigation suggested that an increase in unusual thought content was evident one month before manic relapse (Altman et al., 1992). The same study reported that depressive relapses were preceded by higher levels of conceptual disorganization. Clearly, early detection of these symptoms could help reduce recurrences of affective disorders.

Characterizations of Course and Outcome

Traditionally, bipolar disorder has been viewed as an episodic illness with good outcome and unimpaired psychological functioning between episodes of illness (Kolb, 1968; MacVane, Lange, Brown, & Zayat, 1978; Redlich & Freedman, 1966). Most modern research still supports the idea that bipolar disorder is an episodic illness. Symptomatic remission of adolescent bipolar patients during hospitalized episodes suggest that manic episodes remit more quickly than depressed episodes (Strober et al., 1995). This finding has been replicated in adults, using a 5-year prospective study (Keller et al., 1993).

Although the existence of chronic major depressions and chronic subsyndromal depressions has been acknowledged (Akiskal, King, Rosenthal, Robinson, & Scott-Strauss, 1981), the existence of chronic severe or even subsyndromal mania has received only scant attention. Keller and associates suggest that subsyndromal mania may occur for patients who are treated with lower doses of lithium (Keller et al., 1992). However, these authors also note that subsyndromal affective symptoms were associated with relapse, primarily into a manic episode. In a 10-year study, Winokur and associates found that chronicity during the entire follow-up period was uncommon (Winokur et al., 1994).

Although there is periodicity of the full manic and depressive symptoms in bipolar disorder, modern research is documenting that the interepisodic period is not always characterized by complete remission and return to optimal levels of functioning. Recent longitudinal research, based on modern samples, is providing evidence that many previously hospitalized bipolar patients have poor outcomes, even with modern treatments. This research suggests that a course of persistent poor function over multiple years posthospital is not uncommon (Coryell et al., 1993; Goldberg & Harrow, 1994; Goldberg, Harrow, & Leon, 1996, Goldberg et al., 1995a, 1995b). Interepisodic functioning is often characterized by a variety of psychosocial difficulties and occupational impairments. New research is suggesting that even with treatment, a substantial number of bipolar patients experience chronic psychiatric symptoms, often subsyndromal depression. Compared to patients with unipolar depression, bipolar patients have more affective episodes

and rehospitalizations during the first 5 years of illness (Winokur et al., 1993b).

The episodic nature of bipolar disorder is expressed by recurrences of acute mania or of severe depression. Recurrence risks may vary as a function of age at onset or stage of the disease process (Strober et al., 1995). A controversial issue in the field is whether the periodicity of bipolar disorder changes over time. Winokur and colleagues found that cycle lengths did not change over a 10-year follow-up period (Winokur et al., 1994). Moreover, the same researchers found that patients with multiple episodes before index admission were more likely to have episodes during a posthospital follow-up period (Winokur et al., 1993b). This suggests that the vulnerability to affective episodes is a fairly stable characteristic for individual bipolar patients. Psychosocial factors, such as negative affective style in the family and lower social class, have been associated with outcome in bipolar disorder (O'Connell et al., 1985, 1991).

Psychotic symptoms in bipolar mania are sometimes considered a poor prognostic sign. Research has suggested that bipolar patients with psychotic symptoms or formal thought disorder have poorer social outcomes and higher relapse rates (Tohen et al., 1990; Wilcox, 1992). The presence of mood-incongruent psychotic symptoms is associated with worse prognosis than that of mood-congruent psychotic symptoms (Tohen et al., 1992). Researchers from the Chicago Followup Study have found that, whereas psychotic symptoms during acute hospitalization do not predict subsequent outcome several years after hospitalization (Harrow, Goldberg, Grossman, & Meltzer, 1990), psychotic symptoms during the posthospital period are associated with poorer overall outcome (Grossman et al., 1986). Quite likely, the greater prognostic significance of posthospital psychosis compared to inpatient psychosis is due to the high percentage of hospitalized manic patients with psychotic symptoms.

TREATMENT

Treatment of bipolar disorder has been extensively reviewed (Dieperink & Sands, 1996; Janicak, Davis, Preskorn, & Ayd, 1993, 1995; Keck & McElroy, 1993). Until recently, lithium has been the mainstay for the treatment of bipolar disorder, particularly for acute mania. However, as noted, modern research has revealed much variability of outcome following lithium treatment (Goldberg et al., 1996; O'Connell et al., 1985). The notion that all bipolar patients respond favorably to lithium has been seriously questioned (Goldberg et al., 1995a, 1995b, 1996; Harrow et al., 1990). Still, lithium use has a long history of effectiveness for many bipolar patients, and there continues to be abundant evidence that lithium treatment has a strong prophylactic effect in many, but not all, bipolar patients. For example, Suppes and colleagues report a significantly higher risk for relapse after lithium discontinuation among bipolar I patients compared to those who continued lithium treatment (Suppes, Baldessarini, Faedda, & Tohen, 1991). Maintenance treatment with mood stabilizers early in the course of the illness may help prevent the biological alterations that contribute to an increased vulnerability to more frequent episodes (Keck & McElroy, 1993).

The use of anticonvulsant medications, either alone or in conjunction with lithium, has become much more common in recent years. Augmentation with anticonvulsant medication (especially valproic acid and carbamazepine) is often indicated when response to lithium is poor. Carbamazepine, alone or in conjunction with lithium, may be one treatment of choice for rapid-cycling patients (di Costanzo & Schifano, 1991; Joffe, 1991).

The use of antidepressants in bipolar depression has received less empirical attention than the use of mood stabilizers. Cutting-edge psychopharmacological research is providing new insights into treatment of the depressive phase of bipolar disorder. For example, research has suggested that certain forms of anergic depression among bipolar patients might be more effectively treated with tranylcypromine than with imipramine (Himmelhoch, Thase, Mallinger, & Houck, 1991).

The use of antidepressants in bipolar disorder is somewhat controversial (Goodwin, 1993). There is evidence suggesting that antidepressants may not only induce manic episodes in some vulnerable patients, but also decrease the periodicity of cycles in some patients (Altshuler et al., 1995). Bipolar patients with an early age of onset may have increased vulnerability to cycle acceleration as a result of anti-depressant treatment. Some research has suggested that bipolar patients who suffer a psychotic depression may respond to antidepressant treatment by developing a treatment-resistant mixed state involving both manic and depressive features (Dilsaver & Swann, 1995). However, the association of antidepressant use with an increased frequency of manic or hypomanic episodes is a matter of debate (Rifkin, 1993).

Antipsychotic medication is frequently used in the treatment of acute mania, usually in conjunction with a mood stabilizer (Dieperink & Sands, 1996). Most antipsychotics have a more rapid onset of action than mood stabilizers, and contribute heavily to the initial stabilization of acute mania. Some suggest that acute mania is best treated by initially using antipsychotic medications alone, then adding mood stabilizers only after some stabilization has occurred (Goodwin & Jamison, 1990). Newer atypical antipsychotics have been shown to be effective in the treatment of psychotic stages of bipolar episodes (Banov et al., 1994; Keck et al., 1995).

SUMMARY AND FUTURE DIRECTIONS

Modern research methods have contributed to tremendous growth in our knowledge of bipolar disorder. Although many older concepts continue to be valid, new data are forcing the reconceptualization of fundamental assumptions about the nature of bipolar disorder. Clearly, bipolar disorder is more complex and heterogeneous than heretofore understood. The inclusion of subtypes of bipolar disorder will allow for more homogeneous research and clinical samples, thus facilitating interpretive understanding of new data that are currently being gathered. New developments in brain imaging and biochemical assay are likely to lead to further refinements in understanding this heterogeneity and to move the nosology closer to an etiologically based diagnostic system. Despite these advances, careful attention to clinical phenomenology by the treating physician can never be replaced. Still, with new advances in treatment, it will become increasingly imperative to gather a broad range of clinical and laboratory findings to facilitate the optimal treatment of each individual bipolar patient.

REFERENCES

Abou-Saleh, M.T., & Coppen, A. (1986). Who responds to prophylactic lithium? *Journal of Affective Disorders, 10,* 115–125.

Abrams, R., & Taylor, M.A. (1974). Unipolar mania: A preliminary report. *Archives of General Psychiatry, 30,* 441–443.

Abrams, R., & Taylor, M.A. (1981). Importance of schizophrenic symptoms in the diagnosis of mania. *American Journal of Psychiatry, 138.*

Abrams, R., Taylor, M.A., Hayman, M.A., & Krishna, N.R. (1979). Unipolar mania revisited. *Journal of Affective Disorders, 1,* 59–68.

Akiskal, H.S., King, D., Rosenthal, T.L., Robinson, D., & Scott-Strauss, A. (1981). Chronic depressions: Part 1. Clinical and familial characteristics in 137 probands. *Journal of Affective Disorders, 3,* 297–315.

Akiskal, H.S., Maser, J.D., Zeller, P.J., Endicott, J., et al. (1995). Switching from "unipolar" to bipolar II: An 11-year prospective study of clinical and temperamental predictors in 559 patients. *Archives of General Psychiatry, 52,* 114–123.

Aleksandrowicz, D.R. (1980). Psychoanalytic studies of mania. In R.H. Belmaker & H.M. van Praag (Eds.), *Mania an evolving concept.* Jamaica, NY: Spectrum Publications.

Alexander, J.R., Benjamin, J., Lerer, B., Baron, M., et al. (1995). Frequency of positive family history in bipolar patients in a catchment-area population. *Progress in Neuro-Psychopharmacology and Biological Psychiatry, 19,* 367–373.

Altman, E.S., Rea, M.M., Mintz, J., Miklowitz, D.J., et al. (1992). Prodromal symptoms and signs of bipolar relapse: A report based on prospectively collected data. *Psychiatry Research, 41,* 1–8.

Altshuler, L.L. (1993). Bipolar disorder: Are repeated episodes associated with neuroanatomic and cognitive changes? *Biological Psychiatry, 33,* 563–565.

Altshuler, L.L., Post, R.M., Leverich, G.S., Mikalauskas, K., et al. (1995). Antidepressant-induced mania and cycle acceleration: A controversy revisited. *American Journal of Psychiatry, 152,* 1130–1138.

American Psychiatric Association. (1994). *Diagnostic and statistical manual of mental disorders,* 4th ed. Washington, DC: Author.

Ananth, J., Wohl, M., Ranganath, V., & Beshay, M. (1993). Rapid cycling patients: Conceptual and etiological factors. *Neuropsychobiology, 27,* 193–198.

Andreasen, N. (1979). Thought, language and communications disorders: II. Diagnostic significance. *Archives of General Psychiatry, 36,* 1325–1330.

Andreasen, N., & Grove, W. (1986). Thought, language, and communication in schizophrenia: Diagnosis and prognosis. *Schizophrenia Bulletin, 12,* 348–359.

Andreasen, N.C., & Powers, P.S. (1974). Overinclusive thinking in mania and schizophrenia. *British Journal of Psychiatry, 125,* 452–456.

Andreasen, N.C., & Powers, P.S. (1975). Creativity and psychosis: An examination of conceptual style. *Archives of General Psychiatry, 32,* 70–73.

Andreasen, N.C., Swayze, V.W., Flaum, M., Alliger, R., et al. (1990). Ventricular abnormalities in affective disorder: Clinical and demographic correlates. *American Journal of Psychiatry, 147,* 893–900.

Angst, J. (1992). Epidemiology of depression: Second International Symposium on Moclobemide: RIMA (Reversible Inhibitor of Monoamine Oxidase Type A): A new concept in the treatment of depression (1991, Davos, Switzerland). *Psychopharmacology, 106,* 71–74.

Ballenger, J.C., Reus, V.I., & Post, R.M. (1982). The "atypical" clinical picture of adolescent mania. *American Journal of Psychiatry, 139,* 602–606.

Banov, M.D., Zarate, C.A., Tohen, M., et al. (1994). Clozapine therapy in refractory affective disorders: Polarity predicts response in long-term follow-up. *Journal of Clinical Psychiatry, 55,* 295–300.

Baron, M. (1995). Genes and psychosis: Old wine in new bottles? *Acta Psychiatrica Scandinavica, 92,* 81–86.

Bauer, M.S., & Keller, M.B. (1994). The therapeutic challenge of rapid cycling bipolar disorder. *Psychiatric Annals, 24,* 390–391, 395.

Bauer, M.S., & Whybrow, P.C. (1993). Validity of rapid cycling as a modifier for bipolar disorder in DSM-IV. *Depression, 1,* 11–19.

Bauer, M.S., Whybrow, P.C., Gyulai, L., Gonnel, J.,

et al. (1994). Testing definitions of dysphoric mania and hypomania: Prevalence, clinical characteristics and inter-episode stability. *Journal of Affective Disorders, 32,* 201–211.

Belmaker, R.H., & van Praag, H.M. (1980). *Mania: An evolving concept.* Jamaica, New York: Spectrum Publications.

Berthier, M.L., Starkstein, S.E., Robinson, R.G., & Leiguarda, R. (1990). Limbic lesions in a patient with recurrent mania. *Journal of Neuropsychiatry and Clinical Neurosciences, 2,* 235–236.

Blacker, D., & Tsuang, M.T. (1993). Unipolar relatives in bipolar pedigrees: Are they bipolar? *Psychiatric Genetics, 3,* 5–16.

Borchardt, C.M., & Bernstein, G.A. (1995). Comorbid disorders in hospitalized bipolar adolescents compared with unipolar depressed adolescents. *Child Psychiatry and Human Development, 26,* 11–18.

Bowden, C.L. (1993) The clinical approach to the differential diagnosis of bipolar disorder. *Psychiatric Annals, 23,* 57–63.

Bunney, W.E., Goodwin, F.K., & Murphy, D.L. (1992). Affective illness: Two decades of psychobiological investigations. *Pharmacopsychiatry, 25,* 10–13.

Calabrese, J.R., & Delucchi, G.A. (1989). Phenomenology of rapid cycling manic depression and its treatment with valproate. *Journal of Clinical Psychiatry, 50*(Suppl. 3), 30–34.

Carlson, G., & Goodwin, F. (1973). The stages of mania: A longitudinal analysis of the manic episode. *Archives of General Psychiatry, 28,* 221–228.

Carpenter, W., Strauss, J., & Bartko, J. (1974). The diagnosis and understanding of schizophrenia: Part I. Use of signs and symptoms for the identification of schizophrenic patients. *Schizophrenia Bulletin, 11,* 37–49.

Cassano, G.B., Akiskal, H.S., Savino, M., Musetti, L., et al. (1992). Proposed subtypes of bipolar II and related disorders: With hypomanic episodes (or cyclothymia) and with hyperthymic temperament. *Journal of Affective Disorders, 26,* 127–140.

Chen, Y.W., & Dilsaver, S.C. (1995). Comorbidity of panic disorder in bipolar illness: Evidence from the Epidemiologic Catchment Area Survey. *American Journal of Psychiatry, 152,* 280–282.

Clayton, P.C. (1982). Schizoaffective disorders. *Journal of Nervous and Mental Disease, 170,* 646–650.

Coryell, W., Endicott, J., & Keller, M. (1992). Rapidly cycling affective disorder: Demographics, diagnosis, family history, and course. *Archives of General Psychiatry, 49,* 126–131.

Coryell, W., Keller, M., & Lavori, P., et al. (1990). Affective syndromes, psychotic features, and prognosis: II. Mania. *Archives of General Psychiatry, 47,* 658–662.

Coryell, W., Scheftner, W., Keller, M., Endicott, J., et al. (1993). The enduring psychosocial consequences of mania and depression. *American Journal of Psychiatry, 150,* 720–727.

Coryell, W.H., & Tsuang, M.T. (1985). Major depression with mood-congruent or mood-incongruent psychotic features: Outcome after 40 years. *American Journal of Psychiatry, 142,* 479–482.

Coryell, W., Tsuang, M.T., & McDaniel, J. (1982). Psychotic features in major depression: Is mood congruence important? *Journal of Affective Disorders, 4,* 227–236.

Craddock, N., & Owen, M. (1994). Chromosomal aberrations and bipolar affective disorder. *British Journal of Psychiatry, 164,* 507–512.

Craddock, N., Roberts, Q., Williams, N., McGuffin, P., et al. (1995). Association study of bipolar disorder using a functional polymorphism (Ser311 Cys) in the dopamine D2 receptor gene. *Psychiatric Genetics, 5,* 63–65.

Crow, T.J. (1994). Chromosomal aberration and bipolar affective disorder. *British Journal of Psychiatry, 165,* 693.

Davies, E. W., & Harrow, M. (1994). Does mood congruence of psychotic symptoms matter? *Scientific Proceedings of the 147th Annual Meeting of the American Psychiatric Association,* p. 40.

DellOsso, L., Akiskal, H.S., Freer, P., Barberi, M., et al. (1993). Psychotic and nonpsychotic bipolar mixed states: Comparisons with manic and schizoaffective disorders. *European Archives of Psychiatry and Clinical Neuroscience, 243,* 75–81.

di Costanzo, E., & Schifano, F. (1991). Lithium alone or in combination with carbamazepine for the treatment of rapid-cycling bipolar affective disorder. *Acta Psychiatrica Scandinavica, 83,* 456–459.

Dieperink, M.E., & Sands, J.R. (1996). Bipolar mania

with psychotic features: Diagnosis and treatment. *Psychiatric Annals, 26,* 633–637.

Dilsaver, S.C., & Swann, A.C. (1995). Mixed mania: Apparent induction by a tricyclic antidepressant in five consecutively treated patients with bipolar depression. *Biological Psychiatry, 37,* 60–62.

Docherty, N.M., Hawkins, K.A., Hoffman, R.E., Quinlan, D.M., et al. (1996). Working memory, attention, and communication disturbances in schizophrenia. *Journal of Abnormal Psychology, 105,* 212–219.

Dunner, D.L. (1992). Differential diagnosis of bipolar disorder. *Journal of Clinical Psychopharmacology, 12,* 7–12.

Dunner, D.L., & Fieve, R.R. (1974). Clinical factors in lithium carbonate prophylaxis failure. *Archives of General Psychiatry, 30,* 229–233.

Dunner, D.L., Fliess, J.L., & Fieve, R.R. (1976). Lithium carbonate prophylaxis failure. *British Journal of Psychiatry, 129,* 40–44.

Ehlers, C.L. (1995). Chaos and complexity: Can it help us to understand mood and behavior? *Archives of General Psychiatry, 52,* 960–964.

Ellicott, A., Hammen, C., Gitlin, M., Brown, G., et al. (1990). Life events and the course of bipolar disorder. *American Journal of Psychiatry, 147,* 1194–1198.

Faedda, G.L., Baldessarini, R.J., Suppes, T., Tondo, L., Becker, I., & Lipshultz, D.S. (1995). Pediatric-onset bipolar disorder: A neglected clinical and public health problem. *Harvard Review of Psychiatry, 3,* 171–195.

Fava, G.A., & Kellner, R. (1991). Prodromal symptoms in affective disorders. *American Journal of Psychiatry, 148,* 823–830.

Fennig, S., Bromet, E.J., Karant, M.T., Ram, R., et al. (1996). Mood-congruent versus mood-incongruent psychotic symptoms in first-admission patients with affective disorder. *Journal of Affective Disorders, 37,* 23–29.

Fischer, M. (1980). Twin studies and dual mating studies in defining mania. In R.H. Belmaker & H.M. van Praag (Eds.), *Mania an evolving concept.* Jamaica, New York: Spectrum Publications.

Fitchner, C.G., Grossman, L.S., Harrow, M., & Klein, D.N. (1989). Cyclothymic mood swings in the course of affective disorders and schizophrenia. *American Journal of Psychiatry, 146,* 1149–1154.

Fleming, K., & Green, M.F. (1995). Backward masking performance during and after manic episodes. *Journal of Abnormal Psychology, 104,* 63–68.

Fogarty, F., Russell, J.M., Newman, S.C., & Bland, R.C. (1994). Mania. *Acta Psychiatrica Scandinavica, 89,* 16–23.

Fristad, M.A., Weller, R.A., & Weller, E.B. (1995). The Mania Rating Scale (MRS): Further reliability and validity studies with children. *Annals of Clinical Psychiatry, 7,* 127–132.

Frye, M.A., Altshuler, L.L., Szuba, M.P., et al. (1996). The relationship between antimanic agent for treatment of classic or dysphoric mania and length of hospital stay. *Journal of Clinical Psychiatry, 57,* 17–21.

Geller, B., Fox, L.W., & Clark, K.A. (1994). Rate and predictors of prepubertal bipolarity during follow-up of 6- to 12-year-old depressed children. *Journal of the American Academy of Child and Adolescent Psychiatry, 33,* 461–468.

Gershon, E.S. (1990). Genetics. In F.K. Goodwin & K.R. Jamison (Eds.), *Manic-depressive illness* (pp. 373–401). New York: Oxford University Press.

Gershon, E.S., et al. (1982). A family study of schizoaffective bipolar I, bipolar II, unipolar, and normal control probands. *Archives of General Psychiatry, 39,* 1157–1167.

Glassman, A.H., & Roose, S.P. (1981). Delusional depression: A distinct clinical entity? *Archives of General Psychiatry, 38,* 424–427.

Goldberg, J.F., & Harrow, M. (1994). Kindling in bipolar disorders: A longitudinal follow-up study. *Biological Psychiatry, 35,* 70–72.

Goldberg, J.F., Harrow, M., & Grossman, L.S. (1995a). Course and outcome in bipolar affective disorder: A longitudinal follow-up study. *American Journal of Psychiatry, 152,* 379–384.

Goldberg, J.F., Harrow, M., & Grossman, L.S. (1995b). Recurrent affective syndromes in bipolar and unipolar mood disorders at follow-up. *British Journal of Psychiatry, 166,* 382–385.

Goldberg, J.F., Harrow, M., & Leon, A.C. (1996). Lithium treatment of bipolar affective disorders under naturalistic followup conditions. *Psychopharmacology Bulletin, 32,* 47–54.

Goodnick, P.J., Fieve, R.R., Schlegel, A., et al. (1987). Predictors of interepisode symptoms and relapse in affective disorder patients treated with lithium carbonate. *American Journal of Psychiatry, 144,* 367–369.

Goodwin, F.K. (1993). Predictors of antidepressant response. *Bulletin of the Menninger Clinic, 57,* 146–160.

Goodwin, F.K., & Jamison, K.R. (1990). *Manic-depressive illness.* New York: Oxford University Press.

Gottschalk, A., Bauer, M.S., & Whybrow, P.C. (1995). Evidence of chaotic mood variation in bipolar disorder. *Archives of General Psychiatry, 52,* 947–959.

Grigoroiu, S.M., Nothen, M., Propping, P., & Poustka, F., et al. (1995). Clinical evidence for genomic imprinting in bipolar I disorder. *Acta Psychiatrica Scandinavica, 92,* 365–370.

Grossman, L., Harrow, M., & Sands, J. (1986). Features associated with thought disorder in manic patient at 2–4 year follow-up. *American Journal of Psychiatry, 143,* 306–311.

Harrow, M., Goldberg, J.F., Grossman, L.S., & Meltzer, H.Y. (1990). Outcome in manic disorders: A naturalistic follow-up study. *Archives of General Psychiatry, 47,* 665–671.

Harrow, M., & Grossman, L.S. (1984). Outcome in schizoaffective disorder: A critical review and reevaluation of the literature. *Schizophrenia Bulletin, 10,* 87–108.

Harrow, M., Grossman, L., Silverstein, M., & Meltzer, H. (1982). Thought pathology in manic and schizophrenic patients: Its occurrence at hospital admission and seven weeks later. *Archives of General Psychiatry, 39,* 665–671.

Harrow, M., Grossman, L.S., Silverstein, M., Meltzer, H., & Kettering, R. (1986). A longitudinal study of thought disorder in manic patients. *Archives of General Psychiatry, 43,* 781–785.

Harrow, M., & Marengo, J. (1986). Schizophrenic thought disorder: Its persistence and prognostic significance. *Schizophrenia Bulletin, 12,* 373–392.

Harrow, M., Yonan, C.A., Sands, J.R., & Marengo, J.T. (1994). Depression in schizophrenia: Are neuroleptics, akinesia or anhedonia involved? *Schizophrenia Bulletin, 20,* 327–338.

Heun, R., & Maier, W. (1993). The distinction of bipolar II disorder from bipolar I and recurrent unipolar depression. Results of a controlled family study. *Acta Psychiatrica Scandinavica, 87,* 279–284.

Himmelhoch, J.M., & Garfinkel, M.E. (1986). Sources of lithium resistance in mixed mania. *Psychopharmacology Bulletin, 22,* 613–620.

Himmelhoch, J.M., Thase, M. E., Mallinger, A.G., & Houck, P. (1991). Tranylcypromine versus imipramine in anergic bipolar depression. *American Journal of Psychiatry, 148,* 910–916.

Hoff, A.L., Shukla, S., Aronson, T.A., Cook, B.L., et al. (1990). Failure to differentiate bipolar disorder from schizophrenia on measures of neuropsychological function. *Schizophrenia Research, 3,* 253–260.

Hunt, N., Bruce, J.W., & Silverstone, T. (1992). Life events and relapse in bipolar affective disorder. *Journal of Affective Disorders, 25,* 13–20.

Isometsa, E.T., Henriksson, M.M., Aro, H.M., & Lonnqvist, J.K. (1994). Suicide in bipolar disorder in Finland. *American Journal of Psychiatry, 151,* 1020–1024.

Janicak, P.G., Davis, J.M., Preskorn, S.H., & Ayd, F.J. (1993). *Principles and practice of psychopharmacotherapy.* Baltimore, MD: Williams & Wilkins.

Janicak, P.G., Davis, J.M., Preskorn, S.H., & Ayd, F.J. (1995). *Principles and practice of psychopharmacotherapy—Update.* Baltimore, MD: Williams & Wilkins.

Joffe, R.T. (1991). Carbamazepine, lithium, and life course of bipolar affective disorder. *American Journal of Psychiatry, 148,* 1270–1271.

Jones, B.P., Duncan, C.C., Mirsky, A.F., Post, R.M., et al. (1994). Neuropsychological profiles in bipolar affective disorder and complex partial seizure disorder. *Neuropsychology, 8,* 55–64.

Jurjus, G.J., Nasrallah, H.A., Brogan, M., & Olson, S.C. (1993). Developmental brain anomalies in schizophrenia and bipolar disorder: A controlled MRI study. *Journal of Neuropsychiatry and Clinical Neurosciences, 5,* 375–378.

Kaplan, H.I., & Sadock, B.J. (Eds.). (1981). *Modern synopsis of comprehensive textbook of psychiatry,* 3rd ed. Baltimore, MD: Williams & Wilkins.

Kaprinis, G., Nimatoudis, J., Karavatos, A., Kandylis, D., et al. (1995). Functional brain organization in bipolar affective patients during manic phase and after recovery: A digit dichotic listening study. *Perceptual and Motor Skills, 80,* 1275–1282.

Katz, M.M., Maas, J.W., Frazer, A., Koslow, S.H., et

al. (1994). Drug-induced actions on brain neuro-transmitter systems and changes in the behaviors and emotions of depressed patients. *Neuropsychopharmacology, 11,* 89–100.

Keck, P.E., & McElroy, S.L. (1993). Current perspectives on treatment of bipolar disorder with lithium. *Psychiatric Annals, 23,* 64–69.

Keck, P.E., Wilson, D.R., Stakowski, M.D., et al. (1995). Clinical predictors of acute risperidone response in schizophrenia, schizoaffective disorder and psychotic mood disorder. *Journal of Clinical Psychiatry, 56,* 466–470.

Keller, M.B., & Baker, L.A. (1991). Bipolar disorder: Epidemiology, course, diagnosis, and treatment. *Bulletin of the Menninger Clinic, 55,* 172–181.

Keller, M.B., Lavori, P.W., Coryell, W., Endicott, J., et al. (1993). Bipolar I: A five-year prospective follow-up. *Journal of Nervous and Mental Disease, 181,* 238–245.

Keller, M.B., Lavori, P.W., Kane, J.M., Gelenberg, A.J., et al. (1992). Subsyndromal symptoms in bipolar disorder: A comparison of standard and low serum levels of lithium. *Archives of General Psychiatry, 49,* 371–376.

Kelsoe, J.R., Kristbjanarson, H., Bergesch, P., Shilling, P., et al. (1993). A genetic linkage study of bipolar disorder and 13 markers on chromosome 11 including the D-sub-2 dopamine receptor. *Neuropsychopharmacology, 9,* 293–301.

Khouzam, H.R., Bhat, V.G., Boyer, J., & Hardy, W. (1991). Rapid cycling in a patient with bipolar mood disorder secondary to Graves' disease. *American Journal of Psychiatry, 148,* 1272–1273.

Klerman, G.L. (1981). The spectrum of mania. *Comprehensive Psychiatry, 22,* 11–20.

Kocsis, J.H., Shaw, E.D., Stokes, P.E., Wilner, P., et al. (1993). Neuropsychologic effects of lithium discontinuation. *Journal of Clinical Psychopharmacology, 13,* 268–275.

Kolb, L. (1968). *Noyes' modern clinical psychiatry,* 7th ed. Philadelphia: W.B. Saunders.

Kovacs, M., & Pollock, M. (1995). Bipolar disorder and comorbid conduct disorder in childhood and adolescence. *Journal of the American Academy of Child and Adolescent Psychiatry, 34,* 715–723.

Kraepelin, E. (1919). *Dementia praecox and paraphrenia* (R.M. Barclay, Trans.). Edinbugh: E.S. Livingstone.

Kruger, S., Cooke, R.G., Hasey, G.M., Jorna, T., et al. (1995). Comorbidity of obsessive compulsive disorder in bipolar disorder. *Journal of Affective Disorders, 34,* 117–120.

Kubacki, A. (1986). Male and female mania. *Canadian Journal of Psychiatry, 31,* 70–72.

Kuhs, H., & Reschke, D. (1992). Psychomotor activity in unipolar and bipolar depressive patients. *Psychopathology, 25,* 109–116.

Lewinsohn, P.M., Klein, D.N., & Seeley, J.R. (1995). Bipolar disorders in a community sample of older adolescents: Prevalence, phenomenology, comorbidity, and course. *Journal of the American Academy of Child and Adolescent Psychiatry, 34,* 454–463.

Lohr, J.B., & Caligiuri, M.P. (1995). Motor asymmetry, a neurobiologic abnormality in the major psychoses. *Psychiatry Research, 57,* 279–282.

MacVane, J., Lange, J., Brown, W., & Zayat, M. (1978). Psychological functioning of bipolar manic-depressives in remission. *Archives of General Psychiatry, 35,* 1351–1354.

Maj, M., Del Vecchio, M., Starace, F., et al. (1984). Prediction of affective psychoses response to lithium prophylaxis. *Acta Psychiatrica Scandinavica, 69,* 37–44.

Maj, M., Magliano, L., Pirozzi, R., Marasco, C., et al. (1994). Validity of rapid cycling as a course specifier for bipolar disorder. *American Journal of Psychiatry, 151,* 1015–1019.

Maj, M., Pirozzi, R., & Starace, F. (1989). Previous pattern of course of the illness as a predictor of response to lithium prophylaxis in bipolar patients. *Journal of Affective Disorders, 17,* 237–241.

Marengo, J.T., Galloway, C., Sands, J.R., Koeber, N., & Harrow, M. (1986). *A new index for assessing the course of psychopathology.* Paper presented at the Annual Convention of the Illinois Psychological Association, Chicago.

Marengo, J.T., & Harrow, M. (1987). Schizophrenic thought disorder: A persistent or episodic course? *Archives of General Psychiatry, 44,* 651–659.

Marengo, J.T., Harrow, M., Lanin-Kettering, I., & Wilson, A. (1985). The assessment of bizarre-idiosyncratic thinking: A manual for scoring responses to verbal tests. In M. Harrow & D. Quinlan (Eds.), *Disordered thinking and schizo-*

phrenic psychopathology (pp. 394–449). New York: Gardner Press.

Marshall, E. (1994). Highs and lows on the research roller coaster. *Science, 264,* 1693–1695.

McElroy, S.L., Keck, P.E., Pope, H.G., Hudson, J.I., et al. (1992). Clinical and research implications of the diagnosis of dysphoric or mixed mania or hypomania. *American Journal of Psychiatry, 149,* 1633–1644.

McPherson, H., Herbison, P., & Romans, S. (1993). Life events and relapse in established bipolar affective disorder. *British Journal of Psychiatry, 163,* 381–385.

Mendlewicz, J., Fieve, R.R., & Stallone, F. (1973). Relationship between the effectiveness of lithium therapy and family history. *American Journal of Psychiatry, 130,* 1011–1013.

Mendlewicz, J., & Hirsch, D. (1991). Bipolar manic depressive illness and the fragile X syndrome. *Biological Psychiatry, 29,* 298–299.

Mitchell, P., Parker, G.B., Jamieson, K., Wilhelm, K., et al. (1992). Are there any differences between bipolar and unipolar melancholia? *Journal of Affective Disorders, 25,* 97–105.

Nasrallah, H.A. (1991). Neurodevelopmental aspects of bipolar affective disorder. *Biological Psychiatry, 29,* 1–2.

Nurnberger, J., Roose, S.P., Dunner, D.L., & Fieve, R.R. (1979). Unipolar mania: A distinct clinical entity? *American Journal of Psychiatry, 136,* 1420–1423.

O'Connell, R.A., Mayo, J.A., Eng, L.K., et al. (1985). Social support and long-term lithium outcome. *British Journal of Psychiatry, 147,* 272–275.

O'Connell, R.A., Mayo, J.A., Flatow, L., Cuthbertson, B., et al. (1991). Outcome of bipolar disorder on long-term treatment with lithium. *British Journal of Psychiatry, 159,* 123–129.

Pearlson, G.D., Wong, D.F., Tune, L.E., Ross, C.A., et al. (1995). In vivo D-sub-2 dopamine receptor density in psychotic and nonpsychotic patients with bipolar disorder. *Archives of General Psychiatry, 52,* 471–477.

Pfohl, B., Vasquez, N., & Nasrallah, H.A. (1981). The mathematical case against unipolar mania. *Journal of Psychiatric Research, 16,* 259–265.

Pfohl, B., Vasquez, N., & Nasrallah, H.A. (1982). Unipolar vs. bipolar mania: A review of 247 patients. *British Journal of Psychiatry, 141,* 453–458.

Pichot, P. (1995). The birth of the bipolar disorder. *European Psychiatry, 10,* 1–10.

Pope, H., & Lipinski, J. (1978). Diagnosis in schizophrenia and manic-depressive illness. A reassessment of the specificity of "schizophrenic" symptoms in the light of current research. *Archives of General Psychiatry, 35,* 811–828.

Post, R.M. (1990). Sensitization and kindling perspectives for the course of affective illness: Toward a new treatment with the anticonvulsant carbamazepine. *Pharmacopsychiatry, 23,* 3–17.

Post, R.M. (1992). Transduction of psychosocial stress into the neurobiology of recurrent affective disorders. *American Journal of Psychiatry, 149,* 999–1010.

Post, R.M., Uhde, T.W., Putnam, P.W., et al. (1982). Kindling and carbamazepine in affective illness. *Journal of Nervous and Mental Disease, 170,* 717–731.

Prien, R.F., Caffey, F.M., & Klett, C.J. (1974). Factors associated with treatment success in lithium carbonate prophylaxis. *Archives of General Psychiatry, 31,* 189–192.

Prien, R.F., Himmelhoch, J.M., & Kupfer, D.J. (1988). Treatment of mixed mania. *Journal of Affective Disorders, 15,* 9–15.

Redlich, F., & Freedman, D. (1966). *The theory and practice of psychiatry.* New York: Basic Books.

Retzer, A., Simon, F.B., Weber, G., Stierlin, H., et al. (1991). A followup study of manic-depressive and schizoaffective psychoses after systemic family therapy. *Family Process, 30,* 139–153.

Rifkin, A. (1993). Diagnostic reliability of the history of hypomania in bipolar II patients and patients with major depression. *Psychiatric Annals, 23,* 418.

Rihmer, Z., Barsi, J., Arato, M., & Demeter, E. (1990). Suicide in subtypes of primary major depression. *Journal of Affective Disorders, 18,* 221–225.

Sands, J.R., & Harrow, M. (1994). Psychotic unipolar depression at follow up: Factors related to psychosis in the affective disorders. *American Journal of Psychiatry, 151,* 995–1000.

Sands, J.R., & Harrow, M. (1999). Depression during the longitudinal course of schizophrenia. *Schizophrenia Bulletin, 25,* 157–171.

Sands, J.R., Marengo, J.T., & Harrow, M. (1987). A four-year study of manic thought disorder, *Scientific Proceedings of the 140th Annual Meeting of the American Psychiatric Association* (pp. 234–235). Washington, DC: American Psychiatric Press.

Sax, K.W., Strakowski, S.M., Keck, P.E., Jr., & Upadhyaya, V.H. (1996). Relationships among negative, positive, and depressive symptoms in schizophrenia and psychotic depression. *British Journal of Psychiatry, 168,* 68–71.

Sax, K.W., Strakowski, S.M., McElroy, S.L., Keck, P.E., et al. (1995). Attention and formal thought disorder in mixed and pure mania. *Biological Psychiatry, 37,* 420–423.

Serper, M.R. (1993). Visual controlled information processing resources and formal thought disorder in schizophrenia and mania. *Schizophrenia Research, 9,* 59–66.

Sharma, R., & Markar, H.R. (1994). Mortality in affective disorder. *Journal of Affective Disorders, 31,* 91–96.

Shatzberg, A., & Rothschild, A. (1992). Psychotic (delusional) major depression: Should it be included as a distinct syndrome in DSM-IV? *American Journal of Psychiatry, 149,* 733–745.

Shenton, M., Solovay, M., & Holzman, P. (1987). Comparative studies of thought disorders: II. Schizoaffective disorder. *Archives of General Psychiatry, 44,* 21–30.

Shulman, K.I., & Tohen, M. (1994). Unipolar mania reconsidered: Evidence from an elderly cohort. *British Journal of Psychiatry, 164,* 547–549.

Sinnger, H.K., & Brabender, V. (1993). The use of the Rorschach to differentiate unipolar and bipolar disorders. *Journal of Personality Assessment, 60,* 333–345.

Siris, S.G. (1991). Diagnosis of secondary depression in schizophrenia. *Schizophrenia Bulletin, 17,* 75–98.

Smith, J.A., & Tarrier, N. (1992). Prodromal symptoms in manic depressive psychosis. *Social Psychiatry and Psychiatric Epidemiology, 27,* 245–248.

Starkstein, S.E., Fedoroff, P., Berthier, M.L., & Robinson, R.G. (1991). Manic-depressive and pure manic states after brain lesions. *Biological Psychiatry, 29,* 149–158.

Strakowski, S.M., Tohen, M., Stoll, A.L., Faedda, G.L., et al. (1992). Comorbidity in mania at first hospitalization. *American Journal of Psychiatry, 149,* 554–556.

Stratta, P., Daneluzzo, E., Mattei, P., Casacchia, M., et al. (1995). Phasic asymmetries in phasic affective disorders. *Biological Psychiatry, 38,* 132–133.

Strober, M., Schmidt, L.S., Freeman, R., Bower, S., et al. (1995). Recovery and relapse in adolescents with bipolar affective illness: A five-year naturalistic, prospective follow-up. *Journal of the American Academy of Child and Adolescent Psychiatry, 34,* 724–731.

Suppes, T., Baldessarini, R.J., Faedda, G.L., & Tohen, M. (1991). Risk of recurrence following discontinuation of lithium treatment in bipolar disorder. *Archives of General Psychiatry, 48,* 1082–1088.

Swayze, V.W., Andreasen, N.C., Alliger, R.J., Ehrhardt, J.C., et al. (1990). Structural brain abnormalities in bipolar affective disorder: Ventricular enlargement and focal signal hyperintensities. *Archives of General Psychiatry, 47,* 1054–1059.

Swayze, V.W., Andreasen, N.C., Alliger, R.J., Yuh, W.T., et al. (1992). Subcortical and temporal structures in affective disorder and schizophrenia: A magnetic resonance imaging study. *Biological Psychiatry, 31,* 221–240.

Taylor, M.A., & Abrams, R. (1981). Prediction of treatment response in mania. *Archives of General Psychiatry, 38,* 800–803.

Tohen, M., Tsuang, M.T., & Goodwin, D.C. (1992). Prediction of outcome in mania by mood-congruent or mood-incongruent psychotic features. *American Journal of Psychiatry, 149,* 1580–1584.

Tohen, M., Waternaux, C.M., Tsuang, M.T., et al. (1990). Four-year follow-up of twenty-four first-episode manic patients. *Journal of Affective Disorders, 19,* 79–86.

Tomitaka, S.I., & Sakamoto, K. (1994). Definition and prognosis of rapid cycling affective disorder. *American Journal of Psychiatry, 151,* 1524.

Tsuang, M.T., & Dempsey, G.M. (1979). Long-term outcome of major psychosis: II. Schizoaffective disorder compared with schizophrenia, affective disorders, and a surgical control group. *Archives of General Psychiatry, 36.*

Walker, E.F. (1994). Developmentally moderated expressions of the neuropathology underlying schizophrenia. *Schizophrenia Bulletin, 20,* 453–480.

Walker, E.F., Grimes, K.E., Davis, D.M., & Smith, A.J. (1993). Childhood precursors of schizophrenia: Facial expressions of emotion. *American Journal of Psychiatry, 150,* 1654–1660.

Walker, E.F., Savoie, T., & Davis, D. (1994). Neuromotor precursors of schizophrenia. *Schizophrenia Bulletin, 20,* 441–451.

Weinberger, D.R. (1987). Implications of normal brain development for the pathogenesis of schizophrenia. *Archives of General Psychiatry, 44,* 660–669.

Weissman, M.M., et al. (1984). *The epidemiology of depression: An update on sex differences in rates.* Paper presented at the 22nd Annual Meeting of the American College of Neuropsychopharmacology: Sex-related differences in depression: A reappraisal (1983, San Juan, Puerto Rico). *Journal of Affective Disorders, 7,* 179–188.

Weller, E.B., Weller, R.A., & Fristad, M.A. (1995). Bipolar disorder in children: Misdiagnosis, underdiagnosis, and future directions. *Journal of the American Academy of Child and Adolescent Psychiatry, 34,* 709–714.

West, S.A., McElroy, S.L., Strakowski, S.M., Keck, P.E., et al. (1995). Attention deficit hyperactivity disorder in adolescent mania. *American Journal of Psychiatry, 152,* 271–273.

Wilcox, J.A. (1992). The predictive value of thought disorder in manic psychosis. *Psychopathology, 25,* 161–165.

Winokur, G., Coryell, W., Akiskal, H.S., Endicott, J., et al. (1994). Manic-depressive (bipolar) disorder: The course in light of a prospective ten-year follow-up of 131 patients. *Acta Psychiatrica Scandinavica, 89,* 102–110.

Winokur, G., Coryell, W., Endicott, J., & Akiskal, H. (1993a). Further distinctions between manic-depressive illness (bipolar disorder) and primary depressive disorder (unipolar depression). *American Journal of Psychiatry, 150,* 1176–1181.

Winokur, G., Coryell, W., Keller, M., Endicott, J., et al. (1993b). A prospective follow-up of patients with bipolar and primary unipolar affective disorder. *Archives of General Psychiatry, 50,* 457–465.

Winokur, G., Coryell, W., Keller, M., Endicott, J., et al. (1995). A family study of manic-depressive (bipolar I) disease: Is it a distinct illness separable from primary unipolar depression? *Archives of General Psychiatry, 52,* 367–373.

Winokur, G., & Crowe, R.R. (1983). Bipolar illness: The sex–polarity effect in affectively ill family members. *Archives of General Psychiatry, 40,* 57–58.

Wolpert, E.A., Goldberg, J.F., & Harrow, M. (1990). Rapid cycling in unipolar and bipolar affective disorders. *American Journal of Psychiatry, 147,* 725–728.

Wozniak, J., Biederman, J., Mundy, E., Mennin, D., et al. (1995). A pilot family study of childhood-onset mania. *Journal of the American Academy of Child and Adolescent Psychiatry, 34,* 1577–1583.

Wu, L.H., & Dunner, D.L. (1993). Suicide attempts in rapid cycling bipolar disorder patients. *Journal of Affective Disorders, 29,* 57–61.

Wyatt, R.J., & Henter, I. (1995). An economic evaluation of manic-depressive illness—1991. *Social Psychiatry and Psychiatric Epidemiology, 30,* 213–219.

Young, M., Abrams, R., Taylor, M., & Meltzer, H. (1983). Establishing diagnostic criteria for mania. *Journal of Nervous and Mental Disease, 171,* 676–682.

Young, R.C., & Klerman, G.L. (1992). Mania in late life: Focus on age at onset. *American Journal of Psychiatry, 149,* 867–876.

CHAPTER 15

PERSONALITY DISORDERS

John F. Clarkin
Cynthia Sanderson
Weill Medical College of Cornell University

INTRODUCTION

The creation of the "personality disorders" on Axis II by DSM-III in 1980 was an initiative that has stimulated clinical and research attention to personality pathology as distinguished from symptomatic conditions (e.g., anxiety and depression). This initiative was preceded by an impressive history in psychology of describing and measuring personality traits and their consequences on quality of life, and an extensive history in clinical psychiatry on the diagnosis of abnormalities of personality. The field now faces the daunting task of integrating the best from each of these traditions and deriving descriptions of the personality disorders that provide reliable assessment and construct validity.

DESCRIPTION OF THE PERSONALITY DISORDERS

DSM-IV (American Psychiatric Association [APA], 1994) describes a personality disorder as having four key elements: a pattern of inner experience and behavior (i.e., cognition, affectivity, interpersonal functioning, and impulse control) that (1) deviates markedly from the culture's expectations, (2) develops in adolescence or early adulthood and remains stable across the adult life span, (3) is inflexible and pervades a broad range of personal and social situations; and (4) leads to significant distress or impairment in functioning. The International Classification of Diseases (ICD) system is even more explicit about operational criteria for diagnosing a personality disorder in a yes/no manner before proceeding to assigning a specific personality disorder.

As outlined in DSM-IV, the first decision of the clinician is whether or not the patient meets these criteria for a personality disorder, and the second-order decision is the type of personality disorder manifested. The patterns and types of inner experience and behavior that define specific personality disorders are described in 10 disorders, which, in turn, are grouped for heuristic and content reasons into three clusters of personality disorders. Cluster A includes paranoid, schizoid, and schizotypal personality disorders. Cluster B is composed of the antisocial, borderline, histrionic, and narcissistic personality disorders. Cluster C includes avoidant, dependent, and obsessive-compulsive personality disorders.

Cluster A Personality Disorders

Serious personality disorders such as paranoid, schizoid and schizotypal personality disorder are included in this cluster. These disorders are grouped together because of their central relationship to thought disorder and Axis I schizophrenia.

Schizoid Personality Disorder

The concept of a *schizoid personality* dates to early writings on psychopathology and psychoanalysis. Bleuler (1922, 1929) used the term first to describe a character trait present to some extent in all people, involving a withdrawal from people and turning inward of interests. Schizophrenia was viewed as its most severe form, and a more moderate degree of detachment from people and focus on one's inner life was described as a schizoid personality. Kretschmer (1925) distinguished between those schizoids who withdrew from others as a result of timidity and anxiety and those who withdrew out of lack of interest. Elaborations of the concept of schizoid personality can be found in the work of Fairbairn (1940/1952), Winnicott (1945/1958), and Guntrip (1969).

Patients with schizoid personality disorder as defined in DSM-IV are characterized by a pattern of detachment from social relationships and a restricted range of emotional expression, especially in interpersonal situations. These individuals are solitary, do not desire or enjoy close relationships, have little if any interest in sexual experiences with others, and lack close friends. Their emotions are characterized by coldness and detachment and by flattened affectivity.

The schizoid personality disorder criterion set yields a very low coefficient alpha and, in fact, three of the seven criteria yield convergent correlations below .30 (Morey, 1988). Paranoid personality disorder may frequently overlap with schizoid personality disorder in clinical populations (Kass, Skodol, Charles, Spitzer, & Williams, 1985). In a factor-analytic approach, Livesley and Schroeder (1990) found a first factor composed of generalized hypersensitivity and self-absorption, social apprehensiveness, and ineffective social skills. A second factor, social avoidance, overlaps with schizotypal patients. This two-factor model of schizoid is similar to Kretschmer's (1925) description of both extreme sensitivity and apparent aloofness of schizoid individuals. The Danish adoption studies revealed no relationship between schizoid or inadequate personality (a definition broader than the one in DSM) and schizophrenia (Kety et al., 1975).

Schizotypal Personality Disorder

Both Rado (1962) and Meehl (1962) used a concept of the schizotype in reference to individuals with a genetic predisposition to schizophrenia. Spitzer, Endicott, and Gibbon (1979) established the criteria for schizotypal personality disorder on the basis of the characteristics of the relatives of schizophrenic patients. It is, therefore, quite plausible that these characteristics are related to the genetic background of schizophrenia. However, negative symptoms (social isolation, constricted affect, poor rapport) may be more characteristic of these individuals than positive symptoms (perceptual distortions, magical thinking) (Siever & Kendler, 1988). Furthermore, other criteria sets might also describe and adequately distinguish schizophrenic relatives from controls. The Danish adoption studies (Kety et al., 1975) established the empirical and theoretical background for the diagnosis of schizotypal personality disorder. The biologic relatives of schizophrenics in the study were seen as having borderline or latent schizophrenia characterized by social isolation, eccentricity, and transient psychotic-like symptoms.

The DSM-IV criteria emphasize the pervasive pattern of social and interpersonal deficits and cognitive and perceptual distortions in individuals with schizotypal personality disorder. Cognitive difficulties and distortions can include ideas of reference; odd beliefs or magical thinking; and unusual perceptual experiences, such as bodily illusions, superstitiousness, and odd speech. The social patterns are characterized by a lack of close friends, excessive social anxiety, and odd appearance and/or behavior.

Although this criterion set has good internal consistency, a primary difficulty is the significant overlap and correlation with schizoid personality disorder

(Morey, 1988). Paranoid personality overlaps in clinical populations with schizotypal personality disorder (Kass et al., 1985). Schizotypal personality disorder also overlaps with borderline personality disorder, with 57% of borderlines also schizotypal in one survey (Spitzer et al., 1979). In an attempt to identify factors of structural validity, Livesley and Schroeder (1990) found a factor of schizotypal cognition that included ideas of reference, odd speech, and recurrent delusions. This factor distinguishes between schizotypal and schizoid personality disorder. A second factor, social avoidance, is shared by both schizotypal and schizoid personality disorder.

Meehl's model (1962, 1990) of schizotypy and the development of schizophrenia implies that the liability for schizophrenia is dichotomous, and that genetic influences determine one's membership in a latent class or taxon. There is evidence (Lenzenweger & Korfine, 1992; Korfine & Lenzenweger, 1995) that schizotypy, as assessed by the Perceptual Aberration Scale (PAS) (Chapman, Chapman, & Raulin, 1978), is taxonic at the latent level with a low general population taxon base rate.

Paranoid Personality Disorder

The concept of paranoia goes back to earliest medical literature. It was Kraepelin who narrowed the concept of paranoia to highly systematized and contained delusions in those who otherwise showed no signs of personality deterioration (Millon, 1981). Kraepelin described three different clinical courses of those who manifested paranoia: deterioration to dementia praecox, a mixture of paranoia and dementia praecox, and persistence of paranoia without further deterioration. It was concerning those in the last of these groups that Kraepelin described the premorbid characteristics of the paranoid patient. Whereas Freud conceptualized paranoia as a defense, it was Ferenczi and Abraham who posited the formation of the paranoid character type in the anal period of development.

The individual with paranoid personality disorder in DSM-IV is characterized by a pervasive distrust of others, which may include suspecting that one is being exploited or harmed by others, doubting the loyalty of friends, feeling reluctant to confide in others because of a fear that the information will be used against oneself, reading insults into benign remarks, and taking an unforgiving attitude toward others.

The coefficient alpha for this criterion set is one of the best, but the disorder has poor discrimination from schizotypal, avoidant, and narcissistic personality disorders (Morey, 1988). Factor analysis (Livesley & Schroeder, 1990) indicates that one factor represents the core feature of this diagnosis involving resentfulness toward authority, vindictiveness, externalization, suspiciousness, anger at conditional positive regard, blame/avoidance, a rigid cognitive style, and hypervigilance. A second factor, called *fear of negative appraisal,* does not seem specific to paranoid personality disorder. Some studies suggest a relationship between paranoid personality disorder and schizophrenia. Increased prevalence of paranoid personality disorder has been detected in the biological relatives of schizophrenic adoptees when compared to the biological relatives of control adoptees (Kendler & Gruenberg, 1982). However, the relationship of paranoid personality disorder may be stronger with delusional disorder. For example, Kendler and colleagues (Kendler, Masterson, & Davis, 1985) found a greater prevalence of paranoid personality disorder in the first-degree relatives of patients with delusional disorder than in the first-degree relatives of schizophrenics and controls. In one study (Siever & Kendler, 1988), the risk for paranoid personality disorder or traits was significantly greater in the relatives of those with paranoid psychosis than in relatives of controls or schizophrenics. Thus, the specific familial link may be between paranoid personality disorder and paranoid psychosis.

Cluster B Personality Disorders

This cluster includes the antisocial, borderline, histrionic, and narcissistic personality disorders. These disorders are grouped together because the criteria identify individuals who are dramatic, emotional, and/or erratic in their behavior.

Antisocial Personality Disorder

One can find a clinical literature going back at least to Pinel, Rush, and Prichard, all of whom recognized that some patients without deficits in reasoning are capable of impulsive acts that are socially repugnant, reprehensible, and self-damaging. The German psychiatrist Koch used the term *psychopathic inferiority* to indicate a hypothesized organic cause for antisocial behavior. Kraepelin distinguished a number of psychopaths deficient in affect and/or volition; liars and swindlers, as well as antisocial and quarrelsome persons, are similar to the current conception of the antisocial personality disorder (Millon, 1981).

Cleckley (1941) described the psychopath as an individual without guilt, with egocentricity and superficial charm, but lacking in remorse or shame, the capacity for love, insight, and the ability to learn from past experience. The DSM criteria, based heavily on the research of Robins (1986), are narrower than this definition and would miss many of those with the classic Cleckley behaviors who avoid contact with the legal system (Millon, 1981).

A longstanding pattern of irresponsible behavior that violates the rights of others is most characteristic of antisocial personality disorder as described in DSM-IV. Before the age of 15, there is evidence of behaviors under the diagnosis of conduct disorder. Since age 15, the individual has shown evidence of the following: performing acts that are grounds for arrest; repeatedly lying to or conning others; acting impulsively and failing to plan; and demonstrating irritability and aggressiveness, disregard for the safety of self or others, lack of consistent work behavior, and lack of remorse for own actions.

The internal consistency and discriminative ability of this criterion set is among the strongest (Morey, 1988). There is some difficulty in discriminating this disorder from narcissistic and passive-aggressive personality disorders. There are two factors associated with antisocial personality disorder, interpersonal disesteem and conduct problems (Livesley & Schroeder, 1991). Interpersonal disesteem involves exploitative behaviors that show a lack of concern for others and an absence of guilt about the effects of these actions on others, a group of behaviors that seems quite similar to Cleckley's concept. The second factor, conduct problems, relates to actual behaviors that get individuals into difficulty with the law.

Hare (1983, 1985) has shown that both the DSM criteria and the Cleckley criteria can be reliably assessed in male prison populations. Increased slow-wave activity in antisocial patients may reflect low levels of cortical arousal or a tendency to boredom. Lowered sedation threshold and reduced anticipatory responses to aversive stimuli are also found in psy-

chopaths, suggesting lowered cortical arousal and a reduced sensitivity to environmental stimulation (Hare & Cox, 1978).

Histrionic Personality Disorder

Histrionic personality disorder has its beginnings in the writings by early psychoanalysts on the concept of hysteria. Descriptive psychiatrists such as Kraepelin, Bleuler, Kretschmer, and Schneider identified a type of patient who was prone to overexcitability, impulsivity, flightiness, exaggerated emotional reactions, and volatile emotional outbursts (Millon, 1981). Freud's early formulations for the etiology of hysterical reactions emphasized conflicts generated in later stages of psychosexual development. Reich (1933/1972) made notable contributions to the description of male and female hysterics.

Early clinical literature, especially that of a psychoanalytic perspective, described patients with histrionic characteristics—dependent, infantile, seductive, emotionally labile. The difficulties encountered by early psychotherapists in the treatment of hysterical character led to a reformulation of hysteria as having its routes in a more infantile character structure that is based on oral issues (Kernberg, 1975). Probably one of the most relevant clinical notions in this perspective is the distinction between more mature patients with seductive exhibitionistic behavior, and a more regressed group with impulsive, helpless, and infantile characteristics (Kernberg, 1975; Zetzel, 1968). Current psychoanalytic writers divide the disorder into its less severe form, hysterical personality disorder, and its more severe form, histrionic personality disorder, which is represented in DSM (Gabbard, 1990).

Excessive and pervasive emotional reactivity and attention-seeking behavior are characteristic of the individual with histrionic personality disorder as described in DSM-IV. These generalized orientations are manifested by behaviors such as constant seeking of attention, reassurance, and praise from others; sexual seductiveness; rapidly shifting, shallow, and exaggerated expression of emotion; tendency to be easily influenced by others or the environment; perception that relationships with others are more intimate than the other party would explain; and use of verbal behavior that is impressionistic and lacking in detail.

The internal consistency of this data set is fairly high, but the difficulty is in adequate discrimination from narcissistic and borderline personality disorder (Morey, 1988). There seem to be four factors involved in histrionic personality disorder (Livesley & Schroeder, 1991). Two of these factors, interpersonal exploitation and dependency, overlap with other Axis II personality disorders, namely, borderline and dependent personality disorders. Two other factors, however, appear specific to hysterical personality disorder. These are hysterical affective style (affective overreactivity and lability) and hysterical interpersonal style. In clinical samples, there is overlap between histrionic personality disorder with borderline, and narcissistic personality disorder (Kass et al., 1985).

Narcissistic Personality Disorder

As with histrionic personality disorder, the definition of narcissistic personality disorder does not originate from empirical work but from psychoanalytic writings such as those by Kohut (1984) and Kernberg (1975). Freud considered narcissism an aspect of normal development that occurs when the infant experiences his or her own body as a source of fulfillment, early in the phases of psychosexual development. Freud did not formulate a narcissistic character type, however; that distinction is claimed by Reich (1933/1972) in his writings on the "phallic-narcissistic" character. As noted by Millon (1981), both Freud's and Reich's conceptualizations emphasized the arrogance, self-confidence, leadership, and overt self-interest demonstrated by the narcissistic individual. The more pathological aspects of narcissism were highlighted and developed in later psychoanalytic writings, receiving heightened attention in the last 20 years from Kernberg and Kohut. Kernberg (1974, 1984) hypothesized that narcissistic personality disorder includes a borderline level of personality organization (identity diffusion, primitive defensive operations, tenuous social reality testing). Kernberg also viewed excessive constitutional aggression as a key contributing factor to the development of pathological narcissism; whereas Kernberg posits that the instigation to aggression may lie in the environment (for instance, in the form of rejecting or ambivalent parental figures), the narcissistic individual's primitive defenses and arrogant

misuse of others belie both intense rage toward and envy of others. Kohut (1977, 1984) viewed narcissism as developing from parental shortcomings in the form of empathic failures; he asserted that all individuals need certain responses from others that gratify the self. Narcissistic needs become pathological when parents fail to respond appropriately to a child's needs for validation and admiration or when they fail to give the child themselves as objects of idealization. The child responds by feeling empty and depressed, and seeks an idealized other toward whom the child is self-deprecating and subordinate. The child also seeks to gain the admiration of others by striving to achieve or succeed incessantly. The differences between Kernberg's and Kohut's formulations are striking, and the reader will note that it is Kernberg's formulation that bears the closest resemblance to DSM-III-R criteria.

This clinical entity is characterized in DSM-IV by a pervasive pattern of grandiosity, a need for admiration from others with a lack of empathy for the experience of others. More specifically, these individuals exaggerate their achievements and talents and are preoccupied with fantasies of their own success and brilliance or beauty. They require excessive admiration from others and expect especially favorable treatment from others. They take advantage of others to achieve their own ends and lack empathy for the feelings and needs of others.

In the factor-analytic work of Livesley and Schroeder (1991), three factors were found that relate to narcissistic personality disorder: narcissistic entitlement, exhibitionism, and low self-confidence. However, none of these factors seems specific to narcissistic personality disorder; rather, they overlap substantially with other cluster B diagnoses. This would suggest that narcissism is not a distinct entity but, rather, a dimension that is common to the cluster B disorders.

Borderline Personality Disorder

Historically, there has been recognition of subtypes of borderlines (Grinker, Werble, & Drye, 1968). Prior to DSM-III, there was a conception of a cluster of symptoms not captured clearly in either the schizophrenia category or in the severe neurotic categories. Two major conditions, borderline schizophrenia and borderline personality, were culled from the literature, and a subsequent survey led to the criteria for Axis II schizotypal personality disorder and borderline personality disorder (Spitzer et al., 1979).

The DSM-IV criteria for borderline personality disorder emphasize unstable interpersonal relationships, a shifting self-image, affective instability, and impulsivity. The specific criteria suggest an unstable self-image or sense of oneself; interpersonal behavior characterized by efforts to avoid real or imagined abandonment from others; unstable and intense relationships with others, affective experience marked by intense shifting moods of dysphoria, irritability, or anxiety; chronic feelings of emptiness, and intense anger. These patients may be impulsive in ways that are self-damaging, including excessive spending, promiscuous sexuality, substance abuse, and binge eating. They may experience dissociative symptoms or stress-related paranoid distrust.

This criterion set is among the most internally consistent of the Axis II disorders, but there is difficulty discriminating borderline from histrionic and narcissistic personality disorder (Morey, 1988). In fact, BPD has substantial overlap with histrionic, antisocial, schizotypal, narcissistic, and dependent personality disorders (Widiger & Frances, 1989). This overlap is consistent with the borderline personality organization concept of Kernberg (1984), and suggests once again that the Axis II disorders are not discrete phenomena (Widiger, Frances, Harris, Jacobsberg, Fyer, & Manning, 1991).

The borderline pathology includes three factors (Livesley & Schroeder, 1991): borderline pathology, interpersonal exploitation, and self-harm. The factor of borderline pathology includes diffuse self-concept, unstable moods and interpersonal relations, interpersonal attachment problems, and a tendency to decompensate under stress. In contrast to this factor, which seems distinctive to borderlines, the other two factors are shared by the other diagnoses.

Cluster C Personality Disorders

This cluster includes the avoidant, dependent, obsessive-compulsive, and passive-aggressive personality disorders, grouped together with the hypothesis that fear underlies the behaviors that characterize each of them. Except for obsessive-compulsive personality disorder, cluster C is regarded by many as the weakest of the three clusters in terms of theoretical and empirical support.

Avoidant Personality Disorder

Kretschmer referred to three distinct groups of behaviors in describing the schizoid and considered the first group—unsociable, quiet, shy, reserved, eccentric—as characteristic of all schizoids. The second group of descriptors included timid, sensitive, shy with feelings, nervous, and fond of books and nature; the third group, by contrast, was described as pliable, dull-witted, indifferent, honest, and kindly. Kretschmer hypothesized that unstable schizoids vacillated between the behaviors characteristic of groups 2 and 3. Millon (1981) divided Kretschmer's unified concept into two distinct personality disorders: Group 2 became the avoidant and group 3 the schizoid. Avoidant personality disorder characterizes the person who is overly sensitive and is easily prone to embarrassment and interpersonal humiliation but who desires closeness with others; schizoid personality disorder typifies the individual who is content with his or her solitude and indifferent about closeness with others.

Gunderson (1983) and Livesley et al. (Livesley, West, & Tanney, 1985) criticized Millon's formulation with two major objections. First, Millon's conceptualization of *schizoid* was viewed as impoverished and weakened, robbing the term of its rich development in psychoanalytic theory. Second, Millon's hypothetical avoidant personality disorder had no empirical or theoretical basis on which to stand. Livesley et al. further argued that Millon's measure of personality disorders, the MCMI, demonstrated a high intercorrelation between items on the avoidant scale and the schizoid–asocial scales, indicating that the two scales actually were measuring the more unified concept developed by Kretschmer.

Patients with DSM-IV avoidant personality disorder are characterized by social inhibition, feelings of inadequacy, and a hypersensitivity to what is perceived as negative evaluation by others. This overall orientation may include avoidance of significant interpersonal contact, fear of intimate relationships, preoccupation with the possibility of being criticized or rejected by others, excessive inhibition in new interpersonal situations, fear of risk taking, and view of self as socially inept and fearing.

This criterion set is among the least internally consistent in Axis II. In addition, there is a major problem with discriminability, as almost the entire criterion set is positively correlated with schizotypal, paranoid, dependent, and passive-aggressive personality disorders (Morey, 1988).

Interestingly, more empirical support appears to have been garnered for avoidant personality disorder than for schizoid personality disorder. Schizoid personality disorder appears to be rarely diagnosed, whereas avoidant personality disorder has more practical utility and is diagnosed more frequently by clinicians and by researchers. In a study of inpatients, Trull, Widiger, and Frances (1987) found significant and positive correlations between items for avoidant personality disorder and dependent personality disorder, but no significant correlations between avoidant personality disorder and schizoid personality disorder. Further, they noted that schizoid personality disorder is so rarely diagnosed as to be almost clinically useless. Results from other studies have supported their conclusions (Kass et al., 1985; Pfohl, Coryell, Zimmerman, & Stangl, 1986).

There is a sizable comorbidity of anxiety disorders on Axis I and avoidant personality disorder (Turner & Beidel, 1989). There seem to be important differences, however, between avoidant personality disorder and social phobia. Individuals with avoidant personality disorder appear to be more severely and pervasively disturbed than those with social phobia (Marks, 1985; Turner, Beidel, Dancu, & Keys, 1986). Most important for treatment planning, avoidant personality disorder patients have poorer social skills, and those with social phobia are more skilled interpersonally.

Dependent Personality Disorder

Kraepelin's (1913) "shiftless" individual and Schneider's (1923) "weak-willed" type are early forerunners of the dependent personality diagnosis inasmuch as they describe a person of pliable character who is easily led by the will of others (Millon, 1981). Later psychoanalytic theorists such as Abraham (1921) and Horney (1945), described "oral-sucking" and "compliant" character types, respectively. Their descriptions emphasized the interpersonal behaviors that these individuals employed in their attempts to derive care and sustenance while engaging in a helpless, infantile stance with others.

Millon (1981) describes the dependent personality style as the "submissive pattern" and appears to base his formulation on earlier concepts of the oral character. He hypothesizes that dependent persons may be constitutionally gentle but anxious; he speculates that their neural organization causes them to be overly sensitive to painful emotional arousal without endowing them with the capacity to react adequately to protect themselves.

Gabbard (1990), in contrast, eschews the oral character as an adequate explanation for dependent personality disorder, and views these persons as having been reinforced throughout their childhood and adolescence for dependent behaviors, reinforcement that is not limited to the oral stage of development. Further, he speculates that individuals who exhibit traits of dependent personality disorder may be using defensive operations to mask or suppress anger; they also may be avoiding the reenactment of a painful and traumatic loss suffered earlier in life.

Patients with this DSM-IV disorder are characterized by a pervasive and excessive need to be taken care of, leading to both submissive and clinging behavior and a fear of separation from others. Thus, these patients have difficulty making decisions without advice and reassurance, look to others to take responsibility for major areas of their lives, cannot express disagreement with others, and go to excessive lengths to obtain nurturance and support from others. They may feel uncomfortable when alone because of their fears of being self-sufficient and thus may seek relationships quickly.

There is little empirical support for the dependent personality disorder diagnosis. Trull et al. (1987) noted the overlap between the avoidant and dependent personality disorders in a study of 84 inpatients. The two diagnoses are very similar save for the criterion of social withdrawal in avoidant personality disorder and, most important, it is possible to receive a diagnosis of avoidant personality disorder without meeting that criterion (Gabbard, 1990). It is a diagnosis that is closely related to sexual stereotypes in the culture, given that dependent behavior in women is more tolerated than similar behavior in men (Gunderson, 1988).

Obsessive-Compulsive Personality Disorder

Of the disorders in the C cluster, obsessive-compulsive personality disorder is the one with the greatest empirical support and strongest theoretical background. Psychoanalytic forerunners of obsessive-compulsive disorder can be found in the writings of Freud, Abraham, Jones, and Menninger on anal character (Gabbard, 1990). Psychoanalytic theorists posited that the individual exhibiting perfectionism, emotional constriction, rigid adherence to rules, and a reliance on logic to the exclusion of affect was likely suffering from a punitive superego, which leads to defense against aggressive drives. Later psychoanalytic writers emphasized that the interpersonal style of these individuals—devotion to work, cognitive set, and struggle to contain their emotions—likely reflects self-doubt and a reaction to a childhood in which they were unsure of the love of their parents. Although they long to possess that love, they defend against these wants—and their accompanying disappointment—by being overly self-reliant and counter-dependent. Their striving for perfection is seen as an attempt to finally earn the love they did not receive, and their overcommitment to work reflects conflict about intimacy. Intimate relationships carry a particular danger in that they demand the spontaneous expression of feeling, which the obsessive-compulsive personality type has worked so long to contain.

The DSM-IV criteria for obsessive-compulsive personality disorder focus on a preoccupation with orderliness, perfectionism, and control. This orientation may entail preoccupation with details, order and organization, perfectionism that interferes with completing projects, a devotion to work that excludes pleasurable activities and friendships, a scrupulous orientation to morality and ethics, a reluctance to delegate tasks to others, and a miserly attitude toward money.

This data set shows the lowest internal consistency across Axis II, but relatively good discrimination. A major problem is discriminating it from avoidant personality disorder (Morey, 1988). There is empirical support for obsessive-compulsive personality disorder as distinct from obsessive-compulsive disorder. Rasmussen and Tsuang (1986) demonstrated that fewer than half of the patients with obsessive-compulsive disorder met criteria for the diagnosis of obsessive-compulsive personality disorder. Interestingly, individuals who obtain the former diagnosis are most likely to receive a diagnosis of personality disorder NOS (not otherwise specified) with characteristics from the other cluster C disorders. Unlike obsessive-compulsive disorder, which describes discrete symptoms, obsessive-compulsive personality disorder refers to enduring character traits that pervade individuals' social and professional lives. Whereas the symptoms of obsessive-compulsive disorder are ego-dystonic, the traits of obsessive-compulsive personality disorder are ego-syntonic and often help an individual toward professional success (Gabbard, 1990).

EPIDEMIOLOGY

Using a two-stage procedure (self-report screen followed by a semistructured interview), the point-prevalence estimate for diagnosable personality disorder in a nonclinical population was 11.01% (Lenzenweger, Loranger, Korfine, & Neff, 1997).

Cluster A

From 0.5% to 2.5% of the population meet criteria for paranoid personality disorder (Maier et al., 1992; Samuels et al., 1994; Zimmerman & Coryell, 1989), and more men than women met the criteria for the disorder (Corbitt & Widiger, 1995). The prevalence of schizoid personality disorder is less than 1% in the general population (Zimmerman & Coryell, 1989).

Schizotypal personality disorder may be as prevalent as 3% in the general population (Zimmerman & Coryell, 1989), but studies using semistructured interviews estimate a lower percentage (Maier et al., 1992; Samuels et al., 1994). Schizotypal personality disorder is slightly more prevalent among men (Corbitt & Widiger, 1995; Millon, 1990; Zimmerman & Coryell, 1989). Studies have found evidence for schizotypal personality disorder in relatives of schizophrenic patients (Gunderson, 1983; Kendler, Gruenberg, & Strauss, 1981). The criteria for schizotypal personality disorder (DSM-III) had a prevalence rate of 73% in a sample of relatives of schizophrenics from three different samples (Reider et al., 1975).

There was increased prevalence of schizotypal symptoms in the relatives of schizophrenics as compared to controls in a large U.S. study (Kendler, Gruenberg, & Tsuang, 1983).

Cluster B

Antisocial behavior/personality disorder is probably the only Axis II disorder for which there are data from a number of epidemiologic studies (Merikangas & Weissman, 1986). Rates per 100 vary from 0.2 to 9.4. In the ECA study (Robins et al., 1984), the lifetime prevalence rates for DSM-III antisocial personality disorder ranged from 2.1 to 3.3. The ECA study suggests that 3% of men and 1% of women have antisocial personality disorder (Robins, Tipp, & Przybeck, 1991). Rutter and Giller (1983) have reviewed epidemiological studies of juvenile delinquent behavior and abnormal personality functioning. Multiple causes are seen as active in antisocial behavior/character, including peer group pressure, social control, social learning, biological factors, and situational factors. Given the nature of the criteria of antisocial personality disorder, it is no surprise that the rate of antisocial personality disorder is 50% in prisons (Hare, Hart, & Harpur, 1991; Robins et al., 1991).

Approximately 2% of the general population would meet criteria for borderline personality disorder (Maier et al., 1992; Samuels et al., 1994; Weissman, 1993; Zimmerman & Coryell, 1989). This disorder is the most prevalent of all the personality disorders in the clinical setting, reaching 15% of inpatients and 8% of outpatients (Widiger & Trull, 1993). About 75% of diagnosed BPD patients are female.

From 1% to 3% of the community may meet criteria for histrionic personality disorder (Maier et al., 1992; Nestadt et al., 1990; Zimmerman & Coryell, 1989). At least two-thirds of those meeting the criteria are women. It is striking that in three community studies, covering some 2,000 subjects, not one individual met criteria for narcissistic personality disorder (Maier et al., 1992; Samuels et al., 1994; Zimmerman & Coryell, 1989). In clinical settings, the disorder is diagnosed, but with a low frequency compared to the other personality disorders (Gunderson, Ronningstam, & Smith, 1991).

Cluster C

Avoidant personality disorder is found in only 1% of the general population (Maier et al., 1992; Samuels et al., 1994; Zimmerman & Coryell, 1989) but is one of the most prevalent personality disorders in clinical settings, ranging from 5% to 25% of the patients (Weissman, 1993). From 2% to 4% of the general population may meet criteria for dependent personality disorder (Maier et al., 1992; Samuels et al., 1994; Zimmerman & Coryell, 1989), and this is one of the most prevalent personality disorders in the clinical setting, affecting from 5% to 30% of patients (Hirschfeld, Shea, & Weise, 1991). More females than males are identified with this condition (Corbitt & Widiger, 1995). About 2% of the community met criteria for obsessive-compulsive personality disorder (Maier et al., 1992; Samuels et al., 1994; Zimmerman & Coryell, 1989), and it occurs more often in men than in women (Corbitt & Widiger, 1995).

ETIOLOGY

There are a number of leading theories concerning the etiology and course of personality disorders (see Clarkin & Lenzenweger, 1996) that approach the disorders from different points of view and with varying degrees of theoretical and empirical adequacy. Certainly, the combination of genetic, biological, and environmental factors may contribute to abnormal traits/behaviors related to the personality disorders.

As for the genetic evidence, there is a clear genetic association between schizotypal personality disorder and schizophrenia (McGuffin & Thapar, 1992; Nigg & Goldsmith, 1994; Siever, 1992). This is not surprising, however, given that the diagnostic criteria for schizotypal personality disorder were based on observations of biological relatives of individuals with schizophrenia. There is some evidence to suggest that paranoid personality disorder is related to schizophrenia genetically (Fulton & Winokur, 1993). This result may be due to the overlap between paranoid personality disorder and schizotypal personality disorder. Data from twin family and adoption studies support the hypothesis for a genetic contribution to the etiology of criminal and delinquent behavior that is captured in antisocial personality disorder (Gottesman & Goldsmith, in press; Nigg & Goldsmith, 1994).

A number of studies have examined the incidence of pathology in the first-degree relatives of borderline patients. When probands of borderline patients are compared to probands of schizophrenic patients (Skinner, 1986), borderline patients had significantly higher rates of depression, alcoholism, and antisocial personality disorder. This and other family studies suggest that BPD is related to the affective spectrum and not to the schizophrenic spectrum. The relationship of BPD with concurrent schizotypal personality disorder with the schizophrenic spectrum may exist in a subgroup of patients.

Second, one must consider the evidence for biological and neurotransmitter causality. Low levels of behavioral inhibition may be related to the serotonin system in those with antisocial behaviors (Cloninger, 1987; Cloninger, Svrakic, & Przybeck, 1993; Fowles, 1994). In addition, there is evidence indicating that the electrodermal response in psychopathic individuals is inadequate, especially in anticipation of physically adverse events (Fowles & Missel, 1994). Biologic abnormalities in patients with personality disorders have been associated with dimensional traits of impulsivity, affective instability, anxiety, and cognitive disorganization (Siever & Davis, 1991). For example, abnormalities in dopaminergic function and information processing may be involved in schizotypal personality disorder, and sleep architecture and serotonergic abnormalities implicated in borderline personality disorder. There is speculation as to the role of excessive autonomic arousal, fearfulness, and inhibition (Cloninger, Svrakic, & Przybeck, 1993; Siever & Davis, 1991) in the development of avoidant personality disorder. The potential neurotransmitter systems involved in personality traits are almost countless, so the field needs a theoretical paradigm to guide research. Depue (1996) has formulated such a paradigm around three areas: positive emotion, negative emotion, and constraint.

Finally, environmental variables contribute to the development of personality disorders. Loeber (1990) has articulated a model of the development of antisocial behavior. Also, Patterson (1982) has examined the nature of family interaction in children with conduct disorder. There has been much focus on the role of childhood physical and/or sexual abuse in the development of borderline personality disorder. However, because there are cases of individuals with a history of abuse who are not borderline and of persons who are borderline without such history of abuse, this does not seem to be a sine qua non.

It is primarily psychological theories that have been used to explain the etiology of narcissism. For example, Kohut suggests that parents have failed to mirror the infant's need for idealization. A history of denigrating and embarrassing experiences may likewise play a role. It seems natural to think of the individual's history of insecure attachment to others in the generation of dependent personality disorder (Brown, 1986; Livesley, Schroeder, & Jackson, 1990). This history of insecure attachment may interact with an anxious temperament.

COURSE AND COMPLICATIONS

A central issue for the course of the personality disorders is the stability across time of the criteria and categorical disorder assignment. In fact, as mentioned earlier, an essential defining assumption is that the personality disorders are composed of stable and enduring traits. Because stability of PD diagnoses have only been investigated in BPD and the results are ambiguous, it may be important to emphasize the presence or absence of a personality disorder in future research, rather than focusing primarily on specific personality disorder diagnoses (McDavid & Pilkonis, 1996).

Aside from the stability (or lack thereof) of the criteria and personality disorder diagnostic category membership, others have followed patients with specific personality disorders in their course across time. Because research on psychopathic and antisocial behavior long predates the creation of DSM-III and III-R, there are longitudinal data relevant to this condition. A recent summary and examination of these data (Loeber, 1990) suggests that there are multiple subgroups of antisocial individuals, with multiple developmental pathways to the behavioral clusters. Such a longitudinal approach is most useful in specifying the interaction of genetic dispositions and environmental pressures, and will be most important in tailoring intervention strategies. The longitudinal data in this area make the lack of information on all of the other Axis II disorders painfully clear. There have been four longitudinal studies of outcome in DSM borderlines (Paris, 1988). In all four studies, the patients have clearly improved up to the range of neurotic adjustment. Rehospitalization was uncommon, and on follow-up most had jobs. Rate of suicide varied from 3% to 9.5%, with the mean age of suicide at 27 years. Stone, Hurt, and Stone (1987) followed 188 BPD patients over a 20-year period. There is a high (9%) suicide rate, but those patients who survive do improve. In a review, Stone (1993) points out that the major foci of outcome studies are on borderline, antisocial, and schizotypal disorders. Borderlines have a wide range of outcome, from recovery to suicide; schizoid and schizotypal patients tend to remain isolated. The outcome for those with antisocial personality disorder is bleak if the psychopathic traits are prominent.

TREATMENT IMPLICATIONS

The personality disorders present clinically important and complicated implications for treatment planning. We are referring here to both the treatment of symptom disorders (e.g., Axis I disorders) in the presence of Axis II disorder(s), and treatment of the personality disorder(s) themselves.

Management Issues

The comorbidity of personality disorders and symptom conditions such as anxiety, affective disorders, substance abuse, and eating disorders is extensive. Of course, the complicated (and relatively unexplored) relationship between Axis I and Axis II disorders is intimately related to how one approaches the treatment of Axis I disorders in the presence of Axis II disorders. One might be able to treat the Axis I disorders, while managing the Axis II order, or, if the two are more causally linked, one might be able to treat the Axis I disorder and have some felicitous effect on the Axis II conditions (Bronisch & Klerman, 1991). Alternatively, though not a direct focus of intervention or outcome, the personality disorders may be patient variables that either foster or interfere with a treatment alliance (Shea, Widiger, & Klein, 1992).

Management in the Context of Mood and Anxiety Disorders
Depressed patients, on both inpatient (Brophy, 1994) and outpatient services (Sato et al., 1994), with a per-

sonality disorder improve more slowly with medication treatment. This is not always the case, however, as one study (Peselow, Sanfilipo, Fieve, & Gulbenkian, 1994) suggested that for those patients who responded to desipramine, Axis II cluster I and III personality traits were significantly reduced. The authors concluded that the cluster I and III traits are interwoven with depressive features and, therefore, are subject to change, whereas cluster II traits are more enduring and characteristic modes of thinking and behaving.

A large sample of outpatients with a diagnosis of major depression was randomly assigned to one of four treatment modalities in the NIMH Treatment of Depression Collaborative Research Program (Elkin et al., 1989). Treatments included cognitive-behavioral therapy, interpersonal therapy, imipramine in the context of clinical management, and placebo in the context of clinical management. Those patients who had personality disorders (74% of the total) had a significantly worse outcome in social functioning and were significantly more likely to have residual symptoms of depression when compared to those without personality disorders (Shea et al., 1990).

Several suggestions have been made that personality disorder comorbidity renders the Axis I anxiety disorder less amenable to treatment. For example, AuBuchon and Malatesta (1994) found that OCD patients with personality disorders responded less satisfactorily to comprehensive behavior therapy than did OCD patients without personality disorders; the OCD patients with personality disorders also had more hospitalizations and premature terminations of treatment. In addition, OCD patients with comorbid cluster A personality disorders have been reported to be less responsive than OCD patients without personality disorder in clomipramine treatment (Baer, 1994; Baer et al., 1992).

Unexplored Treatment Issues
The conceptualization of the Axis II personality disorders in terms of more generalized personality traits (Widiger et al., 1994), rather than in the mixture of behaviors, attitudes, and traits of Axis II, is helpful in treatment planning. For example, in treating an Axis I disorder in an individual with paranoid personality disorder, it is especially the trait of hostility that the therapist will encounter and must manage in order to

move the treatment forward. Likewise, clinicians treating individuals with Axis I disorder and comorbid narcissistic personality disorder will be faced with the necessity of dealing with traits of hostility, vulnerability, and extreme assertiveness.

Treatment of Personality Disorders

There is some beginning definition and description in treatment manuals of interventions targeting the personality disorders per se (Beck, Freeman, & Associates, 1990; Benjamin, 1993; Clarkin, Yeomans, & Kernberg, 1998; Linehan, 1993). Treatment begins with a conceptualization of the difficulties the patient is experiencing, and that idea translates into a therapeutic focus shared by therapist and patient. One neither encounters nor treats personality disorder criteria directly. Rather, treatment development for the personality disorders depends on a theory about the interactive nature of the aspects of the disorders, and how these disorders are manifested in daily life.

Traits and Developing a Treatment Alliance

Certain personality traits may be crucial for directing the treatment alliance by choosing the right methods to approach the patient (Beutler & Clarkin, 1990; Sanderson & Clarkin, 1994). We have argued that patient problem complexity relates to the breadth of treatment goals; that patients' coping style relates to the depth of the therapy experience; and that patients' reactance level relates to degree of therapists' directiveness. Any trait instrument that adequately measures patients' coping styles and degree of reactance will be useful to the clinician.

Case Description

(All identifying information has been changed; the case presented is a composite of actual clients the authors have seen in treatment.)

Allison was 27 years old when she first entered the day treatment program. Prior to admission, she had had 12 psychiatric hospitalizations; two of these followed brief stays in intensive care medical units following emergency treatment for near lethal overdoses. She met six criteria for borderline personality disorder and paranoid personality disorder, with traits of narcissistic and antisocial personality disorder. Additionally, she reported symptoms of major depression, recurrent, moderate, alcohol and marijuana abuse,

and some symptoms of posttraumatic stress disorder. Her medical history was significant for carpal tunnel syndrome and mitral valve prolapse. Stressors included unemployment, no close friends in the area, substandard housing, and the recent loss of one of her sisters to AIDS. Her Global Assessment of Functioning (GAF) was 31.

Allison reported that she had been struggling "as long as she could remember." She had started injuring herself by banging her head at age 6. She noted that she did this whenever her parents would get into a "knock down" fight after her father had been drinking. Allison remembered that she, with her two brothers and two sisters, would hide in the basement during the "rampages." Sometimes the father would punch the mother, then search for the children and beat them with his favorite belt. Allison recalled that this only happened when he was intoxicated. After these episodes, her father would become quiet and remorseful and would buy Allison and her sibs gifts. She reported being confused about "which man was my real dad." When Allison was 8, she went to school with bruises on her legs; her math teacher became alarmed and called child protective services. Allison became terrified that she would be blamed and that one of two awful things could happen: Her family could be broken up, or her father would get enraged and beat her again. When the family was investigated, Allison, her siblings, and her parents denied any abuse in the home. Her father was less violent after this event, and his temper outbursts subsided altogether as he entered old age.

When she entered junior high school, Allison met a group of teenagers who were a "little wild"; they invited Allison to join them in smoking marijuana and drinking. She experimented with many illicit drugs but used only alcohol and "pot" with any frequency. Schoolwork came easily to her because she was talented in math and science. Also, many of her teachers were nice to her and provided a haven from the chaos at home. At age 16, Allison fell madly in love with Dan, a senior at the school who was "sort of troubled." By this, Allison meant that Dan was intelligent and an excellent graphic artist, but also depressed and, at times, suicidal. They became intensely involved, and they sometimes skipped school in order to go into a nearby city, hang out, "fool around," and have sex. Allison recalled that Dan treated her better than anyone else she had met and that she was devastated when he was killed in a drunk driving accident a year after they had met. In her opinion, her life quickly went "over the cliff" when Dan died. Her grades dropped, she became severely depressed, and she began thinking of killing herself.

When she stopped going to school for a week and refused to get out of bed, Allison's parents took her to a psychiatrist, who worried that she would kill herself and had her hospitalized for the first time. In the hospital, Allison *was treated with standard antidepressants and sent home, slightly improved. However, she now felt humiliated by having been hospitalized and saw herself as a "real mental case." Her parents were angry with her for having scared them, and her friends at school drifted away. She felt lonely and frightened, as she had most of her life. One night, in the midst of shaving her legs, she got the idea of using the razor to cut herself intentionally. She cut herself on her upper legs and felt immediate relief. She got out of the tub, got into bed, and went soundly to sleep.*

Allison had stumbled on a way to handle her emotional distress. Several days later, when she was upset about how former friends had shunned her at a party, she came home feeling ashamed, lonely, and angry. Her feelings were intolerable to her. She thought of the razor again; this time, she cut herself on her upper arms so that no one would notice. Cutting became a regular way of managing her pain.

Allison graduated from high school with a B average and went to a local community college. She had difficulty making friends and got in and out of relationships with men. Sometimes she would become intoxicated during dates, and on one occasion she was date raped. Allison reported this to her medical doctor but refused his advice to make a police report and also refused his suggestion that she go into therapy. By handling her emotional distress with substance abuse, she barely made it through college and she graduated with a degree in accounting.

Upon entering the job market, Allison discovered that employers were not as tolerant of her behavior as the college had been. From age 22 to 25, she held six different jobs as an accountant. Invariably she would be fired for tardiness, for taking too much sick leave, and for appearing intoxicated on the job. Outside of work, she coupled with a boyfriend who dealt drugs and who slapped her and verbally abused her on occasion. Allison stayed with him for 4 years, until he left her for one of her friends. During her mid-twenties, she was hospitalized several times for inadvertent overdoses of antidepressants and alcohol. By age 26, she could not get a job that paid enough to support her, most of her friends were alcoholics, and she was engaging in unsafe sex with men she met in bars. Each time she was hospitalized, she would be referred to an outpatient therapist, would attend sessions for a few months, and then would drop out. Her therapists often became exasperated: Allison was a talented and educated young woman who appeared capable of having a decent life but who returned, again and again, to self-destructive behaviors. By the time she appeared at our clinic, she was on disability, living in a rooming house, and frequently engaging in self-injurious behaviors. She felt hopeless about her situation, was

ashamed of being a "chronic patient," and she looked much older than 27.

This clinical case, disguised to protect the identity of the individual, illustrates a number of features of the severe personality disorders, as compared to less severe (i.e., more functional) cluster C personality disorders. There is comorbidity for a number of Axis II disorders, and the presence in the early childhood of identifiable disturbances in the family atmosphere and interactions. There is the early identifiable onset of difficulties in school and with peers, and poor choices of friends and intimate companions. An early approach for help in the mental health system was followed by a series of brief interventions. There are early signs of Axis I disorders, in this case substance abuse.

SUMMARY

The concept of personality disorder indicates a long-standing pattern of cognition, affectivity and interpersonal functioning that is inflexible and leads to significant distress. The specific traits that describe the variety of ways this personality dysfunction can be manifested are currently captured in the 10 personality disorders of DSM-IV. There remains controversy over the differentiation, construct validity, and stability of these 10 disorders as currently conceptualized (Livesley, 1995). There is evidence that the personality disorders are a significant clinical issue with a prevalence rate of approximately 11% in nonclinical populations, and a higher prevalence of certain disorders in clinical populations. Most of the existing information is cross-sectional, and longitudinal studies are needed to describe both the long-term stability of these disorders and the mechanism of their impact on psychosocial adjustment and symptom disorders. Treatment approaches have been articulated for the personality disorders themselves, but this effort is in its infancy. It has become clear that the treatment of Axis I conditions in the presence of personality disorders is slower and less beneficial than treatment for those without personality disorders.

REFERENCES

Abraham, K. (1921). Contributions to the theory of anal character. In *Selected papers of Karl Abraham, M.D.* (pp. 370–392). (D. Bryan & A. Strachey, Trans.) London: Hogarth.

American Psychiatric Association. (1980). *Diagnostic and statistical manual of mental disorders,* 3rd ed. Washington, DC: Author.

American Psychiatric Association. (1994). *Diagnostic and statistical manual of mental disorders,* 4th ed. Washington, DC: Author.

AuBuchon, P.G., & Malatesta, V.J. (1994). Obsessive-compulsive patients with comorbid personality disorder: Associated problems and response to a comprehensive behavior therapy. *Journal of Clinical Psychiatry, 55,* 448–453.

Baer, L. (1994). Factor analysis of symptom subtypes of obsessive-compulsive disorder and their relation to personality and tic disorders. *Journal of Clinical Psychiatry, 55*(Suppl.), 18–23.

Baer, L., Jenike, M.A., Black, D.W., et al. (1992). Effect of Axis II diagnoses on treatment outcome with clomipramine in 55 patients with obsessive-compulsive disorder. *Archives of General Psychiatry, 49,* 862–866.

Beck, A.T., Freeman, A., & Associates. (1990). *Cognitive therapy of personality disorders.* New York: Guilford Press.

Benjamin, L.S. (1993). *Interpersonal diagnosis and treatment of personality disorders.* New York: Guilford Press.

Beutler, L.E., & Clarkin, J.F. (1990). *Systematic treatment selection: Toward targeted therapeutic intervention.* New York: Brunner/Mazel.

Bleuler, E. (1922). Die Probleme der Schizoidie und der Syntonie. *Zeitschrift für die Gesamte Neurologie und Psychiatrie, 78,* 373–388.

Bleuler, E. (1929). Syntonie-Schizoidie-Schizophrenie. *Neurologie und Psychopathologie, 38,* 47–64.

Bronisch, T., & Klerman, G.L. (1991). Personality functioning: Change and stability in relationship to symptoms and psychopathology. *Journal of Personality Disorders, 5,* 307–317.

Brown, L.S. (1986). Gender-role analysis: A neglected component of psychological assessment. *Psychotherapy, 23,* 243–248.

Brophy, J.J. (1994). Personality disorder, symptoms and dexamethasone suppression in depression. *Journal of Affective Disorder, 31,* 19–27.

Chapman, L.J., Chapman, J.P., & Raulin, M.L. (1978). Body-image abberation in schizophrenia. *Journal of Abnormal Psychology, 87,* 399–407.

Clarkin, J.F., & Lenzenweger, M.F. (Eds.). (1996). *Major theories of personality disorder.* New York: Guilford Press.

Clarkin, J.F., Yeomans, F., & Kernberg, O.F. (1998). New York: Wiley.

Cleckley, H. (1941). *The mask of sanity.* St. Louis, MO: Mosby.

Cloninger, R.C. (1987). A systematic method for clinical description and classification of personality variants. *Archives of General Psychiatry, 44,* 573–588.

Cloninger, R.C., Svrakic, D.M., & Przybeck, T.R. (1993). A psychobiological model of temperament and character. *Archives of General Psychiatry, 50,* 975–990.

Corbitt, E.M., & Widiger, T.A. (1995). Sex differences among the personality disorders. An exploration of the data. *Clinical Psychology and Science Practice, 2,* 225–238.

Depue, R.A. (1996). A neurobiological framework for the structure of personality and emotion: Implications for personality disorders. In J.F. Clarkin & M.F. Lenzenweger (Eds.), *Major theories of personality disorder* (pp. 347–390). New York: Guilford Press.

Elkin, I., Shea, M.T., Watkins, J.T., et al. (1989). The National Institute of Mental Health Treatment of Depression Collaborative Research Program: General effectiveness of treatments. *Archives of General Psychiatry, 33,* 971–982.

Fairbairn, W.R.D. (1952). Schizoid factors in the personality. In W.R.D. Fairbairn (Ed.), *Psychoanalytic studies of the personality* (pp. 3–27). London: Tavistock. (Original work published 1940.)

Fowles, D.C. (1994). A motivational theory of psychopathology. *Nebraska Symposium on Motivation, 41,* 181–238.

Fowles, D.C., & Missel, K.A. (1994). Electrodermal hyporeactivity, motivation, and psychopathy: Theoretical issues. In D.C. Fowles, P.B. Sutker, & S.H. Goodman (Eds.), *Progress in experimental personality and psychopathology research,* (Vol. 15, pp. 263–283). New York: Springer.

Fulton, M., & Winokur, G. (1993). A comparative study of paranoid and schizoid personality disorders. *American Journal of Psychiatry, 150,* 1363–1367.

Gabbard, G.O. (1990). *Psychodynamic psychiatry in clinical practice.* Washington, DC: American Psychiatric Press.

Gottesman, I.I., & Goldsmith, H.H. (in press). Developmental psychopathology of antisocial behavior: Inserting genes into its ontogenesis and epigenesis. In C. Nelson (Ed.), *Threats of optimal development: Integrating biological, social and psychological risk factors* (Vol. 27). Hillsdale, NJ: Lawrence Erlbaum.

Grinker, R.R., Sr., Werble, B., & Drye, R.C. (1968). *The borderline syndrome: A behavioral study of ego-functions.* New York: Basic Books.

Gunderson, J.G. (1983). DSM-III diagnosis of personality disorders. In J.P. Frosch (Ed.), *Current perspectives in personality disorders* (pp. 20–39). Washington, DC: American Psychiatric Press.

Gunderson, J.G. (1988). Personality disorders. In A.M. Nicholi, Jr. (Ed.), *The new Harvard guide to psychiatry* (pp. 337–357). Cambridge, MA: Belknap Press of Harvard University Press.

Gunderson, J.G., Ronningstam, E., & Smith, L.E. (1991). Narcissistic personality disorder: A review of its current status. *Journal of Personality Disorders, 5,* 167–177.

Guntrip, H. (1969). *Schizoid phenomena, object-relations and the self.* New York: International Universities Press.

Hare, R.D. (1983). Diagnosis of antisocial personality disorder in two prison populations. *American Journal of Psychiatry, 140,* 887–890.

Hare, R.D. (1985). Comparison of procedures for the assessment of psychopathy. *Journal of Consulting and Clinical Psychology, 53,* 7–16.

Hare, R.D., & Cox, D. (1978). Psychophysiological research on psychopathy. In W. Reid (Ed.), *The psychopath: A comprehensive study of antisocial disorders and behaviors* (pp. 209–222). New York: Brunner/Mazel.

Hare, R.D., Hart, S.D., & Harpur, T.J. (1991). Psychopathy and the DSM-IV criteria for antisocial personality disorder. *Journal of Abnormal Psychology, 100,* 391–398.

Hirschfeld, R.M.A., Shea, M.T., & Weise, R. (1991). Dependent personality disorder: Perspectives for DSM-IV. *Journal of Personality Disorders, 5,* 135–149.

Horney, K. (1945). *Our inner conflicts.* New York: Norton.

Kass, F., Skodol, A.E., Charles, E., Spitzer, R.L., & Williams, J.B.W. (1985). Scaled ratings of DSM-III personality disorders. *American Journal of Psychiatry, 142,* 627–630.

Kendler, K.S., & Gruenberg, A. (1982). Genetic relationship between paranoid personality disorder and the "schizophrenic spectrum" disorders. *American Journal of Psychiatry, 139,* 1185–1186.

Kendler, K.S., Gruenberg, A.M., & Strauss, J. (1981). An independent analysis of the Copenhagen sample of the Danish adoption study of schizophrenia: II. The relationship between schizotypal personality disorder and schizophrenia. *Archives of General Psychiatry, 38,* 982–984.

Kendler, K.S., Gruenberg, A.M., & Tsuang, M.T. (1983). *The specificity of DSM-III schizotypal symptoms.* Abstract of the 136th Annual Meeting of the American Psychiatric Association.

Kendler, K.S., Masterson, C.C., & Davis, K.L. (1985). Psychiatric illness in patients with paranoid psychosis, schizophrenia, and medical illness. *British Journal of Psychiatry, 147,* 524–531.

Kernberg, O.F. (1974). Contrasting viewpoints regarding the nature and psychoanalytic treatment of narcissistic personalities: A preliminary communication. *Journal of the American Psychoanalytic Association, 22,* 255–267.

Kernberg, O.F. (1975). *Borderline conditions and pathological narcissism.* New York: Jason Aronson.

Kernberg, O.F. (1984). *Severe personality disorders: Psychotherapeutic strategies.* New Haven: Yale University Press.

Kety, S., Rosenthal, D., Wender, P., et al. (1975). Mental illness in the biological and adoptive families who have become schizophrenic: A preliminary report based on psychiatric interviews. In R. Fieve, D. Rosenthal, & H. Brill (Eds.), *Genetic re-*

search (pp. 147–165). Baltimore, MD: Johns Hopkins University Press.

Kohut, H. (1977). *The restoration of the self*. New York: International Universities Press.

Kohut, H. (1984). *How does analysis cure?* (A. Goldberg, Ed.). Chicago: University of Chicago Press.

Korfine, L., & Lenzenweger, M.F. (1995). The taxonicity of schizotypy: A replication. *Journal of Abnormal Psychology, 104,* 26–31.

Kraepelin, E. (1913). *Psychiatrie: Ein Lehrbuch,* 8th ed. Leipzig: Barth.

Kretschmer, E. (1925). *Korperbau und Charakter* (Physique and character). Berlin: Springer Verlag (London: Kegan Paul).

Lenzenweger, M.F., & Korfine, L. (1992). Confirming the latent structure and base rate of schizotypy: A taxometric analysis. *Journal of Abnormal Psychology, 101,* 567–571.

Lenzenweger, M.F., Loranger, A.W., Korfine, L, & Neff, C. (1997). Detecting personality disorders in a non-clinical population: Application of a two-stage procedure for case identification *Archives of General Psychiatry, 54*(4), 345–351.

Linehan, M.M. (1993). *Cognitive-behavioral treatment of borderline personality disorder*. New York: Guilford Press.

Livesley, W.J. (Ed.). (1995). *The DSM-IV personality disorders*. New York: Guilford Press.

Livesley, W.J., & Schroeder, M.L. (1990). Dimensions of personality disorder: The DSM-III-R cluster A diagnoses. *Journal of Nervous and Mental Disease, 178,* 627–635.

Livesley, W.J., & Schroeder, M.L. (1991). Dimensions of personality disorder: The DSM-III-R cluster B diagnoses. *Journal of Nervous and Mental Disease, 179,* 320–328.

Livesley, W.J., Schroeder, M.L., & Jackson, D.N. (1990). Dependent personality disorder and attachment problems. *Journal of Personality Disorders, 4,* 232–240.

Livesley, W.J., West, M., & Tanney, A. (1985). Historical comment on DSM-III schizoid and avoidant personality disorders. *American Journal of Psychiatry, 142,* 1344–1347.

Loeber, R. (1990). Development and risk factors of juvenile antisocial behavior and delinquency. *Clinical Psychology Review, 10,* 1–42.

Maier, W., Lichtermann, D., Klingler, T., et al. (1992). Prevalence of personality disorders (DSM-III-R) in the community. *Journal of Personality Disorders, 6,* 187–196.

Marks, I.M. (1985). Behavioral treatment of social phobia. *Psychopharmacology Bulletin, 21,* 615–618.

McDavid, J.D., & Pilkonis, P.A. (1996). The stability of personality disorder diagnoses. *Journal of Personality Disorders, 10,* 1–15.

McGuffin, P., & Thapar, A. (1992). The genetics of personality disorder. *British Journal of Psychiatry, 160,* 12–23.

Meehl, P.E. (1962). Schizotaxia, schizotypy, schizophrenia. *American Psychologist, 17,* 827–838.

Meehl, P.E. (1990). Toward an integrated theory of schizotaxia, schizotypy, and schizophrenia. *Journal of Personality Disorders, 4,* 1–99.

Merikangas, K.R., & Weissman, M.M. (1986). Epidemiology of DSM-III Axis II personality disorders. In A.J. Frances & R.E. Hales (Eds.), *Psychiatry update: American Psychiatric Association annual review* (Vol. 5, pp. 258–278). Washington DC: American Psychiatric Association Press.

Millon, T. (1981). *Disorders of personality: DSM-III, Axis-II*. New York: Wiley.

Morey, L.C. (1988). The categorical representation of personality disorder: A cluster analysis of DSM-III-R personality features. *Journal of Abnormal Psychology, 97,* 314–321.

Nestadt, G., Romanoski, A.J., Chahal, R., et al. (1990). An epidemiological study of histrionic personality disorder. *Psychological Medicine, 20,* 413–422.

Nigg, J.T., & Goldsmith, H.H. (1994). Genetics of personality disorders: Perspectives from personality and psychopathology research. *Psychology Bulletin, 115,* 346–380.

Paris, J. (1988). Follow-up studies of borderline personality disorder: A critical review. *Journal of Personality Disorders, 2,* 189–197.

Patterson, G.R. (1982). *A social learning approach: Volume 3. Coercive family process*. Eugene, OR: Castalia Publishing.

Peselow, E.D., Sanfilipo, M.P., Fieve, R.R., & Gulbenkian, G. (1994). Personality traits during depression and after clinical recovery. *British Journal of Psychiatry, 1994,* 349–354.

Pfohl, B., Coryell, W., Zimmerman, W., & Stangl, D. (1986). DSM-III personality disorders: Diagnostic overlap and internal consistency of individual DSM-III criteria. *Comprehensive Psychiatry, 27,* 21–34.

Rado, S. (1962). Schizotypal organization. In *Psychoanalysis of behavior: Volume 2.* New York: Grune & Stratton.

Rasmussen, S.A., & Tsuang, M.T. (1986). Clinical characteristics and family history of DSM-III obsessive-compulsive disorder. *American Journal of Psychiatry, 143,* 317–322.

Reich, W. (1972). *Character analysis.* New York: Farrar, Strauss, & Giroux. (Original work published 1933.)

Reider, R.O., Rosenthal, D., Wender, P.H., et al. (1975). The offspring of schizophrenics: Fetal and neonatal deaths. *Archives of General Psychiatry, 32,* 200–211.

Robins, L. (1986). Epidemiology of antisocial personality disorder. In R. Michels & J. Cavenar (Eds.), *Psychiatry: Volume 3.* Philadelphia: Lippincott.

Robins, L.N., Helzer, J.E., Weissman, M.M., et al. (1984). Lifetime prevalence of specific psychiatric disorders in three sites. *Archives of General Psychiatry, 41,* 949–958.

Robins, L.N., Tipp, J., & Przybeck, T. (1991). Antisocial personality. In L.N. Robins & D.A. Regier (Eds.), *Psychiatric disorders in America* (pp. 258–290). New York: Free Press.

Rutter, M. & Giller, H. (1983). *Juvenile delinquency: Trends and perspectives.* New York: Penguin Books.

Samuels, J.F, Nestadt, G., Romanoski, A.J., et al. (1994). DSM-III personality disorders in the community. *American Journal of Psychiatry, 151,* 1055–1062.

Sanderson, C., & Clarkin, J.F. (1994). Use of the NEO-PI personality dimensions in differential treatment planning. In P.T. Costa & T. Widiger (Eds.), *Personality disorders and the five-factor model of personality* (pp. 219–236). Washington, DC: American Psychological Association.

Sato, T., Sakado, K., Sato, S., et al. (1994). Cluster A personality disorder: A marker of worse treatment outcome of major depression? *Psychiatry Research, 53,* 153–159.

Schneider, K. (1923). *Die psychopathischen Persinlichkeiten.* Vienna: Demticke.

Shea, M.T., Pilkonis, P.A., Beckham, E., Collins, J.F., Elkin, I., Sotsky, S.M., & Docherty, J.P. (1990). Personality disorders and treatment outcome in the NIMH treatment of depression collaborative research program. *American Journal of Psychiatry, 147,* 711–718.

Shea, M.T., Widiger, T.A., & Klein, M.H. (1992). Comorbidity of personality disorders and depression: Implications for treatment. *Journal of Consulting and Clinical Psychology, 60,* 857–868.

Siever, L.J. (1992). Schizophrenia spectrum disorders. In A. Tasman & M.B. Riba (Eds.), *Review of psychiatry* (Vol. II, pp. 25–42). Washington, DC: American Psychiatric Press.

Siever, L.J., & Davis, K.L. (1991). A psychobiological perspective on the personality disorders. *American Journal of Psychiatry, 148,* 1647–1658.

Siever, L.J., & Kendler, K.S. (1988). Schizoid/schizotypal/paranoid personality disorders. In R. Michels & J.O. Cavenar, Jr. (Eds.), *Psychiatry* (Vol. 1, Chap. 16, pp. 1–11). New York: Basic Books.

Skinner, H.A. (1986). Construct validation approach to psychiatric classification. In T. Millon & G. Klerman (Eds.), *Contemporary directions in psychopathology: Toward the DSM-IV* (pp. 307–330). New York: Guilford Press.

Spitzer, R.L., Endicott, J., & Gibbon, M. (1979). Crossing the border into borderline personality and borderline schizophrenia. *Archives of General Psychiatry, 36,* 17–24.

Stone, M.H. (1993). Long-term outcome in personality disorders. *British Journal of Psychiatry, 162,* 299–313.

Stone, M.H., Hurt, S.W., & Stone, D.K. (1987). The PI 500: Long-term follow-up of borderline inpatients meeting DSM-III criteria: I. Global outcome. *Journal of Personality Disorders, 1,* 291–298.

Trull, T.J., Widiger, T.A., & Frances, A. (1987). Co-variation of criteria sets of avoidant, schizoid, and dependent personality disorders. *American Journal of Psychiatry, 144,* 767–771.

Turner, S.M., & Beidel, D.C. (1989). Social phobia:

Clinical syndrome, diagnosis, and comorbidity. *Clinical Psychology Review, 9,* 3–18.

Turner, S.M., Beidel, D.C., Dancu, C.V., & Keys, D.J. (1986). Psychopathology of social phobia and comparison to avoidant personality disorder. *Journal of Abnormal Psychology, 95,* 389–394.

Weissman, M.M. (1993). The epidemiology of personality disorders: A 1990 update. *Journal of Personality Disorders, 7*(Suppl.), 44–62.

Widiger, T.A., & Frances, A.J. (1989). Epidemiology, diagnosis, and comorbidity of borderline personality disorder. In A. Tasman, R.E. Hales, & A.J. Frances (Eds.), *Review of psychiatry* (Vol. 8, pp. 8–23). Washington, DC: American Psychiatric Press.

Widiger, T.A., Frances, A.J., Harris, M., Jacobsberg, L.B., Fyer, M., & Manning, D. (1991). Comorbidity among axis II disorders. In J. Oldham (Ed.), *Personality disorders: New perspectives on diagnostic validity* (pp. 165–194). Washington, DC: American Psychiatric Press.

Widiger, T.A., & Trull, T.J. (1993). Borderline and narcissistic personality disorders. In P.B. Sutker & H.E. Adams (Eds.), *Comprehensive handbook of psychopathology,* 2nd ed. (pp. 181–201). New York: Plenum Publishing.

Widiger, T.A., Trull, T.J., Clarkin, J.F., et al. (1994). A description of the DSM-III-R and DSM-IV personality disorders with the five-factor model of personality. In P.T. Costa & T.A. Widiger (Eds.), *Personality disorders and the five-factor model of personality* (pp. 41–58). Washington, DC: American Psychological Association.

Winnicott, D.W. (1992). Primitive emotional development. In D.W. Winnicott (Ed.), *Through pediatrics to psychoanalysis: Collected papers* (pp. 145–156). New York: Brunner/Mazel.

Zetzel, E.R. (1968). The so-called good hysteric. In E.R. Zetzel (Ed.), *The capacity for emotional growth* (pp. 229–245). New York: International Universities Press.

Zimmerman, M., & Coryell, W. (1989). DSM-III personality disorder diagnosis in a nonpatient sample. *Archives of General Psychiatry, 46,* 682–689.

CHAPTER 16

SUBSTANCE ABUSE

Robert F. Schilling
School of Public Policy and Social Research, UCLA

Steven P. Schinke
Nabila El-Bassel
Columbia University School of Social Work

INTRODUCTION

Alcohol and other psychoactive substances have been used for thousands of years. As early as 1709, opium was prepared commercially and distributed in the United States, and by the latter part of the 18th century opium poppies were grown and harvested in much of the United States and its territories (Inciardi, 1986). By the middle of the next century, there was growing public worry over the smoking of opium. Early concern about the psychiatric implications of substance abuse[1] is evidenced by the linking of alcoholism and depression by 19th-century psychiatrists, and in the use of the term *dope fiend* at the turn of the century (Allen & Frances, 1986; Inciardi, 1986). Since the 1960s, the government, the press, and the nation as a whole have been increasingly concerned with drug abuse. For more than a decade, pollsters have reported that Americans consider drug abuse to be among the nation's most serious problems. Although part of this concern is surely a result of media interest in drug-related crime and violence, it also re-flects a more general perception that illicit drugs as well as alcohol are in some way related to many contemporary social problems.

Many people continue to view chemical dependency as a moral weakness rather than a psychiatric or a social problem, and within the helping professions there remains considerable ambivalence about the wisdom of including substance abuse as a form of mental illness. For example, recent changes in welfare entitlements include sanctions for drug use by welfare recipients, and also exclude social security income benefits based on substance abuse–related disability. Other currents would suggest that the public is beginning to think about drug abuse as a public health problem that is inadequately addressed through law enforcement. Yet another development is the increasing appreciation of the limitations of existing treatment approaches to addiction. Understanding of the social context of substance abuse may give rise to new population- and community-focused roles for prevention and treatment specialists from public health and other disciplines. However chemical dependence is perceived in the years ahead, substance abuse will surely assume greater prominence among the problems attended to by psychiatrists, social workers, psychologists, and other helping professionals.

This chapter defines substance abuse and the criteria for making such a diagnosis, briefly describes the epidemiology and symptoms of specific drug abuse disorders, and discusses the potential causes and nature of such conditions. Last, the authors discuss issues of treatment and control given recent understanding of the chronicity and social context of drug dependence, comment on emerging trends in the epidemiology and comorbidity of substance abuse, and suggest future directions for prevention and treatment policy and research.

DEFINITIONS AND DIAGNOSES

In the *Diagnostic and Statistical Manual of Mental Disorders,* fourth edition (DSM-IV; American Psychiatric Association [APA], 1994), substance-related disorders include "disorders related to the taking of a drug of abuse (including alcohol), to the side effects of a medication, and to toxin exposure" (p. 175). As used in this chapter, *substance* refers to both alcohol and other *psychoactive* chemicals that modify mood or behavior. They may take solid, liquid, or gaseous forms, and often are modified so that they are more readily available to the body. Many substances—legal, illicit, and prescribed—have psychoactive properties. Some, such as tea, are so mild that they are rarely abused. Other psychoactive substances, such as those found in some plants, require the user to endure considerable effort or gastrointestinal distress, and are therefore abused by few. Some other substances, including tobacco and alcohol, are almost always perceived as unpleasant when initially consumed, but are readily acquired tastes. Still other chemical substances, such as heroin, are typically used intravenously, a form of ingestion quite unpalatable to most persons.

General Criteria

The DSM-IV divides substance-related disorders into two groups: substance use disorders (dependence and abuse) and substance-induced disorders (including the following substance-induced conditions: intoxication, withdrawal, delirium, persisting dementia, mood disorder, anxiety disorder, sexual dysfunction, sleep disorder).

Substance dependence is characterized as a "cluster of cognitive, behavioral, and psychological symptoms indicating that the individual continues use of the substance despite significant substance-related problems . . . repeated self-administration . . . usually results in tolerance, withdrawal and compulsive drug-taking behavior." (APA, 1994, p. 176). A diagnosis of substance dependence requires that at least three of the following seven symptom clusters be present at any time during the same 12-month period:

- Tolerance, as defined by either of the following:
  —A need exists for markedly increased amounts of the substance to achieve desired intoxication or desired effects.
  —Markedly diminished effect occurs with continued use of the same amount.
- Withdrawal, as manifested by one of the following:
  —The characteristic withdrawal syndrome for the substance is evident.
  —The same or similar substance is taken to relieve or avoid withdrawal symptoms.
  —The substance is often taken in large amounts or over longer periods than was intended.
- Persistent desire or one or more attempts to reduce or control use exists.
- Considerable time is spent obtaining, taking, or recovering from effects of the substance.
- Important social, occupational, or recreational activities are given up or reduced because of substance use.
- Use is continued despite knowledge of having a persistent or recurrent physical or psychological problem that is caused or exacerbated by the substance.

The diagnosis of substance dependence is further specified as to whether or not physiological dependence is present, as evidenced by tolerance or withdrawal. Substance dependence is further specified by six "course modifiers," including four that apply to remission ("early-full," "early-partial," "sustained-full," and "sustained-partial"), and two others that apply when the individual is on agonist therapy or in a controlled environment.

The *substance abuse* category involves substance use without ". . . tolerance, withdrawal or a pattern of compulsive use and instead includes only harmful consequences of repeated use" (APA, 1994, p. 182). DSM-IV criteria for substance abuse include one or more of the following occurring within a 12-month period:

- Recurrent substance use resulting in a failure to fulfill major role obligations at work, school or home
- Recurrent substance use in hazardous situations (e.g., while operating an automobile or machinery)
- Recurrent substance-related legal problems
- Continued substance use despite having persistent or recurrent social or interpersonal problems caused or exacerbated by effects of substance use

The diagnosis of substance abuse disorder is applied when maladaptive patterns of substance use do not meet criteria for dependence; thus, a diagnosis of *abuse* is preempted by a diagnosis of *dependence*. Although abuse is often diagnosed in individuals with relatively recent experience in taking drugs, some individuals may have substance-related consequences over long periods without meeting criteria of substance dependence.

DSM-IV provides three criteria for *substance intoxication*. The essential feature is "the development of a reversible substance-specific syndrome due to the recent ingestion of (or exposure to) a substance." The diagnosis also requires "clinically significant maladaptive behavioral or psychological changes that are due to the effect of the substance on the central nervous system." (APA, 1994, p. 184). The symptoms must not be due to or better explained by other disorders or conditions. Different substances may produce similar or identical behavior, and the degree to which this behavior places the individual at risk for adverse effects (e.g., accidents, legal difficulties, job jeopardy) is dependent upon the social context.

According to DSM-IV, *substance withdrawal* is "the development of a substance-specific syndrome due to the cessation of (or reduction in) substance use that has been heavy and prolonged . . . [causing] . . . clinically significant distress or impairment in social, occupational, or other important areas of function-

ing . . . not due to a general medical condition and . . . not better accounted for by another mental disorder" (APA, 1994, p. 185).

The material on substance-related disorders was revised substantially in DSM-IV from that in DSM-III-R (when the section was entitled "Psychoactive Substance Use Disorders"). In the earlier manual, the substance-induced disorders and the mental disorders due to a general medical condition were called "organic" and were listed in a separate section. The committees assigned to the fourth revision of DSM believed that the "organic" distinction implied that "functional" mental disorders were unrelated to physical or biological factors. In DSM-IV, the term *organic* is eliminated, and substance-induced mental disorders are distinguished from those attributable to a general medical condition or unknown etiology (APA, 1994). No fewer than eight substance-induced disorders are listed, and the diagnostician is referred to the sections of the manual covering these conditions, which include substance-induced delirium, persisting dementia, persisting amnestic disorder, psychotic disorder, mood disorder, anxiety disorder, sexual dysfunction, and sleep disorder. Another substance-induced disorder, described under the substance-related disorders section of the DSM, is hallucinogen persisting perception disorder (flashbacks).

The writers of DSM-III-R observed that ". . . research and clinical practice would be improved by eliminating many of the diagnostic hierarchies that have prevented giving multiple diagnoses when different syndromes occur together in one episode of the illness" (APA, 1987, p. xxiv). Accordingly, DSM-IV encourages mental health professionals to record disorders related to more than one substance if appropriate, and provides detailed examples to guide clinicians making diagnostic judgments concerning one drug versus another. DSM-IV devotes considerable attention to the temporal juxtaposition of the development of substance-induced disorders. As mental health professionals gain experience with the new criteria, it seems likely that the next revision will attempt to improve on the imprecision of these diagnostic suggestions.

In DSM-III-R, the patterns of use, features, and natural history for each of the specific substances were described for each substance, but essentially the same criteria for dependence and abuse were used to apply generally to all of the specific substances. Variations were described for each class of substances, but separate dependence and abuse criteria for each substance were not delineated. In contrast, criteria for the various substance-induced disorders were specified, for each substance, in the section on organic mental syndromes and disorders. In DSM-IV, each substance is discussed in sequence. The criteria for dependence and abuse are similar for many substances, and the reader is often referred to the general criteria for these phenomena. Intoxication and withdrawal tend to be more substance-specific and are accordingly described for each class of substance. The reader is referred to other sections for other disorders (e.g., amphetamine-induced psychosis, cannabis intoxication delirium). Each section closes with limited additional information on associated features and disorders (e.g., certain substances are often used in combination, and some drugs have similar effects under certain conditions), laboratory findings, physical exam findings, general medical conditions, and information on prevalence, course and differential diagnosis. Thus, the diagnostician who knows or suspects that a given individual has used a particular substance will find readily interpretable diagnostic criteria for that sort of drug.

THE DSM-IV DISORDERS: EPIDEMIOLOGY, PATTERNS OF USE, CRITERIA

DSM-IV defines eleven classes of substances, of which nine are associated with both dependency and abuse. These classes may be grouped into three clusters with similar or related features: (1) alcohol, opioids and sedatives, and other substances with depressant effects; (2) cocaine, amphetamines, and other substances with stimulant properties (including caffeine and nicotine); and (3) hallucinogens, cannabis and phencyclidine (PCP), and similarly acting substances (Table 16-1). The classes of substances are next discussed. Differential attention is given according to the prominence of a given substance, and the correspondent degree of scientific, clinical, and societal attention it has received.

The Legal Drugs: Alcohol, Tobacco, and Caffeine

Alcohol, tobacco, and caffeine are the only legal psychoactive substances available in most Western nations, aside from certain misused nonprescription medicines (e.g. cough syrup, antihistamine sprays), inhalants (e.g., glue, gasoline), and some "natural" foods or health products (e.g. sunflower seeds). Alcohol is the most abused psychoactive substance in all industrialized countries, and in most less developed nations as well. Alcohol's legal status and wide social acceptance belie its toxicity. Continued use of large amounts results in irreversible damage to the central nervous system. Alcohol is responsible for more disease than all other psychoactive substances except tobacco, and its social and economic costs are incalculable. In much of the world, including some industrialized nations, tobacco use is almost universal among men. Although tobacco use continues to decline in the United States and, more recently, in Western Europe, rates of use are rising along with living standards in the developing world. Tobacco remains the number one cause of preventable disease in the developed nations (World Health Organization, 1996), but politicians and the general public have been more concerned with illicit drug use than with alcohol and tobacco. Nonetheless, consumption of tobacco and, more recently, of alcohol is steadily declining among most age groups. Public opinion is turning against alcohol and tobacco, as evidenced by reductions in tobacco-farming subsidies, stricter enforcement of laws combating tobacco sales to youth and driving while intoxicated, and increasing restrictions on places where alcohol and tobacco may be used.

Alcohol

In 1994, approximately 111 million Americans over age 12 were current alcohol users; approximately 52% of the total population age 12 and older—some 32 million adults—reported ingestion of five or more drinks on one occasion during the past month; and 11 million reported ingestion of five or more drinks per occasion on five or more days in the past month. Young adults tend to drink more and are less likely to

TABLE 16-1   Misused psychoactive substances.

General Class Specific Substance	Selected Examples, Commonly Used Names	Comments
Depressant-Acting		
Alcohol	Many varieties intended for consumption, denatured alcohol	Most commonly used substance; involved in half of traffic fatalities.
Sedatives, hypnotics, anxiolytics	Barbiturates, sleeping pills, muscle relaxers, tranquilizers	May be lethal when combined with alcohol.
Opioids, meperidine, methadone	Heroin, codeine, morphine	Injection equipment used with heroin is a major route of HIV infection. Methadone, a prescribed substitute, is often sold on the streets.
Inhalants	Gasoline, glue, paint thinners	Highly toxic
Stimulant-Acting		
Amphetamines and similar-acting sympathamimetics	Speed, methedrine, dexadrine	Rapid tolerance effects
Cocaine	Coke, crack	Crack is inexpensive and widely available.
Hallucinogens and Substances with Related Action		
Lysergic acid diethylamine (LSD), Dimethyltryptamine (DMT)	Acid	True hallucinogens are used by relatively few.
Catecholamine-related substances (mescaline)	Peyote	Nausea and vomiting are common.
Phencyclidine (PCP)	Angel dust	Often used as an adulterant of more expensive drugs.
Cannabis	Marijuana, hashish	Most widely used illegal substance.
Other Mild-Acting Stimulants		
Caffeine	Coffee; No-Doz	Many have reduced intake without major side effects.
Nicotine	Cigarettes, cigars, pipes, chewing tobacco	Cigarettes remain the largest cause of preventable disease and death.

abstain than older adults; about 10 million current drinkers were under age 21 (National Institute on Drug Abuse, 1995). Women drink less than men and are far less likely to be heavy or binge drinkers. Rates of use, dependence, and abuse among most ethnic-racial minority groups tend to be lower than rates of women of white European extraction (Ellickson, McGuigan, Adams, Bell, & Hays, 1996).

As early as 1951, the World Health Organization (WHO) held that alcohol misuse was to some extent defined by the individual's culture. Alcoholism and excessive drinking were defined as a level that inter-fered with an individual's bodily and mental health, interpersonal relationships, and social and economic functioning (WHO, 1952). Though functionally oriented, such a general definition leaves much to be desired in the process of developing descriptive schema useful to both mental health practitioners and researchers. Despite their improved specificity and clarity, the diagnostic procedures for assessing alcohol dependence and abuse within DSM-IV retain many of the problems of all definitional and descriptive schema (Babor, 1995; Kirk and Kutchins, 1992).

DSM-IV provides no specific criteria for *alcohol*

dependence or abuse beyond those listed for substance dependence and abuse in general. *Alcohol intoxication,* as listed under the alcohol-related disorders in DSM-IV, may be characterized by aggressiveness, impaired judgment, irritability, euphoria, depression, and emotional lability. Like most other central nervous system depressants, alcohol may either accentuate or mask a person's normal behavior. Alcohol tends to disinhibit the user; one drink may cause a person to be talkative, energetic, and socially relaxed. Increased amounts result in impaired reasoning and judgment and often belligerent or aggressive behavior. Blackouts, one of the distinguishing features of alcohol abuse and dependence, occur following ingestion of large amounts of alcohol. DSM-IV criteria for alcohol intoxication are similar to the general criteria for substance-induced intoxication. One or more of the following specific signs must be observed: slurred speech, incoordination, unsteady gait, nystagmus, attention or memory impairment, or stupor/coma.

Withdrawal. To meet DSM-IV criteria for alcohol withdrawal, there must be evidence of cessation (or reduction) of heavy and prolonged use, and along with at least two of the following eight physiological or psychological phenomena in the hours or days following: sweating or pulse rate above 100; hand tremor; insomnia; nausea or vomiting; transient visual, tactile, or auditory hallucinations or illusions; psychomotor agitation; anxiety; or grand mal seizures.

Nicotine

Smoking remains the single most preventable cause of disease and death in the United States (L'Abate, Farrar, & Serritella, 1992; U.S. Department of Health and Human Services, 1990). In recognition of the role of nicotine as the critical component in the dependence process, DSM-IV replaced the former term *tobacco dependence* with the term *nicotine dependence*. Although smokers often report positive psychoactive effects, and tobacco use is highly correlated with other drug dependence (Bobo, Schilling, Gilchrist, & Schinke, 1986; Jarvik & Schneider, 1992), smoking appears not to impair social, psychological, or motor functioning as do other substances. However, smoking is associated with depression (Hall, Munoz Reus, & Sees, 1993). Among men in

the United States, smoking rates declined almost by half between 1965 and 1993. Rates for both men (28%) and women (23%) have stabilized in recent years, with general downward trends being offset by increases among persons 18 to 24. Rates of smoking among junior and senior high school students have climbed dramatically since 1991 (National Center for Health Statistics, 1996).

Dependence. Most of the general criteria for dependence apply to tobacco use, except that the wide availability of tobacco products, and their ready portability and ease of use, preclude the criterion of time spent on procurement. In the past, tobacco dependence did not result in reductions in important social, occupational, or recreational activities; however, workplace restrictions and laws curtailing smoking in public areas have made smoking a more inconvenient and socially undesirable habit (Borland & Owen, 1995; Mitchell, 1995; Schilling, Gilchrist, & Schinke, 1985).

Withdrawal. Smokers who attempt to quit or reduce their use experience withdrawal, which may include depressed mood, insomnia, frustration, irritability, anxiety, difficulty concentrating, restlessness, decreased heart rate, and weight gain (APA, 1994). Successful quitters usually have made several earlier attempts, and it is not unusual for relapse to occur months or even years after a period of abstinence (Lichtenstein & Brown, 1982).

Caffeine

Coffee drinking is the most common form of caffeine consumption, but tea, cola, chocolate, "stay alert" products, analgesics and some cold/allergy medicines also contain significant amounts of caffeine. Caffeine has dysfunctional psychological and behavioral effects in some persons. In rare instances, manic episodes, panic, and generalized anxiety may result from ingestion of large doses of caffeine. The mild psychological and neurological effects of caffeine have not been studied extensively, but many people report feeling "less agitated" after reducing their caffeine intake. DSM-IV criteria for caffeine intoxication requires that at least 5 of 12 signs be present. Some of these include restlessness, nervousness, insomnia, diuresis, muscle twitching, and psychomotor agitation. Some individuals who drink large amounts of coffee display aspects of dependence on caffeine and may also exhibit tolerance and perhaps withdrawal. However, the data are insufficient to determine the clinical significance of such symptoms.

Opioids

Heroin and morphine, derivatives of the poppy, are the best known of the natural opioids. Synthetic opioids include codeine, meperidine, and other agents often prescribed for pain or cough suppression. Other substances, such as pentazocine and buprenorphine, have similar effects and are thus included in this class. Opioid use typically begins in late adolescence or the early twenties. Heroin is often mixed with cocaine ("speedballs") and may also be used in combination with many other psychoactive substances.

The prevalence of opioid use is subject to much speculation, in that most of these substances are obtained illegally. According to one recent estimate, there are 1,460,300 injection drug users in the United States (the large majority being heroin users) (Holmberg, 1996). The annual survey of households found 122,000 new heroin users in 1994 (National Institute on Drug Abuse [NIDA], 1995). Use often begins with sniffing ("snorting"), but typically progresses to "skin popping" (injection under the skin) and injection into blood vessels ("mainlining"), which provide more of a "rush" and render more effects per quantum. The number of occasional users, who are more likely to sniff than inject, is open to speculation, but it is clear that many users move from occasional to daily use. Once addiction is established, procurement of one or more daily "fixes" becomes a central activity. Only a small proportion of heroin addicts work regularly, and many support their habit through criminal activity.

Opioid dependence and abuse conform to the general DSM-IV criteria for substance use dependence and abuse. *Opioid-induced intoxication* is observable within a few minutes after use, characterized by psychological or behavioral changes such as "euphoria followed by apathy, dysphoria, psychomotor agitation or retardation, impaired judgment, or impaired social or occupational functioning. Other required criteria include pupillary constriction, and one or more of the following: drowsiness or coma, slurred speech, or impairment in attention or memory" (APA, 1994, p. 250).

Opioid-induced withdrawal is a well-established aspect of opioid addiction: it occurs within 8 hours of last use, peaks within several days, and may last a week or more. DSM-IV requires that three of the following symptoms be observed: dysphoric mood; nausea or vomiting; muscle aches; lacrimation or rhinorrhea; pupillary dilation; piloerection or sweating; diarrhea; yawning; fever; insomnia. Some have observed that the symptoms are similar to those of a bad flu, and may include restlessness, irritability, and depression. Opioid withdrawal and tolerance are clearly evident in heroin users, and there is evidence that some addicts seek treatment in order to lower their daily requirements.

Cocaine

Cocaine, derived from the coca leaf, was a popular patent medicine in Europe and the United States in the late 19th century. It is worth noting that Freud was a regular user of cocaine, which was in the original formulation of Coca-Cola. Reports of the drug's ill effects surfaced in the 19th century, and cocaine was eventually outlawed in Canada in 1911 and in the United States in 1914 (Erickson, Adlaf, Murray, & Smart, 1987; Rosecan & Spitz, 1987). A relatively simple process renders the coca base into cocaine hydrochloride, a white, water-soluble powder that is typically snorted or placed under the tongue, but which may also be injected. In the 1970s, users discovered that cocaine has much more immediate and powerful effects if prepared in a smokeable "free-base" form. Free basing required elaborate preparation with ether, but this process is now done with baking soda, rendering the drug into its "crack" form. In 1994, an estimated 1.5 million Americans were current cocaine users, and 2.5 million were occasional cocaine users. In addition, approximately 400,000 people were current users of crack cocaine (NIDA, 1995). However, crack cocaine use has dropped in recent years.

Cocaine is an extremely short-acting drug; when it is taken in free-base or crack form, its effect on the brain is as rapid as with injection. The search for more cocaine is propelled by a craving rather than a wish to alleviate withdrawal symptoms. Although powdered cocaine is costly and is associated with fast living among the affluent, crack cocaine vials sell for as little as $2.00 apiece in poor neighborhoods. Crack cocaine is associated with street-level sex trade and has been implicated in the transmission of HIV and other sexually transmitted diseases (Edlin et al, 1994). The importation, distribution, and sale and use of cocaine have been blamed as one important dimension in the decline of the quality of life in inner cities.

Cocaine dependence and abuse are established with the general criteria for substance dependence and abuse. *Cocaine intoxication,* is distinguished according to DSM-IV, by "euphoria or affective blunting; changes in sociability; hypervigilence; interpersonal sensitivity; anxiety, tension or anger; stereotyped behaviors; impaired judgment; or impaired social or occupational functioning" (APA, 1994, p. 224). To meet DSM-IV criteria, a diagnosis requires two or more of the following: tachycardia or bradycardia; pupillary dilation; elevated or lowered blood pressure; perspiration or chills; nausea or vomiting; weight loss; psychomotor agitation or retardation; muscular weakness, respiratory depression, chest pain, or cardia arrhythmias; confusion, seizures, dyskinesia, or coma. Tolerance is readily apparent in cocaine abuse and dependence, as users require increasingly larger doses to achieve a pleasurable effect.

Cocaine withdrawal is present if, after cessation of heavy, prolonged use, the individual exhibits two or more of the following symptoms: fatigue; vivid, unpleasant dreams; insomnia or hypersomnia; increased appetite; or psychomotor retardation or agitation. Other cocaine-induced disorders include delirium, psychosis, mood disorder, anxiety disorder, sexual dysfunction, and sleep disorder.

Amphetamine or Amphetamine-like Substances

Although the subjective experience of amphetamine intoxication may be virtually indistinguishable from that of cocaine, these chemical agents tend to last longer and may have more potent side effects. As with cocaine, tolerance and withdrawal are observed; in some instances, delirium and delusions occur. Oral ingestion is most common, but intravenous and nasal routes may also be used. Methamphetamine, in limited use for many decades, has in the past few years become a major street drug in many regions of the country. DSM-IV criteria for dependence, abuse, intoxication, withdrawal and the other amphetamine-induced disorders are nearly identical to that of cocaine.

Sedatives, Hypnotics, and Anxiolytics

Commonly used substances in this class include benzodiazepine (e.g., Valium), barbiturates, and methaqualone. Usually taken orally, they are prescribed to reduce anxiety, induce sleep, and relax muscles. The pharmacological properties of these drugs vary widely, but all share depressant, disinhibitory effects similar to those of alcohol. Thus, intoxicated individuals may evidence increased sexual or occasionally aggressive behavior, and poor judgment in social behavior and coordination across any of life's domains. Tolerance can readily develop to many of these psychoactive substances; withdrawal symptoms are similar to those of alcohol and, in severe cases, can be accompanied by seizures or myoclonic jerks. Even the safest of these agents (e.g., diazepam) can result in death if mixed with alcohol or other substances in this class. The estimated prevalence rate of sedatives or tranquilizers over the past month was 1.2% of American adults (NIDA, 1995). DSM-IV provides no criteria for dependence and abuse unique to this class of substances.

Intoxication is characterized by maladaptive behavioral or psychological changes such as inappropriate sexual or aggressive behavior, mood lability, and impaired judgment and role functioning. One or more of the following signs must be observed to meet DSM-IV criteria for intoxication: slurred speech; incoordination; unsteady gait; nystagmus; attention or memory impairment; or stupor/coma.

Withdrawal criteria are the same as for alcohol.

Inhalants

Vapors in gasoline, glues, paints, thinners, and other volatile compounds are usually breathed through the nose and mouth, typically from a soaked cloth or bag. Intoxicated users, typically adolescents, exhibit behavior similar to persons under the influence of alcohol. As many as one-fifth of high school seniors have tried inhalants over their lifetime. Lower and higher rates of use are found respectively among African American and Native American youth (Beauvais, 1996; Kann et al., 1996). Household surveys indicate that 1.2% of Americans aged 12 and older have used inhalants in the past month (NIDA, 1995). Clinical and correlational findings suggest that users most often exhibit a range of psychosocial, mental, and physical problems (McSherry, 1988; Oetting, Edwards, & Beauvais, 1988). DSM-IV specifies no criteria unique to inhalants, for dependence or abuse.

Inhalant intoxication may be characterized by belligerence, assaultiveness, apathy, impaired judgment, or impaired social or occupational functioning. Two or more of 13 listed signs are required for a diagnosis of intoxication, including almost all of the same signs as for alcohol intoxication, plus dizziness, lethargy, depressed reflexes, psychomotor retardation, tremor, generalized motor weakness, blurred vision or diplopia, and euphoria. Although the latter descriptors may also apply in some instances of alcohol intoxication, they are more typical and pronounced in the case of inhalant use.

Hallucinogens

The numerous substances in this class vary widely in chemical structure and mechanism of action. Lysergic acid diethylamide (LSD) is an "unadulterated" synthetic hallucinogen, which is often mixed with amphetamines or other adulterants when sold. Other substances include phenylalkylamines, one being mescaline, a natural substance found in peyote. Users of phencyclidine (PCP) and delta-9-tetrahydrocannabinol (THC, the active compound in cannabis) also may experience hallucinations, but DSM-IV does not classify these substances as hallucinogens because their primary and usual psychological and behavioral effects are not hallucinogenic. Hallucinogen use is relatively uncommon; according to household surveys in 1995, the rate of current use of hallucinogens was 0.7%; among youth age 12 to 17, the rate increased from 1.1% to 1.7% from 1994 to 1995 (NIDA, 1995). Autonomic nervous system effects include loss of appetite, dizziness, increased body temperature, restlessness, and nausea. Psychological symptoms include a sense of loss of control;

depersonalization; body image changes; feelings of being carefree, elated, or silly; impaired thinking including slowness, impaired sense of time, and loss of meanings; anxiety, depression, fear of becoming crazy, paranoid ideation, intensification of colors, and experiencing sounds as visual burst of color (Milby, Jolly, & Beidleman, 1984; Robbins, Katz, & Stern, 1985).

Hallucinogen dependence and abuse.   Although DSM-IV refers to the general criteria for substance dependence, some of these criteria do not apply to hallucinogens, or require explication. Tolerance may develop rapidly to the euphoric and psychedelic effects, but not to the autonomic effects. Even among individuals meeting criteria for dependence, use is infrequent (not more than several times per week), because of the long duration of action of most hallucinogens, and a long period recovering from the effects. Withdrawal effects have not been established. In DSM-IV, there are no specific criteria for hallucinogen abuse.

Hallucinogen intoxication is characterized by "marked anxiety or depression, ideas of reference, fear of losing one's mind, paranoid ideation, impaired judgment, or impaired social or occupational functioning" (APA, 1994, p. 232). In addition, the individual may demonstrate subjective intensification of perceptions, depersonalization, derealization, illusions, hallucinations, or a blending of sense perceptions. Two or more of the following signs are required: tachycardia, pupillary dilation, sweating, palpitations, blurring of vision, tremors, or incoordination.

DSM-IV describes a hallucinogen persisting perception disorder, which occurs when an individual, sometime after cessation of use, reexperiences one or more of the symptoms without actually taking the hallucinogen.

Phencyclidine (PCP) and Related Substances

PCP and compounds with similar actions may be smoked, inhaled, or taken orally or intravenously. Bingeing is common among users, who initially may experience a euphoric, floating sensation, with intense feelings of being in another world, a fantasy existence (Maxmen & Ward, 1995). In response to low doses, the user may experience disinhibitory effects not unlike those of alcohol, along with numbness and some of the effects of hallucinogens, (e.g., illusions and pseudohallucination). In larger amounts, PCP may result in confusion, disorientation, disorganized thinking, agitation or withdrawal, anxiety, panic, and feelings of isolation. Still larger doses of PCP may produce symptoms similar to those of schizophrenia, including catatonia and paranoid ideation, to the extent that communication is impossible (Robbins, Katz & Stern, 1985).

In the past, as many as 13% of high school seniors had used PCP (Johnson, O'Malley, & Bachman, 1989), but prevalence has been considerably lower in recent years. Lifetime and annual use, as reported in past household surveys, were respectively 3.1% and 0.2% (NIDA, 1989). Although no extensive studies have been done, some observers have suggested that experimenters tend to abandon PCP readily, or quickly develop into dependent users (APA, 1987). Phencyclidine dependence and abuse are not uniquely specified in DSM-IV.

Phencyclidine intoxication is demonstrated via belligerence, assaultiveness, impulsiveness, unpredictability, psychomotor agitation, as well as impaired judgment or social or occupational functioning. A diagnosis requires observance of two or more of the following symptoms, occurring within an hour of use: vertical or horizontal systagmus, hypertension or tachycardia, numbness or diminished responsiveness to pain, ataxia, dysarthria, muscle rigidity, seizures or coma, or hyperacusis.

Other substance-induced disorders associated with PCP use include delirium, psychotic disorder, mood disorder, or anxiety disorder.

Cannabis

Marijuana, in leaf, hashish, or purified forms, has, according to some estimates, been tried by over 60% of adults in the United States (Maxmen & Ward, 1995). The amount of tetrahydrocannabinol (THC) in marijuana has increased substantially in recent years, as foreign and especially domestic producers have developed more sophisticated growing techniques. Household survey data, which tend to underestimate use of illegal substances, indicate that 9.8 million

Americans (4.7%) ages 12 and older have used marijuana in the past month (NIDA, 1995). Since 1992, the rate of use among youths ages 12 to 17 has more than doubled to 8.2% (NIDA, 1995).

Legalization proponents have moderated claims that there are few ill effects from cannabis, and it is known that respiratory problems, acute anxiety states, and flashbacks can occur in some small proportion of users. Panic attacks, which are the most frequently reported symptoms for persons unaccustomed to marijuana, may last for several hours following use. Users commonly experience euphoria, silliness, changes in sensory perception, alteration of visual and color perception, increased appetite, and an overall sense of relaxation and self-awareness. In higher doses, cannabis use may result in suspiciousness or paranoid behavior, and panic. In some instances, paranoid delusions are present. One population-base study found that 4.2% of adults in the United States reported dependence at one point in their life (Anthony, Warner, & Kessler, 1994); in an alcohol-dependent sample, 16% of the higher marijuana use group reported symptoms of cannabis withdrawal (Weisbeck et al., 1996). Nonetheless, both experimental and epidemiological studies have failed to demonstrate adverse intellectual or psychological sequelae, even after years of heavy use (Grinspoon & Bakalar, 1992; Maxmen & Ward, 1995; Roffman & George, 1988).

Unique *dependence and abuse* criteria are not identified in DSM-IV. Physiological dependence is uncommon, although tolerance to most of the effects of cannabis has been reported by chronic users (APA, 1994).

Cannabis intoxication is characterized by "impaired motor coordination, euphoria, anxiety, sensation of slowed time, impaired judgment [or] social withdrawal" (APA, 1994, p. 218).

ETIOLOGY AND COURSE

A brief overview of the causes of substance abuse will be outlined in this chapter. In this discussion, conceptualizations of etiology are divided into developmental/familial/community and ethnic-racial/biological. The multivariate complexity of substance abuse reveals both the limitations of any etiological perspective and the need to avoid attempting to focus simultaneously on too many variables.

Adolescence, the Family, and Social/Community Structures

Drug Use Initiation

The most prominent conceptualizations of drug use initiation include the theory of problem behavior (Donovan & Jessor, 1985), stage theory (Kandel & Logan, 1984), and peer cluster theory (Beauvais & Oetting, 1988; Oetting et al., 1988). Problem behavior theory holds that adolescents who abuse drugs and alcohol exhibit earlier independence, lack of respect for conventional institutions and values, and a critical view of society. According to stage theory, adolescents tend to begin with certain entry drugs, such as cigarettes and liquor, and then move on to marijuana and finally to "harder" drugs. Peer cluster theory argues that religious, school, and familial adjustment variables are related to drug use through mediated peer variables. Other theories which extend these causal notions include parental rejection, social competence, self-efficacy, coping style, and aggression (Botvin, Baker, Renick, Filazzala, & Botvin, 1984; Pentz, 1985; Schinke & Cole, 1995; Schinke & Gilchrist, 1985). Notwithstanding the overlap between these etiological elements, research as yet offers no parsimonious theory as to how children become chemically dependent as adolescents and young adults (Newcomb, 1995; Schilling & McAlister, 1990).

Family Correlates

Although the evidence is mixed (Jacob, Favorini, Meisel, & Anderson, 1978; Russell, Henderson, & Blume, 1984), a large body of evidence points to the association between substance dependence and many indicators of family disadvantage and dysfunction (Hawkins, Catalano, & Miller, 1992; Hesselbrock, 1986). Genetic vulnerability of children of alcoholics is demonstrable, but social learning is at least as plausible in explaining most generational effects of problem drinking. In examining family contributions to adolescent substance abuse, it is possible to generalize across studies with well-defined and relatively large samples; to use instruments with known reliability and validity, and to draw upon established developmental, psychological, and cross-cultural constructs (e.g., Beauvais & Oetting, 1988; Brook, Whiteman, Nomura, Gordon, & Gordon, 1988; Kline, Canter, & Robin, 1987; Simons & Robertson, 1989). Thus, there is little dispute that youths who become problem users often come from families characterized by family disruption, parent–child conflict, nonadherence to traditional values, and use of drugs by older family members. One review of family correlates of alcohol, tobacco, and other drug use in children and adolescents (Kumpfer & Alvarado, 1995) listed no fewer than 10 sets of variables: (1) parental and sibling drug use, (2) poor socialization practices, (3) poor child supervision, (4) poor child discipline, (5) adverse parent–child relationships, (6) family discord and violence, (7) family chaos and stress, (8) poor parental mental health, (9) family social isolation, and (10) differential family acculturation. Although many of these variables overlap with other individual or sociocultural correlates, each of these 10 areas is supported by multiple lines of inquiry.

Family theorists perceive substance abuse as a critical organizing element in a family system. A review of the theories on substance use, particularly alcoholism, finds many creative conceptualizations, often unhampered by attention to such knotty issues as measurement and forming of testable hypotheses. Theory generation has clearly outpaced attempts to validate notions concerning the role of chemical dependency in the family. An incomplete list of the most common themes would include the functional role of alcoholism in the family system; painful family rituals; family secrets; and systems of denial, accommodation, and rationalization.

The notion of *codependence*—family members' responses to living with a substance user—has been extremely well received by clinicians and the public. One advocate claimed that codependence is "any suffering and/or dysfunction that is associated with or results from focusing on the needs and behavior of others. . . . Codependence is not only the most common addiction, it is the *base* out of which all our addictions and compulsions emerge" (Whitfield, 1992, p. 816). According to proponents, codependent family members engage in a range of dysfunctional thoughts, feelings, and behaviors, all in response to the chemically dependent individual. Family members and systems become defined by the relationships to the drug user, manifested by elaborate denial systems, a preoccupation with saving or protecting the drug-dependent individual and the family, submergence of personal needs, self-blame, and unexpressed anger. One outcome is substance abuse in other family members.

The concept of codependency has proved so popular that it has come to be applied to any number of problems, such as sexual abuse, disability, and mental illness. Critics argue, however, that codependence is largely untested, that it is diagnostically imprecise, and that it pathologizes both women's caretaking and all families with an alcoholic member (Anderson, 1994). It may well be that codependency will withstand scientific inquiry leading to demonstrably effective interventions. Until then, however, it may be prudent to consider codependency as an interesting set of speculations about how family members respond to substance abuse.

It is tempting to seek simplistic causes that blame parents whose children experiment with drugs and sometimes develop problems of substance abuse and dependence. But it is useful to remember that not so many years ago, practitioners who "treated" families with schizophrenic members were guided by the then well-accepted, and subsequently discredited, theory of the "schizophrenogenic mother." This example serves as a reminder that treatment practices must be derived from science, particularly in the theory-rich field of family therapy.

Community and Other Macro Influences

Child rearing and adolescent development occur in the context of the influences of communities, regional norms, media and commerce, and the values of the society as a whole. As understanding of the person—alone, in the family, or in the adolescent peer culture—expands, so does awareness that these phenomena occur within the sphere of larger social structures and influences. Although many theorists and reformers have focused on the potential harm caused by macro forces, only in recent decades have addiction researchers begun to measure the nature and extent of such influences. Thus, it can be shown that children in low-income neighborhoods are exposed to more alcohol and tobacco ads; that they have easier access to alcohol, tobacco, and other drugs; and that their exposure to unhealthy role models extends

beyond the family and immediate peer culture. The movement of the black middle class out of urban cores has been well documented; one result is that black youth encounter a disproportionate number of adults who exhibit alcohol and drug dependence. Many users of illicit substances also sell drugs, and some exhibit the rewards of such trade. For impoverished youth in a materialistic society, pairing of drug use and such possessions is indeed a powerful influence. In the years ahead, researchers will likely develop more sophisticated methods for measuring the influence of media, material wants, and macrocultural variables on the initiation and maintenance of substance use. Stanton Peele (1989b), a leading critic of many of the prevailing views about drug addiction, correctly points out that the same sort of disturbed family structure observed in alcoholic families is present in most families that fail to provide nurturing environments for children. For now, this view is far more compelling than the suggestion that any single variable or theoretical perspective will explain the relationship between families and substance abuse (Liddle & Dakof, 1995).

Genetic Predisposition

Genetic markers have long been of interest to addiction researchers. A large, albeit inconclusive and somewhat contradictory body of evidence, based on animal models, twin studies, and case-control investigations, suggests that certain heritable characteristics increase the likelihood that an individual will develop alcoholism or other forms of substance abuse (Tabakoff & Hoffman, 1988; Tarter, 1988). Heritable variables may be demographic (e.g., race-ethnicity, gender) or physiological (e.g., levels of serotonin, hormonal reactions).

Ethnic–Racial Determinants

Patterns of low levels of drinking among some ethnic-racial groups are as intriguing as extremely high rates among other populations. For example, rates of alcohol dependency and abuse are high among persons of Irish background, and lower among Italian descendants, even though drinking is encouraged in both of these cultures. Often cited are the extremely low rates of alcoholism among Jews, and the tragically high rates among most Native American and Alaskan Native peoples.

African Americans tend to drink and smoke less than whites during their adolescent years, but among males, these patterns are reversed in later years (Caetano & Kaskutas, 1995; Kandel, 1995; National Institute on Alcohol Abuse and Alcoholism [NIAAA], 1990). Abstinence rates tend to be high for African Americans, and other indicators also suggest low overall rates of use for most substances among school-age African Americans (U.S. Department of Health and Human Services, 1996). Paradoxically, black Americans also tend to have high rates of drug and alcohol dependence, as evidenced by surveys and secondary indicators, including arrests, emergency room episodes, and medical examiner data (Brown & Alterman, 1992). Together, these findings suggest that although in aggregate drug use is low for African Americans, heavy use beginning in early adulthood often leads to problems of drug dependence.

Beginning in high school, Hispanic males have higher rates of alcohol use and problem use than either white or African American males (Kann et al., 1996; NIAAA, 1990). Previous surveys found that Hispanic women had high abstention rates (Caetano & Kaskutas, 1995; NIAAA, 1990). More recent data, however, indicate that rates of lifetime, current, and heavy episodic drinking among high school Hispanic females are comparable to rates for male and female whites and Hispanic males (Kann et al., 1996). Hispanic male and female students have comparable rates of lifetime cocaine use. About 16% of Hispanic students reported lifetime use of cocaine, at a rate respectively, 2.5 and 8 times that of white and black students (Kann et al, 1996). Thus, recent data on high school students indicate that Hispanics as a group exhibit use rates for most substances comparable to other peer groups, with higher rates of alcohol and crack cocaine use.

Data on use of alcohol among Pacific Islanders are limited, but reports based on arrests and surveys indicate that Native Hawaiians appear to drink more heavily than other ethnic groups in Hawaii. Asians are becoming a substantial proportion of the U.S. population, but as yet there are few national data on their use of alcohol, tobacco and other drugs. Although rates differ across the numerous Asian groups, data from state surveys, national youth polls, and other studies depict the following generalities about drug use in this population. Alcohol use is particularly low, and overall rates of substance use are low relative to other ethnic/racial groups, possibly excepting African Americans. However, men from most Asian backgrounds have high rates of smoking; among some Southeast Asian groups, rates are more than double U.S. national averages. Rates of substance use are extremely low for Asian women, and this gender disparity is the highest among all major ethnic groups (Kim, Coletti, Williams, & Hepler, 1995).

Despite many attempts to explain drug use among minority populations, causal interpretations remain equivocal and controversial. Evidence from many arenas demonstrates that differences within racial groups are at least as important as those between groups, suggesting that race is a poor marker for studying genetic predisposition to substance abuse. Disentangling race/ethnicity from social class and culture has always been difficult, more so with the rapid changes in economic, geographic, and demographic patterns. It is clear that poverty and culture interact in complex ways with patterns of drug use initiation, use, dependence, and substance abuse treatment entry, retention, and relapse (Barr, Farrell, Barnes, & Welte, 1993). Unless ethnic–racial identity can be linked to modifiable characteristics, attempts to establish ethnic–racial determinants of substance abuse will remain of limited utility (Fullilove & Fullilove, 1995).

Biological Determinants

Genetic vulnerability to drug abuse may be approached from at least five perspectives (Pickens & Svikis, 1988). These include animal studies, family pedigree studies, twin studies, adoption studies, and high-risk paradigms. Animal models allow for control of many environmental confounds that plague epidemiological studies of genetic susceptibility to substance abuse. After breeding alcohol-preferring and nonpreferring lines of rats, investigators have found several differences, including: behavioral and electroencephalogram (EEG) and other electrophysiological responses to alcohol, tolerance development, and neurochemical factors (McBride, Murphy, Lumeng, & Li, 1989; NIAAA, 1990). Many animal researchers emphasize that biologically determined preferences involve *predisposition* toward alcoholism or other chemical dependency. Whether that predilection eventually translates into a psychoactive substance disorder is determined by a complex of social, environmental, and psychological variables. Perhaps as a result of these complex factors, human studies, in which investigators have attempted to identify biological markers in drug users, have been at once promising, equivocal, and provocative.

Family pedigrees offer relatively low-cost but methodologically problematic vantage points for studying the genetic-familial basis of drug dependence (Stabenau, 1988). Such studies have shown that children of alcoholic parents are more likely to abuse chemical substances themselves as adolescents and adults. Other variables, such as antisocial personality, also appear to be associated with familial transmission of alcoholism. By themselves, these studies leave unanswered the question as to whether genetic or other factors are the important underlying cause of familial transmission of chemical dependency.

An understanding of the genetic aspects of alcohol and other forms of chemical dependency can also be derived from comparisons of identical and fraternal twins (Pickins & Svikis, 1988). Although not all studies agree, findings from several investigations tend to show that the degree of alcoholic predilection is likely to be more proximate within pairs of monozygotic twins than in dizygotic pairs. Though seemingly the ideal way to control for nature versus nurture, twin studies leave open the possibility that identical twins are subject to environmental influences in ways different from the experiences of fraternal twins. A Swedish study of 862 men and 913 women adopted early in life offers strong evidence of the heritability of substance abuse (Cloninger, 1988). Alcohol abuse in the adoptive parents was unrelated to an increased risk of alcoholism in their adoptive children. Yet biological fathers with histories of alcohol abuse had a twofold excess of sons with alcohol abuse, when compared with those sons of fathers with no alcohol abuse. As with the bulk of the human studies on heritability of substance abuse, observed effects were larger for men than for women.

Tarter and Edwards (1988) have assembled findings to show that virtually any trait or characteristic which predicts substance abuse shares considerable variance with other predictors. In their view, these common characteristics can be described as excesses (e.g. hyperactivity, stealing, an inability to be soothed) which all contain elements of risk taking, compulsivity, and self-destructiveness. Tarter and Edwards observed that intrauterine, perinatal, and postnatal events may account for as much variance as genetic factors. Moreover, the "numerous pathways to a variety of unfavorable outcomes . . . the [changing] parameters of vulnerability . . . external stressors . . . available protective influences of the environment . . . and the mode of expression of outcome (e.g., gambling, alcohol, drugs, etc.) is contingent on macro environment factors which vary from culture to culture. Thus, accurate prediction may not be possible" (p. 78). A decade later, it is now certain that scientists will continue to develop more precise markers that signal risk for subsequent development of substance abuse disorders. The field of molecular genetics has already begun to specify candidate genes associated with susceptibility to alcoholism, raising fears of what Orwellian purpose such information might serve later. However, molecular biology only expands the methods and promise of the search for trait markers that has existed for many decades (Anthenelli & Schuckit, 1992).

Present Understanding of the Biological, Psychological, and Social Determinants of Substance Abuse

Much progress has been made over the past two decades in comprehending how individual, social, and community factors render some persons vulnerable to becoming chemically dependent. Notwithstanding the remarkable advances in the technology of molecular biology, no single trait has been shown to account for even a moderate amount of variance in determining who will abuse drugs. Multivariate approaches can discriminate alcohol abusers with a relatively high degree of consistency, but findings differ according to number and section of variables, samples selected, and definition of drug abuse. Understanding of the many social, psychosocial, and biological correlates of chemical dependency and of the developmental processes that interact with risk taking provides direction for prevention efforts targeted at various age cohorts in high-risk communities

(Botvin, 1995; Hawkins et al., 1992; Schinke & Cole, 1995).

Several long-established facts about drug use remain unchallenged. Variables of race/ethnicity and socioeconomic status are among the most robust correlates of drug use. Predictive indicators share considerable variance with other indicators of psychopathology, deviance, poverty, and social disorganization. Predictive models have thus far not demonstrably increased the efficacy of chemical dependency treatments (Gerstein, Harwood, & Institute of Medicine, 1990). An unknown but likely small proportion of persons who use psychoactive substances become chemically dependent. Abusive patterns of use often lead to dependence; however, many individuals with drug-related problems may function well in the workplace or in other life domains. Once dependence is established, it is extremely difficult to stop using drugs. Most dependent individuals gain sobriety or long-term reduction through their own efforts, and do so only after repeated attempts. Use of alcohol and other substances declines in the fourth decade of life.

NATURE AND TREATMENT OF SUBSTANCE DEPENDENCE DISORDERS

Is chemical dependency a disease, and, if so, is it treatable? How effective are existing treatments for substance use disorders, and to what extent are they responsive to present understanding of chemical dependence? An understanding of the nature of chemical dependency can be approached by considering these questions.

The Disease Model Controversy

Notwithstanding its serious inadequacies (Alexander, 1988; Peele, 1989a, 1989b), the disease model has come to be the prevailing conceptualization of drug abuse among treatment providers, and to a lesser extent in the scientific community (Miller, 1991; Stephens, 1991; Williams, 1988). Dependence on alcohol or drugs is now perceived by most helping professionals, and by an increasing proportion of the public, as an illness rather than a moral weakness. Alcoholics Anonymous (AA) and the 12-step movements that have grown from AA have been extremely influential in advancing the disease concept of addiction. As most societies tend to ascribe labels implying causality to deviant behavior, the illness metaphor is hardly unique to drug and alcohol problems or to industrialized societies.

If substance use disorders are diseases, they are ailments that are to a large extent anchored in culture, yet are found in varying degrees in virtually all societies. These "diseases" seem to peak in the late adolescent and early adult years, and are uncommon in the elderly. In North America and elsewhere, such diseases disproportionately affect the poor and minorities. These diseases seem to have existed as long as humans have known that certain substances alter their state of being; however, they have affected differing proportions of the populace at different periods in history.

The notion of chemical dependence as illness has been useful in shifting the locus of addiction away from one of moral judgment. Unfortunately, however, the disease concept tends to mask the shades of problem use, and approaches addictive behavior as being essentially a within-person phenomena. In a nation with a technologically advanced health care system that has been organized around acute care, the disease concept evokes an image of medical science ridding the body of drugs. Unfortunately, despite all the evidence to the contrary, substance dependence disorders are often treated as if they were acute conditions.

Treatment Efficacy

Almost all forms of treatment produce measurable improvements over short periods, but effectiveness rates decline substantially over time (Gerstein et al., 1990; National Treatment Improvement Evaluation Study, 1996). Treatment effectiveness varies with social class, goals of treatment, and the evaluation methodology employed. Considerable evidence finds that brief, low-cost interventions are generally at least as effective as costlier long-term treatments (Heather, 1989; Miller & Rollnick, 1991). This fact is not lost on managed care providers, and the substance abuse treatment industry is experiencing a rapid shift toward less expensive forms of care. We next describe the major categories of substance abuse treatment.

Methadone maintenance.   Methadone is an opiate substitute provided in oral form in specialty clinics and physicians' offices. Methadone achieves large reductions, often complete, in heroin use among most patients, and first year dropout rates are far below that of other treatment approaches (Lowinson, Marion, Joseph, & Dole, 1992). However, methadone is not a substitute for nonopiate substances, and cocaine and alcohol remain major problems among methadone patients (El-Bassel, Schilling, Turnbull, & Su, 1993; Schilling et al., 1991).

Residential rehabilitation programs.   These programs attempt to alter addictive behavior by isolating individuals from their environments and daily routines. Many operate with elements drawn from the Minnesota Model, a multicomponent program philosophy based on the disease model and 12-step principles. Most "rehab" programs are designed for at least 6 weeks, many for considerably longer for patients with generous insurance coverage. Individual and group counseling, often provided by social workers, may include family therapy; behavioral strategies to cope with anger, rejection, and boredom; and insight therapy to deal with the antecedents of present dysfunction (Geller, 1992). Uncontrolled studies, based on drug and alcohol use prior to and after treatment, are uniformly positive, demonstrating one-year abstinence rates above 40%. The few controlled studies that have been conducted find that inpatients in rehabilitation programs fared better than controls in less structured programs; nevertheless, one-year abstinence rates are a fraction of those reported in uncontrolled studies (Geller, 1992).

Therapeutic communities.   These programs operate on strictly enforced codes including complete abstinence from drugs (and, in recent years, alcohol), confrontational group sessions, and a hierarchy of privileges and governance. Participants benefit from the group living milieu, involving tasks, rules, and interpersonal discourse. Rigorous program requirements preclude many potential applicants from considering therapeutic communities (TCs). Observed declines in drug use for treated participants must be interpreted in light of 75% one-year attrition rates among the self-selected group who enter TCs (DeLeon & Schwartz, 1984). Declining enrollments

and cost-containment pressures have forced some therapeutic communities to reduce their "mandatory" stay from a year or more to stays as short as 6 months.

Outpatient programs.   These are defined here as individual or group counseling delivered by a staff with expertise in chemical dependency. Both day treatment and evening programs (for working clients) require participation for several hours at a time on at least four days per week. Program activities may include groups, individual sessions, education, and recreation. Other approaches include the use of disulfiram, acupuncture, hypnosis, rational emotive therapy, and programs that combine any number of these elements.

Alcoholics Anonymous.   AA and parallel self-help organizations operate without paid staff, in donated space, on small donations from participants. Until the 1970s, all of the research on AA was fraught with sampling problems. Outcomes focused on attendance and abstinence, and tended to rely on self-report. Most studies have found that more than half of respondents have been abstinent for a year or more. As would be expected, increasingly longer periods of abstinence are predictive of successively lower rates of relapse in the future. Participation in AA is associated with any number of positive indicators, including social adjustment, employment adjustment, and concern for others (Nace, 1992; NIAAA, 1987). Few if any studies have examined cohorts of new 12-step participants over time.

Other Treatment and Control Issues

Need for aftercare and follow-up.   Costly inpatient treatments usually do not have lasting effects unless they are successful in linking the client to aftercare. The objective of aftercare programs should be to help the recovering individual integrate a drug-free, or less harmful lifestyle within an environment that holds many of the same temptations and challenges that reinforced earlier patterns of drug use. It would seem that aftercare should be provided as a normal element of treatment, ideally provided by the same treatment organization and perhaps even by the same treatment staff. Until recently, few programs offered full continuities of care; even now, it is difficult to find systems that creatively facilitate the transition from inpatient, to outpatient, to self-help or other maintenance support. The recent and continuing changes in the structure and coverage of substance-dependence treatment have been driven more by cost factors than by concern for quality or effectiveness. Nevertheless, the expansion of health maintenance organizations (HMOs) or similar capitation-based care structures will make it feasible to develop protocols whereby each discharge would invoke standard procedures for referral/transfer and follow-up, carried out for clinical and evaluative purposes.

Treatment matching.   A few studies (e.g., Jaffe et al., 1996; Miller & Hester, 1986) have shown some success in matching patient characteristics (e.g., craving, severity of alcohol dependence) to treatments (e.g., naltrexone or placebo; relapse prevention or supportive therapies). For several reasons, however, the promise of treatment matching remains elusive. As the overall effectiveness of any one treatment episode is low, it is indeed difficult to discern those individuals who will respond better to one treatment than another. Measures of the individual characteristics associated with success in a given type of treatment remain inadequate. Finally, most forms of treatment contain overlapping elements, are inadequately specified, and delivered unevenly (Gerstein, 1994).

Controlled drinking/drug use.   Whether individuals with problematic use patterns can learn to use in moderation remains an issue of debate. On the one hand, the nature of drug dependence would suggest that abstinence is the optimal treatment objective, and most recovered individuals spent years in their own failed "controlled use" experiments prior to abstinence. On the other hand, the insistence on abstinence as the only viable goal of almost all present forms of treatment (save for methadone maintenance) overlooks the low efficacy of abstinence-oriented treatments and ignores the reality that on any one day, only a small proportion of substance-dependent individuals are interested in becoming abstinent.

   Given that so few drug-dependent individuals seek abstinence-based treatment, and considering the high rate of relapse that follows all but a small proportion of abstinence attempts, it would be useful to consider a wide range of treatment objectives, pathways into treatment, and ways of reducing harm associated with drug use. Opposition to expanding the range of responses to drug abuse comes from many quarters, and is based on strong belief systems. There remain strong moral objections to any relaxing of laws against illicit substances, and fears that experiments in decriminalization would result in more, not fewer problems. Holding back changes in treatment approaches are the entrenched beliefs in the abstinence-based treatment community—born of the personal recovery experiences of many who work in the field, the historically ideological perspectives in the chemical dependence field, and the resistance to change that characterizes mature organizations and aging movements.

TRENDS, POINTS OF CONFLICT, AND FUTURE DIRECTIONS

Over the past two decades, two trends—polysubstance use and co-occurrence of substance use and other mental disorders—are clearly evident across urban health, social service, drug abuse treatment, and criminal justice settings. A third development is the realization of the low efficacy and high cost of "one-shot" chemical dependency treatments, and lower cost approaches fostered by managed care pressures.

Polysubstance Use

Polysubstance use is now the rule rather than the exception among substance users. For all psychoactive substances other than alcohol, tobacco, caffeine, and possibly marijuana, use of a single drug is uncommon. Chemically dependent individuals often use substances with similar actions, resulting in cross-tolerance, and infrequently, as in the instance of alcohol and barbiturates, in dangerous and sometimes fatal combinations of drugs. Other users favor combinations of drugs with complementary actions, either ingested simultaneously or timed to counteract the adverse effects that follow the euphoria and sense of well-being. Speedballs—a mixture of heroin and cocaine—have long been used by opiate addicts. More recently, crack cocaine users have taken to using heroin to counteract the "crash" following the short-acting cocaine. Regular alcohol use is reported by users of stimulants and stimulant-like substances, depressants, and substances that have hallucinogenic properties. Heavy use of alcohol is reported by the majority of users of other psychoactive substances (El-Bassel et al., 1993, Gerstein et al., 1990; Wilkinson, Leigh, Cordingley, Martin, & Lei, 1987).

Co-occurrence of Substance Dependence and Other Disorders

A second trend is the increasingly frequent co-occurrence of substance abuse and other psychiatric disorders (Alterman, 1985; Day & Leonard, 1985; Finn, Kleinman, & Pihl, 1990; Kleinman et al., 1990). In part, the increase may be due to clinicians and researchers who now inquire about phenomena which were overlooked in the past, and a concomitant rapprochement between once disparate camps of substance abuse treatment and mental health services. Beyond this phenomena of reporting what was previously disregarded, it is reasonable to assume that chemical dependency and other psychiatric disorders do covary more than in the past. Definitive studies are lacking, but secular trends could readily account for an increase in the covariance of chemical dependency and psychiatric disorders. Some of these trends include deinstitutionalization; homelessness; violence; and a general decline of social, and economic systems within impoverished, decaying communities.

Need for Innovative, Efficacious, and Efficient Approaches to Treatment

Never before has there been a more obvious need for practical solutions to pernicious and problems of substance abuse and related ills of mental disorder, poverty and homelessness, family disorganization, and social disorder. Some of the most convincing arguments in favor of adequate funding across a spectrum of applied investigative arenas can be found in the literature on biological determinants of chemical dependency and other mental disorders. An overarching theme across all of the biological findings is the importance of understanding how genetic and other biologically determined predispositions are expressed as substance dependence and psychiatric dis-

order only in the context of developmental, sociocultural, and environmental influences.

An extensive federally supported program of pharmacological studies will continue, but it may be unreasonable to hope that any single prescribed medicine will achieve results approaching that of lithium used in the management of bipolar disorders, or the expanding array of compounds used in treating depression and psychotic disorders.

As outlined in a landmark report of experts assembled by the Institute of Medicine (Gerstein et al., 1990), more effort should be directed at expanding the range of treatment options. Research directions include patient–treatment matching, graded treatments, and planned aftercare. Because success is quite high for users who remain in treatment, research should emphasize treatment attraction and prevention of attrition and relapse. Studies are also needed that develop and test interventions, maintenance, and harm reduction strategies that attend to the chronic, relapsing, and destructive nature of substance dependence.

At present, treatment is but an incomplete answer to the serious problems of substance use. Therefore, prevention, early intervention and harm reduction studies should receive additional research funding. Unlike cancer and heart disease, addictions do the most harm when young people are becoming adults, beginning careers, and rearing families. Thus, even modest reductions in high-risk behavior among certain age groups and high-risk populations may yield substantial and lifelong returns.

SUMMARY

Recorded declines in the use of alcohol, tobacco, and other drugs over the past decade will translate into reductions in harm related to use of such substances. Smoking rates in general continue to decline, and tobacco use restrictions have reduced "secondhand" tobacco use. Alcohol consumption has also declined, in part as a result of the aging of the population. Overall rates of crack cocaine use have declined. Declines in certain cancers have been attributed to reductions in smoking, and alcohol-related fatalities and injuries have dropped markedly over the past several decades.

Over the past ten years, scientists have made substantial progress in their understanding of the biological, psychological, and social determinants of substance use, abuse, and dependence. Advances in molecular biology offer hope for the development of compounds that would either block the effects of drugs with high abuse/dependence potential, or replenish naturally occurring chemicals where their insufficiency is linked to drug misuse. The discriminative properties of drugs are better understood now than in decades past, as are the relationships between environmental cues and patterns and circumstances of drug use. Constellations of risk and protective factors have been depicted, and these lines of inquiry have influenced the design of prevention programs targeted at youth. Investigators are beginning to describe the relationship between drug abuse and violence. Studies of macro variables, such as neighborhood destabilization, unemployment trends, and community norms have begun to shape perspectives that until recently ignored the influences of broad social forces on drug use initiation, abuse, and dependence.

Such advances notwithstanding, substance abuse will not succumb soon to the inexorable progress of a concerted national effort to understand and attend to the causes and consequences of the problems of alcohol, tobacco, and other drug use. Law enforcement officials have been increasingly candid about the nation's ability to stop the flow of illegal drugs in foreign countries, at the border, or at domestic manufacturing sites. Use of tobacco, alcohol, and some illicit substances appear to be rising among youth, after many years of declining rates (U.S. Department of Health and Human Services, 1996). Large segments of the population—low-income African Americans and Hispanics, and the poor in general—remain affected by the scourge of drug abuse. Still elusive are satisfactory means of intervening in social problems associated with substance abuse: other forms of psychiatric disorder, unwanted pregnancy and ineffectual child rearing, crime and violence, and poverty and homelessness. The expanded understanding of the precursors, nature, correlates, and consequences of drug dependence has thus far not been accompanied by parallel advances in prevention or treatment, via sociobehavioral or biomedical means. Existing substance abuse treatments have been shown to be only modestly efficacious, particularly among indi-

gent persons with few personal or social resources. Insurers have forced changes in the scope and nature of treatment for drug abuse disorders, but the degree to which behavioral health will achieve parity under health maintenance organizations remains to be seen.

In an earlier version of this chapter, we envisioned that helping professionals would spend increasing portions of their time dealing with the threat, existence, and consequences of substance abuse. Five years later, we see little reason to alter that prognostication. By many parameters, the problems of drug dependence in the United States appear to be at least as troublesome, if not more so, than a few years ago. If present trends of increasing economic inequality and instability continue, it seems likely that society will have to contend with still worse problems of drug dependence. It is also possible, of course, that the engine of economic prosperity will create opportunities for disadvantaged groups, resulting in substantial reductions in problems of drug dependence. Under favorable conditions, substantial progress could be realized via modest shifts in the proportions of young persons who experiment with drugs, graduate to abuse and dependence, and remain outside or unaffected by the treatments available. The possibilities for more substantial reductions in the prevalence of substance dependence will depend on overarching social and economic conditions that favorably influence at-risk populations and communities. Even without such developments, it seems plausible that scientists, prevention and treatment advocates, and informed policymakers will together develop improved and enlightened strategies to reduce not only use, but also the harm associated with alcohol, tobacco, and other drugs.

NOTE

1. Laypersons and professionals in the addiction field use the terms *substance abuse, substance dependence, chemical dependency,* and, less often, *addiction* synonymously to describe the habitual or recurrent use of drugs or alcohol characterized by impairment in major life arenas such as work, family lives, or relationships with friends. DSM-IV, of course, differentiates *dependence* and *abuse*.

REFERENCES

Alexander, B. (1988). The disease and adaptive models of addiction: A framework evaluation. In S. Peele (Ed.), *Visions of addiction: Major contemporary perspectives on addiction and alcoholism* (pp. 45–66). Lexington, MA: Lexington Books.

Allen, M., & Frances, R. (1986). Varieties of psychopathology found in patients with addictive disorders: A review. In R. Meyer (Ed.), *Psychopathology and addictive disorders* (pp. 17–38). New York: Guilford Press.

Alterman, A. (1985). Relationships between substance abuse and psychopathology: Overview. In A. Alterman (Ed.), *Substance abuse and psychopathology* (pp. 1–14). New York: Plenum Press.

American Psychiatric Association. (1987). *Diagnostic and statistical manual of mental disorders* (3rd ed., revised). Washington, DC: Author.

American Psychiatric Association. (1994). *Diagnostic and statistical manual of mental disorders* (4th ed.). Washington, DC: Author.

Anderson, S. (1994). A critical analysis of the concept of codependency. *Social Work, 39,* 677–685.

Anthenelli, R., & Schuckit, M. (1992). Genetics. In J. Lowinson, R. Millman, & J. Langrod (Eds.), *Substance abuse: A comprehensive textbook,* 2nd ed. (pp. 39–50). Baltimore, MD: Williams & Wilkins.

Anthony, J., Warner, L., & Kessler, R. (1994). Comparative epidemiology of dependence on tobacco, alcohol, controlled substances, and inhalants: Basic findings from the National Comorbidity Study. *Experimental and Clinical Psychopharmacology, 2,* 244–268.

Babor, T. (1995). The road to DSM-IV: Confessions of an erstwhile nosologist. *Drug and Alcohol Dependence, 38,* 75–79.

Barr, K., Farrell, M., Barnes, G., & Welte, J. (1993). Race, class, and gender differences in substance abuse: Evidence of middle class/underclass polarization among black males. *Social Problems, 40,* 314–327.

Beauvais, F. (1996). Trends in drug use among American Indian students and dropouts, 1975–1994. *American Journal of Public Health, 86,* 1594–1598.

Beauvais, F., & Oetting, E. (1988). *Epidemiology of inhalant abuse: An update.* [Research monograph No. 85, pp. 34–48]. Rockville, MD: National Institute on Drug Abuse.

Bobo, J., Schilling, R., Gilchrist, L., & Schinke, S. (1986). The double triumph: Sustained sobriety and successful cigarette smoking cessation. *Journal of Substance Abuse Treatment, 3,* 21–25.

Borland, R., & Owen, N. (1995). Need to smoke in the context of workplace smoking bans. *Preventive Medicine, 24,* 56–60.

Botvin, G. (1995). Drug abuse prevention in school settings. In G. Botvin, S. Schinke & M. Orlandi (Eds.), *Drug abuse prevention with multiethnic youth* (pp. 169–192). Thousand Oaks, CA: Sage Publications.

Botvin, G., Baker, E., Renick, N., Filazzala, A., & Botvin, E. (1984). A cognitive-behavioral approach to substance abuse prevention. *Addictive Behaviors, 9,* 137–147.

Brook, J., Whitman, M., Nomura, C., Gordon, A., & Cohen, P. (1988). Personality, family, and ecological influences on adolescent drug use: A developmental analysis. *Journal of Chemical Dependency Treatment, 1,* 123–161.

Brown, L., & Alterman, A. (1992). African Americans. In J. Lowinson, R. Millman, & J. Langrod (Eds.), *Substance abuse: A comprehensive textbook,* 2nd ed. (pp. 861–867). Baltimore, MD: Williams & Wilkins.

Caetano, R., & Kaskutas, L. (1995). Changing in drinking patterns among whites, blacks, and Hispanics, 1984–1992. *Journal of Studies on Alcohol, 56,* 558–565.

Cloninger, C. (1988). *Biological vulnerability to drug abuse* [Research monograph No. 89, pp. 52–72]. Rockville, MD: National Institute on Drug Abuse.

Day, N., & Leonard, K. (1985). Alcohol, drug use, and psychopathology in the general population. In A. Alterman (Ed.), *Substance abuse and psychopathology* (pp. 15–44). New York: Plenum Press.

De Leon, G., & Shwartz, S. (1994). Therapeutic communities: What are the retention rates? *American Journal of Drug and Alcohol Abuse, 10,* 267–284.

Donovan, J., & Jessor, R. (1985). Structure of problem behavior in adolescence and young adulthood. *Journal of Consulting and Clinical Psychology, 53,* 890–904.

Edlin, B., Irwin, K., Faruque, S., McCoy, C., Word, C., Serrano, Y., Inciardi, J., Bowser, B., Schilling, R., & Holmberg, S. (1994). Intersecting epidemics—crack cocaine use and HIV infection among inner-city young adults. *New England Journal of Medicine, 331,* 1422–14227.

El-Bassel, N., Schilling, R., Turnbull, J., & Su, K. (1993). Correlates of alcohol use among methadone patients. *Alcoholism: Clinical and Experimental Research, 17,* 681–686.

Ellickson, P., McGuigan, K., Adams, V., Bell, R., & Hays, R. (1996). Teenagers and alcohol misuse in the United States: By any definition, it's a big problem. *Addiction, 91,* 1489–1504.

Erickson, P., Adlaf, E.M., & Smart, R.G. (1987). *The steel drug: Cocaine in perspective.* Lexington, MA: Lexington Books.

Finn, P., Kleinman, I., & Pihl, R. (1990). The lifetime prevalence of psychopathology in men with multigenerational family histories of alcoholism. *Journal of Nervous and Mental Disease, 178,* 500–504.

Fullilove, R., & Fullilove, M. (1995). Conducting research in ethnic minority communities: Considerations and challenges. In G. Botvin, S. Schinke, & M. Orlandi (Eds.), *Drug abuse prevention with multiethnic youth* (pp. 46–56). Thousand Oaks, CA: Sage.

Geller, A. (1992). Rehabilitation programs and halfway houses. In J. Lowinson, R. Millman, & J. Langrod (Eds.), *Substance abuse: A comprehensive textbook,* 2nd ed. (pp. 458–466). Baltimore, MD: Williams & Wilkins.

Gerstein, D. (1994). Outcome research: Drug abuse. In M. Galanter & H. Kleber (Eds.), *The American psychiatric press textbook of substance abuse treatment* (pp. 45–64). Washington, DC: American Psychiatric Press.

Gerstein, D., & Harwood, H. & Institute of Medicine Committee for Substance Abuse Coverage Study. (1990). *Treating drug problems.* Washington DC: National Academy Press.

Grinspoon, L., & Bakalar, J. (1992). Marihuana. In J. Lowinson, R. Millman, & J. Langrod (Eds.), *Substance abuse: A comprehensive textbook,* 2nd ed. (pp. 236–246). Baltimore, MD: Williams & Wilkins.

Hall, S., Munoz, R., Reus, V., & Sees, K. (1993). Nicotine, negative affect, and depression. *Journal of Consulting and Clinical Psychology, 61,* 761–767.

Hawkins, J., Catalano, R., & Miller, J. (1992). Risk and protective factors for alcohol and other drug problems in adolescence and early adulthood: Implications for substance abuse prevention. *Psychological Bulletin, 112,* 64–105.

Heather, N. (1989). Brief intervention strategies. In R. Hester & W. Miller (Eds.), *Handbook of alcoholism treatment approaches: Effective alternatives* (pp. 93–116). Boston: Allyn and Bacon.

Hesselbrock, V. (1986). Family history of psychopathology in alcoholics: A review and issues. In R. Meyer (Ed.), *Psychopathology and addictive disorders* (pp. 41–56). New York: Guilford Press.

Holmberg, S. (1996). The estimated prevalence and incidence of HIV in 96 large U.S. metropolitan areas. *American Journal of Public Health, 86,* 642–654.

Inciardi, J. (1986). *The war on drugs: Heroine, cocaine, crime, and public policy.* Mountain View, CA: Mayfield.

Jacob, T., Favorini, A., Meisel, S., & Anderson, C. (1978). The spouse, children, and family interactions of the alcoholic: Substantive findings and methodological issues. *Journal of the Study of Alcohol, 39,* 1231–1251.

Jaffe, A., Rounsaville, B., Chang, G., Schottenfeld, R., Meyer, R., & O'Malley, S. (1996). Naltrexone, relapse prevention, and supportive therapy with alcoholics: An analysis of patient treatment matching. *Journal of Consulting and Clinical Psychology, 64,* 1044–1053.

Jarvik, M., & Schneider, N. (1992). Nicotine. In J. Lowinson, R. Millman, & J. Langrod (Eds.), *Substance abuse: A comprehensive textbook,* 2nd ed. (pp. 334–356). Baltimore, MD: Williams & Wilkins.

Johnston, L., O'Malley, P., & Bachman, J. (1989). *Drug use, drinking, and smoking: National survey results from high school, college, and young adults populations, 1975–1988.* Rockville, MD: National Institute on Drug Abuse. Washington, DC: U.S. Government Printing Office.

Kandel, D. (1995). Ethnic differences in drug use. In G. Botvin, S. Schinke, & M. Orlandi (Eds.), *Drug abuse prevention with multiethnic youth* (pp. 81–104). Thousand Oaks, CA: Sage Publications.

Kandel, D., & Logan, J. (1984). Patterns of drug use from adolescence to young adulthood: Periods of risk for initiation, continued use and discontinuation. *American Journal of Public Health, 74,* 660–666.

Kann, L., Warren, C., Harris, W., Collins, J., Williams, B., Ross, J., & Kolbe, L. (1996, September). Youth risk behavior surveillance— United States, 1995. *Morbidity and Morality Weekly Report, 45*(SS-4).

Kim, S., Coletti, S., Williams, C., & Hepler, N. (1995). Substance abuse prevention involving Asian/Pacific Islander American Communities. In G. Botvin, S. Schinke, & M. Orlandi (Eds.), *Drug abuse prevention with multiethnic youth* (pp. 295–326). Thousand Oaks, CA: Sage Publications.

Kirk, S., & Kutchins, H. (1992). *The selling of DSM: The rhetoric of science in psychiatry.* New York: Aldine De Gruyter.

Kleinman, P., Miller, A., Millman, R., Woody, G., Todd, T., Kemp, J., & Lipton, D. (1990). Psychopathology among cocaine abusers entering treatment. *Journal of Nervous and Mental Disease, 178,* 442–447.

Kline, R., Canter, W., & Robin, A. (1987). Parameters of teenage alcohol use: A path analytic conceptual model. *Journal of Consulting and Clinical Psychology, 55,* 521–528.

Kumpfer, K., & Alvarado, R. (1995). Strengthening families to prevent drug use in multiethnic youth. In G. Botvin, S. Schinke, & M. Orlandi (Eds.), *Drug abuse prevention with multiethnic youth* (pp. 255–294). Thousand Oaks, CA: Sage Publications.

L'Abate, L., Farrar, J., & Sterritella, D. (1992). *Handbook of differential treatments for addiction.* Boston: Allyn and Bacon.

Lichentenstein, E., & Brown, R. (1982). Current trends in the modification of cigarette dependence. In A. Bellack & M. Hersen (Eds.), *International handbook of behavior modification and therapy* (pp. 575–612). New York: Plenum Press.

Liddle, H., & Dakof, G. (1995). Efficacy of family therapy for drug abuse: Promising but not definitive. *Journal of Marital and Family Therapy, 21,* 511–543.

Lowinson, J., Marion, I., Joseph, H., & Dole, V. (1992). Methadone maintenance. In J. Lowinson, R. Millman, & J. Langrod (Eds.), *Substance abuse: A comprehensive textbook,* 2nd ed. (pp. 550–561). Baltimore, MD: Williams & Wilkins.

Maxmen, J., & Ward, N. (1995). *Essential psychopathology and it's treatment.* New York: Norton.

McBride, W., Murphy, J., Lumeng, L., & Li, T. (1989). Serotonin and ethanol preference. In M. Galanter (Ed.), *Recent developments in alcoholism* (Vol. 7, pp. 187–209). New York: Plenum Press.

McSherry, T. (1988). *Epidemiology of inhalant abuse; An update.* [Research monograph No. 85, pp. 106–120]. Rockville, MD: National Institute on Drug Abuse.

Milby, J., Jolly, P., & Beidleman, W. (1984). Substance abuse: Drugs. In S. Turner & M. Hersen (Ed.), *Adult psychopathology and diagnosis* (pp. 105–139). New York: Wiley.

Miller, N. (1991). Drug and alcohol addiction as a disease. *Alcohol treatment quarterly, 8,* 43–55.

Miller, W., Hester, R. (1986). Matching problem drinkers with optimal treatments. In W. Miller & N. Heather (Eds.), *Treating addictive behaviors: Processes of change* (pp. 175–203). New York: Plenum Press.

Miller, W., & Rollnick, S. (1991). Brief intervention. In W. Miller & S. Rollnick (Eds.), *Motivational interviewing.* New York: Guilford Press.

Mitchell, R. (1995). Smoking in the workplace: A conflict between personal rights and economic realities. *Law and Psychology Review, 19,* 217–237.

Nace, E. (1992). Alcoholics Anonymous. In J. Lowinson, R. Millman, & J. Langrod (Eds.), *Substance abuse: A comprehensive textbook,* 2nd ed. (pp. 486–495). Baltimore, MD: Williams & Wilkins.

National Center for Health Statistics. (1996). *Health United States, 1995.* Hyattsville, MD: U.S. Public Health Service.

National Institute on Alcohol Abuse and Alcoholism. (1987). *Alcohol and health.* Rockville, MD: U.S. Department of Health and Human Services.

National Institute on Alcohol Abuse and Alcoholism. (1990). *Alcohol and health.* Rockville, MD: U.S. Department of Health and Human Services.

National Institute on Drug Abuse. (1989). *National household survey on drug abuse: Population estimates 1988.* Rockville, MD: U.S. Department of Health and Human Services.

National Institute on Drug Abuse. (1995). *National household survey on drug abuse: Population estimates 1994*. Rockville, MD: U.S. Department of Health and Human Services.

National Treatment Improvement Evaluation Study. (1996, September). *Preliminary report: The persistent effects of substance abuse treatment—one year later*. U.S. Department of Health and Human Services, Substance Abuse and Mental Health Services Administration Center for Substance Abuse Treatment.

Newcomb, M. (1995). Drug use etiology among ethnic minority adolescents. In G. Botvin, S. Schinke, & M. Orlandi (Eds.), *Drug Abuse Prevention with multiethnic youth* (pp. 105–129). Thousand Oaks, CA: Sage Publications.

Oetting, E., Edwards, R., & Beauvais, F. (1988). Social and psychological factors underlying inhalant abuse. In R. Crider & B. Rouse (Eds.), *Epidemiology of inhalant abuse: An update* (pp. 172–203). Rockville, MD: National Institute on Drug Abuse.

Peele, S. (1988). Can alcoholism and other drug addiction problems be treated away or is the current treatment binge doing more harm than good? *Journal of Psychoactive Drugs, 20*, 375–383.

Peele, S. (1989). *Diseasing of America: Addiction treatment out of control*. Lexington, MA: Lexington Books.

Peele, S. (1989). A moral vision of addiction: How people's values determine weather they become and remain addicts. In S. Peele (Ed.), *Visions of addiction* (pp. 201–233). Lexington, MA: Lexington Books.

Pentz, M. (1985). Social competence and self-efficacy as determinants of substance use in adolescence. In S. Shiffman & T. Wills (Eds.), *Coping and substance use* (pp. 117–145). New York: Academic Press.

Pickens, R., & Svikis, D. (1988). *Biological vulnerability to drug abuse* [Research monograph No. 89, pp. 1–8]. Rockville, MD: National Institute on Drug Abuse.

Robbins, E., Katz, S., & Stern, M. (1985). Identification and treatment of substance abuse problems in the emergency room. In A. Alterman (Ed.), *Substance abuse and psychopathology* (pp. 239–288). New York: Plenum Press.

Roffman, R., & George, W. (1988). Cannabis abuse. In D. Donovan & G. Marlatt (Eds.), *Assessment of addictive behaviors* (pp. 325–363). New York: Guilford Press.

Rosecan, J., & Spitz, H. (1987). Cocaine reconceptualized: Historical overview. In H. Spitz, & J. Rosecan (Eds.), *Cocaine abuse: New directions in treatment and research* (pp. 5–18). New York: Brunner/Mazel.

Russell, M., Henderson, C., & Blume, S. (1984). *Children of alcoholics: A review of the literature*. New York: Children of Alcoholics Foundation.

Schilling, R., El-Bassel, N., Schinke, S., Nichols, G., Botvin, G., & Orlandi, M. (1991). Sexual behavior, attitudes toward safer sex, and gender among a cohort of 244 recovering IV drug users. *International Journal of the Addictions, 26*, 865–883.

Schilling, R., Gilchrist, L., & Schinke, S. (1985). Smoking in the workplace: Review of critical issues. *Public Health Reports, 100*, 473–479.

Schilling, R., & McAlister, A. (1990). Preventing drug use in adolescents through media interventions. *Journal of Consulting and Clinical Psychology, 58*, 416–424.

Schinke, S., & Cole, K. (1995). Prevention in community settings. In G. Botvin, S. Schinke, & M. Orlandi (Eds.), *Drug abuse prevention with multiethnic youth* (pp. 215–232). Thousand Oaks, CA: Sage Publications.

Schinke, S., & Gilchrist, L. (1985). Preventing substance abuse with children and adolescents. *Journal of Consulting and Clinical Psychology, 53*, 596–602.

Simons, R., & Robertson, J. (1989). The impact of parenting factors, deviant peers and coping styles upon adolescent drug use. *Family Relations, 38*, 273–281.

Stabenau, J. (1988). *Biological vulnerability to drug abuse* [Research monograph No. 89, pp. 25–41]. Rockville, MD: National Institute on Drug Abuse.

Stephens, R. (1991). *The street addict role: A theory of heroin addiction*. Albany: State University of New York Press.

Tabakoff, B., & Hoffman, P. (1988). Genetics and biological markers of risk for alcoholism. *Public Health Reports, 103*, 690–697.

Tarter, R. (1988). Are there inherited behavioral traits

that predispose to substance abuse? *Journal of Consulting and Clinical Psychology, 56,* 189–196.

Tarter, R., & Edwards, K. (1988). Vulnerability to alcohol and drug abuse: A behavioral-genetic view. In S. Peele (Ed.), *Visions of addiction* (pp. 67–84). Lexington, MA: Lexington Books.

U.S. Department of Health and Human Services. (1990). *The health benefits of smoking cessation.* Washington, DC: U.S. Government Printing Office.

U.S. Department of Health and Human Services (Author). (1996). *Monitoring the future study: Summary of findings through 1995.* Washington, DC: U.S. Government Printing Office.

Whitfield, C. (1992). Co-dependence, addictions, and related disorders. In J. Lowinson, R. Millman, & J. Langrod (Eds.), *Substance Abuse: A Comprehensive Textbook,* 2nd ed. (pp. 816–831). Baltimore, MD: Williams & Wilkins.

Wiesbeck, G., Schuckit, M., Kalmijn, J., Tipp, J., Bucholz, K., & Smith, T. (1996). An evaluation of the history of marihuana withdrawal syndrome in a larger population. *Addiction, 91,* 1469–1478.

Wilkinson, D., Leigh, G., Cordingley, J., Martin, G., & Lei, H. (1987). Dimensions of a multiple drug use and a topology of drug users. *British Journal of Addiction, 82,* 259–273.

Williams, R. (1988). Nature, nurture, and family. *New England Journal of Medicine, 318,* 770–771.

World Health Organization. (1952). Expert Committee on Mental Health (Alcoholism Subcommittee). In *World Health Organization Technical Report Series, No. 48.* (pp. 3–39).

World Health Organization. (1996). *Http://www.who .ch/programmes/psu/pres3.htm.*

CHAPTER 17

SEXUAL DYSFUNCTION AND DEVIATION

Gordon C. Nagayama Hall
Kent State University

Barbara L. Andersen and Susan L. Aarestad
Ohio State University

Christy Barongan
Kent State University

INTRODUCTION

Examination of the DSM-IV diagnostic criteria suggest that the sexual dysfunctions can be conceptually grouped using a sexual response cycle framework: specifically, desire, excitement, orgasm, and resolution. There are significant interrelationships among the phases, and dysfunctional responses in one domain may indicate disruptions of other phases as well. However, there are also sufficient data to suggest that each phase has unique aspects too.

As noted by Rosen and Beck (1988), there is "a fundamental assumption underlying most conceptualizations of sexual response," and that is that "sexual arousal processes are likely to follow a predictable sequence of events, and that a cyclical pattern of physiological responding can potentially

be identified" (p. 25). Yet, there has been disagreement about the number and importance of each phase. While popularized by Masters and Johnson (1966), the concept of stages of sexual engagement has early origins (e.g., Ellis, 1906). The number of stages noted by clinicians has ranged from two to four. The phases of desire, plateau, and resolution are inconsistently represented, whereas a two-dimensional model of (1) an arousal/excitement period and (2) an orgasm or orgasm/immediate postorgasm period has been consistent. Historically, researchers have focused on understanding sexual excitement/arousal, and contemporary research focuses on sexual desire (e.g., Beck, 1995) and individual differences (Andersen & Cyranowski, 1994).

The response cycle model offers a physiologic description of the dysfunctions, and the current version of DSM takes a physiologic approach to defining the dysfunctions (American Psychiatric Association [APA], 1994). However, it is often the individual's behavioral disruptions or the affective/emotional concomitants that prompt identification and diagno-

These efforts were supported by research funds to Barbara L. Andersen from the American Cancer Society (PBR-89A) and the U.S. Army Medical Research Acquisition Activity (DAMD17-96-1-6294).

sis of sexual dysfunctions. Thus, descriptive information on the dysfunctions includes the phenomenological context for the physiologic responses.

Central to the discussion on etiology is sexual self-schema theory, a cognitive approach to understanding the importance of one's sexual self-view (Andersen & Cyranowski, 1994; Andersen & Espindle, in preparation). One's sexual self-view is derived from past experience, is manifest in current experience, and guides the processing of domain-relevant social information. Well-articulated schemas may function as a quick referent of one's sexual history, and also as a reference point for information—judgments, decisions, inferences, responses, and behaviors—about the current and future sexual self. In addition to regulating intrapersonal processes, responses, and behaviors, sexual self-schemas mediate interpersonal phenomena, the most obvious being sexual relationships.

For women, cognitive views consist of two positive aspects—an inclination to experience romantic/passionate emotions and a behavioral openness to sexual experiences and/or relationships—and a negative aspect—embarrassment and/or conservatism—which appears to be a deterrent to sexual expression. These important forces can be manifest in four different typologies: positive, negative, aschematic, and coschematic.

Women with a *positive sexual schema* view themselves as emotionally romantic or passionate, and as behaviorally open to romantic and sexual relationships and experiences. These women tend to be liberal in their sexual attitudes and are generally free of such social inhibitions as self-consciousness or embarrassment. This schematic representation is not merely a summary statement of sexual history; it also marks current and future possibilities, as positive-schema women anticipate more sexual partners in the future than do their negative-schema counterparts. Despite this seemingly unrestricted view of sexuality, it is perhaps important to note that affects and behaviors indicative of romantic, loving, and intimate attachments are also central to women with positive sexual schemas, as they report extensive histories of romantic ties. Thus, the positive schematic representation of a sexual woman includes both arousal/drive and romantic/attachment elements.

Conversely, women holding clear *negative self-*

views of their sexuality tend to describe themselves as emotionally cold or unromantic and as behaviorally inhibited in their sexual and romantic relationships. These women tend to espouse conservative and, at times, negative attitudes and values about sexual matters, and may describe themselves as self-conscious, embarrassed, or not confident in a variety of social and sexual contexts.

Women who are *aschematic* appear to lack a coherent framework for guiding sexually relevant perceptions, cognitions, and behaviors. These women have lower rates of sexual behavior and fewer positive sexual affects (e.g., sexual arousability and love for the sexual partner). Alternatively, coschematics are individuals with a schematic representation of their sexuality, yet one that is, in some sense, "conflicted." Their pattern is to experience both positive and negative self-views; these women report low levels of sexual arousal, yet high levels of romantic attachment (love) for their partners.

Not surprisingly, the sexual self-schemas of men and women differ, but there are also similarities. For men, sexual self-schemas consist of three aspects: views that one is compassionate and romantic; aggressive, powerful, and sexually experienced; and liberal and open-minded rather than conservative or reserved about sexuality. Thus, women and men share an important component of their sexual self-views: self-descriptions of being loving, sensual, and arousable. However, men with positive self-views also have sexual self-views that might be construed as characteristically masculine (e.g., Feingold, 1994; Josephs, Markus, & Tafarodi, 1992), views of the self as powerful, independent, and experienced. Conversely, women note that there may be a negative dimension that might be activated for some, acknowledging a self that is embarrassed, timid, and anxious about a sexual self.

HYPOACTIVE SEXUAL DESIRE DISORDERS

Description

It has been suggested that a lack of interest in sexual activity is one of the most prevalent sexual difficulties seen by clinicians (Schreiner-Engel & Schiavi, 1986). Such views are coupled with estimates of base rates in the range of 25% of the adult population, and with estimates in the United States of 33% for women and 16% for men (Laumann, Gagnon, Michael, & Michaels, 1994; see Ernst, Foldenyi, & Angst, 1993, for data from Switzerland). A decade after Masters and Johnson's (1966) formulation proposing sexual excitement as the first phase of the response cycle, Kaplan (1979) and Lief (1977) asserted an expanded model that began with sexual desire, and the term *inhibited sexual desire* was coined for individuals who chronically failed to initiate or respond to sexual cues (Lief, 1977).

In recent DSM definitions (both III-R and IV), a circular statement (i.e., hypoactive desire is deficient desire) is linked to a cognitive symptom—the absence of sexual fantasy—to define sexual desire dysfunction. Correlational data suggest that, in general, individuals distressed about their sexual functioning report fewer spontaneous sexual fantasies, more feelings of guilt about their fantasies, and premature termination of their fantasizing (Zimmer, Borchardt, & Fischle, 1983). Women diagnosed with desire problems fantasize less during a variety of sexual activities in comparison to nondysfunctional women (Nutter & Condron, 1983), and clinicians have found that fantasy can be useful as it plays an important role in women's sex therapies (e.g., directed masturbation, systematic desensitization). Conversely, epidemiologic data indicate that women use sexual fantasies to increase sexual desire and facilitate orgasm (Lunde, Larsen, Fog, & Garde, 1991). Although these data substantiate the importance of fantasy, they do not confirm that the *absence* of fantasy is pathognomonic for low sexual desire.

Data comparing the frequency of internally generated thoughts (fantasies) and externally generated thoughts (sexual urges) among young heterosexual men and women indicate that men report a greater frequency of urges than do women (4.5 vs. 2.0 per day), although the frequency of fantasies was similar (2.5 per day) (Jones & Barlow, 1990). Related data come from Laumann et al. (1994), indicating a normal distribution in the frequency of autoerotic activities (fantasy, masturbation, use of erotica) among women, with an elevated flat distribution for men. This indicates that, on average, men will have higher rates of autoerotic activities and that there will be less variance among men; for women, this indicates that, on average, women have generally lower rates but that there are more individual differences among women in the frequency of autoerotic activity. Regarding the specific content of women's fantasies, data of Ellis and Symons (1990) suggest that touching, partner responses, and emotional responses may be important, in contrast to the characterization of men's fantasies, which emphasizes visual imagery of the sexual partner or the sexual act.

Symptom descriptions follow of individuals complaining of low desire:

- Individuals with low desire report *general lack of interest in sexual activity*. Individuals with low-desire disorder are thought to be indifferent or neutral toward sexual activity. Such an attitude can be manifested behaviorally by never initiating sexual contact and, perhaps, by avoiding or declining a partner's initiations. Importantly, this lower (but nonzero) level of activity is presumably not due to strong negative responses to interpersonal or genital contact. Thus, the absence of strong negative affect can be contrasted with the affective patterns of rule-out diagnoses, such as arousal deficits or sexual aversion (see the discussion that follows; for an early example of the absence of distinction, see McCarthy, 1984).

- Individuals with low desire may report *few or no sexual cognitions*—fantasies or other pleasant, arousing sexual thoughts and mental images. Sexual urges may not occur or may occur only infrequently. Sexual experiences, when they occur, are not memorable.

- In terms of *self-description,* individuals with low desire may have an aschematic self-view (Andersen & Cyranowski, 1994). That is, they do not view themselves as compassionate, loving, or arousable, and they are not open to, and do not willingly approach, sexual venues. Affectively, they are not engaged in the sexual domain, with their neutrality marked by weak positive feelings, and, for women, weak negative feelings as well.

- Disruption in the frequency, focus, intensity, or duration of sexual activity may occur. Individuals with desire problems may continue with sexual activity, albeit at a low frequency (this circumstance might be contrasted to the absence of all sexual activity as may occur with the arousal difficulties noted below). The feelings of low desire may, in turn, result in lower levels of arousal and orgasmic responsiveness.

Etiology

Current theories range from purely dynamic models to ones emphasizing biologic factors. The latter models emphasize hormonal mechanisms, and the data are most consistent for the necessary (but not sufficient) role of androgens, probably testosterone. For this model, supporting data come from men (e.g., O'Carroll, Shapiro, & Bancroft, 1985). Bancroft (1988) proposes that the occurrence of spontaneous erections during sleep are the behavioral manifestations of the androgen-based neurophysiological substrate of sexual desire; in contrast, erections with fantasy or erotic visual cues are seen as evidence for androgen-independent responses.

Hormone/sexual behavior relationships for women are less clear, although estrogen, progesterone, and androgen (testosterone) have been studied. Regarding estrogen effects, it is clear that some amount of estrogen is necessary for normal vaginal lubrication, and receipt of estrogen replacement therapy following menopause may reduce the problematic symptoms (e.g., lack of lubrication, atrophic vaginitis) and allow sexual activity or functioning to proceed unimpaired (Walling, Andersen, & Johnson, 1990). In contrast, progesterone may actually have an inhibitory effect (Bancroft, 1988). Finally, testosterone may have direct effects on sexual functioning; both Bancroft and Wu (1983) and Schreiner-Engle, Schiavi, Smith, and White (1982) have found positive relationships between testosterone levels and frequency of masturbation and vaginal responses to erotic stimuli. In studies of women for whom estrogen therapy was not effective for postmenopausal symptoms, testosterone administration improved sexual desire and related outcomes (Studd et al., 1977; Burger et al., 1984). Perhaps the most direct data on this topic are those from Alexander and Sherwin (1993). In studying 19 oral contraceptive users, they reported that plasma levels of free testosterone were correlated with self-report measures of sexual desire, sexual thoughts, and anticipation of sexual activity. Yet, an interesting and more direct test of the hypothesis

that testosterone is related to sexual cognitions was disconfirmed; using a selective attention (dichotic listening) task, there was no relationship between levels of free testosterone and an attentional bias for sexual stimuli. Finally, a clinical study by Schreiner-Engel, Schiavi, White, and Ghizzani (1989) is relevant. They compared 17 women who met DSM criteria for loss of desire with 13 healthy, sexually active women. Blood samples were drawn every three or four days for one menstrual cycle and were analyzed for testosterone, estradiol, progesterone, prolactin, and luteinizing hormone. No differences between the groups were found, and subgroup analyses (e.g., comparison of women with lifelong versus acquired loss of desire) were also disconfirming. At present, it is unclear whether or not physiologic measures, and hormonal assays in particular, are useful physiologic indicators of sexual desire.

Psychological models of sexual desire do not, in the main, emphasize biological contributors, even as cofactors. For example, Kaplan (1979), in her influential volume *Disorders of Sexual Desire*, reiterated the psychoanalytic position of libido as an innate emotional force that would be expressed in either sexual or nonsexual outlets. It would follow, then, that any inhibition of desire would be due to the unconscious repression or conscious suppression of urges for sexual contact. In either case, such defenses would arise from intrapsychic conflicts surrounding sexuality.

There are interactional models of desire that emphasize other, nondynamic, psychological processes (see also discussion by Beck, 1995). Levine (1992), for example, highlights the role of sexual drive, seen as a biologically based source, and the individual's behavioral and cognitive efforts to seek sexual stimulation. In contrast, Singer and Toates (1987) offer a central nervous system–mediated motivational model. They propose that sexual motivation, like hunger or thirst, emerges from an interaction of external incentives (i.e., a sexual stimulus) and internal states (e.g., sexual deprivation).

We suggest a psychological conceptualization: the sexual self-views of those at risk for sexual desire disorders would, for both women and men, be characterized by an aschematic self-view (Andersen & Cyranowski, 1994; Andersen & Espindle, in preparation). Such individuals, on average, have lower rates of lifetime sexual activity and a narrower range of sexual activities, if involved in a sexual relationship. Affectively, they experience lower levels of positive sexual emotions, such as arousal. Yet, they are not driven from sexual encounters because of negative affect, as they are not incapacitated by sexual anxiety or embarrassment; still, they are not open to (or inviting of) sexual experiences. Finally, their affective ambivalence may be that centered upon love, romance, and compassion for partners—feelings that are notably lacking. Thus, such individuals are less apt to partner, fall in love, or be affectively satisfied with their romantic relationships. In short, these behavioral, cognitive, and affective experiences are consolidated to promote and maintain low levels of sexual desire.

Course and Treatment

Much of the difficulty with this diagnosis stems from the relative dearth of data, but descriptive studies of clinical samples generally confirm the clinical description. In a report of 59 women diagnosed with desire disorder, Stuart, Hammond, and Pett (1987) reported that although no differences were found in the frequency of intercourse in comparisons with nondysfunctional women, the women with desire disorder reported significantly lower levels of sexual arousal. Other important relationship difficulties included women's lower levels of romantic love and compassion for their partners. In a brief diagnostic report with data from 900 patients, Segraves and Segraves (1991) reported on sexual dysfunction comorbidity. Of the 475 women diagnosed, 41% had either accompanying arousal or orgasm dysfunctions, and 18% had both. For the 113 men diagnosed, 47% also had secondary diagnosis of erectile dysfunction. Taken together, these data suggest the problematic relationship context for those with desire dysfunctions, and the potential chronicity and pervasiveness of their sexual difficulties.

O'Carroll (1991), in reviewing the treatment literature for desire disorders, noted that treatment intervention trials have included heterogeneous samples, making it impossible to determine the efficacy of any particular treatment for the disorder. However, Hurlbert and colleagues (Hurlbert, 1993; Hurlbert, White, Powell, & Apt, 1993) provided orgasm consistency training (i.e., using maximally stimulating techniques and intercourse positions to achieve coital orgasm regularly) with 39 women with desire disorder. Women were assigned to conjoint treatment, women-only treatment, or a wait-list control. Measures of sexual arousability, sexual satisfaction, and sexual assertiveness increased significantly for intervention women, and gains were stronger and maintained longer (6-month follow-up) for the women in the conjoint condition. These results underscore the importance of partner factors, and they are consistent with the aschematic conceptualization of the dysfunction.

SEXUAL AVERSION DISORDER

Description

Extreme negative reactions to sexual stimuli have been termed sexual aversions. In DSM-IV, *sexual aversion* is defined as "persistent or recurrent extreme aversion to, and avoidance of, all or almost all, genital contact with a sexual partner" (APA, 1994, p. 500). The behavioral reference of complete (or almost complete) absence of genital contact presumably signifies that all sexual activity is halted, so that the latter stages of the sexual response cycle would thus be circumvented. Aside from specific genital avoidance, there may be wide variation in the clinical pattern of avoidance. Some people proceed up to the point of genital exposure during sex, but others become so avoidant that there is generalization to many stimuli, however sexually vague or intrusive, which become labeled "sexual" and are thus avoided. From an assessment standpoint, aversion may be difficult to distinguish from sexual anxiety with avoidance. At present, there are no experimental or clinical studies that have made the comparison. Finally, the DSM diagnosis is written in a gender-neutral manner, leaving open the possibility that men as well as women could be diagnosed. To date, the literature suggests that the diagnosis is overrepresented among females. For example, on the sexual avoidance subscale of the Katz Sexual Aversion Scale, gender differences were found on 9 of the 10 items, with women scoring in the direction of sexual avoidance (Katz, Gipson, Kearl, & Kriskovich, 1989; Katz, Gipson, & Turner, 1992).

Etiology

Clinicians have noted that sexual aversion disorder poses a diagnostic challenge (Ponticas, 1992), although the key feature is the extreme avoidance of intercourse and related behaviors. Thus, when defined narrowly (i.e., as phobic avoidance), two-factor learning theory explanations can be offered. That is, for the majority of specific-stimulus anxiety-related problems, a single traumatic event or a series of moderately anxiety-provoking events serve as the conditioning stimuli for subsequent fear responses. This first component, the fear response, is then maintained by the second: Avoidance of the feared stimuli is reinforced, and thus maintained, through anxiety reduction. This conceptualization would suggest that the sexual histories of women with sexual aversions might include negative sexual experiences and/or emotions, such as traumatic sexual events (rape), which might have served as the conditioning events. Katz et al. (1992) provide data that support this hypothesis in that women in treatment because of a previous sexual assault scored significantly higher on a questionnaire measure of sexual aversion than a sample of nonassaulted women.

Women without traumatic or conditioning experiences but who have negative sexual self-schemas may be at risk for sexual aversion. Such women are emotionally distant and unromantic, and they are behaviorally inhibited in their sexual and romantic relationships. Their sexually conservative and negative attitudes about sexual matters are pervasive, and they admit to high levels of sexual anxiety and sexual avoidance, and, conversely, to low levels of sexual arousability and sexual satisfaction. They describe themselves as self-conscious, embarrassed, and inadequate in sexual situations. Thus, the negative sexual schema, which guides current and future cognitive processing of sexual behaviors and responses, may provide the diathesis for sexual aversion.

Course and Treatment

At present, only case reports are available on the treatment of sexual aversions. However, anxiety reduction treatments, such as systematic desensitization and sensate focus have been used successfully (e.g., Caird & Wincze, 1974).

MALE AROUSAL (ERECTILE) DISORDER

Description

Among healthy men, the diagnosis of erectile disorder should be made using one primary criterion: partial or complete failure in attaining or maintaining an erection, which interrupts the "completion of sexual activity" (APA, 1994, p. 504). The diagnosis centers around a disruption in the predominant *physiological* response. This is a change from DSM-III-R, which also allowed for a diagnosis if a man persistently lacked feelings of sexual excitement and pleasure during sexual activity. Although many men occasionally fail to achieve an erection, in order for their condition to qualify as a disorder, the frequency of these difficulties should be "persistent" or "recurrent" (APA, 1994, p. 504). Although the onset of the dysfunction does not affect the diagnosis, erectile dysfunction may either be *primary* (i.e., men who report never having had a full erection with sexual activity) or *secondary* (i.e., those who have previously been successful in attaining and maintaining an erection during intercourse). Considering men who seek sexual therapy, erectile difficulty is one of the more common presenting complaints, representing upwards of 40% of male clinical samples (Bancroft & Coles, 1976; Frank, Anderson, & Kupfer, 1976).

When a positive, functional sexual response (erection) would be expected, men evidence physiologic, cognitive, and emotional characteristics that lead to erectile failure. For example, when compared with other men, individuals with erection difficulties do the following:

- Underreport their levels of physiological sexual arousal relative to the magnitude of actual erectile response (Sakheim, Barlow, Abramson, & Beck, 1987)
- Focus their attention on nonerotic rather than erotic cues (Abramson, Barlow, Beck, Sakheim, & Kelly, 1985)
- Report more negative (depressed) feelings (Abramson et al., 1985)
- Report a lack of control over their sexual responses (Beck, Barlow, & Sakheim, 1982)

This dysfunctional process is reiterated and "improved." That is, the dysfunctional individual becomes even more proficient at focusing on the wrong aspects of the sexual context—the consequences of not performing and the continuation of erectile insufficiency. In time, the individual comes to avoid sexual contexts altogether.

Etiology

Historically, anxiety has been the hypothesized mechanism for sexual arousal defects. Wolpe (1958) was the first to emphasize anxiety-based impairment of physiologic responses. In his view, the sympathetic activity characteristic of anxiety inhibits the local (i.e., genital) parasympathetic activity responsible for the initial phases of sexual excitement (erection) in men. Dysfunctional attentional processes and negative affects have been the core of psychological theories. Masters and Johnson (1970) proposed two components: "spectatoring" (i.e., attentional distraction as the individual "watches" for his or her own sexual responding) and negative expectations that the bodily response (e.g., erection) will be inadequate. These components cause anxiety about performance failure (i.e., the absence of the physiologic responses of excitement) to occur. Barlow (1986) provides an overlapping model (see also Beck, 1986).

There may be a variety of predisposing factors for erectile difficulties. Chronic medical conditions and medication side effects are frequent possibilities (Vliet & Meyer, 1982), with the more common conditions including diabetes (Meisler, Carey, Lantinga, & Krauss, 1989), hypertension (Bansal, 1988), vascular inefficiency (Wagner & Metz, 1980), and alcoholism (Fahrner, 1987). In addition, psychiatric patients or other men receiving antipsychotic drug therapy (e.g., phenothiazine tranquilizers) also have erectile difficulties (Fagen, Schmidt, Wise, & Derogatis, 1988; Mitchell & Popkin, 1982). Chronic personality problems and/or antipsychotic drugs are thought to be at the root of their erectile problems. Data are not available on the incidence of erectile difficulties in healthy males. The Kinsey data (Kinsey, Pomeroy, & Martin, 1948) revealed an increasing prevalence of erectile difficulties in men 55 years and older (i.e., 7% at 55 years, 18% at 60 years, 25% at 65 years, 27% at 70 years, 55% at 75 years, and 75% at 80 years), but age and the attendant health conditions are confounded, as the Kinsey study made no medical exclusions. More recent data suggest an overall rate of 10% of men reporting erectile difficulties, with rates consistently in the range of 10% for 20- to 30-year-olds and increasing to the 20% range for 50- to 60-year-olds (Lauman et al., 1994).

Despite extensive study by both psychological and medical researchers, determining the cause(s) of a particular case of erectile disorder remains difficult. Although many clinicians diagnose and treat erectile disorders as *either* psychogenic *or* physiological in origin, research in recent years has revealed that most cases are caused by both psychological and organic factors (Bancroft & Wu, 1985; Hengeveld, 1986). Many psychogenic cases actually have "masked" organic contributors that go undetected by most clinical assessments, and many organic cases require psychological intervention for a complete resolution (Buvat, Buvat-Herbaut, Lemaire, Marcolin, & Quittelier, 1990). Thus, diagnosticians should avoid this rudimentary two-category classification and should exercise great caution when labeling any case as purely psychogenic or purely organic. However, as LoPiccolo and Stock (1986) point out, even a bipolar scale ranging from *primarily organic* to *primarily psychogenic* may not be sufficient. Following the work of Bem (1974), LoPiccolo and Stock propose that organic and psychogenic causation would be more accurately depicted as two orthogonal dimensions. In this way, a case of erectile disorder could have significant contributions from both physiological and psychological factors. Gaining a thorough description of an individual's physiological, cognitive, and emotional history is an essential step in uncovering all contributing factors. This assessment should include questions about the onset of the disorder, rigidity of erections in various situations, and the sexual functioning of the partner.

Several aspects of the diagnostic criteria for erectile disorder merit discussion. First, no mention is made of the presumption of—or necessity for—sexual desire as a prerequisite for sexual arousal. This may be due in part to data dictating that men can respond physically and report subjective arousal under a variety of circumstances, including negative ones (e.g., performance demand, shock treatment; Barlow, Sakheim, & Beck, 1983). However, inclusion of men who regularly have difficulty with their sexual desire results in diagnoses that are heterogeneous on this dimension. Second, although diagnosis only calls for noting the frequency of the impairment ("persistent" and "recurrent"), noting the temporal pattern of the dysfunction may help clinicians and researchers gain a greater understanding of etiology. Research suggests that the distinction between primary and secondary erectile disorder is important etiologically (Buvat et al., 1990; Graber & Kline-Graber, 1981; Magee, 1980). For example, primary erectile dysfunction is usually caused predominantly by psychological factors, and is more typical of the complaints of young men (<20 years) who also report other specific deterrents to sexual activity (e.g., religious prescriptions, early traumatic sexual experiences). Acute versus insidious patterns of onset are often correlated with the presence versus absence of precipitating health factors that may influence erectile potential. These data and the increasing probability that significant health factors may impact erectile responses often yield a heterogeneous clinical sample that can meet the DSM-IV criteria for erectile disorder.

Course and Treatment

Increasingly, medical and surgical treatments are available. These include a wide variety of surgical implants, venous ligation and arterial bypass procedures, vacuum pump devices, and oral medications. However, even in cases where the cause of erectile failure was initially organic, erectile difficulties may become reinforced by psychological factors. Thus, treating the organic cause alone may be insufficient; psychological intervention may be necessary in these cases as well. The most traditional psychological interventions for erectile dysfunction have been sensate focus and nondemand pleasuring (Masters & Johnson, 1970). Both cognitive and behavioral approaches tend to focus on the individual's dysfunctional beliefs and attention processes. As is the case with treating all sexual dysfunctions, helping the sufferer to gain an accurate understanding of the sexual response cycle represents an essential part of the treatment process.

Approximately two-thirds of men treated with behavior sex therapy interventions show improvement. However, despite initial successes in many patients, relapse is a significant problem that couples often must face (Hawton, Catalan, & Fagg, 1992; Levine &

Agle, 1978; Mohr & Beutler, 1990; Munjack et al., 1984). Couples should be encouraged to continue to practice treatment techniques, return for follow-ups, and view "lapses" as opportunities to learn (McCarthy, 1993).

FEMALE AROUSAL DISORDER

Description

Either physical or psychologic sexual stimulation can initiate sexual excitement, and the bodily changes can be considerable. The general physiologic responses are widespread vasocongestion, either superficial or deep, and myotonia, with either voluntary or involuntary muscle contractions. Other changes include increases in heart rate and blood pressure, and deeper and more rapid respiration. For women, sexual excitement is also characterized by the appearance of vaginal lubrication, produced by vasocongestion in the vaginal walls leading to transudation of fluid. Other changes include a slight enlargement of the clitoris and uterus with engorgement. The uterus also rises in position, with the vagina expanding and ballooning out. Maximal vasocongestion of the vagina produces a congested orgasmic platform in the lower one-third of the vaginal barrel. DSM-IV omits affective criteria for arousal disorder in women, whereas subjective arousal had been included in DSM-III-R. The predominant physiologic response of the phase—lubrication and swelling of the genitals—is the single criterion.

Although there is the expectation that physiologic measures will converge with behavioral and subjective reports, examples of dyssynchrony are common (see Turpin, 1991, for a discussion of assessment of anxiety disorders). So too in this area, reports are mixed. Significant correlations have been found between genital measures and women's ratings of their general arousal (e.g., Laan, Everaerd, & Evers, 1995; Morokoff, 1985; Palace & Gorzalka, 1992), yet low to zero correlation has been found between genital measures and women's ratings of genital arousal (e.g., warmth in the genitals, lubrication; Laan et al., 1995; Palace & Gorzalka, 1992). In the U.S. population survey, 19% of the female sample reported difficulties with lubrication, but only 12% of women reported anxiety about performance (Lauman et al.,

1994). Other relevant data indicate that the magnitude of the correlations may be moderated by individual differences among women, such as indications of their sexual responsiveness. For example, Adams, Haynes, and Brayer (1985) found that "infrequently" orgasmic women showed a differential tendency to respond to distracting stimuli; that is, they were less accurate in gauging their physiologic sexual response during a task that was distracting of sexual arousal than were "frequently" orgasmic women. Related examples of this phenomenon have been reported by other investigators (Heiman, 1978; Morokoff & Heiman, 1980). At this time, there are insufficient data to permit a conclusion about the significance (or lack thereof) of this dyssynchrony. Yet, the evidence of the dyssynchrony suggests that awareness of physiologic signs, inadequate lubrication and swelling, may not be pathognomonic.

Etiology

We consider that it is in the balance of affects—both positive (sexual desire and arousal) and negative (sexual anxiety)—that we find the key to understanding sexual excitement difficulties.

Arousal and other positive emotions.   In studies with women, researchers have attempted to assess both physiological and affective aspects of arousal. Although the preceding description notes vasocongestion and lubrication as the predominant bodily responses, psychophysiological research has consisted largely of measures of vaginal vasocongestion—vaginal pulse amplitude (VPA) and/or vaginal blood volume (VBV)—using the vaginal plethesmograph. Other genital measurements (such as those for lubrication) either have not emerged, are unreliable, or are not sensitive to changes in arousal (see Geer & Head, 1990, for a review). As physiological indicators of sexual arousal, it is still unclear what these vaginal signals represent and if they are analogs of distinct vascular processes (Levine, 1992); yet there is evidence for their convergent validity. For example, VPA and VBV are capable of detecting group differences (e.g., differences in absolute levels of arousal between women with and without sexual dysfunctions), and responsiveness to experimental conditions (e.g., novel exposure and habituation to erotic stim-

uli, contrasts between erotic versus nonerotic stimuli; Heiman, Rowland, Hatch, & Gladue, 1991; Laan, Everaerd, van Bellen, & Hanewald, 1994; Meuwissen & Over, 1990). Of the two measures, a variety of data suggest that VPA is the more sensitive and reliable genital measure, particularly because of its *insensitivity* to anxiety-evoking stimuli (Lann et al., 1995).

The construct of arousability is central to understanding cognitive and affective aspects of sexual excitement in women. According to Bancroft (1989), arousability is a cognitive sensitivity to external sexual cues. He suggests that high arousability would imply enhanced perception, awareness, and processing of not only sexual cues but also the bodily responses of sexual excitement. This model seeks to connect cognitive/affective responses with control of genital and peripheral indications of sexual excitement through a neurophysiological substrate for sexual arousal.

It may be useful to consider other positive affects or emotions that may influence sexual excitement/arousal for women. Researchers have found that positive mood, not surprisingly, accompanies sexual arousal in women (Heiman, 1980; Laan et al., 1994). If focused on sexual excitement in the context of an interpersonal relationship, one of the more relevant emotions may be love. Walster and Berscheid (1974) proposed that people may be more apt to experience love whenever they are intensely aroused physiologically (see Hatfield & Rapson, 1993, for a thorough discussion). People then label this arousal as love.

Anxiety and other negative emotions.   Historically, anxiety has been the hypothesized mechanism in many theories of arousal deficits. Psychodynamic hypotheses emphasize fears of phallic-aggressive impulses, castration, rivalry, and/or incestuous object choices (Janssen, 1985). Wolpe's (1958) hypothesis (discussed earlier) was initially offered to explain male arousal deficits, and the model has been applied less satisfactorily to women. There is little experimental support for the contention that the early phases of sexual arousal in women are primarily parasympathetic (Geer & Head, 1990), or even that anxiety will inhibit the physiologic responses of sexual arousal (Palace & Gorzalka, 1990).

Dysfunctional attentional processes and negative

affects have been the core of psychological theories of excitement deficits (see the previous discussion of male arousal disorder). When the Barlow (1986) model of anxiety and cognitive distraction, as discussed earlier, has been examined with women (usually undergraduate females or, perhaps, women recruited from the community), comparisons have been made between "functional" and "dysfunctional" groups. Women are tested in psychophysiology laboratories and presented with stimuli, usually videotapes, representing anxiety-provoking, neutral, and/ or erotic sequences. Vaginal measures as well as self-reports of general or genital arousal are recorded. In tests of the physiologic effects of anxiety, the data have, in general, indicated that genital arousal is *not* inhibited by anxiety. Using individualized, anxiety-provoking audiotaped scenarios, Beggs, Calhoun, and Wolchik (1987), for example, found that genital arousal (VBV) increased during the anxiety-provoking condition, although the levels were not as high as those achieved during an erotic verbal stimulus. Palace and Gorzalka (1990) found that preexposure with an anxiety-provoking video (a threatened amputation) in contrast to a neutral video facilitated VBV responses during subsequent viewing of erotic scenes for both women with and those without sexual dysfunctions. This effect, preexposure to an anxiety-provoking stimulus *increasing* subsequent VBV during erotica, has also been replicated (Palace, 1995).

Other data disconfirming of both the Masters and Johnson and Barlow conceptualizations are those of Laan, Everaerd, van Aanhold, and Rebel (1993). They found that VPA was higher (rather than lower) under experimental "demand" conditions (i.e., "Try to become as sexually aroused as possible within 2 minutes, and try to maintain it for as long as you can. Your level of sexual arousal will be recorded.") in contrast to no-demand conditions. Taken together, these data substantiate neither the physiologic mechanism suggested by Wolpe (arousal may be predominantly a sympathetic rather than a parasympathetic process) nor the psychological mechanism (e.g., performance demand) suggested by Masters and Johnson and by Barlow. For these reasons, it may be important to consider a broader band of negative processes, in addition to anxiety, that also may be relevant determinants of excitement processes for women.

Course and Treatment

Sensate focus and nondemand pleasuring (Masters & Johnson, 1970) form the basis of treatments designed to enhance women's sexual arousal. Both cognitive and behavioral approaches tend to focus on the individual's dysfunctional beliefs and attention processes. Treatment usually focuses on increasing physical stimulation of the genitals and, if appropriate, decreasing performance anxiety.

ORGASMIC DISORDERS

Premature Ejaculation

Description

A second orgasmic dysfunction noted for males is *premature ejaculation*. A "premature" ejaculation occurs "with minimal sexual stimulation before, on, or shortly after penetration and before the person wishes it" (APA, 1994, p. 511). Premature ejaculation is a common presenting complaint for men seeking sex therapy, perhaps accounting for 20% to 40% of all cases (Spector & Carey, 1990). Although data are not available, it is more likely that younger (in their twenties, thirties, and forties) rather than older men will present, as aging slows the ejaculation response. Premature ejaculation may be either *primary* (present from initial attempts at intercourse) or *secondary* (onset occurring after a period of satisfactory sexual functioning).

Etiology

There have been few conceptualizations for premature ejaculation, and the most intuitively appealing viewpoint has not been supported empirically. Kaplan (1974) was the first to suggest that men with this difficulty are extraordinarily sensitive to erotic stimulation (i.e., they respond with higher levels of arousal to more stimuli) and are less adept at monitoring their arousal. However, comparisons of men complaining of premature ejaculation versus men who report normal ejaculatory control reveal few differences (Spiess, Geer, & O'Donohue, 1984; Strassberg, Kelly, Carroll, & Kircher, 1990; Strassberg, Mahoney, Schaugaard, & Hale, 1990). First, the groups do not differ in the rapidity with which they became aroused in response to sexual stimuli (although when prompted to masturbate to ejaculation, premature ejaculators could do so faster). Second, men who ejaculate prematurely do not show higher arousal levels. Third, they do not evidence greater variability in the circumstances in which they become aroused. Finally, they do not report greater sexual anxiety either during intercourse or following in vivo analog exposure. Given this context, we note that there may be a subset of men who "learned" to ejaculate rapidly, with sexual histories that called for expediency. For example, a young man who has several sexual encounters in public or, at least, less private circumstances may learn to ejaculate quickly; he may then continue to exhibit this "skill" in situations where it is not necessary. At present, the etiology of premature ejaculation for the majority of men without specific behavioral histories remains unclear.

Some believe that uncovering the etiology of premature ejaculation has been difficult because scientists have been looking for a single cause (Grenier & Byer, 1995; Godpodinoff, 1989). Premature ejaculation, like many other disorders, may be caused by several interacting factors; thus, the category "premature ejaculation" may include subtypes that vary in etiology, response to treatment, and so on. For example, the distinction between primary and secondary premature ejaculation may be a helpful one (Godpodinoff, 1989; Grenier & Byer, 1995).

Course and Treatment

Premature ejaculation is most often seen in young men and frequently will disappear with sexual experience and age. For these young men, the usual onset is with their first attempts at intercourse. When premature ejaculation occurs later in life, contextual circumstances may be linked to onset. For example, a man's anxiety about performing with a new partner or his attempts to resume sexual activity after a period of abstinence may be influential.

The most common treatment for premature ejaculation is the "pause" technique (Semans, 1956), which was later modified and renamed the "pause–squeeze" technique (Masters & Johnson, 1970). The pause–squeeze technique involves "pausing" when the male reaches high levels of arousal and "squeezing" the frenulum of the penis, which reportedly suspends the ejaculatory impulse. Couples progress from mutual masturbation to vaginal intercourse using this technique. This mechanical technique has had widespread

use and apparent success, but the mechanism for its success remains a mystery. The effectiveness may result from a raised sensory threshold. However, some have speculated that the increased sexual activity that comes from practicing the technique is actually responsible for the success (Kinder & Curtiss, 1988). These researchers posit that *any* increase in sexual activity, not just the pause–squeeze technique, would produce an improvement in the client's condition. Further, despite the high "cure" rates (>95%) initially reported by Masters and Johnson (1970), others have not always reproduced these results. Accurate success rates are difficult to determine, with *success* often being inadequately defined by study reports (St. Lawrence & Madakastra, 1992). A "cure" often seems to reflect an initial improvement in response to therapy, but, long-term follow-up data do not show such unqualified success (Kilman & Auerbach, 1979). Further, most studies do not indicate whether clients need to continue to practice the pause–squeeze technique in order maintain gains (LoPiccolo & Stock, 1986). Still, most clinicians view premature ejaculation as one response amenable to treatment.

Male Orgasmic Disorder

Description

As with female orgasmic disorder, the diagnosis of *male orgasmic disorder* presumes a normal excitement phase and sexual circumstances that are adequate in focus, intensity, and duration. Unlike the female criteria, however, the diagnosis is usually restricted to orgasm failure with a woman during intercourse. The factors resulting in any situational responsiveness (e.g., delayed ejaculation with female partner but not with masturbation) are not elaborated. It is important to note that delayed ejaculation is not isolated among heterosexual couples, as delayed (or "retarded") ejaculation can occur in homosexual males as well (e.g., Wilensky & Myers, 1987). Delayed ejaculation is the least common dysfunction for males, perhaps accounting for only 3% to 8% of the men presenting for treatment (Spector & Carey, 1990).

Etiology

Little is known about delayed ejaculation. Several medical conditions, such as multiple sclerosis (Kedia,

1983) and medication side effects (antihypertensives, sedatives, antianxiety, antipsychotics; Ban & Freyham, 1980) are known physiological causes of delayed ejaculation. With regard to psychological causes, case studies have offered a variety of hypotheses (Dow, 1981; Schull & Sprenkle, 1980). Men with inhibited orgasm may also have other sexual difficulties, such as low desire, arousal deficits, or both. This raises the question: Is it appropriate to diagnose a dysfunction in a later phase of the sexual response cycle when prior ones are only minimally adequate (if not inadequate)?

Course and Treatment

Because of the rarity of the condition and the dearth of information about its etiology, specialized treatments have not emerged. Treatment usually focuses on increasing physical stimulation of the genitals and decreasing performance anxiety. Prognosis may be variable, although Masters and Johnson (1970) reported a success rate of 83%.

Female Orgasmic Disorder

Description

Masters and Johnson (1966) proposed that orgasm is a reflex-like response that occurs once a plateau of excitement has been reached or exceeded, although the specific neurophysiologic mechanisms are not known. The physiologic and behavioral indices of orgasm involve the whole body—facial grimaces, generalized myotonia of the muscles, carpopedal spasms, and contractions of the gluteal and abdominal muscles. For women, orgasm is also marked by rhythmic contractions of the uterus, the vaginal barrel, and the rectal sphincter, beginning at 0.8-second intervals and then diminishing in intensity, duration, and regularity. Attention is focused on internal bodily sensations (concentrated in the clitoris, vagina, and uterus), and the woman's awareness of competing environmental stimuli may be lessened. The subjective experience of orgasm includes feelings of intense pleasure with a peaking and rapid, exhilarating release. These sensations are reported to be singular, regardless of the manner in which orgasm is achieved (Newcomb & Bentler, 1983). Women are unique in their capability to be multiorgasmic; that is, women are capable of a series of distinguishable or-

gasmic responses without a lowering of excitement between them.

The lack of reliable and valid assessment methods for female orgasm (see discussion in Andersen & Cyranowski, 1995) may have contributed to the historical controversy surrounding the diagnostic criteria (Wakefield, 1987, 1988; Morokoff, 1989). The DSM-IV definition emphasizes the importance of an adequate excitement phase. Prior estimates suggested that 5% to 10% of sexually active women have not experienced orgasm, but Laumann and colleagues (Lauman, Gagnon, Michael, & Michaels, 1994) offered data indicating that 24% of the women sampled reported an inability to have orgasm. A second clinical pattern, called secondary orgasmic dysfunction, had been used for women who have orgasms that occur very infrequently or not with the preferred activity, coitus. The latter response often represents a normal variation and is usually not appropriate as a diagnostic entity. In fact, the absence of coital orgasm is common for many adult women early in their sexual relationships, as the rate of coital orgasm increases with experience (Kinsey, Pomeroy, Martin, & Gebhard, 1953). In the survey by Lauman et al. (1994), 10% of women reported that they climaxed too quickly. Other clinical scenarios (e.g., a woman becoming nonorgasmic after being so) are rare. When this does occur, a history may reveal pharmacologic agents as instrumental; for example, anorgasmia in previously responsive women may be associated with the use of tricyclic antidepressants, monoamine oxidase inhibitors, benzodiazepines, and neuroleptics.

Etiology

As noted, the DSM proviso of a normal sexual excitement phase describes only a subgroup of women with orgasm difficulties, as research suggests that women presenting for treatment for inorgasmia vary widely not only in their capacity for sexual arousal but in the presence of accompanying negative affects such as anxiety or aversion to sexual activity (Andersen & Cyranowski, 1995; see Andersen, 1983, for a review). Relatedly, etiological hypotheses for inorgasmia have emphasized the role of anxiety or other distressing affects (Derogatis, Fagen, Schmidt, Wise, & Glidden, 1986; Wolpe, 1958), performance anxiety (Masters & Johnson, 1970), and skills deficits (Barbach, 1975). Hypotheses for coitally inorgasmic women often focus on the role of interpersonal and/or marital satisfaction (e.g. McGovern, Stewart, & LoPiccolo, 1975).

Contrary to current DSM criteria, theoretical and intervention research suggests that subtypes of orgasmic dysfunction exist, and, further, that these subtypes would vary in terms of etiology and, perhaps, treatment. Considering the response cycle conceptualization, prior phases—desire and excitement—both would be expected to have linkages to the occurrence of orgasm. For illustration, consider clinical cases of orgasmic dysfunction in which desire may or may not be regularly present, and excitement may or may not be regularly present (see Table 17-1). Thus, this provides for the delineation of four phasic-based orgasmic dysfunction subtypes, with the diagnostic subtyping tied directly to the response cycle conceptualization. When this conceptualization has been tested empirically with data from women presenting for a treatment outcome study for primary orgasmic dysfunction (Andersen, 1981), 70% of the women scored below the 50th percentile based on normative data for the Hoon, Hoon, and Wincze (1976) Sexual Arousability Index (SAI), a reliable and valid measure of sexual arousal (Andersen, Broffitt, Karlsson, & Turnquist, 1989). Further, 47% of the sample scored below the 25th percentile. Thus, in this sample of women with orgasmic dysfunction, these data suggested that only 30% scored above the 50th percentile on the SAI, with only 7% of the sample above the 75th percentile. These data suggest that the numbers of nonorgasmic women who would report *unimpaired* sexual arousal (i.e., meeting DSM-IV criteria) would be low (only 37%). To summarize, it is probable that there are diagnostically distinct subgroups of women who have difficulty with orgasm.

TABLE 17-1 Orgasmic dysfunction subtypes.

		Excitement Phase Dysfunction	
		Absent	Present
Desire Phase Dysfunction	Absent	No orgasm	Neither excitement nor orgasm
	Present	Neither desire nor orgasm	No desire, excitement, or orgasm

Considering the impact of sexual self-schema, research suggests that women with a coschematic self-view might be at greatest risk for orgasmic difficulties, particularly if the clinical presentation includes reports of sexual arousal with accompanying negative affect, such as sexual anxiety. The competing emotions experienced by coschematic women may be sufficiently disruptive to impair the orgasmic response even though the women experience sexual arousal.

Course and Treatment

Treatment strategies for orgasmic dysfunction, narrowly defined, have historically consisted of sensate focus exercises with couples that incorporate the directed masturbation exercises originally developed for women-only treatment (Andersen, 1983). The phasic conceptualization described here, which includes women with desire and/or excitement difficulties, would suggest that elements of treatments designed specifically for the early phase dysfunctions be incorporated.

SEXUAL PAIN DISORDERS

Vaginismus

Description

Vaginismus is thought to be a relatively rare condition among women. The diagnostic criteria, "a recurrent or persistent involuntary spasm of the outer third of the vagina, sufficient to interfere with intercourse," are similar to Masters and Johnson's original formulation (1970). The spasm usually involves the perineal and levator ani muscles, and, in severe cases, the abductors of the thigh, rectus abdominus, and even the gluteal muscles. With the spasm, localized pain usually occurs. A confirming diagnosis is ordinarily made via a pelvic examination when the spasm can be visually or manually detected, although a successfully completed pelvic exam does not rule out the possibility of vaginismus during sexual intercourse. The simplicity of the criteria belies the heterogeneity that can be found in clinical groups (e.g., Lamont, 1978). From a behavioral standpoint, the spasm may be elicited not only during intercourse but in other contexts as well, ranging from a woman inserting her own finger or a tampon into the vagina to a pelvic examination by a gynecologist. Also, such episodes need not be in vivo to elicit the reflex; vaginismus can occur from imagined or anticipated penetration as well. As the condition is usually disruptive to coitus, it may have prevented all episodes such that a woman comes to treatment as a virgin, with treatment sought because of an unconsummated marriage. Alternatively, the presenting woman may have a long history of "managing" the problem more or less successfully. Although the criteria do not note disruption of phases of the sexual response cycle, women may vary widely, with some women desirous of sex and arousable with sexual activities that do not include penetration, whereas others report lack of interest, nonresponsiveness, and avoidance.

Etiology

There have been two conceptualizations of vaginismus. Dynamic notions regard the spasm as a hysterical symptom of a conversion reaction prompted by prior traumas (e.g., rape, pain with first intercourse experiences) or neurotic processes (e.g., penis envy). At present there is little empirical support for these positions. Alternatively, social learning/behavioral hypotheses trace sexual histories to find episodes of vaginal or penetration traumas to serve as instrumental conditioning episodes. These events may be anticipated—for example, fears that intercourse will be painful—or real, but they are usually of sufficient magnitude that the woman avoids sexual intercourse in particular or sexual contexts in general. This avoidance is maintained, or reinforced, via anxiety reduction. Other predisposing cognitive factors include generalized negative reactions to sexuality, such as guilt or fear, marital distress, or sexual naivete. Primary vaginismus is usually psychosomatic in nature, with a substantial phobic element. In cases of secondary vaginismus, with a previous history of successful functioning, dyspareunia should be considered as a possible cause. In this scenario, possible triggering events could include traumatic childbirth, perineal surgery, or vaginal atrophy with menopause.

Course and Treatment

The aim of treatment is to help a woman gain voluntary control over her pelvic floor muscles. In order for this to occur, the woman's fear of penetration must be gradually desensitized. Vaginismus can be treated ef-

fectively through relaxation training and vaginal self-dilation (Fuchs et al., 1978; Sarrel & Sarrel, 1979). The first step in vaginal self-dilation is for the woman to examine her genitals, and become comfortable with inserting a finger in her vagina. From this point, she begins using glass or plastic vaginal dilators of gradually increasing size. Once the woman has become comfortable inserting the largest dilator, her partner may become involved. Initially, the woman may direct her partner in digital dilation. Eventually, female-directed, nonthrusting sexual intercourse may be attempted. Throughout therapy, relationship issues must be addressed if vaginismus is to be treated effectively. Resistance to treatment may be taken as an indicator of these unaddressed interpersonal or intrapersonal issues.

Dyspareunia

Description

It is important to rule out vaginismus as a cause of dyspareunia in women. The latter is defined for both men and women as "recurrent or persistent genital [emphasis added] pain associated with sexual intercourse" (APA, 1994, p. 513). Of note in this diagnosis, the pain does not need to occur during intercourse. Data suggest that pain at other times, particularly during the resolution phase of painful intercourse, is a common clinical scenario (e.g., Andersen, Anderson, & deProsse, 1989). In addition to vaginismus, the criteria note that lack of lubrication needs to be ruled out as a contributor, as vaginal dryness commonly produces friction and discomfort for the woman.

Etiology

As with vaginismus, there has been relatively little study of dyspareunia, and, interestingly, there are even fewer discussions or data from male samples. An exception is Wabrek and Wabrek's (1975) essay on the most common physical precipitants for dyspareunia in both genders. There are a variety of physical hypotheses for each genital structure, and these hypotheses can be narrowed even further by carefully questioning the client as to the specific localization of the pain, the timing of the pain, and which sexual response cycle phase or sexual technique factors mitigate the pain. For women, lack of lubrication may be difficult to rule out as a cause (Meana & Binik, 1994). First, many women may not be able to provide an accurate report of their degree of lubrication. Second, the comorbidity between dyspareunia and arousal difficulties is thought to be quite high. A woman who is anticipating pain during intercourse might experience fear rather than sexual arousal, and it is hypothesized that she would thus not lubricate adequately. [Interestingly, this clinical view counters the data of Palace and Gorzalka (1990) discussed earlier.] Once physical factors are ruled out via clinical interview, medical history, and gynecological or urological physical examination, psychological factors are more viable as hypotheses. Dynamic and behavioral conceptualizations for dyspareunia often do not differ substantively from those for vaginismus, with primary differences being that the viewpoints refer to psychological antecedents for sexual activity in general rather than only penetration.

Course and Treatment

If the dysfunction is determined to be organic in nature, the appropriate medical or surgical treatment should be administered. However, even in cases of organic origin, especially long-standing ones, sex therapy is often helpful. The most successful forms of psychological treatment are similar to those used for vaginismus (relaxation training and vaginal dilation); the primary treatment goal includes relaxation of the muscles surrounding the vagina and increased lubrication. As with vaginismus, relationship issues will almost always need to be addressed.

Summary

A framework that includes the physiological description and the behavioral and cognitive responses is used to define sexual dysfunctions. DSM uses the specification of the sexual response cycle components—sexual desire, excitement (arousal), orgasm, and resolution—to offer bodily responses (e.g., lubrication and/or vasocongestion for women and erection for men) as markers of dysfunction. However, some dysfunctions (e.g., desire) and aspects of others (e.g., aversion) do not lend themselves to the selection of physiologic markers. Thus, we elaborate the behavioral and cognitive aspects of the dysfunctions.

Continued theoretical and empirical efforts are needed in several areas, and we underscore the central areas. First, sexual desire problems have taken center stage in recent years; yet the research on these phenomena is in its earliest stages (see Beck, 1995, for a discussion). Second, theories have been proposed for the conceptualization of men's sexual excitement and related affects, but the generalization of them to women's arousal processes has been unsuccessful. Although useful data have resulted, the majority of it indicates that the empirical fit is poor. In short, theoretical and diagnostic advances are needed in the understanding of sexual excitement processes, with data for women particularly needed.

Second, we have proposed consideration of affective aspects of the sexual dysfunctions. Toward this end, our discussion includes both positive and negative dimensions, since there is evidence for dyssynchrony. Within the domain of positive affects, emotions such as romantic attachment or love might be considered, as a variety of converging data indicate that for women these feelings are closely tied to sexual arousal. For example, there are gender differences in content of sexual fantasies (currently the marker for sexual desire), with women focusing on personal/emotional feelings, in contrast to men, who focus on the sexual content per se (Ellis & Symons, 1990). Research on women's self-esteem suggests that it comes, in part, from sensitivity and interdependence with others (Joseph, Markus, & Tafarodi, 1992) rather than the more independent orientation common for men. Finally, women's own judgments about a "sexual woman" describe such a woman as one who is passionate as well as romantic and loving (Andersen & Cyranowski, 1994), whereas "a sexual man" is passionate and loving as well as independent and powerful (Andersen & Espindle, in preparation).

Regarding negative affects that may inhibit or lower sexual arousal, there are several that may influence sexual responses, including anxiety (i.e., tension and nervousness), sexual self-criticism and self-consciousness, and global sexual depression (see Andersen & Cyranowski, 1995, for a full discussion). It is also likely that aspects that tap behavioral avoidance are relevant to sexual excitement, including avoidance of sexual activities or stimuli per se.

Third, there is renewed interest in the role of individual differences in predicting and understanding sexual phenomena. The individual difference variable of sexual schema is unique in its cognitive focus, its bandwidth in the prediction of sexual phenomena, and its capability of differentiating topologies of women (positive schema, coschematic, aschematic, and negative schema) and men (positive schema and aschematic) who differ in their sexual behaviors and responses. This variable may lend new clarity to the psychological and etiological factors that may put individuals at risk for the occurrence of sexual dysfunctions.

SEXUAL DEVIATION

Description

Unlike sexual dysfunctions, in which certain disorders are more prominent among women, paraphilias are rarely diagnosed among women (APA, 1994). Sexual masochism, with a sex ratio of 20 males to each female, is the only paraphilia that is typically diagnosed among females (APA, 1994). Women's involvement in some paraphilias (e.g., sexual contact with adolescents) may actually be perceived by male victims as less harmful than it is by female victims (McConaghy, 1994). Men's penchant for impersonal sex may make them more likely to engage in paraphilias, whereas women have more of a tendency to engage in sex in the context of personal relationships (Oliver & Hyde, 1993). Another common component of paraphilias is the abuse of power by the perpetrator (Abel & Rouleau, 1995).

Paraphilias involve sexual arousal, fantasies, or behavior involving nonhuman objects, suffering or humiliation of oneself or one's partner, or children or nonconsenting persons (APA, 1994). Such sexual arousal, fantasies, or behavior must last for at least 6 months and must cause "clinically significant distress or impairment in social, occupational, or other important areas of functioning." Because the DSM-IV definition specifies sexual arousal, fantasies, *or* behavior, it is possible to engage in paraphilic behavior without being sexually aroused by it. For example, some incestuous fathers are not sexually aroused by children (Freund & Watson, 1991). If the behavior causes distress or impairment for a nonconsenting person, it may constitute a paraphilia even if the individual engaging in the behavior does not personally experience distress or impairment (APA, 1994,

p. 525). Unusual sexual behavior that occurs exclusively during the course of other mental disorders (e.g., mental retardation, dementia, substance intoxication, manic episode, schizophrenia) is not considered paraphilic.

Men having paraphilias, particularly those that involve illegal behavior, seldom self-refer to clinicians. Because many persons having paraphilias may be invested in continuing access to their source of sexual arousal (e.g., children), they may deny or be unaware of the effects of their paraphilic behavior on others. Referrals to clinicians are often a result of pressure from a third party (e.g., partner, employer, legal authority) who may view the paraphilia as problematic. Thus, the distress or impairment created by the paraphilia often is best judged by a third party, such as family members, victims and their families, or clinicians.

Exhibitionism

Exhibitionism involves sexual arousal associated with the exposure of one's genitals to an unsuspecting stranger (APA, 1994). The penis is not necessarily erect during exposure, although masturbation may occur during or following exposure (McConaghy, 1994). Exposure usually takes place in secluded areas or from an automobile (McConaghy, 1994). There is typically no attempt at sexual contact with the victim (APA, 1994). Genital exposure in contexts in which strangers are not unsuspecting (e.g., by nightclub strippers) is not necessarily paraphilic. Exhibitionism should be distinguished from public urination, which is occasionally offered as an explanation or excuse for the behavior (APA, 1994).

Fetishism

Fetishism involves sexual arousal associated with nonliving objects (APA, 1994). These objects are commonly women's underpants, bras, stockings, shoes, or boots. Masturbation frequently occurs while holding, rubbing, or smelling the fetish object, or the person may ask the sexual partner to wear the object. In many cases, sexual arousal may not occur in the absence of the object. Fetishism is not diagnosed if the fetish objects are used in cross-dressing or if the objects have been designed for genital stimulation (e.g., a vibrator).

Frotteurism

Frotteurism is touching a nonconsenting person's genitalia or breasts, or rubbing one's genitals against a nonconsenting person's thighs or buttocks (APA, 1994). The behavior usually occurs in crowded public places (e.g., public transportation) where a person can avoid being arrested.

Pedophilia

Pedophilia involves sexual activity between a person who is at least 16 years old and a prepubescent child who is at least 5 years younger (APA, 1994). Very few females meet the DSM-IV criteria for pedophilia (Abel & Rouleau, 1995). Most pedophiles are more sexually aroused by consenting than by coercive pedophilic activity (Hall, Proctor, & Nelson, 1988). Thus, most men who have sexual contact with children would prefer that the child engage in sex willingly. Often men who have sexual contact with children severely distort the meaning of the behavior such that they believe that the child is willingly engaging in sex and may actually be benefiting from it (Abel & Rouleau, 1995). Men who are sexually involved with children often use their position of authority or power over the child to prevent the child from disclosing the sexual abuse.

Sexual attraction in pedophilia can be to male children, female children, or both. Victims may include family members and stepchildren (incest), children outside the family, or both family and nonfamily members. Pedophiles who victimize males who are not family members tend to have the most victims (median number of victims > 50; Abel et al., 1993). Pedophiles who victimize male or female family members and pedophiles who victimize females who are not family members tend to have fewer victims (median for all three groups < 20; Abel et al., 1993). Some pedophiles' sexual attraction is exclusively toward children, whereas others are sexually attracted to both children and adults. Some men who engage in sexual contact with children, particularly those who engage in incestuous contact, do not exhibit sexual arousal in response to children (Freund & Watson, 1991).

Sexual Masochism

Sexual masochism involves sexual arousal associated with the actual act (not simulation) of suffering, including being humiliated, beaten, and bound. Masochism may take place individually (e.g., self-mutilation) or with a partner (e.g., restraint, blindfolding, paddling, spanking, whipping, beating, electrical shocks). One potentially lethal form of sexual masochism is hypoxyphilia (autoerotic asphyxia), in which choking (e.g., via chest compression, noose, plastic bag) is associated with sexual arousal (Friedrich & Gerber, 1994). Sexual masochism may involve cross-dressing, but sexual arousal is associated with being forced to cross-dress, rather than the act of cross-dressing itself (APA, 1994).

Sexual Sadism

Sexual sadism involves sexual arousal associated with actual (not simulated) psychological suffering or physical suffering (including humiliation) of another person (APA, 1994). Sadistic fantasies or behavior include domination (e.g., forcing the victim to act like an animal), restraint, blindfolding, paddling, spanking, whipping, pinching, beating, burning, electrical shocks, cutting, stabbing, strangulation, torture, mutilation, or killing. Although rape may be sadistic, sexual sadism is characteristic of a minority of rapists (Hall & Andersen, 1993; Hall, Shondrick, & Hirschman, 1993b; McConaghy, 1994). Whereas many rapists may be more sexually aroused by rape stimuli than nonrapists are, most rapists are more sexually aroused by consenting than by sadistic or other nonconsenting sexual stimuli. Sadists also commonly practice masochism (McConaghy, 1994).

Transvestic Fetishism

Unlike fetishism, transvestic fetishism involves sexual arousal associated with the act of cross-dressing (APA, 1994). Transvestism may range from wearing a single item of clothing to dressing entirely as a female and wearing makeup. It may be practiced individually, or the person may be involved in a transvestic subculture. Cross-dressing is often accompanied by masturbation during adolescence and by sexual intercourse during adulthood. Most transvestites identify themselves as heterosexual (Zucker & Bradley, 1995). For persons who cross-dress because of persistent discomfort with their gender role or identity, transvestic fetishism with gender dysphoria is specified (APA, 1994).

Voyeurism

Voyeurism involves sexual arousal associated with the act of observing unsuspecting nude individuals in the process of disrobing or engaging in sexual activity (APA, 1994). Although the voyeur may fantasize sexual activity with the person being observed and may masturbate, no sexual activity with the observed person is generally sought. Entering women's lavatories to see or hear women urinating or defecating may be a form of voyeurism (McConaghy, 1994). As with exhibitionism, the victim must be unsuspecting. Thus, situations in which individuals are not unsuspecting (e.g., viewing pornography) are not considered voyeuristic. The co-occurrence of voyeurism and exhibitionism is approximately 70% to 80%, (Abel et al., 1987), perhaps because both paraphilias involve sexual arousal associated with unsuspecting victims.

Paraphilia Not Otherwise Specified

Paraphilias that do not meet the criteria for the other categories are included in this category, which includes obscene phone calls and sexual arousal to corpses, animals, feces, enemas, or urine (APA, 1994).

Epidemiology

Most epidemiological estimates of paraphilias have been based on samples from clinical settings. Those paraphilias that involve illegal behaviors are considered a danger to society; hence, persons having these paraphilias are referred to clinical settings more often than persons having paraphilias that do not involve illegal behaviors. Thus, paraphilias that involve illegal behaviors, such as pedophilia and exhibitionism, are more prevalent in clinical samples than are paraphilias that do not necessarily involve illegal behaviors, such as fetishism (APA, 1994).

Descriptive diagnostic information has recently been reported on large samples of adolescent and adult paraphiliacs who underwent outpatient evaluations (Abel, Osborn, & Twigg, 1993). The frequencies of various paraphilias among adolescents and adults were remarkably consistent. A second recent clinical study included inpatient convicted rapists and child molesters (Barnard, Hankins, & Robbins, 1992).

This inpatient sample appears more pathological than the Abel et al. (1993) outpatient sample.

Recent data from nonclinical samples may provide more accurate estimates than clinical data of the actual prevalence of paraphilias in the general population. One study involved community men in an urban setting (Hall, Hirschman, & Oliver, 1995). Two other studies have included college men (Person, Terestman, Myers, Goldberg, & Salvadori, 1989; Templeman & Stinnett, 1991).

There may exist cultural differences in the incidence and prevalence of paraphilias (Hall, 1996). The majority of the persons in recent studies of paraphilias have been European American men (Abel et al., 1993; Barnard et al., 1992; Hall et al., 1995; Templeman & Stinnett, 1991). Of those arrested in the United States in 1993 for sex offenses other than rape or prostitution (e.g., child molestation, indecent exposure), 77% were European Americans, 21% were African Americans, 1% were American Indians, and 1% were Asian or Pacific Islander Americans (Federal Bureau of Investigation, 1994). Arrest statistics may be misleading because they are a function of victims' willingness to report sex offenses and of police response to such reporting. Nevertheless, it is possible that non-Western collectivist orientations may include protective factors against sexual acting out (Hall, 1996; Hall & Barongan, 1997). The emphasis in Western cultures on individualism and the gratification of personal needs may constitute a risk factor for paraphilias.

Exhibitionism

Among college men, 2% to 4% admit to engaging in exhibitionism (Person et al., 1989; Templeman & Stinnett, 1991). Of the Templeman and Stinnett (1991) sample, 7% indicated a desire to engage in exhibitionism. Exhibitionism may be more common in clinical samples. Among both adolescent and adult outpatients in the Abel et al. (1993) sample, 14% were diagnosed as exhibitionists. In the Barnard et al. (1992) sample, 23% were diagnosed as exhibitionists.

Fetishism

The prevalence of fetishism in nonclinical populations is unknown. Fetishism is not illegal and does not require a partner; thus it may go undetected. In the Abel et al. (1993) outpatient sample, 8% of adolescents and 5% of adults were diagnosed as fetishists. One-quarter of the Barnard et al. (1992) inpatient sample was diagnosed with fetishism.

Frotteurism

Among rural college men, frottage was the second most common paraphilia, following voyeurism (Templeman & Stinnett, 1991). Thirty-five percent of the sample had engaged in touching or rubbing up against a woman in a sexual manner in crowds. This frequency is comparable to the 39% of the Barnard et al. (1992) inpatient sample that was diagnosed with frotteurism. Frottage was relatively uncommon in the Abel et al. (1993) clinical sample, with 6% of adolescents and 4% of adults receiving this diagnosis. However, those who had engaged in frottage did so frequently. Adolescents who engaged in frottage did so a mean of 31 times (range = 1–180). It is possible that the relatively low rate of reporting frottage in the Abel et al. (1993) sample was associated with the sample, including men who were not referred by legal sources (e.g., self-referral, therapist, physician, family, friend; Abel et al., 1987). Frotteurism does not appear to be any more socially undesirable than the other paraphilias for which men sought treatment (e.g., pedophilia). However, it is possible that many men who engage in frotteurism do not view it as sufficiently pathological or harmful to victims to warrant clinical intervention.

Pedophilia

Three percent of college men (Templeman & Stinnett, 1991) and 4% of community men (Hall et al., 1995) admitted to engaging in sexual contact with children. Pedophilia appears to be much more common in clinical populations. The majority of the Abel et al. (1993) sample was diagnosed as pedophilic, with 63% of adolescents and 59% of adults receiving this diagnosis. Similarly, 62% of the Barnard et al. (1992) sample was diagnosed with pedophilia.

Men's sexual arousal to children is more common than their sexual contact with children. In a recent study of a community sample of 80 men, over one-quarter exhibited sexual arousal on genital measures to pedophilic stimuli that equaled or exceeded their sexual arousal to adult stimuli (Hall et al., 1995). These results are consistent with those of other studies in which 12% to 32% of men who had not engaged in sexual contact with children self-reported or exhibited physiological sexual arousal to pedophilic stimuli (Barbaree & Marshall, 1989; Briere & Runtz, 1989; Fedora et al., 1992; Freund & Watson, 1991). However, sexual arousal to pedophilic stimuli is not necessarily equivalent to pedophilic behavior, and most of the men in these studies apparently had not engaged in pedophilic behavior. Nevertheless, these pedophilic fantasies could have met the DSM-IV criteria for pedophilia had they been accompanied by distress or impairment in social, occupational, or other important functioning.

Sexual Masochism

The frequency of masochistic activities in both college and clinical samples ranges from 1% to 3% (Abel et al., 1993; Barnard et al., 1992; Person et al., 1989).

Sexual Sadism

One percent of college men admitted to degrading a partner during sexual activity (Person et al., 1989). In the Abel et al. (1993) sample, 4% of adolescents and 2% of adults were diagnosed with sexual sadism.

Transvestic Fetishism

One percent of college men had dressed in women's clothing in the previous 3 months (Person et al., 1989). Nine percent of adolescents and 5% of adults in the Abel et al. (1993) sample were diagnosed as transvestites. Transvestism was diagnosed in 21% of the Barnard et al. (1992) sample.

Voyeurism

The rates of voyeurism are variable in college and clinical samples. Whereas only 4% of the Person et al. (1989) college male sample admitted to voyeuristic acts, 42% of a sample of rural college men admitted to window peeping on persons having sex, and 54% of the sample indicated a desire to do so (Templeman & Stinnett, 1991). Similarly, 42% of the Barnard et al. (1992) sample was diagnosed with voyeurism. However, only 14% of adolescents and 13% of adults in the Abel et al. (1993) sample were diagnosed as voyeurs.

Paraphilia Not Otherwise Specified

Six percent of adolescents and 4% of adults in the Abel et al. (1993) outpatient sample had made obscene phone calls, and 8% of the Templeman and Stinnett (1991) college sample had done so. Eight percent of both adolescents and adults in the Abel et al. (1993) sample had engaged in bestiality. Fifteen percent of the Barnard et al. (1992) inpatient sample had engaged in bestiality.

Etiology

Sexual victimization during childhood may place a person at risk for developing paraphilias. More than 25% of a sample of 276 sexually abused children from seven clinical settings touched others' "sex parts," whereas only 6% of a sample of 880 nonabused children at a pediatric clinic did so (Friedrich et al., 1992). Male victims of sexual aggression in particular may identify with the aggressor because such identification is more rewarding than a victim identity (Ryan, 1989). Moreover, although sexual victimization is traumatic, it may be accompanied by the victim's sexual arousal. Such pairing of sexual arousal and victimization may cause victimization of boys to become sexually arousing for some male victims (Worling, 1995).

Retrospective studies of paraphiliacs suggest histories of past sexual victimization. Thirty percent of a recent sample of outpatients diagnosed with paraphilias had been physically or sexually abused (Kafka & Prentky, 1994). Sexual victimization particularly appears to be a risk factor for victimizing male children. Whereas 75% of a clinical sample of adolescent males who had molested male children had been sexually abused themselves, only 25% of the sample who had molested female children had been sexually abused (Worling, 1995).

Limited social skills may prevent paraphiliacs from establishing more conventional sexual relationships during their development (Hall, 1996). Those sexual relationships that do develop may be characterized by conflict as a function of poor social skills. Moreover, social skills deficits may also prevent paraphiliacs from developing nonsexual relationships with peers in which corrective feedback concerning inappropriate sexual behavior might be available. Thus, the unavailability or unsatisfying nature of con-

ventional sexual relationships and the lack of input about inappropriate sexual behavior may lead some males to paraphilic behavior.

Many men having paraphilias are more strongly sexually aroused by paraphilic stimuli than by conventional (e.g., consenting adult) stimuli (Hall et al., 1988; Freund & Watson, 1991; Harris, Rice, Quinsey, Chaplin, & Earls, 1992). DSM-IV emphasizes physiological sexual arousal, including sexual urges or fantasies, as the basis of paraphilias. Sexual arousal to paraphilic stimuli may become conditioned (e.g., via masturbation) among men who find conventional sexual stimuli unsatisfying. High rates of sexually impulsive behaviors among paraphiliacs, including compulsive masturbation, promiscuity, and pornography use (Kafka & Prentky, 1994), support sexual arousal as a possible etiological factor in paraphilias.

Sexual arousal to paraphilic stimuli is not characteristic of all men who engage in paraphilic behaviors. These men may engage in paraphilic behavior as a substitute for conventional sexual behavior. Cognitive distortions may allow them to view paraphilic behavior as conventional sexual behavior (Hall, 1996). For example, men who engage in paraphilias involving other persons (e.g., exhibitionism, frotteurism, sadism, pedophilia) may believe that the victims actually enjoy the behavior. As with sexual arousal to paraphilic stimuli, it is possible that cognitive distortions develop as a result of unavailable or unsatisfying conventional sexual behavior and a paucity of corrective feedback from peers.

For some men who engage in paraphilias, paraphilic behavior may represent a maladaptive attempt to cope with dysphoric states (Hall, 1996; Kafka & Prentky, 1994). The physiological high produced by sexual arousal may produce temporary relief from dysphoric states (Hall, 1996). Unlike many peer sexual relationships, paraphilic sexual behavior offers a person a high degree of control over his sexual fantasies, arousal, and behavior. Such feelings of control may also reduce dysphoric states.

Course and Complications

Course

In the Abel et al. (1993) outpatient sample, 42% reported the onset of paraphilias before age 18.

Although paraphilias persist into adulthood for many adolescent paraphiliacs, a prospective study of adolescent paraphiliacs has not been conducted. Thus, the percentages of adolescence-limited versus life-course paraphiliacs (cf. Moffitt, 1993) are unknown.

The Abel et al. (1993) outpatient data suggest that most paraphilias begin during adulthood. Although some males engage in paraphilic behavior multiple times (Abel et al., 1993), frequencies of paraphilic behavior do not necessarily indicate the risk of any individual paraphiliac repeatedly engaging in paraphilic behavior. Recidivism rates among adult child molesters and adult exhibitionists who do not undergo effective treatment interventions average 27% across studies (Hall, 1995b). Because these recidivism rates are based primarily on rearrest data that may underestimate actual behavior, a 27% rate of repeated paraphilic behavior among adults may be conservative.

Sexual arousal tends to decrease as a function of age, which may suggest that paraphilias that are arousal-dependent may also decline with age. Indeed, arrests for exhibitionism decline with age (APA, 1994). However, age is not associated with recidivism for child molestation (Abel et al., 1993; Hanson, Steffy, & Gauthier, 1993). The incidence of child molestation may be a function of access to victims, which may increase with age as a man becomes an uncle, father, and grandfather (Hall, 1996). Children who are relatives and these children's friends constitute the pool of potential victims.

Complications

In a recent outpatient sample of 34 men who had sought treatment for sexual disorders, the most common diagnoses were exhibitionism (38%), pedophilia (29%), and voyeurism (29%; Kafka & Prentky, 1994). These men were diagnosed with a mean of 1.8 paraphilias, with a range of 1 to 3 paraphilias. Lifetime comorbidity with Axis I disorders was common. Seventy-four percent of the sample had experienced mood disorders, including 68% who had experienced dysthymia. Forty-seven percent had experienced anxiety disorders, including 21% with social phobia and 18% with generalized anxiety. Forty-seven percent had experienced substance abuse disorders, including 41% who had abused alcohol and 29% who had abused marijuana.

Exposure to trauma also may be common among pedophiles. In an inpatient sample of convicted rapists and child molesters, 92% had experienced past trauma (Barnard et al., 1992). The most common form of trauma experienced was child sexual abuse (71%), which is consistent with prospective studies of the association between child sexual abuse and sexual acting out (Friedrich et al., 1992). Physical assault was the second most common form of trauma in the Barnard et al. (1992) inpatient sample (58%). Over half of the sample reported experiencing a great deal of emotional disability as a result of past traumatic experiences.

DSM-IV cluster B disorders may be more common among pedophiles than either cluster A or cluster C disorders. Whereas 71% of the Barnard et al. (1992) sample was diagnosed with a cluster B disorder, cluster A and C disorders were diagnosed in 33% and 38% of the sample, respectively. Antisocial (46%) and histrionic (37%) were the most common personality disorders.

Treatment Implications

A literature review by Furby, Weinrott, and Blackshaw (1989) cast serious doubt on the efficacy of the treatment of paraphilias. The conclusion of this review was that there was no evidence for the effectiveness of treatments for sexual offenders. However, the authors acknowledged that many of the programs reviewed were obsolete. Many innovative treatment approaches have been developed since the Furby et al. (1989) review.

The three major contemporary approaches to the treatment of paraphilias that have been most widely discussed are behavioral, cognitive-behavioral, and hormonal (Hall, 1996). The treatment focus of behavioral approaches has been on reducing sexual arousal to inappropriate stimuli (e.g., children). Aversion therapy, which involves the pairing of an inappropriate stimulus (e.g., child) with an aversive stimulus (e.g., aversive fantasy), has been the most common behavioral method used with paraphilias. A few behavioral interventions also include a component to enhance sexual arousal to appropriate stimuli (i.e., adults).

Hormonal treatments have most commonly involved medroxyprogesterone acetate (MPA), an antiandrogen that suppresses sexual arousal to both inappropriate and appropriate stimuli. There is some evidence that cyproterone acetate (CPA) has specific effects in suppressing sexual arousal to inappropriate stimuli (i.e., children) and does not suppress sexual arousal to appropriate stimuli (Bradford, 1990). However, the evidence to support the utility of CPA is from uncontrolled clinical trials.

Cognitive-behavioral programs are comprehensive in that they typically target sexual arousal to inappropriate stimuli, cognitive distortions about paraphilias, and social skills deficits (Marshall & Barbaree, 1990). The effective components of these programs do not necessarily include modification of sexual arousal patterns, which was not associated with recidivism in a major treatment outcome study (Marshall & Barbaree, 1988). Some cognitive-behavioral programs also incorporate relapse prevention strategies to cope with situational temptations to reoffend (Laws, 1989).

The results of recent treatment outcome studies offer reason for optimism in the treatment of paraphilias. In a meta-analysis of recent treatment studies of sexual aggressors (primarily child molesters, rapists, and exhibitionists), cognitive-behavioral and antiandrogen treatments were more effective in reducing recidivism than were behavioral treatments (Hall, 1995b). Both cognitive-behavioral and antiandrogen treatments yielded recidivism rates of 13% versus a recidivism rate of 41% for behavioral treatments. Lasting habituation to sexually arousing stimuli may be difficult to accomplish via behavioral methods, and habituation to one stimulus (e.g., one child) does not necessarily generalize to other stimuli (e.g., other children). Conversely, hormonal methods typically create a suppression of sexual arousal to all stimuli. The effectiveness of cognitive-behavioral programs may be associated with their focus on multiple etiological factors (e.g., sexual arousal, cognitive distortions) involved in paraphilias. Although the recidivism rates for cognitive-behavioral and antiandrogen treatments did not differ, there may be a practical advantage of cognitive-behavioral treatments because of lower dropout rates in cognitive-behavioral (33%) versus antiandrogen (50%–66%) treatment programs (Hall, 1995b).

Given that past paraphilic behavior is the best predictor of future paraphilic behavior (Hall, 1988; Rice et al., 1991), persons having more limited paraphilic histories may have better treatment prognoses than those having more extensive histories. Interventions with sexually acting-out adolescents may prevent the development of paraphilias (Oliver, Hall, & Neuhaus, 1993). Even more effective may be primary prevention, involving sexuality education in schools for all children and adolescents (Hall, 1996). School-based sexuality education programs have typically been oriented toward victim-based strategies of sexual assault prevention. Programs oriented toward perpetrators and potential perpetrators are needed.

Case Description

Mr. W was a 45-year-old man who had engaged in sexual activity with both acquaintance and stranger boys aged 10 to 16 years. At about age 11 or 12, he began to engage in sexual activity with peer males. As he grew older, however, his sexual partners did not. He continued to have sex with minor males after he became an adult, and he did not attempt to establish peer sexual relationships. The sexual activity with minor males typically involved mutual masturbation and oral and anal sex. Mr. W did not engage in sex with female adults or minors, nor did he have any history of nonsexual offenses. He fit the DSM-IV criteria for pedophilia, male, nonincest.

At age 34, Mr. W was arrested and convicted for sexual contact with a minor male. He spent $9\frac{1}{2}$ years in prison. During the final 18 months of his incarceration, he participated in a treatment program. Mr. W reported that the primary lesson he learned from this prison program was that he had come from a "dysfunctional family," but that no one ever told him what a dysfunctional family was.

Mr. W was placed on parole following his prison sentence and participated in an 18-month outpatient cognitive-behavioral treatment program for child molesters (Hall, 1995a). Scales 5 and 4 were elevated on his MMPI profile, which suggests emotional passivity, unrecognized dependency needs, and periods of adequate control alternating with periods of acting out (Graham, 1987). During treatment, Mr. W began to understand the harm that he had perpetrated. He had not viewed his sexual behavior with minors as harmful because he had been sexually active as a minor with peers. However, he realized that although he had not used physical force in any sexual contact, he had psychologically coerced many boys to have sex, and that this sexual contact may have had very negative consequences for many of these boys. He also began to recognize that he had placed himself in situations that created easy access to young boys. For example, he "found himself" purchasing a boat, which subsequently became a method to attract young boys by offering them rides in the boat. Mr. W was also very homophobic. In the treatment group, he was encouraged to accept his gay status and to seek relationships with peer men. He was genuinely surprised to discover that the other men in the treatment group, all of whom were heterosexual, did not derogate him for being gay.

Following the outpatient treatment program, an MMPI profile suggested less overall psychopathology. Mr. W constituted a high risk for reoffense because he had been sexually involved with multiple nonrelative minor males. Nevertheless, he had not reoffended at a follow-up evaluation one year after he had completed the outpatient program.

Summary

Paraphilias are primarily a male phenomenon. Paraphilias that involve illegal behaviors (e.g., pedophilia, exhibitionism) appear to be overrepresented in clinical samples. The prevalence of paraphilias, other than frottage and voyeurism, among nonclinical samples is quite low. Paraphiliacs are often motivated by sexual arousal to deviant stimuli (e.g., children, clothing), although sexual arousal to deviant stimuli is secondary to other motivational factors, such as developmental problems, cognitive distortions, and affective problems, among many other paraphiliacs. Most paraphilias begin during adulthood, although a significant number of paraphilias begin during adolescence. Mood and personality disorders are particularly common among paraphiliacs. Recent evidence suggests that cognitive-behavioral and hormonal treatment interventions are most effective in reducing paraphilic behavior.

REFERENCES

Abel, G.G., Becker, J.V., Mittelman, M.S., Cunningham-Rathner, J., Rouleau, J-L., & Murphy, W.D. (1987). Self-reported sex crimes of nonincarcerated paraphiliacs. *Journal of Interpersonal Violence, 2,* 3–25.

Abel, G.G., Osborn, C.A., & Twigg, D.A. (1993). Sexual assault through the life span: Adult offenders with juvenile histories. In H.E. Barbaree, W.L. Marshall, & S.M. Hudson (Eds.), *The juvenile sex offender* (pp. 104–117). New York: Guilford Press.

Abel, G.G. & Rouleau, J.L. (1995). Sexual abuses. *Psychiatric Clinics of North America, 18,* 139–153.

Abramson, D.J., Barlow, D.H., Beck, J.G., Sakheim, D.K., & Kelly, J.P. (1985). The effects of attentional focus and partner responsiveness on sexual responding: Replication and extension. *Archives of Sexual Behavior, 14,* 361–371.

Adams, A.E., Haynes, S.N., & Brayer, M.A. (1985). Cognitive distraction in female sexual arousal. *Psychophysiology, 22,* 689–696.

Alexander, G.M., & Sherwin, B.B. (1993). Sex steroids, sexual behavior, and selection attention for erotic stimuli in women using oral contraceptives. *Psychoneuroendocrinology, 18,* 91–102.

American Psychiatric Association. (1994). *Diagnostic and statistical manual of mental disorders,* 4th ed. Washington, DC: Author.

Andersen, B.L. (1981). A comparison of systematic desensitization and directed masturbation in the treatment of primary orgasmic dysfunction in females. *Journal of Consulting and Clinical Psychology, 49,* 568–570.

Andersen, B.L. (1983). Primary orgasmic dysfunction: Diagnostic considerations and review of treatment. *Psychological Bulletin, 93,* 105–136.

Andersen, B.L, Anderson, B., & deProsse, C. (1989). Controlled prospective longitudinal study of women with cancer: I. Sexual functioning outcomes. *Journal of Consulting and Clinical Psychology, 57,* 683–691.

Andersen, B.L., Broffitt, B., Karlsson, J.A., & Turnquist, D.C. (1989). A psychometric analysis of the Sexual Arousability Index. *Journal of Consulting and Clinical Psychology, 57,* 123–130.

Andersen, B.L., & Cyranowski, J.C. (1994). Women's sexual self schema. *Journal of Personality and Social Psychology, 67,* 1079–1100.

Andersen, B.L., & Cyranowski, J.C. (1995). Women's sexuality: Behaviors, responses, and individual differences. *Journal of Consulting and Clinical Psychology, 63,* 891–906.

Andersen, B.L., & Espindle, D. (in preparation). *Men's sexual self schema.*

Ban, T.A., & Freyhan, F.A. (1980). *Drug treatment of sexual dysfunction.* New York: Karger.

Bancroft, J. (1988). A physiological approach. In J.H. Geer & W.T. O'Donohue (Eds.), *Theories of human sexuality* (pp. 411–421). New York: Plenum Press.

Bancroft, J. (1989). Sexual desire and the brain. *Sexual and Marital Therapy, 3,* 11–27.

Bancroft, J., & Coles, L. (1976). Three years' experience in a sexual problems clinic. *British Medical Journal, 281,* 1575–1577.

Bancroft, J., & Wu, F. (1985). Erectile impotence. *British Medical Journal, 290,* 1566–1568.

Bancroft, J., & Wu, F.C.W. (1983). Changes in erectile responsiveness during androgen replacement therapy. *Archives of Sexual Behavior, 12,* 59–66.

Bansal, S. (1988). Sexual dysfunction in hypertensive men: A critical review of the literature. *Hypertension, 12,* 1–10.

Barbach, L.G. (1975). *For yourself: The fulfillment of female sexuality.* New York: Doubleday.

Barbaree, H.E. & Marshall, W.L. (1989). Erectile responses among heterosexual child molesters, father–daughter incest offenders, and matched non-offenders. Five distinct age preference profiles. *Canadian Journal of Behavioural Science, 21,* 70–82.

Barlow, D.H. (1986). Causes of sexual dysfunction: The role of anxiety and cognitive interference. *Journal of Consulting and Clinical Psychology, 54,* 140–148.

Barlow, D.H., Sakheim, D.K., & Beck, J.G. (1983). Anxiety increases sexual arousal. *Journal of Abnormal Psychology, 92,* 49–54.

Barnard, G.W., Hankins, G.C., & Robbins, L. (1992). Prior life trauma, posttraumatic stress symptoms, and character traits in sex offenders: An exploratory study. *Journal of Traumatic Stress, 5,* 393–420.

Beck, J.G. (1995). Hypoactive sexual desire disorder: An overview. *Journal of Consulting and Clinical Psychology, 63,* 919–927.

Beck, J.G. (1986). Self-generated distraction in erectile dysfunction: The role of attentional processes. *Advances in Behavior Research and Therapy, 8,* 205–221.

Beck, J.G., Barlow, D.H., & Sakheim, D.K. (1982, August). *Sexual arousal and suppression patterns in function and dysfunctional men.* Paper presented at the annual convention of the American Psychological Association, Washington, DC.

Beggs, V.E., Calhoun, K.S., & Wolchik, S.A. (1987). Sexual anxiety and female sexual arousal: A comparison of arousal during sexual anxiety stimuli and sexual pleasure stimuli. *Archives of Sexual Behavior, 16,* 311–319.

Bem, S.L. (1974) The measurement of psychological androgyny. *Journal of Consulting and Clinical Psychology, 42,* 155–162.

Bradford, J.M.W. (1990). The antiandrogen and hormonal treatments of sex offenders. In W.L. Marshall, D.R. Laws, & H.E. Barbaree, (Eds.), *Handbook of sexual assault: Issues, theories, and treatment of the offender* (pp. 297–310). New York: Plenum Press.

Briere, J., & Runtz, M. (1989). University males' sexual interest in children: Predicting potential indices of "pedophilia" in a nonforensic sample. *Child Abuse and Neglect, 13,* 65–75.

Burger, H.G., Hailes, J., Menelaus, M., Nelson, J., Hudson, B., & Balazs, N. (1984). The management of persistent menopausal symptoms with oestradiol-testosterone implants: Clinical, lipid, and hormonal results. *Maturitas, 6,* 351–358.

Buvat, J., Buvat-Herbaut, M., Lemaire, A., Marcolin, G., & Quittelier, E. (1990). Recent developments in the clinical assessment and diagnosis of erectile dysfunction. *Annual Review of Sex Research, 1,* 265–308.

Caird, W.K., & Wincze, J.P. (1974). Videotaped desensitization of frigidity. *Journal of Behavior Therapy and Experimental Psychiatry, 74,* 175–178.

Condy, S.R., Templer, D.I., Brown, R., & Veaco, L. (1987). Parameters of sexual contact of boys with women. *Archives of Sexual Behavior, 16,* 379–394.

Derogatis, L.R., Fagan, P.J., Schmidt, C.W., Wise, T.N., & Glidden, K.S. (1986). Psychological subtypes of anorgasmia: A marker variable approach. *Journal of Sex and Marital Therapy, 5,* 197–210.

Dow, S. (1981). Retarded ejaculation. *Journal of Sex and Marital Therapy, 7,* 49–53.

Ellis, H. (1906). *Studies in the psychology of sex. Volume V. Erotic symbolism. The mechanism of detumescence. The psychic state in pregnancy.* Philadelphia: FA Davis.

Ellis, B.J., & Symons, D. (1990). Sex differences in sexual fantasy: An evolutionary psychological approach. *Journal of Sex Research, 27,* 527–555.

Ernst, C., Foldenyi, M., & Angst, J. (1993). The Zurich Study: XXI. Sexual dysfunctions and disturbances in young adults. *European Archives of Psychiatry and Clinical Neuroscience, 243,* 179–188.

Fagen, P.J., Schmidt, C.W., Wise, T.N., & Derogatis, L.R. (1988). Sexual dysfunction and dual psychiatric diagnoses. *Comprehensive Psychiatry, 29,* 278–284.

Fahrner, E. (1987). Sexual dysfunction in male alcohol addicts: Prevalence and treatment. *Archives of Sexual Behavior, 16,* 247–257.

Federal Bureau of Investigation. (1994). *Uniform crime reports for the United States, 1993.* Washington, DC: U.S. Government Printing Office.

Fedora, O., Reddon, J.R., Morrison, J.W., Fedora, S.K., Pascoe, H., & Yeudall, L.T. (1992). Sadism and other paraphilias in normal controls and aggressive and nonaggressive sex offenders. *Archives of Sexual Behavior, 21,* 1–15.

Feingold, A. (1994). Gender differences in personality: A meta-analysis. *Psychological Bulletin, 116,* 429–456.

Frank, E., Anderson, C., & Kupfer, D.J. (1976). *American Journal of Psychiatry, 133,* 559–562.

Freund, K., & Watson, R. J. (1991). Assessment of the sensitivity and specificity of a phallometric test: An update of phallometric diagnosis of pedophilia. *Psychological Assessment, 3,* 254–260.

Friedrich, W.N., & Gerber, P.N. (1994). Autoerotic asphyxia: The development of a paraphilia. *Journal of the American Academy of Child and Adolescent Psychiatry, 33,* 970–974.

Friedrich, W.N., Grambsch, P., Damon, L., Hewitt, S.K., Koverola, C., Lang, R.A., Wolfe, V., & Broughton, D. (1992). Child Sexual Behavior Inventory: Normative and clinical comparisons. *Psychological Assessment, 4,* 303–311.

Fuchs, K., Hoch, Z., Paldi, E., Abramovici, H., Brandes, J., Timor-Tritsch, I., & Kleinhaus, M. (1978). Hypnodesensitization therapy of vaginismus: In vitro and in vivo methods. In J. LoPiccolo & L. LoPiccolo (Eds.), *Handbook of sex therapy* (pp. 261–270). New York: Plenum Press.

Furby, L., Weinrott, M.R., & Blackshaw, L. (1989). Sex offender recidivism: A review. *Psychological Bulletin, 105,* 3–30.

Geer, J.H., & Head, S. (1990). The sexual response system. In J.T. Cacioppo & L. Tassinary (Eds.), *Principles of psychophysiology: Physical, social and inferential elements* (pp. 599–630). Cambridge: Cambridge Press.

Godpodinoff, M.L. (1989). Premature ejaculation: Clinical subgroups and etiology. *Journal of Sex and Marital Therapy, 15,* 130–134.

Graber, B., & Kline-Graber, G. (1981). Research criteria for male erectile failure. *Journal of Sex and Marital Therapy, 7,* 37–48.

Graham, J.R. (1987). *The MMPI: A practical guide,* 2nd ed. New York: Oxford University Press.

Grenier, G., & Byers, E.S. (1995). Rapid ejaculation: A review of conceptual, etiological, and treatment issues. *Archives of Sexual Behavior, 24,* 447–472.

Hall, G.C.N. (1988). Criminal behavior as a function of clinical and actuarial variables in a sexual offender population. *Journal of Consulting and Clinical Psychology, 56,* 773–775.

Hall, G.C.N. (1995a). The preliminary development of theory-based community treatment for sexual offenders. *Professional Psychology: Research and Practice, 26,* 478–483.

Hall, G.C.N. (1995b). Sexual offender recidivism revisited: A meta-analysis of recent treatment studies. *Journal of Consulting and Clinical Psychology, 63,* 802–809.

Hall, G.C.N. (1996). *Theory-based assessment, treatment, and prevention of sexual aggression.* New York: Oxford University Press.

Hall, G.C.N., & Andersen, B.L. (1993). Sexual dysfunction and deviation. In A.S. Bellack & M. Hersen (Eds.), *Psychopathology in adulthood* (pp. 295–318). Boston: Allyn and Bacon.

Hall, G.C.N. & Barongan, C. (1997). Prevention of sexual aggression: Sociocultural risk and protective factors. *American Psychologist, 52,* 5–14.

Hall, G.C.N., Hirschman, R., & Oliver, L.L. (1995). Sexual arousal and arousability to pedophilic stimuli in a community sample of "normal" men. *Behavior Therapy, 26,* 681–694.

Hall, G.C.N., Proctor, W.C., & Nelson, G.M. (1988). The validity of physiological measures of pedophilic sexual arousal in a sexual offender population. *Journal of Consulting and Clinical Psychology, 56,* 118–122.

Hall, G.C.N., Shondrick, D.D., & Hirschman, R. (1993a). Conceptually derived treatments for sexual aggressors. *Professional Psychology: Research and Practice, 24,* 62–69.

Hall, G.C.N., Shondrick, D.D., & Hirschman, R. (1993b). The role of sexual arousal in sexually aggressive behavior: A meta-analysis. *Journal of Consulting and Clinical Psychology, 61,* 1091–1095.

Hanson, R.K., Steffy, R.A., & Gauthier, R. (1993). Long-term recidivism of child molesters. *Journal of Consulting and Clinical Psychology, 61,* 646–652.

Harris, G.T., Rice, M.E., Quinsey, V.L., Chaplin, T.C., & Earls, C. (1992). Maximizing the discriminant validity of phallometric assessment data. *Psychological Assessment, 4,* 502–511.

Hatfield, E., & Rapson, R.L. (1993). *Love, sex, and intimacy: Their psychology, biology, and history.* New York: HarperCollins.

Hawton, K., Catalan, J., Fagg, J. (1992). Sex therapy for erectile dysfunction: Characteristics of couples, treatment outcome, and prognostic factors. *Archives of Sexual Behavior, 21,* 161–175.

Heiman, J.R. (1978). Issues in the use of psychophysiology to assess female sexual dysfunction. In J. LoPiccolo & L. LoPiccolo (Eds.), *Handbook of sex therapy* (pp. 123–135). New York: Plenum Press.

Heiman, J.R. (1980). Female sexual response patterns: Interactions of physiological, affective, and contextual cues. *Archives of General Psychiatry, 37,* 1311–1316.

Heiman, J.R., Rowland, D.L., Hatch, J.P., & Gladue, B.A. (1991). Psychophysiological and endocrine responses to sexual arousal in women. *Archives of Sexual Behavior, 20,* 171–186.

Hengeveld, M.W. (1986). Erectile dysfunction: Diagnosis and choice of therapy. *World Journal of Urology, 3,* 249–252.

Hoon, E.F., Hoon, P.W., & Wincze, J.P. (1976). An inventory for the measurement of female sexual arousability: The SAI. *Archives of Sexual Behavior, 5,* 291–300.

Hurlbert, D.F. (1993). A comparative study using orgasm consistency training in the treatment of women reporting hypoactive sexual desire. *Journal of Sex and Marital Therapy, 19,* 41–55.

Hurlbert, D.F., White, L.C., Powell, R.D., & Apt, C. (1993). Orgasm consistency training in the treat-

ment of women reporting hypoactive sexual desire: An outcome comparison of women-only groups and couples-only groups. *Journal of Behavior Therapy and Experimental Psychiatry, 24,* 3–13.

Janssen, P.L. (1985). Psychodynamic study of male potency disorders: An overview. *Psychotherapy and Psychosomatics, 44,* 6–17.

Jones, J.C., & Barlow, D.H. (1990). Self-reported frequency of sexual urges, fantasies, and masturbatory fantasies in heterosexual males and females. *Archives of Sexual Behavior, 19,* 269–279.

Josephs, R.A., Markus, H.R., & Tafarodi, R.W. (1992). Gender and self-esteem. *Journal of Personality and Social Psychology, 63,* 391–402.

Kafka, M.P., & Prentky, R.A. (1994). Preliminary observations of DSM-III-R Axis I comorbidity in men with paraphilias and paraphilia-related disorders. *Journal of Clinical Psychiatry, 55,* 481–487.

Kaplan, H.S. (1974). *The new sex therapy.* New York: Brunner/Mazel.

Kaplan, H.S. (1979). *Disorders of sexual desire.* New York: Brunner/Mazel.

Katz, R.C., Gipson, M.T., Kearl, A., & Kriskovich, M. (1989). Assessing sexual aversion in college students: The Sexual Aversion Scale. *Journal of Sex and Marital Therapy, 15,* 135–140.

Katz, R.C., Gipson, M.T., & Turner, S. (1992). Brief report: Recent findings on the Sexual Aversion Scale. *Journal of Sex and Marital Therapy, 18,* 141–145.

Kedia, K. (1983). Ejaculation and emission: Normal physiology, dysfunction, and therapy. In R.J. Krane, M.B. Siroky, & I. Goldstein (Eds.), *Male sexual dysfunction* (pp. 37–54) Boston: Little, Brown.

Kilmann, P.R., & Auerbach, R. (1979). Treatments of premature ejaculation and psychogenic impotence: A critical review of the literature. *Archives of Sexual Behavior, 8,* 81–100.

Kinder, B.N., & Curtiss, G. (1988). Specific components in the etiology, assessment, and treatment of male sexual dysfunctions. Controlled outcome studies. *Journal of Sex and Marital Therapy, 14,* 40–48.

Kinsey, A.C., Pomeroy, W.B., & Martin, C.E. (1948). *Sexual behavior in the human male.* Philadelphia: W.B. Saunders.

Kinsey, A.C., Pomeroy, W.G., Martin, E.C., & Gebhard, P.H. (1953). *Sexual behavior in the human female*. Philadelphia: W.B. Saunders.

Lann, E., Everaerd, W., & Evers, A. (1995). Assessment of female sexual arousal: Response specificity and construct validity. *Psychophysiology, 32,* 476–485.

Laan, E., Everaerd, W., van Aanhold, M., & Rebel, M. (1993). Performance demand and sexual arousal in women. *Behaviour Research and Therapy, 31,* 25–35.

Laan, E., Everaerd, W., van Bellen, G., & Hanewald, G. (1994). Women's sexual and emotional responses to male- and female-produced erotica. *Archives of Sexual Behavior, 23,* 153–170.

Lamont, J. (1978). Vaginismus. *American Journal of Obstetrics and Gynecology, 131,* 632–636.

Laumann, E.O., Gagnon, J.H., Michael, R.T., & Michaels, S. (1994). *The social organization of sexuality: Sexual practices in the United States*. Chicago: University of Chicago Press.

Laws, D.R. (1989). *Relapse prevention with sex offenders*. New York: Guilford Press.

Levine, R.L. (1992). The mechanisms of human female sexual arousal. In J. Bancroft, C.M. Davis, & H.J. Ruppel (Eds.), *Annual review of sex research* (Vol. 3, pp. 1–48). Lake Mills, IA: Stoyles Graphic Services.

Levine, S.B., & Agle, D. (1978). The effectiveness of sex therapy for chronic secondary psychological impotence. *Journal of Sex and Marital Therapy, 4,* 235–258.

Lief, H.I. (1977). Inhibited sexual desire. *Medical Aspects of Human Sexuality, 7,* 94–95.

LoPiccolo, J., & Stock, W.E. (1986). Treatment of sexual dysfunction. *Journal of Consulting and Clinical Psychology, 54,* 158–167.

Lunde, I., Larsen, G.K., Fog, E., & Garde, K. (1991). Sexual desire, orgasm, and sexual fantasies: A study of 625 Danish women born in 1910, 1936, and 1958. *Journal of Sex Education and Therapy, 17,* 111–115.

Magee, M.C. (1980). Psychogenic impotence: A critical review. *Urology, 15,* 435–442.

Marshall, W.L., & Barbaree, H.E. (1988). The long-term evaluation of a behavioral treatment program for child molesters. *Behaviour Research and Therapy, 26,* 499–511.

Marshall, W.L., & Barbaree, H.E. (1990). Outcome of comprehensive cognitive-behavioral treatment programs. In W.L. Marshall, D.R. Laws, & H.E. Barbaree (Eds.), *Handbook of sexual assault* (pp. 363–385). New York: Plenum Press.

Masters, W.H., & Johnson, V.E. (1966). *Human sexual response*. Boston: Little, Brown.

Masters, W.H., & Johnson, V.E. (1970). *Human sexual inadequacy*. Boston: Little, Brown.

McCarthy, B.W. (1984). Strategies and techniques for the treatment of inhibited sexual desire. *Journal of Sex and Marital Therapy, 10,* 97–104.

McCarthy, B.W. (1993). Relapse prevention strategies and techniques in sex therapy. *Journal of Sex and Marital Therapy, 19,* 142–147.

McConaghy, N. (1994). Sexual deviations. In M. Hersen, R.T. Ammerman, & L.A. Sisson, (Eds.), *Handbook of aggressive and destructive behavior in psychiatric patients* (pp. 261–286). New York: Plenum Press.

McGovern, K.B., Stewart, R.C., & LoPiccolo, J. (1975). Secondary orgasmic dysfunction: I. Analysis and strategies for treatment. *Archives of Sexual Behavior, 4,* 265–275.

Meana, M., & Binik, Y.M. (1994). Painful coitus: A review of female dyspareunia. *Journal of Nervous and Mental Disease, 182,* 264–272.

Meisler, A.W., Carey, M.P., Lantinga, L.J., & Krauss, D.J. (1989). Erectile dysfunction in diabetes mellitus: A biopsychosocial approach to etiology and assessment. *Annals of Behavioral Medicine, 11,* 18–27.

Meuwissen, I., & Over, R. (1990). Habituation and dishabituation of female sexual arousal. *Behaviour Research and Therapy, 28,* 217–226.

Mitchell, J.E., & Popkin, M.K. (1982). Antipsychotic drug therapy and sexual dysfunction in men. *American Journal of Psychiatry, 139,* 633–637.

Moffitt, T.E. (1993). "Life-course-persistent" and "adolescence-limited" antisocial behavior: A developmental taxonomy. *Psychological Review, 100,* 674–701.

Mohr, D.C., & Beutler, L.E. (1990). Erectile dysfunction: A review of diagnostic and treatment procedures. *Clinical Psychology Review, 10,* 123–150.

Morokoff, P.J. (1985). Effects of sex guilt, repression, sexual arousability, and sexual experience on female sexual arousal during erotica and fantasy. *Journal of Personality and Social Psychology, 49,* 177–187.

Morokoff, P.J. (1989). Sex bias and POD. *American Psychologist, 44,* 73–75.

Morokoff, P.J., & Heiman, J.R. (1980). Effects of erotic stimuli on sexually functional and dysfunctional women: Multiple measures before and after sex therapy. *Behaviour Research and Therapy, 18,* 127–137.

Munjack, D.J., Schlaks, A., Sanchez, V.C., Usigli, R., Zulucta, A., & Leonard, M. (1984). Rational-emotive therapy in the treatment of erectile failure: An initial study. *Journal of Sex and Marital Therapy, 10,* 170–175.

Newcomb, M.D., & Bentler, P.M. (1983). Dimensions of subjective female orgasmic responsiveness. *Journal of Personality and Social Psychology, 44,* 862–873.

Nutter, D.E., & Condron, M.K. (1983). Sexual fantasy and activity patterns of females with inhibited sexual desire versus normal controls. *Journal of Sex and Marital Therapy, 9,* 276–282.

O'Carroll, R. (1991). Sexual desire disorders: A review of controlled treatment studies. *Journal of Sex Research, 28,* 607–624.

Oliver, L.L., Hall, G.C.N., & Neuhaus, S. (1993). Personality characteristics of adolescent sex offenders. *Criminal Justice and Behavior, 20,* 359–370.

Oliver, M.B., & Hyde, J.S. (1993). Gender differences in sexuality: A meta-analysis. *Psychological Bulletin, 114,* 29–51.

Palace, E.M. (1995). Modification of dysfunctional patterns of sexual response through autonomic arousal and false physiological feedback. *Journal of Consulting and Clinical Psychology, 63,* 604–615.

Palace, E.M., & Gorzalka, B.B. (1990). The enhancing effects of anxiety on arousal in sexually dysfunctional and functional women. *Journal of Abnormal Psychology, 99,* 403–411.

Palace, E.M., & Gorzalka, B.B. (1992). Differential patterns of arousal in sexually functional and dysfunctional women: Physiological and subjective components of sexual response. *Archives of Sexual Behavior, 21,* 135–159.

Person, E.S., Terestman, N., Myers, W.A., Goldberg,

E.L., & Salvadori, C. (1989). Gender differences in sexual behaviors and fantasies in a college population. *Journal of Sex and Marital Therapy, 15,* 187–198.

Ponticas, Y. (1992). Sexual aversion versus hypoactive sexual desire: A diagnostic challenge. *Psychiatric Medicine, 10,* 273–282.

Rice, M.E., Quinscy, V.L., & Harris, G.T. (1991). Sexual recidivism among child molesters released from a maximum security psychiatric institution. *Journal of Consulting and Clinical Psychology, 59,* 381–386.

Rosen, R.C., & Beck, J.G. (1988). *Patterns of sexual arousal: Psychophysiological processes and clinical applications.* New York: Guilford Press.

Ryan, G. (1989). Victim to victimizer: Rethinking victim treatment. *Journal of Interpersonal Violence, 4,* 325–341.

Sakheim, D.K., Barlow, D.H., Abramson, D.J., & Beck, J.G. (1987). Distinguishing between organogenic and psychogenic erectile dysfunction. *Behavior Research and Therapy, 25,* 379–390.

Sarrel, L.J., & Sarrel, P. (1979). *Sexual unfolding.* Boston: Little, Brown.

Schull, W., & Sprenkle, T. (1980). Retarded ejaculation. *Journal of Sex and Marital Therapy, 6,* 234–246.

Schreiner-Engel, P., & Schiavi, R.C. (1986). Lifetime psychopathology in individuals with low sexual desire. *Journal of Nervous and Mental Diseases, 174,* 646–651.

Schreiner-Engel, P., Schiavi, R.C., Smith, H., & White, D. (1982). Plasma testosterone and female sexual behavior. In Z. Hock & H.I. Lief (Eds.), *Proceedings of the Fifth World Congress of Sexology.* Amsterdam: Excerpta Medica.

Schreiner-Engel, P., Schiavi, R.C., White, D., & Ghizzani, A. (1989). Low sexual desire in women: The role of reproductive hormones. *Hormones and Behavior, 23,* 221–234.

Segraves, K.B., & Segraves, R.T. (1991). Hypoactive sexual desire disorder: Prevalence and comorbidity in 906 subjects. *Journal of Sex and Marital Therapy, 17,* 55–58.

Semans, J.H. (1956). Premature ejaculation: A new approach. *Southern Medical Journal, 49,* 353–357.

Singer, B., & Toates, F.M. (1987). Sexual motivation. *Journal of Sex Research, 23,* 481–501.

Spector, I.P., & Carey, M.P. (1990). Incidence and prevalence of the sexual dysfunctions: A critical review of the empirical literature. *Archives of Sexual Behavior, 19,* 389–408.

Spiess, W.F.J., Geer, J.H., & Donohue, W.T. (1984). Premature ejaculation: Investigation of factors in ejaculatory latency. *Journal of Abnormal Psychology, 93,* 242–245.

St. Lawrence, J.S., & Madakasira, S. (1992). Evaluation and treatment of premature ejaculation: A critical review. *International Journal of Psychiatry in Medicine, 22,* 77–97.

Strassberg, D.S., Kelly, M.P., Carroll, C., & Kircher, J.C. (1990). The psychophysiological nature of premature ejaculation. *Archives of Sexual Behavior, 16,* 327–336.

Strassberg, D.S., Mahoney, J.M., Schaugaard, M., & Hale, V.E. (1990). The role of anxiety in premature ejaculation: Psychophysiological model. *Archives of Sexual Behavior, 19,* 251–257.

Stuart, F.M., Hammond, D.C., & Pett, M.A. (1987). Inhibited sexual desire in women. *Archives of Sexual Behavior, 16,* 91–106.

Studd, J.W., Collins, W.P., Chakravarti, S., Newton, J.R., Oram, D., & Parsons, A. (1977). Oestradiol and testosterone implants in the treatment of psychosexual problems in the postmenopausal women. *British Journal of Obstetrics and Gynecology, 84,* 314–315.

Templeman, T.L., & Stinnett, R.D. (1991). Patterns of sexual arousal and history in a "normal" sample of young men. *Archives of Sexual Behavior, 20,* 137–150.

Turpin, G. (1991). The psychophysiological assessment of anxiety disorders: Three-systems measurement and beyond. *Psychological Assessment, 3,* 366–375.

Vliet, L.W., & Meyer, J.K. (1982). Erectile dysfunction: Progress in evaluation and treatment. *Johns Hopkins Medical Journal, 151,* 246–258.

Wabrek, A.J., & Wabrek, C.J. (1975). Dyspareunia. *Journal of Sex and Marital Therapy, 1,* 234–241.

Wagner, G., & Metz, P. (1980). Impotence (erectile dysfunction) due to vascular disorders: An overview. *Journal of Sex and Marital Therapy, 6,* 223–233.

Wakefield, J.C. (1987). Sex bias in the diagnosis of primary orgasmic dysfunction. *American Psychologist, 42,* 464–471.

Wakefield, J.C. (1988). Female primary orgasmic dysfunction: Masters and Johnson versus DSM-III-R in diagnosis and incidence. *Journal of Sex Research, 24,* 363–377.

Walster, E., & Berscheid, E. (1974). A little bit about love: A minor essay on a major topic. In T.L. Huston (Ed.), *Foundations of interpersonal attraction* (pp. 355–381). New York: Academic Press.

Wilensky, M., & Myers, M.F. (1987). Retarded ejaculation in homosexual patients: A report of nine cases. *Journal of Sex Research, 23,* 85–105.

Wilson, G.D. (1988). Measurement of sex fantasy. *Sexual and Marital Therapy, 3,* 45–55.

Wolpe, J. (1958). *Psychotherapy by reciprocal inhibition.* Stanford, CA: Stanford University Press.

Worling, J.R. (1995). Sexual abuse histories of adolescent male sex offenders: Differences on the basis of the age and gender of their victims. *Journal of Abnormal Psychology, 104,* 610–613.

Zimmer, D., Borchardt, E., & Fischle, C. (1983). Sexual fantasies of sexually distressed and non-distressed men and women: An empirical comparison. *Journal of Sex and Marital Therapy, 9,* 38–50.

Zucker, K.J., & Bradley, S.J. (1995). *Gender identity disorder and psychosexual problems in children and adolescents.* New York: Guilford Press.

CHAPTER 18

EATING DISORDERS

David M. Garner
Toledo Center for Eating Disorders;
Bowling Green State University; University of Toledo

Julie J. Desai
Toledo Center for Eating Disorders

DESCRIPTION OF THE DISORDERS

In recent years, there has been a trend toward understanding both anorexia nervosa and bulimia nervosa as multidetermined disorders in which the symptom patterns represent a final common pathway resulting from a number of distinctly different developmental routes. Biological, psychological, familial, and sociocultural factors have been hypothesized as being relevant to the development of both eating disorders, although the relative contribution of each factor may vary markedly across the heterogeneous patient population.

A complete understanding of anorexia nervosa and bulimia nervosa must account for factors that predispose individuals to each of the eating disorders. Theory should be able to delineate the variety of developmental experiences that interact with these factors to initiate symptom expression as well as accounting for maintaining variables (biological, psychological, and interpersonal) and key variations in the symptom picture. Although current models are

unable to specify all of these elements in precise detail, research and clinical observations in the past two decades have improved the understanding of eating disorders, which, in turn, has led to more sophisticated treatment recommendations. Our chapter will provide an overview of diagnosis, major etiological theories, and associated psychological features for eating disorders.

Diagnosis of Anorexia Nervosa

The current requirements for a diagnosis of anorexia nervosa on the basis of the *Diagnostic and Statistical Manual of Mental Disorders* (DSM-IV; American Psychiatric Association [APA], 1994) are summarized as follows: (1) refusal to maintain a body weight over a minimally normal weight for age and height (e.g., weight loss leading to maintenance of a body weight 15% below norms or failure to achieve expected weight gain during a period of growth); (2) intense fear of gaining weight or becoming fat, even though underweight; (3) disturbance in the way that

419

body weight, size, or shape is experienced; and (4) amenorrhea in females (absence of at least three consecutive menstrual cycles).

DSM-IV (APA, 1994) divides anorexia nervosa into two diagnostic subtypes: (1) restricting type and (2) binge-eating/purging type. The restricting type is defined by rigid restriction of food intake, without bingeing or purging. The binge-eating/purging type is defined by stringent attempts to limit intake, which are punctuated by episodes of binge eating as well as self-induced vomiting and/or laxative abuse. This diverges from previous conventions in which anorexia nervosa was subdivided simply on the basis of the presence or absence of binge eating (Casper et al., 1980; Garfinkel, Moldofsky, & Garner, 1980). The rationale for dividing anorexia nervosa patients on the basis of bingeing *and* purging rather than binge eating alone rests on two observations. First, there are significant medical risks associated with compensatory behaviors, such as self-induced vomiting and laxative abuse (Mitchell, Pomeroy, & Adson, 1997). Second, recent research has indicated that patients who purge, even if they do not engage in objective episodes of binge eating, display significantly more psychosocial disturbance than nonpurging patients (Garner, Garner, & Rosen, 1993). Patients who regularly engage in bulimic episodes report greater impulsivity, social/sexual dysfunction, substance abuse, general impulse control problems (e.g., lying and stealing), family dysfunction, and depression as part of a general picture of more conspicuous emotional disturbance when compared to patients with the restricting subtype of anorexia nervosa (Garner, Garner, & Rosen, 1993; Herzog, Keller, Sacks, Yeh, & Lavori, 1992; Kreipe, 1995) In contrast, restricting anorexia nervosa patients have been described as being overly compliant, but at the same time obstinate, perfectionistic, obsessive-compulsive, shy, introverted, interpersonally sensitive, and stoical (Bastiani, Rao, Weltzin, & Kaye, 1995; Hsu, Kaye, & Weltzin, 1993; Kreipe, 1995).

Diagnosis of Bulimia Nervosa

The criteria for diagnosis of bulimia nervosa according to the DSM-IV (APA, 1994) are summarized as follows: (1) recurrent episodes of binge eating (a sense of lack of control over eating a large amount of food in a discrete period of time, which would be considered unusual under similar circumstances); (2) recurrent inappropriate compensatory behavior(s) in order to prevent weight gain (e.g., vomiting; abuse of laxatives, diuretics, or other medications; fasting or excessive exercise); (3) a minimum average of two episodes of binge eating and inappropriate compensatory behaviors per week for the past 3 months; (4) self-evaluation unduly influenced by body shape and weight; and (5) the disturbance does not occur exclusively during episodes of anorexia nervosa. Bulimia nervosa patients are further divided into purging and nonpurging subtypes based on the regular use of self-induced vomiting, laxatives, or diuretics (APA, 1994). Although binge eating is the key symptom identifying bulimia nervosa, agreement has not been achieved about the definition of this behavior in the disorder. For example, the requirement that binges must be "large" is inconsistent with research indicating that a significant proportion of "binges" reported by bulimia nervosa patients involve small amounts of food (cf. Garner, Shafer, & Rosen, 1992).

Eating Disorders Not Otherwise Specified

DSM-IV (APA, 1994) delineates a large and heterogeneous diagnostic category as "eating disorder, not otherwise specified" (EDNOS) for individuals with clinically significant eating disorders who fail to meet all of the diagnostic criteria for anorexia nervosa or bulimia nervosa. However, the specific terminology of this diagnostic category may result in misinterpretations regarding the clinical significance of such eating problems, as they may mistakenly be perceived as being of less importance. This view is inaccurate, as the clinical picture for individuals diagnosed with EDNOS can be as complex and as serious as for those who meet the diagnostic criteria for anorexia nervosa or bulimia nervosa (Walsh & Garner, 1997).

Binge-eating disorder (BED) is included in the DSM-IV as a category requiring further study. Although there is merit in adopting binge-eating disorder into the diagnostic nomenclature (Spitzer et al., 1993), it is crucial to remain aware that binge eating and associated psychological symptoms, particularly in obese persons, may be attributed to standard weight loss treatments (cf. Garner & Wooley, 1991). This term has been proposed to apply to individuals who suffer from serious distress or impairment as a result of binge eating, but who do not qualify for a diagnosis of bulimia nervosa because they do not regularly engage in inappropriate compensatory behaviors such as self-induced vomiting or the abuse of laxatives and/or medications. Despite those differences, individuals who fit into the separate DSM-IV categories also share many common features, especially pertaining to the degree of emphasis they place on body weight in self-assessment.

DSM-IV criteria in qualifying for BED diagnosis include the following: (1) eating a quantity of food (which most people would consider large under similar circumstances) within a specific period of time, associated with (2) a sense of loss of control with regard to eating behavior. Additionally, it must occur within the context of three of the following five items: (1) eating quickly; (2) eating beyond the point of satiety; (3) eating for reasons other than physical hunger; (4) eating in isolation because of self-consciousness regarding the quantity of food consumed; or (5) experiencing self-depreciating, depressive, or guilty feelings after overeating. Marked distress as a result of binge eating must be present, and the binge eating should occur for 2 days per week for a duration of 6 months (APA, 1994).

Differential Diagnosis

Making a definitive diagnosis of an eating disorder requires careful attention, as there are a plethora of causes to account for weight loss and vomiting, which may be the result of medical complications or occur within the context of other psychological difficulties (Powers, 1997). Although eating disorders may be easily identifiable in many cases, alternative causes of weight loss can be harder to detect, as physical appearance, weight, and other reported symptoms can easily mimic those commonly associated with an eating disorder. Medical disorders that may result in unexplained weight loss include, but are not limited to, oral, pharyngeal, esophageal, metabolic, and gastric complications; malabsorption; Crohn's disease; Addison's disease; inflammatory bowel disease; endocrine disease (hyperthyroidism, diabetes); tuberculosis; AIDS; leukemia, lymphoma; and lung, gastric, esophageal, and pancreatic tumors (Powers, 1997; Szauter & Levine, 1997). Within the psycho-

logical domain, occurrence of mood disturbances (such as depression and anxiety) or psychoses (schizophrenia, paranoid disorder) can provide insight into weight/eating-related difficulties that may closely resemble an eating disorder (Powers, 1997; Szauter & Levine, 1997). Thus, it is essential that individuals assessing, diagnosing, or treating those who presumably have eating disorders thoughtfully evaluate the evidence with which they are presented to prevent misdiagnosis and improper treatment interventions.

Relationship between Different Eating Disorders

There is extraordinary variability within each of the diagnostic subgroups in terms of demographic, clinical, and psychological variables (Welch, Hall, & Renner, 1990). Patients with anorexia and bulimia nervosa have been observed to move between diagnostic categories at different points in time (Russell, 1979). For example, patients move between the two subtypes of anorexia nervosa (restricting and binge-eating/purging types) at different points in time, although the tendency is for restricters to go on to develop the symptoms of binge eating (and purging) more often than binge-eating patients move to an exclusively abstaining mode (Garner, Garner, & Rosen, 1993; Kreipe, 1995).

Even though distinctions between eating disorder syndromes have been emphasized, it is important to recognize that the different diagnostic subgroups tend to share many features in common. For example, even though anorexia nervosa patients are differentiated into "restricting" and "binge-eating/purging" subtypes, all eating disorder patients "restrict their food intake," "diet," and probably "fast" for abnormally long periods of time. Some do this in association with binge eating, some with vomiting and/or purgation, and some with neither of these symptoms. For certain individuals, this occurs at a statistically "normal" body weight (bulimia nervosa); for others, it occurs well over the body weight norms (e.g., binge-eating disorder).

Even the most obvious difference between anorexia and bulimia nervosa, absolute body weight, becomes blurred when one looks at the amount of body weight that bulimia nervosa patients have lost during the course of their disorder. Many bulimia nervosa patients have lost as much weight as those with anorexia nervosa, the difference being that the bulimia nervosa patients have simply lost from higher initial levels (Garner & Fairburn, 1988).

Whether the differences between diagnostic subgroups of eating-disordered patients represent distinctions or simply reflect a pattern of distress associated with binge-eating behaviors is not clear. Eckert, Halmi, Marchi, and Cohen (1987) have indicated that many of the reported differences in overall psychopathology between restricting and bulimic groups disappear with hospital treatment. Nevertheless, it is likely that differences exist between anorexia nervosa and bulimia nervosa with regard to treatment response. Many bulimia nervosa patients respond favorably to treatment, but the prognosis is worse for those with the bulimic subtype of anorexia nervosa (Steinhausen, Rauss-Mason, & Seidel, 1991).

Epidemiology

There are serious limitations to estimates of the incidence and prevalence of eating disorders, because most have been derived exclusively from self-report instruments and on samples that may not reflect important demographic differences in base rates. Nevertheless, there is agreement that both anorexia nervosa and bulimia nervosa may occur in as many as 1% to 4% of female high school and college students (cf. Fairburn & Beglin, 1990, Kreipe, 1995). Suspected cases of clinical eating disorders or subclinical variants are even more common among groups exposed to heightened pressures to diet or maintain a thin shape. Research has confirmed a high incidence of actual or suspected cases among samples of ballet students, professional dancers, wrestlers, swimmers, skaters, and gymnasts (Garner & Rosen, 1991). Although there are case reports of anorexia nervosa in young children (Fosson, Knibbs, Bryant-Waugh, & Lask, 1987), the consensus is that it is very rare in this age group (Jaffe & Singer, 1989). However, some clinicians report seeing children who, although they fail to meet the strict DSM-IV criteria, present with variants of eating disorders (Bryant-Waugh & Lask, 1995). Similarly, though probably rarely, cases of anorexia nervosa also have been observed at the other end of the age spectrum (Kellett, Trimble, & Thorley, 1976).

Eating disorders are less common in men, who account for only 5% to 10% of clinical samples (Hoek, 1995). When eating disorders do occur in males, however, the clinical presentation resembles that of females (Andersen, 1990; Olivardia, Pope, Mangweth, & Hudson, 1995). One of the major differences hypothesized to account for the discrepancy between the genders includes the issues related to cultural values (Garner & Garfinkel, 1980). The expectations of the "ideal" body type represented in society through the media differ significantly for males and females. Females face tremendous pressure to conform to ultrathin, "waiflike" proportions, whereas the standard for males is typically represented in a muscular, V-shaped build that emphasizes strength, not thinness. Males with eating disorders often participate in activities with an emphasis on weight control, such as wrestling, dance, and gymnastics (Andersen, 1990).

Have Eating Disorders Changed over Time?

In the past, anorexia nervosa was typically associated with individuals of the upper socioeconomic classes; currently, however, clinicians and researchers report more heterogeneity with regard to socioeconomic status (Gowers & McMahon, 1989). Similarly, eating disorders have increasingly been identified among populations once thought to be unaffected, such as ethnic minorities and those from non-Western cultures (Srebnik & Saltzberg, 1994). According to Russell (1997), the most dramatic evidence for a transformation in the psychopathology of anorexia nervosa is the increased appearance of binge eating, both in anorexia nervosa and in eating-disordered patients who are not emaciated. However, the extent to which binge eating has actually become more common in anorexia nervosa is unclear, because this symptom may have been identified less reliably in earlier reports (Garner, 1993).

Casper (1983) noted another transformation in the psychopathology of eating disorders, as the motivational theme increasingly turned away from ascetic features commonly identified in "classic cases" toward a "drive for thinness" and associated attempts to achieve the modern cultural ideal of slimness as an expression of beauty for women. Commonly found in earlier writings on anorexia nervosa, the theme of asceticism (Rampling, 1985) is expressed in the conceptions of dieting as purification, thinness as virtue, and fasting as an act of penitence. Nevertheless, there is a subgroup of eating-disordered patients who seem to be motivated by belief in the virtue of oral self-restraint (Garner & Bemis, 1982, 1985; Garner, Vitousek, & Pike, 1997). Banks (1992) describes self-denial as representing a dualistic split between body and spirit, and believes that sexual purity, moral superiority, and fasting are often linked together within particular cultures in the larger context of religious beliefs. Evidence suggests that "oral self-restraint" may be part of a more general theme of renunciation of physical gratification.

NATURE OF THE DISORDERS

Anorexia nervosa, bulimia nervosa, and other eating disorders are characterized by morbid overconcern with weight and shape, often leading to extreme and dangerous weight-controlling behaviors. The clinical features and related psychopathology of anorexia and bulimia nervosa are well documented and widely accepted. As mentioned earlier, both disorders have been conceptualized as final common pathways that derive from a range of potential predisposing factors. Moreover, they have a variety of associated psychological symptoms that may or may not have etiological significance but, in either case, contribute to the heterogeneity in the disorder on presentation. Finally, both anorexia nervosa and bulimia nervosa result in potentially serious physical and psychological sequelae that may perpetuate the eating disorder and also cloud the assessment picture (Mitchell et al., 1997).

Physical Complications

A medical evaluation of patients with eating disorders may be necessary to identify or rule out physical complications of starvation or those associated with certain extreme weight loss behaviors. Occasionally, a medical evaluation will be necessary to determine if weight loss has been precipitated by an underlying physical disorder. Certain symptoms, such as hypotension, hypothermia, bradycardia, and overall reduced metabolic rate, are common to starvation and may be evident in anorexia nervosa. Self-induced vomiting and purgative abuse may cause various symptoms or abnormalities, such as weakness, mus-

cle cramping, edema, constipation, cardiac arrhythmias, and paresthesia. Additionally, general fatigue, constipation, depression, various neurological abnormalities, kidney and cardiac disturbances, swollen salivary glands, electrolyte disturbances, dental deterioration, finger clubbing or swelling, edema, and dehydration have been reported (Mitchell et al., 1997) in those who engage in self-induced vomiting and purgative abuse.

Is Emotional Disturbance Primary or Secondary?

It may not be apparent from an initial assessment whether depression, low self-esteem, psychological distress, personality features, and social maladjustment reported by eating-disordered patients signal fundamental emotional deficits or are secondary elaborations resulting from weight loss and chaotic dietary patterns. These and other symptoms have been identified in human semistarvation studies and in research on the consequences of dieting (Garner et al., 1997). Findings from these studies indicate that striking changes in personality traits can occur with relatively small reductions in body weight.

There also is evidence that patients with good and poor outcome following short-term psychotherapy are indistinguishable at initial assessment on most measures of depression, general psychological distress, and personality disturbance, including traits that would indicate borderline personality disorder (Garner et al., 1990). The speed of the marked improvement in these psychological features, once eating symptoms have been brought under control, suggests that they may be secondary to the eating disorder rather than indicative of enduring emotional deficits.

Nevertheless, although some of the personality observations may be secondary to starvation or chaotic eating patterns, there is compelling evidence that many patients suffer from fundamental emotional deficits that persist long after behavioral symptoms have been ameliorated. Studies of anorexia nervosa have indicated that there is a substantial subgroup of patients with a positive long-term outcome who exhibit anxiety and affective disorders (Toner, Garfinkel, & Garner, 1988), show increased risk avoidance and greater emotional restraint, and are more conforming than age-matched controls (Casper, 1990). Thus, assessment of psychosocial functioning in eating-disordered patients requires an understanding of the potential psychological sequelae of starvation and disturbed eating patterns, as well as the factors that predispose them to the disorder.

Comorbidity

Since the earliest descriptions of anorexia nervosa, there has been considerable controversy as to whether eating disorders represent discrete psychological entities or are simply manifestations of other illnesses (cf. Beumont, Al-Alami, & Touyz, 1987). Anorexia and bulimia nervosa each have been considered variants of affective disorder, obsessive-compulsive disorder, or borderline personality disorder. Traits such as hostility, somatization, social maladjustment, physical anhedonia, affective rigidity, interpersonal sensitivity, anxiety, poor self-esteem, external locus of control, and confused sex-role identity have been observed repeatedly in eating disorder patients (Beumont, George, & Smart, 1976; Rastam, Gillberg, & Gillberg, 1995;). Although there is general acceptance that eating disorders are best considered as discrete clinical entities, there is growing interest in psychological features that may define meaningful subgroups of eating-disordered patients.

Depression and Eating Disorders

Depression has been described as a common theme in eating disorders, but its precise role is controversial. Pope and Hudson (1988) originally argued that bulimia nervosa is a variant of depression based on evidence that the eating disorder patients exhibit (1) a high prevalence of depression, (2) a family history of depression, (3) biological markers of depression, and (4) a positive response to antidepressant medications. Detractors from this view have provided alternative interpretations for these associations and contend that the nature of bulimia nervosa as a variant of depression is "simplistic and theoretically limiting" (Strober & Katz, 1988). Although depression may play an important predisposing role in eating disorders, current evidence fails to support the proposition that eating disorders are simply depressive equivalents (Cooper & Fairburn, 1986). This said, the evidence is over-whelming that depression is one of the most common features experienced by those with eating disorders, and to minimize its significance would be misleading. Moreover, bulimia nervosa patients with a history of affective disorder or substance abuse disorder report significantly more suicide attempts, social impairment, and previous treatment, both before and after the onset of the eating disorder (Hatsukami, Mitchell, Eckert & Pyle, 1986). Hatsukami et al. (1986) found no suicide attempts among the group of patients with bulimia nervosa alone; however, 26.5% of those with concurrent affective disorder and 32.4% with substance abuse had attempted suicide. Bulimia nervosa patients with a history of substance abuse also report a high incidence of stealing, perhaps suggesting a more general problem with impulsivity. Thus, a history of affective disorder may be a foreboding complication for a subgroup of eating-disordered patients who may be particularly resistant to treatment efforts. Unfortunately, this subgroup of patients does not seem to respond more favorably to antidepressant therapy than those without a history of a mood disorder (Brotman, Herzog, & Woods, 1984), so the solution does not seem to be the simple addition of medication to the standard treatment regime for eating disorders.

Personality Disorders

In recent years, there has been intense interest in the relationship between eating disorders and personality disorders. A number of reports have indicated that almost two-thirds of eating-disordered patients sampled received a concurrent diagnosis of personality disorder, with borderline personality disorder being reported as particularly common (Bulik, Sullivan, Joyce, & Carter, 1995; Gillberg, Rastam, & Gillberg, 1995). In an early report, Levin and Hyler (1986) assessed 24 bulimia nervosa patients and found that 15 (63%) met diagnostic criteria for personality disorder, with 6 (25%) fulfilling the diagnosis for borderline personality disorder. In another evaluation of 35 patients with eating disorders, Gartner, Marcus, Halmi, and Loranger (1989) found that 57% met the DSM-III-R (APA, 1987) diagnostic criteria for at least one form of personality disorder, with borderline, self-defeating, and avoidant being the most common. Two or more Axis II diagnostic criteria were met by 40% of the patients, and 17% fulfilled all of the criteria for five to seven personality disorder diagnoses. Wonderlich, Swift, Slotnick, and Goodman (1990) interviewed 46 eating disordered patients and reported that 72% met criteria for at least one personality disorder. Obsessive-compulsive personality disorder was common among restricting anorexic patients. Histrionic and borderline personality disorder diagnoses were common among binge-eating groups. Johnson, Tobin, and Dennis (1990) followed patients one year after an initial assessment and found that those who initially scored above a threshold on the self-report Borderline Syndrome Index had a worse prognosis in terms of eating behavior and general psychiatric symptoms. More recently, Bulik et al. (1995) found at least one personality disorder in 63% of a sample of 76 women with bulimia nervosa. Fifty-one percent of the personality disorders were in cluster C (specifically, avoidant, obsessive-compulsive, or dependent personality disorders), 41% on cluster B (particularly borderline or histrionic), and 33% in cluster A (paranoid, schizoid, or schizotypal). Gill berg et al. (1995) found that obsessive-compulsive and avoidant personality disorders were particularly common in a study comparing 51 anorexia nervosa patients with an age-matched community sample.

Arguing that borderline assessment measures are confounded by certain eating symptoms, Pope and Hudson (1989) challenged the earlier interpretations that borderline personality disorder is overrepresented among eating disorders. For example, binge-eating patterns may be used to satisfy the DSM-III-R (APA, 1987) poor impulse control criterion for borderline personality disorder, making the association between disorders tautological. Nevertheless, the tendency toward poor impulse regulation has been identified as a negative prognostic sign in eating disorders (e.g., Hatsukami et al., 1986; Sohlberg, Norring, Holmgren, & Rosmark, 1989). Results from research on the incidence and prevalence of personality disorders in anorexia nervosa are inconsistent. Some studies indicate remarkably high rates, with avoidant personality disorder occurring in as many as 33% of anorexic restricters and borderline personality disorder occurring in almost 40% of anorexic bulimic patients (Piran, Lerner, Garfinkel, Kennedy, & Brouilette, 1988). Other studies suggest that personality disorders are relatively uncommon in anorexia nervosa

(Herzog et al., 1992; Pope & Hudson, 1989). Impulse control problems, such as self-mutilation, suicide attempts, and stealing, are reported in a subgroup of anorexia nervosa patients, particularly those with purging and/or binge-eating symptoms (Garner, Garner, & Rosen, 1993). Although personality disturbances are not uniform in eating disorders, their presence suggests meaningful subtypes that may be relevant to treatment planning and prognosis.

Sexual Abuse

There has been considerable interest in recent years in the role of sexual abuse as a risk factor for the development of eating disorders. Clinical accounts and the observation in some studies of a high incidence of sexual abuse in eating disorder patient samples (Oppenheimer, Howells, Palmer, & Chaloner, 1985) were followed by further clinical reports and numerous empirical studies yielding conflicting findings (Fallon & Wonderlich, 1997). Fallon and Wonderlich (1997) summarized the literature and concluded that: (1) childhood sexual abuse appears to be positively associated with bulimia nervosa; (2) there is less evidence for this association in anorexia nervosa; (3) childhood sexual abuse does not appear to be a specific risk factor for eating disorders (i.e., it is no higher for eating disorders than in psychiatric controls); (4) childhood sexual abuse does appear to be associated with higher levels of comorbidity among those with eating disorders, but, there is not strong evidence that it predicts a more severe eating disorder; and (5) a more complex approach to the definition of sexual abuse has led to a better prediction of later disturbances in eating. It is indisputable that a significant subgroup of women from some clinical eating disorder samples have a history of sexual abuse, and that careful assessment and treatment is important in the process of dealing with resulting feelings of shame, distrust, and anger (Fallon & Wonderlich, 1997).

ETIOLOGY AND PATHOGENESIS

During the past several decades, single-factor causal theories have been replaced by the view that eating disorders are "multidetermined" (Garfinkel & Garner, 1982). The symptom patterns represent final common pathways resulting from the interplay of three broad classes of predisposing factors shown in Figure 18-1. The roles of cultural, individual (psychological and biological), and familial causal factors are presumed to interact in different ways leading to the development of eating disorders. The precipitants are less clearly understood, except that dieting is invariably an early element. Perhaps the most practical advances in treatment have come from increased awareness of the perpetuating effects of starvation, with its psychological, emotional, and physical consequences (Figure 18-1).

Developmental Theory

Many theories have offered developmental explanations, broadly defined, of eating disorders. Some formulations have emphasized intrapsychic mediation, and others have highlighted interactional factors. Together, they have provided a rich understanding of a range of psychological themes that may account for both anorexia nervosa and bulimia nervosa.

Many of the early psychodynamic writings on eating disorders emphasized anorexia nervosa as a rejection of adult femininity. This theme was refined and extended by Crisp (1997), who contends that the central psychopathology of both anorexia and bulimia nervosa is related to fears of the psychological expectations and biological experiences associated with maintaining an adult weight. According to this view, starvation becomes the mechanism for avoiding psychobiological maturity because it results in a return to prepubertal appearance and hormonal status. This regression is thought to provide relief from adolescent turmoil and conflicts within the family. Moreover, patients report experiencing themselves as younger following extreme weight loss, which may be due to the reversal of mature adolescent hormonal profiles that form the biological substrata for psychological experiences (Crisp, 1997).

Other developmental theorists have attributed eating disorders to various types of parenting failure. Bruch (1973) and Selvini-Palazzoli (1974) provided developmental paradigms in which the mother superimposes her own inaccurate perceptions of the child's needs on the child. Such invalidation of the child's experiences results in an arrest of cognitive development and is manifested in debilitating feelings of ineffectiveness that are later evident in adolescent struggles for autonomy and control of the body. Bruch (1973) postulated that these early parenting failures lead to fundamental deficits in self-awareness, including the way that the body is perceived and experienced.

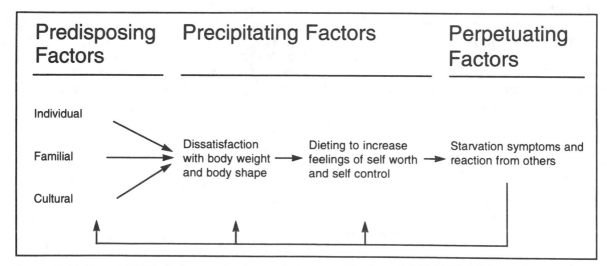

Source: D.M. Garner (1993), Pathogenesis of anorexia nervosa. *The Lancet, 341,* 1631–1635.

FIGURE 18-1. Eating disorders as multidetermined disorders.

Theorists working from an object relations model account for eating disorders in a similar way (Goodsitt, 1997). According to this view, normal development is characterized by the process of separation/individuation, a state achieved by consistent interactions with a primary caretaker who is highly responsive to the needs of the child. Success is reflected by the child's progressive internalization of the ability to accurately recognize, respond, and regulate internal needs and impulses without contact with the immediate caregiver. Accordingly, the different personality structures of eating-disordered patients reflect developmental arrest at particular phases of the process of the separation/individuation. Eating disorder symptoms are an attempt to cope with needs stemming from incomplete self-development or an interruption of the separation/individuation process.

The self-psychology perspective also has been used to account for eating disorders as a reflection of developmental arrest in the separation/individuation process (Goodsitt, 1997). According to this conceptual scheme, the eating-disordered patient's lack of a cohesive sense of self is the direct result of the primary caregiver's failure to provide essential functions during development. These include mirroring, tension regulation, and integration. The obsessive concern about eating and repeated bouts of bingeing and vomiting serve organizing and tension regulation functions in an attempt to modulate basic deficits in "self-structures." These symptoms become an organizing event in one's life and provide intense stimulation that numb the anguish and emptiness that pervade the eating-disordered patient's experience. There is growing empirical evidence to support the clinical view that intense separation distress is common among those with eating disorders and that many patients demonstrate marked separation anxiety in response to mildly as well as severely stressful situations (Armstrong & Roth, 1989).

Others have emphasized the motivation for binge eating as an attempt to escape negative aspects of self-awareness (Heatherton & Baumeister, 1991). According to this view, the binge eater experiences negative self-evaluations and concerns about perceived negative evaluations from others, which are accompanied by anxiety and depression. Binge eating provides a means of avoiding this unpleasant state

of negative self-awareness through the narrowing of attention to one facet of the immediate environment.

Strober (1991) has drawn together developmental theory, psychobiology, and personality genetics in offering a valuable understanding of the adaptive mechanisms behind the range of symptoms seen in eating disorder patients. He integrates modern psychoanalytic concepts of development with constructs indicating (1) that individual differences may be expected in the internal regulators of arousability or temperament that organize self-experiences and (2) that heritable personality traits, and their presumed biological substrata, set limits within which behavior patterns are expressed. Strober (1991) accounts for the differences in traits seen in subgroups of eating disorder patients by incorporating a concept of three bipolar, and primarily genetically determined, dimensions of personality that appear to account for remarkable consistency over time in both normal and psychopathological behavior.

Familial Factors

Some of the earliest descriptions of anorexia nervosa emphasized the role of the family in the development of the disorder (cf. Garfinkel & Garner, 1982). The possible role of the family in the development of anorexia nervosa and bulimia nervosa has been described by writers from a range of theoretical orientations (Bruch, 1973; Dare & Eisler, 1997; Minuchin, Rosman, & Baker, 1978; Selvini-Palazzoli, 1974). A major advancement in family therapy with eating disorders was the formulation of the structural approach of Minuchin and colleagues (1978). They identified a number of characteristics of the interactions encountered in eating-disordered families, including enmeshment, overprotectiveness, rigidity, and poor conflict resolution. The systemic model was applied to eating disorders by Selvini-Palazzoli (1974) and overlaps considerably with the structural model. The systemic approach holds that the identified patient serves an essential homeostatic or stabilizing role within the family. A second generation of family theorists has integrated and greatly elaborated earlier approaches to provide very specific advice regarding the treatment of eating disorders (Dare & Eisler, 1997).

Regardless of their orientation, most individual and family theorists have emphasized that anorexia nervosa often represents a developmental struggle for autonomy, independence, and individuality. These issues are very likely to surface in adolescence, when the vulnerable individual, parents, or entire family is forced to deal with emergent developmental realities. In the only controlled trial examining the efficacy of family therapy for anorexia nervosa, Russell, Szmukler, Dare, and Eisler (1987) found that family therapy was superior to individual therapy for younger patients. This study, as well as clinical experience, suggest that family therapy should be routinely employed as the treatment of choice for young eating disorder patients (Vandereycken, Kog, & Vanderlinden, 1989).

Cultural Values Related to Thinness

A complete understanding of eating disorders requires attention to the cultural forces that have been impinging selectively on women over the past several decades. One of the most pernicious has been the intense pressure to diet and to engage in strict weight control in order to meet unrealistic standards for thinness (Garner, Garfinkel, Schwartz, & Thompson, 1980). Young women today are totally immersed in cultural admiration of a physical form for women that has little to do with the actual shape of most women in our society. The disconcerting result is a norm in which women report being dissatisfied with their shapes and are made to feel guilty about eating even reasonable amounts of food. It has been recognized for some time that dieting can play a direct role in causing a range of symptoms such as binge eating and mood disturbances (Garner, 1997). The relentless pursuit of the "ideal" body through restrictive dieting and disordered eating patterns is endemic to women, and such behaviors have now become "normalized" within Western society. In fact, Polivy and Herman (1987) reported that "normal eating" among North American women is *defined* by restrictive dieting. The values surrounding slenderness have become sufficiently embedded in our cultural value system that many of the symptoms required for eating disorders are not viewed as unusual or abnormal by members of the general public (Huon, Brown, & Morris, 1988). Bruch (1985) suggested that eating disorders

have developed a positive social stereotype and, in some instances, may be spread by social contagion (Bruch, 1985). Eating disorders have been glamorized in the popular media and are associated with "high-status" individuals, such as celebrities. Additionally, some of the traits commonly associated with anorexia nervosa (including intelligence, self-discipline, will power, and control) are highly valued by Western society. Such characteristics are reinforced in the culture and may help perpetuate the maintenance of eating-disordered behaviors. Convincing patients to part with the positive connotations of an "anorexic identity" has been identified as a major impediment in the treatment of anorexia nervosa (Garner et al., 1997).

Just as thinness has acquired a positive valence, being overweight has become a powerful social stigma in society. It is well documented that obese individuals are discriminated against, mocked, and labeled as being lazy, unintelligent, unhygienic, incompetent, and lacking in will power (Garner & Wooley, 1991). Thus, behaviors including dieting and exercising constitute socially acceptable, admirable, and desirable practices that are positively reinforced by society. Recognition of the impact of cultural factors on norms related to dieting and weight control has led to the conclusion that eating disorders may develop in those without underlying personality disturbances or family dysfunction, although secondary disruption in both of these areas may be present by the time the person presents for an assessment (Garner, 1997). Much of the current psychological theorizing related to eating disorders may be criticized for not accounting for these cultural factors, or, when they are mentioned, for not specifying the details of how they must be integrated into the understanding of the psychology of the disorder.

Cognitive-Behavioral Theory

There is now broad agreement that the rationale for cognitive-behavioral therapy (CBT) for eating disorders rests primarily on the assumption that restrictive dieting (largely in response to cultural imperatives to meet unrealistic standards for body weight) is in direct conflict with the internal biological systems responsible for the homeostatic regulation of body weight (Garner et al., 1997). Given the current cultural pressures for thinness, it is easy to understand why women, particularly those with persistent self-doubts, could arrive at the conclusion that personal failings are to some degree related to weight or that the attainment of slenderness would measurably improve self-estimation. It has been asserted that for some who develop eating disorders, the motivating factors do not seem to go beyond a literal or extreme interpretation of the prevailing cultural doctrine glorifying thinness. For others, however, the impetus is more complicated, with the range of psychological and interactional factors playing a role. According to the cognitive-behavioral view, the dieter's steadfast attempts to down-regulate body weight leads to a myriad of compensatory symptoms, including binge eating. Although the cognitive-restructuring component of CBT has taken various forms, most rely on Beck's well-known model, which has been adapted for eating disorders (Fairburn, 1985; Garner & Bemis, 1982; Garner, Vitousek, & Pike, 1997). The initial aim of cognitive restructuring is to challenge specific reasoning errors or self-destructive attitudes toward weight and shape so that the patient can relax restrictive dieting. Behavioral strategies such as self-monitoring, meal planning, and exposure to feared foods serve the overall goal of normalizing food intake. The primary point of emphasis of the cognitive-behavioral view has been the analysis of functional relationships between current distorted beliefs and symptomatic behaviors related to eating, weight, and body shape.

Although it has received relatively little emphasis in theoretical writings, the cognitive-behavioral model is well suited for examining other historical, developmental, and interpersonal themes identified with some eating disorder patients, themes that have been described best by psychodynamic and family theorists. These motifs include fears of separation, engulfment, or abandonment; failures in the separation/individuation process; false-self adaptation; transference, overprotectiveness, enmeshment, or conflict avoidance; inappropriate involvement of the child in parental conflicts, and symptoms as mediators of family stability. All of these involve distorted meaning on the part of the individual, the family, or both. Although the language, style, and specific interpretations may differ sharply between the cognitive-behavioral model and the dynamic models that have

generated these respective formulations, it is notable that both orientations are specifically concerned with meaning and meaning systems. Moreover, the respective therapies are aimed at identifying and correcting misconceptions that are presumed to have developmental antecedents (Garner et al., 1997). The marked social deficits observed in anorexia nervosa, the need to involve the family in many cases, and the longer duration of therapy have formed the basis for the explicit integration of interpersonal themes in early descriptions of CBT for anorexia nervosa (Garner et al., 1997). One of the advantages of the cognitive-behavioral approach is that it allows the incorporation of developmental and interpersonal themes when they apply to a particular patient but does not compel all cases to fit into one restrictive explanatory system.

Although there are now many studies indicating that CBT can achieve good results with many patients, recent research has revealed that other forms of treatment, which do not address eating or weight issues at all, also can lead to the amelioration of binge eating (Fairburn et al., 1995; Garner et al., 1993). In a comparison between CBT, behavioral treatment, and interpersonal psychotherapy, Fairburn et al., (1995) found that CBT was more effective than other treatments in modifying extreme dieting, self-induced vomiting, and disturbed attitudes toward shape and body weight at the end of treatment; however, at a 6-year follow-up there are no meaningful differences between CBT and interpersonal therapy in outcome (Fairburn et al., 1995). This is consistent with results of a study in which CBT and supportive-expressive psychotherapy were compared (Garner et al., 1993). Although CBT was superior to the supportive-expressive modality on measures where group differences were found, both treatments were equally effective in ameliorating binge eating. Identifying the mechanisms of action for CBT as well as for different forms of interpersonal and drug therapy remains an important area for future investigations.

Assessment of Eating Disorder Symptomatology

Assessment should be considered integral to the ongoing treatment process. Various approaches to information gathering have been developed for eating disorders, including standard clinical interviews, semistructured interviews, behavioral observation, standardized self-report measures, symptom checklists, clinical rating scales, self-monitoring procedures, and standardized test means. There are three broad areas of focus in the assessment process: (1) the assessment of specific symptom areas that allow the diagnosis of the eating disorder; (2) the measurement of other attitudes or behaviors characteristic of eating disorders; and (3) the identification and measurement of associated psychological and personality features that are indicative of overall psychosocial functioning (Crowther & Sherwood, 1997).

Assessment should include careful questioning about the duration and frequency of binge eating, as well as extreme measures designed to control body weight such as vomiting, laxative abuse, and excessive exercise. It should also cover weight-controlling behaviors such as other drug or alcohol use to control appetite, chewing and spitting food out before swallowing, prolonged fasting, and vigorous exercise for the purpose of controlling body weight. Diabetic patients may manipulate insulin levels to control weight, and patients taking thyroid replacement may alter their dosage to control their weight (Garfinkel & Garner, 1982).

Marked personality changes mimicking primary personality disorders may actually stem from prolonged undernutrition. The assessment should include a careful evaluation of premorbid personality features. Patients may recall being sociable and more confident prior to the onset of the disorder. As the disorder has progressed, they may have become more sullen and isolated from others. Other patients describe a passive, compliant, and reserved premorbid personality style. Formal personality testing may be useful in some cases; however, the confounding of primary and secondary symptoms is a concern (Crowther & Sherwood, 1997). When primary personality disturbance is identified, it usually means a longer duration of therapy, with a more difficult course. Adaptations are required for patients whose disorder is complicated by substance, physical, or sexual abuse.

In many cases, standardized self-report measures can be efficient in gathering information about eating behavior and other symptoms common in those with eating disorders. The Eating Disorder Inventory–2 (EDI-2, Garner, 1991) is a standardized, multiscale measure that adds three subscales to the original EDI. The EDI-2 is specifically aimed at assessing a range of psychological characteristics clinically relevant to eating disorders. It consists of three subscales for tapping attitudes and behaviors relating to eating, weight, and shape (Drive for Thinness, Bulimia, Body Dissatisfaction), in addition to eight subscales assessing more general organizing constructs or psychological traits clinically relevant to eating disorders (Ineffectiveness, Perfection, Interpersonal Distrust, Interoceptive Awareness, Maturity Fears, Asceticism, Impulse Regulation, and Social Insecurity). In clinical settings, the EDI-2 is designed to provide information helpful in understanding the patient, planning treatment, and assessing progress. In nonclinical settings, the EDI-2 is intended as an economical means of identifying individuals who have "subclinical" eating problems or those who may be at risk for developing eating disorders.

PROTOTYPICAL TREATMENT

General Guidelines

The clinician treating eating disorder patients should possess the accepted qualities of all skilled therapists: warmth, genuineness, empathy, honesty, and acceptance. The fact that many of the symptoms evinced by the eating disorder patient are "ego-syntonic" requires that the therapist have the ability to be firm, authoritative, and directive while maintaining a collaborative therapeutic style. It is important for the clinician to be knowledgeable in certain specific subject domains that are outside typical training in general psychotherapy but are essential in understanding and treating eating disorders. These include (1) the biology of weight regulation, including the effects of restrictive dieting and semistarvation on behavior; (2) the physical complications of extreme weight-controlling methods such as vomiting and laxative abuse; (3) the attitudes and beliefs toward the body and food that are characteristic of eating-disordered patients; and (4) the role of cultural pressures for thinness that impinge on women today and how to address cultural issues meaningfully in psychotherapy.

Establishing a working relationship with the family is essential with younger patients as well as with some older patients who are living at home. However, family therapy may not always be a realistic option because of the unavailability of experienced therapists, insurance limitations, or the family's unwillingness to participate. Reluctant family members may become motivated to participate in family therapy once they recognize that the blame is not being placed on them, or when they find the intervention to be helpful to the overall functioning of the family.

Normalizing Weight and Nutritional Rehabilitation

Education about regular eating patterns, body weight regulation, starvation symptoms, vomiting, and laxative abuse is a strategic element in the treatment of eating disorders. The topic of body weight is approached from an entirely different perspective for anorexia and bulimia nervosa (Garner et al., 1997). While it is commonly accepted that treatment does not have a major effect on body weight for bulimia nervosa, in anorexia nervosa, it is the major target of intervention. The significance of this contrast cannot be overemphasized. It affects motivation to initiate and then to continue treatment, and it also shapes the content of sessions early in treatment. Although patients with both of these eating disorders experience a "morbid fear of becoming fat," in the case of anorexia nervosa, this fear must be addressed while the patient *is actually becoming "fatter."*

Emaciated anorexic patients need to be told that *outpatient treatment can proceed only if their weight does not fall below a certain minimum* (Garner et al., 1997). If the patient is near this minimum at the initial meetings, then this weight needs to be clearly stipulated. However, there are no absolute rules regarding this minimum, which depends on the patient's overall health, the presence of complications, and the ability to make progress in outpatient treatment. Setting a target weight range as a goal in the initial meeting(s) is dependent on the patient's current level of motivation and commitment to treatment. The patient needs to understand the enormous biological significance of reaching a certain minimal body weight threshold and to accept that the achievement of this weight status is essential to recovery. There are individual differences in this threshold, but, it generally corresponds to approximately 90% of expected weight for postmenarcheal women and elicits resumption of normal hormonal functioning and menstruation.

A weight range of 3 to 5 pounds above this threshold has been recommended in order to account for normal weight fluctuations (Garner et al., 1982). It should be explained that this weight is a bit too high for some women and too low for others, but is a good initial estimate. Return to premorbid weight, rather than to a population-average "normal" weight based on normal body mass, has been found to be a better predictor of the return of normal reproductive functioning in anorexia and bulimia nervosa (see Garner et al., 1997, for details). Establishing regular eating patterns is vital to symptom control for both anorexia and bulimia nervosa. Eating should be done *mechanically,* according to set times and a predetermined plan. Food should be thought of as "medication" prescribed to "inoculate" the patient against future extreme food cravings and the tendency to engage in binge eating (Garner et al., 1997). Temporarily taking the decision making out of eating can help patients who are particularly prone to become overwhelmed by anxiety and guilt in problematic eating situations. Deviations from the eating plan, whether undereating or overeating, should be discouraged equally.

Patients need to be encouraged to space meals and snacks rather than try to "save" calories for later in the day. Breakfast should never be omitted, and it is ideal for there to be 3 meals and 1 or 2 snacks spread throughout the day. It is best to confine eating to set times on the clock rather than relying on internal sensations in determining when to eat. The rationale for this type of plan is that it will minimize food cravings, urges to overeat or undereat, and loss of control.

Most eating-disordered patients begin treatment with considerable confusion about what constitutes "normal" eating. Patients tend to severely restrict the amount of food eaten and also to divide food into "good" and "bad" categories. These practices typically are based on "nutritional myths" and extreme interpretations of sensible dietary guidelines. One goal of treatment is learning to feel more relaxed eating a wide range of foods. A weekly meal plan should gradually incorporate small amounts of previously avoided or forbidden foods. Patients should be encouraged to challenge the tendency to divide food into "good" and "bad" categories by recognizing that the calories of those foods previously considered "bad" really have no greater impact on weight than those in calorie-sparing food items. Patients who engage in binge eating should consume small amounts of the foodstuffs they typically reserve for episodes of binge eating.

Challenging specific irrational beliefs about food may require specialized nutritional knowledge, and clinicians need to develop the necessary informational background in this area to help patients combat food myths. Finally, persistent patterns of distorted thinking about food may reflect a more basic tendency toward faulty reasoning. Resistance to experimenting with different types of foods may require the application of more formal cognitive-behavioral therapy methods (Garner et al., 1997).

Educational Material

Psychoeducation has been recommended as a key component in the treatment of both anorexia and bulimia nervosa (Garner, 1997). The rationale for this approach was based on the assumption that eating disorder patients often suffer from misconceptions regarding the factors that cause and then maintain symptoms. It further presumed that patients would be less likely to persist in self-defeating symptoms if they were truly aware of the scientific evidence regarding factors that perpetuate eating disorders. The educational approach imparts a patient-oriented locus of responsibility for change aimed at increasing motivation and reducing defensiveness. The operating assumption is that the patient is a responsible and rational partner in a collaborative relationship. The educational approach is also based on the merits of economy. Education is a relatively inexpensive initial option in the integration and sequencing model of treatment delivery.

Behavioral Principles

Behavioral treatment should be based on a systematic analysis of the contingencies that maintain the eating disorder (Garner & Bemis, 1982). The behavioral principles should be well integrated with other individual and family therapies. Behavioral contingencies should be rational and understandable. Careful inquiry into the patient's understanding of behavioral

contingencies is essential. They should be described as being consistent with the overall goal of recovery and based on the same reinforcement principles that guide most people's behavior. The need for external control in the initial stages of treatment can be explained as a response to the patient's current state of loss of control. This loss of control is evidenced by absence of choice (e.g., the anorexic patient experiences little choice in eating and exercise patterns, just as the bulimic experiences little choice regarding binge-eating and purging behaviors). The patient can be enlisted to participate in treatment planning and may collaborate with the therapist under the assumption that she is valued as an individual and that the goal is to help her return to a state of autonomous functioning. Reasonable objections to contingencies should be met with problem solving and the development of alternative strategies, always with the proviso that more external control is needed if more lenient behavioral objectives are not met. For patients who have the complication of binge eating, it is important to anticipate "slips" and develop a strategy for "getting back on track" after these setbacks (Fairburn, 1985; Fairburn, Marcus, & Wilson, 1993; Garner et al., 1985).

Cognitive-Behavioral Methods

Cognitive-behavioral treatment (CBT) for eating disorders has been described in numerous clinical reports and research articles over the past decade, and the reader is encouraged to consult original sources for detailed descriptions (Agras, Schneider, Arnow, Raeburn, & Telch, 1989; Fairburn, Marcus, & Wilson, 1993; Garner & Bemis, 1982, 1985). Most of these depend heavily on the principles developed originally by Beck and his colleagues for depression and anxiety disorders (Beck, Rush, Shaw, & Emery, 1979). Although there is debate regarding the active ingredients of CBT in the treatment of eating disorders, it is generally recognized that the primary points of emphasis are: (1) the analysis of functional relationships between current distorted beliefs and symptomatic behaviors related to eating, weight, and body shape, and (2) helping the patient challenge inappropriate or distorted beliefs and assumptions that have led to the development and maintenance of the eating symptoms. Although there is general agreement that self-monitoring is an important component of CBT, there are different points of emphasis in the target behaviors for this procedure. Some reports emphasize monitoring of affective and interpersonal antecedents of binge eating, whereas others focus more on dietary management and attitudes toward weight and shape, which are presumed to underlie extreme weight-controlling behaviors. Both of these approaches can play a valuable role in treatment, although there is some consensus that self-monitoring should, at the very least, focus on normalizing food intake.

Descriptions of CBT have typically focused on beliefs and assumptions related to weight and shape, but, cognitive methods also are ideally suited for addressing developmental and interactional themes best described by psychodynamic and family theorists. Themes such as fear of separation, engulfment, or abandonment; failures in the separation/individuation process; false-self adaptation; transference, overprotectiveness, enmeshment, and conflict avoidance; inappropriate involvement of the child in parental conflicts; and symptoms as mediators of family stability all involve distorted meaning on the part of the individual, the family, or both.

Family Therapy

The specific components of family therapy are well beyond the scope of the present chapter and these have been reviewed in detail elsewhere (Dare & Eisler, 1997; Garner et al., 1997; Minuchin et al., 1978; Strober, 1997). However, there are several fundamental issues that are appropriate to most family interventions. These include the following:

1. The identified patient and her parents often need help in overcoming denial regarding the seriousness of the eating disorder. Parents may need assistance in accurately labeling eating-disordered behaviors. For example, behaviors that were previously identified as being "healthy" when they occurred in moderation must be reinterpreted as "eating-disordered" given the current context.

2. Parents may need help in developing an effective parenting style, especially one that is appropriate to the developmental stage of the child. Feelings of guilt and fear may have prohibited them from being firm and effective in establishing guidelines for behaviors that are consistent with recovery. Parents should be encouraged to maintain usual expectations in areas unrelated to food and eating (e.g., bedtime, chores, language, and treatment of siblings) except when unrealistic parental expectations are directly contributing to the problem. Treatment recommendations should be consistent with the family's value system.

3. Parents may need assistance in accepting the patient's intrinsic values as a person irrespective of objective performance standards such as weight, school achievement, or athletic competition.

4. Parental attitudes about weight and shape should be identified, and improper emphasis on thinness or "fitness," which does not take into account the patient's condition, needs to be challenged. Inappropriate family eating patterns, beliefs about food, or eating rituals should be identified, and practical interventions need to be designed to address potential areas of conflict.

5. Problematic family interactional patterns need to be addressed, including "enmeshment," overprotectiveness, the use of inadequate mechanisms for resolving conflicts, and the presence of inappropriate parent–child allegiances that undermine the marital relationship (Minuchin et al., 1978). The identified patient's symptoms may be functional within a disturbed family context, and the meaning systems that underlie the resulting interactional patterns need to be identified and corrected. For example, weight loss, with its effects on shape, emotional maturity, and dependence on the family, may lead to maturational arrest, thereby reducing the fears associated with separation (Crisp, 1997).

Hospitalization

Improvements in outpatient care have reduced the need for hospitalization for most patients with anorexia nervosa. In some circumstances, however, brief or even extended hospitalization is beneficial or necessary. General guidelines for hospitalization include: (1) weight restoration or interruption of steady weight loss in patients who are emaciated; (2) interruption of bingeing, vomiting, and/or laxative abuse that pose medical risks or complications; (3) evaluation and treatment of other potentially serious physical complications; and (4) management of associated conditions such as severe depression, risk of self-harm, or substance abuse. On rare occasions, hospitalization may be required to "disengage" a patient from a social system that both contributes to the maintenance of the disorder and disrupts outpatient treatment.

Most of the objectives of hospitalization can be met with more cost-effective alternatives such as partial hospitalization or intensive outpatient treatment. These treatment options are ideally suited for those who require a degree of structure and a level of intensity that cannot be provided in weekly therapy. It is also helpful for those who have significant health concerns but who do not necessarily require hospitalization. Such a program has many advantages:

1. It allows patients the opportunity to gain control over their symptoms in a safe environment.
2. It is beneficial for younger patients because they do not need to be separated from their families.
3. It is more economical than hospitalization.
4. It allows patients the opportunity to build self-efficacy and develop confidence, as they are responsible for their own recovery in their unique environments, which enables them to be cognizant of areas of vulnerabilities and also aware of their strengths (Kaplan & Olmsted, 1997).

Pharmacotherapy

Medication should be considered for patients with bulimia nervosa or binge-eating disorder who fail an initial trial of cognitive-behavioral therapy, but it is generally not indicated for anorexia nervosa. Many well-controlled trials in the past decade have indicated the effectiveness of some antidepressant medications for bulimia nervosa, and the research evidence will be reviewed in detail in a later section. In reviewing the research in the field, however, Raymond, Mitchell, Fallon, and Katzman (1994) have suggested that medication should not be "the primary mode of therapy with patients with bulimia nervosa" (p. 241). This conclusion is based on the following observations:

1. Psychological interventions have been shown to be very effective.

2. High dropout rates are reported in most medication studies.
3. There are risks of drug side effects.
4. Data suggest high relapse rates with drug discontinuation.

Fluoxetine hydrochloride (Prozac) is currently the first choice for the treatment of bulimia nervosa (daily dosages of 60 mg were generally superior to 20 mg) and probably should be used at least as an adjunct to psychotherapy in many cases failing in a course of adequate psychological treatment (Garfinkel & Walsh, 1997; Walsh et al., 1997).

There is still little evidence for change in earlier recommendations that pharmacotherapy has a very limited value with emaciated anorexia nervosa patients and should never be the sole treatment modality (Garfinkel & Garner, 1982). Occasionally patients may benefit from medication to deal with overwhelming anxiety, severe depression, or intolerable gastric discomfort after meals, but this applies to only a small minority of patients (Garfinkel & Walsh, 1997).

Case Description

K is an 18-year-old Caucasian female initially referred for an evaluation because of a 35-pound weight loss, amenorrhea, severely reduced caloric intake, and fear of weight gain. She exhibited typical complications of weight loss, including dizziness, weakness, and difficulties with concentration. She came for the initial assessment with her mother, who appeared to be appropriately concerned for her daughter's well-being and supportive of her decision to seek treatment.

K communicated openly about her fears of weight gain and was able to provide a detailed chronology of the development of her eating disorder. In high school, K weighed close to 125 pounds. Her first experiences with dieting occurred in her junior year of high school, upon her father's suggestion that she lose a few pounds to improve her speed on the basketball court. K began a weight-loss program that started with eliminating all sweets and snack foods, and increasing her exercise regime with the addition of running. She began weighing herself daily. She recalled being on vacation and feeling increasingly anxious, as she was unable to weigh herself for 2 weeks. K attempted to attenuate her anxiety and guilt around eating by restricting her food intake even further. After returning home from the trip, K felt a tremendous sense of pride and accomplishment upon discovering that her weight had decreased by 4 pounds. When K returned to school in the fall, she was encouraged by her coach to increase her food consumption, since her running ability appeared to have been compromised due to her weight loss. K complied with her coach's request and noticed that her running times improved. However, she noted that the reward associated with improved athletic performance was less potent than the gratification derived from weight loss. Once the season ended, K resumed her highly restrictive eating patterns, and again lost weight. Later in the year, K participated in softball and joined the team. Again, her low weight affected her stamina and endurance, which resulted in decreased performance on the field. Once again, it was advised that she eat more and gain some weight in order to improve her playing ability. Again, K complied with the suggestion by gaining weight, but she reported being angry and resentful at having to make this change. Once the softball season ended, K returned to rigid control of her food intake. She did not allow herself to consume more than 1000 kcal and would not eat any foodstuffs that contained dietary fat. At the time of the initial consultation, K had withdrawn from her family and friends, was running 40 miles every week, and weighed 89 pounds (at 5'4" tall) in light street clothing.

K relayed her weight and eating history in detail, and denied that she had engaged in binge eating or purging. Moreover, she reportedly did not use laxatives, diuretics, emetics, alcohol, or drugs for the purpose of weight control. She described a normal developmental history consisting of a happy childhood within a loving and supportive family. She recalled having positive relationships with her older brother and younger sister. K was an excellent student who always had a supportive network of friends. However, K reported feeling uncomfortable in relationships with young men if she felt that there was any potential for the relationship to develop beyond strict platonic boundaries. She has not had a boyfriend and rarely dated.

It was concluded from the initial assessment that K would be a good candidate for an intensive outpatient program that was designed to assist her in weight gain and in overcoming rigid dietary patterns that she had been unable to change with outpatient therapy. She was terrified at the prospect of weight gain, but was able to see that her condition was deteriorating, and she agreed that withdrawal from school was inevitable without additional treatment.

The intensive outpatient program consisted of seven hours of treatment five days a week in a private clinic setting. There are between 6 and 8 eating disorder patients participating in the program at any given time, with most needing weight restoration. The therapeutic orientation was cognitive-behavioral, and the key components of treatment were supervised eating, meal planning, and psychoeducation. Therapy format is primarily group; however, all patients receive individual therapy with one or more of the program staff. K's participation in the intensive outpatient program allowed her to remain at home with her family, and also did not interfere with her first semester in college.

K's caloric intake began at 1,700 calories per day, which was increased gradually in order to achieve the expected weekly weight gain of 2 or 3 pounds. A great deal of care was taken to explain that the goal of treatment was to restore "control" to her life, not simply to gain weight. She was educated about starvation symptoms and the need to eat in a consistent and predictable manner in order to restore her physical health, emotional well-being, and metabolic functioning. The treatment team assured her that she would not be allowed to gain weight faster than agreed upon since the goal of treatment was predictable change. Her calories would be adjusted either downward or upward to achieve the agreed-upon rate of weight gain. Thus, it was very important to complete all meals and snacks on the meal plan; otherwise, the calculations of caloric need would be meaningless. It was agreed upon that a temporary moratorium should be placed on exercise, with the agreement that it could be gradually reintegrated (in a way that was truly consistent with proper health) once weight restoration was well under way. K ate three meals and two snacks at set times each day in order to normalize her intake and allow her body to adjust to the refeeding process. The primary goals for K were to review starvation symptoms, institute meal planning, provide correct information regarding nutrition, and ensure appropriate weight gain. Her goal weight was 110 pounds, which was considered to be a weight approximately 5 pounds above that necessary for the resumption of normal menstrual periods (Garner et al., 1997). K had to be coached often with accurate nutritional information in order to challenge her rigid rules for avoiding all dietary fat. She was extremely fearful that consumption of dietary fat would turn to body fat, which would accumulate on her stomach and hips.

In the early phases of treatment, K remained extremely tearful and frightened around meal times and when her daily weight was recorded. She required a tremendous amount of support around eating, as she experienced strong feelings of guilt after eating, intensified by the fact that she agreed to refrain from exercise until she had gained an appropriate amount of weight. K found the group atmosphere (with other females recovering from eating disorders) to be of great benefit, as she often questioned the normality of her feelings and thoughts throughout the recovery process.

K was reassured by the structure of the treatment program and the attention to nutritional and dietary details during the refeeding process. She contrasted this with her earlier psychotherapy, in which nutritional issues were not *addressed or were referred to a nutritionist. K was quickly able to develop a trusting therapeutic relationship with staff and other patients. She was highly compliant throughout her treatment, even while experiencing many negative feelings about weight gain and consuming feared foods. One of the most reassuring aspects of the renourishment process, especially in the initial phase of treatment, involved the meal-planning component, as the structure provided K with comfort. While she was in the program, K rigidly adhered to meal planning and carefully followed through, ensuring that she met her daily caloric and fat intake. Initially, K limited herself to "safe" foods, but over time she was gradually able to incorporate more of her "feared, forbidden" foods in small amounts and was able to feel more comfortable about eating them. She was also encouraged to keep notes in a journal and record the foods she ate, her thoughts and feelings around meal times, and her reactions in interpersonal situations at school and at the clinic.*

K steadily gained weight during her treatment, at a rate of about 1 to 3 pounds per week. K struggled excessively with body image–related problems, and had great difficulties learning to adjust to the changing shape of her body. During the course of weight gain, K became more aware of the psychosocial function that her eating disorder had served. It allowed her to avoid social expectations related to dating and it deflected her attention away from uncertainties about her future at school and beyond. She was also able to recognize that her feelings toward her family were not quite as harmonious as they had appeared. She was increasingly able to articulate that she felt angry with her father because she saw him as controlling and demanding.

The day K reached 100 pounds, she became quite distressed because she felt that "there was no turning back." However, with additional support, K remained dedicated to completing her meals and staying on the path of recovery. K participated in the intensive outpatient program until she reached a weight of 103 pounds, at which point a mutual decision was made for K to make the transition to weekly outpatient therapy. She continued in therapy for an additional 6 months, where she was increasingly able to address other psychological issues related to self-esteem, perfectionism, difficulties in accurately identifying and responding to affective states, and fears of addressing the social expectations associated with adulthood that contributed to her eating difficulties. K's weight toward the end of her treatment remained close to 110 pounds, and she was exercising in a responsible and healthful manner. K also resumed menstrual functioning and expressed happiness about the return of her menses, as she had been quite concerned about its effect on her body and its relation to osteoporosis.

K completed her first year at college and fared well academically. She also developed an interest in learning more about proper nutrition, and wrote an academic paper on the need for appropriate amounts of dietary fat. K applied for and accepted a job at a local bank for the summer. She found that she enjoyed spending time with her friends, and she expressed excitement as she started dating. Late in the summer, K began to increase her running distance and lost about 5 pounds. She was able to see that her level of food and weight preoccupations increased dramatically and she became frightened that she was headed for a relapse. Frequency of outpatient meetings was increased, and it was agreed that K should be admitted to the intensive outpatient program if she experienced further weight loss. She was able to reinstitute meal planning and reverse the pattern of weight loss without the level of internal resistance that had characterized the initial treatment phase. She was reassured that periods of vulnerability were common during the course of recovery and that her ability to identify problems early on and make adjustments accordingly were a very positive sign.

Over the next year, K's psychosocial adjustment continued to improve, and she was able to find a healthy balance between academic, athletic, and social activities. The frequency of therapy meetings was gradually reduced, until therapy was terminated. K was encouraged to reinitiate therapy if she developed any concerns about her weight, eating, or exercise, or if other problems emerged.

SUMMARY

A major premise in this chapter has been that eating disorders are multidetermined and heterogeneous syndromes resulting from the interplay of biological, psychological, familial, and sociocultural predisposing factors. In this sense, they are probably best understood as final common pathways that appear to have different psychological points of entry. Within this overall context, the current chapter has selectively reviewed diagnostic issues, major etiological formulations, and associated psychopathology applied to eating disorders.

From research to date, it may be concluded that there has been as considerable resistance to dispelling the "uniformity myth" applied to eating disorders, as has been the case with other disorders with a longer or more visible history in the psychological nomenclature. However, the past decade of research has yielded notable advances in refining the criteria for eating-disordered subgroups and more rigorous research examining psychopathology or psychological topologies associated with diagnostic subtypes. An important direction for future research will be the clearer specification of the relative contribution of particular biological, psychological, and interpersonal predisposing features considered to be relevant to eating disorders. It is to be hoped that the extraordinary clinical and research interest in personality disorders, depression, sexual abuse, and addictive behaviors as they relate to eating disorders will continue to lead to improved understanding. Further research clearly is needed to determine the precise nature and the significance of the observed associations. If past research to date is any indication of future findings, the within-diagnostic-group variability will continue to be as noteworthy as the between-group differences.

It is now evident that certain patients respond relatively quickly to brief interventions, in contrast to others who require more intensive and protracted treatments. Perhaps the most significant goal for future research will be identification of traits, personality features, or background factors that predict differential responses to treatment. Eventually, the development of a taxonomy yielding an accurate match between patient characteristics and treatment type would be a tremendous asset. Recent advances in research on psychopathology and treatment efficacy warrant genuine optimism with regard to bulimia nervosa. Less is known about personality and response to treatment for anorexia nervosa because of the relative absence of controlled treatment research with this eating disorder. It is hoped that controlled treatment research will assume a high priority and that the results will generate the same level of progress as is now evident with bulimia nervosa.

REFERENCES

Agras, W.S., Schneider, J.A., Arnow, B., Raeburn, S.D., & Telch, C.F. (1989). Cognitive-behavioral and response-prevention techniques for bulimia nervosa. *Journal of Consulting and Clinical Psychology, 57,* 215–221.

American Psychiatric Association. (1987). *Diagnostic and statistical manual of mental disorders,* 3rd ed., revised. Washington, DC: American Psychiatric Association.

American Psychiatric Association. (1993). Practice guidelines for eating disorders. *American Journal of Psychiatry, 150,* 212–228.

American Psychiatric Association. (1994). *Diagnostic and statistical manual of mental disorders,* 4th ed. Washington, DC: American Psychiatric Association.

Andersen, A.E. (1990). *Males with eating disorders.* New York: Brunner/Mazel.

Armstrong, J.G., & Roth, D.M. (1989). Attachment and separation difficulties in eating disorders: A preliminary investigation. *International Journal of Eating Disorders, 8,* 141–155.

Banks, C.G., (1992). "Culture" in culture-bound syndromes: The case of anorexia nervosa. *Social Science Medicine, 34,* 867–884.

Bastiani, A.M., Rao, R., Weltzin, T., & Kaye, W.H. (1995). Perfectionism in anorexia nervosa. *International Journal of Eating Disorders, 17,* 147–152.

Beck, A.T., Rush, A.J., Shaw, B.F., & Emery, G. (1979). *Cognitive therapy of depression.* New York: Guilford Press.

Beumont, P.J.V., Al-Alami, M.S., & Touyz, S.W. (1987). The evolution of the concept of anorexia nervosa. In P.V. Beumont, G.D. Burrows, & R.C. Casper (Eds.), *Handbook of eating disorders: Part 1. Anorexia and bulimia nervosa* (pp. 105–116). New York: Elsevier.

Beumont, P.J.V., George, G.G.W., & Smart, D.E. (1976). "Dieters" and "vomiters and purgers" in anorexia nervosa. *Psychological Medicine, 6,* 617–622.

Brotman, A.W., Herzog, D.B., & Woods, S.W. (1984). Antidepressant treatment of bulimia nervosa: The relationship between bingeing and depressive symptomatology. *Journal of Clinical Psychiatry, 45,* 7–9.

Bruch, H. (1973). *Eating disorders: Obesity, anorexia nervosa and the person within.* New York: Basic Books.

Bruch, H. (1985). Four decades of eating disorders. In D.M. Garner & P.E. Garfinkel (Eds.), *Handbook of psychotherapy for anorexia nervosa and bulimia* (pp. 7–18). New York: Guilford Press.

Bryant-Waugh, R., & Lask, B. (1995). Annotation: Eating disorders in children. *Journal of Child Psychological Psychiatry, 36,* 191–202.

Bulik, C., Sullivan, P., Joyce, P., Carter, F. (1995). Temperament character, and personality disorder in bulimia nervosa. *Journal of Nervous and Mental Disease, 183,* 593–598.

Casper, R.C. (1983). On the emergence of bulimia nervosa as a syndrome: A historical view. *International Journal of Eating Disorders, 2,* 3–16.

Casper, R.C. (1990). Personality features of women with good outcome from restricting anorexia nervosa. *Psychosomatic Medicine, 52,* 156–170.

Casper, R.C., Eckert, E.D., Halmi, K.A., Goldberg, S.C., & Davis, J.M. (1980). Bulimia. Its incidence and clinical importance in patients with anorexia nervosa. *Archives of General Psychiatry, 37,* 1030–1034.

Cooper, P.J., & Fairburn, C.G. (1986). The depressive symptoms of bulimia nervosa. *British Journal of Psychiatry, 148,* 268–274.

Cooper, Z., & Fairburn, C.G. (1987). The Eating Disorder Examination: A semistructured interview for the assessment of the specific psychopathology of eating disorders. *International Journal of Eating Disorders, 6,* 1–8.

Crisp, A.H. (1997). Anorexia nervosa as flight from growth: assessment and treatment based on the model. In D.M. Garner & P.E. Garfinkel (Eds.), *Handbook of treatment for eating disorders* (pp. 248–277), New York: Guilford Press.

Crowther, J., & Sherwood, N. (1997). Assessment. In D.M. Garner & P.E. Garfinkel (Eds.), *Handbook of treatment for eating disorders* (pp. 34–49). New York: Guilford Press.

Dare, C., & Eisler, I. (1997). Family therapy for anorexia nervosa. In D.M. Garner & P.E. Garfinkel (Eds.), *Handbook of treatment for eating disorders* (pp. 307–326). New York: Guilford Press.

Eckert, E.D., Halmi, K.A., Marchi, P., & Cohen, J. (1987). Comparison of bulimic and non-bulimic anorexia nervosa patients during treatment. *Psychological Medicine, 17,* 891–898.

Fairburn, C.G. (1985). Cognitive-behavioral treatment for bulimia. In D.M. Garner & P.E. Garfinkel (Eds.), *Handbook of psychotherapy for anorexia nervosa and bulimia* (pp. 160–192). New York: Guilford Press.

Fairburn, C.G. & Beglin, S.J. (1990). Studies of the epidemiology of bulimia nervosa. *American Journal of Psychiatry, 147,* 401–408.

Fairburn, C.G., Marcus, M.D., & Wilson, G.T. (1993) Cognitive-behavioral therapy for binge eating and bulimia nervosa. In C.G. Fairburn & G.T. Wilson (Eds.), *Binge eating: nature, assessment, and treatment* (pp. 361–404). New York: Guilford Press.

Fairburn, C.G., Norman, P.A., Welch, S.L., O'Connor, M.E., Doll, H.A., & Peveler, R.C. (1995). A prospective study of outcome in bulimia nervosa and the long-term effect of three psychological treatments. *Archives of General Psychiatry, 52,* 304–312.

Fallon, P., & Wonderlich, S. (1997). Sexual abuse and other forms of trauma. In D.M. Garner & P.E. Garfinkel (Eds.) *Handbook of treatment for eating disorders* (pp. 394–414). New York: Guilford Press.

Fosson, A., Knibbs, J., Bryant-Waugh, R., & Lask, B. (1987). Early onset anorexia nervosa. *Archives of Disease in Childhood, 62,* 114–118.

Garfinkel, P.E., & Garner, D.M. (1982). *Anorexia nervosa: A multidimensional perspective.* New York: Brunner/Mazel.

Garfinkel, P.E., Moldofsky, H., & Garner, D.M. (1980). The heterogeneity of anorexia nervosa. *Archives of General Psychiatry, 37,* 1036–1040.

Garfinkel, P.E., & Walsh, B. (1997). Drug therapies. In D.M. Garner & P.E. Garfinkel (Eds.), *Handbook of treatment for eating disorders* (pp. 229–247). New York/London: Guilford Press.

Garner, D.M. (1991). *Eating disorder inventory–2: Professional manual.* Odessa, FL: Psychological Assessment Resources.

Garner, D.M. (1993). Binge eating in anorexia nervosa. In C.G. Fairburn & G.T. Wilson (Eds.), *Binge eating: Nature, assessment, and treatment* (pp. 50–76). New York: Guilford Press.

Garner, D.M. (1997). Psychoeducational principles in treatment. In D.M. Garner & P.E. Garfinkel (Eds.), *Handbook of treatment for eating disorders* (pp. 145–177). New York: Guilford Press.

Garner, D.M., & Bemis, K.M. (1982). A cognitive-behavioral approach to anorexia nervosa. *Cognitive Therapy and Research, 6,* 123–150.

Garner, D.M., & Bemis, K.M. (1985). Cognitive therapy for anorexia nervosa. In D.M. Garner & P.E. Garfinkel (Eds.), *Handbook of psychotherapy for anorexia nervosa and bulimia* (pp. 107–146). New York: Guilford Press.

Garner, D.M., & Fairburn, C.G. (1988). Relationship between anorexia nervosa and bulimia nervosa: Diagnostic implications. In D.M. Garner & P.E. Garfinkel (Eds.), *Diagnostic issues in anorexia nervosa and bulimia nervosa* (pp. 56–79). New York: Brunner/Mazel.

Garner, D.M., & Garfinkel, P.E. (1980). Sociocultural factors in the development of anorexia nervosa. *Psychological Medicine, 10,* 647–656.

Garner, D.M., & Garfinkel, P.E. (1997). *Handbook of treatment for eating disorders.* New York: Guilford Press.

Garner, D.M., Garfinkel, P.E., Schwartz, D.M., & Thompson, M.M. (1980). Cultural expectations of thinness in women. *Psychological Reports, 47,* 483–491.

Garner, D.M., Garner, M.V., & Rosen, L.W. (1993). Anorexia nervosa "restricters" who purge: Implications for subtyping anorexia nervosa. *International Journal of Eating Disorders, 13,* 171–185.

Garner, D.M., Olmsted, M.P., Davis, R., Rockert, W., Goldbloom, D., & Eagle, M. (1990). The association between bulimic symptoms and reported psychopathology. *International Journal of Eating Disorders, 9,* 1–15.

Garner, D.M., Rockert, W., Garner, M.V., Davis, R., Olmsted, M.P., & Eagle, M. (1993). Comparison of cognitive-behavioral and supportive-expressive therapy for bulimia nervosa. *American Journal of Psychiatry, 150,* 37–46.

Garner, D.M., Rockert, W., Olmsted, M.P., Johnson, C., & Coscina (1985). Psychoeducational principles in the treatment of bulimia nervosa. In D.M. Garner & P.E. Garfinkel (Eds.), *Handbook of treatment for eating disorders.* New York: Guilford Press.

Garner, D.M., & Rosen, L.W. (1991). Eating disorders in athletes: Research and recommendations. *Journal of Applied Sports Research, 5,* 100–107.

Garner, D.M., Shafer, C.L., & Rosen, L.W. (1992) Critical appraisal of the DSM-III-R personality diagnostic criteria for eating disorders. In S.R. Hooper, G.W. Hynd, & R.E. Mattison (Eds.), *Child psychopathology. diagnostic criteria and clinical assessment.* (pp. 261–303). Hillsdale, NJ: Lawrence Erlbaum.

Garner, D.M., Vitousek, K., & Pike, K. (1997). Cognitive-behavioral therapy for anorexia nervosa. In D.M. Garner & P.E. Garfinkel (Eds.), *Handbook of treatment for eating disorders* (pp. 94–144). New York: Guilford Press.

Garner, D.M., & Wooley, S.C. (1991). Confronting the failure of behavioral and dietary treatments for obesity. *Clinical Psychology Review, 11,* 729–780.

Gartner, A.F., Marcus, R.N., Halmi, K., & Loranger, A.W. (1989). DSM-III-R personality disorders in patients with eating disorders. *American Journal of Psychiatry, 146,* 1585–1591.

Gillberg, G., Rastam, M., & Gillberg, C. (1995). Anorexia nervosa 6 years after onset: Part I. Personality disorders. *Comprehensive Psychiatry, 36,* 61–69.

Goodsitt, A. (1997). Eating disorders a self psychological perspective. In D.M. Garner & P.E. Garfinkel (Eds.), *Handbook of treatment for eating disorders* (pp. 205–228). New York: Guilford Press.

Gowers, S., & McMahon, J.B. (1989). Social class and prognosis in anorexia nervosa. *International Journal of Eating Disorders, 8,* 105–110.

Hatsukami, D., Mitchell, J.E., Eckert, E.D., & Pyle, R. (1986). Characteristics of patients with bulimia only, bulimia with affective disorder, and bulimia with substance abuse problems. *Addictive Behaviors, 11,* 399–406.

Heatherton, T.F., & Baumeister, R.F. (1991). Binge-eating as escape from self-awareness. *Psychological Bulletin, 110,* 86–108.

Herzog, D.B., Keller, M.B., Sacks, N.R., Yeh, C.J., & Lavori, P.W. (1992). Psychiatric morbidity in treatment-seeking anorexics and bulimics. *Journal of the American Academy of Child and Adolescent Psychiatry, 31,* 810–818.

Hoek, H.W. (1995). The distribution of eating disorders. In K.D. Brownell & C.G. Fairburn (Eds.), *Eating disorders and obesity* (pp. 207–211). New York: Guilford Press.

Hsu, L.K.G., Kaye, W. & Weltzin, T.E. (1993). Are the eating disorders related to obsessive compulsive disorder? *International Journal of Eating Disorders, 14,* 305–318.

Huon, G.F., Brown, L., & Morris, S. (1988). Lay beliefs about disordered eating. *International Journal of Eating Disorders, 7,* 239–252.

Jaffe, A.C., & Singer, L.T. (1989). Atypical eating

disorders in young children. *International Journal of Eating Disorders, 8,* 575–582.

Johnson, C., Tobin, D.L., & Dennis, A. (1990). Differences in treatment outcome between borderline and nonborderline bulimics at one-year follow-up. *International Journal of Eating Disorders, 9,* 617–627.

Kaplan, A.S., & Olmsted, M.P. (1997). Partial hospitalization. In D.M. Garner & P.E. Garfinkel (Eds.), *Handbook of Treatment for Eating Disorders* (pp. 354–360). New York: Guilford Press.

Kellet, J., Trimble, M., & Thorley, A. (1976). Anorexia nervosa after the menopause. *British Journal of Psychiatry, 128,* 555–558.

Kreipe, R.E. (1995). Eating disorders among children and adolescents. *Pediatrics in Review, 16,* 370–379.

Levin, A.P., & Hyler, S.E. (1986). DSM-III personality diagnosis in bulimia. *Comprehensive Psychiatry, 27,* 47–53.

Minuchin, S., Rosman, B.L., & Baker, L. (1978). *Psychosomatic families: Anorexia nervosa in context.* Cambridge, MA: Harvard University Press.

Mitchell, J.E., Pomeroy, C., & Adson, D.E. (1997). In D.M. Garner & P.E. Garfinkel (Eds.), *Handbook of treatment for eating disorders* (pp. 383–393). New York: Guilford Press.

Mitchell, J.E., Pyle, R.L., Eckert, E.D., Hatsukami, D., Pomeroy, C., & Zimmerman, R. (1990). A comparison study of antidepressants and structured intensive group psychotherapy in the treatment of bulimia nervosa. *Archives of General Psychiatry, 47,* 149–157.

Olivardia, R., Pope, H., Mangweth, B., Hudson, J. (1995). Eating disorders in college men. *American Journal of Psychiatry, 152,* 1279–1285.

Oppenheimer, R., Howells, K., Palmer, R.L., & Chaloner, D.A. (1985). Adverse sexual experience in childhood and clinical eating disorders: A preliminary description. *Journal of Psychiatric Research, 19,* 357–361.

Piran, N., Lerner, P., Garfinkel, P.E., Kennedy, S.H., & Brouilette, C. (1988). Personality disorders in anorexia patients. *International Journal of Eating Disorders, 5,* 589–599.

Polivy, J., & Herman, C.P. (1987). Diagnosis and treatment of normal eating. *Journal of Consulting and Clinical Psychology, 55,* 635–644.

Pope, H.G., & Hudson, J.I. (1988). Is bulimia nervosa a heterogeneous disorder? Lessons from the history of medicine. *International Journal of Eating Disorders, 7,* 155–166.

Pope, H.G., & Hudson, J.I. (1989). Are eating disorders associated with borderline personality disorder? A critical review. *International Journal of Eating Disorders, 8,* 1–9.

Powers P. (1997). Management of patients with co-morbid medical conditions. In D.M. Garner & P.E. Garfinkel (Eds.), *Handbook of treatment for eating disorders* (pp. 424–436). New York: Guilford Press.

Rampling, D. (1985). Ascetic ideals and anorexia nervosa. *Journal of Psychiatric Research, 19,* 89–94.

Rastam, M., Gillberg, C., Gillberg, C. (1995). Anorexia nervosa 6 years after onset: Part II. Comorbid psychiatric problems. *Comprehensive Psychiatry, 36,* 70–76.

Raymond, N.C., Mitchell, J.E., Fallon, P. & Katzman, M.A. (1994). A collaborative approach to the use of medication. In P. Fallon, M. Katzman, & S.C. Wooley (Eds.). *Feminist perspectives on eating disorders.* (pp. 231–250). New York: Guilford Press.

Russell, G.F.M. (1979). Bulimia nervosa: An ominous variant of anorexia nervosa. *Psychological Medicine, 9,* 429–448.

Russell, G.F.M. (1997). The history of bulimia nervosa. In D.M. Garner & P.E. Garfinkel (Eds.), *Handbook of treatment for eating disorders* (pp. 11–24). New York: Guilford Press.

Russell, G.F.M., Szmukler, G.I., Dare, C., & Eisler, I. (1987). An evaluation of family therapy in anorexia nervosa and bulimia nervosa. *Archives of General Psychiatry, 44,* 1047–1056.

Selvini-Palazzoli, M.P. (1974). *Self-starvation.* London: Chaucer Publishing Company.

Sohlberg, S., Norring, C., Homgren, S., & Rosmark, B. (1989). Impulsivity and long-term prognosis of psychiatric patients with anorexia nervosa/bulimia nervosa. *Journal of Nervous and Mental Disease, 177,* 249–258.

Spitzer, R.L., Yanovski, S., Wadden, T., Wing, R., Marcus, M., Stunkard, A., Delvin, M., Mitchell, J., Hasin, D., & Horne, R.L. (1993). Binge eating disorder: Its further validation in a multisite study.

International Journal of Eating Disorders, 13, 137–153.

Srebnik, D.S., & Saltzberg, E.A. (1994). Feminist cognitive-behavioral therapy for negative body image. *Women and Therapy, 15,* 117–133.

Steinhausen, C.H., Rauss-Mason, C., Seidel, R. (1991). Follow-up studies of anorexia nervosa: A review of four decades of outcome research. *Psychological Medicine, 21,* 447–454.

Strober, M. (1991). Disorders of the self in anorexia nervosa: An organismic-developmental paradigm. In C. Johnson (Ed.), *Psychodynamic theory and treatment for eating disorders* (pp. 354–372). New York: Guilford Press.

Strober, M. (1997). Consultation and therapeutic engagement in severe anorexia nervosa. In D.M. Garner & P.E. Garfinkel (Eds.), *Handbook of treatment for eating disorders* (pp. 229–247). New York: Guilford Press.

Strober, M., & Katz, J.L. (1988). Depression in the eating disorders: A review and analysis of descriptive, family, and biological findings. In D.M. Garner & P.E. Garfinkel (Eds.), *Diagnostic issues in anorexia nervosa and bulimia nervosa* (pp. 80–111). New York: Brunner/Mazel.

Szauter, K., & Levine, R.E. (1997). A case-based review of eating disorders. *Hospital Physician, 33,* 15–28.

Toner, B.B., Garfinkel, P.E., & Garner, D.M. (1988). Affective and anxiety disorders in the long-term follow-up of anorexia nervosa. *International Journal of Psychiatry in Medicine, 18,* 357–364.

Vandereycken, W., Kog, E., & Vanderlinden, J. (1989). *The family approach to eating disorders.* New York: PMA.

Walsh, B.T., & Garner D.M. (1997). Diagnostic issues. In D.M. Garner & P.E. Garfinkel (Eds.), *Handbook of treatment for eating disorders* (pp. 25–33). New York: Guilford Press.

Walsh, B.T., Wilson, G.T., Loeb, K.L., Devlin, M.J., Pike, K.M., Roose, S.P., Fleiss, J., & Waternaux, C. (1997). Medication and psychotherapy in the treatment of bulimia nervosa. *American Journal of Psychiatry, 154,* 523–531.

Welch, G.W., Hall, A., & Renner, R. (1990). Patient subgrouping in anorexia nervosa using psychologically-based classification. *International Journal of Eating Disorders, 9,* 311–322.

Wonderlich, S.A., Swift, W.J., Slotnick, H.B., & Goodman, S. (1990). DSM-III-R personality disorders in eating-disorder subtypes. *International Journal of Eating Disorders, 9,* 607–616.

GLOSSARY

action potential: The all-or-none rapid change in electrical potential that is propagated down an axon conducting information along the extent of the neuron.

adaptation: In Piaget's theory, the process by which a person changes in order to function more effectively in a given situation. Also, John Bowlby formulated *adaptational theory*, which integrates evolutionary, psychoanalytic, information-processing, and social learning models.

aggression: A wide range of assertive and intrusive behaviors and/or characteristics.

agonist: A drug that simulates the effect of a particular neurotransmitter or acts to enhance that transmitter's effect.

agoraphobia: The fear of being alone in public places, especially in situations from which a rapid exit would be difficult. Agoraphobic dread and avoidance behavior are primarily focused on concern about physical sensations and losing control, rather than features of a phobic

disorder. Often occurs in conjunction with panic disorder. Situations commonly associated with agoraphobia include being in crowds, going out alone, tunnels, bridges, and using public transportation.

amenorrhea: The loss of menses (*secondary amenorrhea*) or the failure to menstruate when expected (*primary amenorrhea*), typically resulting from low body weight, inadequate food intake, excessive exercise, and/or stress, all of which are potential causes of insufficient estrogen production.

amphetamine: A group of drugs, usually but not always in tablet form, with stimulant properties. Depending on the dose, effects of this class of drugs range from feelings of alertness and energy, to a euphoric "rush," to hallucinations, delusions, paranoia, and psychosis.

analytic epidemiology: The level of epidemiology focused on the study of the determinants or correlates of disorder, or on the reasons for strong or weak associations between disorder occurrence and other variables.

anorexic eating: Eating in a manner stereotypic of eating disorders, such as dividing foods into "good" and "bad" categories, cutting food into minuscule pieces, taking a very long time to eat, eating excessively small portions of food, manipulating food, and maintaining rigidity

Glossary terms are adapted from various sources, including Cacioppo and Tassinary (1990) (see Chapter 5 References) and the DSM-IV (APA, 1994) (see Chapter 17 References).

around the consumption of certain food items. These patterns have also been observed as common among victims of severe dietary restriction or semistarvation.

anorexic identity: The tendency for someone with an eating disorder to see the disorder itself as having favorable connotations because of its ostensible association with positive traits such as self-discipline, intelligence, determination, and control. Eating disorders have been repeatedly misrepresented and glamorized in the popular media (e.g., magazines, books, and talk shows) and linked to high-status individuals (e.g., models, athletes, and other celebrities). When the eating disorder itself is ego-syntonic and confers secondary gain, it poses a special challenge to psychotherapy.

antagonist: A drug that inhibits or counteracts the effect of a particular neurotransmitter.

antiobsessional agents: Medications prescribed to reduce obsessions or compulsions.

anxiety sensitivity: The fear of anxiety symptoms, which reflects a consistent belief that anxiety symptoms are harmful.

attachment: The enduring emotional tie between infant and caregiver that is established through repeated interaction over time.

autonomic nervous system (ANS): The branch of the peripheral nervous system that is concerned with the regulation of smooth muscle, cardiac muscle, and glands. The ANS consists of three separate systems: the *sympathetic* nervous system (SNS), the *parasympathetic* nervous system (PNS), and the *enteric* nervous system (ENS).

behavioral inhibition: A temperamental precursor to shyness and the development of anxiety disorders.

Berkson's bias: A referral bias in which cases with two disorders are more likely to be referred than individuals with only one disorder.

binge eating: Consuming a large amount of food in a short period of time when this behavior is associated with feelings of loss of control. It is contrasted with "overeating," which does not involve a loss of control. Many eating disorder patients experience their behavior as "binge eating" even on occasions when they do not consume an objectively large amount of food (see Garner, 1993, cited in Chapter 18, for a full discussion).

bipolar depression: One of the major subtypes of affective disorders delineated by DSM-IV; a psychological disorder characterized by both manic and depressive episodes, either separately or concurrently. To be diagnosed with bipolar depression requires the presence of at least one manic episode.

brain ventricles: Deep brain structures filled with cerebrospinal fluid (CSF). They enlarge to fill space left by atrophic changes in the brain, so their size provides an indirect index of losses in neuronal tissue. Ventricle enlargement can reflect degenerative or developmental perturbations.

cannabis: Marijuana, in leaf, hashish, or purified forms; its use results in feelings of euphoria, silliness, changes in sensory perception, increased appetite, and an overall sense of relaxation and self-awareness. In high doses, cannabis use may result in suspiciousness or paranoid behavior, and in panic.

case: An individual with the defined characteristic of interest (e.g., a disorder, a score exceeding a certain level on a test).

cell body: Also known as *soma,* the part of the neuron that contains the nucleus and other organelles necessary for sustaining normal cell function.

cell membrane: A thin lipid bilayer surrounding the organelles and substances that make up a cell and separating them from external surroundings.

clinical phenomenology: Description of the overt, observable, clinical characteristics (signs and symptoms) of a patient, without assumption about the underlying disease process.

cocaine: A stimulant, made from the coca leaf, which can be injected or sniffed in powder form, or smoked when in a solid form called "crack." Cocaine's principal effects are exhilaration, elation, euphoria, grandiosity, and a sense of confidence.

cognitive-behavioral therapy: A therapeutic approach that combines cognitive and behavioral theoretical approaches. The several psychotherapeutic treatments that derive from this theoretical viewpoint use multiple strategies to reduce symptoms. Cognitive-behavioral therapists use cognitive techniques to identify patients' dysfunctional beliefs, guide them in real-life experiments to test the validity of these beliefs, and then correct erroneous or maladaptive ways of thinking. At the same time, they use behavioral strategies to enhance the effectiveness of the treatment.

coherence: Qualitative similarities in behavior over time (e.g., similarity in approach or process versus content).

cohort: A group of individuals defined on the basis of one or more shared characteristics.

comorbidity: The occurrence of at least two different disorders in the same individual.

comorbidity: Psychiatric disorders that commonly co-occur in a population, such as PTSD and substance abuse disorders.

compulsion: A repetitive behavior or sets of behaviors (overt or covert) that a person feels compelled or driven to perform.

computed transaxial tomography (CT) scanning: A

neuroimaging technique for evaluating brain anatomy. Older than clinical MRI imaging, it relies on ionizing radiation to generate brain images. CT scans typically provide lower resolution images of brain anatomy than do MRI scans.

continuity: Behavioral (quantitative) stability across time.

cross-sectional survey: A research strategy in which individuals are sampled from one or more populations at one point in time, and associations between a wide range of characteristics possessed by the individuals are examined.

culture: Nonmaterial aspects of a society, including its norms, values, belief, rituals, and symbols.

dendrite: Treelike processes that extend from the cell body of the neuron and receive information from other neurons.

dendritic spines: Tiny mushroom-shaped extensions of dendrites that form synapses with axon terminals of other neurons.

depolarization: A change in membrane potential that reduces the negativity and rendering the cell more excitable.

descriptive epidemiology: The level of epidemiology focused on the study of the rates and distribution of a disorder in a population or in subsets of the population.

developmental psychopathology: The study of the origin and course of disordered behavior (e.g., the time at which the behavior initially appears, what form it takes, and how this form changes over time).

deviance: Behavior that violates the commonly accepted standards of a culture.

diathesis–stress: A model of psychopathology that proposes that an individual possesses an underlying predisposition for a disorder but will not manifest the clinical symptoms unless this vulnerability is activated by acute or extreme stress.

discontinuity: Behavioral change over time.

disease model of addiction: A belief system based on a conviction that drug abuse and dependence (particularly maladaptive use of alcohol) are best conceived of as diseases, rather than as learned behaviors or as evidence of moral weakness.

dissociation: Sudden, transient alienation in consciousness marked by diminished responsiveness to environmental stimuli and, in severe instances, by an interruption of memory for events occurring during the dissociative episode.

dopamine (DA): A major neurotransmitter in the brain distributed via three different systems, all originating in brainstem structures. Implicated in schizophrenia, Parkinson's disease, and reward. It is believed to be important in schizophrenia because of its role in cognitive

processes, and because blocking activity at certain specific dopamine receptor sites appears to be an important mechanism of action of antipsychotic drugs.

dyspareunia (not due to a general medical condition): Recurrent or persistent genital pain associated with sexual intercourse in either a male or a female, and not caused exclusively by vaginismus or lack of lubrication.

dysthymia: One of the major subtypes of affective disorders delineated by DSM-IV; a chronic, nonpsychotic disturbance that includes the presence of sustained or intermittent depressed mood for at least two years, as well as the presence of at least two major symptoms of depression.

eating-disordered behavior: Engaging in symptomatic patterns that include, but are not limited to, "anorexic eating," in that patients' ways of thinking and behaving also serve to maintain and perpetuate certain features of the disorder (e.g., ruminating on pervasive thoughts pertaining to weight, size, and caloric intake, and partaking in weight-compensatory behaviors).

electrode: A device that permits the recording or transmission of electrical signals. Common electrodes used in psychophysiological research include cups, needles, disks, and pads, and assist in the transmission of electrical signals from an organism to an amplification source. Some electrodes may be used in combination with electrolytic substances to assist in the transmission of the signals.

electrodermal activity (EDA): The measurement of electrical activity on the skin. This general term encompasses, among others, skin conductance response (SCR), skin conductance level (SCL), electrodermal response (EDR), electrodermal level (EDL), and skin potential. The term EDA replaces the original term for this type of measurement, galvanic skin response (GSR).

electroencephalogram (EEG): The continuous measurement of electrical activity produced by the brain. The measurement may take place on the surface of the brain or on the surface of the scalp.

electromyogram (EMG): The continuous measurement of electrical activity produced by muscle tissue contraction. The measurement may take place over the muscle on the surface of the skin or through the insertion of electrodes directly into the muscle tissue.

endogenous depression: A subtype of depression that, historically, demarcated a biological etiology of depression that was independent of precipitating life events. More recently, this term is used to refer to depressions, regardless of etiology, that exhibit a particular symptom cluster, including severely depressed mood; depressive delusions and/or hallucinations; psychomotor retardation or agitation; pathological guilt; and disorders of sleep, appetite, and other bodily functions. This subtype is generally contrasted with *reactive depression*.

epidemiology: The study of the rates of occurrence and distribution of disease or disorder in the population and the factors that affect this distribution.

event-related potential (ERP): A change in electrical activity related to discrete internal or external stimuli; usually measured through EEG recordings. ERPs are classified according to the stimuli that produced them. *Exogenous* ERPs are produced by stimuli external to the organism, *endogenous* ERPs by internal stimuli, and *mesogenous* ERPs by a combination of external and internal stimuli.

excitatory postsynaptic potential (EPSP): A graded potential representing the sum of small depolarizations.

experimental epidemiology: The level of epidemiology focused on manipulation of identified risk factors to determine their effects on the occurrence of disorder or its components.

exposure therapy: A cognitive-behavioral technique in which a feared stimulus or event is reviewed imaginally and repeatedly until a significant reduction or cessation in anxiety responding is evident.

exposure with response prevention: A behavioral therapy technique used to treat anxiety disorders, whereby the patient is exposed to the anxiety-producing stimulus and prevented from avoiding or escaping the anxiety.

expressed emotion: When interaction with a patient within a family takes on the character of being intrusive, emotionally controlling, and highly critical, the family is considered to have a high level of expressed emotion that increases risk for episodes of psychosis.

female orgasmic disorder: Persistent or recurrent delay in, or absence of, orgasm following a normal sexual excitement phase, diagnosed on the basis of the clinician's judgment that the woman's orgasmic capacity is less than would be reasonable for her age, her degree of sexual experience, and the adequacy of sexual stimulation she receives.

female sexual arousal disorder: Persistent or recurrent inability to attain, or to maintain until completion of the sexual activity, an adequate lubrication–swelling response of sexual excitement.

fetishism: Sexual arousal associated with nonliving objects.

first messenger: Refers to the chemical messengers that are involved in the first step of neural activation by affecting receptors on the cell membrane.

flashback: Acting or feeling as if a traumatic event were recurring; a sense of reliving the experience.

follow-back study: A research strategy in which a cohort is selected on the basis or archival or historical records. The rate of disorder during the period from the time the records were compiled until a later point in time is examined and compared to rates in other cohorts or populations.

food phobias: Intense fears of foods commonly assumed to be "fattening" or of food items consumed during binge-eating episodes. Often, these foods are avoided completely, and irrational beliefs regarding the consequences of consuming them are perceived as the truth.

formal thought disorder: Disruption in the cohesion of thought process, often manifest by loose associations, cognitive slippage, tangentiality, and a variety of other descriptors.

functional magnetic resonance imaging (fMRI): A new brain-imaging technique that allows regional changes in brain activation during different kinds of cognitive activity to be studied noninvasively in single subjects at high spatial resolution.

generalized anxiety disorder: A disorder characterized by excessive and impairing worry occurring more days than not for at least 6 months. The worry may concern a number of different domains or activities (e.g., work, finances, family, health) and must be difficult to control. In addition, the worry or anxiety must be associated with a number of physiological symptoms, including restlessness, fatigue, impaired concentration, irritability, muscle tension, or sleep disturbance.

genetic heterogeneity: Characteristic of a disorder or clinical syndrome that is the product of more than one genetic factor.

genetic marker variables: Measurements used to distinguish at-risk patients for psychiatric illnesses with complex phenotypes (clinical expressions), which may be difficult to link to particular genetic abnormalities because of possible etiologic heterogeneity.

glia: Nonneuronal cells thought to provide structural support and "housekeeper" functions such as clearing away excess or debris materials.

hallucinogens: A class of drugs containing various substances that vary widely in chemical structure and mechanism of action, but that, in general, induce feelings that include a sense of loss of control, depersonalization, feelings of being carefree or silly, impaired thinking including slowness and loss of meanings, anxiety, depression, fear of becoming crazy, and paranoid ideation.

haloperidol: An antipsychotic drug that binds to dopamine receptors and is used to treat schizophrenia.

harm reduction: As applied to drug and alcohol addiction, refers to approaches that seek to reduce individual, familial, and societal harm related to chemical abuse and dependence; based on an underlying belief that it is desirable to help an individual move to a less harmful state, without assuming an objective of abstinence or even reduction in drug use.

heart rate (HR): The reciprocal transformation of the heart's interbeat interval, typically expressed in beats per minute (bpm) and often assessed as a general measure of arousal. Like many other measures of psychophysiology, HR may be measured as tonic activity (heart rate level, or HRL) or as phasic activity (heart rate response, or HRR).

hyperarousal: A state of increased psychological responsiveness to sensory stimulation; PTSD Criterion D symptoms indicating increased arousal such as difficulty falling asleep and irritability.

hyperpolarization: A change in membrane potential *increasing* the negativity inside the cell and rendering the cell less excitable.

hypervigilance: PTSD Criterion D symptom indicating an excessive preoccupation with the identification of threat from the environment, manifesting as a pattern of exaggerated self-protective behaviors.

hypoactive sexual desire disorder: Persistent or recurrent deficiency in (or absence of) sexual fantasies and desire for sexual activity. The judgment of deficiency or absence is made by the clinician, taking into account factors that affect sexual functions, such as age, sex, and the context of the person's life.

hypoxyphilia: Also known as autoerotic asphyxia, in which choking (e.g., via chest compression, noose, plastic bag) is associated with sexual arousal.

incidence rate: The ratio of newly diagnosed cases during a given time period to the population at risk for developing a first episode of the disorder.

inhalants: Vapors in gasoline, glues, and other volatile compounds, usually breathed through the nose and mouth. Intoxicated users exhibit behavior similar to that of persons under the influence of alcohol.

inhibited sexual desire: The chronic failure to initiate or respond to sexual cues. A precursor to the DSM-IV diagnosis of hypoactive sexual desire disorder.

inhibitory postsynaptic potential (IPSP): A graded potential representing the sum of small hyperpolarizations.

interoceptive conditioning: A process whereby internal stimuli of panic-like symptoms come to elicit the full panic response when sensations that may present as panic symptoms (e.g., palpitations due to any cause) serve as a conditioning stimulus, cueing the onset of other anxiety symptoms (e.g., dizziness) as a conditioning response.

interpersonal psychotherapy: A psychotherapeutic treatment, growing out of the psychodynamic tradition, that focuses specifically on interpersonal relationships, although it is typically conducted in a one-on-one format.

Interpersonal psychotherapy attempts to guide patients in identifying and understanding their interpersonal problems and conflicts, and to help them relate to others in a more adaptive manner.

interpersonal violence: Violence that targets people exclusively.

intrusive thoughts: Unwanted, unwelcome, distressing thoughts or images that are very difficult to block out of consciousness or to interrupt once present; a reexperiencing symptom of posttraumatic stress disorder (PTSD).

kindling: A model of neurophysiological excitation, originally proposed as a model for epilepsy but now being applied to bipolar disorder to account for variations of this illness (e.g., rapid cycling).

law of initial values: (LIV): This "law" is actually a principle and refers to the observation that the higher the physiological tonic activity, the lower the tendency of the physiological response to change. In other words, there is an inverse relation between the physiological response to a stimulus and the prestimulus level of physiological activity.

limbic system: A group of nuclei involved in emotion and motivation. Structures include the amygdala, hippocampus, adjacent cortex, septal nuclei, and parts of the thalamus and hypothalamus.

locus coeruleus: Nucleus of cells located in brainstem, containing nearly half of the brain's noradrenergic neurons and producing 70% of the brain's norepinephrine. The locus coeruleus controls alarm, fear, and anxiety reactions.

longitudinal study: The study of a phenomenon over time, often using multiple data points and repeated measures.

macroparadigm: An overarching framework that functions to coordinate various theoretical modes that emphasize particular subsets of variables, methods, and explanations.

magnetic resonance imaging (MRI): An imaging technique that provides high-resolution anatomical images of the brain to permit the study of abnormalities in anatomy and structure.

magnetic resonance spectroscopy (MRS): An application of MR that provides information about brain neurochemistry in a noninvasive manner. For example, MRS can provide information about the rate of degradation of neuronal membranes and about metabolic byproducts of energy consumption.

major depressive disorder: The most common of the subtypes of depression described in DSM-IV; refers to the presence of one or more major depressive episodes. Patients must exhibit at least 5 of a list of 9 symptoms most of the day, nearly every day, for at least 2 weeks. At least one of these symptoms must be either depressed mood or anhedonia.

male erectile disorder: Persistent or recurrent inability to attain, or to maintain until completion of the sexual activity, an adequate erection.

male orgasmic disorder: Persistent or recurrent delay in, or absence of, orgasm following a normal sexual excitement phase during sexual activity that the clinician, taking into account the person's age, judges to be adequate in focus, intensity, and duration.

meal planning: A structured approach to eating that involves selecting food items in advance in order to decrease the amount of time spent surrounding decision making about eating and food choiccs. Mcal planning involves selecting foods based on a set plan that takes into consideration the number of calories needed to achieve therapeutic goals as well as the proportion of fat grams needed to ensure adequate nutrition. Meal planning is a particularly useful alternative to "self-monitoring" that has been recommended for bulimia nervosa.

medroxyprogesterone acetate (MPA): An antiandrogen hormone that suppresses sexual arousal to both inappropriate and appropriate stimuli.

muscarinic receptor: Type of acetylcholine receptor that is found in the autonomic nervous system and response to the poison "muscarine."

National Crime Victimization Survey: Survey conducted every year by the Bureau of the Census, in cooperation with the Bureau of Justice Statistics, based on reports by victims; violent crimes included are robbery, rape, and assault.

neurodevelopmental models: Models of etiology that propose that abnormalities in brain development, rather than pathological processes that occur at the time of illness onset, are the primary cause of illnesses such as schizophrenia.

neuron: Basic building block of the nervous system; specialized cell for integration and transmission of information.

neurotransmitter chemicals: Substances released from an axon terminal into a synapse. Neurotransmitters diffuse across the synapse to cause excitation or inhibition of the adjacent neuron.

nicotinic receptor: Type of acetylcholine receptor found at neuromuscular junctions. Also recognizes and response to nicotine.

nosological: Pertaining to the theory of diagnostic classification of diseases and the relationships between diagnostic groups.

nutritional rehabilitation: The process of gaining weight slowly and learning to eat in a more normal manner

(e.g., eating moderate amounts of food periodically throughout the day).

obsession: A repetitive, intrusive, and persistent thought or image that does not respond easily to suppression.

opioids: The group of narcotic substances derived from opium, including heroin, which is derived from morphine, which, in turn, is derived from opium. In addition to several alkaloid products of opium, there are a number of synthetic narcotics that have many of the same effects as heroin. All of these substances reduce sensory feeling and, in sufficient doses, induce drowsiness and feelings of euphoria.

orienting response (OR): A physiological pattern of responses that occur in the presence of a novel stimulus. A typical OR may include, among other responses, increased skin conductance, decreased HR, increased muscle tone, movement of the eyes toward the object, and changes in respiration. Upon repeated presentations of a stimulus, OR may habituate.

panic attack: A discrete period of intense fear or discomfort that is accompanied by a number of somatic or cognitive symptoms including difficulty breathing, heart palpitations, dizziness, trembling, terror, and feelings of dread.

panic disorder: A disorder in which the individual has spontaneous panic attacks. There may be extreme apprehension about the possibility of having an attack. In addition, the panic disorder patient may develop avoidance behavior that could lead to a diagnosis of panic disorder with agoraphobia.

paraphilia: Sexually arousing fantasies, urges, or behaviors to deviant stimuli, including nonhuman objects, the suffering or humiliation of oneself or one's partner, or children or other nonconsenting partners.

pause–squeeze technique: A technique designed by Masters and Johnson for the treatment of premature ejaculation. Involves "pausing" when the male reaches high levels of arousal and "squeezing" the frenulum of the penis, which reportedly suspends the ejaculatory impulse.

pedophilia: Sexual activity between a person who is at least 16 years old and a prepubescent child who is at least 5 years younger.

personality disorder: A pattern of inner experience and behavior, which develops in adolescence or early adulthood, that is inflexible and leads to significant distress or functional impairment.

perturbation: A disturbance in or challenge to the status quo.

phasic: Referring to a relatively brie change in physiological activity when compared to ongoing baseline activity. The change, often a response to some identifiable external or internal stimuli, is typically characterized by a rapid onset followed by a return to baseline.

polarity: The characteristic valence of mood, typically characterized as either manic or depressed.

polygenic multifactorial models: Models that describe the situation in which different genetic abnormalities work in concert to cause a disorder that no single abnormality alone would be necessary and sufficient to cause.

population at risk: The group of individuals from which the cases of disorder are identified.

positron emission tomography (PET): A neuroimaging technique using emission of two photons for measurement of the structure and function of the brain. This strategy has some sensitivity to neurotransmitter receptors and provides data about regional cerebral blood flow, glucose metabolism, and neurotransmitter receptors in different areas of the brain using radioactive tracers.

premature ejaculation: Persistent or recurrent ejaculation with minimal sexual stimulation before, on, or shortly after penetration and before the person wishes it. The clinician must take into account factors that affect duration of the excitement phase, such as age, novelty of the sexual partner or situation, and recent frequency of sexual activity.

prevalence rate: The ratio of all existing cases of disorder during a given time period to the defined population from which the cases were identified.

primary depression: A full depressive syndrome that meets the criteria for major depression in the absence of other psychiatric or medical disorders, as distinguished from *secondary depression,* which refers broadly to depressive symptoms occurring subsequent to, or superimposed on, any other psychiatric or medical disorder.

prognosis: The prediction of outcome based on a specified set of clinical characteristics.

prophylaxis: Maintenance treatment with the goal of prevention of relapse.

prospective study: A research strategy in which one or more cohorts of individuals are identified prior to onset of the outcome of interest (e.g., a disorder) and are followed over time.

protective factor: An event, circumstance, condition, or characteristic that promotes or maintains healthy development and/or resilience.

psychiatric epidemiology: The study of the distribution of psychiatric disorders and symptoms in the population and the factors that affect these distributions.

psychogenic amnesia: Inability to recall a trauma or significant aspects of the trauma; an avoidance/numbing symptom of posttraumatic stress disorder (PTSD).

psychomotor retardation: Motor behavior that is slow

and lethargic, involving a great deal of effort; a common symptom of depression.

psychophysiological arousal: Physical signs of arousal, such as increased heart rate, sweating, and blood pressure, that are associated with concurrent cognitive or emotional states.

psychophysiology: The study of cognitive, emotional, and behavioral events as they relate to and are revealed through physiological principles and events. A scientific method for studying organism environment inter actions for both internal and external environments.

psychosis: A gross disturbance of reality testing, typically manifest by delusions or hallucinations. Some theorists incorporate formal thought disorder or bizarre behavior as manifestations of psychosis.

reactive depression: A subtype of depression in which a stressful environmental event likely played an important role in the development of symptoms; not typically characterized by the constellation of symptoms seen with *endogenous depression,* the subtype of depression with which it is contrasted.

receptor: A protein molecule typically embedded within the cell membrane that recognizes and binds a particular chemical messenger.

response specificity: The relationship between psychophysiological response patterns and independent variables. Response specificity can be classified into three general categories: *stimulus–response specificity,* the tendency of a stimulus to evoke a relatively consistent pattern of physiological responses; *individual-response specificity,* the tendency of an individual to respond physiologically across situations and stimuli in a relatively consistent pattern; and *motivational-response specificity,* a relatively consistent interaction between stimulus–response specificity and individual-response specificity that produces a relatively consistent pattern of physiological responses.

resting potential: The potential difference across the membrane when there is dynamic equilibrium, approximately −70 mV inside relative to outside.

retrospective cohort study: A research strategy in which a cohort of individuals with a disorder (and a comparison group of individuals without the disorder) are selected on the basis of existing records and then studied to determine whether they possessed certain risk factors prior to onset of the disorder.

risk factor: An event, circumstance, condition, or characteristic that, when present, increases a person's vulnerability and the likelihood of developing a disorder.

schizophrenia: A severe debilitating disorder that typically has its onset between the ages of 15 and 30, and is typically characterized by episodes of psychosis with either hallucinations or delusions (positive symptoms) and persistent disturbances in role function, emotional responsivity, and volition (negative symptoms).

second messenger: A substance (e.g., cAMP) that produces a transmitter-like action from within a postsynaptic cell, usually resulting from changes within the cell following activation by a first messenger.

sedatives, hypnotics, and anxiolytics: Substances, usually taken orally, that are prescribed to reduce anxiety, induce sleep, and relax muscles. These drugs, which include benzodiazepine, barbiturates, and methaqualone, have widely varying pharmacological properties but all share depressant, disinhibitory effects similar to those of alcohol.

selective serotonin reuptake inhibitors (SSRIs): Antidepressant medications that are selective for the neurotransmitter serotonin (5-hydroxytryptamine or 5-HT) in the brain.

self-monitoring (as it pertains to the treatment of eating disorders): A useful tool for therapists and eating-disordered patients, which involves recording journal entries about the behaviors, thoughts, and feelings that one experiences throughout the day. It is often helpful to initiate this upon completion of meals, and it is essential to keep track of any symptomatic behavior (e.g., food restriction, binge eating, purging, excessive exercise, or the use of laxatives or diuretics). The purpose of this activity is twofold, as it allows the patient and therapist to specify potential "triggers" for engaging in symptomatic behaviors (and to follow any particular themes or patterns that emerge), and it provides a base from which the patient can learn to identify feelings accurately and respond appropriately to various affective states. Additionally, if done regularly, self-monitoring can provide a context from which the progressive movement of therapy can be tracked, which can be useful in patient motivation, as it enables one to look at the positive aspects and changes within recovery, which can be self-reinforcing.

set point theory: The concept of *set point* has been proposed to account for data from human and animal studies showing that there is remarkable stability in body weight over time. According to the set point concept, body weight is regulated by physiological mechanisms that oppose the displacement of body weight caused by either over- or underfeeding.

sexual aversion disorder: Persistent or recurrent extreme aversion to and avoidance of all or almost all genital sexual contact with a sexual partner.

sexual disorder not otherwise specified: A sexual disturbance that does not meet the criteria for any specific sexual disorder and is neither a sexual dysfunction nor a paraphilia.

sexual dysfunction not otherwise specified: Sexual dysfunctions that do not meet criteria for any specific sexual dysfunction.

sexual self-schema: The cognitive generalizations one makes about the sexual aspects of oneself that are derived from past experience, manifest in current experience, influential in the processing of sexually relevant social information, and guide sexual behavior.

single photon emission computerized tomography (SPECT): A noninvasive electrophysiological technique using the emission of a single photon to measure the structure and function of the brain. SPECT has high sensitivity to neurotransmitter receptors.

smooth-pursuit eye movement (SPEM): Low-velocity movements of the eyes that are elicited by external stimuli and serve to maintain visual contact by keeping the fovea focused on an object that is moving slowly with respect to the head. Patients with schizophrenia and their relatives often have slow pursuit movements.

social norms: Standards for behavior in society; may be folkways, mores, or laws. Folkways are customs that can be violated with relatively few sanctions; mores are strongly held expectations whose violation carries severe sanctions; laws are norms whose violation may potentially involve the criminal justice system.

social phobia: A disorder marked by persistent fear of situations in which the phobic stimulus is perceived scrutiny by others or exposure to unfamiliar people and in which the person fears displaying anxiety symptoms or behaving in a manner that would be embarrassing or humiliating.

sociology: The study of human interpersonal behavior, behavior in groups, and institutional behavior; the study of the effects of society on the individual and the effects of the individual on society.

specific phobia: Previously named "simple phobia," this disorder is marked by two components: intense anxiety when exposed to a specific stimulus and persistent fear and/or avoidance of that stimulus between exposures.

spectatoring: A term coined by Masters and Johnson in their 1970 study to refer to a person's tendency to "watch" for his or her own sexual responding.

stressor: An event, activity, or other stimulus that causes stress.

subculture: Subsection of a culture that shares the culture's dominant institutionalized values but differs on some specific belief, norms, and/or values.

subplate neuron: A special type of neuron that guides

cells and developing fibers destined for cortex and dies out as cortex is established.

substance abuse: Substance use involving only the harmful consequences of repeated use, but without the development of tolerance, withdrawal, or a pattern of compulsive use.

substance dependence: Development of a "cluster of cognitive, behavioral, and psychological symptoms indicating that the individual continues use of the substance despite significant substance-related problems . . . repeated self-administration . . . usually results in tolerance, withdrawal and compulsive drug-taking behavior" (DSM-IV).

substance intoxication: ". . . the development of a reversible substance-specific syndrome due to the recent ingestion of (or exposure to) a substance. . . ." The diagnosis also requires "clinically significant maladaptive behavioral or psychological changes that are due to the effect of the substance on the central nervous system" (DSM-IV).

substance-related disorders: ". . . disorders related to the taking of a drug of abuse (including alcohol), to the side effects of a medication, and to toxin exposure" (DSM-IV).

substance withdrawal: ". . . the development of a substance-specific syndrome due to the cessation of (or reduction in) substance use that has been heavy and prolonged . . . [causing] . . . clinically significant distress or impairment in social, occupational, or other important areas of functioning . . . not due to a general medical condition and . . . not better accounted for by another mental disorder" (DSM-IV).

synapse: The communication point between the axon terminal of one neuron and the dendrite or cell body of another neuron. A chemical synapse is one in which communication is achieved by chemical signal. An electrical synapse is one in which communication is achieved by inducing an electric field in the postsynaptic cell.

syndrome: A coherent set of clinical signs and symptoms that suggest the presence of a disease entity or illness.

tonic: A general term for ongoing, baseline physiological activity.

trait: A distinguishing personal characteristic indicating a proclivity to act in a certain way across environmental situations.

transvestic fetishism: Sexual arousal associated with the act of cross-dressing.

Uniform Crime Reports: Data compiled by the Federal Bureau of Investigation, based on police reports of crimes known to the police; violent crimes included are aggravated assault, robbery, nonnegligent manslaughter, murder, and forcible rape.

unipolar depression: A psychological disorder characterized by one depressive episode or a history of only depressive episodes, with no evidence of mania; one of the major subtypes of affective disorders described in DSM-IV.

vaginal blood volume (VBV): A measure of vaginal vasocongestion obtained from a vaginal photoplethysmograph.

vaginismus (not due to a general medical condition): Recurrent or persistent involuntary spasm of the musculature of the outer third of the vagina that interferes with sexual intercourse.

violence: Application of force that is intended to cause injury or destruction to property or another person

worry: A predominantly verbal, linguistic, and repetitive thought process that is aimed at problem-solving anxiety-producing concerns. It is often concerned with future events where there is uncertainty in outcome.

Yale-Brown Obsessive-Compulsive Scale: A clinician-administered measure for the assessment of obsessive-compulsive severity.

AUTHOR INDEX

453

SUBJECT INDEX